A digest of reported cases

In the Supreme court, Court of insolvency, and courts of
mines of the state of Victoria, and appeals therefrom to the
High court of Australia and the Privy council.

For the years 1906 to 1912 inclusive

L. F. S. Robinson

Alpha Editions

This edition published in 2019

ISBN : 9789353867805

Design and Setting By
Alpha Editions
email - alphaedis@gmail.com

A DIGEST

OF

REPORTED CASES

IN THE

SUPREME COURT, COURT OF INSOLVENCY, AND COURTS OF
MINES OF THE STATE OF VICTORIA, AND APPEALS
THEREFROM TO THE HIGH COURT OF AUSTRALIA
AND THE PRIVY COUNCIL.

FOR THE YEARS

1906 TO 1912

INCLUSIVE.

By

L. F. S. ROBINSON, B.A., LL.B.

(JOINT COMPILER OF THE VICTORIAN DIGESTS, 1890-1895, AND 1895-1900, AND COMPILER OF THE
VICTORIAN DIGEST 1901-1905.

BARRISTER-AT-LAW.

Melbourne:
CHARLES F. MAXWELL,
LAW BOOKSELLER AND PUBLISHER,
458 CHANCERY LANE.
LONDON: SWEET & MAXWELL LIMITED.

PREFACE.

In the preparation of this work the system of classification adopted in previous Victorian Digests has not been departed from in any material particular. This Digest includes the decisions of the Privy Council and of the High Court sitting as Courts of Appeal, and also decisions of the High Court sitting in the exercise of its original jurisdiction in cases in which the cause of action arose within the State of Victoria. There are the usual double indexes of cases and of decisions over-ruled, &c., and an index of references to Statutes. The compiler is indebted to Mr. Maurice Blackburn, Barrister-at-Law, for much valuable assistance.

Selborne Chambers,
May 22nd, **1916.**

CORRIGENDA.

Col. 32.—The reference to the case of *Jenkins'* v. *Lanfranchi* should be under the sub-heading "(e) Costs."

Col. 198.—In the first reference to the case of *Re Rogers and Rodd's Contract*, insert the figures "13" before the letters "A.L.R."

Col. 384.—In the fifteenth line from the bottom the word "Register" should be substituted for the word "Registrar."

Col. 406.—In the reference to *In re Summons for Directions and Interrogatories; Statement on behalf of the Judges of the Supreme Court*, insert immediately after the word "Court" the figures and letters "(1909 V.L.R., 393."

Col. 408.—Immediately before the sub-heading "(b) *Privileged Communications*" insert a reference to the case of "*Boulton v. Robinson*," in Col. 410.

Col. 478.—At the foot of the column add a reference to the case of "*Davis v. Davis and Hattrick*" in Col. 482.

Col. 498.—In the second line from the top substitute the word "Suitor's" for the word "Solicitors'."

Col. 512.—After the sub-heading "(b) *Affidavits*" add a reference to "*Practice and Pleading*," Cols. 1064, 1065.

Col. 543.—Immediately before the sub-heading "(l) *Parties*" add a reference to the case of "*Boulton v. Robinson*," in Col. 410.

Col. 561.—Immediately after the sub-heading "(d) *Commission*," add "*See also, post (f) Passing Accounts*."

Col. 618.—In the reference to the case of *Bloxham* v. *Bloxham*, the words "*Marriage Act*" should be substituted for the words "*Justices Act*."

Col. 658.—In the reference to the case of *Davis* v. *Davis and Hattrick*, after the word "Evidence" insert the letters and figures, "Col. 482."

Col. 716.—In the last line substitute the figures "29" for the figures "30."

Col. 889.—In the reference to the case of *Bloxham* v. *Bloxham*, the words "*Marriage Act*" should be substituted for the words "*Justices Act*."

Col. 1196.—After the second reference to the case of *In re Moore; Fanning* v. *Fanning*, add a reference to the case of "*Perpetual Executors and Trustees Association* v. *Simpson*," Col. 1272.

Col. 1204.—Immediately after the reference to the case of *Macartney* v. *Macartney*, add another reference to the same case at col. 1268.

TABLE OF CASES.

CASES

FOLLOWED, NOT FOLLOWED, APPROVED, OVER-RULED, QUESTIONED, EXPLAINED, DISTINGUISHED, AND COMMENTED UPON.

Aarons, In re, 6 V.L.R. (I.P. & M.), 56 ; 2 A.L.T., 51, distinguished. *In re Hickman,* 31 A.L.T. (Supplement), 10 ; 15 A.L.R. (C.N.) 21.

Abbott v. Morris, 24 A.L.T., 228 ; 9 A.L.R., 96, not followed as to costs of trustee in regard to his commission. *Macartney v. Kesterson,* (1907) V.L.R., 226 ; 28 A.L.T., 170 ; 13 A.L.R., 14.

Adcock, In re, 26 A.L.T., 127 ; 10 A.L.R., 268, approved and applied. *In re Simeon,* (1910) V.L.R., 335 ; 32 A.L.T., 25 ; 16 A.L.R., 362.

Adie, Clark v., 2 App. Cas., 315, applied. *Moore v. Phillips,* 4 C.L.R., 1411 ; 13 A.L.R., 424.

Agar-Ellis, In re, 10 Ch. D., 49, considered and applied. *Goldsmith v. Sands,* 4 C.L.R., 1648 ; 13 A.L.R., 601.

Ahern v. Cathcart, (1909) V.L.R., 132 ; 30 A.L.T., 156 ; 15 A.L.R., 67, overruled. *President &c. of Shire of Tungamah v. Merrett,* 15 C.L.R., 407 ; 18 A.L.R., 511.

Ah Loey, Montgomery v., 2 A.L.R., 207, distinguished. *English v. Potter,* (1908) V.L.R., 632 ; 30 A.L.T., 91 ; 14 A.L.R., 559.

Ainslie, Murphy v., (1905) V.L.R., 350 ; 26 A.L.T., 202 ; 11 A.L.R., 163, applied. *In re Buckhurst ; Equity Trustees Executors and Agency Co. v. Buckhurst,* (1907) V.L.R., 252 ; 28 A.L.T., 190 ; 13 A.L.R., 74. Also, *In re Staughton ; Oliver v. Staughton,* (1910) V.L.R., 415 ; 32 A.L.T., 63 ; 16 A.L.R., 443.

Akeroyd's Settlement, In re ; Roberts v. Akeroyd, (1893) 3 Ch., 363, distinguished. *In re Lyons ; Grant v. Trustees Executors &c. Co. Ltd.,* (1908) V.L.R., 190 ; 29 A.L.T., 202 ; 14 A.L.R., 147.

Alexander v. Jenkins, (1892) 1 Q.B., 571, considered. *Livingston v. M'Cartin,* (1907) V.L.R., 48 ; 28 A.L.T., 131 ; 12 A.L.R., 524.

Alexander v. Steinhardt, Walker & Co., (1903) 2 K.B., 208, applied by *Isaacs, J. Muntz v. Smail,* 8 C.L.R., 262 ; 15 A.L.R., 162.

Allen v. Flood, (1898) A.C., followed. *Bond v. Morris,* (1912) V.L.R., 351 ; 34 A.L.T., 52 ; 18 A.L.R., 348.

Allen, Sprague v., 15 T.L.R., 150, followed. *In re Bennett Brothers,* (1910) V.L.R., 51 ; 31 A.L.T., 148 ; 16 A.L.R., 30.

Amos v. Fraser, 4 C.L.R., 78 ; 12 A.L.R., 481, considered. *Lever Brothers Ltd. v. G. Mowling & Son,* 30 A.L.T., 144 ; 15 A.L.R., 40.

Anderson v. Carter, 20 V.L.R., 246 ; 16 A.L.T., 49, distinguished. *International Harvester Co. of America v. Rowe,* (1909) V.L.R., 244 ; 30 A.L.T., 201 ; 15 A.L.R., 212.

Anderson, Wilson v., 26 A.L.T. (Supplement), 5 ; 11 A.L.R. (C.N.), 35, explained. *Townsing v. Egan,* 29 A.L.T. (Supplement), 29 ; 14 A.L.R. (C.N.), 18.

Andrew, Gower v., 43 Am. R., 242, approved. *Prebble v. Reeves,* (1910) V.L.R., 88 ; 31 A.L.T., 114 ; 15 A.L.R., 631.

Anglo-American Brush Electric Light Corporation v. King, Brown & Co., (1892) A.C., 367, applied. *N. Guthridge Ltd.* v. *Wilfley Ore Concentrator Syndicate Ltd.,* 3 C.L.R., 583 ; 12 A.L.R., 398.

Antony v. Dillon, 15 V.L.R., 240, discussed. *Bell* v. *Clarke,* (1906) V.L.R., 567 ; 28 A.L.T., 24 ; 12 A.L.R., 308.

Armitage, Clarazite Manufacturing Co. Ltd. v. (No. 1), 30 A.L.T. (Supplement), 21 ; 15 A.L.R. (C.N.), 6, disapproved. *Clarazite Manufacturing Co. Ltd.* v. *Armitage* (No. 2), 30 A.L.T. (Supplement), 22 ; 15 A.L.R. (C.N.), 6. Also, not followed, *Lee* v. *Cunningham,* 32 A.L.T. (Supplement), 4 ; 16 A.L.R. (C.N.), 1.

Armytage, Davidson v., 4 C.L.R., 205 ; 12 A.L.R., 538, discussed. *Kelly* v. *Collector of Imposts,* 29 A.L.T., 91 ; 13 A.L.R., 613, discussed. *Kelly* v. *Collector of Imposts,* 29 A.L.T., 91 ; 13 A.L.R., 613.

Armytage, Davidson v., 4 C.L.R., 205 ; 12 A.L.R., 538, explained and distinguished. *Davidson* v. *Chirnside,* 7 C.L.R., 324 ; 14 A.L.R., 686.

Arnold, Booth v., (1895) 1 Q.B., 571, considered. *Livingston* v. *M'Cartin,* (1907) V.L.R., 48 ; 28 A.L.T., 131 : 12 A.L.R., 524.

Artificial Manure Board, In re, (1905) V.L.R., 19 ; 26 A.L.T., 87 ; 10 A.L.R., 230, approved. *In re the Fellmongers Board,* 15 A.L.R., 225.

Ashforth, In re, (1905) 1 Ch., 535, followed. *In re Malin ; National Trustees &c. Co.* v. *Loughnan,* (1912) V.L.R., 259 ; 34 A.L.T., 30 ; 18 A.L.R., 274.

Ashley v. Ashley, 24 V.L.R., 220 ; 4 A.L.R., 154, explained. *The King* v. *Watt ; Ex parte Slade,* (1912) V.L.R., 225 ; 33 A.L.T., 222 ; 18 A.L.R., 158.

Asten v. Asten, (1894) 3 Ch., 260, followed. *In re Leaf; Donaldson* v. *Leaf,* (1907) V.L.R., 278; 29 A.L.T., 54 ; 13 A.L.R., 148.

Atkinson v. Morris, (1897) P., 40, followed. *Gair* v. *Bowers,* 9 C.L.R., 510 ; 15 A.L.R., 494.

Attorney-General for New South Wales v. Brewery Employees Union of New South Wales, 6 C.L.R., 469 ; 14 A.L.R., 565, applied. *Huddart Parker & Co. Proprietary Ltd.* v. *Moorehead ; Appleton* v. *Moorehead,* 8 C.L.R., 330 ; 15 A.L.R., 241

Attorney-General v. Dean of Christ Church, (1826) 2 Russ., 321, distinguished. *Fomsgard* v. *Fomsgard,* (1912) V.L.R., 209 ; 34 A.L.T., 11 ; 18 A.L.R., 220.

Attorney-General v. Hooper, (1893) 3 Ch., 483, distinguished. *Bremner* v. *New Normanby Quartz Mining Co., No Liability,* (1910) V.L.R., 72 ; 31 A.L.T., 140 ; 16 A.L.R., 25.

Attorney-General, Monkton v., 2 R. & My., 147, not followed. *In re Osmand ; Bennett* v. *Booty,* (1908) V.L.R., 67 ; 29 A.L.T., 168 ; 13 A.L.R., 728. F.C., affirming *Cussen, J.,* (1906) V.L.R., 455 ; 27 A.L.T., 218 ; 12 A.L.R., 256.

Bagot, In re ; Paton v. Ormerod, (1893) 3 Ch., 348, followed. *In re Stead,* (1908) V.L.R., 10 ; 29 A.L.T., 155 ; 13 A.L.R., 683.

Ball, In re, L.R. 8 C.P., 104, explained. *Pope* v. *Peacock,* (1906) V.L.R., 667 ; 28 A.L.T., 63 ; 12 A.L.R., 440.

Bank of New Zealand v. Simpson, (1900) A.C., 182, followed. *Bruton* v. *Farm and Dairy Machinery Co. Proprietary Ltd.,* (1910) V.L.R., 196 ; 31 A.L.T., 200 ; 16 A.L.R., 241.

Bank of Scotland, Logan v. (No. 2), (1906) 1 K.B., 141, considered and applied. *Maritime Insurance Co. Ltd.* v. *Geelong Harbour Trust Commissioners,* 6 C.L.R., 194 ; 14 A.L.R., 424.

Banks v. Hollingsworth, (1893) 1 Q.B., 442, followed. *Ronald* v. *Harper,* (1908) V.L.R., 674 ; 30 A.L.T., 72 ; 14 A.L.R., 472.

Barber, R. v., 3 A.L.R. (C.N.), 21, approved. *R.* v. *Turnbull,* (1907) V.L.R., 11 ; 28 A.L.T., 103 ; 12 A.L.R., 551.

Barger, The King v., 6 C.L.R., 41 ; 14 A.L.R., 374, applied. *Huddart Parker & Co. Proprietary Ltd.* v. *Moorehead ; Appleton* v. *Moorehead,* 8 C.L.R., 330 ; 15 A.L.R., 241.

Barker v. Henty, 29 V.L.R., 293; 25 A.L.T., 34; 9 A.L.R., 160, distinguished. *Annear v. Inskip*, (1910) V.L.R., 235; 31 A.L.T., 220; 16 A.L.R., 276.

Barns v. Queensland National Bank, 3 C.L.R., 925, followed. *Pendlebury* v. *Colonial Mutual &c. Society Ltd.*, 13 C.L.R., 676; 18 A.L.R., 124.

Bartley, Peterswald v., 1 C.L.R., 497, principles of interpretation applied. *Huddart Parker & Co. Proprietary Ltd.* v. *Moorehead*; *Appleton* v. *Moorehead*, 8 C.L.R., 330; 15 A.L.R., 241.

Baseley, Huguenin v., 14 Ves., 273, considered. *Union Bank of Australia Ltd.* v. *Whitelaw*, (1906) V.L.R., 711; 28 A.L.T., 17; 12 A.L.R., 393.

Bayne v. Blake, (1908) A.C., 371; 14 A.L.R., 317, explained. *In re Transfer of Land Act*; *Ex parte Equity Trustees Executors &c. Co. Ltd. and O'Halloran*, (1911) V.L.R., 197; 32 A.L.T., 183; 17 A.L.R., 154.

Beecham & Co., The King v., (1910) V.L.R., 204; 31 A.L.T., 183; 16 A.L.R., 173, applied. *Annear v. Inskip*, (1910) V.L.R., 235; 31 A.L.T., 220; 16 A.L.R., 276.

Beissel, Crout v., (1909) V.L.R., 211; 30 A.L.T., 185; 16 A.L.R., 636, followed. *Grunden v. Nissen*, (1911) V.L.R., 97; 32 A.L.T., 117; 16 A.L.R., 636.

Bell, Gates v., (1902) 2 K.B., 38, distinguished. *McKinnon* v. *Gange*, (1910) V.L.R., 32; 31 A.L.T., 112; 15 A.L.R., 640.

Bence, In re, (1891) 3 Ch., 242, followed. *Milligan v. Shaw*, (1907) V.L.R., 668; 29 A.L.T., 75; 13 A.L.R., 545.

Benson, Wilson v., (1905) V.L.R., 229; 26 A.L.T., 144; 11 A.L.R., 85, approved. *Wilson v. Travers*, (1906) V.L.R., 734; 28 A.L.T., 56; 12 A.L.R., 413.

Best, In re, 9 A.L.T., 32, approved. *In re McConnell*, 29 A.L.T. (Supplement), 8; 13 A.L.R. (C.N.), 32.

Betts v. Menzies, 10 H.L.C., 117, applied. *N. Guthridge Ltd.* v. *Wilfley Ore Concentrator Syndicate Ltd.*, 3 C.L.R., 583; 12 A.L.R., 398.

Bevan v. Moore, 24 V.L.R., 729 20; A.L.T., 238; 5 A.L.R., 100, explained. *McCallum* v. *Purvis*, (1906) V.L.R., 578; 28 A.L.T., 31; 12 A.L.R., 329.

Bible, Knox v., (1907) V.L.R., 485; 29 A.L.T., 23; 13 A.L.R., 252, approved. *Macmanamny v. King*, (1907) V.L.R., 535; 28 A.L.T., 250; 13 A.L.R., 258.

Biggs v. Kelly, 24 V.L.R., 402; 20 A.L.T., 105; 4 A.L.R., 153, distinguished. *Annear v. Inskip*, (1910) V.L.R., 235; 31 A.L.T., 220; 16 A.L.R., 276.

Binko, In re, 2 Morr., 45, followed. *In re McConnell*, 29 A.L.T. (Supplement), 26; 14 A.L.R. (C.N.), 19.

Blake, Bayne v., (1908) A.C., 371; 14 A.L.R., 317, explained. *In re Transfer of Land Act*; *Ex parte Equity Trustees Executors &c. Co. Ltd. and O'Halloran*, (1911) V.L.R., 197; 32 A.L.T., 183; 17 A.L.R., 154.

Bloomfield v. Dunlop Tyre Co. Ltd., 28 V.L.R., 72; 23 A.L.T., 227; 8 A.L.R., 103, followed. *Chomley v. Watson*, (1907) V.L.R., 502; 29 A.L.T., 46; 13 A.L.R., 380.

Booth v. Arnold, (1895) 1 Q.B., 571, considered. *Livingston v. M'Cartin*, (1907) V.L.R., 48; 28 A.L.T., 131; 12 A.L.R., 524.

Bouche v. Sproule, 12 App. Cas., 385, at pp. 397, 401, considered. *In re Longley*; *Reid v. Silke*, (1906) V.L.R., 641; 28 A.L.T., 82; 12 A.L.R., 499, applied. *In re Smith*; *Edwards v. Smith*, 29 A.L.T., 173; 14 A.L.R., 22.

Bourke, Palmer v., 28 V.L.R., 275; 24 A.L.T., 11; 8 A.L.R., 151, distinguished. *Doig v. Keating*, (1908) V.L.R., 118; 29 A.L.T., 171; 14 A.L.R., 20.

Bowden v. Little, 4 C.L.R., 1364; 13 A.L.R., 689, followed. *H. Beecham & Co. v. R. W. Cameron & Co.*, (1910) V.L.R., 19; 31 A.L.T., 100; 15 A.L.R., 598.

Bowman, Chadwick v., 16 Q.B.D., 561, followed. *Shaw v. David Syme & Co.*, (1912) V.L.R., 336; 34 A.L.T., 68; 18 A.L.R., 345.

Bradford, Mayor &c. of, Chamberlain & Hookham Ltd. v., 20 R.P.C., 673, followed.

Minerals Separation Ltd. v. *Potter's Sulphide Ore Treatment Ltd.*, 8 C.L.R., 779 ; 13 A.L.R., 332.

Brand v. Lawrence, 1 Q.B.D., 344, followed. *L. Osborn & Co. Ltd.* v. *Davidson Brothers,* (1911) V.L.R., 416 ; 33 A.L.T., 66 ; 17 A.L.R., 448.

Brewery Employees Union of New South Wales, Attorney-General for New South Wales v., 6 C.L.R., 469 ; 14 A.L.R., 565, applied. *Huddart Parker & Co. Proprietary Ltd.* v. *Moorehead ; Appleton* v. *Moorehead,* 8 C.L.R., 330 ; 15 A.L.R., 241.

Brewster, Rochdale Canal Co. v., (1894) 2 Q.B., 852, followed. *Mayor &c. of City of Melbourne* v. *Howard Smith Co. Ltd.,* 13 C.L.R., 253 ; 17 A.L.R., 437.

Bricknell, Christie v., 21 V.L.R., 71 ; 17 A.L.T., 59 ; 1 A.L.R., 59, applied. *O'Connor* v. *Bini,* (1908) V.L.R., 567 ; 30 A.L.T., 74 ; 14 A.L.R., 537.

Brimacombe, Wimmera, Shire of, v., 23 V.L.R., 217 ; 19 A.L.T., 12 ; 3 A.L.R., 146, explained. *Poowong, Shire of,* v. *Gillen,* (1907) V.L.R., 37 ; 28 A.L.T., 123 ; 12 A.L.R., 522.

Brisac & Scott, R. v., 4 East, 164, followed. *R.* v. *Kellow,* (1912) V.L.R., 162 ; 33 A.L.T., 203 ; 18 A.L.R., 170.

Bristol Steam Navigation Co., Speller v., 13 Q.B.D., 96, distinguished. *Edwards* v. *Edwards,* (1913) V.L.R., 30 ; 34 A.L.T., 103 ; 18 A.L.R., 580.

British Homes Assurance Corporation v. Paterson, (1902) 2 Ch., 404, distinguished. *Reid* v. *Silberberg,* (1906) V.L.R., 126.

Brooks, Robinson & Co. v. Smith, 16 V.L.R., 245 ; 11 A.L.T., 168, applied. *H. Beecham & Co.* v. *R. W. Cameron & Co.,* (1910) V.L.R., 19 ; 31 A.L.T., 100 ; 15 A.L.R., 598.

Broughton v. Broughton, 5 DeG. M. & G., 160, at p. 164, applied. *Macartney* v. *Macartney,* (1909) V.L.R., 183 ; 30 A.L.T., 172 ; 15 A.L.R., 139.

Brown, Dalgety & Co. Ltd. v., 24 V.L.R., 161 ; 20 A.L.T., 45 ; 4 A.L.R., 170, commented on. *Riggall* v. *Muirhead,* 13 C.L.R., 436.

Browne, Ex parte ; Re Sandilands, 4 V.L.R. (L.) 318, followed. *Pope* v. *Peacock,* (1906) V.L.R., 667 ; 28 A.L.T., 63 ; 12 A.L.R., 440.

Brown, R. v., 24 Q.B.D., 357, followed. *Rex* v. *Turnbull,* (1907) V.L.R., 11 ; 28 A.L.T., 103 ; 12 A.L.R., 551.

Brown v. Victorian Railways Commissioners, 3 C.L.R., 316 ; 12 A.L.R., 1, applied. *Crouch* v. *Victorian Railways Commissioners,* (1907) V.L.R., 80 ; 28 A.L.T., 141 ; 12 A.L.R., 574.

Burdett, R. v., 4 B. & A., 95, discussed. *R.* v. *Waugh,* (1909) V.L.R., 379 ; 31 A.L.T., 37 ; 15 A.L.R., 366.

Busk, Jewry v., 5 Taunt, 302, distinguished. *Griffith* v. *O'Donoghue,* (1906) V.L.R., 548 ; 28 A.L.T., 31 ; 12 A.L.R., 357.

Butler v. Rice, (1910) 2 Ch., 277, applied. *Cuddigan* v. *Poole,* 33 A.L.T., 210 ; 18 A.L.R., 120.

Butler, Ex parte ; Ex parte Wylie, 4 A.L.T., 41, explained and distinguished. *Mooney* v. *Still,* (1909) V.L.R., 227 ; 30 A.L.T., 191 ; 15 A.L.R., 197.

Butters v. Durham G. M. Co., 11 V.L.R., 375 ; 7 A.L.T., 30, followed. *Brisbane* v. *Stewart,* (1906) V.L.R., 608 ; 28 A.L.T., 110 ; 12 A.L.R., 549.

Callwell v. Callwell, 3 Sw. & Tr., 259, considered. *Forster* v. *Forster,* (1907) V.L.R., 159 ; 28 A.L.T., 144 ; 13 A.L.R., 33.

Carberry v. Cook, 3 C.L.R., 995 ; 12 A.L.R., 265, applied. *Le Cocq* v. *McErvale,* (1908) V.L.R., 69 ; 29 A.L.T., 134 ; 13 A.L.R., 699.

Carew, In re, 25 A.L.T., 117 ; 9 A.L.R., 266, followed. *In re Cotter,* (1907) V.L.R., 78 ; 28 A.L.T., 106 ; 12 A.L.R., 550.

Carr, In re, 85 L.T., 552, distinguished. *In re Camp,* (1910) V.L.R., 42 ; 31 A.L.T., 126 ; 15 A.L.R., 642, followed. *In re Knights ; Ex parte Purcell,* (1910) V.L.R., 188 ; 31 A.L.T., 178 ; 16 A.L.R., 184.

Cartman, Commissioners of Police v., (1896) 1 Q.B., 655, followed. *Davies* v. *Young,* (1910) V.L.R., 369 ; 32 A.L.T., 39 ; 16 A.L.R., 368.

Carter, Anderson v., 20 V.L.R., 246; 16 A.L.T., 49, distinguished. *International Harvester Co. of America v. Rowe,* (1909) V.L.R., 244; 30 A.L.T., 201; 15 A.L.R., 212.

Cash v. Cash. 22 V.L R, 110; 17 A.L.T., 326; 2 A.L.R., 153, approved. *Hines v. Phillips,* (1906) V.L.R., 417; 28 A.L.T., 1; 12 A.L.R., 249.

Cathcart, Ahern v., (1909) V.L.R., 132; 30 A.L.T., 156; 15 A.L.R., 67, overruled. *President &c. of Shire of Tungamah v. Merrett,* 15 C.L.R., 407; 18 A.L.R., 511.

Caulfield, In re, 27 V.L.R., 588; 23 A.L.T., 133; 7 A.L.R. (C.N.), 94, considered. *In re Cohen,* 13 A.L.R. (C.N.), 33.

Cave-Brown-Cave, In re, (1906) V.L.R., 283; 27 A.L.T., 183; 12 A.L.R., 167, explained. *In re Cavin,* (1906) V.L.R., 517; 28 A.L.T., 39; 12 A.L.R., 333.

Ceylon, Governor of, and Mitchell and Izard, In re, 21 Q.B.D., 408, followed. *Re Freeman and Kempster,* (1909) V.L.R., 394; 31 A.L.T., 42; 15 A.L.R., 444.

Chadwick v. Bowman, 16 Q.B.D., 561, followed. *Shaw v. David Syme & Co.,* (1912) V.L.R., 336; 34 A.L.T., 68; 18 A.L.R., 345.

Chamberlain & Hookham Ltd. v. Mayor &c. of Bradford, 20 R.P.C., 673, followed. *Minerals Separation Ltd. v. Potter's Sulphide Ore Treatment Ltd.,* 8 C.L.R., 779; 13 A.L.R., 332.

Chantler v. Chantler, 4 C.L.R., 585; 13 A.L.R., 540, discussed. *Ross v. Ross,* (1909) V.L.R., 318; 30 A.L.T., 220; 15 A.L.R., 305.

Chapman v. Fylde Waterworks Co., (1894) 2 Q.B., 599, followed. *Frencham v. Melbourne and Metropolitan Board of Works,* (1911) V.L.R., 363; 33 A.L.T., 30; 17 A.L.R., 333.

Charter v. Charter, L.R. 7 H.L., 364, applied. *In re Loughlin; Acheson v. O'Meara,* (1906) V.L.R., 597; 28 A.L.T., 28; 12 A.L.R., 411.

Chidley, May v., (1894) 1 Q.B., 451, followed. *Colonial Bank of Australia Ltd. v. Nicholl,* (1907) V.L.R., 402; 13 A.L.R., 297.

Christie v. Bricknell, 21 V.L.R., 71; 17 A.L..T., 59; 1 A.L.R., 59, applied. *O'Connor v. Bini,* (1908) V.L.R., 567; 30 A.L.T., 74; 14 A.L.R., 537.

Chia Gee v. Martin, 3 C.L.R., 649; 12 A.L.R., 425, discussed and distinguished. *Ah Sheung v. Lindberg,* (1906) V.L.R., 323; 27 A.L.T., 189; 12 A.L.R., 190.

Church Wardens of St. Saviour's, Southwark v. Smith, 1 Wm. Bl., 351, followed. *Renshaw v. Maher,* (1907) V.L.R., 520; 29 A.L.T., 237; 13 A.L.R., 265.

Clarazite Manufacturing Co. Ltd. v. Armitage (No. 1), 30 A.L.T. (Supplement), 21; 15 A.L.R. (C.N.), 6, disapproved. *Clarazite Manufacturing Co. Ltd. v. Armitage (No. 2),* 30 A.L.T. (Supplement), 22; 15 A.L.R. (C.N.), 6. Also, not followed, *Lee v. Cunningham,* 32 A.L.T. (Supplement), 4; 16 A.L.R. (C.N.), 1.

Clark v. Adie, 2 App. Cas., 315, applied. *Moore v. Phillips,* 4 C.L.R., 1411; 13 A.L.R., 424.

Clark, Fisher v., 2 A.L.R. (C.N.), 321, considered. *Russ v. Carr,* (1909) V.L.R., 78; 30 A.L.T., 131; 15 A.L.R., 24.

Clutterbuck v. Curry, 11 V.L.R., 810, followed. *McKinnon v. Gange,* (1910) V.L.R., 32; 31 A.L.T., 112; 15 A.L.R., 640.

Cohen v. MacDonough, (1906) V.L.R., 521; 28 A.L.T., 97; 12 A.L.R., 447, dictum of *Cussen, J.,* disapproved. *Cohen v. MacDonough,* (1907) V.L.R., 7; 28 A.L.T., 119; 12 A.L.R., 566.

Collector of Imposts, Moffat v., 22 V.L.R., 164; 18 A.L.T., 144; 2 A.L.R., 255, approved. *Davidson v. Armytage,* 4 C.L.R., 205; 12 A.L.R., 538.

Collector of Imposts, Wiseman v., 21 V.L.R., 743; 17 A.L.T., 251, overruled. *Davidson v. Chirnside,* 7 C.L.R., 324; 14 A.L.R., 686.

Collett v. Collett, 1 Curt. Eccl. Rep., 678, considered. *Isles v. Isles,* (1906) V.L.R., 86; 12 A.L.R. (C.N.), 26.

Collins, R. v.; Ex parte Collins, 7 V.L.R., 74; 2 A.L.T., 118, followed. *Ross v. Ross,* (1909) V.L.R., 318; 30 A.L.T., 220; 15 A.L.R., 305.

Colonial Bank of Australia Ltd. v. Nicholl, (1907) V.L.R., 402; 28 A.L.T., 222; 13 A.L.R., 297, followed. *Australian Widows' Fund &c. Society Ltd.* v. *Story*, (1907) V.L.R., 594; 29 A.L.T., 110; 13 A.L.R., 588.

Commissioners of Police v. Cartman, (1896) 1 Q.B., 655, followed. *Davies* v. *Young*, (1910) V.L.R., 369; 32 A.L.T., 39; 16 A.L.R., 368.

Connors v. McCarthy, 17 A.L.T., 187; 2 A.L.R., 10, discussed. *In re Lamrock, Brown and Hall's Costs*, (1908) V.L.R., 238; 29 A.L.T., 214; 14 A.L.R., 81.

Constable v. Constable, 1 W.W. & A'B. (I. E. & M.), 88, applied. *Maddock* v. *Maddock*, (1911) V.L.R., 127; 32 A.L.T., 124; 17 A.L.R., 66.

Cook, Carberry v., 3 C.L.R., 995; 12 A.L.R., 265, applied. *Le Cocq* v. *McErvale*, (1908) V.L.R., 69; 29 A.L.T., 134; 13 A.L.R., 699.

Cooper v. Cooper, L.R. 7 H.L., 53, followed. *Bayne* v. *Blake*, (1908) A.C., 371; 14 A.L.R., 317. Also, *In re Transfer of Land Act; Ex parte Equity Trustees Executors &c. Co. Ltd. and O'Halloran*, (1911) V.L.R., 197; 32 A.L.T., 183; 17 A.L.R. 154.

Cooper v. Cooper, 26 V.L.R., 649; 22 A.L.T., 215; 7 A.L.R., 147, explained and followed. *Macartney* v. *Macartney*, 33 A.L.T., 183; 18 A.L.R., 1, applied. *Holmes* v. *Holmes*, 28 A.L.T., 22; 12 A.L.R., 409.

Cooper, Falkner v., Carter's Cases, 55, followed. *Chomley* v. *Watson*, (1907) V.L.R., 502; 29 A.L.T., 46; 13 A.L.R., 380.

Cooper v. Wandsworth District Board of Works, 14 C.B. N.S., 180, followed. *Bremner* v. *New Normanby Quartz Mining Co., No Liability*, (1910) V.L.R., 72; 31 A.L.T., 140; 16 A.L.R., 25.

Cork and Bandon Railway v. Goode, 13 C.B., 826, distinguished. *Land Mortgage Bank of Victoria Ltd.* v. *Reid*, (1909) V.L.R., 284; 31 A.L.T., 9; 15 A.L.R., 234.

Corsellis, In re, 34 Ch. D., 675, followed. *Macartney* v. *Macartney*, (1909) V.L.R., 183; 30 A.L.T., 172; 15 A.L.R., 139.

Cowan & Sons v. Lockyer, 1 C.L.R., 460; 10 A.L.R. (C.N.), 63, distinguished. *Sargood Brothers* v. *Commonwealth*, 11 C.L.R., 258; 16 A.L.R., 483.

Cox, Eyre v., 24 W.R., 317, not followed. *Cameron* v: *Cameron*, (1906) V.L.R., 13; 28 A.L.T., 169; 13 A.L.R., 10.

Crabb v. Crabb, L.R. 1 P. & D., 601, followed. *Jordan* v. *Jordan*, (1906) V.L.R., 414; 27 A.L.T., 229; 12 A.L.R., 252.

Crane, Crowley v., 21 V.L.R., 258; 17 A.L.T., 43; 1 A.L.R., 101, followed. *Macartney* v. *Macartney*, 33 A.L.T., 183; 18 A.L.R., 1.

Crawshaw, Mitchell v., (1903) 1 K.B., 701, considered. *O'Connor* v. *Anderson*, (1909) V.L.R., 1; 30 A.L.T., 145; 15 A.L.R., 22.

Crepps v. Durden, 1 S.L.C. (9th ed.), p. 692, distinguished. *Knox* v. *Bible*, (1907) V.L.R., 485; 29 A.L.T., 23; 13 A.L.R., 352.

Crook v. Crook, 23 A.L.T., 123; 8 A.L.R., 2, over-ruled. *Forster* v. *Forster*, (1907) V.L.R., 159; 28 A.L.T., 144; 13 A.L.R., 33.

Crooke v. Smith, 4 V.L.R. (L.), 95, applied. *H. Beecham & Co.* v. *R. W. Cameron & Co.*, (1910) V.L.R., 19; 31 A.L.T., 100; 15 A.L.R., 598.

Cropley, Re, 4 V.L.R. (I. P. & M.), 61, distinguished. *In re Ghillmetei*, (1907) V.L.R., 657; 29 A.L.T., 81; 13 A.L.R., 519.

Cronch v. Victorian Railways Commissioners, (1907) V.L.R., 80; 28 A.L.T., 141; 12 A.L.R., 574, followed. *In re Hilliard, Ex parte Tinkler*, (1907) V.L.R., 375; 28 A.L.T., 204; 13 A.L.R., 138.

Crout v. Beissel, (1909) V.L.R., 211; 30 A.L.T., 185; 16 A.L.R., 636, followed. *Grunden* v. *Nissen*, (1911) V.L.R., 97; 32 A.L.T., 117; 16 A.L.R., 636.

Crowley v. Crane, 21 V.L.R., 258; 17 A.L.T., 43; 1 A.L.R., 101, followed. *Macartney* v. *Macartney*, 33 A.L.T., 183; 18 A.L.R., 1.

Crown Hotel, In re; Ex parte Waxman, 28 V.L.R., 710; 24 A.L.T., 234; 9 A.L.R., 108, not followed. *Mooney* v. *Lucas*, (1909) V.L.R., 333; 31 A.L.T., 3; 15 A.L.R., 296.

Culverwell, Brooks & Co., Palmer v., 85 L.T., 758, applied by *Isaacs, J. Muntz v. Smail,* 8 C.L.R., 262 ; 15 A.L.R., 162.

Cundy v. Le Cocq, 13 Q.B.D., 207, followed. *Davies* v. *Young,* (1910) V.L.R., 369 ; 32 A.L.T., 39 ; 16 A.L.R., 368.

Curry, Clutterbuck v., 11 V.L.R., 810, followed. *McKinnon* v. *Gange,* (1910) V.L.R., 32 ; 31 A.L.T., 112 ; 15 A.L.R., 640.

Cussen v. MacPherson, 6 A.L.T., 205, followed. *Kelsey* v. *Caselberg,* (1909) V.L.R., 347 ; 31 A.L.T., 31 ; 15 A.L.R., 362.

Cutts v. Gilbert, 9 Moo. P.C.C., 131, considered. *Gair* v. *Bowers,* 9 C.L.R., 510 ; 15 A.L.R., 494.

Dalgety & Co. Ltd. v. Brown, 24 V.L.R., 161 ; 20 A.L.T., 45 ; 4 A.L.R., 170, commented on. *Riggall* v. *Muirhead,* 13 C.L.R., 436.

Davidson v. Armytage, 4 C.L.R., 205 ; 12 A.L.R., 538, discussed. *Kelly* v. *Collector of Imposts,* 29 A.L.T., 91 ; 13 A.L.R., 613.

Davidson v. Armytage, 4 C.L.R., 205 ; 12 A.L.R., 538, explained and distinguished. *Davidson* v. *Chirnside,* 7 C.L.R., 324 ; 14 A.L.R., 686.

Davidson, Weedon v., 4 C.L.R., 895 ; 13 A.L.R., 87, explained. *Richardson v. Austin,* 12 C.L.R., 463 ; 17 A.L.R., 324.

Davies, R. v., (1906) 1 K.B., 32, discussed. *Packer* v. *Peacock,* 13 C.L.R., 577 ; 18 A.L.R., 70.

Davis v. Hamlin, 48 Am. R., 541, approved. *Prebble* v. *Reeves,* (1910) V.L.R., 88 ; 31 A.L.T., 114 ; 15 A.L.R., 631.

Dawson, Higgins v., (1902) A.C., 1, applied. *In re Longley* ; *Reid* v. *Silk.* (1906) V.L.R., 641 ; 28 A.L.T., 82 ; 12 A.L.R., 499.

Deakin v. Webb, 1 C.L.R., 585, approved and applied. *Baxter* v. *Commissioners of Taxation* ; *Flint* v. *Webb,* 4 C.L.R., 1087 ; 1178 ; 13 A.L.R., 313.

Deane, Reid v., (1906) V.L.R., 138, 27 A.L.T., 153 ; 12 A.L.R., 46, followed. *In re Tong,* (1907) V.L.R., 338 ; 28 A.L.T., 200 ; 13 A.L.R., 119, not followed as regards liability for sewerage expenses. *Macartney* v. *Macartney,* 33 A.L.T., 183 ; 18 A.L.R., 1.

Dean of Christ Church, Attorney-General v., (1826) 2 Russ., 321, distinguished. *Fomsgard* v. *Fomsgard,* (1912) V.L.R., 209 ; 34 A.L.T., 11 ; 18 A.L.R., 220.

Death, Roberts v., 8 Q.B.D., 319, followed. *Richards* v. *Jager,* (1909) V.L.R., 140 ; 30 A.L.T., 163 ; 15 A.L.R., 119.

Deeley v. Perkes, 13 R.P.C., 581, followed on question of amendment. *Moore* v. *Phillips,* 4 C.L.R., 1411 ; 13 A.L.R., 424.

D'Emden v. Pedder, 1 C.L.R., 91 ; 10 A.L.R. (C.N.), 30, application of considered. *Federated Engine Drivers and Firemen's Association of Australasia v. Broken Hill Proprietary Co. Ltd.,* 12 C.L.R., 398 ; 17 A.L.R., 285.

Dennis v. Victorian Railways Commissioners, 28 V.L.R., 576 ; 24 A.L.T., 196 ; 9 A.L.R., 69, applied. *Victorian Railways Commissioners* v. *Campbell,* 4 C.L.R., 1446 ; 13 A.L.R., 403.

De Trafford, Kennedy v., (1897) A.C., 180, followed. *Pendlebury* v. *Colonial Mutual &c. Society Ltd.,* 13 C.L.R., 676 ; 18 A.L.R., 124.

Dickinson v. Dodds, 2 Ch. D., 463, distinguished. *Patterson* v. *Dolman,* (1908) V.L.R., 354 ; 29 A.L.T., 256 ; 14 A.L.R., 240.

Dillet, In re, 12 App. Cas., 459, at p. 467, principle as to granting special leave to appeal in criminal cases, applied. *Hope* v. *The King,* 9 C.L.R., 257.

Dillon, Antony v., 15 V.L.R., 240, discussed. *Bell* v. *Clarke,* (1906) V.L.R., 567 ; 28 A.L.T., 24 ; 12 A.L.R., 308.

Dodds, Dickinson v., 2 Ch. D., 463, distinguished. *Patterson* v. *Dolman,* (1908) V.L.R., 354 ; 29 A.L.T., 256. ; 14 A.L.R., 240.

Doherty v. Thompson, 94 L.T., 626, followed. *Harrison San Miguel Proprietary Ltd.* v. *Alfred Lawrence & Co.,* (1912) V.L.R., 367 ; 34 A.L.T., 88 ; 18 A.L.R., 394.

Downey, In re, 5 V.L.R. (I. P. & M.), 72, distinguished. *In re Johnson,* (1909) V.L.R., 324 ; 31 A.L.T., 2 ; 15 A.L.R., 304.

Doyle v. Ferne, 25 V.L.R., 291; 5 A.L.R. (C.N.), 93, followed. *Harney v. Huntley, President &c. of Shire of*, (1910) V.L.R., 455; 32 A.L.T., 82; 16 A.L.R., 582.

Drake, London &c. Discount Co. v., 6 C.N.B.S., 798, followed. *Armstrong v Duke of Wellington G. M. Co., No Liability*, 3 C.L.R., 1028; 12 A.L.R., 316.

Dublin, Wicklow and Wexford Ry. Co. v. Slattery, 3 A.C., 1155, at p. 1201, applied. *Farrands v. Mayor &c. of Melbourne*, (1909) V.L.R., 531; 31 A.L.T., 78; 15 A.L.R., 520. distinguished. *Fraser v. Victorian Railways Commissioners*, 8 C.L.R., 54; 15 A.L.R., 93.

Dunbar, Rees v., 14 V.L.R., 645; 10 A.L.T., 147, followed. *Davis v. Davis and Hattrick*, (1912) V.L.R., 23; 33 A.L.T., 108; 17 A.L.R., 607.

Dunlevie, Dungey v., 31 A.L.T. (Supplement), 3; 15 A.L.R. (C.N.), 13, followed. *Ormond v. Joske*, 16 A.L.R. (C.N.), 1.

Dunlop Tyre Co. Ltd., Bloomfield v., 28 V.L.R., 72; 23 A.L.T., 227; 8 A.L.R., 103, followed. *Chomley v. Watson*, (1907) V.L.R., 502; 29 A.L.T., 46; 13 A.L.R., 380.

Dun, Macintosh v., (1908) A.C., 390, distinguished. *Howe v. Lees*, 11 C.L.R., 361; 16 A.L.R., 605.

Durden, Crepps v., 1 S.L.C. (9th ed.), p. 692, distinguished. *Knox v. Bible*, (1907) V.L.R., 485; 29 A.L.T., 23; 13 A.L.R., 352.

Durham, Earl of, Wood v., 21 Q.B.D., 501, followed. *Wilson v. Dun's Gazette*, (1912) V.L.R., 342; 34 A.L.T., 77; 18 A.L.R., 327.

Durham G. M. Co., Butters v., 11 V.L.R., 375; 7 A.L.T., 30, followed. *Brisbane v. Stewart*, (1906) V.L.R., 608; 28 A.L.T., 110; 12 A.L.R., 549.

Eager, In re, 32 A.L.T., 145; 17 A.L.R., 90, approved. *In re Bloom*, (1911) V.L.R., 313; 33 A.L.T., 26; 17 A.L.R., 331.

Eames, Lambe v, L.R. 6 Ch., 597, followed. *In re Lawn; Ballarat Trustees &c. Co. v. Perry*, (1911) V.L.R., 318; 33 A.L.T., 25; 17 A.L.R., 311.

Earl of Chesterfield's Estate, In re, 24 Ch. D., 643, distinguished. *Holmes v. Holmes*, 28 A.L.T., 22; 12 A.L.R., 409.

Edwards, Stroud v., 77 L.T. N.S., 280, followed. *Trustees Executors and Agency Co. Ltd. v. Webster*, (1907) V.L.R., 318; 28 A.L.T., 225; 13 A.L.R., 188.

Egbert v. Short, (1907) 2 Ch., 207, considered and applied. *Maritime Insurance Co. Ltd. v. Geelong Harbour Trust Commissioners*, 6 C.L.R., 194; 14 A.L.R., 424.

Ellis, R. v., (1899) 1 Q.B., 230, discussed. *R. v. Waugh*, (1909) V.L.R., 379; 31 A.L.T., 37; 15 A.L.R., 366.

Ellison v. Ivanhoe Gold Mining Co., No Liability, 23 V.L.R., 224; 19 A.L.T., 104; 3 A.L.R., 209, distinguished. *Manning v. Tewksbury Freehold Gold Dredging Co., No Liability*. (1908) V.L.R., 50; 29 A.L.T., 78; 13 A.L.R., 547.

Ely, Re; Tottenham v. Ely, 65 L.T., 452, distinguished. *In re Loughlin; Acheson v. O'Meara*, (1906) V.L.R., 597; 28 A.L.T., 28; 12 A.L.R., 411.

England, Ex parte; R. v. Templeton, 3 V.L.R. (L.), 305, followed. *Burvett v. Moody*, (1909) V.L.R., 126; 30 A.L.T., 160; 15 A.L.R., 91.

Equitable Life Assurance Society, Warnecke v., (1906) V.L.R., 482; 27 A.L.T., 236; 12 A.L.R., 254, approved. *National Mutual Life Association of Australasia Ltd. v. Godrich*, 10 C.L.R., 1; 16 A.L.R., 110.

Equity Trustees &c. Co., Wilkie v., (1909) V.L.R., 277; 30 A.L.T., 211; 15 A L.R., 208, followed. *Macartney v. Macartney*, 33 A.L.T., 183; 18 A.L.R., 1.

Evans v. Evans and Elford, (1906) P., 125, followed. *Mulder v. Mulder*, (1906) V.L.R., 388; 27 A.L.T., 216; 12 A.L.R., 210, and approved. *McRae v. McRae*, (1906) V.L.R., 778; 28 A.L.T., 90; 14 A.L.R., 479.

Evans v. Sneddon, 28 V.L.R., 396; 24 A.L.T., 79; 8 A.L.R., 215, explained. *Smith v. Chisholm*, (1908) V.L.R., 579; 30 A.L.T., 48; 14 A.L.R., 471.

Eyre v. Cox, 24 W.R., 317, not followed. *Cameron v. Cameron*, (1906) V.L.R., 13; 28 A.L.T., 169; 13 A.L.R., 10.

D

Falkner v. Cooper, Carter's Cases, 55, followed. *Chomley v. Watson,* (1907) V.L.R., 502; 29 A.L.T., 46; 13 A.L.R., 380

Farrer v. Lowe, 5 T.L.R., 234, followed. *Ronald v. Harper,* (1908) V.L.R., 674; 30 A.L.T., 72; 14 A.L.R., 472.

Feary, Vestry of St. James and St. John v., 24 Q.B.D., 703, distinguished. *Bremner v. New Normanby Quartz Mining Co., No Liability,* (1910) V.L.R., 72; 31 A.L.T., 140; 16 A.L.R., 25.

Fellows, Re, 5 V.L.R. (I. P. & M.), 82; 1 A.L.T., 53, followed. *In re Winter; Winter-Irving v. Winter,* (1907) V.L.R., 546; 29 A.L.T., 4; 13 A.L.R., 298.

Fenessy, In re, 8 A.L.R., 211 (n), distinguished. *Ex parte Edmonds and Harrison,* 34 A.L.T., 105; 18 A.L.R., 41.

Fenton v. Nevin, 31 L.R. Ir., 478, followed. *In re Lewis; Gollan v. Pyle,* 29 A.L.T., 36; 13 A.L.R., 431.

Ferne, Doyle v., 25 V.L.R., 291; 5 A.L.R. (C.N.), 93, followed. *Harney v. Huntley, President &c. of Shire of,* (1910) V.L.R., 455; 32 A.L.T., 82; 16 A.L.R., 582.

Field, In re, 21 V.L.R., 278; 16 A.L.T., 162; 1 A.L.R., 26, followed. *In re Hamilton,* 28 A.L.T., 124; 12 A.L.R., 523.

Firkins v. Firkins, 23 A.L.T., 122; 4 A.L.R., 74, over-ruled. *Forster v. Forster,* (1907) V.L.R., 159; 28 A.L.T., 144; 13 A.L.R., 33.

Fisher v. Clark, 2 A.L.R. (C.N.), 321, considered. *Russ v. Carr,* (1909) V.L.R., 78; 30 A.L.T., 131; 15 A.L.R., 24.

Fitzgerald, R. v., 15 V.L.R., 40; 10 A.L.T., 241, followed. *Rex v. Turnbull,* (1907) V.L.R., 11; 28 A.L.T., 103; 12 A.L.R., 551.

Fletcher, Rylands v., L.R., 3 H.L., 330, distinguished. *Rickards v. Lothian,* (1913) A.C., 263.

Flood, Allen v., (1898) A.C., 1, followed. *Bond v. Morris,* (1912) V.L.R., 351; 34 A.L.T., 52; 18 A.L.R., 348.

Foley v. Monaghan, 14 A.L.T., 240, discussed. *Adams v. Rogers,* (1907) V.L.R., 245; 28 A.L.T., 180; 13 A.L.R., 71.

Folk, In re, 6 W.W. & A'B. (Eq.), 171, disapproved. *In re Tong,* (1907) V.L.R., 338; 28 A.L.T., 200; 13 A.L.R., 199.

Foulkes, Re, (1909) V.L.R., 76; 30 A.L.T., 108; 14 A.L.R., 729, followed. *Re Garrett; Smith v. Garrett,* (1910) V.L.R., 287; 31 A.L.T., 203; 16 A.L.R., 215.

Fraser, Amos v., 4 C.L.R., 78; 12 A.L.R., 481, considered. *Lever Brothers Ltd. v. G. Mowling & Son,* 30 A.L.T., 144; 15 A.L.R., 40.

Fraser, In re; Lowther v. Fraser, (1904) 1 Ch., 726, followed. *In re Stead,* (1908) V.L.R., 10; 29 A.L.T., 155; 13 A.L.R., 683.

Friendly Society of Operative Stonemasons, Read v., (1902) 2 K.B., 732, distinguished. *Bond v. Morris,* (1912) V.L.R., 351; 34 A..L.T., 52; 18 A.L.R., 348.

Frost, In re, 43 Ch. D., 246, followed. *In re Malin; National Trustees &c. Co. v. Loughnan,* (1912) V.L.R., 259; 34 A.L.T., 30; 18 A.L.R., 274.

Fylde Waterworks Co., Chapman v., (1894) 2 Q.B., 599, followed. *Frencham v. Melbourne and Metropolitan Board of Works,* (1911) V.L.R., 363; 33 A.L.T., 30; 17 A.L.R., 333

Gaffee, Re, 1 Mac. & G., 541, discussed. *Trustees Executors and Agency Co. Ltd. v. Webster,* (1907) V.L.R., 318; 28 A.L.T., 225; 13 A.L.R., 188.

Gates v. R. Bell & Son, (1902) 2 K.B., 38, distinguished. *McKinnon v. Gange,* (1910) V.L.R., 32; 31 A.L.T., 112; 15 A.L.R., 640.

Gibson, R. v., 18 Q.B.D., 537, considered. *Knox v. Bible,* (1907) V.L.R., 485; 29 A.L.T., 23; 13 A.L.R., 352.

Gilbert, In re; Gilbert v. Huddlestone, 28 Ch. D., 549, applied. *Alexander Ferguson & Co. v. Daniel Crawford & Co.,* 10 C.L.R., 207.

Gilbert, Cutts v., 9 Moo. P.C.C., 131, considered. *Gair v. Bowers,* 9 C.L.R., 510; 15 A.L.R., 494.

Glamorgan Coal Co., South Wales Miners' Federation v., (1905) A.C., 239, distinguished. *Bond v. Morris,* (1912) V.L.R., 351; 34 A.L.T., 52; 18 A.L.R., 348.

Goddard, Robins v., (1905) 1 K.B., 294, distinguished. *Briscoe & Co. v. Victorian Railways Commissioners,* (1907) V.L.R., 523 29 A.L.T., 17 ; 13 A.L.R., 308.

Goldsmith v. Sands, 4 C.L.R., 1648 ; 13 A.L.R., 601, applied. *Moule v. Moule,* 13 C.L.R., 267 ; 17 A.L.R., 446.

Goode, Cork and Bandon Railway v., 13 C.B., 826, distinguished. *Land Mortgage Bank of Victoria Ltd. v. Reid,* (1909) V.L.R., 284 ; 31 A.L.T., 9 ; 15 A.L.R., 234.

Goodman's Trust, In re, 6 V.L.R. (E.), 181, followed. *In re Connell,* (1910) V.L R., 471 ; 32 A.L.T., 83 ; 16 A.L.R., 504.

Goodyear v. Mayor, &c. of Weymouth, 35 L.J. N.S. C.P., 12, discussed and applied. *Briscoe & Co. v. Victorian Railways Commissioners,* (1907) V.L.R., 523 ; 29 A.L.T., 17 ; 13 A.L.R., 308.

Gossling, In re, (1902) 1 Ch., 945 ; (1903) 1 Ch., 448, applied. *In re Munro ; National Trustees Executors &c. Co. of Australasia Ltd. v. Dunbar,* (1910) V.L.R., 395 ; 32 A.L.T., 41 ; 16 A.L.R., 363.

Gower v. Andrew, 43 Am. R., 242, approved. *Prebble v. Reeves,* (1910) V.L.R., 88 ; 31 A.L.T., 114 ; 15 A.L.R., 631.

Graham, In re, (1910) V.L.R., 466 ; 32 A.L.T., 68 ; 16 A.L.R., 512, followed. *In re Martin,* (1912) V.L.R., 206 ; 34 A.L.T., 1 ; 18 A.L.R., 216.

Graves v. Panam, (1905) V.L.R., 297 ; 26 A.L.T., 232 ; 11 A.L.R., 180, discussed. *Graham v. Matoorekos,* (1907) V.L.R., 270 ; 28 A.L.T., 173 ; 13 A.L.R., 113.

Great Northern Ry. Co., Harwood v., 11 H.L.C., 654, applied. *Linotype Co. Ltd. v. Mounsey,* 9 C.L.R., 194 ; 15 A.L.R., 310.

Greatorex v. Shackle, (1895) 2 Q.B., 249, followed. *Looker v. Mercer,* 28 A.L.T. (Supplement), 15 ; 13 A.L.R. (C.N.), 13.

Green, Grescot v., 1 Salk, 198, followed. *Renshaw v. Maher,* (1907) V.L.R., 520 ; 29 A.L.T., 237 ; 13 A.L.R., 265.

Grescot v. Green, 1 Salk., 198, followed. *Renshaw v. Maher,* (1907) V.L.R., 520 ; 29 A.L.T., 237 ; 13 A.L.R., 265.

Grumley v. Webb, 100 Am. Dec., 304, approved. *Prebble v. Reeves,* (1910) V.L.R., 88 ; 31 A.L.T., 114 ; 15 A.L.R., 631.

Gyngall, R. v., (1893) 2 Q.B., 232, considered and applied. *Goldsmith v. Sands,* 4 C.L.R., 1648 ; 13 A.L.R., 601, explained. *The King v. Lennie ; The King v. Mackenzie,* 29 A.L.T. 56 ; 13 A.L.R., 505.

Hambrough v. Mutual Life &c. of New York, 72 L.T., 141, disapproved. *Dalgety & Co. Ltd. v. Australian Mutual Provident Society,* (1908) V.L.R., 481 ; 30 A.L.T., 4 ; 14 A.L.R., 299.

Hamlin, Davis v., 48 Am. R., 541, approved. *Prebble v. Reeves,* (1910) V.L.R., 88 ; 31 A.L.T., 114 ; 15 A.L.R., 631.

Hancock v. Watson, (1902) A.C., 14, at p. 22, applied. *In re Watson ; Cain v. Watson,* (1910) V.L.R., 256 ; 31 A.L.T., 212 ; 16 A.L.R., 76.

Handley v. London Edinburgh and Glasgow Assurance Co., (1902) 1 K.B., 350, commented on. *Armstrong v. Great Southern G. M. Co. No Liability,* 12 C.L.R., 382 ; 17 A.L.R., 377.

Harford, Neilson v., 1 Web. Pat. Cas., 295, distinguished. *Gillies v. Hartnett Patent Milking Machine Co. Ltd.,* 31 A.L.T., 164 ; 16 A.L.R., 88.

Harrison San Miguel & Co. v. Maddern, (1905) V.L.R., 400 ; 26 A.L.T., 215 ; 11 A.L.R., 178, over-ruled. *The King v. Beecham ; Ex parte Cameron,* (1910) V.L.R., 204 ; 31 A.L.T., 183 ; 16 A.L.R., 173.

Harter v. Harter, L.R. 3 P. & D., 11, applied. *In re Green ; Crowson v. Wild,* (1907) V.L.R., 284 ; 28 A.L.T., 206 ; 13 A.L.R., 121.

Harwood v. Great Northern Ry. Co., 11 H.L.C., 654, applied. *Linotype Co. Ltd. v. Mounsey,* 9 C.L.R., 194 ; 15 A.L.R., 310.

Hastings Pier Co., Laidlaw v. (referred to in Hudson on Building Contracts), discussed and applied. *Briscoe & Co. v. Victorian Railways Commissioners,* (1907) V.L.R., 523 ; 29 A.L.T., 17 ; 13 A.L.R., 308.

Hayes, Heffernan v., 25 V.L.R., 156 ; 21 A.L.T., 118 ; 5 A.L.R., 269, followed. *Wilson v. Dun's Gazette,* (1912) V.L.R., 342 ; 34 A.L.T., 77 ; 18 A.L.R., 327.

Hayward, In re, 19 Ch. D., 470, distinguished. *In re Gleeson,* (1910) V.L.R., 181 ; 31 A.L.T., 194 ; 16 A.L.R., 143.

Hearne, Ward v., 10 V.L.R. (L.), 163 ; 6 A.L.T., 49, explained. *The King v. Watt ; Ex parte Slade,* (1912) V.L.R., 225 ; 33 A.L.T., 222 ; 18 A.L.R., 158.

Hedley's Trusts, In re, 25 W.R., 529, distinguished. *In re Vickers,* (1912) V.L.R., 385 ; 34 A.L.T., 133 ; 18 A.L.R., 521.

Heffernan v. Hayes, 25 V.L.R., 156 ; 21 A.L.T., 118 ; 5 A.L.R., 269, followed. *Wilson v. Dun's Gazette,* (1912) V.L.R., 342 ; 34 A.L.T., 77 ; 18 A.L.R., 327.

Hensler, R. v., 11 Cox, 573, discussed. *R. v. Waugh,* (1909) V.L.R., 379 ; 31 A.L.T., 37 ; 15 A.L.R., 366.

Henty, Barker v., 29 V.L.R., 293 ; 25 A.L.T., 34 ; 9 A.L.R., 160, distinguished. *Annear v. Inskip,* (1910) V.L.R., 235 ; 31 A.L.T., 220 ; 16 A.L.R., 276.

Hernaman, Tucker v., 1 Sm. & G., 394 ; 4 DeG. M. & G., 395, followed. *In re Poole,* 31 A.L.T. (Supplement) ; 13 ; 15 A.L.R. (C.N.), 25.

Heward v. The King, 3 C.L.R., 117 ; 11 A.L.R., 494, followed. *In re Draper ; Graham v. Draper,* (1910) V.L.R., 376 ; 32 A.L.T., 34 ; 16 A.L.R., 370.

Heywood, Justices of, Regina v., 21 V.L.R., 654 ; 17 A.L.T., 238, distinguished. *Richards v. Jager,* (1909) V.L.R., 140 ; 30 A.L.T., 163 ; 15 A.L.R., 119.

Hickling v. Todd, 15 V.L.R., 154 ; 10 A.L.T., 236, followed. *In re Stamps Acts,* (1906) V.L.R., 364 ; 27 A.L.T., 204 ; 12 A.L.R., 186.

Higgins v. Dawson, (1902) A.C., 1, applied. *In re Longley ; Reid v. Silk,* (1906), V.L.R., 641 ; 28 A.L.T., 82 ; 12 A.L.R., 499.

Hill v. Hill, 19 V.L.R., 187 ; 14 A.L.T., 269, distinguished. *Buttle v. Hart,* (1906) V.L.R., 195 ; 27 A.L.T., 184 ; 12 A.L.R. (C.N.), 5, and *Goodman v. Jonas,* (1909) V.L.R., 308 ; 31 A.L.T., 16 ; 15 A.L.R., 308.

Hinds, Quan Yick v., 2 C.L.R., 345 ; 11 A.L.R., 223, considered. *Ex parte Dunn ;*

Ex parte Aspinall, (1906) V.L.R., 584 ; 28 A.L.T., 72 ; 12 A.L.R., 418.

Hingeston v. Sidney ; In re Sidney, (1908) 1 Ch., 126, 488, distinguished. *In re Wallace ; Trustees Executors and Agency Co. Ltd. v. Fatt,* (1908) V.L.R., 636 ; 30 A.L.T., 100 ; 14 A.L.R., 502.

Ho-a-Mie v. Ho-a-Mie, 6 V.L.R. (I. P. & M.), 113, over-ruled. *Forster v. Forster,* (1907) V.L.R., 159 ; 28 A.L.T., 144 ; 13 A.L.R., 33.

Hohenzollern, Re, and City of London Corporation, 54 L.T. N.S., 596, distinguished. *Briscoe & Co. v. Victorian Railways Commissioners,* (1907) V.L.R., 523 ; 29 A.L.T., 17 ; 13 A.L.R., 308.

Holford v. Melbourne Tramway and Omnibus Co. Ltd., (1909) V.L.R., 497 ; 29 A.L.T., 112 ; 13 A.L.R., at p. 677, doubted. *Armstrong v. Great Southern G.M. Co., No. Liability,* 12 C.L.R., 382 ; 17 A.L.R., 377.

Hollingsworth, Banks v., (1893) 1 Q.B., 442, followed. *Ronald v. Harper,* (1908) V.L.R., 674 ; 30 A.L.T., 72 ; 14 A.L.R., 472,

Hollingworth, Permezel v., (1905) V.L.R., 321 ; 26 A.L.T., 213 ; 11 A.L.R., 217, followed. *In re Ralston ; Perpetual Executors and Trustees Association v. Ralston,* (1906) V.L.R., 689 ; 28 A.L.T., 45 ; 12 A.L.R., 365, distinguished. *Cattanach v. Macpherson,* (1908) V.L.R., 390 ; 29 A.L.T., 259 ; 14 A.L.R., 214.

Hooper, Attorney-General v., (1893) 3 Ch., 483, distinguished. *Bremner v. New Normanby Quartz Mining Co., No Liability,* (1910) V.L.R., 72 ; 31 A.L.T., 140 ; 16 A.L.R., 25.

Hosken, Marriott v., (1911) V.L.R., 54 ; 32 A.L.T., 115 ; 16 A.L.R., 604, explained. *Lambourn v. Hosken,* (1912) V.L.R., 394 ; 34 A.L.T., 101 ; 18 A.L.R., 371.

Hosken, Perpetual Executors and Trustees Association of Australia v., 14 C.L.R., 286 ; 18 A.L.R., 201, followed. *Mahoney v. Hosken,* 14 C.L.R., 379 ; 18 A.L.R., 205.

Hotchkys, In re, 32 Ch. D., 408, followed. *In re Tong,* (1907) V.L.R., 338 ; 28 A.L.T., 200 ; 13 A.L.R., 119.

Howard v. Jones, 18 V.L.R., 578; 14 A.L.T., 106, distinguished. *Davis* v. *Davis and Hattrick,* (1912) V.L.R., 427; 34 A.L.T., 66; 18 A.L.R., 398.

Howell, Re, (1906) V.L.R., 223; 27 A.L.T., 172; 12 A.L.R., 92, over-ruled. *In re Winter; Winter-Irving* v. *Winter,* (1907) V.L.R., 546; 29 A.L.T., 4; 13 A.L.R., 298.

Huddlestone, Gilbert v.; In re Gilbert, 28 Ch. D., 549, applied. *Alexander Ferguson & Co.* v. *Daniel Crawford & Co.,* 10 C.L.R., 207.

Huguenin v. Baseley, 14 Ves., 273, considered. *Union Bank of Australia Ltd.* v. *Whitelaw,* (1906) V.L.R., 711; 28 A.L.T., 17; 12 A.L.R., 393.

Hunt, Wilkie v., 1 W.W. & a'B. (L.), 66, distinguished. *Bruton* v. *Farm and Dairy Machinery Co. Proprietary Ltd.,* (1910) V.L.R., 196; 31 A.L.T., 200; 16 A.L.R., 241.

Hutchinson, Re, 32 W.R., 392, approved and applied. *In re Winter; Winter-Irving* v. *Winter,* (1908) V.L.R., 74; 29 A.L.T., 144; 13 A.L.R., 701.

Huxley and Walsh, R. v., 8 V.L.R. (L.), 15; 3 A.L.T., 96, followed. *McLiney* v. *Minster,* (1911) V.L R , 347; 33 A.L.T., 33; 17 A.L.R., 336.

Income Tax Acts, In re, 28 V.L.R., 203; 24 A.L.T., 38; 8 A.L.R., 157, approved. *In re Income Tax Acts; The Seven Hills Estate Company's Case,* (1906) V.L.R., 225; 27 A.L.T., 175; 12 A.L.R., 188.

Income Tax Acts, In re; Hydraulic Company's Case, (1905) V.L.R., 185; 26 A.L.T., 177; 11 A.L.R., 65, commented on. *Re Income Tax Acts,* (1907) V.L.R., 327; 28 A.L.T., 196; 13 A.L.R., 154.

Income Tax Act 1902, In re, Queensland S.R. (1904), 57, distinguished. *Re Income Tax Acts,* (1907) V.L.R., 358; 28 A.L.T., 215; 13 A.L.R., 151.

Inman, In re, (1893) 3 Ch., 518, followed. *In re Thompson; Brahe* v. *Mason,* (1910) V.L.R., 251; 31 A.L.T., 210; 16 A.L.R., 215

International Harvester Co. of America v. Mullavey, (1906) V.L.R., 659; 28 A.L.T., 51; 12 A.L.T., 380, approved. *Colonial Bank of Australasia Ltd.* v. *Martin,* (1912) V.L.R., 383; 34 A.L.T., 47; 18 A.L.R., 325.

Ivanhoe Gold Mining Co., No Liability, Ellison v., 23 V.L.R., 224; 19 A.L.T., 104; 3 A.L.R., 209, distinguished. *Manning* v. *Tewksbury Freehold Gold Dredging Co., No Liability,* (1908) V.L.R., 50; 29 A.L.T., 78; 13 A.L.R., 547.

Ivey, Thomas v., 13 A.L.T., 190, distinguished. *Riely* v. *Biggs,* 28 A.L.T. (Supplement), 11; 13 A.L.R. (C.N.), 5.

Jackson v. Napper, 35 Ch. D., 162, at p. 172, cited and approved. *Equity Trustees Executors and Agency Co. Ltd.* v. *Harston,* (1908) V.L.R., 23; 29 A.L.T., 131; 13 A.L.R., 686.

Jager, Richards v., (1909) V.L.R., 140; 30 A.L.T., 163; 15 A.L.R., 119, approved. *Swinburne* v. *David Syme & Co.,* (1909) V.L.R., 550; 31 A.L.T., 81; 15 A.L.R., 579.

James, In re, 13 V.L.R., 154, followed. *In re Moriarty,* (1907) V.L.R., 315; 29 A.L.T., 65; 13 A.L.R., 307.

James Gillespie & Co. Ltd. v. Reid, (1905) V.L.R., 101; 26 A.L.T., 154; 11 A.L.R., 12, considered. *Land Mortgage Bank of Victoria Ltd.* v. *Reid,* (1909) V.L.R., 284; 31 A.L.T., 9; 15 A.L.R., 234.

Jeffryes, Smith v., 15 M. & W., 561, distinguished. *Bruton* v. *Farm and Dairy Machinery Co. Proprietary Ltd.* (1910) V.L.R., 196; 31 A.L.T., 200; 16 A.L.R., 241.

Jenkins, Alexander v., (1892) 1 Q.B., 571, considered. *Livingston* v. *McCartin,* (1907) V.L.R., 48; 28 A.L.T., 131; 12 A.L.R., 524.

Jenner, Trustees Executors and Agency Co. v., 22 V.L.R., 584; 18 A.L.T., 255; 3 A.L.R., 138, followed. *England* v. *Bayles,* (1906) V.L.R., 94; 27 A.L.T., 181; 12 A.L.R., 122.

Jewell v. Jewell, 2 W. & W. (I.E. & M.), 136, distinguished. *Maddock* v. *Maddock,* (1911) V.L.R., 127; 32 A.L.T., 124; 17 A.L.R., 66.

Jewry v. Busk, 5 Taunt, 302, distinguished. *Griffith* v. *O'Donoghue*, (1906) V.L.R., 548; 28 A.L.T., 31; 12 A.L.R., 357.

Jones, Howard v., 18 V.L.R., 578; 14 A.L.T., 106, distinguished. *Davis* v. *Davis and Hattrick*, (1912) V.L.R., 427; 34 A.L.T., 66; 18 A.L.R., 398.

Jope, Trustees Executors &c. Co. v., 27 V.L.R., 706; 24 A.L.T., 30; 8 A.L.R. (C.N.), 21, followed. *In re Tong*, (1907) V.L.R., 338; 28 A.L.T., 200; 13 A.L.R., 119.

Joske, Stiggants v., 12 C.L.R., 549; 17 A.L.R., 526, discussed and applied. *Joske* v. *Strutt*, (1912) V.L.R., 118; 33 A.L.T., 189; 18 A.L.R., 84. Also, explained, 14 C.L.R., 180; 18 A.L.R., at p. 90.

Joske v. Strutt, (1912) V.L.R., 110; 33 A.L.T., 189; 18 A.L.R., 84, not followed. *Joske* v. *Blitz*, (1912) V.L.R., 256; 34 A.L.T., 15; 18 A.L.R., 352.

Justices of the County of London and the London County Council, R. v., (1893) 2 Q.B., 476, followed. *Mooney* v. *Anderson*, (1907) V.L.R., 623; 29 A.L.T., 42; 13 A.L.R., 471.

Kay v. Kay, (1904) P., 382, at p. 397, followed and applied. *Garrick* v. *Garrick*; *Sutton, co-respondent*, (1908) V.L.R., 420; 30 A.L.T., 21; 14 A.L.R., 312.

Keates v. Woodward, (1902) 1 K.B., 532, followed. *Harrison San Miguel Proprietary Ltd.* v. *Alfred Lawrence & Co.*, (1912) V.L.R., 367; 34 A.L.T., 88; 18 A.L.R., 394.

Keighley, Maxsted &c. Co., Re, (1893) 1 Q.B., 405, followed. *In re Bennett Brothers*, (1910) V.L.R., 51; 31 A.L.T., 148; 16 A.L.R., 30.

Kelly, Biggs v., 24 V.L.R., 402; 20 A.L.T., 105; 4 A.L.R., 153, distinguished. *Annear* v. *Inskip*, (1910) V.L.R., 235; 31 A.L.T., 220; 16 A.L.R., 276.

Kelly v. Lonsdale, (1906) 2 K.B., 486, distinguished. *Rider* v. *Dunn*, (1908) V.L.R., 377; 29 A.L.T., 279; 14 A.L.R., 245.

Kempton Park Racecourse Co. Ltd., Powell v., (1899) A.C., 143, followed as to " user." *McCann* v. *Morgan*, (1912) V.L.R., 303; 34 A.L.T., 43; 18 A.L.R., 334.

Kennedy v. DeTrafford, (1897) A.C., 180, followed. *Pendlebury* v. *Colonial Mutual &c. Society Ltd.*, 13 C.L.R., 676; 18 A.L.R., 124.

Kennedy v. Miller, 4 W.W. & A'B. (L.), 255, followed. *Equity Trustees Executors and Agency Co. Ltd.* v. *Harston*, (1908) V.L.R., 23; 29 A.L.T., 131; 13 A.L.R., 686.

Kennedy v. Purser, 23 V.L.R., 530; 19 A.L.T., 192; 4 A.L.R., 54, followed. *O'Donnell* v. *McKelvie*, (1906) V.L.R., 207; 27 A.L.T., 164; 12 A.L.R., 39.

Kickham v. The Queen, 8 V.L.R. (E.), 1 6; 3 A.L.T., 86, followed. *The King* v. *Dale*, (1906) V.L.R., 662; 28 A.L.T., 140; 12 A.L.R., 549.

King, The v. Barger, 6 C.L.R., 41; 14 A.L.R., 374, applied. *Huddart Parker & Co. Proprietary Ltd.* v. *Moorehead*; *Appleton* v. *Moorehead*, 8 C.L.R., 330; 15 A.L.R., 241.

King, The v. Beecham & Co., (1910) V.L.R., 204; 31 A.L.T., 183; 16 A.L.R., 173, applied. *Annear* v. *Inskip*, (1910) V.L.R., 235; 31 A.L.T., 220; 16 A.L.R., 276.

King, The, Heward v., 3 C.L.R., 117; 11 A.L.R., 494, followed. *In re Draper*; *Graham* v. *Draper*, (1910) V.L.R., 376; 32 A.L.T., 34; 16 A.L.R., 370.

King, The, Trainer v., 4 C.L.R., 156; 13, A.L.R., 53, discussed. *R.* v. *Schiffman*, (1910) V.L.R., 348; 32 A.L.T., 28; 16 A.L.R., 346.

King, Brown & Co., Anglo-American Brush Electric Light Corporation v., (1892) A.C., 367, applied. *N. Guthridge Ltd.* v. *Wilfley Ore Concentrator Syndicate Ltd.*, 3 C.L.R., 583; 12 A.L.R., 398.

King, Toronto Ry. Co. v., (1908) A.C., 260, distinguished. *Fraser* v. *Victorian Railways Commissioners*, 8 C.L.R., 54; 15 A.L.R., 93.

King, Weekes v., 15 Cox C.C., 733, followed. *Rider* v. *M'Kell*, (1908) V.L.R., 110; 29 A.L.T., 77; 13 A.L.R., 513.

Kingsbury v. Walter, (1901) A.C., 187, distinguished. *In re Jones*; *Harris* v. *Jones*, (1910) V.L.R., 306; 32 A.L.T., 3; 16 A.L.R., 266.

Knapp's Settlement, In re ; Knapp v. Vassall, (1895) 1 Ch., 91, plan of distribution adopted. *In re Hobson ; Hobson v. Sharp,* (1907) V.L.R., 724 ; 29 A.L.T., 125 ; 13 A.L.R., 703.

Knox v. Bible, (1907) V.L.R., 485 ; 29 A.L.T., 23 ; 13 A.L.R., 352, approved. *Macmanamny v. King,* (1907) V.L.R., 535 ; 28 A.L.T., 250 ; 13 A.L.R., 258.

Laidlaw v. Hastings Pier Co. (referred to in Hudson on Building Contracts), discussed and applied. *Briscoe & Co. v. Victorian Railways Commissioners,* (1907) V.L.R., 523 ; 29 A.L.T., 17 ; 13 A.L.R., 308.

Lambe v. Eames, L.R. 6 Ch., 597, followed. *In re Lawn ; Ballarat Trustees &c. Co. v. Perry,* (1911) V.L.R., 318 ; 33 A.L.T., 25 ; 17 A.L.R., 311.

Lawrence, Brand v., 1 Q.B.D., 344, followed. *L. Osborn & Co. Ltd. v. Davidson Brothers,* (1911) V.L.R., 416 ; 33 A.L.T., 66 ; 17 A.L.R., 448.

Leapingwell, Page v., 18 Ves., 463, distinguished. *a'Beckett v. Trustees Executors &c. Co. Ltd.,* 5 C.L.R., 512.

Le Cocq, Cundy v., 13 Q.B.D., 207, followed. *Davies v. Young,* (1910) V.L.R., 369 ; 32 A.L.T., 39 ; 16 A.L.R., 368.

Lee, Re, 28 V.L.R., 510 ; 22 A.L.T., 117 ; 6 A.L.R., 235, approved. *In re Howell,* (1906) V.L.R., 223 ; 27 A.L.T., 172 ; 12 A.L.R., 29.

Lehane, Trent Brewery v., 21 V.L.R., 283 ; 1 A.L.R., 89, followed. *Sack v. Wolstencroft,* 29 A.L.T., 85 ; 13 A.L.R., 588.

Le Mesurier v. Le Mesurier, (1895) A.C., 517, followed. *Forster v. Forster,* (1907) V.L.R., 159 ; 28 A.L.T., 144 ; 13 A.L.R., 33.

Lester v. Torrens, 2 Q.B.D., 403, followed. *McKinnon v. Colborne,* (1911) V.L.R., 486 ; 33 A.L.T., 117 ; 17 A.L.R., 524.

Lindley, Porteous v., 28 V.L.R., 606 ; 24 A.L.T., 139 ; 9 A.L.R., 25, distinguished. *Annear v. Inskip,* (1910) V.L.R., 235 ; 31 A.L.T., 220 ; 16 A.L.R., 276.

Little, Bowden v., 4 C.L.R., 1364 ; 13 A.L.R., 689, followed. *H. Beecham & Co. v.*

R. W. Cameron & Co., (1910) V.L.R., 19 ; 31 A.L.T., 100 ; 15 A.L.R., 598.

Liverpool, Corporation of, Scott v., 3 DeG. & J., at p. 368, discussed and explained. *Briscoe & Co. v. Victorian Railways Commissioners,* (1907) V.L.R., 523 ; 29 A.L.T., 17 ; 13 A.L.R., 308.

Lockyer, Cowan & Sons v., 1 C.L.R., 460 ; 10 A.L.R. (C.N.), 63, distinguished. *Sargood Brothers v. Commonwealth,* 11 C.L.R., 258 ; 16 A.L.R., 483.

Logan v. Bank of Scotland (No. 2), (1906) 1 K.B., 141, considered and applied. *Maritime Insurance Co. Ltd. v. Geelong Harbour Trust Commissioners,* 6 C.L.R., 194 ; 14 A.L.R., 424.

Londesborough, Scholefield v., (1896) A.C., 514, followed. *Colonial Bank of Australasia v. Marshall,* (1906) A.C., 559.

London and Brighton Railway Co. v. Watson, 3 C.P.D., 429, followed. *Borsum v. Smith,* (1907) V.L.R., 72 ; 28 A.L.T., 89 ; 12 A.L.R., 495.

London and South-Western Ry. Co., Wakelin v., 12 App. Cas., 41, applied. *Fraser v. Victorian Railways Commissioners,* 8 C.L.R., 54 ; 15 A.L.R., 93.

London, Corporation of City of and Hohenzollern, Re, 54 L.T.N.S., 596, distinguished. *Briscoe & Co. v. Victorian Railways Commissioners,* (1907) V.L.R., 523 ; 29 A.L.T., 17 : 13 A.L.R., 308.

London &c. Discount Co. v. Drake, 6 C.B.N.S., 798, followed. *Armstrong v. Duke of Wellington G. M. Co. No Liability,* 3 C.L.R., 1028 : 12 A.L.R., 316.

London, Edinburgh and Glasgow Assurance Co., Handley v., (1902) 1 K.B., 350, commented on. *Armstrong v. Great Southern G.M. Co. N.L.,* 12 C.L.R., 382 ; 17 A.L.R., 377.

Long & Co., In re, 20 Q.B.D., 316, applied. *In re Nolan* (No. 1), 30 A.L.T. (Supplement), 1 ; 14 A.L.R. (C.N.), 21.

Lonsdale, Kelly v., (1906) 2 K.B., 486, distinguished. *Rider v. Dunn,* (1908) V.L.R., 377 ; 29 A.L.T., 279 ; 14 A.L.R., 245.

Loring, Millington v., 6 Q.B.D., 190, not followed. *Wilson* v. *Dun's Gazette,* (1912) V.L.R., 342 ; 34 A.L.T., 77 ; 18 A.L.R., 327.

Lowe, Farrer v., 5 T.L.R., 234, followed. *Ronald* v. *Harper,* (1908) V.L.R., 674 ; 30 A.L.T., 72 ; 14 A.L.R., 472

Lowther v. Fraser : In re Fraser, (1904) 1 Ch., 726, followed. *In re Stead,* (1908) V.L.R., 10 ; 29 A.L.T., 155 ; 13 A.L.R., 683.

Lyell, Ex parte : In re Premier Permanent Building Society, 25 V.L.R., 77 ; 21 A.L.T., 67 ; 5 A.L.R., 209, overruled. *Fink* v. *Robertson,* 4 C.L.R., 864 ; 13 A.L.R., 157.

MacGregor, Vinnicombe v., 29 V.L.R., 32 ; 28 V.L.R., 144 ; 24 A.L.T., 200 ; 24 A.L.T., 15 : 9 A.L.R., 60 ; 8 A.L.R., 141, discussed and disapproved. *Nelson* v. *Walker,* 10 C.L.R., 560 ; 16 A.L.R., 285.

MacDonough, Cohen v., (1906) V.L.R., 521 ; 28 A.L.T., 97 : 12 A.L.R., 447, dictum of *Cussen, J.,* disapproved. *Cohen* v. *Mac-Donough,* (1907) V.L.R., 7 ; 28 A.L.T., 119 ; 12 A.L.R., 566.

Macintosh v. Dun, (1908) A.C., 390, distinguished. *Howe* v. *Lees,* 11 C.L.R., 361 ; 16 A.L.R., 605.

Mackay, In re, 3 A.J.R., 10, discussed and distinguished. *In re Cooper,* 30 A.L.T. (Supplement), 13 ; 14 A.L.R. (C.N.), 43.

Macmanamny v. McCulloch (or McMahon), 18 A.L.T., 164 : 3 A.L.R., 14, approved. *Rogerson* v. *Phillips and O'Hagan,* (1906) V.L.R., 272 ; 27 A.L.T., 166 ; 12 A.I.R., 147.

MacPherson, Cussen v., 6 A.L.T., 205, followed. *Kelsey* v. *Caselberg,* (1909) V.L.R., 347 ; 31 A.L.T., 31 ; 15 A.L.R., 362.

McAlinden v. McAlinden, 11 Ir. R. Eq., 219, followed. *In re Lawn ; Ballarat Trustees &c. Co.* v. *Perry,* (1911) V.L.R., 318 ; 33 A.L.T., 25 ; 17 A.L.R., 311.

McCarthy, Connors v., 17 A.L.T., 187 ; 2 A.L.R., 10, discussed. *In re Lamrock, Brown and Hall's Costs,* (1908) V.L.R., 238 ; 29 A.L.T., 214 ; 14 A.L.R., 81.

M'Cormick, R. v., 4 V.L.R. (L.), 46, discussed. *Adams* v. *Rogers,* (1907) V.L.R., 245 ; 28 A.L.T., 180 ; 13 A.L.R., 71.

McCracken, Natonal Trustees Executors &c. Co. v., 19 A.L.T., 175 ; 4 A.L.R., 31, discussed. *In re Black ; Black* v. *Melbourne Hospital,* (1911) V.L.R., 280 ; 33 A.L.T., 2 ; 17 A.L.R., 240.

McCulloch (or McMahon), Macmanamny v., 18 A.L.T., 164 ; 3 A.L.R., 14, approved. *Rogerson* v. *Phillips and O'Hagan,* (1906) V.L.R., 272 ; 27 A.L.T., 166 ; 12 A.I.R., 147.

McCulloch v. Maryland, 4 Wheat., 316, approved and applied by majority of Court. Held, by *Higgins, J.,* inapplicable. *Baxter* v. *Commissioners of Taxation ; Flint* v. *Webb,* 4 C.L.R., 1087, 1178 ; 13 A.L.R., 313.

McGaw, In re, 4 N.S.W. S.R., 591, discussed and disapproved. *In re Moore ; Fanning* v. *Fanning,* (1907) V.L.R., 639 ; 29 A.L.T., 138 ; 13 A.L.R., 507.

McGee v. Wolfenden, (1907) V.L.R., 195 ; 28 A.L.T., 163 ; 13 A.L.R., 51, distinguished. *Biggs* v. *Lamley,* (1907) V.L.R., 300 : 28 A.L.T., 202 ; 13 A.L.R., 144.

McGinnis, Whiting v., (1909) V.L.R., 250 ; 30 A.L.T., 207 ; 15 A.L.R., 203, approved. *In re Rosenthal ; Rosenthal* v. *Rosenthal.* 11 C.L.R., 87 ; 16 A.L.R., 455.

McKenzie, Stephens v., 29 V.L.R., 652 ; 25 A.L.T., 239 ; 10 A.L.R., 106, approved. *Swinburne* v. *David Syme & Co.,* (1909) V.L.R., 550 ; 31 A.L.T., 81 ; 15 A.L.R., 579.

McKenzie, Thompson v., (1908) 1 K.B., at p. 908, dictum of Lord *Alverstone* approved. *McKinnon* v. *Colborne,* (1911) V.L.R., 486 ; 33 A.L.T., 117 ; 17 A.L.R., 524.

McKie v. McKie, 23 V.L.R., 489 ; 19 A.L.T., 190 ; 4 A.L.R., 98, followed. *Stuckey* v. *Trustees, Executors and Agency Co. Ltd.,* (1910) V.L.R., 55 ; 31 A.L.T., 157 ; 16 A.L.R., 65.

M'Kinley, Steele v., 5 A.C., 754, discussed. *Ferrier* v. *Stewart,* 15 C.L.R., 32 ; 18 A.L.R., 262.

Maddern, Harrison San Miguel & Co. v., (1905) V.L.R., 400 ; 26 A.L.T., 215 ; 11 A.L.R., 178, over-ruled. *The King* v. *Beecham ; Ex parte Cameron,* (1910) V.L.R., 204 ; 31 A.L.T., 183 ; 16 A.L.R., 173.

Mailes, In re, (1908) V.L.R., 269 ; 29 A.L.T., 263 ; 14 A.L.R., 181, explained. *In re Bennett,* (1909) V.L.R., 205 ; 30 A.L.T., 181 ; 15 A.L.R., 141.

Marks v. Pett, 10 V.L.R. (L.), 342, commented on. *Ambler & Co. Proprietary Ltd. v. Clayton,* (1909) V.L.R., 56 ; 30 A.L.T., 113 ; 14 A.L.R., 730

Marriott v. Hosken, (1911) V.L.R., 54 ; 32 A.L.T., 115 ; 16 A.L.R., 604, explained. *Lambourn v. Hosken,* (1912) V.L.R., 394 ; 34 A.L.T., 101 ; 18 A.L.R., 371.

Martin, In re, 2 A.L.T., 48, discussed. *In re Ross,* 31 A.L.T. (Supplement), 3 ; 15 A.L.R. (C.N.), 13.

Martin, Chia Gee v., 3 C.L.R., 649 ; 12 A.L.R., 425, discussed and distinguished. *Ah Sheung v. Lindberg,* (1906) V.L.R., 323 ; 27 A.L.T., 189 ; 12 A.L.R., 190.

Maryland, McCulloch v., 4 Wheat. 316, approved and applied by majority of Court. *Held,* by *Higgins,* J., inapplicable. *Baxter v. Commissioners of Taxation ; Flint v. Webb,* 4 C.L.R., 1087, 1178 ; 13 A.L.R., 313.

May v. Chidley, (1894) 1 Q.B., 451, followed. *Colonial Bank of Australia Ltd. v. Nicholl,* (1907) V.L.R., 402 ; 13 A.L.R., 297.

Maynard, Re, 12 V.L.R., 313, followed. *In re Hoarey,* (1906) V.L.R., 437 ; 28 A.L.T., 93 ; 12 A.L.R., 450.

Melbourne Tramway and Omnibus Co. Ltd., Holford v., (1909) V.L.R., 497 : 29 A.L.T., 112 : 13 A.L.R., at p. 677, doubted. *Armstrong v. Great Southern G. M. Co., No Liability,* 12 C.L.R , 382 : 17 A.L.R., 377.

Menzies, Betts v., 10 H.L.C., 117, applied. *N. Guthridge Ltd. v. Wilfley Ore Concentrator Syndicate Ltd.,* 3 C.L.R., 583 ; 12 A.L.R., 398.

Miller, Kennedy v., 4 W.W. & A'B. (L.), 255, followed. *Equity Trustees Executors and Agency Co. Ltd. v. Harston,* (1908) V.L.R., 23 ; 29 A.L.T., 131 ; 13 A.L.R., 686.

Millin, Re. 2 V.L.R. (I. P. & M.), 58, 86, explained. *In re Winter ; Winter-Irving v. Winter,* (1907) V.L.R., 546 ; 29 A.L.T., 4 ; 13 A.L.R., 298, approved. *In re Howell,* (1906) V.L.R., 223 ; 27 A.L.T., 172 ; 12 A.L.R., 29.

Millington v. Loring, 6 Q.B.D., 190, not followed. *Wilson v. Dun's Gazette,* (1912) V.L.R., 342 ; 34 A.L.T., 77 ; 18 A.L.R., 327.

Mills, Re, 58 L.T., 871, followed. *M'Donald v. Bank of Victoria,* (1906) V.L.R., 199 ; 27 A.L.T., 177 ; 12 A.L.R., 120.

Mills, R. v., 7 Cox C.C., 263, followed. *R. v. Perera,* (1907) V.L.R., 240 ; 28 A.L.T., 176 ; 13 A.L.R., 116

Mitchell v. Crawshaw, (1903) 1 K.B., 701, considered. *O'Connor v. Anderson,* (1909) V.L.R., 1 ; 30 A.L.T , 145 ; 15 A.L.R., 22.

Mitchell and Izard and the Governor of Ceylon, In re, 21 Q.B.D., 408, followed. *Re Freeman and Kempster,* (1909) V.L.R., 394 ; 31 A.L.T., 42 ; 15 A.L.R., 444.

Moffatt v. Collector of Imposts, 22 V.L.R., 164 ; 18 A.L.T., 144 ; 2 A.L.R., 255, approved. *Davidson v. Armytage,* 4 C.L.R., 205 : 12 A.L.R., 538.

Monaghan, Foley v., 14 A.L.T., 240, discussed. *Adams v. Rogers,* (1907) V.L.R., 245 : 28 A.L.T., 180 : 13 A.L.R., 71.

Monkton v. Attorney-General, 2 R. & My., 147, not followed. *In re Osmand : Bennett v. Booty,* (1908) V.L.R., 67 ; 29 A.L.T., 168 ; 13 A.L.R., 728. F.C., affirming *Cussen, J.,* (1906) V.L.R., 455 ; 27 A.L.T., 218 ; 12 A.L.R., 256.

Montgomery v. Ah Loey, 2 A.L.R., 207, distinguished. *English v. Potter,* (1908) V.L.R., 632 ; 30 A.L.T., 91 : 14 A.L.R., 559.

Mooney v. Still, (1909) V.L.R., 227 ; 30 A.L.T., 191 ; 15 A.L.R., 197, followed. *Mooney v. McKeand,* (1909) V.L.R., 294 ; 30 A.L.T., 225 ; 15 A.L.R., 280.

Moore, Bevan v., 24 V.L.R., 792 : 20 A.L.T., 238 ; 5 A.L.R., 100, explained. *McCallum v. Purvis,* (1906) V.L.R., 578 ; 28 A.L.T., 31 ; 12 A.L.R., 329.

Moore v. Moore, (1892) P., 382, applied. *Strong v. Strong,* (1910) V.L.R., 122 ; 31 A.L.T., 156 ; 16 A.L.R., 62.

Moore, R. v. ; Ex parte Myers, 10 V.L.R. (L.), 322 : 6 A.L.T., 151, followed. *Equity Trustees Executors and Agency Co. Ltd. v. Harston,* (1908) V.L.R., 23 ; 29 A.L.T., 131 ; 13 A.L.R., 686.

Morgan, In re, 24 Ch. D., 114, followed. *In re Cheke or Akehurst ; Cheke v. Hamilton,* (1910) V.L.R., 310 : 32 A.L.T., 5 ; 16 A.L.R., 246.

Morgan & Co. v. Windover & Co., 7 R.P.C., 131, applied. *Linotype Co. Ltd. v. Mounsey,* 9 C.L.R., 194 : 15 A.L.R., 310.

Morley, In re, (1895) 2 Ch., 738, followed. *Macartney v. Macartney,* 33 A.L.T., 183 ; 18 A.L.R., 1.

Morrice v. Morrice, 14 N.S.W.L.R. (Eq.), 211, followed. *In re Connell,* (1910) V.L.R., 471 ; 32 A.L.T., 83 : 16 A.L.R., 504

Morris, Abbott v., 24 A.L.T., 228 : 9 A.L.R., 96, not followed as to costs of trustee in regard to his commission. *Macartney v. Kesterson,* (1907) V.L.R., 226 ; 28 A.L.T., 170 ; 13 A.L.R., 14.

Moubray v. Riordan, 15 V.L.R., 354 ; 11 A.L.T., 19, followed. *Kelsey v. Caselberg,* (1909) V.L.R., 347 ; 31 A.L.T., 31 : 15 A.L.R., 362.

Moylan v. Nolan, 27 A.L.T. (Supplement), 16 ; 12 A.L.R. (C.N.), 13, approved. *Townsing v. Egan,* 29 A.L.T. (Supplement), 29 ; 14 A.L.R. (C.N.), 18.

Mullavey, International Harvester Co. of America v., (1906) V.L.R., 659 ; 28 A.L.T., 51 : 12 A.L.R., 380, approved. *Colonial Bank of Australasia Ltd. v. Martin,* (1912) V.L.R., 383 ; 34 A.L.T., 47 : 18 A.L.R., 325.

Murphy v. Ainslie, (1905) V.L.R., 350 ; 26 A.L.T., 202 ; 11 A.L.R., 163, applied. *In re Buckhurst : Equity Trustees Executors and Agency Co. v. Buckhurst,* (1907) V.L.R., 252 ; 28 A.L.T., 190 ; 13 A.L.R., 74. Also, *In re Staughton ; Oliver v. Staughton,* (1910) V.L.R., 415 ; 32 A.L.T., 63 ; 16 A.L.R., 443.

Municipal Corporation of Toronto v. Virgo, (1896) App. Cas., 88, followed. *Co-operative Brick Co. Proprietary Ltd. v. Hawthorn, Mayor &c. of City of,* 9 C.L.R., 301 ; 15 A.L.R., 479.

Muntz v. Smail, 8 C.L.R., 262 : 15 A.L.R., 162, discussed. *In re McConnell ; Macfarlane v. McDonald,* (1912) V.L.R., 102 ; 33 A.L.T., 195 ; 18 A.L.R., 90.

Murray, Ritchie v. : In re Ritchie, 28 V.L.R., 255 ; 24 A.L.T., 62 ; 8 A.L.R., 211, distinguished. *Ex parte Edmonds and Harrison,* 34 A.L.T., 105 : 18 A.L.R., 41.

Mutch, Rogers v., 10 Ch. D., 25, followed. *In re Thompson ; Brahe v. Mason,* (1910) V.L.R., 251 ; 31 A.L.T., 210 : 16 A.L.R., 266.

Mutual Life &c. of New York, Hambrough v., 72 L.T., 141, disapproved. *Dalgety & Co. Ltd. v. Australian Mutual Provident Society,* (1908) V.L.R., 481 ; 30 A.L.T., 4 ; 14 A.L.R., 299.

Myers, Ex parte ; R. v. Moore, 10 V.L.R. (L.), 322 ; 6 A.L.T., 151, followed. *Equity Trustees Executors and Agency Co. Ltd. v. Harston,* (1908) V.L.R., 23 ; 29 A.L.T., 131 ; 13 A.L.R., 686. .

Napper, Jackson v., 35 Ch. D., 162, at p. 172, cited and approved. *Equity Trustees Executors and Agency Co. Ltd. v. Harston,* (1908) V.L.R., 23 ; 29 A.L.T., 131 ; 13 A.L.R., 686.

National Trustees Executors &c. Co. v. McCracken, 19 A.L.T., 175 ; 4 A.L.R., 31, discussed. *In re Black ; Black v. Melbourne Hospital,* (1911) V.L.R., 280 ; 33 A.L.T., 2 ; 17 A.L.R., 240.

National Trustees Executors &c. Co. v. O'Hea, 29 V.L.R., 814 ; 25 A.L.T., 230 ; 10 A.L.R., 81, followed and applied. *In re Draper ; Graham v. Draper,* (1910) V.L.R., 376 ; 32 A.L.T., 34 ; 16 A.L.R., 370.

Naylor, Slattery v., 13 App. Cas., 446, distinguished. *Co-operative Brick Co. Proprietary Ltd. v. Hawthorn, Mayor, &c. of City of,* 9 C.L.R., 301 : 15 A.L.R., 479.

Neale, Pasquier v., (1902) 2 K.B., 287, observations of Lord *Alverstone* distinguished. *Mooney v. McKeand,* (1909) V.L.R., 294 ; 30 A.L.T., 225 ; 15 A.L.R., 280.

Neilson v. Harford, 1 Web. Pat. Cas., 295, distinguished. *Gillies v. Hartnett Patent Milking Co. Ltd.,* 31 A.L.T., 164 ; 16 A.L.R., 88.

Nevin, Fenton v., 31 L.R. Ir., 478, followed. *In re Lewis ; Gollan v. Pyle,* 29 A.L.T., 36 ; 13 A.L.R., 431.

New, In re, (1901) 2 Ch., 534, applied. *Fomsgard v. Fomsgard,* (1912) V.L.R., 209; 34 A.L.T., 11; 18 A.L.R., 220.

New Koh-i-noor Co. v. Williams, 13 V.L.R., 435; 8 A.L.T., 169, discussed. *In re Lamrock, Brown and Hall's Costs,* (1908) V.L.R., 238; 29 A.L.R., 214; 14 A.L.R., 81 .

Nicholl, Colonial Bank of Australia Ltd. v., (1907) V.L.R., 402; 28 A.L.T., 222; 13 A.L.R., 297, followed. *Australian Widows' Fund &c. Society Ltd. v. Story,* (1907) V.L.R., 594; 29 A.L.T., 110; 13 A.L.R., 588.

Nicholls, Shanahan v., 27 A.L.T. (Supplement), 8; 11 A.L.R. (C.N.), 65, followed. *Ambler & Co. Proprietary Ltd. v. Clayton,* 29 A.L.T. (Supplement), 28; 14 A.L.R. (C.N.), 17.

Nicholson, Sanderson v., (1906) V.L.R., 371; 27 A.L.T., 215; 12 A.L.R., 208, not followed. *Honeybone v. Glass,* (1908) V.L.R., 466; 30 A.L.T., 54; 14 A.L.R., 345.

Nolan, Moylan v., 27 A.L.T. (Supplement), 16; 12 A.L.R. (C.N.), 13, approved. *Townsing v. Egan,* 29 A.L.T. (Sup.); 29; 14 A.L.R. (C.N.), 18

Northcote, Skrymsher v., 1 Swanst., 566, distinguished. *In re Stead,* (1908) V.L.R., 10; 29 A.L.T., 155; 13 A.L.R., 683.

Norton, Re, 3 V.L.R. (I.P. & M.), 58, distinguished. *In re Ghillmetei,* (1907) V.L.R., 657; 29 A.L.T., 81; 13 A.L.R., 519.

O'Farrell v. Syme, 16 V.L.R., 422; 12 A.L.T., 11, approved. *Orchard v. Oriental Timber Corporation Ltd.,* (1910) V.L.R., 192; 31 A.L.T., 198; 16 A.L.R., 213.

Ogle v. Lord Sherborne : In re Whorwood, 34 Ch. D., 446, distinguished. *In re Loughlin ; Acheson v. O'Meara,* (1906) V.L.R., 597; 28 A.L.T., 28; 12 A.L.R., 411.

O'Grady, In re, 26 V.L.R., 171; 6 A.L.R., 162, followed. *In re Cavin,* (1906) V.L.R., 517; 28 A.L.T., 39; 12 A.L.R., 333.

O'Hea, National Trustees Executors &c. Co. v., 29 V.L.R., 814; 25 A.L.T., 230; 10 A.L.R., 81, followed and applied. *In re Draper ; Graham v. Draper,* (1910) V.L.R., 376; 32 A.L.T., 34; 16 A.L.R., 370.

O'Neill, In re, (1905) V.L.R., 64; 26 A.L.T., 108, discussed. *In re Nolan,* 33 A.L.T. (Supplement), 2; 17 A.L.R. (C.N.), 14

Ormerod, Paton v. · In re Bagot, (1893) 3 Ch., 548, followed. *In re Stead,* (1908) V.L.R., 10; 29 A.L.T., 155; 13 A.L.R., 683.

Ormiston, In re : Young v. Ormiston, 11 V.L.R., 285, followed. *In re Reed,* (1911) V.L.R., 232; 32 A.L.T., 168; 17 A.L.R., 164.

Osborne, Peacock v., 4 C.L.R., 1564; 13 A.L.R., 565, applied. *Bayne v. Blake,* 5 C.L.R., 497; 14 A.L.R., 103.

Osborne, R. v., (1905) 1 K.B., 551. Observations at p. 556 doubted by *Madden, C.J. R. v. McNeill,* (1907) V.L.R., 265; 28 A.L.T., 182; 13 A.L.R., 99.

Outtrim, Webb v., (1907) A.C., 81, not followed. *Baxter v. Commissioners of Taxation ; Flint v. Webb,* 4 C.L.R., 1087, 1178; 13 A.L.R., 313.

Page v. Leapingwell, 18 Ves. 463, distinguished. *a'Beckett v. Trustees Executors &c. Co. Ltd.,* 5 C.L.R., 512.

Palmer v. Bourke, 28 V.L.R., 275; 24 A.L.T., 11; 8 A.L.R., 151, distinguished. *Doig v. Keating,* (1908) V.L.R., 118; 29 A.L.T., 171; 14 A.L.R., 20.

Palmer v. Culverwell, Brooks & Co., 85 L.T., 758, applied by *Isaacs, J. Muntz v. Smail,* 8 C.L.R., 262; 15 A.L.R., 162.

Panam, Graves v., (1905) V.L.R., 297; 26 A.L.T., 232; 11 A.L.R., 180, distinguished. *Graham v. Matoorekos,* (1907) V.L.R., 270; 28 A.L.T., 173; 13 A.L.R., 113.

Papworth, Williams v. ,(1900) A.C., p. 566, followed. *In re Stevens ; Trustees Executors and Agency Co. Ltd. v. Teague,* (1912) V.L.R., 194; 33 A.L.T., 233; 18 A.L.R., 195.

Parke, R. v., (1903) 2 K.B., 432, discussed. *Packer v. Peacock,* 13 C.L.R., 577; 18 A.L.R., 70.

Parker, Suckling v., (1906) 1 K.B., 527, distinguished. *Gunner v. Payne,* (1908) V.L.R., 363; 29 A.L.T., 264; 14 A.L.R., 243

Parkin, R. v., 1 Mood. C.C., 45, approved. *David Syme & Co. v. Swinburne,* 10 C.L.R., 43 ; 16 A.L.R., 93.

Pasquier v. Neale, (1902) 2 K.B., 287, observations of Lord *Alverstone* distinguished. *Mooney v. McKeand,* (1909) V.L.R., 294 ; 30 A.L.T., 225 : 15 A.L.R., 280.

Paterson, British Homes Assurance Corporation v., (1902) 2 Ch., 404, distinguished. *Reid v. Silberberg,* (1906) V.L.R., 126

Paton v. Ormerod : In re Bagot, (1893) 3 Ch., 548, followed. *In re Stead,* (1908) V.L.R., 10 ; 29 A.L.T., 155 ; 13 A.L.R., 683.

Peacock v. Osborne, 4 C.L.R., 1564 ; 13 A.L.R., 565, applied. *Bayne v. Blake,* 5 C.L.R., 497 ; 14 A.L.R., 103.

Peatling v. Watson, (1909) V.L.R., 198 ; 30 A.L.T., 176 ; 15 A.L.R., 150, overruled. *Howe v. Lees,* 11 C.L.R., 361 ; 16 A.L.R., 605

Pedder, D'Emden v., 1 C.L.R., 91 ; 10 A.L.R. (C.N.), 30, application of considered. *Federated Engine-Drivers and Firemen's Association of Australasia v. Broken Hill Proprietary Co. Ltd.,* 12 C.L.R., 398 ; 17 A.L.R , 285

Perkes, Deeley v., 13 R.P.C., 581. followed on question of amendment. *Moore v. Phillips,* 4 C.L.R., 1411 ; 13 A.L.R., 424.

Permezel v. Hollingworth, (1905) V.L.R., 321 ; 26 A.L.T., 213 ; 11 A.L.R., 217, followed. *In re Ralston ; Perpetual Executors and Trustees Association v. Ralston,* (1906) V.L.R., 689 ; 28 A.L.T., 45 ; 12 A.L.R., 365, distinguished. *Cattanach v. Macpherson,* (1908) V.L.R., 390 ; 29 A.L.T., 259 : 14 A.L.R.. 214.

Perpetual Executors and Trustees Association of Australia v. Hosken, 14 C.L.R., 286 ; 18 A.L.R., 201, followed. *Mahoney v. Hosken,* 14 C.L.R., 379 ; 18 A.L.R., 205.

Peterswald v. Bartley, 1 C.L.R., 497, principles of interpretation applied. *Huddart Parker & Co. Proprietary Ltd. v. Moorehead ; Appleton v. Moorehead,* 8 C.L.R., 330 ; 15 A.L.R., 241.

Pett, Marks v., 10 V.L.R. (L.), 342, commented on. *Ambler & Co. Proprietary Ltd. v. Clayton,* (1909) V.L.R., 56 ; 30 A.L.T., 113 ; 14 A.L.R., 730.

Porteous v. Lindley, 28 V.L.R., 606 ; 24 A.L.T., 139 ; 9 A.L.R., 25, distinguished. *Annear v. Inskip,* (1910) V.L.R., 235 ; 31 A.L.T., 220 ; 16 A.L.R., 276.

Powell v. Kempton Park Racecourse Co. Ltd., (1899) A.C., 143, followed as to " user." *McCann v. Morgan,* (1912) V.L.R., 303 ; 34 A.L.T., 43 · 18 A.L.R., 334.

Power, In re, 26 A.L.T. (Supplement), 10 ; 11 A.L.R. (C.N.), 37, disapproved and not followed. *In re Alderman,* 28 A.L.T. (Supplement), 13 : 13 A.L.R. (C.N.), 6.

Premier Permanent Building Society, In re ; Ex parte Lyall, 25 V.L.R., 77 ; 21 A.L.T., 67 ; 5 A.L.R., 209, overruled. *Fink v. Robertson,* 4 C.L.R., 864 ; 13 A.L.R., 157.

Price v. Williamson · In re Williamson, 26 A.L.T., 91 ; 10 A.L.R., 197, distinguished. *In re Reed,* (1911) V.L.R., 232 ; 32 A.L.T., 168 ; 17 A.L.R., 164.

Prideaux, Sweeting v., 2 Ch. D., 413, distinguished. *In re Green ; Crowson v. Wild,* (1907) V.L.R., 284 ; 28 A.L.T., 206 : 13 A.L.R., 121.

Prior v. Sherwood, 3 C.L.R., 1054, followed as to "user." *McCann v. Morgan,* (1912) V.L.R., 303 ; 34 A.L.T., 43 ; 18 A.L.R., 334.

Public Trustee, The, Rathbone v., 24 L.R. N.Z., 801, distinguished. *Re Income Tax Acts,* (1907) V.L.R., 358 ; 28 A.L.T., 215 ; 13 A.L.R., 151.

Purser, Kennedy v., 23 V.L.R., 530 ; 19 A.L.T., 192 ; 4 A.L.R., 54, followed. *O'Donnell v. McKelvie,* (1906) V.L.R., 207 ; 27 A.L.T., 164 ; 12 A.L.R., 39.

Quan Yick v. Hinds, 2 C.L.R., 345 ; 11 A.L.R., 223, considered. *Ex parte Dunn ; Ex parte Aspinall,* (1906) V.L.R., 584 ; 28 A.L.T., 72 ; 12 A.L.R., 418.

Queensland National Bank, Barns v., 3 C.L.R., 925, followed. *Pendlebury v. Colonial Mutual &c. Society Ltd.,* 13 C.L.R., 676 ; 18 A.L.R., 124.

Queen, The, Kickham v., 8 V.L.R. (E.), 1, 6; 3 A.L.T., 86, followed. *The King v. Dale,* (1906) V.L.R., 662; 28 A.L.T., 140; 12 A.L.R., 549.

Raikes v Ward, 1 Hare, 445, commented on. *In re Lawn; Ballarat Trustees &c. Co. v. Perry,* (1911) V.L.R., 318; 33 A.L.T., 25; 17 A.L.R., 311

Rajah of Faridkote, Sirdar Gurdyal Singh v., (1894) A.C., 670, distinguished. *Kelsey v. Caselberg,* (1909) V.L.R., 347; 31 A.L.T., 31; 15 A.L.R., 362.

Randt Gold Mining Co. Ltd. v. Wainwright, (1901) 1 Ch., 184, doubted. *Land Mortgage Bank of Victoria Ltd. v. Reid,* (1909) V.L.R., 284; 31 A.L.T., 9; 15 A.L.R., 234.

Rathbone v. The Public Trustee, 24 L.R. N.Z., 801, distinguished. *Re Income Tax Acts,* (1907) V.L.R., 358; 28 A.L.T., 215; 13 A.L.R., 151.

Rawlins' Trusts, In re, 45 Ch., 299; (1892) A.C., applied. *In re Munro; National Trustees Executors &c. Co. of Australasia Ltd. v. Dunbar,* (1910) V.L.R., 395; 32 A.L.T., 41: 16 A.L.R., 363.

Read v. Friendly Society of Operative Stonemasons, (1902) 2 K.B., 732, distinguished. *Bond v. Morris,* (1912) V.L.R., 351; 34 A.L.T., 52; 18 A.L.R., 348.

Rees v. Dunbar, 14 V.L.R., 645; 10 A.L.T., 147, followed. *Davis v. Davis and Hattrick,* (1912) V.L.R., 23; 33 A.L.T., 108; 17 A.L.R., 607.

Reid v. Deane, (1906) V.L.R., 138; 27 A.L.T., 153; 12 A.L.R., 46, followed. *In re Tonq,* (1907) V.L.R., 338; 28 A.L.T., 200; 13 A.L.R., 119. Not followed as regards liability for sewerage expenses. *Macartney v. Macartney,* 33 A.L.T., 183: 18 A.L.R., 1.

R. v. Barber, 3 A.L.R. (C.N.), 21, approved. *R. v. Turnbull,* (1907) V.L.R., 11; 28 A.L.T., 103; 12 A.L.R., 551.

R. Bell & Son, Gates v., (1902) 2 K.B., 38, distinguished. *McKinnon v. Gange,* (1910) V.L.R., 32; 31 A.L.T., 112; 15 A.L.R., 640.

R. v. Brisac & Scott, 4 East., 164, followed. *R. v. Kellow,* (1912) V.L.R., 162; 33 A.L.T., 203; 18 A.L.R., 170.

R. v. Brown, 24 Q.B.D., 357, followed. *Rex v. Turnbull,* (1907) V.L.R., 11; 28 A.L.T., 103: 12 A.L.R., 551.

R. v Burdett, 4 B. & A., 95, discussed. *R. v. Waugh,* (1909) V.L.R., 379; 31 A.L.T., 37: 15 A.L.R., 366.

R. v. Collins; Ex parte Collins, 7 V.L.R., 74; 2 A.L.T., 118, followed. *Ross v. Ross,* (1909) V.L.R., 318: 30 A.L.T., 220; 15 A.L.R., 305.

R. v. Davies, (1906) 1 K.B., 32, discussed. *Packer v. Peacock,* 13 C.L.R., 577; 18 A.L.R., 70.

R. v. Ellis, (1899) 1 Q.B., 230, discussed. *R. v. Waugh,* (1909) V.L.R., 379; 31 A.L.T., 37; 15 A.L.R., 366.

R. v. Fitzgerald, 15 V.L.R., 40; 10 A.L.T., 241, followed. *Rex v. Turnbull,* (1907) V.L.R., 11; 28 A.L.T., 103; 12 A.L.R., 551.

R. v. Gibson, 18 Q.B.D., 537, considered. *Knox v. Bible,* (1907) V.L.R., 485; 29 A.L.T., 23; 13 A.L.R., 352.

R. v. Gyngall, (1893) 2 Q.B., 232, considered and applied. *Goldsmith v. Sands,* 4 C.L.R., 1648; 13 A.L.R., 601. Explained. *The King v. Lennie; The King v. Mackenzie,* 29 A.L.T., 56; 13 A.L.R., 505.

R. v. Hensler, 11 Cox, 573, discussed. *R. v. Waugh,* (1909) V.L.R., 379; 31 A.L.T., 37; 15 A.L.R., 366.

R. v. Huxley and Walsh, 8 V.L.R. (L.), 15; 3 A.L.T., 96, followed. *McLiney v. Minster,* (1911) V.L.R., 347; 33 A.L.T., 33; 17 A.L.R., 336.

R. v. Justices of the County of London and the London County Council, (1893) 2 Q.B., 476, followed. *Mooney v. Anderson,* (1907) V.L.R., 623; 29 A.L.T., 42; 13 A.L.R., 471.

Regina v. Justices of Heywood, 21 V.L.R., 654; 17 A.L.T., 238, distinguished. *Richards v. Jager,* (1909) V.L.R., 140; 30 A.L.T., 163; 15 A.L.R., 119.

R. v. M'Cormick, 4 V.L.R. (L.), 46, discussed. *Adams v. Rogers,* (1907) V.L.R., 245; 28 A.L.T., 180; 13 A.L.R., 71.

R. v. Mills, 7 Cox C.C., 263, followed. *R. v. Perera,* (1907) V.L.R., 240; 28 A.L.T., 176; 13 A.L.R., 116.

R. v. Moore ; Ex parte Myers, 10 V.L.R. (L.), 322 : 6 A.L.T., 151, followed. *Equity Trustees Executors and Agency Co. Ltd. v. Harston,* (1908) V.L.R., 23 ; 29 A.L.T., 131 : 13 A.L.R., 686.

R. v. Osborne, (1905) 1 K.B., 551, observations at p. 556, doubted by *Madden, C.J. R. v. McNeill,* (1907) V.L.R., 265 ; 28 A.L.T., 182 : 13 A.L.R., 99.

R. v. Parke, (1903) 2 K.B., 432, discussed. *Packer v. Peacock,* 13 C.L.R., 577 : 18 A.L.R., 70

R. v. Parkin, 1 Mood. C.C., 45, approved. *David Syme & Co. v. Swinburne,* 10 C.L.R., 43 ; 16 A.L.R., 93.

R. v. Reynolds, 2 Cox C.C., 170, followed. *R. v. Hill and Marshall,* (1909) V.L.R., 491 ; 31 A.L.T., 76 ; 15 A.L.R., 523.

R. v. Roche, 13 V.L.R., 150 ; 8 A.L.T., 193, discussed. *R. v. Schiffman,* (1910) V.L.R., 348 ; 32 A.L.T., 28 ; 16 A.L.R., 346.

R. v. Sayers, 4 W.W. & a'B. (L.), 46, applied. *Porter v. Martin,* (1910) V.L.R., 38 ; 31 A.L.T., 105 ; 16 A.L.R., 12., followed 32 A.L.T. (Supplement), 8 ; 16 A.L.R. (C.N.), 18.

R. v. Stowers, 24 A.L.T., 52 ; 8 A.L.R., 134, considered. *R. v. Downey,* (1910) V.L.R., 361 ; 32 A.L.T., 14 ; 16 A.L.R., 319.

R. v. Templeton ; Ex parte England, 3 V.L.R. (L.), 305, followed. *Burvett v. Moody,* (1909) V.L.R., 126 ; 30 A.L.T., 160 ; 15 A.L.R., 91.

R. v. Tolson, 23 Q.B.D., 168, applied. *Billingham v. Oaten,* (1911) V.L.R., 44 ; 32 A.L.T., 170 ; 17 A.L.R., 36.

R. v. Vodden, Dears., 229, approved. *David Syme & Co. v. Swinburne,* 10 C.L.R., 43 ; 16 A.L.R., 93.

R. v. Webb, (1896) 1 Q.B., 487, followed. *Rees v. Downer,* (1910) V.L.R., 5 ; 31 A.L.T., 97 ; 15 A.L.R., 360.

Reid, James Gillespie & Co. Ltd. v., (1905) V.L.R., 101 ; 26 A.L.T., 154 ; 11 A.L.R., 12, considered. *Land Mortgage Bank of Victoria Ltd. v. Reid,* (1909) V.L.R., 284 ; 31 A.L.T., 9 ; 15 A.L.R., 234.

Reuter Hufeland & Co. v. Sala & Co., 4 C.P.D., 239, distinguished. *L. Osborn & Co. Ltd. v. Davidson Brothers,* (1911) V.L.R., 416 ; 33 A.L.T., 66 ; 17 A.L.R., 448.

Reynolds, R. v., 2 Cox C.C., 170, followed. *R. v. Hilland Marshall,* (1909) V.L.R., 491 ; 31 A.L.T., 76 : 15 A.L.R., 523.

Rice, Butler v., (1910) 2 Ch., 277, applied. *Cuddigan v. Poole,* 33 A.L.T., 210 ; 18 A.L.R., 120.

Richards v. Jager, (1909) V.L.R., 140 ; 30 A.L.T., 163 ; 15 A.L.R., 119, approved. *Swinburne v. David Syme & Co.,* (1909) V.L.R., 550 ; 31 A.L.T., 81 ; 15 A.L.R., 579.

Richards v. Richards, 17 V.L.R., 758 ; 13 A.L.T., 133, approved. *Kemp v. Kemp,* (1907) V.L.R., 718 ; 29 A.L.T., 92 ; 13 A.L.R., 615.

Rickerby v. Rickerby, 25 A.L.T., 95 ; 10 A.L.R., 30, followed. *Farrer v. Farrer,* (1907) V.L.R., 382 ; 28 A.L.T., 221 ; 13 A.L.R., 236.

Ridge v. Ridge, 22 A.L.T., 44 ; 6 A.L.R., 149, applied. *Maddock v. Maddock,* (1911) V.L.R., 127 ; 32 A.L.T., 124 ; 17 A.L.R., 66.

Riordan, Moubray v., 15 V.L.R., 354 ; 11 A.L.T., 19, followed. *Kelsey v. Caselberg,* (1909) V.L.R., 347 ; 31 A.L.T., 31 : 15 A.L.R., 362.

Ritchie, In re ; Murray v. Ritchie, 28 V.L.R., 255 ; 24 A.L.T., 62 ; 8 A.L.R., 211, distinguished. *Ex parte Edmonds and Harrison,* 34 A.L.T., 105 : 18 A.L.R., 41.

Roberts v. Akeroyd : In re Akeroyd's Settlement, (1893) 3 Ch., 363, distinguished. *In re Lyons : Grant v. Trustees Executors &c. Co. Ltd.,* (1908) V.L.R., 190 ; 29 A.L.T., 202 ; 14 A.L.R., 147

Roberts v. Death, 8 Q.B.D., 319, followed. *Richards v. Jager,* (1909) V.L.R., 140 ; 30 A.L.T., 163 ; 15 A.L.R., 119

Roberts v. Roberts, 29 V.L.R., 158 ; 25 A.L.T., 54 ; 10 A.L.R., 20, distinguished and (by *Cussen, J.*) doubted. *Lobley v. Lobley,* (1909) V.L.R., 383 ; 31 A.L.T., 46 ; 15 A.L.R., 443.

Robins v. Goddard, (1905) 1 K.B., 294, distinguished. *Briscoe & Co. v. Victorian Railways Commissioners,* (1907) V.L.R., 523; 29 A.L.T., 17; 13 A.L.R., 308.

Rochdale Canal Co. v. Brewster, (1894) 2 Q.B., 852, followed. *Mayor, &c. of City of Melbourne v. Howard Smith & Co Ltd.,* 13 C.L.R., 253; 17 A.L.R., 437.

Roche, R. v., 13 V.L.R., 150; 8 A.L.T., 193, discussed. *R. v. Schiffman,* (1910) V.L.R., 348; 32 A.L.T., 28: 16 A.L.R., 346.

Rogers and Rodd's Contract, In re, (1907) V.L.R., 511; 29 A.L.T., 30; 13 A.L.R., 312, followed. *In re Crook's Contract,* (1909) V.L.R., 12; 30 A.L.T., 108; 14 A.L.R., 698.

Rogers v. Mutch, 10 Ch. D., 25, followed. *In re Thompson; Brahe v. Mason,* (1910) V.L.R., 251; 31 A.L.T., 210; 16 A.L.R., 266.

Rooney, Webb v., 1 A.L.R., 83, discussed. *Le Cocq v. McErvale,* (1908) V.L.R., 69; 29 A.L.T., 134; 13 A.L.R., 699.

Rylands v. Fletcher, L.R. 3 H.L., 330, distinguished. *Rickards v. Lothian,* (1913) A.C., 263.

Sala & Co., Reuter Hufeland & Co. v., 4 C.P.D., 239, distinguished. *L. Osborn & Co. Ltd. v. Davidson Brothers,* (1911) V.L.R., 416; 33 A.L.T., 66; 17 A.L.R., 448.

Sanderson v. Nicholson, (1906) V.L.R., 371; 27 A.L.T., 215; 12 A.L.R., 208, not followed. *Honeybone v. Glass,* (1908) V.L.R., 466; 30 A.L.T., 54: 14 A.L.R., 345.

Sandilands, Re; Ex parte Browne, 4 V.L.R. (L.), 318, followed. *Pope v. Peacock,* (1906) V.L.R., 667; 28 A.L.T., 63; 12 A.L.R. 440.

Sands, Goldsmith v., 4 C.L.R., 1648; 13 A.L.R., 601, applied. *Moule v. Moule,* 13 C.L.R., 267: 17 A.L.R., 446.

Saunders v. Saunders, (1897) P., at p. 104, principle laid down by *Rigby, L.J.,* adopted. *Richards v. Richards,* (1911) V.L.R., 42; 32 A.L.T., 101; 16 A.L.R., 579.

Sayers, R. v., 4 W.W. & A'B. (L.), 46, applied. *Porter v. Martin,* (1910) V.L.R., 38; 31 A.L.T., 105: 16 A.L.R., 12. followed. 32 A.L.T. (Supplement), 8; 16 A.L.R. (C.N.), 18.

Scholefield v. Londesborough, (1896) A.C., 514, followed. *Colonial Bank of Australasia v. Marshall,* (1906) A.C., 559.

Scott, In re, 4 A.J.R., 50, distinguished. *In re Ross,* 31 A.L.T. (Supplement), 3; 15 A.L.R. (C.N.), 13.

Scott v. Corporation of Liverpool, 3 DeG. & J., at p. 368, discussed and applied. *Briscoe & Co. v. Victorian Railways Commissioners,* (1907) V.L.R., 523; 29 A.L.T., 17; 13 A.L.R., 308.

Scott, Wilson v., 3 A.L.R. (C.N.), 87, explained. *Hopkins v. Forster,* 32 A.L.T. (Supplement), 5; 16 A.L.R. (C.N.), 6. And distinguished, *Ambler & Co. Proprietary Ltd. v. Clayton,* 31 A.L.T. (Supplement), 5; 15 A.L.R. (C.N.), 15.

Sealey, In re; Tomkins v. Tucker, 85 L.T., 451, applied. *In re Stroud; Bell v. Stroud,* (1908) V.L.R., 33; 29 A.L.T., 104; 13 A.L.R., 645.

Shackle, Greatorex v., (1895) 2 Q.B., 249, followed. *Looker v. Mercer,* 28 A.L.T. (Supplement), 15; 13 A.L.R. (C.N.), 13.

Shanahan v. Nicholls, 27 A.L.T. (Supplement), 8; 11 A.L.R. (C.N.), 65, followed. *Ambler & Co. Proprietary Ltd. v. Clayton,* 29 A.L.T. (Supplement), 28; 14 A.L.R. (C.N.), 17.

Shankland, Trotman v., 7 V.L.R. (L.), 16, adopted. *McLaren v. Bradley,* (1908) V.L.R., 318; 29 A.L.T., 239; 14 A.L.R., 252.

Sherborne, Lord, Ogle v., In re Whorwood, 34 Ch. D., 446, distinguished. *In re Loughlin; Acheson v. O'Meara,* (1906) V.L.R., 597; 28 A.L.T., 28; 12 A.L.R., 411.

Sherwood, Prior v., 3 C.L.R., 1054, followed as to "user." *McCann v. Morgan,* (1912) V.L.R., 303; 34 A.L.T., 43; 18 A.L.R., 334.

Short, Egbert v., (1907) 2 Ch., 207, considered and applied. *Maritime Insurance Co. Ltd. v. Geelong Harbour Trust Commissioners,* 6 C.L.R., 194; 14 A.L.R., 424.

Sidney, Re; Hingeston v. Sidney, (1908) 1 Ch., 126, 488, distinguished. *In re Wallace;*

Trustees Executors and Agency Co. Ltd. v. *Fatt*, (1908) V.L.R., 636 ; 30 A.L.T., 100 ; 14 A.L.R., 502.

Simpson, In re, (1897) 1 Ch., 256, form of order adopted. *In re Weir*, (1912) V.L.R., 77 ; 33 A.L.T., 162 ; 18 A.L.R., 26.

Simpson, Bank of New Zealand v., (1900) A.C., 182, followed. *Bruton* v. *Farm and Dairy Machinery Co. Proprietary Ltd.*, (1910) V.L.R., 196 ; 31 A.L.T., 200 ; 16 A.L.R., 241.

Sirdar Gurdyal Singh v. Rajah of Faridkote, (1894) A.C., 670, distinguished. *Kelsey* v. *Caselberg*, (1909) V.L.R., 347 ; 31 A.L.T., 31 ; 15 A.L.R., 362.

Skrymsher v. Northcote, 1 Swanst., 566, distinguished. *In re Stead*, (1908) V.L.R., 10 ; 29 A.L.T., 155 ; 13 A.L.R., 683.

Slattery, Dublin, Wicklow and Wexford Ry. Co. v., 3 A.C., 1155, at p. 1201, applied. *Farrands* v. *Mayor &c. of Melbourne*, (1909) V.L.R., 531 ; 31 A.L.T., 78 ; 15 A.L.R., 520, distinguished. *Fraser* v. *Victorian Railways Commissioners*, 8 C.L.R., 54 ; 15 A.L.R., 93.

Slattery v. Naylor, 13 App. Cas., 446, distinguished. *Co-operative Brick Co. Proprietary Ltd.* v. *Hawthorn, Mayor &c. of City of*, 9 C.L.R., 301 ; 15 A.L.R., 479.

Smail, Muntz v., 8 C.L.R., 262 ; 15 A.L.R., 162, discussed. *In re McConnell* ; *Macfarlane* v. *McDonald*, (1912) V.L.R., 102 ; 33 A.L.T., 195 ; 18 A.L.R., 90.

Smith, Brooks Robinson & Co. v., 16 V.L.R., 245 ; 11 A.L.T., 168, applied. *H. Beecham & Co.* v. *R. W. Cameron & Co.*, (1910) V.L.R., 19 ; 31 A.L.T., 100 ; 15 A.L.R., 598.

Smith, Church Wardens of St. Saviour's, Southwark v., 1 Wm. Bl., 351, followed. *Renshaw* v. *Maher*, (1907) V.L.R., 520 ; 29 A.L.T., 237 ; 13 A.L.R., 265.

Smith, Crooke v., 4 V.L.R. (L.), 95, applied. *H. Beecham & Co.* v. *R. W. Cameron & Co.*, (1910) V.L.R., 19 ; 31 A.L.T., 100 ; 15 A.L.R., 598.

Smith v. Jeffryes, 15 M. & W., 561, distinguished. *Bruton* v. *Farm and Dairy Machinery Co. Proprietary Ltd.*, (1910) V.L.R., 196 ; 31 A.L.T., 200 ; 16 A.L.R., 241.

Smith v. South Eastern Ry. Co., (1896) 1 Q.B., 178, distinguished. *Fraser* v. *Victorian Railways Commissioners*, 8 C.L.R., 54 ; 15 A.L.R., 93.

Smith v. Syme, 20 V.L.R., 56 ; 15 A.L.T., 193, approved. *Orchard* v. *Oriental Timber Corporation Ltd.*, (1910) V.L.R., 192 ; 31 A.L.T., 198 ; 16 A.L.R., 213.

Smith, Wadsworth v., L.R. 6 Q.B., 332, discussed and explained. *Briscoe & Co.* v. *Victorian Railways Commissioners*, (1907) V.L.R., 523 ; 29 A.L.T., 17 ; 13 A.L.R., 308.

Sneddon, Evans v., 28 V.L.R., 396 ; 24 A.L.T., 79 ; 8 A.L.R., 215, explained. *Smith* v. *Chisholm*, (1908) V.L.R., 579 ; 30 A.L.T., 48 ; 14 A.L.R., 471.

Snelling, In re, 24 V.L.R., 753 ; 20 A.L.T., 256 ; 5 A.L.R., 102, not followed. *In re Allen*, (1908) V.L.R., 20 ; 29 A.L.T., 164 ; 14 A.L.R., 28.

Solomons, In re, 10 Man. 369, discussed and followed. *In re Moulton*, 30 A.L.T. (Supplement), 4 ; 14 A.L.R. (C.N.), 29.

South Eastern Ry. Co., Smith v., (1896) 1 Q.B., 178, distinguished. *Fraser* v. *Victorian Railways Commissioners*, 8 C.L.R., 54 ; 15 A.L.R., 93.

South Wales Miners' Federation v. Glamorgan Coal Co., (1905) A.C., 239, distinguished. *Bond* v. *Morris*, (1912) V.L.R., 351 ; 34 A.L.T., 52 ; 18 A.L.R., 348.

Speller v. Bristol Steam Navigation Co., 13 Q.B.D., 96, distinguished. *Edwards* v. *Edwards*, (1913) V.L.R., 30 ; 34 A.L.T., 103 ; 18 A.L.R., 580.

Sprague v. Allen, 15 T.L.R., 150, followed. *In re Bennett Brothers*, (1910) V.L.R., 51 ; 31 A.L.T., 148 ; 16 A.L.R., 30.

Sproule, Bouche v., 12 App. Cas., 385, at pp. 397, 401, considered. *In re Longley* ; *Reid* v. *Silke*, (1906) V.L.R., 641 ; 28 A.L.T., 82 ; 12 A.L.R., 499, applied. *In re Smith* ; *Edwards* v. *Smith*, 29 A.L.T., 173 ; 14 A.L.R., 22.

Stanford v. Stanford, 34 Ch. D., 362, distinguished. *In re Lyons* ; *Grant* v. *Trustees Executors &c. Co. Ltd.*, (1908) V.L.R., 190 ; 29 A.L.T., 202 ; 14 A.L.R., 147.

Steele v. M'Kinley, 5 A.C., 754, discussed. *Ferrier* v. *Stewart,* 15 C.L.R., 32 : 18 A.L.R., 262.

Steinhardt, Walker & Co., Alexander v., (1903) 2 K.B., 208, applied by *Isaacs, J. Muntz* v. *Smail,* 8 C.L.R., 262 ; 15 A.L.R., 162.

Stephens v. McKenzie, 29 V.L.R., 652 ; 25 A.L.T., 239 ; 10 A.L.R., 106, approved. *Swinburne* v. *David Syme & Co.,* (1909) V.L.R., 550 ; 31 A.L.T., 81 ; 15 A.L.R., 579.

Sterious, Taddy v., (1904) 1 Ch., 358, judgment of *Swinfen Eady J.* approved. *National Phonograph Co. of Australia Ltd.* v. *Menck,* (1911) A.C., 336, at p. 347 ; 17 A.L.R., 94, at p. 96.

Stevenson, In re, 19 V.L.R., 660 ; 15 A.L.T., 119, overruled. *In re Whitelaw ; Savage* v. *Union Bank of Australia Ltd. ; Whitelaw* v. *The Same,* 3 C.L.R., 1170 ; 12 A.L.R., 285.

Stewart and Park's Contract, Re, (1907) V.L.R., 31 ; 28 A.L.T., 133 ; 12 A.L.R., 553 ; followed. *Re Rogers and Rodd's Contract,* (1907) V.L.R., 511 ; 29 A.L.T., 13 ; 13 A.L.R., 312. Also, *In re Crook's Contract,* (1909) V.L.R., 12 ; 30 A.L.T., 108 ; 14 A.L.R., 698.

Stiggants v. Joske, 12 C.L.R., 549 ; 17 A.L.R., 526, discussed and applied. *Joske* v. *Strutt,* (1912) V.L.R., 118 ; 33 A.L.T., 189 ; 18 A.L.R., 84. Also, explained, 14 C.L.R., 180 ; 18 A.L.R., at p. 90.

Still, Mooney v., (1909) V.L.R., 227 ; 30 A.L.T., 191 ; 15 A.L.R., 197, followed. *Mooney* v. *McKeand,* (1909) V.L.R., 294 : 30 A.L.T., 225 · 15 A.L.R., 280

Storey, In re, 28 V.L.R., 336 ; 24 A.L.T., 80 ; 8 A.L.R., 210, followed. Announcement, *per Hood, J.,* after consulting the other Judges, 34 A.L.T., 86 ; 18 A.L.R. (C.N.), 20.

Stowers, R. v., 24 A.L.T., 52 ; 8 A.L.R., 134, considered. *R.* v. *Downey,* (1910) V.L.R., 361 ; 32 A.L.T., 14 ; 16 A.L.R., 319.

Stray, In re, L.R. 2 Ch., 374, commented on. *In re Knights ; Ex parte Purcell,* (1910) V.L.R., 188 ; 31 A.L.T., 178 ; 16 A.L.R., 184.

Stroud v. Edwards, 77 L.T. N.S., 280, followed. *Trustees Executors and Agency Co. Ltd.* v. *Webster,* (1907) V.L.R., 318 ; 28 A.L.T., 225 ; 13 A.L.R., 188.

Strutt, Joske v., (1912) V.L.R., 110 ; 33 A.L.T., 189 ; 18 A.L.R., 84, not followed. *Joske* v. *Blitz,* (1912) V.L.R., 256 ; 34 A.L.T., 15 ; 18 A.L.R., 352.

Suckling v. Parker, (1906) 1 K.B., 527, distinguished. *Gunner* v. *Payne,* (1908) V.L.R., 363 : 29 A.L.T., 264 ; 14 A.L.R., 243.

Sweeting v. Prideaux, 2 Ch. D., 413, distinguished. *In re Green ; Crowson* v. *Wild,* (1907) V.L.R., 284 ; 28 A.L.T., 206 ; 13 A.L.R., 121.

Syme, O'Farrell v., 16 V.L.R., 422 ; 12 A.L.T., 11, approved. *Orchard* v. *Oriental Timber Corporation Ltd.,* (1910) V.L.R., 192 ; 31 A.L.T., 198 ; 16 A.L.R., 213.

Syme, Smith v., 20 V.L.R., 56 ; 15 A.L.T., 193, approved. *Orchard* v. *Oriental Timber Corporation Ltd.,* (1910) V.L.R., 192 ; 31 A.L.T., 198 ; 16 A.L.R., 213.

Syme, Re, Ex parte Worthington, 28 V.L.R., 552 ; 24 A.L.T., 123 ; 8 A.L.R., 239, overruled. *Packer* v. *Peacock,* 13 C.L.R., 577 ; 18 A.L.R., 70.

Taddy v. Sterious, (1904) 1 Ch., 358, judgment of *Swinfen Eady, J.,* approved. *National Phonograph Co. of Australia Ltd.* v. *Menck,* (1911) A.C., 336, at p. 347 ; 17 A.L.R., 94, at p. 96.

Templeton, R. v. ; Ex parte England, 3 V.L.R. (L.), 305, followed. *Burvett* v. *Moody,* (1909) V.L.R. 126 ; 30 A.L.T., 160 ; 15 A.L.R., 91.

Templeton, Warr v., 3 V.R. (L.), 57, discussed. *Cross* v. *Daffy,* (1910) V.L.R., 316 ; 32 A.L.T., 10 · 16 A.L.R., 279.

Thomas v. Ivey, 13 A.L.T., 190, distinguished. *Riely* v. *Biggs,* 28 A.L.T. (Supplement), 11 ; 13 A.L.R. (C.N.), 5.

Thompson v. McKenzie, (1908) 1 K.B., at p. 908, dictum of Lord *Alverstone,* approved. *McKinnon* v. *Colborne,* (1911) V.L.R., 486 ; 33 A.L.T., 117 ; 17 A.L.R., 524.

E

Thompson, Doherty v., 94 L.T., 626, followed. *Harrison San Miguel Proprietary Ltd.* v. *Alfred Lawrence & Co.,* (1912) V.L.R., 367 ; 34 A.L.T., 88 ; 18 A.L.R., 394.

Thompson, Whiting v., 29 V.L.R., 89 ; 21 A.L.T., 231 ; 6 A.L.R., 132, followed. *In re Rosenthal ; Rosenthal* v. *Rosenthal,* (1911) V.L.R., 55 ; 32 A.L.T., 46 ; 16 A.L.R., 399.

Thornhill, In re, 3 W.W. & A'B. (E.), 110, followed. *In re Vance ; Ex parte Carr,* (1906) V.L.R., 664 ; 28 A.L.T., 62 ; 12 A.L.R., 439

Threlkeld, Wilson v., 3 W.W. & A'B. (L.), 158, applied. *Kelsey* v. *Caselberg,* (1909) V.L.R., 347 ; 31 A.L.T., 31 . 15 A.L.R., 362.

Todd's Application, In re, 9 R.P.C., 487, applied. *Linotype Co. Ltd.* v. *Mounsey,* 9 C.L.R., 194 ; 15 A.L.R., 310.

Todd, Hickling v., 15 V.L.R., 154 ; 10 A.L.T., 236, followed. *In re Stamps Acts,* (1906) V.L.R., 364 ; 27 A.L.T., 204 ; 12 A.L.R., 186.

Tolson, R. v., 23 Q.B.D., 168, applied. *Billingham* v. *Oaten,* (1911) V.L.R., 44 ; 32 A.L.T., 170 ; 17 A.L.R., 36.

Tomkins v. Tucker, In re Sealey, 85 L.T., 451, applied. *In re Stroud ; Bell* v. *Stroud,* (1908) V.L.R., 33 ; 29 A.L.T., 104 ; 13 A.L.R., 645.

Toronto Ry. Co. v. King, (1908) A.C., 260, distinguished. *Fraser* v. *Victorian Railways Commissioners,* 8 C.L.R., 54 : 15 A.L.R., 93.

Torrens, Lester v., 2 Q.B.D., 403, followed. *McKinnon* v. *Colborne,* (1911) V.L.R., 486 ; 33 A.L.T., 117 ; 17 A.L.R., 524.

Tottenham v. Ely : In re Ely, 65 L.T., 452, distinguished. *In re Loughlin : Acheson* v. *O'Meara,* (1906) V.L.R., 597 ; 28 A.L.T., 28 ; 12 A.L.R., 411.

Towns v. Wentworth, 11 Moo. P.C., 526, applied. *In re Green ; Crowson* v. *Wild,* (1907) V.L.R., 284 ; 28 A.L.T., 206 ; 13 A.L.R., 121.

Trainer v. The King, 4 C.L.R., 156 ; 13 A.L.R., 53, discussed. *R.* v. *Schiffman,* (1910) V.L.R., 348 ; 32 A.L.T., 28 ; 16 A.L.R., 346.

Tredwell, In re, (1891) 2 Ch., 640, distinguished. *In re Nilen ; Kidd* v. *Nilen,* (1908) V.L.R., 332 ; 29 A.L.T., 284 ; 14 A.L.R., 277.

Trent Brewery v. Lehane, 21 V.L.R., 283 ; 1 A.L.R., 89, followed. *Sack* v. *Wolstencroft,* 29 A.L.T., 85 ; 13 A.L.R., 588.

Trequair, Willis v., 3 C.L.R., 912 ; 12 A.L.R., 507, applied. *National Mutual Life Association of Australasia Ltd.* v. *Australian Widows' Fund &c. Society Ltd.,* (1910) V.L.R., 411 ; 32 A.L.T., 51 ; 16 A.L.R., 460.

Trotman v. Shankland, 7 V.L.R. (L.), 16, adopted. *McLaren* v. *Bradley,* (1908) V.L.R., 318 ; 29 A.L.T., 239 : 14 A.L.R., 252

Trustees Executors and Agency Co. v. Jenner, 22 V.L.R., 584 ; 18 A.L.T., 255 ; 3 A.L.R., 138, followed. *England* v. *Bayles,* (1906) V.L.R., 94 ; 27 A.L.T., 181 ; 12 A.L.R., 122.

Trustees Executors &c. Co. v. Jope, 27 V.L.R., 706 ; 24 A.L.T., 30 ; 8 A.L.R. (C.N.), 21, followed. *In re Tong,* (1907) V.L.R., 338 ; 28 A.L.T., 200 ; 13 A.L.R., 119.

Tucker v. Hernaman, 1 Sm. & G., 394 ; 4 DeG. M. & G., 395, followed. *In re Poole,* 31 A.L.T. (Supplement), 13 ; 15 A.L.R. (C.N.), 25

Tucker, Tomkins v. In re Sealey, 85 L.T., 451, applied. *In re Stroud ; Bell* v. *Stroud,* (1908) V.L.R., 33 ; 29 A.L.T., 104 ; 13 A.L.R., 645.

Twist v. Tye, (1902) P., 92, considered. *In re Keane,* (1909) V.L.R., 231 ; 30 A.L.T., 216 ; 15 A.L.R., 198.

Tye, Twist v., (1902) P., 92, considered. *In re Keane,* (1909) V.L.R., 231 ; 30 A.L.T., 216 : 15 A.L.R., 198.

Vallentine v. Vallentine, (1901) P., 283, followed. *Mackay* v. *Mackay,* (1910) V.L.R., 50 ; 31 A.L.T., 138 ; 16 A.L.R., 29

Vassall, Knapp v. ; In re Knapp's Settlement, (1895) 1 Ch., 91, plan of distribution adopted. *In re Hobson ; Hobson* v. *Sharp,* (1910) V.L.R., 724 ; 29 A.L.T., 125 ; 13 A.L.R., 703.

Vestry of St. James and St. John v. Feary, 24 Q.B.D., 703, distinguished. *Bremner v. New Normanby Quartz Mining Co., No Liability,* (1910) V.L.R., 72 ; 31 A.L.T., 140 ; 16 A.L.R., 25.

Victorian Railways Commissioners, Brown v., 3 C.L.R., 316 ; 12 A.L.R., 1, applied. *Crouch v. Victorian Railways Commissioners,* (1907) V.L.R., 80 ; 28 A.L.T., 141 ; 12 A.L.R., 574.

Victorian Railways Commissioners, Crouch v., (1907) V.L.R., 80 ; 28 A.L.T., 141 : 12 A.L.R., 574, followed. *In re Hilliard ; Ex parte Tinkler,* (1907) V.L.R., 375 ; 28 A.L.T., 204 ; 13 A.L.R., 138.

Victorian Railways Commissioners, Dennis v., 28 V.L.R., 576 ; 24 A.L.T., 196 : 9 A.L.R., 69, applied. *Victorian Railways Commissioners v. Campbell,* 4 C.L.R., 1446 ; 13 A.L.R., 403.

Vinnicombe v. MacGregor, 29 V.L.R., 32 ; 28 V.L.R., 144 ; 24 A.L.T., 200 ; 24 A.L.T., 15 ; 9 A.L.R., 60 ; 8 A.L.R., 141, discussed and disapproved. *Nelson v. Walker,* 10 C.L.R., 560 ; 16 A.L.R., 285.

Virgo, Municipal Corporation of Toronto v., (1896) App. Cas., 88, followed. *Co-operative Brick Co. Proprietary Ltd. v. Hawthorn, Mayor, &c. of City of,* 9 C.L.R., 301 ; 15 A.L.R., 479.

Vodden, R. v., Dears., 229, approved. *David Syme & Co. v. Swinburne,* 10 C.L.R., 43 ; 16 A.L.R., 93.

Vogt v. Vogt, 25 V.L.R., 283 ; 21 A.L.T., 109 ; 5 A.L.R. (C.N.), 77, followed. *Kidd v. Kidd,* (1908) V.L.R., 409 ; 30 A.L.T., 29 ; 14 A.L.R., 274.

Wadsworth v. Smith, L.R. 6 Q.B., 332, discussed and explained. *Briscoe & Co. v. Victorian Railways Commissioners,* (1907) V.L.R., 523 ; 29 A.L.T., 17 ; 13 A.L.R., 308.

Wainwright, Randt Gold Mining Co. Ltd. v., (1901) 1 Ch., 184, doubted. *Land Mortgage Bank of Victoria Ltd. v. Reid,* (1909) V.L.R., 284 ; 31 A.L.T., 9 ; 15 A.L.R., 234.

Wakelin v. London and South Western Railway Co., 12 App. Cas., 41, applied. *Fraser v. Victorian Railways Commissioners,* 8 C.L.R., 54 ; 15 A.L.R., 93.

Walter, Kingsbury v., (1901) A.C., 187, distinguished. *In re Jones ; Harris v. Jones,* (1910) V.L.R., 306 ; 32 A.L.T., 3 ; 16 A.L.R., 266.

Wandsworth District Board of Works, Cooper v. 14 C.B.N.S., 180, followed. *Bremner v. New Normanby Quartz Mining Co., No Liability,* (1910) V.L.R., 72 ; 31 A.L.T., 140 ; 16 A.L.R., 25.

Ward v. Hearne, 10 V.L.R. (L.), 163 : 6 A.L.T., 49, explained. *The King v. Watt ; Ex parte Slade,* (1912) V.L.R., 225 ; 33 A.L.T., 222 ; 18 A.L.R., 158.

Ward, Raikes v., 1 Hare, 445, commented on. *In re Lawn ; Ballarat Trustees &c. Co. v. Perry,* (1911) V.L.R., 318 ; 33 A.L.T., 25 ; 17 A.L.R., 311.

Warnecke v. Equitable Life Assurance Society, (1906) V.L.R., 482 ; 27 A.L.T., 236 ; 12 A.L.R., 254, approved. *National Mutual Life Association of Australasia Ltd. v. Godrich,* 10 C.L.R., 1 ; 16 A.L.R., 110.

Warr v. Templeton, 3 V.R. (L.), 56, discussed. *Cross v. Duffy,* (1910) V.L.R., 316 ; 32 A.L.T., 10 ; 16 A.L.R., 279.

Watson, Hancock v., (1902) A.C., 14, at p. 22, applied. *In re Watson ; Cain v. Watson,* (1910) V.L.R., 256 ; 31 A.L.T., 212 ; 16 A.L.R., 76.

Watson, London and Brighton Railway Co. v., 3 C.P.D., 429, followed. *Borsum v. Smith.* (1907) V.L.R., 72 ; 28 A.L.T., 89 : 12 A.L.R., 495.

Watson, Peatling v., (1909) V.L.R., 198 ; 30 A.L.T., 176 ; 15 A.L.R., 150, overruled. *Howe v Lees,* 11 C.L.R., 361 ; 16 A.L.R., 605.

Waxman, Ex parte : In re Crown Hotel, 28 V.L.R., 710 ; 24 A.L.T., 234 ; 9 A.L.R., 108, not followed. *Mooney v. Lucas,* (1909) V.L.R., 333 ; 31 A.L.T., 3 ; 15 A.L.R., 296.

Wayth, In re, 5 V.L.R. (L.), 389 ; 1 A.L.T., 97, followed. *In re Simpson and Fricke ; Ex parte Robinson,* (1910) V.L.R., 177 ; 31 A.L.T., 163 ; 16 A.L.R., 125.

Webb, Deakin v., 1 C.L.R., 585, approved and applied. *Baxter v. Commissioners of Taxation ; Flint v. Webb,* 4 C.L.R., 1087, 1178 ; 13 A.L.R., 313.

Webb, Grumley v., 100 Am. Dec., 304, approved. *Prebble v. Reeves*, (1910) V.L.R., 88; 31 A.L.T., 114; 15 A.L.R., 631.

Webb v. Outtrim, (1907) A.C., 81, not followed. *Baxter v. Commissioners of Taxation; Flint v. Webb*, 4 C.L.R., 1087, 1178; 13 A.L.R., 313.

Webb, R. v., (1896) 1 Q.B., 487, followed. *Rees v. Downer*, (1910) V.L.R., 5; 31 A.L.T., 97; 15 A.L.R., 360.

Webb v. Rooney, 1 A.L.R., 83, discussed. *Le Cocq v. McErvale*, (1908) V.L.R., 69; 29 A.L.T., 134; 13 A.L.R., 699.

Weedon v. Davidson, 4 C.L.R., 895; 13 A.L.R., 87, explained. *Richardson v. Austin*, 12 C.L.R., 463; 17 A.L.R., 324.

Weekes v. King, 15 Cox C.C., 733, followed. *Rider v. M'Kell*, (1908) C.L.R., 110; 29 A.L.T., 77; 13 A.L.R., 513.

Wentworth, Towns v., 11 Moo. P.C., 526, applied. *In re Green: Crowson v. Wild*, (1907) V.L.R., 284; 28 A.L.T., 206; 13 A.L.R., 121.

Weymouth, Mayor &c. of, Goodyear v., 35 L.J. N.S. C.P., 12, discussed and applied. *Briscoe & Co. v. Victorian Railways Commissioners*, (1907) V.L.R., 523; 29 A.L.T., 17; 13 A.L.R., 308.

Whiting v. McGinnis, (1909) V.L.R., 250; 30 A.L.T., 207; 15 A.L.R., 203, approved. *In re Rosenthal; Rosenthal v. Rosenthal*, 11 C.L.R., 87; 16 A.L.R.. 455.

Whiting v. Thompson, 29 V.L.R., 89; 21 A.L.T., 231; 6 A.L.R., 132, followed. *In re Rosenthal; Rosenthal v. Rosenthal*, (1911) V.L.R., 55; 32 A.L.T., 46· 16 A.L.R., 399.

Whorwood, In re · Ogle v. Lord Sherborne, 34 Ch. D., 446, distinguished. *In re Loughlin: Acheson v. O'Meara*, (1906) V.L.R., 597; 28 A.L.T., 28; 12 A.L.R., 411.

Wilkie v. Equity Trustees &c. Co., (1909) V.L.R., 277; 30 A.L.T., 211; 15 A.L.R., 208, followed. *Macartney v. Macartney*, 33 A.L.T., 183: 18 A.L.R., 1.

Wilkie v. Hunt, 1 W.W. & A'B. (L.), 66, distinguished. *Bruton v. Farm and Dairy Machinery Co. Proprietary Ltd.*, (1910) V.L.R., 196; 31 A.L.T., 200; 16 A.L.R., 241

Williams, New Koh-i-noor Co. v., 13 V.L.R., 435; 8 A.L.T., 169, discussed. *In re Lamrock, Brown and Hall's Costs*, (1908) V.L.R., 238; 29 A.L.T., 214; 14 A.L.R., 81.

Williams v. Papworth, (1900) A.C., p. 566, followed. *In re Stevens; Trustees Executors and Agency Co. Ltd. v. Teague*, (1912) V.L.R., 194; 33 A.L.T., 233; 18 A.L.R., 195

Williamson, In re: Price v. Williamson, 26 A.L.T., 91; 10 A.L.R., 197, distinguished. *In re Reed*, (1911) V.L.R., 232; 32 A.L.T., 168; 17 A.L.R., 164.

Willis v. Trequair, 3 C.L.R., 912; 12 A.L.R., 507, applied. *National Mutual Life Association of Australasia Ltd. v. Australian Widows' Fund &c. Society Ltd.*, (1910) V.L.R., 411; 32 A.L.T., 51; 16 A.L.R., 460.

Wilson, Re, 24 A.L.T., 168; 9 A.L.R., 36, doubted. *In re McCracken; Webb v. McCracken*, 3 C.L.R., 1018; 12 A.L.R., 313.

Wilson v. Anderson, 26 A.L.T. (Supplement), 5; 11 A.L.R. (C.N.), 35, explained. *Townsing v. Egan*, 29 A.L.T. (Supplement), 29: 14 A.L.R. (C.N.), 18.

Wilson v. Benson, (1905) V.L.R., 229; 26 A.L.T., 144: 11 A.L.R., 85, approved. *Wilson v. Travers*, (1906) V.L.R., 734; 28 A.L.T., 56: 12 A.L.R., 413.

Wilson v. Scott, 3 A.L.R. (C.N.), 87, explained. *Hopkins v. Forster*, 32 A.L.T. (Supplement), 5; 16 A.L.R. (C.N.), 6. And distinguished, *Ambler & Co. Proprietary Ltd. v. Clayton*, 31 A.L.T. (Supplement), 5; 15 A.L.R. (C.N.), 15

Wilson v. Threlkeld, 3 W.W. & A'B. (L.), 158, applied. *Kelsey v. Caselberg*, (1909) V.L.R., 347; 31 A.L.T., 31; 15 A.L.R., 362.

Wilson v. Wilson, 17 A.L.T., 154, followed. *Kidd v. Kidd*, (1908) V.L.R., 409; 30 A.L.T., 29; 14 A.L.R., 274.

Wimmera, Shire of v. Brimacombe, 23 V.L.R., 217; 19 A.L.T., 12; 3 A.L.R., 146, explained. *Poowong, Shire of v. Gillen*, (1907) V.L.R., 37; 28 A.L.T., 123: 12 A.L.R., 522.

Windover & Co., Morgan & Co. v., 7 R.P.C., 131, applied. *Linotype Co. Ltd. v. Mounsey,* 9 C.L.R., 194 ; 15 A.L.R.. 310.

Wiseman v. Collector of Imposts. 21 V.L.R., 743 ; 17 A.L.T., 251, overruled. *Davidson v. Chirnside,* 7 C.L.R., 324 ; 14 A.L.R., 686.

Wisewould, Ex parte, 16 V.L.R., 149 ; 11 A.L.T., 182, approved. *In re Transfer of Land Act ; Ex parte Danaher,* (1911) V.L.R., 214 ; 32 A.L.T., 190 ; 17 A.L.R., 160.

Wolfenden, McGee v., (1907) V.L.R., 195 ; 28 A.L.T., 163 ; 13 A.L.R., 51, distinguished. *Biggs* v. *Lamley,* (1907) V.L.R., 300 ; 28 A.L.T., 202 ; 13 A.L.R., 144.

Wood v. Earl of Durham, 21 Q.B.D., 501, followed. *Wilson v. Dun's Gazette,* (1912) V.L.R., 342 ; 34 A.L.T., 77 ; 18 A.L.R., 327.

Woodward, Keates v., (1902) 1 K.B., 532, followed. *Harrison San Miguel Proprietary Ltd.* v. *Alfred Lawrence & Co.,* (1912) V.L.R., 367 ; 34 A.L.T., 88 ; 18 A.L.R., 394.

Worthington, Ex parte ; Re Syme, 28 V.L.R., 552 ; 24 A.L.T., 123 ; 8 A.L.R., 239, overruled. *Packer v. Peacock,* 13 C.L.R., 577 ; 18 A.L.R., 70.

Wotton, In the Goods of, L.R. 3 P. & D., 159, followed. *In re Hall,* (1910) V.L.R., 14 ; 31 A.L.T., 132 ; 16 A.L.R., 15.

Wyke v. Wyke, (1904) P., 149, disapproved. *Mulder* v. *Mulder,* (1906) V.L.R., 388 ; 27 A.L.T., 216 ; 12 A.L.R., 210.

Wylie, Ex parte ; Ex parte Butler, 4 A.L.T., 41 ; explained and distinguished. *Mooney* v. *Still,* (1909) V.L.R., 227 ; 30 A.L.T., 191 ; 15 A.L.R., 197.

Young v. Ormiston ; In re Ormiston, 11 V.L.R., 285, followed. *In re Reed,* (1911) V.L.R., 232 ; 32 A.L.T., 168 ; 17 A.L.R., 164.

Zanoni v. Zanoni, 24 V.L.R., 940 ; 5 A.L.R., 206, followed. *Farrer* v. *Farrer,* (1907) V.L.R., 382 ; 28 A.L.T., 221 ; 13 A.L.R., 236

INDEX OF REFERENCES TO STATUTES.

The numbers after the Sections refer to the Columns.

IMPERIAL STATUTES.

A DIGEST

OF

REPORTED CASES

IN THE

SUPREME COURT, COURT OF INSOLVENCY, AND COURTS OF MINES,
OF THE STATE OF VICTORIA.

◆◆◆

For the years 1906 to 1912 inclusive.

ABATEMENT

Settlement—Trustee and cestui que trust—Appointment—Gifts out of specific fund—Gift of residue—Failure of fund—Abatement.] —*See* SETTLEMENTS. *a'Beckett* v. *Trustees Executors &c. Co. Ltd.*, (1908) 5 C.L.R., 512.

ABUSE OF PROCESS

Malicious arrest—Abuse of process of Court.]—The distinction between an action for malicious arrest and an action founded on an abuse of the process of the Court discussed. *Varawa* v. *Howard Smith & Co. Ltd.*, (1911) 13 C.L.R., 35; 17 A.L.R., 499. H.C., *Griffith, C.J., O'Connor* and *Isaacs, JJ.*

Abuse of process—Insolvency proceedings to stifle litigation—Action by non-trader—No actual damage.]—*Quaere*, whether proceedings in insolvency taken to stifle litigation between the parties amount to an abuse of the process of the Court in respect of which an action will lie. *Quaere*, also, whether such an action, if it will lie at all, will lie by a non-trader without proof of actual damage. *Bayne* v. *Baillieu*; *Bayne* v. *Riggall*, (1908) 6 C.L.R., 382; *sub nom., Bayne* v. *Blake*,

14 A.L.R., 426. H.C., *Griffith, C.J., Barton* and *O'Connor, JJ.*

Abuse of process of Court—Insolvency proceedings to stifle litigation—Action for damages in respect of—Special damage, whether necessary to prove.]—*See* INSOLVENCY. *Bayne* v. *Blake*, (1909) 9 C.L.R., 347; 15 A.L.R., 486.

Abuse of process of Court—Petition in insolvency during pendency of action between parties—Good petitioning creditor's debt.]—*See* INSOLVENCY. *Bayne* v. *Blake*, (1909) 9 C.L.R., 360.

Order XIV. (A) (Rules of 1906)—Frivolous or vexatious action, what is—Order for arrest of witness in insolvency proceedings—Purpose of order not to discover assets but to hamper appeal to High Court—Action for damages in respect of such order—Conspiracy to oppress—No actual damage.]—*See* PRACTICE AND PLEADING. *Bayne* v. *Baillieu*; *Bayne* v. *Riggall*, (1908) 6 C.L.R., 382; *sub nom., Bayne* v. *Blake*, 14 A.L.R., 426.

Order XIV. (A) (Rules of 1906)—Stay of action—Inherent jurisdiction—Abuse of process—Action frivolous or vexatious—Summary judgment.] — *See* PRACTICE AND PLEADING. *Burton* v. *Bairnsdale, President, &c., of Shire of*, (1908) 7 C.L.R., 76; 14 A.L.R., 529.

ACCOUNTS

See EXECUTORS AND ADMINISTRATORS, PRACTICE AND PLEADING, TRUSTS AND TRUSTEES.

ADEMPTION.

Evidence — Legacy — Ademption — Gift made for same purpose as legacy—Statements by donor made subsequently to gifts as to intention in making gifts.]—*See* EVIDENCE. *In re Leggatt ; Griffith* v. *Calder*, (1908) V.L.R., 385 ; 30 A.L.T., 34 ; 14 A.L.R., 314.

Ademption—Pecuniary legacy to be applied in uncontrolled discretion of trustees to several purposes—Subsequent gift by testatrix towards one of such purposes which was only imperfectly accomplished at death—Statements as to her intention made by testatrix subsequently to gifts.]—*See* WILL. *In re Leggatt ; Griffith* v. *Calder*, (1908) V.L.R., 385 ; 30 A.L.T., 34 ; 14 A.L.R., 314.

ADMINISTRATION OF ESTATES OF DECEASED PERSONS

See also, DUTIES ON THE ESTATES OF DECEASED PERSONS ; EXECUTORS AND ADMINISTRATORS ; TENANT FOR LIFE AND REMAINDERMAN ; TRUSTS AND TRUSTEES ; WILL.

Order II., r. 3—Form of writ—Administration action—Heading.]—*See* PRACTICE AND PLEADING. *Cameron* v. *Cameron*, (1906) V.L.R., 13.

ADULTERY

See HUSBAND AND WIFE.

ADVANCEMENT

Parent and child—Purchase by parent in name of child—Presumption of advancement, when rebutted—Retention of life interest by parent—Real property, rule applicable to.]—Where property is purchased by a parent in the name of a child the presumption that the purchase is by way of advancement of the child is rebutted if it be shown that the parent intended to reserve a life interest to himself. This applies to both real and personal property. *McKie* v. *McKie*, 23 V.L.R., 489 ; 19 A.L.T. 190 ; 4 A.L.R., 98, followed. *Stuckey* v. *Trustees, Executors and Agency Co. Ltd.*, (1910) V.L.R., 55 ; 31 A.L.T., 157 ; 16 A.L.R., 65. *Madden, C.J.*

ADVERSE POSSESSION

Adverse possession—Land under operation of Transfer of Land Act 1890 (No. 1149)—Land of several owners—Enclosed by common fence—Common use—Presumption of possession—Equivocal acts of possession—Intention—Real Property Act 1890 (No. 1136), Part II.—Transfer of Land Act 1904 (No. 1931), secs. 10 and 11.]—*See* LIMITATIONS (STATUTES OF). *Clement* v. *Jones*, 8 C.L.R., 133 ; 15 A.L.R., 158.

Possession—Adverse possession—Land of two owners within one fence—Re-entry of registered proprietor—Cutting firewood—Renewal of survey marks on boundaries—Effect of.]—*See* LIMITATIONS (STATUTES OF). *Clement* v. *Jones*, 8 C.L.R., 133 ; 15 A.L.R., 158.

Possession—Land of two owners within one fence—Presumption of possession—Possession follows title—Equivocal acts of possession.]—*See* LIMITATIONS (STATUTES OF). *Clements* v. *Jones*, 8 C.L.R., 133 ; 15 A.L.R., 158.

Real Property Act 1890 (No. 1136), sec. 23 —Adverse possession—Statutory period, when time begins to run—Tenancy at will—Creation of new tenancy—Permission of owner, acknowledgement of tenant that he holds by.]—*See* LIMITATIONS (STATUTES OF). *Wilson* v. *Equity Trustees, Executors, &c. Co. Ltd.*, (1911) V.L.R., 481 ; 33 A.L.T., 89 ; 17 A.L.R., 523.

Real Property Act 1890 (No. 1136), secs. 18, 23—Adverse possession—Period of limitation, commencement of—New tenancy at will, what will create—Request for transfer of land.]—*See* LIMITATIONS (STATUTES OF). *Wilson* v. *Equity Trustees, Executors, &c. Co. Ltd.*, (1911) V.L.R., 481 ; 33 A.L.T., 89 ; 17 A.L.R., 523.

Transfer of Land Act 1904 (No. 1931), secs. 10, 11—Land alienated after 1st October 1862—Crown grant not registered—Adverse possession.]—*See* LIMITATIONS (STATUTES OF). *Burns* v. *Registrar of Titles*, (1912) V.L.R., 29 ; 18 A.L.R., 47.

Transfer of Land Act 1904 (No. 1931), sec. 10—Supreme Court Rules 1906, Chapter VIII., r. 2—Adverse possession, title by—Vesting order—Registered proprietor deceased —Practice.]—*See* TRANSFER OF LAND ACT. *Marriott* v. *Hosken*, (1911) V.L.R., 54 ; 32 A.L.T., 115 ; 16 A.L.R., 604.

Transfer of Land Act 1904 (No. 1931), sec. 10—Rules of the Supreme Court 1906, Chapter VIII., r. 2—Adverse possession against registered proprietor—Procedure—Registered proprietor deceased.]—*See* LIMITATIONS (STATUTES OF). *Lambourn* v. *Hosken*, (1912) V.L.R., 394 ; 34 A.L.T., 101 ; 18 A.L.R., 371.

Transfer of Land Act 1904 (No. 1931), sec. 10 — Adverse possession — Registered proprietor dead before commencement of adverse possession—No administration of his estate— Next of kin unknown—Duration of adverse possession.]—*See* LIMITATIONS (STATUTES OF). *Lambourn* v. *Hosken*, (1912) V.L.R., 394 ; 34 A.L.T., 101 ; 18 A.L.R., 371.

Transfer of Land Act 1904 (No. 1931), sec. 10—Title by adverse possession against registered proprietor—Declaratory judgment sought—Action brought too soon—Liberty to apply at future date.]—*See* LIMITATIONS (STATUTES OF). *Lambourn* v. *Hosken*, (1912) V.L.R., 394 ; 34 A.L.T., 101 ; 18 A.L.R., 371.

AFFIDAVITS

See also, HABEAS CORPUS.

Instruments Act 1890 (No. 1103), secs. 133, 144—Declarations and Affidavits Act 1890 (No. 1191), sec. 6—Bill of sale—Registration —Affidavit verifying bill—Affidavit of renewal —Such affidavits to be made before commissioners for taking declarations and affidavits — Affidavits — Commissioners of Supreme Court—Restriction of authority.]—*See* BILL

OF SALE. *Wrigglesworth* v. *Collis* ; *Spencer, claimant*, 33 A.L.T. (Supplement), 13 ; 18 A.L.R. (C.N.), 6.

Affidavits filed but not used—Whether a part of the proceedings.]—The mere filing of an answering affidavit by one of the parties does not make it part of the proceedings. *Manson* v. *Ponninghaus*, (1911) V.L.R., 239 ; 33 A.L.T., 1 ; 17 A.L.R., 238. *Madden, C.J.* (1911).

Order XXXVIII., r. 3 (Rules of 1906)— Affidavit as to belief—Grounds of belief not stated—Admissibility.]—*See* PRACTICE AND PLEADING. *Manson* v. *Ponninghaus*, (1911) V.L.R., 239 ; 33 A.L.T., 1 ; 17 A.L.R., 238.

Supreme Court Act 1890 (No. 1142), secs. 185, 186—Order XXXVIII., r. 3 (Rules of 1906)—Charging stock and shares—Charging order, whether final or interlocutory—Affidavit of information and belief, admissibility of.]—*See* PRACTICE AND PLEADING. *Manson* v. *Ponninghaus*, (1911) V.L.R., 239 ; 33 A.L.T., 1 ; 17 A.L.R., 238.

Petition by company for winding up of another company—Affidavit supporting petition—Companies Act 1890 (No. 1074), secs. 252, 253—Mines Act 1890 (No. 1120), sec. 180.]—*See* MINING. *Re Mount Lyell Consols Mining Corporation No Liability* (*No.* 2), 30 A.L.T. (Supplement), 17 ; 14 A.L.R. (C.N.), 41.

Order to review—Affidavits of justices— Duty of Justices as to—Facts to which Justices may properly depose.]—*See* JUSTICES OF THE PEACE. *Larkin* v. *Penfold*, (1906) V.L.R., 535 ; 28 A.L.T., 42 ; 12 A.L.R., 337.

Order to review—Affidavits in reply, when they may be used.]—*See* JUSTICES OF THE PEACE. *Larkin* v. *Penfold*, 12 A.L.R., 337.

Order to review—Practice—Order nisi and affidavit in support—How brought to the knowledge of Justices—Subsequent affidavits, suggested practice as to.]—*See* JUSTICES OF THE PEACE. *Larkin* v. *Penfold*, (1906) V.L.R. 535 ; 28 A.L.T., 42 ; 12 A.L.R., 337.

Lotteries Gaming and Betting Act 1906 No. 2055), sec. 38—Application for declaration

that premises are a common gaming house—
Affidavit of police officer showing reasonable
grounds for suspecting — Whether police
officer may be cross-examined thereon.]—
See GAMING AND WAGERING. *In re Lotteries
Gaming and Betting Act* 1906; *In re
Shanghai Club*; *In re Ah Pow*; *Ex parte
Gleeson*, (1907) V.L.R., 463; 29 A.L.T., 31;
13 A.L.R., 360.

Lotteries Gaming and Betting Act 1906
(No. 2055), sec. 38—Application for declaration that premises are a common gaming
house—Affidavits in reply to affidavits of
party opposing—Cross-examination of deponents.]—*See* GAMING AND WAGERING.
In re Lotteries Gaming and Betting Act
1906; *In re Shanghai Club*; *In re Ah
Pow*; *Ex parte Gleeson*, (1907) V.L.R., 463;
29 A.L.T., 31; 13 A.L.R., 360.

Interpleader summons—Affidavit in support—County Court Rules 1891, r. 230.]—*See*
COUNTY COURT. *Looker* v. *Mercer*, 28
A.L.T. (Supplement), 15; 13 A.L.R. (C.N.),
13.

AFFILIATION

See MAINTENANCE AND MAINTEN-
ANCE ORDERS.

AGENT

See PRINCIPAL AND AGENT.

AGISTMENT

Agister—Negligence — Liability — Horse
placed among horned cattle—Horse injured
by bull—Scienter.]—*See* CATTLE. *Sanderson*
v. *Dunn*, 32 A.L.T. (Supplement), 14; 17
A.L.R. (C.N.), 9.

ALIENS ACT

Licensing—British subject—Licensing Act
1890 (No. 1111), sec. 177—Aliens Act 1890

(No. 1063), sec. 6—Naturalization Act 1903
(No. 11 of 1903), secs. 9, 10.]—*See* LICENSING.
In re Hall, 18 A.L.R. (C.N.), 20.

ALLEGIANCE

The Aliens Statute 1865 (No. 256)—Letters
of naturalization issued under, effect of.]—
For a discussion on the extra-territorial
effect of naturalization under a Victorian
law, see *Ah Sheung* v. *Lindberg*, (1906)
V.L.R., 323; 27 A.L.T., 189; *sub nom.*,
Rex v. *Ah Sheung*, 12 A.L.R., 190. *Cussen*,
J. (1906). (*See* 4 C.L.R., 949).

Immigration Restriction Acts 1901-1905—
"Immigrant," meaning of—Naturalised subject domiciled in Victoria—Return to Victoria
from China.]—*See* IMMIGRATION RESTRICTION
ACTS. *Ah Sheung* v. *Lindberg*, (1906)
V.L.R. 323; 27 A.L.T., 189; *sub nom.*, *Rex*
v. *Ah Sheung*, 12 A.L.R., 190. (*See* 4 C.L.R.,
949).

AMENDMENT

See COUNTY COURT, GENERAL SES-
SIONS, INSOLVENCY, JUSTICES OF
THE PEACE, MINING, PRACTICE
AND PLEADING.

ANIMALS

See CATTLE, CRIMINAL LAW, STOCK
DISEASES ACT.

APPEAL

I. TO THE PRIVY COUNCIL.

A. FROM THE HIGH COURT.

1. *Where Appeal Lies.*

(a) Certificate of the High Court.

Commonwealth of Australia Constitution Act (63 & 64 Vict. c. 12)— The Constitution sec. 74—Appeal to King in Council—Certificate of High Court—Reasons for granting, sufficiency of—Conflicting decisions of Privy Council and High Court.]—*Per Griffith, C.J. Barton, O'Connor, Isaacs* and *Higgins, JJ.*, The fact that there are conflicting decisions of the Privy Council and the High Court on the question is not a sufficient reason for granting a certificate that the question is one which ought to be determined by His Majesty in Council. *Per O'Connor. J.*: It is the duty of the High Court to refuse the certificate where, if the certificate were given, the Privy Council would be likely to decide the question in a manner contrary to the true intent of the Constitution as interpreted by the High Court. *Per Isaacs, J.*: Australian considerations should have a weighty, perhaps a dominant force, in guiding the judgment of the High Court in granting or refusing a certificate. *Baxter* v. *Commissioners of Taxation*; *Flint* v. *Webb*, 4 C.L.R., 1087, 1178; 13 A.L.R., 313 (1907).

Commonwealth of Australia Constitution Act (63 & 64 Vict. c. 12)—The Constitution, secs. 74, 109—Appeal to Privy Council—Question as to limits inter se of powers of Commonwealth and State, nature of—How distinguished from question of inconsistency between law of State and law of Commonwealth.]—*Per Griffith, C.J., Barton, O'Connor* and *Isaacs, JJ.*: Section 109 of the Constitution deals with the case of two admitted powers of legislation meeting on a concurrent field, and provides that in the event of inconsistency the one shall prevail over the other. The cases dealt with by section 74 are cases in which the question is whether an attempted exercise of the powers of either a State or the Commonwealth in such a manner as to interfere with the free exercise of the powers of the other of the two authorities is or is not within the limits prescribed by the Constitution. The question whether a State *Income Tax Act* applied to the salaries of Federal officers is or is not to be considered as trespassing upon a region exclusively assigned to the Commonwealth is a question of the kind referred to in sec. 74. *Per Isaacs, J.* : The question whether or not a State *Income Tax Act* levying tax upon federal officers proportioned to their Federal salaries clashes *pro tanto* with the Federal enactment that their remuneration shall be the full sum granted them by the Commonwealth is a question coming under sec. 109. *Baxter* v. *Commissioners of Taxation* ; *Flint* v. *Webb*, 4 C.L.R., 1087, 1178 ; 13 A.L.R., 313 (1907).

Commonwealth of Australia Constitution Act (63 & 64 Vict. c. 12)—The Constitution, sec. 74—Questions as to the limits inter se of constitutional powers of Commonwealth and State—Conflicting decisions of Privy Council and High Court—Whether High Court final arbiter upon such questions—9 Geo. IV. c. 83 ; 7 & 8 Vict. c. 79 and Orders in Council thereunder.]—*Per Griffith, C.J., Barton, O'Connor* and *Isaacs, JJ., Higgins. J.,* dissenting : Upon all questions of the classes referred to in sec. 74 of the Constitution, except those in regard to which the High Court may by granting a certificate under that section have submitted itself to the guidance of the Privy Council, it is the High Court and not the Privy Council which is the ultimate arbiter. The High Court is not bound to follow a decision of the Privy Council given upon such a question without the certificate of the High Court and in conflict with a previous decision of the High Court with regard to which the grant of such a certificate was refused. *Baxter* v. *Commissioners of Taxation* ; *Flint* v. *Webb*, 4 C.L.R., 1087, 1178 ; 13 A.L.R., 313 (1907).

Commonwealth of Australia Constitution Act (63 & 64 Vict.) c. 12—The Constitution, sec. 74—"Decision . . . upon any question," meaning of—Appeal to Privy Council.]—*Per Griffith, C.J., Barton, O'Connor* and *Isaacs, JJ.* : " Decision of the High Court upon any question " means what the Court decides to be the law with regard to that question. It does not refer to the judgment

inter partes in the cause. *Baxter* v. *Commissioners of Taxation* ; *Flint* v. *Webb*, 4 C.L.R., 1087, 1178 ; 13 A.L.R., 313 (1907).

Commonwealth of Australia Constitution Act (63 & 64 Vict. c. 12)—The Constitution, sec. 74—Interpretation, principles of—History of Constitution, whether it may be considered—Appeal to Privy Council.]—*Per Griffith, C.J., Barton* and *O'Connor, JJ.* : The duty of the High Court in regard to questions under sec. 74 is to be determined upon consideration of the whole purview and history of the Constitution. *Baxter* v. *Commissioners of Taxation* ; *Flint* v. *Webb*, 4 C.L.R., 1087, 1178 ; 13 A.L.R., 313 (1907).

(b) Special Leave.

Appeal to Privy Council—Special leave—Decree of High Court.]—Where petitioners for special leave have elected to appeal to the High Court of Australia, from which it is known that there is no further appeal without special leave, their Lordships will not, except in a very special case, entertain their petition. *Victorian Railways Commissioners* v. *Brown*, (1906) A.C., 381. (Privy Council).

Practice—Special leave to appeal to Privy Council—Decree of High Court of Australia.]—Where on a petition for special leave to appeal from the High Court of Australia it appeared that the law as laid down by that Court could not be objected to. *Held,* that the question of the application of the law to the particular case involving simply the construction of a document, however substantial as between the parties, was not one of public importance, and that there was not sufficient ground for granting the petition. *Wilfley Ore Concentrator Syndicate Ltd.* v. *N. Guthridge Ltd.*, (1906) A.C., 548. (Privy Council).

Practice—Special leave to appeal to Privy Council from judgment of High Court—State Income Tax—Liability of Commonwealth officers.]—The High Court, having decided contrary to the decision of the Privy Council, that a State had no power to impose income tax upon a salary paid by the Commonwealth to its officers, or to a member of the Commonwealth Parliament, resident in such

State, the Commonwealth Parliament thereafter passed an Act expressly authorizing the States to impose such taxation. *Held*, that petitions for special leave to appeal from the High Court decisions must be refused, the amount at stake being inconsiderable and the controversy having been closed. *Webb* v. *Crouch*; *Same* v. *Flint*, (1908) A.C., 214; (1907) 5 C.L.R., 398. (Privy Council).

2. *Practice.*

(*a*) Where Judgment Reversed on Appeal.

Appeal to Privy Council from Order of High Court—Order of High Court in two parts—One part only appealed from—The whole order discharged—Re-affirmance of previous decision of High Court as to the part of the order not appealed from.]—Decision of the High Court in *Cock* v. *Smith*, 9 C.L.R., 773; 15 A.L.R., 526, on a question of apportionment between tenant for life and remainderman, followed, notwithstanding the decision of the Privy Council in *Smith* v. *Cock*, (1911) A.C., 317; 12 C.L.R., 30, reversing the previous judgment of the High Court, as this part of the judgment had not in fact been appealed from. *Cock* v. *Aitken*, (1911) 13 C.L.R., 461; 18 A.L.R., 337. H.C., *Griffith, C.J., Barton* and *O'Connor, JJ.*

Trustee—Life tenant and remainderman——Corpus and income—Costs paid by trustees under order of High Court—Decision of High Court reversed on appeal by one party to Privy Council—Effect on rights of parties not appealing—Indemnity of trustees—Rights of assignee of life tenant.]—*See* TENANT FOR LIFE AND REMAINDERMAN. *Cock* v. *Aitken*, (1912) 15 C.L.R., 373; 18 A.L.R., 576.

Appeal to Privy Council—Judgment of High Court reversed—Judgment of State Court restored—Practice—Order of Privy Council made order of High Court—Costs.]—*See Cock* v. *Smith*, 13 C.L.R., 129; 18 A.L.R., 139. *Griffith, C.J.*

(*b*) Stay of Proceedings.

Practice—Appeal to Privy Council from decision of High Court—Stay of proceedings—Special circumstances—Danger of loss of evidence by delay.]—Where special leave has been given by the Judicial Committee of the Privy Council to appeal from a decision of the High Court in its appellate jurisdiction directing inquiries to be made in the Supreme Court of a State, the High Court will, pending the appeal, stay proceedings under its judgment, unless special circumstances be shown, *e.g.*, the danger of necessary evidence being lost by delay. *Bayne* v. *Blake*, (1907) 4 C.L.R., 944; 13 A.L.R., 101. *Griffith, C.J.* (1907)

B. FROM THE FULL COURT OF THE STATE.

1. *Jurisdiction Generally.*

Commonwealth of Australia Constitution (63 & 64 Vict. c. 12)—Power of Victorian Legislature (18 & 19 Vict. c. 55)—Income tax—Right of appeal from Supreme Court to Privy Council—Whether Commonwealth Parliament may take away.]—*Held*, that a petition by the Commonwealth for the dismissal on the ground of incompetency of an appeal from an order of the Supreme Court of Victoria relating to the assessment of an officer of the Commonwealth, resident in Victoria and receiving his official salary in that State, for income tax in respect of such salary, the income tax being imposed by an Act of the Victorian Legislature, should be dismissed. The Constitution Act does not authorise the Commonwealth Parliament to take away the right of appeal to the Privy Council existing in such case. *Webb* v. *Outtrim*, (1907) A.C., 81; 13 A.L.R. (C.N.), 1. (Privy Council).

Judiciary Act 1903 (No. 6 of 1903), sec. 39—Federal jurisdiction of State Courts — Validity of grant of — Right of appeal to High Court—Prerogative right of appeal to Privy Council, whether affected — Commonwealth of Australia Constitution Act (63 & 64 Vict. c. 12—The Constitution, secs. 71, 77—Colonial Laws Validity Act (28 & 29 Vict. c. 63.]—*Per Griffith, C.J., Barton, O'Connor* and *Isaacs. JJ.*: Even if sec. 39 (2) (*a*) of the *Judiciary Act* 1903 purports to take away the prerogative right of appeal to the Privy Council, and the section is to that extent *ultra vires* and inoperative, its failure in that respect does not affect the validity of the grant of federal jurisdiction to State Courts contained in the rest of the section and the consequent right of appeal to the High Court. *Sed Quaere*, whether sub-section (2) (*a*) should be construed as affecting the prerogative. *Baxter* v. *Commissioners of Taxation*; *Flint* v. *Webb*, 4 C.L.R., 1087, 1178; 13 A.L.R., 313 (1907).

Appeal—Supreme Court Act 1890 (No. 1142), sec. 231—Whether ultra vires the Parliament of Victoria.]—The Full Court of the State refused to go into the question whether sec. 231 of the *Supreme Court Act* 1890 is *ultra vires* the Parliament of Victoria—the validity of that section having been assumed in a long series of decisions. *In re " Maizo " and " Maizena " Trade Marks*; *Robert Harper & Co.* v. *National Starch Co.* (1906) V.L.R., 246; 27 A.L.T., 168; 12 A.L.R., 164. F.C. *Holroyd, A.C.J., a' Beckett* and *Hodges, JJ.* (1906).

2. *Appealable Amount.*

Privy Council—Supreme Court Act 1890 (No. 1142), sec. 231—Appealable amount— " Matter in issue," what is—Assumption that contention of unsuccessful party was correct —Res judicata—Uncontradicted affidavits.]— An application by R. for the registration as a trade mark of a pictorial label containing the word " Maizo " was opposed by N. on the ground that the word " Maizo " so resembled N.'s trade mark and trade name " Maizena " as to be likely to deceive and to create confusion in trade by causing R.'s goods to be passed off and mistaken for N.'s goods; N. did not dispute that the word " Maizo " as used in the label could not deceive, but he contended that upon the true construction of sec. 17 of the *Trade Marks Act* 1890 (No. 2) registration should be refused if the word " Maizo " might by any means or in any connection be used so as to deceive. The Court decided against this contention and granted the application. On motion for leave to appeal to the Privy Council, *Held* that in order to determine what was the matter in issue within the meaning of sec. 231 of the *Supreme Court Act* 1890 not only must

the decision be assumed to be erroneous but that the said contention of N. must be assumed to be correct; and that, on the uncontradicted affidavit of N. " that the average sales of Maizena in Victoria amounted to about £8,000 per annum " and " that the matter in issue—namely whether R.'s trade mark should be registered and whether the opposition should be allowed—amounts to more than the sum of £1,000 " leave to appeal should be granted. *In re " Maizo " and " Maizena " Trade Marks*; *Robert Harper & Co.* v. *National Starch Co.*, (1906) V.L.R., 246; 27 A.L.T., 168; 12 A.L.R., 164. F.C. *Holroyd, A.C.J., a' Beckett* and *Hodges, JJ.* (1906).

Order in Council 9th June 1860—Supreme Court Act 1890 (No. 1142), sec. 231—Appealable amount—Judgment respecting property of value of £500—Trade Mark.]—On motion by L. to expunge a trade mark of M., and a cross motion by M. to expunge or limit a trade mark of L., the Court dismissed the motion of L., and on M.'s motion limited the trade mark of L. to the class of goods in respect of which alone it was then being used by L. L. applied for leave to appeal to the Privy Council under the Order in Council of 9th June 1860. *Held*, that the fact that L.'s trade mark was worth over £500 did not entitle L. to have leave to appeal. Where the circumstances are such as to preclude the Court from forming, not a guess, but a reasonable conclusion as to the amount at stake, leave should not be given to appeal. *Amos* v. *Fraser*, 4 C.L.R., 78; 12 A.L.R., 481, considered. *Lever Bros. Ltd.* v. *G. Mowling & Son*, 30 A.L.T., 144; 15 A.L.R., 40. *a' Beckett, J.* (1908).

II. TO THE HIGH COURT.

A. THE COMMONWEALTH COURT OF CONCILIA-
   TION AND ARBITRATION; PROHIBITION;
   SPECIAL CASE.

The Constitution (No. 63 & 64 Vict. c. 12), sec. 73—Appellate jurisdiction of High Court— Court of Conciliation and Arbitration—Commonwealth Conciliation and Arbitration Act 1904 (No. 13 of 1904), sec. 31.]—An appeal lies to the High Court from a decision of the President of the Commonwealth Court of Conciliation and Arbitrarion dismissing an appeal to him from a decision of the Industrial Registrar disallowing objections to the registration of an Association under the *Commonwealth Conciliation and Arbitration Act* 1904. *Jumbunna Coal Mine No Liability* v. *Victorian Coal Miners' Association,* (1908) 6 C.L.R., 309 ; 14 A.L.R., 701. H.C., *Griffith, C.J., O'Connor, Barton* and *Isaacs, JJ.*

Commonwealth of Australia Constitution Act (63 & 64 Vict. c. 12)—The Constitution secs. 71, 73, 75 (v)—Commonwealth Conciliation and Arbitration Act 1904 (No. 13 of 1904), sec. 31—Judiciary Act 1903 (No. 6 of 1903), secs. 30, 33 (b), 38—Prohibition—Jurisdiction of High Court to issue to Commonwealth Court of Conciliation and Arbitration—Whether prohibition original or appellate jurisdiction.]—*Per Griffith, C.J., Barton* and *O'Connor, JJ.*—The High Court has jurisdiction to issue prohibition to the Commonwealth Court of Conciliation and Arbitration either under sec. 75 (v) of the Constitution, the President of the Court being an officer within the meaning of that sub-section, or under sec. 33 of the *Judiciary Act* 1903, and whether an appeal does or does not lie to the High Court *Per Isaacs, J.*—Prohibition to revise or correct the proceedings instituted in another Court is appellate not original jurisdiction, and is therefore not within sec. 75 (v.). But the High Court has jurisdiction to issue prohibition to the Commonwealth Court of Conciliation and Arbitration because sec. 31 of the *Commonwealth Conciliation and Arbitration Act* 1904 has not taken away that part of the appellate power granted by the Constitution. *The King and the Commonwealth Court of Conciliation and Arbitration and the President thereof and the Boot Trade Employees Federation, Ex parte Whybrow & Co.,* (1910) 11 C.L.R., 1 ; 16 A.L.R., 373.

High Court—Practice—Motion for prohibition to restrain Commonwealth Court of Conciliation and Arbitration—Finding by President that dispute exists, whether High Court

bound by—The Commonwealth Constitution, sec. 51 (xxxv.).]—*See* PROHIBITION. *The King and the Commonwealth Court of Conciliation and Arbitration and the President thereof and the Boot Trade Employees Federation, Ex parte Whybrow & Co.,* (1910) 11 C.L.R., 1 ; 16 A.L.R., 373.

Commonwealth Court of Conciliation and Arbitration—Power of President to state case for opinion of High Court.]—For observations of the President of the Commonwealth Court of Conciliation and Arbitration as to his power to state a case for the opinion of the High Court, *See Jumbunna Coal Mine No Liability* v. *Victorian Coal Miners' Association,* (1908) 6 C.L.R., 309 ; 14 A.L.R., 701.

Commonwealth Conciliation and Arbitration Act 1904 (No. 13 of 1904), sec. 31—Case stated for opinion of High Court—Duties of High Court and President respectively.]—*See* EMPLOYER AND EMPLOYEE. *Federated Engine Drivers and Firemen's Association of Australasia* v. *Broken Hill Proprietary Co. Ltd.,* (1911) 12 C.L.R., 398 ; 17 A.L.R., 285.

B. IN TRADE MARKS AND PATENT MATTERS.

Trade Mark—Practice—Costs—Award of costs by Law Officer—Discretion—Appeal to High Court—Trade Marks Act 1905 (No. 20 of 1905), secs. 95, 96.]—The High Court has jurisdiction to entertain an appeal as to the costs awarded by the Law Officer on an appeal to him from the Registrar of Trade Marks. But on such an appeal the Court will not over-rule his order unless there has been a disregard of principle or a misapprehension of facts. *In re Gilbert ; Gilbert* v. *Hudlestone,* 28 Ch. D., 549, applied. *Alexander Ferguson & Co.* v. *Daniel Crawford & Co.,* (1909) 10 C.L.R., 207 ; H.C. *Griffith, C.J., O'Connor* and *Isaacs, JJ.*

Patents Act 1903 (No. 21 of 1903) sec. 58 — Appeal from decision of Commissioner of Patents—Directions as to procedure—The Patents Regulations 1904, r. 80—Appeal book.]—In a pending appeal from a decision of the Commissioner of Patents a Justice of the High Court, upon an application under Rule 80 of *The Patents Regulations* 1904, directed that the appeal should be set down for hearing at the then current sittings of the Court, and that it be heard before the Full Court but not until ten days after the delivery of the appeal book. His Honor also gave directions as to the preparation and printing of the appeal book. *Moore v. Phillips*, 13 A.L.R., 66. *Isaacs, J.* (1907).

Patents Act 1903 (No. 21 of 1903) secs. 14, 58, 111—Appeal against decision of Commissioner of Patents — Costs of opposition to grant of patent before Commissioner.]—The costs of a successful appellant's opposition before the Commissioner were allowed on the lower Supreme Court scale. *Moore v. Phillips*, 4 C.L.R., 1411 ; 13 A.L.R., 424. H.C., *Griffith, C.J., Barton, Isaacs* and *Higgins, JJ.* (1907).

C. FROM INFERIOR COURTS EXERCISING FEDERAL JURISDICTION.

Commonwealth of Australia Constitution Act (63 & 64 Vict. c. 12)—The Constitution, secs. 73, 74, 76, 77—Question as to limits inter se of constitutional powers of Commonwealth and State, what is—Question raised by defence whether State tax on federal salary an interference with powers of Commonwealth — Exercise of federal jurisdiction by Court of Petty Sessions — Appeal to High Court, competency of—Judiciary Act 1903 (No. 6 of 1903), sec. 39.]—In proceedings in a Court of Petty Sessions to recover income tax from a federal officer in respect of his official salary, the defendant claimed to be exempt on the ground that taxation of his official salary by the State was an interference with the free exercise of the powers of the Commonwealth within the meaning of the rule in *D'Emden v. Pedder*, 1 C.L.R., 91 ; 10 A.L.R. (C.N.), 30, and therefore impliedly prohibited by the Constitution. The Court of Petty Sessions, following *Webb v. Outtrim*, (1907) A.C., 81, made an order for the amount claimed against the defendant, who thereupon appealed to the High Court. *Held*, that the question raised by the defence was a question as to the limits *inter se* of the Constitutional powers of the Commonwealth and

a State within the meaning of sec. 74 of the Constitution, that the Court of Petty Sessions was exercising federal jurisdiction under sec. 39 of the *Judiciary Act* 1903, and that the appeal was competent by virtue of sub-sec. (2) (*b*) of that section as well as by section 73 of the Constitution. *Baxter v. Commissioners of Taxation* ; *Flint v. Webb*, 4 C.L.R., 1087, 1178 ; 13 A.L.R., 313. H.C. *Griffith, C.J., Barton, O'Connor* and *Isaacs, JJ.* (1907).

Federal Jurisdiction—Exercise of, what is —Two questions decided, one federal and the other not—Each decision sufficient to sustain judgment—Court of Petty Sessions—Appeal to High Court, whether it lies—Judiciary Act 1903 (No. 6), sec. 39 (2) (d)—Commonwealth of Australia Constitution Act (63 & 64 Vict. c. 12), The Constitution, sec. 77.]—A Court of Petty Sessions exercises federal jurisdiction within the meaning of sec. 39 (2) (*d*) of the *Judiciary Act* 1903, if it be necessary in the particular case for the Court to decide any question arising under the Constitution or involving its interpretation. If, however, whether that question is answered rightly or wrongly, the Court answers another question not arising under the Constitution or involving its interpretation, and the Court's answer to such other question enables it to decide the case, the Court does not exercise federal jurisdiction, and therefore no appeal lies to the High Court. *Miller v. Haweis*, (1907) 5 C.L.R. 89 ; 13 A.L.R., 583. H.C. *Griffith, C.J., Barton, O'Connor, Isaacs* and *Higgins, JJ.*

Court of Petty Sessions—Federal jurisdiction—Exercise of, what is—Commonwealth of Australia Constitution, secs. 31, 76—Constitution Act Amendment Act 1890 (No. 1075), sec. 282—Judiciary Act 1903 (No. 6), sec. 39 (2) (d)—Question decided involving interpretation of sec. 31 of Constitution—Other question decided involving interpretation of Commonwealth Electoral Act 1902 (No. 19 of 1902)—Appeal to High Court, whether it lies.] —On a complaint for work and labour done at an election for the House of Representatives of the Commonwealth Parliament, the defence being that sec. 282 of the *Constitution Act*

Amendment Act 1890 was a bar to the complaint, the Court of Petty Sessions held that sec. 282 was a "law relating to elections" and by virtue of sec. 31 of the Commonwealth Constitution applied to elections for the House of Representatives until Parliament otherwise provided, but also held that Parliament had otherwise provided by passing the *Commonwealth Electoral Act* 1902 and had thereby repealed sec. 282, and the Court therefore gave judgment for the complainant. *Held*, that in determining the second point the Court of Petty Sessions had not exercised federal jurisdiction, and therefore that no appeal lay to the High Court from the judgment of the Court of Petty Sessions. *Miller* v. *Haweis*, (1907) 5 C.L.R., 89 ; 13 A.L.R., 583. H.C. *Griffith, C.J., Barton, O'Connor, Isaacs* and *Higgins, JJ.*

Appeal from Court of Petty Sessions exercising federal jurisdiction—Order to review— No appeal under State law—Rules of High Court 1911, Part II., Sec. IV., r. 1—Justices Act 1904 (No. 1959), sec. 21.]—An appeal to the High Court from a decision of a Court of Petty Sessions exercising federal jurisdiction in the case of a civil debt recoverable summarily when the sum involved does not exceed £5 may under the *Rules of the High Court*, Part II., Sec. IV., r. 1, be brought by way of order to review notwithstanding that by section 21 of the *Justices Act* 1904 in such a case the granting of an order to review is prohibited. *Prentice* v. *Amalgamated Mining Employees Association of Victoria and Tasmania*, (1912) 15 C.L.R., 235 ; 18 A.L.R., 343. H.C. *Griffith, C.J., Barton* and *Isaacs, JJ.*

D. FROM THE COURTS OF THE STATE.

1. *Where Appeal Lies.*

(a) Jurisdiction Generally.

Appeal—High Court—Jurisdiction to hear appeal from single Judge.]—The High Court has jurisdiction to entertain an appeal from a single Judge of the State Supreme Court whether sitting in Chambers or in Court. *Blake* v. *Bayne*, (1908) A.C., 371, at p. 374. (Privy Council).

Appeal to High Court—Chambers, order of Judge of Supreme Court in—Whether appeal lies from.]—An appeal lies to the High Court from an order in Chambers of a Judge of the Supreme Court staying proceedings in a cause remitted to the Supreme Court for the execution of the judgment of the High Court pronounced on appeal from the Supreme Court. *Peacock* v. *Osborne*, (1907) 4 C.L.R., 1564 ; 13 A.L.R., 565. H.C. *Griffiths, C.J., Barton, O'Connor, Isaacs* and *Higgins, JJ.*

Appeal—Order on habeas corpus—Jurisdiction of High Court.]—The High Court has jurisdiction to entertain an appeal from the Supreme Court in a case of *habeas corpus*. *Attorney-General for the Commonwealth* v. *Ah Sheung*, (1907) 4 C.L.R., 949. H.C. *Griffith, C.J., Barton* and *O'Connor, JJ.*

Trade Marks Act 1905 (No. 20 of 1905), secs. 6, 14—Trade Marks Act 1890 (No. 2), (No. 1183), sec. 13—Application for registration pending at passing of Federal Act—Transfer of administration—Appeal to Federal Attorney-General— Reference of Appeal to Supreme Court by Federal Attorney-General —Appeal from Supreme Court, jurisdiction to hear — Whether Supreme Court exercised administrative jurisdiction only.]—An application for the registration of a trade mark was pending at the time the *Trade Marks Act* 1905 (Commonwealth) came into operation and pursuant to sec. 6 of that Act and sec. 13 of the *Trade Marks Act* 1890 (*No.* 2) an appeal from the Commonwealth Registrar of Trade Marks to the Attorney-General of the Commonwealth was by him referred to the Supreme Court. *Held*, that the reference to the Supreme Court was authorized and that an appeal lay from a decision of that Court to the High Court. *Lever Bros.* v. *G. Mowling & Son*, (1908) 6 C.L.R., 136 ; 14 A.L.R., 296. H.C. *Griffith, C.J., Barton, Isaacs* and *Higgins, JJ.*

Appeal—Costs—Order directing trustee to pay costs—Supreme Court Act 1890 (No. 1142), sec. 60.]—An appeal lies from an order directing a trustee to pay costs in an action for administration, because it is a settled rule that such an order cannot be made unless the occasion of the suit has arisen from something in the nature of the trustee's own misconduct. It is also settled that the question, whether a trustee has been guilty of such misconduct as to justify the Court in ordering him to pay costs, is appealable. *Amos* v. *Fraser*, 4 C.L.R., Pt. I., 78; 12 A.L.R., 481. H.C. *Griffith, C.J., Barton* and *O'Connor, JJ.* (1906).

Practice — Appeal to High Court—Special leave—Decision of inferior Court of State— Right of appeal to Supreme Court—Judiciary Act 1903 (No. 6 of 1903), sec. 35—The Constitution (63 & 64 Vict. c. 12), sec. 73.]— Special leave to appeal to the High Court from a decision of the Court of Mines refused on the ground that there was a right of appeal to the Supreme Court. The question whether the High Court has jurisdiction under sec. 73 of the Constitution to entertain an appeal direct from such a decision should not be raised in a case in which there is an appeal to another Court. *Kamarooka Gold Mining Co.* v. *Kerr*, (1908) 6 C.L.R., 255. H.C. *Griffith, C.J., Barton, Isaacs* and *Higgins, JJ.*

High Court, jurisdiction of—Case remitted to Supreme Court on appeal to High Court— Accounts and inquiries directed by High Court—Determination of questions arising on taking of accounts.]—On appeal from the Supreme Court the High Court with a declaration of rights and an order for accounts and inquiries. *Held*, that the High Court had no jurisdiction to determine questions arising on the taking of the accounts by the Chief Clerk of the Supreme Court as to the extent of the accounts and inquiries actually directed. *Cock* v. *Smith*, (1910) 12 C.L.R., 11; 17 A.L.R., 467. *Griffith, C.J.*

(b) Appealable Amount.

Judiciary Act 1903 (No. 6 of 1903), sec. 35—Appeal from Supreme Court of State — Appealable Amount — Amount at issue, how to be determined.]—In order to determine the amount at issue for purposes of appeal, the judgment is to be looked at as it affects the interests of the party prejudiced by it, and who seeks to relieve himself from it by appeal. *Jenkins* v. *Lanfranchi*, 10 C.L.R., 595; 16 A.L.R., 275. H.C., *Griffith, C.J., O'Connor, Isaacs* and *Higgins, JJ.* (1910).

Appeal to High Court—Appealable amount —Judiciary Act 1903 (No. 6 of 1903), sec. 35 (1), (a) (2)—Judgment involving claim respecting to property amounting to or of the value of three hundred pounds.]—A remainderman sued trustees, in form, for administration, but in substance for a declaration that the defendants were bound to keep farm buildings and fences in repair during the life of the tenant for life. *Madden, C.J.* made the declaration sought, but the Full Court reversed his judgment. *Held*, that an appeal lay to the High Court as of right. *Amos* v. *Fraser*, 4 C.L.R., Pt. I., 78; 12 A.L.R., 481. H.C. *Griffith, C.J., Barton* and *O'Connor, JJ.* (1906).

Appeal to High Court—Appealable amount —Order nisi for probate—Interest of Caveator less than £300—Judiciary Act 1903 (No. 6 of 1903), sec. 35.]—On a rule *nisi* for probate of a will in respect of property amounting in value to over £1,000 it appeared that the interest of the caveator, one of three sons of testatrix, none of whom took any benefit under the will, would on an intestacy have amounted to less than £300. The Supreme Court had decided in favour of the validity of the will. *Held*, that, under sec. 35 (1) of the *Judiciary Act* 1903, the judgment was one for or in respect of a matter at issue of the value of over £300, and that an appeal by the caveator to the High Court would be without special leave. *Tipper* v. *Moore*, (1911) 13 C.L.R., 248; 18 A.L.R., 341. H.C. *Griffith, C.J., Barton* and *O'Connor, JJ.*

(c) Special Leave.

Breach of Statute charged—No serious wrong committed—Dismissal of charge— Special leave to appeal, Grant of in terms.]— Where a man is said to have committed a technical breach of a Statute, but has done nothing seriously wrong, and it is sought to punish him for it, special leave to appeal from a dismissal of the charge against him is not granted without imposing terms. *Pemberton* v. *Banfield*, (1912) 15 C.L.R., 323 ; 18 A.L.R., 486. H.C., *Griffith, C.J., Barton* and *Isaacs, JJ.*

Appeal from Supreme Court—Special leave —Time for appealing expired—Conditional leave.]—An order was made by the Supreme Court on an originating summons determining that the daughters of a settlor, to the exclusion of his sons, were entitled to an uncertain portion of a trust fund. The sons did not within the time limited for appealing, appeal either to the State Full Court or to the High Court, and until that time had expired they believed that the portion of the trust fund affected by the order would not exceed a certain sum. A claim was then made by the daughters that the order affected a much larger sum. On application by the sons for special leave to appeal. *Held*, that special leave should be granted, on the undertaking by the appellants that, in the event of the appeal being allowed, they should not claim a refund of moneys paid by the trustees on the faith of the order not having been appealed from within time, and to indemnify the trustees against any such payments. *a' Beckett* v. *Backhouse*, (1907) 4 C.L.R., 1334. *Griffith, C.J., O'Connor, Isaacs* and *Higgins, JJ.*

High Court Practice—Criminal Case— Special leave to appeal—Evidence—Dying declaration.]—Principle laid down by Privy Council in *In re Dillet*, 12 App. Cas., 459, at p. 467, as to granting special leave to appeal in criminal cases applied (*Isaacs, J.*, dissentiente). *Hope* v. *The King*, (1909) 9 C.L.R., 257. *Griffith, C.J., Isaacs* and *Higgins, JJ.* (High Court).

Practice—Appeal to High Court from Supreme Court—Special leave—Stay by Supreme Court of proceedings under judgment—Conditions—Order LVIII., r. 16.]—It is only in very exceptional circumstances that the High Court will grant special leave to appeal from an order made by a Judge of the Supreme Court in the exercise of his discretion staying proceedings under a judgemnt of the Supreme Court subject to conditions. *Howard Smith*

& Co. Ltd. v. *Varawa*, (1910) 10 C.L.R., 607. H.C. *Griffith, C.J., O'Connor, Isaacs* and *Higgins, JJ.*

Leave to appeal to High Court—Applicant in prison—Appearance in person—Whether High Court has jurisdiction to order that it be allowed.]—Where a person is detained in the State gaol under a sentence of the State Court, the High Court has no jurisiction to order him to be allowed to come before the High Court in order that he may personally apply for leave to appeal from a judgment of the Court of the State. *Horwitz* v. *Connor*, (1908) 6 C.L.R., 38 ; 14 A.L.R., 342. H.C., *Griffith, C.J., Barton, O'Connor, Isaacs* and *Higgins, JJ.*

2. *Practice.*

(a) Notice : Parties.

Practice—Appeal from Supreme Court of State—Extension of time for giving notice— Rules of the High Court 1903, Part I., Order XLV., r. 6 ; Part II., Sec. 1, r. 4, Sec. 3, r. 4.]— *Semble*, Part I., Order XLV., r. 6 (*Rules of the High Court* 1903) does not apply to an appeal from the Supreme Court of the State, and the High Court has no jurisdiction to extend the time for giving notice of such an appeal. *Lever Bros. Ltd.* v. *G. Mowling & Son*, (1908) 5 C.L.R., 510 ; 14 A.L.R., 73. *Griffith, C.J.*

High Court Practice—Appeal to High Court —Cross appeal—Rules of the High Court 1903, Part II., Sec. III., Rule 13.]—Where in one action two distinct causes of action are sued upon, and one judgment is given for the plaintiff as to one cause of action and for the defendant as to the other, the fact that special leave to appeal to the High Court in respect of one of the causes of action is given to one of the parties does not entitle the other party to give a cross notice of appeal under *Rules of the High Court* 1903, Part II., Sec. III., Rule 13 in respect of the other cause of action. *Wilson* v. *Moss*, 8 C.L.R., 146 ; 15 A.L.R., 131. H.C. *Griffith, C.J., Barton, O'Connor* and *Isaacs, JJ.* (1909).

Practice—Joinder of parties—Administration action—Trustee sued as representative—

Refusal of trustee to appeal—Judgment not yet drawn up—Joinder of cestuis que trustent—Order XVI., r. 8 (Rules of 1906).]—Where a trustee is sued as a representative of his *cestui que trustent*, and a judgment adverse to them is given from which the trustee refuses to appeal, the *cestui que trustent* before the judgment is drawn up are entitled *ex debito justitial* to be added as parties so that they may appeal. *Connolly* v. *Macartney*, (1908) 7 C.L.R., 48; 14 A.L.R., 558. H.C., *Griffith, C.J., Barton, O'Connor* and *Isaacs, JJ.*

(b) Pendency of Appeal, Effect of; Stay of Execution of Judgment appealed from; Bail, etc.

Practice—Money paid into Court under Order XIV., r. 6—Defendant successful at trial—Order for payment out of money to defendant—Appeal to High Court—" Execution of the judgment appealed from "—Stay of execution—High Court Appeal Rules 1903, Sec. III., r. 19.]—The defendant obtained leave to defend under Order XIV., r. 6 upon payment into Court of £500. Subsequently on 17th October 1906 judgment in the action was given for the defendant, and an order was made that he be at liberty after the expiration of fourteen days to take out of Court the said sum of £500. On the 29th October 1906 the plaintiff duly instituted an appeal against the judgment to the High Court. *Held*, that the order for payment out of the money was not "execution of the judgment appealed from " within the meaning of Rule 19 of Sec. III. of the *High Court Appeal Rules* 1903, and that in any case the due institution of the appeal against the judgment did not operate as a stay of such order. *Christie* v. *Robinson*, (1907) V.L.R., 118. *Hodges, J.*

Fugitive Offenders Act 1881 44 & 45 Vict. c. 69), secs. 5, 6—Fugitive committed to prison to await return—Legality of detention affirmed by Supreme Court—Appeal to High Court—Bail.]—*See* FUGITIVE OFFENDERS. *Re McKelvey*, (1906) V.L.R., 304; 12 A.L.R., 209.

Insolvency — Order nisi for sequestration based on judgment for costs of prior action —Appeal before High Court from prior judgment—Adjournment of insolvency proceedings.]—*See* INSOLVENCY. *Bayne* v. *Baillieu or Blake*, (1907) 5 C.L.R., 64; 13 A.L.R., 503.

Application to annul sequestration—Sequestration based on judgment for costs ordered to be paid in prior action—Judgment in prior action set aside on appeal—Judgment for costs in subsequent action still standing.]—*See* INSOLVENCY. *Bayne* v. *Baillieu or Blake*, (1907) 5 C.L.R., 64; 13 A.L.R., 503.

(c) Matters which may be Considered; Further Evidence; New Trial.

Appeal from Supreme Court—Admission of further evidence—Jurisdiction of High Court—Verdict obtained on perjured evidence.]—On an appeal from the Supreme Court of a State, the High Court has no jurisdiction to receive further evidence. *Held*, therefore, that leave to read affidavits for the purpose of showing that the evidence on which an original judgment in the Supreme Court of Victoria had been obtained was perjured should be refused. *Ronald* v. *Harper*, (1910) 11 C.L.R., 63; 16 A.L.T., 415. H.C. *Griffith, C.J., Barton* and *O'Connor, JJ.*

Appeal—Point not raised in Court below—Whether party bound by course deliberately adopted at trial.]—Where the conduct of a party at the trial has been such that certain questions have been left to the jury and have been determined, he cannot on appeal raise totally different questions even though upon the pleadings and the evidence they might have been open to him. *Varawa* v. *Howard Smith Co. Ltd.*, (1911) 13 C.L.R., 35; 17 A.L.R., 499. H.C. *Griffith, C.J., O'Connor* and *Isaacs, JJ.*

Appeal—Pleadings—Amendment to raise new case.]—The High Court refused to allow an amendment of the pleadings to raise a new case. *Trengrove & Co.* v. *Story*, (1908) 6 C.L.R., 10; 14 A.L.R., 420. H.C., *Griffith, C.J., O'Connor* and *Higgins, JJ.*

Appeal—Exercise of discretion as to costs—Whether High Court will interfere where there is no other foundation for appeal.]—

It would require a case of very extreme circumstances to justify the High Court in reviewing the discretion of the Supreme Court on a question of costs, where there is no other foundation for the appeal. *Jenkins* v. *Lanfranchi*, 10 C.L.R., 595 ; 16 A.L.R., 275. H.C. *Griffith*, *C.J.*, *O'Connor*, *Isaacs* and *Higgins*, *JJ*. (1910).

New trial—Trial by jury—Observations made by Judge in summing up—Whether directions to the jury.]—Whether observations made by the Judge in the course of his summing up are directions to the jury is a question of fact depending on all the circumstances of the case. *Ronald* v. *Harper*, (1910) 11 C.L.R., 63 ; 16 A.L.R., 415. H.C. *Griffith*, *C.J.*, *Barton* and *O'Connor*, *JJ*.

New trial—Several issues—Wrong finding by jury on one issue.]—A wrong finding by a jury on one issue does not necessarily vitiate their findings on other issues. *Ronald* v. *Harper*, (1910) 11 C.L.R., 63 ; 16 A.L.R., 415. H.C. *Griffith*, *C.J.*, *Barton* and *O'Connor*, *JJ*.

County Court—New trial—Notice of application served out of time—Refusal of Judge to enlarge time—Jurisdiction of Court of Appeal to enlarge—Misdirection—No objection taken at trial—Jurisdiction of Judge to grant new trial—Refusal of Judge to grant new trial—Whether High Court will grant new trial—Infinitesimal hope of success if new trial granted—County Court Act 1890 (No. 1078), sec. 96—County Court Rules, 188, 424.]—Assuming that the High Court and the Supreme Court have jurisdiction to review the exercise by a Judge of County Courts of the discretion given him by rule 424 of the *County Court Rules* 1891 to enlarge the time for serving notice of an application for a new trial, and that a Judge of County Courts has jurisdiction under sec. 96 of the *County Court Act* 1890 to grant a new trial on the ground of misdirection in law where objection has not been taken at the trial to the misdirection (as to both of which questions, *quaere*), the High Court will not grant a new trial where the Judge of County Courts has refused it and the party asking

for it would, in the opinion of the Court, only have a problematical and infinitesimal hope of success if a new trial were had. *Holford* v. *Melbourne Tramway and Omnibus Co. Ltd.*, (1909) V.L.R., 497 ; 29 A.L.T., 112 ; 13 A.L.R., at p. 677, doubted ; *Handley* v. *London, Edinburgh and Glasgow Assurance Co.*, (1902) 1 K.B., 350, commented on. *Armstrong* v. *Great Southern Gold Mining Co. No Liability*, (1911) 12 C.L.R., 382 ; 17 A.L.R., 377. H.C. *Griffith*, *C.J.*, *Barton* and *O'Connor*, *JJ*.

Criminal Law—New trial, when to be granted after quashing of conviction—Circumstances to be considered in exercise of discretion—Failure to warn jury against convicting on uncorrobotated evidence of accomplice—Evidence improperly admitted and afterwards withdrawn from jury—Crimes Act 1890 (No. 1079), sec. 482.]—*See* CRIMINAL LAW. *Peacock* v. *The King*, (1911) 13 C.L.R., 619 ; 17 A.L.R., 566.

(d) Execution of Judgment of High Court.

Judgment of High Court on appeal from Supreme Court—Duty of Supreme Court to execute—Judiciary Act 1903 (No. 6 of 1903), sec. 37, whether ultra vires—The Constitution, sec. 51 (xxxix.)—Commonwealth of Australia Constitution Act (63 & 64 Vict. c. 12), sec. v.]—Sec. 37 of the *Judiciary Act* 1903 in so far as it authorizes the High Court in the exercise of its appellate jurisdiction to remit a cause to the Supreme Court for the execution of the judgment of the High Court, and imposes upon the Supreme Court the duty of executing the judgment of the High Court in the same manner as if that judgment were the judgment of the Supreme Court is a valid exercise by Parliament of the power conferred by sec. 51 (xxxix.) of the Constitution. *Bayne* v. *Blake*, 5 C.L.R., 497 ; 14 A.L.R., 103. H.C. *Griffith*, *C.J.*, *Barton* and *O'Connor*, *JJ*. (1908).

Judiciary Act 1903 (No. 6), sec. 37—Appeal to High Court from Supreme Court—Cause remitted to Supreme Court for execution of judgment of High Court—Duty of Supreme Court—Staying proceedings.]—When the High Court on the hearing of an appeal from the

Supreme Court has remitted the case to the Supreme Court for the execution of the judgment of the High Court pursuant to sec. 37 of the *Judiciary Act* 1903 the Supreme Court is authorized to make any order for the purpose of executing the judgment of the High Court but not to make an order which has the effect of preventing or obstructing the execution of that order. Where, therefore, a cause was remitted to the Supreme Court for an inquiry as to damages an order by the Supreme Court staying proceedings as to the inquiry was on appeal to the High Court discharged. *Peacock* v. *Osborne*, (1907) 4 C.L.R., 1564; 13 A.L.R., 565. H.C. *Griffith, C.J., Barton, O'Connor, Isaacs* and *Higgins, JJ.*

Judgment of High Court on appeal from Supreme Court—Judgment remitted to Supreme Court for execution—Officer of Supreme Court—Whether subject to control of High Court.]—The High Court may directly order an officer of the Supreme Court to obey a judgment of the High Court. *Bayne* v. *Blake*, (1908) 5 C.L.R., 497; 14 A.L.R., 103. H.C. *Griffith, C.J., Barton* and *O'Connor, JJ.*

Judgment of High Court on appeal from Supreme Court—Judgment remitted to Supreme Court—Stay of proceedings, jurisdiction of Supreme Court to order.]—On an appeal from the Supreme Court to the High Court, the High Court, in allowing the appeal ordered the judgment appealed from to be discharged, and that in lieu thereof there should be substituted a declaration that the plaintiffs were entitled to recover a sum to be thereafter ascertained, and further ordered that the cause " be remitted to the Supreme Court to do therein what is right in pursuance of the judgment." Leave to appeal to the Privy Council from the judgment of the High Court having been obtained by the defendants, and a stay of proceedings having been granted by the High Court and subsequently renewed, an application to the Supreme Court to proceed with the inquiry directed by the High Court was made by the plaintiff. *Held,* that an order made by the Supreme Court, that the matter should be deferred until the decision of the Privy

Council should be made known, was a stay of proceedings, and therefore was an order which the Supreme Court had no authority to make. *Peacock* v. *D. M. Osborne & Co.,* 4 C.L.R., 1564; 13 A.L.R., 565., applied. *Bayne* v. *Blake*, (1908) 5 C.L.R., 497; 14 A.L.R., 103. H.C. *Griffith, C.J., Barton* and *O'Connor, JJ.*

Appeal—Dismissal on the ground that it is incompetent—No notice of objection before hearing—Costs.]—Where an appeal is dismissed on the ground that it is incompetent, the respondent if he has not given the appellant notice of such ground before the hearing, may not be allowed costs. *Jenkins* v. *Lanfranchi*, 10 C.L.R., 595; 16 A.L.R., 275. H.C. *Griffith, C.J., O'Connor, Isaacs* and *Higgins, JJ.* (1910).

(e) Costs.

Costs— Trustees— Unsuccessful appeal.]—The costs of trustees, unsuccessful appellants, were in the special circumstances allowed out of the estate. *In re Rosenthal; Rosenthal* v. *Rosenthal*, (1910) 11 C.L.R., 87; 16 A.L.R., 455. H.C. *Griffith, C.J.* and *Isaacs, J.* (*Higgins, J.,* dissenting).

Costs—Appeal in administration action—Costs of trustee—Whether trustee entitled to be indemnified out of the estate.]—Trustees who have been guilty of breaches of trust in respect of which an order has been made in an administration action by a Court of first instance, but who, in respect of the matters in question upon an appeal from that order, are blameless, are entitled to be indemnified out of the estate for their costs of such appeal. *Nissen* v. *Grunden*, (1912) 14 C.L.R., 297; 18 A.L.R., 254. H.C. *Griffith, C.J., Barton* and *Isaacs, JJ.*

Costs—Taxation—Appeal from Court of Petty Sessions to High Court—Order to review—Limitation of amount of costs—Justices Act 1890 (No. 1105), sec. 148—Rules of the High Court 1903, Part I., Order XLVI., r. 14; Part II., sec. IV., r. 1; Rules of the High Court of 12th October, 1903, r. 3.]—Order XLVI., r. 14 of Part I. of the Rules of the High Court 1903, which prescribes the scale for taxation of costs does not refer to any maximum amount of costs to be allowed, and, therefore, the provision in sec. 148 of the *Justices Act* 1890, which limits the total amount of costs that can be allowed in the Supreme Court upon an order to review a decision of a Court of Petty Sessions to £20, does not apply to the costs of an appeal by way of order to review from a Court of Petty Sessions exercising Federal jurisdiction to the High Court. *Lyons* v. *Smart*, (1908) 6 C.L.R., 285; 14 A.L.R., 619. H.C., *Griffith*, *C.J.*, *Barton*, *O'Connor*, *Isaacs* and *Higgins*, *JJ.*

Order XLVI., r. 13 (High Court)—Costs—Proceedings of an unnecessarily expensive character—" Taking proceedings " meaning of—Printing or type-writing documents and evidence.]—Preparing type-written or printed copies of documents or evidence for an appeal is not taking a proceeding within the meaning of Order XLVI., r. 13. *Peacock* v. *Osborne & Co.*, 13 A.L.R., 254. *Barton*, *J.* (1907).

High Court—Appeal Rules, Section IV., r. 16—Costs—Printing evidence for purpose of appeal—" Printing," whether it includes type-writing.]—Type-writing is not " printing " within the meaning of Section IV., r. 16 of the Appeal Rules under the *High Court Procedure Act*. *Peacock* v. *Osborne & Co.*, 13 A.L.R., 254. *Barton*, *J.* (1907).

III. To the Supreme Court of the State.
A. JURISDICTION.

Patent, application for—Opposition—State Patents Act—Transfer of administration to Commonwealth pending proceedings—Appeal to State Supreme Court—Jurisdiction—Patents Act 1890 (No. 1123), sec. 33—Patents Act 1903 (No. 21 of 1903).]—At the date of the proclamation by the Governor-General under sec. 18 of the Federal *Patents Act* 1903 transferring the administration of the State *Patents Act* 1890 to the Commonwealth, the hearing of an opposed application for a patent was pending before the Commissioner of Patents. After that date the hearing was continued and concluded by the same officer acting as a Deputy Commissioner of Patents appointed under the *Patents Act*

1903, and he refused the application. The applicant then appealed to the Crown Solicitor of the Commonwealth as a Federal Law Officer, and he granted the patent. From that decision the opponent appealed to the Supreme Court of Victoria under sec. 33 of the *Patents Act* 1890. *Held*, that the State *Patents Act* having ceased to be administered by the State by reason of sec. 19 (a) of the *Patents Act* 1903, the Supreme Court had no jurisdiction to entertain the appeal. *In re McLeod's Patent*; *Burton* v. *McLeod*, (1906) V.L.R., 483; 12 A.L.R., 335. *a'Beckett*, *J.* (1906).

Appeal—Reference—Reference as to law applicable on findings of fact—Right of appeal notwithstanding reference.]—Where on the trial of an action the primary Judge finds the facts and refers the question of the law applicable to the facts so found to the Full Court, the reference does not affect the right of a party to appeal against the findings of fact. *Glass* v. *Pioneer Rubber Works of Australia Ltd.*, (1906) V.L.R., 754; 28 A.L.T., 64; 12 A.L.R., 529. F.C. *a'Beckett*, *A.C.J.*, *Hodges* and *Chomley*, *JJ.*

Appeal—County Court—Action struck out for want of jurisdiction—Jurisdiction to deal with defendant's application for costs declined by Judge—Whether appeal lies—County Court Act 1890 (No. 1078), sec. 133.]—An action having been brought in a County Court which the Court had no jurisdiction to try the Judge ordered the case to be struck out and refused to consider the defendant's application for costs on the ground that he had no jurisdiction to do so, *Held*, that an appeal lay from such refusal. *The King* v. *Beecham*; *Ex parte Cameron*, (1910) V.L.R., 204; 31 A.L.T., 183; 16 A.L.R., 173. F.C. *Madden*, *C.J.* and *a'Beckett*, *J.* (*Cussen*, *J.*, doubting).

Appeal—Judgment of Supreme Court—Notice of appeal to High Court—Subsequent notice of appeal to Full Court—Jurisdiction—High Court Procedure Rules 1903, Part II., Section IV., r. 19.]—The pendency of an appeal to the High Court does not deprive the State Full Court of jurisdiction to hear an appeal to it in respect of the same matter. *O'Sullivan* v. *Morton*, (1911) V.L.R., 235 ; 32 A.L.T., 172 ; 17 A.L.R., 140. F.C. *Madden, C.J., Hodges* and *Hood, JJ.* (1911).

County Court Act 1890 (No. 1078), sec. 133—County Court Rules 1891, rr. 378, 379—Practice—Appeal—Case settled by Judge—Transmission to Supreme Court—Enlargement of time—Failure of Judge to indorse—Effect of.]—The indorsement of enlargement of the time for transmitting a case on appeal from an order of the County Court to the Supreme Court, directed by rule 379 to be made by the Judge in cases falling within the rule, is not a condition of the jurisdiction of the Supreme Court to hear the appeal ; and failure on the part of the Judge to make such indorsement will not prevent the Supreme Court from hearing the appeal if, in fact, the case is transmitted within fourteen days from the day on which the Judge shall have returned the case settled and signed by him to the appellant. *Ryan* v. *Muir & Co.*, (1912) V.L.R., 411 ; 34 A.L.T., 64 ; 18 A.L.R., 396. F.C. *Madden, C.J., Hood* and *Cussen, JJ.* (1912).

Supreme Court Act 1890 (No. 1142), sec. 37—" Civil or mixed matter "—Appeal from mandamus.]—A proceeding by mandamus granted on the application of a private person ordering the Treasurer to comply with the mandatory provisions of a public Statute imposing a duty upon him is a " civil or mixed matter " within the meaning of sec. 37 of the *Supreme Court Act* 1890 although the refusal to so comply may be an indictable misdemeanour. There may therefore be an appeal to the Full Court from the order of a Judge granting such a mandamus. *The King* v. *Watt* ; *Ex parte Slade*, (1912) V.L.R., 225 ; 33 A.L.T., 222 ; 18 A.L.R., 158. F.C. *Madden, C.J., Hodges* and *Cussen, JJ.*

Crimes Act 1890 (No. 1079), secs. 481, 482—Crown cases reserved—Question of difficulty in point of law—Arising " on the trial," meaning of—Whether case may be stated after termination of sittings.]—If there was an existing point of law which arose on the materials at the trial, and which might

have been taken, such point of law has arisen " on the trial " within the meaning of sec. 481 of the *Crimes Act* 1890, although at the trial no question was raised and the Judges attention was not directed to it, and the Court may, even after the completion of the sittings at which the trial took place, state a case under sec. 482 of the said Act. *R.* v. *Fitzgerald*, 15 V.L.R., 40 ; 10 A.L.T., 241, and *R.* v. *Brown*, 24 Q.B.D., 357, followed. *Rex* v. *Turnbull*, (1907) V.L.R., 11 ; 28 A.L.T., 103 ; 12 A.L.R., 551. *Cussen, J.*

Mandamus—Remedy by appeal available—Discretion of Court, matters to be considered in exercise of—Comparative advantage of applying one remedy rather than the other—County Court—Case struck out for want of jurisdiction—Jurisdiction to entertain defendant's application for costs declined by Judge.]—A Judge of County Courts, having ordered a case to be struck out for want of jurisdiction, refused to consider the defendant's application for costs on the ground that he had no jurisdiction to do so. *Held*, *Per a' Beckett* and *Cussen, JJ.* (*Madden, C.J.,* dissenting), that notwithstanding the existence of the remedy by appeal, the Court should exercise its discretion in favour of granting a writ of *mandamus* ordering the Judge to consider the question of costs, as in all the circumstances that remedy was more appropriate, less expensive, and more desirable from a judicial point of view than the remedy by appeal. *The King* v. *Beecham, Ex parte Cameron*, (1910) V.L.R., 204 ; 31 A.L.T., 183 ; 16 A.L.R., 173.

B. PRACTICE.

1. Notice ; Setting Down of Appeal.

Order LVIII., r. 6—Appeal to Full Court—Cross appeal, notice of—Practice.]—*Semble*, where a judgment deals with two causes of action, and an appeal in respect to one only of such causes of action is brought, the respondent cannot raise an appeal in respect of the other cause of action without having given notice. *Prebble* v. *Reeves*, (1910) V.L.R., 88 ; 31 A.L.T., 114 ; 15 A.L.R., 631. F.C. *Madden, C.J., Hood* and *Cussen, JJ.*

Patent—Application for—Law Officer's decision—Appeal, setting down—Whether order by Judge necessary—Patents Act 1890 (No. 1123), sec. 33.]—When notice has been given of an appeal to the Supreme Court from a decision of the Law Officer, under sec. 33 of the *Patents Act* 1890, an order from a Judge is not necessary before the appeal can be set down by the Prothonotary in the list for hearing before a Judge. *In re McLeod's Patent*; *Burton* v. *McLeod*, (1906) V.L.R., 488; 12 A.L.R., 307. *a'Beckett, A.C.J.*

2. *Constitution of Bench*; *Over-ruling Previous Decision.*

Practice—Over-ruling previous Full Court decision—Summoning Full Bench.]—The Full Court will not summon a Full Bench to consider a previous decision of the Full Court unless it doubts the correctness of that decision. *McKinnon* v. *Gange*, (1910) V.L.R., 32; 31 A.L.T., 112; 15 A.L.R., 640. *Madden, C.J., Hood* and *Cussen, JJ.*

3. *The Hearing*; *Right to Begin*; *Evidence to be Considered.*

Administration and Probate Act 1890 (No. 1060), sec. 98—Case stated—Right to begin.]—On a case stated by the Master-in-Equity under sec. 98 of the *Administration and Probate Act* 1890 the Crown should begin. *In re McCracken*, 27 A.L.T., 233; 12 A.L.R., 303. F.C. *a'Beckett, A.C.J., Hodges* and *Hood, JJ.* (1906).

Special case—Right to begin—Stamps Act 1890 (No. 1140), sec. 71.]—Upon a special case stated under the *Stamps Act* 1890 the alleged tax-payer has the right to begin. *Armytage* v. *Collector of Imposts*, (1906) V.L.R., 504; 28 A.L.R., 9; 12 A.L.R., 305. F.C. *a'Beckett, A.C.J., Hodges* and *Hood, JJ.* (1906).

Criminal law—Practice—Crown case reserved—Right to begin—Crimes Act 1890 (No. 1079), sec. 481.]—Upon the argument of points of law reserved upon a criminal trial at the instance of a prisoner, his counsel is entitled to begin. *Rex* v. *Shuttleworth*, (1909) V.L.R., 431; 31 A.L.T., 50; 15 A.L.R., 492. F.C. *Madden, C.J., a'Beckett, Hodges, Hood* and *Cussen, JJ.*

Certiorari to Judge of a County Court—Evidence—Conflict of evidence as to proceedings in County Court—Unsworn statement of Judge, whether admissible.]—*See* County Court. *A.Macrow & Sons Proprietary Ltd.* v. *Macartney* or *McCartney*, (1911) V.L.R., 393; 33 A.L.T., 64; 17 A.L.R., 397.

Order LVIII., r. 4—Appeal—Fresh evidence—Discretion to receive.]—*Semble*, (*per Hodges* and *Cussen, JJ.*) the rules laid down in *Ward* v. *Hearne*, (1884) 10 V.L.R. (L.), 163; 6 A.L.T., 49, and *Ashley* v. *Ashley*, 24 V.L.R., 220; 4 A.L.R., 154, though sound, and to be followed in most cases, may not apply in cases where the rights of others than the immediate parties are concerned, *e.g.* in cases of trustees, guardians of infants, committees of lunatics, and where the action of the person tendering the fresh evidence is really brought in the interests of the public at large. *The King* v. *Watt*; *Ex parte Slade*, (1912) V.L.R., 225; 33 A.L.T., 222; 18 A.L.R., 158. F.C. *Madden, C.J., Hodges* and *Cussen, JJ.*

Order LVIII., r. 4—Appeal from order granting mandamus—"Judgment after trial or hearing of cause or matter on the merits"—Discretion to receive further evidence.]—An appeal from an order granting a mandamus is not an appeal from "a judgment after trial or hearing of a cause or matter on the merits" within Order LVIII., r. 4 of the *Rules of the Supreme Court* 1906, and the Court has full discretion to receive further evidence. *The King* v. *Watt*; *Ex parte Slade*, (1912) V.L.R., 225; 33 A.L.T., 222; 18 A.L.R., 158. F.C. *Madden, C.J., Hodges* and *Cussen, JJ.*

Appeal—Evidence, admissibility of—Application for new trial on ground of misconduct of juryman—Evidence as to such misconduct given before primary Judge—Affidavit as to such evidence.]—During the trial of an action by a Judge and jury one of the juryman was charged with misconduct in making a certain statement to a clerk of the defendant's solicitor. After hearing the clerk's sworn testimony as to what had occurred and the denial of the juryman not on oath, the Judge accepted the denial of the juryman and directed the case to proceed On defendant's application to the State Full Court for a new trial, an affidavit was tendered setting out the evidence of their solicitor's clerk as given before the primary Judge. The Full Court (*Hood, J.,* dissenting) rejected the affidavit. On appeal to the High Court, *Held, per O'Connor J.*—The affidavit should have been admitted, but (*per Isaacs, J.,*) it was rightly rejected. *David Syme & Co.* v. *Swinburne,* 10 C.L.R., 43 ; 16 A.L.R., 93 (1909).

4. *New Trial.*

Order XXXIX. (Rules of 1906), r. 6—New trial—Misdirection—Substantial wrong or miscarriage.]—*See* PRACTICE AND PLEADING. *Holford and Wife* v. *Melbourne Tramway and Omnibus Co.,* (1909) V.L.R., 497 ; 29 A.L.T., 112 ; 13 A.L.R., 667.

Order XXXIX. (Rules of 1906)—Supreme Court Act 1890 (No. 1142), sec. 58—New trial —Misdirection as to law—No objection taken at trial—Relevancy of evidence, misdirection as to.]—*See* PRACTICE AND PLEADING. *Holford and Wife* v. *Melbourne Tramway and Omnibus Co.,* (1909) V.L.R., 497 ; 29 A.L.T., 112 ; 13 A.L.R., 667.

County Court Act 1890 (No. 1078), secs. 96, 133, 148—Order XXXIX., r. 7 (Rules of 1906) —County Court—New trial—Whether issues to be tried may be limited—Full Court, power of on appeal.]—In the case of an action in a County Court involving the determination of several issues the Full Court on appeal (and, *semble,* the County Court on an application for a new trial) may order a new trial on some only of the issues tried in the case to the exclusion of others. *Holford and Wife* v. *Melbourne Tramway and Omnibus Co.,* (1909) V.L.R., 497 ; 29 A.L.T., 112 ; 13 A.L.R., 667. F.C. *Madden, C.J., a' Beckett* and *Cussen, JJ.*

New trial—Limitation of issues to be tried —Verdict finding negligence and amount of damages—New trial as to issue of negligence only—County Court—Appeal to Full Court— County Court Act 1890 (No. 1078), secs. 96, 133, 148—Order XXXIX. (Rules of 1906), r. 7.]—In an action for damages for negligence tried in a County Court, the jury having found for the plaintiffs and awarded them damages and a new trial having been refused by the Judge of the County Court, on appeal to the Full Court a new trial before a Judge of the Supreme Court of the question of negligence or no negligence was ordered, leaving the finding as to the amount of damages standing. *Holford and Wife* v. *Melbourne Tramway and Omnibus Co.,* (1909) V.L.R., 497 ; 29 A.L.T., 112 ; 13 A.L.R., 667. F.C. *Madden, C.J., a' Beckett* and *Cussen, JJ.*

Order XXII. (Rules of 1906)—Action tried in County Court—Appeal to Full Court— Re-trial ordered in Supreme Court—Payment into Court.]—*See* PRACTICE AND PLEADING. *Fitzgerald* v. *Murray,* (1907) V.L.R., 715 ; 29 A.L.T., 158 ; 13 A.L.R., 645.

Appeal—Evidence, admissibility of—Application for new trial on ground of misconduct of juryman—Evidence as to such misconduct given before primary Judge—Affidavit as to such evidence.]—*See* SUB-DIVISION ; THE HEARING ; RIGHT TO BEGIN ; EVIDENCE TO BE CONSIDERED. *David Syme & Co.* v. *Swinburne,* 10 C.L.R., 43 ; 16 A.L.R., 93.

5. *Stay of Execution.*

Order LVIII., r. 16 (Rules of 1906)—Stay of proceedings pending appeal—Application for stay—Whether Full Court may entertain.] —An application for a stay of proceedings pending an appeal to the Full Court may under Order LVIII., r. 16 be made to the Full Court. *O'Sullivan* v. *Morton,* (1911) V.L.R., 235 ; 32 A.L.T., 172 ; 17 A.L.R., 140. F.C. *Madden, C.J., Hodges* and *Hood, JJ.* (1911).

6. *Parties.*

" **Actio personalis moritur cum persona** " **—Action for personal injuries—Judgment for plaintiff—Death of plaintiff pending appeal —Survival of action to executor—Executor** added as respondent to appeal.]—*See* MAXIMS. *Farrands* v. *Melbourne, The Mayor, &c. of the City of;* (1909) V.L.R., 531.

7. *Costs.*

Practice—Costs—Taxation—Appeal from County Court—Order dismissing Appeal with costs to be taxed by Taxing Master.]—Where the Full Court has made an order that an appeal from the County Court be dismissed with costs, such costs to be taxed by the Taxing Master of the Supreme Court, the Taxing Master has power to tax only the costs of the appeal, and has no power to tax the costs incurred in the County Court prior to the institution of the appeal. *Marks* v. *Pett,* 10 V.L.R. (L.), 342, commented on. *Ambler & Co. Proprietary Ltd.* v. *Clayton,* (1909) V.L.R., 56; 30 A.L.T., 113; 14 A.L.R., 730. *a' Beckett, J.* (1908).

IV. COURT OF INDUSTRIAL APPEALS.

[For the principles to be applied in determining the lowest prices or rates, *see, post,* FACTORIES AND SHOPS ACTS.]

Factories and Shops Act 1905 (No. 1975), sec. 122—Court of Industrial Appeals—Whether the determination may prejudice the progress maintenance of or scope of employment in the trade concerned—What to be considered.]—*See* FACTORIES AND SHOPS ACTS. *In re the Starch Board,* 13 A.L.R., 558.

Factories and Shops Act 1905 (No. 1975), secs. 83, 122—Reference of determination to Court of Industrial Appeals—Average prices paid by reputable employers insufficient to afford a reasonable limit—Principles upon which Court should act—Whether determination would prejudice the progress, &c., of the trade.]—*See* FACTORIES AND SHOPS ACTS. *In re the Starch Board,* 13 A.L.R., 558.

Court of Industrial Appeals—Purpose of its existence—Principles governing its determination—Absence of absolute discretion.]—*See* FACTORIES AND SHOPS ACTS. *In re Fellmongers Board,* 15 A.L.R., 225.

Factories and Shops Act 1905 (No. 1975), sec. 122—Determination alleged to prejudice progress maintenance of or scope of em- ployment in industry—Appeal to Court of Industrial Appeal, in respect of what matters it may be brought.]—*See* FACTORIES AND SHOPS ACTS. *In re Boilermakers Board,* 18 A.L.R., 399.

Court of Industrial Appeals — Appeal, whether in the nature of a re-hearing—Factories and Shops Act 1905 (No. 1975), Part X.] —An appeal from a determination of a Wages Board to the Court of Industrial Appeals is an appeal by way of re-hearing on any evidence procurable, and the Court is not limited to dealing with the determination on the materials which were before the Board. *In re the Bread Board,* 13 A.L.R., 589. *Hood, J.* (1907).

Factories and Shops Act 1905 (No. 1975), sec. 122—Court of Industrial Appeals—Factories and Shops Act 1907 (No. 2137), sec. 33—Appeal, nature of—Re-hearing—Whether Court confined to materials before Wages Board.]—An appeal to the Court of Industrial Appeals from the determination of a Wages Board is in the nature of a re-hearing, and the Court is not confined to a consideration of the materials which were before the Board in coming to a conclusion as to what should be the minimum wage in the process trade or business for which the Board was appointed. *In re the Ice Board.* 16 A.L.R., 46. *Hodges, J.* (1909).

Court of Industrial Appeals—Evidence on hearing of appeal.]—For observations as to the evidence to be given on the hearing of industrial appeals, *see, In re the Bread Board,* 13 A.L.R., 589. *Hood, J.* (1907).

Minimum wage, what is—Matters to be considered in determining—Factories and Shops Act 1905 (No. 1975), sec. 75—Court of Industrial Appeals.]—*See* FACTORIES AND SHOPS ACTS. *In re the Bread Board,* 13 A.L.R., 589.

V. TO GENERAL SESSIONS.

Appeal to General Sessions—Increase of fine to facilitate, propriety of—Justices Act 1890 (No. 1105), secs. 59 (1), 127.]—*See* JUSTICES OF THE PEACE. *Kane* v. *Dureau,* (1911) V.L.R., 293; 33 A.L.T., 15; 17 A.L.R., 277.

Marriage Act 1890 (No. 1166), secs. 51, 52
—Maintenance order—Disobedience by husband—Proceedings to enforce—Dismissal by Justices—Appeal to General Sessions.]—See MAINTENANCE AND MAINTENANCE ORDERS. *Bloxham* v. *Bloxham*, 33 A.L.T. (Supplement), 11 ; 18 A.L.R. (C.N.), 1.

General Sessions—Notice of Appeal— Recognizance, when it must be entered into—Recognizance entered into after service of notice on clerk of Petty Sessions but before service on respondent—Justices Act 1890 (No. 1105), sec. 128.]—See GENERAL SESSIONS. *Ormond* v. *Joske*, 16 A.L.R. (C.N.), 1.

Justices Act 1890 (No. 1105), sec. 128 (5)—Appeal—Recognizance—Notice of Appeal—Time for entering into recognizance.]—See GENERAL SESSIONS. *Martin* v. *Rowden*, 32 A.L.T. (Supplement), 8 ; 16 A.L.R. (C.N.), 10.

Marriage Act 1890 (No. 1166), sec. 52—Justices Act 1890 (No. 1105), sec. 131—Maintenance appeals — Notice of intention to appeal—Statement of grounds of appeal—Filing notices.]—See GENERAL SESSIONS. *Gavey* v. *Gavey*, 31 A.L.T. (Supplement), 6 ; 15 A.L.R. (C.N.), 17.

Marriage Act 1890 (No. 1166), sec. 52—Marriage Act 1900 (No. 1684), sec. 7—Practice—Applications to quash, &c.—Orders under the Marriage Acts—Service of notice.] —See GENERAL SESSIONS. *In re Applications to Quash, &c.*, 31 A.L.T. (Supplement), 10 ; 15 A.L.R. (C.N.), 25.

Justices Act 1890 (No. 1105), secs. 128, 132—Notice of appeal—Security for appearance of appellant—Recognizance entered into before notice of appeal given—Invalidity of recognizance—Refusal to hear appeal.]—See GENERAL SESSIONS. *Dungey* v. *Dunlevie*, 31 A.L.T. (Supplement), 3 ; 15 A.L.R. (C.N.), 13.

Justices Act 1890 (No. 1105), sec. 139—General Sessions—Invalidity of recognizance—Refusal to hear appeal—Power to state a case.]—See GENERAL SESSIONS. *Dungey* v. *Dunlevie*, 31 A.L.T. (Supplement), 3 ; 15 A.L.R. (C.N.), 13.

General Sessions—Appeal against conviction—Information—Whether Court may amend

—Justices Act 1890 (No. 1105), secs. 73 (4), 128 (7), 133.]—See GENERAL SESSIONS. *Delaney* v. *Napthine*, 32 A.L.T. (Supplement), 10 ; 16 A.L.R. (C.N.), 19.

Appeal from Court of Petty Sessions—Conviction—Amendment, powers of—Justices Act 1890 (No. 1105), secs. 133, 185.]—See GENERAL SESSIONS. *Li Wan Quai* v. *Christie*, (1906) 3 C.L.R., 1125 ; 12 A.L.R., 429.

Justices Act 1890 (No. 1105), sec. 139—General Sessions—Special case, contents of—What should be stated.]—See GENERAL SESSIONS. *Russell* v. *Sheehan*, (1911) V.L.R., 81 ; 32 A.L.T., 181 ; 17 A.L.R., 83.

Justices Act 1890 (No. 1105), secs. 117, 119, 128 (12), 141—Attachment of debt—Judgment debt—Order of General Sessions—Garnishee order—Petty Sessions—Effect of—Jurisdiction—Order to review—" Person aggrieved."] —See JUSTICES OF THE PEACE. *Brown* v. *Gunn* ; *McKay* (*Garnishee*), (1912) V.L.R., 463 ; 34 A.L.T., 113 ; 18 A.L.R., 462.

Attachment of debts—Money ordered to be paid by Court of General Sessions—Attachment by Court of Petty Sessions—Jurisdiction.] —See JUSTICES OF THE PEACE. *Brown* v. *Gunn* ; *McKay* (*Garnishee*), (1913) V.L.R., 60 ; 34 A.L.T., 115 ; 18 A.L.R. (C.N.), 21.

VI.—TO THE BOARD OF PUBLIC HEALTH.

Noxious trade establishment—Refusal of Council to register—Appeal to Board of Public Health—Right of appellant to be heard and to know what he has to answer—Audi alteram partem—Health Act 1890 (No. 1098), sec. 225.]—See HEALTH (PUBLIC). *The King* v. *Prahran, Mayor, &c. of* ; *Ex parte Morris*, (1910) V.L.R., 460 ; 32 A.L.T., 92 ; 16 A.L.R., 507.

APPORTIONMENT.

See also LICENSING, TENANT FOR LIFE AND REMAINDERMAN.

Life tenant and remainderman—Investment on mortgage—Apportionment of proceeds of

realization—Interest on cost of sewerage—
Rate of interest upon mortgage.]—Trust
moneys having been lent on mortgage by the
trustees, and the mortgagor being unable to
pay the interest, the trustees took possession
of the mortgaged property, and expended
out of the income of the estate certain sums
in sewering the property pursuant to *The
Melbourne and Metropolitan Board of Works
Act.* The trustees subsequently sold the
property for less than the principal sum
advanced and interest thereon. On apportionment of the proceeds of sale between
corpus and income. *Held,* that before
apportionment corpus was chargeable with
interest on the sums so expended out of
income up to the date of repayment to the
life tenants. *In re Morley,* (1895) 2 Ch.,
738, followed. On such apportionment the
life tenant is entitled to interest on the
principal owing under the mortgage from the
date when the mortgagor ceased paying
interest, at the rate (but not the penal rate)
fixed by the mortgage, unless it is shown
that such rate of interest was higher than
the current rates during the period over
which the arrears extend. *Cooper v. Cooper,*
26 V.L.R., 649 ; 22 A.L.T.. 215 ; 7 A.L.R.,
147, explained and followed. *Macartney v.
Macartney,* 33 A.L.T., 183 ; 18 A.L.R., 1.
Madden, C.J. (1912).

ARBITRATION.

I.—Generally.

**Arbitration—Agreement to submit to—
Intention to make, how to be ascertained.**]—No
special words are essential to create a stipulation for a formal arbitration, provided the
intention can be gathered from the words
in fact used, or is reasonably to be intended
from them, or from the nature and purpose
of the stipulation. *Briscoe & Co. Ltd.* v.
The Victorian Railways Commissioners,
(1907) V.L.R., 523 ; 29 A.L.T., 17 ; 13
A.L.R., 308. *Madden, C.J.*

**Contract for sale of goods—Condition that
goods may be rejected if not to satisfaction of
purchaser's storekeeper—Condition that disputes shall be determined by storekeeper—
Arbitration clause not providing for or implying a judicial inquiry.**]—The plaintiff contracted to supply the defendant with stores,
of the kind specified in a schedule, to the order
of the defendant's storekeeper under agreed
conditions and in strict accordance with the
prescribed samples (if any). Condition 10
provided that, if in respect of any item in the
schedule no particular brand of stores was
specified, the contractor might supply stores
of any brand, provided that the whole of the
stores supplied were, in the judgment of the
storekeeper, of the very best quality and
strictly in accordance with the specified
sample (if any) and in every respect to the
satisfaction of the storekeeper. Condition 12
provided that, notwithstanding that stores
had been provisionally signed for or accepted
by the receiving officer or that they had been
paid for, the storekeeper should have full
power to reject any of such stores which were
in his judgment not in every respect in accordance with the contract, and that such rejection might take place at any time until the
storekeeper should have expressly certified
in writing that the stores so supplied under
the particular order had been found, after
complete examination and testing, in every
respect in accordance with the contract.
The condition also provided that notice in
writing of the rejection should be given to
the contractor by the storekeeper, and that
the contractor should remove the rejected
stores within a certain time and replace
them with stores in every respect in accordance with the contract, failing which the
storekeeper might purchase stores which in
his opinion were suitable at the contractor's
risk. Condition 13 provided that payments
should be made on the storekeeper's certi-
cate. Condition 19 was in the following
terms :—All questions and disputes relating
to the construction of this contract, or otherwise arising thereunder, shall be determined
by the storekeeper, and his decision shall be
final and binding on the corporation (*i.e.*, the
defendant) and the contractor respectively.

Certain stores supplied by the plaintiff were not in the storekeeper's opinion within the meaning of condition 10 of the very best quality, nor strictly in accordance with the order and the sample, and were not in every respect to the satisfaction of the storekeeper, and they were in consequence rejected by him under condition 12. The plaintiff requested the defendant and the defendant refused, to submit the question and dispute in reference to the rejected stores to the determination of the storekeeper, and the plaintiff brought an action to recover damages from the defendant for so refusing. *Held*, that condition 19 was not intended to provide for a judicial inquiry, but merely to emphasise and complete the right of the defendant to demand that the stores supplied should be such as should satisfy the storekeeper after he had examined and tested them, and did not entitle the plaintiff to insist on an inquiry by the storekeeper in the nature of an arbitration in respect of matters which he had already considered and dealt with under condition 12. *Laidlaw v. Hastings Pier Co.* (referred to in *Hudson on Building Contracts*); *Scott v. Corporation of Liverpool*, 3 DeG. & J., at p. 368; *Goodyear v. Mayor, &c., of Weymouth*, 35 L.J. N.S. C.P., 12; and *Wadsworth v. Smith*, L.R. 6 Q.B., 332, discussed and applied. *Robins v. Goddard*, (1905) 1 K.B., 294, and *Re Hohenzollern, &c., and the City of London Corporation*, 54 L.T. N.S., 596, distinguished. *Briscoe & Co. Ltd.* v. *Victorian Railways Commissioners*, (1907) V.L.R., 523; 29 A.L.T., 17; 13 A.L.R., 308. *Madden, C.J.*

Arbitration—Building contract—Extension of time fixed for completion—Determination of contract by employer during currency of further time allowed for completion—Arbitration provision, whether applicable—Stay of action—Supreme Court Act 1890 (No. 1142), sec. 152.]—One of the conditions of a contract between a Shire council and a contractor for building a bridge provided that the contractor should complete the whole of the works on a certain day. Another condition provided that if the contractor should, in the opinion of the engineer, fail to make such progress with the works as the engineer should deem sufficient to ensure their completion within the specified time, and should fail or neglect to rectify such cause of complaint for seven days after being thereunto required in writing by the engineer, it should be lawful for the council to determine the contract. A third condition provided should " any doubt dispute or difference arise or happen touching or concerning the said works . . . or in relation to the exercise of any of the powers of the council or the engineer under this contract or any claim made by the contractor in consequence thereof or in any way arising therefrom or in relation to any impediment prevention or obstruction to or in the carrying on of the works of this contract or any part thereof (or any extras additions enlargements deviations or alterations thereon or thereof) by the council or the engineer . . . . or any claim made by the contractor in consequence thereof or in any way arising therefrom or touching or concerning the meaning or intention of this contract or of the specifications or conditions or any other part thereof . . . or respecting any other matter or thing not hereinbefore left to the decision or determination of the engineer " every such doubt dispute and difference should from time to time be referred to and settled and decided by the engineer. Subsequently the council agreed to extend the time for completion, and, by an indenture between the parties, the condition for completion on a certain day was rescinded, and a new condition was substituted, identical in terms except that a new date for completion was inserted. The council, after the original date for completion and before the new date purported to determine the contract in pursuance of the conditions in that behalf. An action having been brought by the contractor claiming (*inter alia*) damages for breach of contract, for wrongful prevention of due and complete performance, and for wrongful determination of the contract, and upon a *quantum meruit* for work and labour done. *Held*, that the matters in dispute were referable to the arbitration of the engineer, notwithstanding that the original time for completion had passed when the contract was determined, and, therefore, that the action should be stayed under sec. 152 of the *Supreme Court Act* 1890. *Burton v. Bairnsdale, President, &c., of Shire of*, (1908) 7 C.L.R., 76 ; 14 A.L.R., 529. H.C., *Barton, O'Connor, Isaacs* and *Higgins, JJ.*

Arbitration — Submission — Revocation — Incorporation of laws of Victoria—Bankruptcy of one of the parties to the agreement for reference—Leave to revoke submission—Supreme Court Act 1890 (No. 1142), secs. 141, 160.]—A contract in writing provided that all differences arising between the contracting parties should be referred to two arbitrators, one to be appointed by each party. The contract did not expressly provide that the submission should be made a rule of Court, but provided (*inter alia*) that the arbitration should take place in Melbourne and should be " subject to the provisions of the law in that behalf for the time being in force in Victoria," or failing Melbourne, in such other place as the principal business should then be carried on. After differences had arisen between the parties, and one of them had been adjudged bankrupt, he appointed an arbitrator, whereupon the other party applied to the Court for leave to revoke the appointment, power and authority of the arbitrator appointed. *Held*, that the provision in the contract that the arbitration should be subject to the laws of Victoria amounted to an agreement that the submission should be made a rule of Court, and that under sec. 141 of the *Supreme Court Act* 1890 the arbitrator's authority was not revocable without the leave of the Court. *In re Mitchell and Izard and the Governor of Ceylon*, 21 Q.B.D., 408, followed. *Held*, further, that in view of the bankruptcy of the party appointing, such leave should be given. *Re Freeman and Kempster*, (1909) V.L.R., 394 ; 31 A.L.T., 42 ; 15 A.L.R., 444. *a' Beckett, J.* [But see *Arbitration Act* 1910 (No. 2265).]

Arbitration—Award, validity of — Uncertainty—Refusal to hear evidence—Specific performance of agreement ordered—Lease, time of commencement—Covenant not to alter will.]—On a reference to arbitration to determine all disputes between A. and B.,

the deed of submission gave the arbitrators or their umpire power to order what they or he should think fit to be done by either of the parties. By his award the umpire found that on a certain day an agreement had been entered into between the parties to the effect (*inter alia*) that A. should pay to B. a certain sum in settlement of all claims between them up to the date of the agreement, that A. should lease to B. certain premises for a certain term at a certain rent, and that A. should not alter the terms of her will. He also found that the agreement had been partly performed by B. having on a certain day been admitted by A. into possession of the premises agreed to be leased, and that B. had altered his position and incurred expense on the faith of the agreement. He then ordered and determined that A. should specifically perform her part of such agreement, including a covenant that she would not alter her will, and that B. should execute all leases and documents, and do all such things as might be necessary to effectuate the observance by him of the agreement. On motion by A. to set aside the award. *Held*, that the award was not uncertain, for (1) by reference to the agreement as to the lease and the finding that possession had been taken pursuant to that agreement on a particular day, the proper inference was that the lease was to begin on that day ; (2) it was not necessary that the deeds and documents directed to be executed should be further specified ; and (3) that it was not necessary to set out the terms of the will referred to. *Held*, further, that as by the award it was found that an agreement had been made between the parties for the payment of a certain sum in settlement of all disputes between them, and specific performance of that agreement was directed, it was not necessary to go into evidence as to what were the disputes, and, therefore, that there had been no such refusal to hear evidence as would invalidate the award, *Jopling* v. *Jopling*, (1908) 8 C.L.R., 33. H.C., *Griffith, C.J., O'Connor* and *Isaacs, JJ.*

Arbitration—Publication of award—Amendment of award—Power of arbitrator—Remission of award by Court.]—An arbitrator has no power to amend an award after publication to the parties, but where he has purported to make an amendment the Court may remit the subject matter of such amendment for consideration. *In re Bennett Brothers*, (1910) V.L.R., 51 ; 31 A.L.T., 148 ; 16 A.L.R., 30. *Madden, C.J.*

Arbitration—Discovery of fresh evidence since publication of award—Remitting award to arbitrator for reconsideration—Jurisdiction.]—The Court has jurisdiction to remit an award to the arbitrator for reconsideration on the ground of the discovery of fresh evidence, notwithstanding that such evidence might by due diligence have been discovered and produced at the former inquiry by the party in whose favour it is. *Re Keighley, Maxsted & Co.*, (1893) 1 Q.B., 405, and *Sprague v. Allen*, 15 T.L.R., 150, followed. *In re Bennett Brothers*, (1910) V.L.R., 51 ; 31 A.L.T., 148 ; 16 A.L.R., 30. *Madden, C.J.*

County Court—Action on insurance policy—Arbitration a condition precedent to right of action—Stay of proceedings—Adjournment—Jurisdiction—County Court Act 1890 (No. 1078), sec. 71.]—An action was brought against the assurer by the person assured upon a policy of insurance which provided that the determination of any dispute or question by arbitration should be a condition precedent to the liability of the assurer, and to the right of the assured to recover. Upon an application by the assurer for a stay of all proceedings, *Held*, that the trial of the action should, under section 71 of the *County Court Act* 1890, be adjourned until arbitration under the terms of the policy had taken place. *Borrett* v. *Norwich and London Accident Insurance Association*, 29 A.L.T. (Supplement), 1 ; 13 A.L.R. (C.N.), 22. *Judge Chomley* (1907).

II.—UNDER WATER ACT AND RAILWAYS ACT.

Water Act 1905 (No. 2016), sec. 231—Compensation for land taken for works—Principles in awarding compensation—Municipal valuation of block of land as a whole—Part only of block taken.]—Where land taken as a site for a channel for the conveyance and distribution of water forms portion of a block of land of the same owner which has been valued as a whole by the municipal authority, the value of the land so taken must, for the purpose of ascertaining the compensation payable in respect of such land, be estimated at an amount bearing the same proportion to the value of the whole block as the area of such land bears to that of such block. *In re Godfrey and Board of Land and Works*, (1910) V.L.R., 83 ; 31 A.L.T., 152 ; 16 A.L.R., 51. *Madden, C.J.* (1910).

Water Act 1905 (No. 2016), sec. 231—Compensation in respect of land taken—Injury to other land of same owner—Compensation in respect of, whether it may be given.]—In assessing compensation in respect of land taken under the *Water Act* 1905 compensation may be awarded for other land of the same owner injuriously affected by the taking of the land required. *In re Godfrey and the Board of Land and Works*, (1910) V.L.R., 83 ; 31 A.L.T., 152 ; 16 A.L.R., 51. *Madden, C.J.* (1910).

Water Act 1905 (No. 2016), sec. 231—Compensation in respect of land taken—Principles in awarding—" Channels for the conveyance and distribution of water."]—In section 231 of the *Water Act* 1905, the words " channels for the conveyance and distribution of water " include main irrigation channels as well as distributing channels. *In re Godfrey and the Board of Land and Works*, (1910) V.L.R., 83 ; 31 A.L.T., 152 ; 16 A.L.R., 51. *Madden, C.J.* (1910).

Arbitration—Railways Act 1896 (No. 1439), sec. 21—Action against Railways Commissioners for losses caused by sparks from railway engines—Practice—Summons for directions—Order on summons—Order XXX., r. 2 (Rules of 1906).]—*See* RAILWAYS. *Roach* v. *Victorian Railways Commissioners*, (1910) V.L.R., 314 ; 32 A.L.T., 10 ; 16 A.L.R., 302.

ARREST.

See also, SERVICE AND EXECUTION OF PROCESS ACT.

Bail—Prisoner charged with murder—Preliminary hearing before Justices pending—

Granting bail before committal.]—*See* CRIMINAL LAW. *Rex v. Peacock*, 33 A.L.T., 84 ; 17 A.L.R., 452.

Bail—Person charged with capital offence—Whether bail should be allowed—Matters to be considered in determining.]—*See* CRIMINAL LAW. *Rex v. Peacock*, 33 A.L.T., 84 ; 17 A.L.R., 452.

Arrest—Person found offending by laymen—Arrest by laymen—Delivery to constable—Duty of constable—Police Offences Act 1890 (No. 1126), sec. 82.]—*See* POLICE OFFENCES ACTS. *McLiney v. Minster*, (1911) V.L.R., 347 ; 33 A.L.T., 33 ; 17 A.I.R., 336.

Police Offences Act 1890 (No. 1126), sec. 82—Apprehension of person found offending—Apprehension, what amounts to—Whether actual manual arrest necessary.]—*See* POLICE OFFENCES ACTS. *McLiney v. Minster*, (1911) V.L.R., 347 ; 33 A.L.T., 33 ; 17 A.L.R., 336.

Police Offences Act 1890 (No. 1126), sec. 94—Person unlawfully arrested by constable—Whether justified in resisting arrest.]—*See* POLICE OFFENCES ACTS. *McLiney v. Minster*, (1911) V.L.R., 347 ; 33 A.L.T., 33 ; 17 A.L.R., 336.

Fugitive Offenders Act 1881 (44 & 45 Vict. c. 69), secs. 3, 5, 9—Warrant for apprehension of fugitive—Statement of offence charged, sufficiency of.] — An endorsed warrant sufficiently mentions within the meaning of sec. 5 of the *Fugitive Offenders Act* 1881, the offence charged if the charge be substantially sufficient according to the law of the State where the warrant was issued. *McKelvey v. Meagher*, 4 C.L.R., 265 ; 12 A.L.R., 483 ; H.C., *Griffith*, *C.J.*, *Barton* and *O'Connor*, *JJ.* (1906).

Fugitive Offenders Act 1881 (44 & 45 Vict. c. 69), sec. 5—Endorsed warrant—Statement of offence, sufficiency of.]—*See* FUGITIVE OFFENDERS. *McKelvey v. Meagher*, 4 C.L.R., 265 ; 12 A.L.R., 483.

Malicious Arrest—Abuse of process of Court.]—The distinction between an action for malicious arrest, and an action founded on an abuse of the process of the Court

discussed. *Varawa v. Howard Smith Co. Ltd.*, (1911) 13 C.L.R., 35 ; 17 A.L.R., 499. H.C., *Griffith*, *C.J.*, *O'Connor* and *Isaacs*, *JJ.*

Malicious Arrest—Arrest under process of foreign Court—Termination of proceedings in favour of plaintiff before action brought—Setting aside of order to hold to bail and writ of ca. re.—Reasonable and probable cause.]—*See* MALICIOUS PROSECUTION. *Varawa v. Howard Smith Co.*, (1911) 13 C.L.R., 35 ; 17 A.L.R., 499.

Supreme Court Act 1890 (No. 1142), sec. 110—Arrest and bail—Order to hold to bail, effect of.]—*See* PRACTICE AND PLEADING. *Varawa v. Howard Smith Co. Ltd.*, (1911) 13 C.L.R., at p. 53 ; 17 A.L.R., at pp. 504-5.

Service and Execution of Process Act 1901 (No. 11), sec. 18 (4)—Application for discharge of person apprehended—Procedure—Form of order.]—*See* SERVICE AND EXECUTION OF PROCESS ACT. *In re George*, (1908) V.L.R., 734 ; 30 A.L.T., 113 ; 14 A.L.R., 699.

ARTICLED CLERK.
See SOLICITOR.

ARTICLES OF ASSOCIATION.
See COMPANY.

ARTIFICIAL MANURES ACT.

Artificial Manures Act 1904 (No. 1930), secs. 11, 16, 17—Manure—Offence—Deficiency in chemical constituents—Manure in possession of Purchaser—Manure taken and collected by chemist without consent of Purchaser—Meaning of " place where manure is stored "—Manure kept or offered for sale.]—It is not an offence under sec. 16 of the *Artificial Manures Act* 1904 (which makes it an offence on the part of the vendor of " manure " within the meaning of the Act if such manure is deficient to a prescribed extent in respect of certain chemical constituents), where the manure in question has not been submitted for analysis by a purchaser of the same under sec. 11, but has been collected and taken by the chemist on his own initiative from the premises of the purchaser without the consent of the latter. Sec. 17 of that Act (which section gives power to the chemist or his deputy to enter shops, etc., examine manure collect and take for analysis portions thereof) refers to manure which in fact is kept or offered for sale by a person dealing in such manure, and is in the custody of such person. The expression in sec. 17 " the place where manure is stored," means a place where manure is stored by any manufacturer, importer or vendor of or dealer in manure, and does not mean a place where a person who has purchased it for the purpose of using it may have deposited it on his land or premises. *Robertson* v. *Rohs*, (1909) V.L.R., 68; 30 A.L.T., 110; 14 A.L.R., 731. *Madden, C.J.* (1908).

ASSAULT.

Police Offences Act 1890 (No. 1126), sec. 94 —Person unlawfully arrested by constable— Whether justified in resisting arrest.]—A person unlawfully arrested by a constable is justified in resisting and endeavouring to escape from such constable, provided he does not use undue voilence in so doing. *McLiney* v. *Minster*, (1911) V.L.R., 347; 33 A.L.T., 33; 17 A.L.R., 336. F.C., *Madden, C.J., Hood* and *Cussen, JJ.*

Autrefois acquit—Arrest by two constables —Dismissal of charge of assaulting one constable in execution of his duty—Whether an answer to charge of assaulting other constable in execution of his duty.]—*See* CRIMINAL LAW. *McLiney* v. *Minster*, (1911) V.L.R., 347; 33 A.L.T., 33; 17 A.L.R., 336.

ASSIGNEE.

See INSOLVENCY.

ASSIGNMENT.

See, also, INSOLVENCY.

I.—WHAT MAY BE ASSIGNED.

Railways Act 1890 (No. 1135), sec. 93— Railway employee — Retiring allowance, whether assignable—Liability to be recalled to service—Civil Service Act 1862 (No. 160), secs. 42, 43, 44.]—An employee of the Victorian Railways Commissioners, who held office before the passing of *The Victorian Railways Commissioners Act* 1883, was permitted by the Governor-in-Council to retire from the service, on the ground of incapacity to discharge the duties of his office by reason of infirmity of body. *Held,* that the employee was not liable to be recalled to service, and that the allowance was therefore assignable. *Brown* v. *Victorian Railways Commissioners,* 3 C.L.R., 316; 12 A.L.R., 1, applied. *Crouch* v. *Victorian Railways Commissioners,* (1907) V.L.R., 80; 28 A.L.T., 141; 12 A.L.R., 574. F.C., *a'Beckett, A.C.J., Hodges* and *Cussen, JJ.*

Pension—Police officer—Whether assignable—Liability of pensioner to be recalled to duty—Police Regulation Act 1890 (No. 1127), secs. 20, 24.]—A pension granted to a police officer under Part III. of the *Police Regulation Act* 1890 is not assignable, inasmuch as under sec. 24 it is subject to the condition that the officer shall remain in the service of the Government to the extent that, though he is not for the time being employed, he may be recalled to his duties and be actively employed. *Crouch* v. *Victorian Railways Commissioners,* (1907) V.L.R., 80; 28 A.L.T., 141; 12 A.L.R., 574, followed. *In re Hilliard*; *Ex parte Tinkler*, (1907) V.L.R., 375; 28 A.L.T., 204; 13 A.L.R., 138. F.C., *Madden, C.J., Hodges* and *Hood, JJ.*

Chose in action consisting of right against the Crown—Assignment—Petition of right by assignee—Crown Remedies and Liability Act

1890 (No. 1080), sec. 20]—A chose in action consisting of a right against the Crown can be assigned so as to entitle the assignee to present a petition of right under the *Crown Remedies and Liability Act* 1890, sec. 20, in respect of it. *The King* v. *Brown* (1912) 14 C.L.R., 17; 18 A.L.R., 111. H.C., *Griffith, C.J., Barton* and *Isaacs, JJ.*

II.—EQUITABLE ASSIGNMENTS.

Contract—Interpretation—Agreement to deposit time-payment agreements as security—Depositor allowed to collect debts due—Deposit of additional time-payment agreements equal in value to those discharged by payment—Equitable assignment—Book Debts Act 1896 (No. 1424), secs. 2, 3—Non-registration.] —J., who had in the ordinary course of his business sold furniture under time-payment agreements, in consideration of advances made to him by M., agreed in writing to deposit with M. as security for such advances certain time-payment agreement forms signed and complete, which were to remain the property of M. until the full amount of the advances with interest had been repaid to him; and it was further provided that if any of the time-payment agreements should be fully paid up by the " hirer," J. should replace them with others of equal value. In pursuance of the agreement J. delivered to M. the time-payment agreement forms. The agreement between J. and M. was not registered under the *Book Debts Act* 1896. The estate of J. was sequestrated. *Held*, that the transaction gave to M. not a mere security over, and right to retain the documents deposited, but amounted to an equitable assignment to him of the debts due to J. under the time-payment agreements, and that the assignment was void for want of registration under the *Book Debts Act* 1896. *In re Jones*, (1906) V.L.R., 432; 27 A.L.T., 230; 12 A.L.R., 279. F.C., *a'Beckett, A.C.J., Hodges* and *Chomley, JJ.* (1906).

Book debt—Assignment—Future debt—Money to become payable by agent to principal on sale of goods—Book Debts Act 1896 (No. 1424), secs. 2, 3.]—A wool-grower consigned wool to a firm of woolbrokers to be sold. Before the wool was sold the wool-grower bought sheep from A, and in payment for them gave A a written order directing the firm to pay to A. a certain sum when his wool should be sold, and to deduct that sum from the proceeds of the sale of the wool. The wool having been sold, the wool-grower became insolvent, and subsequently the firm paid to A the sum as directed by the order. In an action by the trustees of the wool-grower against A to recover the money so paid, *Held*, that the order given by the wool-grower to A was an assignment to A to the extent therein mentioned of the debt, which was not invalidated by its non-registration under the *Book Debts Act* 1896, and, therefore, that the trustee was not entitled to recover. *Shackell* v. *Howe, Thornton & Palmer*, (1909) 8 C.L.R., 170; 15 A.L.R., 176. H.C., *Griffith, C.J., O'Connor* and *Isaacs, JJ.*

Equitable assignment of future fund—Registration—Book Debts Act 1896 (No. 1424), sec. 2—Instruments Act 1890 (No. 1103), Part VI.]—A, a cattle salesman, sold cattle on behalf of a principal to B., advancing the purchase money himself and receiving from B. a promissory note for the amount of the advance, and also entering into a verbal agreement with B. that B. should resell the cattle through A., who might repay himself the amount of the advance out of the purchase money. *Quaere* (*per Griffith, C.J., Barton* and *O'Connor, JJ.*), whether the agreement as to the re-sale of the cattle through A. amounted to an assignment to A. of the purchase money which might be paid on the re-sale of the cattle, and, if so, whether the agreement should have been in writing and registered under the *Book Debts Act* 1896. *Per Isaacs, J.*—The agreement amounted to an equitable assignment, and did not require registration either under the *Instruments Act* 1890 or the *Book Debts Act* 1896. *Muntz* v. *Smail*, (1909) 8 C.L.R., 262; 15 A.L.R., 162.

Assignment—Deposit of Savings Bank pass book and order for payment out of money in bank—Debt due in connection with business carried on by assignor—Book Debts Act 1896 (No. 1424), sec. 2 (a).]—A., having entered into a contract with the Commonwealth to erect a post-office, and being required by the conditions of tendering to give security for the due and proper performance of the contract deposited with the proper officer of the Commonwealth a Savings Bank pass-book showing an amount of money to his credit together with a duly signed order for withdrawal by means of which the said amount might be withdrawn from the Savings Bank. By means of an H. order he authorized the Commonwealth to hand over the pass-book and withdrawal order to B. and notice of the giving of the H. order was duly given to the Commonwealth by B. *Held*, that the H. order constituted a good assignment of the debt due in respect of the deposit by the Commonwealth to A., but that it was not an assignment of a debt within the meaning of the *Book Debts Act* 1896. *Cox* v. *Smail*, (1912) V.L.R., 274 ; 18 A.L.R., 299. *Cussen*, *J.*

Supreme Court Act 1890 (No. 1142), sec. 63 (6)—Order III., r. 6 (Rules of 1906)—Order XIV.—" Debt or liquidated demand "—Assignment of debt—No written notice of assignment.]— *Quaere*, whether in the case of an assignment of a debt the assignee's claim is for a " debt or liquidated demand " within the meaning of Order III., r. 6, unless the assignment is a legal assignment completed by written notice under the *Supreme Court Act* 1890, section 63 (6). *Caddy* v. *Beattie*, (1908) V.L.R., 17 ; 29 A.L.T., 165 ; 13 A.L.R., 643. *Cussen*, *J.* (1907).

Assignment of debt—No written notice of assignment—Proceedings by assignee—Parties.—For a discussion of the question whether, in proceedings by the assignee of a debt, it is necessary that the assignor should be before the Court, where the assignment is not a legal assignment. *See Caddy* v. *Beattie*, (1908) V.L.R., 17 ; 29 A.L.T., 165 ; 13 A.L.R., 643. *Cussen*, *J.* (1907).

Mortgage—Equitable security—Amount secured re-paid by a stranger—Preservation of encumbrances.]—*See* MORTGAGOR AND MORTGAGEE. *Cuddigan* v. *Poole*, 33 A.L.T., 210 ; 18 A.L.R., 120.

III.—BOOK DEBTS.

Contract—Interpretation—Agreement to deposit time-payment agreements as security—Depositor allowed to collect debts due—Deposit of additional time-payment agreements equal in value to those discharged by payment—Equitable assignment—Book Debts Act 1896 (No. 1424), secs. 2, 3—Non-registration.]—*See* Sub-heading, EQUITABLE ASSIGNMENTS. *In re Jones*, (1906) V.L.R., 432 ; 27 A.L.T., 230 ; 12 A.L.R., 279.

Book debt—Money to become payable by agent to principal on sale of goods—" On account of or in connection with . . . business "—Book Debts Act 1896 (No. 1424), secs. 2, 3.]—Money which will become payable by an agent to his principal, a trader, as purchase money on the sale of goods of the principal consigned to the agent for sale, constitutes a debt to become due by the agent to the principal, but not a debt on account of or in connection with the business of the principal within the meaning of the *Book Debts Act* 1896, and is therefore not a " book debt " within the meaning of that Act. *Shackell* v. *Howe, Thornton & Palmer*, (1908) 8 C.L.R., 170 ; 15 A.L.R., 176. H.C., *Griffith, C.J., O'Connor* and *Isaacs, JJ.*

Equitable assignment of future fund—Registration—Book Debts Act 1896 (No. 1424), sec. 2—Instruments Act 1890 (No. 1103), Part VI.]—*See* sub-heading, EQUITABLE ASSIGNMENTS. *Muntz* v. *Smail*, (1909) 8 C.L.R., 262 ; 15 A.L.R., 162.

Assignment—Deposit of Savings Bank pass-book and order for payment of money in bank—Debt due in connection with business carried on by assignor—Book Debts Act 1896 (No. 1424), sec. 2 (a).]—*See* sub-heading, EQUITABLE ASSIGNMENTS. *Cox* v. *Smail*, (1912) V.L.R., 274 ; 18 A.L.R., 299.

Book Debts Act 1896 (No. 1424), sec. 2 (a)—" Business," meaning of—Engagement in particular kind of transaction with intention to continue therein—Isolated transactions.]—*See* BOOK DEBTS. *Schroder* v. *Hebbard*, (1907) V.L.R., 107 ; 29 A.L.T., 1 ; 13 A.L.R., 141.

Book Debts Act 1896 (No. 1424), sec. 2 (a)— " Business," meaning of—Three contracts for the supply of firewood entered into at different times.]—*See* Book Debts. *Schroder* v. *Hebbard*, (1907) V.L.R., 107 ; 29 A.L.T., 1 ; 13 A.L.R., 141.

IV.—Other Points.

Lessor and lessee—Breach of covenant by lessee—Subsequent assignment of lease— Liability of assignee.]—*See* Landlord and Tenant. *Renshaw* v. *Maher*, (1907) V.L.R., 520 ; 29 A.L.T., 237 ; 13 A.L.R., 265.

Illegal Contract—Transfer of land to defeat creditors—No proof that creditors defeated— Resulting trust.]—*See* Trusts and Trustees. *Payne* v. *McDonald*, (1908) 6 C.L.R., 208 ; 14 A.L.R., 366.

Trustee—Life tenant and remainderman— Corpus and income—Costs paid by trustees under order of High Court—Decision of High Court reversed on appeal by one party to Privy Council—Effect on rights of parties not appealing—Indemnity of trustees—Rights of assignee of life tenant.]—*See* Tenant for Life and Remainderman. *Cock* v. *Aitken*, (1912) 15 C.L.R., 373 ; 18 A.L.R., 576.

ATTACHMENT.

I.—Attachment of Debts.

Attachment of debts—Money ordered to be paid by Court of General Sessions—Attachment by Court of Petty Sessions—Jurisdiction.]—*See* Justices of the Peace. *Brown* v. *Gunn* ; *McKay, Garnishee*, (1913) V.L.R., 60 ; 34 A.L.T., 115 ; 18 A.L.R. (C.N.), 21.

Justices Act 1890 (No. 1105), secs. 117, 119, 128, 141—Attachment of debt—Judgment debt—Order of General Sessions— Garnishee order—Petty Sessions—Effect of— Jurisdiction—Order to review—" Person ag-

grieved."]—*See* Justices of the Peace. *Brown* v. *Gunn* ; *McKay, Garnishee*, (1912) V.L.R., 463 ; 34 A.L.T., 113 ; 18 A.L.R., 462.

Attachment of debts—Garnishee order— Judgment debtor trustee of moneys attached— Appearance of judgment debtor before Justices to protect fund—Justices Act 1890 (No. 1105), sec. 117.]—A judgment debtor, who is a trustee of moneys sought to be attached by a garnishee order *nisi* for payment of a judgment debt due by him personally, has a right, and is under a duty, to appear before the Justices on the garnishee proceedings to show that the moneys are trust moneys and ought not therefore be attached. *Roberts* v. *Death*, 8 Q.B.D., 319, followed. *Regina* v. *Justices of Heywood*, 21 V.L.R., 654 ; 17 A.L.T., 238, distinguished. *Richards* v. *Jager*, (1909) V.L.R., 140 ; 30 A.L.T., 163 ; 15 A.L.R., 119. *Madden, C.J.*

Attachment of debts—Action for unlawfully attaching trust funds.]—No action will lie for unlawfully causing moneys standing to the credit of a trust account in the name of the plaintiff to be attached for his personal debt. *Jager* v. *Richards*, (1909) V.L.R., 181 ; 30 A.L.T., 199 ; 15 A.L.R., 123. *Cussen, J.*

County Court—Attachment of debts—Service of garnishee order nisi—Notice of order directed to be sent by telegram to garnishee, to be followed by personal service upon him of a copy of such order—Order nisi made returnable before a Judge of a County Court sitting in place other than where judgment obtained—County Court Act 1890 (No. 1078), secs. 108, 109.]—*Greenwood* v. *McCormack, Blakeley Garnishee*, 28 A.L.T. (Supplement), 5 ; 12 A.L.R. (C.N.), 24. *Judge Eagleson* (1906).

II.—Foreign Attachment.

Supreme Court Act 1890 (No. 1142), sec. 91—Foreign attachment—Affidavit to be filed.]—The conditions prescribed by sec. 91 of the *Supreme Court Act* 1890 as precedent to the issue of a writ of foreign attachment must be strictly observed. The affidavit must set forth facts from which the Court can judge whether or not the cause of action arose wholly within Victoria, and what the nature and character of the action is. It is not sufficient for the affidavit to state generally the cause of action, and that it arose in Victoria. If made on information and belief the affidavit must set out the source of the deponent's knowledge and the facts on which it is based. *Henderson* v. *Ward*, (1912) V.L.R., 289; 34 A.L.T., 13; 18 A.L.R., 218. *Madden, C.J.*

III.—ATTACHMENT OF THE PERSON.

a. IN CIVIL MATTERS.

Order XLIV., r. 2 (Rules of 1884)—Order XLII., rr. 3, 6, 7, 17 (Rules of 1884)—Attachment—Disobedience of order to pay costs—Imprisonment of Fraudulent Debtors Act 1890 (No. 1100)—Whether power to attach for disobedience affected by.]—Notwithstanding the provisions of the *Imprisonment of Fraudulent Debtors Act* 1890, the Court has power to issue a writ of attachment for disobedience of its order to pay costs. *Re Sandilands; Ex parte Browne*, 4 V.L.R. (L.), 318, followed. *Pope* v. *Peacock*, (1906) V.L.R., 667; 28 A.L.T., 63; 12 A.L.R., 440. *Hodges, J.*

Attachment—Contempt of Court—Mandamus—Statutory public duty—Minister of the Crown.]—*Semble*, there is no privilege in a Minister of the Crown entitling him to immunity from attachment for contempt of Court for his disobedience of a mandamus calling upon him to perform a statutory public duty. *The King* v. *Watt; Ex parte Slade*, (1912) V.L.R., 225; 33 A.L.T., 222; 18 A.L.R., 158. F.C., *Madden, C.J., Hodges and Cussen, JJ.*

Contempt of Court—Ecclesiastical privilege—Presbyterian Church of Victoria—Refusal of Presbytery Clerk to produce documents in civil action.]—*See* CONTEMPT. *Ronald* v. *Harper*, 15 A.L.R. (C.N.), 5.

Contempt of Court—Nature of offence—Publication of statements concerning a Judge of the High Court.]—*See* CONTEMPT. *Rex* v. *Nicholls*, (1911) 12 C.L.R., 280; 17 A.L.R., 309.

Insolvency Act 1890 (No. 1102), secs. 76, 113—Execution of process or judgment, stay of—Debt due by insolvent to creditor—Trust moneys which are or ought to be in hands of trustee—Trustee ordered to pay moneys into Court.—Disobedience of order—Attachment.]—Secs. 76 and 113 of the *Insolvency Act* 1890 are both directed to process for the enforcement of the payment of money as a debt due by the insolvent to a creditor. The insolvency of a person, who in the position of a trustee, has not accounted for money he once had and still ought to have, and who has been ordered to pay the money into Court, does not operate as a stay upon process of attachment against him for non-compliance with the order for payment into Court. *Peterson* v. *M'Lennan*, (1907) V.L.R., 94; 28 A.L.T., 135: 12 A.L.R., 577. *Cussen, J.*

Order XLII., rr. 3, 17 (Rules of 1884)—Order XLIV., r. 2—Order for payment of money—Execution under fi. fa.—Attachment for disobedience—Election of remedy, whether creditor bound by.]—A writ of attachment for disobedience of an order of the Court for payment of a sum of money may issue, although a writ of *fi. fa.* to enforce such payment has been issued previously. *In re Ball*, L.R. 8 C.P., 104, explained. *Pope* v. *Peacock*, (1906) V.L.R., 667; 28 A.L.T., 63; 12 A.L.R., 440. *Hodges, J.*

Order LII., r. 11—Order LXVII.* r. 9—Writ of attachment—Sheriff, refusal of to execute—Execution, how enforced—Whether mandamus may issue.]—Whether the Sheriff refuses to execute a writ of attachment he should be called upon to return the writ or bring in the body within a given time, and on his non-compliance application should be made under Order LII., r. 11, for his committal. A writ of mandamus will not issue, there being an alternative remedy. *Peterson* v. *M'Lennan*, (1907) V.L.R., 94; 28 A.L.T., 135; 12 A.L.R., 577. *Cussen, J.*

Attachment of person—Sheriff, duty of—Writ of attachment regular on its face.]—*Quaere*, whether under a writ of attachment the Sheriff is not bound, in every case in which the writ of attachment is regular on its face, to attach the person named in the writ, leaving it to the Court to say whether he ought to be discharged. *Peterson* v. *M'Lennan*, (1907) V.L.R., 94 ; 28 A.L.T., 135 ; 12 A.L.R., 577. *Cussen, J.*

Insolvency Act 1890 (No. 1102), sec. 149—Insolvency Act 1897 (No. 1513), s. 91—Insolvency Rules 1898, Appendix of Forms, No. 64—Contempt of Court—Certificate—Compulsory appearance—Refusal of insolvent to be sworn—Power of committal—Form of notice of motion to insolvent.]—*See* CONTEMPT. *In re Hickman*, 31 A.L.T. (Supplement) 10 ; 15 A.L.R. (C.N.), 21.

"The County Court Rules 1891," rr. 333, 334, 335, 343—Judgment that defendant deliver certain chattel to plaintiff—Warrant of delivery under r. 343 returned unsatisfied—Warrant of attachment, issue of—Jurisdiction.]—*See* COUNTY COURT. *Macrow & Sons Co. Proprietary Ltd.* v. *Davidson*, 27 A.L.T. (Supplement), 11 ; 12 A.L.R. (C.N.), 9.

B. IN CRIMINAL MATTERS.

Attachment of the person—Contempt of Court — Jurisdiction of Supreme Court — Criminal Charge — Publication of matters tending to prevent fair trial — Publication before committal for trial—Extent to which publication in a newspaper is lawful.]—*See* CONTEMPT. *Packer* v. *Peacock* ; *Burrell* v. *Peacock* ; *Smart* v. *Peacock*, (1902) 13 C.L.R., 577 ; 18 A.L.R., 70.

Contempt of Court—Criminal trial—Disagreement of jury—Remand of prisoner—Petition against second trial—Presentation to Attorney-General—Publication in newspapers.]—On the trial of a prisoner charged with murder at the Supreme Court at Ballarat, the jury disagreed, and the prisoner was remanded for trial at the next sitting of the Court. While the prisoner was on remand his solicitors' managing clerk prepared a petition to the Attorney-General, assisted in obtaining signatures to it of some of the jurymen, sent it to the Attorney-General, and supplied a copy of it to a Ballarat newspaper in which extracts from the petition were published. The petition, which was signed by ten of the twelve jurymen, set out certain facts and matters which in their opinion justified an acquittal, and expressed their opinion that it was undesirable and unfair to put the prisoner on his trial a second time on the same evidence. *Held*, a contempt as tending to defeat the due course of justice. *In re Mann* ; *In re King*, (1911) V.L.R., 171 ; 32 A.L.T., 156 ; 16 A.L.R., 598. *Cussen, J.*

Contempt of Court—Pending criminal trial—Petition to Attorney-General in relation to—Whether a contempt.]—*Semble.*—Communications to the Attorney-General in relation to a pending criminal trial constitute contempt of Court if they contain deliberate mis-statements or threats, or otherwise display an intention to defeat the due course of justice. *In re Mann* ; *In re King*, (1911) V.L.R., 171 ; 32 A.L.T., 156 ; 16 A.L.R., 598. *Cussen, J.*

Contempt of Court—Nature of offence.]—*See* CONTEMPT. *Ex parte Dunn* ; *Ex parte Aspinall*, (1906) V.L.R., 493 ; 28 A.L.T., 3 ; 12 A.L.R., 358.

Contempt of Court—Attempt to influence juryman—Juryman not yet empanelled for trial of accused person in whose favour attempt is made.]—*See* CONTEMPT. *Ex parte Dunn* ; *Ex parte Aspinall*, (1906) V.L.R., 493 ; 28 A.L.T., 3 ; 12 A.L.R., 358.

Criminal contempt—Attempt to interfere with the course of justice—Nature of offence.]—*See* CONTEMPT. *Ex parte Dunn* ; *Ex parte Aspinall*, (1906) V.L.R., 493 ; 28 A.L.T., 3 ; 12 A.L.R., 358.

Inferior Court of Record—Power to commit for contempt.]—*See* CONTEMPT. *Ex parte Dunn* ; *Ex parte Aspinall*, (1906) V.L.R., 493 ; 28 A.L.T., 3 ; 12 A.L.R., 358.

Contempt of Court—Extent of powers of Court of General Sessions—Justices Act 1890 (No. 1105), sec. 184.]—*See* CONTEMPT. *Ex parte Dunn* ; *Ex parte Aspinall*, (1906) V.L.R., 493 ; 28 A.L.T., 3 ; 12 A.L.R., 358.

General Sessions—Attempt to influence juryman—Contempt of Court—Power of

Supreme Court to punish.]—*See* CONTEMPT. *Ex parte Dunn* ; *Ex parte Aspinall*, (1906) V.L.R., 493 ; 28 A.L.T., 3 ; 12 A.L.R., 358.

Supreme Court Act 1890 (No. 1142), sec. 25—Criminal causes and matters—Proceedings by way of certiorari in case of criminal contempt.] — *See* CERTIORARI. *Ex parte Dunn* ; *Ex parte Aspinall*, (1906) V.L.R., 584 ; 28 A.L.T., 72 ; 12 A.L.R., 418.

Certiorari—Court of General Sessions—Person committed for contempt by warrant of Chairman—No jurisdiction — Whether act judicial or administrative—Party aggrieved—Whether entitled ex debito justitiae.]—*See* CERTIORARI. *Ex parte Dunn* ; *Ex parte Aspinall*, (1906) V.L.R., 584 ; 28 A.L.T., 72 ; 12 A.L.R., 418.

Justices Act 1890 (No. 1105), sec. 198—Contempt of Court—Wilful misbehaviour in a Court of Petty Sessions—Insulting language to witness after case decided.]—*See* JUSTICES OF THE PEACE. *Westcott* v. *Lord*, (1911) V.L.R., 452 ; 33 A.L.T., 54 ; 17 A.L.R., 433.

Justices Act 1890 (No. 1105), sec. 198—Contempt of Court—Misbehaviour not witnessed by Court itself—Formal adjournment of Court before occurrence of misbehaviour, effect of.]—*See* JUSTICES OF THE PEACE. *Westcott* v. *Lord*, (1911) V.L.R., 452 ; 33 A.L.T., 54 ; 17 A.L.R., 433.

ATTORNEY.

See POWER OF ATTORNEY, SOLICITOR.

ATTORNEY-GENERAL.

See COSTS ; CROWN.

AUCTION AND AUCTIONEER.

Conveyancing Act 1904 (No. 1953), sec. 4 (6)—Auction Sales Act 1890 (No. 1065), secs. 3, 29—Sale of land by Sheriff under fi. fa.—Whether a " sale by auction "—Sheriff's costs of perusal of conveyance—Stipulation in contract of sale for payment by purchaser, legality of.]—*See* VENDOR AND PURCHASER. *Re Rogers and Rodd's Contract*, (1907) V.L.R., 511 ; 29 A.L.T., 13 ; 13 A.L.R., 312.

Insolvency—Surcharges—Auctioneer's fees —Commission allowed to auctioneer on advertising charges—Out of pocket expenses— Appendix of forms to Insolvency Rules 1898, Part 4.]—*See* INSOLVENCY. *In re McBain*, 32 A.L.T. (Supplement), 2 ; 16 A.L.R. (C.N.), 9.

AUSTRALIAN INDUSTRIES PRE-SERVATION ACT.

Questions asked by Comptroller-General of Customs—Duty to answer—Prosecution pending—Person interrogated not charged—Corporation—Australian Industries Preservation Act 1906-1909 (No. 9 of 1906—No. 26 of 1909), sec. 15b.]—When the Attorney-General has formally instituted a prosecution in the High Court in respect of an alleged offence against the *Australian Industries Preservation Act* 1906-1909, the power conferred by section 15B is exhausted so far as regards the persons whom the Attorney-General alleges to have committed the offence for which he prosecutes, whether they are made parties to the suit or not, and that section therefore cannot be used for the purpose of a pending suit. So *held* by *Griffith*, C.J. and *Barton*, J. (*Isaacs*, J., dissenting). *Per Isaacs*, J.—The limit of the power conferred by section 15B is that where the Crown has arraigned before the Court a particular person on a particular charge, the power cannot be exercised as to that person in relation to that particular charge. *Per Griffith*, C.J.—When a public officer entrusted with a power to be used for a particular purpose avowedly seeks to use it for another and unauthorized purpose, the persons against whom it is sought to be so used may object to its exercise. Consequently, if questions are avowedly put for an unauthorized purpose the person interrogated is justified in refusing to answer. *Semble per Griffith*, C.J.—When a question demanding a categorical answer is put under section 15B, and is so framed as to include matters concerning which the questioner is not entitled, as well as matters concerning which he is entitled to ask, it is for the questioner, and not for the person questioned, to modify it so as to confine it within permitted limits. *Held,* also, *per Griffith, C.J.* and *Barton, J.* (*Isaacs, J.* dissenting), that sec. 15B does not authorize the Comptroller-General of Customs to require an incorporated company to answer questions. *Melbourne Steamship Co.* v. *Moorehead,* (1912) 15 C.L.R., 333 ; 18 A.L.R., 533.

AUTREFOIS ACQUIT.

See CRIMINAL LAW.

BAIL.

See CRIMINAL LAW; FUGITIVE OFFENDERS ; SERVICE AND EXECUTION OF PROCESS ACT.

BAKERS AND MILLERS ACT.

Bakers and Millers Act 1893 (No. 1332), secs. 5, 6—Baker—Inspector—Weighing Bread— Customer's Premises—Power to enter.]— An inspector appointed under sec. 5 of the *Bakers and Millers Act* 1893 weighed five loaves of bread taken by him from a baker's cart and one loaf obtained by him from the premises of a customer to whom it had been delivered by the baker ; and as the weighing in each case disclosed a deficiency in the weight of the loaves, the inspector laid an information against the baker for an offence under sec. 6 of the Act. *Held,* that as the Act gave no power to the inspector to enter on the premises of and weigh bread delivered to the customer, the weight had not been taken as to the minimum number of six loaves, in accordance with the provisions of the Act, and consequently no offence had been established. *Brown* v. *Webb,* (1912) V.L.R., 347 ; 34 A.L.T., 63 ; 18 A.L.R., 320. F.C. *Madden, C.J., Hodges* and *Hood, JJ.* (1912).

BANKER AND CUSTOMER.

Banker and customer—Cheques drawn with spaces afterwards fraudulently filled up— Liability of bank—Duty of customer—Negligence.]—The mere fact that a cheque is drawn with spaces which can be utilised for the purpose of fraudulent alteration, is not by itself any violation of duty by the customer to his banker. Five cheques were drawn on the defendant bank by the two plaintiffs and defendant M. to the debit of their joint account. After they were signed by the plaintiffs M. enhanced their apparent amounts by adding words and figures in the blank spaces to the left of those originally written. In a suit to recover the balance of account, the bank claimed to debit it with the enhanced amounts of the cheques, and the jury found that the bank could not, by the exercise of ordinary care and caution, have avoided paying the cheques as altered, and that the cheques were drawn by the plaintiffs in neglect of their duty to the bank. *Held,* that there was no evidence of negligence on the part of the respondents proper to be left to the jury. *Scholefield* v. *Londesborough,* (1896) A.C., 514, followed. *Colonial Bank of Australasia* v. *Marshall,* (1906) A.C., 559. Privy Council.

Deposit receipt, security by way of—Contract to supply goods to Crown—Security for due performance of contract—Deposit receipt in name of servant of the Crown procured by contractor and delivered to such servant— Contractor's account with bank overdrawn— Contract duly performed—Whether amount of deposit receipt a debt due by Crown to contractor—Money had and received—Set-off of bank's claim against contractor, whether justifiable.]—In May, 1892, the Government of Victoria called for tenders for the supply of coal to certain Government Departments for the period 1st July, 1892, to 30th June, 1893, one of the conditions being that :— " Security will be required in cash Government debentures or bank deposit receipt in favour of the Secretary, Tender Board." P., acting for B., his undisclosed principal, tendered ; his tender was accepted, and two contracts were entered into between him and

" W. Kemp, Secretary to the Tender Board of Victoria for and on behalf of Her Majesty and Her Majesty's Government of the said Colony." The amount of the security in respect of the two tenders was £710. Each contract provided that in the event of the contractor failing to carry out the contract " the contract security money will in that case be absolutely forfeited " and each contained a condition that deductions might be made from the " security money " for certain breaches of the contract. P., who had an overdrawn account at the L. C. Bank, into which he paid moneys received by him for the sale of coal on behalf of B., drew a cheque on that account for £710, and received in exchange for it from the bank a deposit receipt for £710 in favour of Kemp, repayable in twelve months with interest, and purporting to be not transferable. This deposit receipt P. handed to Kemp as security for and until the completion of the contracts, and received a receipt for it which he transmitted to B. Before the contract was completed the L. C. Bank suspended payment, and that suspension was continued until after the contracts were completed. On their completion P. signed an order in Form H to the Regulations under the *Audit Act* 1890 requesting Kemp to pay to R., an agent of B., the amount of the deposit receipt. R. presented the order to Kemp and asked for the money. Kemp refused to pay it, but offered to hand the deposit receipt to R., who refused to accept it. In 1898 the Crown handed the deposit receipt to the L. C. Bank, which had then been reconstructed, and to which P. was still indebted to an amount exceeding the amount of the deposit receipt, receiving from the bank an indemnity, and the bank destroyed the deposit receipt. In 1906 P. by deed assigned and confirmed to B. all his claim against Kemp or the Crown in respect of the sum represented by the deposit receipt, and in 1910 notice of the assignment was given to the Crown. On a petition by B. to recover the amount of the deposit receipt from the Crown. *Held*, by *Griffith, C.J.* and *Barton, J.* (*Isaacs, J.* dissenting) that on the due completion of the contracts the Crown was under a legal obligation to pay

to P. a sum representing the amount of the deposit receipt, which P. could recover from the Crown by a petition as money had and received, and that by virtue of the assignment of 1906 B. was now entitled to recover that sum from the Crown. *The King* v. *Brown*, (1912) 14 C.L.R., 17 ; 18 A.L.R., 111.

Savings bank—Lost pass-book—Payment by bank on forged order to person other than depositor before notice of loss given—Whether bank liable—Rules, General Order No. 26, rr. 45, 48.]—Where the Commissioners of Savings Banks, on production of a depositor's pass-book and of a forged order in his name, pay out to a third person moneys standing to the credit of the depositor, the loss falls on the depositor by reason of the provisions of the Savings Banks Rules, unless, prior to payment, notice of the loss of the pass-book has been given. *Levy* v. *The Commissioners of Savings Banks*, (1906) V.L.R., 299 ; 27 A.L.T., 171 ; 12 A.L.R., 140. F.C. *Holroyd, A.C.J., a'Beckeet* and *Hodges, JJ.* (1906).

" The manager " of a bank, meaning of.]—The expression " the manager " of a bank held to mean the manager of a branch of the bank. See *Union Bank of Australia Ltd.* v. *Whitelaw*, (1906) V.L.R., 711 ; 28 A.L.T., 17 ; 12 A.L.R., 393.

Fraudulent Preference—Transfer with intent to defeat or delay creditors—Desire to protect sureties—Banker and customer—Payments made in the ordinary course of banking business—Insolvency Act 1890 (No. 1105), ss. 37 (ii.), 73.]—M. an hotelkeeper bought an hotel and in order to carry on the business obtained an overdraft from a bank which was guaranteed by two sureties to the extent of £450. He was not successful in the business and with the intention made known by him to the bank of protecting the sureties but with the belief, also made known by him to the bank, that he was still solvent he sold the hotel and business which were substantially all his assets. The overdraft at this time amounted to £576. The purchase money consisted of £350 in cash and three promissory notes of £200 each. One of the notes was by M.'s desire and with the consent of the bank discounted and after payment of £140, the amount due to one of M.'s creditors, the balance of the proceeds together with the £350 was paid into M.'s account in the ordinary way and the remaining two notes were lodged with the bank for collection. Cheques drawn on M.'s account for small amounts were paid and another of the notes was discounted and after payment of £57, the amount due to another of M.'s creditors, the balance of the proceeds was paid into M.'s account. The bank discounted the remaining note paid the proceeds into M.'s account, thereby extinguishing the overdraft, and released the sureties. Within three months of the payment of the purchase money into the bank, M.'s estate was compulsorily sequestrated. The debts remaining unpaid amounted to £335 and the assets were practically nothing. *Held,* that the payment to the Bank was neither a fraudulent preference nor a transfer made with intent to defeat or delay creditors. *Re Mills,* 58 L.T., 871, followed. *M'Donald* v. *Bank of Victoria,* (1906) V.L.R., 199; 27 A.L.T., 177; 12 A.L.R., 120. *a'Beckett, J.* (1906).

BARRISTER AND SOLICITOR.

See COUNSEL, SOLICITOR.

BASTARDY.

See MAINTENANCE AND MAINTENANCE ORDERS.

BENEFICIARY.

See WILL.

BEQUEST.

See WILL.

BETTING.

See GAMING AND WAGERING; POLICE OFFENCES ACTS; STREET BETTING SUPPRESSION ACT.

BILL OF COSTS.

See COSTS.

BILLS OF SALE.

I.—FILING.

Bill of sale given by way of security—Consideration—Statement of in notice of intention to file, whether sufficient—Instruments Act 1890 (No. 1103), secs. 134, 135, Schedule V.]—A bill of sale given by way of security cannot be attacked on the ground that the consideration has been wrongly stated in the notice of intention to file, so long as the statement of the consideration given in such notice is substantially accurate. *O'Connor* v. *Quinn,* (1911) 12 C.L.R., 239; 17 A.L.R., 345. H.C., *Griffith, C.J., Barton* and *O'Connor, JJ.*

Instruments Act 1890 (No. 1103), secs. 134, 135, Schedule V.—Notice of intention to file—Statement of consideration, whether sufficient—Past debt.]—A. in 1908 gave to B. a bill of sale over certain chattels and a mortgage of his interest under a will to secure the advance of £800 then made to him by B. with interest thereon, the principal being made repayable under each instrument on a certain date in 1911. The bill of sale contained a provision that in case any caveat should be lodged against the filing thereof it should be lawful for B. to sell the chattels and that as the right should arise under the bill of sale to sell the chattels the whole of the principal and other moneys secured and for the time being due and payable under the bill of sale should immediately become " due payable and recoverable." Caveats were lodged against the filing of the bill of sale and it was not filed and became void. Three months afterwards A. gave B. a second bill of sale which recited that A. was indebted to B. in the sum of £800 and that " the same is now due and owing " and that A. had requested B. not to press for the immediate repayment thereof which request B. had agreed to grant upon A. giving the bill of sale. The consideration was stated as being "the sum of £800 now due and owing" by A. to B., and the time for repayment of the principal was the same date as under the first bill of sale and mortgage. In the notice of intention to file the second bill of sale, the consideration was stated under the sub-heading "Past Debt" as being "the sum of £800 now due and owing by A. to B. and in consideration of B. agreeing not to press for immediate payment thereof." The second bill of sale was subsequently filed. *Held*, that the notice of intention to file was sufficient and that the second bill of sale was valid. *O'Connor v. Quinn*, (1911) 12 C.L.R., 239; 17 A.L.R., 345. H.C., *Griffith, C.J., Barton* and *O'Connor, JJ.*

Instruments Act 1890 No. 1103), secs. 133, 144—Declarations and Affidavits Act 1890 (No. 1191), sec. 6—Bill of Sale—Registration——Affidavit verifying Bill—Affidavit of Renewal—Such affidavits to be made before Commissioners for taking Declarations and Affidavits—Affidavits—Commissioners of the Supreme Court—Restriction of authority.]— The filing or the renewing of a bill of sale under the *Instruments Act* 1890 is not a "proceeding in the Supreme Court" within the meaning of those words in sec. 6 of the *Declarations and Affidavits Act* 1890. Consequently, the affidavits required to be filed under sections 133 and 144 of the *Instruments Act* 1890, must be sworn before a Commissioner for taking declarations and affidavits appointed under the *Declarations and Affidavits Act* 1890, and not before a Commissioner of the Supreme Court for taking affidavits. Commissioners of the Supreme Court for taking affidavits are restricted by their commission to matters connected with the Supreme Court, except where special provision is made by Act of Parliament. *Wrigglesworth v. Collis; Spencer,* claimant, 33 A.L.T. (Supplement), 13; 18 A.L.R. (C.N.), 6. *Judge Moule* (1912).

II.—Caveats.

Instruments Act 1890 (No. 1103), sec. 142—Bill of sale—Removal of caveat—Summons,
form of.]—An objection, that the summons in an application for an order for the removal of a caveat lodged against the filing of a bill of sale did not call upon the caveator to show cause why the caveat should not be removed, was overruled. *In re Coburn*, 28 A.L.T. (Supplement), 3; 12 A.L.R. (C.N.), 17. *Judge Eagleson* (1906).

Instruments Act 1890 (No. 1103), sec. 142—Bill of sale—Caveat—Tender of amount due to caveator—Refusal to accept—Removal of caveat—Jurisdiction of Judge to order.]— Where the grantor of a bill of sale had tendered to a caveator the amount of his debt, which the caveator refused to accept, *Held*, that the Judge had jurisdiction under sec. 142 of the *Instruments Act* 1890 to order the removal of the caveat. *In re Coburn*, 28 A.L.T. (Supplement), 3; 12 A.L.R. (C.N.), 17. *Judge Eagleson* (1906).

III.—Foreign Bills of Sale.

Bill of Sale—Given and registered in New South Wales over goods in New South Wales—Goods subsequently brought to Victoria—Bill of sale valid in Victoria.]— *Taylor v. Lovegrove; Original Mont de Piete Ltd.*, claimant, 18 A.L.R. (C.N.), 22. *Hodges, J.* (1912).

IV.—Stock Mortgage.

Instruments Act 1890 (No. 1103), secs. 169, 170, 171—Stock mortgage—"Other chattels," meaning of.]— The words "other chattels on any station in Victoria" in secs. 169, 170 and 171 of the *Instruments Act* 1890 include all other chattels whatever may be their nature, and whatever be the purpose for which they are used on such station. *Anderson v. Carter*, 20 V.L.R., 246; 16 A.L.T., 49, distinguished. *International Harvester Co. of America v. Rowe*, (1909) V.L.R., 244; 30 A.L.T., 201; 15 A.L.R., 212. F.C., *Madden, C.J., a'Beckett* and *Hood, JJ.*

BILLS OF EXCHANGE AND PROMISSORY NOTES.

Promissory note—Liability of indorser—Order in time of indorsement—Indorsement by payee—Holder in due course—Estoppel—

Instruments Act 1890 (No. 1103), secs. 21, 38, 55, 56, 57 and 90.]—A promissory note made by A. in favour of B., bore the indorsements " B. without recourse," " C.," " B.," above one another and in that order. It appeared that C. took the note, which had already been signed by A., and was intended to be used by way of renewal of a promissory note and indorsed in the same way, to B., who refused to take it unless C. herself first endorsed it. C. accordingly signed her name on the back of the note with the intention of endorsing it, and of being liable as an indorser to B., and then B. took it. B. subsequently placed his indorsements on the note in the order in which they appeared. In an action by B. against C. on the note. *Held,* that the indorsements were in the order which they were intended by C. to appear, and that C. was estopped from denying that she was an indorser or that B. was a holder in due course. *Held,* therefore, that C. was liable to B. either as an actual indorser or as having under sec. 57 of the *Instruments Act* 1890 incurred the liability of an indorser. *Semble, per Griffith, C.J.*—The promissory note was a " bill wanting in a material particular " which the persons in possession of it were entitled to fill up under sec. 21 of the *Instruments Act* 1890. *Steele v. M'Kinlay,* 5 A.C., 754, discussed. *Ferrier v. Stewart,* (1912) 15 C.L.R., 32 ; 18 A.L.R., 262. H.C., *Griffith, C.J., Barton* and *Isaacs, JJ.*

(The corresponding sections of the Commonwealth *Bills of Exchange Act* are secs. 25, 43, 60, 61, 62 and 96).

Promissory note—Material alteration, what is—Place of payment, what is—Instruments Act 1890 (No. 1103), sec. 65 (2).]—A promissory note, when made, contained nothing indicating the place of payment other than the printed words " Payable at " followed by a blank. After delivery and without the authority or assent of the maker, the blank was filled in with the words and figures " 15 Queen's Bridge Street, Melbourne." In proceedings against the maker for money due on the note. *Held,* that it had been materially altered, and was accordingly avoided as against the maker. *Semble,* that it was an alteration of the " place of payment " within the meaning of sec. 65 (2) of the *Instruments Act* 1890. *Sims v. Anderson,* (1908) V.L.R., 348 ; 29 A.L.T., 241 ; 14 A.L.R., 210. *Cussen, J.*

Negotiable instrument—Material alteration, nature of—Instruments Act 1890 (No. 1103), sec. 65—Enumeration of material alterations, whether exhaustive.]—The enumeration of material alterations in section 65 of the *Instruments Act* 1890 is not exhaustive. An alteration is a material alteration if it makes the instrument operate differently. *Sims v. Anderson,* (1908) V.L.R., 348 ; 29 A.L.T., 241 ; 14 A.L.R., 210. *Cussen, J.* (1908)

Banker and Customer—Cheques drawn with spaces afterwards fraudulently filled up—Liability of bank—Duty of customer—Negligence.]—*See* BANKER AND CUSTOMER. *Colonial Bank of Australasia v. Marshall,* (1906) A.C., 559.

Sale of land—Principal and agent—Deposit payable to agent on named day—Payment to agent by way of promissory note—Authority to receive.]—Where the conditions of sale provided that " the purchaser shall on 1/10/1907 pay to the vendor's agent a deposit of one hundred pounds of the purchase money," *Held,* that the agent had no authority to receive payment by way of promissory note. *Walder v. Cutts,* (1909) V.L.R., 261 ; 31 A.L.T., 19 ; 15 A.L.R., 352. F.C., *Hodges, Hood* and *Cussen, JJ.*

Money-lender—Re-opening transactions—" Agreement or security "—Money Lenders Act 1906 (No. 2061), sec. 4.]—*See* MONEY LENDERS ACT. *Wilson v. Moss,* 8 C.L.R., 146 ; 15 A.L.R., 131.

Instruments Act 1890 (No. 1103), secs. 92, 93—" Resides " meaning of, in sec. 93—A writ under the Act may be served on a person temporarily resident in Victoria, who is permanently domiciled and resident in another State.]—*Philips v. Cooper,* (1906) V.L.R., 31 ; 12 A.L.R. (C.N.), 5. *a'Beckett, J.*

Bill of exchange—Action upon, under the Instruments Act 1890—Writ—Service out of jurisdiction—Indorsement by Prothonotary—Necessity for Judge's order for such indorsement—Instruments Act 1890 (No. 1103), sec. 92—Service and Execution of Process Act 1901 (No. 11 of 1901), secs. 5, 8.]—*Sternberg v. Egan*, 18 A.L.R. (C.N.), 20. *Hood, J.* (1912).

Stamps Act 1890 (No. 1140), sec. 81, Third Schedule—Stamps Act 1892 (No. 1274), Schedule—" Promissory note "—Mortgage debenture charging property and providing means for enforcement of security.]—*See* STAMPS ACTS. *In re Stamps Acts*, (1906) V.L.R., 364 ; 27 A.L.T., 204 ; 12 A.L.R., 186.

Insolvency Act 1890 (No. 1102), sec. 37—Insolvency Act 1897 (No. 1513), sec. 106 (2)—Sequestration—Petitioning creditor's debt—Current promissory note.]—*See* INSOLVENCY. *David v. Malouf*, (1908) 5 C.L.R., 749 ; 14 A.L.R., 297.

BIRTH

See EVIDENCE.

BOND

See EXECUTORS AND ADMINISTRATORS ; WILL.

BOOK DEBTS

Contract—Interpretation—Agreement to deposit time-payment agreements as security—Depositor allowed to collect debts due—Deposit of additional time-payment agreements equal in value to those discharged by payment—Equitable assignment—Book Debts Act 1896 (No. 1424), secs. 2, 3—Non-registration.]—J., who had in the ordinary course of his business sold furniture under time-payment agreements, in consideration of advances made to him by M. agreed in writing to deposit with M. as security for such advances certain time-payment agreement forms signed and complete which were to remain the property of M. until the full amount of the advances with interest had been repaid to him ; and it was further provided that if any of the time-payment agreements should be fully paid up by the " hirer," J. should replace them with others of equal value. In pursuance of the agreement J. delivered to M. the time-payment agreement forms. The agreement between J. and M. was not registered under the *Book Debts Act* 1896. The estate of J. was sequestrated. *Held*, that the transaction gave to M. not a mere security over and right to retain the documents deposited, but amounted to an equitable assignment to him of the debts due to J. under the time-payment agreements, and that the assignment was void for want of registration under the *Book Debts Act* 1896. *In re Jones*, (1906) V.L.R., 432 ; 27 A.L.T., 230 ; 12 A.L.R., 279. F.C., *a'Beckett, A.-C.J., Hodges* and *Chomley, JJ.* (1906).

Book Debts Act 1896 (No. 1424), sec. 2 (*a*)—" Business," meaning of—Engagement in particular kind of transaction with intention to continue therein—Isolated transaction.]—The engagement in a particular kind of transaction continuously, with the intention of continuing that line of transaction for the purpose of profit, is " business " within the meaning of the *Book Debts Act* 1896. Engagement in a transaction in one particular instance without any intention that it shall be the first of several similar transactions would not be " business " within the meaning of the Act. *Schroder v. Hebbard*, (1907) V.L.R., 107 ; 29 A.L.T., 1 ; 13 A.L.R., 141. *Cussen, J.*

Book Debts Act 1896 (No. 1424), s. 2 (*a*)—" Business," meaning of—Three contracts for the supply of firewood entered into at different times.]—A. entered into a contract to supply firewood to a hospital. The performance of the contract was not completed at once in one single specific act but extended over some time. Prior to this A. had had two other contracts for the supply of firewood to the hospital, but there was no evidence as to the time at which these contracts were had or as to what their nature was or whether they were isolated transactions or extended over some time. A. assigned the moneys due under the first-mentioned contract, but the assignment was not registered under the *Book Debts Act* 1896. On the question of the validity of the assignment being raised before Justices, they decided that the debt had not become due in connexion with any trade or business, and therefore that the assignment did not require registration. *Held,* that it was open to Justices to take a view of the facts which would justify them in holding that the debt had not become due in connexion with any trade or business. *Schroder* v. *Hebbard,* (1907) V.L.R., 107; 29 A.L.T., 1; 13 A.L.R., 141. *Cussen, J.*

Equitable assignment of future fund— Registration—Book Debts Act 1896 (No. 1424), sec. 2—Instruments Act 1890 (No. 1103), Part VI.]—A., a cattle salesman, sold cattle on behalf of a principal to B., advancing the purchase money himself and receiving from B. a promissory note for the amount of the advance, and also entering into a verbal agreement with B. that B. should re-sell the cattle through A., who might repay himself the amount of the advance out of the purchase money. *Quaere,* (*per Griffith, C.J., Barton* and *O'Connor, JJ.*) whether the agreement as to the re-sale of the cattle through A. amounted to an assignment to A. of the purchase money which might be paid on the re-sale of the cattle, and, if so, whether the agreement should have been in writing and registered under the *Book Debts Act* 1896. *Per Isaacs, J.*: The agreement amounted to an equitable assignment and did not require registration either under the *Instruments Act* 1890 or the *Book Debts Act* 1896. *Muntz* v. *Smail,* (1909) 8 C.L.R., 262; 15 A.L.R., 162.

Book debt—Money to become payable by agent to principal on sale of goods—" On account of or in connection with . . . business "—Book Debts Act 1896 (No. 1424), secs. 2, 3.]—Money which will become payable by an agent to his principal, a trader, as purchase money on the sale of goods of the principal consigned to the agent for sale, constitutes a debt to become due by the agent to the principal, but not a debt on account of or in connection with the business of the principal within the meaning of the *Book Debts Act* 1896, and is therefore not a " book debt " within the meaning of that Act. *Shackell* v. *Howe, Thornton & Palmer,* (1909) 8 C.L.R., 170; 15 A.L.R., 176. H.C., *Griffith, C.J., O'Connor* and *Isaacs, JJ.*

Book debt—Assignment—Future debt— Money to become payable by agent to principal on sale of goods—Book Debts Act 1896 (No. 1424), secs. 2, 3.]—A woolgrower consigned wool to a firm of woolbrokers to be sold. Before the wool was sold the woolgrower bought sheep from A., and in payment for them gave A. a written order directing the firm to pay to A. a certain sum when his wool should be sold, and to deduct that sum from the proceeds of the sale of the wool. The wool having been sold, the woolgrower became insolvent, and subsequently the firm paid to A. the sum as directed by the order. In an action by the trustee of the woolgrower against A. to recover the money so paid. *Held,* that the order given by the woolgrower to A. was an assignment to A. to the extent therein mentioned of the debt, which was not invalidated by its non-registration under the *Book Debts Act* 1896, and, therefore, that the trustee was not entitled to recover. *Shackell* v. *Howe, Thornton & Palmer,* (1909) 8 C.L.R., 170; 15 A.L.R., 176. H.C., *Griffith, C.J., O'Connor* and *Isaacs, JJ.*

Assignment—Debt arising by deposit of Savings Bank pass-book and order for payment out of money in bank—Debt due in connection with business carried on by assignor—Book Debts Act 1896 (No. 1424), sec. 2 (a).]—A. having entered into a contract with the Commonwealth to erect a Post Office and being required by the conditions of tendering to give security for the due and proper performance of the contract deposited with the proper officer of the Commonwealth a Savings Bank pass-book, showing an amount of money to his credit together with a duly signed order for withdrawal by means of which the said amount might be withdrawn from the Savings Bank. By means of an H. order he authorized the Commonwealth to hand over the pass-book and withdrawal order to B. and notice of the giving of the H. order was duly given to the Commonwealth by B. *Held*, that the H. order constituted a good assignment of the debt due in respect of the deposit by the Commonwealth to A. but that it was not an assignment of a debt within the meaning of the *Book Debts Act* 1896. *Cox v. Smail*, (1912) V.L.R., 274 ; 18 A.L.R., 299. *Cussen, J.*

BREAD

See BAKERS AND MILLERS ACT.

BOUNDARIES

Boundary of States—Letters Patent creating province—Degree of longitude stated as boundary—Implied authority of Executives to locate.]—*See* COMMONWEALTH OF AUSTRALIA CONSTITUTION. *State of South Australia v. Victoria*, (1914) A.C., 283.

The Constitution (63 & 64 Vict. c. 12), sec. 75—Original jurisdiction of High Court—" Matters " between States, what are—Dispute as to boundary between two States—Boundary fixed by Act of Imperial Parliament.]—*See* COMMONWEALTH OF AUSTRALIA CONSTITUTION. *State of South Australia v. State of Victoria*, (1911) 12 C.L.R., 667 ; 17 A.L.R., 206.

BURDEN OF PROOF

See also, EVIDENCE.

Burden of proof—Land held in fee simple to be used only for a public racecourse—Member of public claiming right to enter land—Victoria Racing Club Act 1871 (No. 398), secs. 7, 20.]—*See* EVIDENCE. *Colman v. Miller*, (1906) V.L.R., 622 ; 28 A.L.T., 35 ; 12 A.L.R., 386.

Patent—Burden of proof—Want of novelty by reason of prior sales—Identity of articles so sold with articles made in accordance with patent—Identity proved by circumstantial evidence only—Facts within exclusive knowledge of other party, failure to prove.]—*See* EVIDENCE. *Cullen v. Welsbach Light Co. of Australasia Ltd.*, 4 C.L.R. 990 ; 13 A.L.R., 194.

Evidence—Burden of proof—Husband and wife living in same house—Wife tenant of house—Possession of goods in the house—Possession prima facie evidence of title.]—*See* EVIDENCE. *McKenzie v. Balchin* ; *McKenzie (claimant)*, (1908) V.L.R., 324 ; 29 A.L.T., 246 ; 14 A.L.R., 238.

Husband and wife—Maintenance—Former marriage—Husband not heard of for more than seven years—Proof of invalidity of second marriage—Onus—Marriage Act 1890 (No. 1166), sec. 46.]—*See* EVIDENCE. *Ousley v. Ousley*, (1912) V.L.R., 32 ; 33 A.L.T., 155 ; 18 A.L.R., 5.

Infant—Custody of—Father's rights—Child in custody of others—Abdication—Welfare of child— Burden of proof.]—*See* INFANT. *Goldsmith v. Sands*, 4 C.L.R., 1648 ; 13 A.L.R., 601.

Local Government Act 1903 (No. 1893), sec. 455, 456—Contract—Consideration—Tender—Deposit—Forfeiture—Withdrawal of tender before acceptance—Mode of making contract —Burden of proof.]—*See* CONTRACT OR AGREEMENT. *Stafford v. South Melbourne, Mayor, &c. of*, (1908) V.L.R., 584 ; 30 A.L.T., 43 ; 14 A.L.R., 464.

Defamation — Privileged occasion — Presumption that speaker had a proper motive—Burden of proof.]—*See* DEFAMATION. *Ronald v. Harper*, (1910) 11 C.L.R., 63 ; 16 A.L.R., 415.

Burden of proof—Evidence of negligence—Level crossing on railway—Neglect of engine-driver to whistle—Duty of persons using road to look for approaching trains.]—*See* NEGLIGENCE. *Fraser v. Victorian Railways Commissioners*, 8 C.L.R., 54 ; 15 A.L.R., 93.

Police Offences Act 1890 (No. 1126), secs. 49, 51—" Business," assisting in conducting— Club incorporated as company—Shareholders in company members of Club—Totalisator— Whether conducted as a business—Percentage of stakes retained—Burden of proof—Moneys received as consideration for an assurance to pay moneys on contingencies relating to horse races.]—*See* GAMING AND WAGERING. *O'Donnell* v. *Solomon*, (1906) V.L.R., 425 ; 27 A.L.T., 237 ; 12 A.L.R., 283.

Lotteries Gaming and Betting Act 1906 (No. 2055), sec. 38—Application for declaration that premises are a common gaming house— Affidavit of police officer showing reasonable grounds for suspecting—Suspicion, whether in mind of officer or Court—Prima facie case, how established—Prima facie case, how answered.]—*See* GAMING AND WAGERING. *In re Lotteries Gaming and Betting Act* 1906 ; *In re Shanghai Club* ; *In re Ah Pow* ; *Ex parte Gleeson*, (1907) V.L.R., 463 ; 29 A.L.T., 31 ; 13 A.L.R., 360.

Licensing Act 1890 (No. 1111), secs. 134, 135—Licensing Act 1906 (No. 2068), sec. 78 (2)—Unlawful sale of liquor—Prima facie evidence of sale of liquor—Presence of two or more persons on licensed premises—Onus of proof as to lodgers, &c.]—*See* EVIDENCE. *Biggs* v. *Cunningham*, (1907) V.L.R., 344 ; 29 A.L.T., 14 ; 13 A.L.R., 244.

Licensing Act 1890 (No. 1111), secs. 134, 135—Licensing Act 1906 (No. 2068), sec. 78 (2)—Unlawful sale of liquor—Evidence— Presence on licensed premises of two or more persons—Onus of proof as to bona fide lodgers, &c.]—*See* LICENSING. *Cahill* v. *Millett*, (1907) V.L.R., 605 ; 29 A.L.T., 16 ; 13 A.L.R., 375.

Secret Commission Prohibition Act 1905 (No. 1974), secs. 2, 14—Giving money to agent without principal's knowledge—Burden of proof.]—*See* CRIMINAL LAW. *Rex* v. *Stevenson*, (1907) V.L.R., 475 ; 29 A.L.T., 62 ; 13 A.L.R., 383.

Health Act 1890 (No. 1098), secs. 53, 54— Unwholesome food—Prosecution for having such food under control for purpose of sale for human consumption—Prima facie case

proved by informant—Burden of proof that food not intended for sale—Effect of statements made by defendant elicited on cross-examination of informant's witnesses.]—*See* HEALTH (PUBLIC). *Mellis* v. *Jenkins*, (1910) V.L.R., 380 ; 32 A.L.T., 36 ; 16 A.L.R., 430.

Factories and Shops Act 1905 (No. 1975), sec. 134—Factories and Shops Act 1905 (No. 2) (No. 2008), secs. 22, 24—Weekly half-holiday—Whether time of closing on Wednesday 1 o clock or 6 o clock—Choice of shop-keeper, burden of proof of.]—*See* FACTORIES AND SHOPS ACTS. *Billingham* v. *Gaff*, (1907) V.L.R., 691 ; 29 A.L.T., 159 ; 13 A.L.R., 474.

BUTCHERS AND ABATTOIRS ACT

Butchers and Abattoirs Act 1890 (No. 1069), sec. 26—Slaughtering cattle without licence—" Contrary to the provisions of this Act."]—The words " contrary to the provisions of this Act " in section 26 of the *Butchers and Abattoirs Act* 1890 mean " in circumstances other than those in which this Act allows slaughtering." They do not mean " contrary to any direct prohibition in this Act." Accordingly, although the Act contains no direct prohibition against slaughtering elsewhere than in an abattoir or without a licence, the act of slaughtering without a licence or in any improper place is a penal offence. *Dugdale* v. *Charles Dight* ; *Same* v. *West* ; *Same* v. *George Dight*, (1906) V.L.R., 783 ; 28 A.L.T., 186 ; 13 A.L.R., 15. *Chomley, J.* (1907).

Butchers and Abattoirs Act 1890 (No. 1069), sec. 26—Slaughtering cattle without licence—Mens rea.]—In order to establish an offence under sec. 26 of the *Butchers and Abattoirs Act* 1890, it is not necessary to prove *mens rea*. *Dugdale* v. *Charles Dight* ; *Same* v. *West* ; *Same* v. *George Dight*, (1906) V.L.R., 783 ; 28 A.L.T., 186 ; 13 A.L.R., 15. *Chomley, J.* (1907).

Butchers and Abattoirs Act 1890 (No. 1069), sec. 26—Slaughtering cattle without licence—Several persons joining in same act —Whether offence severable.]—*Prima facie* two or more persons who join in the commission of an offence are severally liable, unless the words of the Act creating the offence are such as to compel the Judge to hold that it is joint. Accordingly, where two or more persons join in committing an offence under section 26 of the *Butchers and Abattoirs Act 1890*, each is separately and severally liable. *Dugdale* v. *Charles Dight* ; *Same* v. *West* ; *Same* v. *George Dight*, 1906 V.L.R., 783 ; 28 A.L.T., 186 ; 13 A.L.R., 15. *Chomley, J.* (1907).

BY-LAWS

I. Validity.

By-law made under statutory safeguards—Validity of, whether Court may consider—Victoria Racing Club Act 1871 (No. 398), secs. 14, 15, 17.]—The Court is not deprived of its power to determine the question of the validity of a by-law by the fact that the Statute under which the by-law is made provides (*a*) that no by-law shall be of any force or effect until the expiration of one month after a copy has been sent to the Chief Secretary ; (*b*) that at any time within such month the Governor-in-Council may disallow such by-law, and (*c*) that the Governor-in-Council may at any time by a six months' notice published in the *Government Gazette* repeal any by-law made under the Statute. *Colman* v. *Miller*, (1906) V.L.R., 622 ; 28 A.L.T., 35 ; 12 A.L.R., 386. F.C., *Hodges, Hood* and *Chomley, JJ.* (1906).

By-law—Validity—Repugnancy to Act of Parliament.]—Where by an Act of Parliament the doing of an Act with a fraudulent intent is made punishable, a by-law imposing a penalty on the doing of the same act irrespective of the intent is repugnant to the Act of Parliament and therefore invalid. *London and Brighton Railway Co.* v. *Watson*, 3 C.P.D., 429, followed. *Borsum* v. *Smith*,

(1907) V.L.R., 72 ; 28 A.L.T., 89 ; 12 A.L.R., 495. F.C., *Hodges, Hood* and *Chomley, JJ.* (1906).

Mildura Irrigation Trusts Act 1895 (No. 1409), sec. 69—Regulation—Regulation imposing penalty upon person without reference to his connection with forbidden Act—Power to make such regulation.]—A regulation which purports to impose a penalty on a person without reference to his connection with an act that is forbidden by the regulation as framed, and might impose liability on a person even though he has done his best to prevent a breach of the regulation, is invalid, unless the power of making such a regulation is exercised by Parliament, or under some enactment of Parliament whereby this exceptional power is given to a subordinate body either expressly or by necessary implication. *Brown* v. *Burrow*, 30 A.L.T., 102 ; 14 A.L.R., 460. *Cussen, J.* (1908).

" Bookmaking " on racecourse—How far lawful—By-law regulating " bookmaking "—Validity of.]—*Per Hood, J.*—Provided that in doing so he violates no Statute law nor interferes unduly with others, any person lawfully on a racecourse may make wagers either privately with his friends or publicly as a business. Public betting as a business may become a nuisance or an annoyance, and by-laws designed to prevent this should be supported if possible, but, like all by-laws interfering with private rights, they must be reasonable and certain. *Colman* v. *Miller*, (1906) V.L.R., 622 ; 28 A.L.T., 35 ; 12 A.L.R., 386.

By-law—Validity — Unreasonableness and uncertainty—Regulation of " bookmaking " on public racecourse—Victoria Racing Club Act 1871 (No. 398), secs. 7, 20.]—Certain land was by Statute vested in an officer of a racing club to be held only for the purpose of its being maintained and used for a public racecourse, and the committee of the club was empowered by such Statute to make by-laws for regulating the admission of persons to the land, the expulsion of persons from the land, the rates and charges to be paid for admission, and for the general management of the racecourse. Purporting to act under this power the committee made a by-law forbidding any person to carry on upon any part of the land the vocation of a bookmaker unless he was approved of by the committee, and paid to the committee in advance such registration fee as the committee should from time to time determine, and unless he complied with such directions as might from time to time be given by or on behalf of the committee. A person offending against the by-law incurred a penalty of £5, and was liable to be removed from the land. *Held*, that, in the method prescribed for fixing fees, and in its requirements as to the approval of the committee, and as to compliance with directions, the by-law was unreasonable and uncertain, and was therefore invalid. *Colman* v. *Miller*, (1906) V.L.R., 622; 28 A.L.T., 35; 12 A.L.R., 386. F.C., *Hodges, Hood* and *Chomley, JJ.* (1906).

Local Government Act 1903 (No. 1893), sec. 197—By-law—Validity—Power to regulate or control—Power to prohibit.]—*See* LOCAL GOVERNMENT. *Co-operative Brick Co. Pty. Ltd.* v. *Hawthorn, Mayor &c. of City of,* (1909) 9 C.L.R., 301; 15 A.L.R., 479.

Local Government — By-law — Validity— Power to " regulate or control quarrying or blasting operations "—Local Government Act 1903 (No. 1893), sec. 197 (21).]—*See* LOCAL GOVERNMENT. *Co-operative Brick Co. Pty. Ltd.* v. *Hawthorn, Mayor &c. of,* (1909) 9 C.L.R., 301; 15 A.L.R., 479.

Local Government—By-law—Public highway—Traction engine—Power to regulate— Restrictions on construction and user—Local Government Act 1903 (No. 1893), secs. 197, 594.]—*See* LOCAL GOVERNMENT. *Tungamah President, &c. of Shire of* v. *Merrett,* (1912) 15 C.L.R., 407; 18 A.L.R., 511.

Local Government Act 1903 (No. 1893), secs. 203, 213, 222, 232, 609, 610, 613, 635— By-law, validity of—Licensing yards for sale of cattle—Prohibition of use of unlicensed premises—Penalty—Wilfulness—Limiting Locality of licensed yards—Differentiation between kinds of cattle.]—Under sec. 635 (c) of the *Local Government Act* 1903, which authorizes a municipal council to make by-laws for licensing yards and premises for the sale of cattle, a council has no power to prohibit the use of unlicensed yards and premises for the sale of cattle. So held by *a'Beckett* and *Cussen, JJ.* (*Hood, J.* dissenting). Sec. 222 of the *Local Government Act* 1903 authorizes the imposition by a by-law of a penalty for a "wilful act or default contrary thereto." *Held*, by *a'Beckett* and *Cussen, JJ.* (*Hood, J.* dissenting), that a by-law imposing a penalty on "every person offending against or committing any breach of" the by-law was invalid. A municipal council may by a by-law made under sec. 635 (c) define a particular area of the municipality within which alone yards and premises will be licensed for the sale of cattle. *Per a'Beckett* and *Hood, JJ.,* a municipal council may by such a by-law differentiate between different kinds of cattle. *In re City of Bendigo ; Ex parte Edwards,* (1908) V.L.R., 609; 30 A.L.T., 63; 14 A.L.R., 475.

By-law, regulation made under—By-law made under Act subsequently repealed— Provision that by-law continue in force notwithstanding repeal—Regulation purporting to be made under repealing Act—Clear intention to exercise a power—Effect of mis-recital of authority—Local Government Act 1874 (No. 506), Schedule XIII., Part V., sec. 1— Local Government Act 1890 (No. 1112), sec. 2, Schedule XIII., Part V., sec. 1—Local Government Act 1903 (No. 1893), secs. 2, 232.]—*See* LOCAL GOVERNMENT. *Ex parte Swan ; In re Mayor, &c., of the City of Hawthorn,* (1907) V.L.R., 16; 28 A.L.T., 113; 12 A.L.R., 611.

Melbourne Harbour Trust Act 1890 (No. 1119), sec. 142 (xix.)—Carter plying for hire without licence from Harbour Trust Commissioners—Regulation in prohibition thereof, how far valid—Licence from City of Melbourne.]—*See* MELBOURNE HARBOUR TRUST. *Vincent* v. *Curran,* (1909) V.L.R., 370; 31 A.L.T., 24; 15 A.L.R., 359.

By-law, validity of—By-law regulating privies, &c., generally—Penalty not following the words of the by-law—Penalty not imposed

on person responsible for existence of the thing prohibited—Health Act 1890 (No. 1098), secs. 32, 35.]—*See* HEALTH (PUBLIC). *Charlton, President, &c., of Shire of* v. *Ruse,* (1912) 14 C.L.R., 220 ; 18 A.L.R., 207.

By-law, validity of—Power to make by-laws as to the position and construction of privies, &c., generally—Retrospective operation of by-law—Health Act 1890 (No. 1098), secs. 32, 35.]— *See* HEALTH (PUBLIC). *Charlton, President, &c., of Shire of* v. *Ruse* (1912) 14 C.L.R., 220 ; 18 A.L.R., 207.

Pure Food Act 1905 (No. 2010), sec. 41 (2)—Cleanliness and freedom from contamination of articles of food—Regulation, validity of—Reasonableness—Certainty.]—*See* HEALTH (PUBLIC). *Robertson* v. *Abadee* (1907) V.L.R., 235 ; 28 A.L.T., 184 ; 13 A.L.R., 137.

Post and Telegraph Act 1901 (No. 12) secs. 80, 97 (r.)—Telephone Regulations (Statutory Rules 1908, No. 87)—Telephone system—Lists of subscribers—Whether Postmaster-General has exclusive right to publish —Publication by private persons—Regulation, whether ultra vires.]—*See* POST AND TELEGRAPH ACTS. *Commonwealth* v. *Progress Advertising and Press Agency Co. Pty. Ltd.,* (1910) 10 C.L.R., 457 ; 16 A.L.R., 305.

II. INTERPRETATION.

Mines—By-laws—Maryborough mining district—Prospector discovering payable gold—Prospector's claim, extent of—" Other alluvial gold workings," what are—Abandoned gold workings.]—*See* MINING. *Pelletier* v. *Porter,* (1907) V.L.R., 213 ; 28 A.L.T., 211 : 13 A.L.R., 68.

Highway—Obstruction—Standing or loitering in street and not moving on when requested — Collecting a crowd—Interference with traffic—By-law—Police Offences Act 1890 (No. 1126), sec. 6.]—*See* POLICE OFFENCES ACTS. *Haywood* v. *Mumford,* (1908) 7 C.L.R., 133 ; 14 A.L.R., 555.

Carriages Act 1890 (No. 1070), secs. 3, 4—Licensed Carriages Statute 1864 (No. 217), secs. 3, 4—By-law, validity of—City of Melbourne By-Laws, No. 78, sec. 8—Hackney carriage—Vehicle plying for hire, licensing of.]—*See* CARRIAGES ACT. *Montgomery* v. *Gerber,* (1907) V.L.R., 428 ; 28 A.L.T., 230 ; 13 A.L.R., 219.

III.—LEGAL PROCEEDINGS ; PRESUMPTIONS AND INFERENCES.

Local Government—By-law — Validity — Evidence Act 1890 (No. 1088), sec. 48—Local Government Act 1903 (No. 1893), sec. 197.]— The right to apply to quash a by-law of a municipality under sec. 48 of the *Evidence Act* 1890 has not been impliedly repealed by sec. 232 of the *Local Government Act* 1903. *Merrett & Whiteman* v. *President, &c., of the Shire of Tungamah,* (1912) V.L.R., 248 ; 34 A.L.R., 35 ; 18 A.L.R., 214. F.C., a' Beckett, Hood and Cussen, JJ.

Actual legal possession—Disturbance of, how far permissible—Rights of true owner, how to be asserted—Person in possession of ground as a claim under prima facie title—Claim registered—Failure to observe mining by-laws.]—*See* MINES AND MINING. *Bell* v. *Clarke,* (1906) V.L.R., 567 ; 28 A.L.T., 24 ; 12 A.L.R., 308.

Licensed carriage—Negligence of driver—Liability of owner—By-law No. 78 of City of Melbourne— Regulation prohibiting owner from entrusting licensed carriage to any person except as his servant—Prima facie presumption of relation of master and servant.] *See* CARRIER. *McKinnon* v. *Gange,* (1910) V.L.R., 32 ; 31 A.L.T., 112 ; 15 A.L.R., 640.

CALLS.

See COMPANY.

CAPIAS

See PRACTICE AND PLEADING.

CARRIAGES ACT

Carriages Act 1890 (No. 1070), secs. 3, 4 (Licensed Carriages Statute 1864 (No. 217), secs. 3, 4)—By-law, validity of—City of Melbourne By-Laws, No. 78, sec. 8—Hackney carriage—Vehicle plying for hire, licensing of.]—By sec. 4 of the *Carriages Act* 1890 the council of the City of Melbourne is empowered to make by-laws " for licensing and regulating hackney carriages plying for hire . . . and the owners and drivers of such hackney carriages." The council made a by-law by sec. 2 of which the words " hackney carriage " were defined to mean and include a vehicle which by the Act the council was empowered to license. Sec. 3 provided that no carriage should ply for hire as a hackney carriage until licensed, and secs. 5, 6 and 7 provided for the mode of licensing and the form of licence. Sec. 8 provided that :—" No person shall keep, use, employ, or let for hire for the carrying of passengers, any hackney carriage, or act as driver or conductor thereof . . . unless he shall have a licence . . ." *Held*, that although not expressly limited in its operation to vehicles plying for hire, sec. 8, when read with the rest of the by-law, was by necessary implication so limited, and was not in excess of the powers conferred on the council by the *Carriages Act* 1890. *Montgomery* v. *Gerber*, (1907) V.L.R., 428 ; 28 A.L.T., 230 ; 13 A.L.R., 219. *a'Beckett, J.* (1907).

Licensed carriage—Negligence of driver—Liability of owner—By-law 78 of the City of Melbourne—Regulation prohibiting owner from entrusting licensed carriage to any person except as his servant—Prima facie presumption of relation of master and servant.]—Every owner licensed under by-law 78 of the City of Melbourne, which provides that no owner of a licensed carriage shall entrust it to any person as driver except as his servant, is presumed until the contrary is shown to have obeyed the by-law, and therefore the fact that a person other than the owner is driving such carriage is not conclusive that such person is the servant of the owner. *Clutterbuck* v. *Curry*, (1885) 11 V.L.R., 810, followed. *Gates* v. *R. Bell & Son*, (1902) 2 K.B., 38, distinguished. *McKinnon* v. *Gange*, (1910) V.L.R., 32 ; 31 A.L.T., 112 ; 15 A.L.R., 640. F.C., *Madden, C.J., Hood and Cussen, JJ.*

CASE STATED

See also, COUNTY COURT, GENERAL SESSIONS.

Administration and Probate Act 1890 (No. 1060), sec. 98—Case stated—Right to begin.]—*See* DUTIES ON THE ESTATES OF DECEASED PERSONS. *In re McCracken*, 27 A.L.T., 233 ; 12 A.L.R., 303.

Special case—Right to begin—Stamps Act 1890 (No. 1140), sec. 71.]—*See* STAMPS ACTS. *Armytage* v. *Collector of Imposts*, (1906) V.L.R., 504 ; 12 A.L.R., 305.

CATTLE

See also, BUTCHERS AND ABATTOIRS ACT.

Agister—Negligence — Liability — Horse placed among horned cattle—Horse injured by bull—Scienter.]—An agister for reward of a horse, who had put the horse in a paddock where there were a bull and cows, was held liable in damages for injuries caused by the bull to the horse, though the agister did not know the bull was of a mischievous disposition. *Sanderson* v. *Dunn*, 32 A.L.T. (Supplement), 14 ; 17 A.L.R. (C.N.), 9. *Judge Moule* (1911).

Highway—Open drain lawfully constructed by municipal authority—Liability of municipal authority—Damages, whether too remote—Wandering horse entering drain at shallow part and walking along drain to deep part—Horse unable to extricate itself.]—*See* LOCAL GOVERNMENT. *Benalla, President, &c., of (defendants appellants)* v. *Cherry (plaintiff respondent)*, (1911) 12 C.L.R., 642 ; 17 A.L.R., 537.

Crimes Act 1890 (No. 1079), sec. 74—Using another person's cattle without his consent—Unlawful user by person in lawful possession.] *See* CRIMINAL LAW. *Wimble* v. *Foulsham*, (1908) V.L.R., 98 : 29 A.L.T., 158 ; 13 A.L.R., 727.

Stock Diseases Act 1890 (No. 1141), sec. 74—Travelling sheep—Meaning of " on each day "—Offence by person in charge of such sheep for part of a day.]—*See* STOCK DISEASES ACT. *West* v. *Armstrong*, (1908) V.L.R., 685 ; 30 A.L.T., 92 ; 14 A.L.R., 562.

Stock Diseases Act 1890 (No. 1141), sec. 74
—Travelling sheep—Minimum daily distance
not travelled—Lawful excuse—Condition of
sheep.]—*See* STOCK DISEASES ACT. *McCure*
v. *Fraser*, (1908) V.L.R., 678; 30 A.L.T., 94;
14 A.L.R., 561.

CAVEAT

See BILL OF SALE, TRANSFER OF LAND
ACT.

CERTIFICATE

See TRANSFER OF LAND ACT.

CERTIORARI

Certiorari—Court of General Sessions—
Person committed for contempt by warrant
of Chairman—No jurisdiction—Whether act
judicial or administrative—Party aggrieved—
Whether entitled ex debito justitiae.]—The
Chairman of General Sessions by warrant
under his hand committed to prison a woman
for a contempt, and on the return of a writ of
habeas corpus the woman was discharged
on the ground that there was no jurisdiction
to commit her. In proceedings for a writ
of *certiorari*, *Held*, that the Court of General
Sessions having assumed to exercise jurisdiction over a person thought to be subject
thereto, there was a judicial act controllable
by *certiorari*, and that the woman was a
party aggrieved, and would on proper
materials, be entitled to the issue of the
writ *ex debito justitiae*. *Ex parte Dunn*;
Ex parte Aspinall, (1906) V.L.R., 584;
28 A.L.T., 72; 12 A.L.R., 418. *Cussen, J.*

Supreme Court Act 1890 (No. 1142), sec. 25
Criminal causes and matters—Proceedings
by way of certiorari in case of criminal contempt.]—A proceeding by way of *certiorari* in
the case of a criminal contempt is itself a
criminal cause or matter in the broad sense
of that phrase, and, *semble*, is a criminal
cause or matter within the meaning of sec.
25 of the *Supreme Court Act* 1890. *Ex parte*
Dunn; *Ex parte Aspinall*, (1906) V.L.R.,
584; 28 A.L.T., 72; 12 A.L.R., 418. *Cussen, J.*

Certiorari—13 Geo. II. c. 18—Whether Act
in force in Victoria as regards Justices and
Courts of General Sessions.]—So far as relates
to Justices the Act 13 Geo. II., c. 18, is in
force in Victoria. *Quaere*, whether the Act
is not also in force in regard to Courts of
General Sessions, notwithstanding the fact
that when the Act 9 Geo. IV. c. 83 was passed
there were no Courts of Quarter or General
Sessions in New South Wales. *Ex parte*
Dunn; *Ex parte Aspinall*, (1906) V.L.R.,
584; 28 A.L.T., 72; 12 A.L.R., 418. *Cussen, J.*

Certiorari—Court of General Sessions—
Notice of proceedings to Chairman and Justices, necessity for—13 Geo. II. c. 18, sec. 5—
9 Geo. IV. c. 83—Supreme Court Act 1890
(No. 1142), secs. 25, 31.]—Even assuming
that sec. 5 of the Act 13 Geo. II. c. 18 is not
in force with regard to Courts of General
Sessions by virtue of 9 Geo. IV. c. 83, the
same result as if it were in force is brought
about by secs. 25 and 31 of the *Supreme Court*
Act 1890 or one of them, and consequently
in proceedings to remove any criminal matter
from a Court of General Sessions by way of
certiorari, it is necessary to show that the
notice required by sec. 5 has been duly given.
The notice must be given before the application even though an order *nisi* only is granted
in the first instance. *Ex parte Dunn*; *Ex*
parte Aspinall, (1906) V.L.R., 584; 28
A.L.T., 72; 12 A.L.R., 418. *Cussen, J.*

Certiorari to Judge of a County Court—
Evidence—Conflict of evidence as to proceedings in County Court—Unsworn statement of Judge, whether admissible.]—*Per*
a' Beckett, J.—On the hearing of an order *nisi*
for *certiorari* directed to the Judge of a
County Court and a party to an action tried
before him, the Supreme Court may obtain
and act upon a statement, though not on
oath, by the Judge as to what took place at
the trial, if the affidavits are in conflict
upon that matter. *A. Macrow & Sons*
Pty. Ltd. v. *Macartney*, (1911) V.L.R., 393;
33 A.L.T., 64; 17 A.L.R., 397.

CESTUI QUE TRUST

See TRUSTS AND TRUSTEES, WILL.

CHAMBERS

See COUNTY COURT, PRACTICE AND PLEADING.

CHARGE AND CHARGING ORDERS.

Will—Land subject to an equitable charge—Charge created by parol—Conveyancing Act 1904 (No. 1953), sec. 75.]—An equitable charge on land under this section can be created by parol. When any person in a fiduciary position, including an agent, has invested trust money in the purchase of land, the beneficial owner may have a charge on the property for the amount of the trust money, and trust money may be followed into land upon parol evidence. *In the Will of David Smith; Smith v. Smith*, (1909) V.L.R., 91; 30 A.L.T., 214; 15 A.L.R., 25. *Hood, J.* (1908).

Will—Power of appointment of certain land to testator's children—Appointment to testator's sons—Legacies to daughters out of his own estate—If such estate insufficient to pay legacies, payment to extent of deficiency charged on land—Validity of charge.]—*See* WILL. *In re Connell; National Trustees, Executors, &c., Co. of Australasia Ltd. v. Connell*, (1910) V.L.R., 471; 32 A.L.T., 83; 16 A.L.R., 504.

Will — Settlement — Annuity — Charge, whether on corpus or income—Order of Court—Transfer of Land Statute 1866 (No. 301), sec. 86.]—*See* SETTLEMENT. *Brown v. Abbott*, (1908) 5 C.L.R., 487.

Equitable incumbrance—Legal estate got in pendente lite.]—A legal estate may be got in by an equitable incumbrancer and may be used against persons having equitable interests, although it has been got in *pendente lite*. *Crout v. Beissel*, (1909) V.L.R., 207; 30 A.L.T., 185; 15 A.L.R., 143. *a'Beckett, J.*

Local Government Act 1903 (No. 1893), secs. 324 to 328, 340 to 343—Rates—Enforcement of charge upon land—County Court practice—Special defence, notice of—County Court Act 1890 (No. 1078), sec. 66.]—*See* LOCAL GOVERNMENT. *Mayor, &c., of Malvern v. Johnson*, 28 A.L.T. (Supplement), 7; 12 A.L.R. (C.N.), 28.

Local Government Act 1903 (No. 1893), secs. 324 to 328, 340 to 343—Rates, interest and costs, how far a charge upon land—Costs of removing an order from Petty Sessions to Supreme Court.]—*See* LOCAL GOVERNMENT. *Mayor, &c., of Malvern v. Johnson*, 28 A.L.T. (Supplement) 7; 12 A.L.R. (C.N.), 28.

Local Government Act 1903 (No. 1893), secs. 2, 341—Local Government Act 1891 (No. 1243,) sec. 64—Real Property Act 1890 (No. 1136), sec. 47—Rates—Charge upon land—Statutes of Limitations.]—*See* LOCAL GOVERNMENT. *Richmond, Mayor, &c., of v. Federal Building Society*, (1909) V.L.R., 413; 31 A.L.T., 52; 15 A.L.R., 439.

Application to bring land under the Transfer of land Act—Sale of land for non-payment of rates under decree of County Court—Dead owner made defendant—Order for substituted service—Commissioner of Titles acting upon records in Office—Refusal to issue certificate—Local Government Act 1903 (No. 1893), secs. 324, 341, 342, 343, 704.]—*See* TRANSFER OF LAND ACT. *In re Transfer of Land Act; Ex parte Anderson*, (1911) V.L.R., 397; 33 A.L.T., 78; 17 A.L.R., 399.

Local Government Act 1903 (No. 1893), secs. 341, 342—County Court Rules 1891, r. 103—Rates—Charge on land—Proceedings to enforce—Death of owner—Parties—Executor of executor—Order for sale—Title.]—*See* LOCAL GOVERNMENT. *Moorabbin, Shire of v. Soldi*, (1912) V.L.R., 389; 34 A.L.T., 93; 18 A.L.R., 493.

Action to enforce charge upon lands for rates—County Court—Scale of costs, how determined—Value of land.]—*See* COUNTY COURT. *Mayor, &c., of Malvern v. Johnson*, 28 A.L.T. (Supplement), 7; 12 A.L.R. (C.N.), 28.

CHARITY

Will—Charity, gift of—Compromise, jurisdiction of Court to sanction—Attorney-General, consent of.]—By his will testator left a house and land known as " Goodrest " together with the furniture therein to the Melbourne Hospital upon trust " to be used for hospital purposes and as a convalescent home for the convalescent patients of the said hospital " with power to the trustees of the hospital from time to time to alter repair erect and re-erect buildings on such land, provided however that such land and the tenements at any time erected thereon should be maintained and kept by the trustees of the hospital " for hospital purposes and as a convalescent home as hereinbefore specified and for such purposes only." There was a gift of the testator's residuary real and personal estate. To make " Goodrest " suitable for hospital purposes or for a convalescent home, would have required a good deal of money. The trustees of the Melbourne Hospital had no money for these purposes, and, being engaged in erecting new hospital buildings, were unable to make up their minds whether to take the gift or not. They then entered into an agreement with the persons entitled under the gift of the residue to sell " Goodrest " and divide the proceeds of the sale into two moieties—one to go to the Melbourne Hospital to be applied for hospital purposes, and the other to go into the residuary estate. *Held*, that the Court had jurisdiction to sanction the compromise, and, the compromise being modified so as to provide that the moiety going to the Melbourne Hospital should be spent in the erection of a building for convalescent hospital patients, that the sanction of the Court should be given. *In re Buckhurst*; *Melbourne Hospital v. Equity Trustees, Executors &c. Co. Ltd.*, (1911) V.L.R., 61; 32 A.L.T., 165; 17 A.L.R., 63. *Cussen, J.*

Will — Construction — Charitable trust — Trust to pay passage money for immigrants — Relief of poverty—Validity of trust.]—*See* WILL. *In re Wallace*; *Trustees, Executors and Agency Co. Ltd. v. Fatt*, (1908) V.L.R., 636; 30 A.L.T., 100; 14 A.L.R., 502.

Will—Construction—Gift of residue—Trust for " charitable purposes "—Trust for " religious purposes "—Whether valid—Uncertainty.]—*See* WILL. *In re Dobinson*; *Maddock v. Attorney-General*, (1911) V.L.R., 300; 33 A.L.T., 20; 17 A.L.R., 280.

Administration and Probate Duties Act 1907 (No. 2089), sec. 3—Exemption from duty —Public charitable bequest or settlement— Institution for the promotion of science and art, what is.]—*See* DUTIES ON THE ESTATES OF DECEASED PERSONS. *Edgar v. Greenwood*, (1910) V.L.R., 137; 31 A.L.T., 132; 16 A.L.R., 6.

CHEQUE

See BANKER AND CUSTOMER; BILLS OF EXCHANGE AND PROMISSORY NOTES.

CHILDREN

I.—LEGITIMACY; DOMICIL.

Evidence—Legitimacy, presumption as to— Father and mother living together as man and wife—European woman and Chinese man.]— *Potter v. Minahan*, 7 C.L.R., 277; 14 A.L.R., 635.

Child born in wedlock—Presumption of legitimacy.]—*See* EVIDENCE. *In re Osmand*; *Bennett v. Booty*, (1908) V.L.R., 67; 29 A.L.T., 168; 13 A.L.R., 728.

Prohibited immigrant—Infant—Domicil of father in Australia—Immigration Restriction

Act 1905 (No. 17 of 1905), sec. 4—Immigration Restriction Act 1901 (No. 17 of 1901), sec. 3.]—*See* IMMIGRATION RESTRICTION ACTS. *Ah Yin* v. *Christie*, 4 C.L.R., 1428; 13 A.L.R., 372.

II. CUSTODY.

Infant—Custody—Rights of father—Benefit of infant—Power of Court.]—*See* INFANT. *The King* v. *Lennie*; *The King* v. *Mackenzie*, 29 A.L.T., 56; 13 A.L.R., 505.

Infant—Custody of—Father's rights—Child in custody of others—Abdication—Welfare of child—Burden of proof.]—*See* INFANT. *Goldsmith* v. *Sands*, 4 C.L.R., 1648; 13 A.L.R., 601.

Infant, custody of—Right to custody, how determined—Welfare of child, importance of—Marriage Act 1890 (No. 1166), secs. 31, 33.]—*See* INFANT. *Moule* v. *Moule*, (1911) 13 C.L.R., 267; 17 A.L.R., 446.

Infant, custody of—Infant a girl of three years in custody of mother—Mother a fit person—Right of father—Welfare of child—Marriage Act 1890 (No. 1166), secs. 31, 33.]—*See* INFANT. *Moule* v. *Moule*, (1911) 13 C.L.R., 267; 17 A.L.R., 446.

Custody of infant—Father outside jurisdiction—Order which cannot be enforced—Whether Court will make.]—*See* INFANT. *Knipe* v. *Alcock*, (1907) V.L.R., 611; 29 A.L.T., 98; 13 A.L.R., 433.

Custody of infant—Procedure—Habeas corpus—Who may apply by—Application to Court for appointment of guardian, where necessary.]—*See* INFANT. *The King* v. *Waters*, (1912) V.L.R., 372; 34 A.L.T., 48; 18 A.L.R., 304.

Custody of child—Jurisdiction of Justices to determine—Marriage Act 1890 (No. 1166), secs. 42, 43.]—Justices have no power under section 43 of the *Marriage Act* 1890 to deal with the question of the custody of an illegitimate child at the hearing of a complaint under section 43 by or with the authority of the mother of the child against the father. *Fisher* v. *Clack*, 2 A.L.R. (C.N.), 321, considered. *Russ* v. *Carr*, (1909) V.L.R., 78; 30 A.L.T., 131; 15 A.L.R., 24. *Hodges, J.*

Custody of infant—Procedure—Habeas corpus—Who may apply by—Application to Court for appointment of guardian, where necessary.]—*See* INFANT. *The King* v. *Waters*, (1912) V.L.R., 372; 34 A.L.T., 48; 18 A.L.R., 304.

III.—MAINTENANCE.

(a) *Breaking into Corpus.*

Breaking into corpus—Trusts Act 1896 (No. 1421), sec. 19 — Infant — Maintenance and education—Trust fund—Breaking into corpus—Advancement.]—*See* INFANT. *In re English*, (1909) V.L.R., 430; 31 A.L.T., 74; 15 A.L.R., 517.

Trust—Corpus in trust for infant—Breaking into in order to provide University fees—Trusts Act 1896 (No. 1421), sec. 19.]—*See* TRUSTS AND TRUSTEES. *Re Keam (or Kean)*, (1911) V.L.R., 165; 32 A.L.T., 159; 17 A.L.R., 130.

Infant—Application for maintenance by breaking into corpus—Heading of papers, form of.]—*See* TRUSTS AND TRUSTEES. *Re Smith*, 12 A.L.R. (C.N.), 5.

(b) *Under the Widows' and Young Children Maintenance Act.*

Widows' and Young Children Maintenance Act 1906 (No. 2074), sec. 3—Disposition of property by will—Provision for widow and children—" Sufficient means for their maintenance and support," what are.]—*See* WIDOWS AND YOUNG CHILDREN MAINTENANCE ACT. *In re Read*, (1910) V.L.R., 68; 31 A.L.T., 154; 16 A.L.R., 60.

Widows and Young Children Maintenance Act 1906 (No. 2074), sec. 3—Disposition of property by will—Widow and children left without sufficient means for maintenance—Provision for maintenance by order of Court—Discretion, how exercised.]—*See* WIDOWS AND YOUNG CHILDREN MAINTENANCE ACT *In re Read*, (1910) V.L.R., 68; 31 A.L.T., 154; 16 A.L.R., 60.

Widows and Young Children Maintenance Act 1906 (No. 2074)—Purpose of Act—Capricious and unreasonable testamentary dispositions.]—*See* WIDOWS' AND YOUNG

CHILDREN MAINTENANCE ACT. *In re Mc-Goun*, (1910) V.L.R., 153; 31 A.L.T., 193; 16 A.L.R., 141.

(c) Maintenance Orders.

See also, MAINTENANCE AND MAINTENANCE ORDERS.

Marriage Act 1890 (No. 1166), secs. 42, 43—Order for maintenance of child—Subsequent return of child to father—Order still valid.]—*See* MAINTENANCE AND MAINTENANCE ORDERS *Lobley* v. *Lobley*, (1909) V.L.R., 383; 31 A.L.T., 46; 15 A.L.R., 443.

Marriage Act 1890 (No. 1166), secs. 42, 43—Illegitimate child without adequate means of support—Offer by father to provide home for child—Right to custody of child—Agreement by mother to support child.]—*See* MAINTENANCE AND MAINTENANCE ORDERS. *Russ* v. *Carr*, (1909) V.L.R., 78; 30 A.L.T., 131; 15 A.L.R., 24.

Marriage Act 1890 (No. 1166), secs. 42, 43—Illegitimate child without adequate means of support—Dismissal of previous complaint—Res judiciata.]—*See* MAINTENANCE AND MAINTENANCE ORDERS. *Russ* v. *Carr*, 30 A.L.T., 131.

Marriage Act 1890 (No. 1166), secs. 42, 43—Maintenance order—Summons to appear before Court of Petty Sessions—Order in fact made by two Justices—Jurisdiction of Justices—Justices Act 1896 (No. 1458), sec. 4.]—*See* MAINTENANCE AND MAINTENANCE ORDERS. *Shee* v. *Larkin*, (1907) V.L.R., 295; 28 A.L.T., 188; 13 A.L.R., 97.

IV.—WILLS AND SETTLEMENTS, INTERESTS OF CHILDREN UNDER ADVANCEMENT.

Settlement by widow on children—Non-registration—Validity of settlement—Insolvency Act 1897 (No. 1513), sec. 100.]—*See* INSOLVENCY. *Lorimer* v. *Smail*, (1911) 12 C.L.R., 504; 17 A.L.R., 441.

Will—Construction—Rule against perpetuities—Gift to father for life—Gift over to " all his children " who shall attain the age of twenty-five years—Context showing intention to benefit only certain children then in being.]

—*See* WILL. *In re Hobson*; *Hobson* v. *Sharp*, (1907) V.L.R., 724; 29 A.L.T., 125; 13 A.L.R., 703.

Will — Construction — Perpetuities, rule against—Remoteness—Trust for maintenance and education—Validity.]—*See* WILL. *In re Stevens*; *Trustees, Executors and Agency Co. Ltd.* v. *Teague*, (1912) V.L.R., 194; 33 A.L.T., 233; 18 A.L.R., 195.

Will — Construction — Accumulations — Income of residuary estate, direction to accumulate beyond period allowed—Gift to grandchildren upon youngest attaining twenty-one—After-born grandchildren—Intestacy—Wills Act 1890 (No. 1159), sec. 35.]—*See* WILL. *In re Stevens*; *Trustees, Executors &c. Co. Ltd.* v. *Teague*, (1912) V.L.R., 194; 33 A.L.T., 233; 18 A.L.R., 195.

Wills Act 1890 (No. 1159), sec. 36—Restriction upon accumulations—Exceptions—Provision for raising portions for children of person taking interest under will, what is—Accumulation of uncertain portion of income from share of residue—Accumulated fund to be added to such share and aggregate fund divided amongst children—Parent of children entitled to interest in such share.]—*See* WILL; *In re Watson*; *Cain* v. *Watson*, (1910) V.L.R., 256; 31 A.L.T., 212; 16 A.L.R., 76.

Will—Power of appointment of certain land to testator's children—Appointment to testator's sons—Legacies to daughters out of his own estate—If such estate insufficient to pay legacies payment to extent of deficiency charged on land—Validity of charge.]—*See* WILL. *In re Connell*; *National Trustees. Executors, &c., Co. of Australasia Ltd.* v. *Connell*, (1910) V.L.R., 471; 32 A.L.T., 83; 16 A.L.R., 504.

Will — Construction — Gift to testator's widow—" To be used by her as she may think proper for the benefit of herself and our children " — Whether trust created.]—*See* WILL. *In re Lawn*; *Ballarat Trustees, &c., Co.* v. *Perry*, (1911) V.L.R., 318; 33 A.L.T., 25; 17 A.L.R., 311.

Will—Construction—Trust to hold for infants until they shall have attained 21—Interest of infants.]—*See* WILL. *In re Vickers*; *Vickers* v. *Vickers*, (1912) V.L.R., 385; 34 A.L.T., 133; 18 A.L.R., 521.

Will—Interpretation—No devise in express terms—Devise by implication—Whether intention of testator on the whole will sufficiently declared to justify implication—Devise of property for life with remainder to children of life tenant—Gift of other properties to life tenant "upon the same condition" as properties hereinbefore mentioned are to be given—Whether children take in remainder.]—*See* WILL. *In re Green*; *Crowson* v. *Wild*, (1907) V.L.R., 284; 28 A.L.T., 206; 13 A.L.R., 121.

Gift by implication—Gift to parent—Postponement of gift over until child attains twenty-one—Whether child entitled contingently on attaining twenty-one.]—*See* WILL. *In re Munro*; *National Trustees, Executors, &c., Co. of Australasia* v. *Dunbar*, (1910) V.L.R., 395; 32 A.L.T., 41; 16 A.L.R., 363.

Will—Construction—Real estate devised to son for life on attaining twenty-five—Subsequent direction as to son acquiring profession before getting possession of estate—Whether condition precedent—Direction to trustees to see that son acquires profession, effect of.]—*See* WILL. *In re Meagher*; *Trustees, Executors and Agency Co. Ltd.* v. *Meagher*, (1910) V.L.R., 407; 32 A.L.T., 69; 16 A.L.R., 551.

Will—Construction—Contingent legacies—Interim interest, whether infant contingent legatees entitled to—Trusts Act 1896 (No. 1421), sec. 18.]—*See* WILL. *In the Will of Thompson*; *Brahe* v. *Mason*, (1910) V.L.R., 407; 31 A.L.T., 210; 16 A.L.R., 215.

Will—Construction—Maintenance of infants out of income—Whether to be treated as a common fund or separate shares—Income directed to form part of the capital of the share when it arose.]—*See* WILL. *In re Munro*; *National Trustees, Executors, &c., Co. of Australasia Ltd.* v. *Dunbar*, (1910) V.L.R., 395; 32 A.L.T., 41; 16 A.L.R., 363.

Will—Construction—Gift to class—Gift to testator's brother and his sister's children—Division per capita.]—*See* WILL. *In re Jones*; *Harris* v. *Jones*, (1910) V.L.R., 306; 32 A.L.T., 3; 16 A.L.R., 266.

Will—Gift to daughter with remainder to her children—Gift over in default of children—Forfeiture of daughter's share—Daughter childless and past child-bearing—When share distributable.]—*See* WILL. *In re Lyons*; *Grant* v. *Trustees, Executors and Agency Co. Ltd.*, (1908) V.L.R., 190; 29 A.L.T., 202; 14 A.L.R., 147.

Parent and child—Purchase by parent in name of child—Presumption of advancement, when rebutted—Retention of life interest by parent—Real property, rule applicable to.]—*See* ADVANCEMENT. *Stuckey* v. *Trustees, Executors and Agency Co. Ltd.*, (1910) V.L.R., 55; 31 A.L.T., 157; 16 A.L.R., 65.

V.—LEGAL PROCEEDINGS.

Infant complainant in Court of Petty Sessions—Claim for wages—Order to review obtained by infant—Next friend, whether infant must proceed by—Justices Act 1890 (No. 1105), sec 72—Rules of Supreme Court 1884, Order XVI., r. 16.]—*See* INFANT. *Hines* v. *Phillips*, (1906) V.L.R., 417; 28 A.L.T., 1; 12 A.L.R., 249.

Order to review — Infant respondent—Guardian ad litem—Practice.]—*See* INFANT. *Brown* v. *Gunn*; *McKay, Garnishee*, (1913) V.L.R., 60; 34 A.L.T., 114; 18 A.L.R. (C.N.), 21.

County Court Act 1890 (No. 1078), sec. 60—County Court Rules 1891, r. 107—Infant, action by—Appointment of next friend.]—*See* COUNTY COURT. *Thompson* v. *Peach*, 28 A.L.T. (Supplement) 10; 13 A.L.R. (C.N.), 5.

Administration and Probate Act 1890 (No. 1060), sec. 18—Will—Caveat, who may lodge—Infant, next friend—Appointment of guardian as—Form of caveat where both infant and next friend interested in estate.]—*See* INFANT. *In re Simeon*, (1910) V.L.R., 335; 32 A.L.T., 25; 16 A.L.R., 362.

Settled Estates and Settled Lands Act 1909 (No. 2235), secs. 127, 128—Contract of sale——Purchase in names of infants—Settled estate—Tenant for life—Settlement—Appointment of trustees—Trustees to exercise powers of infant tenant for life.]—*See* SETTLED ESTATES AND SETTLED LANDS ACT. *In re Weir*, (1912) V.L.R., 77; 33 A.L.T., 162; 18 A.L.R., 26.

Settled Estates and Settled Lands Act 1909 (No. 2235), secs. 50, 51, 98, 101, 117, 118, 121, 124, 127, 128, 132—Will—Devise to trustees—Power of sale to trustees—Power to carry on testator's business—Settled estate—Settlement—Persons with power of tenant for life—Infants.]—*See* SETTLED ESTATES AND SETTLED LANDS ACT. *In re Snowball*, (1912) V.L.R., 176; 33 A.L.T., 172; 18 A.L.R., 65.

Settled Estates and Settled Lands Act 1909 (No. 2235), secs. 51, 124, 127—Sale of settled land—Infant being person with powers of tenant for life—Appointment of persons to exercise such powers.]—*See* INFANT. *In re Cheke or Akehurst*; *Cheke v. Hamilton*, (1910) V.L.R., 310; 32 A.L.T., 5; 16 A.L.R., 246.

Order XXX. (Rules of 1906)—Summons for directions—Claim for appointment of guardian of infant—Infant not a party—Whether a ward of Court—Order for examination of witnesses as to infants' whereabouts—Whether order may be made.]—*See* INFANT. *Knipe v. Alcock*, (1907) V.L.R., 611; 29 A.L.T., 98; 13 A.L.R., 433.

Infant—When a ward of the Court.]—*See* INFANT. *Knipe v. Alcock*, (1907) V.L.R., 611; 29 A.L.T., 98; 13 A.L.R., 433.

County Court Act 1890 (No. 1078), secs. 81, 148—Infant, whether interrogatories may be administered to—Rules of Supreme Court 1906, Order XXXI., r. 29.]—*See* COUNTY COURT. *Brock v. Victorian Railways Commissioners*, 29 A.L.T. (Supplement), 3; 13 A.L.R. (C.N.), 21.

VI.—OTHER POINTS

Local Government Act 1903 (No. 1893), secs. 119, 120, 143, 149—Election of councillors—Infant's name inscribed on roll—

Voting by infant—Validity of election.]—*See* LOCAL GOVERNMENT. *In re Hollins*; *Ex parte Daly*, (1912) V.L.R., 87; 33 A.L.T., 157; 18 A.L.R., 43.

Infant—Intended marriage—Goods supplied—Necessaries.]—*See* INFANT. *Quiggan Brothers v. Baker*, (1906) V.L.R., 259; 27 A.L.T., 174; 12 A.L.R., 168.

CHILDREN'S COURTS.

Justices Act 1890 (No. 1105), sec. 141—Order to review—Order which may be reviewed, what is—Order remanding accused to custody—Remand not for convenience of hearing but for another purpose—Neglected Children's Act 1890 (No. 1121), secs. 18, 19—Children's Court Act 1906 (No. 2058).]—*See* JUSTICES OF THE PEACE. *McSweeney v. Haggar*, (1911) V.L.R., 130; 32 A.L.T., 194; 17 A.L.R., 70.

CHOSE IN ACTION.

See also, ASSIGNMENT.

Chose in action consisting of right against the Crown—Assignment—Petition of right by assignee—Crown Remedies and Liability Act 1890 (No. 1080), sec. 20.]—*See* CROWN REMEDIES AND LIABILITY ACT. *The King v. Brown*, (1912) 14 C.L.R., 17; 18 A.L.R., 111.

CHURCH OF ENGLAND.

Church of England Acts, 18 Vict. No. 45 and 36 Vict. No. 454—Diocese of Wangaratta—"Removal of Clerks Act" (No. 3 of 1907)—Validity of—Removal of clerk from benefice without formulation or hearing of any charge.]—The *Removal of Clerks Act* (No. 3 of 1907 of the Diocese of Wangaratta) is a valid exercise of the powers conferred by the Church of England Acts, 18 Vict. No. 45 and 36 Vict. No. 454, although it has not received the consent of the Archbishop of Canterbury. *Gladstone v. Armstrong*, (1908) V.L.R., 454; 29 A.L.T., 285; 14 A.L.R., 270. *a' Beckett, J.* (1908).

Church of England—Diocese of Wangaratta
—Act of Church Assembly—How far examin-
able by Court—Act empowering Bishop to
remove clerk without trial—No interference
with standards of faith or doctrine—Church
of England Acts, 18 Vict. No. 45, sec. 5, and
36 Vict. No. 454, sec. 2.]—The Church
Assembly of the Diocese of Wangaratta has,
subject to the limitations imposed by the
Act, 18 Vict. No. 45, full power to legislate
on all purely Church matters, so as to bind
all members of the Church. An Act of the
Assembly, which does not infringe those
limitations, will not be examined by the
Court in order to find whether it sufficiently
respects vested rights, whether it is unjustly
retrospective, whether it destroys the inde-
pendence of the clergy, or whether it deprives
the Bishop of administrative authority. An
Act which empowers the Bishop, without any
charge being formulated or heard, to remove
a clerk from his office upon his failure to
resign within a certain time from the service
upon him of a written request by the Bishop
for his resignation, does not exceed the powers
conferred by the Act 18 Vict. No. 45, which
preserves adherence only to standards of
faith and doctrine. *Gladstone* v. *Armstrong*,
(1908) V.L.R. 454; 29 A.L.T., 285; 14
A.L.R., 270. *a'Beckett, J.* (1908).

CLIENT.

See SOLICITOR.

CLUB.

See also, VICTORIA RACING CLUB.

**Police Offences Act 1890 (No. 1126), secs.
49, 51—" Business," assisting in conducting
—Club incorporated as company—Shareholders in company members of club—Totalisator—Whether conducted as a business—
Percentage of stakes retained—Burden of
proof—Moneys received as consideration for
an assurance to pay moneys on contingencies
relating to horse races.]—*See* GAMING AND
WAGERING. *O'Donnell* v. *Solomon*, (1906)
V.L.R., 425; 27 A.L.T., 237; 12 A.L.R.,
283.

CODICIL.

See WILL.

COMMISSION.

See CONTRACT OR AGREEMENT;
EXECUTORS AND ADMINISTRA-
TORS; INSOLVENCY.

COMMONWEALTH CONCILIATION AND ARBITRATION ACT.

See also, CONSTITUTIONAL LAW; EMPLOYER
AND EMPLOYEE.

**Commonwealth Conciliation and Arbitra-
tion Act 1904 (No. 13 of 1904), sec. 68—
Association registered as organization—Rules
—Levies imposed on branches—Liability of
members of Association.]**—By the rules of a
voluntary Association which was registered
as an organization under the *Commonwealth
Conciliation and Arbitration Act* 1904 it was
provided that the executive council might
make levies upon the various branches
of the Association, the amount of which
should be in accordance with the number of
financial members of the branches. *Held*,
that a member of a branch was not liable to
the Association for any portion of a levy
made on the branch, and, therefore, that
the Association could not recover it from
him under sec. 68 of the *Commonwealth
Conciliation and Arbitration Act* 1904.
Prentice v. *Amalgamated Mining Employees
Association of Victoria and Tasmania*, (1912)
15 C.L.R., 235; 18 A.L.R., 343. H.C.,
Griffith, C.J., Barton and *Isaacs, JJ.*

**Commonwealth Conciliation and Arbitra-
tion Act 1904 (No. 13 of 1904), secs. 4, 9, 55,
58, 60, 65, 73—Registration of Association—
Validity of legislation—Association of employees in one State—Incorporation of organization—The Constitution (63 & 64 Vict. c. 12),
sec. 51 (xxxv.) (xxxix.).]**—*See* EMPLOYER AND
EMPLOYEE. *Jumbunna Coal Mine, No
Liability* v. *Victorian Coal Miners Association*, (1908) 6 C.L.R., 309; 14 A.L.R., 701.

The Constitution (63 & 64 Vict. c. 12), sec. 73—Appellate jurisdiction of High Court—Court of Conciliation and Arbitration—Commonwealth Conciliation and Arbitration Act 1904 (No. 13 of 1904), sec. 31.]—*See* EMPLOYER AND EMPLOYEE. *Jumbunna Coal Mine, No Liability* v. *Victorian Coal Miners Association,* (1908) 6 C.L.R., 309 ; 14 A.L.R., 701.

The Constitution (63 & 64 Vict. c. 12), sec. 51 (xxxv.)—" Industrial dispute "—" Extending beyond the limits of any one State."]—*See* EMPLOYER AND EMPLOYEE. *Jumbunna Coal Mine, No Liability* v. *Victorian Coal Miners Association,* (1908) 6 C.L.R., 309 ; 14 A.L.R., 701.

Operation of the Constitution and laws of the Commonwealth — Commonwealth Conciliation and Arbitration Act 1904 (No. 13 of 1904) —Jurisdiction of Court of Conciliation and Arbitration — Industrial dispute — " Ships whose first port of clearance and whose port of destination are in the Commonwealth "—Commonwealth of Australia Constitution Act (63 & 64 Vict. c. 12), sec. v.]—*See* EMPLOYER AND EMPLOYEE. *Merchant Service Guild of Australasia* v. *Archibald Currie & Co.,* (1908) 5 C.L.R., 737 ; 14 A.L.R., 438.

COMMONWEALTH ELECTORAL ACTS.

See also ELECTION LAW.

Election—Ballot paper—Necessity for placing cross within square—Commonwealth Electoral Act 1902 (No. 19 of 1902), secs. 151.]—The decision of the High Court in *Chanter* v. *Blackwood* (*No.* 1), 1 C.L.R., 39, viz., that the provision requiring the cross indicating a voter's preference to be placed within the square printed on a ballot-paper opposite to a candidate's name is directory only and not mandatory, is not affected by the *Commonwealth Electoral Act 1905. Kennedy* v. *Palmer,* (1907) 4 C.L.R., 1481. *Barton, J.*

Election— Ballot-paper — Marks enabling voter to be identified—Commonwealth Electoral Act 1902 (No. 19 of 1902), sec. 158 (d).]—

In the absence of any evidence of an improper practice or plan, the mere fact that there is upon a ballot-paper a mark which may possibly enable someone to identify the voter, does not necessarily invalidate the vote. *Kennedy* v. *Palmer,* (1907) 4 C.L.R., 1481. *Barton, J.*

For a consideration of the questions to be determined before acceptance of a ballot-paper, *See Kennedy* v. *Palmer,* (1907) 4 C.L.R., 1481. *Barton, J.*

Agent—Liability of candidate for acts of.]—Where a candidate at an election is sought to be made responsible for illegal acts done during the election by his agent, it must be proved that the candidate either countenanced or directed the doing of the acts. *Crouch* v. *Ozanne,* (1910) 12 C.L.R., 539. *O'Connor, J.*

Commonwealth Electoral Acts (No. 19 of 1902) (No. 26 of 1905), sec. 182 (a)—Electoral offences—Canvassing for votes at entrance of polling booth, what is.]—*Semble,* that canvassing for votes on or at the top of the steps leading to a polling booth is within the prohibition in sec. 182 (A) of the *Commonwealth Electoral Acts* 1902-1909 against canvassing for votes at the entrance to a polling booth, but canvassing between the gate of the land on which the polling booth is and the building itself is not within the prohibition. *Crouch* v. *Ozanne,* (1910) 12 C.L.R., 539. *O'Connor, J.*

Commonwealth Electoral Acts (No. 19 of 1902) (No. 26 of 1905), sec. 198 (a)—Illegal practices—Voiding election—Scrutineers of defeated candidates prevented from entering polling booth—Majority of successful candidate at such booth greater than total majority.]—The presiding officers at certain booths wrongly prevented scrutineers for the defeated candidate from entering the polling booths. *Held,* that the mere fact that at those booths the majority of votes polled for the successful candidate was larger than his total majority was not a sufficient ground for avoiding the election, in the absence of reasonable grounds for concluding that the result of the election

was affected by the exclusion of the scrutineers. *Crouch* v. *Ozanne*, (1910) 12 C.L.R.,
539. *O'Connor, J.*

**Commonwealth Electoral Act 1902-1909,
sec. 109 (b) (1)—Application for postal vote
certificate—Witnessing signature — Application not signed by Elector.**]—Section 109 (B)
(1) of the *Commonwealth Electoral Art* 1902-
1909 provides that a witness shall not witness
the signature of an elector to an application
for a postal vote certificate unless he has
seen the applicant sign the application in the
applicant's own handwriting. The respondent signed an application form as witness,
but the application was never signed by the
elector, the space for the signature of the
elector in the form being left blank. *Held,*
that, as the application had never been
signed, the respondent had not witnessed a
signature, and was not liable to a penalty
under this section. *Hearn* v. *Hill*, (1910)
13 C.L.R., 128. H.C., *Griffith, C.J., Barton*
and *O'Connor, JJ.*

COMMONWEALTH OF AUSTRALIA
CONSTITUTION.

I.—INTERPRETATION GENERALLY.

**Commonwealth of Australia Constitution
Act (63 & 64 Vict. c. 12)—The Constitution—
Principles of interpretation.**]—*Per Griffith,
C.J., Barton* and *O'Connor, JJ.*—In construing the Constitution regard must be had
to the fact that it is an instrument of government calling into existence a new State with
all such attributes of sovereignty as are
consistent with its being still " under the
Crown." *Baxter* v. *Commissioners of Taxation*; *Flint* v. *Webb*, 4 C.L.R., 1087, 1178;
13 A.L.R., 313 (1907).

II.—POWERS OF PARLIAMENT.

(a) *Validity of Legislation Generally.*

**Powers of Commonwealth Parliament—
Validity of legislation—Part of Act invalid—
Whether whole Act invalidated—Test for
determining whether invalid part severable.**]—
Per Griffith, C.J., Barton and *O'Connor, JJ.*
—The test to be applied in determining
whether the invalid part of an Act is severable is whether the Act with the invalid
portions omitted would be substantially
a different law as to the subject matter dealt
with by the portion which remains from the
law as it would be with the omitted portions
forming part of it. *Per Isaacs, J.*—The test
of invalidity is this : If good and bad provisions are included in the same words or
expression the whole must fail. Where they
are contained in separate words or expressions,
then, if the good and bad parts are so mutually connected with and dependent upon each
other as to lead the Court, upon applying
the language to the subject matter, to believe
that Parliament intended them as a whole,
and did not pass the good parts as independent provisions, all the provisions so
connected and dependent must fall together.
*The King and the Commonwealth Court of
Conciliation and Arbitration and the President*

thereof and the Boot Trade Employees Federation, Ex parte Whybrow & Co., (1910) 11 C.L.R., 1 ; 16 A.L.R., 373.

The Constitution (63 & 64 Vict. c. 12), sec. 51—Legislative power of Commonwealth— Validity of Act, principles to be observed in determining question of—Form of Act— Substance of Act—Direct and indirect effect— Motive and object of legislation—Interference with domestic affairs of State—Excise Tariff 1906 (No. 16 of 1906)—Taxation.]—*Per Griffith, C.J., Barton* and *O'Connor, JJ.*—In determining whether a particular law is or is not within the power of the Commonwealth Parliament to enact, regard must be had to its substance rather than to its literal form. The circumstance that an indirect effect may be produced by the exercise of an admitted power of legislation is irrelevant to the question whether the legislature is competent to prescribe the same effect by direct law. So are the motives which actuated the legislature and the ultimate end desired to be attained. So long as the limits of the power of taxation are not transgressed, Parliament may select the persons or things in respect of which the exercise of the power is to operate. If the control of the domestic affairs of the States is in any particular forbidden by the Constitution either expressly or by necessary implication, the power of taxation cannot be exercised so as to operate as a direct interference with those affairs in that particular. The selection of a particular class of goods produced in Australia for taxation by a method which makes the liability to taxation dependent upon conditions to be observed in the industry in which they are produced is as much an attempt to regulate those conditions as if the regulation were made by distinct enactment. *Per Isaacs* and *Higgins, JJ.*—The powers substantially granted to the Commonwealth by the Constitution may be exercised to their utmost extent, and in as plenary a manner as if the Commonwealth were a unitary State, subject only to the express limitations found in the Constitution itself and (*per Isaacs, J.*) to the necessary freedom of the States to exercise without interference the

powers reserved to them. *Held*, further (*per Isaacs* and *Higgins, JJ.*), the Commonwealth powers are not to be limited by first assuming the extent of the State powers. The reserved powers of the States are those which remain after full effect is given to the powers granted to the Commonwealth, and cannot control the extent of those constitutional grants. If a legislative power is once granted, neither its abuse nor its consequences nor any purpose, motive, or object of the legislature can render its exercise illegal ; any remedy for abuse, so long as the limits of the power are not exceeded, must rest with the electors and not with the Court. The objections raised to the validity of the Excise Tariff 1906 (No. 16) on the ground alleged that it in substance regulates conditions of remuneration of labour, are in reality objections based on abuse of power, consequences, and the purpose, motive and object of Parliament, and are therefore beyond the competency of the Court to entertain. Compulsory contribution to the consolidated revenue, demanded irrespective of any legality or illegality in the circumstances upon which the liability depends, is taxation. Pecuniary penalties, imposed as a punishment for an unlawful act or omission, are regulation. *The King* v. *Barger ; The Commonwealth* v. *McKay*, (1908) 6 C.L.R., 41 ; 14 A.L.R., 374.

(*h*) *Taxation and Tax Bills*

The Constitution (63 & 64 Vict. c. 12), secs. 51 (ii.), 99—Taxation, power of Commonwealth with respect to—Discrimination between States or parts of States—Preference to one State over another State—Excise Tariff 1906 (No. 16 of 1906), whether ultra vires.]— The Excise Tariff (No 16) 1906, if otherwise valid, is invalid on the ground that it authorizes discrimination, and therefore discriminates, between States or parts of States within the meaning of sec 51 (II) of the Constitution, and authorizes the giving, and therefore gives, preference to one State or a part thereof over another State or a part thereof within the meaning of sec 99 of the Constitution *Held*, therefore (*per Griffith, C J, Barton* and *O'Connor, JJ. Isaacs* and

Higgins, JJ , dissenting), that the Excise Tariff 1906 (No 16) is invalid   *Per Isaacs* and *Higgins, JJ* —The proviso to the Excise Tariff 1906 (No 16) does not discriminate between localities at all, but describes standards applicable to Australia generally, irrespective of its division into States or parts of States, and does not offend against the prohibition contained in sec 51 (II) of the Constitution   *Per Isaacs, J* —The discrimination forbidden by sec. 51 (II.) is between localities considered and treated as States and parts of States, and not as mere Australian localities or parts of the Commonwealth considered as a single country.   *The King* v. *Barger ;   The Commonwealth* v. *McKay,* (1908) 6 C.L.R., 41 ; 14 A.L.R., 374.

The Constitution (63 & 64 Vict. c. 12), sec. 51 (ii.)—Legislative powers of the Commonwealth — Taxation — Regulative legislation, what is—Excise Tariff 1906 (No. 16 of 1906), whether a taxing or a regulative Act.]—*Per Griffith, C.J., Barton* and *O'Connor, JJ.—* The Excise Tariff 1906 (No. 16) is not an Act imposing duties of excise, but is an Act to regulate the conditions of manufacture of agricultural implements, and is therefore not an exercise of the power of taxation conferred by the Constitution. Even if the term " taxation," uncontrolled by any context, were capable of including the indirect regulation of the domestic affairs of the States by means of taxation, its meaning in the Constitution is limited by the implied prohibition- against direct interference with matters reserved exclusively to the States. *Per Isaacs* and *Higgins, JJ.—*The Excise Tariff 1906 (No. 16), should be construed according to the natural meaning of the language used by the legislature, and should not be turned by an argument of equivalence of effect into an enactment of a totally different character. Properly construed, the Act imposes taxation upon implements which are not in fact manufactured under prescribed conditions to be ascertained in prescribed modes, but does not render any conditions unlawful. It is consequently not a regulative Act which a State could pass

in the same terms, but an exercise of the power of excise taxation, and, if passed by a State legislature would be invalid. *The King* v. *Barger ;   The Commonwealth* v. *McKay,* (1908) 6 C.L.R., 41 ; 14 A.L.R., 374.

The Constitution (63 & 64 Vict. c. 12), sec 55—Laws imposing taxation—To deal only with imposition of taxation—Excise Tariff 1906 (No. 16 of 1906), whether it deals with matters other than excise duty.]—*Per Griffith, C.J., Barton* and *O'Connor, JJ.—*Even if it were otherwise within the competence of the Commonwealth Parliament to deal with the conditions of labour, the Excise Tariff 1906 (No. 16) which, if valid, would have the effect of regulating the conditions of manufacture, would be invalid as dealing with matters other than duties of excise contrary to sec. 55 of the Constitution. *Per Isaacs* and *Higgins, JJ.—*As the Excise Tariff 1906 (No. 16) merely imposes excise taxation, sec. 55 of the Constitution is not contravened. *The King* v. *Barger ;   The Commonwealth* v. *McKay,* (1908) 6 C.L.R., 41 ; 14 A.L.R., 374.

Customs Tariff 1908 (No. 7 of 1908), secs. 3, 4, 5, 7—Duties collected under proposed tariff—Proposed tariff different from tariff enacted by Parliament—Right to recover money back—" Duties of Customs collected pursuant to any tariff or tariff alteration "—Commonwealth Constitution, sec. 55—Imposing taxation.] — *See* CUSTOMS. *Sargood Brothers* v. *The Commonwealth,* (1910) 11 C.L.R., 258 ; 16 A.L.R., 483.

(c) Corporations.

Commonwealth of Australia Constitution (63 & 64 Vict. c. 12), sec. 51 (xx.)—Power to make laws with respect to foreign corporations and trading and financial corporations formed within the limits of the Commonwealth—Limits of power.]—Section 51 (xx.) of the Constitution does not confer on the Commonwealth Parliament power to create corporations, but the power is limited to legislation as to foreign corporations and trading and financial corporations created by State law. *Huddart Parker & Co. Proprietary Ltd.* v.

Moorehead; *Appleton* v. *Moorehead*, (1909) 8 C.L.R., 330; 15 A.L.R., 241. H.C., *Griffith, C.J., Barton, O'Connor. Isaacs* and *Higgins, JJ.*

Commonwealth of Australia Constitution (63 & 64 Vict. c. 12), sec. 51 (xx.)—Interference with internal trade and commerce—Power to make laws with respect to " foreign corporations and trading or financial corporations formed within the limits of the Commonwealth "—Limits of power—Control of corporations, their status, capacity and contracts.]—*Held*, by *Griffith, C.J.* and *Barton J.*—Sec. 51 (xx.) of the Constitution confers upon the Commonwealth Parliament power to prohibit foreign corporations and trading and financial corporations formed under State laws from engaging in trade and commerce within a State, as distinguished from trade and commerce between States or with foreign countries, or to impose conditions subject to which they may engage in such trade and commerce, but does not confer upon the Commonwealth Parliament power to control the operations of such corporations which lawfully engage in such trade and commerce. By *O'Connor, J.*—The power conferred by sec. 51 (xx.) of the Constitution is limited to the making of laws with respect to the recognition of corporations as legal entities within the Commonwealth, and does not include a power to make laws for regulating and controlling the business of corporations when once they have been so recognized, and are exercising their corporate functions by carrying on business in the Commonwealth. By *Isaacs, J.*—Sec. 51 (xx.) confers on the Commonwealth Parliament, power to control the conduct of the specified corporations in relation to outside persons, but not the powers and capacities of corporations. By *Higgins, J.*—The power conferred by sec. 51 (xx.) of the Constitution is a power to legislate with respect to the classes of corporations named as corporations—that is, to regulate the status and capacity of such corporations, and the conditions upon which they may be permitted to carry on business; but does not include a power to regulate the contracts into which corporations may enter

within the scope of their permitted powers. *Huddart Parker & Co. Proprietary Ltd.* v. *Moorehead*; *Appleton* v. *Moorehead*, (1909) 8 C.L.R., 330; 15 A.L.R., 241.

Commonwealth of Australia Constitution (63 & 64 Vict. c. 12), sec. 51 (xx.)—Power to make laws with respect to " foreign corporations, and trading and financial corporations formed within the limits of the Commonwealth "—Australian Industries Preservation Act 1906 (No. 9 of 1906), secs. 5 and 8, whether intra vires.]—Secs. 5 and 8 of the *Australian Industries Preservation Act* 1906 are *ultra vires* the Commonwealth Parliament and invalid. *Huddart Parker & Co. Proprietary Ltd.* v. *Moorehead*; *Appleton* v. *Moorehead*, (1909) 8 C.L.R., 330; 15 A.L.R., 241. H.C., *Griffith, C.J., Barton, O'Connor,* and *Higgins, JJ.* (*Isaacs, J. dissentiente*).

(d) *Immigration and Emigration.*

The Constitution (63 & 64 Vict. c. 12), sec. 51 (xxvii.)—" Immigrant," meaning of—Member of Australian community returning from abroad.]—A person whose permanent home is Australia and who, therefore, is a member of the Australian community, is not, on arriving in Australia from abroad, an immigrant in respect of whose entry the Parliament of the Commonwealth can legislate under the power conferred by sec. 51 (xxvii.) of the Constitution to make laws with respect to immigration, and, therefore, such a person is not an immigrant within the meaning of the *Immigration Restriction Acts* 1901-1905. *Potter* v. *Minahan*, (1908) 7 C.L.R., 277; 14 A.L.R., 635. H.C., *Griffith, C.J., Barton, O'Connor. Isaacs* and *Higgins, JJ.*

Immigration Restriction Act 1901 (No. 17 of 1901)—Prohibited immigrant—Application of Act to Australian citizen—Commonwealth Constitution, sec. 51.]—*Semble*, there is no Australian nationality, as distinguished from British nationality, so as to limit the power of the Commonwealth under sec. 51 of the Constitution to exclude persons from Australia. *Quaere*, whether the power of the Parliament under sec. 51 to deal with " immigration " extends to the case of

Australians absent from Australia on a visit *animo revertendi*. *Attorney-General of the Commonwealth* v. *Ah Sheung*, (1907) 4 C.L.R., 949. H.C., *Griffith, C.J., Barton* and *O'Connor, JJ.*

(e) *External Affairs.*

Commonwealth of Australia Constitution Act (63 & 64 Vict. c. 12)—The Constitution, sec. 51 (xxix.)—External affairs—Surrender of fugitive offenders—Power of Commonwealth Parliament with regard to.]—*Semble*, sec. 51 (xxix.) of the Constitution empowers the Parliament of the Commonwealth to make laws with respect to the surrender of fugitive offenders between the Commonwealth and other parts of the British dominions. *McKelvey* v. *Meagher*, 4 C.L.R., 265 ; 12 A.L.R., 483. H.C., *Griffith, C.J., Barton* and *O'Connor, JJ.* (1906).

(f) *Conciliation and Arbitration.*

Commonwealth of Australia Constitution Act (63 & 64 Vict. c. 12)—The Constitution, sec. 51 (xxxv.)—Arbitration in regard to industrial disputes—Extent of power of Commonwealth.]—*Per Griffith, C.J., Barton* and *O'Connor, JJ.*—Under the Constitution the only arbitral power which can be conferred upon the Commonwealth Court of Conciliation and Arbitration is a power of judicial determination between the parties to a dispute. *The King and the Commonwealth Court of Conciliation and Arbitration and the President thereof and the Boot Trade Employees Federation, Ex parte Whybrow & Co.*, (1910) 11 C.L.R., 1 ; 16 A.L.R., 373.

Commonwealth Conciliation and Arbitration Act 1904 (No. 13 of 1904), secs. 4, 55, 58, 60, 65, 73—Registration of Association—Validity of legislation—Association of employees in one State—Incorporation of organization—The Constitution (63 & 64 Vict. c. 12), sec. 51 (xxxv.) (xxxix.).]—The provisions of the *Commonwealth Conciliation and Arbitration Act* 1904 in respect of the registration of Associations as organizations, particularly in so far as they permit the registration of an Association of employers or employees in an industry in one State only, and provide for the incorporation of organiza-

tions when registered, are valid as being incidental to the power conferred on the Commonwealth Parliament by sec. 51 (xxxv.) of the Constitution. *Jumbunna Coal Mine, No Liability* v. *Victorian Coal Miners' Association*, (1908) 6 C.L.R., 309 ; 14 A.L.R., 701 ; H.C., *Griffith, C.J., Barton, O'Connor* and *Isaacs, JJ.*

Commonwealth of Australia Constitution Act (63 & 64 Vict. c. 12)—The Constitution, sec. 51 (xxxv.)—Conciliation and arbitration for prevention and settlement of industrial disputes—Commonwealth Conciliation and Arbitration Act 1904 (No. 13 of 1904)—Validity.]—The *Commonwealth Conciliation and Arbitration Act* is not *ultra vires* the Constitution, either on the ground that under that Act the reference to the Court of Conciliation and Arbitration is compulsory, or on the ground that the tribunal for the determination of such disputes is not chosen by the disputants. *The King and the Commonwealth Court of Conciliation and Arbitration and the President thereof and the Boot Trades Employees Federation, Ex parte Whybrow & Co.*, (1910) 11 C.L.R., 1 ; 16 A.L.R., 373. H.C., *Griffith, C.J., Barton, O'Connor* and *Isaacs, JJ.*

" Conciliation and arbitration for the prevention and settlement of industrial disputes "—Powers of the Commonwealth—Common rule—The Constitution (63 & 64 Vict. c. 12), sec. 51 (xxxv.) (xxxix.)—Commonwealth Conciliation and Arbitration Act (No. 13 of 1904), secs. 19, 38 (f), (g)—Commonwealth Conciliation and Arbitration Act (No. 7 of 1910).]—The provisions of the *Commonwealth Conciliation and Arbitration Act* 1904-1910, which purport to authorize the Commonwealth Court of Conciliation and Arbitration to declare a common rule in any particular industry, and direct that the common rule shall be binding upon the persons engaged in the industry, are *ultra vires* the Parliament of the Commonwealth and invalid. *Australian Boot Trade Employees Federation* v. *Whybrow*, (1910) 11 C.L.R., 311 ; 16 A.L.R., 513. H.C., *Griffith, C.J., Barton, O'Connor, Isaacs* and *Higgins, JJ.*

Operation of the Constitution and laws of the Commonwealth—Commonwealth Conciliation and Arbitration Act 1904 (No. 13 of 1904)—Jurisdiction of Court of Conciliation and Arbitration—Industrial dispute—" Ships whose first port of clearance and whose port of destination are in the Commonwealth "—Commonwealth of Australia Constitution Act (63 & 64 Vict. c. 12), sec. v.]—A joint stock company registered in Victoria were owners of a line of ships registered in Melbourne and engaged in trade between Australia, Calcutta and South Africa. The officers of the company's ships resided in Australia, and were engaged there, but the ships' articles were filled in and signed in Calcutta. The officers, though not entitled to be discharged in Australian ports, were allowed to leave at such ports if they wished, with the consent of the master. The ships did no inter-State trade, but occasionally made short trips to other Indian ports. The organization of employees to which the officers belonged filed a claim in the Commonwealth Court of Conciliation and Arbitration for the settlement of a dispute between the officers and their employers as to wages, hours, and conditions of labour during the voyages of their ships. *Held,* that the Court had no jurisdiction to settle the dispute. Ships engaged in such trade are not ships " whose first port of clearance and whose port of destination are in the Commonwealth " within the meaning of sec. v. of the *Commonwealth of Australia Constitution Act. Merchant Service Guild of Australasia* v. *Archibald Currie & Co.,* (1908) 5 C.L.R., 737 ; 14 A.L.R., 438. H.C., *Griffith, C.J., Barton, O'Connor, Isaacs* and *Higgins, JJ.*

The Constitution (63 & 64 Vict. c. 12), sec. 51 (xxxv.)—" Industrial dispute "— " Extending beyond the limits of any one State."]—For observations as to the meaning of " industry," " industrial dispute " and " Extending beyond the limits of any one State," *See Jumbunna Coal Mine, No Liability* v. *Victorian Coal Miners' Association,* (1908) 6 C.L.R., 309 ; 14 A.L.R., 701. H.C.

Commonwealth Constitution, sec. 51 (xxxv.) — Industrial dispute extending beyond the limits of any one State.]—What constitutes evidence of an industrial dispute extending beyond the limits of any one State considered. *The King and the Commonwealth Conciliation and Arbitration Court and the President thereof and the Boot Trade Employees Federation, Ex parte Whybrow & Co.,* (1910) 11 C.L.R., 1 ; 16 A.L.R., 373. H.C.

Commonwealth Conciliation and Arbitration Act 1904 (No. 13 of 1904)—Industrial dispute, what is—Commonwealth Constitution, sec. 51 (xxxv.).]—*See* EMPLOYER AND EMPLOYEE. *The King and the Commonwealth Court of Conciliation and Arbitration and the President thereof and the Boot Trade Employees Federation, Ex parte Whybrow & Co.,* (1910) 11 C.L.R., 1 ; 16 A.L.R., 373.

Commonwealth Conciliation and Arbitration Act 1904 (No. 13 of 1904)—Whether ultra vires of Parliament.]—The provisions of the *Commonwealth Conciliation and Arbitration Act 1904,* dealing with the regulation of industries generally, if invalid, are severable. *The King and the Commonwealth Court of Conciliation and Arbitration and the President thereof and the Boot Trade Employees Federation, Ex parte Whybrow & Co.,* (1910) 11 C.L.R., 1 ; 16 A.L.R., 373. H.C., *Griffith, C.J., Barton, O'Connor* and *Isaacs, JJ.*

Commonwealth Conciliation and Arbitration Act 1904 (No. 13 of 1904)—Claims in regard to matters in dispute—Joinder of claims in regard to matters not in dispute—Jurisdiction of Court of Conciliation and Arbitration—The Commonwealth Constitution, sec. 51 (xxxv.).]—*See* EMPLOYER AND EMPLOYEE. *The King and the Commonwealth Court of Conciliation and Arbitration and the President thereof and the Boot Trade Employees Federation, Ex parte Whybrow & Co.,* (1910) 11 C.L.R., 1 ; 16 A.L.R., 373.

Commonwealth Court of Conciliation and Arbitration—Award, validity of—Higher rate awarded than that demanded by claimants—Demand that wage of apprentice be based on experience—Wage awarded based on age and experience — Industrial dispute.]—*See* EMPLOYER AND EMPLOYEE. *The King and the Commonwealth Court of Conciliation and*

Arbitration and the President thereof and the Boot Trade Employees Federation, Ex parte Whybrow & Co., (1910) 11 C.L.R.. 1 ; 16 A.L.R., 373.

(y) Elections.

Parliamentary election—Political article in newspaper during election—Signature of author —Validity of Commonwealth legislation—The Constitution (63 & 64 Vict. c. 12), secs. 10, 51 (xxxvi.)—Commonwealth Electoral Act 1902-1911 (No. 19 of 1902—No. 17 of 1911), sec. 181aa.]—The Commonwealth Parliament has power under the Constitution to make laws regulating Federal Parliamentary elections, and, therefore, sec. 181aa of the *Commonwealth Electoral Act* 1902-1911 is within the powers of the Commonwealth Parliament to enact. *Smith* v. *Oldham,* (1912) 15 C.L.R., 355 ; 18 A.L.R., 448. H.C., *Griffith, C.J., Barton* and *Isaacs, JJ.*

III.—THE JUDICATURE.

(a) Judicial Power Generally.

Commonwealth of Australia Constitution (63 & 64 Vict. c. 12), sec. 71—" Judicial power."]—*Per Griffith, C.J.*—The power which, by sec. 71 of the Constitution, is to be exercised by the Courts is a power of such a nature that an appeal will lie to the High Court from anything done in its exercise. It means the power which every sovereign authority must of necessity have to decide controversies between its subjects, or between itself and its subjects, whether the rights relate to life, liberty or property. The exercise of this power does not begin until some tribunal which has power to give a binding and authoritative decision (whether subject to appeal or not) is called upon to take action. *Per Isaacs, J.*—The expression " judicial power " understood as the power which the State exercises in the administration of justice in contradistinction from the power it possesses to make laws and the power of executing them, is not in the least ambiguous. *Huddart Parker & Co. Proprietary Ltd.* v. *Moorehead* ; *Appleton* v. *Moorehead,* (1909) 8 C.L.R., 330 ; 15 A.L.R., 241. H.C.

Commonwealth legislation, validity of— Anti-trust laws—Inquiry by Comptroller-General of Customs—Compulsory answers— Judicial power of Commonwealth—Trial by jury— Inter-State Commission — Australian Industries Preservation Act 1906 (No. 9 of 1906) amended by Australian Industries Preservation Act 1907 (No. 5 of 1908), sec. 15b —The Constitution (63 & 64 Vict. c. 12), secs. 51 (1) (xx.), 71, 80, 101.]—Sec. 15b of the *Australian Industries Preservation Act* 1906 (as amended by the *Australian Industries Preservation Act* 1907) is *intra vires* the Commonwealth Parliament and valid. The inquiry authorised by that section is not inconsistent with the right to trial by jury conferred by sec. 80 of the Constitution, nor is such inquiry an exercise of the judicial power of the Commonwealth, nor an incident of the execution and maintenance of the provisions of the Constitution relating to trade and commerce within the meaning of sec. 101 of the Constitution. Such inquiry need not therefore be entrusted to the inter-State Commission. *Huddart Parker & Co. Proprietary Ltd.* v. *Moorehead* ; *Appleton* v. *Moorehead,* (1909) 8 C.L.R., 330 ; 15 A.L.R., 241. H.C., *Griffith, C.J., Barton, O'Connor, Isaacs* and *Higgins, JJ.*

(b) Original Jurisdiction.

The Constitution (63 & 64 Vict. c. 12), sec. 75—Original jurisdiction of High Court— " Matters " between States, what are— Dispute as to boundary between two States— Boundary fixed by Act of Imperial Parliament.]—The " matters " between States, in respect of which original jurisdiction is, by sec. 75 of the Commonwealth Constitution conferred on the High Court, are matters which are of a like nature to those which can arise between individuals, and which are capable of determination upon principles of law. *Held,* accordingly, in a case in which the boundary between two States had been fixed by an Imperial Act of Parliament before Federation, that the High Court had jurisdiction to entertain an action by one of such States against the other seeking a declaration that certain land adjoining that boundary, and in the *de facto* occupation of the latter State, formed part of the territory of the former State. *State of South Australia* v. *State of Victoria*, (1911) 12 C.L.R., 667 ; 17 A.L.R., 206. H.C., *Griffith, C.J., Barton, O'Connor, Isaacs* and *Higgins, JJ.*

[This point was not considered by the Privy Council.]

(c) *Appellate Jurisdiction.*

Judiciary Act 1903 (No. 6 of 1903), sec, 39 — Federal jurisdiction of State, Courts—Validity of grant of—Right of appeal to High Court—Prerogative right of appeal to Privy Council, whether affected—Commonwealth of Australia Constitution Act (63 & 64 Vict. c. 12)—The Constitution, secs. 71, 77—Colonial Laws Validity Act (28 & 29 Vict. c. 63.]—*Per Griffith, C.J., Barton, O'Connor* and *Isaacs, JJ.*—Even if sec. 39 (2) (a) of the *Judiciary Act* 1903 purports to take away the prerogative right of appeal to the Privy Council, and the section is to that extent *ultra vires* and inoperative, its failure in that respect does not affect the validity of the grant of Federal jurisdiction to State Courts contained in the rest of the section, and the consequent right of appeal to the High Court. *Sed Quaere*, whether sub-sec. (2) (a) should be construed as affecting the prerogative. *Baxter* v. *Commissioners of Taxation* ; *Flint* v. *Webb*, 4 C.L.R., 1087, 1178 ; 13 A.L.R., 313 (1907).

The Constitution (63 & 64 Vict. c. 12), sec. 73—Appellate jurisdiction of High Court—Court of Conciliation and Arbitration—Commonwealth Conciliation and Arbitration Act 1904 (No. 13 of 1904), sec. 31.]—An appeal lies to the High Court from a decision of the President of the Commonwealth Court of Conciliation and Arbitration dismissing an appeal to him from a decision of the Industrial Registrar disallowing objections to the registration of an Association under the *Commonwealth Conciliation and Arbitration Act* 1904. *Jumbunna Coal Mine, No Liability* v. *Victorian Coal Miners' Association*, (1908) 6 C.L.R., 309 ; 14 A.L.R., 701. H.C., *Griffith, C.J., Barton, O'Connor* and *Isaacs, JJ.*

Commonwealth of Australia Constitution Act (63 & 64 Vict. c. 12)—The Constitution, secs. 71, 73, 75 (v.)—Commonwealth Conciliation and Arbitration Act 1904 (No. 13 of 1904), sec. 31—Judiciary Act 1903 (No. 6 of 1903), secs. 30, 33 (b), 38—Prohibition—Jurisdiction of High Court to issue to Commonwealth Court of Conciliation and Arbitration—Whether prohibition original or appellate jurisdiction.]—*Per Griffith, C.J., Barton* and *O'Connor, JJ.*—The High Court has jurisdiction to issue prohibition to the Commonwealth Court of Conciliation and Arbitration either under sec. 75 (v.) of the Constitution, the President of the Court being an officer within the meaning of that sub-section, or under sec. 33 of the *Judiciary Act* 1903 and whether an appeal does or does not lie to the High Court. *Per Isaacs, J.*—Prohibition to revise or correct the proceedings instituted in another Court is appellate, not original, jurisdiction, and is therefore not within sec. 75 (v.). But the High Court has jurisdiction to issue prohibition to the Commonwealth Court of Conciliation and Arbitration because sec. 31 of the *Commonwealth Conciliation and Arbitration Act* 1904 has not taken away that part of the appellate power granted by the Constitution. *The King and the Commonwealth Court of Conciliation and Arbitration and the President thereof and the Boot Trade Employees Federation, Ex parte Whybrow & Co.*, (1910) 11 C.L.R.; 1 ; 16 A.L.R., 373.

Federal jurisdiction—Exercise of, what is—Two questions decided, one Federal and the other not—Each decision sufficient to sustain judgment—Court of Petty Sessions—Appeal to High Court, whether it lies—Judiciary Act 1903 (No. 6), sec. 39 (2) (d)—Commonwealth of Australia Constitution Act (63 & 64 Vict. c. 12)—The Constitution, sec. 77.]—A Court of Petty Sessions exercises Federal jurisdiction within the meaning of sec. 39 (2) (d) of the *Judiciary Act* 1903, if it be necessary in the particular case for the Court to decide any question arising under the Constitution or involving its interpretation. If, however, whether that question is answered rightly or wrongly, the Court answers another question not arising under the Constitution or involving its interpretation, and the Court's answer to such other question enables it to decide the case, the Court does not exercise Federal jurisdiction, and therefore no appeal lies to the High Court. *Miller* v. *Haweis,* (1907) 5 C.L.R., 89 ; 13 A.L.R., 583. H.C., *Griffith, C.J., Barton, O'Connor, Isaacs* and *Higgins, JJ.*

Court of Petty Sessions—Federal jurisdiction—Exercise of, what is—Commonwealth of Australia Constitution, secs. 31, 76—Constitution Act Amendment Act 1890 (No. 1075), sec. 282—Judiciary Act 1903 (No. 6), sec. 39 (2) (d)—Question decided involving interpretation of sec. 31 of Constitution—Other question decided involving interpretation of Commonwealth Electoral Act 1902 (No. 19)—Appeal to High Court, whether it lies.]—On a complaint for work and labour done at an election for the House of Representatives of the Commonwealth Parliament, the defence being that sec. 282 of the *Constitution Act Amendment Act* 1890 was a bar to the complaint, the Court of Petty Sessions held that sec. 282 was a " law relating to elections " and by virtue of sec. 31 of the Commonwealth Constitution, applied to elections for the House of Representatives until Parliament otherwise provided, but also held that Parliament had otherwise provided by passing the *Commonwealth Electoral Act* 1902, and had thereby repealed sec. 282, and the Court therefore gave judgment for the complainant. *Held,* that in determining the second point the Court of Petty Sessions had not exercised Federal jurisdiction, and therefore that no appeal lay to the High Court from the judgment of the Court of Petty Sessions. *Miller* v. *Haweis,* (1907) 5 C.L.R., 89 ; 13 A.L.R., 583. H.C., *Griffith, C.J., Barton, O'Connor, Isaacs* and *Higgins, JJ.*

Appeal—Order on habeas corpus—Jurisdiction of High Court.]—The High Court has jurisdiction to entertain an appeal from the Supreme Court in a case of *habeas corpus. Attorney-General for the Commonwealth* v. *Ah Sheung,* (1907) 4 C.L.R., 949. H.C., *Griffith, C.J., Barton* and *O'Connor, JJ.*

High Court—Practice—Declaratory judgment—Abstract question of law in decision of which rights of parties are not involved—Whether High Court will decide—Rules of High Court 1903, Part I., Order III., r. 1—Trade Marks Act 1905 (No. 20), Part VII., constitutionality of.]—*See* HIGH COURT (PRACTICE). *Bruce* v. *Commonwealth Trade Marks Label Association,* (1907) 4 C.L.R., 1569 ; 13 A.L.R., 582.

Practice—Appeal to High Court—Special leave—Decision of inferior Court of State—Right of appeal to Supreme Court—Judiciary Act 1903 (No. 6 of 1903), sec. 35—The Constitution (63 & 64 Vict. c. 12), sec. 73.]—*See* APPEAL. *Kamarooka Gold Mining Co.* v. *Kerr,* (1908) 6 C.L.R., 255.

(b) Appeal to King in Council.

Commonwealth of Australia Constitution Act (63 & 64 Vict. c. 12)—The Constitution, sec. 74—Interpretation, principles of—History of the Constitution, whether it may be considered—Appeal to Privy Council.]—*Per Griffith, C.J., Barton* and *O'Connor, JJ.*—The duty of the High Court in regard to questions under sec. 74 is to be determined upon consideration of the whole purview and history of the Constitution. *Baxter* v. *Commissioners of Taxation ; Flint* v. *Webb,* 4 C.L.R., 1087, 1178 ; 13 A.L.R., 313 (1907).

Commonwealth of Australia Constitution Act (63 & 64 Vict. c. 12)—The Constitution, sec. 74—Questions as to limits inter se of constitutional powers of Commonwealth and State—Conflicting decisions of Privy Council and High Court—Whether High Court final arbiter upon such questions—9 Geo. IV. c. 83 ; 7 & 8 Vict. c. 69 and Orders in Council thereunder.]—*Per Griffith, C.J., Barton, O'Connor* and *Isaacs, JJ., Higgins, J.,* dissenting.—Upon all questions of the classes referred to in sec. 74 of the Constitution, except those in regard to which the High Court may by granting a certificate under that section have submitted itself to the guidance of the Privy Council, it is the High Court and not the Privy Council which is the ultimate arbiter. The High Court is not bound to follow a decision of the Privy Council given upon such a question without the certificate of the High Court and in conflict with a previous decision of the High Court with regard to which the grant of such a certificate was refused. *Baxter* v. *Commissioners of Taxation* ; *Flint* v. *Webb*, 4 C.L.R., 1087, 1178 ; 13 A.L.R., 313 (1907).

Commonwealth of Australia Constitution Act (63 & 64 Vict. c. 12)—The Constitution, sec. 74—Appeal to King in Council—Certificate of High Court— Reasons, for granting, sufficiency of—Conflicting decisions of Privy Council and High Court.]—*Per Griffith, C.J., Barton, O'Connor. Isaacs* and *Higgins, JJ.*—The fact that there are conflicting decisions of the Privy Council and the High Court on the question is not a sufficient reason for granting a certificate that the question is one which ought to be determined by His Majesty in Council. *Per O'Connor, J.*—It is the duty of the High Court to refuse the certificate where, if the certificate were given, the Privy Council would be likely to decide the question in a manner contrary to the true intent of the Constitution as interpreted by the High Court. *Per Isaacs, J.*—Australian considerations should have a weighty, perhaps a dominant force, in guiding the judgment of the High Court in granting or refusing a certificate. *Baxter* v. *Commissioners of Taxation* ; *Flint* v. *Webb*, 4 C.L.R., 1087, 1178 ; 13 A.L.R., 313. (1907).

Commonwealth of Australia Constitution Act (63 & 64 Vict. c. 12)—The Constitution, sec. 74—" Decision . . . upon any question," meaning of—Appeal to Privy Council.]—*Per Griffith, C.J., Barton, O'Connor* and *Isaacs, JJ.*—" Decision of the High Court upon any question " in sec. 74 of the Constitution means what the Court decides to be the law with regard to that question. It does not refer to the judgment *inter partes* in the cause. *Baxter* v. *Commissioners of Taxation* ; *Flint* v. *Webb*, 4 C.L.R., 1087, 1178 ; 13 A.L.R., 313 (1907).

Commonwealth of Australia Constitution Act (63 & 64 Vict. c. 12)—The Constitution, secs. 74, 109—Question as to limits inter se of powers of Commonwealth and State, nature of—How distinguished from question of inconsistency between law of State and law of Commonwealth.]—*Per Griffith, C.J., Barton. O'Connor* and *Isaacs, JJ.*—Sec. 109 of the Constitution deals with the case of two admitted powers of legislation meeting on a concurrent field, and provides that in case of inconsistency the one shall prevail over the other. The cases dealt with by sec. 74 are cases in which the question is whether an attempted exercise of the powers of either a State or the Commonwealth in such a manner as to interfere with the free exercise of the powers of the other of the two authorities is or is not within the limits prescribed by the Constitution. The question whether a State *Income Tax Act* applied to the salaries of Federal officers is or is not to be considered as trespassing upon a region exclusively assigned to the Commonwealth is a question of the kind referred to in sec. 74. *Per Isaacs, J.*—The question whether or not a State *Income Tax Act* levying tax upon Federal officers proportioned to their Federal salaries clashes *pro tanto* with the Federal enactment that their remuneration shall be the full sum granted them by the Commonwealth is a question coming under sec. 109. *Baxter* v. *Commissioners of Taxation* ; *Flint* v. *Webb*, 4 C.L.R., 1087 ; 1178 ; 13 A.L.R., 313 (1907).

Commonwealth of Australia Constitution Act (63 & 64 Vict. c. 12))—The Constitution, secs. 73, 74, 76, 77—Question as to limits inter se of constitutional powers of Commonwealth and State, what is—Question raised by defence whether State tax on Federal salary an interference with powers of the Commonwealth—Exercise of Federal jurisdiction by Court of Petty Sessions—Appeal to High Court, competency of—Judiciary Act 1903 (Commonwealth) (No. 6 of 1903), sec. 39.]— In proceedings in a Court of Petty Sessions to recover income tax from a Federal officer in respect of his official salary, the defendant claimed to be exempt on the ground that taxation of his official salary by the State was an interference with the free exercise of the powers of the Commonwealth within the meaning of the rule in *D'Emden* v. *Pedder*, 1 C.L.R., 91, and therefore impliedly prohibited by the Constitution. The Court of Petty

Sessions, following *Webb* v. *Outtrim*, (1907) A.C., 81, made an order for the amount claimed against the defendant, who thereupon appealed to the High Court. *Held*, that the question raised by the defence was a question as to the limits *inter se* of the Constitutional powers of the Commonwealth, and a State within the meaning of sec. 74 of the Constitution, that the Court of Petty Sessions was exercising Federal jurisdiction under sec. 39 of the *Judiciary Act* 1903, and the appeal was competent by virtue of sub-sec. (2) (*b*) of that section as well as by sec. 73 of the Constitution. *Baxter* v. *Commissioners of Taxation*; *Flint* v. *Webb*, 4 C.L.R., 1087, 1178; 13 A.L.R., 313. H.C., *Griffith*, *C.J.*, *Barton*, *O'Connor* and *Isaacs*, JJ. (1907).

Commonwealth of Australia Constitution (63 & 64 Vict. c. 12)—Power of Victorian Legislature (18 & 19 Vict. c. 55)—Income tax —Right of appeal from Supreme Court to Privy Council—Whether Commonwealth Parliament may take away.]—*Held*, that a petition by the Commonwealth for the dismissal on the ground of incompetency of an appeal from an order of the Supremo Court of Victoria relating to the assessment of an officer of the Commonwealth, resident in Victoria and receiving his official salary in that State, for income tax in respect of such salary, the income tax being imposed by an Act of the Victorian Legislature, should be dismissed. The *Constitution Act* does not authorise the Commonwealth Parliament to take away the right of appeal to the Privy Council existing in such case. *Webb* v. *Outrim*, (1907) A.C., 81; 13 A.L.R., C.N., 1. Privy Council.

IV.—The Executive Government; Finance and Trade.

Commonwealth of Australia Constitution (62 & 63 Vict. c. 12), secs. 51 (i.) (xx.) (xxxix.) 61, 101—Inter-State Commission—Execution and maintenance of provisions of Constitution relating to trade and commerce and of all laws made thereunder.]—Subject to any laws that may be made by Parliament as to the Inter-State Commission and its powers, the powers for the execution and maintenance within the Commonwealth of the provisions of the Constitution relating to trade and commerce, and of all laws made thereunder may be exercised by the Commonwealth Executive. *Huddart Parker & Co. Proprietary Ltd.* v. *Moorehead*; *Appleton* v. *Moorehead*, (1909) 8 C.L.R., 330; 15 A.L.R., 241. H.C., *Griffith*, *C.J.*; *Barton*, *O'Connor*, *Isaacs* and *Higgins*, JJ.

Immigration Restriction Acts 1901-1905— " Immigrants " and " prohibited immigrants," who are—Whether administrative officers of the Commonwealth may determine such questions.]—For a discussion of the question whether the officers administering the Immigration Restriction Acts are the final arbiters as to who are, and who are not, " immigrants " or " prohibited immigrants," see *Ah Sheung* v. *Lindberg*, (1906) V.L.R., 323; 27 A.L.T., 189; *sub nom.*, *Rex* v. *Ah Sheung*, 12 A.L.R., 190. *Cussen*, J. (1906).

Officer of department transferred to Commonwealth—Whether Commonwealth Parliament may reduce salary—" Existing rights " —Public Service Act 1900 (No. 1721), sec. 19—Commonwealth Constitution, sec. 84.]— Sec. 19 of the *Public Service Act* 1900 was merely a temporary provision to fix the status of the officers therein referred to when they should be transferred with their departments to the Commonwealth. That section therefore does not, notwithstanding sec. 84 of the Constitution, restrict the power of the Commonwealth Parliament to reduce the salaries of officers of Victorian Government departments transferred with those departments to the Commonwealth. *Cousins* v. *The Commonwealth*, 3 C.L.R., 529; 12 A.L.R., 175. H.C., *Griffith*, *C.J.*, *Barton* and *O'Connor*, JJ. (1906).

Commonwealth Public Service Act 1902 (No. 5 of 1902), secs. 8, 51, 60, 80—Officer of department transferred to Commonwealth— Whether salary altered—" Existing rights " Commonwealth Constitution, sec. 84.]—The provisions of the *Commonwealth Public Service Act* 1902 purporting to affect the salaries of officers in the public service of the Commonwealth apply to officers transferred with their departments from the several States to the Commonwealth as well as to other officers in that service, even if the effect in particular cases is to reduce the salaries those officers were entitled to receive when such departments were so transferred. *Cousins v. The Commonwealth*, 3 C.L.R., 529 ; 12 A.L.R., 175. H.C., *Griffith, C.J., Barton* and *O'Connor*, J.J. (1906).

Public Service Act 1900 (No. 1721), sec. 19—Post and Telegraph Department—Transfer to Commonwealth—" Any Australian colony."]—*See* PUBLIC SERVICE. *Curley* v. *The King*, (1906) V.L.R., 633 ; 28 A.L.T., 12 ; 12 A.L.R., 555.

Public Service Act 1900 (No. 1721), sec. 19—Post and Telegraph Department—Transfer to Commonwealth—" Officers of corresponding position "—Identity of duties.]—*See* PUBLIC SERVICE. *Curley* v. *The King*, (1906) V.L.R., 633 ; 28 A.L.T., 12 ; 12 A.L.R., 555.

V.—THE STATES.

(a) *Reserved Powers of State Parliament.*

Commonwealth of Australia Constitution (62 & 63 Vict. c. 12))—Trade and commerce—Internal trade of State, interference with—Implied prohibition.]—The Commonwealth Constitution is to be construed as if it contained a declaration that power to make laws with respect to trade and commerce within the limits of the various States is reserved to the States exclusively except so far as the exercise of that power by the Commonwealth is incidental to the execution of some other power of the Commonwealth. *Huddart Parker & Co. Proprietary Ltd.* v. *Moorehead* ; *Appleton* v. *Moorehead*, (1909) 8 C.L.R., 330 ; 15 A.L.R., 241. H.C., *Griffith, C.J., Barton* and *O'Connor, JJ.* (*Isaacs* and *Higgins, JJ., dissententibus*).

(b) *Inconsistency of Laws.*

Rendition of fugitive offenders—Law of Victoria—Effect of establishment of Commonwealth—Commonwealth of Australia Constitution Act (63 & 64 Vict. c. 12)—The Constitution, secs. 108, 109—Fugitive Offenders Act 1881 (44 & 45 Vict. c. 69).]—The *Fugitive Offenders Act* 1881 was a law in force in Victoria at the time of the establishment of the Commonwealth within the

meaning of sec. 108 of the Constitution, and, the Parliament of the Commonwealth not having exercised the powers (if any) which it possesses to make provision in that behalf, the law of Victoria remains exactly the same as it was and the powers of the Governor, the Judges and the Magistrates of Victoria under the *Fugitive Offenders Act* 1881 are exactly as they were before the establishment of the Commonwealth. *McKelvey* v. *Meagher*, 4 C.L.R., 265 ; 12 A.L.R., 483. H.C., *Griffith, C.J., Barton* and *O'Connor, JJ.* (1906).

Fugitive Offenders Act 1881 (44 & 45 Vict. c. 69)—Commonwealth of Australia Constitution Act (63 & 64 Vict. c. 12)—Authority of State of Victoria with regard to fugitive offenders—How far affected by establishment of Commonwealth.]—Unless the Commonwealth Parliament has power under the Constitution to make laws under sec. 32 of the *Fugitive Offenders Act* 1881 or to deal with the surrender of fugitive offenders between the Commonwealth and other parts of the British dominions, the establishment of the Commonwealth has had no effect whatever upon the position and authority of the State of Victoria with regard to that Act. *McKelvey* v. *Meagher*, 4 C.L.R., 265 ; 12 A.L.R., 483. H.C., *Griffith, C.J., Barton* and *O'Connor, JJ.* (1906).

Conciliation and arbitration — Commonwealth Court—Jurisdiction—Award inconsistent with determination of Wages Board—The Constitution, sec. 51 (xxxv.).]—*Per Griffith, C.J., Barton* and *O'Connor, JJ.* (*Isaacs* and *Higgins, JJ.,* dissenting).—The Commonwealth Court of Conciliation and Arbitration has no jurisdiction to make an award inconsistent with the determination of a Wages Board. But (*per totam curiam*), the Court may make an award fixing the minimum wage payable to journeymen at a higher rate than that fixed by the Wages Board. *Australian Boot Trade Employees Federation* v. *Whybrow*, (1910) 10 C.L.R., 266. 16 A.L.R., 185.

Factories and Shops Act 1909 (No. 2241), sec. 39—No person compellable to pay more

than the minimum wage unless he contract so to do—**Jurisdiction of Commonwealth Court of Conciliation and Arbitration—How far affected by State legislation.**]—The *Factories and Shops Act* 1909 (No. 2241), sec. 39 does not affect the power of the Commonwealth Court of Conciliation and Arbitration to fix wages and conditions of labour which are otherwise within its jurisdiction. *Australian Boot Trade Employees Federation* v. *Whybrow*, (1910) 10 C.L.R., 266: 16 A.L.R., 185. H C., *Griffith, C.J., Barton, O'Connor, Isaacs* and *Higgins, JJ.* (1910).

(c) *Interference with Instruments of Government.*

Commonwealth of Australia Constitution Act (63 & 64 Vict. c. 12)—The Constitution— —Doctrine of implied prohibition of interference with Commonwealth instrumentalities —Whether implied in Constitution.]—*Per Griffith, C.J., Barton, O'Connor* and *Isaacs, JJ., Higgins, J.,* dissenting.—The rule laid down in *D'Emden* v. *Pedder*, 1 C.L.R., 91, at p. 111, that when a State attempts to give its legislative or executive authority an operation which, if valid, would fetter, control, or interfere with the free exercise of the legislative or executive power of the Commonwealth, the attempt, unless expressly authorised by the Constitution, is to that extent invalid and inoperative—is included by necessary implication in the Australian Constitution. *Webb* v. *Outtrim*, (1907) A.C., 81, not followed. *McCulloch* v. *Maryland*, 4 Wheat., 316, and *Deakin* v. *Webb*, 1 C.L.R., 585, approved and followed. *Per Higgins, J.*—The doctrine of *McCulloch* v. *Maryland* is inapplicable to the Australian Constitution. *Baxter* v. *Commissioners of Taxation*; *Flint* v. *Webb*, 4 C.L.R., 1087, 1178; 13 A.L.R., 313 (1907).

Commonwealth of Australia Constitution (63 & 64 Vict. c. 12)—Income of Federal officer —Whether liable to income tax imposed by State—Power of State Legislature—Whether restricted by Commonwealth Constitution.]— *Held*, that the respondent, an officer of the Commonwealth resident in Victoria and receiving his official salary in that State, is liable to be assessed in respect thereof for income tax imposed by an Act of the Victorian Legislature. No restriction on the power of the Victorian Legislature in favour of such officer is expressly enacted by the Commonwealth *Constitution Act*, nor can one be implied on any recognised principle of interpretation applicable thereto. *Webb* v. *Outtrim*, (1907) A.C., 81; 13 A.L.R. (C.N.), 1. Privy Council.

Commonwealth of Australia Constitution Act (63 & 64 Vict. c. 12)—Interference by State with legislative or executive authority of Commonwealth—Implied prohibition—Income Tax Acts, validity of.]—*Per Griffith, C.J., Barton* and *O'Connor, JJ.*—The Income Tax Acts in so far as they purport to tax the emoluments of Federal officers, are inoperative and void. *Per Isaacs, J.*—These Acts do not infringe the doctrine of non-interference inasmuch as they cannot by any fair and reasonable intendment be read as impairing the usefulness or efficiency of the officers concerned to serve the Federal Government. *Per Isaacs* and *Higgins, JJ.*— It is not an improper interference with a Federal agent for a State to collect from him a tax upon his income, on the same scale as from other citizens of the State, even though his salary as a Federal agent has to be included in his return. *Baxter* v. *Commissioners of Taxation*; *Flint* v. *Webb*, 4 C.L.R., 1087, 1178; 13 A.L.R., 313 (1907).

Commonwealth of Australia Constitution (62 & 63 Vict. c. 12)—Power of Parliament— Federal nature of Constitution—Interference with domestic affairs of State—Implied prohibition.] — Principles of interpretation adopted in *Peterswald* v. *Bartley*, 1 C.L.R., 497, and (by the majority of the Court) in *The King* v. *Barger*, 6 C.L.R., 41; 14 A.L.R., 374, and *Attorney-General for New South Wales* v. *Brewery Employees Union of New South Wales (Union Label Case)*, 6 C.L.R., 469; 14 A.L.R., 565, applied. *Huddart Parker & Co. Proprietary Ltd.* v. *Moorehead*; *Appleton* v. *Moorehead*, (1909) 8 C.L.R., 330; 15 A.L.R., 241. H.C., *Griffith, C.J., Barton* and *O'Connor, JJ.* (*Isaacs* and *Higgins, JJ., dissentientibus*).

Instrumentality of State Government, what is—Municipal corporation engaging in trading enterprise.]—*Semble* (*per Griffith, C.J., Barton, O'Connor, Isaacs* and *Higgins, JJ.*). *Semble*, assuming that a municipal corporation is an instrument of State government, if the corporation engages in a trading enterprise, *e.g.*, the supply of electricity to those who choose to buy it, it is not in respect of such enterprise exempt from Federal legislation under the rule laid down in *D'Emden* v. *Pedder*, 1 C.L.R., 91; 10 A.L.R. (C.N.), 30. *Federated Engine-Drivers and Firemen's Association of Australasia* v. *Broken Hill Proprietary Co. Ltd.*, (1911) 12 C.L.R., 398; 17 A.L.R., 285.

(d) Legislation in Respect of Religion.

Defence—Compulsory military training—Religious objection to bear arms—Validity of Act—Exemption—Excuse—Defence Act 1903-1910 (No. 12 of 1904—No. 37 of 1910), secs. 61, 125, 135, 138, 143—The Constitution (63 & 64 Vict. c. 12), sec. 116.]—The provision of the *Defence Act* 1903-1910 imposing obligations on all male inhabitants of the Commonwealth in respect of military training do not prohibit the free exercise of any religion, and, therefore, are not an infringement of sec. 116 of the Constitution. A person who is forbidden by the doctrines of his religion to bear arms is not thereby exempted or excused from undergoing the military training and rendering the personal service required by Part XII. of the *Defence Act* 1903-1910. *Krygger* v, *Williams*, (1912) 15 C.L.R., 366; 18 A.L.R., 518. H.C., *Griffith, C.J.* and *Barton, J.*

(e) The State Courts.

Judgment of High Court on appeal from Supreme Court—Duty of Supreme Court to execute—Judiciary Act 1903 (No. 6 of 1903), sec. 37, whether ultra vires—The Constitution, sec. 51 (xxxix.)—Commonwealth of Australia Constitution Act (63 & 64 Vict. c. 12), sec. v.]—Sec. 37 of the *Judiciary Act* 1903 in so far as it authorises the High Court in the exercise of its appellate jurisdiction to remit a cause to the Supreme Court for the execution of the judgment of the High Court, and imposes upon the Supreme Court the duty of executing the judgment of the High Court in the same manner as if that judgment were the judgment of the Supreme Court is a valid exercise by Parliament of the power conferred by sec. 51 (xxxix.) of the Constitution. *Bayne* v. *Blake*, (1908) 5 C.L.R., 497; 14 A.L.R., 103. H.C., *Griffith, C.J., Barton* and *O'Connor, JJ.*

Judgment of High Court on appeal from Supreme Court — Judgment remitted to Supreme Court for execution—Officer of Supreme Court—Whether subject to control of High Court.]—The High Court may directly order an officer of the Supreme Court to obey a judgment of the High Court. *Bayne* v. *Blake*, (1908) 5 C.L.R., 497; 14 A.L.R., 103. H.C., *Griffith, C.J., Barton* and *O'Connor, JJ.*

Judgment of High Court on appeal from Supreme Court—Judgment remitted to Supreme Court—Stay of proceedings, jurisdiction of Supreme Court to order.]—*See* APPEAL. *Bayne* v. *Blake*, (1908) 5 C.L.R., 497; 14 A.L.R., 103.

Patent, application for—Opposition—State Patents Act—Transfer of administration to Commonwealth pending proceedings—Appeal to State Supreme Court—Jurisdiction—Patents Act 1890 (No. 1123), sec. 33—Patents Act (Federal) (No. 21 of 1902).]—*See* APPEAL. *In re McLeod's Patent*; *Burton* v. *McLeod*, (1906) V.L.R., 488; 12 A.L.R., 335.

Supreme Court—Jurisdiction—Habeas corpus—Applicant held under restraint under authority of Commonwealth—Immigration Restriction Amendment Act 1905 (No. 17), sec. 14 (13b)—Judiciary Act 1903 (No. 6) Part VI.]—*See* HABEAS CORPUS.— *Ah Sheung* v. *Lindberg*, (1906) V.L.R., 323; 27 A.L.T., 189; *sub nom.*, *Rex* v. *Ah Sheung*, 12 A.L.R., 190.

_____

COMMONWEALTH PUBLIC SERVICE ACTS.

See PUBLIC SERVICE.

COMPANY.

COMPANY.

I.—REGISTRATION : NAME.

Companies Act 1896 (No. 1482), Div. VIII.—Defunct companies—Restoration of name to Register—No secretary or directors—Directions for calling meeting of shareholders.]—Order made for the restoration to the register of the name of a company which had been struck off the register. Directions given for calling a meeting of shareholders there being no secretary and no directors. *In re Great Southern Land Investment Co. Ltd.,* (1910) V.L.R. 150 ; 31 A.L.T., 129 ; 16 A.L.R., 14. *Hodges, J.*

Company—Name struck off Register—Motion to restore name—Parties—Registrar-General—Companies Act 1896 (No. 1482), Div. VIII.—Defunct companies.]—The Regis-trar-General should be served with notice of a motion that the name of a company, which has been struck off the Register of Companies should be restored thereto. *In re Great Southern Land and Investment Co. Ltd.,* (1910) V.L.R. 150 ; 31 A.L.T., 129 ; 16 A.L.R., 14. *Hodges, J.*

Trade name—Name adopted by company—Similarity to name of another company—Both companies carrying on the same business—Likelihood of confusion—Burden of proof.]— In an action by one company to prevent another company from using a name so like that of the plaintiff company as to be likely to deceive, the plaintiff company must show that it is reasonably certain that what the defendant company is about to do will cause imminent and substantial damage to the plaintiff company. *Royal Insurance Co. Ltd. v. Midland Insurance Co. Ltd.,* 26 R.P.C., 95, followed. *Held,* that the name of the appellant company was not so like that of the respondent company as to render it reasonably certain that anyone intending to employ the respondent company and make them trustees under a will or settlement or employ them as agents, would be led to believe that the appellant company was the respondent company. *The Bendigo and Country Districts Trustees &c Co. Ltd. v. The Sandhurst. and Northern District Trustees, &c., Co. Ltd.,* (1909) 9 C.L.R., 474 ; 15 A.L.R., 565. *Griffith, C.J., O'Connor* and *Isaacs, JJ.*

Trade Marks Act 1905 (No. 20 of 1905)—Trade mark—Infringement—User not as a trade mark—Trade name—Name adopted by company—Similarity to name of another company—Likelihood of confusion—Class of business carried on—Actual and prospective—Injunction.]—*See* TRADE MARKS AND TRADE NAMES. *Austral Canning Co. Proprietary Ltd. v. Austral Grain and Produce Proprietary Ltd.,* 34 A.L.T., 37 ; 18 A.L.R., 354.

II.—SHARES.

(a) *Liability of Shareholders Generally.*

Companies Act 1890 (No. 1074)—Company—Agreement to take shares—Contract thereby implied.]—*Per Cussen, J.—*" Where a person agrees to become a member of a company under the Act, either by subscribing the memorandum and articles, or by allotment, or transfer, or after transmission, or otherwise, I think there must be taken to be implied, so far as it is not expressed, a contract to fulfil any obligation imposed by, or in pursuance of the Act, the conditions of the memorandum or the regulations in the articles, involving the payment of money by him to the company. Other obligations may be of so direct a nature as between the company and the individual as to be implied also, but the obligation to pay moneys to the company is all I am at present concerned with. *The Land Mortgage Bank of Victoria Ltd. v. Reid*, (1909) V.L.R. 284, at p. 292; 31 A.L.T., 9, at p. 12; 15 A.L.R., 234, at p. 237. (But see *Goldsmith v. The Colonial Finance, Mortgage, Investment and Guarantee Corporation Ltd.*, 8 C.L.R. 241; 15 A.L.R., 431.

Companies Act 1890 (No. 1074), sec. 16— Articles of association—Registration of—Effect thereof—" Shall bind the Company and its members "—Meaning of members.]—The provision in sec. 16 of the *Companies Act 1890* which provides that the articles of association " when registered shall bind the company and the members thereof to the same extent as if each member had subscribed his name and affixed his seal thereto, and there were in such articles contained a covenant on the part of himself his heirs executors and administrators to conform to all the regulations contained in such articles subject to the provisions of this part of the Act " is to be limited to binding members while they are members. *The Land Mortgage Bank of Victoria Ltd. v. Reid*, (1909) V.L.R., 284; 31 A.L.T., 9; 15 A.L.R., 234. *Cussen, J.*

Company — Shares — Certificate stating shares fully paid up—Incorrectness of Statement—Purchaser without actual notice—Estoppel—Constructive notice—Articles of Association.]—Where a Company has issued a certificate for shares which states that such shares are fully paid up, the Company and the liquidator of the Company are estopped from alleging any mistake or inaccuracy in such statement as against a person who has been thereby induced to believe that such shares were fully paid up, and, acting on that belief and without knowledge of any liability on the shares, purchased them as fully paid up shares. Such estoppel applies even where the Company has acted *ultra vires* in issuing the shares as fully paid up. Such purchaser is not to be presumed to have had notice from the articles of association that such shares were not fully paid up; nor, where there is nothing to excite suspicion, is there any obligation on him to search the Articles in order to see if the statement in the certificate was true or false. *In re Victoria Silicate Brick Co. Ltd. (in liquidation); Ex parte Martin*, (1913) V.L.R., 71; 34 A.L.T., 110; 18 A.L.R., 557. F.C., *a' Beckett, Hodges* and *Cussen, JJ.*

Companies Act 1890 (No. 1074), sec. 16, — Company — Calls — Shares—Reduction of Capital—Cancellation of forfeited Shares—Effect on liability.]— *Quaere*, whether the fact of the cancellation of shares extinguishes the liability of their former holder under the Articles of Association. *Randt Gold Mining Co. Ltd. v. Wainwright*, (1901) 1 Ch., 184, doubted. *The Land Mortgage Bank of Victoria Ltd. v. Reid*, (1909) V.L.R., 284; 31 A.L.T., 9; 15 A.L.R., 234. *Cussen, J.*

(b) Calls.

Companies Act 1890 (No. 1074), sec. 16— Company—Calls—Forfeited shares, liability upon—Articles of association—Statute of Limitations — Cancellation of shares — Specialty debt.]—L. was a shareholder in a company limited by shares, incorporated under the Companies Acts. In 1896 a call was made which was not paid. In December, 1900, the shares were forfeited for non-payment of the first call. In 1901 the capital of the company was reduced and the shares in question cancelled. Clause 30 of the articles of association provided that any member whose shares were forfeited should be liable to pay all calls, instalments, interest and expenses, owing upon or in respect of such shares at the time of forfeiture, together with interest at ten per cent. per annum. In

1908 an action was brought for the recovery of the amount of the calls with interest thereon. *Held*, that the liability of L. in her character as a member was extinguished by the forfeiture; that her liability was one arising by virtue of an implied contract made when she became a member, to fulfil any obligations imposed by or in pursuance of the Act, the conditions of the memorandum or the regulations in the articles of association involving the payment of money to the company; that this was *prima facie* a liability arising on a simple contract; and that as the Act did not provide that a liability arising upon forfeiture should be deemed to be or to give rise to a specialty debt, the action was barred after six years from the date of forfeiture. *The Land Mortgage Bank of Victoria Ltd.* v. *Reid*, (1909) V.L.R., 284; 31 A.L.T., 9; 15 A.L.R., 234. *Cussen, J.* (And see *Goldsmith* v. *The Colonial Finance, Mortgage, Investment and Guarantee Corporation Ltd.*, 8 C.L.R., 241; 15 A.L.R., 431.

Companies Act 1890 (No. 1074), sec. 16—Articles of association, registration of—Effect thereof—Moneys payable by any member to be deemed a specialty debt—Provision in articles of association that members whose shares are forfeited shall continue liable for calls and interest thereon due at forfeiture—Whether such liability is a specialty debt.]— Where the registered Articles of Association of a Company contained a provision that any member whose shares shall be forfeited shall, notwithstanding be liable to pay all calls, instalments, interest and expenses owing upon or in respect of such shares at the time of forfeiture together with interest at ten per cent. per annum. *Held* that the liability under such provision, in respect of calls and interest owing on shares at the date of forfeiture is not a specialty debt within sec. 16 of the *Companies Act* 1890, inasmuch as the provision in that section making such liability a specialty debt applies to only those moneys which are payable by a member in his character of member. *The Land Mortgage Bank of Victoria Ltd.* v. *Reid*, (1909) V.L.R., 284; 31 A.L.T., 9; 15 A.L.R., 234. *Cussen, J.* [See *Gillespie & Co. Ltd.* v.

Reid, (1905) V.L.R., 101; 26 A.L.T., 154; 11 A.L.R., 12.]

Calls on shares in no-liability company—Power in will to postpone sale of personal property—Retention of shares by trustees—Whether liable for calls paid by them.]—See TRUSTS AND TRUSTEES. *Grunden* v. *Nissen*, (1911) V.L.R., 267; 33 A.L.T., 11; 17 A.L.R., 260.

(c) Dividends.

Will—Construction—Shares in company owned by testator—Bequest to life tenant of dividends and to remainderman absolutely—Bonus declared by company on shares—New shares issued and offered to shareholders—Bonus applicable in payment therefor—Whether bonus capital or income.]—See TENANT FOR LIFE AND REMAINDERMAN. *In re Smith*; *Edwards* v. *Smith*, 29 A.L.T., 173; 14 A.L.R., 22.

Tenant for life and remainderman—Dividends declared by company, whether capital or income.]—See WILL. *In re Longley*; *Reid* v. *Silke*, (1906) V.L.R., 641; 28 A.L.T., 82; 12 A.L.R., 499.

(d) Transfer.

Companies Act 1890 (No. 1074), sec. 23—Transfer of shares—How far right of transfer may be restricted.]—Sec. 23 of the *Companies Act* 1890 does not prevent restrictions being placed on the right to transfer shares in a company, even very general restrictions, so long as, possibly, the right of transfer is not altogether stopped. *In re Australian Mont de Piete Loan, &c., Co. Ltd.*; *Ex parte Alexander*, (1907) V.L.R., 660; 29 A.L.T., 58; 13 A.L.R., 513. *Cussen, J.*

Companies Act 1890 (No. 1074), secs. 23, 36—Transfer of shares—Power to refuse to register transfer conferred in absolute terms—How such power limited.]—A power to refuse to register any transfer of shares, although the terms in which it is conferred upon the directors are absolute and general, is to be controlled in the interests of the shareholders and of the transferees and possibly, also, in the interests of the creditors of the company and of the transferrers. Where the directors in the exercise of such a power have declined to register a transfer, the Court, upon application to it by the transferee to rectify the register of the company, will not set aside the decision of the directors if they have acted honestly and within their powers. *In re Australian Mont de Piete Loan, &c., Co. Ltd.; Ex parte Alexander* (1907) V.L.R., 660; 29 A.L.T., 58; 13 A.L.R., 513. *Cussen, J.*

Company—Transfer of shares—Powers of directors— Refusal to register transfer — Shares purchased by business rivals of company.]—One of the articles of association of a trading company provided that " The directors may, if they think fit, decline to register any transfer of shares, except transfers by operation of law." *Held,* that the directors had power to refuse to register transfers of shares in the company to persons engaged in and conducting a rival business, and who were stated to be actually desirous of purchasing the company's business. *In re Australian Mont de Piete Loan, &c., Co. Ltd.: Ex parte Alexander,* (1907) V.L.R., 660; 29 A.L.T., 58; 13 A.L.R., 513. *Cussen, J.*

Transfer of share—Unnecessary delay in registration—Ante-dating registration to date upon which shares should have been registered—Jurisdiction of Court.]—*Semble,* the Court has power, where there has been unnecessary delay in rectifying the register, to direct that the date on which the transfer of shares in a company should have been registered shall be entered as the date of the transfer. *In re Blackwood; Power v. Melbourne Flour Milling Co. Proprietary Ltd.,* (1908) V.L.R., 517; 30 A.L.T., 14; 14 A.L.R., 368. *Cussen, J.*

Companies Act 1896 (No. 1482), sec. 168 (2) —Transfer of shares for nominal consideration in order to avoid liability—Shares of deceased testator—Liability of executor.]—Sec. 168 (2) of the *Companies Act* 1896 applies to a transfer by an executor of shares in a company belonging to the estate of his testator. *In re Blackwood; Power v. Melbourne Flour Milling Co. Proprietary Ltd.,* (1908) V.L.R.,

517; 30 A.L.T., 14; 14 A.L.R., 368. *Cussen, J.*

Trusts Act 1901 (No. 1769), sec. 2—Shares not fully paid up held by testator at death—Distribution of assets of estate by executor—Whether necessary to reserve portion for payment of calls—Transfer of shares for nominal consideration to avoid liability—Whether executor liable—Companies Act 1896 (No. 1482), sec. 168 (2)]—Sec. 2 of the *Trusts Act* 1901 is a special enabling section for the benefit of executors, and is intended to apply to every case falling naturally within the words, so that in certain cases it may, so far as an executor's personal liability is concerned, cut down the effect which, standing alone, sec. 168 (2) of the *Companies Act* 1896 would have. *In re Blackwood; Power v. Melbourne Flour Milling Co. Proprietary Ltd.,* (1908) V.L.R., 517; 30 A.L.T., 14; 14 A.L.R., 368. *Cussen, J.* (1908).

Transfer of shares by executor—Registration delayed—Distribution of assets of testator's estate—Facts insufficient to justify determination on originating summons.]—Where the question to be determined on an originating summons was whether, having regard to certain facts, the executor of a will could safely and properly, and should he, hand over the remaining assets in the testator's estate to the sole beneficiary under the will without making any provisions for any liability for calls made after a certain date on shares not fully paid up in an incorporated company, of which shares the testator was the registered holder, and which the executor had previously to such date transferred, in order to free the estate from contingent liability, for a nominal consideration to the executor and for a consideration to be paid to the transferee upon the transfer being registered, which transfer was not registered till subsequently to such date: *Held,* that no order or declaration could be made which would justify the executor, on the facts as they then stood, in distributing the assets: *In re Blackwood; Power v. Melbourne Flour Milling Co. Proprietary Ltd.,* (1908) V.L.R., 517; 30 A.L.T., 14; 14 A.L.R., 368. *Cussen, J.*

III.—MANAGEMENT AND ADMINISTRATION.

(a) Interference by Court.

Company—Management of internal affairs —Injunction—When Court will interfere by.] —The rule in *Foss* v. *Harbottle*, 2 Hare, 461, does not apply to a case where a company in regard to the management of its internal affairs does or attempts to do that which it is not lawful for the company to do ; in such a case the Court will interfere by way of injunction. *Oliver* v. *North Nuggetty Ajax Co. No Liability*, (1912) V.L.R. 416 ; 34 A.L.T., 58 ; 18 A.L.R., 309. *Madden, C.J.*

(b) Meetings.

Companies Act 1890 (No. 1074), sec. 67— Proceedings at meetings of company, how proved—Minutes not entered in minute book]—Sec. 67 of the *Companies Act* 1890 is an enabling section, and, although no minutes have been entered in a minute book, the proceedings of the company can be proved otherwise by any admissible evidence. *McLean Brothers & Rigg Ltd.* v. *Grice*, 4 C.L.R., 835 ; 13 A.L.R., 77. H.C., *Griffith, C.J., Barton* and *O'Connor, JJ.* (1907).

Companies Act 1890 (No. 1074), sec. 54— Printed copy of resolution of shareholders forwarded to Registrar-General—Presumption against fraud—Validity of resolution, prima facie evidence of]—By reason of the presumption against fraud in the carrying out of duties to be performed under an Act of Parliament, a certified copy of a printed copy of a resolution for the voluntary winding-up of a company forwarded to the Registrar-General by the company in pursuance of sec. 54 is *prima facie* evidence of a valid resolution. *McLean Brothers & Rigg Ltd.* v. *Grice*, 4 C.L.R., 835 ; 13 A.L.R., 77. H.C., *Griffith, C.J., Barton* and *O'Connor, JJ.* (1907).

Evidence—Proceedings of corporation— Resolution passed at meeting of shareholders —Presumption that quorum present at meeting.]—Where an Act is done which can be done legally only after the performance of some prior act, proof of the latter carries with it a presumption of the due performance of the prior act. This presumption applies to the proceedings of corporations, and, therefore, proof of the passing of a resolution for the voluntary winding-up of a company is *prima facie* evidence that, if a quorum was necessary at the meeting at which the resolution was passed, such quorum was present. *McLean Brothers & Rigg Ltd.* v. *Grice*, 4 C.L.R., 835 ; 13 A.L.R., 77. H.C., *Griffith, C.J., Barton* and *O'Connor, JJ.* (1907).

Omnia praesumuntur rite esse acta—Presumption afforded by the records of transactions required by law to be kept—Proceedings at meeting of shareholders, validity of— Printed copy of resolution forwarded to Registrar-General—Notice of winding-up resolution—Publication in Government Gazette— Companies Act 1890 (No. 1074), ss. 54. 118.]— It was proved that a resolution for the voluntary winding-up of a company was recorded in writing, and signed by the chairman of the meeting of shareholders at which the resolution was passed, and that a copy was sent to the Registrar-General and recorded by him, and that a copy was published in the *Government Gazette*. Held, that there was *prima facie* evidence that all that took place at the meeting was done lawfully, and, therefore, if a quorum was requisite at such meeting, that there was such a quorum present. *McLean Brothers & Rigg Ltd.* v. *Grice*, 4 C.L.R., 835 ; 13 A.L.R., 77 ; H.C., *Griffith, C.J., Barton* and *O'Connor, JJ.* (1907).

Company—General meeting—Election of Directors—Nominations—Informality — Error in Company's name—Mode of election— Chairman's powers—Right of meeting to discuss and to complete business]—Part of the business at a general meeting of a gold-mining company named " North Nuggetty Ajax Co. No Liability " was the election of directors to fill three vacancies on the Board ; the chairman rejected the nominations of two of the candidates on the ground that in their nomination papers the company for which they were nominated was called the " North Nuggetty G. M. Co. No Liability," and then, after refusing to accept a motion that his ruling be disagreed with and also refusing to permit any discussion on the matter, he, without putting to the vote of the meeting the names of the remaining candidates (who were three in number) declared that they were elected to fill the vacancies, and he thereupon announced that the business was concluded and that the meeting was closed, and together with some other shareholders, left the meeting : *Held,* that the chairman should not have rejected such nominations, as it was reasonably clear to what company and to what vacancy they related. *Held,* also, that the election of the three candidates declared by such chairman to be elected was invalid, as the articles of the company contained no provision that where the number of candidates duly nominated was equal to the number of vacancies, the chairman was to have power to declare them elected without submitting their names to the vote of the meeting. *Held,* further, that as long as there remained to be dealt with any business reasonably and properly pertinent to the business of the meeting, the shareholders thereat were entitled to put their views and to have the vote of the meeting with regard thereto ; and that the chairman could not, by leaving the chair, terminate the meeting before such business was disposed of. *Oliver v. North Nuggetty Ajax Co. No Liability,* (1912) V.L.R., 416 ; 34 A.L.T., 58 ; 18 A.L.R., 309 ; *Madden, C.J.*

Company—Election of directors—General meeting improperly declared closed by chairman—Right of meeting to discuss and complete business—Names of candidates for directorships not separately put to and voted on by meeting.]—Part of the business of a general meeting of a gold mining company was the election of directors. The chairman improperly rejected the nominations of certain candidates, refused to accept a motion that his ruling be disagreed with, and declared the remaining candidates elected. He then announced that the business was completed and that the meeting was closed, and, together with certain other shareholders, left the meeting. After the departure of the chairman and such other shareholders, the remaining shareholders elected a new chairman and thereupon elected three persons as directors to fill the vacancies above referred to . *Held* (but not without doubt), that such persons were, for the time being, to be regarded as duly elected although their names were not separately put to and voted upon by the meeting. *Oliver v. North Nuggetty Ajax Co. No Liability,* (1912) V.L.R., 416 ; 34 A.L.T., 58 ; 18 A.L.R., 309. *Madden, C.J.* (1912).

(c) *Contracts.*

Director with contractual rights against company—Concurrence in acts rendering company unable to perform contract—Whether a waiver of rights of director.]—The mere concurrence of a person in his capacity as director of a company in acts, which render such company unable to perform a contract then existing between him and the company, does not amount to a waiver by him of his personal rights in respect of a breach of contract by the company resulting from such acts. *Glass v. Pioneer Rubber Works of Australia Ltd.,* (1906) V.L.R., 754 ; 28 A.L.T., 64 ; 12 A.L.R., 529. F.C., a' Beckett, A.C.J., *Hodges* and *Chomley, JJ.*

Contract with company—Implied from articles of association and conduct of the parties.]—The articles of association of a company may express the terms upon which a person may contract with the company, and, if acted upon, an agreement between such person and the company on which either party may sue may be implied, partly from the articles and partly from the conduct of the parties. *Glass v. Pioneer Rubber Works of Australia Ltd.,* (1906) V.L.R., 754 ; 28 A.L.T., 64 ; 12 A.L.R., 529. F.C., a Beckett, A.-C.J., *Hodges* and *Chomley, JJ.*

Instruments Act 1890 (No. 1103), sec. 208—Memorandum of contract contained in several documents—Agreement to act as manager of company—Agreement implied from articles of association and conduct of parties.]—See CONTRACT OR AGREEMENT. *Glass v. Pioneer Rubber Works of Australia Ltd.,* (1906) V.L.R., 754 ; 28 A.L.T., 64 ; 12 A.L.R., 529.

(d) Mortgages.

Company—Mortgage—Over uncalled capital—Indenture containing recitals—Insertion by mistake—Rectification—Companies Act 1896 (No. 1482), sec. 53.]—A company registered under the *Companies Act* 1890 executed a mortgage over its uncalled capital. The requirements of section 53 of the *Companies Act* 1896 were complied with. The indenture contained recitals which were held by the Court to have been inserted by mutual mistake. *Held,* that the Court was not precluded from rectifying the instrument merely because of the incidents attached to it by Statute. *Caulfield, Elsternwick and Malvern Tramway Co.* v. *The Royal Bank of Australia Ltd.,* 33 A.L.T., 14; 17 A.L.R., 91. *a' Beckett, J.* (1911).

Companies Act 1890 (No. 1074), sec. 235—Transfer of Land Act 1890 (No. 1149), sec. 59—Mortgage by mining company — Registration, sufficiency of—Land under general law.]—Where a mining company gives a mortgage over land under the *Transfer of Land Act,* registration of the instrument under that Act is the only registration necessary in order to comply with the requirements of sec. 235 of the *Companies Act* 1890. The provision requiring registration with the Registrar-General applies only to land under the general law. *In re Transfer of Land Act; Ex parte Coronation Syndicate Mining Co. No Liability,* (1911) V.L.R., 78; 32 A.L.T., 129; 17 A.L.R., 39. *F.C., a' Beckett, Hodges and Hood, JJ.*

(e) Sale of Assets.

Mining company—No liability company—Sale of assets by majority of shareholders—Payment to be taken in part by shares in another company in another State—Companies Act 1890 (No. 1074), Part II.]—A Victorian No Liability mining company has no authority to sell its assets by resolution of a majority of its shareholders and take payment in part by shares in a Limited Liability company in another State. *Ellison* v. *Ivanhoe Gold Mining Co. No Liability,* 23 V.L.R., 224; 19 A.L.T., 104; 3 A.L.R., 209, distinguished. *Manning* v. *Tewksbury*

Freehold Gold Dredging Co. No Liability, (1908) V.L.R., 50; 29 A.L.T., 78; 13 A.L.R., 547. *Hood, J.*

(f) Notice by Company.

Landlord and Tenant Act 1890 (No. 1108), sec. 92—Eighth Schedule—Notice of intention to apply to justices to recover possession—Signature of notice, sufficiency of—Application by corporation—Name of corporation signed by agent authorised so to do.]—*See* LANDLORD AND TENANT. *Equity Trustees Executors and Agency Co. Ltd.* v. *Harston,* (1908) V.L.R., 23; 29 A.L.T., 131; 13 A.L.R., 686.

IV.—INCOME TAX.

(a) Profits.

Company—Income tax—" Profits " of company, what are—Income Tax Act 1903 (No. 1819), sec. 9.]—Sec. 9 of the *Income Tax Act* 1903 has not the effect of rendering taxable as income profits of a company which would not be income in the ordinary sense of that term. *Webb* v. *Australian Deposit and Mortgage Bank Ltd.,* (1910) 11 C.L.R., 223; 16 A.L.R., 446. *H.C., Griffith, C.J., O'Connor, Isaacs and Higgins, JJ.*

Income Tax Act 1903 (No. 1819), sec. 9—Companies Act 1896 (No. 1482), sec. 88—Profits of company—Reduction of capital—Receipts in excess of amount of reduced capital—Whether such receipts may be capital.]—The fact of the reduction of the capital of a company, pursuant to sec. 88 of the *Companies Act* 1896, is not by itself decisive of the question of what are the profits of the company for the purposes of the Income Tax Acts. Receipts beyond the honestly estimated value of assets representing the reduced amount of capital may for such purposes be capital moneys and not profits. *Webb* v. *Australian Deposit and Mortgage Bank Ltd.,* (1910) 11 C.L.R., 223; 16 A.L.R., 446. *H.C., Griffith, C.J., O'Connor, Isaacs and Higgins, JJ.*

Income Tax Act 1903 (No. 1819), sec. 9 (1), (2)—Whether tax payable by trading company only—" Profits," meaning of—Income Tax Act 1895 (No. 1374), ss. 2, 7 (e).]—The use of the word " profits " in sec. 9 (1) of the *Income Tax Acts* 1903 does not confine the payment of income tax to trading companies only. *Quaere*, whether the " profits " referred to in the section are those from which dividends might legally be payable. *In re Income Tax Acts* (1907) V.L.R., 185 ; 28 A.L.T., 168 ; 13 A.L.R., 31. F.C., *Hood, Cussen* and *Chomley, JJ.*

Income Tax Act 1903 (No. 1819), sec. 9 (1)— " Profits " of company, what are—Mutual benefit association incorporated as a company —Profits of club established for benefit of members and other persons—Subscriptions by members to benefit funds—Interest on investment of benefit funds—Income Tax Act 1895 (No. 1374), secs. 2, 7 (e)—Companies Act 1890 (No. 1074), sec. 181.]—The taxpayer was an association registered under the *Companies Act* 1890 whose main object was the promotion of the welfare of persons carrying on a certain specified business, which was achieved by the establishment of an ordinary club to which persons other than members of the association (called club members) might belong, and also by the establishment of certain benefit funds participation in which was confined to members of the association and their families. By the rules of the association its clear net profits for each financial year were to be paid into the benefit funds, and in addition a fixed part of the subscriptions of members of the association was to be paid into such funds. *Held*, that income tax was payable on the whole of the profits of the taxpayer ; that not only should the profits of the club be included, but that in estimating the profits the entrance fees and subscriptions of members of the association, and all moneys received by way of interest from the investment of the benefit funds, should also be taken into consideration. *In re Income Tax Acts*, (1907) V.L.R., 185 ; 28 A.L.T., 168 ; 13 A.L.R., 31. F.C., *Hood, Cussen* and *Chomley, JJ.*

Income Tax Act 1903 (No. 1819), sec. 11 (1) —Companies Act 1890 (No. 1074), sec. 334— Income of life assurance company—Premiums in respect of " insurances or assurances "—Consideration for annuities.]—An-nuities granted by a company carrying on the business of life assurance are within the term " insurances or assurances " in sec. 11 (1) of the *Income Tax Act* 1903, and the considerations received by the company for them are premiums in respect of insurances or assurances and form part of the amount which under that section is the basis of ascertaining the taxable amount of the income of the company. *In re Income Tax Acts* ; *In re Australian Mutual Provident Society*, (1913) V.L.R., 42 ; 34 A.L.T., 118 ; 18 A.L.R., 524. F.C., *a' Beckett, Hodges* and *Cussen, JJ.* (1912).

Income Tax Act 1903 (No. 1819), sec. 9— Company—Registered in Victoria—Purchase and sale of land in New South Wales on behalf of Company to be formed—Transactions of company in Victoria—Profit, whether earned in Victoria—Re-sale of land by promoter of company—Contracts taken over by company —Purchase money payable by instalments— Tax on sums not yet received.]—*See* INCOME TAX ACTS. *In re Income Tax Acts* ; *Ex parte Quat Quatta Co.*, (1907) V.L.R., 54 ; 28 A.L.T., 100 ; 12 A.L.R., 526.

Income Tax—Company—Profits—Company formed to realize assets of companies in liquidation—Surplus proceeds of realization—Business of company—Income Tax Act 1903 (No. 1819), sec. 9.]—*See* INCOME TAX ACTS. *Melbourne Trust Limited* v. *Commissioner of Taxes*, (1912) 15 C.L.R., 274 ; 18 A.L.R., 497.

(b) Deductions.

Income Tax—Deductions—Company formed for one venture—Profits from venture—Deduction of promotion expenses.]—Law costs and preliminary expenses incurred in the promotion of a company formed for one venture may, in assessing income, be deducted from the gross profits of the venture. *In re Income Tax Acts* ; *Ex parte Quat Quatta Co.*, (1907) V.L.R., 54 ; 28 A.L.T., 100 : 12 A.L.R., 526. F.C., *a' Beckett, A.C.J., Hodges* and *Chomley, JJ.*

Income Tax Act 1903 (No. 1819), secs. 5, 9—Taxation of company—Deductions, authority for making—Income Tax Act 1895 (No.

1374), sec. 9—Income Tax Act 1896 (No. 1467), sec. 6.]—*See* INCOME TAX ACTS. *Re Income Tax Acts*, (1907) V.L.R., 327; 28 A.L.T., 196; 13 A.L.R., 154.

Income Tax Act 1903 (No. 1819), secs. 5, 9—Taxation of company—Deductions—Depreciation of machinery.]—*See* INCOME TAX ACTS. *Re Income Tax Acts*, (1907) V.L.R., 327; 28 A.L.T., 196; 13 A.L.R., 154.

Income Tax Act 1903 (No. 1819), secs. 5, 9—Taxation of company—Interest on borrowed capital—Interest on bills given for purchase of stock in trade.]—*See* INCOME TAX ACTS, (1907) V.L.R., 327; 28 A.L.R., 196; 13 A.L.R., 154.

V.—SECURITY FOR COSTS.

Security for costs—Foreign company—Registered office and agent in Victoria—Companies Act 1896 (No. 1482), sec. 70—Rules of Supreme Court 1884, Order LXV., r. 6.]—A foreign company suing as plaintiff in Victoria, will not be relieved from giving security for costs upon proof only that it has an agent in and is carrying on business in Victoria, and has complied with sec. 70 of the *Companies Act* 1896. *Norton or Horton & Sons Ltd.* v. *Sewell*, (1906) V.L.R., 401; 27 A.L.T., 214; 12 A.L.R., 209. *a'Beckett, A.C.J.* (1906).

VI.—CRIMINAL LIABILITY.

Company—Liability for criminal offences—Mens rea—Liability to presentment on charge of conspiracy—Capacity to conspire.]—*See* CORPORATION. *R.* v. *Kellow*, (1912) V.L.R., 162; 33 A.L.T., 203; 18 A.L.R., 170. *Cussen, J.*

Questions asked by Comptroller-General of Customs—Duty to answer—Prosecution pending—Person interrogated not charged—Corporation—Australian Industries Preservation Act 1906-1909 (No. 9 of 1906—No. 26 of 1909), sec. 15B.]—*See* AUSTRALIAN INDUSTRIES PRESERVATION ACT. *Melbourne Steamship Co.* v. *Moorehead*, (1912) 15 C.L.R., 333; 18 A.L.R., 533.

VII.—TRUSTEE COMPANIES.

" Equity Trustees Executors and Agency Company Limited Act " (No. 978), sec. 9—Appointment of company under, effect of.]—*Quaere*, whether under sec. 9 of the *Equity Trustees Executors and Agency Company Limited Act* (No. 978) an executor administrator or trustee can permanently appoint the company to act in his stead. *In re Hoarey*, (1906) V.L.R., 437; 28 A.L.T., 93; 12 A.L.R., 450. *Cussen, J.*

Executors—Renunciation—Appointment of a trustee company—Power of sole remaining executor—" The Union Trustees Executors and Administrators' Co. Act " (No. 839), sec. 3.]—*See* WILL. *In the Will of Gilbert*, 27 A.L.T., 241; 12 A.L.R., 528.

Intestacy—Next of kin entitled to administration resident abroad—Authority to trustee company to obtain administration—Form of grant to company.]—*See* EXECUTORS AND ADMINISTRATORS. *In the Estate of Morris*, (1909) V.L.R., 425; 31 A.L.T., 61; 15 A.L.R., 446.

Administration and Probate Act 1907 (No. 2120), sec. 7—Authority to trustee company to apply for probate—Revocation—Form of authority—Form of application.]—*See* EXECUTORS AND ADMINISTRATORS. *In the Will of Synot*, (1912) V.L.R., 99; 33 A.L.T., 182; 18 A.L.R., 82.

National Trustees Executors and Agency Co. of Australasia Ltd. Act (No. 938), sec. 10—Appointment with consent of Court of company to perform administrator's duties—Title of administrator not perfected—Letters of administration not issued.]—*See* EXECUTORS AND ADMINISTRATORS. *In re Moriarty*, (1907) V.L.R., 315; 29 A.L.T., 65; 13 A.L.R., 307.

VIII.—INSURANCE COMPANIES.

Companies Act 1890 (No. 1074), sec. 335—Purpose of this section—Protection of funds of life assurance branch of company transacting other business besides life assurance.]—Sec. 335 of the *Companies Act* 1890 was intended to protect the funds of the life assurance branch of a company, carrying on life assurance and also other business, from claims arising in connection with such other business, and the section applies only to a company which is carrying on life assurance business as well as other business. *In re Longley*; *Reid* v. *Silke*, (1906) V.L.R., 641 ; 28 A.L.T., 82 ; 12 A.L.R., 499. *Cussen, J.*

Income Tax Act 1903 (No. 1819), sec. 11 (1)—Companies Act 1890 (No. 1074), sec. 334—Income of life assurance company—Premiums in respect of " insurances or assurances "—Consideration for annuities.]—*See ante*, IV.—INCOME TAX. A. PROFITS. *In re Australian Mutual Provident Society*, (1913) V.L.R., 42 ; 34 A.L.T., 118 ; 18 A.L.R., 524.

IX.—WINDING-UP.

(a) *Jurisdiction* ; *Resolutions*.

Companies Act 1890 (No. 1074), sec. 76—Companies Act 1896 (No. 1482), secs. 1, 2, 70—Company—Incorporated outside Victoria—Registered in Victoria as a foreign company—Winding-up—Jurisdiction.]—The Court has jurisdiction to make an order for the winding-up under Part I. of the *Companies Act* 1890 of a company incorporated elsewhere than in Victoria and registered as a foreign company under sec. 70 of the *Companies Act* 1896. *In re the Egerton and Gordon Consolidated Gold Mines Co. No Liability*, (1908) V.L.R., 22 ; 29 A.L.T., 165 ; 14 A.L.R., 7. *a'Beckett, J.* (1907).

Companies Act 1890 (No. 1074), sec. 54—Printed copy of resolution of shareholders forwarded to Registrar-General—Presumption against fraud—Validity of resolution, prima facie evidence of.]—*See ante*, III. MANAGEMENT AND ADMINISTRATION. B. MEETINGS. *McLean Brothers & Rigg Ltd.* v. *Grice*, 4 C.L.R., 835 ; 13 A.L.R., 77.

Evidence—Proceedings of corporation—Resolution passed at meeting of shareholders—Presumption that quorum present at meeting.]—*See ante*, III. MANAGEMENT AND ADMINISTRATION. B. MEETINGS. *McLean Brothers & Rigg Ltd.* v. *Grice*, 4 C.L.R., 835 ; 13 A.L.R., 77.

Omnia praesumuntur rite esse acta—Presumption afforded by the records of transactions required by law to be kept—Proceedings at meeting of shareholders, validity of—Printed copy of resolution forwarded to Registrar-General—Notice of winding-up resolution—Publication in Government Gazette—Companies Act 1890 (No. 1074), secs. 54, 118.]—*See ante*, III. MANAGEMENT AND ADMINISTRATION. B. MEETINGS. *McLean Brothers & Rigg Ltd.* v. *Grice*, 4 C.L.R., 835 ; 13 A.L.R., 77.

(b) *Liquidators*.

Liquidation — Voluntary liquidation — Liquidator—Appointment of liquidator jointly with liquidator appointed by company—Resolution of creditors authorizing application to Court—Non-appointment by creditors of any person to make application—Application to Court by company and company's liquidator—Jurisdiction—Companies Act 1910 (No. 2293), sec. 189.]—Where at a meeting of creditors in a voluntary winding-up it has been determined under sec. 189 (2) of the *Companies Act* 1910 than an application shall be made to the Court for the appointment of a named person as liquidator jointly with the liquidator appointed by the company, the application may be made by a person other than a creditor appointed in accordance with that sub-section for the purpose of making the application. Therefore, where the creditors of a company in a voluntary winding up had duly determined that such an application should be made, but had not appointed any person to make the application, the Court, having regard to these and other circumstances, made an order in conformity with the determination of the creditors, upon the application of the company and the liquidator appointed by the company. *In re G. C. Meader Pty. Ltd. (in Liquidation)*, (1912) V.L.R., 471 ; 34 A.L.T., 86 ; 18 A.L.R., 461. *Cussen, J.*

Practice—Summons by official liquidator for directions—Summons served on secretary of company at time of passing of winding-up resolution—Matter directed to be taken to be in same position as if service on secretary had been ordered.]—*In re Australian Producers and Traders Ltd.*, 29 A.L.T., 185 (1908).

(c) Examination of Witnesses.

Companies Act 1896 (No. 1482), sec. 133 (1)—Company—Winding up—Public examination of promoters, directors, and others—Application for order—Materials—Fraud.]—The Court has no jurisdiction to direct any person to be publicly examined under sec. 133 (1) of the *Companies Act* 1896 where facts suggestive of fraud are not shown. *In re Rubber Inventions Co. Ltd.*, (1908) V.L.R., 414 ; 30 A.L.T., 41 ; 14 A.L.R., 350. *Madden, C.J.*

Companies Act 1890 (No. 1074), sec. 109—Practice—Winding up—Examination of persons capable of giving information concerning the trade dealings of the company—Jurisdiction.]—The Court has no power to summons before it under sec. 109 of the *Companies Act* 1890 a person claiming to be a creditor of a debtor of a company which is being compulsorily wound up by the Court, where it is not shown that such person knows anything of the trade dealings estate or effects of the company. *In re City of Melbourne Bank Ltd.*, (1910) V.L.R., 282 ; 32 A.L.T., 20 ; 16 A.L.R., 283. *Hodges, J.* (1910).

(d) Contributories.

See also, *ante*, II.—SHARES.

Companies Act 1890 (No. 1074), secs. 24, 39, 71—Liquidation—List of contributories—Contract to take shares with agreement that something is to be done after membership completed—Contract that there shall be no membership unless condition performed—Waiver.]—A person who has entered into a contract *in praesenti* to take shares, with an agreement that something is to be done after membership has been completed, is liable to be settled on the list of contributories in a winding-up, even though such agreement has not been performed ; so also is a person whose application to take shares is subject to the condition that it is not to be perfected until something has been done, if by his subsequent conduct he shows an intention to waive any right he had to insist on the condition, and he makes a new agreement to take and hold shares without any condition. *In re The Australian Producers and Traders*

Ltd., (1906) V.L.R., 511 ; 28 A.L.T., 80 ; 12 A.L.R., 445. *Cussen, J.*

(e) Debts ; Expenses of Liquidation ; Priorities.

Voluntary liquidation—Liquidation by the Court—Wages—Preferential claim—Period of four months, how calculated—Date of commencement of liquidation—Companies Act 1896 (No. 1482), sec. 148.]—After a resolution for the voluntary liquidation of a company had been passed, an order for compulsory winding-up was made by the Court. Among the creditors were servants of the company with claims for wages. *Held*, that for the purpose of ascertaining the period of four months in respect of which such claims would have priority under sec. 148 of the *Companies Act* 1896, the presentation of the petition to the Court was the commencement of the liquidation. *Re Australian Producers and Traders Ltd.*, (1908) V.L.R., 227 ; 29 A.L.T., 185 ; 14 A.L.R., 118. *Hodges, J.* (1908).

Companies Act 1890 (No. 1074), sec. 104—Assets insufficient to satisfy liabilities—Costs charges and expenses of winding-up—Order as to priority of payment of.]—Upon an application in a compulsory winding-up of a company for an order as to the priority and payment out of the estate of the company of the costs charges and expenses incurred in the winding-up, the Court ordered payment in the order of priority provided by rule 31 of the English rules of 1890. *In re People's Daily Co-operative Newspaper &c. Co. Ltd.*, (1907) V.L.R., 666 ; 29 A.L.T., 111 ; 13 A.L.R., 504. *a'Beckett, J.* (1907).

Mines Act 1897 (No. 1514), sec. 168—Mines Act 1904 (No. 1961), sec. 64—Mining company—Winding-up—Assets insufficient to satisfy liabilities—Miners' wages—" Costs of administration or otherwise "—Priority of payment.]—*See* MINING. *In re Egerton and Gordon Consolidated Gold Mines, No Liability*, (1908) V.L.R., 526 ; 30 A.L.T., 27 ; 14 A.L.R., 372.

Mines Act 1897 (No. 1514), sec. 168—Insolvency Act 1890 (No. 1102), sec. 115—Insolvency Act 1897 (No. 1513), sec. 79—

Companies Act 1890 (No. 1074), secs. 250, 303—Mining company—Assignment for benefit of creditors—Workmen's wages—Payment —Priority.]—*See* MINING. *In re Old Jubilee Gold Mines, No Liability*, 34 A.L.T. (Supplement), 2 ; 18 A.L.R. (C.N.), 21.

Solicitor's lien—Solicitor ordered to deliver to liquidator documents of company, although company indebted to him for costs—Companies Act 1890 (No. 1074), sec. 274.]— *In re Mount Murphy Wolfram Co., No Liability*, 29 A.L.T. (Supplement), 19 ; 14 A.L.R. (C.N.), 6. *Judge Box.*

(f) Distribution of Surplus Assets.

Companies Act 1890 (No. 1074), secs. 124, 301—Mines Act 1890 (No. 1120), sec. 135— Winding-up mining company—Unclaimed dividends in liquidator's hands—Payment into Court—Costs.]—Order made for payment into Court of the amount of the unclaimed dividends in the hands of the liquidator of a mining company in the course of winding-up under Part II. of the *Companies Act* 1890 after deducting therefrom the costs of the liquidator. *In re The Lyell Tharsis Mining Co. No Liability*, 29 A.L.T. (Supplement), 5 ; 13 A.L.R. (C.N.), 27. *Judge Eagleson* (1907).

Company—Liquidation—Voluntary Liquidation—Surplus after discharge of liabilities—Distribution—Rights of " A " and " B " contributories—Interest on unpaid calls—Companies Act 1910 (No. 2293), sec. 194.]— Twenty years after a company had gone into voluntary liquidation, the liquidators, having in the meanwhile discharged its liabilities out of moneys obtained from calls made by them upon the " A " and " B " contributories and from the realization of the company's assets, had in hand a large surplus over and above what had been received from the " B " contributories : *Held*, that the " B " contributories were entitled to be repaid the whole of their contributions with six years' interest at four per cent. *Held*, further, that for the purpose of distributing amongst the " A " contributories the surplus then remaining, the amount paid in respect of any share by a " B " contributory should be deducted

from the total amount paid up on such share. *Held*, further, that where a contributory was the holder of shares in respect of which a dividend was payable out of such surplus and also of shares in respect of which calls remained unpaid, his right to receive such dividend was subject to the liquidator's right to deduct therefrom the amount of such unpaid calls. *Held*, further, that contributories should, in respect of any dividend payable to them, be debited with interest at the rate of six per cent. upon their unpaid calls (if any). *In re Metropolitan Bank Ltd.*, (1912) V.L.R., 449 ; 34 A.L.T., 138 ; 18 A.L.R., 463. *a' Beckett, J.*

Company—Liquidation—Surplus after discharge of liabilities—Distribution—Shareholder with fully paid up and contributing shares—Sequestration of estate—Composition with creditors—Release, effect of.]—A company went into voluntary liquidation and, after payment of the liabilities of the company out of the moneys obtained from calls upon the " A " and " B " contributories and from the realization of the assets of the company, there remained a large surplus in the hands of the liquidators. At the time the company went into liquidation, one of the shareholders owned some fully paid up shares and other shares partly paid up ; subsequently, before the call was made, his estate was sequestrated —the liquidators proving in the insolvency for the amount of the call ; his creditors accepted a composition, and he was released from his debts, and gave up by transfer (which was in the hands of the liquidators) the shares, in consideration of the release from liability which he then obtained : Held, that he was entitled to a dividend on the fully paid up shares without any deduction being made in respect of the amount unpaid on the other shares. *In re Metropolitan Bank Limited (in Liquidation)*, (1912) V.L.R., 449 ; 34 A .L.T., 138 ; 18 A.L.R., 463. *a' Beckett, J.*

Companies Act 1890 (No. 1074), Part II.— Mining companies—Company in liquidation— Proposed plan of distribution of surplus— Distribution between holders of paid up and contributing shares—Power of shareholders to make and to amend rules—Amendment providing that all holders of shares whether paid up or contributing entitled to share in surplus in proportion to the number of shares held, declared to be valid, and not unfair to or in breach of the contract with certain of the holders of paid up shares who were original vendors to the company and had taken the purchase money partly in cash and partly in paid up shares.]— *In re Quartz Hill Gold Mining Company, No Liability,* 27 A.L.T., (Supplement), 13 ; 12 A.L.R. (C.N.), 11. *Judge Eagleson* (1906).

COMPLAINT.

See INFORMATION, JUSTICES OF THE PEACE.

COMPROMISE.

See CHARITY.

CONDITION.

See also, CONTRACT OR AGREEMENT.

County Court—Action on insurance policy —Arbitration a condition precedent to right of action—Stay of proceedings—Adjournment —Jurisdiction—County Court Act 1890 (No. 1078), sec. 71.]—*See* ARBITRATION, col. 51. *Borrett v. Norwich and London Accident Insurance Association,* 29 A.L.T. (Supplement), 1 ; 13 A.L.R. (C.N.), 22. *Judge Chomley* (1907).

Condition restrictive of use or sale of goods —Running with goods.]—*See* SALE OF GOODS. *National Phonograph Co. v. Menck,* L.R. [1911] A.C., 336 (P.C.) ; 17 A.L.R., 94.

CONFINEMENT EXPENSES.

See HUSBAND AND WIFE.

CONSIDERATION.

See CONTRACT OR AGREEMENT.

CONSTABLE.

See POLICE AND POLICE REGULATION ACT ; POLICE OFFENCES ACTS.

CONSPIRACY.

Conspiracy—Corporation—Liability to presentment on charge of conspiracy—Capacity to conspire.]—*See* CRIMINAL LAW. *R.* v. *Kellow,* (1912) V.L.R., 162 ; 33 A.L.T., 203 ; 18 A.L.R., 170. *Cussen, J.*

CONSTITUTIONAL LAW.

I.—GENERALLY.

(a) Crown Liability.

Relief against forfeiture for non-payment of rent—Crown, relief against—Settlement of Lands Act 1893 (No. 1311), secs. 5, 10—Lease by Board of Land and Works—Supreme Court Act 1890 (No. 1142), sec. 202.]—See LAND-LORD AND TENANT. *The King* v. *Dale*, [1906] V.L.R., 662; 28 A.L.T., 140; 12 A.L.R., 549.

Chose in action consisting of right against the Crown—Assignment—Petition of right by assignee—Crown Remedies and Liability Act 1890 (No. 1080), sec. 20]—See CROWN REME-DIES AND LIABILITY ACT. *The King* v. *Brown*, (1912) 14 C.L.R., 17; 18 A.L.R., 111.

Deposit receipt, security by way of—Contract to supply goods to Crown—Security for due performance of contract—Deposit receipt in name of servant of the Crown procured by contractor and delivered to such servant—Contractor's account with bank overdrawn—Contract duly performed—Whether amount of deposit receipt a debt due by Crown to contractor—Money had and received—Set-off of bank's claim against contractor, whether justifiable.]—See BANKER AND CUSTOMER, cols. 70, 71, 72. *The King* v. *Brown*, (1912) 14 C.L.R., 17; 18 A.L.R., 111.

Commonwealth Public Service Act 1902 (No. 5 of 1902), sec. 78 (1)—Salary not appropriated by Parliament—Whether public servant entitled to.]—See PUBLIC SERVICE. *Cousins* v. *The Commonwealth*, 3 C.L.R., 529; 12 A.L.R., 175.

Commonwealth Public Service Act 1902 (No. 5 of 1902), sec. 78—Public servant—Wrongful dismissal—Claim for damages—Money not voted by Parliament—Whether a defence.]—See PUBLIC SERVICE. *Williamson* v. *The Commonwealth*, (1907) 5 C.L.R., 174; 14 A.L.R., 1.

Action against Commonwealth—Right to discovery from Commonwealth—Judiciary Act 1903 (Commonwealth) No. 6), secs. 56, 64.]—See DISCOVERY. *Commonwealth* v. *Miller*, 10 C.L.R., 742; 16 A.L.R., 424.

(b) Legislative Power.

Subordinate legislature—Power in criminal matters, territorial limits of—"Quitting Natal," whether legislature may make it a criminal offence.]—Section 76 of Law No. 47 of the Colony of Natal provides :—"If any person who is adjudged insolvent or has his affairs liquidated by arrangement after the presentation of an insolvency petition by or against him or the commencement of the liquidation or within four months before such presentation or commencement quits Natal and takes with him . . . . any part of his property to the amount of £20 or upwards which ought by law to be divided amongst his creditors he shall (unless the jury is satisfied that he had no intent to defraud) be guilty of an offence punishable with imprisonment for a time not exceeding two years with or without hard labour." *Held*, that the law was not *ultra vires* of the legislature of Natal. *McKelvey* v. *Meagher*, 4 C.L.R., 265; 12 A.L.R., 483. H.C., *Griffith, C.J., Barton* and *O'Connor, JJ.* (1906).

Appeal—Supreme Court Act 1890 (No. 1142), sec. 231—Whether ultra vires the Parliament of Victoria.]—The Full Court refused to go into the question whether sec. 231 of the *Supreme Court Act* 1890 is *ultra vires* the Parliament of Victoria—the validity of that section having been assumed in a long series of cases. *In re* "*Maizo*" *and* "*Maizena*" *Trade Marks*; *Robert Harper & Co.* v. *National Starch Co.*, (1906) V.L.R., 246; 27 A.L.T., 168; 12 A.L.R., 164. F.C., *Holroyd, A.C.J., a'Beckett* and *Hodges, JJ.* (1906).

(c) Discretion of Governor in Council.

Discretion of Governor in Council—Prisoner under sentence—Remission of sentence—Mandamus.]—Mandamus will not lie to the Governor in Council of the State, and no Court has jurisdiction to review his discretion in the exercise of the prerogative of mercy. *Horwitz* v. *Connor*, (1908) 6 C.L.R., 38; 14 A.L.R., 342. H.C., *Griffith, C.J., Barton, O'Connor, Isaacs* and *Higgins, JJ.*

CONSTITUTIONAL LAW.

(d) State Boundaries.

Boundary of States—Letters patent creating province—Degree of longitude stated as boundary—Implied authority of executive to locate.]—By letters patent dated February 19, 1836, and made in exercise of powers given by 4 & 5 Will. IV., c. 95, the King in Council erected and established the province of South Australia (now the appellant State) and declared that its boundary on the east on which side it adjoined New South Wales should be the 141st degree of east longitude. Under an agreement between the Governments of New South Wales and South Australia the supposed position of that longitude was marked upon the ground for 123 miles north from the sea, and proclamations were issued in the two Colonies publishing the line so marked as the boundary. This marked line was afterwards extended under agreement between the two Governments as far as the river Murray. The Secretary of State for the Colonies approved of what had been done. The line so marked was subsequently found to be about 2¼ miles to the west of the true position of the 141st degree. The Colony of Victoria (now the respondent State) was created in 1850 out of part of New South Wales and so that on the west it adjoined South Australia as far north as the river Murray. The appellant State brought an action in the High Court of Australia claiming possession of the land between the boundary agreed and marked as above stated and the 141st degree of east longitude, and for ancillary relief. *Held*, that upon the true construction of the letters patent, it was contemplated that the 141st degree of east latitude should be ascertained and represented upon the surface of the earth, and that there was implied authority given to the executives of the two Colonies to do such acts as were necessary to that end ; that, upon the facts, the executives of the two Colonies had acted within that implied authority, and that the line agreed and marked became and was the boundary between the States ; and that the action was, accordingly, rightly dismissed. *State of South Australia v. State of Victoria*, (1914) A.C., 283. (Privy Council).

II.—COMMONWEALTH OF AUSTRALIA CONSTITUTION.

(a) Interpretation Generally.

Commonwealth of Australia Constitution Act 63 & 64 Vict. c. 12, The Constitution—Principles of interpretation.]—*See* COMMONWEALTH OF AUSTRALIA CONSTITUTION, col. 114. *Baxter v. Commissioners of Taxation; Flint v. Webb*, 4 C.L.R., 1087, 1178 ; 13 A.L.R., 313.

(b) Powers of Parliament.

(1) Validity of Legislation Generally.

Powers of Commonwealth Parliament—Validity of legislation—Part of Act invalid—Whether whole Act invalid—Test for determining whether invalid part severable.]—*See* COMMONWEALTH OF AUSTRALIA CONSTITUTION, cols. 114, 115. *The King and the Commonwealth Court of Conciliation and Arbitration and the President thereof and the Boot Trade Employes Federation ; Ex parte Whybrow & Co.*, (1910) 11 C.L.R., 1 ; 16 A.L.R., 373.

The Constitution (63 & 64 Vict. c. 12), sec. 51—Legislative powers of Commonwealth—Validity of Act, principles to be observed in determining question of—Form of Act—Substance of Act—Direct and indirect effect—Motive and object of legislation—Interference with domestic affairs of State—Taxation—Excise Tariff 1906 (No. 16 of 1906).]—*See* COMMONWEALTH OF AUSTRALIA CONSTITUTION, cols. 115, 116. *The King v. Barger; The Commonwealth v. McKay*, (1908) 6 C.L.R., 41 ; 14 A.L.R.. 374.

(2) Taxation and Tax Bills.

The Constitution (63 & 64 Vict. c. 12), secs. 51 (II.), 99—Taxation, power of Commonwealth with respect to—Discrimination between States or parts of States—Preference to one State over another State—Excise Tariff 1906 (No. 16 of 1906), whether ultra vires.]—*See* COMMONWEALTH OF AUSTRALIA CONSTITUTION, cols. 116, 117. *The King v. Barger; The Commonwealth v. McKay*, (1908) 6 C.L.R., 41 ; 14 A.L.R., 374.

The Constitution (63 & 64 Vict. c. 12), sec. 51 (ii.)—Legislative powers of the Com-

monwealth—Taxation—Regulative legislation, what is—Excise Tariff 1906 (No. 16 of 1906), whether a taxing or a regulative Act.]—*See* COMMONWEALTH OF AUSTRALIA CONSTITUTION, cols. 117, 118. *The King* v. *Barger; The Commonwealth* v. *McKay*, (1908) 6 C.L.R., 41; 14 A.L.R., 374.

The Constitution (63 & 64 Vict. c. 12), sec. 55—Laws imposing taxation—To deal only with imposition of taxation— Excise Tariff 1906 (No. 16 of 1909), whether it deals with matters other than excise duty.]—*See* COMMONWEALTH OF AUSTRALIA CONSTITUTION col. 118. *The King* v. *Barger; The Commonwealth* v. *McKay*, (1908) 6 C.L.R., 41; 14 A.L.R., 374.

Customs Tariff 1908 (No. 7 of 1908), secs. 3, 4, 5, 7—Duties collected under proposed tariff—Proposed tariff different from tariff enacted by Parliament—Right to recover money back—" Duties of Customs collected pursuant to any Tariff or Tariff alteration " —Commonwealth Constitution, sec. 55—Imposing taxation.]—*See* CUSTOMS. *Sargood Bros.* v. *The Commonwealth*, (1910) 11 C.L.R., 258; 16 A.L.R., 483.

(3) Corporations.

Commonwealth of Australia Constitution (63 & 64 Vict. c. 12), sec. 51 (xx.)—Power to make laws with respect to " foreign corporations and trading and financial corporations formed within the limits of the Commonwealth" —Limits of power.]—*See* COMMONWEALTH OF AUSTRALIA CONSTITUTION, cols. 118, 119. *Huddart Parker & Co. Proprietary Ltd.* v. *Moorehead; Appleton* v. *Moorehead*, (1909) 8 C.L.R., 330; 15 A.L.R., 241.

Commonwealth of Australia Constitution (63 & 64 Vict. c. 12), sec. 51 (i.) (xx.)—Interference with internal trade and commerce— Power to make laws with respect to " foreign corporations, and trading or financial corporations formed within the limits of the Commonwealth"—Limits of power—Control of corporations, their status, capacities and contracts.]—*See* COMMONWEALTH OF AUSTRALIA CONSTITUTION, cols. 119, 120. *Huddart*

Parker & Co. Proprietary Ltd. v. *Moorehead; Appleton* v. *Moorehead*, (1909) 8 C.L.R., 331; 15 A.L.R., 241.

Commonwealth of Australia Constitution (63 & 64 Vict. c. 12), sec. 51 (xx.)—Power to make laws with respect to " foreign corporations, and trading and financial corporations formed within the limits of the Commonwealth "—Australian Industries Preservation Act 1906 (No. 9 of 1906), secs. 5 and 8, whether intra vires.]—*See* COMMONWEALTH OF AUSTRALIA CONSTITUTION, col. 120. *Huddart Parker & Co. Proprietary Ltd.* v. *Moorehead; Appleton* v. *Moorehead*, (1909) 8 C.L.R., 330; 15 A.L.R., 241.

(4) Immigration and Emigration.

The Constitution (63 & 64 Vict. c. 12), sec. 51 (xxvii.)—" Immigrant," meaning of— Member of Australian community returning from abroad.]—*See* COMMONWEALTH OF AUSTRALIA CONSTITUTION, col. 120. *Potter* v. *Minahan*, (1908) 7 C.L.R., 277; 14 A.L.R., 635.

Immigration Restriction Act 1901 (No. 17 of 1901)—Prohibited immigrant—Application of Act to Australian citizen—Commonwealth Constitution, sec. 51.]—*See* COMMONWEALTH OF AUSTRALIA CONSTITUTION, col. 120, 121. *Attorney-General of the Commonwealth* v. *Ah Sheung*, (1907) 4 C.L.R., 949.

(5) External Affairs.

Commonwealth of Australia Constitution Act (63 & 64 Vict. c. 12)—The Constitution, sec. 51 (xxix.)—External affairs—Surrender of fugitive offenders—Power of Commonwealth Parliament with regard to.]—*See* COMMONWEALTH OF AUSTRALIA CONSTITUTION, col. 121. *McKelvey* v. *Meagher*, 4 C.L.R., 265; 12 A.L.R., 483.

(6) Conciliation and Arbitration.

Commonwealth of Australia Constitution Act (63 & 64 Vict. c. 12)—The Constitution, sec. 51 (xxxv.)—Arbitration in regard to industrial disputes—Extent of power of Commonwealth.]—*See* COMMONWEALTH OF AUSTRALIA CONSTITUTION, col. 121. *The King and Commonwealth Court of Conciliation and*

Arbitration and the President thereof, and the Boot Trade Employes Federation ; *Ex parte Whybrow & Co.*, (1910) 11 C.L.R., 1 ; 16 A.L.R., 373.

Commonwealth Conciliation and Arbitration Act 1904 (No. 13 of 1904), secs. 4, 55, 58, 60, 65, 73—Registration of association—Validity of legislation—Association of employes in one State—Incorporation of organization—The Constitution (63 & 64 Vict. c. 12), sec. 51 (xxxv.) (xxxix.).]—See COMMONWEALTH OF AUSTRALIA CONSTITUTION, cols. 121, 122. *Jumbunna Coal Mine N. L.* v. *Victorian Coal Miners' Association*, (1908) 6 C.L.R., 309 ; 14 A.L.R., 701.

Commonwealth of Australia Constitution Act (63 & 64 Vict. c. 12),—The Constitution sec. 51 (xxxv.)—Conciliation and arbitration for the prevention and settlement of industrial disputes—Commonwealth Conciliation and Arbitration Act 1904 (No. 13 of 1904)—Validity.]—See COMMONWEALTH OF AUSTRALIA CONSTUTITION, col. 122. *The King and the Commonwealth Court of Conciliation and Arbitration and the President thereof and the Boot Trade Employes Federation* ; *Ex parte Whybrow & Co.*, (1910) 11 C.L.R., 1 ; 16 A.L.R., 373.

" Conciliation and arbitration for the prevention and settlement of industrial disputes "—Powers of the Commonwealth—Common rule—The Constitution (63 & 64 Vict. c. 12), sec. 51 (xxxv.), (xxxix.)—Commonwealth Conciliation and Arbitration Act (No. 13 of 1904), secs. 19, 38 (f), (g) ; Commonwealth Conciliation and Arbitration Act (No. 7 of 1910).]—*See* COMMONWEALTH OF AUSTRALIA CONSTITUTION col. 122. *Australian Boot Trade Employees Federation* v. *Whybrow*, (1910) 11 C.L.R., 311 ; 16 A.L.R., 513.

Operation of the Constitution and laws of the Commonwealth—Commonwealth Conciliation and Arbitration Act 1904 (No. 13 of 1904)—Jurisdiction of Court of Conciliation and Arbitration—Industrial dispute—" Ship whose first port of clearance and whose port of destination are in the Commonwealth "—Commonwealth of Australia Constitution Act (63 & 64 Vict. c. 12), sec. V.]—See COMMON-WEALTH OF AUSTRALIA CONSTITUTION, col. 123. *Merchant Service Guild of Australasia* v. *Archibald Currie & Co.*, (1908) 5 C.L.R., 737 ; 14 A.L.R., 438.

The Constitution (63 & 64 Vict. c. 12), sec. 51 (xxxv.)—" Industrial dispute "—" Extending beyond the limits of any one State."]—See COMMONWEALTH OF AUSTRALIA CONSTITUTION, col. 123. *Jumbunna Coal Mine N.L.* v. *Victorian Coal Miners' Association*, (1908) 6 C.L.R., 309 ; 14 A.L.R., 701.

Commonwealth Constitution, sec. 51 (xxxv.)—Industrial dispute extending beyond the limits of any one State.]—See COMMONWEALTH OF AUSTRALIA CONSTITUTION, cols. 123, 124. *The King and the Commonwealth Conciliation and Arbitration Court and the President thereof and the Boot Trade Employees Federation* ; *Ex parte Whybrow & Co.*, (1910) 11 C.L.R., 1 ; 16 A.L.R., 373.

Commonwealth Conciliation and Arbitration Act 1904 (No. 13 of 1904)—Industrial dispute, what is—Commonwealth Constitution, sec. 51 (xxxv.).]—See EMPLOYER AND EMPLOYEE. *The King and the Commonwealth Court of Conciliation and Arbitration and the President thereof, and the Boot Trade Employees Federation* ; *Ex parte Whybrow*, (1910) 11 C.L.R., 1 ; 16 A.L.R., 373.

Commonwealth Conciliation and Arbitration Act 1904 (No. 13 of 1904),—Whether ultra vires of Parliament.]—See COMMONWEALTH OF AUSTRALIA CONSTITUTION, col. 124. *The King and the Commonwealth Court of Conciliation and Arbitration and the President thereof and the Boot Trade Employees Federation* ; *Ex parte Whybrow & Co.*, (1910) 11 C.L.R., 1 ; 16 A.L.R., 373.

Commonwealth Conciliation and Arbitration Act 1904 (No. 13 of 1904)—Claims in regard to matters in dispute—Joinder of claims in regard to matters not in dispute—Jurisdiction of Court of Conciliation and Arbitration—The Commonwealth Constitution, sec. 51 (xxxv.).]—See EMPLOYER AND EMPLOYEE, col. 124. *The King and the Commonwealth Court of Conciliation and Arbitra-*

tion and the President thereof and the Boot Trade Employees Federation ; *Ex parte Whybrow & Co.*, (1910) 11 C.L.R., 1 ; 16 A.L.R., 373.

Commonwealth Court of Conciliation and Arbitration—Award, validity of—Higher rate awarded than that demanded by claimants— Demand that wage of apprentice be based on experience—Wage awarded based on age and experience— Industrial dispute.]— *See* EM- PLOYER AND EMPLOYEE. *The King and the Commonwealth Court of Conciliation and Arbitration and the President thereof and the Boot Trade Employees Federation* ; *Ex parte Whybrow & Co.*, (1910) 11 C.L.R., 1 ; 16 A.L.R., 373.

(7) Elections.

Parliamentary election—Political article in newspaper during election — Signature of author—Validity of Commonwealth legislation —The Constitution (63 & 64 Vict. c. 12), secs. 10, 51 (xxxvi.)—Commonwealth Elec- toral Act 1902-1911 (No. 19 of 1902—No. 17 of 1911), sec. 181 A.A.]—*See* COMMON- WEALTH OF AUSTRALIA CONSTITUTION, col. 125. *Smith v. Oldham*, (1912) 15 C.L.R., 355 : 18 A.L.R., 448.

(c) The Judicature.

(1) Judicial Power Generally.

Commonwealth of Australia Constitution (63 & 64 Vict. c. 12), sec. 71—" Judicial power."]—*See* COMMONWEALTH OF AUS- TRALIA CONSTITUTION, col. 125. *Huddart Parker v. Moorehead* ; *Appleton v. Moore- head*, (1909) 8 C.L.R., 330 : 15 A.L.R., 241.

Commonwealth legislation, validity of— Trade and Commerce — Anti-trust laws— Inquiry by Comptroller-General of Customs —Compulsory answers—Judicial power of Commonwealth — Trial by jury — Inter-State Commission—Australian Industries Preserva- tion Act 1906 (No. 9 of 1906) amended by Australian Industries Preservation Act 1907 (No. 5 of 1908), sec. 15b—The Constitu- tion (63 & 64 Vict. c. 12), secs. 51 (i.) xx.), 71, 80, 101.]—*See* COMMONWEALTH OF AUSTRALIA CONSTITUTION, col. 126. *Huddart*

Parker & Co. Proprietary Ltd. v. Moore- head ; *Appleton v. Moorehead*, (1909) 8 C.L.R., 330 ; 15 A.L.R., 241.

(2) Original Jurisdiction.

The Constitution (63 & 64 Vict. c. 12), sec. 75—Original jurisdiction of High Court —" Matters " between States, what are— Dispute as to boundary between two States— Boundary fixed by Act of Imperial Parlia- ment.]—*See* COMMONWEALTH OF AUSTRALIA CONSTITUTION, cols. 126, 127. *State of South Australia v. State of Victoria*, (1911) 12 C.L.R., 667 ; 17 A.L.R., 206.

(3) Appellate Jurisdiction.

Judiciary Act 1903 (No. 6 of 1903), sec. 39 —Federal jurisdiction of State Courts—Valid- ity of grant of—Right of appeal to High Court —Prerogative right of appeal to Privy Council, whether affected—Commonwealth of Aus- tralia Constitution Act (63 & 64 Vict. c. 12)— The Constitution, secs. 71, 77—Colonial Laws Validity Act (28 & 29 Vict. c. 63).]—*See* COM- MONWEALTH OF AUSTRALIA CONSTITUTION col. 127. *Baxter v. Commissioners of Taxa- tion* ; *Flint v. Webb*, 4 C.L.R., 1087, 1178 : 13 A.L.R., 313.

The Constitution (63 & 64 Vict. c. 12), sec. 73—Appellate jurisdiction of High Court— Court of Conciliation and Arbitration—Com- monwealth Conciliation and Arbitration Act 1904 (No. 13 of 1904), sec. 31.]—*See* COMMON- WEALTH OF AUSTRALIA CONSTITUTION, col. 127. *Jumbunna Coal Mine No Liability v. Victorian Coal Miners' Association*, (1908) 6 C.L.R., 309 ; 14 A.L.R., 701.

Commonwealth of Australia Constitution Act (63 & 64 Vict. c. 12)—The Constitution, secs. 71, 73, 75 (v.)—Commonwealth Concilia- tion and Arbitration Act 1904 (No. 13 of 1904), sec. 31—Judiciary Act 1903 (No. 6 of 1903), secs. 30, 33 (b), 38—Prohibition—Juris- diction of High Court to issue to Common- wealth Court of Conciliation and Arbitration— Whether prohibition original or appellate jurisdiction.]—*See* COMMONWEALTH OF AUS- TRALIA CONSTITUTION, col. 128. *The King and the Commonwealth Court of Conciliation and Arbitration and the President thereof and the*

Boot Trade Employees' Federation; Ex parte Whybrow & Co., (1910) 11 C.L.R., 1; 16 A.L.R., 373.

Federal jurisdiction—Exercise of, what is—Two questions decided, one Federal and the other not—Each decision sufficient to sustain judgment—Court of Petty Sessions—Appeal to High Court, whether it lies—Judiciary Act 1903 (No. 6), sec. 39 (2) (d)—Commonwealth of Australia Constitution Act (63 & 64 Vict. c. 12),—The Constitution, sec. 77.]—*See* APPEAL, col. 20. *Miller* v. *Haweis*, (1907) 5 C.L.R., 89; 13 A.L.R., 583.

Court of Petty Sessions—Federal jurisdiction—Exercise of, what is—Commonwealth of Australia Constitution, secs. 31, 76—Constitution Act Amendment Act 1890 (No. 1075), sec. 282—Judiciary Act 1903 (No. 6), sec. 39 (2) (d)—Question decided involving interpretation of sec. 31 of Constitution—Other question decided involving interpretation of Commonwealth Electoral Act 1902 (No. 19)—Appeal to High Court, whether it lies.]—*See* COMMONWEALTH OF AUSTRALIA CONSTITUTION, col. 129. *Miller* v. *Haweis*, (1907) 5 C.L.R., 89; 13 A.L.R., 583.

Appeal—Order on habeas corpus—Jurisdiction of High Court.]—*See* APPEAL, col. 22. *Attorney-General of the Commonwealth* v. *Ah Sheung*, (1907) 4 C.L.R., 949.

High Court—Practice—Declaratory judgment—Abstract question of law in decision of which rights of parties are not involved—Whether High Court will decide—Rules of High Court 1903, Part I., Order III., r. 1—Trade Marks Act 1905 (No. 20), Part VII., constitutionality of.]—*See* HIGH COURT (PROCEDURE). *Bruce* v. *Commonwealth Trade Marks Label Association*, (1907) 4 C.L.R., 1569; 13 A.L.R., 582.

Practice—Appeal to High Court—Special leave—Decision of inferior Court of State—Right of appeal to Supreme Court—Judiciary Act 1903 (No. 6 of 1903), sec. 35—The Constitution (63 & 64 Vict. c. 12), sec. 73.]—*See* APPEAL, col. 23. *Kamarooka Gold Mining Co.* v. *Kerr*, (1908) 6 C.L.R., 255.

(4) Appeal to King in Council.

Commonwealth of Australia Constitution Act (63 & 64 Vict. c. 12)—The Constitution, sec. 74—Interpretation, principles of—History of Constitution, whether it may be looked at—Appeal to Privy Council.]—*See* COMMONWEALTH OF AUSTRALIA CONSTITUTION, col. 130. *Baxter* v. *Commissioners of Taxation; Flint* v. *Webb*, 4 C.L.R., 1087, 1178; 13 A.L.R., 313.

Commonwealth of Australia Constitution Act (63 & 64 Vict. c. 12)—The Constitution, sec. 74—Questions as to the limits inter se of constitutional powers of Commonwealth and State—Conflicting decisions of Privy Council and High Court—Whether High Court final arbiter upon such questions—9 Geo. IV. c. 83; 7 & 8 Vict. c. 69, and Orders in Council thereunder.]—*See* COMMONWEALTH OF AUSTRALIA CONSTITUTION, cols. 130, 131. *Baxter* v. *Commissioners of Taxation; Flint* v. *Webb*, 4 C.L.R., 1087, 1178; 13 A.L.R., 313.

Commonwealth of Australia Constitution Act (63 & 64 Vict. c. 12)—The Constitution, sec. 74—Appeal to King in Council—Certificate of High Court—Reasons for granting, sufficiency of—Conflicting decisions of Privy Council and High Court.]—*See* COMMONWEALTH OF AUSTRALIA CONSTITUTION, col. 131. *Baxter* v. *Commissioners of Taxation; Flint* v. *Webb*, 4 C.L.R., 1087, 1178; 13 A.L.R., 313.

Commonwealth of Australia Constitution Act (63 & 64 Vict. c. 12)—The Constitution, sec. 74—" Decision . . . upon any question," meaning of—Appeal to Privy Council.] —*See* COMMONWEALTH OF AUSTRALIA CONSTITUTION, col. 131. *Baxter* v. *Commissioners of Taxation; Flint* v. *Webb*, 4 C.L.R., 1087, 1178; 13 A.L.R., 313.

Commonwealth of Australia Constitution Act (63 & 64 Vict. c. 12)—The Constitution, secs. 74, 109—Question as to limits inter se of powers of Commonwealth and State, nature of—How distinguished from question of inconsistency between law of State and law of Commonwealth.]—*See* COMMONWEALTH OF AUSTRALIA CONSTITUTION, cols. 131, 132.

Baxter v. *Commissioners of Taxation* ; *Flint* v. *Webb*, 4 C.L.R., 1087, 1178 ; 13 A.L.R., 313.

Commonwealth of Australia Constitution Act (63 & 64 Vict. c. 12)—The Constitution, secs. 73, 74, 76, 77—Question as to limits inter se of constitutional powers of Commonwealth and State what is—Question raised by defence whether State tax on Federal salary an interference with powers of Commonwealth—Exercise of Federal jurisdiction by Court of Petty Sessions—Appeal to High Court, competency of—Judiciary Act 1903 (Commonwealth) (No. 6 of 1903), sec. 39.]—*See* COMMONWEALTH OF AUSTRALIA CONSTITUTION cols. 132, 133. *Baxter* v. *Commissioners of Taxation* ; *Flint* v. *Webb*, 4 C.L.R., 1087, 1178 ; 13 A.L.R., 313.

Commonwealth of Australia Constitution (63 & 64 Vict. c. 12)—Power of Victorian Legislature (18 & 19 Vict. c. 55)—Income tax—Right of appeal from Supreme Court to Privy Council — Whether Commonwealth Parliament may take away.]—*See* APPEAL. col. 14. *Webb* v. *Outrim*, (1907) A.C., 81 ; 13 A.L.R., (C.N.), 1.

(d) The Executive Government ; Finance and Trade.

Commonwealth of Australia Constitution (62 & 63 Vict. c. 12), secs. 51 (1) (xx.) (xxxix.), 61, 101—Inter-State Commission—Execution and maintenance of provisions of Constitution relating to trade and commerce and of all laws made thereunder.]—*See* COMMONWEALTH OF AUSTRALIA CONSTITUTION, cols. 133, 134. *Huddart Parker & Co. Proprietary Ltd.* v. *Moorehead* ; *Appleton* v. *Moorehead*, (1909) 8 C.L.R., 330 ; 15 A.L.R., 241. H.C., *Griffith, C.J., Barton O'Connor, Isaacs* and *Higgins, JJ.*

Immigration Restriction Acts 1901-1905— " Immigrants " and " prohibited immigrants," who are—Whether administrative officers of the Commonwealth may determine such questions.]—For a discussion of the question whether the officers administering the Immigration Restriction Acts are the final arbiters as to who are, and who are not,

" immigrants " or " prohibited immigrants," see *Ah Sheung* v. *Lindberg*, (1906) V.L.R., 323 ; 27 A.L.T., 189 ; *sub nom.*, *Rex* v. *Ah Sheung*, 12 A.L.R., 190. *Cussen, J.* (1906).

Officer of Department transferred to Commonwealth—Whether Commonwealth Parliament may reduce salary—" Existing rights "—Public Service Act 1900 (No. 1721), sec. 19—Commonwealth Constitution, sec. 84.]—*See* COMMONWEALTH OF AUSTRALIA CONSTITUTION, col. 134. *Cousins* v. *The Commonwealth*, 3 C.L.R., 529 ; 12 A.L.R., 175.

Commonwealth Public Service Act 1902 (No. 5 of 1902), secs. 8, 51, 60, 80—Officer of department transferred to Commonwealth—Whether salary altered—" Existing rights "—Commonwealth Constitution, sec. 84.]—*See* COMMONWEALTH OF AUSTRALIA CONSTITUTION, cols. 134, 135. *Cousins* v. *The Commonwealth*, 3 C.L.R., 529 ; 12 A.L.R., 175.

Public Service Act 1900 (No. 1721), sec. 19—Post and Telegraph Department—Transfer to Commonwealth—" Any Australian colony."]—*See* PUBLIC SERVICE. *Curley* v. *The King*, (1906) V.L.R., 633 ; 28 A.L.T., 12 ; 12 A.L.R., 555.

Public Service Act 1900 (No. 1721), sec. 19—Post and Telegraph Department—Transfer to Commonwealth— " Officers of corresponding position " —Identity of duties.]—*See* PUBLIC SERVICE. *Curley* v. *The King*, (1906) V.L.R., 633 ; 28 A.L.T., 12 ; 12 A.L.R., 555.

(e) The States.

(1) Reserved Powers of State Parliament.

Commonwealth of Australia Constitution (62 & 63 Vict. c. 12)—Federal nature of Constitution—Interference with domestic affairs of State—Implied prohibition.]—*See* COMMONWEALTH OF AUSTRALIA CONSTITUTION, col. 135. *Huddart Parker & Co. Proprietary Ltd.* v. *Moorehead* ; *Appleton* v. *Moorehead*, (1909) 8 C.L.R., 330 ; 15 A.L.R., 241.

(2) Inconsistency of Laws.

Rendition of Fugitive offenders—Law of Victoria—Effect of establishment of the

Commonwealth—Commonwealth of Australia Constitution Act (63 & 64 Vict. c. 12)—The Constitution, secs. 108, 109—Fugitive Offenders Act 1881 (44 & 45 Vict. c. 69).]—*See* COMMONWEALTH OF AUSTRALIA CONSTITUTION, cols 135, 136. *McKelvey* v. *Meagher*, 4 C.L.R., 265; 12 A.L.R., 483.

Fugitive Offenders Act 1881 (44 & 45 Vict. c. 69)—Commonwealth of Australia Constitution Act (63 & 64 Vict. c. 12)—Authority of State of Victoria with regard to fugitive offenders—How far affected by establishment of Commonwealth.]—*See* COMMONWEALTH OF AUSTRALIA CONSTITUTION, col. 136. *McKelvey* v. *Meagher*, 4 C.L.R., 265; 12 A.L.R., 483.

Conciliation and arbitration— Commonwealth Court—Jurisdiction—Award inconsistent with determination of Wages Board—The Constitution, sec. 51 (xxxv.)]—*See* COMMONWEALTH OF AUSTRALIA CONSTITUTION, col. 136. *Australian Boot Trade Employees Federation* v. *Whybrow & Co.*, [1910] 10 C.L.R., 266; 16 A.L.R., 185.

Factories and Shops Act 1909 (No. 2241), sec. 39—No person compellable to pay more than the minimum wage unless he contract so to do—Jurisdiction of Commonwealth Court of Conciliation and Arbitration—How far affected by State legislation.]—*See* COMMONWEALTH OF AUSTRALIA CONSTITUTION, cols. 137, 138. *Australian Boot Trade Employees Federation* v. *Whybrow & Co.*, [1910] 10 C.L.R., 266; 16 A.L.R., 185.

(3) Interference with Instruments of Government.

Commonwealth of Australia Constitution Act (63 & 64 Vict. c. 12)—The Constitution—Doctrine of implied prohibition of interference with Commonwealth instrumentalities — Whether implied in Constitution.]—*See* COMMONWEALTH OF AUSTRALIA CONSTITUTION col. 137. *Baxter* v. *Commissioners of Taxation*; *Flint* v. *Webb*, 4 C.L.R., 1087, 1178; 13 A.L.R., 313.

Commonwealth of Australia Constitution (63 & 64 Vict. c. 12)—Income of Federal officer—Whether liable to income tax imposed by State—Power of State Legislature—Whether restricted by Commonwealth Constitution.]—*See* COMMONWEALTH OF AUSTRALIA CONSTITUTION, cols. 137, 138. *Webb* v. *Outtrim*, (1907) A.C., 81; 13 A.L.R. (C.N.), 1.

Commonwealth of Australia Constitution Act (63 & 64 Vict. c. 12)—Interference by State with legislative or executive authority of Commonwealth —Implied prohibition —Income Tax Acts, validity of.]—*See* COMMONWEALTH OF AUSTRALIA CONSTITUTION, col. 138. *Baxter* v. *Commissioners of Taxation*; *Flint* v. *Webb*, 4 C.L.R., 1087, 1178; 13 A.L.R., 313 (1907).

Commonwealth of Australia Constitution (63 & 64 Vict. c. 12)—Power of Parliament— Federal nature of Constitution—Interference with domestic affairs of State—Implied prohibition.]—*See* COMMONWEALTH OF AUSTRALIA CONSTITUTION, col. 138. *Huddart Parker & Co. Proprietary Ltd.* v. *Moorehead*; *Appleton* v. *Moorehead*, (1909) 8 C.L.R., 330; 15 A.L.R., 241.

Instrumentality of State Government, what is—Municipal corporation engaging in trading enterprise.]—*See* COMMONWEALTH OF AUSTRALIA CONSTITUTION, col. 139. *Federated Engine-Drivers and Firemen's Association of Australasia* v. *Broken Hill Proprietary Co. Ltd.*, (1911) 12 C.L.R., 398; 17 A.L.R., 285.

(4) Legislation in respect of Religion.

Defence—Compulsory military training— Religious objection to bear arms—Validity of Act—Exemption—Excuse—Defence Act 1903-1910 (No. 12 of 1904—No. 37 of 1910), ss. 61, 125, 135, 138, 143—The Constitution (63 & 64 Vict. c. 12), sec. 116.]—*See* COMMONWEALTH OF AUSTRALIA CONSTITUTION, col. 139. *Krygger* v. *Williams*, (1912) 15 C.L.R., 366; 18 A.L.R., 518.

(5) The State Courts.

Judgment of High Court on appeal from Supreme Court—Duty of Supreme Court to execute—Judiciary Act 1903 (No. 6 of 1903), sec. 37, whether ultra vires—The Constitution, sec. 51 (xxxix.)—Commonwealth of Australia Constitution Act (63 & 64 Vict. c. 12), sec. 5.]—*See* Appeal, col. 30. *Bayne* v. *Blake*, (1908) 5 C.L.R., 497 ; 14 A.L.R., 103.

Judgment of High Court on appeal from Supreme Court—Judgment remitted to Supreme Court for execution—Officer of Supreme Court—Whether subject to control of High Court.]— *See* Appeal, col. 31. *Bayne* v. *Blake*, (1908) 5 C.L.R., 497 ; 14 A.L.R., 103.

Judgment of High Court on appeal from Supreme Court—Judgment remitted to Supreme Court—Stay of proceedings, jurisdiction of Supreme Court to order.]—*See* Appeal, cols. 31, 32. *Bayne* v. *Blake*, (1908) 5 C.L.R., 497 ; 14 A.L.R., 103.

Patent, application for—Opposition—State Patents Act—Transfer of administration to Commonwealth pending proceedings—Appeal to State Supreme Court—Jurisdiction—Patents Act 1890 (No. 1123), sec. 33—Patents Act (No. 21 of 1903).]—*See* Appeal, cols. 33, 34. *In re McLeod's Patent* ; *Burton* v. *McLeod*, (1906) V.L.R., 483 ; 12 A.L.R., 335.

Supreme Court—Jurisdiction—Habeas corpus—Applicant held under restraint under authority of Commonwealth—Immigration Restriction Act 1905 (No. 17), sec. 14 (13b)—Judiciary Act 1903 (No. 6), Part VI.]—*See* Habeas Corpus. *Ah Sheung* v. *Lindberg*, (1906) V.L.R., 323 ; 27 A.L.T., 189 ; *sub nom.*, *Rex* v. *Ah Sheung*, 12 A.L.R., 190.

CONTEMPT.

I.—Criminal Contempt.

Contempt of Court—Jurisdiction of Supreme Court—Criminal charge—Publication of matters tending to prevent fair trial—Publication before committal for trial—Extent to which publication in a newspaper is lawful.]—When a person has been arrested and charged on information with an offence in respect of which Justices may commit him for trial in the Supreme Court, the publication after his arrest and before he has been so committed, of matter tending to prejudice his fair trial in the Supreme Court is a contempt of the Supreme Court which that Court has jurisdiction to punish. A publication, which on a consideration of the whole matter published, tends to prejudice and bias the public mind, either on one side or the other, and so to endanger the fair trial of an accused person, is unlawful and contempt of Court. The publication in respect of a pending criminal charge of extrinsic ascertained facts to which any eye-witness could bear testimony, such as in the case of a charge of murder, the finding of a body and its condition, the place where it was found, the persons by whom it was found the arrest of the person accused, is lawful. But the publication of alleged facts depending upon the testimony of some particular person, which may not be true and may or may not be admissible in a Court of justice, and the publication of comments on alleged facts are unlawful, if such publication is likely to interfere with the fair trial of the person charged. *Re Syme* ; *Ex parte Worthington*, 28 V.L.R., 552 ; 24 A.L.T., 123 ; 8 A.L.R., 239, overruled. *R.* v. *Parke*, (1903) 2 K.B., 432, and *R.* v. *Davies*, (1906) 1 K.B., 32, discussed. *Packer* v. *Peacock* ; *Burrell* v. *Peacock* ; *Smart* v. *Peacock*, (1912) 13 C.L.R., 577 ; 18 A.L.R., 70. H.C., *Griffith*, C.J. and *Barton*, J.

Contempt of Court—Criminal trial—Disagreement of jury—Remand of prisoner—Petition against second trial—Presentation to Attorney-General—Publication in newspapers.] On the trial of a prisoner charged with murder at the Supreme Court at Ballarat, the jury disagreed, and the prisoner was remanded for trial at the next sittings of the Court. While the prisoner was on remand his solicitor's managing clerk prepared a petition to the Attorney-General assisted in obtaining signatures to it of some of the jurymen, sent it to the Attorney-General, and supplied a copy of it to a Ballarat newspaper in which extracts from the petition were published, The petition which was signed by ten of the twelve jurymen, set out certain facts and matters which in their opinion justified an acquittal, and expressed their opinion that it was undesirable and unfair to put prisoner on his trial a second time on the same evidence. *Held,* a contempt as tending to defeat the due course of justice. *In re Mann* ; *In re King,* (1911) V.L.R., 171 ; 32 A.L.T., 156 ; 16 A.L.R., 598. *Cussen, J.*

Contempt of Court—Pending criminal trial —Petition to Attorney General in relation to— Whether a contempt.]—*Semble.*—Communications to the Attorney-General in relation to a pending criminal trial constitute contempt of Court if they contain deliberate mis-statements or threats, or otherwise display an intention to defeat the due course of justice. *In re Mann* ; *In re King,* (1911) V.L.R., 171 ; 32 A.L.T., 156 ; 16 A.L.R., 598. *Cussen, J.*

Contempt of Court—Attempt to influence juryman—Juryman not yet empanelled for trial of accused person in whose favour attempt is made.]—Where a juryman has been sworn to act at the sessions of the Court at which an accused person is to be tried, it is a contempt of Court to attempt to influence him in the verdict he would be called upon to give if he should be empanelled upon the trial of such accused person. *Ex parte Dunn* ; *Ex parte Aspinall,* (1906) V.L.R., 493 ; 28 A.L.T., 3 ; 12 A.L.R., 358. *Cussen, J.* (1906).

Contempt of Court—Nature of offence.]— The essence of contempt is action or inaction amounting to an interference with or obstruction to or having a tendency to interfere with or obstruct the due administration of justice. *Ex parte Dunn* ; *Ex parte Aspinall,* (1906) V.L.R., 493 ; 28 A.L.T., 3 ; 12 A.L.R., 358. *Cussen, J.* (1906).

Contempt of Court—Extent of powers of Court of General Sessions—Justices Act 1890 (No. 1105), sec. 184.]—The Court of General Sessions has no power to punish for contempt of Court except in the cases specified, and to the extent limited in the *Justices Act* 1890. *Ex parte Dunn* ; *Ex parte Aspinall,* (1906) V.L.R., 493 ; 28 A.L.T., 3 ; 12 A.L.R., 358. *Cussen, J.*

Inferior Court of Record—Power to commit for contempt.]—*Semble.*—Apart from statutory authority an inferior Court of Record can punish only for contempt committed in the

face of the Court. *Ex parte Dunn* ; *Ex parte Aspinall,* (1906) V.L.R., 493 ; 28 A.L.T., 3 ; 12 A.L.R., 358. *Cussen, J.*

General Sessions—Attempt to influence juryman—Contempt of Court—Power of Supreme Court to punish.]—*Semble.*—An attempt to influence a juror in the Court of General Sessions is a contempt punishable by the Supreme Court *brevi manu. Ex parte Dunn* ; *Ex parte Aspinall,* (1906) V.L.R. 493 ; 28 A.L.T., 3 ; 12 A.L.R., 358. *Cussen, J.*

Criminal contempt—Attempt to interfere with the course of justice—Nature of offence.] —*Semble.*—All attempts to interfere with the course of justice are criminal contempts and are misdemeanours. *Ex parte Dunn* ; *Ex parte Aspinall,* (1906) V.L.R., 493 ; 28 A.L.T., 3 ; 12 A.L.R., 358. *Cussen, J.*

Certiorari—Court of General Sessions— Person committed for contempt by warrant of Chairman—No jurisdiction — Whether act judicial or administrative—Party aggrieved— Whether entitled ex debito justitiae.]—*See* CERTIORARI, col. 95. *Ex parte Dunn* ; *Ex parte Aspinall,* (1906) V.L.R., 584 ; 28 A.L.T., 72 ; 12 A.L.R., 418.

Supreme Court Act 1890 (No. 1142), sec. 25—Criminal causes and matters—Proceedings by way of certiorari in case of criminal contempt.]—*See* CERTIORARI, cols. 95, 96. *Ex parte Dunn* ; *Ex parte Aspinall,* (1906) V.L.R., 584 ; 28 A.L.T., 72 ; 12 A.L.R., 418.

Contempt of Court—Nature of offence— Publications of statements concerning a Judge of the High Court.]—Statements made concerning a Judge of the High Court do not amount to contempt unless calculated to obstruct or interfere with the course of justice in the High Court or the due administration of the law by that Court. *Rex v. Nicholls,* (1911) 12 C.L.R., 287 ; 17 A.L.R., 309. H.C., *Griffith, C.J., Barton* and *O'Connor, JJ.*

Contempt of Court—Ecclesiastical privilege —Presbyterian Church of Victoria—Refusal of Presbytery Clerk to produce documents in civil action.]—Where the clerk of a Presbytery or Court of the Presbyterian Church of Victoria being served with a *subpoena duces tecum* to produce at the hearing of a civil action certain documents relevant to the issue which were in his possession as clerk to the Presbytery, refused to produce them on the ground that he had taken an oath to the Presbytery not to hand over any document in his possession as clerk without the Presbytery's authority, the Court ordered him to be imprisoned until he should purge his contempt, and adjourned the hearing of the case. *Semble*, that if, on the application for release of the clerk, the parties had asked the Court for the expenses occasioned by the clerk's conduct, he would not have purged his offence until he had paid such expenses. *Ronald* v. *Harper*, 15 A.L.R. (C.N.), 5. *Hodges, J.* (1909).

Insolvency Act 1890 (No. 1102), sec. 149—Insolvency Act 1897 (No. 1513), sec. 91—Insolvency Rules 1898 (Appendix of Forms, No. 64)—Contempt of Court—Certificate—Compulsory appearance—Refusal of insolvent to be sworn—Power of committal—Form of notice of motion to insolvent.]—*Semble.*—By virtue of sec. 91 of the *Insolvency Act* 1897, the Insolvency Court has power to compel an insolvent who has been required to appear before it under sec. 149 of the *Insolvency Act* 1890 to be sworn and give evidence, although such evidence might tend to render him liable to imprisonment. *In re Aarons*, 6 V.L.R. I.P. & M., 56 ; 2 A.L.T., 51, distinguished. The notice required under sec. 149 of the *Insolvency Act* 1890 requiring the insolvent to attend before the Court to have the question of the grant or refusal of his certificate dealt with, should direct attention to the fact that the insolvent may be punished or otherwise dealt with as if the certificate had been applied for by him. *In re Hickman*, 31 A.L.T. (Supplement) 10 ; 15 A.L.R. (C.N.), 21. *Judge Moule* (1909).

Justices Act 1890 (No. 1105), sec. 198—Contempt of Court—Wilful misbehaviour in a Court of Petty Sessions—Insulting language to a witness after case decided.]—*See* Jus-TICES OF THE PEACE. *Westcott* v. *Lord*, (1911) V.L.R., 452 ; 33 A.L.T., 54 ; 17 A.L.R., 433.

Justices Act 1890 (No. 1105), sec. 198—Contempt of Court—Misbehaviour not witnessed by Court itself—Formal adjournment of Court before occurrence of misbehaviour, effect of.]—*See* JUSTICES OF THE PEACE. *Westcott* v. *Lord*, (1911) V.L.R., 452 ; 33 A.L.T., 54 ; 17 A.L.R., 433.

II.—CONTEMPT IN PROCEDURE.

Order XLIV., r. 2 (Rules of 1884)—Order XLII., rr. 3, 6, 7, 17 (Rules of 1884)—Attachment—Disobedience of order to pay costs—Imprisonment of Fraudulent Debtors Act 1890 (No. 1100)—Whether power to attach for disobedience affected by.]—Notwithstanding the provisions of the *Imprisonment of Fraudulent Debtors Act* 1890, the Court has power to issue a writ of attachment for disobedience of its order to pay costs. *Re Sandilands ; Ex parte Browne*, 4 V.L.R. (L.), 318, followed. *Pope* v. *Peacock*, (1906) V.L.R., 667 ; 28 A.L.T., 63 ; 12 A.L.R., 440. *Hodges, J.*

Insolvency Act 1890 (No. 1102), secs. 76, 113—Execution of process or judgment, stay of—Debt due by insolvent to creditor—Trust moneys which are or ought to be in hands of trustee—Trustee ordered to pay moneys into Court—Disobedience of order—Attachment.]—Secs. 76 and 113 of the *Insolvency Act* 1890 are both directed to process for the enforcement of the payment of money as a debt due by the insolvent to a creditor. The insolvency of a person, who in the position of a trustee, has not accounted for money he once had and still ought to have, and who has been ordered to pay the money into Court, does not operate as a stay upon process of attachment against him for non-compliance with the order for payment into Court. *Peterson* v. *M'Lennan*, (1907) V.L.R., 94 ; 28 A.L.T., 135 ; 12 A.L.R., 577. *Cussen, J.*

Order XLII., rr. 3, 17 (Rules of 1884)—Order XLIV., r. 2—Order for payment of money—Execution under fi. fa.—Attachment for disobedience—Election of remedy, whether creditor bound by.]—A writ of attachment for disobedience of an order of the Court for payment of a sum of money may issue, although a writ of *fi. fa.* to enforce such payment has been issued previously. *In re Ball*, L.R. 8

C.P., 104, explained. *Pope* v. *Peacock*, (1906) V.L.R., 667; 28 A.L.T., 63; 12 A.L.R., 440. *Hodges, J.*

Order LII., r. 11—Order LXVII.* r. 9— Writ of attachment—Sheriff, refusal of to execute—Execution, how enforced—Whether mandamus may issue.]—Whether the Sheriff refuses to execute a writ of attachment he should be called upon to return the writ or bring in the body within a given time, and on his non-compliance application should be made under Order LII., r. 11, for his committal. A writ of mandamus will not issue, there being an alternative remedy. *Peterson* v. *M'Lennan*, (1907) V.L.R., 94; 28 A.L.T., 135; 12 A.L.R., 577. *Cussen, J.*

Attachment of person—Sheriff, duty of— Writ of attachment regular on its face.]— *Quaere*, whether under a writ of attachment the Sheriff is not bound, in every case in which the writ of attachment is regular on its face, to attach the person named in the writ, leaving it to the Court to say whether he ought to be discharged. *Peterson* v. *M'Lennan*, (1907) V.L.R., 94; 28 A.L.T., 135; 12 A.L.R., 577. *Cussen, J.*

"The County Court Rules 1891," rr. 333, 334, 335, 343—Judgment that defendant deliver certain chattel to plaintiff—Warrant of delivery under r. 343 returned unsatisfied— Warrant of attachment, issue of—Jurisdiction.]—*See* County Court. *Macrow & Sons Co. Proprietary Ltd.* v. *Davidson*, 27 A.L.T. (Supplement), 11; 12 A.L.R. (C.N.), 9.

Attachment—Contempt of Court—Mandamus—Statutory public duty—Minister of the Crown.]—*Semble*, there is no privilege in a Minister of the Crown entitling him to immunity from attachment for contempt of Court for his disobedience of a mandamus calling upon him to perform a statutory public duty. *The King* v. *Watt*; *Ex parte Slade*, (1912) V.L.R., 225; 33 A.L.T., 222; 18 A.L.R., 158. F.C., *Madden, C.J., Hodges* and *Cussen, JJ.*

Mandamus—Minister of Crown—Disobeienced of public Statute—Criminal contempt— Attachment—Privilege.]—Disobedience to a public Statute for disobedience to which no other penalty is provided by the Legislature, is an indictable misdemeanour; therefore, contempt in refusing to obey a writ of mandamus ordering compliance with the Statute, is of a criminal or quasi-criminal nature, and, *semble*, there is no privilege in a Minister of the Crown or in anyone else from attachment for such contempt. *The King* v. *Watt*; *Ex parte Slade*, (1912) V.L.R., 225; 33 A.L.T., 222; 18 A.L.R., 159. F.C., *Madden, C.J., Hodges* and *Cussen, JJ.*

CONTRACT OR AGREEMENT.

I.—Offer and Acceptance.

Contract, formation of—Offer—Acceptance —Offer to one person and acceptance by such person and others.]—Where an offer made by A. to B. is accepted by B. and C., or is accepted by B. as agent for B. and C., the acceptance is not an acceptance of the original offer, but is a new offer by B. and C. to make a contract on the terms of the original offer, and none of the parties are bound by the new offer until it is accepted. *Lang* v. *Morrison & Co. Ltd.*, (1911) 13 C.L.R., 1 ; 17 A.L.R., 530. H.C. *Griffith, C.J., Barton* and *O'Connor, JJ.*

Contract—Formation—Offer and Acceptance—Offer to sell goods—Goods sold to third party before acceptance of offer—Offer by post—Acceptance by post.]—A. made and sent by post a written offer to sell certain goods to B. A. also offered to sell the same goods to C. Both B. and C. wrote and posted acceptances of A.'s offer, C.'s acceptance being posted first. The two acceptances were received by A. by the same post. A. carried out his contract with C. In an action by B. against A. for breach of contract. *Held,* that there was a contract between A. and B. notwithstanding the prior contract between A. and C. *Dickinson* v. *Dodds,* 2 Ch. D., 463, distinguished. *Patterson* v. *Dolman,* (1908) V.L.R., 354 ; 29 A.L.R., 256 ; 14 A.L.R., 240. F.C. *a'Beckett, Hodges* and *Cussen, JJ.*

Sale of land—Contract—Offer—Acceptance —Formal contract to be signed.]—Plaintiff wrote to defendant—" As I am anxious to dispose of my property in Faraday Street, Carlton, I should be glad if you would favour me with an offer by return post." Four days afterwards the defendant wrote in reply—" In answer to yours I can offer you £1,450 for your property in Faraday Street, Carlton." On the same day the plaintiff wrote in reply—" I accept your offer of this day's date to purchase my properties, No. 156-162 Faraday Street, Carlton, for the sum of £1,450 cash, formal contract to be signed." *Held,* that the defendant's letter amounted to an offer, and that the plaintiff's second letter was in acceptance of that offer, the words " formal contract to be signed " not being a term of the assent, and therefore that there was a binding contract enforceable by the plaintiff. *Bruen* v. *Smith,* 30 A.L.T., 149 ; 14 A.L.R., 700. *a'Beckett, J.* (1908).

Contract—Breach in performance of— Steps taken by party not in default to minimise loss—Whether new contract to be inferred from—Waiver.]—Steps taken by a party not in default for the purpose of minimising loss should not of themselves be taken as evidencing any intention to enter into any new agreement or to waive any of his rights. *Alexander Cross & Sons Ltd.* v. *Hasell,* (1908) V.L.R., 194 ; 29 A.L.T., 179 ; 14 A.L.R., 44. *Cussen, J.*

Contract with company—Implied from Articles of Association and conduct of the parties.]—The Articles of Association of a company may express the terms upon which a person may contract with the company, and, if acted upon, an agreement between such person and the company on which either party may sue may be implied, partly from the articles and partly from the conduct of the parties. *Glass* v. *Pioneer Rubber Works of Australia Ltd.* (1906) V.L.R., 754 ; 28 A.L.T., 64 ; 12 A.L.R., 529. F.C. *a'Beckett, A.-C.J., Hodges* and *Chomley, JJ.*

Contract — Work and labour—Wages— Promise to pay express or implied—Evidence, sufficiency of.]—The complainant at the age of nine years was, out of charity, taken by the defendant to live with her on her farm and was fed, clothed and sent to school. He lived with the defendant on her farm for about ten years, and was set to do such work as he was able to do. On one occasion during this period he ran away from the defendant's home and was forcibly brought back. On another occasion when the complainant was a grown lad he asked to be paid wages, and was told by the defendant that she would give him a foal and would remember him in her will, but that he would get no wages. In a complaint for wages, *Held*, that there was no evidence of any agreement express or implied to pay wages to the complainant. *Jewry* v. *Busk*, 5 Taunt., 302, distinguished. *Griffith* v. *O'Donoghue*, (1906) V.L.R., 548; 28 A.L.T., 31; 12 A.L.R., 357. *Hood, J.*(1906).

II.—CONSIDERATION.

Local Government Act 1903 (No. 1893), ss. 455, 456—Contract—Consideration—Tender—Deposit—Forfeiture—Withdrawal of tender before acceptance—Mode of making contract—Burden of proof.]—In response to an advertisement by a municipal council for tenders for certain work the plaintiff made a tender in which he stated :—" I herewith make a preliminary deposit of £50 . . such sum to be absolutely forfeited to the council as liquidated damages and not by way of penalty in the event of withdrawing cancelling or rescinding this tender or failing to enter into a properly executed contract for the performance of the work within 48 hours after being called upon so to do." The plaintiff deposited £50 with the tender accordingly. Before acceptance of the tender the plaintiff withdrew it. In an action by the plaintiff against the municipality to recover the £50. *Held,* that there was a binding contract under which the council could retain the £50 in the event of the plaintiff withdrawing . his tender before acceptance ; that the promise of the council to consider the tender was a sufficient consideration to support the contract, notwithstanding section 456 of the *Local Government Act* 1903 ; and that the burden of proving that the contract was not made in the manner prescribed by section 455 of that Act was upon the plaintiff. *Stafford* v. *City of South Melbourne*, 30 A.L.T., 43 ; (1908) V.L.R., 584; 14 A.L.R., 464. F.C., *a'Beckett, Hood* and *Cussen, JJ.*

III.—CONTRACTS REQUIRED TO BE IN WRITING.

(a) Statute of Frauds.

(1) Memorandum, Sufficiency of.

Instruments Act 1890 (No. 1103), ss. 208, 209—Statute of Frauds (29 Car. II. c. 3)—Contract for sale of land—Signature to note or memorandum—Signature by amanuensis in presence and by direction of party to be charged, whether sufficient.]—To satisfy the requirements of sections 208 and 209 of the *Instruments Act* 1890, there must be a personal signature by the hand of the party to be charged, or a signature by an agent authorised in writing by the party to be charged, and the signature by an amanuensis, in the presence by the direction and with the name of the party to be charged, cannot be regarded as a signature by that party with his own hand, and is therefore insufficient. *Thomson* v. *McInnes*, (1911) 12 C.L.R., 562 ; 17 A.L.R., 354. H.C., *Griffith, C.J., Barton* and *O'Connor, JJ.*

Sale of goods—Memorandum of agreement, whether necessary—Contract itself in writing—Sale of Goods Act 1896 (No. 1422), sec 9.]—A signed and sent to B a letter offering to sell him goods of the value of £10 and upwards on conditions therein specified. B, by a subsequent letter, accepted A's offer. *Held,* that the provisions of sec. 9 (1) of the *Sale of Goods Act* 1896 requiring a note or memorandum of the contract did not preclude B from enforcing the agreement to sell. *Patterson* v. *Dolman*, (1908) V.L.R., 354 ; 29 A.L.T., 256 ; 14 A.L.R., 240. F.C., *a'Beckett, Hodges* and *Cussen, JJ.*

Instruments Act 1890 (No. 1103), sec. 208—Memorandum of contract contained in several documents—Agreement to act as manager of company—Agreement implied from articles of Association and conduct of parties.]—Article 55 of the P company's Articles of Association was to the following effect :—" B.G. shall be the first managing director of the P company and shall hold such office for the term of ten years from August 1st, 1900. B.G. shall be entitled as such managing director to receive out of the funds of the company during his tenure of office the sum of £500 per annum payable by weekly instalments. The remuneration of B.G. after the expiration of the said term of ten years from August 1st 1900 or any other managing director appointed in his stead shall be fixed by the directors." For a period of over four years B.G. acted as managing director of the P company, without any objection by any director or officer or member of the company, and during all that period from August 1st, 1900, was paid for his services at the rate mentioned in the Articles of Association. B.G. signed a consent to act and in the directors' report was returned as managing director. On February 15th, 1905, B.G. wrote a letter to the secretary of the P company in the following terms :—" Take notice that I claim by virtue of clause 55 of the Articles of Association of the above company and every other right enabling me so to do to be retained in my position as managing director of the P company for the period of ten years from August 1st, 1900, at the remuneration of £500 as therein provided and that any sale of the company's business assets and goodwill to the D company must be subject to my claim or its equivalent in money." On the next day the secretary wrote in reply as follows :—" In reply to your letter of the 15th which was submitted to my board of directors at their meeting held to-day I am instructed to inform you that the contemplated sale of this company's assets to the D company will carry with it the obligation to carry out the contract with you so far as regards the salary of £500 per annum for the balance of the term of ten years from August 1st, 1900." The minutes of the P company showed that the secretary was instructed by the board of directors to write the above letter, and that a copy of that letter was submitted to the board on March 2nd and again approved. In an action by B.G. against the P company for breach of contract to employ him, *Held*, that there was sufficient evidence that a contract was in fact made between the P company and B.G. to employ him for the time and on the terms stated in Article 55 of the Articles of Association, and that a memorandum of such contract sufficient to comply with the *Statute of Frauds* (*Instruments Act* 1890, sec. 208) was contained in the various documents referred to. *Glass v. Pioneer Rubber Works of Australia Ltd.* (1906) V.L.R., 754; 28 A.L.T., 64; 12 A.L.R., 529. F.C., *a'Beckett, A.-C.J., Hodges* and *Chomley, JJ.*

(2) Parol Evidence.

Instruments Act 1890 (No. 1103), sec. 208— Sale of Land—Note or memorandum—Several documents—Parol evidence, when admissible to connect—Reference to document—Reference to transaction in which document may or may not have been written.]—Where the memorandum of a contract is sought to be constituted from several documents, the reference in the document signed by the party to be charged must be to some other document the identity of which may be proved by parol evidence, and not merely to some transaction in the course of which another document may or may not have been written. *Held*, therefore, that the words " purchase money " in a receipt given by the vendor of land for a sum of money " being a deposit and first part purchase money " could not refer to another document and that parol evidence was not admissible. *Thomson v. McInnes*, (1911) 12 C.L.R., 562; 17 A.L.R., 354. H.C., *Griffith, C.J., Barton* and *O'Connor, JJ.*

Written contract—Parol evidence to identify subject matter, admissibility of—Latent ambiguity—Language apt to express a specific article of a class or any article of that class—Statute of Frauds.]—Where a written contract for the sale of a particular chattel is couched in general terms equally apt to express the sale of any article of a certain class or the sale of a specific article of that class, parol evidence is admissible to show that a specific article was contracted for and to ascertain and identify that specific article. *Bank of New Zealand v. Simpson*, (1900) A.C., 182, followed. *Smith v. Jeffryes*, 15 M. & W., 561, and *Wilkie v. Hunt*, 1 W.W. & a'B. (L.), 66, distinguished. *Bruton v. Farm and Dairy Machinery Co. Proprietary Ltd.*, (1910) V.L.R., 196; 31 A.L.T., 200; 16

A.L.R., 241. F.C., *Madden, C.J., a' Beckett* and *Hood, JJ.*

Instruments Act 1890 (No. 1103), sec. 208—Parol lease for less than three years—Lessee in possession of premises under existing tenancy.]—An agreement to lease for less than three years premises of which the lessee is already in possession under an existing tenancy, may be proved by parol, and is not affected by the *Statute of Frauds*. The eixsting tenancy is surrendered by operation of law and the possession of the lessee is referable to the new tenancy. *Knott v. McKendrick,* 28 A.L.T. (Supplement), 4; 12 A.L.R. (C.N.), 23. *Judge Box* (1906).

(b) *Under Mines Act.*

Mines Act 1897 (No. 1514), sec. 75—Mining on private property—Compensation—Agreement with owner—Necessity for writing—Waiver.]—*Semble.*—Sec. 75 (2) of the *Mines Act* 1897 which provides that no agreement between the applicant for a mining lease on private property and the owner thereof as to compensation shall have any force or validity unless it is in writing signed by the parties thereto is for the benefit of the owner and may be waived by him. *Armstrong v. The Duke of Wellington G.M. Co. No Liability,* (1906) V.L.R., 145; 27 A.L.T., 146; 12 A.L.R., 67. *Madden, C.J.*

IV.—CAPACITY.

Infant—Intended marriage— Goods supplied—Necessaries.]—An infant about to marry may make himself liable for things reasonably required for the marriage, or for the joint establishment .after marriage. *Quiggan Brothers v. Baker,* (1906) V.L.R., 259; 27 A.L.T., 174; 12 A.L.R., 168. *a' Beckett, J.* (1906).

V.—LEGALITY OF OBJECT.

Conveyancing Act 1904 (No. 1953), secs. 1, 3, 4 (6), (9)—Vendor and purchaser—Perusal fees, legality of contract for payment of by purchaser—Land under Transfer of Land Act—Transfer.]—Sub-sec. 6 of sec. 4 of the *Conveyancing Act* 1904, is effective, notwithstanding sub-sec. 9, and it applies to all land sold by auction whether under the

Transfer of Land Act or under the general law. *Re Stewart and Park's Contract,* (1907) V.L.R., 31; 28 A.L.T., 133; 12 A.L.R., 553. *Hood J.* (1906).

Conveyancing Act 1904 (No. 1953), sec. 4 (6), (9)—Interpretation—Repugnant clauses—Insertion of words to give effect to clear intention of Statute.]—Sub-sec. 9 of sec. 4 of the *Conveyancing Act* 1904 should be read as though it contained some words excluding sub-sec. 6 from its operation. *Re Stewart and Park's Contract,* (1907) V.L.R., 31; 28 A.L.T., 133; 12 A.L.R., 553. *Hood, J.* (1906).

Conveyancing Act 1904 (No. 1953), sec. 4 (6)—Whether applicable to land under Transfer of Land Act—" Conveyance," " transfer "—Contract of sale by auction—Stipulation that purchaser shall pay vendor's costs of perusal of conveyance.]—Sec. 4 (6) of the *Conveyancing Act* 1904 applies to sales by auction of land under the *Transfer of Land Act* 1890. *Re Stewart and Park's Contract,* (1907) V.L.R., 31; 28 A.L.T., 133; 12 A.L.R., 553, followed. *Re Rogers aud Rodd's Contract,* (1907) V.L.R., 511; 29 A.L.T., 13; A.L.R., 312. *Madden, C.J.* (1907).

Conveyancing Act 1904 (No. 1953), sec. 4 (6)—Auction Sales Act 1890 (No. 1065), secs. 3, 29—Sale of land by Sheriff under fi. fa.—Whether a " sale by auction "—Sheriff's costs of perusal of conveyance—Stipulation in contract of sale for payment by purchaser, legality of.]—A sale of land by auction conducted by the Sheriff under a writ of *fi. fa.* is, notwithstanding the provisions of the *Auction Sales Act* 1890, excusing the Sheriff from the responsibilities imposed by that Act, a sale by auction within the meaning of sec. 4 (6) of the *Conveyancing Act* 1904, and a clause in the contract of sale charging the purchaser with the payment of the Sheriff's costs of perusal of the conveyance is accordingly illegal. *Re Rogers' and Rodd's Contract,* (1907) V.L.R., 511; 29 A.L.T., 13; 13 A.L.R., 312. *Madden, C.J.* (1907).

Conveyancing Act 1904 (No. 1953), secs. 4 (6), (9), 10—Auction—Sale of land—Con-

tract of sale—Costs of perusal and of obtaining execution of conveyance—Stipulation for payment by purchaser—Waiver by signing contract—Procedure for declaration of illegality of stipulation—Existence of contract.]—A clause in a contract of sale by auction of land stating that sec. 4 (6) of the *Conveyancing Act* 1904 did not apply to the contract and stipulating for the payment by the purchaser to the vendor or his solicitor of the costs of perusal of the conveyance or of obtaining the execution thereof is illegal, and the purchaser does not waive the benefit of the provision in that section of the Act by signing a contract containing such a clause. Where a purchaser has signed a contract containing such a clause he may apply on summons under sec. 10 of the *Conveyancing Act* 1904 for a declaration that the clause is illegal and void, as the illegal stipulation may be disregarded and the contract still subsists. *In re Stewart and Park's Contract*, (1907) V.L.R., 31 ; 28 A.L.T., 133 ; 12 A.L.R., 553, and *In re Rogers and Rodd's Contract*, (1907) V.L.R., 511 ; 29 A.L.T., 30 ; 13 A.L.R., 312, followed. *In re Crook's Contract*, (1909) V.L.R., 12 ; 30 A.L.T., 108 ; 14 A.L.R., 698. *a'Beckett, J.* (1908).

Conveyancing Act 1904 (No. 1953), sec. 4 (6)—Contract for sale of land—Sale by auction—Costs—Exclusive of perusal and obtaining execution of transfer—Purchaser to pay—Validity—Condition.]—A provision in a contract made at the sale of land by auction " that the purchaser shall pay the vendor's costs and expenses of and incidental to the transfer exclusive of perusal and of obtaining the execution of the transfer " is not void under sec. 4 (6) of the *Conveyancing Act* 1904. The expression " costs of perusal of the conveyance or of obtaining the execution thereof " in sec. 4 (6) of the *Conveyancing Act* 1904 does not include the costs of all matters connected with the transfer of the land sold. Perusal means reading the conveyance to see if it expresses what it is intended to express. *In re Sutton and the Federal Building Society's Contract*, (1909) V.L.R., 473 ; 31 A.L.T., 75 ; 15 A.L.R., 560. *Cussen, J.*

Vendor and purchaser—Contract of sale—Provision for apportionment of federal land tax—Validity—Interpretation—Land Tax Assessment Act 1910 (No. 22 of 1910), secs. 37, 63.]—*See, post* 220, 221. *Patterson* v. *Farrell*, (1912) 14 C.L.R., 348 ; 18 A.L.R., 237.

Illegal contract—Transfer of land to defeat creditors—No proof that creditors defeated—Resulting trust.]—*See* TRUSTS AND TRUSTEES. *Payne* v. *McDonald*, (1908) 6 C.L.R., 208 ; 14 A.L.R., 366.

VI.—MISREPRESENTATION ; NON-DISCLOSURE.

Representation made during negotiation for contract—Whether deemed to be a continuing representation until altered—Life insurance.] —A representation once made in the course of negotiations for a contract, *prima facie* continues in force until it is withdrawn or altered, and such a representation is construed to mean that the facts represented are then true, and, when made by a proponent for life assurance, that no other facts are then known to him. *Dalgety & Co. Ltd.* v. *Australian Mutual Provident Society*, (1908) V.L.R., 481; 30 A.L.T., 4 ; 14 A.L.R., 299. *Cussen, J.* (1908).

Contract—When contracting party bound to disclose all material facts known to him—Innocent failure to disclose material fact, effect of—Life insurance.]—When the circumstances show that confidence is reposed in one party to a contract by the other, the former is bound to disclose all material facts which he knows, unless the latter knows those facts or is presumed to know them, or takes on himself knowledge or waives information about them, and, if this disclosure is not made, whether from design, accident, inadvertence, or mistake the contract is voidable at the option of the party misled. This rule applies as well to contracts of life assurance as to those of marine insurance. *Hambrough* v. *Mutual Life &c. of New York*, 72 L.T., 141, disapproved. *Dalgety & Co. Ltd.* v. *Australian Mutual Provident Society*, (1908) V.L.R., 481; 30 A.L.T., 4 ; 14 A.L.R., 299. *Cussen, J.* (1908).

Contract—Life Assurance—Statements by party proposing to insure to be basis of contract—**Whether a warranty.**]—The statement in a proposal for life assurance that " the proponent agrees that answers or statements shall be the basis of the contract " does not amount to a warranty. *Dalgety & Co. Ltd.* v. *Australian Mutual Provident Society*, (1908) V.L.R., 481 ; 30 A.L.T., 4 ; 14 A.L.R., 299. *Cussen, J.* (1908).

Contract—Insurance—Innocent non-disclosure of material fact discovered before completion of contract.]—H., having made a proposal for assurance on his life with a company, received from the company a notice stating that the proposal was accepted and a policy would issue on payment of the premium, and that the company reserved the right of cancelling the notice " should anything to the prejudice of the life transpire in the meantime." On the next day from certain circumstances that then happened H. knew and believed that a growth on his neck was possibly malignant, and that his medical advisers suspected it of being so. H. without fraud, made no disclosure of this matter to the company, and three days afterwards the premium was paid. *Held*, that the contract was revocable at the option of the company. *Dalgety & Co. Ltd.* v. *Australian Mutual Provident Society*, (1908) V.L.R., 481 ; 30 A.L.T., 4 ; 14 A.L.R., 299. *Cussen, J.* (1908).

Composition with creditors—Debtor's Duty to disclose assets—Non-disclosure of valueless assets of a deceased person—Assets subsequently becoming valuable—Rights of creditors and next of kin.]—In inducing his creditors to accept a composition and to release him from all liability in respect of the debts due by him to them, a debtor should disclose everything which would affect the judgment of a rational creditor governing himself by the principles and calculations on which creditors do in practice act. Certain shares in building societies that were part of the estate of a deceased person, which was insolvent, were not disclosed to the creditors of such estate on their agreeing by deed to accept a composition (which they did accept) and on payment thereof to discharge his estate (which they did discharge) from

all liability in respect of his debts. Such shares were valueless at that time, but some considerable time subsequently became valuable : *Held*, that the creditors were not entitled to the proceeds of the sale of such shares, as against the next of kin of the deceased, because the creditors' judgment would not, under the circumstances of the case, have been affected by the disclosure of the shares. *In re Warren* ; *National Trustees Executors and Agency Co. of Australasia Ltd.* v. *Daniel White & Co. Ltd.*, (1909) V.L.R., 6 ; 30 A.L.T., 129 ; 14 A.L.R., 683. *Cussen, J.*

VII.—OPERATION OF CONTRACT.

(a) Rights and Obligations of Third Parties.

Partnership—Contract with individual who afterwards takes another into partnership—Liability of firm in respect of contract.]—Where A. has a contract with B. and B. takes C. into partnership, A. may elect to abide by his contract with B. alone, or may accept the liability of the partnership. The mere fact that he prefers, in connection with his contract, to see and consult the partner who had previously acted for him does not prove an election not to deal with the firm. *Reid* v. *Silberberg*, (1906) V.L.R., 126. *a' Beckett, J.*

Partnership—Contract with individual who afterwards takes another into partnership—Election to hold firm liable on contract—Solicitors—Liability for fraud of co-partner.]—*See* PARTNERS AND PARTNERSHIP. *Reid* v. *Silberberg*, (1906) V.L.R., 126.

Contract of life assurance—Parties—Policy for benefit of assured only—Refusal of executors of will of assured to sue on policy—Action by beneficiaries under will of insured—Cause of action.]—*See* INSURANCE. *Miller* v. *National Mutual Life Assurance Association of Australasia Ltd.*, (1909) V.L.R., 193 ; 30 A.L.T., 193,; 15 A.L.R., 141.

Partnership—Formation of—Contract made before partnership in existence.]—In an action by the plaintiffs to recover damages for breach of contract from the three defendants, who, it was alleged, were partners, and as such had entered into a joint adventure with the plaintiffs. *Held*, on the evidence, that the existence of the partnership was not established, and that, even if the partnership existed, it had not been formed at the time when the contract was alleged to have been made. *Lang* v. *Morrison & Co. Ltd.*, (1911) 13 C.L.R., 1; 17 A.L.R., 530. H.C. *Griffith, C.J., Barton* and *O'Connor, JJ.*

(b) *Assignment.*

See also, Bills of Exchange and Promissory Notes.

Chose in action consisting of right against the Crown—Assignment—Petition of right by assignee—Crown Remedies and Liability Act 1890 (No. 1080), sec. 20.]—*See* ASSIGNMENT, cols. 56, 57. *The King* v. *Brown*, (1912) 14 C.L.R., 17; 18 A.L.R., 111.

Contract—Interpretation—Agreement to deposit time-payment agreements as security—Depositor allowed to collect debts due—Deposit of additional time payment agreements equal in value to those discharged by payment—Equitable assignment—Book Debts Act 1896 (No. 1424), secs. 2, 3—Non-registration.]—J., who had in the ordinary course of his business sold furniture under time payment agreements in consideration of advances made to him by M. agreed in writing to deposit with M. as security for such advances certain time payment agreement forms signed and complete which were to remain the property of M. until the full amount of the advances with interest had been repaid to him; and it was further provided that, if any of the time payment agreements should be fully paid up by the "hirer," J. should replace them with others of equal value. In pursuance of the contract J. delivered to M. the time payment agreement forms. The contract was not registered under the *Book Debts Act* 1896. The estate of J. was sequestrated. *Held*, that the transaction gave to M. not a mere security over and right to retain the documents deposited, but amounted to an equitable assignment to him of the debts due to J. under the time payment agreements, and that the assignment was

void for want of registration under the *Book Debts Act* 1896. *In re Jones*, (1906) V.L.R., 432; 27 A.L.T., 230; 12 A.L.R., 279. F.C. *a'Beckett, A.-C.J., Hodges* and *Chomley, JJ.* (1906).

Book debt—Assignment—Future debt—Money to become payable by agent to principal on sale of goods—Book Debts Act 1896 (No. 1424), secs. 2, 3.]—*See* ASSIGNMENT, cols. 57, 58. *Shackell* v. *Howe Thornton & Palmer*, (1909) 8 C.L.R., 170; 15 A.L.R., 176.

Book debt—Money to become payable by agent to principal on sale of goods—"On account of or in connection with . . . business "—Book Debts Act 1896 (No. 1424), secs. 2, 3.]—Money which will become payable by an agent to his principal, a trader, as purchase money on the sale of goods of the principal consigned to the agent for sale, constitutes a debt to become due by the agent to the principal, but not a debt on account of or in connection with the business of the principal within the meaning of the *Book Debts Act* 1896, and is therefore not a "book debt" within the meaning of that Act. *Shackell* v. *Howe, Thornton & Palmer*, (1909) 8 C.L.R., 170; 15 A.L.R., 176. H.C., *Griffith, C.J., O'Connor* and *Isaacs, JJ.*

Equitable assignment of future fund—Registration—Book Debts Act 1896 (No. 1424), sec. 2—Instruments Act 1890 (No. 1103), Part VI.]—*See* ASSIGNMENT, col. 58. *Muntz* v. *Smail*, (1909) 8 C.L.R., 262; 15 A.L.R., 162.

Assignment—Deposit of Savings Bank passbook and order for payment of money in bank—Debt due in connection with business carried on by assignor—Book Debts Act 1896 (No. 1424), sec. 2 (a).]—*See* ASSIGNMENT, cols. 58, 59. *Cox* v. *Smail*, (1912) V.L.R., 274; 18 A.L.R., 299.

Book Debts Act 1896 (No. 1424), sec. 2 (a)—"Business," meaning of—Engagement in particular kind of transaction with intention to continue therein—Isolated transactions.]—*See* BOOK DEBTS. *Schroder* v. *Hebbard*, (1907) V.L.R., 107; 29 A.L.T., 1; 13 A.L.R., 141.

Book Debts Act 1896 (No. 1424), sec. 2 (a)—
" Business," meaning of—Three contracts for
the supply of firewood entered into at different
times.]—*See* BOOK DEBTS. *Schroder* v. *Hebbard*, (1907) V.L.R., 107; 29 A.L.T., 1;
13 A.L.R., 141.

Supreme Court Act 1890 (No. 1142), sec.
63 (6)—Order III., r. 6 (Rules of 1906)—
Order XIV.—" Debt or liquidated demand "
—Assignment of debt—No written notice of
assignment.]— *See* ASSIGNMENT, col. 59.
Caddy v. *Beattie*, (1908) V.L.R., 17; 29
A.L.T., 165; 13 A.L.R., 643.

Assignment of debt—No written notice of
assignment—Proceedings by assignee—Parties.].*See* ASSIGNMENT, col. 59. *Caddy* v.
Beattie, (1908) V.L.R., 17; 29 A.L.T., 165;
13 A.L.R., 643.

VIII.—DISCHARGE OF CONTRACT.

(a) Waiver.

Director with contractual rights against
company—Concurrence in acts rendering
company unable to perform contract—Whether
a waiver of rights of director.]—The mere
concurrence of a person in his capacity of
director of a company in acts, which render
such company unable to perform a contract
then existing between him and the company
does not amount to a waiver by him of his
personal rights in respect of a breach of
contract by the company resulting from such
acts. *Glass* v. *Pioneer Rubber Works of
Australia Ltd.*, (1906) V.L.R., 754; 28 A.L.T.,
64; 12 A.L.R., 529. F.C., *a' Beckett, A.-C.J.,
Hodges* and *Chomley, JJ.*

Contract—Banker and customer— Acceptance of drafts—Condition precedent—Performance rendered impossible—Part performance, acceptance of benefits of.]—The
appellant, who carried on business in Australia, agreed to buy from a merchant in
Buenos Ayres a cargo of wheat for delivery
at a named Australian port, payment to be
" by London banker's acceptance of seller's
drafts at 90 days sight under confirmed credit
with documents attached as usual which are
to be given up on acceptance. Seller to give
policies and/or certificates of insurance for

2 per cent. over invoice value." For the
purpose of carrying out the provisions as to
payment the appellant by letter requested
the respondent bank to issue to him a credit
authorizing the seller to draw on London at
90 days sight for the value of the wheat.
The letter continued :—" Insurance to be
effected by shippers. Drafts to be accompanied by bills of lading, policy of insurance,
merchant's certificate of weight and quality.
Separate documents for each 100 tons of
wheat and the certificate of your agents at
Buenos Ayres that the conditions of the
credit have been complied with." The appellant then undertook that in consideration of
the bank issuing such credit he would provide
funds by purchasing the bank's drafts on
London at the exchange of the day to retire
all bills drawn under the credit in time to
meet the bills before maturity. On the same
day, respondents at appellant's instance
sent to their London house a cable message
summarizing the request. A credit was
subsequently opened by the bank in London
under which the seller drew certain drafts
on the bank in London and negotiated them
in Buenos Ayres. The drafts were subsequently accepted by the bank in London,
but there were not attached to them policies
of insurance, and the policies were not
delivered to the bank until a fortnight
afterwards. Prior to his requesting the bank
to issue the credit the appellant had sold
the wheat by a contract by which he bound
himself to deliver with the wheat separate
policies of insurance for each 100 tons, and
this fact was communicated to the bank in
London before the issue of the credit. It
appeared that under these circumstances
the separate policies could only be issued
in London, and would not be issued until
after the arrival of the bills of lading. When
the wheat arrived in Melbourne the appellant
refused to accept delivery of the wheat. In
an action by the bank against the appellant
to enforce his liability in respect of the drafts,
Held (per Griffith, C.J., Barton and *O'Connor, JJ., Isaacs, J.,* dissenting), on the construction of the documents and the facts
that it was not a condition precedent to
the contract between the bank and the appel-

ant that the drafts should at the time of presentment for acceptance be accompanied by policies of insurance and that, if it was, the appellant had rendered its performance impossible, and so had excused the bank from performance of it. *Held*, also (*per totam curiam*), on the evidence, that if the bank by accepting the drafts unaccompanied by policies of insurance had failed to perform a condition precedent of the contract, the appellant by his conduct after the arrival of the wheat in Australia had elected to take advantage of the acceptance of the drafts and was therefore liable to provide for them. *Friedlander* v. *Bank of Australasia*, (1909) 8 C.L.R., 85.

(b) Agreement: Breach.

Vendor and Purchaser—Contract for sale of land—Requisition on title—Vendor unable or unwilling to comply with requisition—Right of vendor to annul sale—Transfer of Land Act 1890 (No. 1149), Schedule XXV. Table A. (4).] Where the purchaser under a contract of sale of land in his requisitions on title persists in making requisitions of such a nature that the vendor by complying or partly complying therewith may complicate matters, the vendor may avail himself of a condition in the contract entitling him to annul a sale which is substantially the same as condition 4 in Schedule XXV. Table A. of the *Transfer of Land Act* 1890. *West* v. *Hedgeland*, (1909) V.L.R., 178; 30 A.L.T., 175; 15 A.L.R., 123. *a'Beckett, J.*

Contract of sale of land—Construction—Provisions for annulment and compensation, whether mutually exclusive—Objections to title or matter in particulars—Power to annul if objection to title " or otherwise "—Error in particulars—Deficiency in frontage.]—In a contract of sale of land the particulars described the property as " having a frontage of about 40 feet." As a matter of fact the frontage was 33 feet 3 inches. One of the conditions of sale contained in the contract required the purchaser within a certain time to deliver to the vendor a statement in writing of all objections to the title or " concerning any matter appearing on the particulars."

In the next condition the vendor was empowered. to annul the sale if the purchaser made any objection to the title " or otherwise" which the vendor was unable or unwilling to remove; and then followed a condition providing that any mistake in the description or error in the particulars of the property should not annul the sale, but that compensation, to be settled by arbitration, should be given or taken as the case might require. *Held*, that the conditions as to annulment and compensation were not mutually exclusive, and that, objection having been raised by the purchaser as to the deficiency of frontage, such objection was an objection concerning a " matter appearing on the particulars," and that, consequently, the vendor was entitled. to annul the contract. *In re Cook and Preece's Contract*, (1910) V.L.R., 328; 32 A.L.T., 17; 16 A.L.R., 324. *Hodges, J.* (1910).

Title with apparent flaw—Existence of flaw negatived by proof of facts—Whether purchaser may be compelled to accept title—Transfer of Land Act—Land under, whether same rule applicable to.]—By the general law a title having what would appear to be a flaw until negatived by proof of disputable facts, can be forced on an unwilling purchaser, and that rule applies to land under the *Transfer of Land Act*. *In re Kenna and Ritchie's Contract*, (1907) V.L.R., 386; 28 A.L.T., 218; 13 A.L.R., 191. *a'Beckett, J.*

Sale of land—Restrictive covenant running with land—Covenant notified as an encumbrance on certificate of title—Purchaser of part of land not in fact affected by covenant—Whether purchaser bound to accept title—Proof of facts showing covenant does not affect part of land sold—Costs of, how borne.] —R., who owned an estate, as to which there existed a restrictive covenant running with the land limiting the amount of water which might be discharged from it on to adjoining land, subdivided the estate and sold part of it to K. The rights of the persons claiming under the deed creating this restrictive covenant were notified as an encumbrance on the certificate of title to the whole estate. A requisition was made for an undertaking by R. that a certificate of title to the part sold should issue to K. free from the incumbrance. R. refused to give his undertaking and K. took out a summons claiming recission. The Judge found that by reason of the contour and natural features of the part purchased by K. and of the adjoining lands, the restrictive covenant would not in fact affect such part. *Held*, that K. was entitled to demand satisfactory evidence that the covenant in question did not affect the land purchased by him, which evidence should have been furnished at the cost of R., but that the encumbrance on the certificate of title did not constitute a valid objection to title. *In re Kenna and Ritchie's Contract*, (1907) V.L.R., 386; 28 A.L.T., 218; 13 A.L.R., 191. *a' Beckett, J.*

Vendor and purchaser—Specific performance—Time limited for production of title—Notice to produce—Deficiency of area—Annulment of contract—Land Act 1901 (No. 1749), secs. 35, 49 (6), 56 (6)]—By a contract of sale of seven specified Crown allotments of land described therein as containing 2,131 acres or thereabouts, the titles to which were Crown leases of grazing areas granted under the *Land Act* 1901, the vendors agreed that they would apply to select two of the allotments as agricultural allotments and a third as a grazing allotment, and to have issued to them a lease under section 49 (6) of the Act in respect of such two allotments, and a lease under sec. 56 (6) in respect of such third allotment. It was also agreed that " the two last-mentioned leases " and the leases of the other grazing areas should be produced " to the purchaser or his solicitor within eight months from the day of sale and a copy thereof may be made by the purchaser or his solicitor on application in that behalf to the vendors or their solicitor," and that in the event of non-production of the leases it shall be lawful for either the vendors or the purchaser to annul the sale. It was further provided that if any mistake should be made in the description or area of the property or any other error should appear in the particulars, such mistake or error

should not annul the sale, but compensation should be fixed by referees. It was finally provided that time should be of the essence of the contract in all respects. The two allotments agreed to be selected as agricultural allotments were comprised in a single Crown lease and together contained more land by about 30 acres than could under the Act be so selected, and the allotment agreed to be selected as a grazing allotment contained more land by about 3 acres than could under the Act be so selected, and the leases issued in respect of such selections were of correspondingly smaller areas. The price was at the rate of 5s. per acre for the land agreed to be selected as agricultural allotments, and 10s. per acre for the rest. *Held*, that in order to enable the vendors to rely on the non-production of the leases within the specified period, they must before the expiration of that period have asked for production. *Held*, also, that the deficiency in the area of the land selected was not a ground for resisting specific performance of the contract, but was a matter for compensation under the contract. *Cox* v. *Hoban* (1911) 12 C.L.R., 256; 17 A.L.R., 195. H.C., *Griffith, C.J., O'Connor* and *Isaacs, JJ.*

Vendor and purchaser—Agreement to give possession on a certain day—Condition that vendor may annul sale if unable or unwilling to comply with requisition—Inability or unwillingness, what is—Knowledge by vendor of his inability to comply with term of contract—Specific performance so far as possible, with compensation—Whether purchaser entitled to —Transfer of Land Act 1890 (No. 1149), Schedule XXV., Table A., Condition 4.]—The vendor under a contract for the sale of land made in April, 1909, agreed to give possession to the purchaser on May 17th, 1910. The contract contained the following condition :—In case the purchaser shall . . . make any objection to or requisition on the title or otherwise which the vendor shall be unable or unwilling to remove or comply with and such objection or requisition be insisted on it shall be lawful for the vendor (whether he shall have attempted to remove such objection or to comply with such requisition or not) at any time by notice in writing to annul the sale, and within one week after giving such notice to repay to the purchaser the amount of the purchase money or so much thereof as shall have been paid in full satisfaction of all claims and demands whatsoever by the purchaser, and also to return all unpaid acceptances given by the purchaser, but without any interest, costs, or damages of any description." At the time the contract was made a tenant was in possession of the premises under a lease expiring on May 13th, 1910, with an option of renewal for a term of eleven years. The purchaser at the time of entering into the contract was unaware of this option, and the vendor who never made any real effort to procure possession had been refused vacant possession by the lessee at the end of her then current term. The lessee exercised her option and obtained a renewal of her lease for a term of eleven years from May 13th, 1910. The purchaser made requisitions on title including a demand for vacant possession on May 17th, 1910. This demand was refused by the vendor, and the purchaser persisting in it the vendor gave formal notice that he annuled the sale purporting to act under the condition above set forth. In an action by the purchaser against the vendor claiming specific performance or specific performance so far as possible with damages, *Held*, that the vendor's inability or unwillingness to give possession was not covered by the condition above set out and that he was not entitled to annul the sale ; and that the purchaser was entitled to specific performance, so far as possible, with compensation for loss of possession. *McGavin* v. *Gerraty*, 32 A.L.T., 151 ; 17 A.L.R., 85. *Madden, C.J.* (1911).

Companies Act 1890 (No. 1074), secs. 24, 39, 71—Liquidation—List of contributories—Contract to take shares with condition that something is to be done after membership completed—Contract that there shall be no membership unless condition performed—Waiver.]—A person who has entered into a contract *in praesenti* to take shares, with an agreement that something is to be done after membership has been completed, is liable to be settled upon the list of contributories in a winding-up, even though such agreement has not been performed ; so also is a person whose application to take shares is subject to the condition that it is not to be perfected until something has been done, if by his subsequent conduct he shows his intention to waive any right he had to insist on the condition, and he makes a new agreement to take and hold shares without any condition. *In re Australian Producers and Traders' Ltd.*, (1906) V.L.R., 511 ; 28 A.L.T., 80 ; 12 A.L.R., 445. *Cussen, J.*

(c) Alteration of Instrument in Writing.

Promissory note—Material alteration, what is—Place of payment, what is—Instruments Act 1890 (No. 1103), sec. 65 (2).]—A promissory note, when made, contained nothing indicating the place of payment other than the printed words " Payable at " followed by a blank. After delivery and without the authority or assent of the maker, the blank was filled in with the words and figures " 15 Queen's Bridge Street, Melbourne." In proceedings against the maker for money due on the note. *Held*, that it had been materially altered, and was accordingly avoided as against the maker. *Semble*, that it was an alteration of the " place of payment " within the meaning of sec. 65 (2) of the *Instruments Act* 1890. *Sims* v. *Anderson*, (1908) V.L.R., 348 ; 29 A.L.T., 241 ; 14 A.L.R., 210. *Cussen, J.*

Negotiable instrument—Material alteration, nature of—Instruments Act 1890 (No. 1103), sec. 65—Enumeration of material alterations, whether exhaustive.]—The enumeration of material alterations in sec. 65 of the *Instruments Act* 1890 is not exhaustive. An alteration is a material alteration if it makes the instrument operate differently. *Sims* v. *Anderson*, (1908) V.L.R., 348 ; 29 A.L.T., 241 ; 14 A.L.R., 210. *Cussen, J.* (1908).

(d) Lapse of Time.

Statute of Limitations—Simple contract debt—Acknowledgment—Letter from debtor's solicitors expressing debtor's inability to pay—

Promise as to payment by debtor's wife.]— On an application for judgment in an action for the recovery of a simple contract debt which the defendant opposed on the ground that the debt was barred by the *Statute of Limitations*, the plaintiff relied upon two letters which, according to him, were written by the defendant's solicitors. In the first letter, after stating that the defendant had no means whatever, the writers expressed their opinion that if the plaintiff delayed the matter for a few weeks they might be able to persuade the defendant's wife to pay the plaintiff's account and in the second letter, after explaining why the defendant's wife had been unable to settle the account as promised, they stated that if the plaintiff would wait for a certain further time, within which the wife would be likely to receive the balance of her usual quarter's income the whole amount of the income would be paid, and they asked plaintiff to send them the exact amount of the account as it had been mislaid. *Held*, that such letters did not constitute such an acknowledgment of the debt that a promise by or on behalf of the defendant to pay it should be inferred therefrom, and that therefore, the *Statute of Limitations* was not prevented from running. *Quaere*, whether a mere general statement that solicitors are acting for a client in connection with a certain claim, and nothing more, is sufficient evidence that such solicitors are agents of the debtor to make an acknowledgment. *Holden* v. *Lawes-Wittewronge*, (1912) V.L.R., 82; 33 A.L.T., 153; 18 A.L.R., 28. *Cussen* J.

IX.—INTERPRETATION; INCIDENTS OF CONTRACTS RELATING TO VARIOUS SUBJECTS.

(a) Principal and Agent.

Agent—Disclosed principal—Liability of agent—Question of fact.]—An agent who contracts personally though on behalf of his principal is personally liable, and may be sued in his own name on the contract, whether the principal is named therein or is known to the other contracting party or not. Whether an agent who discloses his principal contracts personally is a question of intention to be decided on the facts, where there is

nothing in the language employed in making the contract which expressly declares the intention. *Cooper* v. *Fisken*, 33 A.L.T., 231; 18 A.L.R., 155. *a'Beckett, J.* (1912).

Principal and agent—Agent for foreign shipping company—Sale of passenger's ticket —Failure of principal to carry passenger on terms mentioned in ticket—Liability of agent. —No undertaking by agent that passenger should be so carried.]—In an action for breach of contract the Court found on the evidence that the plaintiff approached the defendant's firm as a medium through which to obtain contracts for the carriage of passengers by the N.D.L., a shipping company, incorporated and having its head office in Germany, the contracts to be represented by tickets to be used in the ordinary way; that the defendant's firm agreed to provide the contracts and did so as to certain tickets actually issued; that the defendant's firm never undertook that the passengers should be carried by the route or on the terms mentioned in the tickets; and that the plaintiff looked to the N.D.L. as alone bound to provide the passages. *Held*, that the defendant was not liable to the plaintiff for the failure of the N.D.L. to carry the passengers. *Cheong* v. *Lohmann*, (1907) V.L.R., 571; 28 A.L.T., 252; 13 A.L.R., 269. *a'Beckett, J.*

Principal and agent—Agent contracting on behalf of disclosed foreign principal—Whether agent personally liable on contract.]—In determining whether an agent contracting on behalf of a disclosed foreign principal is personally liable on the contract, the Court will take into consideration the character of the transaction in which the parties are engaged, and the subject of the contract resulting from their negotiations. *Cheong* v. *Lohmann*, (1907) V.L.R., 571; 28 A.L.T., 252; 13 A.L.R., 269. *a'Beckett, J.* (1907).

Principal and agent—Breach of warranty of authority, nature of action for—Breach of duty as agent.]—An action for breach of warranty of authority lies only where a person having in fact no authority purports to bring his supposed principal into legal relations with the plaintiff. If an agent alleges that he has concluded a contract on behalf of his principal with a third party, and he has not in fact done so, the principal's cause of action is for breach of duty by the agent, and not for breach of warranty of authority. *Gosman* v. *Ockerby*, (1908) V.L.R., 298; 29 A.L.T., 266; 14 A.L.R., 186. *Cussen, J.*

Master and servant—Business—Attempted sale of as a going concern—Servant assisting—Lease of premises procured by servant for himself—Fiduciary relation—Whether servant a trustee of lease for master—Transfer of lease, whether master entitled to.]—*See* TRUSTS AND TRUSTEES. *Prebble* v. *Reeves*, (1910) V.L.R., 88; 31 A.L.T., 114; 15 A.L.R., 631.

Book debt—Money to become payable by agent to principal on sale of goods—" On account of or in connection with . . . business "—Book Debts Act 1896 (No. 1424), secs. 2, 3.]—*See* PRINCIPAL AND AGENT. *Shackell* v. *Howe, Thornton & Palmer*, (1909) 8 C.L.R., 170; 15 A.L.R., 176.

Principal and agent—Landlord and Tenant Act 1890 (No. 1108), sec. 92—Eighth Schedule—Notice of intention to apply to justices to recover possession—Signature of notice, sufficiency of—Application by corporation—Name of corporation signed by agent authorised so to do.]—*See* PRINCIPAL AND AGENT. *Equity Trustees Executors and Agency Co. Ltd.* v. *Harston*, (1908) V.L.R., 23; 29 A.L.T., 131; 13 A.L.R., 686.

Agent—Liability of candidate for acts of.]—*See* COMMONWEALTH ELECTORAL ACTS, col. 112. *Crouch* v. *Ozanne*, (1910) 12 C.L.R., 539.

Husband and wife—Agency—Destitute wife—Sale of husband's goods for purchase of necessaries—Authority of wife.]—*See* HUSBAND AND WIFE. *Moreno* v. *Slinn*, (1910) V.L.R., 457; 32 A.L.T., 66; 16 A.L.R., 503.

Insolvency Act 1890 (No. 1102), sec. 37—Compulsory sequestration—Petitioning creditor—Power of attorney—Authority of attorney to present petition.]—*See* INSOLVENCY. *In re Anderson*, (1909) V.L.R., 465; 31 A.L.T., 72; 15 A.L.R., 518.

Statute of Limitations—Acknowledgment—Solicitor acting in connection with claim—Whether debtor's agent to make an acknowledgment.]—*See* PRINCIPAL AND AGENT. *Holden* v. *Lawes-Wittewronge*, (1912) V.L.R., 82; 33 A.L.T., 153; 18 A.L.R., 28.

Supreme Court Act 1890 (No. 1142), sec. 85—Where cause of action arises—Agent outside jurisdiction—Goods improperly sold by agent—Action by principal for money had and received—Place of payment—Rule that debtor must seek out creditor.]—If an agent abroad acting for a principal within the jurisdiction deals with goods in a manner not authorised by the principal and receives the proceeds thereof and the principal, waiving the tort, sues for money had and received, the cause of action does not arise within the jurisdiction. The rule that the debtor must seek out his creditor particularly applies to cases where the question depends upon an excuse alleged for non-payment of money within a jurisdiction. *Gosman* v. *Ockerby*, (1908) V.L.R., 298; 29 A.L.T., 266; 14 A.L.R., 186. *Cussen, J.*

Principal and agent—Contract of agency—Agent to procure purchaser—Right to commission—Statement by vendor that he is ready to sell for a certain sum " net."]—The respondents who were cork and general merchants, and as such had had previous dealings with the appellant, a brewer, wrote to the appellant as follows :—" The writer is under the impression that he heard somewhere that you were inclined to sell your business. If such is the case we should be glad to hear from you stating what amount you require for same and any particulars that are likely to help us to make a sale. We have an inquiry for a small brewery and shall be glad to hear from you on the subject." The appellant wrote in reply :—" In reference to sale of brewery, I want £2,500 net for the business. If I can't get that I don't sell. The only reason for selling I am getting too old, if I was 20 years younger I would not think of selling. Any further particulars you can have by applying." The respondents brought the business under the notice of S. who subsequently purchased it directly from the appellant for £2,500. *Held*, that the letters did not establish a contract between the appellant and respondents that the appellant would employ the respondents as his agents to introduce a purchaser on a promise by the appellant that, if the respondents did so, he would pay them commission ; and, therefore, that the respondents were not entitled to recover commission on the sale. *Dolphin* v. *Harrison, San Miguel Proprietary Ltd.*, (1911) 13 C.L.R., 271 ; 17 A.L.R., 444. H.C., *Griffith, C.J., Barton* and *O'Connor, J.J*

Contract—Agency—Order to supply goods—Condition for cancellation—Authority of agent.]—The plaintiff employed an agent to obtain signed orders on a printed form for certain machines. On the form was printed in special black type immediately above the place for the signatures the following statement :—" No conditions, representations or promises are authorized and shall not be binding except such as are printed or written hereon." Another provision was that the order was not to be binding on the plaintiff until ratified by him. The defendant signed an order and at the same time the plaintiff's agent signed and handed to the defendant a document stating that the defendant might cancel the order before a certain date if he did not have a fair average crop to his satisfaction. The plaintiff, without knowing of the arrangement for cancellation, ratified the order. The Full Court of the State decided that the defendant might nevertheless cancel the order before the date mentioned. The amount claimed was £23 10s. *Held*, that the case was not one for special leave to appeal. *House* v. *Whitelock*, (1911) 13 C.L.R., 334. H.C., *Griffith, C.J., Barton* and *O'Connor, JJ.*

Principal and agent—Estate agent—Contract to " introduce a buyer "—" Effect a sale."]—The defendant by writing authorised the plaintiffs, who were estate agents, to sell a property for " £550 or offer," and also to accept a deposit and sign contracts of sale on his behalf, and agreed ". to pay their usual commission if they effect a sale or introduce a buyer." The plaintiffs obtained an offer of £450 from P. and communicated it to the defendant, without disclosing who made it. The offer was declined, and whilst the plaintiffs were endeavouring to induce P. to offer £500, he bought the property for that amount through another agent. *Held* (per *Hodges* and *Hood, JJ., Madden, C.J.*, doubting), that the plaintiffs had not " introduced a buyer " within the meaning of the contract. *Semble* (per *Hodges, J.*), that in such contract the words " effect a sale " meant " sign a valid contract." *Looker & Sons* v. *Doveton*, (1911) V.L.R., 23 ; 32 A.L.T., 95 ; 16 A.L.R., 592. F.C.,

Vendor and purchaser—Contract for sale of land—Deposit to be paid to G. " as agent for vendor "—Deposit to be paid over to vendor on acceptance of title—Contract rescinded by mutual consent—Title not accepted—Whether vendor liable to repay deposit to purchaser—Money had and received—Stakeholder.]—One of the conditions of a contract in writing for the sale of certain land and stock provided that the purchasers should on the signing of the contract pay " a deposit of £500 " to G. " as agent for the vendor." Another condition provided that as soon as the purchasers accepted the title " the deposit shall be paid over to the vendor." There was another condition enabling the vendor in certain circumstances to annul the sale and prescribing that he should " repay " the purchase money already paid. The £500 deposit was paid by the purchasers to G. but was not paid by him to the vendor. Subsequently the purchasers and the vendor by agreement in writing rescinded the contract, title never having been accepted. In an action by the purchasers against the vendor to recover the £500 deposit as money had and received, *Held* (by *Griffith, C.J., O'Connor* and *Higgins, JJ.* (*Isaacs, J.*, dissenting) that G. was the agent of the vendor and not a stakeholder, and that the purchasers were entitled to recover the £500 from the vendor. *Christie* v. *Robinson*, 4 C.L.R., Pt. II., 1338 ; 13 A.L.R., 288 (1907).

Vendor and purchaser—Principal and agent —Sale of land—Deposit payable to agent on named day—Authority of agent to receive

deposit after due date—Payment to agent by way of promissory note—Payment to agent by way of set-off—Cancellation of contract by principal after receipt of deposit by agent—Commission, right of agent to—" Total amount realised "—Right of agent to deduct commission from moneys coming to his hands.]—*See* PRINCIPAL AND AGENT. *Walder* v. *Cutts*, (1909) V.L.R., 261; 31 A.L.T., 19; 15 A.L.R., 352.

Principal and agent—Commission—Sale of property—Property for sale at fixed price in hands of two agents—Offer by one of agents to a probable purchaser at price fixed refused—No communication as to such negotiation by agent to principal—Sale of property to same person subsequently by other agent for less sum after conferring with principal—Whether first agent may claim commission.]—*See* PRINCIPAL AND AGENT. *Overton* v. *Phillips*, (1912) V.L.R., 143; 33 A.L.T., 188; 18 A.L.R., 95.

Landlord and Tenant Act 1890 (No. 1108), secs. 81, 83—Distress for rent—Proceeds of sale—Overplus in hands of landlord's agent—Claim by tenant against landlord—Money had and received—Jurisdiction of Court of Petty Sessions.]—*See* LANDLORD AND TENANT. *Rhodes* v. *Parrott*, (1912) V.L.R. 333; 34 A.L.T., 90; 18 A.L.R., 353.

Conveyancing Act 1904 (No. 1953), sec. 75—Equitable charge upon land, how created—Investment of trust money by agent in purchase of land—Parol evidence.]—*See* TRUSTS AND TRUSTEES. *In re Smith*; *Smith* v. *Smith*, (1909) V.L.R., 91; 30 A.L.T., 214; 15 A.L.R., 25.

County Court Rules 1891, r. 230—Action for commission—Claim of third party—Interpleader by defendant—Claims arising out of same subject matter—Whether claims for one and the same debt.]—*See* COUNTY COURT. *Looker* v. *Mercer*, 28 A.L.T. (Supplement), 15; 13 A.L.R. (C.N.), 13.

Larceny—Fraudulent conversion by agent—Secretary of Friendly Society—Trustees—No relation of Agency—Crimes Act 1890 Amendment Act 1896 (No. 1478), sec. 2].—*See* CRIMINAL LAW. *Rex* v. *Buckle*, 31 A.L.T., 43; 15 A.L.R., 372.

Secret Commissions Prohibition Act 1905 (No. 1974), sec. 2—Giving of valuable consideration to agent—Tendency to influence agent to show favour.]—*See* CRIMINAL LAW. *Rex* v. *Scott*, (1907) V.L.R., 471; 29 A.L.T., 60; 13 A.L.R., 143.

Secret Commissions Prohibition Act 1905 (No. 1974), sec. 2—Corruptly giving valuable consideration to agent—Secret giving, presumption as to corruptness arising from.]—*See* CRIMINAL LAW. *Rex* v. *Scott*, (1907) V.L.R., 471; 29 A.L.T., 60; 13 A.L.R., 143.

Secret Commissions Prohibition Act 1905 (No. 1974), secs. 2, 14—Giving money to agent without principals' knowledge—Burden of proof.]—*See* CRIMINAL LAW. *Rex* v. *Stevenson*, (1907) V.L.R., 475; 29 A.L.T., 62; 13 A.L.R., 383.

Secret Commissions Prohibition Act 1905 (No. 1974), sec. 2—" Corruptly," meaning of.]—*See* CRIMINAL LAW. *Rex* v. *Stevenson*, (1907) V.L.R., 475; 29 A.L.T., 62; 13 A.L.R., 383.

Factories and Shops Act 1905 (No. 1975), sec. 119 (1)—Employing person at lower rate than rate determined by Special Board—Mens rea, whether a necessary element of offence—Employer, liability of, for act of agent.]—*See* FACTORIES AND SHOPS ACTS. *Billingham* v. *Oaten*, (1911) V.L.R., 44; 32 A.L.T., 170; 17 A.L.R., 36.

Insolvency Act 1890 (No. 1102), sec. 141 (xii.)—Trustee, agent or broker—Unlawful appropriation of property held as agent—Principal's goods sold by agent on commission—Relationship of debtor and creditor—Insolvency of agent—Whether agent liable for offence.]—*See* INSOLVENCY. *In re James*, 32 A.L.T. (Supplement), 12; 17 A.L.R. (C.N.), 5.

(b) *Vendor and Purchaser.*

See also; preceding sub-headings.

Vendor and purchaser—Contract of sale—Provision for apportionment of Federal land tax—Validity—Interpretation—Land Tax Assessment Act 1910 (No. 22 of 1910), secs. 37, 63.]—The owner of certain land sold it shortly before the coming into operation of the *Land Tax Assessment Act* 1910, and the purchaser entered into possession shortly after that date. One of the conditions of the contract of sale provided that the purchaser should be liable for " all rates and taxes and insurance premiums accruing or falling due from or after the date of possession " but that " all annual outgoings and insurance premiums in respect of the property sold " should be " apportioned between the vendor and purchaser up to such date." The vendor, who also owned other land, having paid the Federal land tax in respect of the whole of his land, including the land so sold for the year during which the purchaser went into possession. *Held*, that the Federal land tax was an outgoing within the meaning of the condition ; that the agreement that the land tax for that year should be apportioned was not affected by sec. 63 of the Act ; and therefore that the vendor was entitled to recover from the purchaser a sum which would represent a portion of the Federal land tax payable in respect of land whose unimproved value was equivalent to that of the land sold proportionate to the period of the year during which the purchaser had been in possession. *Held*, further, that the purchaser was not liable to pay at the higher rate at which the vendor was liable to pay because of his owning other land. *Patterson* v. *Farrell*, (1912) 14 C.L.R., 348 ; 18 A.L.R., 237. *Griffith. C.J., Barton and Isaacs, JJ.*

Vendor and purchaser—Conditions of sale—Production of certificate of title—Place of production.]—One of the conditions in a contract for the sale of land situated in the neighbourhood of Kerang provided that " the certificate of title to the property sold shall be produced and a copy thereof may be made by the purchaser or his solicitor on application in that behalf to the vendor or his solicitor." No place for the production of the certificate of title was specified. The vendor lived near Kerang, and it was a condition of the contract that the vendor's solicitor

was M. O. of Kerang. *Held*, that the certificate of title should be produced at some place reasonably convenient to Kerang, it might be the land itself or the place of residence or business of the vendor or his solicitor, and that the production of the certificate of title at Melbourne was not a compliance with the condition. *Morrison* v. *Richardson*, (1907) V.L.R., 218 ; 28 A.L.T., 166 ; 13 A.L.R., 94. *Hodges, J.*

Contract of sale—Construction—Sale of land under name by which it is known—Words stating measurements, whether words of estimate or of warranty.]—In a contract of sale of land the particulars described the property sold as being " that property known as Nos. 420 and 422 Church Street, Richmond, Victoria, and having a frontage of about 40 feet by a depth of 130 feet to a right of way on which are erected two shops." *Semble*, what was sold by the contract was the property known as Nos. 420 and 422 Church Street, Richmond, and the words " about 40 feet " were words of estimate and not of warranty. *In re Cook and Preece's Contract*, (1310) V.L.R., 328 ; 32 A.L.T., 17 ; 16 A.L.R., 324. (*Hodges, J.* (1910).

Vendor and purchaser—Sale of part of a parcel of land—Retention by vendor of balance —Implied grant of easement.]—*See* VENDOR AND PURCHASER. *Nelson* v. *Walker*, 10 C.L.R., 560 ; 16 A.L.R., 285.

Quasi-easement—Severance of unity of possession and title—Implied grant—Derogation from grant.]—*See* VENDOR AND PURCHASER. *Nelson* v. *Walker*, 10 C.L.R., 560 ; 16 A.L.R., 285.

Vendor and purchaser—Title—Executor or administrator—Conveyance by—Devolution of estate—Administration and Probate Act 1890 (No. 1060), sec. 6.]—*See* VENDOR AND PURCHASER. *In re Thomas and McKenzie's Contract*, (1912) V.L.R., 1 ; 33 A.L.T., 141 ; 17 A.L.R., 451.

Vendor and purchaser—Deposit paid to agent of vendor—Rescission of contract—Recovery of deposit from vendor — Stakeholder—Money had and received.]—By the conditions of a contract in writing for the sale of land and stock it was provided that a deposit of £500 should bo paid by the purchasers to A. " as agent for the vendor." By another condition it was provided that as soon as the purchasers had accepted title " the deposit should be paid over to the vendor." The £500 was paid by the purchasers to A., and was never paid by him to the vendor. Subsequently in writing the contract was— " cancelled by mutual consent " of the vendor and purchasers, title never having been accepted. *Held* (per *Griffith*, *C.J.*, *O'Connor* and *Higgins*, *JJ.*, *Isaacs*, *J.*, dissenting), that the purchasers were entitled to recover the £500 from the vendor. *Christie v. Robinson*, (1907) 4 C.L.R., 1338; 13 A.L.R., 288.

(c) *Bills of Lading.*

Ship—Bill of lading—Exceptions, construction of—Heat of holds—Neglect of master, mariners or others in service of owners—Fruit damaged by negligent omission to admit air to hold.]—Fruit was shipped at Naples in good order and condition fit for travelling and properly packed to be delivered under the bill of lading at Melbourne " in like good order and condition," but arrived in a damaged condition owing to the negligence of the servants of the shipowners in not admitting sufficient air to the hold in which the fruit was carried. The bill of lading exempted the shipowners from any liability for any loss or damage from certain causes or perils, including *inter alia* " effects of climate," " heat of holds " and " neglect, default, or error in judgment of the master, mariners, engineers or others in the service of the owners." In an action by the shippers against the shipowners, *Held*, that on the true construction of the bill of lading the " neglect " should not be limited to subject matters other than those previously specified and that the shipowners were exempted from liability for any neglect or default of any of their servants in the discharge of any of their duties connected with bringing the ship and its cargo from port to port. *Henty v. Orient Steam Navigation Co. Ltd.*, 29 A.L.T., 48; 13 A.L.R., 516. *Hodges, J.* (1907).

Agreement to sell goods—Goods to be shipped from Glasgow and delivered at a certain place at Melbourne—Price payable in London on receipt of proper bill of lading—Place of delivery in bill of lading different from place provided by agreement—Place of completion of contract—Delivery of shipping documents in accordance with agreement—Whether a condition precedent—Right of recission.]— C. in Glasgow agreed to sell to H. in Melbourne superphosphates on (*inter alia*) the following terms :—Shipment at Glasgow, price 70s. per ton c.i.f., destination Sydney and/or Melbourne *railway wharves*, buyer's option to be declared by buyer before sailing ; terms cash against documents in London against letter of credit provided by buyer in London. H. forwarded to C. a letter of credit on a bank in London payable on C. delivering to the bank shipping documents in accordance with the contract. C. shipped the goods, but the bills of lading merely provided for delivery at wharves in Melbourne and not at *railway wharves* in Melbourne. On C. presenting the letter of credit together with the shipping documents, the bank refused to pay under the letter of credit. The documents, together with the draft on H., were forwarded to him in Melbourne. He refused to accept the same. *Held*, that the contract was to have been completed in London by C. delivering to the bank proper shipping documents (*i.e.*, documents in accordance with the contract) and the bank paying the price therefor. *Held*, further, that the delivery of shipping documents in strict accordance with the contract was a condition precedent, and that as the bill of lading did not provide for the contractual destination of the goods, the defendant was entitled to rescind the contract. *Alexander Cross & Sons Ltd. v. Hasell*, (1908) V.L.R., 194 ; 29 A.L.T., 179; 14 A.L.R., 44. *Cussen, J.*

Sale of goods to be shipped from one port to another—Price payable at certain place on delivery of shipping documents—Bill of lading stating goods shipped by vendor and deliverable to his order or assigns—Property in goods, passing of—Delivery, when effected.]—In a c.i.f. contract for the shipment of goods from one port to another, where payment is to be made at a certain place on the surrender of the shipping documents, and the seller takes a bill of lading which states that the goods are shipped by him and deliverable to his order or assigns, there is no sale or delivery of the goods or the symbol of the goods until the indorsement and delivery of the bill of lading to the buyer or his agents. *Alexander Cross & Sons Ltd.* v. *Hasell*, (1908) V.L.R., 194; 29 A.L.T., 179; 4 A.L.R., 44. *Cussen, J.*

Stipulations as to place of delivery—Whether conditions precedent or warranties—Symbolical delivery elsewhere than place of actual delivery.]—In the absence of express agreement, stipulations as to place of delivery or as to place of consignment, where there is to be symbolical delivery elsewhere, are conditions precedent. *Alexander Cross & Sons Ltd.* v. *Hasell*, (1908) V.L.R., 194; 29 A.L.T., 179; 14 A.L.R., 44. *Cussen, J.*

Contract—Sale of goods to be shipped abroad—" C.i.f.e." contract—Place of delivery—County Court Practice—Jurisdiction—Part of cause of action arising out of jurisdiction.]—A contract for the sale of timber was made in Melbourne between the plaintiffs, a Melbourne firm, and the defendants, who were described as of " Melbourne," but who had their principal place of business in New York, with a branch house in Melbourne. The contract provided that the price should be £18 15s. per 1,000 feet super., c.i.f.e. Melbourne; that the terms should be " sellers' New York house on shipment to draw on buyers at 90 days' sight "; that shipment should be " at New York by sailing vessel—May shipment "; and that " sellers reserve the right to insure against war risk, the cost of which to be paid for by buyers in addition to the price above-named." *Held*, that the place of delivery under the contract was New York, and that, therefore, as the whole cause of action did not arise in Victoria, the County Court had no jurisdiction in an action for non-delivery of the timber in accordance with the contract. *Bowden* v. *Little*, (1907) 4 C.L.R., 1364; 13 A.L.R., 689, followed. *Crooke* v. *Smith*,

(1878) 4 V.L.R. (L.), 95, and *Brooks, Robinson & Co.* v. *Smith*, (1890) 16 V.L.R., 245; 11 A.L.T., 168, applied. *H. Beecham & Co.* v. *R. W. Cameron & Co.*, (1910) V.L.R., 19; 31 A.L.T., 100; 15 A.L.R., 598. F.C., *Madden, C.J., Hood* and *Cussen, JJ.*

Place of performance—Variation thereof—Course of dealing.]—The place of performance of a contract may be varied by a course of dealing between the parties thereto. *Kelsey* v. *Caselberg*, (1909) V.L.R., 347; 31 A.L.T., 31; 15 A.L.R., 362. *Madden, C.J.*

Sale of goods—Divisibility of contract—Delivery " spread "—Right of vendor to deliver in more than one instalment—Duty of purchaser to pay for each instalment as delivered.]—On 8th December, 1910, the plaintiffs and the defendants agreed that the plaintiffs should sell and the defendants should buy, 2,000 bags of maize at 2s. 7d. per bushel, delivered f.o.b. Melbourne, shipment spread over January and February, 1,000 bags each month, terms net cash against documents. On 12th January, 1911, before any shipments were made, the defendants suggested to the plaintiffs that the plaintiffs should ship 500 bags in January, and delay the second 500 bags till early in February. Plaintiffs agreed to this course. On 28th January the plaintiffs shipped 296 bags at Melbourne, but was prevented from shipping more by reason of a strike of wharf labourers. Plaintiffs forwarded the shipping documents to the defendants. No more maize was shipped during January. Defendants refused to accept or to pay for the 296 bags. *Held*, that the word " spread " still applied to the contract as altered; that, having regard to it, the plaintiffs were at liberty to deliver in more than one instalment; that the contract was divisible, and that the defendants were bound to pay against the documents for each instalment as delivered, and were not entitled to reject the 296 bags. *Brand* v. *Lawrence*, 1 Q.B.D., 344, followed; *Reuter Huleland & Co.* v. *Sala & Co.*, 4 C.P.D., 239, distinguished. *L. Osborn & Co. Ltd.* v. *Davidson Bros.*, (1911) V.L.R., 416; 33 A.L.T., 66; 17 A.L.R., 448. *Hodges, J.* (1911).

(d) Arbitration.

Arbitration—Agreement to submit to—Intention to make, how to be ascertained.]—No special words are essential to create a stipulation for a formal arbitration, provided the intention can be gathered from the words in fact used, or is reasonably to be intended from them, or from the nature and purpose of the stipulation. *Briscoe & Co. Ltd.* v. *The Victorian Railways Commissioners*, (1907) V.L.R., 523; 29 A.L.T., 17; 13 A.L.R., 308. *Madden, C.J.*

Sale of goods—Goods to be in every respect to the satisfaction of the purchaser's storekeeper—Condition that all disputes arising under contract shall be determined by storekeeper—Goods rejected by storekeeper—Goods sold and delivered—Goods bargained and sold—Non-acceptance of goods—Arbitration so-called and arbitration proper—Whether vendor entitled to have dispute dealt with by storekeeper as arbitrator.]—The plaintiff by contract under seal covenanted to supply the defendant with stores, of the kind specified in a schedule, to the order in writing of the defendant's storekeeper under agreed conditions and in strict accordance with the prescribed samples (if any). Condition 10 provided that in the case of any item in the schedule in which no particular brand of stores is specified the contractor may at his option supply the stores of any brand, provided that the whole of the stores supplied under the contract be in the judgment of the storekeeper of the very best quality and strictly in accordance with the prescribed sample if any and in every respect to the satisfaction of the storekeeper. Condition 12 provided that notwithstanding that any of the stores supplied may have been previsionally signed for or accepted by the receiving officer, or that they may have been paid for, the storekeeper shall have full power to reject any of such stores which in his judgment are not in every respect in accordance with this contract and such rejection may take place at any time until the storekeeper shall have expressly certified in writing that the whole of such stores so supplied under the particular order have been found, after complete examination and testing, to be in every respect in accordance with this contract. The condition also provided that notice of rejection should be given to the contractor in writing by the storekeeper, and that the contractor should remove the rejected stores within a certain time and replace them with stores in every respect in accordance with the contract, failing which the storekeeper might purchase stores which in his opinion were suitable at the contractor's risk. Condition 13 provided that payments should be made on the certificate in writing of the storekeeper. Condition 19 was in the following terms :—All questions and disputes relating to the construction of this contract, or otherwise arising thereunder, shall be determined by the storekeeper, and his decision shall be final and binding on the corporation (*i.e.*, the defendant) and the contractor respectively. Stores were supplied by the plaintiff which were not in the opinion of the storekeeper within the meaning of condition 10 of the very best quality, nor strictly in accordance with the order and the sample, and were not in every respect to the satisfaction of the storekeeper, and they were in consequence rejected by him under condition 12, and no certificate in writing under conditions 12 or 13 was given by him. *Held*, that the plaintiff could not recover the price of the goods in an action for goods sold and delivered or for goods bargained and sold, and was precluded from recovering damages against the defendant for not accepting the stores supplied. *Held*, further, that the plaintiff was not entitled under condition 19 to insist on an inquiry in the nature of an arbitration by the storekeeper in respect of a matter which he had already considered and dealt with under condition 12. *Laidlaw* v. *Hastings Pier Co.* (referred to in *Hudson on Building Contracts*); *Scott* v. *Corporation of Liverpool*, 3 DeG. & J., at p. 363; *Goodyear* v. *Mayor, &c., of Weymouth*, 35 L.J. N.S. C.P., 12; and *Wadsworth* v. *Smith*, L.R. 6 Q.B., 332, discussed and applied. *Robins* v. *Goddard*, (1905) 1 K.B., 294, and *Re Hohenzollern, &c., and the City of London Corporation*, 54 L.T. N.S., 596, distinguished. *Briscoe & Co. Ltd.* v. *The Victorian Railways*

Commissioners, (1907) V.L.R., 523 ; 29 A.L.T., 17 ; 13 A.L.R., 308. *Madden, C.J.*

Arbitration—Building contract—Extension of time fixed for completion—Determination of contract by employer during currency of further time allowed for completion—Arbitration provision, whether applicable—Supreme Court Act 1890 (No. 1142), sec. 152.]—One of the conditions of a contract between a shire council and a contractor for building a bridge provided that the contractor should complete the whole of the works on a certain day. Another condition provided that if the contractor should, in the opinion of the engineer, fail to make such progress with the works as the engineer should deem sufficient to ensure their completion within the specified time, and should fail or neglect to rectify such cause of complaint for seven days after being thereunto required in writing by the engineer, it should be lawful for the council to determine the contract. A third condition provided should " any doubt dispute or difference arise or happen touching or concerning the said works . . . or in relation to the exercise of any of the powers of the council or the engineer under this contract or any claim made by the contractor in consequence thereof or in any way arising therefrom or in relation to any impediment prevention or obstruction to or in the carrying on of the works of this contract or any part thereof (or any extras additions enlargements deviations or alterations thereon or thereof) by the council or the engineer . . . or any claim made by the contractor in consequence thereof or in any way arising therefrom or touching or concerning the meaning or intention of this contract or of the specifications or conditions or any other part thereof . . . or respecting any other matter or thing not hereinbefore left to the decision or determination of the engineer " every such doubt, dispute and difference should from time to time be referred to and settled and decided by the engineer. Subsequently the council agreed to extend the time for completion, and, by an indenture between the parties, the condition for completion on a

certain day was rescinded, and a new condition was substituted identical in terms except that a new date for completion was inserted. The council, after the original date for completion and before the new date, purported to determine the contract in pursuance of the conditions in that behalf. An action having been brought by the contractor claiming (*inter alia*) damages for breach of contract, for wrongful prevention of due and complete performance, and for wrongful determination of the contract, and upon a *quantum meruit* for work and labour done, *Held,* that the matters in dispute were referable to the arbitration of the engineer, notwithstanding that the original time for completion had passed when the contract was determined, and, therefore, that the action should be stayed under sec. 152 of the *Supreme Court Act* 1890. *Burton* v. *Bairnsdale, President, &c., of Shire of,* (1908) 7 C.L.R., 76 ; 14 A.L.R., 529. H.C., *Barton, O'Connor, Isaacs* and *Higgins, JJ.*

County Court—Action on insurance policy—Arbitration a condition precedent to right of action—Stay of proceedings—Adjournment—Jurisdiction — County Court Act 1890 (No. 1078), sec. 71.]—*See* COUNTY COURT. *Borrett* v. *Norwich and London &c. Association,* 29 A.L.T. (Supplement) 1 ; 13 A.L.R. (C.N.), 22.

Arbitration — Submission — Revocation — Incorporation of laws of Victoria—Bankruptcy of one of the parties to the agreement for reference—Leave to revoke submission—Supreme Court Act 1890 (No. 1142), secs. 141, 160.]—A contract in writing provided that all differences arising between the contracting parties should be referred to two arbitrators, one to be appointed by each party. The contract did not expressly provide that the submission should be made a rule of Court, but provided (*inter alia*) that the arbitration should take place in Melbourne and should be " subject to the provisions of the law in that behalf for the time being in force in Victoria," or failing Melbourne, in such other place as the principal business should then be carried on. After differences had arisen between the parties, and one of them had been adjudged bankrupt, he appointed an arbitrator, whereupon the other party applied to the Court for leave to revoke the appointment, power and authority of the arbitrator appointed. *Held*, that the provision in the contract that the arbitration should be subject to the laws of Victoria amounted to an agreement that the submission should be made a rule of Court, and that under sec. 141 of the *Supreme Court Act* 1890 the arbitrator's authority was not revocable without the leave of the Court. *In re Mitchell and Izard and the Governor of Ceylon,* 21 Q.B.D., 408, followed. *Held,* further, that in view of the bankruptcy of the party appointing, such leave should be given. *Re Freeman and Kempster,* (1909) V.L.R., 394 ; 31 A.L.T., 42 ; 15 A.L.R., 444. *a' Beckett, J.* (But see *Arbitration Act* 1910 (No. 2265).]

(e) *Patent Rights.*

Patents Act 1903 (No. 21 of 1903), sec. 62— Sales of patented articles to jobbers and dealers—Infringement by dealer of patentee's rights—Rights of patentee—Condition imposed upon dealer.]—The appellants held patents under the *Commonwealth Patents Act* 1903 for improvements in phonographs, sound records or blanks, and in the production of the two latter articles, and under sec. 62 were entitled, by way of monopoly by themselves, their agents and licensees " to make, use, exercise and vend the invention . . . in such manner as to him seems meet." It appeared that their course of business was to sell their patented articles to jobbers, who in turn sold to dealers, the dealers' contracts being made with the appellants. The main object of those contracts was to prevent the undercutting of trade prices and also the introduction of rival goods by way of exchange The respondent held various dealers' contracts made in April and May, 1906, and was entered on the appellant's dealers' list under a dealers' contract, which rendered him liable to be withdrawn therefrom on violating any of the conditions of sale therein expressed or any other reasonable conditions which might from time to time be imposed. If so withdrawn he undertook that he would in no way " handle sell or deal in or use, either directly

or indirectly " the patented articles unless authorised to do so in writing by the appellants. In an action to restrain the respondent whom the appellants had removed from their dealers' list from (1) acting in breach of contract ; (2) infringing their patent rights, their Lordships approved the finding by the High Court that no violation by the respondent of his contract had been established. *Held,* therefore, that he was free from those contractual obligations to the appellants, resulting from the withdrawal of his name from the dealers' list, which imposed upon him a comprehensive restraint on his conduct as a trader. But, *held,* also, that the appellants were entitled under the Statute to impose conditions in transactions of making, using, and vending their patented articles ; that knowledge of those conditions was brought home to the respondent by the said contract : and that he could not deal therewith as ordinary articles of commerce free from the conditions so imposed. *National Phonograph Co. of Australia Ltd.* v. *Menck,* (1911) A.C., 336 : 17 A.L.R , 94. P.C.

(f) *Insurance.*

Insurance—Re-insurance—Construction of policy—Statements basis of contract—Settlement of claim by re-insured—Liability of re-insurers.]—By a policy dated 2nd January, 1908, the respondents insured the life of M. for £5,000 with profits, the policy providing that certain written statements made by M. as to his health, should be the basis of the contract, and that the policy would be void if they were untrue. By a proposal form of the same date the respondents applied to the appellants to re-insure M's life for £5,000. This proposal contained a provision that in accepting the risk the appellants did so on the same terms and conditions as those on which the policy had been granted by the respondents " by whom, in the event of claim, the settlement will be made." The appellants on 28th January, 1908, issued a policy of re-insurance for £5,000, but limited to the amount which the respondents should pay irrespective of any bonus. The policy recited that the written statement of M. was the basis of the contract, also that the appellants had agreed to accept the respondents' proposal. M. died in May, 1909, and a claim was made against the respondents by his executrix. The appellants informed the respondents that they had reason to believe that some of the statements made by M. were untrue, and warned them thet they would not acquiesce in a settlement. The respondents, however, paid £5,000 in settlement of the claim, and sued the appellants upon the policy of re-insurance. The jury found that certain of M.'s statements were untrue, and that he had been guilty of concealment and mis-representation, but that the respondents, in settling the claim, had acted reasonably and *bona fide*. *Held*, that, assuming that the provision in the proposal form that a settlement should be affected by the respondents was incorporated in the policy of re-insurance, that provision could not alter the express terms of the policy, which warranted the truth of M.'s statements, and that, the jury having found those statements to he false, the appellants were not liable. *Australian Widows' Fund Life Assurance Society Ltd. v. National Mutual Life Association of Australasia Ltd.,* (1914) A.C., 634. P.C.

County Court—Action on insurance policy—Arbitration a condition precedent to right of action—Stay of proceedings — Adjournment—Jurisdiction—County Court Act 1890 (No. 1078), sec. 71.]—*See* COUNTY COURT. *Borrett v. Norwich and London Accident Insurance Association,* 29 A.L.T. (Supplement), 1 ; 13 A.L.R. (C.N.), 22.

Contract—Life assurance—Statements by party proposing to insure to be basis of contract — Whether a warranty.]—*See, ante,* VI. MISREPRESENTATION ; NON-DISCLOSURE. *Dalgety & Co. Ltd. v. Australian Mutual Provident Society,* (1908) V.L.R., 481; 30 A.L.T., 4 ; 14 A.L.R., 299.

Contract— Insurance — Innocent non-disclosure of material fact discovered before completion of contract.]—*See, ante,* VI. MISREPRESENTATION ; NON-DISCLOSURE. *Dalgety & Co. Ltd. v. Australian Mutual Provident Society,* (1908) **V.L.R.**, 481; 30 A.L.T., 4 ; 14 A.L.R., 299.

Contract of life assurance—Parties—Policy for benefit of assured only—Refusal of executors of will of assured to sue on policy—Action by beneficiaries under will of assured—Cause of action.]—*See* INSURANCE. *Miller v. National Mutual Life Assurance Association of Australasia Ltd.,* (1909) V.L.R., 193 ; 30 A.L.T., 193 ; 15 A.L.R., 141.

(g) *Building Contract.*

Building contract—Provision for appointment of architect to certify for payments to contractor—No architect appointed—Waiver—Payment of whole of contract price—Subsequent discovery of defects—Architect's certificate, effect of.]—A contract to build a house provided that the work should be carried out to the full intent and meaning of the drawings and specifications and to the satisfaction of such architect as should be appointed by the proprietor to give certificates for payments to the contractor, and that no payments should be made except on the certificate of the architect. It also provided that the whole was to be completed in a workmanlike and thorough manner, and to the satisfaction of the proprietor. No architect was in fact appointed, and after the house had been built and the whole of the contract price paid, the proprietor discovered that in certain particulars the specifications had not been complied with. He accordingly brought an action for breach of contract against the contractor. *Held*, (1) that the parties had by their conduct waived the right to have an architect appointed ; (2) that the fact of the payment of the whole of the purchase money was not conclusive proof that the work had been done to the proprietor's satisfaction. *Semble,* the provision for the appointment of an architect was for the benefit of the proprietor in the first instance, and not for the advantage or protection of the contractor. *Semble,* the architect's certificate, if given, would not have been conclusive against the proprietor. *Hopper v. Meyer,* (1906) V.L.R., 235 ; 27 A.L.T., 185 ; 12 A.L.R., 146. F.C., Holroyd, A.-C.J., a' Beckett and Hodges, JJ. (1906).

(h) Contract of Employment.

See also EMPLOYER AND EMPLOYEE, FACTORIES AND SHOPS ACTS, PUBLIC SERVICE AND RAILWAYS.

Indentures of apprenticeship, what are—Writing not under seal.]—The term indentures of apprenticeship has no specific legal significance, and will include a writing not under seal. *Hines* v. *Phillips,* (1906) V.L.R., 417; 28 A.L.T., 1; 12 A.L.R., 249. *a' Beckett, A.-C.J.* (1906).

Factories and Shops Act 1903 (No. 1857), sec. 7—Factories and Shops Act 1900 (No. 1654), secs. 4, 15, 22—Indentures of apprenticeship binding employer to instruct, what are.—Agreement to employ an " apprentice " in connection with employer's business—No clause binding employer to instruct—Nature of business not described.]—*See* FACTORIES AND SHOPS ACTS. *Hines* v. *Phillips,* (1906) V.L.R., 417; 28 A.L.T., 1; 12 A.L.R., 249.

Action, cause of—Inducing employer to discharge employee from his employment—Interference—Lawful justification or excuse—Intention to injure—Malice—Self-interest—Trades union—Secretary.]—*See* EMPLOYER AND EMPLOYEE. *Bond* v. *Morris,* (1912) V.L.R., 351; 34 A.L.T., 52; 18 A.L.R., 348.

(i) Trustees and Executors.

Trusts Act 1896 (No. 1421), sec. 11—Trustee—Power to compromise—Agreement between trustee and tenant for life—Compromise as to future liability of tenant for life for repairs—Disadvantage of the estate—Mistake of law, effect of.]—*See* TRUSTS AND TRUSTEES. *In re Tong*; *Tong* v. *Trustees, &c., Co. Ltd.,* (1910) V.L.R. 110; 31 A.L.T., 169; 16 A.L.R., 87.

Executor—Commission—Probate in Scotland and Victoria—Victorian executors also attorneys of trustees of will in Scotland—Agreement as to commission—Costs of executors passing accounts—Administration and Probate Act 1890 (No. 1060), sec. 26.]—*See* EXECUTORS AND ADMINISTRATORS. *Cattanach* v. *Macpherson,* (1908) V.L.R., 390; 29 A.L.T., 259; 14 A.L.R., 214.

(j) Deeds of Separation.

Judicial separation—Suit for—Deed of separation—Covenants—Dum casta clause—Maintenance clause—Duration of allowance to wife.]—*See* HUSBAND AND WIFE. *Woods* v. *Woods,* (1913) V.L.R., 39; 34 A.L.T., 104; 18 A.L.R., 460.

Divorce—Alimony pendente lite—Deed of separation containing covenant by wife not to require payment for her maintenance and support—Petition by wife for dissolution of marriage.]—*See* HUSBAND AND WIFE. *Brooker* v. *Brooker,* (1910) V.L.R., 488; 32 A.L.T. 108; 16 A.L.R., 580.

(k) Banker and Customer.

Banker and customer—Cheques drawn with spaces afterwards fraudulently filled up—Liability of bank—Duty of customer—Negligence.]—*See* BANKER AND CUSTOMER, col. 70. *Colonial Bank of Australasia* v. *Marshall,* (1906) A.C., 559.

Deposit receipt, security by way of—Contract to supply goods to Crown—Security for due performance of contract—Deposit receipt in name of servant of Crown procured by contractor and delivered to such servant—Contractor's account with bank overdrawn—Contract duly performed—Whether amount of deposit receipt a debt due by Crown to contractor—Money had and received—Set-off of bank's claim against contractor, whether justifiable.]—*See* BANKER AND CUSTOMER, cols. 70, 71, 72. *The King* v. *Brown,* 14 C.L.R., 17; 18 A.L.R., 111.

Savings Bank—Lost pass-book—Payment by bank on forged order to person other than depositor before notice of loss given—Whether bank liable—Rules, General Order No. 26, rr. 45, 48.]—*See* BANKER AND CUSTOMER, col. 72. *Levy* v. *Commissioners of Savings Banks,* (1906) V.L.R., 299; 27 A.L.T., 171; 12 A.L.R., 140.

" The Manager " of a bank, meaning of.]—*See* BANKER AND CUSTOMER, col. 72. *Union Bank of Australia* v. *Whitelaw,* (1906) V.L.R., 711; 28 A.L.T., 17; 12 A.L.R., 393.

(*l*) *Other Contracts.*

Particular contract — Interpretation — "Theatre," meaning of.]—The registered proprietor of the performing rights in a play gave to X. " the exclusive licence to perform the said play in any theatre in any part of Australia." ·*Held*, that the word " theatre " was not restricted in meaning to licensed theatres, but meant the places where the play was performed. *Meynell* v. *Pearce*, (1906) V.L.R., 447 ; 27 A.I..T., 226 ; 12 A.L.R., 282. *Cussen, J.* (1906).

Partnership agreement — Construction — Share payable on death of partner—Whether at his absolute disposal or in trust for widow and children.]—*See* PARTNERS AND PARTNER-SHIP. *England* v. *Bayles*, (1906) V.L.R., 94 ; 27 A.L.T., 181 ; 12 A.L.R., 122.

Contract—Transmission of cablegrams by company—Agreement between company and Government—Powers of Government to reduce rates—Abolition of rates—Rights of company — Post and Telegraph Rates Act 1902 (No. 13 of 1902) — Tasmanian Cable Rates Act 1906 (No. 10 of 1906).]—By various agreements made between a telegraph company, which had laid a telegraph cable between Tasmania and Victoria and the Tasmanian Government, to whose rights and liabilities under the agreements the Commonwealth succeeded, the company was given a monopoly of submarine telegraph communications between Tasmania and Victoria for a fixed period, a scale of charges for the transmission of telegrams was fixed, and it was provided that the Government should pay a subsidy of £4,200 a year. It was further provided that the Government should have " full power at any time to reduce " the scale of charges for telegrams, that in each year the company should be entitled to take " the whole of the proportion of the moneys collected and receivable by them from all sources in respect of such telegrams," called " message receipts," and, that " if, after such reduction in the scale of charges, the message receipts shall not in any year . . . by reason of such reduction or otherwise amount to the sum of £5,600, the Tasmanian Government shall guarantee and pay to the Telegraph Company, and their assigns, the difference between the message receipts and the said sum of £5,600." *Held*, (per *Griffith, C.J., Barton* and *O'Connor, JJ., Higgins, J.*, dissenting), that the power to reduce the rates did not authorize the Commonwealth to abolish them. The Commonwealth, after a previous reduction, purported to abolish the rates altogether, and thereupon the Company protested, and for some time after there business was carried on uninterruptedly so far as the carrying of telegrams was concerned. *Held*, that the Company was entitled in respect of telegrams carried after the date of the attempted abolition to be paid as if no such abolition had been attempted *Higgins, J.* concurring on the ground that the defendant, by agreeing to the special case in its existing form, had precluded themselves from contending to the contrary. *Held*, further, that the *Post and Telegraph Rates Act* 1902 as amended by the *Tasmania Cable Rates Act* 1906, did not affect the rights of the parties under the agreements. *Eastern Extension Australasia &c. Co.* v. *The Commonwealth*, (1908) 6 C.L.R., 647 ; 14 A.L.R., 542.

X.—DAMAGES.

Damages—Sale of specific chattel—Special measure of damages prescribed by warranty —Whether special measure of damages applies where the specific chattel is not delivereed Loss of profits—Purpose for which chattel purchased disclosed to vendor.]—Where in a warranty, part of a written contract for the sale of a specific chattel, a special measure of damages is provided, that special measure of damages does not apply if the specific chattel purchased under the contract is not delivered. Damages may be recovered for loss of profits occasioned by the non-delivery, the purpose for which the specific chattel was purchased being known to the seller. *Bruton* v. *Farm and Dairy Machine Co. Proprietary Ltd.*, (1910) V.L.R., 196 ; 31 A.L.T., 200 ; 16 A.L.R., 241. F.C., *Madden, C.J., a'Beckett* and *Hood, JJ.*

Contract—Breach—Cause of action—quantum of damages, whether part of.]—The quantum of damages is no part of the cause of action. *Railton* v. *Fleming*, (1912) V.L.R., 113; 33 A.L.T., 180; 18 A.L.R., 24. *a'Beckett, Hodges* and *Cussen, JJ.* F C.

XI.—Money Had and Received; Money Paid.

Rates—Payment without protest after due notice and demand—Rates not lawfully demandable—Money had and received.]—Money paid, without protest and after due notice and demand, for municipal rates not lawfully demandable is not recoverable as money had and received. *Geelong Mechanics' Institute Incorporated* v. *Geelong, Mayor, &c. of*, (1907) V.L.R., 580; 29 A.L.T., 33; 13 A.L.R., 377. *a'Beckett, J.* (1907).

Vendor and purchaser—Contract for sale of land—Deposit to be paid to G. " as agent for vendor "—Deposit to be paid over to vendor on acceptance of title—Contract rescinded by mutual consent—Title not accepted —Whether vendor liable to pay deposit to purchaser—Money had and received—Stakeholder.]—*See ante,* ix. (*a*). *Christie* v. *Robinson*, 4 C.L.R., Pt. II., 1338; 13 A.L.R., 288.

Supreme Court Act 1890 (No. 1142), sec. 85 —Where cause of action arises—Agent outside jurisdiction—Goods improperly sold by agent—Action by principal for money had and received—Place of payment—Rule that debtor must seek creditor.]—*See ante,* ix. (*a*) *Gosman* v. *Ockerby*, (1908) V.L.R., 298; 29 A.L.T., 266; 14 A.L.R., 186.

Deposit receipt, security by way of—Contract to supply goods to Crown—Security for due performance of contract—Deposit receipt in name of servant of the Crown procured by contractor and delivered to such servant—Contractor's account with bank over-drawn — Contract duly performed — Whether amount of deposit receipt a debt due by Crown to contractor—Money had and received—Set-off of bank's claim against contractor, whether justifiable.]—*See* BANKER AND CUSTOMER, *The King* v. *Brown*, (1912) 14 C.L.R., 17; 18 A.L.R., 111.

Customs Act 1901 (No. 6), sec. 167—Customs Tariff 1908 (No. 7), sec. 7—Duties collected under proposed tariff—Proposed tariff different from tariff enacted—Payment without protest—Recovery back of money paid—Money exacted colore officii—Deposit of amount demanded under section 167 of the Customs Act 1901—Whether the only remedy —" Dispute," what is.]**—*See* CUSTOMS. *Sargood Bros.* v. *The Commonwealth*, (1910) 11 C.L.R., 258; 16 A.L.R., 483.

Landlord and Tenant Act 1890 (No. 1108), secs. 81, 83—Distress for rent—Proceeds of sale—Overplus in hands of landlord's agent—Claim by tenant against landlord—Money had and received—Jurisdiction of Court of Petty Sessions.]—*See* LANDLORD AND TENANT. *Rhodes* v. *Parrott*, (1912) V.L.R., 333; 34 A.L.T., 90; 18 A.L.R., 353.

Mistake—Money paid under mistake of fact—Effect of payer's neglect or misconduct —Conditions precedent to right to recover such money.]—*See* MONEY PAID TO USE OF ANOTHER. *Morton & Son* v. *Smith*, 34 A.L.T., 79; 18 A.L.R., 322.

XII.—Legal Proceedings; Jurisdiction.

Supreme Court Act 1890 (No. 1142), sec. 85—Foreign procedure—Contract made in Queensland—Part performance by plaintiff in Victoria—Breach by defendant in Queensland.]—*See* PRACTICE AND PLEADING. *J. E. Lindley & Co.* v. *Pratt*, (1911) V.L.R., 444; 33 A.L.T., 50; 17 A.L.R., 404.

Supreme Court Act 1890 (No. 1142), sec. 85—Writ for service outside jurisdiction— Breach outside jurisdiction—Substantial performance within jurisdiction—" A cause of action which arose within the jurisdiction."] —*See* PRACTICE AND PLEADING. *Kelsey* v. *Caselberg*, (1909) V.L.R., 347; 31 A.L.T., 31; 15 A.L.R., 362.

Supreme Court Act 1890 (No. 1142), sec. 85—Where cause of action arises—Agent outside jurisdiction—Goods improperly sold by agent—Action by principal for money had and received—Place of payment—Rule that debtor must seek creditor.]—*See ante,* ix. (*a*). *Gosman* v. *Ockerby*, (1908) V.L.R., 298; 29 A.L.T., 266; 14 A.L.R., 186.

**Contract for sale of goods—Breach in Victoria—Cause of action—County Court—Jurisdiction.]—*See* COUNTY COURT. *Railton* v. *Fleming*, (1912) V.L.R., 113; 33 A.L.T., 180; 18 A.L.R., 24.

Contract—Sale of goods to be shipped abroad—C.i.f. contract—Place of delivery—County Court practice—Jurisdiction—Part of cause of action arising out of jurisdiction.]—*See* COUNTY COURT. *H. Beecham* v. *R. W. Cameron & Co.*, (1910) V.L.R., 19; 31 A.L.T., 100; 15 A.L.R., 598.

CONTRIBUTORY.

See COMPANY.

CONTRIBUTORY NEGLIGENCE.

See NEGLIGENCE.

CONVERSION.

Conversion—Sale of stolen goods—Recovery of value of goods from purchaser—Payment by cheque—Proceeds afterwards coming to hands of owner of goods—Obligation to elect to affirm or disaffirm sale.]—*See* SALE OF GOODS. *Creak* v. *James Moore & Sons Proprietary Ltd.*, (1912) 15 C.L.R., 426; 18 A.L.R., 542.

CONVEYANCING ACT.

Conveyancing Act 1904 (No. 1953), secs. 1, 3, 4 (6), (9)—Vendor and purchaser—Perusal fees, legality of contract for payment of by purchaser—Land under Transfer of Land Act—Transfer.]—Sub-section 6 of section 4 of the *Conveyancing Act* 1904 is effective, notwithstanding sub-section 9, and it applies to all land sold by auction whether under the *Transfer of Land Act* or under the general law. *Re Stewart and Park's Contract*, (1907) V.L.R., 31; 28 A.L.T., 133; 12 A.L.R., 553. *Hood, J.* (1906).

Conveyancing Act 1904 (No. 1953), sec. 4 (6)—Whether applicable to land under Transfer of Land Act—" Conveyance," " transfer "—Contract of sale by auction—Stipulation that purchaser shall pay vendor's costs of perusal of conveyance.]—Section 4 (6) of the *Conveyancing Act* 1904 applies to sales by auction of land under the *Transfer of Land Act* 1890. *Re Stewart and Park's Contract*, (1907) V.L.R., 31; 28 A.L.T., 133; 12 A.L.R., 553, followed. *Re Rogers and Rodd's Contract*, (1907) V.L.R., 511; 29 A.L.T., 13; 13 A.L.R., 312. *Madden, C.J.*

Conveyancing Act 1904 (No. 1953), sec. 4 (6), (9)—Interpretation—Repugnant clauses —Insertion of words to give effect to clear intention of Statute.]—Sub-section 9 of section 4 of the *Conveyancing Act* 1904 should be read as though it contained some words excluding sub-section 6 from its operation. *Re Stewart and Park's Contract*, (1907) V.L.R., 31; 28 A.L.T., 133; 12 A.L.R., 553. *Hood, J.* (1906).

Conveyancing Act 1904 (No. 1953), sec. 4 (6)—Auction Sales Act 1890 (No. 1065), secs. 3, 29—Sale of land by Sheriff under fi. fa.—Whether a " sale by auction "—Sheriff's costs of perusal of conveyance—Stipulation in contract of sale for payment by purchaser, legality of.]—A sale of land by auction conducted by the Sheriff under a writ of *fi. fa.* is, notwithstanding the provisions of the *Auction Sales Act* 1890 excusing the Sheriff from the responsibilities imposed by that Act, a " sale by auction " within the meaning of sec. 4 (6) of the *Conveyancing Act* 1904, and a clause in the contract of sale charging the purchaser with the payment of the Sheriff's costs of perusal of the conveyance is accordingly illegal. *Re Rogers and Rodd's Contract*, (1907) V.L.R., 511; 29 A.L.T., 13; 13 A.L.R., 312. *Madden, C.J.* (1907).

Conveyancing Act 1904 (No. 1953), secs. 4 (6), (9), 10—Auction—Sale of land—Contract of sale—Costs of perusal and of obtaining execution of conveyance—Stipulation for payment by purchaser—Waiver by signing contract—Procedure for declaration of illegality of stipulation—Existence of Contract.]—A clause in a contract of sale of land by auction stating that section 4 (6) of the *Conveyancing Act* 1904 did not apply to the contract and stipulating for the payment by the purchaser to the vendor or his solicitor of the costs of perusal of the conveyance or of obtaining the execution thereof is illegal, and the purchaser does not waive the benefit of the provision in that section of the Act by signing a contract containing such a clause. Where a purchaser has signed a contract containing such a clause he may apply on summons under sec. 10 of the *Conveyancing Act* 1904 for a declaration that the clause is illegal and void, as the illegal stipulation may be disregarded and the contract still subsists. *In re Stewart and Park's Contract*, (1907) V.L.R., 31; 28 A.L.T., 133; 12 A.L.R., 553, and *In re Rogers and Rodd's Contract*, (1907) V.L.R., 511; 29 A.L.T., 13; 13 A.L.R., 312, followed. *In re Crook's Contract*, (1909) V.L.R., 12; 30 A.L.T., 108; 14 A.L.R., 698. *a'Beckett, J.* (1908).

Conveyancing Act 1904 (No. 1953), sec. 4 (6)—Contract for sale of land—Sale by auction—Costs—Exclusive of perusal and obtaining execution of transfer—Purchaser to pay—Validity of condition.]—*See* CONTRACT OR AGREEMENT. Col. 199. *In re Sutton and the Federal Building Society's Contract*, (1909) V.L.R., 473; 31 A.L.T., 75; 15 A.L.R., 560.

Conveyancing Act 1904 (No. 1953), sec. 6—Transfer of Land Act 1890 (No. 1149), sec. 89—Vendor and Purchaser—Former unity of title and possession—Implied grant—Quasi—Easement—Rainwater flowing over surface—Adjoining owners—Natural servitude—Alteration of surface.]—Upon transfer by A. to B. of one of two allotments owned by A. subject to the *Transfer of Land Act* and so situated that rainwater flowed from the allotment sold to B. upon the allotment retained by A., there being no grant expressed in the transfer or implied from the circumstances attending the transfer of a servitude *ne facias* or a negative easement restraining A. from preventing the rainwater from flowing on to the allotment retained by him. *Held*, that such a servitude or easement was not passed by virtue of the general words in sec.

6 of the *Conveyancing Act* 1904, and sec. 89 of the *Transfer of Land Act* 1890. *Nelson v. Walker*, (1909) 10 C.L.R., 560; 16 A.L.R., 285. H.C., *Griffith, C.J., O'Connor, Isaacs* and *Higgins, JJ.*

Statute of Frauds—Conveyancing Act 1904 (No. 1593), sec. 75—Charge—Parol declaration.]—*See* STATUTE OF FRAUDS. *In the Will of Smith*; *Smith v. Smith*, (1909) V.L.R., 91; 30 A.L.T., 214; 15 A.L.R., 25.

CONVICTION.

Police Offences Act 1890 (No. 1126), secs. 49, 51, 89—Fine in default imprisonment—No time fixed for payment of fine.]—Where justices do not in their order name a time for payment of a fine, the fine is to be treated as having been ordered to be paid immediately. *Rogerson v. Phillips & O'Hagan*, (1906) V.L.R., 272; 27 A.L.T., 166; 12 A.L.R., 147. *a'Beckett, J.* (1906).

Factories and Shops Act 1905 (No. 1975), sec. 162 (c), (d)—Factories and Shops Act 1905 (No. 2), (No. 2008), sec. 9.]—Conviction against firm in firm name—Rules under the Justices Act 1890, rr. 18, 20—Information, form of.]—In proceedings against a firm for an offence under the Act No. 1975, the conviction ought to be against the individual members of the firm, and a conviction in the firm name is bad. *Quaere*, whether in such proceedings the information should be against the individuals, and not against the firm. *Bishop v. Chung Brothers*, 4 C.L.R., 1262; 13 A.L.R., 412. H.C., *Griffith, C.J., Barton* and *Isaacs, JJ., Higgins, J.*, dissenting (1907). (See Act No. 2137, sec. 39].

Justices—Court of Petty Sessions—Conviction—Sentence—Remand for sentence after determination of guilt of accused—Justices Act 1890 (No. 1105), sec. 18.]—Where Justices sitting in Petty Sessions are satisfied that the person charged before them is guilty of the alleged offence, but, in the absence of evidence as to prior convictions, are unable at once to fix the quantum of punishment, they may remand the prisoner, and at a future date, after hearing evidence as to prior convictions, formally record the conviction and pass sentence. *Quaere*, whether a Court of Petty Sessions has any jurisdiction to adjourn a case after pronouncing judgment. *Mc Innes* v. *King*; *De La Rue* v. *Everett*, (1909) V.L.R., 368; 31 A.L.T., 27; 15 A.L.R., 356. *Hodges, J.*

Informations heard together—Same defendant—Conviction, validity of.]—*See* JUSTICES OF THE PEACE. *Joske* v. *Lubrano*, (1906) V.L.R., 407; 28 A.L.T. 40.; 12 A.L.R., 311.

Marriage Act 1890 (No. 1166), sec. 43—Maintenance order—Direction to pay to Clerk of Petty Sessions at particular place—Whether clerk is a " person."]—*See* MAINTENANCE AND MAINTENANCE ORDERS. *Cohen* v. *MacDonough* (*or* *O'Donough*), (1906) V.L.R., 521; 28 A.L.T., 97; 12 A.L.R., 447.

" Second offence," what is—Pure Food Act 1905 (No. 2010), sec. 36.]—*See* CRIMINAL LAW. *O'Connor* v. *Bini*, (1908) V.L.R., 567; 30 A.L.T., 74: 14 A.L.R., 537.

Court of Petty Sessions—Jurisdiction—Discretion as to sentence—Evidence of character—Prior convictions.]—*See* JUSTICES OF THE PEACE. *O'Donnell* v. *Perkins*; *Tognini* v. *Hargreaves*, (1907) V.L.R., 537; 30 A.L.T., 45; 14 A.L.R., 435.

Appeal from Court of Petty Sessions—Conviction—General Sessions, powers of amendment of—Justices Act 1890 (No. 1105). secs. 133, 185.]—*See* GENERAL SESSIONS. *Li Wan Quai* v. *Christie*, (1906) 3 C.L.R., 1125; 12 A.L.R., 429.

General Sessions—Appeal against conviction — Information — Whether Court may amend—Justices Act 1890 (No. 1105), secs. 73 (4), 128 (7), 133.]—*See* INFORMATION. *Delaney* v. *Napthine*, 32 A.L.T. (Supplement) 10; 16 A.L.R. (C.N.), 19.

Justices Act 1890 (No. 1105), sec. 141—Information disclosing no offence—Conviction thereon—Amendment on return of order to review—Powers of Court—Defendant never charged with an offence.]—*See* JUSTICES OF THE PEACE. *Knox* v. *Thomas Bible*; *Knox* v. *J. L. Bible*, (1907) V.L.R., 485, 29 A.L.T., 23; 13 A.L.R., 352.

Justices Act 1890 (No. 1105), sec. 141—Return of order to review conviction—Amendment of information and conviction—Altering the offence charged in information to different offence.]—*See* JUSTICES OF THE PEACE. *Knox* v. *Thomas Bible*; *Knox* v. *J. L. Bible*, (1907) V.L.R., 485; 29 A.L.T., 23; 13 A.L.R., 352.

Amendment—Order to review—Conviction under Police Offences Act 1890 (No. 1126), sec. 40 (vi.)—No substantial disadvantage to defendant—Justices Act 1890 (No. 1105), sec. 147.]—*See* JUSTICES OF THE PEACE. *Hickling* v. *Skerritt*, (1912) V.L.R., 322; 34 A.L.T., 72; 18 A.L.R., 329.

COPYRIGHT.

Title to a play—Proprietary rights in—Injunction restraining infringement— Performing rights, assignment of—" Theatre," meaning of.]—*See* TRADE MARKS AND TRADE NAMES. *Meynell* v. *Pearce*, (1906) V.L.R., 447; 27 A.L.T., 226; 12 A.L.R., 282.

CO-RESPONDENT.

See HUSBAND AND WIFE.

CORPORATION.

See also, COMPANY.

Corporation—Liability for criminal offences—Mens rea—Liability to presentment on charge of conspiracy—Capacity to conspire.]— A corporation cannot conspire nor (*semble*) can it be conspired with. It cannot, therefore, be presented on a charge of conspiracy to defraud, nor (*semble*) can an individual be presented on a charge of conspiracy with a corporation to defraud. *Semble*, the criminal liability of a corporation for the criminal acts of its servants does not at common law extend beyond cases in which the criminal acts (*a*) create a public nuisance or (*b*) constitute a criminal libel. *R.* v. *Kellow*, (1912) V.L.R., 162; 33 A.L.T., 203; 18 A.L.R., 170. *Cussen, J*

Commonwealth of Australia Constitution (63 & 64 Vict. c. 12), sec. 51 (xx.)—Power to make laws with respect to " foreign corporations and trading and financial corporations formed within the limits of the Commonwealth "—Limits of power.]—*See* COMMONWEALTH OF AUSTRALIA CONSTITUTION. *Huddart Parker & Co. Proprietary Ltd.* v. *Moorehead*; *Appleton* v. *Moorehead,* (1909) 8 C.L.R., 330; 15 A.L.R., 241.

Commonwealth of Australia Constitution (63 & 64 Vict. c. 12), sec. 51 (1) (xx.)—Interference with internal trade and commerce—Power to make laws with respect to " foreign corporations and trading and financial corporations formed within the limits of the Commonwealth "—Limits of power—Control of corporations, their status, capacity and contracts.]—*See* COMMONWEALTH OF AUSTRALIA CONSTITUTION. *Huddart Parker & Co. Proprietary Ltd.* v. *Moorehead*; *Appleton* v. *Moorehead,* (1909) 8 C.L.R., 330; 15 A.L.R., 241.

Administration cum testamento annexo—Right of corporation aggregate, a beneficiary to administer—Grant to Syndic of corporation aggregate.]—*See* WILL. *In the Will of Basse,* (1909) V.L.R., 313; 31 A.L.T., 17; 15 A.L.R., 302. *Madden, C.J.*

CORPUS.

See TENANT FOR LIFE AND REMAINDERMAN; TRUSTS AND TRUSTEES; WILL.

CORROBORATION.

See EVIDENCE.

COSTS.

I.—JURISDICTION.

(a) *Of High Court and of Supreme Court.*

See, also, DIVORCE, Sub-heading II.

(1) To Hear Appeals as to Costs.

Appeal—Costs—Order directing trustee to pay costs—Supreme Court Act 1890 (No. 1142), sec. 60.]—An appeal lies from an order directing a trustee to pay costs in an action for administration, because it is a settled rule that such an order cannot be made unless the occasion of the suit has arisen from something in the nature of the trustee's own misconduct. It is also settled that the question, whether a trustee has been guilty of such misconduct as to justify the Court in ordering him to pay costs, is appealable. *Amos* v. *Fraser*, 4 C.L.R., Pt. I., 78 ; 12 A.L.R., 481. H.C., *Griffith, C.J., Barton* and *O'Connor, JJ.* (1906).

Trade Mark—Practice—Costs—Award of costs by Law Officer—Discretion—Appeal to High Court—Trade Marks Act 1905 (No. 20 of 1905), secs. 95, 96.]—The High Court has jurisdiction to entertain an appeal as to the costs awarded by the Law Officer on an appeal to him from the Registrar of Trade Marks. But on such an appeal the Court will not over-rule his order unless there has been a disregard of principle or a misapprehension of facts. *In re Gilbert* ; *Gilbert* v. *Hudlestone*, 28 Ch. D., 549, applied. *Alexander Ferguson & Co.* v. *Daniel Crawford & Co.*, (1909) 10 C.L.R., 207. H.C., *Griffith, C.J., O'Connor* and *Isaacs, JJ.*

Appeal—Exercise of discretion as to costs —Whether High Court will interfere where there is no other foundation for appeal.]—It would require a case of very extreme circumstances to justify the High Court in reviewing the discretion of the Supreme Court on a question of costs, where there is no other foundation for the appeal. *Jenkins* v. *Lanfranchi*, 10 C.L.R., 595 ; 16 A.L.R., 275. H.C., *Griffith, C.J., O'Connor, Isaacs* and *Higgins, JJ.* (1910).

Appeal—County Court—Action struck out for want of jurisdiction—Jurisdiction to deal with defendant's application for costs declined by Judge—Whether appeal lies—County Court Act 1890 (No. 1078), sec. 133.]—An action having been brought in a County Court which the Court had no jurisdiction to try the Judge ordered the case to be struck out and refused to consider the defendant's application for costs on the ground that he had no jurisdiction to do so. *Held*, that an appeal lay from such refusal. *The King* v. *Beecham* ; *Ex parte Cameron*, (1910) V.L.R., 204 ; 31 A.L.T., 183 ; 16 A.L.R., 173. F.C., *Madden, C.J.* and *a'Beckett, J.* (*Cussen, J.*, doubting).

(2) To Award Costs.

Service and Execution of Process Act 1901 (No. 11 of 1901), sec. 18—Execution of warrant issued in another State—Order of Justice of Peace directing return of accused—Review of order by Judge—Costs, jurisdiction to award.]—Upon review of the decision of a justice of the peace ordering an accused person to be returned to the State in which the warrant for his apprehension was issued a Judge has no jurisdiction to award costs. *In re George*, (1909) V.L.R., 15 ; 30 A.L.T., 141 ; 15 A.L.R., 27. *a'Beckett, J.*

Costs — Probate — Will — Caveat — Withdrawal before motion—Costs against caveator.]—Where a caveat against a grant of probate has been withdrawn prior to the motion for probate occasioned by the lodging of such caveat, the Court has no power to award costs against the caveator. *In re Downey*, 5 V.L.R. (I.P. & M.), 72, distinguished. *In the Will of Johnson*, (1909) V.L.R., 324 ; 31 A.L.T., 2 ; 15 A.L.R., 304. *Madden, C.J.*

(b) Of Inferior Courts.

County Court Act 1890 (No. 1078), secs. 48, 94—No jurisdiction to try action—Costs, whether Court may award.]—The power conferred by sec. 94 of the *County Court Act* 1890 to order a case to be struck out for want of jurisdiction, and to award costs extends to all cases in which the Court has no jurisdiction, and is not limited to those cases in which, under sec. 48 the want of jurisdiction might be cured by consent of parties. *Harrison, San Miguel & Co.* v. *Maddern*, (1905) V.L.R., 400 ; 26 A.L.T., 215 ; 11 A.L.R., 178, over-ruled. *The King* v. *Beecham* ; *Ex parte Cameron*, (1910) V.L.R., 204 ; 31 A.L.T., 183 ; 16 A.L.R., 173. F.C., *Madden, C.J., a'Beckett* and *Cussen, JJ.*

County Court Act 1890 (No. 1078), sec. 45—Costs—Amount recovered not exceeding ten pounds—Injunction a material part of the action—Professional costs.]—*Semble*, the provision in sec. 45 of the *County Court Act* 1890 as to professional costs where the amount recovered does not exceed £10, does not apply to cases where an injunction is a material part of the relief sought. *Harrison San Miguel Proprietary Ltd.* v. *Alfred Lawrence & Co.*, 1912) V.L.R., 367 ; 34 A.L.T., 88 ; 18 A.L.R., 394. *Madden, C. J.* (1912).

County Court Act 1890 (No. 1078), secs. 45, 64—Costs—Proposed action—Claims not not exceeding £10—Certificate for costs—Plaintiff's costs of employing an attorney—

Time for making application.]—An application for a certificate that a person who intends to issue a special summons under sec. 64 of the *County Court Act* 1890 shall be allowed the costs of employing an attorney in the proposed action cannot be made under section 45 of that Act. *Semble*, when the plaintiff in an action commenced by a special summons under sec. 64 is about to sign final judgment in default of notice to defend for an amount not exceeding £10 he should apply to the Judge sitting in Chambers to be allowed costs under Scale A. and for a direction that the Registrar so fix them. *Clarazite Manufacturing Co. Ltd.* v. *Armitage* (*No.* 1), 30 A.L.T. (Supplement), 21 ; 15 A.L.R. (C.N.), 6. *Judge Eagleson* (1909).

County Court Act 1890 (No. 1078), secs. 45, 62, 64—County Court Rules 1891, r. 200—Costs—Action—Claim not exceeding £10—Payment into Court by Dependant of debt and costs—Plaintiff's costs of employing attorney—Time for making application.]—Where the defendant in an action commenced by special summons under sec. 64 of the *County Court Act* 1890 duly pays into Court the amount of the debt and costs indorsed on the summons, and such debt does not exceed £10, a Judge of the County Court has no jurisdiction to allow the plaintiff the costs of employing an attorney—such costs not being mentioned in the summons. The plaintiff to be entitled to the costs of employing an attorney should have endorsed them on the summons at the time of issuing and before service. *Clarazite Manufacturing Co. Ltd.* v. *Armitage* (*No.* 1), 30 A.L.T. (Supplement), 21 ; 15 A.L.R. (C.N.), 6, disapproved. *Clarazite Manufacturing Co. Ltd.* v. *Armitage* (*No.* 2), 30 A.L.T. (Supplement), 22. 15 A.L.R. (C.N.), 6. *Judge Chomley* (1909).

County Court Act 1890 (No. 1078), secs. 45, 64—Costs— Proposed action — Claim not exceeding £10—Plaintiff's costs of employing attorney—Time for making application that costs be allowed.]—An order may be made under sec. 45 of the *County Court Act* 1890 prior to the issue of a special summons under sec. 64 that the Registrar on issuing such summons shall indorse thereon the

COSTS.

plaintiff's costs of employing an attorney. *Clarazite Manufacturing Co. Ltd.* v. *Armitage* (*No.* 1), 30 A.L.T. (Supplement), 21 ; 15 A.L.R. (C.N.), 6, not followed. *Lee* v. *Cunningham*, 32 A.L.T. (Supplement), 4 ; 16 A.L.R. (C.N.), 1. *Judge Box* (1910).

County Court Act 1890 (No. 1078), sec. 62— Payment into Court—Costs fixed by Registrar —Whether plaintiff may be allowed additional costs.]—The fixation of costs by the Registrar under sec. 62 of the *County Court Act* 1890 is final and conclusive for all purposes, and there is no power to allow the plaintiff any costs beyond the amount so fixed. *Armstrong* v. *Cuming Smith & Co. Proprietary Ltd.*, 29 A.L.T. (Supplement), 17 ; 13 A.L.R. (C.N.), 34. *Judge Chomley* (1907).

Imprisonment of Fraudulent Debtors Act 1890 (No. 1100), sec. 15—County Court, Rules of 1891, interpretation clause, r. 354— Schedule of Scale of Costs, Item 2—Judgment summons— Judgment under £10 — Practitioners' costs—Attending at hearing—Instructions.]—On granting leave to withdraw a judgment summons issued on a judgment for less than £10, a Judge of the County Court may order payment by the judgment creditor of the judgment debtor's practitioner's costs for instructions from his client ; but he may not allow the costs of the practitioner for attending on such summons. *Coppel* v. *Anderson*, 28 A.L.T. (Supplement), 8 ; 12 A.L.R. (C.N.), 22. *Judge Box* (1906). ·

County Court Act 1890 (No. 1078), secs. 68, 70, 71—Discontinuance of action—Costs not paid—Subsequent action for same cause of action—Stay of proceedings until costs paid—Jurisdiction.]—A Judge of a County Court has power to stay an action until payment by the plaintiff of the costs ordered to be paid by him in a prior action for the same cause of action against the same defendant. *Leeder* v. *Ballarat East, Mayor, &c., of*, 29 A.L.T. (Supplement), 6 ; 13 A.L.R. (C.N.), 25. *Judge Eagleson* (1907).

County Court Act 1890 (No. 1078), sec. 47— Costs of chamber application—Jurisdiction of Judge to fix.]—A Judge of a County Court has jurisdiction under sec. 47 of the *County Court Act* 1890 to fix the amount of the costs of an application before him in Chambers. *Leeder* v. *Ballarat East, Mayor, &c., of*, 29 A.L.T. (Supplement), 6 ; 13 A.L.R. (C.N.), 25. *Judge Eagleson* (1907).

Notice of intention to present a petition for the winding up of a mining company—Service of notice—Petition not presented—Power of Court to award costs—Companies Act 1890 (No. 1074), sec. 252—Mines Act 1890 (No. 1120), sec. 179.]—Courts of Mines have jurisdiction to award costs where notice of intention to present a petition on a certain day for the winding up of a mining company has been given, although no such petition is presented. *Re The Mount Lyell Consols Mining Corporation, No Liability* (*No.* 1), 30 A.L.T. (Supplement), 13 ; 14 A.L.R. (C.N.), 40. *Judge Eagleson* (1908).

II.—DIVORCE.

(a) *Generally.*

Marriage Act 1890 (No. 1166), sec. 111— Divorce—Petition by husband—No substance in wife's case— Counter-charges without reasonable basis—Wife's costs, how to be borne.]—In a suit for dissolution of marriage a wife will not be allowed her costs unless her case has substance and the costs have been reasonably incurred ; and if charges are presented which have no reasonable basis, the costs are treated as costs which are incurred at the risk of those who have incurred them *Kay* v. *Kay*, (1904) P., 382, at p. 397, followed and applied. *Garrick* v. *Garrick* ; *Sutton, co-respondent*, (1908) V.L.R., 420 ; 30 A.L.T., 21 ; 14 A.L.R., 312. *Hood, J.*

Marriage Act 1890 (No. 1166), sec. 111— Wife's costs, how to be borne—Petition by husband on ground of adultery—Wife's denial withdrawn — Unfounded counter-charges against husband.]—In answer to a husband's petition for dissolution of marriage on the ground of his wife's adultery, the wife pleaded a denial of the adultery and set up counter-charges of cruelty, connivance, and misconduct. The denial of the adultery was withdrawn shortly before the hearing of the petition, and at the hearing the Court found that in the face of the facts the counter-charges ought never to have been made, and certainly ought never to have been carried into Court. *Held,* that the wife's costs be not allowed, and that the £20 paid into Court by the petitioner under sec. 111 of the *Marriage Act* 1890 be returned to him or his proctor. *Garrick* v. *Garrick* ; *Sutton, co-respondent,* (1909) V.L.R., 420 ; 30 A.L.T., 21 ; 14 A.L.R., 312. *Hood, J.* (1908).

(b) *Under Section* 111 *of the Marriage Act* 1890.

Marriage Act 1890 (No. 1166), sec. 111—Divorce—Money for investigation of Wife's case — Merits of her case — Demerits of Husband's Case.]—A wife who is respondent in a suit for dissolution of marriage on the ground of adultery, is not entitled under sec. 111 of the *Marriage Act* 1890 to an order for the payment into Court by her husband, the petitioner, of a sum of money merely for the purpose of enabling her to have investigated by her proctor a countercharge of adultery which she intends to make against him in the suit. *Rackham* v. *Rackham* ; *Stokes (co-respondent),* (1913) V.L.R., 120 ; 34 A.L.T., 141 ; 18 A.L.R., 581. *Hodges, J.* (1912).

Divorce—Practice—Application for investigation money—Time for making—Answer already filed by wife respondent—Marriage Act 1890 (No. 1166), sec. 111.]—An order, that the husband, petitioner, shall pay into Court a sum of money for the investigation of the respondent's case, may be made after the respondent has filed her answer ; but the application should be made promptly and before any further steps are taken. *Goodman* v. *Goodman,* (1906) V.L.R., 671 ; 28 A.L.T., 122 ; 12 A.L.R., 548. *Hodges, J.*

Marriage Act 1890 (No. 1166), sec. 111—Costs of preliminary investigation—Application after investigation made—Whether too late.]—An application by the respondent for the costs of having the merits of her case investigated is too late if made after the work of investigation has been done. *Wilson*

v. *Wilson,* 17 A.L.T., 154, and *Vogt* v. *Vogt,* 25 V.L.R., 283 ; 21 A.L.T,, 109 ; 5 A.L.R. (C.N.), 77, followed. *Kidd* v. *Kidd,* (1908) V.L.R., 409 ; 30 A.L.T., 29 ; 14 A.L.R., 274. *Hood, J.*

Marriage Act 1890 (No. 1166), s. 111—Costs of investigating case of wife—Time for making application—Petition by wife—Respondent's answer filed—Case already investigated.]—An application, in a suit in which the wife is petitioner, for an order under sec. 111 of the *Marriage Act* 1890 for payment into Court of a sum of money sufficient to enable her to have the merits of her case investigated is not too late, although made after the respondent has filed his answer. But no order will be made if, prior to such application, an investigation of the merits of the petitioner's case has been made by her proctor. *Ruddell* v. *Ruddell,* (1911) V.L.R., 277; 33 A.L.T., 10 ; 17 A.L.R., 276. *Cussen, J.*

Marriage Act 1890 (No. 1166), sec. 111—Wife's costs—Sum fixed by Taxing Master on proctor's certificate—Order to pay sum so fixed into Court—Jurisdiction—No preliminary order as to investigation of merits of case.]—Where the wife's proctor, no order having being obtained with reference to having the merits of her case investigated, filed a certificate that she had a good cause of action on the merits, and the Taxing Master thereupon fixed the sum which was to be paid into Court, an order was made that the husband should forthwith pay such sum into Court. *Zanoni* v. *Zanoni,* 24 V.L.R., 940 ; 5 A.L.R., 206, and *Rickerby* v. *Rickerby,* 25 A.L.T., 95 ; 10 A.L.R., 30, followed. *Farrer* v. *Farrer,* (1907) V.L.R., 382 ; 28 A.L.T., 221 ; 13 A.L.R., 236. *Cussen, J.*

Marriage Act 1890 (No. 1166), secs. 111, 118—Divorce—Wife's costs—No preliminary order as to investigation—Suit by husband in forma pauperis—Payment into Court of Wife's costs—Jurisdiction to order.]—Under sec. 111 of the *Marriage Act* 1890 an order may be made for payment into Court by a husband of the sum fixed by the Taxing Master as the amount of the wife's costs, although no order has been obtained for payment by him of money to enable her to have her case investigated. Under that section a husband who has been granted leave under sec. 118 to sue in *forma pauperis* may be ordered to pay into Court the sum so fixed. *Howard* v. *Howard*, (1913) V.L.R., 47; 34 A.L.T., 116; 18 A.L.R., 528. *a' Beckett, J.*

Marriage Act 1890 (No. 1166), sec. 111— Wife respondent not appearing at trial—Order that £20 paid into Court be paid out to wife's proctor.]—Where under sec. 111 of the *Marriage Act* 1890 the sum of £20 had been paid into Court, but the wife respondent did not appear at the trial, the money was ordered to be paid out to the wife's proctor on account of his costs for preparing her defence. *Montgomery* v. *Montgomery and Andrews*, 12 A.L.R. (C.N.), 1. *Madden, C.J.* (1906).

Marriage Act 1890 (No. 1166), sec. 111— Order for payment into Court of wife's costs— Failure to obey order—Stay of proceedings— Jurisdiction.]—Whether an order will be made staying all proceedings in a suit for dissolution of marriage until the husband who is petitioner therein shall have paid into Court the sum so fixed for the wife's costs is a matter of discretion. Where proceedings in a suit by a husband against his wife for dissolution of marriage had been stayed until payment into Court of the respondent's costs under sec. 111, and the petitioner subsequently instituted in *forma pauperis* another suit on the same ground, the petitioner was ordered in the latter suit to pay into Court the sum of £20 for the respondent's costs, but, in view of the circumstances of the case, the hearing of this suit was not to be stayed pending payment into Court under this order or by reason of the order made in the previous suit. *Howard* v. *Howard*, (1913) V.L.R., 47; 34 A.L.T., 116; 18 A.L.R., 528. *a' Beckett, J.* (1912).

No appearance by respondent—Service of summons by filing—Divorce Rules 1907, rr. 36, 38, 39, 59—Marriage Act 1890 (No. 1166), sec. 111.]—Where the husband respondent has not appeared in the suit, a summons to obtain an order that he pay into Court the sum fixed by the taxing officer for his wife's costs may be served by filing with the Prothonotary. *Farrer* v. *Farrer*, (1907) V.L.R., 382; 28 A.L.T., 221; 13 A.L.R., 236. *Cussen, J.* (1907).

III.—DISCRETION OF COURT, HOW EXERCISED.

(a) Public Officers.

Licences Reduction Board—Procedure on deprivation of victualler's licences—Mistaken refusal to hear owners and occupiers of other licensed premises who are interested—Erroneous belief in absence of jurisdiction to hear them—Prohibition—Costs.]— Notwithstanding the existence of a fund under the control of the Licences Reduction Board out of which the costs of all parties in *The King* v. *Licences Reduction Board*; *Ex parte Martin and Godfrey*, (1908) V.L.R., 721; 30 A.L.T., 133; 14 A.L.R., 675, had been ordered to be paid, where the error of the Board was in holding that they had no power to permit the relator to intervene, the order *nisi* for a writ of prohibition was made absolute, without costs. *The King* v. *Licences Reduction Board*; *Ex parte Miller*, (1909) V.L.R., 327; 30 A.L.T., 223; 15 A.L.R., 282. F.C., *Hodges*, and *Hood, JJ.* (*a' Beckett, J.*, dissenting).

Patent—Appeal from Commissioner—Right of Commissioner when unsuccessful to his costs—Patents Act 1903 (No. 21 of 1903), sec. 111.]—Where the Commissioner of Patents is represented upon the hearing of an appeal from his decision and the appeal succeeds, the costs of the Commissioner are in the discretion of the Court, and ordinarily the successful appellant will not be ordered to pay them. *Re McKay's Application*, (1909) V.L.R., 423; 31 A.L.T., 63; 15 A.L.R., 445. *a' Beckett, Hodges* and *Hood, JJ.*

Trustee in insolvency—Certificate of discharge—Compulsory application—Power of trustee—Costs.]—*See* INSOLVENCY. *In re McConnell*, 29 A.L.T. (Supplement), 26; 14 A.L.R. (C.N.), 19. *Judge Moule* (1908).

(b) Where Trial with Jury.

Order LXV., r. 1—Costs—Trial by a jury— Wrongful dismissal—One farthing damages— "Good cause."]—In an action for wrongful

9

dismissal, the jury awarded the plaintiff a farthing damages. The Judge was of opinion that the verdict was attributable to disapproval of the plaintiff's conduct and disbelief of his denials on the part of some at least of the jury, and His Honor also disapproved of such conduct, and disbelieved such denials. *Held*, that there was "good cause" for depriving the plaintiff of his costs. *Galsworthy v. Reid*, 32 A.L.T., 189; 17 A.L.R., 144. *a'Beckett, J.* (1911).

Order LXV., r. 1 (Rules of 1906)—Costs—Trial by jury—"Event," meaning of—Several causes of action—Taxation.]—Where in an action for several causes of action tried before a jury the plaintiff succeeds on some causes of action, and fails on others, the result of each cause of action is an "event" within the meaning of Order LXV., r. 1, and, unless there is good cause shown, judgment should be given for the plaintiff for the amount recovered by him with costs on the causes of action on which he succeeded, and for the defendant for the costs of the causes of action on which he has succeeded, and the costs of each cause of action should be taxed as if it were a separate action. *O'Sullivan v. Morton*, (1911) V.L.R., 249; 32 A.L.T., 198; 17 A.L.R., 201. F.C., *Madden, C.J., Hodges* and *Hood, JJ.* (1911). [Leave to appeal refused], (1911) 12 C.L.R., 390.]

Order XXIII., r. 5a—Order XXXVI., r. 7 (c)—Jury fees—Action—Trial with a jury—Memorandum of close of pleadings—Statement therein of number of jurors—Payment of jury fees on entering case for trial.]—*See* PRACTICE AND PLEADING. *Moss v. Donnelly*, (1909) V.L.R., 443; 31 A.L.T., 49; 15 A.L.R., 516.

(c) Defendants in Same Interest or Joining in Defence.

Order LXV.—Costs of two parties appearing in same interest.]—For observations on the allowance of costs to two parties appearing in the same interest, *see In re Hobson*; *Hobson v. Sharp*, (1907) V.L.R., 724; 29 A.L.T., 125; 13 A.L.R., 703. *Cussen, J.*

Costs—Two defendants joining in one defence—One succeeding, the other failing—

Order that each abide his own costs.]—*See Crout v. Beissel*, (1909) V.L.R., 207; 30 A.L.T., 185; 15 A.L.R., 143. *a'Beckett, J.*

(d) Set-off.

Order LXV., r. 14 (Rules of 1906)—Several causes of action—Set-off of costs recovered by defendant against damages and costs recovered by plaintiff—Complication of evidence and argument on several causes of action.]—Where in an action for several causes of action which crossed one another in evidence and argument, the plaintiff obtained judgment for damages on one cause of action with the costs thereof, and the defendant obtained judgment for costs on the other causes of action, *Held*, that the costs of the defendant in respect of the causes of action on which he succeeded should be set off against the damages and costs in respect of the cause of action on which the plaintiff succeeded. *O'Sullivan v. Morton*, (1911) V.L.R., 249; 32 A.L.T., 198; 17 A.L.R., 201. F.C., *Madden, C.J., Hodges* and *Hood, JJ.* (1911). [Leave to appeal refused, (1911) 12 C.L.R., 390].

(e) Special Scales of Costs.

Patents Act 1903 (No. 21 of 1903) (Commonwealth), ss. 14, 58, 111—Appeal against decision of Commissioner of Patents—Costs of opposition to grant of patent before Commissioner.]—The costs of a successful appellant's opposition before the Commissioner were allowed on the lower Supreme Court scale. *Moore v. Phillips*, 4 C.L.R., 1411; 13 A.L.R., 424. H.C., *Griffith, C.J., Barton, Isaacs* and *Higgins JJ.* (1907).

Taxation—Scale of costs—Action for recovery of land—No monetary claim—Order LXV., r. 29 (a), Appendix N. (Rules of 1904), whether applicable.]—Order LXV., r. 29 (a) (Rules of 1904) applies only to cases where a plaintiff is seeking to recover a sum of money, which sum does not exceed £500, and does not apply to an action for the recovery of land. *Griffin v. Millane*, (1907) V.L.R., 46; 28 A.L.T., 97; 12 A.L.R., 494. *Hood, J.* (1906).

Order LXV., r. 29 (a) (Rules of 1906)—Special scale of costs in Appendix N.—Application that costs be taxed on ordinary scale—When application to be made—Discretion of Judge.—An application by a successful party that his costs may be allowed on the ordinary scale, notwithstanding that the notice under Order LXV., r. 29 (a) has been given, should be made at the conclusion of the trial to the Judge who has tried the action. Such an application will not be granted unless definite special reasons are shown why the scale of costs in Appendix N. should be departed from. *Bloomfield* v. *Dunlop Tyre Co. Ltd.*, 28 V.L.R., 72; 23 A.L.T., 227; 8 A.L.R., 103, followed. *Chomley* v. *Watson*, (1907) V.L.R., 502; 29 A.L.T., 46; 13 A.L.R., 380. *Madden, C.J.* (1907).

Order LXV., r. 29 (a)—Costs—Special scale in Appendix N.—Notice of intention to proceed under, given by defendant on entry of appearance—Judgment for plaintiff—Application by plaintiff that the Judge should "otherwise order" as to scale of costs—When such application should be made.]—When either party to an action has given notice under Order LXV. r. 29 (a) that he intends to proceed under the special scale of costs in Appendix N., an application by the other party for an order that the costs of the action shall not be taxed under that scale must be made at the trial and before judgment. *Leviston* v. *Douglas*, (1912) V.L.R., 318; 34 A.L.T., 15; 18 A.L.R., 309. *Hodges, J.*

Order LXV., r. 12—Costs—Action of tort—Judgment for damages under £50 and injunction—Supreme Court costs—"Sum recovered"—Impossibility of valuing injunction.]—Order LXV., rule 12, of the Rules of the Supreme Court 1906 does not apply to an action where the plaintiff, in addition to damages, obtains judgment for an injunction which is a substantial part of his action. The principle determined in *Doherty* v. *Thompson*, 94 L.T., 626, and *Keates* v. *Woodward*, (1902) 1 K.B., 532, followed. An injunction is not, nor can its value be estimated so as to make it a "sum recovered." *Harrison San Miguel Proprietary Ltd.* v. *Alfred*

Lawrence & Co., (1912) V.L.R., 367; 34 A.L.T., 88; 18 A.L.R., 394. *Madden, C.J.*

(f) *Omission to Deal with Costs at Hearing.*

Order XXXI., r. 3* (Rules of 1900)—Interrogatories—Costs—No application as to at trial—Application for after trial.]—Where a party had omitted to apply at the trial for the costs of interrogatories, an order was made allowing such costs after the lapse of two years from the trial, no special circumstances being shown why the order should not be made. *General Finance &c. Co.* v. *National Trustees &c. Co.*, 12 A.L.R. (C.N.), 1. *a' Beckett, J.* (1906).

Commission to examine witnesses—Costs reserved until trial—Judgment for general costs of action—No mention at hearing of costs of commission—Jurisdiction to amend—Order XXVIII., r. 11—"Accidental slip or omission" in judgment, correction of after appeal—Special circumstances—Complicated issues and lengthy trial.]—*See* PRACTICE AND PLEADING, Order XXVIII. *Melbourne Harbour Trust Commissioners* v. *Cuming Smith & Co. Proprietary Ltd.*, (1906) V.L.R. 192; 27 A.L.T., 186; 12 A.L.R., 142.

County Court — Costs — Taxation — Conference with counsel—No application made at hearing—Discretion of Registrar—County Court Rules 1891, Schedule of Scale of Costs, Item 13.]—Where no application has been made at the hearing of an action to be allowed for a conference with counsel under Item 13 of the Schedule of Scale of Costs, the allowance of such a charge is a matter for the discretion of the Registrar. *Hopkins* v. *Forster*, 32 A.L.T. (Supplement), 5; 16 A.L.R. (C.N.), 6; *Judge Chomley* (1910).

(g) *Application for Final Judgment.*

Order XIV., r. 8 (Rules of 1900)—Costs—Application for liberty to enter final judgment dismissed—Order made as on summons for directions.]—No general rule will be laid down as to the costs of an application for liberty to enter final judgment where the application is dismissed, and the matter is treated as a summons for directions. *International Har-*

vester Co. of America Ltd. v. Mullavey, (1906) V.L.R., 659 ; 28 A.L.T., 51 ; 12 A.L.R., 380. Hodges, J.

Order XIV., rr. 1, 8—Dismissal of summons for final judgment—Directions given after dismissal—Costs.]—See PRACTICE AND PLEADING. Colonial Bank of Australasia Ltd. v. Martin, (1912) V.L.R., 383 ; 34 A.L.T., 47 ; 18 A.L.R., 325.

(h) Contested Wills.

Will—Probate—Caveat— Costs — Administration and Probate Act 1890 (No. 1060), sec. 21.]—In cases of contested wills, costs should follow the event unless there are adequate reasons for an order of a different character. Where the testator by his conduct, habits or mode of life has given the opponent of the will reasonable grounds for questioning his testamentary capacity, the costs of the opponent, although he is unsuccessful, should be paid out of the estate. Where that is not so, but the opponent after due inquiry entertains a bona fide belief in the existence of a state of things, which, if it did exist, would justify the litigation, the unsuccessful party must bear his own costs. In re Millar, (1908) V.L.R., 682 ; 30 A.L.T., 106 ; 14 A.L.R., 564. Hood, J.

Will — Probate — Practice — Costs — Order nisi to revoke probate—Costs of unsuccessful propounder of will—Reasonable belief in validity of will.]—An executor who has obtained probate of an instrument which he reasonably and bona fides believes to be a valid will, but which is afterwards revoked on the ground of want of testamentary capacity, should be allowed out of the estate his costs as between solicitor and client, both of propounding the will and of opposing the application for revocation of probate. Twist v. Tye, (1902) P., 92, considered. In re Keane, (1909) V.L.R., 231 ; 30 A.L.T., 216 ; 15 A.L.R., 198. Hodges, J.

Will—Party supporting invalid revocation—Costs.]—Semble, the costs of a party supporting an apparently valid but really invalid revocation of a will by destruction, are governed by the same considerations as govern the costs of an executor propounding an apparently valid but really invalid will. In re Richards, (1911) V.L.R., 284 ; 33 A.L.T., 38. a' Beckett, J.

(i) Administration of Estates ; Interpretation of Wills, &c.

Costs— Originating summons — Litigation arising out of plaintiff's mistake as executor.]—Plaintiff, executor of a will, ordered to bear his own costs of an originating summons, the main purpose of which was to adjust a difference between the plaintiff and a beneficiary arising out of a mistake made by the plaintiff as executor. Perpetual Executors and Trustees Association v. Simpson, 27 A.L.T., 179 ; 12 A.L.R., 95. a' Beckett, J. (1905).

Will—Construction—Validity of Trusts—Originating summons—Costs.]—" The cases to which counsel referred on the question of costs show that at all events since 1908 it has been the practice in cases like the present to grant costs out of the estate as between solicitor and client to all parties, and as there are here no circumstances to justify a departure from that practice I accordingly make that order. The costs are to be paid one half out of the accumulation within the twenty-one years and the other half out of the accumulations since." In re Stevens ; The Trustees Executors &c. Co. Ltd. v. Teague, (1912) V.L.R., 194 ; 33 A.L.T., 233 ; 18 A.L.R., 195. Hood, J.

Costs—Trustees—Unsuccessful Appeal.]— The costs of trustees, unsuccessful appellants, were in the special circumstances allowed out of the estate. In re Rosenthal ; Rosenthal v. Rosenthal, (1910) 11 C.L.R., 87 ; 16 A.L.R., 455. H.C., Griffith, C.J. and Isaacs, J. (Higgins, J., dissenting).

Costs — Originating — summons — King's Counsel appearing with junior—Certificate for counsel.]—On an originating summons in which King's Counsel appeared with a junior, the Judge, upon an application that he should certify for one counsel only, left the matter to the discretion of the Taxing Officer. In re Jamieson ; Christensen v. Jamieson, (1907) V.L.R., 103 ; 28 A.L.T., 138 ; 12 A.L.R., 570. Cussen, J.

Costs—Trustees—Passing accounts and allowance of commission—Order for in action—Trustees' costs of obtaining commission—Whether chargeable against estate—Administration and Probate Act 1890 (No. 1060), sec. 26.]—Where, under an order in an action, trustees are authorised to pass their accounts and apply for commission, they are entitled to charge the estate with the costs incurred by them in relation to commission, as well as in regard to passing their accounts. *Abbott v. Morris*, 24 A.L.T., 228; 9 A.L.R., 96, not followed on this point. *Macartney v. Kesterson*, (1907) V.L.R., 226; 28 A.L.T., 170; 13 A.L.R., 14. *Hodges, J.*

Trustees—Passing Accounts and Allowance of Commission—Costs of trustee—Summons for sole purpose of obtaining leave to pass accounts and commission.]—Trustees seeking leave by originating summons to pass their accounts and obtain commission out of the testator's estate on passing accounts, may be allowed their costs out of the estate, even though no other questions are asked by the summons. *In re Foulkes* ; *Ford v. Foulkes*, 30 A.L.T., 108; 14 A.L.R., 729. *Madden, C.J.* (1908).

Executor or trustee passing accounts—Costs—Whether payable out of estate.]—Although ordinarily an executor or trustee is entitled to have his costs of passing his accounts and obtaining his discharge paid out of the estate, yet, if in so doing he seeks to cast an unnecessary burden on the estate, he must abide those costs himself. *Cattenach v. Macpherson*, (1908) V.L.R., 390; 29 A.L.T., 259; 14 A.L.R., 214. *Madden, C.J.*

Administration and Probate Act 1890 (No. 1060), sec. 26—Practice—Executors and Trustees—Passing Accounts before Chief Clerk—Costs of executors and trustees—Objection to allowance thereof—Time to take.]—Where beneficiaries desire to object that executors and trustees should not be allowed their costs of the proceedings before the Chief Clerk for the passing of accounts and allowance of commission, they should ask the Chief Clerk to certify specially upon the matter, and then raise the question upon further consideration before the Judge on the certificate. *In re Dingwall* ; *Ross v. Ross*, 34 A.L.T., 137; 18 A.L.R., 584. *a'Beckett, J.* (1912).

Trustees—Corpus and income interested—Mathematical adjustment of the burden of costs impossible—Burden divided equally.]—See *Macartney v. Macartney*, (1909) V.L.R., 183; 30 A.L.T., 172; 15 A.L.R., 139. *Hodges, J.*

Practice—Originating summons—Payment of costs out of estate—Order for sale of settled properties.]—An originating summons was taken out asking for certain directions affecting several properties settled by the will of the testator and seeking the sale of such properties. The sale was refused on the ground on which it was asked for, but there being no part of the testator's estate other than the properties in question out of which the costs of the summons could properly be taken the Court in the circumstances directed a sale of the whole of the properties for the payment of the costs, though the sale of some only of such properties would have been sufficient for the purpose. *In re Lees* ; *Lees v. National Trustees Co.*, (1908) V.L.R., 211; 30 A.L.T., 26; 14 A.L.R., 147. *a'Beckett, J.*

(j) Conveyancing.

Vendor and purchaser—Apparent flaw on title—Costs of proving existence of facts negativing existence of flaw.]—The costs of proving facts negativing the existence of what, on the face of the documents, appeared to be a flaw in the title, were ordered to be paid by the vendor. *In re Kenna and Ritchie's Contract*, (1907) V.L.R., 386; 28 A.L.T., 218; 13 A.L.R., 191. *a'Beckett, J.*

(k) In Patent Matters.

Patents Act 1890 (No. 1123), sec. 50—Costs —Defendant's particulars of objections—Certificate of reasonableness.]—For a case in which, for the purposes of taxation of costs under the special circumstances of the case, a certificate was granted that the particulars of the defendant under sec. 50 of the *Patents Act* 1890 were reasonable, *see Potter*

v. *Broken Hill Proprietary Co. Ltd.*, 13
A.L.R. (C.N.), 3. *a' Beckett, J.* (1907).

Patent—Practice—Application to Court for indulgence—Attendance of Commissioner of Patents—Costs.]—Where an applicant for a patent applies to the High Court for an indulgence on notice to the Commissioner of Patents it is the duty of the Commissioner to attend the hearing and the applicant, whether he is successful or not, must pay the costs of the Commissioner. *In re Stanley's Application*, (1908) 5 C.L.R., 508 ; 14 A.L.R., 238. *Isaacs, J.*

(*l*) *Other Cases.*

Appeal—Dismissal on the ground that it is incompetent—No notice of objection before hearing.—Costs]—Where an appeal is dismissed on the ground that it is incompetent, the respondent, if he has not given the appellant notice of such ground before the hearing, may not be allowed costs. *Jenkins* v. *Lanfranchi*, (1910) 10 C.L.R., 595 ; 16 A.L.R., 275. H.C., *Griffith, C.J., O'Connor, Isaacs* and *Higgins, JJ.*

Costs—Attorney-General necessary party—Attorney-General not joined until after proceedings instituted—Special order as to costs.]—The Attorney-General having been held to be a necessary party, and having accordingly been joined as a party to proceedings after they had been instituted against a municipal council, a special order was made as to costs. *Attorney-General (ex rel. Dodd)* v. *Ararat, Mayor, &c., of Borough of*, (1911) V.L.R., 489 ; 33 A.L.T., 99 ; 17 A.L.R., 474. *Madden, C.J.*

IV. BILLS OF COSTS.

Supreme Court Act 1890 (No. 1142), sec. 209—Solicitor—Client—Bill of costs—Order for delivery—Discretion of Court.]—Under sec. 209 of the *Supreme Court Act* 1890 the Court has discretion to refuse to order the delivery of a bill of costs. *Bear* v. *Waxman*, (1912) V.L.R., 292 ; 34 A.L.T., 6 ; 18 A.L.R., 269. F.C., *Madden, C.J., Hood* and *Cussen, JJ.*

Taxation—Solicitor and client—Bill of costs, what is—Moneys paid to solicitors in England in respect of appeal to Privy Council—Account of balance of lump sum so paid attached to bill of costs—" Moderation " of charges—Whether amount paid to English solicitors " moderated " or " taxed "—Jurisdiction to review decision of Taxing Master.]—Attached to B. and H.'s bill of costs, which was signed and dated, was a cash account in which the balance of a lump sum was charged as payment to solicitors in England acting in connection with an application for leave to appeal to the Privy Council from the decision in the action in which the costs set out in the bill were incurred. The order of the Court directing taxation did not expressly provide for liberty to charge all sums paid by the solicitors to or on account of the client. The Taxing Master during the taxation in fact dealt with the payment made to the English solicitors, and, to enable him to do so, B. and H. gave him details of the charges of those solicitors. The client had provided the moneys to pay the costs of the English solicitors. *Held*, that the balance charged as payment to the English solicitors did not form part of the bill of costs. *Held*, also, that, under the circumstances, the Taxing Master had not taxed the English solicitor's charges as part of the bill, but had " moderated " them as if they had been charges made by a commission agent. *Semble*, the Court had no jurisdiction to review the Taxing Master's decision. *In re Lamrock, Brown and Hall's Costs*, (1908) V.L.R., 238 ; 29 A.L.T., 214 ; 14 A.L.R., 81. *Cussen, J.*

V. TAXATION.

(*a*) HIGH COURT AND SUPREME COURT.
(1) *Review of Taxation.*

Order LXV., r. 27 (38a) (Rules of 1906)—Taxation—Costs increased by misconduct or negligence of solicitor—Report of Taxing officer—Duty of Judge, nature of.]—On a report by the Taxing Officer under Order LXV., r. 27 (38A) the jurisdiction of the Judge is not disciplinary, but in the nature of a review of taxation. *Woolf* v. *Willis*, (1911) 13 C.L.R., 23 ; 17 A.L.R., 454. H.C., *Griffith, C.J., Barton* and *O'Connor, JJ.*

Order LXV., r. 28 (Rules of 1906)—Whether applicable to probate matters — Appeal from

Taxing Officer's decision on item " Instructions for brief "—Discretion of Judge.]—*Quaere,* whether Order LXV., r. 28, applies to probate matters, or to any proceedings other than actions *Re Duke's Will,* (1907) V.L.R., 632; 29 A.L.T., 50; 13 A.L.R., 477. *Cussen, J.* (1907).

Taxation—Solicitor and client—Bill of costs, what is—Money paid to solicitors in England in respect of appeal to Privy Council—Account of balance of lump sum so paid attached to bill of costs—" Moderation " of charges—Whether amount paid to English solicitors " moderated " or " taxed."—Jurisdiction to review decision of Taxing Master.]—*See, ante,* Sub-heading, BILL OF COSTS. *In re Lamrock, Brown and Hall's Costs,* (1908) V.L.R., 238; 29 A.L.T., 214; 14 A.L.R., 81.

(2) Costs of Order to Review Heard by High Court.

Costs—Taxation—Appeal from Court of Petty Sessions to High Court—Order to review—Limitation of amount of costs—Justices Act 1890 (No. 1105), sec. 148—Rules of the High Court 1903, Part I., Order XLVI., r. 14; Part II., Sec. IV., r. 1; Rules of the High Court of 12th October, 1903, r. 3.]—Order XLVI., r. 14 of Part I., of the *Rules of the High Court* 1903 which prescribes the scale for taxation of costs does not refer to any maximum amount of costs to be allowed, and, therefore, the provision in sec. 148 of the *Justices Act* 1890, which limits the total amount of costs that can be allowed in the Supreme Court upon an order to review a decision of a Court of Petty Sessions to £20, does not apply to the costs of an appeal by way of order to review from a Court of Petty Sessions exercising federal jurisdiction to the High Court. *Lyons* v. *Smart,* (1908) 6 C.L.R., 285; 14 A.L.R., 619. H.C., *Griffith, C.J., Barton, O'Connor, Isaacs* and *Higgins, JJ.*

(3) Costs of Appeal from County Court.

Practice—Costs — Taxation — Appeal from County Court—Order dismissing appeal with costs to be taxed by Taxing Master.]—Where the Full Court has made an order that an appeal from the County Court be dismissed with Costs, such costs to be taxed by the Taxing Master of the Supreme Court, the Taxing Master has power to tax only the costs of the appeal, and has no power to tax the costs incurred in the County Court prior to the institution of the appeal. *Marks* v. *Pett,* 10 V.L.R. (L.), 342, commented on. *Ambler & Co. Proprietary Ltd.* v. *Clayton,* (1909) V.L.R., 56; 30 A.L.T., 113; 14 A.L.R., 730. *a' Beckett, J.*

(4) Instructions for Brief.

Instructions for brief—Total amount allowed by Taxing Officer not excessive—Item in such amount not properly chargeable—Reduction of total amount.]—Where the total amount allowed for " Instructions for brief " appears to the Court to be reasonable, having regard to the nature of the case, but the taxing officer has shown how he makes up the amount and the Court disagrees with the allowance of an item, the total amount will be reduced by the amount of that item. *Re Duke's Will,* (1907) V.L.R., 632; 29 A.L.T., 50; 13 A.L.R., 477. *Cussen, J.*

" Instructions for Brief "—What included therein—Typing notes of evidence.]—*Quaere,* whether the charge for typing notes of evidence for the use of counsel is properly included under " Instructions for Brief." *In re Duke's Will,* (1907) V.L.R., 632; 29 A.L.T., 50; 13 A.L.R., 477. *Cussen, J.*

(5) Drawing Documents.

Taxation—Appendix N.—Drawing pleadings and other documents—Accounts, statements, &c. for Judges' Chambers—Statement for duty.]—A statement for duty is not included under the item in Appendix N. " Accounts, statements and other documents for the Judge's Chambers, when required, and fair copy to leave." *In re Duke's Will,* (1907) V.L.R., 632; 29 A.L.T., 50; 13 A.L.R., 477. *Cussen, J.*

(6) Copies.

High Court—Appeal Rules, Section IV., r. 16—Printing evidence for purpose of appeal—" Printing," whether it includes type-writing.]—Type-writing is not " printing " within the meaning of section IV., r. 16 of the Appeal Rules under the *High Court Procedure Act. Peacock* v. *Osborne & Co.*, 13 A.L.R., 254. *Barton, J.* (1907).

Order XLVI., r. 13 (High Court)—Costs—Proceedings of an unnecessarily expensive character—" Taking proceedings," meaning of—Printing or type-writing documents and evidence.]—Preparing type-written or printed copies of documents or evidence for an appeal is not taking a proceeding within the meaning of Order XLVI., r. 13. *Peacock* v. *Osborne & Co.*, 13 A.L.R., 254. *Barton, J.* (1907).

Order LXV., r. 31—Taxation—Solicitor and client—Copies of documents brought from opposite party—Costs of.]—Order LXV., r. 31 does not apply where copies of documents are bought from the other side. *In re Lamrock Brown & Hall's Costs*, (1908) V.L.R., 238 ; 29 A.L.T., 214 ; 14 A.L.R., 81. *Cussen, J.*

Taxation—Solicitor and Client—Firm of solicitors carrying on business in Melbourne and country town—Correspondence between Melbourne and country office—Close copies for country office—Whether costs may be allowed.]—Where two solicitors in partnership practise both at Melbourne and at a country town, one partner having the entire management of the Melbourne business and the other of the country business, charges for correspondence between the two offices and of close copies for the use of the country office are not allowable on taxation. *The New Kohinoor Co.* v. *Williams*, 13 V.L.R., 435 ; 8 A.L.T., 169 ; and *Connors* v. *McCarthy*, 17 A.L.T., 187 ; 2 A.L.R., 10 ; discussed. *In re Lamrock, Brown & Hall's Costs*, (1908) V.L.R., 238 ; 29 A.L.T., 214 ; 14 A.L.R., 81. *Cussen, J.*

Taxation—Solicitor and client—Copy of notes of proceedings at hearing for use in Appeal Court.]—A charge for a copy of the notes of the proceedings at the hearing for use of counsel on appeal was allowed. *Semble*, such a charge is not affected by the decision : *In re Duke's Will*, (1907) V.L.R., 632 ; 29 A.L.T., 50 ; 13 A.L.R., 477. *In re Lamrock Brown & Hall's Costs*, (1908) V.L.R., 238 ; 29 A.L.T., 214 ; 14 A.L.R., 81. *Cussen, J.*

Costs—Taxation—Party and party—Copy of Judge's notes—No agreement that costs be costs in the cause—No order of Court.]—Costs of obtaining a copy of the Judge's notes are not allowed in a taxation between party and party in the absence of any agreement that they shall be costs in the cause or an order of the Court. *Semble*, such an agreement should be embodied in an order of the Court. *National Trustees &c. Co.* v. *Hassett*, (1908) V.L.R., 282 ; 29 A.L.T., 229 ; 14 A.L.R., 154. *Cussen, J.*

Taxation—Notes of evidence—Duty of counsel.]—Where one counsel alone is conducting a complicated and technical case, neither he nor the clerk in attendance can be expected to take full notes of the evidence given. *National Trustees &c. Co.* v. *Hassett*, (1908) V.L.R., 282 ; 29 A.L.T., 229 ; 14 A.L.R., 154. *Cussen, J.*

(7) Attendances ; Consultations.

Taxation—Attendance on Registrar of Probates—What should be allowed for.]—*Quaere*, whether an allowance of 10s. for attendance on the Registrar of Probates should not have been 6s. 8d. *In re Duke's Will*, (1907) V.L.R., 632 ; 29 A.L.T., 50 ; 13 A.L.R., 477. *Cussen, J.*

Order LXV., r. 31 (Rules of 1906)—Attendance to deliver documents—What included in such item—Attendances on counsel with brief, &c.]—Order LXV., r. 31 does not apply to attendances on counsel with brief, to appoint consultations, or to mark refreshers. *In re Duke's Will*, (1907) V.L.R., 632 ; 29 A.L.T., 50 ; 13 A.L.R., 477. *Cussen, J.*

Taxation—Scale N.—Necessary attendance where no other provision made—Consultation with solicitor for purpose of getting advice.]—The item in Scale N. " For any other necessary attendance where no other provision is made, per hour 6s. 8d." does not apply to attendances in the nature of consultations by the client with the solicitor for the purpose of getting legal advice in connection with the management of an estate of which the client is executrix. *In re Duke's Will*, (1907) V.L.R., 632; 29 A.L.T., 50; 13 A.L.R., 477. *Cussen, J.*

Taxation—Solicitor and client—Country solicitor—Attendance at trial at Melbourne—Costs of, when allowed.]—The expenses of the attendance of a country solicitor at the trial of an action in Melbourne are allowed in exceptional cases only. *In re Lamrock Brown & Hall's Costs*, (1908) V.L.R., 238; 29 A.L.T., 214; 14 A.L.R., 81. *Cussen, J.*

Taxation—Solicitor and client—" Attendance "—Client interviewing solicitor — No specific information as to advice given—Discretion of Taxing Master to disallow costs.]—Though *prima facie* where a client calls and takes up the time of a solicitor about the client's business, an attendance should be allowed for, yet, if the solicitor can say nothing more than that there were a number of attendances in the course of preparing for the hearing of an action, and can give no specific information as to the advice given, the Taxing Officer may properly disallow charges for such attendances. *In re Lamrock Brown & Hall's Costs*, (1908) V.L.R., 238; 29 A.L.T., 214; 14 A.L.R., 81. *Cussen, J.*

Taxation—Solicitor and client—" Attendance " where letter would have been sufficient—Discretion of Taxing Master to allow for costs of letter only.]—Where there are two courses open to a solicitor and he chooses the less economical one, the Taxing Officer has power to allow for the more economical course only. Accordingly, charge for letter allowed, and not for attendance. *In re Lamrock Brown & Hall's Costs*, (1908) V.L.R., 238; 29 A.L.T., 214; 14 A.L.R., 81. *Cussen, J.*

(8) *Counsel's Fees.*

Taxation — Refreshers — Refresher claimed for each day instead of for each period of five hours—Claim remodelled by Taxing Master.]—Where the refreshers to counsel were marked at the beginning of each day and some days exceeded five hours and some of the refreshers were, accordingly, for periods of more than five hours, the Taxing Master was justified in remodelling the claim so that in the total the party was allowed the amount he was entitled to under the rules, which was less than he actually claimed, but more than it would have been had the number of refreshers been calculated according to the number of days for which refreshers were marked and not according to the number of periods of five hours each, during which counsel was engaged. *National Trustees &c. Co. v. Hassett*, (1908) V.L.R., 282; 29 A.L.T., 229; 14 A.L.R., 154. *Cussen, J.*

Order LXV., r. 27 (48), (Rules of 1884 and 1906)—Taxation—" Leading counsel "—Absence of senior counsel.]—" Leading counsel " in Order LXV., r. 27 (48) means the counsel who was on the record as conducting the case. The second counsel while conducting the case from time to time in the absence of the senior counsel is not " leading counsel." *National Trustees &c. Co. v. Hassett*, (1908) V.L.R., 282; 29 A.L.T., 229; 14 A.L.R., 154. *Cussen, J.*

Rules of Supreme Court 1884, Order LXV., r. 27—Fee on brief marked after hearing concluded—Discretion.]—The Taxing Master may allow counsel's fee on brief although not marked before the conclusion of the hearing if satisfied that the omission to mark was accidental and that the solicitor had bound himself to pay the fee. *Re " Maizo " and " Maizena " Trade Marks; Robert Harper & Co. v. National Starch Co.*, (1906) V.L.R., 262; 27 A.L.T., 173; 12 A.L.R., 166. *a' Beckett, J.*

(9) *Witnesses.*

Costs—Witness—Permanent residence at place of trial—Temporary residence at another place—Scale applicable—Allowance for attendance at trial—Time occupied in travelling—Travelling expenses.] — Under Schedule XXXVIII. of the *Common Law Procedure Act 1865* a witness whose permanent residence is at the place of trial or in the neighbourhood is entitled to fees on the lower scale only, although he happens to be temporarily resident at another place. In such a case he is entitled to his expenses of travelling from and back to the place of his temporary residence, and to the scale allowance for the time occupied in travelling in addition to the time he is actually engaged at the trial. *Jarrett* v. *Strempel*, (1911) V.L.R., 179 ; 32 A.L.T., 160 ; 17 A.L.R., 141. *Hodges, J.*

Taxation—Service of subpoena—Discretion of Taxing Master to disallow costs of.]— Where he comes to the conclusion that a witness would have attended as well without as with a subpoena, and that the party making a charge for service of the subpoena upon such witness could not have been under any other belief on the subject, the Taxing Master is justified in disallowing such charge ; but if there is any doubt the charge should be allowed. *National Trustees &c. Co.* v. *Hassett*, (1908) V.L.R., 282 ; 29 A.L.T., 229 ; 14 A.L.R., 154. *Cussen, J.*

(10) *Procuring Evidence ; Cause not Brought on for Trial ; No Evidence Given as to Particular Defence.*

Taxation—Procuring Evidence before case set down for trial—Whether any special obligation to justify.]—There is no general rule that the procuring of evidence should not take place until after the action is set down for trial, and that a party who procures evidence at an earlier stage must satisfy the Taxing Master as to the necessity for so doing. *Etheridge* v. *President, &c. of the Shire of Berwick*, (1906) V.L.R., 746 ; 28 A.L.T., 77 ; 12 A.L.R., 442. *Cussen, J.*

Action not brought to trial—Whether costs prematurely incurred—Facts to be considered —Evidence procured before case set down for trial—Action for flooding land—Contour survey—Parties at issue—Summons for directions Order LXV., r. 27 (9), (49), (Rules of 1884).] —An action, in which the plaintiff claimed damages for the flooding of his land and an injunction, never came to trial but was put an end to by an order awarding the plaintiff his costs of the action to the date of the order and giving him liberty to take out of Court in satisfaction of his claim money which had been paid in with a denial of liability. The

defence, which was the only pleading ordered on the summons for directions, the endorsement on the writ being accepted as a statement of claim, denied the allegations in the indorsement. Immediately after the delivery of the defence, and before the action was set down for trial, the plaintiff caused a contour map of the land to be made. On the question whether the costs of the map should be disallowed on the ground that they were incurred prematurely. *Held*, that the Taxing Master should have regard to all the circumstances of the case at the time the costs were incurred, including the facts that it was an action for flooding, that the surveyor's report and evidence would have to be considered by the plaintiff's advisers as a source of information possibly affecting the future conduct of the case, that a plan would have to be prepared, that there had been a summons for directions, that on the delivery of the defence the parties were at issue, and that the action might be heard in a month. *Etheridge* v. *President &c. of the Shire of Berwick*, (1906) V.L.R., 746 ; 28 A.L.T., 77 ; 12 A.L.R., 442. *Cussen, J.*

Order LXV., r. 27 (9), (49), (Rules of 1884) —"Procuring evidence "—"Preparation and delivery of briefs "—Appendix N., Instructions for brief.]— *Quaere*, whether the costs incurred in " procuring evidence " within the meaning of sub-rule 9 of Order LXV., r. 27 are costs " of and consequent on the preparation and delivery of briefs " within the meaning of sub-rule 49. *Etheridge* v. *The President, &c. of the Shire of Berwick*, (1906) V.L.R., 746 ; 28 A.L.T., 77 ; 12 A.L.R., 442. *Cussen, J.*

Order LXV., r. 2 (Rules of 1884)—Costs of issues—Judgment for defendant with costs, effect of—" Follow the event "—" Otherwise ordered "—Several defences—No evidence called as to one defence.]—The defendant pleaded three different defences but called evidence as to two only. Judgment was given for the defendant with costs. *Held*, that the defendant was entitled to the costs of preparing for the defence as to which no evidence was called, the form of the judgment amounting to an order " otherwise," so as to exclude the operation of Order LXV., r. 2. *McLean Bros. & Rigg Ltd.* v. *Grice*, (1907) V.L.R., 28; 28 A.L.T., 120; 12 A.L.R., 474. F.C., *a' Beckett, A.-C.J., Hodges* and *Chomley, JJ.*

(11) *Unusual Expenses.*

Taxation—Order giving party his costs of action—Taxing Master, jurisdiction of to disallow.]—Although an order gives a party his costs of an action the Taxing Master is not thereby deprived of his jurisdiction to disallow costs not properly or reasonably incurred. *Etheridge* v. *President &c. of the Shire of Berwick*, (1906) V.L.R., 746; 28 A.L.T., 77; 12 A.L.R., 442. *Cussen, J.*

Taxation—Discretionary items—Duty of Taxing Master—Order LXV., r. 27 (9), (29), (38), (49), (Rules of 1884).]—Where there are costs which may possibly be allowed, the Taxing Master has to decide whether such costs in fact incurred are necessary or proper for the attainment of justice or defending the rights of the party, or whether they have been incurred through over-caution, negligence or mistake, or merely at the desire of the party. In deciding this question he is to take into consideration, *inter alia*, the nature of the cause or matter, the general conduct of the proceedings, and all other circumstances, including other fees and allowances made. *Etheridge* v. *The President &c. of the Shire of Berwick*, (1906) V.L.R., 746; 28 A.L.T., 77; 12 A.L.R., 442. *Cussen, J.*

Taxation—Solicitor and client—Unusual charges, payment of by solicitor—Client's knowledge of unusual character of charges—Knowledge not obtained from solicitor.]—Where an amount above the ordinary or scale fees is paid by a solicitor on behalf and with the sanction of his client, who knows that the amount is unusual and may not or will not be allowed on taxation between party and party, such payment may be properly chargeable by the solicitor against the client although the client's knowledge was not based on the information of the solicitor. *Re Duke's Will*, (1907) V.L.R., 632; 29 A.L.T., 50; 13 A.L.R., 477. *Cussen, J.*

Taxation—Solicitor and client—Country solicitor—Attendance at trial at Melbourne—Costs of, when an unusual expense—Knowledge of client that they may not be allowed as between party and party—Necessity of proving.]—B. and H. were a firm of solicitors carrying on business at Melbourne and Benalla. H. resided in Melbourne and did the firm's business there and B. did the firm's business at Benalla. H. attended at the trial of an action in Melbourne and the scale fee for such attendance was claimed in the bill of costs and allowed. B., also, attended at the trial. *Held*, that the costs of B.'s attendance and travelling expenses were an unusual expense and that such costs should not be allowed unless the solicitor proved that before they were incurred the client knew that they would not or might not be allowed as between solicitor and client. *In re Lamrock Brown & Hall's Costs*, (1908) V.L.R., 238; 29 A.L.T., 214; 14 A.L.R., 81. *Cussen, J.*

Taxation—Unusual work—Making copy of witness's evidence for his use—Request of client—Charge for unusual work—When client protected against.]—A charge for making a copy, at the client's request, of a statement made by a very old and important witness for the use of such witness, is not the kind of charge against which the client needs protection as being for unusual work. That kind of charge usually relates to some matter suggested by the solicitor, and which the client may regard as so much part of the controversial proceedings that success will usually mean an order for payment by the other side. *In re Duke's Will*, (1907) V.L.R., 632; 29 A.L.T., 50; 13 A.L.R., 477. *Cussen, J.*

Notes of evidence—Duty of junior counsel to take—Typing notes—Unusual expense.]—Where junior counsel's fees are allowable on taxation, it is his duty and that of the clerk in attendance to take sufficient notes of the evidence given at the hearing. A sum paid for typing notes is, accordingly, an unusual expense. *Re Duke's Will*, (1907) V.L.R., 632; 29 A.L.T., 50; 13 A.L.R., 477. *Cussen, J.*

(12) *Costs Increased by Misconduct or Negligence.*

Order LXV., r. 27 (38a), (Rules of 1906)— Taxation—Costs increased by misconduct or negligence of solicitor—Burden of proof.]— Where it is alleged under Order LXV., r. 27 (38A) that costs have been increased by the misconduct or negligence of the solicitor the onus is upon the client to establish that he has been damnified and to what extent. *Woolf* v. *Willis*, (1911) 13 C.L.R., 23 ; 17 A.L.R., 454. H.C., *Griffith, C.J., Barton* and *O' Connor, JJ.*

(13) *Conveyancing.*

Conveyancing Act 1904 (No. 1953), s. 4 (6) —Auction Sales Act 1890 (No. 1065), ss. 3, 29—Sale of land by Sheriff under fi. fa.— Whether a " sale by auction "—Sheriff's costs of perusal of conveyance—Stipulation in contract of sale for payment by purchaser, legality of.]—A sale of land by auction conducted by the Sheriff under a writ of *fi. fa.* is, notwithstanding the provisions of the *Auction Sales Act* 1890 excusing the Sheriff from the responsibilities imposed by that Act, a sale by auction within the meaning of section 4 (6) of the *Conveyancing Act* 1904, and a clause in the contract of sale charging the purchaser with the Sheriff's costs of perusal of the conveyance is accordingly illegal. *Re Rogers' and Rodd's Contract*, (1907) V.L.R., 511 ; 29 A.L.T., 13 ; 13 A.L.R., 312., *Madden, C.J.*

Conveyancing Act 1904 (No. 1593), s. 4 (6) —Contract for sale of land—Sale by auction —Costs—Exclusive of perusal and obtaining execution of transfer—Purchaser to pay— Validity of condition.]—A provision in a contract made at the sale of land by auction that the purchasers shall pay the vendors' costs and expenses of and incidental to obtaining the execution of the transfer is not void under section 4 (6) of the *Conveyancing Act* 1904. The expression " costs of perusal of the conveyance or of obtaining the execution thereof " in section 4 (6) of the *Conveyancing Act* 1904, does not include the costs of all matters connected with the transfer of the land sold. " Perusal " means reading

the conveyance to see if it expresses what it is intended to express. *In re Sutton and the Federal Building Society's Contract*, (1909) V.L.R., 473 ; 31 A.L.T., 75 ; 15 A.L.R., 560.

Conveyancing Act 1904 (No. 1953), s. 4 (6) —Whether applicable to land under Transfer of Land Act—" Conveyance," " transfer " —Contract of sale by auction—Stipulation that purchaser shall pay vendor's costs of perusal of conveyance.]—*See* VENDOR AND PURCHASER. *Re Rogers and Rodd's Contract*, (1907) V.L.R., 511 ; 29 A.L.T., 13 ; 13 A.L.R., 312.

(14) *Term Fee.*

" Term fee "—Letters necessary in interest of client.]—On a taxation between solicitor and client charges for letters necessary in the interests of the client as executrix under a will are not covered by the allowance of a term fee. *In re Duke's Will*, (1907) V.L.R., 632 ; 29 A.L.T., 50 ; 13 A.L.R., 477. *Cussen, J.*

(15) *Court Fees.*

Appendix O* Rules of Supreme Court 1884— Trustees—Passing accounts—Accounts agreed upon between parties—Fees chargeable.]— Where trustees are ordered by the Court to pass their accounts before the Chief Clerk the fees prescribed for " taking accounts " by Appendix O* to the *Rules of the Supreme Court* 1884 are chargeable although the parties agree amongst themselves not to dispute the accounts presented by the trustees and the Chief Clerk accordingly accepts them as proper accounts. There is also chargeable 10s. per hour for each hour occupied by the Chief Clerk in inquiring as to the commission to be allowed the trustees. *Re Hutchinson*, 32 W.R., 392, approved and aplied ; *In re Winter* ; *Winter- Irving* v. *Winter*, (1908) V.L.R., 74 ; 29 A.L.T., 144 ; 13 A.L.R., 701. F.C., *Madden, C.J., a' Beckett* and *Cussen, JJ.*

Rules of the Supreme Court 1884, Order LXXIII.—Appendix O—Court fees and percentages—Attendance of officer on production of document.]—The fee of £1 provided by Appendix O must be paid whenever, at the request of the solicitor, a document from the Prothonotary's Office is produced in Court by an officer. *Daniel* v. *McNamara*, 17 A.L.R. (C.N.), 9. *Madden, C.J.* (1911).

(b) INFERIOR COURTS.

(1) County Court.

(a) Scale of Costs.

(i.) Where Scale in the Rules Applicable.

County Court—Scale of Costs—Rule 446 (Rules of 1891)—" Value of property in litigation "—Judgment for 1s. damages and injunction restraining defendant from breaking his covenant with the plaintiff not to carry on business within a certain area—Scale of costs regulated, not by the amount of damages, but by the value of the plaintiff's right preserved from infringement by the injunction.]— *Moylan* v. *Nolan*, 27 A.L.T. (Supplement), 16; 12 A.L.R. (C.N.), 13. *Judge Box* (1906).

County Court—Action to enforce charge upon land for rates—Scale of costs, how determined—Value of land.]—In actions to enforce by sale a charge for municipal rates over land, the value of the land and not the amount of the charge fixes the scale upon which costs should be taxed. *Mayor, &c. of Malvern* v. *Johnson*, 28 A.L.T. (Supplement) 7; 12 A.L.R. (C.N.), 28. *Judge Box* (1906).

County Court—Scale of Costs—Review of taxation—" The value of the property in litigation "—County Court Rules 1891, Rules 448, 450.]—The true test of " the value of the property in litigation " in Rule 446 of *County Court Rules* 1891 is the value of the right in the property claimed by the plaintiff and not the value of the whole property in which the right is claimed. *Wilson* v. *Anderson*, 26 A.L.T. (Supplement), 5; 11 A.L.R., (C.N.), 35, explained. *Moylan* v. *Nolan*, 27 A.L.T. (Supplement), 16; 12 A.L.R. (C.N.), 13, approved. *Townsing* v. *Egan*, 29 A.L.T. (Supplement), 29; 14 A.L.R. (C.N.), 18. *Judge Moule* (1908).

County Court—Costs of issues—Rule 446 (Rules of 1891).]—Where a plaintiff recovers judgment for a smaller amount than he claimed with costs on certain of the issues,

his costs as between party and party are regulated by the scale of costs applying to the amount for which he has obtained judgment; but the costs of the defendant, who obtains judgment with costs on the other issues, are regulated by the amount sought to be recovered in the action. *Lynch* v. *Tognini*, 28 A.L.T. (Supplement), 1; 12 A.L.R. (C.N.), 14. *Judge Box* (1906).

County Court—Costs—Plaintiff successful on both claim and counter-claim—Scale upon which costs to be taxed—County Court Rules 1891, Schedule of Scale of Costs.]—Where an item under the Schedule of Scale of Costs applies both to the claim and counter-claim, and is not divisible, and where the plaintiff is successful on both claim and counterclaim, the higher scale of costs relating to such item should be allowed. *Wilson* v. *Scott*, 3 A.L.R. (C.N.), 87, explained. *Hopkins* v. *Forster*, 32 A.L.T. (Supplement), 5; 16 A.L.R. (C.N.), 6. *Judge Chomley* (1910).

County Court—Application for new trial—Scale of costs applicable.]—For the scale of costs adopted in fixing the costs of an application for a new trial, see *Levey* v. *Parker*, 28 A.L.T. (Supplement), 6; 12 A.L.R. (C.N.), 21. *Judge Box* (1906).

(ii.) In Other Cases.

Costs—Taxation—Solicitor and Client—County Court — Proposed action which is never commenced—Action commenced but proceedings dropped without order as to costs—Scale of costs applicable—County Court Rules 1891, Schedule of Scale of costs.]—In taxing the costs as between solicitor and client for work done in relation to a proposed County Court action which is never commenced, or in relation to a County Court action which is commenced but in which, by reason of the proceedings being dropped, no order is made as to costs, the Scale of Costs in the Schedule to the *County Court Rules* 1891 is not the governing and only guide in determining the amount to be allowed, but the Taxing Master may obtain assistance from it in the exercise of his discretion. *In re Brown*, (1911) V.L.R., 39; 32 A.L.T., 133; 16 A.L.R., 602. *a'Beckett, J.*

County Court—Costs—Items not included in Schedule of Scale of Costs—Jury fees and expenses—View—Travelling and other expenses—Juries Act 1890 (No. 1104), sec. 77, Tenth Schedule.]—By virtue of sec. 77 of the *Juries Act* 1890 and the Tenth Schedule thereto, jury fees and travelling and other expenses paid by one of the parties to an action, in respect to a view by the jury, are allowable on the taxation of his costs under an order giving him the costs of the action. *Reid* v. *Panton*, 32 A.L.T. (Supplement), 7; 16 A.L.R. (C.N.), 13. *Judge Eagleson* (1910).

County Court—Costs—Items not included in Schedule of Scale of Costs—Conduct of parties at trial—Implied agreement not to take objection—Expenses incurred on faith of such agreement.]—On the taxation of costs the unsuccessful party will be precluded from taking objection to the allowance of items on the ground that they are not comprised in those set out in the Schedule of Scale of Costs, where the parties have during the trial entered into an implied agreement that no such objection will be raised. *Reid* v. *Panton*, 32 A.L.T. (Supplement),. 7; 16 A.L.R. (C.N.), 13. *Judge Eagleson* (1910).

(b) Instructions to Sue, &c.

Schedule of Scale of Costs—Items 2, 35—Plaintiff's costs on claim and counterclaim—Two sets of costs—Instructions on claim—Instructions on counterclaim.]—Where a defendant's counterclaim raises matter different from that which arises upon the plaintiff's claim, the plaintiff should, on taxation of his bill of costs as against the defendant, be allowed under Item 35 of the Schedule of the Scale of Costs for his solicitors' attendance upon him to advise or receive instructions from him in regard to the counterclaim, as well as under Item 2, for instructions to sue in regard to the claim. *Ambler & Co. Proprietary Ltd.* v. *Clayton*, 31 A.L.T. (Supplement), 5; 15 A.L.R. (C.N.), 15. *Judge Johnston.*

County Court Rules 1891—Schedule of Scale of Costs, Item 2, and Schedule of Forms, Form 3—Form of summons.]—Professional costs provided by Item 2 of the Schedule of Scale of Costs to the *County Court Rules* 1891 are not to be allowed on taxation where the summons issued consists of two separate sheets of paper, one of which sheets contains the plaintiff's particulars of demand. *Lawson* v. *Batchelor*, 29 A.L.T. (Supplement), 29; 14 A.L.R. (C.N.), 17. *Judge Eagleson* (1908).

County Court—Scale of Costs, Item 2—" Instructions to sue "—Costs allowed for obtaining further particulars, drawing, engrossing, &c. in connection therewith in addition to allowance for " Instructions to sue "—Discretion of Registrar.]—*Moylan* v. *Nolan*, 27 A.L.T. (Supplement), 16; 12 A.L.R. (C.N.), 13. *Judge Box* (1906).

(c) Perusing; Attendance on Client.

County Court—Costs—Solicitor plaintiff—Acting professionally on his own behalf—Costs of perusing documents—Perusing interrogatories—Schedule of Scale of Costs, Item 28.]—Where the plaintiff, a solicitor, obtains judgment with costs in an action wherein he acted as solicitor on his own behalf, he is entitled to the fee fixed by the Schedule of Scale of Costs for the perusal of all necessary documents, and he accordingly may charge under Item 28 for perusing the defendant's interrogatories. *Hopkins* v. *Forster*, 32 A.L.T. (Supplement), 5; 16 A.L.R. (C.N.), 6. *Judge Chomley* (1910).

County Court—Scale of Costs, Item 28—Costs of perusing further and better answers to interrogatories may be allowed.]—*Moylan* v. *Nolan*, 27 A.L.T. (Supplement), 16; 12 A.L.R. (C.N.), 13. *Judge Box* (1906).

Schedule of Scale of Costs—Item 35—Proceedings taken by opposite party—Payment into Court by defendant—Plaintiff's solicitor's attendance upon his client thereon.]—Payment into Court by a defendant is a " proceeding taken by the opposite party " within the meaning of Item 35 of the Schedule of Scale of Costs, and, consequently, the plaintiff may be allowed under that item for his solicitor's attendance upon him to advise or get instructions from him on receiving notice from him of such payment in. *Ambler & Co. Proprietary Ltd.* v. *Clayton*, 31 A.L.T. (Supplement), 5; 15 A.L.R. (C.N.), 15. *Judge Johnston.*

COSTS.

(d) Attending Court.

County Court—Scale of Costs, Items 15 and 16—" Attending on trial with counsel." —" On trial," meaning of—Attending Court to hear the judgment of the Court reserved from one day to a subsequent day is not attending " on trial "—The Scale does not provide for such an attendance.]—*Moylan* v. *Nolan*, 27 A.L.T. (Supplement), 16; 12 A.L.R. (C.N.), 13. *Judge Box* (1906).

County Court—Costs—Taxation—Solicitor party to action acting professionally on own behalf—Solicitor called as witness—" Attending Court "—Witnesses' expenses—Schedule of Scale of Costs (The County Court Rules 1891), Items 14, 15, 16.]—A solicitor was party to an action in which he acted professionally on his own behalf and was also called as a witness. *Held*, that he was entitled to be allowed his charge for " attending Court " under Items 14, 15 and 16 of the Schedule of Scale of Costs, or his expenses as a witness, whichever allowance was the higher, but not both. *Hopkins* v. *Forster*, 32 A.L.T. (Supplement), 5; 16 A.L.R. (C.N.), 6. *Judge Chomley* (1910).

County Court—Costs — Counsel's fees—Practitioner conducting trial on behalf of his client.]—*See post* (e) COUNSEL'S FEES; DRAWING BRIEF, &c. *O'Brien* v. *Victorian Railways Commissioners*, 27 A.L.T. (Supplement), 11; 12 A.L.R. (C.N.), 6.

(e) Counsel's Fees; Drawing Brief, &c.

County Court—Practice—Costs—Application for liberty to sign final judgment—Scale of costs.]—Items 30, 31 and 32 of the Schedule of Scale of Costs apply to applications for final judgment. Consequently the following items were allowed :—" Drawing and engrossing brief for counsel £1; Fee to counsel and clerk £2 4s. 6d.; Attending with counsel 10s." *Mackay* v. *Burley*, 27 A.L.T. (Supplement), 10; 12 A.L.R. (C.N.), 2. *Judge Chomley* (1905)

County Court—Costs—Counsel's fees—Practitioner conducting trial on behalf of his client.]—Where a party's practitioner attends Court and conducts the trial on behalf of his client he is not entitled to counsel's fee on brief as set out in Item 11 of the Scale of Costs. His fees for the first and subsequent days of the trial are governed by Items 17 and 44 of such Scale. *O'Brien* v. *Victorian Railways Commissioners*, 27 A.L.T. (Supplement), 11; 12 A.L.R., 6. *Judge Eagleson* (1906).

County Court Act 1890 (No. 1078), sec. 64 (4), (8)—Summons for final judgment—Rule 84—Attendance of counsel—Costs—Allowances under Schedule of Scale of Costs to counsel and attorney—Items 30, 31 and 32— " Drawing and engrossing brief "—" Fee to counsel and clerk "—" Attending with counsel."]—There is nothing in Rule 84 to preclude counsel from appearing for the parties on applications for final judgment. In referring the costs of such an application to the Registrar for taxation, His Honor Judge Box, intimated that in the majority of the applications for final judgment which had come before him, if he had had to deal with the fixing of the costs, he would have allowed the costs of " Drawing and engrossing brief for counsel," " Fee for counsel and clerk" and " Attending with counsel." *Watson* v. *Watson*, 27 A.L.T. (Supplement), 14; 12 A.L.R. (C.N.), 9 (1906).

(f) Costs of Warrants.

County Court Rules 1891, r. 441—Costs—Warrant of execution to satisfy a County Court judgment—Bailiff's fees—County Court Rules 1891, r. 441—Scale of Costs, Item 24.]—The only costs of warrants against the goods which may be allowed against the defendant under *County Court Rules* 1891, r. 441, are the costs of issuing such warrant and the bailiff's fee for execution thereof. *In re Luke Nolan, deceased* (*No.* 1), 29 A.L.T. (Supplement), 31; 14 A.L.R. (C.N.), 21. *Judge Moule* (1908).

" Taxed costs incurred in an action "—Costs of warrant of execution—Effect of sequestration—County Court Rules 1891, r. 441—Insolvency Act 1890 (No. 1102), sec. 77.]—The term " taxed costs " in sec. 77 of the *Insolvency Act* 1890 does not include costs of execution of a County Court judgment other than the costs of issuing the warrant of execution (including the bailiff's fee for executing the warrant). *In re Luke Nolan*, 29 A.L.T. (Supplement), 31; 14 A.L.R. (C.N.), 21.

(g) Witnesses' Expenses.

County Court—Witnesses present until close of trial.]—A party is entitled to have his witnesses present until the close of the trial, and to be allowed, as part of his costs of the action, the expenses of having them so present. *Lynch* v. *Tognini*, 28 A.L.T. (Supplement), 1; 12 A.L.R. (C.N.), 14. *Judge Box* (1906)

County Court—Witnesses in attendance—Case in printed list—No defended cases to be taken—Discretion of Registrar.]—Plaintiff's expenses and those of his witnesses were allowed for the day on which the case was in the printed list for hearing, but no defended cases were to be taken. *Lynch* v. *Tognini*, 28 A.L.T. (Supplement), 1; 12 A.L.R. (C.N.), 14. *Judge Box* (1906).

County Court—Costs—Taxation—Solicitor party to action acting professionally on own behalf—Solicitor called as witness—" Attending Court "—Witnesses' expenses—Schedule of Scale of Costs (The County Court Rules 1891), Items 14, 15, 16.]—*See ante (d)* ATTENDING COURT. *Hopkins* v. *Forster*, 32 A.L.T. (Supplement), 5; 16 A.L.R. (C.N.), 6.

(2) *Court of Insolvency.*

(a) Authority of Taxing Officer.

Costs—Insolvency—Taxation—Allocatur—Objection thereto by official accountant—Insolvency Rules 1898, r. 151.]—The Taxing Officer's decision as to an item in a solicitor's bill of costs cannot be questioned by the official accountant in exercise of his powers under r. 151 of the *Insolvency Rules* 1898. *Re Schutze*, 29 A.L.T. (Supplement), 20; 14 A.L.R. (C.N.), 5. *Judge Moule* (1908).

(b) Proceedings Relating to Deeds of Assignment ; Scale of Costs.

Insolvency Act 1897 (No. 1513), Part VI.—Deed of assignment—Costs of preparation of—Taxation—Scale of costs—Rules of Supreme Court 1906, App. N., Conveyancing.]—The costs of a deed of assignment should be taxed under the Conveyancing Scale in Appendix N. to the *Rules of the Supreme Court* 1906. *In re Hipper and Butcher*, 28 A.L.T. (Supplement), 17; 13 A.L.R. (C.N.), 9. *Judge Molesworth* (1907).

Insolvency Act 1897 (No. 1513), Part VI.—Insolvency Rules 1898—Deeds of assignment—Solicitor's costs.]—Solicitors' costs in connection with deeds of assignment are not governed by the *Insolvency Rules* 1898. *In re Power*, 26 A.L.T. (Supplement), 10; 11 A.L.R. (C.N.), 37, disapproved and not followed. *In re Alderman*, 28 A.L.T. (Supplement), 13; 13 A.L.R. (C.N.), 6. *Judge Molesworth* (1907).

Insolvency Act 1897 (No. 1513), Part VI.—Deed of assignment—Costs of trustee—Costs of taxation—Insolvency Rules 1898, r. 152.]—Rule 152 of the *Insolvency Rules* 1898 does not apply to the costs of taxation of a bill of costs of a solicitor acting for a trustee of an estate assigned by deed. *In re Hipper and Butcher*, 28 A.L.T. (Supplement), 17; 13 A.L.R. (C.N.), 9. *Judge Molesworth* (1907).

(c) Trustee : Costs of Instructing Solicitor.

Costs—Insolvency—Certificate application —Trustee's report—Offences charged in report—Costs of employing solicitor to frame, &c. such charges—Trustee's statutory duties, delegation of—Insolvency Act 1897 (No. 1513), secs. 27 (1), 91 (4)—Insolvency Rules 1898, r. 297.]—A trustee must perform all the ordinary statutory duties himself; he cannot delegate those duties so as to cast an extra burden on the estate. But where there are legal difficulties as to the form of the charges to be laid against the insolvent for offences against the insolvency law in the report required to be filed by the trustee under sec. 91 of the *Insolvency Act* 1897, the trustee will be allowed his costs of instructing a solicitor to frame such charges, and of the drawing, copying and engrossing by the solicitor of so much of the report as relates to such charges. *In re Early*, 32 A.L.T. (Supplement), 9; 17 A.L.R. (C.N.), 9. *Judge Moule* (1911).

(d) Partnership Matters.

Costs—Assignments of Joint and separate estates—Costs of administration—Apportionment—Solicitor's costs—Trustees' duties.]—Where it is provided in a deed of assignment of the joint and separate estates of persons trading as partners, that in the administration of the separate estates, the separate creditors are to get advantage of the separate assets after deducting therefrom the costs of and incidental to the administration of the separate estates, the costs distinctly referable to the separate estates should be paid thereout, and not out of the assets of the joint estate. Bills of costs are not rendered to trustees as a matter of form merely, but in order that the trustees may have the necessary opportunity of duly protecting the interests of the creditors whom they represent. *In re Hipper and Butcher*, 30 A.L.T. (Supplement), 18; 15 A.L.R. (C.N.), 1. *Judge Moule* (1909).

Insolvency Act 1890 (No. 1102), sec. 41—Insolvency Rules 1898, rr. 166, 167, 168, 169,—Appendix to Rules, Part 2, Scale of solicitor's costs—" Instructions for Schedule "—Sequestration of partnership estate—Estates of partners—Separate Schedules, whether solicitor entitled to charge in respect of.]—In the case of the sequestration of a partnership estate, where the schedule of the firm has been filed, a solicitor is not entitled, in addition to the allowance of the item " instructions for Schedule " in respect of the partnership schedule, to charge for " instructions for schedule " in respect of the individual members of the partnership. *In re Day and Sloan*, 32 A.L.T. (Supplement), 3; 16 A.L.R. (C.N.), 9. *Judge Moule* (1910).

(e) Drawing; Engrossing.

Insolvency—Deed of assignment—Printed form—Costs of preparing—" Engrossing."]—Where a deed of assignment was on a printed form, *Held*, that the solicitor should be allowed a fair charge for " engrossing " the deed, which was fixed at 3d. per folio, and that the allowance should not be restricted to the part of the deed which was in writing. *In re Hipper and Butcher*, 28 A.L.T. (Sup-

plement), 17; 13 A.L.R. (C.N.), 9. *Judge Molesworth* (1907).

Taxation—" Drawing " deeds of assignment—Meaning thereof—Allowances where printed forms of deeds of assignment are used—Rules of the Supreme Court, Appendix N—Conveyancing Scale.]—The drawing or drafting of a deed means " composing and writing it." The mere production of a printed document does not by itself carry with it the conclusion that the person producing it " drafted " it or that it was " drafted " for him. *In re Moylan*, 30 A.L.T. (Supplement), 10; 14 A.L.R. (C.N.) 37. *Judge Moule* (1908).

Taxation—" Engrossing "—Use of printed forms as engrossments—Rules of the Supreme Court—Appendix N.—Conveyancing sale.]—*Semble*, no allowance should be made for " engrossing " except for the actual writing contained in the document. *In re Moylan*, 30 A.L.T. (Supplement), 10; 14 A.L.R. (C.N.), 37. *Judge Moule* (1908).

Insolvency—Costs—Trustee's solicitor—Deed of assignment—Charge for drawing bill of costs and copy for Chief Clerk—Allowance on taxation—Insolvency Act 1890 (No. 1102), secs. 12, 153, 154—Insolvency Act 1897 (No. 1513), sec. 27 (3)—Insolvency Act 1903 (No. 1836), sec. 10—Insolvency Rules 1890, Schedule of Fees and Costs.]—Owing to the repeal by sec. 10 of the *Insolvency Act* 1903 of the provision in sec. 27 (3) of the *Insolvency Act* 1897 prohibiting the allowance of any costs " for preparing or taxing " bills of costs, a solicitor acting for the trustee under a deed of assignment, which provides for payment by the trustee of all costs charges and expenses out of the assigned estate, is entitled on the taxation of his bill of costs by the Chief Clerk to charge against the estate for drawing the bill of costs for taxation, and a copy for the Chief Clerk. *In re Nicholls and Skelton*, 32 A.L.T. (Supplement), 10; 17 A.L.R. (C.N.), 2. *Judge Moule* (1911).

(f) Auctioneer's Charges.

Insolvency — Surcharges — Auctioneer's fees—Commission allowed to auctioneer on

advertising charges—Out-of-pocket expenses —Appendix of Forms to Insolvency Rules 1898, Part 4.]—Where an auctioneer engaged in the sale of property of an insolvent estate incurs expenses in advertising the sale in the newspapers and pays the proprietors of the newspapers their account, less a commission or rebate, he is not entitled to charge the estate with the full amount, *i.e.*, without deducting the commission or rebate. *In re McBain*, 32 A.L.T. (Supplement), 2 ; 16 A.L.R. (C.N.), 9. *Judge Moule* (1910).

VI.—SECURITY FOR COSTS.

Commonwealth Trade Marks Act 1905 (No. 20 of 1905), sec. 46—Registration of Trade mark—Notice of opposition to person not resident in Australia—Security for costs—High Court —Jurisdiction.]—The Court has no jurisdiction under sec. 46 of the *Trade Marks Act* 1905 to order security for costs of an application pending before the Registrar of Trade Marks to be given by a person not resident in Australia who has given notice of opposition to the application. *Ex parte Carroll*, 15 A.L.R., 295. *Isaacs, J.* (1909).

Service and Execution of Process Act 1901 (No. 11 of 1901), sec. 10—Writ of summons served in another State—Security for costs— Discretion to order.]—Sec. 10 of the *Service and Execution of Process Act* 1901 leaves the Court or Judge entirely at large as to the ground upon which it or he may exercise or ought to exercise its or his discretion to order that security for costs of a defendant who has been served under that Act with a writ of summons should be given by the plaintiff, and the Court or Judge must be guided in each particular case by the facts. In *Evans* v. *Sneddon*, 28 V.L.R., 396 ; 24 A.L.T., 79 ; 8 A.L.R., 215, the Full Court did not attempt to enumerate all the circumstances which might influence the Court in granting or refusing an application under that section. *Smith* v. *Chisholm*, (1908) V.L.R., 579 ; 30 A.L.T., 48 ; 14 A.L.R., 471 (*Hodges, J.*).

Security for costs—Foreign company— Registered office and agent in Victoria— Companies Act 1896 (No. 1482), sec. 70—

Rules of Supreme Court 1884, Order LXV., r. 6.]—A foreign company, suing as plaintiff in Victoria, will not be relieved from giving security for costs upon proof only that it has an agent in Victoria, and is carrying on business in Victoria, and has complied with sec. 70 of the *Companies Act* 1896. *Norton or Horton & Sons Ltd.* v. *Sewell*, (1906) V.L.R., 401 ; 27 A.L.T., 214 ; 12 A.L.R., 209. *a' Beckett, A.-C.J.* (1906).

Court of Mines—Petition to wind up mining company—Practice — Security for costs— Mines Act 1890 (No. 1120), sec. 180.]—Under sec. 180 of the *Mines Act* 1890, a Court of Mines has jurisdiction to deal with an application that a petitioner resident out of the jurisdiction of the Court should be required to give security for costs before proceeding with the petition. The usual practice is that where a petitioner resides out of the jurisdiction of the Court, and the respondent would, if successful, have great difficulty in recovering the costs incurred by the presentation of a petition, security for such costs should be required. The exception is where the petitioner is clearly a creditor of the respondent company to such an amount as to sufficiently secure all probable costs occasioned by the presentation of the petition to wind up. *Re The Mount Lyell Consols Mining Corporation, No Liability* (*No.* 2), 30 A.L.T. (Supplement), 17 ; 14 A.L.R. (C.N.), 41. *Judge Chomley* (1908).

VII.—AGREEMENTS FOR REMUNERATION OF SOLICITOR.

Supreme Court Act 1890 (No. 1142), sec. 262—Solicitor—Client—Costs—Agreement as to so.icitor's remuneration—Agreement to pay lump sum for work wholly past.]—Sec. 262 of the *Supreme Court Act* 1890 does not relate to agreements between solicitor and client as to the amount of the solicitors, professional remuneration for work wholly past. Such agreements are governed by the rules of common law and equity. *Bear* v. *Waxman*, (1912) V.L.R., 292 ; 34 A.L.T., 6 ; 18 A.L.R., 269. F.C., *Madden, C.J., Hood* and *Cussen, JJ.*

VIII.—RECOVERY OF COSTS.

See also, EXECUTION.

(a) *Attachment of the Person.*

Order XLII., rr. 3, 6, 7, 17 (Rules of 1884)—Order XLIV., r. 2 (Rules of 1884)—Attachment—Disobedience of order to pay costs—Imprisonment of Fraudulent Debtors Act 1890 (No. 1100)—Whether power to attach for disobedience affected by.]—Notwithstanding the provisions of the *Imprisonment of Fraudulent Debtors Act* 1890 the Court has power to issue a writ of attachment for disobedience of its order to pay costs. *Re Sandilands; Ex parte Browne,* 4 V.L.R. 'L.), 318, followed. *Pope* v. *Peacock,* (1906) V.L.R., 667; 28 A.L.T., 63; 12 A.L.R., 440. *Hodges, J.*

(b) *Solicitor's Lien.*

Solicitor to trustee of deceased person's estate—Lien for costs.]—A solicitor to the trustee under a will is not a solicitor to the estate, and therefore does not acquire a lien over the trust property for his costs. *In re Luke Nolan, deceased (No. 2),* 30 A.L.T. (Supplement), 1; 14 A.L.R. (C.N.), 25. *Judge Moule* (1908).

Court of Mines—Company in liquidation—Delivery up of Company's property to the liquidator— Costs — Solicitor's lien — Companies Act 1890 (No. 1074), sec. 274.]—An order made under sec. 274 of the *Companies Act* 1890 for delivery up to the liquidator of any books, documents or property belonging or relating to the company in the possession of a solicitor deprives the solicitor of his lien thereon for costs. *Re Mount Murphy Wolfram Co. No Liability,* 29 A.L.T (Supplement), 19; 14 A.L.R. (C.N.), 6. *Judge Box* (1908).

(c) *Payment of Costs a Condition.*

County Court—Chamber application—Costs of, whether payment should be made a condition precedent.]—Payment of costs of a Chamber application will not be made a condition precedent. *Ambler & Co. Proprietary Ltd.* v. *Clayton,* 29 A.L.T. (Supplement), 28; 14 A.L.R., 17. *Judge Eagleson* (1908).

Insolvency—Costs of trustee, what are——Costs of examination summons—Insolvency Act 1897 (No. 1513), sec. 93—Insolvency Act 1903 (No. 1836), sec. 16.]—The trustee's costs of an examination summons are "costs, charges, expenses, &c." of the trustee within the meaning of sec. 93 of the *Insolvency Act* 1897, as amended by sec. 16 of the *Insolvency Act* 1903. *In re Ostberg,* 33 A.L.T. (Supplement), 10; 17 A.L.R. (C.N.), 28. *Judge Moule* (1911).

Court of Mines—Company in liquidation—Delivery up of Company's property to the liquidator—Costs—Solicitor's lien—Companies Act 1890 (No. 1074), sec. 274.]—An order under sec. 274 of the *Companies Act* 1890 for delivery to the liquidator of any books, documents or property belonging or relating to the Company in the possession of a solicitor cannot be made conditionally on the payment of, or on the undertaking by the liquidator to pay the solicitor's costs. *Re Mount Murphy Wolfram Co. No Liability,* 29 A.L.T. (Supplement), 19; 14 A.L.R. (C.N.), 6. *Judge Box* (1908).

Insolvency—Certificate of discharge—Trustee's costs, dispute as to—Practice—Application for Judge's signature to certificate—Insolvency Act 1890 (No. 1102), sec. 145—Insolvency Act 1897 (No. 1513), sec. 93—Insolvency Act 1903 (No. 1836), sec. 16.]—*See* INSOLVENCY. *In re Ostberg,* 33 A.L.T. (Supplement), 10; 17 A.L.R. (C.N.), 28.

(d) *Priority of Payment.*

Taxed costs incurred in action—Party and Party costs—Costs of warrant of execution to satisfy a judgment of the County Court—Party and party costs—Effect of sequestration on warrant of execution—Expenses of execution—prior to sequestration—Insolvency Act 1890 (No. 1102), sec. 77—County Court Rules 1891, r. 441.]—The term "taxed costs" in sec. 77 of the *Insolvency Act* 1890 refers to costs taxed in the ordinary way between party and party, and does not include the costs of execution of a County Court judgment other than the costs of issuing the warrant, and, perhaps, the bailiff's fee for executing it. *In re Luke Nolan, deceased (No. 1),* 29

A.L.T. (Supplement), 31 ; 14 A.L.R. (C.N.), 21. *Judge Moule* (1908).

Insolvency Act 1890 (No. 1102), sec. 123 (iii.)—Insolvency Act 1897 (No. 1513), sec. 113 —Sequestration of estate of deceased person— Testamentary expenses incurred by the representative of a deceased person in or about the debtor's estate—Right of trustee to payment as a preferential debt.]—*See* INSOLVENCY. *In re Luke Nolan, deceased* (*No.* 2), 30 A.L.T. (Supplement), 1 ; 14 A.L.R. (C.N.), 25. *Judge Moule.*

"Taxed costs incurred in an action"—A preferential debt—Insolvency Act 1890 (No. 1102), secs. 77, 115, 123 (3).]—*See* INSOLVENCY. *In re Luke Nolan* (*No.* 1), 29 A.L.T. (Supplement), 31 ; 14 A.L.R. (C.N.), 21. *Judge Moule* (1908).

Mines Act 1897 (No. 1514), sec. 168— Mining company—Winding up—Distribution of assets—Priorities—"Costs of administration or otherwise," what are.]—The phrase "costs of administration or otherwise" in sec. 168 of the *Mines Act* 1897 means something similar to "costs of winding up." *In re Egerton and Gordon Consolidated Gold Mines, No Liability,* (1908) V.L.R., 526 ; 30 A.L.T., 27 ; 14 A.L.R., 372. *Madden, C.J.*

Companies Act 1890 (No. 1074), sec. 104— Assets insufficient to satisfy liabilities—Costs, charges and expenses of winding-up—Order as to priority of payment of.]—*See* COMPANY. *In re People's Daily Co-operative Newspaper, &c., Co. Ltd.,* (1907) V.L.R., 666 ; 29 A.L.T., 111 ; 13 A.L.R., 504.

(e) *Indemnity.*

Insolvency—Costs of examination summons —Trustee indemnified against by creditor— Whether trustee entitled to be paid by insolvent or out of estate—Insolvency Act 1897 (No. 1513), sec. 111.]—Although a trustee holds an indemnity from a creditor against the costs of an examination summons, he is entitled (unless the Court otherwise order) to have them paid by the insolvent or out of the insolvent estate. *In re Ostberg,* 33 A.L.T. (Supplement), 10 ; 17 A.L.R. (C.N.), 28. *Judge Moule* (1911).

Costs—Appeal in administration action— Costs of trustee—Whether trustee entitled to be indemnified out of the estate.]—Trustees who have been guilty of breaches of trust in respect of which an order has been made in an administration action by a Court of first instance, but who, in respect of the matters in question upon an appeal from that order, are blameless, are entitled to be indemnified out of the estate for their costs of such appeal. *Nissen* v. *Grunden,* (1912) 14 C.L.R., 297 ; 18 A.L.R., 254. H.C., *Griffith, C.J., Barton* and *Isaacs, JJ.*

Trustee—Life tenant and remainderman— Corpus and income—Costs paid by trustee under order of High Court—Decision of High Court reversed on appeal by one party to Privy Council—Effect on rights of parties not appealing—Indemnity of trustees—Rights of assignee of life tenant.]—*See* TENANT FOR LIFE AND REMAINDERMAN. *Cock* v. *Aitken,* (1912) 15 C.L.R., 373 ; 18 A.L.R., 576.

(*f*) *Other Points.*

Local Government Act 1903 (No. 1893), secs. 324 to 328, 340 to 343—Rate, interest, and costs, how far a charge upon land—Costs of removing an order from Petty Sessions to Supreme Court.]—*See* LOCAL GOVERNMENT. *Mayor, &c., of Malvern* v. *Johnson,* 28 A.L.T. (Supplement), 7 ; 12 A.L.R. (C.N.), 28.

Trustee—Bringing land under Transfer of Land Act 1890—Mortgage of trust estate to pay costs of—Breach of trust.]—*See* TRUSTS AND TRUSTEES. *Crout* v. *Beissel,* (1909) V.L.R., 207 ; 30 A.L.T., 185 ; 15 A.L.R., 143.

COUNCILLOR.

See LOCAL GOVERNMENT.

COUNSEL.

See also, COSTS ; SOLICITOR AND CLIENT.

Income Tax Act 1895 (No. 1374), sec. 27— Special case for opinion of Supreme Court— Number of counsel who may be heard.]—As a general rule one counsel only will be heard on the argument of a special case. *Re Income Tax Acts*, (1907) V.L.R., 358. F.C.

Costs—Originating summons—King's Counsel appearing with junior—Certificate for counsel.]—*See* COSTS. *In re Jamieson*; *Christensen* v. *Jamieson*, (1907) V.L.R., 103; 28 A.L.T., 138; 12 A.L.R., 570.

Notes of evidence—Duty of junior counsel to take—Typing notes—Unusual expense.]—Where junior counsel's fees are allowable on taxation, it is his duty and that of the clerk in attendance to take sufficient notes of the evidence given at the hearing. A sum paid for typing notes is, accordingly, an unusual expense. *Re Duke's Will*, (1907) V.L.R., 632; 29 A.L.T., 50; 13 A.L.R., 477. *Cussen, J.*

Order XXXIX. (Rules of 1906)—New trial—Misconduct of counsel.]—Misconduct of counsel, where such conduct has taken place in open Court, is not a ground for granting a new trial. *David Syme & Co.* v. *Swinburne*, 10 C.L.R., 43; 16 A.L.R., 93. H.C., *Griffith, C.J.*, *Barton, O'Connor* and *Higgins, JJ.* (1909).

Legal Profession Practice Act 1891 (No. 1216),—Solicitor, responsibility of—Whether protected by counsel's advice.]—*Quaere*, whether counsel's advice is any protection to a solicitor since the *Legal Profession Practice Act* 1891, even on points of law. *Garrick* v. *Garrick*; *Sutton, co-respondent*, (1908) V.L.R., 420; 30 A.L.T., 21; 14 A.L.R., 312. *Hood, J.*

Justices Act 1890 (No. 1105), sec. 77 (11)—Ordering witnesses out of Court at request of party—Discretion of Justices—Counsel and solicitor of opposite party subpoenaed as witnesses—Permission to remain in Court, effect of.]—*See* EVIDENCE. *Barry* v. *Cullen*, (1906) V.L.R., 393; 27 A.L.T., 227; 12 A.L.R., 235.

Clause empowering trustees to act on advice of counsel—Liability of trustees so acting.]—*See* WILL. *In the Will of Thompson*; *Brahe* v. *Mason*, (1910) V.L.R., 251; 31 A.L.T., 210; 16 A.L.R., 215.

COUNTY COURT.

I.—JURISDICTION.

Contract—Sale of Goods to be shipped abroad—" C.i.f." contract—Place of delivery —County Court practice—Jurisdiction—Part of cause of action arising out of jurisdiction.]— A contract for the sale of timber was made in Melbourne between the plaintiff, a Melbourne firm, and the defendants, who were described as of Melbourne, but who had their principal place of business in New York, with a branch house in Melbourne. The contract provided that the price should be " £18 5s. per 1,000 feet super, c.i.f. Melbourne," that the terms should be " sellers' New York house on shipment to draw on buyers at 90 days' sight," that shipment should be " at New York by sailing vessel—May shipment," and that " sellers reserve the right to insure against war risk, the cost of which to be paid for by buyers in addition to the price above-named." *Held*, that the place of delivery under the contract was New York, and that, therefore, as the whole cause of action did not arise in Victoria, the County Court had no jurisdiction in an action for non-delivery of the timber in accordance with the contract. *Bowden* v. *Little*, (1907) 4 C.L.R., 1364; 13 A.L.R., 689, followed. *Crooke* v. *Smith*, (1878) 4 V.L.R. (L.), 95, and *Brooks, Robinson & Co.* v. *Smith*, (1890) 16 V.L.R., 245; 11 A.L.T., 168, applied. *H. Beecham* v. *R. W. Cameron & Co.*, (1910) V.L.R., 19; 31 A.L.T., 100; 15 A.L.R., 598. F.C., *Madden, C.J., Hood* and *Cussen, JJ.*

County Court—Jurisdiction—Contract for sale of goods—Breach in Victoria—Cause of action—Quantum of damages—County Court Act 1890 (No. 1078), sec. 5.]— Plaintiff, a Melbourne resident, contracted in Melbourne with F., another Melbourne resident, for the sale of certain peas to be delivered f.o.b. Tasmania. Defendant, when required to do so, refused to name a ship to take delivery and announced his intention of not accepting the goods. Plaintiff brought an action in the County Court at Melbourne for this breach of contract. *Held*, that the County Court had jurisdiction, as the whole cause of action arose in Victoria, the breach being the failure in Melbourne to nominate a ship as the defendant was bound to do under the contract. The quantum of damages is no part of the cause of action, and it was immaterial on the question of jurisdiction that evidence of the price of peas in Tasmania had to be given to fix the damages. *Railton* v. *Fleming*, (1912) V.L.R., 113; 33 A.L.T., 180; 18 A.L.R., 24. F.C., *a' Beckett, Hodges* and *Cussen, JJ.*

County Court—Jurisdiction—Libel circulating throughout Australia—Claim for damages and injunction.]— *Semble.*—An action cannot be brought in the County Court where the plaintiff's claim is for damages and an injunction in respect of the publication of a libel in a newspaper circulating throughout Australia. *Harrison San Miguel Proprietary Ltd.* v. *Alfred Lawrence & Co.*, (1912) V.L.R., 367; 34 A.L.T., 88; 18 A.L.R., 394. *Madden, C.J.*

County Court Act 1890 (No. 1078), secs. 61, 64—Fourth and Fifth Schedules—Practice —Liquidated money demand—Ordinary summons— Necessity for special summons — Amendment.]— Where for a liquidated money demand an ordinary summons in the form of the Fourth Schedule of the *County Court Act* 1890, pursuant to sec. 61 of that Act, is issued, and both parties appear at the hearing, the Judge should not, on the objection of the defendant that the summons should be in the form of the Fifth Schedule pursuant to section 64, strike out the case, but should proceed to hear it, either with or without an amendment of the summons. *Best* v. *Best*, (1908) V.L.R., 1; 29 A.L.T., 82; 13 A.L.R., 608. F.C., *Madden, C.J., Hodges* and *Hood, JJ.*

Judgment recovered in Petty Sessions— Death of complainant—Enforcement of judgment by executors—County Court action.]— *Semble.*—Where an order is made by Court of Petty Sessions for the payment to the complainant of a sum of money, which remains unsatisfied at his death, the complainant's executors may sue in the County Court on such order. *Goodman* v. *Jonas*, (1909) V.L.R., 307; 31 A.L.T., 16; 15 A.L.R., 308. *Cussen, J.*

County Court Act 1890 (No. 1078), secs. 48, 94—No jurisdiction to try action—Costs, whether Court may award.]—The power conferred by sec. 94 of the *County Court Act* 1890 to order a case to be struck out for want of jurisdiction and to award costs extends to all cases in which the Court has no jurisdiction, and is not limited to those cases in which under sec. 48 the want of jurisdiction might be cured by consent of the parties. *Harrison San Miguel & Co.* v. *Maddern*, (1905) V.L.R., 400 ; 26 A.L.T., 215 ; 11 A.L.R., 178, over-ruled. *The King* v. *Beecham & Co., Ex parte Cameron*, (1910) V.L.R., 204 ; 31 A.L.T., 183 ; 16 A.L.R., 173. F.C., *Madden, C.J., a' Beckett* and *Cussen, JJ.*

County Court Act 1890 (No. 1078), sec. 121 (1)—Equitable jurisdiction—Action by creditor of deceased person against beneficiaries—Jurisdiction of County Court.]—Even though the assets of the estate of a deceased person have been distributed among the beneficiaries under his will, County Courts have jurisdiction under sec 121 (1) of the *County Court Act* 1890 to hear an action brought against such beneficiaries by a creditor of the deceased claiming payment of the debt due to him by the deceased. *Smart* v. *Buchanan*, 31 A.L.T. (Supplement), 8 ; 15 A.L.R. (C.N.), 25. *Judge Chomley* (not without doubt) (1909).

Instruments Act 1890 (No. 1103), sec. 142—Bill of sale—Caveat—Tender of amount due to caveator—Refusal to accept—Removal of caveat—Jurisdiction of Judge to order.]—Where the grantor of a bill of sale had tendered to a caveator the amount of his debt, which the caveator refused to accept. *Held*, that the Judge had jurisdiction under sec. 142 of the *Instruments Act* 1890 to order the removal of the caveat. *In re Coburn*, 28 A.L.T. (Supplement), 3 ; 12 A.L.R. (C.N.), 17. *Judge Eagleson* (1906).

II.—Practice.

(a) service.

Practice—Service of summons—Time — Whether time for service may be abridged— Defendant, whether a party to action before service of plaint summons.]—A Judge of the County Court has no power to abridge the time fixed by r. 11 of the *County Court Rules* 1891 for the service of an ordinary plaint summons. Until served with such summons the person named therein as defendant is not a party to the action. *Newnham* v. *Lobb*, 27 A.L.T. (Supplement), 15 ; 12 A.L.R. (C.N.), 10. *Judge Box* (1906).

(b) proceedings at chambers generally.

Forms—Rules — Effect thereof — County Court Act 1890 (No. 1078), sec. 148.]—The forms set out in the schedule of forms are part of the Rules and have the same force as the Rules themselves. By virtue of sec. 148 of the *County Court Act* 1890 these Rules have the same force and effect as an Act of Parliament. *Devlin* v. *Tredrea*, 30 A.L.T. (Supplement), 19 ; 14 A.L.R. (C.N), 42. *Judge Chomley* (1908).

Practice—Country cause — Summons in Chambers—When it may be heard in Melbourne—Rule 210.]—A Chamber summons issued during the progress of a country cause cannot be heard in Melbourne, unless a Judge has previously directed such summons to be made returnable in Melbourne. *Perpetual Executors and Trustees Association of Australia* v. *Watts*, 27 A.L.T. (Supplement), 12 ; 12 A.L.R. (C.N.), 6. *Judge Eagleson* (1906).

Instruments Act 1890 (No. 1103), sec. 142—Bill of sale—Removal of caveat—Summons, form of.]—An objection, that the summons in an application for an order for the removal of a caveat lodged against the filing of a bill of sale did not call upon the caveator to show cause why the caveat should not be removed, was overruled. *In re Coburn*, 28 A.L.T. (Supplement), 3 ; 12 A.L.R. (C.N.), 17. *Judge Eagleson* (1906).

County Court—Filing of documents — Notice of an application for an extension of time within which to appeal—County Court Rules of 1891, r. 375.]—Notice of an application for an extension of time within which to appeal, should be in the proper form and filed with the Registrar of the Court. *Shan-*

ahan v. *Nicholls*, 27 A.L.T. (Supplement), 8 ;
11 A.L.R. (C.N.), 65, followed. *Ambler &
Co. Proprietary Ltd.* v. *Clayton*, 29 A.L.T.
(Supplement), 28 ; 14 A.L.R. (C.N.), 17.
Judge Eagleson (1908).

**County Court.—Chamber application—Costs
of, whether payment should be made condition
precedent.**]—Payment of costs of a Chamber
application will not be made a condition
precedent. *Ambler & Co. Proprietary Ltd.*
v. *Clayton*, 29 A.L.T. (Supplement), 28 ; 14
A.L.R. (C.N.), 17. *Judge Eagleson* (1908).

(c) UNDER SECTION 64 OF THE ACT.

**County Court Act 1890 (No. 1078), sec.
64 (3), (4)—Summons for final judgment—
Issue before giving of notice of intention to
defend.**]—Summonses under sec. 64 (4) of the
County Court Act 1890 must not be issued
before the notice of intention to defend has
been given. *Densham* v. *Quirk*, 28 A.L.T.
(Supplement), 6 ; 12 A.L.R. (C.N.), 22.
Judge Eagleson (1906).

**Practice—Liberty to sign final judgment—
The summons should be filed with the Registrar of the Court prior to the hearing.**]—
Mackay v. *Burley*, 27 A.L.T. (Supplement),
10 ; 12 A.L.R. (C.N.), 2. *Judge Chomley*
(1905).

**Summons for final judgment—Filing with
Registrar—Rule 209 (Rules of 1891).**]—A
summons in an application for leave to sign
final judgment should, under r. 209, be filed.
Densham v. *Quirk*, 28 A.L.T. (Supplement),
6 ; 12 A.L.R. (C.N.), 22. *Judge Eagleson*
(1906).

**County Court Act 1890 (No. 1078), secs. 5,
64—Final judgment, application for—Objection to Court—Nearer Court to defendant and
cause of action.**]—The objection which may
be raised by a defendant by virtue of sec. 5
of the *County Court Act* 1890 as to the Court
in which the plaint was entered, can be raised
only at the trial of the action. Therefore,
such an objection is no answer to an application for final judgment under sec. 64 of that
Act. *Pearson, Rowe, Smith & Co.* v.
Crispin, 32 A.L.T. (Supplement), 6 ; 16
A.L.R. (C.N.), 14. *Judge Chomley* (1910).

**County Court Act 1890 (No. 1078), sec. 146,
148—Rules 82, 416—Form 9—Practice—
Defective summons—Power of amendment.**]—
A County Court Judge has jurisdiction to
allow amendment of a summons for final
judgment where the same has been issued
in the terms of Form 9 of the Schedule of
Forms to the *County Court Rules* 1891,
although such summons does not comply
with the requirements of r. 82 of the said
Rules. *Devlin* v. *Tredrea*, 30 A.L.T. (Supplement), 19 ; 14 A.L.R. (C N.), 42. *Judge
Chomley* (1908).

**County Court Act 1890 (No. 1078), secs.
64, 98—Special summons—Judgment signed
on default by defendant—Application in
Chambers—Order for payment by instalments.**]
—Under sec. 98 of the *County Court Act* 1890
a Judge in Chambers has power to make
an order that a judgment debtor be at liberty
to pay by instalments the judgment debt,
where, on a summons under sec. 64 of that
Act, the plaintiff has signed judgment in
default of notice of intention to defend.
*Carlton and United Breweries Proprietary
Ltd.* v. *Sheahan*, 30 A.L.T. (Supplement), 20 ;
15 A.L.R. (C.N.), 5. *Judge Eagleson* (1909).

**County Court Act 1890 (No. 1078), sec. 64
(4)—Summons for final judgment—Supple-
mentary affidavit.**]—On the return of a
summons for final judgment, an application
by the plaintiff to be allowed to file a further
affidavit was refused. *Woolf* v. *Rae*, 28
A.L.T. (Supplement), 5 ; 12 A.L.R. (C.N.),
18. *Judge Neighbour* (1906).

(d) PARTIES.

**County Court Act 1890 (No. 1078), sec. 133
—Action for personal injuries—Judgment for
plaintiff—Appeal from refusal of new trial—
Death of plaintiff pending appeal—Survival of
action to executor—Executor added as respondent to appeal.**]—The plaintiff had
succeeded in the County Court in an action
for damages for personal injuries. Judgment was entered for her. The defendant
moved for a new trial, which was refused,
and then appealed from such refusal. Before
the appeal came on for hearing the plaintiff
died. *Held*, that the maxim *actio personalis*

moritur cum persona did not apply, and that the rights under the judgment survived to her executor, who was added as a party respondent to the appeal. *Farrands* v. *Mayor, &c., of Melbourne,* (1909) V.L.R., 531 ; 31 A.L.T., 78 ; 15 A.L.R., 520. F.C., *Madden, C.J., Hodges* and *Cussen, JJ.*

County Court Act 1890 (No. 1078), sec. 60 —County Court Rules 1891, r. 107—Infant, action by—Appointment of next friend.]—A County Court has no power to allow the appointment of a next friend during the course of the trial of an action brought by an infant in his own name. *Thompson* v. *Peach,* 28 A.L.T. (Supplement), 10 ; 13 A.L.R. (C.N.), 5. *Judge Box* (1906).

Local Government Act 1903 (No. 1893), secs. 341, 342—County Court Rules 1891, r. 103—Rates—Charge on land—Proceedings to enforce—Death of owner—Parties—Executor of executor—Order for sale—Title.]—See LOCAL GOVERNMENT. *Moorabbin, Shire of* v. *Soldi,* (1912) V.L.R., 389 ; 34 A.L.T., 93 ; 18 A.L.R., 493.

(e) SPECIAL DEFENCES ; PAYMENT INTO COURT.

County Court—Practice—Slander—Special defence that slander is true—Limitation of such defence at trial to part only of the words complained of.]—The defendant, who had given notice that he relied on the defence that the slander complained of was true in substance and in fact, was allowed at the trial to limit such defence to part only of the words complained of, and as to the whole of such words to set up the defence that they were not spoken and published of and concerning the plaintiff. *Griffiths* v. *Barry,* 27 A.L.T. (Supplement), 12 ; 12 A.L.R. (C.N.), 9. *Judge Johnston* (1906).

County Court Act 1890 (No. 1078), s. 51— County Court Rules 1891, rr. 155, 424— Wrongs Act 1890 (No. 1160), sec. 3—Remitted action—Action for libel—Notice of special defence under Wrongs Act 1890—Enlargement of time for serving and filing such notice— Power of Court to grant.]—Where an action for libel has been remitted under section 51 of the *County Court Act* 1890 to be tried in a County Court, such Court has power under rule 424 of the *County Court Rules* 1891 to allow the defendant to serve and file a notice of special defence under the *Wrongs Act* 1890 after the expiration of the time allowed or appointed for so doing by rule 155. *Bayne* v. *Wilson & Mackinnon,* 31 A.L.T. (Supplement), 2 ; *Judge Box* (1909).

County Court Act 1890 (No. 1078), s. 66— Special defence, notice of—Rates—Enforcement of charge upon land—Local Government Act 1903 (No. 1893), ss. 324 to 328, 340 to 343.]—Section 66 of the *County Court Act* 1890 requiring notice of special defences applies to actions for enforcing charges upon land for rates. *Mayor, &c. of Malvern* v. *Johnson,* 28 A.L.T. (Supplement), 7 ; 12 A.L.R. (C.N.), 28. *Judge Box* (1906).

County Court Act 1890 (No. 1078), s. 62— County Court Rules 1891, rr. 197, 200— Payment into Court—Several claims or causes of action—Payment into Court on one claim or cause of action only with denial of liability —Taking out of Court the amount paid in— Abatement of action.]—Where a defendant, under section 62 of the *County Court Act* 1890 and rule 197 of the *County Court Rules* 1891, pays into Court a sum of money in full satisfaction of one of several claims or causes of action set out in the particulars of plaintiff's demand in the action, with a denial of liability, the plaintiff is not entitled under rule 200 or at all to take out of Court before the determination of the action the amount so paid in unless he accepts the same in full satisfaction of all such claims or causes of action. *Kelly* v. *Trimble,* 31 A.L.T. (Supplement), 1 ; 15 A.L.R. (C.N.), 7. *Judge Chomley* (1909).

County Court Act 1890 (No. 1078), s. 62— County Court Rules 1891, rr. 197, 200— Payment into Court—Action against defendants as executors and as beneficiaries— Payment into Court by executors—Acceptance in satisfaction of claim against executors— Survival of claim against beneficiaries.]—Where the defendants in an action who are sued as executors and also as beneficiaries, pay money into Court under section 62 of the *County Court Act* 1890 and rule 197 of the *County Court Rules* 1891 as executors merely, the action does not abate as against them as beneficiaries on the plaintiff electing to accept and taking out of Court such money in full satisfaction of his claim against them as executors. *Smart* v. *Buchanan*, 31 A.L.T. (Supplement), 8; 15 A.L.R. (C.N.), 25. *Judge Chomley* (1909).

County Court Rules 1891, rr. 197, 199—Payment into Court with a denial of liability—Delay of plaintiff in furnishing particulars—Payment after expiration of prescribed time.]—Where the plaintiff failed to deliver particulars of his claim until after the expiration of the time prescribed for payment of money into Court. *Held*, that the defendant was entitled to wait till the further particulars were delivered before deciding whether or not to pay money into Court, and that he should be allowed to pay money into Court with a denial of liability although the prescribed time had expired. *Armstrong* v. *Cuming Smith & Co. Proprietary Ltd.*, 29 A.L.T. (Supplement), 17; 13 A.L.R. (C.N.), 31. *Judge Box* (1907).

(*f*) INTERROGATORIES AND DISCOVERY OF DOCUMENTS.

County Court Act 1890 (No. 1078), ss. 81, 148—Infant, whether interrogatories may be administered to—Rules of Supreme Court 1906, Order XXXI., r. 29.]—A party to an action in the County Court cannot object to answer interrogatories delivered under section 81 of the *County Court Act* 1890 merely on the ground of infancy. Order XXXI., r. 29 (*Supreme Court Rules* 1906) applies. *Brock* v. *Victorian Railways Commissioners*, 29 A.L.T. (Supplement), 3; 13 A.L.R. (C.N.), 21. *Judge Johnston* (1907).

Interrogatories—Form of order—County Court Act 1890 (No. 1078), sec. 81 (1).]—The following form of order (omitting formal parts) was settled by His Honor Judge Eagleson—" I do order that the above-named —— to deliver to the —— the interrogatories in writing, a copy of which is hereunto annexed marked A, and that the —— do within seven days from the service hereof answer the said interrogatories as prescribed by section 81 of the *County Court Act* 1890."

Spence v. *Simpson*, 33 A.L.T. (Supplement), 11; 18 A.L.R. (C.N.), 1. (1912).

Interrogatories—Form of order—An order directing a party to answer interrogatories should set out specifically the time for answering—It is not sufficient if the order merely directs the party to answer " as prescribed by section 81 of the County Court Act 1890."]—*Crouch* v. *Victorian Railways Commissioners*, 27 A.L.T. (Supplement), 11; 12 A.L.R. (C.N.), 2. *Judge Box* (1905).

Interrogatories—Order for interrogatories, form of—" Upon reading the interrogatories."]—An order granting leave to deliver interrogatories should not state that it was made " upon reading the interrogatories." *Naylor* v. *Kelly*, 27 A.L.T. (Supplement), 14; 12 A.L.R. (C.N.), 17. *Judge Box* (1906).

County Court Act 1890 (No. 1078), s. 81—Interrogatories—Leave to deliver—Application by solicitor's clerk—Form of order.]—Where on the application of a solicitor's clerk leave is granted to deliver interrogatories, the order should not state that it was made after hearing the solicitor. *Gobetti* v. *Harris*, 28 A.L.T. (Supplement), 9; 12 A.L.R. (C.N.), 28. *Judge Eagleson* (1906).

Interrogatories—County Court Act 1890 (No. 1078), s. 81 (4)—Shortening time for answering—Affidavit in support of application, necessity for.]—An application for an order that answers to interrogatories be filed within a period less than seven days should be supported by affidavit showing the necessity for curtailing the time. *Williams* v. *Alcock*, 28 A.L.T. (Supplement), 5; 12 A.L.R. (C.N.). 18. *Judge Eagleson* (1906).

Discovery—County Court Rules 1891, r. 93—Written communications by servant to master—Affidavit, sufficiency of—Privilege.]—The defendants by their affidavit of documents refused to disclose certain written communications by one of their servants to another which defendants swore were made " for the purpose of assisting the defendants to resist or settle " anticipated litigation by the plaintiff. *Held*, that, though it was not in terms sworn that the communications were made to the defendants, it sufficiently appeared that they were made for the purpose of reaching the defendants ultimately and that the communications were accordingly privileged. *Connan* v. *Victorian Railways Commissioners*, 28 A.L.T. (Supplement), 19 ; 13 A.L.R. (C.N.), 14. *Judge Chomley* (1907).

County Court Act 1890 (No. 1078), s. 78—Production and inspection of documents—Materiality of documents—Objection to produce—Rectification of affidavit in support.] —A party in his affidavit of documents made in pursuance of an order for discovery disclosed his possession of certain books, describing them in such a way that they appeared to be material to the case, but objecting to produce them on the ground that he had been advised that the entries contained therein in no way related to the matters in dispute in the action and were not material to the other party's claim. *Held*, that leave to rectify the affidavit should not be given, and that the entries in the books should be produced. *Choon* v. *Beecham*, 29 A.L.T. (Supplement), 2 ; 13 A.L.R. (C.N.), 18. *Judge Box* (1907).

(g) EVIDENCE.

County Court—Evidence—Action for trial before Judge and jury—Examination of witnesses before trial—Jurisdiction.]—In an action to be tried before a Judge and jury in the County Court at Palmerston an application was made in Melbourne to the Judge of County Courts, who was to preside at the trial, that in order to avoid the expense of taking them to Palmerston the evidence of certain witnesses might be taken before His Honor in Melbourne and be read to the jury at the trial. *Held*, that there was no jurisdiction to grant the application. *Ferris* v. *Litchfield*, 28 A.L.T. (Supplement), 14 ; 13 A.L.R. (C.N.), 10. *Judge Box* (1907).

(h) JURIES.

County Court Act 1890 (No. 1078), s. 89—Jury, right to trial by—Common law claim for liquidated amount—Claim for declaration that plaintiff entitled to that amount—Whether action equitable.]—In an action in the County Court, by the particulars of demand it was alleged that the parties agreed that the plaintiff should prepare building plans for a competition to be sent in in the name of the defendant on condition that the plaintiff should receive one quarter of the prize or reward which the plans might win ; that the plans were prepared and sent in and won the prize or reward which was the amount of the architect's commission on the building estimated by the plaintiff at £720 ; and that the defendant refused to pay the plaintiff one quarter or any proportion of the commission or to return the plans. The plaintiff claimed a declaration that he was entitled to one quarter of the prize or reward, viz., £180, or alternatively return of the plans or damages £180 ; and he also claimed an injunction restraining the defendant from using the plans. *Held*, that the particulars of demand set out no circumstances to which a Court of Equity attaches its jurisdiction, and that the claim for a declaration did not in itself make the claim an equitable one, and that the plaintiff was entitled by section 89 of the *County Court Act* 1890 to have the action tried by a jury. *Biggs* v. *Kelly*, 24 V.L.R., 402 ; 20 A.L.T., 105 ; 4 A.L.R., 153 ; *Barker* v. *Henty*, 29 V.L.R., 293 ; 25 A.L.T., 34 ; 9 A.L.R., 160 ; and *Porteous* v. *Lindley*, 28 V.L.R., 606 ; 24 A.L.T., 139 ; 9 A.L.R., 25, distinguished. *Annear* v. *Inskip*, (1910) V.L.R., 235 ; 31 A.L.T., 220 ; 16 A.L.R., 276. F.C., *Madden, C.J., a'Beckett* and *Hood, JJ.*

County Court Act 1890 (No. 1078), s. 89—Jury, right of party to trial by—Whether limited to cases where claim is for liquidated amount.]—Under section 89 of the *County Court Act* 1890 the right of either party to have the case tried by a jury is not limited to actions other than those for the recovery of unliquidated damages, but extends to all actions in which the amount claimed exceeds twenty pounds. *The King* v. *Beecham & Co.*, (1910) V.L.R., 204 ; 31 A.L.T., 183 ; 16 A.L.R., 173, applied. *Annear* v. *Inskip*, (1910) V.L.R., 235 ; 31 A.L.T., 220 ; 16 A.L.R., 276. F.C., *Madden, C.J., a'Beckett* and *Hood, JJ.*

(i) LOCAL GOVERNMENT ACT, PROCEEDINGS UNDER.

See also, STAY OF PROCEEDINGS.

Local Government Act 1903 (No. 1893), ss. 324 to 328, 340 to 343—Rates, interest and costs, how far a charge upon land—Costs of removing an order from Petty Sessions to the Supreme Court.]—The statutory charge over lands for the payment of municipal rates, interest and costs, includes the costs of removing an order for rates, interest and costs, obtained in a Court of Petty Sessions, into the Supreme Court and of issuing execution thereon. *Mayor, &c. of Malvern v. Johnson,* 28 A.L.T. (Supplement), 7 ; 12 A.L.R. (C.N.), 28. *Judge Box* (1906).

Local Government Act 1903 (No. 1893), s. 708—Notice of injury—Sufficiency—Place at which the accident took place—" Bridge "— " Approach."]—*See* LOCAL GOVERNMENT. *Daniel v. Benalla, President &c. of Shire of,* (1906) V.L.R., 101 ; 27 A.L.T., 141 ; 12 A.L.R., 16.

(j) INTERPLEADER.

County Court Rules 1891, r. 230—Action for commission—Claim by third party— Interpleader by defendant—Claims arising out of same subject matter—Whether claims for one and same debt.]—The plaintiff, an estate agent, sued the defendant for commission alleged to be due to him on the sale of a house of the defendant. Another estate agent claimed from the defendant commission in respect of the same sale of the same house. *Held,* that the defendant was not entitled to relief by way of interpleader. *Greatorex v. Shackle,* (1895) 2 Q.D., 249, followed. *Looker v. Mercer,* 28 A.L.T. (Supplement), 15 ; 13 A.L.R. (C.N.), 13. *Judge Eagleson* (1907).

Interpleader—Grounds of claim, statement of—Alternative and inconsistent grounds— Rule 236 (Rules of 1891).]—A claimant in an interpleader by bailiff under section 103 of the *County Court Act* 1890 may rely upon alternative and inconsistent grounds of claim. *Moorhead v. Chauncey, Hays* (claimant), 28 A.L.T. (Supplement), 7 ; 12 A.L.R.

(C.N.), 27. *Judge Eagleson* (affirmed on appeal to Full Court) (1906)

County Court Rules 1891, r. 236—Interpleader—Particulars of claim—Grounds of claim—Defective Particulars—Amendment.] —Where in his particulars of claim to goods seized by the County Court bailiff under a warrant of execution, the claimant merely states that he claims certain of such goods, " the same being my property," such particulars of claim are defective as they do not set out the " grounds of claim " as required by Rule 236 of the *County Court Rules* 1891. An application made on the return of an interpleader summons, for leave to amend the particulars in notices of claim which were defective in this respect, was refused, and the claims were dismissed. *Rogers v. Metters ; Metters* (claimants), 34 A.L.T. (Supplement), 4 ; 18 A.L.R. (C.N.), 21. *Judge Eagleson* (1912).

Interpleader—Grounds of claim—Order giving leave to amend—Whether necessary to draw up.]—An order giving leave to amend the grounds of his claim in a claimant's particulars of claim need not be drawn up. *Moorhead v. Chauncey, Hays* (claimant), 28 A.L.T. (Supplement), 7 ; 12 A.L.R (C.N.), 27. *Judge Eagleson* (1906).

Interpleader summons—Affidavit in support—County Court Rules 1891, r. 230.]—An interpleader summons under rule 230 of the *County Court Rules* 1891 should be supported by an affidavit. *Looker v. Mercer,* 28 A.L.T. (Supplement), 15 ; 13 A.L.R. (C.N.), 13. *Judge Eagleson* (1907).

(k) IMPRISONMENT OF FRAUDULENT DEBTORS ACT.

Judgment summons—Proceedings in Supreme Court—Judgment signed in Supreme Court on judgment of County Court—Damages awarded in action of tort—" Sum of money recoverable under any judgment of the Supreme Court "—Imprisonment of Fraudulent Debtors Act 1890 (No. 1100), ss. 4, 5— County Court Act 1890 (No. 1078), sec. 104 ; Ninth and Tenth Schedules.]—Where a judgment has been signed in the Supreme Court

under section 104 of the *County Court Act*
1890 on a County Court judgment awarding
damages in an action of tort, the amount for
which such judgment is signed is a " sum of
money recoverable under any judgment of
the Supreme Court " within the meaning of
section 4 of the *Imprisonment of Fraudulent
Debtors Act* 1890,, and a summons to debtor
may be issued in the Supreme Court under
section 4 and an order thereon may be made
under section 5 (iv.) (*d*) of that Act. *Tipper*
v. *Wathen*, (1911) V.L.R., 464 ; 33 A.L.T.,
85 ; 17 A.L.R., 543. *Hood, J.*

—Imprisonment of Fraudulent Debtors Act
1890 (No. 1100), sec. 15—The County Court
Rules 1891, Schedule of Forms, Form 14—
Judgment summons—Statement of matters
for examination of judgment debtor.]—A
judgment summons should not include as
matters as to which the judgment debtor is
to be examined matters which are not intended
to be relied on at the hearing. *Lawson* v
Lang, 32 A.L.T. (Supplement), 4 ; 16 A.L.R.
(C.N.), 9. *Judge Eagleson* (1910).

Imprisonment of Fraudulent Debtors Act
1890 (No. 1100), sec. 15—County Court Act
1890 (No. 1078), sec. 31—Judgment debtor's
summons—Service of judgment—Sufficiency
of certified extract from Register.]—*See
Royal Finance Company* v. *Summers*, 30
A.L.T. (Supplement), 24 ; 15 A.L.R. (C.N.),
9. *Judge Box* (1909).

Imprisonment of Fraudulent Debtors Act
1890 (No. 1100), s. 16—Sequestration of
judgment debtor's estate—Liability contracted
by fraud.]—*See* DEBTORS ACT. *Davies* v.
Burley, 29 A.L.T. (Supplement), 18 ; 13
A.L.R. (C.N.), 34.

Imprisonment of Fraudulent Debtors Act
1890 (No. 1100), sec. 16 (iv. A)—Liability
contracted by fraud—Jurisdiction.]—The fraud
referred to in section 16 (IV. A) of the *Imprisonment of Fraudulent Debtors Act* 1890
means fraud going to the whole subject
matter of the judgment. *Weeks* v. *Mayhew*,
28 A.L.T. (Supplement), 9 ; 12 A.L.R.
(C.N.), 27. *Judge Box.*

(*l*) ENFORCEMENT OF JUDGMENTS.

The County Court Rules 1891, rr. 333, 334,
335, 343—Judgment that defendant deliver a
certain chattel to plaintiff—Warrant of delivery
under Rule 343 returned unsatisfied—Warrant
of attachment, issue of—Jurisdiction.]—A
County Court Judge has jurisdiction to order
a warrant of attachment to issue under
Rule 335 of *The County Court Rules* 1891
when a warrant of delivery under Rule 343
has proved ineffectual. *Macrow & Sons Co.
Proprietary Ltd.* v. *Davidson*, 27 A.L.T.
(Supplement), 11 ; 12 A.L.R. (C.N.), 9.
Judge Johnston (1906).

County Court Act 1890 (No. 1078), sec. 104
—County Court judgment—Loss of certificate
of judgment—Issue of duplicate certificate.]
—Where a certificate of a County Court judgment, after having been granted and delivered
by the Registrar to a judgment creditor
under section 104 of the *County Court Act*
1890, has not been filed in the Supreme Court,
but has been lost, the County Court has
jurisdiction to direct the Registrar to issue
a duplicate certificate to such creditor.
Ireland v. *Floate*, 28 A.L.T. (Supplement),
16 ; 13 A.L.R. (C.N.), 13. *Judge Eagleson*
(1907).

Execution of judgment, difficulty in or
about—Attendance and examination of judgment debtor—Rule 323 (Rules of 1891).]—
Where a judgment debtor had in his possession at the time of the trial of the action
goods which could not be found when the
warrant of execution upon the judgment
was attempted to be enforced, *Held*, that
under Rule 323 of *The County Court Rules*
1891 the Judge had power to order the
attendance and examination of the judgment
debtor. *Tye & Co. Proprietary Ltd.* v.
Presland, 28 A.L.T. (Supplement), 3 ; 12
A.L.R. (C.N.), 17. *Judge Eagleson* (1906).

Attachment of debts—Service of garnishee
order nisi—Notice of order directed to be
sent by telegram to the garnishee, to be
followed by personal service upon him of a
copy of such order—Order nisi made returnable before a Judge of a County Court sitting
in a place other than where judgment obtained—County Court Act 1890 (No. 1078),
secs. 108, 109.]—*Greenwood* v. *Cormack*,

Blakely (Garnishee), 28 A.L.T. (Supplement), 5; 12 A.L.R. (C.N.), 24. *Judge Eagleson* (1906).

(m) STAY OF PROCEEDINGS.

Local Government Act 1903 (No. 1893), secs. 708, 710—Non-compliance with conditions of section 708—Whether application for stay of action imperative.]—In order that a municipality may take advantage of the plaintiff's non-compliance with the conditions of section 708 it is not imperative that an application should be made under section 710 for a stay of the action. If no such application has been made the municipality may raise the defence of non-compliance at the trial of the action. *Daniel* v. *Benalla, President, &c. of Shire of*, (1906) V.L.R., 101. F.C., *Madden, C.J., Holroyd* and *Hodges, JJ.*

Local Government Act 1903 (No. 1893), secs. 708, 710—Notice of action against municipality—Failure to comply with conditions—Stay of action—Judge in Chambers —Jurisdiction.]—A Judge in Chambers has under section 710 of the *Local Government Act* 1903 a discretion, where the facts relating to the injury its nature and extent and the consequent suffering are in dispute, to say that he will not stay the action at that juncture. In such a case it is for the Judge who presides at the trial, after hearing the evidence, to say whether the plaintiff has shown sufficient reason why he was unable to give the notice required by section 708 (1). *Leeder* v. *Ballarat East, Mayor &c. of*, 29 A.L.T. (Supplement), 6; 13 A.L.R. (C.N.), 25. *Judge Eagleson* (1907).

County Court—Action on insurance policy —Arbitration a condition precedent to right of action—Stay of proceedings—Adjournment —Jurisdiction—County Court Act 1890 (No. 1078), sec. 71.]—An action was brought against the assurer by the person assured upon a policy of insurance which provided that the determination of any dispute or question by arbitration should be a condition precedent to the liability of the assurer and to the right of the assured to recover. Upon an application by the assurer for a stay of all proceedings. *Held,* that the trial of the action should, under section 71 of the *County Court Act* 1890, be adjourned until arbitration under the terms of the policy had taken place. *Borrett* v. *Norwich and London Accident Insurance Association,* 29 A.L.T. (Supplement), 1; 13 A.L.R. (C.N.), 22. *Judge Chomley* (1907).

County Court Act 1890 (No. 1078), secs. 68, 70, 71—Discontinuance of action—Costs not paid—Subsequent action for same cause of action—Stay of proceedings until costs paid—Jurisdiction.]—A Judge of a County Court has power to stay an action until payment by the plaintiff of the costs ordered to be paid by him in a prior action for the same cause of action against the same defendant. *Leeder* v. *Ballarat East, Mayor &c. of*, 29 A.L.T. (Supplement), 6; 13 A.L.R. (C.N.), 25. *Judge Eagleson* (1907).

Stay of action—Notice of action, when necessary—Local Government Act 1903 (No. 1893), secs. 491, 708 (1), (4), 710.]—Section 708 refers only to accidents arising through the improper maintenance of roads. Accordingly, where the cause of action alleged was the negligence of a driver of a water-cart of the defendant municipality, an application to stay proceedings on the ground that no notice of action had been given was dismissed. *Gordon* v. *Ballarat, Mayor &c. of*, 29 A.L.T. (Supplement), 4; 13 A.L.R. (C.N.), 19. *Judge Johnston.*

(n) NEW TRIAL.

County Court—New trial—Notice of application served out of time—Refusal of Judge to enlarge time—Jurisdiction of Court of appeal to enlarge—Misdirection—No objection taken at trial—Jurisdiction of Judge to grant new trial—Refusal of Judge to grant new trial —Whether High Court will grant new trial —Infinitesimal hope of success if new trial granted—County Court Act 1890 (No. 1078), sec. 96—County Court Rules 188, 424.]— Assuming that the High Court and the Supreme Court have jurisdiction to review the exercise by a Judge of County Courts of the discretion given him by Rule 424 of the *County Court Rules* 1891 to enlarge the time for serving notice of an application for a new trial, and that a Judge of County Courts has jurisdiction under section 96 of the *County Court Act* 1890 to grant a new trial on the ground of misdirection in law where objection has not been taken at the trial to the misdirection (as to both of which questions, *quaere*), the High Court will not grant a new trial where the Judge of County Courts has refused it and the party asking for it would, in the opinion of the Court, only have a problematical and infinitesimal hope of success if a new trial were had. *Holford* v. *Melbourne Tramway and Omnibus Co. Ltd.,* (1909) V.L.R., 497; 29 A.L.T., 112; 13 A.L.R., at p. 677, doubted; *Handley* v. *London, Edinburgh and Glasgow Assurance Co.,* (1902) 1 K.B., 350, commented on. *Armstrong* v. *Great Southern Gold Mining Co. No Liability,* (1911) 12 C.L.R., 382; 17 A.L.R., 377. H.C., *Griffith, C.J., Barton* and *O'Connor, JJ.*

County Court—New trial—Service of notice of application—Time—" Clear days "—County Court Rules 1891, r. 188, Interpretation clause.]—The definition of " clear days " in the interpretation clause of the *County Court Rules* 1891 does not apply to Rule 188 and, therefore, service of a copy of a notice of application for a new trial on the eighth day after the last day of the trial is out of time. *Armstrong* v. *Great Southern Gold Mining Co. No Liability,* (1911) 12 C.L.R., 382; 17 A.L.R., 377. H.C., *Griffith, C.J., Barton* and *O'Connor, JJ.*

County Court Act 1890 (No. 1078), secs. 96, 133, 148—Order XXXIX., r. 7 (Rules of 1906)—County Court—New trial—Whether issues to be tried may be limited.]—*Semble,* on an application for a new trial, a County Court may order a new trial on some only of the issues tried in the case to the exclusion of others. *Holford and Wife* v. *Melbourne Tramway and Omnibus Co.,* (1909) V.L.R., 497; 29 A.L.T., 112; 13 A.L.R., 667. F.C., *Madden, C.J., a' Beckett* and *Cussen, JJ.*

New trial—Exercise of discretion to grant a new trial.]—For a case in which the discretion to be exercised in granting a new trial was considered. *See Farrands* v. *Mayor &c.*

of Melbourne, (1909) V.L.R., 531; 31 A.L.T., 78; 15 A.L.R., 520.

(*o*) COSTS.

(1) *Jurisdiction.*

See also *post.* (2) *Amount Recovered not Exceeding Ten Pounds.*

County Court Act 1890 (No. 1078), sec. 47 —Costs of chamber application—Jurisdiction of Judge to fix.]—A Judge of a County Court has jurisdiction under section 47 of the *County Court Act* 1890 to fix the amount of the costs of an application before him in Chambers. *Leeder* v. *Ballarat East, Mayor &c. of,* 29 A.L.T. (Supplement), 6; 13 A.L.R. (C.N.), 25. *Judge Eagleson* (1907).

County Court Act 1890 (No. 1078), sec. 62 —Payment into Court—Costs fixed by Registrar—Whether plaintiff may be allowed additional costs.]—The fixation of costs by the Registrar under section 62 of the *County Court Act* 1890 is final and conclusive for all purposes, and there is no power to allow the plaintiff any costs beyond the amount so fixed. *Armstrong* v. *Cuming Smith & Co. Proprietary Ltd.,* 29 A.L.T. (Supplement), 17; 13 A.L.R. (C.N.), 34. *Judge Chomley* (1907).

(2) *Amount Recovered not Exceeding Ten Pounds.*

County Court Act 1890 (No. 1078), secs. 45, 64—Costs—Proposed actions—Claims not exceeding £10—Certificate for costs—Plaintiff's costs of employing an attorney—Time for making application.]—An application for the allowance of professional costs under section 45 cannot be made before the summons in the action is issued. *Semble,* when the plaintiff in an action commenced by a special summons under section 64 is about to sign final judgment in default of notice to defend, for an amount not exceeding £10, he should apply to the Judge sitting in Chambers to be allowed costs under Scale A. and for a direction that the Registrar so fix them. *Clarazite Manufacturing Company Limited* v. *Armitage* (*No.* 1), 30 A.L.T. (Supplement), 21; 15 A.L.R. (C.N.), 6. *Judge Eagleson* (1909).

County Court Act 1890 (No. 1078), secs. 45, 62, 64—County Court Rules 1891, r. 200—Costs—Action—Claim not exceeding £10—Payment into Court by defendant of debt and costs—Plaintiff's costs of employing attorney—Time for making application.]—Where the defendant in an action commenced by special summons under section 64 of the *County Court Act* 1890 duly pays into Court the amount of the debt and costs indorsed on the summons and such debt does not exceed £10, a Judge of the County Court has no jurisdiction to allow the plaintiff the cost of employing an attorney—such costs not being mentioned in the summons. *Clarazite Manufacturing Company Limited* v. *Armitage* (*No.* 1), 30 A.L.T. (Supplement), 21 ; 15 A.L.R. (C.N.), 6, disapproved. *Clarazite Manufacturing Company Limited* v. *Armitage* (*No* 2), 30 A.L.T. (Supplement), 22 ; 15 A.L.R. (C.N.), 6. *Judge Chomley* (1909).

County Court Act 1890 (No. 1078), secs. 45, 64—Costs—Proposed action—Claim not exceeding £10—Plaintiff's costs of employing attorney—Time for making application that costs be allowed.]—An order may be made under section 45 of the *County Court Act* 1890 prior to the issue of a special summons under section 64 that the Registrar on issuing such summons shall indorse thereon the plaintiff's costs of employing an attorney. *Clarazite Manufacturing Co. Ltd.* v. *Armitage* (*No.* 1), 30 A.L.T. (Supplement), 21 ; 15 A.L.R. (C.N.), 6, not followed. *Clarazite Manufacturing Co. Ltd.* v. *Armitage* (*No.* 2), 30 A.L.T. (Supplement), 22 ; 15 A.L.R. (C.N.), 6, approved. *Lee* v. *Cunningham*, 32 A.L.T. (Supplement), 4 ; 16 A.L.R. (C.N.), 1. *Judge Box* (1910).

County Court Act 1890 (No. 1078), sec. 45 —Costs—Amount recovered not exceeding Ten pounds—Injunction a material part of the action—Professional costs.]—*Semble* : The provision in section 45 of the *County Court Act* 1890 as to professional costs where the amount recovered does not exceed £10, does not apply to cases where an injunction is a material part of the relief sought. *Harrison San Miguel Proprietary Ltd.* v. *Alfred Law-*rence & Co., (1912) V.L.R., 367 ; 34 A.L.T., 88 ; 18 A.L.R., 394. *Madden, C.J.*

(3) *Taxation.*

(a) Scale of Costs.

(i.) Under Scale in Rules under the Act.

Scale of costs—Rule 446 (Rules of 1891)— " Value of property in litigation "—Judgment for 1s. damages and injunction restraining defendant from breaking his covenant with plaintiff not to carry on business within a certain area—Scale of costs regulated, not by the amount of damages, but by the value of the plaintiff's right preserved from infringement by the injunction.]—*Moylan* v. *Nolan*, 27 A.L.T. (Supplement), 16 ; 12 A.L.R. (C.N.), 13. *Judge Box* (1906).

Action to enforce charge upon land for rates—County Court—Scale of costs, how determined—Value of land.]—In actions to enforce by sale a charge for municipal rates over land, the value of the land and not the amount of the charge fixes the scale upon which costs should be taxed. *Mayor &c. of Malvern* v. *Johnson*, 28 A.L.T. (Supplement, 7 ; 12 A.L.R. (C.N.), 28. *Judge Box* (1906).

County Court—Scale of costs—Review of taxation—" The value of the property in litigation "—County Court Rules 1891, rr. 446, 450.]—The true test of " the value of the property in litigation " in Rule 446 of *County Court Rules* 1891 is the value of the right in the property claimed by the plaintiff and not the value of the whole property in which the right is claimed. *Wilson* v. *Anderson*, 26 A.L.T. (Supplement), 5 ; 11 A.L.R. (C.N.), 35, explained. *Moylan* v. *Nolan*, 27 A.L.T. (Supplement), 16 ; 12 A.L.R. (C.N.), 13, approved. *Townsing* v. *Egan*, 29 A.L.T. (Supplement), 29 ; 14 A.L.R. (C.N.), 18. *Judge Moule* (1908).

Costs—Application for new trial—Scale of costs applicable—Schedule of scale of costs Items, 28, 29, 30, 31, 32.]—For the scale of costs applicable upon an application for a new trial, see *Levey* v. *Parker*, 28 A.L.T. (Supplement), 6 ; 12 A.L.R. (C.N.), 21. *Judge Box* (1906).

Costs of issues—Rule 446 (Rules of 1891).]—Where the plaintiff recovers judgment for a smaller amount than he claimed with costs on certain of the issues, his costs as between party and party are regulated by the scale of costs applying to the amount for which he has obtained judgment ; but the costs of the defendant, who obtains judgment on the other issues, are regulated by the amount sought to be recovered in the action. *Lynch* v. *Tognini*, 28 A.L.T. (Supplement), 1 ; 12 A.L.R. (C.N.), 14. *Judge Box* (1906).

County Court—Costs—Plaintiff successful on both claim and counterclaim—Scale upon which costs to be taxed—County Court Rules 1891, Schedule of Scale of Costs.]—Where an item under the Schedule of Scale of Costs applies both to the claim and the counterclaim, and is not divisible, and where the plaintiff is successful on both claim and counterclaim, the higher scale of costs relating to such item should be allowed. *Wilson* v. *Scott*, 3 A.L.R. (C.N.), 87, explained. *Hopkins* v. *Forster*, 32 A.L.T. (Supplement), 5 ; 16 A.L.R. (C.N.), 6. *Judge Chomley* (1910).

(ii.) In Other Cases.

See, also, *post* (*h*) Jury Fees and Expenses.

Costs—Taxation—Solicitor and client— County Court—Proposed action which is never commenced—Action commenced but proceedings dropped without order as to costs —Scale of costs applicable—County Court Rules 1891, Schedule of Scale of Costs.]— In taxing the costs as between solicitor and client for work done in relation to a County Court action which is never commenced, or in relation to a County Court action which is commenced but in which, by reason of the proceedings being dropped, no order is made as to costs, the Scale of Costs in the Schedule to the *County Court Rules* 1891 is not the governing and only guide in determining the amount to be allowed, but the Taxing Master may obtain assistance from it in the exercise of his discretion. *In re Brown*, (1911) V.L.R., 39 ; 32 A.L.T., 133 ; 16 A.L.R., 602. *a'Beckett, J.*

County Court—Costs—Items not included in Schedule of Scale of Costs—Conduct of trial—Implied agreement not to take objection **—Expenses incurred on faith of such agreement.]**—On the taxation of costs the unsuccessful party will be precluded from taking objection to the allowance of items on the ground that they are not comprised in those set out in the Schedule of Scale of Costs, where the parties have during the trial entered into an implied agreement that no such objection will be raised. *Reid* v. *Panton*, 32 A.L.T. (Supplement), 7 ; 16 A.L.R. (C.N.), 13. *Judge Eagleson.* (1910).

(*b*) Costs of Appeal.

Practice—Costs—Taxation — Appeal from County Court—Order dismissing appeal with costs to be taxed by Taxing Master.]—Where the Full Court has made an order that an appeal from the County Court be dismissed with costs, such costs to be taxed by the Taxing Master of the Supreme Court, the Taxing Master has power to tax only the costs of the appeal, and has no power to tax the costs incurred in the County Court prior to the institution of the appeal. *Marks* v. *Pett*, 10 V.L.R. (L.), 342, commented on. *Ambler & Co. Proprietary Ltd.* v. *Clayton*, (1909) V.L.R., 56 ; 30 A.L.T., 113 ; 14 A.L.R., 730. *a'Beckett, J.*

(*c*) Instructions ; Attendances on Client ; Preparation of Documents.

County Court Rules 1891—Schedule of Scale of Costs, Item 2, and Schedule of Forms, Form 3—Form of summons.]—Professional costs provided by Item 2, Schedule of Scale of Costs to the *County Court Rules* 1891 are not to be allowed on taxation where a summons is issued consisting of two separate sheets of paper, one of which sheets contains the plaintiff's particulars of demand. *Lawson* v. *Batchelor*, 29 A.L.T. (Supp.), 29 ; 14 A.L.R. (C.N.), 17. *Judge Eagleson* (1908).

Scale of Costs, Item 2—" Instructions to sue "—Costs for obtaining further particulars, drawing, engrossing, &c., in connection therewith allowed in addition to allowance for " Instructions to sue "—Discretion of Registrar.]—*Moylan* v. *Nolan*, 27 A.L.T. (Supplement), 16 ; 12 A.L.R. (C.N.), 13. *Judge Box* (1906).

Imprisonment of Fraudulent Debtors Act 1890 (No. 1100), sec. 15—Rules of 1891, Interpretation clause, r. 354—Schedule of Scale of Costs, Item 2—Judgment summons—Judgment under £10—Practitioner's costs—Attending at hearing—Instructions.]—On granting leave to withdraw a judgment summons issued on a judgment for less than £10 a Judge of the County Court may order payment by the judgment creditor of the judgment debtor's practitioner's costs for instructions from his client ; but he may not allow the costs of the practitioner for attending on such summons. *Coppel* v. *Anderson*, 28 A.L.T. (Supplement), 8 ; 12 A.L.R. (C.N.), 22. *Judge Box* (1906).

Schedule of Scale of Costs—Items 2, 35—Plaintiff's costs on claim and counterclaim—Two sets of costs—Instructions on claim—Instructions on counterclaim.]—Where a defendant's counterclaim raises matter different from that which arises upon the plaintiff's claim, the plaintiff should, on taxation of his bill of costs as against the defendant, be allowed under item 35 of the Schedule of the Scale of Costs for his solicitor's attendance upon him to advise or receive instructions from him in regard to the counterclaim, as well as under Item 2 for instructions to sue in regard to the claim. *Wilson* v. *Scott*, 3 A.L.R. (C.N.), 87, distinguished. *Ambler & Co. Proprietary Ltd.* v. *Clayton*, 31 A.L.T. (Supplement), 5 ; 15 A.L.R. (C.N.), 15 *Judge Johnson* (1909).

Schedule of Scale of Costs—Item 35—" Proceeding taken by opposite party "—Payment into Court by defendant—Plaintiff's Solicitor's attendance upon his client thereon.]—Payment into Court by a defendant is a " proceeding taken by the opposite party " within the meaning of Item 35 of the Schedule of Scale of Costs ; and, consequently, the plaintiff may be allowed under that Item for his solicitor's attendance upon him to advise or receive instructions from him on receiving notice of such payment in. *Ambler & Co. Proprietary Ltd.* v. *Clayton*, 31 A.L.T. (Supplement), 5 ; 15 A.L.R. (C.N.), 15. *Judge Johnson* (1909).

(d) Attending Court on Trial.

—Scale of Costs, Items 15 and 16—" Attending on trial with counsel "—" On trial " meaning of—Attending Court to hear the judgment of the Court reserved from one day to a subsequent day is not attending " on trial "—The Scale does not provide for such an attendance.]—*Moylan* v. *Nolan*, 27 A.L.T. (Supplement), 16 ; 12 A.L.R. (C.N.), 13. *Judge Box* (1906).

County Court—Costs—Taxation—Solicitor party to action acting professionally on own behalf—Solicitor called as witness—" Attending Court "—Witnesses' expenses—Schedule of Scale of Costs, Items 14, 15, 16.]—A solicitor was party to an action in which he acted professionally on his own behalf and was also called as a witness. *Held*, that he was entitled to be allowed his charge for " attending Court " under Items 14, 15 and 16 of the Schedule of Scale of Costs, or his expenses as a witness, whichever allowance was the higher, but not both. *Hopkins* v. *Forster*, 32 A.L.T. (Supplement), 5 ; 16 A.L.R. (C.N.), 6. *Judge Chomley* (1910).

(e) Perusing.

County Court—Scale of Costs, Item 28—Costs of perusing further and better answers to interrogatories may be allowed.]—*Moylan* v. *Nolan*, 27 A.L.T. (Supplement), 16 ; 12 A.L.R. (C.N.), 13. *Judge Box* (1906).

County Court—Costs—Solicitor plaintiff—Acting professionally on his own behalf—Costs of perusing documents—Perusing interrogatories—Schedule of Scale of Costs, Item 28.]—Where the plaintiff a solicitor obtains judgment with costs in an action wherein he acts as solicitor on his own behalf, he is entitled to the fee fixed by the Schedule of Scale of Costs for the perusal of all necessary documents, and he accordingly may charge under Item 28 for perusing the defendant's interrogatories. *Hopkins* v. *Forster*, 32 A.L.T. (Supplement), 5 ; 16 A.L.R. (C.N.), 6. *Judge Chomley* (1910).

(f) Counsel's Fees ; Drawing and Engrossing Brief ; Conference.

County Court—Practice—Costs—Application for liberty to sign final judgment—Scale of Costs.]—Items 30, 31 and 32 of the Schedule of Scale of Costs apply to applications for final judgment. Consequently the following items were allowed :—" Drawing and engrossing brief for counsel £1 ; Fee for counsel and clerk £2 4s. 6d. ; attending with counsel 10s." *Mackay* v. *Burley*, 27 A.L.T. (Supplement), 10 ; 12 A.L.R. (C.N.), 2. *Judge Chomley* (1905).

County Court Act 1890 (No. 1078), sec. 64 (4), (8)—Summons for final judgment—Rule 84 ; attendance of counsel—Costs—Allowances under Schedule of Scale of Costs to counsel and attorney—Items 30, 31 and 32— " Drawing and engrossing brief "—" Fee to counsel and clerk "—" Attending with counsel."]—There is nothing in r. 84 to preclude counsel from appearing for the parties on applications for final judgment. In referring the costs of such an application to the Registrar for taxation, His Honor Judge Box intimated that in the majority of the applications for final judgment which had come before him, if he had had to deal with the fixing of the costs, he would have allowed the costs of " drawing and engrossing brief for counsel," " Fee to counsel and clerk," and " attending with counsel." *Watson* v. *Watson*, 27 A.L.T. (Supplement), 14 ; 12 A.L.R. (C.N.), 9 (1906).

County Court—Costs — Counsel's fees— Practitioner conducting trial on behalf of his client.]—Where a party's practitioner attends Court and conducts the trial on behalf of his client he is not entitled to counsel's fee on brief as set out in Item 11 of the Scale of Costs. His fees for the first and subsequent days of the trial are governed by Items 17 and 44 of such scale. *O'Brien* v. *Victorian Railways Commissioners*, 27 A.L.T. (Supplement), 11 ; 12 A.L.R. (C.N.), 6. *Judge Eagleson* (1906).

County Court—Costs—Taxation—Conference with counsel—No application made at hearing—Discretion of Registrar—County Court Rules 1891, Schedule of Scale of Costs. Item 13.]—Where no application has been made at the hearing of an action to be allowed for a conference with Counsel under Item 13 of the Schedule of Scale of Costs, the allowance of such a charge is a matter for the

discretion of the Registrar. *Hopkins* v. *Forster*, 32 A.L.T. (Supplement), 5 ; 16 A.L.R. (C.N.), 6. *Judge Chomley*. (1910).

(g) Witnesses' Expenses.

Costs—Witnesses present until close of trial.] A party is entitled to have his witnesses present until the close of the trial, and to be allowed, as part of his costs of the action, the expenses of having them so present. *Lynch* v. *Tognini*, 28 A.L.T. (Supplement), 1 ; 12 A.L.R. (C.N.), 14. *Judge Box* (1906).

Costs—Witnesses in attendance—Case in printed list—No defended cases to be taken— Discretion of Registrar.]—Plaintiff's expenses and those of his witnesses were allowed for the day on which the case was in the printed list for hearing, but no defended cases were taken. *Lynch* v. *Tognini*, 28 A.L.T., (Supplement), 1 ; 12 A.L.R. (C.N.), 14. *Judge Box* (1906).

County Court—Costs—Taxation—Solicitor's party to action acting professionally on own behalf—Solicitor called as witness—" Attending Court "—Witnesses' expenses—Schedule of Scale of Costs, Items 14, 15, 16.]—*See, ante,* (d) ATTENDING COURT ON TRIAL. *Hopkins* v. *Forster*, 32 A.L.T. (Supplement), 5 ; 16 A.L.R. (C.N.), 6.

(h) Jury Fees and Expenses.

County Court—Costs—Items not included in Schedule of Scale of Costs—Jury fees and expenses—View—Travelling and other expenses—Juries Act 1890 (No. 1104), sec. 77, Tenth Schedule.]—By virtue of sec. 77 of the *Juries Act* 1890 and the Tenth Schedule thereto, jury fees and travelling and other expenses paid by one of the parties to an action tried with a jury, in respect to a view by the jury, are allowable on the taxation of his costs under an order giving him the costs of the action. *Reid* v. *Panton*, 32 A.L.T. (Supplement), 7 ; 16 A.L.R. (C.N.), 13. *Judge Eagleson* (1910).

(i) Costs of Warrants.

Costs—Warrant of execution to satisfy a County Court judgment—Bailiff's fees— County Court Rules 1891, r. 441.]—The only " costs of warrants against the goods " which may be allowed against the defendant under

County Court Rules 1891, r. 441, are the costs of issuing such warrant and the bailiff's fee for execution thereof. *In re Luke Nolan, deceased* (*No.* 1), 29 A.L.T. (Supplement), 31 ; 14 A.L.R. (C.N.), 21. *Judge Moule* (1908).

III.—REMITTING ACTIONS TO COUNTY COURT.

County Court Act 1890 (No. 1078), sec. 51—Action of tort brought in Supreme Court—Remission to County Court—Action fit to be tried in Supreme Court, what is.]—In determining that the plaintiff has, within the meaning of sec. 51 of the *County Court Act* 1890 a cause of action fit to be prosecuted in the Supreme Court, the Judge should be satisfied that difficulties of law or in the application of the law and complexity of fact are likely to arise at the trial. *O'Farrell* v. *Syme*, 16 V.L.R., 422 ; 12 A.L.T., 11, and *Smith* v. *Syme*, 20 V.L.R., 56, 15 A.L.T., 193, approved. *Orchard* v. *Oriental Timber Corporation Ltd.*, (1910) V.L.R., 192 ; 31 A.L.T., 198 ; 16 A.L.R., 213. F.C., *Madden, C.J., Hood* and *Cussen, JJ.*

County Court Act 1890 (No. 1078), sec. 51—Action brought in Supreme Court—Remission to County Court—" Cause of action fit to be prosecuted in the Supreme Court "—Matters to be taken into consideration.]—The words in the *County Court Act* 1890, sec. 51, " a cause of action fit to be prosecuted in the Supreme Court " mean a cause which is more fit to be tried in the Supreme Court than in the County Court, or which ought to be tried in the Supreme Court. *Farrer* v. *Lowe*, 5 T.L.R., 234, and *Banks* v. *Hollingsworth*, (1893) 1 Q.B., 442, followed. In determining whether the plaintiff has, within the meaning of that section, " a cause of action fit to be prosecuted in the Supreme Court," consideration should be given to the magnitude of the issues to be tried, and to the complexity of the facts and the difficulty of unravelling them, and to the difficulty of the questions of law involved. *Ronald* v. *Harper*, (1908) V.L.R., 674 ; 30 A.L.T., 72 ; 14 A.L.R., 472. *Hodges, J.*

County Court Act 1890 (No. 1078), sec. 51—Action brought in Supreme Court—Application to remit to County Court—Right of plaintiff to fix place of trial—Alteration on ground of convenience—Onus on defendant.]—Where in an application under sec. 51 of the *County Court Act* 1890 the defendant applies to have an action remitted for trial before a County Court at a place other than that fixed by the plaintiff in his writ, the onus is on the defendant to show that the alteration will effect a real and substantial advantage on the ground of convenience. Such an alteration of the place of trial will not be made on the mere ground that the parties reside nearer to the Court at which the defendant desires the trial to take place. *Mason* v. *Kelly*, 31 A.L.T., 121. *Madden, C.J.* (1910).

IV.—APPEALS ; CERTIORARI ; MANDAMUS.

Appeal—Jurisdiction—Discretion of Judge of County Court—Order enlarging time for taking any step—County Court Rules 1891, r. 424.]—*Quaere*, whether the High Court and the Supreme Court have jurisdiction to review the exercise by a Judge of County Courts of the discretion given him by r. 424 of the *County Court Rules* 1891 to enlarge the time for serving notice of an application for a new trial. *Armstrong* v. *Great Southern Gold Mining Co., No Liability*, (1911) 12 C.L.R., 382 ; 17 A.L.R., 377. H.C., *Griffith, C.J., Barton* and *O'Connor, JJ.*

Appeal—County Court—Action struck out for want of jurisdiction—Jurisdiction to deal with defendant's application for costs declined by Judge—Whether appeal lies—County Court Act 1890 (No. 1078), sec. 133.]—An action having been brought in a County Court which the Court had no jurisdiction to try, the Judge ordered the case to be struck out and refused to consider the defendant's application for costs on the ground that he had no jurisdiction to do so. *Held*, that an appeal lay from such refusal. *The King* v. *Beecham & Co., Ex parte Cameron*, (1910) V.L.R., 204 ; 31 A.L.T., 183 ; 16 A.L.R., 173. F.C., *Madden, C.J.* and *a'Beckett, J.* (*Cussen, J.*, doubting).

County Court Act 1890 (No. 1078), sec. 133—County Court Rules 1891, rr. 378, 379—Practice—Appeal—Case settled by Judge—Transmission to Supreme Court—Enlargement of time—Failure of Judge to indorse.]—The indorsement of enlargement of the time for transmitting a case on appeal to the Supreme Court, directed by r. 379 to be made by the Judge in cases falling within the rule, is not a condition of the jurisdiction of the Supreme Court to hear the appeal; and failure on the part of the Judge to make such indorsement will not prevent the Supreme Court from hearing the appeal if, in fact, the case is transmitted within fourteen days from the day on which the Judge shall have returned the case settled and signed by him to the appellant. *Ryan* v. *Muir & Co.*, (1912) V.L.R., 411; 34 A.L.T., 64; 18 A.L.R., 396. F.C., *Madden, C.J., Hood* and *Cussen, JJ.*

Action in County Court—Appeal to Full Court—Re-trial ordered in Supreme Court—Payment into Court—Order XXII. (Rules of 1906).]—When the Full Court on appeal from the County Court has directed the cause to be re-heard before a Judge of the Supreme Court, and has ordered that the costs of the first trial shall abide the result of the re-hearing, leave will not be given to the defendant to pay money into Court. Order XXII. does not apply to such a case. *Fitzgerald* v. *Murray*, (1907) V.L.R., 715; 29 A.L.T., 158; 13 A.L.R., 645. *Cussen, J.*

County Court Act 1890 (No. 1078), sec. 135—Special case for opinion of Supreme Court—Announcement by Judge of his intention to state—Change of intention before case actually stated.]—*Per Hodges* and *Hood, JJ.* —A Judge of a County Court, who has expressed his intention to state a special case under sec. 135 of the *County Court Act* 1890, may, before he has actually stated the question in the form of a special case, change his mind and deliver judgment. *Macartney* v. *A. Macrow & Sons Proprietary Ltd.*, (1911) V.L.R., 393; 33 A.L.T., 64; 17 A.L.R., 397.

Certiorari to Judge of a County Court—Evidence—Conflict of evidence as to proceedings in County Court——Unsworn statement of Judge, whether admissible.]—*Per a' Beckett, J.*—On the hearing of an order *nisi* for *certiorari* directed to the Judge of a County Court and a party to an action tried before him, the Supreme Court may obtain and act upon a statement, though not an oath, by the Judge as to what took place at the trial, if the affidavits are in conflict upon that matter. *Macartney* v. *A. Macrow & Sons Proprietary Ltd.*, (1911) V.L.R., 393; 33 A.L.T., 64; 17 A.L.R., 397.

Mandamus—Remedy by appeal available—Discretion of Court, matters to be considered in exercise of—Comparative advantage of applying one remedy rather than the other—County Court—Case struck out for want of jurisdiction—Jurisdiction to entertain defendant's application for costs declined by Judge.]—*See* APPEAL. *The King* v. *Beecham, Ex parte Cameron*, (1910) V.L.R., 204; 31 A.L.T., 183; 16 A.L.R., 173.

V.—OTHER POINTS.

Insolvency Act 1890 (No. 1102), sec. 37, sub-sec. viii.—Creditors' petition—Act of insolvency—Execution on a judgment obtained in " any Court "—County Court judgment.]—The words " any Court " in section 37 (viii.) of the *Insolvency Act* 1890 include a County Court. *In re Anderson*, (1909) V.L.R., 465; 31 A.L.T., 72; 15 A.L.R., 518. *Cussen, J.*

" Clear days."]—*See* TIME. *Armstrong* v. *Great Southern Gold Mining Co. No Liability.* (1911) 12 C.L.R., 382; 17 A.L.R., 377.

COURT.

See APPEAL; COUNTY COURT; INSOLVENCY; JUSTICES OF THE PEACE; MINING; PRACTICE AND PLEADING.

COURT FEES.

See COSTS.

CREDITOR.

See INSOLVENCY.

CRIMINAL LAW.

See also, *Police Offences Act* and the various Statutes creating offences punishable summarily.

I.—CARNALLY KNOWING ; INDECENT ASSAULT.

Crimes Act 1891 (No. 1231), sec. 6—Unlawfully and carnally knowing girl under age of sixteen—Consent—Girl of " same age as the defendant."]—The girl and the defendant are not " of the same age," if there be any difference, however slight, in their ages. If the defendant be a day older than the girl that is sufficient to take the case out of the proviso in section 6. *Rex* v. *Hibbert*, (1906) V.L.R., 198 ; 12 A.L.R. (C.N.), 5. *Hodges, J.* (1906).

Crimes Act 1891 (No. 1231), sec. 33—Evidence Act 1890 (No. 1088), sec. 50—Unsworn evidence of child of tender years—Corroboration—Indecent assault.]—*See post*, XXII.—PRACTICE ; (a) EVIDENCE ; (3) *Corroboration. The King* v. *O'Brien*, (1912) V.L.R., 133 ; 33 A.L.T., 177 ; 18 A.L.R., 38.

Evidence—Indecent assault—Statement or complaint by female assaulted—First reasonable opportunity—Statement or complaint in answer to questions.]—*See post*, XXII.—

PRACTICE; (*a*) EVIDENCE; (10) *Evidence of Other Acts of Accused and of Collateral Matters.* Rex v. *McNeill*, (1907) V.L.R., 265; 28 A.L.T., 182; 13 A.L.R., 99.

II.—CONSPIRACY.

Conspiracy—Corporation—Liability to presentment on charge of conspiracy—Capacity to conspire.]—A corporation cannot conspire nor (*Semble*) can it be conspired with. It cannot therefore be presented on a charge of conspiracy to defraud nor (*Semble*) can an individual be presented on a charge of conspiracy with a corporation to defraud. *R.* v. *Kellow*, (1912) V.L.R., 162; 33 A.L.T., 203; 18 A.L.R., 170. *Cussen, J.*

Conspiracy—Jurisdiction of Court—Agreement made outside overt acts within.]—The Court has jurisdiction to hear a charge of conspiracy to defraud if any overt act is done, in pursuance of the conspiracy, within the jurisdiction, although the original agreement between the conspirators is made outside the jurisdiction. *Rex* v. *Brisac & Scott*, (1803) 4 East., 164, followed. *R.* v. *Kellow*, (1912) V.L.R., 162; 33 A.L.T., 203; 18 A.L.R., 170. *Cussen, J.*

III.—CONTEMPT OF COURT.

Contempt of Court—Jurisdiction of Supreme Court—Criminal charge—Publication of matters tending to prevent a fair trial—Publication before committal for trial—Extent to which publication in newspaper is lawful.]—Where a person has been arrested and charged on information with an offence in respect of which Justices may commit him for trial in the Supreme Court, the publication after his arrest and before he has been so committed of matter tending to prejudice his fair trial in the Supreme Court is a contempt of the Supreme Court which that Court has jurisdiction to punish. The publication, in respect of a pending criminal charge of extrinsic ascertained facts to which any eye-witness could bear testimony, such as, in the case of a charge of murder, the finding of a body and its condition, the place where it was found, the persons by whom it was found, the arrest of the person accused, is lawful. But the publication of alleged facts depending upon the testimony of some particular person, which may or may not be true and may or may not be admissible in a Court of justice, and the publication of comments on alleged facts are unlawful, if such publication is likely to interfere with the fair trial of the person charged. *Packer* v. *Peacock*; *Burrell* v. *Peacock*; *Smart* v. *Peacock*, (1912) 13 C.L.R., 577; 18 A.L.R., 70. H.C., *Griffith, C.J.* and *Barton, J.*

Contempt of Court—Nature of offence—Publication of statements concerning a Judge of the High Court.]—Statements made concerning a Judge of the High Court do not amount to contempt unless calculated to obstruct or interfere with the course of justice in the High Court in the due administration of the law by that Court. *Rex* v. *Nicholls*, (1911) 12 C.L.R., 280; 17 A.L.R., 309. H.C., *Griffith, C.J.*, *Barton* and *O'Connor, JJ.*

Contempt of Court—Nature of offence.]—The essence of contempt is action or inaction amounting to an interference with or obstruction to or having a tendency to interfere with or obstruct the due administration of justice. *Ex parte Dunn*; *Ex parte Aspinall*, (1906) V.L.R., 493; 28 A.L.T., 3; 12 A.L.R., 358. *Cussen, J.* (1906).

Criminal contempt—Attempt to interfere with the course of justice—Nature of offence.] —*Semble.*—All attempts to interfere with the course of justice are criminal contempts and are misdemeanours. *Ex parte Dunn*; *Ex parte Aspinall*, (1906) V.L.R., 493; 28 A.L.T., 3; 12 A.L.R., 358. *Cussen, J.*

Contempt of Court—Attempt to influence juryman—Juryman not yet empanelled for trial of accused person in whose favour attempt is made.]—Where a juryman has been sworn to act at the sessions of the Court at which an accused person is to be tried, it is a contempt of Court to attempt to influence him in the verdict he would be called upon to give if he should be empanelled upon the trial of such accused person. *Ex parte Dunn*; *Ex parte Aspinall*, (1906) V.L.R., 493; 28 A.L.T., 3; 12 A.L.R., 358. *Cussen, J.* (1906).

Mandamus—Minister of Crown—Disobedience of public Statute—Criminal contempt—Attachment—Privilege.]—Disobedience to a public Statute for disobedience to which no other penalty is provided by the Legislature, is an indictable misdemeanour; therefore contempt in refusing to obey a writ of mandamus ordering compliance with the Statute is of a criminal or quasi-criminal nature, and (*semble*) there is no privilege in a Minister of the Crown or anyone else from attachment for such contempt. *The King* v. *Watt; Ex parte Slade*, (1912) V.L.R., 225; 33 A.L.T., 222; 18 A.L.R., 158. F.C., *Madden, C.J., Hodges* and *Cussen, JJ.*

Contempt of Court—Pending criminal trial—Petition to Attorney-General in relation to—Whether a contempt.]—See CONTEMPT. *In re Mann; In re King*, (1911) V.L.R., 171; 32 A.L.T., 156; 16 A.L.R., 598.

Contempt of Court—Criminal trial—Disagreement of jury—Remand of prisoner—Petition against second trial—Presentation to Attorney-General—Publication in newspapers.]—See CONTEMPT. *In re Mann; In re King*, (1911) V.L.R., 171; 32 A.L.T., 156; 16 A.L.R., 598.

Court of General Sessions—Contempt of Court—Extent of powers of Court of General Sessions—Justices Act 1890 (No. 1105), sec. 184.]—The Court of General Sessions has no power to punish for contempt of Court except in the cases specified, and to the extent limited in the *Justices Act* 1890. *Ex parte Dunn; Ex parte Aspinall*, (1906) V.L.R., 493; 28 A.L.T., 3; 12 A.L.R., 358. *Cussen, J.*

Inferior Court of Record—Power to commit for contempt.]—*Semble.*—Apart from statutory authority an inferior Court of Record can punish only for contempt committed in the face of the Court. *Ex parte Dunn; Ex parte Aspinall*, (1906) V.L.R., 493; 28 A.L.T., 3; 12 A.L.R., 358. *Cussen, J.*

IV.—DEMANDING MONEY BY LETTER WITH MENACES.

Crimes Act 1890 (No. 1079), sec. 113—Letter demanding with menaces money or other valuable thing—Uttering—Felonious intent, whether necessary—What acts will constitute an offence.]—A felonious intent is a necessary ingredient of the offence of " uttering " a letter demanding with menaces money or other valuable thing under sec. 113 of the *Crimes Act* 1890. It is not, however, an essential part of the offence that that which is done with the letter should be an act tending to the letter being sent to or reaching the hands of the person against whom the menaces are directed. *Rex* v. *Crowe*, (1906) V.L.R., 476; 27 A.L.T., 239; 12 A.L.R., 253. F.C., *a'Beckett, A.-C.J., Hodges* and *Chomley, JJ.* (1906).

V.—EMBEZZLEMENT.

Embezzlement—Secretary of friendly Society—Moneys of trustees—No relation of master and servant.]—The prisoner was the secretary of a Branch of a Friendly Society registered under the *Friendly Societies Act* 1890, having being appointed by the Branch under the rules of the Society, and held office during the pleasure of the Branch. It was his duty to receive all moneys on behalf of the Branch and immediately after the close of each meeting to hand over to the treasurer all moneys he might have received, and also to balance the books every quarter and present the balance-sheet duly audited to the Branch. It was the duty of the treasurer to receive all moneys paid to the Branch through the secretary, and to pay all moneys into the Bank to the credit of the trustees. It was the duty of the trustees to hold in trust for the Branch all moneys of the Branch which might come into their possession, and to invest the same and collect all interest and pay the same to that Branch. Money which had been thus invested by the trustees fell due, and with the interest due thereon was paid by the borrowers to the prisoner, and was by him misappropriated. The prisoner was charged as clerk and servant of the trustees with embezzlement of the money so paid to him. *Held*, that he was not a clerk or servant of the trustees, but of the Branch. *Rex* v. *M'Auslan*, (1907) V.L.R., 710; 29 A.L.T., 83; 13 A.L.R., 609. F.C., *Madden, C.J., Hodges* and *Hood, JJ.*

VI.—EMBRACERY.

Embracery—Juryman sworn to act—Attempt to induce him to give false verdict if he should be impanelled.]—*Quaere*, whether an attempt to induce a person sworn to act as a juryman to give a false verdict if he should be impanelled is embracery. *Ex parte Dunn; Ex parte Aspinall*, (1906) V.L.R., 493; 28 A.L.T., 3; 12 A.L.R., 358. *Cussen, J.*

VII.—FALSE PRETENCES.

Attempting to obtain money by false pretence—Falsity known to person to whom pretence made—Money obtained but not by false pretence.]—Where the person to whom a false pretence is made for the purpose of obtaining money, knows of its falsity, but nevertheless parts with his money, a charge of attempting to obtain money with intent to defraud will lie against the person making such pretence. *Reg.* v. *Mills*, 7 Cox. C.C., 263, followed. *Rex* v. *Perera*, (1907) V.L.R., 240; 28 A.L.T., 176; 13 A.L.R., 116. F.C., *Madden, C.J., a' Beckett* and *Hood, JJ.*

Criminal law—Jurisdiction—False pretences made in Tasmania—Attempt to obtain money in Victoria—Crimes Act 1890 (No. 1079), sec. 165.]—An Act done in Victoria forming part of a series of acts which, if uninterrupted, would result in the obtaining of money in Victoria as a consequence of false representations made out of Victoria, is an attempt to obtain money by false pretences which the Victorian Courts have jurisdiction to try. W. wrote and posted a letter in Victoria addressed to C. in Tasmania; the letter contained false representations by means of which W. hoped to induce C. to send the money to him in Victoria. *Held*, that the Victorian Courts had jurisdiction to convict W. of attempting to obtain money by false pretences. *R.* v. *Burdett*, 4 B. & A.., 95; *R.* v. *Hensler*, 11 Cox., 573; and *R.* v. *Ellis*, (1899) 1 Q.B., 230, discussed. *Rex* v. *Waugh*, (1909) V.L.R., 379; 31 A.L.T., 37; 15 A.L.R., 366. F.C., *Madden, Hodges* and *Cussen, JJ.*

VIII.—FORGERY.

Criminal law—Forgery—Fraudulent intent —Intent of forger to gain advantage.]—It is sufficient on a charge of forgery to prove an intention on the part of the accused to gain an advantage to himself without proving any intent to defraud anyone. *The King* v. *Elton*, (1910) V.L.R., 1; 31 A.L.T., 98; 15 A.L.R., 596. F.C., *Madden, C.J., Hood* and *Cussen, JJ.* (1909).

Criminal law—Forgery—Fraudulent intent —Public document—Intention of forger to gain advantage—Permission of Justice to Marriage being clebrated without notice—Marriage Act 1909 (No. 2192), secs. 2, 3.]—A permission by a Justice of the Peace under sec. 2 of the *Marriage Act* 1909 that a marriage may be celebrated without notice is a document of a public nature, and may be the subject of forgery without proving an intent to defraud. *The King* v. *Elton*, (1910) V.L.R., 1; 31 A.L.T., 98: 15 A.L.R., 596. F.C., *Madden, C.J., Hood* and *Cussen, JJ.*

IX.—INCITING TO COMMIT CRIME.

Inciting to steal goods—Delivery of stolen goods by prisoner to third person to be sold or pawned—Evidence of, whether admissible—Accomplice's evidence—Corroboration.]—See *post*, XXII.—PRACTICE; (a) EVIDENCE; (10) *Evidence. of other Acts of Accused and of Collateral Matters. Rex* v. *Campbell*, (1908) V.L.R., 136; 29 A.L.T., 196; 14 A.L.R., 41.

X.—LARCENY.

See also, post RECEIVING.

Larceny — Innocent taking — Subsequent fraudulent misappropriation—Intention to part with property.]—Where without coercion or trick money is given to a person with the intention that he shall retain the amount of a debt due to himself, and give change, and he keeps the money but refuses to give change, he is not guilty of larceny. *R.* v. *Reynolds*, 2 Cox C.C., 170, followed. *Rex* v. *Hill and Marshall*, (1909) V.L.R., 491; 31 A.L.T., 76; 15 A.L.R., 523. F.C., *Madden, C.J., a' Beckett* and *Hood, JJ.*

Larceny—Money of friendly society—Money in possession of treasurer—Felonious taking by trustee—In whom property should be laid—Friendly Societies Act 1890 (No. 1094), sec. 16 (iii.), (vi.).]—The treasurer of a friendly society received on behalf of the society moneys which, under the rules of the society, it was his duty within twenty-four hours to pay into a Bank to the credit of the trustees. By the rules the trustees were to hold all property of the society which came into their possession in trust for the society. The treasurer placed the moneys in a safe and, within twenty-four hours of their being received by the treasurer, one of the trustees broke into the safe, abstracted the moneys, and applied them to his own use. The trustee was charged on presentment with larceny of the moneys of the treasurer and found guilty. *Held*, that, as the moneys had not within the rules of the society come into the possession of the trustees, but were at the time of the asportation in the lawful possession of the treasurer, they were rightly laid in the presentment as the moneys of the treasurer and the trustee was rightly convicted. *Rex* v. *Watson*, (1908) V.L.R., 103; 29 A.L.T., 146; 13 A.L.R., 724. F.C., *Madden, C.J., Hodges* and *Hood, JJ.* (1907).

Friendly Societies Act 1890 (No. 1094), sec. 16 (iii.), (vi.)—Property of society, legal proceedings concerning—Owners, who to be named as—Trustees.]—Sec. 16 (vi.) of the *Friendly Societies Act* 1890, which provides that in legal proceedings all property of a friendly society shall be stated to be the property of the trustees in their proper names as trustees for the society, does not apply unless the property in question has actually become the property of the trustees. *Rex* v. *Watson*, (1908) V.L.R., 103; 29 A.L.T., 146; 13 A.L.R., 724. F.C., *Madden, C.J., Hodges* and *Hood, JJ.* (1907).

Criminal law—Larceny—Property, in whom to be laid—Trustees of friendly society—Friendly Societies Act 1890 (No. 1094), sec. 16 (vi.).]—*Per Hood, J.*—*Quaere*, whether a prosecution for theft is a " proceeding concerning property " within the meaning of sec. 16 (vi.) of the *Friendly Societies Act*, which provides that in such a proceeding the property of a friendly society shall be stated to be the property of the trustees in their proper names as trustees for the society. *Rex* v. *Watson*, 13 A.L.R., at p. 725.

Larceny—Fraudulent conversion by agent—Secretary of friendly society—Trustees—No relation of agency—Crimes Act 1896 (No. 1478), sec. 2.]—The rules of a friendly society provided in substance that the secretary was authorised to receive moneys on behalf of the society at lodge meetings, and that he should pay all such moneys either to the treasurer or into the society's Bank to the credit of the trustees. The secretary having received moneys on behalf of the society at other times and places than a lodge meeting applied them to his own use. *Held*, that there was no relation of agency between the trustees and the secretary, and therefore that the secretary could not be convicted under sec. 2 of the *Crimes Act* 1896 of fraudulent conversion of moneys received as agent of the trustees. *Rex* v. *Buckle*, 31 A.L.T., 43; 15 A.L.R., 372. F.C., *Madden, C.J., a'Beckett* and *Hodges, JJ.* (1909).

Larceny — Receiving — Similarity between goods found in possession of prisoner and goods alleged to have been stolen—Failure of prisoner to give satisfactory account of how goods came into his possession—Evidence of stealing and identity of goods, sufficiency of.]—*See, post,* XXII.—PRACTICE; (*a*) EVIDENCE; (9) *Identification of Persons and Property*. *Rex* v. *Schiffman*, (1910) V.L.R., 348; 32 A.L.T., 28; 16 A.L.R., 346. [Leave to appeal refused by High Court, 11 C.L.R., 255; 17 A.L.R., 150.]

Evidence—Larceny—Recent possession — Offences against the Commonwealth—Judiciary Act 1903 (No. 6), sec. 80.]—*See, post,* XXII. PRACTICE; (*a*) EVIDENCE; (8) *Recent Possession*. *Rex* v. *Forrest*, 34 A.L.T., 95; 18 A.L.R., 495.

XI.—MALICIOUS INJURIES TO PROPERTY.

Crimes Act 1890 (No. 1079), sec. 185— " Crop of grass," what is—Setting fire to crops, &c.]—The words " crop of grass " in sec. 185 of the *Crimes Act* 1890 mean grass sown or cultivated for the purpose of getting a crop of hay or seed, and not a natural growth of grass. *Rex* v. *Philbey*, (1906) V.L.R., 290; 27 A.L.T., 186; 12 A.L.R., 188. F.C., *Holroyd, A.-C.J., Hood* and *Cussen, JJ.* (1906).

Crimes Act 1890 (No. 1079), sec. 194—
Unlawfully destroying fence—Actual malice.]
Actual malice is an essential element in the
offence of wilfully and maliciously cutting,
breaking, &c., or otherwise destroying a fence
under section 194 of the *Crimes Act* 1890.
Trotman v. *Shankland*, 7 V.L.R. (L.), 16,
adopted. *McLaren* v. *Bradley*, (1908) V.L.R.,
318; 29 A.L.T., 239; 14 A.L.R., 252.
a' Beckett, J.

Crimes Act 1890 (No. 1079), sec. 194—
Maliciously destroying fence—Question of
title—Jurisdiction of Justices—Justices Act
1890 (No. 1105), sec. 69.]—The jurisdiction
of Justices under sec. 194 of the *Crimes Act*
1890 is ousted by a *bona fide* claim by the
defendant that the land whereon the fence
stood belongs to him solely, although the
Justices may think that he is in fact only
jointly interested with some other person.
McLaren v. *Bradley*, (1908) V.L.R., 318;
29 A.L.T., 239; 14 A.L.R., 252.   *a' Beckett,
J.*

XII.—MURDER.

Criminal law—Murder—Evidence, sufficiency of—Circumstantial evidence—Proof of
fact of death—Proof that prisoner caused
death—Reasonable hypothesis consistent with
innocence—Direction to jury—Accomplice,
evidence of—Corroboration of part of his
evidence, sufficiency of.]—*See, post*, XXII.
PRACTICE; (a) EVIDENCE; (3) *Corroboration; Nature of Evidence Necessary to
Justify Conviction. Peacock* v. *The King*,
(1911) 13 C.L.R., 619; 17 A.L.R., 566.

XIII.—NUISANCE.

Nuisance—Drain on highway constructed by
municipal authority.]—A drain constructed by
a municipal authority on a highway for the
purpose of draining the highway is not in
itself an indictable offence. *Benalla, President. &c., of* v. *Cherry*, (1911) 12 C.L.R.,
642; 17 A.L.R., 537. H.C., *Griffith, C.J.,
Barton* and *O'Connor, JJ.*

XIV.—PERJURY.

Perjury—Administration of oath—Acting
clerk of Petty Sessions—Justices Act 1890
(No. 1105), secs. 41, 64, 77 (7).]—A witness

sworn by an acting clerk of Petty Sessions
may be guilty of perjury. *Reg.* v. *Barber*,
3 A.L.R. (C.N.), 21, approved. *Rex* v.
Turnbull, (1907) V.L.R., 11; 28 A.L.T., 103;
12 A.L.R., 551.   *Cussen, J.*

Perjury—Administration of oath—Clerk of
Petty Sessions, who is—Justices Act 1890 (No.
1105), sec. 77 (7).]—*Quaere*, whether under
section 77 (7) of the *Justices Act* 1890 a
person who *de facto* acts as a clerk of Petty
Sessions may not lawfully administer the
oath to a witness. *Rex* v. *Turnbull*, (1907)
V.L.R., 11; 28 A.L.T., 103; 12 A.L.R., 551.
Cussen, J.

XV.—PUBLIC STATUTE, DISOBEDIENCE TO.

Disobedience to public Statute—No penalty
prescribed—Misdemeanour—Mandamus to enforce obedience, disregard of—Criminal contempt.]—Disobedience to a public Statute
for disobedience to which no other penalty
is provided by the Legislature, is an indictable
misdemeanour. Therefore contempt in refusing to obey a writ of mandamus ordering
compliance with the Statute is of a criminal
or quasi-criminal nature. *The King* v.
Watt; Ex parte Slade, (1912) V.L.R., 225;
33 A.L.T., 222; 18 A.L.R., 158. F.C.,
Madden, C.J., Hodges and *Cussen, JJ.*

XVI.—RECEIVING.

See also, ante, LARCENY.

Crimes Act 1890 (No. 1079), sec. 307—
Receiving property knowing the same to have
been feloniously stolen—Stolen articles deposited in a certain place by pre-existing
arrangement—No knowledge by accused that
particular goods stolen or deposited—No act
of dominion.]—A. agreed with B. that if B.
would deposit any articles he might steal in a
certain place A. would pay B. for any articles
so deposited. B. afterwards stole and deposited in the agreed place certain articles.
A. did not know that any property had been
stolen and did not know that the articles had
been so deposited, and made no payment
and did no act in regard to such articles.
Held, that A. was not guilty of receiving
property knowing it to have been feloniously
stolen within the meaning of section 307 of

the *Crimes Act* 1890. *Per Hodges* and *Chomley, JJ.*—There was no evidence that A. " received " the property, or that he knew it was stolen. *Per Cussen, J.*—Although guilty knowledge and receiving need not always be simultaneous, there must at some time be a combination of receipt and guilty knowledge—not a general guilty knowledge but a guilty knowledge with respect to the particular goods received. *Rex* v. *Merriman*, (1907) V.L.R., 1; 28 A.L.T., 108; 12 A.L.R., 571. F.C.

Receiving stolen goods—Guilty knowledge, evidence of—Anticipated defence of innocent receipt—Evidence to rebut—Course of dealing —Finding of " burglar's kit " on prisoner's premises.]—*See post*, XXII.—PRACTICE; (*a*) EVIDENCE; (11) *Evidence to Meet Anticipated Defence*. *Rex* v. *O'Kane*, (1910) V.L.R., 8; 31 A.L.T., 110; 15 A.L.R., 628.

Recent possession—Possession of skirt and blouse nine months after their being stolen— False statements made by person found in possession of such articles—Evidence, admissibility of.]—*See post*, XXII.—PRACTICE; (*a*) EVIDENCE; (8) *Recent Possession*. *Rex* v. *McCaffery*, (1911) V.L.R., 92; 32 A.L.T., 105; 17 A.L.R., 40.

XVII.—SECRET COMMISSION, OFFENCES RELATING TO.

Secret Commissions Prohibition Act 1905 (No. 1974), secs. 2, 14—Giving money to agent without principal's knowledge—Burden of proof.]—Where, without his principal's knowledge, money is given to an agent the receipt of which would tend to influence the agent to show favour to the donor in relation to the principal's business, the donor is guilty of an offence under section 2 of the *Secret Commission Prohibitions Act* 1905, unless he proves that when he gave the money he did not intend to influence the agent. *Rex* v. *Stevenson*, (1907) V.L.R., 475; 29 A.L.T., 62; 13 A.L.R., 383. *Hood, J.* (1907).

Secret Commissions Prohibition Act 1905 (No. 1974), sec. 2—" Corruptly," meaning of.]—" Corruptly " in the *Secret Commissions Prohibition Act* 1905 does not mean merely the doing of an act prohibited by the Statute but the doing of that act with some wrongful intention. *Rex* v. *Stevenson*, (1907) V.L.R., 475; 29 A.L.T., 62; 13 A.L.R., 383. *Hood, J.* (1907).

Secret Commissions Prohibition Act 1905 (No. 1974), sec. 2—Corruptly giving valuable consideration to agent—Secret giving, presumption as to corruptness arising from.]— The fact that a secret commission has been given raises the presumption that it was given " corruptly " within the meaning of section 2 of the *Secret Commissions Prohibition Act* 1905. *Rex* v. *Scott*, (1907) V.L.R., 471; 29 A.L.T., 60; 13 A.L.R., 143. *Cussen, J.*

Secret Commissions Prohibition Act 1905 (No. 1974), sec. 2—Giving of valuable consideration to agent—Tendency to influence agent to show favour.]—On a presentment for an offence under section 2 of the *Secret Commissions Prohibition Act* 1905 charging the prisoner with unlawfully and corruptly giving a valuable security to an agent the receipt of which would tend to influence the agent to show favour to the prisoner in relation to his principal's affairs or business, it is for the jury to decide whether the giving of the valuable security would not so tend to influence the agent. *Rex* v. *Scott*, (1907) V.L.R., 471; 29 A.L.T., 60; 13 A.L.R., 143. *Cussen, J.*

XVIII.—USING CATTLE WITHOUT OWNER'S CONSENT.

Crimes Act 1890 (No. 1079), sec. 74—Using another person's cattle without his consent— Unlawful user by person in lawful possession.] —A person who is entrusted by the owner with the possession of a horse for the purpose of grazing it commits an offence under section 74 of the *Crimes Act* 1890 if he uses it for his own purposes without the consent of the owner. *Wimble* v. *Foulsham*, (1908) V.L.R., 98; 29 A.L.T., 158; 13 A.L.R., 727. *Hodges, J.* (1907).

XIX.—VARIOUS STATUTORY OFFENCES; LIABILITY FOR JOINT OFFENCE.

Butchers and Abattoirs Act 1890 (No. 1069), sec. 26—Slaughtering cattle without licence—

Several persons joining in same act—Whether offence severable.]—*Prima facie* two or more persons who join in the commission of an offence are severally liable, unless the words of the Act creating the offence are such as to compel the Judge to hold that it is joint. Accordingly where two or more persons join in committing an offence under section 26 of the *Butchers and Abattoirs Act* 1890, each is separately and severally liable. *Dugdale* v. *Charles Dight*; *Same* v. *West*; *Same* v. *George Dight*, (1906) V.L.R., 783; 28 A.L.T., 186; 13 A.L.R., 15. *Chomley, J.* (1907).

Questions asked by Comptroller-General of Customs—Duty to answer—Prosecution pending—Person interrogated not charged—Corporation—Australian Industries Preservation Act 1906-1909 (No. 9 of 1906)—No. 26 of 1909, sec. 15B.]—*See* AUSTRALIN INDUSTRIES PRESERVATION ACT. *Melbourne Steamship Co.* v. *Moorehead*, (1912) 15 C.L.R., 333; 18 A.L.R., 533.

Insolvency Act 1890 (No. 1102), sec. 141 (xii.)—Trustee agent or broker—Unlawful appropriation of property held as agent—Principal's goods sold by agent on commission—Relationship of debtor and creditor—Insolvency of agent—Whether agent liable for offence.]—*See* INSOLVENCY. *In re James*, 32 A.L.T. (Supplement), 12; 17 A.L.R. (C.N.), 5.

XX.—WIFE DESERTION.

Marriage Act 1901 (No. 1737), sec. 3—Criminal law—Wife desertion—Leaving her without adequate means of support—Meaning of " adequate."]—To a charge under section 3 of the *Marriage Act* 1901 against a husband of deserting his wife without lawful or reasonable cause or excuse and leaving her without adequate means of support, and going to reside or being resident out of Victoria, the fact that the husband has left his wife with means which were adequate to support her in her condition of life during the period preceding the date of the charge is not an answer, but the means must be adequate to support the wife in her condition of life during the period over which the desertion is intended to extend. *Rex* v. *Mackie*, (1908) V.L.R., 689; 30 A.L.T., 60; 14 A.L.R., 488. F.C., *a' Beckett, Hodges* and *Cussen, JJ.* (1908).

Evidence—Wife, whether competent witness against husband—Wife desertion—Neglect to comply with order for maintenance—Marriage Act 1901 (No. 1737), secs. 3, 4—Crimes Act 1891 (No. 1231), sec. 34.]—*See post*, XXII.—PRACTICE; (a) EVIDENCE; (2) *Witness, Competency of*. *Rex* v. *Jacono*, (1911) V.L.R., 326; 33 A.L.T., 28; 17 A.L.R., 340.

XXI.—MENS REA.

Mens rea—Meaning of—Definition of offence created by Statute—How to be ascertained.]—*Mens rea* means no more than that the definition of all or nearly all crimes contains not only an outward and visible element, but a mental element, varying according to the different nature of the different crimes. If in a section creating an offence the language is not clear as to what is the outward and visible element and what the mental element that is to enter into the offence and impose responsibility, the rest of the Statute should be examined, and the subject matter with which it deals and the character of the punishment for the offence should be considered. *Moffat* v. *Hassett*, (1907) V.L.R., 515; 29 A.L.T., 87; 13 A.L.R., 266 *Hodges, J.* (1907).

Corporation—Liability for criminal offences —Mens rea.]—(*Semble*) the criminal liability of a corporation for the criminal acts of its servants does not at common law extend beyond cases in which the criminal acts (a) create a public nuisance or (b) constitute a criminal libel. *R.* v. *Kellow*, (1912) V.L.R., 162; 33 A.L.T., 203; 18 A.L.R., 170. *Cussen, J.*

Butchers and Abattoirs Act 1890 (No. 1069), sec. 26—Slaughtering cattle without licence —Mens rea.]—In order to establish an offence under section 26 of the *Butchers and Abattoirs Act* 1890 it is not necessary to prove *mens rea*. *Dugdale* v. *Charles Dight*; *Same* v. *West*; *Same* v. *George Dight*, (1906) V.L.R., 783; 28 A.L.T., 186; 13 A.L.R., 15. *Chomley, J.*

Mens rea—Selling liquor without licence—
Ignorance of nature of liquid sold, whether a
defence—Licensing Act 1890 (No. 1111), sec.
182.]—*Quaere*, whether in a prosecution
under section 182 of the *Licensing Act* 1890
the ignorance of the seller of the fact, that
the liquid sold was "liquor" within the
meaning of the Act, is a defence. *Gleeson* v.
Hobson, (1907) V.L.R., 148; 28 A.L.T., 151;
13 A.L.R., 10.   *Cussen, J.*

Licensing Act 1890 (No. 1111), sec. 124—
Supplying liquor to person in state of intoxication—Knowledge of intoxicated state of person
supplied—Whether a necessary ingredient of
offence.]—*See* LICENSING. *Davies* v. *Young*,
(1910) V.L.R., 369; 32 A.L.T., 39; 16 A.L.R.,
368.

Licensing Act 1890 (No. 1111), sec. 124—
Licensing Act 1906 (No. 2068), sec. 73—
Licensee, liability for act of servant—Supply-
ing liquor to person in state of intoxication—
Supply by servant in absence without know-
ledge and contrary to instructions of licensee.]
—*See* LICENSING. *Davies* v. *Young*, (1910)
V.L.R., 369; 32 A.L.T., 39; 16 A.L.R., 368.

Factories and Shops Act 1905 (No. 1975),
sec. 119 (1)—Employing person at lower rate
than rate determined by Special Board—Mens
rea, whether a necessary element of offence—
Employer, liability of for act of agent.]—
See FACTORIES AND SHOPS ACT. *Billingham*
v. *Oaten*, (1911) V.L.R., 44; 32 A.L.T.,
170; 17 A.L.R., 36.

Tramways Act 1890 (No. 1148), Second
Schedule, Part II., Clause 17—"Avoiding"
payment of fare—Refusal to pay full fare—
Honest belief that full fare not payable—Mens
rea.]—*Sec* LOCAL GOVERNMENT. *Cochrane*
v. *Tuthill*, (1908) V.L.R., 549; 30 A.L.T.,
50; 14 A.L.R., 453.

XXII.—PRACTICE.

(a) EVIDENCE.

(1) *Judicial Notice.*

Justices—Local jurisdiction—Objection that
offence committed outside jurisdiction—How
Justices may satisfy themselves on the question
—Whether formal evidence necessary—Effect
of erroneous conclusion—Justices Act 1890
(No. 1105), sec. 73 (3).]—*See* EVIDENCE.
Le Cocq v. *McErvale*, (1908) V.L.R., 69;
29 A.L.T., 134; 13 A.L.R., 699.

(2) *Witness, Competency of.*

Evidence—Wife, whether competent witness
against husband—Wife desertion—Neglect to
comply with order for maintenance—Marriage
Act 1901 (No. 1737), secs. 3, 4—Crimes Act
1891 (No. 1231), sec. 34.]—The prisoner's wife
is a competent witness against him on an
indictment for wife desertion under section
3 (1) (*a*) of the *Marriage Act* 1901, but not
on an indictment for wilfully neglecting to
comply with an order for maintenance under
section 4 of that Act. *Rex* v. *Jacono*, (1911)
V.L.R., 326; 33 A.L.T., 28; 17 A.L.R.,
340. F.C., *Madden, C.J., Hodges* and *Hood,
JJ.* (1911).

Crimes Act 1891 (No. 1231), sec. 34 (3)—
Witness on own behalf—Cross-examination
as to credit, when admitted—Evidence as to
good character in the particular class of transaction in issue — Prosecution under Health
Acts.]—At the hearing of an information
under the Health Acts for selling adulterated
food the defendant in giving evidence said:
—"I always take every precaution." *Held*,
that this statement was evidence of good
character as applied to the trade in question,
and that cross-examination directed to
impeaching it was permissible under section
34 (3) of the *Crimes Act* 1891. *Gunner* v.
Payne, (1910) V.L.R., 45; 31 A.L.T., 138;
16 A.L.R., 29. *Madden, C.J.*

(3) *Corroboration; Nature of Evidence Neces-*
sary to Justify Conviction.

Criminal law—Evidence of accomplice—
Warning by Judge to jury against convicting
on uncorroborated evidence—Whether Judge
under positive duty to give warning—Omission
to give warning, effect of—Quashing conviction—Entry on record that party ought not
to have been convicted—Corroboration, sufficiency of—Crimes Act 1890 (No. 1079), sec.
482.]—*Per Griffith, C.J.*—It is now settled
law in England that if the Judge omits to
give the jury the usual warning as to convicting upon the evidence of an accomplice,

and such evidence is not in fact corroborated, the conviction will be quashed. As to whether this is a new rule established under the *Criminal Appeal Act* 1907 (7 Edw. VII. c. 22), or a modern statement of the common law introduced into Australia, *quaere*. *Per Barton J.*—(1) When the evidence of the accomplice is not substantially corroborated, the duty of the Judge to warn the jury against acting upon it has not yet become a positive rule of law, although it is a matter of settled practice; (2) In England if there is an absence of substantial corroboration, and the Judge has failed to warn the jury according to the usual practice, the Court will treat the conviction as a "miscarriage of justice" within the meaning of the *Criminal Appeal Act*, sec. 41 (1) and set it aside; *quaere*, whether in such a case in Victoria there should be an entry on the record that "the party ought not to have been convicted" under sec. 482 of the *Crimes Act* 1890; (3) The corroboration will be deemed sufficient if it is substantial, and is upon a material part of the case, and it need not amount to independent evidence implicating the prisoner. *Per O'Connor, J.*—The omission to give warning, where the evidence of the accomplice is not in fact corroborated, is not an error in law entitling the prisoner to have the conviction quashed, under the *Crimes Act* 1890. *Peacock* v. *The King*, (1911) 13 C.L.R., 619; 17 A.L.R., 566.

Crimes Act 1891 (No. 1231), sec. 33— Evidence Act 1890 (No. 1088), sec. 50—Unsworn evidence of child of tender years— Corroboration—Indecent assault.]—In all cases of the nature provided for in sec. 33 (1) of the *Crimes Act* 1891 the testimony admitted by virtue of that section must, notwithstanding sec. 50 of the *Evidence Act* 1890, be corroborated by some other material evidence in support thereof implicating the accused. Such implication of the accused ought to be by evidence of some direct kind which would show that he more probably than any other person was the man who committed the offence charged. *Per a'Beckett, J.*—A Judge or Justice may, in such cases, if the provisions of sec. 33 (2) of the *Crimes Act* 1891 are fulfilled, disre-

gard the requirements of sec. 50 of the *Evidence Act* 1890. *The King* v. *O'Brien*, (1912) V.L.R., 133; 33 A.L.T., 177; 18 A.L.R., 38. F.C., *Madden, C.J., a'Beckett* and *Hodges, JJ.*

Criminal law—Murder— Evidence, sufficiency of—Circumstantial evidence—Proof of fact of death—Proof that prisoner caused death—Reasonable hypothesis consistent with innocence—Direction to jury—Accomplice, evidence of—Corroboration of part of his evidence, sufficiency of.]—The appellant, a medical practitioner, was convicted of the murder of M. D., an unmarried woman. The case presented by the Crown was that M. D., being pregnant, in pursuance of an arrangement previously made between the appellant, M. D., and a man named Poke, who was responsible for her condition, and who then represented himself to be her husband, entered a private hospital kept by the appellant, and which was used only by women, on 9th or 10th August, for the purpose of having an operation performed by the appellant with a view to procuring abortion; that an operation was performed by the appellant, and a miscarriage procured, that on 21st or 22nd August M. D. died from the results of the miscarriage, and that the appellant secretly disposed of her body, of which no trace was afterwards found. The evidence in nearly all branches of the case was circumstantial. Poke was called as a witness for the Crown, and gave evidence of conversations he alleged had taken place between himself and the appellant. He said that before M. D. died he had admitted to the appellant that he was not her husband, and that the appellant said—"If you are not married you had better leave it to me. Do not come to this house again, it might draw suspicion"; that on 22nd August the appellant told him M. D. was dead; that they discussed the disposal of the body; that the appellant said he would dispose of her clothes by burning them at his farm in the country, and that on 29th August the appellant told him the body was buried, and the clothes were burnt. Some jewellery belonging to M. D. was found in the appellant's possession, and evidence was given that on

27th August the appellant had taken a bag to his farm in the country, and had afterwards lit a fire in the scrub. In the ashes of the fire certain articles were discovered, which it was suggested by the Crown had formed part of the wearing apparel, or had belonged to M.D. Various other circumstances were relied upon in support of the Crown case. The trial took place before *Madden, C.J.,* who, in his direction to the jury, did not give them the usual caution against convicting upon the evidence of the accomplice, Poke, if uncorroborated. *Held,* that, upon a trial for murder, the fact of death, and the fact that the prisoner caused the death, may be proved by circumstantial evidence. Where the evidence is circumstantial, it is the usual practice to direct the jury that it is their duty to acquit the prisoner if there is any reasonable hypothesis consistent with his innocence. In this case there was evidence of the fact of death. *Held,* also, by *Barton* and *O'Connor, JJ.,* that upon the whole of the evidence it was open to the jury to find that the appellant caused the death. *Held,* by *Griffith, C.J.,* that there was a reasonable hypothesis consistent with the appellant's innocence. *Held,* by *Barton* and *O'Connor, JJ., Griffith, C.J.,* dissenting, that there was evidence in corroboration of Poke's testimony as to his alleged conversation with the appellant. *Peacock* v. *The King,* (1911) 13 C.L.R., 619; 17 A.L.R., 566.

Evidence—Admissible evidence—Evidence such that no reasonable man could form a conclusion—Direction to acquit.]—*Per Cussen, J.*—" I am of opinion that if at the end the evidence is such that the Court thinks no reasonable man could form a conclusion on it the Court would be bound to direct a jury to acquit the prisoner. *R.* v. *Parker,* (1912) V.L.R., 152; 33 A.L.T., 215; 18 A.L.R., 150.

(4) *Foreign Law.*

Evidence—Foreign law—Fugitive Offenders Act 1881 (44 & 45 Vict. c. 69)—Law of other country, whether a question of fact—How Magistrate may be satisfied as to.]—*See*

FUGITIVE OFFENDERS. *McKelvey* v. *Meagher,* 4 C.L.R., 265; 12 A.L.R., 483.

Evidence—Foreign law—Rendition of fugitive offender—Fugitive Offenders Act 1881 (44 & 45 Vict. c. 69), secs. 5, 29.]—*See* FUGITIVE OFFENDERS. *McKelvey* v. *Meagher,* 4 C.L.R., 265; 12 A.L.R., 483.

(5) *Evidence not on Oath.*

Unsworn statement of prisoner—Evidentiary nature of—Evidence Act 1890 (No. 1088), sec. 52—Crimes Act 1891 (No. 1231), sec. 38.]—When a prisoner makes a statement of facts under sec. 52 of the *Evidence Act* 1890 the jury should be directed to take the statement as *prima facie* a possible version of the facts, and to consider it with the sworn evidence, giving it such weight as it appears to be entitled to in comparison with the facts established by evidence. *Peacock* v. *The King,* (1911) 13 C.L.R., 619; 17 A.L.R., 566. H.C., *Griffith, C.J., Barton* and *O'Connor, JJ.*

Crimes Act 1891 (No. 1231), sec. 38—Evidence Act 1890 (No. 1088), sec. 52—Statement by accused person not on oath—Proper time to announce intention to make such statement.]—Where an accused person calls no evidence, the proper time for him to announce whether he will make a statement under sec. 38 of the *Crimes Act* 1891 is at the conclusion of the case for the Crown; otherwise he will lose his right to make such statement. *R.* v. *Kellow,* (1912) V.L.R., 162; 33 A.L.T., 203; 18 A.L.R., 170. *Cussen, J.*

(6) *Expert Evidence.*

Criminal law—Evidence—Expert witnesses —Finger prints.]—*Semble.*—*Per Cussen, J.* : Expert witnesses may give in evidence statements based upon their own experience or study; but they cannot be permitted (*a*) to attempt to point out to the jury matters which the jury could determine for themselves, or (*b*) to formulate their empirical knowledge as a universal law. Thus, experts may depose that there are certain broadly marked differences in character between the finger prints of different people; that these differences can be classified; and that it can be illustrated from their expert knowledge what those broad characteristics are. But they may not (a) point out similarities between the finger mark of the accused and a finger mark alleged to be his, nor (b) state that there cannot be two finger marks alike. *R.* v. *Parker*, (1912) V.L.R., 152 ; 33 A.L.T., 215 ; 18 A.L.R., 150. F.C., *Madden, Hodges* and *Cussen, JJ.*

(7) *Dying Declarations.*

Criminal law—Evidence—Dying declarations in case of homicide—Impending death—Expectation of death—Form of deposition.]— In order that the declaration of persons *in extremis* may be admitted as evidence in cases of homicide against an accused person, the person making the declaration must be at the time in actual danger of death, must have an unqualified belief and a clear apprehension that he will not recover from his injury or illness, and death must follow from that injury directly or indirectly caused by the accused. The length of time elapsing between the making of the declarations and death is an element to be considered in determining whether they were made in the definite and full expectation of death. Where the circumstances are such that a dying declaration is admissible, a witness may state a conversation (amounting to such a declaration) between himself and the declarant, although the effect of the conversation is reduced to writing and the written statement is afterwards read over, assented to and signed by the declarant. There is no rule requiring that the statement shall or shall not be by question and answer. *Rex* v. *Hope*, (1909) V.L.R., 149 ; 30 A.L.T., 167 ; 15 A.L.R., 87. F.C., *Madden, C.J., Hodges* and *Cussen, JJ.* (1909). Special leave to appeal refused by High Court. *Hope* v. *The King*, (1909) 9 C.L.R., 257. *Griffith, C.J., Higgins, J.* (*Isaacs, J.,* dissentiente).

Criminal law—Evidence—Dying declarations in case of homicide—Impending death—Expectation of death.]—*Per Madden, C.J.—* " Therefore, some Judges have said he must be ' in hopeless expectancy of immediate death '—of death ' immediately impending,' or ' in *articulo mortis* ' or ' *moriens* ' as dis-

tinguished from ' *moriturus.*' All these expressions are rather an effort to be emphatic as to the importance of exactitude in the determination of the essential things which make declarations admissible than any determination on the part of the Judges that the declaration must have been made within some given distance from the death which afterwards undoubtedly occurred." *Per Hodges, J.—*I do not feel it possible to define the word " impending " beyond saying that it means " near " as distinguished from " remote," " imminent," as distinguished from " deferred." But it is not, in my opinion, possible to say that " impending " means any number of hours, or any number of days." *Rex* v. *Hope*, (1909) V.L.R., 149, pp. 158, 163 ; 30 A.L.T., 167, pp. 169, 171 ; 15 A.L.R., pp. 88, 90. F.C.

Criminal law—Evidence—Dying depositions in case of homicide—" Settled hopeless expectation of immediate death."]—*Per Cussen, J.—*" It has been sometimes said that the declarant must have a settled hopeless expectation of immediate death. I think there is some possibility of difficulty arising from the use of each of those words. " Hope " is generally compounded of expectation and desire. What I really think is meant in the language of many Judges is simply " expectation." A person may desire his recovery very much, and in that sense not have abandoned hope, although he has abandoned all expectation and humanly speaking has no hope . . . So with the word ' settled.' ' Settled ' may mean either ' absolutely unalterable,' or ' non-fluctuating.' In the latter case, proof of change would merely be evidence that the expectation or belief was not firm and unqualified. So the expression ' immediate death ' is distinctly ambiguous." *Rex* v. *Hope*, (1909) V.L.R., 149, at p. 164 ; 30 A.L.T., 167, at p. 171 ; 15 A.L.R., 87, at p. 90. F.C.

Criminal law—Evidence—Dying declarations in case of homicide—Impending death—Expectation of death.]—*Per Cussen, J.—* " The language of the declarant in this case fluctuates to some extent. She said ' I am sure I cannot recover,' and also said ' I don't think I will recover.' It has been pointed out that the medical man also said ' think.' That is ambiguous. Sometimes it means ' I think it probable '; sometimes it means ' I believe.' If those expressions stood alone, I should have doubted whether they were by themselves sufficient; but taking them with the other circumstances, I think they may be read as—' I believe I shall not recover '." *Rex* v. *Hope*, (1909) V.L.R., 149, p. 165; 30 A.L.T., 167, p. 172; 15 A.L.R., 87, p. 91.

(8) *Recent Possession.*

Recent possession—Possession of skirt and blouse nine months after their being stolen—False statements made by person found in possession of such articles—Evidence, admissibility.]—On the trial of a prisoner charged with receiving a skirt and blouse which had been stolen nine months previously, evidence was tendered by the Crown that the prisoner when found in possession of the goods, and again on a subsequent occasion, had made statements as to her possession of them. These statements were contradictory in themselves, and suggestive of guilt. On objection raised by prisoner's counsel that such statements were inadmissible, inasmuch as the prisoner might lawfully be called upon to explain her possession of the articles alleged to have been stolen only when such possession was recent and that possession of the skirt and blouse nine months after the theft was not recent, the Chairman of General Sessions over-ruled the objection and admitted the evidence. *Held*, that such statements were rightly admitted in evidence. *Held*, also, that the prisoner's possession of the skirt and blouse was sufficiently recent to be within the doctrine of recent possession, and to throw on her the obligation of satisfactorily explaining her possession of them. *Rex* v. *McCaffery*, (1911) V.L.R., 92; 32 A.L.T., 105; 17 A.L.R., 40. F.C., *Madden, C.J., a' Beckett* and *Hodges, JJ.*

Evidence—Larceny—Recent possession—Offences against the Commonwealth—Judiciary Act 1903 (No. 6), sec. 80.]—*Semble.*—The doctrine of recent possession of stolen goods applies to offences against the Commonwealth. *Rex* v. *Forrest*, 34 A.L.T., 95; 18 A.L.R., 495. *Cussen, J.* (1912).

(9) *Identification of Persons and Property.*

Criminal law—Circumstantial evidence—Identification—Finger prints, similarity of.]—The resemblance between the finger print of an accused person and a finger print found on an article may be sufficient evidence to justify a jury in finding that the finger print found on the article was made by the accused. *R.* v. *Parker*, (1912) V.L.R., 152; 33 A.L.T., 215; 18 A.L.R., 150. F.C., *Hodges* and *Cussen, JJ.* (*Madden, C.J.,* dissentiente). (Leave to appeal refused by High Court, (1912) 14 C.L.R., 681; 18 A.L.R., 157. *Griffith, C.J., Barton* and *Isaacs, JJ.*]

Larceny—Receiving—Similarity of goods found in possession of prisoner with goods alleged to have been stolen—Failure of prisoner to give satisfactory account of how goods came into his possession—Evidence of stealing and of identity of goods, sufficiency of.]—On a charge of receiving stolen property belonging to the Victorian Railways Commissioners, the evidence showed that three kegs of cream of tartar, part of a large consignment, had been missed by the Victorian Railways Commissioners, that within a fortnight kegs which contained or had contained cream of tartar and were similar to those lost in size, shape, colour and dimensions, were found in the possession of the prisoners, who gave a false account as to their possession of such goods. In the one case there was evidence that marks had been obliterated from the kegs. In the other case there was evidence of an attempt to bribe a constable. *Held, per a' Beckett* and *Hood, JJ.* (*Cussen, J.* dissenting), that there was evidence on which the jury might properly convict. *Held, per Cussen, J.,* that there was not sufficient evidence to identify the goods with those lost by the Victorian Railways Commissioners. *Trainer* v. *The King*, 4 C.L.R., 156; 13 A.L.R., 53, and *R.* v. *Roche*, 13 V.L.R., 150; 8 A.L.T., 193, discussed. *Rex* v. *Schiffman*, (1910) V.L.R., 348; 32 A.L.T., 28; 16 A.L.R., 346. In this case leave to appeal was refused by the

High Court ; *see* 11 C.L.R., 255 ; 17 A.L.R., 150.

(10) *Evidence of Other Acts of Accused and of Collateral Matters.*

Inciting to steal goods—Delivery of stolen goods by prisoner to third persons to be sold or pawned—Evidence of, whether admissible—Accomplice's evidence—Corroboration.]—The prisoner was charged with inciting M. to steal certain goods from his employer. M. gave evidence, which was not objected to, that the prisoner requested him to steal the goods, that he accordingly stole the goods and that he handed them to the prisoner. Evidence, objected to by prisoner's counsel, was admitted which showed that, shortly after receiving the stolen goods, the prisoner gave portions of them to various persons, who, at his request, pawned or sold them. The prisoner was convicted. *Held*, that the evidence objected to was admissible and that the prisoner was rightly convicted. *Per a'Beckett, J.*—Although that evidence did not corroborate the actual inciting, yet it was corroborative of M.'s statement that he handed the goods to the prisoner, and might be considered by the jury in coming to a conclusion as to the truthfulness of the whole of M.'s story. *Per Hodges, J.*—What was said when M. handed the goods to the prisoner and what the latter then did with them formed part of the *res gestae,* and the evidence was admissible in support of the proposition upon which the prosecution was based. *Per Cussen, J.*—The prisoner's conduct after receiving the goods was an admission that they were stolen for him, and therefore showed a motive why he should incite M., and tended to support M.'s statement that the prisoner did incite him to steal the goods. *Rex* v. *Campbell,* (1908) V.L.R., 136 ; 29 A.L.T., 196 ; 14 A.L.R., 41.   F.C. (1908).

Evidence—Indecent assault—Statement or complaint by female assaulted—First reasonable opportunity—Statement or complaint in answer to questions.]—On a trial for indecent assault upon a female child, a statement made by the child to the mother with regard to the alleged assault is not admissible in evidence unless it is shown that the statement was made at the first reasonable opportunity under the circumstances after the assault. *Per Madden, C.J.*—As to the observations in *R.* v. *Osborne,* (1905) 1 K.B., 551, at p. 556, that a statement is inadmissible where but for questions put to her the child or woman assaulted would not have made the statement, *Quaere,* whether it is not merely a dictum, and whether it correctly states the law. *Rex* v. *McNeill,* (1907) V.L.R., 265 ; 28 A.L.T., 182 : 13 A.L.R., 99. F.C., *Madden, C.J., a'Beckett, Hood* and *Cussen, JJ.* (1907).

Opium Smoking Prohibition Act 1905 (No. 2003), sec. 10—Conviction of principal offender of smoking opium—Whether evidence against person charged with being privy to offending.]— *See* EVIDENCE. *Stapleton* v. *Davis* ; *Stapleton* v. *Bell,* (1908) V.L.R., 114 ; 29 A.L.T., 162 ; 14 A.L.R., 26.

Court of Petty Sessions—Jurisdiction—Discretion as to sentence—Evidence of character—Prior convictions.]—*See* EVIDENCE. *O'Donnell* v. *Perkins* ; *Tognini* v. *Hargreaves,* (1908) V.L.R., 537 ; 30 A.L.T., 45 ; 14 A.L.R., 435.

(11) *Evidence to Meet Anticipated Defence.*

Receiving stolen goods—Guilty knowledge, evidence of—Anticipated defence of innocent receipt—Evidence to rebut—Course of dealing—Finding of " burglar's kit " on prisoner's premises.]—On a charge of receiving goods knowing them to have been stolen, a conversation which took place between a detective and the prisoner with respect to a " burglar's kit " found with part of the stolen goods under the counter in the prisoner's shop was admitted in evidence. *Held*, that the evidence was wrongly admitted, and that the conviction should be quashed. *Rex* v. *O'Kane,* (1910) V.L.R., 8 ; 31 A.L.T., 110 ; 15 A.L.R., 628. F.C., *Madden, C.J., Hood* and *Cussen, JJ.*

Receiving stolen goods—Guilty knowledge, evidence of—Anticipated defence of innocent receipt—Evidence to rebut—Admissibility of—Course of dealing—Finding of burglar's kit on prisoner's premises—Judge's duty as to evidence temporarily admitted.]—The prisoner was convicted of receiving stolen goods knowing them to have been stolen. At the trial evidence that the police had found in the prisoner's shop near the tools in question a " burglar's kit," was admitted as showing guilty knowledge. *Held*, that the evidence was inadmissible to show guilty knowledge. If evidence is admitted of an act which if followed by other similar acts might show a course of dealing on the part of the person doing the act, and no evidence of such subsequent acts is given, it is the duty of the Judge to strike out the evidence so given, and to warn the jury to disregard it. *The King* v. *O'Kane*, (1910) V.L.R., 8 ; 31 A.L.T., 110 ; 15 A.L.R., 628. F.C., *Madden, C.J., Hood* and *Cussen, JJ.*

(12) *Improper Admission of Evidence, Effect of.*

See, also, ante (11) *Evidence to Meet Anticipated Defence* ; and, *post,* (*f*) NEW TRIAL.

Justices Act 1890 (No. 1105), sec. 141— Order to review conviction—Evidence improperly admitted—Whether Court bound either to set aside conviction or remit case for re-hearing.]—*See* EVIDENCE. *Knox* v. *Thomas Bible* ; *Knox* v. *J. L. Bible,* (1907) V.L.R., 485 ; 29 A.L.T., 23 ; 13 A.L.R., 352.

Justices Act 1890 (No. 1105), secs. 141— Order to review conviction—Improper admission of evidence—Whether duty of Court either to set aside conviction or remit for re-hearing.]—*See* JUSTICES OF THE PEACE. *Macmanamny* v. *King,* (1907) V.L.R., 536 ; 28 A.L.T., 250 ; 13 A.L.R., 258.

(B) BAIL.

Bail—Person charged with capital offence— Whether bail should be allowed—Matters to be considered in determining.]—On an application to admit to bail a person charged with a capital offence, the matters to be considered are the nature of the charge, the character of the evidence that is before the Court, and the punishment that may be inflicted for the offence. *Rex* (or *Coonan*) v. *Peacock,* 33 A.L.T., 84 ; 17 A.L.R., 452.

Bail—Prisoner charged with murder—Preliminary hearing before Justices pending—

Granting bail before committal.]—Where a person, charged before Justices with the murder of a woman whose body had not yet been found, had been remanded on the application of the prosecution, for the purpose of enabling further searches and investigations to be made, a Judge of the Supreme Court allowed, on terms, the liberation of the accused on bail until the conclusion of the hearing before Justices. *Rex* (or *Coonan*) v. *Peacock,* 33 A.L.T., 84 ; 17 A.L.R., 452. *Hodges, J.* (1911).

(c) LEGAL ASSISTANCE FOR DEFENCE.

Judiciary Act 1903 (No. 6 of 1903), sec. 69 (3)—Indictable offences against the Commonwealth—Committal for trial—Appointment of counsel for defence—Application— Materials in support—" Interests of justice "] —In an application under sec. 69 (3) of the *Judiciary Act* 1903 the affidavit in support should state the facts with regard to the means of the accused in such a way as to enable the Judge to decide that the applicant is without adequate means to provide for his defence. A mere general statement by the solicitor for the accused, that he believes it would be unsafe for the accused to be tried without being represented by counsel to argue points of law which deponent believes can be raised in favour of accused, is not sufficient to enable the Judge to decide whether it is desirable in the interests of justice than an appointment of counsel for the defence should be made. In deciding whether such appointment should be made, the Judge should contrast what would or might occur if counsel were not present at the trial, with what might be expected to arise if counsel were present. Facts and circumstances which may render the appointment of counsel for the defence desirable in the interests of justice considered. *Rex* v. *Forrest,* (1912) V.L.R., 466 ; 34 A.L.T., 95 ; 18 A.L.R., 495. *Cussen, J.* (1912).

Judiciary Act 1903 (No. 6 of 1903), sec. 69— (3)—Legal assistance for defence of prisoner— Whether solicitor as well as counsel may be provided.]—*Semble.*—Under sec. 69 (3) the Attorney-General has power to provide not only counsel for the defence, but also a

CRIMINAL LAW.

solicitor to instruct such counsel. *Rex* v *Forrest*, (1912) V.L.R., 466 ; 34 A.L.T., 95 ; 18 A.L.R., 495. *Cussen, J.* (1912).

(d) TRIAL GENERALLY.

(1) *Venue.*

Crimes Act 1890 (No. 1079), sec. 406—Venue—Application to change—Trial on criminal charge—Disagreement of jury—Remand of prisoner—Publication of statements by jurymen in favour of acquittal—Venue of second trial changed to another place—"Expedient to the ends of justice."]—On the trial of a prisoner charged with murder at the Supreme Court at Ballarat the jury disagreed, and the prisoner was remanded for trial at the next sittings of that Court. A letter was subsequently prepared, without the prisoner's knowledge, by his solicitor's managing clerk, and signed by ten of the jurymen, and forwarded to the Attorney-General. That letter set out the number of the jurymen who had been in favor of an acquittal, certain facts and matters that they considered justified an acquittal, and contained an expression of their opinion that it was undesirable and unfair to put the prisoner on his trial a second time unless further evidence against him was forthcoming. The main portion of this letter was published in several Ballarat newspapers. On an application by the Crown for a change of venue to Melbourne. *Held*, that it was expedient to the ends of justice that the second trial should take place in Melbourne, and that the application should, accordingly, be granted. *Rex* v. *Peter Long*, (1911) V.L.R., 30 ; 32 A.L.T., 130 ; 17 A.L.R., 68. *Cussen, J.* (1911).

(2) *Special Jury.*

Juries Act 1890 (No. 1104), sec. 39—Jury—Criminal cases—Trial by special jury—Discretion of Court.]—The power conferred upon the Court by sec. 39 of the *Juries Act* 1890 to order that a criminal inquest shall be tried by a special jury is discretionary. *Rex* v. *Milburn*, (1908) V.L.R., 591 ; 30 A.L.T., 59 ; 14 A.L.R., 474. *Hodges, J.*

(3) *Presentment.*

Presentment, sufficiency of—Wrong date alleged—Amendment not asked for—Jury not misled—Crimes Act 1890 (No. 1079), sec. 422.]—A presentment charged the prisoner with larceny of a cow on 29th December, 1906. The evidence showed that he had taken possession of the cow in November, 1905, and had kept and used it till 29th December, when he purported to sell it. The evidence for the prosecution at the trial was substantially the same as that given in the Police Court before the prisoner was committed for trial, and the attention of the jury was directed, both by counsel for the prosecution and for the prisoner, and also by the Judge in charging the jury, to the conduct of the prisoner in November 1905. Objection was taken on behalf of the prisoner that the wrong date was assigned in the presentment but the Crown refused to ask for an amendment. The prisoner was convicted. *Held*, that the assignment of a wrong date was an immaterial circumstance, and that the conviction should be affirmed. *Rex* v. *Tieman*, (1908) V.L.R., 4 ; 29 A.L.T., 136 ; 13 A.L.R., 681. F.C., *Madden, C.J., a' Beckett* and *Cussen, JJ.*

Presentment—Amendment of—Power of Court to amend—Crimes Act 1890 (No. 1079), secs. 444, 457.]—The powers of amendment conferred by section 444 and 457 of the *Crimes Act* 1890 are not limited to cases of prosecutions for offences mentioned in such Act. *R.* v. *Kellow*, (1912) V.L.R., 162 ; 33 A.L.T., 203 ; 18 A.L.R., 170. *Cussen, J.*

The charge, what is—Presentment, whether the charge itself or a record thereof.]—The presentment upon which a man is tried is the charge and is not merely the record of the charge. *Powell* v. *Wilson and Mackinnon*, (1908) V.L.R., 574 ; 30 A.L.T., 84 ; 14 A.L.R., 458. *Hodges, J.*

(4) *Mode of Trial where Several Accused Persons or Several Charges.*

Criminal trial—Practice—Prisoners presented jointly—Separate trials, whether Court may order.]—The Court in its discretion has power to order the separate trial of persons who have been jointly presented on a criminal charge. *R.* v. *Stowers*, 24 A.L.T., 52 ; 8 A.L.R., 134, considered. *R.* v. *Downey*, (1910) V.L.R., 361 ; 32 A.L.T., 14 ; 16

A.L.R., 319. F.C., a'Beckett, Hodges and Cussen, JJ.

Criminal or quasi-criminal cases—Practice —Several persons charged with similar offences —Consent to be tried together and to be absent from Court—Several persons tried separately —Agreement to be bound by evidence taken in one case, effect of.]—For observations as to the effect in criminal or quasi-criminal cases of the consent by several persons charged with similar offences to be tried together and to be absent from Court during the whole or part of the proceedings, and also as to the effect, where persons charged with similar offences are tried separately, of an agreement to be bound by the evidence taken in the case of one of such persons and by the view taken by the Court of that evidence, see Larkin v. Penfold, (1906) V.L.R., 535; 28 A.L.T., 44; 12 A.L.R., 337. Cussen, J. (1906).

Informations heard together—Same defendant—Conviction, validity of.]—See JUSTICES OF THE PEACE. Joske v. Lubrano, (1906) V.L.R., 407; 28 A.L.T., 40; 12 A.L.R., 311.

(5) Pleading.

Autrefois acquit—When a good plea— Evidence on second charge sufficient to procure conviction on first.]—The true test whether a plea of autrefois acquit or autrefois convict is a sufficient bar in any particular case is whether the evidence necessary to support the second charge would have been sufficient to procure a legal conviction on the first. Li Wan Quai v. Christie, (1906) 3 C.L.R., 1125; 12 A.L.R., 429. H.C., Griffith, C.J., Barton and O'Connor, JJ.

Autrefois acquit—Arrest by two constables —Dismissal of charge of assaulting one constable in execution of his duty—Whether an answer to charge of assaulting other constable in execution of his duty.]—The dismissal of a charge of assaulting constable A. in the execution of his duty is no bar to a charge of assaulting Constable B. in the execution of his duty even though the two charges arise out of the same set of facts and the evidence on both is substantially the same.

McLiney v. Minster, (1911) V.L.R., 347; 33 A.L.T., 33; 17 A.L.R., 336. F.C., Madden, C.J., Hood and Cussen, JJ.

(6) Witness, Power of Judge to Call.

Witness—Whether Judge may call—Request by jury—Further proceedings.]—A Judge for the better ascertainment of truth has a discretion, whether in a civil or criminal case, to call a fresh witness, particularly where the jury requests it, and this is so in a trial before a jury even when the jury has retired to consider its verdict. The Judge also has a discretion, after hearing the evidence of such fresh witness and having regard to all the circumstances of the case, to say what further proceedings if any should be taken, e.g., he may permit counsel to cross-examine, or to again address the jury, or may allow further evidence to be called. Rex v. Collins, (1907) V.L.R., 292; 28 A.L.T., 222; 13 A.L.R., 184. Cussen, J.

(7) Reserving Decision.

Two charges against one defendant—Reserving decision in first case pending hearing of second charge.]—For observations as to the propriety of justices reserving their decision upon one information until they have heard the evidence upon a second information against the same defendant, where such evidence might influence their decision upon the first information, see Hunter v. Stewart, (1907) V.L.R., 619; 29 A.L.T., 39; 13 A.L.R., 440. a'Beckett, J.

(e) APPEAL; CROWN CASES RESERVED; CERTIORARI.

Criminal law—Appeal to High Court in criminal case—Special leave— Evidence — Dying declarations.]—On the trial of a woman for murder of a girl, statements made by the deceased girl within 24 hours of her death, which had been reduced to writing and signed by her, and also conversations between her and the persons to whom she made the statements which were reduced to writing, were admitted in evidence. The accused was convicted. A question as to the admissibility of this evidence having been referred to the Full Court, the conviction was affirmed. Rex v. Florence Hope, (1909) V.L.R., 149;

30 A.L.T., 167; 15 A.L.R., 87. Special leave to appeal to the High Court was sought on the grounds that the principle upon which dying declarations are admissible had been wrongly stated, and that where such declarations are reduced to writing, oral evidence of what the deceased said is inadmissible. *Held* (*Isaacs, J.*, dissenting), applying the principle in *In re Dillet*, 12 App. Cas., 459, at p. 467, that the case was not one in which special leave should be granted. *Hope* v. *The King*, (1909) 9 C.L.R., 257. H.C., *Griffith, C.J., Isaacs* and *Higgins, JJ.*

Leave to appeal to High Court—Applicant in prison—Appearance in person—Whether High Court has jurisdiction to order that it be allowed.]—Where a person is detained in the State gaol under a sentence of the State Court, the High Court has no jurisdiction to order him to be allowed to come before the High Court in order that he may personally apply for leave to appeal from a judgment of the Court of the State. *Horwitz* v. *Connor*, (1908) 6 C.L.R., 38; 14 A.L.R., 342. H.C., *Griffith, C.J., Barton, O'Connor, Isaacs* and *Higgins, JJ.*

Crimes Act 1890 (No. 1079), secs. 481, 482—Crown cases reserved—Question of difficulty in point of law—Arising "on the trial," meaning of—Whether case may be stated after termination of sittings.]—If there was an existing point of law which arose on the materials at the trial, and which might have been taken, such point of law has arisen " on the trial " within the meaning of sec. 481 of the *Crimes Act* 1890, although at the trial no question was raised, and the Judge's attention was not directed to it, and the Court may, even after the completion of the sittings at which the trial took place, state a case under sec. 482 of the said Act. *R.* v. *Fitzgerald*, 15 V.L.R., 40; 10 A.L.T., 241, and *R.* v. *Brown*, 24 Q.B.D., 357, followed. *Rex* v. *Turnbull*, (1907) V.L.R., 11; 28 A.L.T., 103; 12 A.L.R., 551. *Cussen, J.*

Criminal law—Practice—Crown case reserved—Right to begin—Crimes Act 1890 (No. 1079), sec. 481.]—Upon the argument of points of law reserved upon a criminal trial at the instance of the prisoner, his counsel is entitled to begin. *Rex* v. *Shuttleworth*, (1909) V.L.R., 431; 31 A.L.T., 50; 15 A.L.R., 492. F.C., *Madden, C.J., a' Beckett, Hodges, Hood* and *Cussen, JJ.*

Supreme Court Act 1890 (No. 1142), sec. 25 —Criminal causes and matters—Proceedings by way of certiorari in case of criminal contempt.]—A proceeding by way of *certiorari* in the case of a criminal contempt is itself a criminal cause or matter in the broad sense of that phrase, and, *semble*, is a criminal cause or matter within the meaning of sec. 25 of the *Supreme Court Act* 1890. *Ex parte Dunn; Ex parte Aspinall*, (1906) V.L.R., 584; 28 A.L.T., 72; 12 A.L.R., 418. *Cussen, J.*

—Certiorari—Court of General Sessions—Person committed for contempt by warrant of Chairman—No jurisdiction—Whether act judicial or administrative—Party aggrieved—Whether entitled ex debito justitiæ.]—*See* CERTIORARI, col. 95. *Ex parte Dunn; Ex parte Aspinall*, (1906) V.L.R., 584; 28 A.L.T., 72; 12 A.L.R., 418.

(f) NEW TRIAL.

Criminal law—New trial, when to be granted after quashing of conviction—Circumstances to be considered in exercise of discretion—Failure to warn jury against convicting on uncorroborated evidence of accomplice—Evidence improperly admitted and afterwards withdrawn from jury—Crimes Act 1890 (No. 1079), sec. 482.]—*Per Griffith, C.J.*—Assuming that the Court has power to grant a new trial in capital cases, under the *Crimes Act* 1890, sec. 482, this power should be used with great caution and should not be exercised as of course in every case where a conviction is set aside on the ground of irregularity at the trial. If there was evidence to go to the jury, and the error was of such a nature that if it had not been made, the verdict would probably have been the same, a new trial may be granted. If on the whole case it is reasonably probable that, but for the error complained of, the verdict would or might have been different, a new trial should not be granted. The failure of the Judge at the trial to give the jury the usual warning as to the convicting upon the uncorroborated evidence of an accomplice, and the mere formal withdrawal of evidence which was admitted after objection and put an entirely different complexion on the whole case, but which was afterwards held to be inadmissible, are matters to be considered in the exercise of the Court's discretion to grant a new trial. *Per O'Connor, J.*—When the facts proved at the trial would have been sufficient to support the conviction, if the jury had been properly directed, a new trial may in general be granted. *Peacock v. The King*, (1911) 13 C.L.R., 619 ; 17 A.L.R., 566.

(*g*) PUNISHMENT AND THE REMISSION THEREOF.

Criminal law—Indeterminate Sentences Act 1907 (No. 2106), secs. 3, 6, 32—Construction—Jurisdiction—Discretionary powers of Court.] —It is a condition precedent to the exercise by the Supreme Court of jurisdiction under sec. 6 of the *Indeterminate Sentences Act* 1907, that there shall have been an order of a Court of Petty Sessions in the form prescribed by regulations made by the Governor in Council. *Rex v. Marsden*, 31 A.L.T., 144 ; 15 A.L.R., 643. *Cussen, J.* (1909).

Criminal law—Indeterminate Sentences Act 1907 (No. 2106), sec. 6—Prior convictions —Evidence—Justices Act 1890 (No. 1105), sec. 65—Crimes Act 1891 (No. 1231), sec. 45.]— *Quaere*, whether the fact that the admission or proof of prior convictions of a prisoner is entered in the register of a Court of Petty Sessions makes those entries *prima facie* evidence of those convictions on an application to the Supreme Court under sec. 6 of the *Indeterminate Sentences Act* 1907. *Rex v. Marsden*, 31 A.L.T., 144 ; 15 A.L.R., 643. *Cussen, J.* (1909).

" Second offence," what is—Pure Food Act 1905 (No. 2010), sec. 36.]—Where a Statute fixes one penalty for a first offence, and another penalty for a second offence, the accused must have been convicted of the first offence before the commission of the second offence in order to justify a conviction and penalty in the latter case as for a second offence. *Christie v. Bricknell*, 21 V.L.R., 71 ; 17 A.L.T., 59 ; 1 A.L.R., 59,

applied. *O'Connor v. Bini*, (1908) V.L.R., 567 ; 30 A.L.T., 74 ; 14 A.L.R., 537. *Hodges, J.* (1908).

" First offence "—" Second offence "— Meaning of—Police Offences Act 1890 (No. 1126), sec. 51—Street Betting Suppression Act 1896 (No. 1436), sec. 7—Using house for betting purposes.]—*See* POLICE OFFENCES ACTS. *Knox v. Thomas Bible ; Knox v. J. L. Bible*, (1907) V.L.R., 485 ; 29 A.L.T., 23 ; 13 A.L.R., 352.

Discretion of Governor in Council—Prisoner under sentence—Remission of sentence— Mandamus.]—Mandamus will not lie to the Governor in Council of the State, and no Court has jurisdiction to review his discretion in the exercise of the prerogative of mercy. *Horwitz v. Connor*, (1908) 6 C.L.R., 38 ; 14 A.L.R., 342. H.C., *Griffith, C.J., Barton, O'Connor, Isaacs* and *Higgins, JJ.*

Crimes Act 1890 (No. 1079), sec. 540— Regulations providing for mitigation of sentence as incentive for good conduct—Habeas corpus by prisoner alleging right to liberty under regulations.]—Where a writ of *habeas corpus*, which had been obtained by a prisoner alleging that he was entitled to his liberty under regulations made pursuant to sec. 540 of the *Crimes Act* 1890, had been discharged by the Supreme Court, the High Court refused special leave to appeal. *Horwitz v. Connor*, (1908) 6 C.L.R., 38 ; 14 A.L.R., 342. H.C., *Griffith, C.J., Barton, O'Connor. Isaacs* and *Higgins, JJ.*

Offences against Customs laws—Intent to defraud the revenue—Reduction of penalty— Customs Act 1901 (No. 6 of 1901), secs. 234, 240, 241.]—*See* CUSTOMS. *Lewis v. The King*, (1912) 14 C.L.R., 183 ; 18 A.L.R., 239.

Court of Petty Sessions—Jurisdiction— Discretion as to sentence—Evidence of character—Prior convictions.]—*See* EVIDENCE. *O'Donnell v. Perkins ; Tognini v. Hargreaves*, (1908) V.L.R., 537 ; 30 A.L.T., 45 ; 14 A.L.R., 435.

XXIII.—FUGITIVE OFFENDERS.

Fugitive Offenders Act 1881 (44 & 45 Vict.

CRIMINAL LAW.

c. 69)—**Commonwealth of Australia Constitution Act (63 & 64 Vict. c. 12)—Authority of State of Victoria with regard to fugitive offenders—How far affected by establishment of Commonwealth.**]—*See* COMMONWEALTH OF AUSTRALIA CONSTITUTION, col. 136. *McKelvey* v. *Meagher*, 4 C.L.R., 265; 12 A.L.R., 483.

Rendition of fugitive offenders—Law of Victoria—Effect of establishment of the Commonwealth—Commonwealth of Australia Constitution Act (63 & 64 Vict. c. 12)—The Constitution, secs. 108, 109—Fugitive Offenders Act 1881 (44 & 45 Vict. c. 69).]—*See* COMMONWEALTH OF AUSTRALIA CONSTITUTION, cols. 135, 136. *McKelvey* v. *Meagher*, 4 C.L.R., 265; 12 A.L.R., 483.

Commonwealth of Australia Constitution Act (63 & 64 Vict. c. 12)—The Constitution, sec. 51 (xxix.)—External affairs—Surrender of fugitive offenders—Power of Commonwealth Parliament with regard to.]—*See* COMMONWEALTH OF AUSTRALIA CONSTITUTION, col. 121. *McKelvey* v. *Meagher*, 4 C.L.R., 265; 12 A.L.R., 483.

Subordinate legislature—Power in criminal matters, territorial limits of—"Quitting Natal," whether legislature may make it a criminal offence—Fugitive Offenders Act 1881 (44 & 45 Vict. c. 69), secs. 2, 9—Offences to which Act applies—Criminality dependent upon event happening after "quitting Natal."]—Sec. 76 of Law No. 47 of the Colony of Natal provides:—"If any person who is adjudged insolvent or has his affairs liquidated by arrangement after the presentation of an insolvency petition by or against him or the commencement of the liquidation or within four months before such presentation or commencement quits Natal and takes with him . . . any part of his property to the amount of £20 or upwards which ought by law to be divided amongst his creditors he shall (unless the jury is satisfied that he has no intent to defraud) be guilty of an offence punishable with imprisonment for a term not exceeding two years with or without hard labor." In proceedings under the *Fugitive Offenders Act* 1881 for the rendition of a fugitive accused of the crime of contravening the above Law it appeared that the

fugitive had not been adjudged insolvent until after he had left Natal. *Held*, that the Law was not *ultra vires* of the legislature of Natal. *Held*, also, that the acts which the law of Natal made an offence had been completed so far as they rested with the fugitive if he, being a person whose financial position was such, and who within Natal had done or suffered such an act as rendered him liable to be adjudged insolvent, had left Natal, taking with him property to the said amount divisible amongst his creditors, and that the fact that he had not actually been adjudged insolvent was not material. *McKelvey* v. *Meagher*, 4 C.L.R., 265; 12 A.L.R., 483. H.C., *Griffith, C.J., Barton* and *O'Connor, JJ.* (1906).

Fugitive Offenders Act 1881 (44 & 45 Vict. c. 69)—"Judge of a superior Court"—"Magistrate."—*See* FUGITIVE OFFENDERS. *McKelvey* v. *Meagher*, 4 C.L.R., 265; 12 A.L.R., 483.

Fugitive Offenders Act 1881 (44 & 45 Vict. c. 69), secs. 3, 5, 9—Warrant for apprehension of fugitive—Statement of offence charged, sufficiency of.]—*See* FUGITIVE OFFENDERS. *McKelvey* v. *Meagher*, 4 C.L.R., 265; 12 A.L.R., 483.

Fugitive Offenders Act 1881 (44 & 45 Vict. c. 69), sec. 5—Endorsed warrant—Statement of offence, sufficiency of.]—*See* FUGITIVE OFFENDERS. *McKelvey* v. *Meagher*, 4 C.L.R., 265; 12 A.L.R., 483.

Justices Act 1890 (No. 1105), sec. 141—Fugitive Offenders Act 1881 (44 & 45 Vict. c. 69)—Order by Victorian Magistrate exercising powers conferred by Imperial Act—Whether it may be dealt with by order to review.]—*See* FUGITIVE OFFENDERS. *O'Donnell* v. *McKelvey*, (1906) V.L.R., 207; 27 A.L.T., 164; 12 A.L.R., 39.

Fugitive Offenders Act 1881 (44 & 45 Vict. c. 69), secs. 5, 6—Fugitive committed to prison to await return—Legality of detention affirmed by Supreme Court—Bail, whether Court may grant.]—*See* FUGITIVE OFFENDERS. *Re McKelvey*, (1906) V.L.R., 304; 12 A.L.R., 168.

Fugitive Offenders Act 1881 (44 & 45 Vict. c. 69), secs. 5, 6—Fugitive committed to

prison to await return—Legality of detention affirmed by Supreme Court—Appeal to High Court—Bail.]—*See* FUGITIVE OFFENDERS. *Re McKelvey*, (1906) V.L.R., 304; 12 A.L.R., 209.

Service and Execution of Process Act 1901 (No. 11), sec. 18—Person arrested on warrant issued in another State—Duty of Justice of Peace before whom such person is brought.]—*See* SERVICE AND EXECUTION OF PROCESS ACT. *O'Donnell* v. *Heslop*; *The King* v. *Cresswell, Ex parte Heslop*, (1910) V.L.R., 162; 31 A.L.T., 173; 16 A.L.R., 168.

Service and Execution of Process Act 1901 (No. 11), sec. 18—Warrant endorsed for execution in another State—Apprehension of accused on unsustainable charge—Exercise of discretion by Justice—Jurisdiction of Judge —Review of Justice's discretion by Judge.]— *See* SERVICE AND EXECUTION OF PROCESS ACT. *In re George*, (1909) V.L.R., 15; 30 A.L.T., 141; 15 A.L.R., 27.

Service and Execution of Process Act 1901 (No. 11), sec. 18 (4)—Application to Judge— Jurisdiction—Whether original or appellate.] —*See* SERVICE AND EXECUTION OF PROCESS ACT. *O'Donnell* v. *Heslop*; *The King* v. *Cresswell, Ex parte Heslop*, (1910) V.L.R., 162; 31 A.L.T., 173; 16 A.L.R., 168.

Service and Execution of Process Act 1901 (No. 11), sec. 18—Person charged with offence in another State—Execution of warrant in Victoria — Power to discharge accused— Whether it may be exercised after his admission to bail to appear and answer the charge.] —*See* SERVICE AND EXECUTION OF PROCESS ACT. *O'Donnell* v. *Heslop*; *The King* v. *Cresswell, Ex parte Heslop*, (1910) V.L.R., 162; 31 A.L.T., 173; 16 A.L.R., 168.

Service and Execution of Process Act 1901 (No. 11), sec. 18 (4)—Person arrested on warrant issued in another State—Return of such person to such other State, whether unjust or oppressive—Dispute as to facts alleged in defence—Bona fide assurance of dispute by prosecutor.]—*See* SERVICE AND EXECUTION OF PROCESS ACT. *O'Donnell* v. *Heslop*; *The King* v. *Cresswell, Ex parte Heslop*,

(1910) V.L.R., 162; 31 A.L.T. 173; 16 A.L.R., 168.

Service and Execution of Process Act 1901 (No. 11), sec. 18 (4)—Practice—Application to Judge for discharge of prisoner, how made.]— *See* SERVICE AND EXECUTION OF PROCESS ACT. *O'Donnell* v. *Heslop*; *The King* v. *Cresswell, Ex parte Heslop*, (1910) V.L.R., 162; 31 A.L.T., 173; 16 A.L.R., 168.

Service and Execution of Process Act 1901 (No. 11), sec. 18 (4)—Warrant—Execution— Application for discharge of person apprehended—Procedure—Form of order.]—*See* FUGITIVE OFFENDERS. *In re George*, (1908) V.L.R., 734; 30 A.L.T., 113; 14 A.L.R., 699.

Service and Execution of Process Act 1901 (No. 11), sec. 18—Execution of warrant issued in another State—Order of Justice of Peace directing return of accused—Review of order by Judge—Costs, jurisdiction to award.]—*See* SERVICE AND EXECUTION OF PROCESS ACT. *In re George*, (1909) V.L.R., 15; 30 A.L.T., 141; 15 A.L.R., 27.

XXIV.—STOLEN PROPERTY.

See also, POLICE AND POLICE REGULATION ACT.

Conversion—Sale of stolen goods—Recovery of value of goods from purchaser—Payment by cheque—Proceeds afterwards coming to hands of owner of goods—Obligation to elect to affirm or disaffirm sale.]—*See* SALE OF GOODS. *Creak* v. *James Moore & Co. Proprietary Ltd.*, (1912) 15 C.L.R., 426; 18 A.L.R., 542.

CROSS-EXAMINATION.

See EVIDENCE.

CROWN.

See also COMMONWEALTH OF AUSTRALIA CONSTITUTION; CONSTITUTIONAL LAW; MINING; PUBLIC SERVICE.

Minister of the Crown—Attachment—Contempt of Court—Mandamus—Statutory public duty.]—*Semble.*—There is no privilege in a

Minister of the Crown entitling him to immunity from attachment for contempt of Court for his disobedience of a mandamus calling upon him to perform a statutory public duty. *The King* v. *Watt, Ex parte Slade*, (1912) V.L.R., 225; 33 A.L.T., 222; 18 A.L.R., 158. F.C., *Madden, C.J., Hodges* and *Cussen, JJ.*

Relief against forfeiture for non-payment of rent—Crown, relief against—Settlement of Lands Act 1893 (No. 1311), secs. 5, 10—Lease by Board of Lands and Works—Supreme Court Act 1890 (No. 1142), sec. 202.]—*See* LANDLORD AND TENANT. *The King* v. *Dale*, (1906) V.L.R., 662; 28 A.L.T., 140; 12 A.L.R., 549.

Chose in action consisting of right against the Crown—Assignment—Petition of right by assignee—Crown Remedies and Liability Act 1890 (No. 1080), sec. 20.]—*See* CROWN REMEDIES AND LIABILITY ACT. *The King* v. *Brown*, (1912) 14 C.L.R., 17; 18 A.L.R., 111.

Will—Charity, gift to—Compromise, jurisdiction of Court to sanction—Attorney-General, consent of.]—*See* CHARITY, col. 99. *In re Buckhurst; Melbourne Hospital* v. *Equity Trustees, Executors, &c. Ltd.*, (1911) V.L.R., 61; 32 A.L.T., 165; 17 A.L.R., 63.

Deposit receipt, security by way of—Contract to supply goods to Crown—Security for due performance of contract—Deposit receipt in name of servant of the Crown procured by contractor and delivered to such servant—Contractor's account with bank over-drawn—Contract duly performed—Whether amount of deposit receipt a debt due by Crown to contractor—Money had and received—Set-off of bank's claim against contractor, whether justifiable.]—*See* BANKER AND CUSTOMER, cols. 70, 71, 72. *The King* v. *Brown*, (1912) 14 C.L.R., 17; 18 A.L.R., 111.

CROWN GRANT.

Crown grant—Evidence of the land to which it relates—Long and unchallenged occupancy.]—In the absence of survey marks there can be no better indication of the land to which

a Crown grant relates than long and unchallenged occupancy. *National Trustees Executors &c. Co. of Australasia Ltd.* v. *Hassett and the Registrar of Titles*, (1907) V.L.R., 404; 28 A.L.T., 232; 13 A.L.R., 208. *Cussen, J.*

CROWN REMEDIES AND LIABILITY ACT.

Chose in action consisting of right against the Crown—Assignment—Petition of right by assignee—Crown Remedies and Liability Act 1890 (No. 1080), sec. 20.]—A chose in action consisting of a right against the Crown can be assigned so as to entitle the assignee to present a petition of right under the *Crown Remedies and Liability Act* 1890, section 20, in respect of it. *The King* v. *Brown*, (1912) 14 C.L.R., 17; 18 A.L.R., 111. H.C., *Griffith, C.J., Barton* and *Isaacs, JJ.*

CRUELTY.

See HUSBAND AND WIFE.

CUSTODY OF CHILDREN.

See INFANT.

CUSTOMS.

Customs Tariff 1908 (No. 7 of 1908), secs. 3, 4, 5, 7—Duties collected under proposed tariff—Proposed tariff different from Tariff enacted by Parliament—Right to recover money back—" Duties of Customs collected pursuant to any Tariff or Tariff alteration "—Commonwealth Constitution, sec. 55—Imposing taxation.]—The words " duties of Customs " in section 7 of the *Customs Tariff* 1908 include moneys demanded by the Collector of Customs and paid in respect of imported goods under such circumstances that, if the Tariff proposed in Parliament on 8th August 1907 or any proposed amendment thereof had, at the time of the demand and payment, been a lawfully imposed Tariff, the moneys would have been properly collected as Customs duties. *Cowan & Sons*

v. *Lockyer*, 1 C.L.R., 460; 10 A.L.R. (C.N.), 63, distinguished. *Sargood Bros.* v. *The Commonwealth*, (1910) 11 C.L.R., 258; 16 A.L.R., 483. H.C., *O'Connor, Isaacs* and *Higgins, JJ.*, (*Griffith, C.J.*, dissenting).

Customs Act 1901 (No. 6)—Whether a taxing Act.]—*Per Griffith, C.J.* and *Higgins, J.*—The *Customs Act* 1901 is not a taxing Act and does not make any goods liable to duty. *Sargood Bros.* v. *The Commonwealth*, (1910) 11 C.L.R., 258; 16 A.L.R., 483.

Customs Act 1901 (No. 6), sec. 167—Customs Tariff 1908 (No. 7), sec. 7—Duties collected under proposed Tariff—Proposed Tariff different from Tariff enacted—Payment without protest—Recovery back of money paid—Money exacted colore officii—Deposit of amount demanded under section 167 of the Customs Act 1901—Whether the only remedy —" Dispute," what is.]—Where importers in order to obtain possession of imported goods pay the moneys demanded by Customs officers as and for duties of Customs under a Tariff proposed in Parliament. *Held*, (*Per Griffith, C.J., O'Connor* and *Higgins, JJ., Isaacs, J.* dissenting) (1) that in the absence of some statutory provision to the contrary such payments, even though no actual protest be made, do not deprive the importers of their right to recover the moneys, if the proposal is not adopted by Parliament. (2) That under such circumstances there is no " dispute " within the meaning of section 167 of the *Customs Act* 1901. *Per Isaacs, J.*—Section 167 is applicable, and unless made use of the payments are voluntary. If made use of, there is an implied agreement when the money is paid that if the proposed Tariff shall not eventually become law, the money collected in pursuance of it shall be returned. *Sargood Bros.* v. *The Commonwealth*, (1910) 11 C.L.R., 258; 16 A.L.R., 483.

Customs duties—Tariff—Manufactures of paper for advertising purposes—" Pictures (not being advertising) "—Customs Tariff 1902 (No. 14 of 1902) Schedule, Division XIII., Items 122, 123 and exemption (k)—Construction of Taxing Statute.]—By Item 122 of Division XIII. of the Schedule to the *Customs Tariff* 1902 under the heading " Paper and Stationery " a customs duty at the rate of 3d. per lb. is charged on " Paper, viz. :—Manufactures of, unframed, for advertising purposes, including price lists catalogues and all printed or lithographed matter for such purposes." By special exemption (K) to that Division there are exempted from duty. " Pictures (not being advertising) viz. :—Auto-types, chromographs, engravings, etchings, oleographs, oil paintings, photographs, photogravures and water colours." *Held*, (*Griffith, C.J.* and *Barton, J.*, dissenting) that pictures printed on paper by a mechanical process, some being chromographs and others photogravures, which when imported bore on their faces no advertisements, but which were chiefly used for advertising purposes, in which case advertisements were printed on the margins or mounts, or on the pictures themselves, were within Item 122 and not within the special exemption (K), and were therefore liable to duty at 3d. per lb. *Per O'Connor, Isaacs* and *Higgins, JJ.*—Where goods are made liable to Customs duty as being for particular purposes, the principal or predominant use of them determines their classification. *Per Griffith, C.J.* and *Barton, J.*—Where goods, described as being for certain named purposes, are made liable to Customs duty, there must be apparent in the goods themselves, to those who know their character, a quality which shows them to be specially fit for the particular purpose specified, rather than for any other. *Chandler* v. *Collector of Imposts*, 4 C.L.R., 1719; 13 A.L.R., 617. (1907).

Customs Act 1901 (No. 6), sec. 154 (a)—Value of goods for purposes of duty—Outside packages containing goods dutiable ad valorem —Whether packages accessories to goods—Whether value of packages to be included in that of goods.]—The value of outside packages in which goods subject to duty according to their value are imported is not included in the value of those goods as defined by section 154 (a) of the *Customs Act* 1910. *Sargood Bros.* v. *The Commonwealth*, (1910) 11 C.L.R., 258; 16 A.L.R., 483. *Griffith, C.J.*,

and *Higgins, J.* (*O'Connor,* and *Isaacs JJ.,*
dissenting).

Customs Act 1901 (No. 6 of 1901), secs. 229, 233—Unlawful possession of goods—Unlawful importation—Possession unconnected with importation—Knowledge—Prohibited imports.]—Section 233 of the *Customs Act* 1901 does not impose a penalty on a person who is in possession of goods which have been unlawfully imported, but who was in no way connected with their importation, although he knows that they have been so imported. *Lyons* v. *Smart,* (1908) 6 C.L.R., 143 ; 14 A.L.R., 328. H.C., *Griffith, C.J., Barton, O'Connor* and *Higgins, JJ.* (*Isaacs, J.,* dissenting).

Offences against Customs laws—Intent to defraud the revenue—Reduction of penalty—Customs Act 1901 (No. 6 of 1901), secs. 234, 240, 241.]—A person convicted of an offence against the *Customs Act* and convicted also of intent to defraud the revenue is liable to a maximum penalty of six times the value of the goods. *Held,* upon an appeal from the imposition of the maximum penalties amounting in all to £1212 that in the circumstances of the case the penalties should be reduced to £300. *Per Griffith, C.J.—* "The Legislature has allowed a very large discretion in offences committed with intent to defraud the revenue. The range is from £10 as a minimum to six times the value of the goods as a maximum unless indeed six times the value of the goods is less than £200 and then that is the maximum. When the legislature allows a large range like that, I read it as an instruction that the Court should consider the nature of the offence, and if it is a very bad one—of course, you cannot classify offences in categories—but if it is deliberate and systematic, the Court may impose the maximum penalty ; and if it is an isolated offence, not likely to be repeated, the Court may apply a different rule. It is impossible to lay down any precise rule, but all the circumstances of the case must be taken into consideration." *Lewis* v. *The King,* (1912) 14 C.L.R., 183 ; 18 A.L.R., 239. H.C., *Griffith, C.J., Barton* and *Isaacs, JJ.*

DAMAGES.

I.—WHETHER AN ELEMENT IN CAUSE OF ACTION.

Abuse of process—Insolvency proceedings to stifle litigation—Action by non-trader—No actual damage.]—*Quaere,* whether proceedings in insolvency taken to stifle litigation between the parties amount to an abuse of the process of the Court in respect of which an action will lie. *Quaere,* also, whether such an action, if it will lie at all, will lie by a non-trader without proof of actual damage. *Bayne* v. *Baillieu* ; *Bayne* v. *Riggall,* (1908) 6 C.L.R., 382 ; *sub nom., Bayne* v. *Blake,* 14 A.L.R., 426. H.C., *Griffith, C.J., Barton* and *O'Connor, JJ.*

Words spoken of a man in the way of his office—Office of credit or honour and not of profit—Special damage, whether necessary to prove—Words which would not justify removal from office—Municipal councillor charged with using office for benefit of friends.]—Words charging misconduct of any substantial character in the performance of the duties of an office of credit or honour though not of profit, *e.g.,* words charging a municipal councillor with using his office and powers as a councillor to get the ratepayers' money expended for the benefit of his friends and not of the ratepayers, are actionable without proof of special damage and it is immaterial whether or not the charge, if true, would justify removal from the office. *Alexander* v. *Jenkins,* (1892) 1 Q.B., 797, and *Booth* v. *Arnold,* (1895) 1 Q.B., 571 considered. *Livingston* v. *M'Cartin,* (1907) V.L.R., 48 ; 28 A.L.T., 131 ; 12 A.L.R., 524. *Hodges, J.*

Slander—Words actionable without proof of special damage—Words spoken in way of

person's office, trade or business—**Words not expressly directed to office, trade or business—Tendency to prejudice therein.**]—The mere fact that defamatory words tend to prejudice a person in relation to his office, trade or business does not give him a right of action without proof of special damage. To be actionable *per se* the words must have been spoken of him in relation to his office, trade or business. *Chomley* v. *Watson*, (1907) V.L.R., 502 ; 29 A.L.T., 46 ; 13 A.L.R., 380. *Madden, C.J.*

Contract—Breach—Cause of action—Quantum of damages, whether part of.]—The quantum of damages is no part of the cause of action. *Railton* v. *Fleming*, (1912) V.L.R., 113 ; 33 A.L.T., 180 ; 18 A.L.R., 24. F.C., *a'Beckett, Hodges* and *Cussen, JJ.*

II.—AMOUNT AND MEASURE OF DAMAGES.

Libel—Damages, whether excessive.]—The plaintiff, an ex-Minister of the Crown, sued the defendants, the proprietors of a newspaper having a large circulation, for libel contained in an article in the newspaper capable of being interpreted as alleging that the plaintiff dishonestly wasted public moneys on his own favourites, and was a person of habitual mendacity, whose presence in Parliament was a disgrace. The defence was fair comment, and the jury awarded the plaintiff £3,250 damages. *Held*, that under the circumstances of the case the damages were not excessive. *David Syme & Co.* v. *Swinburne*, 10 C.L.R., 43 ; 16 A.L.R., 93. H.C., *Griffith, C.J., Barton, O'Connor* and *Higgins, JJ.* (1909).

Damages—Sale of specific chattel—Special measure of damages prescribed by warranty—Whether special measure of damages applies where the specific chattel is not delivered—Loss of profits—Purpose for which chattel purchased disclosed to vendor.]—Where in a warranty, part of a written contract for the sale of a specific chattel, a special measure of damages is provided, that special measure of damages does not apply if the specific chattel purchased under the contract is not delivered. Damages may be recovered for loss of profits occasioned by the non-delivery, the purpose for which the specific chattel was purchased being known to the seller. *Bruton* v. *Farm and Dairy Machinery Co. Proprietary Ltd.*, (1910) V.L.R., 196 ; 31 A.L.T., 200 ; 16 A.L.R., 241. F.C., *Madden, C.J.. a'Beckett* and *Hood, JJ.*

Wrongful dismissal of public servant—Damages—Liability to be dismissed rightfully—Whether an element in determining amount of damages—Commonwealth Public Service Act 1902 (No. 5 of 1902), sec. 46.]—Where a public servant has been dismissed without the observance of the conditions precedent to rightful dismissal prescribed by the *Commonwealth Public Service Act* 1902, the Court, in assessing damages for such wrongful dismissal, will take into consideration the fact that the public servant was liable to be dismissed rightfully under the process prescribed by the Act. *Williamson* v. *The Commonwealth*, (1907) 5 C.L.R., 174 ; 14 A.L.R., 1. *Higgins, J.*

III.—REMOTENESS.

Highway—Open drain lawfully constructed by municipal authority—Liability of municipal authority—Damages, whether too remote—Wandering horse entering drain at shallow part and walking along drain to deep part—Horse unable to extricate itself.]—*See* LOCAL GOVERNMENT. *Benalla, President, &c., of* v. *Cherry*, (1911) 12 C.L.R., 642 ; 17 A.L.R., 537.

IV.—NEW TRIAL.

Negligence—General damages—No sufficient evidence of particular items of damage—New trial motion—Exercise of discretion to grant a new trial—" Substantial wrong or miscarriage "—Order XXXIX., r. 6.]—Subsequently to injuries caused to a woman by the negligence of the defendants, she had a miscarriage, and that was left to the jury as a matter in respect of which they might award her damages. The jury gave a verdict in her favour. After notice of appeal and pending appeal, the woman died. The Court being of opinion that it was at least doubtful whether there was evidence fit to be submitted to a jury that the miscarriage was the result of the accident. *Held* (*Hodges, J.* dissenting), that under the circumstances, as there had been no substantial wrong or miscarriage, neither a new trial nor a new assessment of damages should be ordered. *Farrands* v. *Mayor, &c., of Melbourne,* (1909) V.L.R., 531; 31 A.L.T., 78; 15 A.L.R., 520. F.C., *Madden, C.J., Hodges* and *Cussen, JJ.*

V.—INSOLVENCY, EFFECT OF.

Insolvency Act 1890 (No. 1102),—Certificate of discharge—Effect of—Order or judgment in matrimonial cause—Insolvent as co-respondent ordered to pay damages—Certificate subject to condition—Statutory dividend.]— *See* INSOLVENCY. *In re Ware,* 34 A.L.T., (Supplement), 1; 18 A.L.R. (C.N.), 5.

VI.—PLEADING.

Order XIX., r. 3 (Rules of 1906)—Set off or counterclaim—Claim sounding in damages —Extent of right of set off—Whether affected by rule 3.]—Rule 3 of Order XIX. does not create any new right, but merely enables the defendant to plead any right to set-off which he may otherwise possess. *Held,* accordingly, that the defendant was not entitled to raise as a set-off a claim for damages which he could not have so raised before the *Judicature Act,* but that his proper course was to raise it by way of counterclaim. *Smail* v. *Zimmerman,* (1907) V.L.R., 702; 29 A.L.T., 63; 13 A.L.R., 587. (*Hood, J.*).

Order XIX., r. 27—Order XXXVI., r. 37— Pleading—Tendency to embarrass—Libel— Defence—Matters in mitigation of damages.] In an action for libel a defendant may not in his defence allege matters merely in mitigation of damages. *Wood* v. *Earl of Durham,* 21 Q.B.D., 501; *Heffernan* v. *Hayes,* 25 V.L.R., 156; 21 A.L.T., 118; 5 A.L.R., 269, followed; *Millington* v. *Loring,* 6 Q.B.D., 190, not followed. *Wilson* v. *Dun's Gazette Ltd.,* (1912) V.L.R., 342; 34 A.L.T., 77; 18 A.L.R., 327. *Madden, C.J.*

DEATH.

" **Actio personalis moritur cum persona "— Action for personal injuries—Judgment for plaintiff—Death of plaintiff pending appeal—**

Survival of action to executor—Executor added as respondent to appeal.]—*See* MAXIMS. *Farrands* v. *Melbourne, The Mayor, &c., of City of,* (1909) V.L.R., 531.

DEBENTURE.

See STAMPS ACTS.

DEBTORS ACT.

I.—NATURE OF PROCEEDINGS GENERALLY.

Imprisonment of Fraudulent Debtors Act 1890 (No. 1100), Part III.—Court of Petty Sessions—Proceedings upon summons to debtor, nature of—Whether a mere method of enforcing judgment.]—The procedure upon a summons to debtor issued under sec. 22 of the *Imprisonment of Fraudulent Debtors Act* 1890 is nothing more than a stringent or severe method of bringing pressure to bear upon the debtor to pay his debt. *Caldecott* v. *Cunningham,* (1908) V.L.R., 38; 29 A.L.T., 94; 13 A.L.R., 639. F.C., *Hodges, Hood* and *Cussen, JJ.* (1907).

Order XLIV., r. 2 (Rules of 1884)—Order XLII., rr. 3, 6, 7, 17 (Rules of 1884)—Attachment—Disobedience of order to pay costs— Imprisonment of Fraudulent Debtors Act 1890 (No. 1100)—Whether power to attach for disobedience affected by.]—Notwithstanding the provisions of the *Imprisonment of Fraudulent Debtors Act* 1890, the Court has power to issue a writ of attachment for disobedience of its order to pay costs. *Re Sandilands; Ex parte Browne,* 4 V.L.R. (L.) 318 followed. *Pope* v. *Peacock,* (1906) V.L.R., 667; 28 A.L.T., 63; 12 A.L.R., 440. *Hodges, J.*

II.—JURISDICTION.

Judgment summons—Proceedings in Supreme Court—Judgment signed in Supreme Court on judgment of County Court—Damages awarded in action of tort—" Sum of money recoverable under any judgment of the Supreme Court "—Imprisonment of Fraudulent Debtors Act 1890 (No. 1100), secs. 4, 5—County Court Act 1890 (No. 1078), sec. 104 Ninth and Tenth Schedules.]—Where judgment has been signed in the Supreme Court under sec. 104 of the *County Court Act* 1890 on a County Court judgment awarding damages in an action of tort, the amount for which such judgment is signed is a " sum of money recoverable under any judgment of the Supreme Court " within the meaning of sec. 4 of the *Imprisonment of Fraudulent Debtors Act* 1890, and a summons to debtor may be issued in the Supreme Court under sec. 4, and an order thereon may be made under sec. 5 (IV.) (D.) of that Act. *Tipper* v. *Wathen*, (1911) V.L.R., 464 ; 33 A.L.T., 85 ; 17 A.L.R., 543. *Hood, J.*

Imprisonment of Fraudulent Debtors Act 1890 (No. 1100), Part III.—Court of Petty Sessions — Jurisdiction — Judgment debtor served with summons to debtor—Whether he may also be served with summons to witness——Non-attendance as witness, power to fine upon—Justices Act 1890 (No. 1105), secs. 20 (2), 36 (4).]—A judgment debtor served with a summons to debtor issued under Part III. of the *Imprisonment of Fraudulent Debtors Act* 1890 may also be served with a summons to witness, and, if he neglects or refuses to obey the latter summons, he may be fined for non-attendance as a witness under sec. 36 (4) of the *Justices Act* 1890. *Caldecott* v. *Cunningham*, (1908) V.L.R., 38 ; 29 A.L.T., 94 ; 13 A.L.R., 639. F.C., *Hodges, Hood* and *Cussen, JJ.* (1907).

Imprisonment of Fraudulent Debtors Act 1890 (No. 1100), sec. 16 (v.) (a)—" Means and ability "—Payment of ordinary debts.]—Where since a County Court judgment was obtained the judgment debtor has had sufficient money to pay the judgment debt and has chosen to pay other debts therewith, he has had sufficient means and ability to pay the judgment debt within the meaning of sec. 16 (v.) (a) of the *Imprisonment of Fraudulent Debtors Act* 1890. *Hamer* v. *Dowdney*, 29 A.L.T. (Supp.), 19 ; 14 A.L.R., (C.N.), 15. *Judge Box* (1908).

Imprisonment of Fraudulent Debtors Act 1890 (No. 1100), sec. 16 (iv.) (a)—Liability contracted by fraud—Part only of subject of judgment contracted by fraud.]—An order will not be made on the ground that the judgment debtor contracted the liability which was the subject of the judgment by fraud, unless it be shown that the whole of such liability was so contracted. *Weeks* v. *Mayhew*, 28 A.L.T. (Supplement), 9 ; 12 A.L.R. (C.N.), 27. *Judge Box* (1906).

Imprisonment of Fraudulent Debtors Act 1890 (No. 1100), sec. 16—Sequestration of judgment debtor's estate—Liability contracted by fraud.]—Where a judgment debtor's estate had been sequestrated, a judgment summons under Part II. of the *Imprisonment of Fraudulent Debtors Act* 1890 was dismissed, although the ground alleged was that he had contracted the liability which was the subject of the judgment by fraud. *Davies* v. *Burley*, 29 A.L.T. (Supplement), 18 ; 13 A.L.R. (C.N.), 34. *Judge Box* (1907).

III.—PRACTICE.

(a) Service of Judgment or Order.

Imprisonment of Fraudulent Debtors Act 1890 (No. 1100), sec. 15—County Court Act 1890 (No. 1078), sec. 31—Judgment Debtor's summons—Service of judgment—Certified extract from Registrar.]—To satisfy the requirement that the judgment or a copy thereof should be served upon the judgment debtor prior to the issue of a summons under sec. 15 of the *Imprisonment of Fraudulent Debtors' Act* 1890, it is sufficient to serve him with a certified copy of the entry of the judgment in the register which complies with section 31 of the *County Court Act* 1890. *The Royal Finance Co.* v. *Summers*, 30 A.L.T. (Supplement), 24 ; 15 A.L.R. (C.N.), 9. *Judge Box* (1909).

(b) Summons to Debtor, Form of.

Imprisonment of Fraudulent Debtors Act 1890 (No. 1100), sec. 15—The County Court

Rules 1891, Schedule of Forms, Form 14—
Judgment summons—Statement of matters
for examination of judgment debtor.]—A
judgment summons should not include as
matters as to which the judgment debtor
is to be examined matters which are not
intended to be relied on at the hearing. *Lawson* v. *Lang*, 32 A.L.T. (Supplement), 4 ;
16 A.L.R. (C.N.), 9. *Judge Eagleson* (1910).

(c) *Adjournment.*

Imprisonment of Fraudulent Debtors Act
1890 (No. 1100), Part III.—Proceedings upon
summons to debtor—Adjournment—Whether
witness bound to attend without issue or service
of further summons—Justices Act 1890 (No.
1105), sec. 78 (4).]—Sub-sec. 4 of sec. 78
of the *Justices Act* 1890 applies to all
adjournments made by Justices, *e.g.*, to the
adjournment of proceedings upon a summons
to debtor issued under the *Imprisonment of
Fraudulent Debtors Act* 1890. *Caldecott* v.
Cunningham, (1908) V.L.R., 38 ; 29 A.L.T.,
94 ; 13 A.L.R., 639. F.C., *Hodges, Hood*
and *Cussen, JJ.* (1907).

Justices Act 1890 (No. 1105), secs. 20, 36,
78 (4)—Witness who has been paid his expenses
failing to attend—Adjournment—Whether
witness entitled to expenses of attending
adjourned hearing.]—See JUSTICES OF THE
PEACE. *Caldecott* v. *Cunningham*, (1908)
V.L.R., 38 ; 29 A.L.T., 94 ; 13 A.L.R., 639.

(d) *Sequestration of Debtor's Estate.*

Insolvency Act 1890 (No. 1102)—Imprisonment of Fraudulent Debtors Act 1890 (No.
1100)—Insolvency—Effect of upon existing
order on fraud summons—Payments made
thereunder after insolvency.] — *Quaere.* —
Whether, once a person's estate is sequestrated, he should continue to make payments
under an existing order made under the
Imprisonment of Fraudulent Debtors Act
1890. *In re Watts*, 33 A.L.T. (Supplement),
1 ; 17 A.L.R. (C.N.), 13. *Judge Moule*
(1911).

Insolvency—Imprisonment of Fraudulent
Debtors Act 1890 (No. 1100)—Order on fraud
summons in force—Duty of trustee in insolvency.]—Whenever trustees in insolvency

know that orders under the *Imprisonment of
Fraudulent Debtors Act* 1890 are outstanding
and in full force, they should warn insolvents
that they are not to use their money (that is
the money of the trustees) to discharge such
orders. *In re Watts*, 33 A.L.T. (Supplement),
1 ; 17 A.L.R. (C.N.), 13. *Judge Moule* (1911).

Satisfaction after insolvency of orders made
on judgment summonses.]—For comments
on the state of the law which permits orders
made upon judgment summonses just prior
to the insolvency of judgment debtors to be
satisfied in full after insolvency. *See In re
Summers*, 32 A.L.T. (Supplement), 1 ; 16
A.L.R. (C.N.), 15. *Judge Moule* (1910).

Imprisonment of Fraudulent Debtors Act
1890 (No. 1100), sec. 16—Sequestration of
judgment debtor's estate—Liability contracted
by fraud.]—See, *ante*, II. JURISDICTION.
Davies v. *Burley*, 29 A.L.T. (Supplement),
18 ; 13 A.L.R. (C.N.), 34.

(e) *Costs.*

Imprisonment of Fraudulent Debtors Act
1890 (No. 1100), sec. 15—County Court Rules
Rules of 1891, interpretation clause, r. 354—
Schedule of Scale of Costs, Item 2—Judgment
summons—Judgment under £10 — Practitioner's costs—Attending at hearing—Instructions.]—On granting leave to withdraw
a judgment summons issued on a judgment
for less than £10 a Judge of the County Court
may order payment by the judgment creditor
of the judgment debtor's practitioner's costs
for instructions from his client ; but he may
not allow the costs of the practitioner for
attending on such summons. *Coppel* v.
Anderson, 28 A.L.T. (Suplement), 8 ; 12
A.L.R. (C.N.), 22. *Judge Box* (1906).

DECEIT.

See FRAUD AND MISREPRESENTATION.

DECIDED CASES.

Decision of Divisional Court followed.]—
The case of *Weekes* v. *King*, 15 Cox. C.C.,
733, a decision of two Judges sitting as a

Divisional Court, was followed by *Hood, J.,* in *Rider* v. *M'Kell*, (1908) V.L.R., 110 ; 29 A.L.T., 77 ; 13 A.L.R., 543 (1907).

Practice—Over-ruling previous decision of Full Court—Summoning full Bench.]—The Full Court will not summon a full Bench to consider a previous decision of the Full Court unless it doubts the correctness of that decision. *McKinnon* v. *Gange*, (1910) V.L.R., 32 ; 31 A.L.T., 112 ; 15 A.L.R., 640. *Madden, C.J., Hood* and *Cussen, JJ.*

Foreign Statute—Adoption in Victoria—Principle of interpretation—Foreign decisions.] Sec. 55 of the *Evidence Act* 1890 having been taken from a Statute of the State of New York, which had been judicially interpreted by the Courts of that State before its adoption in Victoria, the Parliament of Victoria is to be regarded as having legislated with reference to such interpretation.—*Warnecke* v. *Equitable Life Assurance Society of the United States*, (1906) V.L.R., 482 ; 27 A.L.T., 236 ; 12 A.L.R., 254. F.C., *a' Beckett, A.-C.J., Hodges* and *Chomley, JJ.*

Commonwealth of Australia Constitution Act (63 & 64 Vict. c. 12)—The Constitution, sec. 74—Questions as to the limits inter se of constitutional powers of Commonwealth and State—Conflicting decisions of Privy Council and High Court—Whether High Court final arbiter upon such questions—9 Geo. IV. c. 83 ; 7 & 8 Vict. c. 69, and Orders in Council thereunder.]—*See* COMMONWEALTH OF AUSTRALIA CONSTITUTION, col. 130. *Baxter* v. *Commissioners of Taxation* ; *Flint* v. *Webb*, 4 C.L.R., 1087, 1178 ; 13 A.L.R., 313.

DEFAMATION.

I. THE STATEMENT ; WORDS ACTIONABLE PER SE ; PUBLICATION.

Slander—Words spoken impartially of either of two persons.]—Defamatory words spoken impartially in relation to either of two persons do not give a right of action to either. Accordingly, where the words complained of were, " Either D. or C. must have suppressed or delayed the letter," *Held*, that C. had no cause of action. *Falkner* v. *Cooper*, Carter's Cases, 55, followed. *Chomley* v. *Watson*, (1907) V.L.R., 502 ; 29 A.L.T., 46 ; 13 A.L.R., 380. *Madden, C.J.*

Slander—Words actionable without proof of special damage—Words spoken in way of person's office, trade or business—Words not expressly directed to office, trade or business—Tendency to prejudice therein.]—The mere fact, that defamatory words tend to prejudice a person in relation to his office, trade or business, does not give him a right of action without proof of special damage. To be actionable *per se* the words must have been spoken of him in relation to his office, trade or business. *Chomley* v. *Watson*, (1907) V.L.R., 502 ; 29 A.L.T., 46 ; 13 A.L.R., 380. *Madden, C.J.*

Slander—Words tending to injure a person in respect of his business or profession—Whether actionable without proof of special damage—Imputation not connected with such business or profession.]—In order that defamatory words which tend to injure a person in respect of his business or profession may be actionable without proof of special damage, they must be spoken of him in the way of that business or profession. *Ronald* v. *Harper*, (1910) 11 C.L.R., 63 ; 16 A.L.R., 415 ; H.C., *Griffith, C.J., Barton* and *O'Connor, JJ.*

Slander—Defamatory words spoken of a person who was both a politician and a Minister of religion—Whether words spoken of him in one character only—Privilege.]—*See,* *post.* DEFENCES ; (*b*) PRIVILEGE. *Ronald* v. *Harper,* (1910) 11 C.L.R., 63 ; 16 A.L.R., 415.]

Words spoken of a man in the way of his office—Office of credit or honour and not of profit—Special damage, whether necessary to prove—Words which would not justify removal from office—Municipal councillor charged with using office for benefit of friends.]
Words charging misconduct of any substantial character in the performance of the duties of an office of credit or honour though not of profit, *e.g.,* words charging a municipal councillor with using his office and powers as a councillor to get the ratepayer's money expended for the benefit of his friends and not of the ratepayers, are actionable without proof of special damage, and it is immaterial whether or not the charge, if true, would justify removal from the office. *Alexander* v. *Jenkins,* (1892) 1 Q.B., 797, and *Booth* v. *Arnold,* (1895) 1 Q.B., 571, considered. *Livingston* v. *M'Cartin,* (1907) V.L.R., 48 ; 28 A.L.T., 131 ; 12 A.L.R., 524. *Hodges,* J.

Slander—Publication—Words uttered in answer to plaintiff's questions and in presence of witness present at his request—Privilege.]—In an action for slander, publication is proved by evidence showing that the words complained of were uttered in answer to the plaintiff's questions and in the presence of a third party who attended, at the request of the plaintiff, in order to hear what the defendant might say. The occasion is not privileged if the defendant's answers contain defamatory matter going beyond the questions put by the plaintiff. *Misson* v. *McOwan,* (1906) V.L.R., 280 ; 27 A.L.T., 197 ; 12 A.L.R., 478. F.C., *Holroyd,* A.-C.J., *Hood* and *Cussen,* JJ.

County Court—Jurisdiction—Libel circulating throughout Australia—Claim for damages and injunction.]—*Semble* : An action cannot be brought in the County Court where the plaintiff's claim is for damages and an injunction in respect of the publication of a libel in a newspaper circulating throughout Australia. *Harrison San Miguel Proprietary Ltd.* v. *Alfred Lawrence & Co.,* (1912)

V.L.R., 367 ; 34 A.L.T., 88 ; 18 A.L.R., 394. *Madden, C.J.*

II.—DEFENCES.

(a) *Justification.*

See also, *post,* IV.—PRACTICE. (*a*) *Pleading* ; *Notices of Defence in County Court.*

Defamation — Repetition of defamatory words—Circumstances showing that speaker did not give defamatory statement his own authority—Truth of speaker's statement that he had heard such defamatory words, whether a defence.]—Where one says that he has heard ·a defamatory statement of another, repeating it, if the circumstances of the repetition are such as to show that the speaker does not give the defamatory statement his own authority, the speaker may, in an action against him for defamation, if the repetition is justifiable, rely on the truth of the actual words spoken by him although the defamatory statement is untrue. *Ronald* v. *Harper,* (1910) 11 C.L.R., 63 ; 16 A.L.R., 415. H.C., *Griffith, C.J., Barton* and *O'Connor,* JJ.

Defamation—Privilege—Justification not pleaded—Evidence of truth of libel, admissibility of.]—If justification is not pleaded, the words complained of are admitted to be false, and evidence as to their truth cannot be given. *Peatling* v. *Watson,* (1909) V.L.R., 198 ; 30 A.L.T., 176 ; 15 A.L.R., 150. F.C., *Madden, C.J., Hodges* and *Hood,* JJ.

(b) *Privilege.*

Defamation—Slander — Privilege — Association of traders—Report as to non-payment for goods purchased by customer—Communication to members—Common interest—Duty.]—The defendants, a firm of stock salesmen, were members of an association of stock salesmen who carried on their business in the Bendigo saleyards. By the rules of the association it was provided that stock sold by members at the yards were to be settled for within four days after sale ; that if a purchaser did not pay within that time, the member effecting the sale should, subject to a penalty in case of his not doing so, report (that fact to the secretary of the association who should report the names of all purchasers' in default to the other members ; and that no member should deliver stock to a purchaser in default except on a legal tender of the price being made. The plaintiff, a stock dealer, who had been dealing at the Bendigo saleyards for some years, bought cattle from the defendants and paid cash for them, but the defendants reported him to the secretary as being in default, and the secretary informed the other members accordingly. In an action by the plaintiff against the defendants for defamation, *Held*, that the occasion was privileged, and, there having been no misuse of the occasion, that the action would not lie. *Peatling* v. *Watson*, (1909) V.L.R., 198 ; 30 A.L.T., 176 ; 15 A.L.R., 150, overruled. *Macintosh* v. *Dun*, (1908) A.C., 390, distinguished. *Howe* v. *Lees*, (1910) 11 C.L.R., 361 ; 16 A.L.R., 605. H.C., *Griffith, C.J., Barton, O'Connor* and *Higgins, JJ.* (*Isaacs, J.*, dissenting).

Libel—Privileged occasion—Inquiry by domestic tribunal of Presbyterian Church—Letter written in answer to request for information by tribunal.]—A tribunal of the Presbyterian Church being about to inquire as to the truth of defamatory statements concerning R., one of the Ministers of the Church, said to have been made by S. on the authority, as alleged by him, of H., requested H. to attend the inquiry. H. wrote refusing to attend, and setting out what he had said to S., including a statement defamatory of R. *Held*, that the letter was written on a privileged occasion. *Ronald* v. *Harper*, (1910) 11 C.L.R., 63 ; 16 A.L.R., 415. H.C., *Griffith, C.J., Barton* and *O'Connor, JJ.*

Slander—Defamatory words spoken of a person who was both a politician and a Minister of religion—Whether words spoken of him in one character only—Privilege.]—R., who was a member of Parliament and also a Minister of the Presbyterian Church, was about to stand for re-election. During a discussion as to his chances of re-election, H. said that he had been informed that R. had been rebuked by some members of the Labour Party for using improper language, or words to that effect. In an action by R. against

H. for slander R. alleged that the words were spoken of him as a Minister. *Held*, that the jury might properly find that the words were spoken of R. in his character of a politician and not in that of a Minister, and further (*Barton, J.* doubting), that had it been alleged that the words were spoken of R. in his character of a politician, the occasion was privileged. *Ronald* v. *Harper*, (1910) 11 C.L.R., 63 ; 16 A.L.R., 415. H.C., *Griffith, C.J., Barton* and *O'Connor, JJ.*

Privilege—Association for protection of traders—List of defaulting customers circulated amongst members—Publication to head clerk of member.]—Certain stock salesmen agreed for their protection to form an association according to the rules of which each member had from time to time to forward to the secretary of the association the names of such of his customers as had failed to settle their accounts, and the secretary had to compile a list of such defaulters and forward copies thereof to the members of the association. The secretary handed a copy of such a list to the head clerk of one of the members. *Held*, that even on the assumption that the publication to the member would be privileged, the publication by the secretary under these circumstances was not within the privilege. *Peatling* v. *Watson*, (1909) V.L.R., 198 ; 30 A.L.T., 176 ; 15 A.L.R., 150. F.C., *Madden, C.J., Hodges* and *Hood, JJ.*

Defamation — Privilege — Privileged Occasion—Common interest—Social or moral duty.]—Certain stock salesmen for their own protection formed themselves into an association and adopted a set of rules under which it was provided that each member should give to the secretary of the association every week the names of all buyers of stock who had not settled their accounts with such member for the preceding week and that the secretary should communicate the names of all such defaulters to the members of the association. *Held*, that a communication made under these circumstances by the secretary to a member was not made on a privileged occasion. *Peatling* v. *Watson*, (1909) V.L.R., 198 ; 30 A.L.T., 176 ; 15

A.L.R., 150. F.C., *Madden, C.J., Hodges and Hood, JJ.* (But *see Howe* v. *Lees*, 11 C.L.R., 361 ; 16 A.L.R., 605).

Defamation — Privileged occasion — Presumption that speaker had a proper motive— Burden of proof.]—Where defamatory words are spoken on a privileged occasion, the presumption arising from the occasion that the speaker had a proper motive will continue until displaced by proof of the presence of an improper motive. *Ronald* v. *Harper*, (1910) 11 C.L.R., 63 ; 16 A.L.R., 415. H.C., *Griffith, C.J., Barton and O'Connor, JJ.*

Defamation—Malice, actual—Evidence — Erroneous statement—Discovery of error— Failure to correct, whether evidence of malice.] —Before any actual damage had resulted from the erroneous defamatory statement uttered by the defendant on a privileged occasion, he discovered his error, but omitted to correct it, as he had power to do. *Held*, not evidence that the statement had been uttered with actual malice. *Howe* v. *Lees*, (1910) 11 C.L.R., 361 ; 16 A.L.R., 605. H.C., *Griffith, C.J., Barton, O'Connor and Higgins, JJ.*

Privilege—Actual malice, evidence of— Defamatory allegations persisted in at trial— Invitation to withdraw.]—Where words are uttered on a privileged occasion, the fact that their use is persisted in at the trial of an action brought in respect of them, notwithstanding an invitation to withdraw, is evidence of actual malice. *Livingston* v. *M'Cartin*, (1907) V.L.R., 48 ; 28 A.L.T., 131 ; 12 A.L.R., 524. *Hodges, J.*

Slander—Publication—Words uttered in answer to plaintiff's questions and in presence of witness present at his request.]—*See, ante,* I.—THE STATEMENT ; WORDS ACTIONABLE PER SE ; PUBLICATION. *Misson* v. *McOwen*, (1906) V.L.R., 280 ; 27 A.L.T., 197 ; 12 A.L.R., 478.

(c) *Fair Comment.*

See, post, IV.—PRACTICE. *Pleading : Notices of Defence in County Court.*

(d) *Other Defences.*

Libel—Publication of copy of record kept by Registrar-General—Mistake in record owing to agent of plaintiff—Whether a defence.]— The solicitor acting for the grantee of a bill of sale, by an error in the notice of intention to file the instrument stated that his client was the grantor. The proprietor of a trade circular copied the information from the records of the Registrar-General, and published it in the circular. In an action for libel by reason of the publication, *Held*, that the allegation that the defendant was misled and induced to publish the erroneous matter by the error of the plaintiff's solicitor and agent was no defence. *Wilson* v. *Dun's Gazette Ltd.*, (1912) V.L.R., 342 ; 34 A.L.T., 77 ; 18 A.L.R., 327. *Madden, C.J.* (1912).

III.—DAMAGES.

See also, ante, I. THE STATEMENT ; WORDS ACTIONABLE PER SE : PUBLICATION.

Libel—Damages, whether excessive.]—The plaintiff, an ex-Minister of the Crown, sued the defendants, the proprietors of a newspaper having a large circulation, for libel contained in an article in the newspaper capable of being interpreted as alleging that the plaintiff dishonestly wasted public money on his own favourites and was a person of habitual mendacity whose presence in Parliament was a disgrace. The defence was fair comment, and the jury awarded the plaintiff £3,250 damages. *Held*, that under the circumstances of the case the damages were not excessive. *David Syme & Co.* v. *Swinburne*, 10 C.L.R., 43 ; 16 A.L.R., 93. H.C., *Griffith, C.J., Barton, O'Connor and Higgins, JJ.* (1909).

IV.—PRACTICE.

(a) *Pleading ; Notices of Defence in County Court.*

Defamation—Justification—Fair comment —Particulars of defence properly given— Undertaking given by plaintiff on suggestion of Judge—Particulars struck out—Jurisdiction.]—Plaintiff sued defendant for libel in respect of the whole of an article published by the defendant and reflecting on the plaintiff. The defendant pleaded justification and fair comment, and under his defence gave certain particulars which, as the statement of claim and defence stood, were unobjectionable, but might have prolonged the trial greatly. On summons to strike out these particulars the Judge in Chambers ordered that upon the plaintiff giving an undertaking to make certain admissions, and not to rely on the parts of the article to which the particulars related, the particulars should be struck out, and on such undertaking being given they were struck out accordingly. *Held*, that the Judge had no power to strike out particulars on such terms, and that the proper course was for the plaintiff to amend his statement of claim. *Clarke v. Norton*, (1911) V.L.R., 83 ; 32 A.L.T., 126 ; 17 A.L.R., 59. F.C., *Madden, C.J., a' Beckett, and Hood, JJ.* [Leave to appeal refused, (1910) 12 C.L.R., 13].

Defamation—Pleading—Matter of public interest—" True in substance and in fact "— " Comment "—Meaning of, whether ambiguous.]—In a libel action respecting words published in regard to an alleged subject of public interest, the defence that the words are " true in substance and in fact " may mean that they are " true " in the ordinary sense or that they are a true statement concerning or a true or correct description of such subject. The word " comment " in a defence of fair comment to such an action may mean something which is or can reasonably be inferred to be a deduction, inference, conclusion, criticism, judgment, remark, observation, &c. or it may be used as inclusive of a direct statement concerning or description of the subject of public interest. *Clarke v. Norton,* (1910) V.L.R., 494 ; 32 A.L.T., 109 ; 16 A.L.R., 544. *Cussen, J.*

Defamation — Libel — Defence — Justification—Fair comment—Particulars of meaning of expressions used in defence—Particulars of facts relied on—Relevant facts not mentioned in the libel—Particulars and right to prove.]—In his defence to an action for libel in respect of an article published in his newspaper the defendant pleaded that " in so far as such words consist of statements of fact they are true in substance and in fact, and in so far as such words consist of comment, they are fair and *bona fide* comment on matters of public interest " ; and he gave particulars of facts he intended to rely upon in support of that plea. *Held*, that the defendant must state the sense in which he used the expressions " true in substance and in fact " and " comment," and must give particulars of all the facts he intended to rely upon in support of the plea ; that the plaintiff was not entitled to particulars stating definitely which portions of the matter complained of were statements of fact and which were comment ; that the defendant on giving particulars of all the facts on which he intended to rely in support of the allegations in such plea might say, that as regards statements in the publication complained of which may be found to be defamatory statements of fact, the defence is to be given the same effect as an ordinary plea that the matters complained of are true in substance and in fact, and that as regards statements in such publication which may be found to be defamatory comments, the defence is relied on as warranting the proof of any additional relevant facts forming a basis for such comment ; and that the defendant being entitled to prove relevant facts, whether mentioned in the alleged libel or not, particulars of all the facts relied upon must be given. *Clarke v. Norton*, (1910) V.L.R., 494 ; 32 A.L.T., 109 ; 16 A.L.R., 544. *Cussen, J.*

Order XVIII., r. 6—Order XVI., r. 1— Joinder of parties—Joinder of causes of action —Slander actions—Joint and separate claims —Arising out of " the same transaction or series of transactions "—" The same publication or series of publications."]—*See* PRACTICE AND PLEADING. *Smith v. Foley*, (1912) V.L.R., 314 ; 34 A.L.T., 75 ; 18 A.L.R., 333.

Order XIX., r. 27—Order XXXVI., r. 37— —Pleading—Tendency to embarrass—Libel— Defence—Matters in mitigation of damages.]— In an action for libel a defendant may not in his defence allege matters merely in mitigation of damages. *Wood v. Earl of Durham*, 21 Q.B.D., 501 ; *Heffernan v. Hayes*, 25 V.L.R., 156 ; 21 A.L.T., 118 ; 5 A.L.R., 269, followed. *Millington v. Loring*, 6 Q.B.D., 190, not followed. *Wilson v. Dun's Gazette*

Ltd., (1912) V.L.R., 342 ; 34 A.L.T., 77 ; 18 A.L.R., 327. *Madden, C.J.*

Order XIX., r. 27—Pleading—Tendency to embarrass—Libel contained in public newspaper—Allegation of apology and absence of malice and gross negligence—No payment into Court—Wrongs Act 1890 (No. 1160), sec. 5.]— In an action for libel against a newspaper, a defence stating defendant's intention to rely on sec. 5 of the *Wrongs Act* 1890, and alleging the absence of malice and gross negligence and the publication of an apology, is embarrassing, and will be struck out, where no money is paid into Court by the defendant. *Wilson* v. *Dun's Gazette Ltd.*, (1912) V.L.R., 342 ; 34 A.L.T., 77 ; 18 A.L.R., 327. *Madden, C.J.*

Wrongs Act 1890 (No. 1160), sec. 5—Rules of the Supreme Court 1906, XXII., r. 1— Practice—Libel action against newspaper proprietor—Defence—Payment into Court with Denial of liability—Defence under Wrongs Act and Payment into Court thereunder.]— In an action against a proprietor of a newspaper for the recovery of damages for libel, the defendant pleaded in one paragraph of his defence payment into Court of £10 with a denial of liability, and in another paragraph thereof, whilst denying the meanings ascribed by the plaintiff to the words complained of, he pleaded a defence and a payment into Court as under sec. 5 of the *Wrongs Act* 1890. Only one sum of £10 was paid into Court by the defendant. *Held*, that the words denying the innuendoes should be struck out of the latter paragraph, and a second sum of £10 should be brought into Court as under that paragraph. *Kiel* v. *Clark*, (1908) V.L.R., 627 ; 30 A.L.T., 86 ; 14 A.L.R., 500. *Madden, C.J.*

County Court Act 1890 (No. 1078), sec. 51— County Court Rules 1891, rr. 155, 424— Wrongs Act 1890 (No. 1160), — Remitted action—Action for libel—Notice of special defence under Wrongs Act 1890—Enlargement of time for serving and filing such notice— Power of Court to grant.]— Where an action for libel has been remitted under sec. 51 of the *County Court Act* 1890 to be tried in a County Court, such Court has power under r.

424 of the *County Court Rules* 1891 to allow the defendant to serve and file a notice of special defence under the *Wrongs Act* 1890 after the expiration of the time allowed or appointed for so doing by r. 155. *Bayne* v. *Wilson and Mackinnon*, 31 A.L.T. (Supplement), 2 ; *Judge Box* (1909).

County Court—Practice—Slander—Special defence that slander is true—Limitation of such defence at trial to part only of the words complained of.]— The defendant, who had given notice that he relied on the defence that the slander complained of was true in substance and in fact, was allowed at the trial to limit such defence to part only of the words complained of, and as to the whole of such words to set up the defence that they were not spoken and published of and concerning the plaintiff. *Griffiths* v. *Barry*, 27 A.L.T. (Supplement), 12 ; 12 A.L.R. (C.N.), 9. *Judge Johnson* (1906).

(b) Interrogatories.

Libel — Interrogatories — Practice—Interrogatories as to fresh cause of action.]— Where in an action for libel the plaintiff alleges specific instances of publication of the libel he will not be permitted to interrogate the defendant in order to discover other instances of publication of which he is unaware. *Mutual Life and Citizens Assurance Co. Ltd.* v. *National Mutual Fire Association of Australia Ltd.*, (1909) V.L.R., 445 ; 31 A.L.T., 60 ; 15 A.L.R., 476. *Hood, J.*

Order XXXI.—Libel—Intention of defendant in using words complained of—Interrogatories as to, whether permissible.]— Where there is a dispute as to whether the words complained of by the plaintiff as libellous of him referred to him, the plaintiff is entitled to interrogate the defendant as to whether he intended such words to apply to the plaintiff, and whether he meant or intended the words to have the meaning ascribed to them in the statement of claim. *Powell* v. *Wilson and Mackinnon*, (1908) V.L.R., 574 ; 30 A.L.T., 84 ; 14 A.L.R., 458. *Hodges J.*

Order XXXI., r. 11—Interrogatories—Libel —Further and better answers—Contents of

written document—Criminal presentment.]— In an action for libel based upon a statement published by the defendants that the plaintiff had been found guilty of a criminal offence, the plaintiff interrogated the defendants as to whether he had been tried on a certain charge (specifying it) or upon some other and what charge, and as to whether certain things had not taken place at the trial in respect of "such charge." *Held*, that the defendants could refuse to answer such interrogatories on the ground that it was sought thereby to make the defendants disclose or admit the contents of a written document—namely, the presentment on which the plaintiff was tried. *Powell* v. *Wilson and Mackinnon*, (1908) V.L.R., 574; 30 A.L.T., 84; 14 A.L.R., 458. *Hodges, J.*

(c) *Jury.*

Order XXXVI., r. 2—Action of libel—Right to jury.]—*See* PRACTICE AND PLEADING. *North* v. *Jamieson*, (1908) V.L.R., 533; 30 A.L.T., 47; 14 A.L.R., 410.

DEFAULT.

See PRACTICE AND PLEADING.

DEFENCE.

Defence—Compulsory military training— Religious objection to bear arms—Validity of Act—Exemption—Excuse—Defence Act 1903-1910, secs. 61, 125, 135, 138, 143—The Constitution (63 & 64 Vict. c. 12), sec. 116.]—The provisions of the *Defence Act* 1903-1910 imposing obligations on all male inhabitants of the Commonwealth in respect of military training do not prohibit the free exercise of any religion, and, therefore, are not an infringement of sec. 116 of the Constitution. A person who is forbidden by the doctrines of his religion to bear arms is not thereby exempted or excused from undergoing the military training and rendering the personal service required by Part XII. of the *Defence Act* 1903-1910. *Krygger* v. *Williams*, (1912) 15 C.L.R., 366; 18 A.L.R., 518. H.C., *Griffith, C.J.*, and *Barton, J.*

DEFRAUD.

See FRAUD AND MISREPRESENTATION.

DELIVERY.

See CONTRACT OR AGREEMENT.

DENTIST.

Dentists Act 1898 (No. 1595), sec. 7—Using words at place of business implying that practice of dentistry is carried on—Placards outside place of business—Witnesses aware that person referred to in placards is not the person actually practising.]—L., who was neither a legally qualified medical practitioner nor a registered dentist, practised dentistry in a house on the outside of which were placards bearing the words " D., Dentist," and other placards bearing the [words " Teeth Extracted." D. was a registered dentist, who was absent from Victoria. L.'s name did not appear on the outside of the house, but he was the only person who practised dentistry there. *Held*, that L. was properly convicted of the offence of using at his place of business words implying that he was carrying on the practice of dentistry, notwithstanding the evidence of the witnesses for the prosecution that upon visiting the house and asking for D. they were informed by L. that D. was absent, that his name was L., and that he acted for D., and was carrying on business for him. *Joske* v. *Lubrano*, 4 C.L.R., 71; 12 A.L.R., 423. H.C., *Griffith, C.J., Barton* and *O'Connor, JJ.* (1906).

Dentists Act 1898 (No. 1595), sec. 7— " Taking the title of ' dentist ' "—Assertion by word of mouth.]—An unqualified person, who is engaged for profit in the business of operating upon teeth in any way, may by a direct assertion by word of mouth commit the offence of taking the title of "dentist" within the meaning of the first part of sec. 7 of the *Dentists Act* 1898, *e.g.*, if, upon being asked by an intending patient " Are you a dentist ? " he replies " Yes." *Joske* v. *Lubrano*, (1906) V.L.R., 407; 28 A.L.T., 40; 12 A.L.R., 311. *a'Beckett, A.-C.J.* (1906).

Dentist—Person " recorded " by the Dental Board—Use of word " dentist "—Words implying that he is practising dentistry—Dentists Act 1898 (No. 1595), sec. 7—Dentists Act 1910 (No. 2257), sec. 13.]—The prohibition in sec. 7 of the *Dentists Act* 1898 against the use by any person other than a legally qualified medical practitioner or a person registered under the Dentists Acts, of the title " dentist " or " dental practitioner " or " dental surgeon " or " surgeon dentist," applies to persons recorded by the Dental Board under sec. 13 of the *Dentists Act* 1910. But, notwithstanding the prohibition in section 7 of the Act of 1898 against the use by any person other than those specified of any name, title, etc., implying or tending to the belief that he is registered, or that he is qualified to practice dentistry, or is carrying on the practice of dentistry, a person recorded under sec. 13 of the Act of 1910 is entitled to use, in addition to the words " Recorded by the Dental Board of Victoria," words which will explain to the public what it is that he is recorded as being permitted to do, provided that those words do not imply that he is registered. *Stiggants* v. *Joske*, (1910-11) 12 C.L.R., 549 ; 17 A.L.R., 526. H.C., *Griffith*, *C.J.*, *Barton* and *O'Connor*, *JJ.*

Dentist—Recorded by the Dental Board of Victoria—What words may be used by " recorded " men—Dentists Act 1898 (No. 1595), sec. 7—Dentists Act 1910 (No. 2257), secs. 4, 5, 13.]—A person " Recorded by the Dental Board of Victoria," under sec. 13 of the *Dentists Act* 1910, exhibited on his place of business words, to wit, " Dentistry," " Painless Dentistry," &c., tending to the belief that he was carrying on the practice of dentistry. *Held* (*Cussen*, *J.*, *dissentiente*), that the defendant was entitled to use such words. *Stiggants* v. *Joske*, 12 C.L.R., 549 ; 17 A.L.R., 526, discussed and applied. *Joske* v. *Strutt*, (1912) V.L.R., 118 ; 33 A.L.T., 189 ; 18 A.L.R., 84. F.C., *Hodges*, *Hood* and *Cussen*, *JJ.* [Leave to appeal refused by High Court (*Griffith*, *C.J.*, *Barton* and *Isaacs*, *JJ.*), 14 C.L.R., 180 ; 18 A.L.R., at p. 90, but *Stiggants* v. *Joske*, explained. In *Joske* v. *Blitz*, (1912) V.L.R., 256 ; 34 A.L.T., 15 ; 18 A.L.R., 352, *Hood*, *J.*, withdrawing his opinion, *Joske* v. *Strutt* (*supra*) was not followed by the Full Court consisting of *a'Beckett*, *Hood* and *Cussen*, *JJ.*].

Dentist—Recorded by the Dental Board of Victoria—What words may be used by " recorded " men—Dentists Act 1898 (No. 1595), sec. 7—Dentists Act 1910 (No. 2257), secs. 4, 5, 13.]—Decision of Full Court, *Hodges*, *Hood*, *JJ.* (*Cussen*, *J.*, *dissentiente*), in *Joske* v. *Strutt*, (1912) V.L.R., 110 ; 33 A.L.T., 189 ; 18 A.L.R., 84, not followed, *Hood*, *J.*, withdrawing his opinion. *Joske* v. *Blitz*, (1912) V.L.R., 256 ; 34 A.L.T., 15 ; 18 A.L.R., 352. F.C., *a'Beckett*, *Hood* and *Cussen*, *JJ.*

DEVISE.

See WILL.

DIRECTOR.

See COMPANY.

DISCOVERY.

I.—INTERROGATORIES.

(a) *Who May be Interrogated.*

Order XXXI., rr. 1, 5, 12—Judiciary Act 1903 (Commonwealth) (No. 6), secs. 56, 64—Judicature Act—Commonwealth party to action—Discovery—Right to, from Commonwealth.]—In an action to which the Commonwealth is a party, by the joint effect of the *Judiciary Act*, secs. 56 and 64, of the *Supreme Court Act* 1890, and of Order XXXI., rr. 1 and 12 of the *Rules of the Supreme Court*

1906, discovery can be obtained from the Commonwealth by the opposite party. *Commonwealth* v. *Miller*, 10 C.L.R., 742 ; 16 A.L.R., 424. H.C., *Griffith, C.J., Barton, O'Connor, Isaacs* and *Higgins, JJ.* (1910).

Action against Commonwealth—Right to discovery from the Commonwealth—Judiciary Act 1903 (Commonwealth) (No. 6), secs. 56, 64.]—The " rights " referred to in sec. 64 of the *Judiciary Act* 1903 include the " right to discovery." *Commonwealth* v. *Miller*, 10 C.L.R., 742 ; 16 A.L.R., 424. H.C., *Griffith, C.J., Barton, O'Connor, Isaacs,* and *Higgins, JJ.* (1910).

County Court Act 1890 (No. 1078), secs. 81, 148—Infant, whether interrogatories may be administered to—Rules of Supreme Court 1906, Order XXXI., r. 29.]—Interrogatories may be administered to an infant party to an action in a County Court. *Brock* v. *Victorian Railways Commissioners*, 29 A.L.T. (Supplement), 3 ; 13 A.L.R. (C.N.), 21. *Judge Johnston.*

(b) What Interrogatories are Admissible.

Order XXXI.—Interrogatories—What questions may be asked.]—A party is entitled in his interrogatories to ask the same questions of the opposite party as he could ask the latter if called by him as a witness at the trial. *Powell* v. *Wilson and Mackinnon*, (1908) V.L.R., 574 ; 30 A.L.T., 84 ; 14 A.L.R., 458. *Hodges, J.* (1908).

Interrogatories—Practice — Libel — Interrogatories as to fresh cause of action.]—In an action for libel in which the plaintiff alleges specific instances of publication of libel he is not allowed to interrogate the defendant for the purpose of finding out whether there have been other instances of publication by the defendant, of which the plaintiff is unaware. *Mutual Life, &c., Co. Ltd.* v. *National Mutual Fire Association, &c., Ltd.,* (1909) V.L.R., 445 ; 31 A.L.T., 60 ; 15 A.L.R., 476. *Hood, J.*

Order XXXI.—Libel—Intention of defendant in using words complained of—Interrogatories as to, whether permissible.]—Where there is a dispute whether the words complained of by the plaintiff as libellous of him referred to him, the plaintiff is entitled to interrogate the defendant as to whether he intended such words to apply to the plaintiff, and whether he meant or intended the words to have the meaning ascribed to them in the statement of claim. *Powell* v. *Wilson and Mackinnon,* (1908) V.L.R., 574 ; 30 A.L.T., 84 ; 14 A.L.R., 458. *Hodges, J.* (1908).

Divorce—Practice—Petition on ground of adultery—Discovery of documents and interrogatories directed to fact of adultery—Divorce Rules 1906, rr. 26, 126.]—In a suit for dissolution of marriage on the ground of adultery neither the respondent nor the co-respondent can be compelled to answer interrogatories as to the fact of adultery, or to make discovery of documents relating to that fact. *Davis* v. *Davis; Hattrick, co-respondent,* (1912) V.L.R., 12 ; 33 A.L.T., 109 ; 17 A.L.R., 552. F.C., *Hodges, Hood* and *Cussen, JJ.*

(c) Answers.

Interrogatories — Privilege — Communications between solicitor and client—Abuse of process—Allegation of fraud.]—The plaintiff sued the defendants for malicious arrest and for abuse of the process of the Court. The plaintiff administered interrogatories to the defendants as to whether the defendants had obtained from their solicitor before they arrested the plaintiff any advice as to his liability. *Held,* that if the arrest was unlawful, the unlawful proceeding did not begin until after the advice had been given, and that as the communications between the defendants and their solicitor were not shown to have been made in furtherance of an illegal object, they were privileged, and that leave to appeal from the decision of the Supreme Court (reported at (1910) V.L.R., 289 ; 31 A.L.T., 179 ; 16 A.L.R., 137) should be refused. *Varawa* v. *Howard Smith & Co. Ltd.,* (1910) 10 C.L.R., 382 ; 16 A.L.R., 526. H.C., *Griffith, C.J., O'Connor* and *Isaacs, JJ.*

**Order XXXI.—Sufficiency of answer to interrogatories—Assumption that allegations in pleadings are true—Whether such assumption extends to matters not alleged in pleadings.]—*Semble, per Cussen, J.*—The assumption for the purposes of discovery that an allegation in a pleading is true cannot be extended to warrant the assumption that everything, which, though not pleaded, a party suggests would go to prove an allegation in his pleading, is also true. *Varawa v. Howard Smith & Sons,* (1910) V.L.R., 289 ; 31 A.L.T., 179 ; 16 A.L.R., 137.

Order XXXI., r. 11—Interrogatories—Action for libel—Further and better answers to interrogatories—Contents of written document—Criminal presentment.]—In an action for libel based upon a statement published by the defendants that the plaintiff had been found guilty of a criminal offence, the plaintiff interrogated the defendants as to whether he had been tried on a certain charge (specifying it) or upon some other and what charge, and as to whether certain things had not taken place at the trial in respect of " such charge." *Held*, that the defendants could refuse to answer such interrogatories on the ground that it was sought thereby to make the defendants disclose or admit the contents of a written document—namely, the presentment on which the plaintiff was tried. *Powell v. Wilson and Mackinnon,* (1908) V.L.R., 574 ; 30 A.L.T., 84 ; 14 A.L.R., 458. *Hodges, J.* (1908).

(d) Practice.

Divorce—Discovery and interrogatories—Adultery—Objection that discovery of documents or answering interrogatories may tend to criminate—How objection properly raised.]—The proper way of raising the objection, that compliance with an order for discovery and interrogatories obtained against a corespondent would disclose or tend to disclose adultery on his part and would or might criminate him, is upon oath in his affidavit of documents and his answers to interrogatories. *Davis v. Davis and Hattrick,* (1912) V.L.R., 23 ; 33 A.L.T., 108 ; 17 A.L.R., 607. *Hood, J.*

Husband and Wife—Divorce—Practice—Discovery—Jurisdiction to order ex parte—Divorce Rules 1906, rr. 126, 128—Rules of the Supreme Court 1906, Order XXXI., rr. 1, 1a, 12.]—In a divorce suit an order for discovery and interrogatories may be made *ex parte. Rees v. Dunbar,* 14 V.L.R., 645 ; 10 A.L.T., 147, followed. *Davis v. Davis and Hattrick,* (1912) V.L.R., 23 ; 33 A.L.T., 108 ; 17 A.L.R., 607. *Hood, J.*

Order XXXI., r. 3* (Rules of 1900)—Interrogatories—Costs—No application as to at trial—Application for after trial.]—Where a party had omitted to apply at the trial for the costs of interrogatories, an order was made allowing such costs after the lapse of two years from the trial, no special circumstances being shown why the order should not be made. *General Finance &c. Co. v. National Trustees &c. Co.,* 12 A.L.R. (C.N.), 1. *a' Beckett, J.* (1906).

Order XXXI., r. 3 (a)—Order XXXII.—Interrogatories—Notice to admit—Costs.]—In granting an order for interrogatories *ex parte* weight will be given to the presence or absence of notices to admit under Order XXXII., and a like consideration may affect the allowance of costs of interrogatories if opposed at the trial under Order XXXI., r. 3 (a). *In re Summons for Directions and Interrogatories ; Statement on behalf of the Judges of the Supreme Court,* 31 A.L.T., 49 ; 15 A.L.R. (C.N.), 17.

County Court—Costs—Solicitor plaintiff—Acting professionally on his own behalf—Costs of perusing documents—Perusing interrogatories—Schedule of Scale of Costs, Item 28.]—Where the plaintiff, a solicitor, obtains judgment with costs in an action wherein he acts as solicitor on his own behalf, he is entitled to the fee fixed by the Schedule of Scale of Costs for the perusal of all necessary documents, and he accordingly may charge under Item 28 for perusing the defendant's interrogatories. *Hopkins v. Forster,* 32 A.L.T. (Supplement), 5 ; 16 A.L.R. (C.N.), 6.

County Court—Interrogatories—Form of order—An order directing a party to answer interrogatories should set out specifically the time for answering. It is not sufficient if the order merely directs the party to answer " as prescribed by section 81 of the County Court Act 1890."]—*Crouch* v. *Victorian Railways Commissioners*, 27 A.L.T. (Supplement), 11 ; 12 A.L.R. (C.N.), 2. *Judge Box* (1905).

County Court—Order for interrogatories, form of—" Upon reading the interrogatories."]—An order granting leave to deliver interrogatories should not state that it was made " upon reading the interrogatories." *Naylor* v. *Kelly*, 27 A.L.T. (Supplement), 14 ; 12 A.L.R. (C.N.), 17. *Judge Box* (1906).

County Court Act 1890 (No. 1078), sec. 81 —Interrogatories—Leave to deliver—Application by solicitor's clerk—Form of order.]—Where on the application of a solicitor's clerk leave is granted to deliver interrogatories, the order should not state that it was made after hearing the solicitor. *Gobetti* v. *Harris*, 28 A.L.T. (Supplement), 9 ; 12 A.L.R. (C.N.), 28. *Judge Eagleson* (1906).

County Court — Practice — Interrogatories —Shortening time for answering—Affidavit in support of application, necessity for.]—An application for an order that answers to interrogatories be filed within a period less than seven days should be supported by affidavit showing the necessity for curtailing the time. *Williams* v. *Alcock*, 28 A.L.T. (Supplement), 5 ; 12 A.L.R. (C.N.), 18. *Judge Eagleson* (1906).

Interrogatories—Form of order—County Court Act 1890 (No. 1078), sec. 81 (1).]—The following is the form of order for leave to deliver interrogatories (omitting formal parts) settled by His Honour Judge Eagleson : —" I do order that the above-named plaintiff be at liberty to deliver to the defendant the interrogatories in writing a copy of which is hereunto annexed marked " A," and that the defendant do within seven days from the service hereof answer the said interrogatories as prescribed by section 81 of the *County Court Act 1890*." *Spence* v. *Simpson*, 33 A.L.T. (Supplement), 11 ; 18 A.L.R. (C.N.), 1.

II.—DOCUMENTS.

(a) *In Probate Matters.*

Practice — Probate — Discovery — Testa- mentary scripts—English practice, whether applicable—Supreme Court Act 1890 (No. 1142), secs. 20, 21.]—In proceedings to show cause why a caveat against the grant of probate should not be removed, the Court may order the discovery of testamentary scripts. *Semble*, the terms of sections 20 and 21 of the *Supreme Court Act* 1890 are wide enough to introduce the English practice in probate matters where no other provision has been made. *In re Carew*, 25 A.L.T., 117 ; 9 A.L.R., 266 ; followed. *In the Will of Cotter*, (1907) V.L.R., 78 ; 28 A.L.T., 106 ; 12 A.L.R., 550. *Cussen, J.*

Discovery of documents—Probate—Caveat —Testamentary incapacity and undue influence alleged—Discovery by caveator, how limited—Rules of Supreme Court 1906 (Probate), Rule 32.]—In a case in which testamentary incapacity and undue influence were alleged by a caveator opposing the grant of probate, the Court refused to order discovery by the caveator generally ; but directed him to make discovery of all documents or letters signed by or in the handwriting of the testator and of all letters or documents addressed to the testator. *Re Baker*, (1907) V.L.R., 234 ; 28 A.L.T., 189 ; 13 A.L.R., 121. *a'Beckett, J.* (1907).

(b) *Privileged Communications.*

Discovery of documents—Privilege—Documents brought into existence prior to and not for purposes of litigation—Solicitor in possession for purposes of litigation—Order XXXI., r. 12 (Rules of 1906).]—Documents brought into existence before and not for the purposes of litigation are not privileged from inspection merely because possession of them has been obtained by a party or his solicitor for the purposes of the litigation. *O'Sullivan* v. *Morton*, (1911) V.L.R., 70 ; 32 A.L.T., 104 ; 17 A.L.R., 12. F.C., *Madden, C.J., a'Beckett* and *Hodges, JJ.*

Order XXXI., r. 12—Discovery—Documents —Professional privilege.]—The petitioners in their affidavit of documents objected to produce certain documents on the ground that they were communications between various branches of their business for the purpose of submitting matters to their solicitors or for the purpose of obtaining advice. *Held*, that as the documents were not alleged to be for the purpose of being submitted to the solicitors they were not privileged from inspection. *Brown* v. *The King*, (1911) V.L.R., 159; 32 A.L.T., 150; 17 A.L.R., 131. *Hodges, J.*

County Court Rules 1891, r. 91—Rules of Supreme Court 1906, Order XXXI., r. 15— Practice—Discovery and inspection—Privilege —Shorthand report of proceedings in Court— Transcript obtained for purposes of subsequent litigation.]—An action of libel was threatened to be brought against the proprietors of a newspaper in respect of a report published in the newspaper of proceedings in a Court of Petty Sessions. The defendants obtained a transcript of a shorthand note of the said proceedings for the purpose of enabling their solicitors to advise them in relation to the threatened libel action. The possession of the transcript was disclosed by the defendants in an affidavit of documents and inspection of the transcript was sought by the plaintiff in the libel action subsequently brought, but the defendants refused to produce it for inspection on the ground of privilege. *Held*, that the transcript was not privileged from inspection. *Chadwick* v. *Bowman*, 16 Q.B.D., 561, followed. *Shaw* v. *David Syme & Co.*, (1912) V.L.R., 336; 34 A.L.T., 68; 18 A.L.R., 345. F.C., *Madden, C.J., Hodges* and *Hood, JJ.* (1912).

Discovery—County Court Rules 1891, r. 93 —Written communications by servant to master—Affidavit, sufficiency of—Privilege.] —Defendants, by their affidavit of documents, refused to disclose certain written communications by one of their servants to another which defendants swore were made "for the purpose of assisting the defendants to resist or settle" anticipated litigation by the plaintiff. *Held*, that though it was not in terms sworn that the communications were made to the defendants, it sufficiently appeared that they were made for the purpose of reaching the defendants ultimately, and that the communications were accordingly privileged. *Connan* v.

Victorian Railways Commissioners, 28 A.L.T (Supplement), 19; 13 A.L.R. (C.N.), 14. *Judge Chomley* (1907).

(c) *Practice.*

Order XXXI., r. 12 (Rules of 1906)—Summons for directions—Action by beneficiary against executrix for accounts and administration—Discovery of documents before statement of claim.]—A testator had, by his will, given a life interest in his estate to the defendant, his widow, who was also executrix, with remainder in fee to the plaintiff, his daughter. At testator's death the plaintiff was a child of tender years, and after his death the defendant, as life tenant and executrix, had enjoyed and managed the estate. In an action in which the plaintiff sought declarations that certain real and personal property belonged to the estate and should be vested in trustees, the removal of the defendant and the appointment of a new trustee, and all necessary accounts and inquiries. *Held*, on summons for directions, in which the plaintiff asked for general discovery of documents before delivery of statement of claim, that discovery before such delivery should be limited to documents relating to the estate of the testator. *Boulton* v. *Robinson*, 32 A.L.T., 35; 16 A.L.R., 367. *a'Beckett, J.* (1910).

County Court Act 1890 (No. 1078), sec. 78 —Production and inspection of documents— Materiality of documents—Objection to produce—Rectification of affidavit in support.] —*See* COUNTY COURT, col. 309. *Choon* v. *Beecham*, 29 A.L.T. (Supplement), 2; 13 A.L.R. (C.N.),, 18.

DISCRETION.

See also, APPEAL ; GAMING AND WAGERING ; PRACTICE AND PLEADING.

Discretion of public body—Exercise of— What may be considered in such exercise— When Court will interfere therewith—Mandamus—Local Government Act 1903 (No. 1893), sec. 197, Thirteenth Schedule, Part VI.]—A municipal council had adopted Part

VI. of the Thirteenth Schedule to the *Local Government Act* 1903 which requires the occupier of any ground in which public amusements are conducted to register the ground each year, imposes a penalty upon the causing or permitting of any public amusement on an unregistered ground, and provides that the Council on the application of the occupier, may, if they see fit, cause any ground to be registered and grant a certificate of registration thereof. *Held*, that mandamus would lie to compel the Council to exercise their discretion as to granting or refusing an application for registration. *Held*, also, that in exercising their discretion the Council might properly take into consideration the fact that the ground, sought to be registered adjoined a public house of which the applicant was licensee that the applicant intended to use the ground for the purpose of making money for himself, and that the ground, if licensed, would enter into competition with a public recreation ground of which some of the cuuncillors were trustees and on which the Council had spent money of the municipality. *Per O'Connor, J.*—Where it is sought to prove that a discretion vested in a public body has been exercised on a ground which in law is deemed to be no ground at all, it must be shown that the alleged ground really affected the exercise of the discretion. It is not necessary that that circumstance should appear on the face of the resolution expressing the determination of the public body. It is enough if the Court, on consideration of the whole of the material before it, come to the conclusion that the public body has acted on a ground which it was not open to it to consider. *Per Higgins, J.*—No duty is imposed on the councillors to hear and determine in the judicial sense ; and *Semble*, if the councillors took grounds into consideration which ought not to have been taken, mandamus to hear and determine is not the appropriate remedy. The councillors are in a position analogous to that of trustees. *Randall* v. *The Council of the Town of Northcote*, 11 C.L.R., 100 ; 16 A.L.R., 249. H.C., *Griffith, C.J., O'Connor, Isaacs* and *Higgins, JJ.* (1910).

DISSOLUTION OF MARRIAGE.

See HUSBAND AND WIFE.

DIVIDEND.

See COMPANY.

DIVORCE.

See HUSBAND AND WIFE.

DOCTOR.

See MEDICAL MAN.

DOMESTIC TRIBUNAL.

See CHURCH OF ENGLAND ; COMPANY ; FRIENDLY SOCIETY.

DOMICIL.

See also, INTER-STATE AND INTERNATIONAL LAW.

Domicil—Commonwealth Public Servant—Voluntary removal from domicil of choice to take up similar duties in the same department in another State—Whether he acquires new domicil of choice.]—H., whose domicil of origin was outside the Commonwealth had, in February 1907, a Victorian domicil of choice. In that month and year he was an officer in the Commonwealth Customs Department, residing and performing all his duties in Melbourne. He there answered a departmental call for applications from Victorian officers willing to go to Adelaide on temporary work in connection with a re-organization of the Custims Department there. He was chosen and went to Adelaide. There existed reasons which made it probable that he was not sorry to leave Victoria. Soon after he reached Adelaide he applied for and was appointed to the position there corresponding to that which he had previously occupied in Melbourne. The evidence showed that he intended to remain in South Australia indefinitely, though if he could get promotion he would go to any of the other States. *Held*, that H. was domiciled in South Australia. *Semble*, if H. had gone to South Australia under orders or if his work in South Australia had been of the temporary character which it at first was the decision would have been different. Case of soldier or sailor distinguished. *Bailey* v. *Bailey*, (1909) V.L.R., 299; 30 A.L.T., 217; 15 A.L.R., 237. *Cussen, J.*

Domicile of origin—Change of, what constitites.]—*See* HUSBAND AND WIFE. *Forster* v. *Forster*, (1907) V.L.R., 159; 28 A.L.T., 144; 13 A.L.R., 33.

Domicile, change of—Evidence—Statements of intention, weight to be attached to—Contrary inference from conduct and acts.]—*See* HUSBAND AND WIFE. *Forster* v. *Forster*, (1907) V.L.R., 159; 28 A.L.T., 144; 13 A.L.R., 33.

Marriage Act 1890 (No. 1166), secs. 74, 75, 76—" Any wife," " any husband," meaning of—Domicile—Wife domiciled in Victoria at time of desertion.]—*See* HUSBAND AND WIFE. *Forster* v. *Forster*, (1907) V.L.R., 159; 28 A.L.T., 144; 13 A.L.R., 33.

Domicile—Dissolution of marriage—Victoria the domicile of origin of both parties—Victorian marriage—Change of domicile and subsequent desertion—Jurisdiction of Victorian Court.]—*See* HUSBAND AND WIFE. *Forster* v. *Forster*, (1907) V.L.R., 159; 28 A.L.T., 144; 13 A.L.R., 33.

Dissolution of marriage—Jurisdiction—Domicile—Submission to jurisdiction by respondent, effect of.]—*See* HUSBAND AND WIFE. *Forster* v. *Forster*, (1907) V.L.R., 159; 28 A.L.T., 144; 13 A.L.R., 33.

Marriage Act 1890 (No. 1166), sec. 74—Divorce—Wife deserted in Victoria when domiciled there—Husband subsequently becoming domiciled elsewhere—Jurisdiction of Court on cross-petition by husband.]—*See* HUSBAND AND WIFE. *Bailey* v. *Bailey*, (1909) V.L.R., 299; 30 A.L.T., 217; 15 A.L.R., 237.

Immigration Restriction Acts 1901-1905—" Immigrant," meaning of—Naturalised subject domiciled in Victoria—Return to Victoria from China.]—*See* IMMIGRATION RESTRICTION ACTS. *Ah Sheung* v. *Lindberg*, (1906) V.L.R., 323; 27 A.L.T., 189; *sub nom.*, *Rex* v. *Ah Sheung*, 12 A.L.R., 190.

Prohibited immigrant—Infant—Domicile of father in Australia—Immigration Restriction Act 1905 (No. 17 of 1905), sec. 4—Immigration Restriction Act 1901 (No. 17 of 1901), sec. 3.]—*See* IMMIGRATION RESTRICTION ACTS. *Ah Yin* v. *Christie*, 4 C.L.R., 1428; 13 A.L.R., 372.

DURESS.

Customs Act 1901 (No. 6), sec. 167—Customs Tariff 1908 (No. 7), sec. 7—Duties collected under proposed Tariff—Proposed Tariff different from Tariff enacted—Payment without protest—Recovery back of money paid—Money exacted colore officii—Deposit of amount demanded under section 167 of the Customs Act 1901—Whether the only remedy —" Dispute," what is.]—*See* CUSTOMS. *Sargood Bros.* v. *The Commonwealth*, (1910) 11 C.L.R., 258; 16 A.L.R., 483.

DUTIES ON THE ESTATES OF DECEASED PERSONS.

I.—PROPERTY IN RESPECT OF WHICH DUTY IS PAYABLE.

Administration and Probate Act 1903 (No. 1815), sec. 13—Duty—General power of appointment—By will only—Property subject to power, whether dutiable.]—Property, over which a deceased person had at the time of his death a general power of appointment by will only, is subject to duty by virtue of section 13 of the *Administration and Probate*

Act 1903. *Semble*, *Re Wilson*, 24 A.L.T., 168; 9 A.L.R., 36, was wrongly decided. *In re McCracken*; *Webb* v. *McCracken*, 3 C.L.R., 1018; 12 A.L.R., 313. H.C., *Griffith*, *C.J.*, *Barton* and *O'Connor*, *JJ.* (1906).

Administration and Probate Duties Act 1907 (No. 2089), sec. 3—Exemption from duty—Public charitable bequest or settlement—Institution for the promotion of science and art, what is.]—An institution is not an "institution for the promotion of science and art" within the meaning of section 3 of the *Administration and Probate Duties Act* 1907 unless the promotion of science and art is the chief object of the institution. *Held*, accordingly, on the evidence, that Queen's College, which is affiliated with the University of Melbourne, is not an institution for the promotion of science and art within the meaning of the above section, although in fact it does promote science and art. *Commissioners of Inland Revenue* v. *Forrest*, 15 App. Cas., 334, followed. *Edgar* v. *Greenwood*, (1910) V.L.R., 137; 31 A.L.T., 132; 16 A.L.R., 6. F.C., *Madden*, *C.J.*, *Hood* and *Cussen*, *JJ.*

Settlement, duty on—Trusts or dispositions to take effect after the death of the settlor—Trust to come into operation on death of survivor of settlor or his wife—Death of settlor before his wife—Administration and Probate Act 1890 (No. 1060), sec. 112—Administration and Probate Act 1903 (No. 1815), sec. 8.]—Section 112 of the *Administration and Probate Act* 1890 provides that "every settlement of any property made . . . . by any person containing trusts or dispositons to take effect after his death shall upon the death of the settlor be registered within the prescribed time . . . and no such trusts or dispositions shall be valid unless such settlement be so registered." The section also requires that the trustees of the settlement shall before registration pay the duty fixed by the Statute. *Held*, that a settlement containing trusts which are directed to come into operation upon the death of the settlor and his wife is a settlement containing trusts to take effect after the settlor's death, notwithstanding that the settlor dies before his wife, and is liable to duty accordingly. *Whiting* v. *McGinnis*, (1909) V.L.R., 250; 30 A.L.T., 207; 15 A.L.R., 203, approved. *In re Rosenthal*; *Rosenthal* v. *Rosenthal*, (1910) 11 C.L.R., 87; 16 A.L.R., 455. H.C., *Griffith*, *C.J.*, *Isaacs* and *Higgins*, *JJ.*

Administration and Probate Act 1890 (No. 1060), sec. 112—Administration and Probate Act 1903 (No. 1815), secs. 8 and 9—Settlement—Duty—Trusts and dispositions to take effect after death.]—Settlements which fall within the exceptions of section 112 of the *Administration and Probate Act* 1890 are, as a result of the repeal of such exceptions by Act No. 1815, section 9, liable to duty although made prior to such repeal. A settlement upon trust for the settlor's wife for life and after her death upon trust for the children of the marriage must, even where the settlor predeceases his wife, be registered under section 112 of the *Administration and Probate Act* 1890, and is liable to duty on the value of the whole property comprised in the settlement. *Whiting* v. *McGinnis*, (1909) V.L.R., 250; 30 A.L.T., 207; 15 A.L.R., 203. F.C., *Madden*, *C.J.*, *Hodges*, *J.* (*a'Beckett*, *J.* as to the latter point doubting). [Approved by the High Court in *Rosenthal* v. *Rosenthal*, (1910) 11 C.L.R., 87; 16 A.L.R., 455.]

Administration and Probate Act 1903 (No. 1815), sec. 11—Probate duty—Liability for—Gift purporting to act as immediate gift inter vivos—Donor continuing in possession under lease at full rental from donee—Whether bona fide possession and enjoyment immediately assumed and retained to exclusion of donor or of any benefit to him by contract or otherwise.]—On September 25th 1908 testatrix, for natural love and affection, transferred to her three sons portions of certain lands of which she was the owner in fee simple. The sons in pursuance of an arrangement previously made thereupon immediately executed leases of the property so transferred to them to the testatrix, who remained in possession under the leases till her death in January 1910, working the property as a whole in the same manner as prior to September 1908. The rent reserved by the leases was fair and reasonable, and was regularly paid without any remission refund or allowance being made to the lessee down to the date of her death, and there was no fraud imputed. *Held*, that the sons could not be regarded as having immediately upon the gift assumed *bona fide* possession and enjoyment and thenceforward retained it to the entire exclusion of the donor or of any benefit to her by contract or otherwise, and that therefore the lands so transferred were by virtue of section 11 (*b*) of the *Administration and Probate Act* 1903 chargeable with duty as part of the deceased's estate. *Lang* v. *Webb*, (1911) 13 C.L.R., 503; 18 A.L.R., 49. H.C., *Griffith, C.J., Barton* and *Isaacs, JJ.*

Administration and Probate Act 1890 (No. 1060), sec. 112—Settlement containing trusts which may take effect either before or after settlor's death—Property transferred in lifetime of settlor—Whether duty payable in respect of.]—A settlor settled property for the benefit of various persons, and in the settlement made provisions which might take effect either before or after his death; some of the property was disposed of in accordance with the settlement and transferred to the beneficiaries before the death of the settlor. *Held*, that duty was payable under the *Administration and Probate Acts* only upon the property which was subject to the provisions at the time of the death of the settlor. *Whiting* v. *Thompson*, 29 V.L.R., 89; 21 A.L.T., 231; 6 A.L.R., 132, followed. *In re Rosenthal; Rosenthal* v. *Rosenthal*, (1911) V.L.R., 55; 32 A.L.T., 46; 16 A.L.R., 399. *Hodges, J.*

II.—DUTY; PAYMENT AND APPORTIONMENT OF; RATE OF.

Will—Probate duty—Voluntary transfer by testator during lifetime—Duty chargeable on property transferred, how to be paid—Administration and Probate Act 1903 (No. 1815), sec. 11.]—The duty chargeable under section 11 of the *Administration and Probate Act* 1903 on property the subject matter of a voluntary transfer made by the testator during his lifetime, is not chargeable upon the estate of the testator disposed of by his will unless a contrary intention appears in the will. *National Trustees Executors &c. Co.* v. *O'Hea*, 29 V.L.R., 814; 25 A.L.T., 230; 10 A.L.R., 81, followed. *In re Draper; Graham* v. *Draper*, (1910) V.L.R., 376; 32 A.L.T., 34; 16 A.L.R., 370. *a'Beckett, J.* (1910).

Administration and Probate Act 1907 (No. 2120), sec. 3—Administration and Probate Act 1903 (No. 1815), sec. 11—Probate duty on property voluntarily transferred in lifetime of deceased—Whether payable out of residue.]—Section 3 of the Act No. 2120, which provides for the payment by the executor or administrator of the estate of any deceased person of any duty payable on the whole or any part thereof under the provisions of the *Administration and Probate Acts* out of the residue of such estate unless a contrary intention appears in the will, does not apply to the duty chargeable under section 11 of the Act No. 1815, on property voluntarily transferred by the deceased during his lifetime. *Heward* v. *The King*, 3 C.L.R., 117; 11 A.L.R., 494, followed. *In re Draper; Graham* v. *Draper*, (1910) V.L.R., 376; 32 A.L.T., 34; 16 A.L.R., 370. *a'Beckett, J.* (1910).

Will—Construction—Direction to pay funeral and testatmentary expenses and debts—Probate duty in respect of property transferred by testator in his lifetime—Administration and Probate Act 1903 (No. 1815), sec. 11.]—A direction by a testator to his executors to pay his funeral and testamentary expenses and debts out of his residuary estate does not authorize the payment of probate duty on property the subject of a voluntary transfer made chargeable with that duty under section 11 of the *Administration and Probate Act* 1903. *National Trustees Executors &c. Co.* v. *O'Hea*, 29 V.L.R., 814; 25 A.L.T., 230; 10 A.L.R., 81, applied. *In re Draper; Graham* v. *Draper*, (1910) V.L.R., 376; 32 A.L.T., 34; 16 A.L.R., 370. *a'Beckett, J.* (1910).

Probate duty, how payment to be apportioned—Direction that each beneficiary shall

pay duty payable in respect of his interest—
Tenants for life and remaindermen.]—The
testator by his will made certain specific
bequests and devises and created various life
estates with remainders. He also directed
that each beneficiary should " pay the legacy
probate or succession duty payable in respect
of his or her interest." Held, that the direction as to payment of duty meant no more
than that one beneficiary should not be
called upon to pay the duty assessed in
respect of the gift to another, and that this
would be attained by following the rules
laid down in the case of *Murphy* v. *Ainslie*,
(1905) V.L.R., 350; 26 A.L.T., 202; 11
A.L.R., 163. *In re Buckhurst*; *Equity
Trustees Executors and Agency Co.* v.
Buckhurst, (1907) V.L.R., 252; 28 A.L.T.,
190; 13 A.L.R., 74. *Cussen, J.*

**Administration and Probate Act 1907 (No.
2120), sec. 3—Administration and Probate
Act 1890 (No. 1060), sec. 103—Probate duty—
Apportionment — Tenant for life and remainderman—Whether legislation retrospective.]—**Sec. 3 of the *Administration and Probate Act* 1907 is not retrospective. *In re
Staughton*; *Oliver* v. *Staughton*, (1910) V.L.R.,
415; 32 A.L.T., 63; 16 A.L.R., 443.
a'Beckett, J.

**Probate Duty—Apportionment—Tenant for
life and remainderman—Mistake of law—
Agreement between executors and tenant for
life as to apportionment of duty based on
wrong principle—Duty of executors.]—**A
testator by his will left a life interest in the
bulk of his estate to his widow and specifically
devised to her certain properties. The probate duty having been paid on the testator's
estate by his executors, they obtained an
actuarial valuation of the widow's life interest,
and took this valuation as the basis of her
contribution to probate duty in respect to
such life interest. The widow not being able
to provide for immediate payment of the
share of duty apportioned on such basis, an
arrangement, which was embodied in a deed,
was made between her and the executors for
payment by her of her proportion of the duty
by instalments. At that time the law as to
how the burden of probate duty should be

borne and apportioned was not settled. Subsequently the case of *Murphy* v. *Ainslie*,
(1905) V.L.R., 350; 26 A.L.T., 202; 11
A.L.R., 163, was decided. *Held*, that the
executors should exercise their powers under
sec. 103 of the *Administration and Probate
Act* 1890 as interpreted by the judgment in
Murphy v. *Ainslie*, notwithstanding the
execution of the deed by the widow, and
without reference to any payment they had
received thereunder attributable to the
amount she was charged in respect of her
life interest, and that the moneys she had so
paid should be returned to her out of the
money raised by the exercise of the powers
conferred by section 103. *In re Staughton*;
Oliver v. *Staughton*, (1910) V.L.R., 415; 32
A.L.T., 63; 16 A.L.R., 443. *a'Beckett, J.*

**Will and codicil—General direction in will
exempting legacies from probate duty—
Further legacies given in codicil without
reference to exemption from probate duty.]**
—*See* WILL. *In re Stroud*; *Bell* v. *Stroud*,
(1908) V.L.R., 33; 29 A.L.T., 104; 13
A.L.R., 645.

**Probate duty—Testamentary expenses—
Estate for life devised subject to payment
thereof—Tenant for life, refusal of payment
by—No income from realty available—Payment by trustees of probate duty and testamentary expenses out of personalty bequeathed
to other beneficiaries—Mortgage of real estate
to recoup such beneficiaries—Whether a
breach of trust.]**—*See* TRUSTS AND TRUSTEES.
Crout v. *Beissel*, (1909) V.L.R., 207; 30
A.L.T., 185; 15 A.L.R., 143.

**Administration and Probate Act 1890 (No.
1060), secs. 100, 112, 116—Administration
and Probate Act 1903 (No. 1815), secs. 9 (2),
15 (2)—Second Schedule—" Total value of
the property "—Settlement—Rate at which
duty payable—Whether based on the value of
all the settled property.]**—Part II. of the
Second Schedule to the *Administration and
Probate Act* 1903 provides that on all settlements of property " where the person taking
the property is a brother or sister . . .
and the total value of the property exceeds "
so much duty shall be payable at the rates

there set out. *Held*, that the words " the total value of the property " mean the value of the whole of the property settled by the settlement, and not the value of the part taken by each beneficiary. *Edgar* v. *Greenwood*, (1910) V.L.R., 137; 31 A.L.T., 132; 16 A.L.R., 6. F.C., *Madden, C.J., Hood* and *Cussen, JJ.*

III.—LEGAL PROCEEDINGS ; PRACTICE ; COSTS.

Function imposed upon tribunal by Legislature—No machinery provided—Power of Court—Ascertainment of amount of duty payable—Administration and Probate Act 1903 (No. 1815), secs. 9 (2), 15 (2)—Second Schedule.]—Where the Legislature imposes a function upon a tribunal but prescribes no machinery for the discharge of that function, *e.g.*, where there is no machinery provided by which the calculation of the amount of duty payable may be worked out, the Court will prescribe the machinery. *Edgar* v. *Greenwood*, (1910) V.L.R., 137; 31 A.L.T., 132; 16 A.L.R., 6. F.C., *Madden, C.J., Hood* and *Cussen, JJ.*

Administration and Probate Act 1890 (No. 1060), sec. 99—Probate duty—Procedure on assessment—Valuation of assets—Summons by Master, when it may be issued.]—Where the Commissioner is dissatisfied with the executors' valuation of the assets of an estate, and appoints a valuer who fixes a higher value to which the executors agree, the Commissioner, if he disagrees with such higher valuation, is not precluded by the valuation of his valuer or by the assent thereto of the executors from issuing a summons under sec. 99 of the *Administration and Probate Act* 1890 for the determination of the value. *Brookes* v. *The King*, (1911) V.L.R., 371; 33 A.L.T., 91; 17 A.L.R., 402 (1911).

Administration and Probate Act 1890 (No. 1060), sec. 98—Case stated—Right to begin.]—On a case stated by the Master-in-Equity under sec. 98 of the *Administration and Probate Act* 1890 the Crown should begin. *In re McCracken*, 27 A.L.T., 233; 12 A.L.R., 303. F.C., *a'Beckett, A.-C.J., Hodges* and *Hood, JJ.* (1906).

Costs—Taxation—Appendix N.—Drawing pleadings and other documents—Accounts, statements, &c., for Judge's Chambers—Statement for duty.]—*See* COSTS. *In re Duke's Will*, (1907) V.L.R., 632; 29 A.L.T., 50; 13 A.L.R., 477.

EASEMENTS.

—Easement—Implied grant of—Sale of part of a parcel of land—Retention by vendor of balance.]—In order that the grant to a purchaser of a right in the nature of an easement in respect of land of the vendor may be implied from a conveyance of part of a parcel of land of which the vendor retains the balance it must appear, having regard to all the circumstances of the case, to have been in the contemplation of the parties that the grantor should not use the land which he retains in a manner inconsistent with the enjoyment of the alleged easement. *Nelson* v. *Walker*, (1910) 10 C.L.R., 560; 16 A.L.R., 285. High Court, *Griffith, C.J., O'Connor, Isaacs* and *Higgins, JJ.*

Quasi-easement—Severance of unity of possession and title—Implied grant—Derogation from grant.]—The foundation of the doctrine of implied grant in the case of conveyance of part of a parcel of land, the vendor retaining the rest, is that having regard to all the circumstances of the case it must (not may) have been in the contemplation of the parties that the grantor should not use the land which he retains in such a way as to preclude any use of the land which he sells or that use for which he knows he is selling it to the purchaser. *Semble* : No such grant is to be implied (so as to bind successors in title) from circumstances not referred to in the transfer or conveyance. *Nelson* v. *Walker*, (1910) 10 C.L.R., 560; 16 A.L.R., 285. High Court, *Griffith, C.J., O'Connor, Isaacs* and *Higgins, JJ.*

Vendor and Purchaser—Derogation from grant—Implied grant—Quasi-easement—Rain water flowing over surface—Adjoining owners —Natural servitude—Alteration of surface— Transfer of Land Act 1890 (No. 1149), sec. 89

—Conveyancing Act 1904 (No. 1953), sec. 6.]— Where the proprietor of land under the *Transfer of Land Act* 1890, comprising two adjoining town allotments, and lying upon a slope, sells and transfers the upper allotment, the rain water falling on which naturally flowed at the time of transfer on to the other or lower allotment, no grant of a quasi-easement to allow the rain-water to continue so to flow is implied from the transfer in favour of the transferee as against the transferror. By creating an embankment to prevent the flow, the transferror is not derogating from his grant. *Vinnicombe* v. *MacGregor*, 29 V.L.R., 32 ; 28 V.L.R., 144 ; 24 A.L.T., 200 ; 24 A.L.T., 15 ; 9 A.L.R., 60 ; 8 A.L.R., 141, disapproved, *per Griffith, C.J.*, and *O'Connor, J.* *Nelson* v. *Walker*, (1910) 10 C.L.R., 560 ; 16 A.L.R., 285. High Court, *Griffith, C.J.*, *O'Connor, Isaacs* and *Higgins, JJ.*

Flow of water—Owners of adjoining lands—Upper and lower—Former unity of title and possession—Country and town—Artificial alteration of natural surface—Obligation to receive—Transfer of Land Act 1890 (No. 1149).]—By *Griffith, C.J.* and *O'Connor, J.* (*contra* by *Isaacs, J.* and *Higgins, J.*) :— If the principle that an owner is bound to receive the rain water naturally flowing over the surface of the adjoining higher land is part of the common law, it applies to the case of land the surface of which has been altered by the hand of man or otherwise during the unity of title and possession, and before severance, as well as to land the original natural surface of which has not been altered. By *Griffith, C.J.* and *O'Connor, J.* : That principle, if it is part of the common law, applies only to country lands and not to town lands. By *O'Connor, J.* (*Semble* by *Griffith, C.J.*) :—That principle is not part of the common law, and the owner of the lower land may prevent such water from flowing on to his land. *Quaere, per Higgins, J.*, whether land held under the *Transfer of Land Act* 1890 is subject to a natural right on the part of the proprietor of adjoining land to the flow of water. By *Higgins, J.* :— If there is any right such as is declared in *Vinnicombe* v. *MacGregor*, it must be confined, as in the case of a defined stream, to

water spreading over the natural surface of the land ; but under the word "natural" surfaces (or river beds) which have been changed beyond living memory should be included. *Vinnicombe* v. *MacGregor*, 29 V.L.R., 32 ; 28 V.L.R., 144 ; 24 A.L.T., 200 ; 24 A.L.T., 15 ; 9 A.L.R., 60 ; 8 A.L.R., 141 discussed, and (*per Griffith, C.J.* and *O'Connor, J.*), disapproved. *Nelson* v. *Walker*, (1910) 10 C.L.R., 560 ; 16 A.L.R., 285. High Court, *Griffith, C.J.*, *O'Connor, Isaacs* and *Higgins, JJ.*

EDUCATION.

Failing to cause child to attend a State School—Reasonable excuse—Efficient and regular instruction according to regulations—Failure to define efficient and regular instruction by regulations—Parent alleging his child to be under efficient and regular instruction—Whether he may be convicted—Education Act 1905 (No. 2005), secs. 3, 4, 5—Education Act 1890 (No. 1086), sec. 23.]—Sec. 5 of the *Education Act* 1905 imposes a penalty upon a parent of any child who not having a reasonable excuse, neglects to cause such child to attend a State School as required by the Act. It is provided by sub-section 4 of section 3 of that Act that it shall be a reasonable excuse that such child is under efficient and regular instruction in some other manner, and is complying with the like conditions of attendance as are prescribed, and by sub-sec. 6 that "efficient and regular instruction" means such instruction in the subjects of the standard of education as may be prescribed by regulations under the Education Acts. Under sec. 23 of the *Education Act* 1890 regulations may be made by the Governor-in-Council. An Order-in-Council was passed specifying the subjects in which instruction was to be given, and providing that the programme of instruction in such subjects shall be as from time to time prescribed by the Director and approved by the Minister. The Minister and the Director adopted a certain programme of instruction, but it was not made an Order-in-Council. *Held*, that inasmuch as there were no regulations under the Education Acts which, within the meaning of sec. 3, sub-sec. 6 of the *Education Act 1905*, prescribed the instruction in the standard of education, there could be no conviction under sec. 5 of a parent alleging that his child was " under efficient and regular instruction in some other manner." *Fleming* v. *Greene*, (1907) V.L.R., 394 ; 28 A.L.T., 212 ; 13 A.L.R., 185. *Madden, C.J., Hodges* and *Hood, JJ.*

EJECTMENT.

Landlord and Tenant Act 1890 (No. 1108), sec. 92—Eighth Schedule—Notice of intention to apply to Justices to recover possession—Signature of notice, sufficiency of—Application by corporation—Name of corporation signed by agent authorised so to do.]—*See* LANDLORD AND TENANT. *Equity Trustees Executors and Agency Co. Ltd.* v. *Harston,* (1908) V.L.R., 23 ; 29 A.L.T., 131 ; 13 A.L.R., 686.

Landlord and Tenant Act 1890 (No. 1108), sec. 92—Eighth Schedule—Notice of owner's intention to apply to justices to recover possession—Statement that tenement held over and detained from purchaser—Legal estate still in vendor—Whether equitable owner might himself obtain warrant.]—*See* LANDLORD AND TENANT. *Equity Trustees Executors and Agency Co. Ltd.* v. *Harston,* (1908) V.L.R., 23 ; 29 A.L.T., 131 ; 13 A.L.R., 686.

Landlord and Tenant Act 1890 (No. 1108), secs. 92, 93—Justices Act 1890 (No. 1105), secs. 4, 29—Recovery of possession—Justices—Jurisdiction to issue summons to witness—Notice of intention to apply, service of—" Complaint."]—*See* LANDLORD AND TENANT. *Lesser* v. *Knight,* 29 A.L.T., 111 ; 13 A.L.R., 708.

Landlord and Tenant Act 1890 (No. 1108), sec. 92—Eighth Schedule—Ninth Schedule—Notice of intention to apply to justices to recover possession—Complaint—Immaterial matters contained in, effect of.]—*See* LANDLORD AND TENANT. *Equity Trustees Executors and Agency Co. Ltd.* v. *Harston,* (1908) V.L.R., 23 ; 29 A.L.T., 131 ; 13 A.L.R., 686.

Landlord and Tenant Act 1890 (No. 1108), secs. 92, 93—Notice to quit—Second notice,

effect of—Offer of new tenancy—Non-acceptance—Whether second notice a waiver of first.]—*See* LANDLORD AND TENANT. *Green* v. *Summons,* 29 A.L.T., 245 ; 14 A.L.R., 218.

Notice to quit—Monthly tenancy—Length of notice.]—*See* LANDLORD AND TENANT. *Bayne* v. *Love,* (1909) 7 C.L.R., 748.

Lease—Power to re-enter and determine tenancy on non-payment of rent—Necessity for demand of rent made upon the land not dispensed with—Termination of tenancy—Whether demand of rent essential.]—*See* LANDLORD AND TENANT. *Sandhurst and Northern District, &c., Agency Co. Ltd.* v. *Canavan,* (1908) V.L.R., 373 ; 30 A.L.T., 1 ; 14 A.L.R., 250.

Relief against forfeiture for non-payment of rent—Crown, relief against—Settlement of Lands Act 1893 (No. 1311), secs. 5, 10—Lease by Board of Land and Works—Supreme Court Act 1890 (No. 1142), sec. 202.]—*See* LANDLORD AND TENANT. *The King* v. *Dale,* (1906) V.L.R., 662 ; 28 A.L.T., 140 ; 12 A.L.R., 549.

ELECTION (DOCTRINE OF)

Order XLII., rr. 3, 17 (Rules of 1884)—Order XLIV., r. 2—Order for payment of money—Execution under fi. fa.—Attachment for disobedience—Election of remedy, whether creditor bound by.]—*See* ATTACHMENT. *Pope* v. *Peacock,* (1906) V.L.R., 667 ; 28 A.L.T., 63 ; 12 A.L.R., 440. *Hodges, J.*

Conversion—Sale of stolen goods—Recovery of value of goods from purchaser—Payment by cheque—Proceeds afterwards coming to hands of owner of goods—Obligation to elect to affirm or disaffirm sale.]—*See* SALE OF GOODS. *Creak* v. *James Moore & Sons Proprietary Ltd.,* (1912) 15 C.L.R., 426 ; 18 A.L.R., 542.

ELECTION LAW.

Parliamentary Election (Commonwealth)—Political article in newspaper during election—Signature of author—Validity of Commonwealth legislation—The Constitution (63 & 64 Vict. c. 12), sec. 10, 51 (xxxvi.)—Commonwealth Electoral Act 1902-1911 (No. 19 of 1902—No. 17 of 1911), sec. 181 AA.]—The Commonwealth Parliament has power under the Constitution to make laws regulating federal parliamentary elections, and, therefore, section 181 AA of the *Commonwealth Electoral Act* 1902-1911 is within the powers of the Commonwealth Parliament to enact. *Smith* v. *Oldham*, (1912) 15 C.L.R., 355 ; 18 A.L.R., 448. H.C., *Griffith*, *C.J.*, *Barton* and *Isaacs*, *JJ*.

Election—Ballot paper—Necessity for placing cross within square—Commonwealth Electoral Act 1902, sec. 151.]—See COMMONWEALTH ELECTORAL ACTS, col. 111. *Kennedy* v. *Palmer*, (1907) 4 C.L.R., 1481.

Election—Ballot paper—Marks enabling voter to be identified—Commonwealth Electoral Act 1902 (No. 19 of 1902), sec. 158 (d).]—See COMMONWEALTH ELECTORAL ACTS, cols. 111, 112. *Kennedy* v. *Palmer*, (1907) 4 C.L.R., 1481.

For a consideration of the questions to be determined before acceptance of a ballot-paper.]—See *Kennedy* v. *Palmer*, (1907) 4 C.L.R., 1481. *Barton*, *J*.

Agent—Liability of candidate for acts of.]—See COMMONWEALTH ELECTORAL ACTS, col. 112. *Crouch* v. *Ozanne*, (1910) 12 C.L.R., 539.

Commonwealth Electoral Acts (No. 19 of 1902) (No. 26 of 1905), sec. 182 (a)—Electoral offences—Canvassing for votes at entrance to polling booth, what is.]—See COMMONWEALTH ELECTORAL ACTS, col. 112. *Crouch* v. *Ozanne*, (1910) 12 C.L.R., 539.

Commonwealth Electoral Acts (No. 19 of 1902) (No. 26 of 1905), sec. 198 (a)—Illegal practices—Voiding election—Scrutineers of defeated candidate prevented from entering polling booth—Majority of successful candidate at such booth greater than total majority.] See COMMONWEALTH ELECTORAL ACTS, col. 112. *Crouch* v. *Ozanne*, (1910) 12 C.L.R., 539.

Commonwealth Electoral Acts 1902-1909,

sec. 109 (B) (b)—Application for postal certificate—Witnessing signature—Application not signed by elector.]—See COMMONWEALTH ELECTORAL ACTS, col. 113. *Hearn* v. *Hill*, (1910) 13 C.L.R., 128.

Local Government Act 1903 (No. 1893), secs. 120, 143—Council election—Persons whose names are on roll—Infant voters.]—See LOCAL GOVERNMENT. *In re Hollins Ex parte Daly*, (1912) V.L.R., 87 ; 33 A.L.T. 157 ; 18 A.L.R., 43.

Local Government Act 1903 (No. 1893) secs. 119, 120, 143, 149—Election of councillors—Infant's name inscribed on roll—Voting by infant—Validity of election.]—See LOCAL GOVERNMENT. *In re Hollins* ; *Ex parte Daly*, (1912) V.L.R., 87 ; 33 A.L.T., 157 ; 18 A.L.R., 43.

———

ELECTRIC LIGHT AND POWER ACT.

Electric Light and Power Act 1896 (No. 1413), secs. 38, 39—Electric Light and Power Act 1901 (No. 1775), sec. 3—Construction—Powers of undertakers to vary rates of charge.]—Under the *Electric Light and Power Act* 1896, the respondents supply electricity within the City of Melbourne under two different systems of charge, one at a fixed rate, the other at a rate varying with the amount consumed. The system adopted is at the choice of the customer. Within each system no preference is given to one customer over another. *Held*, that by the true construction of sections 38 and 39 of the said Act they were authorized so to do, and were not restricted to one uniform rate for all electricity supplied by them. The preference prohibited by section 39 is not as between customers dealing under two different systems, but only as between customers dealing under the same system. *Held*, also, that section 3 of the *Electric Light and Power Act* 1901, in authorizing a specified variation in rates of charge after a judicial decision to the effect that they must in all cases be uniform, did not either expressly or impliedly declare that, except in the special instance, the judicial decision must be upheld. *Attorney-General for Victoria* v. *Melbourne, Mayor &c. of,* (1907) A.C., 469 ;(1907) 5 C.L.R., 257. Privy Council.

Local Government Act 1903 (No. 1893), repealing effect of—Electric Light and Power Act 1896 (No. 1413), Electric Light and Power Act 1900 (No. 1694).]—The *Local Government Act* 1903 does not by implication repeal the *Electric Light and Power Act* 1896 or the *Electric Light and Power Act* 1900. *Attorney-General (ex rel. Dodd)* v. *Ararat, Mayor, &c. of Borough of,* (1911) V.L.R., 489 ; 33 A.L.T., 99 ; 17 A.L.R., 474. *Madden, C.J.*

Municipality, powers of—Supply of electricity for public or private purposes within municipal district—Whether municipality entitled as of right to Order-in-Council authorising—Electric Light and Power Act 1896 (No. 1413), secs. 8, 9, 10, 11, 13, 16, 17, 18.]— Under the *Electric Light and Power Act* 1896 a municipal council is not entitled as of right to obtain an order in Council free from conditions authorizing it to supply electricity within its municipal district. *Attorney-General (ex rel. Dodd)* v. *Ararat, Mayor &c. of Borough of,* (1911) V.L.R., 489 ; 33 A.L.T., 99 ; 17 A.L.R., 474. *Madden, C.J.*

Municipality, powers of—Supply of electricity, Order in Council authorising—Borrowing money for purpose of erecting works— Order in Council, whether a condition precedent to publication of notice of intention to borrow—Electric Light and Power Act 1896 (No. 1413), secs. 5, 10—Local Government Act 1903 (No. 1893), sec. 355.]—The Order in Council authorising a municipal council to supply electricity must be obtained before the Council publishes the notice prescribed by section 355 of the *Local Government Act* 1903. *Attorney-General (ex rel. Dodd)* v. *Ararat, Mayor &c. of Borough of,* (1911) V.L.R., 489 ; 33 A.L.T., 99 ; 17 A.L.R., 474. *Madden, C.J.*

Municipality, powers of—Supply of electricity for light, heat and power—Power to borrow money to construct necessary works— Electric Light and Power Act 1896 (No. 1413), secs. 5, 10, 16, 17 ; Electric Light and Power Act 1900 (No. 1694), secs. 2, 3—Local Government Act 1890 (No. 1112), secs. 304, 311 ; Local Government Act 1891 (No. 1243), sec. 77 (xi.) ; Local Government Act 1903 (No. 1893),secs. 345, 346, 347 (6), 595.]—A municipal council which has obtained an Order in Council authorising it to supply electricity for light, heat and power, may borrow money on the credit of the municipality to enable it to construct the necessary works. *Attorney-General (ex rel. Dodd)* v. *Ararat, Mayor, &c. of Borough of,* (1911) V.L.R., 489 ; 33 A.L.T., 99 ; 17 A.L.R., 474. *Madden, C.J.*

EMBEZZLEMENT.

See CRIMINAL LAW.

EMBRACERY.

See CRIMINAL LAW.

EMPLOYER AND EMPLOYE.

See also, PUBLIC SERVICE.

I.—RIGHTS AND LIABILITIES OF EMPLOYER AND EMPLOYE.

(a) Contract of Employment.

Contract—Work and Labour—Wages—Promise to pay, express or implied—Evidence, sufficiency of.]—*See* CONTRACT OR AGREEMENT, cols. 192-193. *Griffith* v. *O'Donoghue*, (1906) V.L.R., 548 ; 28 A.L.T., 31 ; 12 A.L.R., 357.

(b) Injuries to Employe in Course of Employment.

Negligence—Employer and Employe—Evidence—Employers and Employes Act 1890 (No. 1087), sec. 38.]—Section 38 of the *Employers and Employes Act* 1890 provides that where personal injury is caused to a workman (*inter alia*) : " (2) by reason of the negligence of any person in the service of the employer who has any superintendence entrusted to him whilst in the exercise of such superintendence ; or (3) by reason of the negligence of any person in the service of the employer to whose orders or directions the workman at the time of the injury was bound to conform and did conform, where such injury resulted from his having so conformed ; or (4) by reason of the act or omission of any person in the service of the employer done or made . . . in obedience to particular instructions given by any person delegated with the authority of the employer in that behalf " the workman or his representative " shall have the same right of compensation and remedies against the employer as if the workman had not been a workman of or not in the service of the employer nor engaged in his work." In an action under that section by the representative of a man who was killed by the explosion of a charge during blasting operations at a quarry. *Held*, on the evidence (*per Griffith, C.J.* and *Barton, J.* (*Isaacs, J.* dissenting) that the plaintiff was properly non-suited. *Footscray Quarries Proprietary Ltd.* v. *Nicholls*, (1912) 14 C.L.R., 321.

Mines Act 1904 (No. 1961), sec. 45 (36) (37)—General rules to be observed in mines—Parts of machinery to be kept in fit condition—Temporary platform used for convenience in cleaning tank—Dangerous parts of machinery to be fenced—Machinery not in itself dangerous—Danger arising from height above the ground and not from nature of machinery itself.]—A tank used for supplying water to a battery at the defendant's mine rested on a permanent scaffolding which stood at the height of 25 feet on poppet legs. It was necessary that the tank should be cleaned out at intervals of several years. Rungs fastened to the poppet legs formed a permanent ladder to the top. Except the cross beams of the scaffolding there was nothing to afford a footing for a person employed in cleaning out the tank, nor was there any fencing of any kind. The plaintiff, an employe of the defendant at the mine and another employe having been ordered to clean out the tank ascended the ladder and placed laths across the cross-beams of the scaffolding so as to form a temporary platform. The platform was formed to provide a place on which to deposit the dirt taken out of the tank, so as to prevent it from falling on the pump which supplied the tank with water. The laths projected beyond the cross beams and were not nailed or fastened in any way. The plaintiff stepped on the projecting end of one of the laths which tipped up and so caused him to fall to the ground and suffer damage. *Held*, that the temporary platform did not fall within section 45 (36) as a part of the " machinery " used for any mining purpose and required to be kept in a fit state and condition ; and that neither the cross beams nor the temporary platform nor the tank were within the meaning of section 45 (37) " dangerous or exposed parts of the machinery " which had to be kept securely and safely fenced, the machinery contemplated by sub-section (37) being machinery which is in itself dangerous to those who come in contact with it. *Eames* v. *Birthday Tunnel G.M. Co.*, (1906) V.L.R., 293 ; 27 A.L.T., 164 ; 12 A.L.R., 37. F.C., *a' Beckett, Hodges* and *Hood, JJ.*

(c) *Fiduciary Nature of Employe's Position.*

Employe under contract to devote whole time to employer's service—Employe entering service of another person—Duties towards other person inconsistent with service of employer—Knowledge and consent of employer—Right of employer to remuneration received by employe from other person—Constructive trust.]—A., a manufacturer of refrigerating machinery at Adelaide, having other establishments elsewhere, employed B. at a yearly salary as his manager at Adelaide. B. agreed to devote his whole time and ability to his duties. One of these duties was to promote syndicates or companies which should purchase refrigerating machinery from A. B. promoted an ice skating rink company in Melbourne, and, with A.'s knowledge and consent, was appointed consulting engineer of the company. As such consulting engineer he was called upon by the company to draw plans and specifications of refrigerating machinery, prepare the conditions of the contract for its supply and erection and superintend its erection on their behalf. A. tendered for the supply of the machinery in accordance with the plans and specifications prepared by B., his tender was accepted, and the machinery was erected under the supervision of B. B. received from the company as remuneration for his services to the company as consulting engineer 2,000 paid up shares in the company. *Held*, that A. was not entitled to claim the shares from B. *Reid* v. *MacDonald*, (1907) 4 C.L.R., 1572. H.C., *Griffith, C.J., Barton, O'Connor, Isaacs* and *Higgins, JJ.*

Employer and employe—Fiduciary relationship—Servant employed to sell business as a going concern—Servant secretly procuring determination of master's tenancy and lease for himself—Constructive trustee.]—The plaintiff who carried on business in premises held on a monthly tenancy, requested the defendant, his manager, who lived upon the premises, to help him in finding a purchaser for the business as a going concern. While so employed, acting secretly as regards the plaintiff and in breach of his duty to the plaintiff and in his own interest, the defendant procured the landlord to determine the plaintiff's tenancy, and to give the defendant a lease of the premises for six years. *Held* that the defendant was a trustee for the plaintiff of the lease thus obtained. *Davis* v. *Hamlin*, 48 Am. R., 541 ; *Gower* v. *Andrew*, 43 Am. R., 242, and *Grumley* v. *Webb*, 100 Am. Dec., 304, approved. *Prebble* v. *Reeves*, (1910) V.L.R., 88 ; 31 A.L.T., 114 ; 15 A.L.R., 631. F.C., *Madden, C.J., Hood* and *Cussen, JJ.*

(d) *Wrongful Dismissal.*

Employer and employe—Dismissal—Without notice—Dishonesty of servant prior to employment no ground of dismissal.]—A master is not, in the absence of express provision in the contract of employment, justified in summarily discharging a servant on the ground that he has been guilty of dishonesty before entering the master's employment. *Gill* v. *Colonial Mutual Life Assurance Society Limited*, (1912) V.L.R., 146 ; 33 A.L.T., 201 ; 18 A.L.R., 140. *Hood, J.*

Commonwealth Public Service Act 1902 (No. 5 of 1902), sec. 46—Public servant—Dismissal — Procedure prescribed by Act, failure to observe—Effect of—Suspension—Dismissal based on charge on which public servant not suspended.]—*See* PUBLIC SERVICE. *Williamson* v. *The Commonwealth*, (1907) 5 C.L.R., 174 ; 14 A.L.R., 1.

Commonwealth Public Service Act 1902 (No. 5 of 1902), sec. 46—Tenure of office of public servant—Conditions of exercise of power to dismiss—Civil servant dismissed

without observance of conditions—Whether entitled to declaration that he is still in the Service—Wrongful dismissal, remedy for.]— See PUBLIC SERVICE. ·Williamson v. The Commonwealth, (1907) 5 C.L.R., 174 ; 14 A.L.R., 1.

Wrongful dismissal of public servant— Damages—Liability to be dismissed rightfully—Whether an element in determining amount of damages—Commonwealth Public Service Act 1902 (No. 5 of 1902), sec. 46.]— See PUBLIC SERVICE. Williamson v. The Commonwealth, (1907) 5 C.L.R., 174 ; 14 A.L.R., 1.

Commonwealth Public Service Act 1902 (No. 5 of 1902), sec. 78—Public servant— Wrongful dismissal—Claim for damages— Money not voted by Parliament—Whether a defence.]—See PUBLIC SERVICE. Williamson v. The Commonwealth, (1907) 5 C.L.R., 174 ; 14 A.L.R., 1.

Railways Act 1890 (No. 1135), secs. 70, 86-88, 93 — Compensation, when employe entitled to—Employe not ready and willing to perform his contract—Removal of such employe — Ways in which contract with employe may be terminated.] — See RAILWAYS. Noonan v. Victorian Railways Commissioners, 4 C.L.R., Pt. 2, 1668 ; 13 A.L.R., 593.

Railways Act 1890 (No. 1135), sec. 93— Compensation, meaning of—Who entitled to— Employe deprived of his office through no fault of his own.]—See RAILWAYS. Noonan v. Victorian Railways Commissioners, 4 C.L.R., Pt. 2, 1668 ; 13 A.L.R., 593.

(e) Preferential Claims for Wages.

Mines Act 1897 (No. 1514), sec. 168—Mines Act 1904 (No. 1961), sec. 64—Mining company —Winding up—Assets insufficient to satisfy liabilities—Miners' wages—" Costs of administration or otherwise "—" Priority of payment."]—See MINING. In re Egerton and Gordon Consolidated Gold Mines, No Liability, (1908) V.L.R., 526 ; 30 A.L.T., 27 ; 14 A.L.R., 372.

Mines Act 1897 (No. 1514), sec. 168—Insolvency Act 1890 (No. 1102), sec. 115—Insol-

vency Act 1897 (No. 1513), sec. 79—Companies Act 1890 (No. 1074), secs. 250, 303— Mining Company—Assignment for benefit of creditors—Workmen's wages—Priority.]—See MINING. In re Old Jubilee Gold Mines, No Liability, 34 A.L.T. (Supplement), 2 ; 18 A.L.R. (C.N.), 21.

Company—Voluntary liquidation—Liquidation by the Court—Wages—Preferential claim —Period of four months, how calculated— Date of commencement of liquidation—Companies Act 1896 (No. 1482), sec. 148.]—See COMPANY. Re Australian Producers and Traders Ltd., (1908) V.L.R., 227 ; 29 A.L.T., 185 ; 14 A.L.R., 118.

Insolvency—Preferential claims—Wages— Small sum in hand—Question considered whether such money to be expended in payment of preferential claims or in costs of examination summons—Insolvency Act 1890 (No. 1102), secs. 40, 115, 123—Insolvency Act 1897 (No. 1513), sec. 111.]—See In re Wilson, 16 A.L.R. (C.N.), 17. Judge Moule (1910).

(f) Under Commonwealth Conciliation and Arbitration Acts.

(1) Validity of Legislation.

Commonwealth of Australia Constitution Act (63 & 64 Vict. c. 12)—The ˙Constitution, sec. 51 (xxxv.)—Arbitration in regard to industrial disputes—Extent of power of Commonwealth.]—See COMMONWEALTH OF AUSTRALIA CONSTITUTION, col. 121. The King and the Commonwealth Court of Conciliation and Arbitration and the President thereof and the Boot Trade Employes Federation ; Ex parte Whybrow & Co., (1910) 11 C.L.R., 1 ; 16 A.L.R., 373.

Commonwealth Conciliation and Arbitration Act 1904 (No. 13 of 1904)—Whether ultra vires of Parliament.]—See COMMONWEALTH OF AUSTRALIA CONSTITUTION, col. 124. The King and the Commonwealth Court of Conciliation and Arbitration and the President thereof and the Boot Trade Employes Federation ; Ex parte Whybrow & Co., (1910) 11 C.L.R., 1 ; 16 A.L.R., 373.

" Conciliation and Arbitration for the prevention and settlement of industrial disputes "

—Powers of Commonwealth—Common rule
—The Constitution (63 & 64 Vict. c. 12), sec.
51 (xxxv.), (xxxix.)—Commonwealth Conciliation and Arbitration Act (No. 13 of 1904),
secs. 19, 38 (f), (g) ; do. No. 7 of 1910).]—*See*
COMMONWEALTH OF AUSTRALIA CONSTITU-
TION, col. 122. *Australian Boot Trade
Employes' Federation* v. *Whybrow*, (1910)
11 C.L.R., 311 ; 16 A.L.R., 513.

**Commonwealth of Australia Constitution
Act (63 & 64 Vict. c. 12)—The Constitution,
sec. 51 (xxxv.)—Conciliation and arbitration
for prevention and settlement of industrial
disputes—Commonwealth Conciliation and
Arbitration Act 1904 (No. 13 of 1904)—
Validity.]**—*See* COMMONWEALTH OF AUS-
TRALIA CONSTITUTION, col. 122. *The King
and the Commonwealth Court of Conciliation
and Arbitration and the President thereof, and
the Boot Trade Employes Federation, Ex
parte Whybrow & Co.*, (1910) 11 C.L.R., 1 ;
16 A.L.R., 373.

**Commonwealth Conciliation and Arbitra-
tion Act 1904 (No. 13 of 1904), secs. 4, 9, 55,
58, 60, 65, 73—Registration of Association—
Validity of legislation—Association of employees in one State—Incorporation of organization—The Constitution (63 & 64 Vict. c.
12), sec. 51 (xxxv.), xxxix.).]**—The provisions
of the *Commonwealth Conciliation and Arbitration Act* 1904 in respect of the registration
of Associations as organizations, particularly
in so far as they permit the registration of
an Association of employers or employes in
an industry in one State only, and provide for
the incorporation of organizations when
registered, are valid as being incidental to the
power conferred on the Commonwealth
Parliament by sec. 51 (xxxv.) of the Constitution. *Jumbunna Coal Mine No Liability* v.
Victorian Coal Miners' Association, (1908)
6 C.L.R., 309 ; 14 A.L.R., 701. H.C.,
*Griffith, C.J., Barton. O'Connor and Isaacs,
JJ.*

(2) Commonwealth Court of Conciliation
and Arbitration.

(*a*) Jurisdiction.

**Commonwealth Conciliation and Arbitra-
tion Act 1904 (No. 13 of 1904), secs. 4, 7, 55—**

"Industry," meaning of.]—An " industry "
contemplated by the *Commonwealth Conciliation and Arbitration Act* 1904, means an
enterprise in which both employers and
employes are associated, and does not
include the vocation of persons doing a particular kind of work in connection with
several different classes of such enterprises.
Held, therefore (*per Griffith, C.J., Barton
and Isaacs, JJ., O'Connor and Higgins, JJ.,*
dissenting), that an Association of land
engine-drivers and firemen, whose members
were employed indiscriminately in mines, in
timber yards, in tanneries, in soap and
candle works, etc., was not under sec. 55 (1)
(*b*) entitled to be registered as an organization. *Federated Engine-Drivers and Firemen's Association of Australasia* v. *Broken
Hill Proprietary Co. Ltd.*, (1911) 12 C.L.R.,
398 ; 17 A.L.R., 285.

**Operation of the Constitution and laws of
the Commonwealth—Commonwealth Conciliation and Arbitration Act 1904 (No. 13
of 1904)—Jurisdiction of Court of Conciliation and Arbitration—Industrial dispute—
" Ships whose first port of clearance and whose
port of destination are in the Commonwealth "
—Commonwealth of Australia Constitution
Act (63 & 64 Vict. c. 12), sec. v]**—A joint
stock company registered in Victoria were
owners of a line of ships registered in Melbourne and engaged in trade between Australia, Calcutta and South Africa. The
officers of the company's ships resided in
Australia, and were engaged there, but the
ships' articles were filled in and signed in
Calcutta. The officers, though not entitled
to be discharged in Australian ports, were
allowed to leave at such ports if they wished,
with the consent of the master. The ships
did no inter-State trade, but occasionally
made short trips to other Indian ports. The
organization to which the officers belonged
filed a claim in the Commonwealth Court of
Conciliation and Arbitration for the settlement of a dispute between the officers and
their employers as to wages, hours, and conditions of labour during the voyages of their
ships. *Held*, that the Court had no jurisdiction to settle the dispute. Ships engaged
in such trade are not ships " whose first port

of clearance and whose port of destination are in the Commonwealth " within the meaning of sec. v. of the *Commonwealth of Australia Constitution Act. Merchant Service Guild of Australasia* v. *Archibald Currie & Co.,* (1908) 5 C.L.R., 737 ; 14 A.L.R., 438. H.C., *Griffith, C.J., Barton, O'Connor, Isaacs* and *Higgins, JJ.*

Commonwealth Conciliation and Arbitration Act 1904 (No. 13 of 1904)—Industrial dispute, what is—Commonwealth Constitution, sec. 51 (xxxv.).]—*Per Griffith, C.J.,* and *Barton, J.* :—A demand and a refusal is not of itself sufficient to establish the existence of a dispute. *Per Isaacs, J.* :—A dispute raised in a formal and complete way is to be taken *prima facie* as genuine and real. *The King and the Commonwealth Court of Conciliation and Arbitration and the President thereof and the Boot Trade Employes Federation* ; *Ex parte Whybrow,* (1910) 11 C.L.R., 1 ; 16 A.L.R., 373.

The Constitution (63 & 64 Vict. c. 12), sec. 51 (xxxv.)—Industrial dispute—" Extending beyond the limits of any one State."]—For observations as to the meaning of " Industry," " Industrial dispute " and " extending beyond the limits of any one State," see *Jumbunna Coal Mine No Liability* v. *Victorian Coal Miners' Association,* (1908) 6 C.L.R., 309 ; 14 A.L.R., 701.

Commonwealth Conciliation and Arbitration Act 1904 (No. 13 of 1904)—Claims in regard to matters in dispute—Joinder of claims in regard to matters not in dispute—Jurisdiction of Court of Conciliation and Arbitration—The Commonwealth Constitution, sec. 51 (xxxv.)]—A letter signed by the Secretary of the Australian Boot Trade Employes' Federation was sent to employers in four States, alleging that the persons employed by the respective employers were dissatisfied with their conditions of employment, and demanding that the conditions mentioned in a log annexed to the letter should be granted by the employer. These conditions had been previously adopted by the branches of the Federation in all the four States, and constituted a complete code for the regulation of the industry. Various dates were given

for replying to the demand. The conditions demanded not having been conceded within the time limited, the applicant Federation filed a plaint, alleging the pendency of a dispute extending beyond the limits of any one State as to various matters, and claiming in the terms of the log. The President found that only two of the twenty-three claims were really in dispute between the parties. *Held,* that the claim was severable, and that the Court of Conciliation and Arbitration had jurisdiction to deal with the matters found to be in dispute. *The King and the Commonwealth Court of Conciliation and Arbitration and the President thereof and the Boot Trade Employes Federation* ; *Ex parte Whybrow & Co.,* (1910) 11 C.L.R., 1 ; 16 A.L.R., 373. H.C., *Griffith, C.J., Barton, O'Connor* and *Isaacs, JJ.*

Conciliation and arbitration—Commonwealth Court—Jurisdiction—Award inconsistent with determination of Wages Board—The Constitution, sec. 51 (xxxv.).]—*Per Griffith, C.J., Barton* and *O'Connor, JJ.* (*Isaacs* and *Higgins, JJ.,* dissenting). The Commonwealth Court of Conciliation and Arbitration has no jurisdiction to make an award inconsistent with the determination of a Wages Board. But (*per totam curiam*) the Court may make an award fixing the minimum wage payable to journeymen at a higher rate than that fixed by the Wages Board. *Australian Boot Trade Employes Federation* v. *Whybrow,* (1910) 10 C.L.R., 266 ; 16 A.L.R., 185.

Factories and Shops Act 1909 (No. 2), (No. 2241), sec. 39—No person compellable to pay more than minimum wage unless he contract so to do—Jurisdiction of Commonwealth Court of Conciliation and Arbitration—How far affected by State legislation.]—The *Factories and Shops Act* 1909 (No. 2241), sec. 39, does not affect the power of the Commonwealth Court of Conciliation and Arbitration to fix wages and conditions of labour which are otherwise within its jurisdiction. *Australian Boot Trade Employes Federation* v. *Whybrow,* (1910) 10 C.L.R., 266 ; 16 A.L.R., 185. H.C., *Griffith, C.J., Barton, O'Connor, Isaacs* and *Higgins, JJ.*

Factories and Shops Acts—Determination of special board—Commonwealth Court of Conciliation and Arbitration, award of—Inconsistency with determination—Commonwealth of Australia Constitution Act (62 & 63 Vict. c. 12), sec. 51 (xxxv.).]—*See* FACTORIES AND SHOPS ACTS. *The Federated Sawmill, Timberyard and General Woodworkers Employes Association of Australasia* v. *James Moore & Sons Proprietary Ltd.*, 8 C.L.R., 465; 15 A.L.R., 374. [And see *Australian Boot Trade Employes Federation* v. *Whybrow & Co.*, (1910) 10 C.L.R., 266; 16 A.L.R., 185.]

Commonwealth Court of Conciliation and Arbitration—Award, validity of—Delegation of powers of Court to board of reference.]—An award of the Commonwealth Court of Conciliation and Arbitration provided that "persons bound under a deed of apprenticeship shall, if the subject of the apprenticeship is approved by the board of reference, be deemed to have been duly apprenticed." *Held*, (*Per Griffith, C.J., Barton, O'Connor* and *Isaacs, JJ.*), that the President could not delegate to the board of reference the question of the validity of the deeds of apprenticeship. *Per Isaacs, J.*—The President could not delegate to the Board the final decision as to the classification of the trade, which was one of the issues to be tried by the Court. *The King and the Commonwealth Court of Conciliation and Arbitration and the President thereof, and the Boot Trade Employes Federation; Ex parte Whybrow & Co.*, (1910) 11 C.L.R., 1; 16 A.L.R., 373.

Commonwealth Court of Conciliation and Arbitration—Award, validity of—Higher rate awarded than that demanded by claimants—Demand that wage of apprentice be based on experience—Wage awarded based on age and experience—Industrial dispute.]—In an industrial dispute brought before the Commonwealth Court of Conciliation and Arbitration the claimants demanded a rate of wages for apprentices fixed upon the basis of experience. *Held*, that the President had no jurisdiction to award a higher rate than was asked for. *Held*, also, (*per Griffith, C.J., Barton* and *O'Connor, JJ.*) that the payment of wages could not be fixed upon an age basis. *Per*

Isaacs, J.—In fixing the wage for apprentices the President had regarded both the age and experience of the apprentice, and the award in this respect was valid. *The King and the Commonwealth Court of Conciliation and Arbitration and the President thereof and the Boot Trade Employes Federation; Ex parte Whybrow & Co.*, (1910) 11 C.L.R., 1; 16 A.L.R., 373.

(b) Evidence.

Commonwealth Constitution, sec. 51 (xxxv.)—Industrial dispute extending beyond the limits of any one State.]—What constitutes evidence of an industrial dispute extending beyond the limits of any one State, considered. *The King and the Commonwealth Court of Conciliation and Arbitration and the President thereof and the Boot Trade Employes Federation; Ex parte Whybrow*, (1910) 11 C.L.R., 1; 16 A.L.R., 373. H.C.

Commonwealth Conciliation and Arbitration Act 1904 (No. 13 of 1904), sec. 21—Evidence—Registrar's certificate as to existence and extent of dispute—Whether evidence of existence of dispute.]—A certificate given by the Registrar under section 21 of the *Commonwealth Conciliation and Arbitration Act* 1904 that a dispute relating to industrial matters is an industrial dispute extending beyond the limits of one State is not evidence of the existence of an industrial dispute within the meaning of the Act. *Federated Engine-Drivers and Firemen's Association of Australasia* v. *Broken Hill Proprietary Co. Ltd.*, (1911) 12 C.L.R., 398; 17 A.L.R., 285. *Griffith, C.J., Barton, O'Connor, Isaacs* and *Higgins, JJ.*

Commonwealth Conciliation and Arbitration Act 1904 (No. 13 of 1904), sec. 57—Registrar's certificate of registration of organization—Whether conclusive evidence of validity of registration.]—A certificate of the Registrar of the Commonwealth Court of Conciliation and Arbitration of the registration of an organization given under section 57 of the *Commonwealth Conciliation and Arbitration Act* 1904 is not conclusive evidence of the validity of such registration. *Federated Engine Drivers and Firemen's Associa-*

tion of Australasia v. *Broken Hill Proprietary Co. Ltd.*, (1911) 12 C.L.R., 398 ; 17 A.L.R., 285. *Griffith, C.J., Barton, O'Connor, Isaacs* and *Higgins, JJ.*

(c) Prohibition ; Appeal ; Case Stated.

Commonwealth of Australia Constitution Act (63 & 64 Vict. c. 12)—The Constitution, secs. 71, 73, 75 (v.)—Commonwealth Conciliation and Arbitration Act 1904 (No. 13 of 1904), sec. 31—Judiciary Act 1903 (No. 6 of 1903), secs. 30, 33 (b), 38—Prohibition—Jurisdiction of High Court to issue to Commonwealth Court of Conciliation and Arbitration—Whether prohibition original or appellate jurisdiction.]—*See* APPEAL, col. 17. *The King and the Commonwealth Court of Conciliation and Arbitration and the President thereof and the Boot Trade Employes Federation ; Ex parte Whybrow & Co.*, (1910) 11 C.L.R., 1 ; 16 A.L.R., 373.

High Court—Practice—Motion for prohibition to restrain Commonwealth Court of Conciliation and Arbitration—Finding by President that dispute existed, whether High Court bound by—Commonwealth Constitution, sec. 51 (xxxv).]—*See* APPEAL, cols. 17, 18. *The King and the Commonwealth Court of Conciliation and Arbitration and the President thereof and the Boot Trade Employes Federation ; Ex parte Whybrow & Co.*, (1910) 11 C.L.R., 1 ; 16 A.L.R., 373.

The Constitution (63 & 64 Vict. c. 12), sec. 73—Appellate jurisdiction of High Court— Court of Conciliation and Arbitration—Commonwealth Conciliation and Arbitration Act 1904 (No. 13 of 1904), sec. 31.]—An appeal lies to the High Court from a decision of the President of the Commonwealth Court of Conciliation and Arbitration dismissing an appeal to him from a decision of the Industrial Registrar disallowing objections to the registration of an association under the *Commonwealth Conciliation and Arbitration Act 1904. Jumbunna Coal Mine N. L.* v. *Victorian Coal Miners Association*, (1908) 6 C.L.R., 309 ; 14 A.L.R., 701. H.C., *Griffith, C.J., Barton, O'Connor* and *Isaacs, JJ.*

Commonwealth Conciliation and Arbitra-

tion Act 1904 (No. 13 of 1904), sec. 31—Case stated for opinion of High Court—Duties of High Court and President respectively.]—*Per Higgins, J.*—It is the duty of the Court on a case stated under section 31 of the *Commonwealth Conciliation and Arbitration Act* 1904 to answer judicially the questions asked in pursuance of that section, and to leave the consequences of the answers to the President of the Court of Conciliation and Arbitration to determine. *Federated Engine Drivers and Firemen's Association of Australasia* v. *Broken Hill Proprietary Co. Ltd.*, (1911) 12 C.L.R., 398 ; 17 A.L.R., 285.

Commonwealth Court of Conciliation and Arbitration—Power of President to state case for opinion of High Court.]—For observations of the President of the Commonwealth Court of Conciliation and Arbitration as to his power to state a case for the opinion of the High Court, see *Jumbunna Coal Mine N. L.* v. *Victorian Coal Miners' Association*, (1908) 6 C.L.R., 309 ; 14 A.L.R., 701.

(y) *Under Factories and Shops Acts.*

(1) Factory, What is.

Factories and Shops Act 1905 (No. 1975), secs. 5, 14 (3)—" Factory or workroom "— "Preparing or manufacturing articles for sale "—Sorting weighing and packing goods.]—*See* FACTORIES AND SHOPS ACTS. *Alderson* v. *Gold*, (1909) V.L.R., 219 ; 30 A.L.T., 189 ; 15 A.L.R., 180.

(2) Special Boards ; Matters to be Considered in Making Determination.

See also, *post*, (c) COURT OF INDUSTRIAL APPEALS.

Factories and Shops Act 1905 (No. 1975), Parts IX. and X.—Special Boards—Court of Industrial Appeals—Minimum wage, determination of—Matters to be taken into consideration.]—*See* FACTORIES AND SHOPS ACTS. *In re the Starch Board*, 13 A.L.R., 558.

Factories and Shops Act 1905 (No. 1975), Pt. IX.—Minimum wage, determination of— Consideration of the merits of each particular case—Whether every adult male entitled as of right to at least £2 a week.]—*See* FACTORIES

AND SHOPS ACTS. *In re the Starch Board*, 13 A.L.R., 558.

Factories and Shops Act 1905 (No. 1975), Parts IX. and X.—Minimum wage, determination of—Matters to be taken into consideration —Competition amongst employers—State of trade.]—*See* FACTORIES AND SHOPS ACTS. *In re the Starch Board*, 13 A.L.R., 558.

Minimum wage, what is—Matters to be considered in determining—Factories and Shops Act 1905 (No. 1975), sec. 75—Court of Industrial Appeals.]—*See* FACTORIES AND SHOPS ACTS. *In re the Bread Board*, 13 A.L.R., 589.

Wages Boards—Factories and Shops Acts—Alterations of industrial conditions—Principles upon which they should be made.]—*See* FACTORIES AND SHOPS ACTS. *In re the Bread Board*. 13 A.L.R., 589.

Minimum wage, how to be determined—Alteration of—Matters to be considered—Circumstances of a temporary or fluctuating nature.]—*See* FACTORIES AND SHOPS ACTS. *In re the Bread Board*, 13 A.L.R., 589.

Wages Boards—Minimum wage, how to be determined—Cost of living, general increase in.]—*See* FACTORIES AND SHOPS ACTS. *In re the Bread Board*, 13 A.L.R., 589.

Minimum wage, how to be determined—Comparison with rates of wages paid in Victoria and in other States.]—*See* FACTORIES AND SHOPS ACTS. *In re the Bread Board*, 13 A.L.R., 589.

Factories and Shops Act 1905 (No. 1975), sec. 75—"Lowest prices or rates" what are —Principles of determination.]—*See* FACTORIES AND SHOPS ACTS. *In re Fellmongers' Board*, 15 A.L.R., 225.

Factories and Shops Act 1905 (No. 1975), sec. 75—"Lowest prices or rates" what are —Mode of ascertaining.]—*See* FACTORIES AND SHOPS ACTS. *In re Fellmongers' Board*, 15 A.L.R., 225.

Factories and Shops Act 1905 (No. 1975), sec. 75—"Lowest prices or rates which may be paid to persons employed in factories"— Provisions not confined to protected indus-

tries.]—*See* FACTORIES AND SHOPS ACTS. *In re Fellmongers' Board*, 15 A.L.R., 225.

Factories and Shops Acts—Minimum wage —Matters to be considered in determining.] —*See* FACTORIES AND SHOPS ACTS. *In re the Ice Board*, 16 A.L.R., 46.

Wages board—Lowest price or rates, how to be determined—Classification of work with regard to skill and onerousness &c.—Nature kind and class of work and mode and manner in which it is to be done.]—*See* FACTORIES AND SHOPS ACTS. *In re Boilermakers' Board*, 18 A.L.R., 399.

Wages board—Lowest prices or rates, how to be determined—Ability of individual worker. *See* FACTORIES AND SHOPS ACTS. *In re Boilermakers' Board*, 18 A.L.R., 399.

Wages board—Determination of lowest price or rate—Matters affecting—Cost of living —Evidence as to.]—*See* FACTORIES AND SHOPS ACTS. *In re Boilermakers' Board*, 18 A.L.R., 399.

Wages board—Lowest prices or rates— Current rate of wages—Agreement between employers and employes as evidence of.]— *See* FACTORIES AND SHOPS ACTS. *In re Boilermakers' Board*, 18 A.L.R., 399.

Factories and Shops Act 1905—Maximum number of hours.]—*See* FACTORIES AND SHOPS ACTS. *In re Fellmongers' Board*, 15 A.L.R., 225.

(3) Court of Industrial Appeals.

Court of Industrial Appeals — Appeal, whether in the nature of a re-hearing—Factories and Shops Act 1905 (No. 1975), sec. 122.] —*See* FACTORIES AND SHOPS ACTS. *In re the Bread Board*, 13 A.L.R., 589.

Factories and Shops Act 1905 (No. 1975), sec. 122—Court of Industrial Appeals—Factories and Shops Act 1907 (No. 2137), sec. 33 —Appeal, nature of—Re-hearing—Whether Court confined to materials before Wages Board.]—*See* FACTORIES AND SHOPS ACTS. *In re the Ice Board*, 16 A.L.R., 46.

Court of Industrial Appeals—Evidence on hearing of appeal.]—*See* FACTORIES AND

SHOPS ACTS. *In re the Bread Board*, 13 A.L.R., 589.

Court of Industrial Appeals—Purpose of its existence—Principles governing its administration—Absence of absolute discretion.]—*See* FACTORIES AND SHOPS ACTS. *In re Fellmongers' Board*, 15 A.L.R., 225.

Factories and Shops Act (No. 1975), sec. 122—" Living wage "—How to be estimated.] —*See* FACTORIES AND SHOPS ACTS. *In re the Starch Board*, 13 A.L.R., 558.

Factories and Shops Act 1905 (No. 1975), sec. 122—" Living wage "—Personal not family wage.]—*See* FACTORIES AND SHOPS ACTS. *In re Fellmongers' Board*, 15 A.L.R., 225.

Factories and Shops Act 1905 (No. 1975), secs. 83, 122—Reference of determination to Court of Industrial Appeals—Average prices paid by reputable employers insufficient to afford a reasonable limit—Principles upon which Court should act—Whether determination may prejudice the progress &c. of the trade.]—*See* FACTORIES AND SHOPS ACTS. *In re the Starch Board*, 13 A.L.R., 558.

Factories and Shops Act 1905 (No. 1975), sec. 122—Court of Industrial Appeals— Whether the determination may prejudice the progress, maintenance of or scope of employment in the trade concerned—What to be considered.]—*See* FACTORIES AND SHOPS ACTS. *In re the Starch Board*, 13 A.L.R., 558.

Factories and Shops Act 1905 (No. 1975), sec. 122—Determination alleged to prejudice progress maintenance of or scope of employment in industry—Appeal to Court of Industrial Appeals—In respect of what matters it may be brought.]—*See* FACTORIES AND SHOPS ACTS. *In re Boilermakers' Board*, 18 A.L.R., 399.

(4) Weekly Half-Holiday; Conditions of Employment in Shops.

Factories and Shops Act 1905 (No. 1975), sec. 134—Suspension of provisions as to closing—Who may revoke.]—*See* FACTORIES AND SHOPS ACTS. *Billingham* v. *Gaff*, (1907) V.L.R., 691 ; 29 A.L.T., 159 ; 13 A.L.R., 474.

Factories and Shops Act 1905 (No. 1975), sec. 134—Keeping shop open when it should be closed—Whether necessary to prove a sale of goods.]—*See* FACTORIES AND SHOPS ACTS. *Billingham* v. *Gaff*, (1907) V.L.R., 691 ; 29 A.L.T., 159 ; 13 A.L.R., 474.

Factories and Shops Act 1905 (No. 1975), sec. 149—Sitting accommodation for employes—Sufficiency of—Seats provided for customers—Employes at liberty to use.]— *See* FACTORIES AND SHOPS ACTS. *Trainor* v. *Younger*, 28 A.L.T., 171 ; 13 A.L.R., 50.

(5) Hours of Labour.

Factory—Restriction of hours of labour— " Work," meaning of—Factories and Shops Act 1905 (No. 1975), secs. 5, 42.]—*See* FACTORIES AND SHOPS ACTS. *Ingham* v. *Hie Lee*, (1912) 15 C.L.R., 267 ; 18 A.L.R., 453.

Factories and Shops—Carters and drivers— Carting during prohibited hours—Empties carted back to stable—Carting goods " from outside a city "—Factories and Shops Act 1907 (No. 2137), sec. 40—Factories and Shops Act 1909 (No. 2184), sec. 12—Factories and Shops Act 1910 (No. 2305), sec. 38.]—*See* FACTORIES AND SHOPS ACTS. *Pemberton* v. *Banfield*, (1912) 15 C.L.R., 323 ; 18 A.L.R., 486.

(6) Apprentices and Improvers.

Indentures of apprenticeship, what are— Writing not under seal—Factories and Shops Act 1903 (No. 1857), sec. 7.]—The term " indentures of apprenticeship" have no specific legal significance, and will include a writing not under seal. *Quaere*, whether such term in sec. 7 of the *Factories and Shops Act* 1903 is limited to agreements under seal. *Hines* v. *Phillips*, (1906) V.L.R., 417 ; 28 A.L.T., 1 ; 12 A.L.R., 249. *a' Beckett, A.-C.J.* (1906).

Factories and Shops Act 1900 (No. 1654), secs. 4, 15—Factories and Shops Act 1903 (No. 1857), sec. 7—" Improver," who is— Apprentice under indentures or agreement not binding employer to instruct for not less than three years.]—*See* FACTORIES AND SHOPS ACTS. *Hines* v. *Phillips*, (1906) V.L.R., 417 ; 28 A.L.T., 1 ; 12 A.L.R., 249.

Factories and Shops Act 1903 (No. 1857), sec. 7—Factories and Shops Act 1900 (No. 1654), secs. 4, 15, 22—Indentures of apprenticeship binding employer to instruct, what are—Agreement to employ an " apprentice " in connection with employer's business—No clause binding employer to instruct—Nature of business not described.]—*See* FACTORIES AND SHOPS ACTS. *Hines* v. *Phillips*, (1906) V.L R., 417; 28 A.L.T., 1; 12 A.L.R., 249.

(7) Legal Proceedings.

Factories and Shops Act 1905 (No. 1975), sec. 162 (c)—Factories and Shops Act 1905 (No. 2) (No. 2008), sec. 9—Conviction against firm in firm name—Rules under the Justice Act 1890, rr. 18, 20—Information, form of.]— *See* CONVICTION. *Bishop* v. *Chung Brothers*, 4 C.L.R., 1262; 13 A.L.R., 412.

Factories and Shops Act 1905 (No. 1975), sec. 119 (1)—Employing person at lower rate than rate determined by Special Board—Mens rea, whether a necessary element of offence— Employer, liability of for act of agent.]—*See* FACTORIES AND SHOPS ACT. *Billingham* v. *Oaten*, (1911) V.L.R., 44; 32 A.L.T., 170; 17 A.L.R., 36.

II.—RIGHTS AND LIABILITIES OF EMPLOYER AND THIRD PARTY.

(a) *Negligence of Employe.*

Licensed carriages—By-law 78 of the City of Melbourne—Regulation prohibiting owner from entrusting licensed carriage to any person except as his servant—Prima facie presumption of relation of master and servant.]— Although every owner licensed under by-law 78 of the City of Melbourne, which provides that . no owner of a licensed carriage shall entrust it to any person as driver except as his servant, is presumed to have obeyed the by-law, the presumption is not irrebuttable, and, therefore, the fact that a person other than the owner is driving such carriage is not conclusive evidence that such person is the servant of the owner. *Clutterbuck* v. *Curry*, 11 V.L.R., 810, followed; *Gates* v. *Bill*, (1902) 2 K.B., 38, distinguished. *McKinnon* v. *Gange*, (1910) V.L.R., 32; 31 A.L.T., 112; 15 A.L.R., 640. *Madden, C.J., Hood* and *Cussen, JJ.*

Pounds Act 1890 (No. 1129), secs. 4 to 9, 18 to 22, 28—Duties imposed by Act on poundkeeper—Liability of municipality—Master and servant.]—When performing the duties imposed upon him by the *Pounds Act* 1890, a poundkeeper duly appointed by a municipality is acting as a public officer, and not as a servant of the municipality, and consequently the municipality is not liable for his acts in discharging such duties. *Ryan* v. *Swan Hill, President, &c., of*, 28 A.L.T. (Supplement), 17; 13 A.L.R. (C.N.), 17. *Judge Eagleson* (1907).

(b) *Criminal Liability of Employer.*

See also, FACTORIES AND SHOPS ACT.

Poisons Act 1890 (No. 1125), secs. 4, 11— Sale of poison by unqualified person—Sale by assistant—Offence by master.]—*See* POISONS ACT. *Shillinglaw* v. *Redmond*, (1908) V.L.R., 427; 30 A.L.T., 37; 14 A.L.R., 343.

Pure Food Act 1903 (No. 2010), secs. 32, 35, 36—Adulterated article of food, sale of—Sale by servant—Reasonable precautions by master against committing offence.]—*See* HEALTH (PUBLIC). *O'Connor* v. *Jenner*, (1909) V.L.R. 468; 31 A.L.T., 71; 15 A.L.R., 519.

Licensing Act 1890 (No. 1111), sec. 124— Licensing Act 1906 (No. 2068), sec. 73—Licensee, liability for act of servant—Supplying liquor to person in state of intoxication— Supply by servant in absence without the knowledge and contrary to instructions of licensee.] *See* LICENSING. *Davies* v. *Young*, (1910) V.L.R., 369; 32 A.L.T., 39 ;16 A.L.R., 368.

III.—RIGHTS AND LIABILITY OF EMPLOYE AND THIRD PARTY.

(a) *Discharge of Employe*; *Liability for Procuring.*

Action, cause of—Inducing employer to discharge employe from his employment— Interference—Lawful Justification or excuse Intention to injure—Malice—Self-interest— Trade Union—Secretary.]—It is not actionable for one person acting in his own interest and without malice, merely to induce another not to employ a particular individual, without procuring a breach of contract and without threats, coercion, violence or other unlawful

15

means. The plaintiff was employed by the hour in discharging cargo from a ship. He had a reasonable expectation of being continued in such employment until the work upon which he was engaged was completed. The defendant was secretary of a trade union which had an agreement with the plaintiff's employer providing that members of the union only should be employed in certain events in discharging cargo from certain ships. The plaintiff was not a member of that union. The defendant informed the plaintiff's employer that the plaintiff was not a member of the union, and advised him to cease to employ the plaintiff further. In consequence of that advice the employer did not re-employ the plaintiff. The defendant acted in the interests and for the benefit of his union and to save the plaintiff's employer from the consequences of a breach of his contract with the union, and not with the intention of injuring the plaintiff. *Held*, that the plaintiff had no cause of action against the defendant. *Allen* v. *Flood*, (1898) A.C., 1, followed. *Read* v. *Friendly Society of Operative Stonemasons*, (1902) 2 K.B., 732, and *South Wales Miners' Federation* v. *Glamorgan Coal Co.*, (1905) A.C., 239, distinguished. *Bond* v. *Morris*, (1912) V.L.R., 351; 34 A.L.T., 52; 18 A.L.R., 348. F.C., *Madden, C.J., Hodges* and *Hood, JJ.*

(b) *Criminal Liability of Employe.*

See also, CRIMINAL LAW, X.—LARCENY.

Embezzlement—Secretary of Friendly Society—Moneys of trustees—No relation of master and servant.]—*See* CRIMINAL LAW. *Rex* v. *M'Auslan*, (1907) V.L.R., 710; 29 A.L.T., 83; 13 A.L.R., 609.

EQUITABLE ASSIGNMENT.

Contract—Interpretation—Agreement to deposit time-payment agreements as security—Depositor allowed to collect debts due—Deposit of additional time-payment agreements equal in value to those discharged by payment—Equitable assignment—Book Debts Act 1896 (No. 1424), secs. 2, 3—Non-registration.]—*See* ASSIGNMENT, col. 57. *In re Jones*, (1906)

V.L.R., 432; 27 A.L.T., 230; 12 A.L.R., 279.

Book debt—Assignment—Future debt—Money to become payable by agent to principal on sale of goods—Book Debts Act 1896 (No. 1424), secs. 2, 3.]—*See* ASSIGNMENT, cols. 57, 58. *Shackell* v. *Howe, Thornton & Palmer*, (1909) 8 C.L.R., 170: 15 A.L.R., 176.

Equitable assignment—Advance of purchase money by salesman to purchaser—Agreement that advance shall be deducted from proceeds of future re-sale by salesman on purchaser's behalf.]—X., a cattle salesman, for a principal sold cattle to A., a dealer, advancing purchase money himself and receiving from A. a promissory note for the amount of the advance. As part of the transaction, it was agreed that A. would re-sell the cattle through X., who might repay himself the amount of the advance out of the proceeds of the re-sale. *Quaere*, whether such agreement amounted to an assignment to X. of the purchase money which might be paid on the re-sale of the cattle. *Per Isaacs, J.* :— "It was in my opinion an equitable assignment to secure X. Being verbal, it is not struck by Part VI. of the *Instruments Act* 1890. Applying not to any "debt" owing by a possible purchaser, but to the proceeds when either in the hands of A or his agent, it was not concerning a "book debt" within the meaning of the *Book Debts Act* 1896. Consequently, it was an assignment which, on the principle of *Alexander* v. *Steinhardt, Walker & Co.*, (1903) 2 K.B., 208, and *Palmer* v. *Culverwell, Brooks & Co.*, 85 L.T., 758, and other cases of that class, gave as between X. and A., an equitable security to X." *Muntz* v. *Smail*, 8 C.L.R., 262; 15 A.L.R., 162. High Court, *Griffith, C.J., Barton, O'Connor* and *Isaacs, JJ.* (1909).

Assignment—Deposit of Savings Bank pass book and order for payment out of money in Bank—Debt in connection with business carried on by assignor—Book Debts Act 1896 (No. 1424), sec. 2 (a).]—*See* ASSIGNMENT, cols. 58, 59. *Cox* v. *Smail*, (1912) V.L.R., 274; 18 A.L.R., 299.

Supreme Court Act 1890 (No. 1142), sec. 63 (6)—Order III., r. 6 (Rules of 1906)—Order XIV.—Debt or liquidated demand—Assignment of debt—No written notice of assignment.]—*See* ASSIGNMENT, col. 59. *Caddy* v. *Beattie*, (1908) V.L.R., 17; 29 A.L.T., 165; 13 A.L.R., 643.

Assignment of debt—No written notice of assignment—Proceedings by assignee—Parties.]—*See* ASSIGNMENT, col. 59. *Caddy* v. *Beattie*, (1908) V.L.R., 17; 29 A.L.T., 165; 13 A.L.R., 643.

Equitable assignment of mortgage—Amount repaid by stranger—Preservation of incumbrance.]—Where a mortgage is paid off by a stranger to the mortgagor, and no re-conveyance is executed, the mortgage may, in certain circumstances, be presumed to be kept alive in favour of the person paying off. *Butler* v. *Rice*, (1910) 2 Ch., 277, applied. *Cuddigan* v. *Poole*, 33 A.L.T., 210; 18 A.L.R., 120. *a' Beckett, J.* (1912).

EQUITABLE CHARGE.

See CHARGE.

EQUITABLE ESTATES AND INTERESTS.

See ASSIGNMENT; MORTGAGOR AND MORTGAGEE; TRUSTS AND TRUSTEES; WILL.

EQUITABLE MORTGAGE.

Life assurance—Equitable mortgage of policy—Evidence—Pleading—Amendment to raise new case.]—*See* MORTGAGOR AND MORTGAGEE. *Trengrouse & Co.* v. *Story*, (1908) 6 C.L.R., 10; 14 A.L.R., 420.

Mortgage — Equitable security — Amount repaid by a stranger—Preservation of incumbrance.]—*See* MORTGAGOR AND MORTGAGEE. *Cuddigan* v. *Poole*, 33 A.L.T., 210; 18 A.L.R., 120.

ESTATE.

See also, TENANT FOR LIFE AND REMAINDERMAN; TRUSTS AND TRUSTEES; WILL.

Station property—Management of by trustees—Tenant for life and remainderman—Capital and income, distinction between—Preservation of capital.]—*See* TRUSTS AND TRUSTEES. *In re Moore*; *Fanning* v. *Fanning*, (1907) V.L.R., 639; 29 A.L.T., 138; 13 A.L.R., 507.

Improvements to station property—Expenditure, adjustment between capital and income—Tenant for life and remainderman.]—*See* TRUSTS AND TRUSTEES. *In re Moore*; *Fanning* v. *Fanning*, (1907) V.L.R., 639; 29 A.L.T., 138; 13 A.L.R., 507.

Excess of expenditure over income—Deficiency met by drawing on capital—Life tenant entitled to income of capital so used—Recoupment of capital out of income—Tenant for life and remainderman.]—*See* TRUSTS AND TRUSTEES. *In re Moore*; *Fanning* v. *Fanning*, (1907) V.L.R., 639; 29 A.L.T., 138; 13 A.L.R., 507.

Settlement, construction of—Life estate to A.—Remainder to children of A.—Gift over of share of child dying without issue—Rule against perpetuities—Gift void by—Subsequent limitation whether also void—Gift over in default of grandchildren—Whether it includes gift over in default of children.]—*See* SETTLEMENT. *Milligan* v. *Shaw*, (1907) V.L.R., 668; 29 A.L.T., 75; 13 A.L.R., 545.

ESTOPPEL.

Res judicata—Judgment—Finding of fact, whether conclusive in other proceedings against another party—Finding of fact as to status—Prohibited immigrant—Immigration Restriction Act 1901 (No. 17).]—*See* EVIDENCE. *Christie* v. *Ah Sheung*, (1906) 3 C.L.R., 998; 12 A.L.R., 432.

Supreme Court Act 1890 (No. 1142), sec. 231—Privy Council—Appealable amount— " Matter in issue," what is—Assumption that contention of unsuccessful party was correct—Res judicata—Uncontradicted affidavits.]—See APPEAL, cols. 15, 16. *In re "Maizo" and "Maizena" Trade Marks; Robert Harper & Co. v. National Starch Co.* (1906) V.L.R., 246 ; 27 A.L.T., 168 ; 12 A.L.R., 164.

Marriage Act 1890 (No. 1166), secs. 42, 43—Illegitimate child without adequate means of support—Dismissal of previous complaint.]—*Semble.*—That the mere fact that a complaint against a father for leaving his child without adequate means of support has been dismissed, does not entitle the defendant to plead *res judicata* to a similar complaint subsequently laid against him. *Russ v. Carr*, 30 A.L.T., 131. *Hodges, J.* (1908).

Justices Act 1890 (No. 1105), secs. 4, 59 (3)—Complaint for detention of goods—Refusal to make order—Dismissal—Second complaint for same cause of action—Estoppel.]—*See* JUSTICES OF THE PEACE. *McMahon v. Johnston*, (1909) V.L.R., 376 ; 31 A.L.T., 36 ; 15 A.L.R., 371.

Director with contractual rights against company—Concurrence in acts rendering company unable to perform contract—Whether a waiver of rights of director.]—The mere concurrence of a person in his capacity of director of a company in acts which render such company unable to perform a contract then existing between him and the company, does not amount to a waiver by him of his personal rights in respect of a breach of contract by the company resulting from such acts. *Glass v. Pioneer Rubber Works of Australia Ltd.*, (1906) V.L.R., 754 ; 28 A.L.T., 64 ; 12 A.L.R., 529. F.C., *a' Beckett, A.-C.J., Hodges* and *Chomley, JJ.*

Company — Shares — Certificate stating shares fully paid up—Incorrectness of statement—Purchaser without actual notice—Estoppel—Constructive notice—Articles of Association.]—Where a company has issued a certificate for shares which states that such shares are fully paid up, the company and the liquidator of the Company are estopped from alleging any mistake or inaccuracy in such statement as against a person who has been thereby induced to believe that such shares were fully paid up, and, acting on that belief and without knowledge of any liability on the shares, purchased them as fully paid up shares. Such estoppel applies even where the Company has acted *ultra vires* in issuing the shares as fully paid up. Such purchaser is not to be presumed to have had notice from the Articles of Association that such shares were not fully paid up ; nor, where there was nothing to excite suspicion, was there any obligation on him to search the Articles in order to see if the statement in the certificate was true or false. *In re Victoria Silicate Brick Co. Ltd. (in Liquidation); Ex parte Martin*, (1913) V.L.R., 71 ; 34 A.L.T., 110 ; 18 A.L.R., 557. F.C., *a' Beckett, Hodges* and *Cussen, JJ.* (1912).

Insolvency Act 1890 (No. 1102), sec. 37 (1)—Act of insolvency—Assignment for benefit of creditors generally—No objection raised by creditor—Whether estopped from treating assignment as act of insolvency.]—*See* INSOLVENCY. *In re Knights; Ex parte Purcell*, (1910) V.L.R., 188 ; 31 A.L.T., 178 ; 16 A.L.R., 184.

Estoppel—Insolvency—Act of insolvency—Deed of assignment for the benefit of creditors generally—Creditor acquiescing in deed—Delay, effect of—Insolvency Act 1890 (No. 1102), sec. 37 (1).]—*See* INSOLVENCY. *In re Camp*, (1910) V.L.R., 42 ; 31 A.L.T., 126 ; 15 A.L.R., 642.

Promissory note—Liability of indorser—Indorsement by payee—Holder in due course—Estoppel—Instruments Act 1890 (No. 1103), secs. 20, 38, 55, 56, 57 and 90.]—*See* BILLS OF EXCHANGE AND PROMISSORY NOTES, cols. 76, 77. *Ferrier v. Stewart*, (1912) 15 C.L.R., 32 ; 18 A.L.R., 262.

Surrender of tenancy by operation of law—Acceptance of fresh lease.]—*See Knott v. McKendrick*, 28 A.L.T. (Supplement) 4 ; 12 A.L.R. (C.N.), 23. *Judge Box* (1906).

EVIDENCE.

I.—Function of Judge and Jury.

Patent—Prior publication—Document, interpretation of—Duty of Court—Evidence, admissibility of.]—Where a patent is challenged on the ground of alleged prior publication contained in a document, the interpretation of the document is, subject to proof of the state of common knowledge amongst persons familiar with the subject-matter at the time of publication, and of the meaning of technical terms, a question of law for the Court. *Betts* v. *Menzies*, 10 H.L.C., 117, and *Anglo-American Brush Electric Light Corporation* v. *King, Brown & Co.*, (1892) A.C., 367, applied. *N. Guthridge Ltd.* v. *Wilfley Ore Concentrator Syndicate Ltd.*, 3 C.L.R., 583; 12 A.L.R., 398. H.C., *Griffith, C.J., Barton* and *O'Connor, JJ.* (1906).

Evidence—Guilty knowledge, evidence of—Course of dealing—Isolated acts only proved—Judge's duty.]—Where, to show guilty knowledge, evidence is admitted of an act which, if followed by other similar acts might show a course of dealing on the part of the person doing the act, but no evidence of such subsequent acts is given, it is the duty of the Judge to strike out the evidence so given and to warn the jury to disregard it. *Rex* v. *O'Kane*, (1910) V.L.R., 8; 31 A.L.T., 110; 15 A.L.R., 628. F.C., *Madden, C.J., Hood* and *Cussen, JJ.*

Evidence, uncontradicted—Obligation of Court to accept—When obligation arises.]— Where uncontradicted evidence, which is inherently reasonable, probable, and conclusive of the matter, has been given, the Court is bound to accept it; but it is not bound to accept evidence, even though uncontradicted, which is in itself inherently unreasonable and improbable, or is hesitating, doubting, shuffling, inconclusive and unconvincing. *Stephens* v. *Mc Kenzie*, 29 V.L.R., 652; 25 A.L.T., 239; 10 A.L.R., 106, and *Richards* v. *Jager*, (1909) V.L.R., 140; 30 A.L.T., 163; 15 A.L.R., 119, approved. *Swinburne* v. *David Syme & Co.*, (1909) V.L.R., 550; 31 A.L.T., 81; 15 A.L.T., 579. F.C., *Madden, C.J., a' Beckett* and *Hood, JJ.*

Uncontradicted evidence—Decision of Justices against—Duty to give reasons.]—Justices are not at liberty, by disregarding uncontradicted evidence before them, to find a verdict against it unless they at the same time give some definite reasons justifying their decision. *Richards* v. *Jager*, (1909) V.L.R., 140; 30 A.L.T., 163; 15 A.L.R., 119. *Madden, C.J.*

Insolvency—Evidence of insolvent—Weight to be attached to.]—When an insolvent is intelligent, honest and desirous of telling the truth, his statement that the transaction attacked was not entered into with a view to prefer the particular creditor should be treated as of great weight. *Cox* v. *Smail*, (1912) V.L.R., 274; 18 A.L.R., 299.

Evidence—Trial by jury—Credibility of witnesses—Jury entitled to believe part only of a witness's evidence.]—Where the accuracy of a witness's testimony is disputed, the jury is not bound to believe the evidence of any witness, or to believe the whole of the evidence of any witness. Rule laid down by Lord *Blackburn* in *Dublin, Wicklow and Wexford Railway Co.* v. *Slattery*, (1878) 3 A.C., 1155, at p. 1201. *Farrands* v. *Mayor, &c., of Melbourne*, (1909) V.L.R., 531; 31 A.L.T., 78; 15 A.L.R., 520. F.C., *Madden, C.J., Hodges* and *Cussen, JJ.*

II.—Burden of Proof.

Patent—Burden of proof—Want of novelty by reason of prior sales—Identity of articles so sold with articles made in accordance with patent—Identity proved by circumstantial evidence only—Facts within exclusive knowledge of other party, failure to prove.]—In an action for infringement of a patent for an improved hood for incandescent gas burners, the defendant raised the defence of want of novelty by reason of sales by the inventor to the public prior to the grant of the patent. The evidence for the defence to establish the identity of hoods sold prior to the grant of the patent with hoods manufactured in accordance therewith did not include any chemical analysis of the hoods, but consisted of the testimony of a salesman engaged in the trade who had sold on behalf of the plaintiff's agent many hoods before the grant of the patent, and who since the grant had been for a long time engaged in the sale of hoods which were undoubtedly manufactured in accordance with the patent, and who said there was not so far as he could see any difference in the shape of the hoods or in the brilliancy of the light they gave or the quantity of the light they diffused. *Held*, that the natural inference from the evidence was that hoods made in accordance with plaintiff's patent were in use before the grant thereof; and therefore that in the absence of evidence by the plaintiff that the hoods supplied before the grant of the patent were of a different kind and made according to different specification, the defence of want of novelty had been sustained. *Cullen* v. *Welsbach Light Co. of Australasia Ltd.*, 4 C.L.R., Pt. 2, 990; 13 A.L.R., 194. H.C., *Griffith, C.J., Barton, O' Connor* and *Higgins, JJ.* (1907).

Burden of proof—Evidence of negligence—Level crossing on railway—Neglect of engine-driver to whistle—Duty of persons using road to look for approaching trains.]—In an action for negligence where the evidence called for the plaintiff is equally consistent with the wrong complained of having been caused by the negligence of the plaintiff, and with its having been caused by the negligence of the defendant, the case should not be left to a jury. Where a railway crosses a road at a level crossing without gates, and an approaching train is visible from all material positions to persons about to pass over the crossing, although it is the duty of the owners of the railway to take reasonable precautions to prevent such persons from being injured by trains, it is equally the duty of such persons to look for approaching trains, and they are not excused from looking by the omission of precautions on the part of the owners of the railway. *Fraser* v. *The Victorian Railways Commissioners*, 8 C.L.R., 54 ; 15 A.L.R., 93. High Court, *Griffith, C.J., Barton, O'Connor* and *Isaacs, JJ.* (1909).

Burden of proof—Land held in fee simple to be used only for a public racecourse—Member of public claiming right to enter land—Victoria Racing Club Act 1871 (No. 398), secs. 7-20.]—As to the burden of proof, where the plaintiff, a member of the public, claims the right to enter on race days land on which a racecourse is situated, and the defendant is the legal owner in fee simple, but, under a Statute, holds the land to be used as a public racecourse, and for that purpose only. *See Colman* v. *Miller*, (1906) V.L.R., 622 ; 28 A.L.T., 35 ; 12 A.L.R., 386. F.C., *Hodges, Hood* and *Chomley, JJ.*

Husband and wife—Maintenance—Former marriage—Husband not heard of for more than seven years—Proof of invalidity of second marriage—Onus—Marriage Act 1890 (No. 1166), secs. 43, 46.]—Where upon the hearing, under sec. 43 of the *Marriage Act* 1890, of a complaint by a woman that she had been left by her husband, the defendant, without means of support, the complainant proves a marriage with the defendant which would be valid if a former husband were not in existence, the onus of proving the invalidity of such marriage is on the defendant, who denies its validity. *Ousley* v. *Ousley*, (1912) V.L.R , 32 ; 33 A.L.T., 155 ; 18 A.L.R., 5. *a'Beckett, J.*

Infant—Custody of—Father's rights—Child in custody of others—Abdication—Welfare of child — Burden of proof.]—*See* INFANT.

Goldsmith v. *Sands*, 4 C.L.R., 1648 ; 13 A.L.R., 601.

Defamation — Privileged occasion — Presumption that speaker had a proper motive—Burden of proof.]—*See* DEFAMATION. *Ronald* v. *Harper*, (1910) 11 C.L.R., 63 ; 16 A.L.R., 415.

Local Government Act 1903 (No. 1893), secs. 455, 456—Contract—Consideration—Tender—Deposit—Forfeiture—Withdrawal of tender before acceptance—Mode of making contract—Burden of proof.]—*See* CONTRACT OR AGREEMENT, col. 193. *Stafford* v. *South Melbourne, Mayor, &c., of*, (1908) V.L.R., 584 ; 30 A.L.T., 43 ; 14 A.L.R., 464.

Licensing Act 1890 (No. 1111), secs. 134, 135—Licensing Act 1906 (No. 2068), sec. 78 (2)—Unlawful sale of liquor—Prima facie evidence of sale of liquor—Presence of two or more persons on licensed premises—Onus of proof as to lodgers, &c.]—Where in a prosecution for a breach of sec. 134 of the *Licensing Act* 1890 the informant relies on sec. 78 (2) of the *Licensing Act* 1906, which makes the presence of two or more persons on licensed premises *prima facie* evidence of a sale of liquor having taken place, the onus is on the informant to prove that the persons shown to have been upon the licensed premises of the defendant did not come within the excepted classes mentioned in section 78 (2). *Semble.*—Evidence that such persons resided in the locality of the licensed premises will *prima facie* discharge that onus. *Biggs* v. *Cunningham*, (1907) V.L.R., 344 ; 29 A.L.T., 14 ; 13 A.L.R., 244. *Cussen, J.* (1907).

Licensing Act 1890 (No. 1111), secs. 134, 135—Licensing Act 1906 (No. 2068), sec. 78 (2)—Unlawful sale of liquor—Evidence—Presence on licensed premises of two or more persons—Onus of proof as to bona fide lodgers, &c.]—Where on an information against a licensed person for selling liquor on Sunday, the informant does not prove that any individual was supplied with liquor, but relies on sec. 78 (2) of the *Licensing Act* 1906, he must prove not only the presence on the licensed premises of two or more persons, but also that such persons were persons other than *bona fide* lodgers, weekly or other boarders, travellers, inmates or servants. The provision as to burden of proof contained in the first part of sec. 135 of the *Licensing Act* 1890 applies only where the prosecution proves that some individual was supplied with liquor. *Cahill* v. *Millett*, (1907) V.L.R., 605 ; 29 A.L.T., 16 ; 13 A.L.R., 375. *Hodges, J.* (1907).

Factories and Shops Act 1905 (No. 1975), sec. 134—Factories and Shops Act 1905 (No. 2) (No. 2008), secs. 22, 24—Weekly half-holiday—Whether time of closing on Wednesday 1 o'clock or 6 o'clock—Choice of shop-keeper, burden of proof of.]—By the conjoint operation of secs. 22 and 24 of the *Factories and Shops Act* 1905 (No. 2) 1 o'clock on Wednesday is to be deemed to be the closing time for shops (other than Fourth Schedule shops) except those in respect of which the shopkeeper may have chosen 6 o'clock as the time of closing on that day, and in a prosecution for keeping his shop open after 1 o'clock on that day the onus is on the shopkeeper to show that he has made that choice. *Billingham* v. *Gaff*, (1907) V.L.R., 691 ; 29 A.L.T., 159 ; 13 A.L.R., 474. *Hodges, J.* (1907).

Police Offences Act 1890 (No. 1126), secs. 49, 51—" Business," assisting in conducting—Club incorporated as company—Shareholders in company members of Club—Totalisator—Whether conducted as a business—Percentage of stakes retained—Burden of proof—Moneys received as consideration for an assurance to pay moneys on contingencies relating to horse races.]—*See* GAMING AND WAGERING. *O'Donnell* v. *Solomon*, (1906) V.L.R., 425 ; 27 A.L.T., 237 ; 12 A.L.R., 283.

Lotteries Gaming and Betting Act 1906 (No. 2055), sec. 61—Evidence of certain facts made prima facie evidence of commission of offence—Procedural provision—Whether applicable to offences committed before passing of Act.]—*Quaere*, whether sec. 61 of the *Lotteries Gaming and Betting Act* 1906, being procedural, would not apply to offences committed before that Act. *Knox* v. *Thomas Bible* ; *Knox* v. *J. L. Bible*, (1907) V.L.R., 485 ; 29 A.L.T., 23 ; 13 A.L.R., 352. *Cus-*

sen, J. Special leave to appeal to High Court refused, 4 C.L.R., 1462].

Police Offences Act 1890 (No. 1126), sec. 64—Scope of section—Prima facie evidence that place is a common gaming house.]—Sec. 64 applies only where the charge is one of keeping a common gaming house. *O'Donnell* v. *Dodd*, (1910) V.L.R., 482 ; 32 A.L.T., 87 ; 16 A.L.R., 539. *Madden, C.J., Hodges* and *Hood, JJ.*

Secret Commission Prohibition Act 1905 (No. 1974), secs. 2, 14—Giving money to agent without principal's knowledge—Burden of proof.]—*See* CRIMINAL LAW, col. 343. *Rex* v. *Stevenson*, (1907) V.L.R., 475 ; 29 A.L.T., 62 ; 13 A.L.R., 383.

Health Act 1890 (No. 1098), secs. 53, 54—Unwholesome food—Prosecution for having such food under control for purpose of sale for human consumption—Prima facie case proved by informant—Burden of proof that food not intended for sale—Effect of evidence of statements made by defendant elicited on cross-examination of informant's witnesses.]—*See* HEALTH (PUBLIC). *Mellis* v. *Jenkins*, (1910) V.L.R., 380 ; 32 A.L.T., 36 ; 16 A.L.R., 430.

Fraudulent preference—Burden of proof—Nature of offence—Motive of insolvent—Knowledge of insolvent as to his insolvent condition—Insolvency Act 1890 (No. 1102), secs. 73, 141 (xiii.)—Insolvency Act 1897 (No. 1513), sec. 116.]—*See* INSOLVENCY. *Re Cohen*, (1908) V.L.R., 171 ; 29 A.L.T., 187 ; 14 A.L.R., 74.

III.—FACTS WHICH MAY BE PROVED.

(a) *Similar Facts ; Surrounding Circumstances.*

Evidence—Criminal law—Receiving stolen goods—Guilty knowledge, evidence of—Course of dealing — Isolated acts do not prove.]—The prisoner was convicted of receiving certain carpenter's tools knowing them to have been stolen. At the trial evidence that the police had found in the prisoner's shop near the tools in question a " burglar's kit " was admitted as showing guilty knowledge. *Held*, that the evidence was inadmissable to show guilty knowledge. *Rex* v. *O'Kane*, (1910) V.L.R., 8 ; 31 A.L.T., 110 ; 15 A.L.R., 628. F.C., *Madden, C.J., Hood* and *Cussen, JJ.*

Receiving stolen goods—Guilty knowledge, evidence of—Anticipated defence of innocent receipt—Evidence to rebut, admissibility of—Course of dealing—Finding of " burglar's kit " on prisoner's premises.]—On a charge of receiving goods knowing them to be stolen, a conversation which took place between a detective and the prisoner with respect to a " burglar's kit " found with part of the stolen goods under the counter in the prisoner's shop was admitted in evidence. *Held*, that the evidence was wrongly admitted, and that the conviction should be quashed. *Rex* v. *O'Kane*, (1910) V.L.R., 8 ; 31 A.L.T., 110 ; 15 A.L.R., 628. F.C., *Madden, C.J., Hood* and *Cussen, JJ.*

Factories and Shops Act 1905 (No. 1975), sec. 134—Closing of shop—Carrying on business of a kind necessitating closing of shop—Evidence of the carrying on of such business before and after the day stated in information—Admissibility of.]—In support of a charge that a particular business was carried on in a shop on a particular day, evidence is admissible of sales of goods pertaining to such business shortly before and after such day. *Billingham* v. *Gaff*, (1907) V.L.R., 691 ; 29 A.L.T., 159 ; 13 A.L.R., 474. *Hodges, J.* (1907).

Lotteries Gaming and Betting Act 1906 (No. 2055), secs. 10, 17—Evidence—Use as a common gaming house—Acts of persons other than defendant—Acts prior to the date of the alleged offence.]—To establish the fact that on the date named in the information a house was used as a common gaming house, the informant may give evidence of the acts showing such user of persons other than the defendant, and of acts showing such user previous to the date so named, and of facts from which a continuance of that user might fairly be inferred. *Macmanamny* v. *King*, (1907) V.L.R., 535 ; 28 A.L.T., 250 ; 13 A.L.R., 258. F.C., *a' Beckett, Hood* and *Cussen, JJ.*

Licensed victualler—Permit to sell liquor after hours—Evidence of effect of previous permits on good order of district—Admissibility of—Licensing Act 1890 (No. 1111), sec 7.]—In opposition to an application for a special permit under sec. 7 of the *Licensing Act* 1890, evidence is not admissible as to the effect of permits previously granted to other licensed houses upon the peace and good order of the city and upon the consumption of liquor, and the drinking habits of the public. *Mooney* v. *Lucas*, (1909) V.L.R., 333 ; 31 A.L.T., 3 ; 15 A.L.R., 296. F.C., *a' Beckett, Hodges* and *Hood, JJ.*

Land—Valuation—Inquiry as to Value at a particular time—Evidence as to sales of the same and similar land—Admissibility.]—Upon an inquiry as to the amount which would have been produced by the sale of certain land on a certain date, evidence as to the prices which had been obtained on sales of the same land and of similar land in its vicinity about or shortly after such date, is admissible. *Pendlebury* v. *Colonial Mutual Life Assurance Society Ltd.*, (1912) V.L.R., 319 ; 34 A.L.T., 67 ; 18 A.L.R., 324. *Madden, C.J.*

Opium Smoking Prohibition Act 1905 (No. 2003), sec. 10—Conviction of principal offender of smoking opium—Whether evidence against person charged with being " privy " to offending.]—D. was charged with being " privy " to offending against a provision of the *Opium Smoking Prohibition Act* 1905. The evidence showed that D. was found locked in a small room in which J., another man, was smoking opium. *Held*, that the fact that J. had been convicted of smoking opium at the time and place in question was not evidence against D. *Stapleton* v. *Davis* ; *Stapleton* v. *Bell*, (1908) V.L.R., 114 ; 29 A.L.T., 162 ; 14 A.L.R., 26. *Hodges, J.* (1907).

Adultery—Evidence—Communication of a venereal disease — Surrounding circumstances, whether they may be considered.]—*See* HUSBAND AND WIFE. *Isles* v. *Isles*, (1906) V.L.R., 86 ; 12 A.L.R. (C.N.), 26.

Criminal law—Inciting to steal goods—Delivery of stolen goods by prisoner to be pawned or sold—Evidence of, whether admissible — Accomplice's evidence — Corroboration.]—*See, post, (d)* MALICE; MOTIVE; INTENTION. *Rex* v. *Campbell,* (1908) V.L.R., 136; 29 A.L.T., 196; 14 A.L.R., 41.

(b) Identification ; Recent Possession of Stolen Property.

Criminal law—Circumstantial evidence—Identification—Finger prints, similarity of.]—The resemblance between the finger print of an accused person and a finger print found on an article may be sufficient evidence to justify a jury in finding that the finger print found on the article was made by the accused. *R.* v. *Parker,* (1912) V.L.R., 152; 33 A.L.T., 215; 18 A.L.R., 150. F.C., *Hodges* and *Cussen, JJ.* (*Madden, C.J.* dissentiente). Leave to appeal refused by High Court, (1912) 14 C.L.R., 681; 18 A.L.R., 157. *Griffith, C.J., Barton* and *Isaacs, JJ.*]

Larceny—Receiving—Similarity of goods found in possession of prisoner with goods alleged to have been stolen—Failure of prisoner to give satisfactory account of how goods came into his possession—Evidence of stealing and of identity of goods, sufficiency of.]—On a charge of receiving stolen property belonging to the Victorian Railways Commissioners, the evidence showed that three kegs of cream of tartar part of a large consignment, had been missed, by the Victorian Railways Commissioners, that within a fortnight kegs which contained or had contained cream of tartar and were similar to those lost in size, shape, colour and dimensions, were found in the possession of the prisoners who gave a false account as to their possession of such goods. In one case there was evidence that marks had been obliterated from the kegs. In the other case there was evidence of an attempt to bribe a constable. *Held, per a'Beckett* and *Hood, JJ.* (*Cussen, J.* dissenting), that there was evidence on which the jury might properly convict. *Held, per Cussen, J.,* that there was not sufficient evidence to identify the goods with those lost by the Victorian Railways Commissioners. *Trainer* v. *The King,* 4 C.L.R.,

126; 13 A.L.R., 53, and *R.* v. *Roche,* 13 V.L.R., 150; 8 A.L.T., 193, discussed. *Rex* v. *Schiffman,* (1910) V.L.R., 348; 32 A.L.T., 28; 16 A.L.R., 346. In this case leave to appeal was refused by the High Court, 17 A.L.R., 150.]

Criminal law—Receiving—Recent possession—Possession of skirt and blouse nine months after their being stolen—False statements made by person found in possession of such articles—Evidence, admissibility.]—On the trial of a prisoner charged with receiving a skirt and blouse which had been stolen nine months previously, evidence was tendered by the Crown that the prisoner when found in possession of the goods and again on a subsequent occasion had made statements as to her possession of them. These statements were contradictory in themselves and suggestive of guilt. On objection raised by prisoner's counsel that such statements were inadmissible, inasmuch as the prisoner might be lawfully called upon to explain the possession of the articles alleged to have been stolen only when such possession was recent, and that possession of the skirt and blouse nine months after the theft was not recent, the Chairman of General Sessions overruled the objection and admitted the evidence. *Held,* that such statements were rightly admitted. *Held,* also, that the prisoner's possession of the skirt and blouse was sufficiently recent to be within the doctrine of recent possession, and to throw on her the obligation of satisfactorily explaining her possession of them. *Rex* v. *McCaffery,* (1911) V.L.R., 92; 32 A.L.T., 105; 17 A.L.R., 40. F.C., *Madden, C.J., a'Beckett* and *Hodges, JJ.*

Evidence — Larceny — Recent Possession—Offences against the Commonwealth—Judiciary Act 1903 (No. 6 of 1903), sec. 80.]—*Semble.*—The doctrine of recent possession of stolen goods applies to offences against the Commonwealth. *Rex* v. *Forrest,* 34 A.L.T., 95; 18 A.L.R., 495. *Cussen, J.* (1912).

(c) Possession ; Acts of Ownership.

Evidence—Burden of proof—Husband and wife living in same house—Wife tenant of the

house—**Possession of goods in the house—Possession prima facie evidence of title.**]—Under an execution for a judgment debt against a husband goods were seized in a house of which his wife was the tenant and in which she lived with her husband. On an interpleader issue in which the wife claimed the goods. *Held,* that the fact of the goods being on property of which the wife was tenant was *prima facie* evidence that she was in possession of the goods ; that a *prima facie* title to the goods was to be inferred from her possession of them ; and, therefore, that the burden of showing that the goods were the property of the husband was upon the judgment creditor. *McKenzie* v. *Balchin* ; *McKenzie, claimant,* (1908) V.L.R., 324 ; 29 A.L.T., 246 ; 14 A.L.R., 238. F.C., *a' Beckett, Hodges* and *Cussen, JJ.* (1908).

Landlord and tenant—Evidence of tenancy—Promise to pay rent and request for time to pay.]—A. had been in possession of land as a monthly tenant, but there was no evidence as to who was then the owner. Subsequently B. became the owner, and A. continued in possession, and, on rent being demanded from her, promised B. to pay it and asked for time. *Held,* that there was evidence of a tenancy between A. and B. *Bayne* v. *Love,* (1909) 7 C.L.R., 748. H.C., *Griffith, C.J., Barton, O'Connor* and *Isaacs, JJ.*

Weights and Measures Act 1890 (No. 1158), sec. 54—False Weights, &c.—"Possession," meaning of—Prima facie evidence of use.]—The word " possession " in sec. 54 of the *Weights and Measures Act* 1890 (which makes it an offence for any person to have in his possession certain weights) means " possession for the purpose of use." The possession of weights and scales in the ordinary way in a shop on the counter is *prima facie* evidence of use. *Montgomery* v. *Ah Loey,* 2 A.L.R., 207, distinguished. *English* v. *Potter,* (1908) V.L.R., 632 ; 30 A.L.T., 91 ; 14 A.L.R., 559. *Hood, J.*

Evidence—Possession—Adverse possession—Land of two owners within one fence—Re-entry of registered proprietor—Cutting firewood—Renewal of survey marks on bound-aries—**Effect of.**]—*See* LIMITATIONS (STATUTES OF). *Clements* v. *Jones,* 8 C.L.R., 133 ; 15 A.L.R., 158.

Evidence—Possession—Land of two owners within one fence—Presumption of possession—Possession follows title—Equivocal acts of possession — Intention.] — *See* LIMITATIONS (STATUTES OF). *Clement* v. *Jones,* 8 C.L.R., 133 ; 15 A.L.R., 158.

(d) Malice ; Motive ; Intention.

Defamation—Malice, actual—Evidence — Erroneous statement—Discovery of error—Failure to correct, whether evidence of malice.] Before any actual damage had resulted from the erroneous defamatory statement uttered by the defendant on a privileged occasion, he discovered his error, but omitted to correct it as he had power to do. *Held,* not evidence that the statement had been uttered with actual malice. *Howe* v. *Lees,* (1910) 11 C.L.R., 361 ; 16 A.L.R., 605. H.C., *Griffith, C.J., Barton, O'Connor* and *Higgins, JJ.*

Privileged occasion—Actual malice, evidence of—Defamatory allegations persisted in at trial—Invitation to withdraw.]—Where words are uttered on a privileged occasion, the fact that their use is persisted in at the trial of an action brought in respect of them, is evidence of actual malice. *Livingston* v. *M'Cartin,* (1907) V.L.R., 48 ; 28 A.L.T., 131 ; 12 A.L.R., 524. *Hodges, J.*

Criminal law—Inciting to steal goods—Delivery of stolen goods by prisoner to third person to be pawned or sold—Evidence of, whether admissible—Accomplice's evidence—Corroboration.]—The prisoner was charged with inciting M. to steal certain goods from his employer. M. gave evidence, which was not objected to, that the prisoner had requested him to steal the goods, that he accordingly stole the goods and that he handed them to the prisoner. Evidence, objected to by prisoner's counsel, was admitted which showed that, shortly after receiving the stolen goods, the prisoner gave portions of them to various persons, who, at his request, pawned or sold them. The prisoner was convicted. *Held,* that the evidence objected to was admissible, and that the prisoner was rightly convicted. *Per a' Beckett J.*—Although that evidence did not corroborate the actual inciting, yet it was corroborative of M.'s statement that he handed the goods to the prisoner, and might be considered by a jury in coming to a conclusion as to the truthfulness of the whole of M.'s story. *Per Hodges, J.*—What was said when M. handed the goods to the prisoner and what the latter then did with them, formed part of the *res gestae*, and the evidence was admissible in support of the proposition upon which the prosecution was based. *Per Cussen, J.* The prisoner's conduct after receiving the goods was an admission that they were stolen for him, and therefore showed a motive why he should incite M., and tended to support M.'s statement that the prisoner did incite him to steal the goods. *Rex v. Campbell*, (1908) V.L.R., 136; 29 A.L.T., 196; 14 A.L.R., 41. F.C., (1908).

Divorce—Repeated cruel beatings alleged in petition—No misconduct charged in answer —Justification—Evidence of improprieties on part of petitioner, admissibility of—Beatings not result of altercation as to alleged improprietaries.]—Upon the hearing of a petition by the wife for dissolution of marriage on the ground that the respondent had repeatedly within a year previous to the presentation of the petition assaulted and cruelly beaten her, the Court refused to receive certain evidence tendered on behalf of the respondent to show laxity of conduct on the part of the petitioner, as no misconduct was charged in the answer, and the alleged improprieties would have afforded no excuse or justification for beatings on occasions when no impropriety occurred and on which no altercation as to alleged impropriety had arisen. *Hocking v. Hocking*, 32 A.L.T., 134; 17 A.L.R., 13. *a' Beckett, J.* (1911).

Fixture, nature of—Purpose with which chattel attached to freehold—Attachment for better enjoyment of freehold—Evidence as to purpose, admissibility of.]—*See* LANDLORD AND TENANT. *Love v. Bloomfield*, (1906) V.L.R., 723; 28 A.L.T., 52.; 12 A.L.R., 383.

Domicile, change of—Evidence—Statements of intention, weight to be attached to—Contrary inference from conduct and acts.]—For a case in which, upon a question of change of domicile, statements of intention made by the person, whose domicile was in issue, were not allowed to countervail the inference drawn from his conduct and acts. *See Forster v. Forster*, (1907) V.L.R., 159; 28 A.L.T., 144; 13 A.L.R., 33. F.C., *Hood, Cussen* and *Chomley, JJ.*

(e) *Opinions of Expert Witnesses.*

Evidence—Expert witnesses—Finger prints *Semble, per Cussen, J.*—Expert witnesses may give in evidence statements based upon their own experience or study; but they cannot be permitted (*a*) to attempt to point out to the jury matters which the jury could determine for themselves or (*b*) to formulate their empirical knowledge as a universal law. Thus experts may depose that there are certain broadly marked differences in character between the finger prints of different people; that these differences can be classified; and that it can be illustrated from their expert knowledge what those broad characteristics are. But they may not (*a*) point out similarities between the finger mark of the accused and a finger mark alleged to be his, nor (*b*) state that there cannot be two finger marks alike. *R. v. Parker*, (1912) V.L.R., 152; 33 A.L.T., 215; 18 A.L.R., 150. F.C., *Madden, C.J., Hodges* and *Cussen, JJ.*

(f) *Complaint by Female Alleging Indecent Assault.*

Indecent assault—Statement or complaint by female assaulted—First reasonable opportunity—Statement or complaint in answer to questions, admissibility of.]—On a trial for indecent assault upon a female child a statement made by the child to her mother with regard to the alleged assault is not admissible in evidence, unless it is shown that the statement was made at the first reasonable opportunity under the circumstances after the assault. *Per Madden, C.J.*—As to the observation in *R. v. Osborne*, (1905) 1 K.B., 551, at p. 556, that a statement is inadmissible where but for questions put to her the child or woman assaulted would not have made the statement, *Quaere*, whether it is not merely a dictum and whether it correctly states the law. *Rex* v. *McNeill*, (1907) V.L.R., 265; 28 A.L.T., 182; 13 A.L.R., 99. F.C., *Madden, C.J., a'Beckett, Hood* and *Cussen, JJ.* (1907).

(g) Character of Accused Person.

Police Offences Act 1907 (No. 2093), sec. 8 (a), (b)—Vagrancy—Evidence of bad character, when it must be tendered—Evidence as to general character, what is—Evidence to rebut.]—The defendant was charged under sec. 40 (VI.) of the *Police Offences Act* 1890 with being an idle and disorderly person. He gave evidence in his defence and described the nature of his employment and added that he was living respectably and earning an honest living. *Held,* that the latter statements did not amount to evidence as to general character such as to permit the informant to give evidence in rebuttal under the *Police Offences Act* 1907 (No. 2093), sec. 8 (*b*). *Held,* also, that the evidence permitted by sec. 8 (*a*) of the *Police Offences Act* 1907 as to the defendant's bad character cannot be given after the informant has closed his case, unless the defendant has in his defence given evidence as to his general character. *Hickling* v. *Skerritt,* (1912) V.L.R., 322; 34 A.L.T., 72; 18 A.L.R., 329. *Madden, C.J.* (1912).

Court of Petty Sessions—Jurisdiction—Discretion as to sentence—Evidence of character—Prior convictions.]—Where, on the hearing of an information before a Court of Petty Sessions, the justices have convicted the defendant, they have jurisdiction to receive evidence on oath as to the character of the defendant, and particularly of prior convictions, in order to assist them in the exercise of their discretion as to the amount of punishment they will award. *O'Donnell* v. *Perkins; Tognini* v. *Hargreaves,* (1908) V.L.R., 537; 30 A.L.T., 45; 14 A.L.R., 435. F.C., *a'Beckett, Hood* and *Cussen, JJ.* (1908).

(h) Declarations of Dying Persons.

Criminal law—Evidence—Dying declarations in case of homicide—Impending death—Expectation of death—Form of deposition.]—In order that the declaration of persons *in extrmis* may be admitted as evidence in cases of homicide against an accused person, the person making the declaration must be at the time in actual danger of death, must have an unqualified belief and a clear apprehension that he will not recover from his injury or illness, and death must follow from that injury directly or indirectly caused by the accused. The length of time elapsing between the making of the declarations and death is an element to be considered in determining whether they were made in the definite and full expectation of death. Where the circumstances are such that a dying declaration is admissible, a witness may state a conversation (amounting to such a declaration) between himself and the declarant, although the effect of the conversation is reduced to writing and the written statement is afterwards read over, assented to and signed by the declarant. There is no rule requiring that the statement shall or shall not be by question and answer. *Rex* v. *Hope,* (1909) V.L.R., 149; 30 A.L.T., 167; 15 A.L.R., 87. F.C., *Madden, C.J., Hodges* and *Cussen, JJ.* (1909). Special leave to appeal refused by High Court. *Hope* v. *The King,* (1909) 9 C.L.R., 257. *Griffith, C.J., Higgins, J.* (*Isaacs, J.,* dissentiente).

Criminal law—Evidence — Dying declarations in case of homicide—Impending death—Expectation of death.]—*Per Madden, C.J.—* "Therefore, some Judges have said he must be 'in hopeless expectancy of immediate death'—of death 'immediately impending,' or 'in *articulo mortis*' or '*moriens*' as distinguished from '*moriturus.*' All these expressions are rather an effort to be emphatic as to the importance of exactitude in the determination of the essential things which make declarations admissible than any determination on the part of the Judges that the declaration must have been made within some given distance from the death which afterwards undoubtedly occurred." *Per Hodges, J.—*I do not feel it possible to define the word "impending" beyond saying that it means "near" as distinguished from

" remote," " imminent," as distinguished from " deferred." But it is not, in my opinion, possible to say that " impending " means any number of hours, or any number of days." *Rex* v. *Hope*, (1909) V.L.R., 149, pp. 158, 163 ; 30 A.L.T., 167, pp. 169, 171 ; 15 A.L.R., pp. 88, 90. F.C.

Criminal law—Evidence—Dying depositions in case of homicide—" Settled hopeless expectation of immediate death."]—*Per Cussen, J.*—" It has been sometimes said that the declarant must have a settled hopeless expectation of immediate death. I think there is some possibility of difficulty arising from the use of each of those words. " Hope " is generally compounded of expectation and desire. What I really think is meant in the language of many Judges is simply " expectation." A person may desire his recovery very much, and in that sense not have abandoned hope, although he has abandoned all expectation and humanly speaking has no hope . . . So with the word ' settled.' ' Settled ' may mean either ' absolutely unalterable,' or ' non-fluctuating.' In the latter case, proof of change would merely be evidence that the expectation or belief was not firm and unqualified. So the expression ' immediate death ' is distinctly ambiguous." *Rex* v. *Hope*, (1909) V.L.R., 149, at p. 164 ; 30 A.L.T., 167, at p. 171 ; 15 A.L.R., 87, at p. 90. F.C.

Criminal law — Evidence — Dying declarations in case of homicide—Impending death—Expectation of death.]—*Per Cussen, J.*— " The language of the declarant in this case fluctuates to some extent. She said ' I am sure I cannot recover,' and also said ' I don't think I will recover.' It has been pointed out that the medical man also said ' think.' That is ambiguous. Sometimes it means ' I think it probable ' ; sometimes it means ' I believe.' If those expressions stood alone, I should have doubted whether they were by themselves sufficient ; but taking them with the other circumstances, I think they may be read as—' I believe I shall not recover '." *Rex* v. *Hope*, (1909) V.L.R., 149, p. 165 ; 30 A.L.T., 167, p. 172 ; 15 A.L.R., 87, p. 91.

(i) Declarations as to Pedigree ; Public Reputation.

Evidence—Pedigree—Declarations by deceased members of family—Alleged member of family—Declarations by deceased relative of alleged member.]—In pedigree cases declarations of deceased relatives of the family concerning which inquiries are being made are admissible as to the state of the family, but not declarations of deceased persons proved to be connected with someone else who they say is a member of the family being inquired about. *Monkton* v. *Attorney-General*, 2 R. & My., 147, not followed. *In re Osmand* ; *Bennett* v. *Booty*, (1908) V.L.R., 67 ; 29 A.L.T., 168 ; 13 A.L.R., 728. F.C., *a' Beckett, Hodges* and *Hood, JJ.* (1908), affirming *Cussen, J.* (1906) V.L.R., 455 ; 27 A.L.T., 218 ; 12 A.L.R., 256.

Evidence—Pedigree—Declarations by deceased relative of family—Whether evidence of circumstances leading up to alleged illegitimacy.]—Declarations by A., a deceased relative of a family, are admissible to show that B. was not a member of the family, but, *quaere*, whether such declarations are admissible for the purpose of showing the circumstances leading up to the alleged illegitimacy of B. *In re Osmand* ; *Bennett* v. *Booty*, (1906) V.L.R., 455 ; 27 A.L.T., 218 ; 12 A.L.R., 256. *Cussen, J.*

Evidence—Pedigree—Declarations by deceased relatives of family—Ante litem motam.] —For a discussion of the question whether or not under the circumstances of the case certain declarations of a deceased relative of a family were made *ante litem motam*, see, *In re Osmand* ; *Bennett* v. *Booty*, (1906) V.L.R., 455 ; 27 A.L.T., 218 ; 12 A.L.R., 256.

Evidence—Pedigree—Marriage—Legitimacy or illegitimacy—Public reputation, when admissible.]—Public reputation is evidence on the question whether a man and a woman are married, but is not admissible as to legitimacy or illegitimacy. *In re Osmand* ; *Bennett* v. *Booty*, (1908) V.L.R., 67 ; 29 A.L.T., 168 ; 13 A.L.R., 728. F.C., *a' Beckett, A.-C.J., Hodges* and *Hood, JJ.*, affirming

Cussen, J., (1906) V.L.R., 455 ; 27 A.L.T., 218 ; 12 A.L.R., 256.

(j) *Other Cases.*

Husband and wife—Divorce—Service on respondent—Evidence in proof of—Nature of.] In undefended divorce suits the Court has to be satisfied by the best evidence procurable that service on the respondent has been duly effected. *Maddock* v. *Maddock*, (1911) V.L.R., 127 ; 32 A.L.T., 124 ; 17 A.L.R., 66. *Hood, J.*

Companies Act 1890 (No. 1074), sec. 67—Proceedings at meetings of company, how proved—Minutes not entered in minute book.]—Sec. 67 of the *Companies Act* 1890 is an enabling section, and, although no minutes have been entered in a minute book, the proceedings of the company can be proved otherwise by any admissible evidence. *McLean Brothers & Rigg Ltd.* v. *Grice*, 4 C.L.R., 835 ; 13 A.L.R., 77. H.C., *Griffith, C.J., Barton* and *O'Connor, JJ.* (1907).

Marriage Act 1890 (No. 1166), sec. 74 (c)— " Frequent " convictions for crime—Test of frequency—Criminal tendency—Evidence of, what is.]—*See* HUSBAND AND WIFE. *Kemp* v. *Kemp*, (1907) V.L.R., 718 ; 29 A.L.T., 92 ; 13 A.L.R., 615.

Contract—Work and labour — Wages— Promise to pay, express or implied—Evidence, sufficiency of.]—*See* CONTRACT OR AGREEMENT, cols. 192, 193. *Griffith* v. *O'Donoghue*, (1906) V.L.R., 548 ; 28 A.L.T., 31 ; 12 A.L.R., 357.

IV.—MODE OF PROOF.

(a) *Judicial Notice* ; *Information Obtained Otherwise than from Evidence.*

See, also, post (d) *Foreign Law.*

Evidence—Foreign law—Fugitive Offenders Act 1881 (44 & 45 Vict. c. 69)—Law of other country, whether a question of fact—How Magistrate may be satisfied as to.]—*Semble.*— The law of another part of the dominions is, for the purposes of the *Fugitive Offenders Act* 1881, not a matter of fact required to be legally proved, but is a matter as to which a Magistrate may satisfy himself by any available means. *McKelvey* v. *Meagher*, 4 C.L.R., 265 ; 12 A.L.R., 483. H.C., *Griffith, C.J. Barton* and *O'Connor, JJ.* (1906).

Justices—Local limits of jurisdiction, how to be ascertained—Judicial notice.]—Where the local limits of a Court of Petty Sessions are described in a public Statute, the Court may take judicial notice of the area enclosed in those limits, and that the place described in an information is within or without those limits. *Le Cocq* v. *McErvale*, (1908) V.L.R., 69 ; 29 A.L.T., 134 ; 13 A.L.R., 699. F.C., *per a'Beckett* and *Cussen, JJ.*

Justices—Local jurisdiction—Objection that offence committed outside jurisdiction—How justices may satisfy themselves on the question —Whether formal evidence necessary—Effect of erroneous conclusion—Justices Act 1890 (No. 1105), sec. 73 (3).]—Where on the hearing of an information before a Court of Petty Sessions an objection is taken that the offence was committed at a place outside the local jurisdiction of the Court, it is not necessary that formal evidence should be called to show that such place is within such jurisdiction, and the Court if otherwise satisfied of that fact should proceed with the hearing. The decision of the Court may be nullified if it be afterwards shown that the Court was wrong in concluding that it was acting within its jurisdiction. *Carberry* v. *Cook*, 3 C.L.R., 995 ; 12 A.L.R., 265, applied. *Webb* v. *Rooney*, 1 A.L.R., 83, discussed. *Le Cocq* v. *McErvale*, (1908) V.L.R., 69 ; 29 A.L.T., 134 ; 13 A.L.R., 699. F.C., *a'Beckett* and *Cussen, JJ.* (*Madden, C.J.,* doubting).

Order XXXVIII., r. 6 (Rules of 1906)— Supreme Court Act 1890 (No. 1142), sec. 90— Judicial notice—Certificate of notary public authenticating signature of party to document —Signature of notary, whether sufficient.]— The Court will take judicial notice of the certificate of a notary public in the United Kingdom authenticating the signature of a party to a document, and in such a case the signature of the notary to the certificate is sufficient without his official notarial seal. *In re Sutherland*, (1910) V.L.R., 118 ; 31 A.L.T., 150 ; 16 A.L.R., 63. *Cussen, J.*

Licensing Act 1890 (No. 1111), sec. 55—
Licensing Court—Evidence, how to be taken—
Evidence not on oath, whether Court may
receive.]—A Licensing Court has no authority to determine questions on materials
not proved before it on the oath of a witness
or by documents which prove themselves.
Ex parte Hunter Brothers, (1911) V.L.R.,
138; 32 A.L.T., 143; 17 A.L.R., 92.
Hodges, J. (1911).

Evidence—Information in possession of
Magistrates but not in evidence before them—
Whether Magistrates may act upon—Licensing
—Prohibition order—Licensing Act 1890 (No.
1111), sec. 125.]—In making a prohibition
order under sec. 125 of the *Licensing Act
1890*, the Magistrates acted on certain special
and peculiar information with regard to the
defendant possessed by one of their number,
who communicated it to them, but not to
the defendant. *Held*, that a Magistrate
possessing such information was not at
liberty to use it himself, or to influence his
fellow Magistrates by it in coming to a determination on the matter before them. *Strange
v. Strange*, (1908) V.L.R., 187; 29 A.L.T.,
177; 14 A.L.R., 42. *Hodges, J.* (1908).

Money-lender—Excessive interest—Res ipsa
loquitur—Money Lenders Act 1906 (No. 2061),
sec. 4.]—The rate of interest charged by a
money-lender may on its face appear excessive, particularly if unexplained, and in such
a case the Court may act without requiring
extrinsic evidence to be given on the subject.
Wilson v. Moss, 8 C.L.R., 146; 15 A.L.R.,
131. High Court, *Griffith, C.J., Barton,
O' Connor* and *Isaacs, JJ.* (1909).

(b) *Admissions.*

Divorce—Adultery, evidence of—Admissions—Registration by husband of birth of
illegitimate child—Certified copy of entry
in register of births—Admission therein of
paternity.]—On the hearing of a petition by a
wife for dissolution of marriage on the ground
of a repeated act of adultery by her husband,
the only evidence tendered in support of
such ground was a certified copy of an entry
in the Register of Births in Brisbane, showing
that the husband had registered the birth

of an illegitimate child of which he therein
described himself as the father. *Held*, that
the Court might act upon the admission of
adultery contained in such entry, as set out
in the certified copy thereof, there being
no reasonable doubt that the husband was
the person who registered the birth, and no
circumstances of suspicion. *Wright v. Wright*,
(1911) V.L.R., 28; 32 A.L.T., 114; 16
A.L.R., 602. *a' Beckett, J.*

Negligence—Level crossing on railway—
Neglect of engine-driver to whistle—Regulation issued by owners of railway directing
engine-driver to whistle when approaching
level crossing — Evidence.] — A regulation
issued by the owners of the railway directing
their engine drivers to sound a whistle when
approaching a level crossing without gates is
evidence that the sounding of the whistle is
a reasonable precaution to be taken in such
circumstances, and the omission to sound a
whistle is evidence of negligence. *Fraser v.
The Victorian Railways Commissioners*, 8
C.L.R., 54; 15 A.L.R., 93. High Court,
Griffith, C.J., Barton, O' Connor and *Isaacs,
JJ.* (1909).

Evidence—Defamation—No plea of justi-
fication—Evidence of truth, admissibility of.]
—If justification is not pleaded, the words
complained of are admitted to be false, and
evidence as to their truth cannot be given.
Peatling v. Watson, (1909) V.L.R., 198; 30
A.L.T., 176; 15 A.L.R., 150. F.C., *Madden,
C.J., Hodges* and *Hood, JJ.*

Police Offences Act 1890 (No. 1126), secs.
49, 51—Use of room for purpose of betting—
User, sufficiency of evidence to prove—
Repeated acts, whether necessary to show—
Character of use, proof of by admission express
or implied.]—*See* POLICE OFFENCES ACTS,
Knox v. Thomas Bible; *Knox v. J. L. Bible*.
(1907) V.L.R., 485; 29 A.L.T., 23; 13
A.L.R., 252. [Leave to appeal to High Court
refused, 4 C.L.R., 1462].

Criminal or quasi-criminal cases—Practice
—Several persons charged with similar
offences—Consent to be tried together and
to be absent from Court—Several persons tried
separately—Agreement to be bound by evi-

dence taken in one case, effect of.]—*See* CRIM-INAL LAW. *Larkin* v. *Penfold*, (1906) V.L.R., 535; 28 A.L.T., 42; 12 A.L.R., 337.

Medical Act 1890 (No. 1118), sec. 12—Justices Act 1890 (No. 1105), sec. 59—Justices Act 1904 (No. 1959), sec. 17, Third Schedule — Default summons—Evidence—Proof of registration of medical man, whether necessary.]—*See* JUSTICES OF THE PEACE. *Iredell* v. *Skinner*, (1909) V.L.R., 108; 30 A.L.T., 154; 15 A.L.R., 41.

(c) *Presumptions.*

(1) As to Legitimacy

Evidence—Legitimacy, presumption as to—Father and mother living together as man and wife—European woman and Chinese man.]—No presumption of legitimacy arises in the case of a child born in Victoria in 1876 to a white woman and a Chinese who lived together as man and wife for several years. *Potter* v. *Minahan*, (1908) 7 C.L.R., 277; 14 A.L.R., 635. High Court, *Griffith, C.J., Barton, O'Connor* and *Isaacs, JJ.* (*Higgins, J.,* dissenting).

Child born in wedlock—Presumption of legitimacy.]—For an application of the rule that a child born in wedlock will be presumed to be the child of the husband unless non-access is proved, *see In re Osmand*; *Bennett* v. *Booty*, (1908) V.L.R., 67; 29 A.L.T., 168; 13 A.L.R., 728. F.C., *a' Beckett, Hodges* and *Hood, JJ.* (1908), affirming *Cussen, J.,* (1906) V.L.R., 455; 27 A.L.T., 218; 12 A.L.R., 256.

(2) As to Death.

Husband and wife—Maintenance—Former marriage—Husband not heard of for seven years—Presumption—Validity of second marriage—Proof of invalidity—Onus—Marriage Act 1890 (No. 1166), secs. 43, 46.]—Upon the hearing under sec. 43 of the *Marriage Act* 1890 of a complaint of a woman that she had been left by the defendant, her husband, without means of support, evidence was given that she had previously to her marriage with the defendant, been married to a man who had disappeared about fifteen years ago, and of whom she had not heard since his disappearance; that after the lapse of seven years from his disappearance she had obtained a decree *nisi* for dissolution of marriage with him on the ground of desertion, which decree had not been made absolute; and that she was subsequently married to the defendant who was then aware of her previous marriage and of the divorce proceedings. *Held,* that the evidence raised the presumption of the first husband's death before the second marriage, and that, even if it did not, the second marriage should not have been treated as bad by the Justices until it was proved to be so. *Ousley* v. *Ousley*, (1912) V.L.R., 32; 33 A.L.T., 155; 18 A.L.R., 5. *a'Beckett, J.*

(3) As to Official Acts.

Public office—Person acting in discharge of—Presumption of due appointment.]—A public officer who is proved to have acted as such is presumed to have been validly appointed, and the burden of proving the invalidity of his appointment lies on the persons alleging it. *Rex* v. *Turnbull*, (1907) V.L.R., 11; 28 A.L.T., 103; 12 A.L.R., 551. *Cussen, J.*

Marriage Act 1890 (No. 1166), sec. 126—Supreme Court Act 1890 (No. 1142), sec. 90—Evidence—Affidavits sworn outside Victoria—Notary Public—Judicial notice of signature.]—Where an affidavit purports to be sworn out of Victoria, but within the King's dominions, before a person who therein subscribes his name and describes himself as a notary public, the Court assumes that he is acting within his jurisdiction as such, and takes judicial notice of the signature. *Howard* v. *Jones*, 14 A.L.T., 106; 18 V.L.R., 578, distinguished. *Davis* v. *Davis, Hattrick, Co-respondent*, (1912) V.L.R., 427; 34 A.L.T., 66: 18 A.L.R., 398. *Hood, J.* (1912).

(4) As to Due Performance of Legal Requisites.

Will — Execution — Evidence — Will not produced—Presumption of due execution.]—The *prima facie* presumption that a will with a regular attestation clause has been duly executed, even when the attesting witnesses deny or cannot remember, the due execution, does not apply to a document which is not produced after the testator's death and as to which the fact of the signature of the deceased is not established *aliunde*. *Gair* v. *Bowers*; *Falconar* v. *Bowers*; *Gair* v. *Falconar*, (1909) 9 C.L.R., 510; 15 A.L.R., 494. High Court, *Griffith*, *C.J.*, *O'Connor*, *Isaacs* and *Higgins*, *JJ.*

Omnia praesumuntur rite esse acta—Presumption afforded by the records of transactions required by law to be kept—Proceedings at meetings of shareholders of company, validity of—Printed copy of resolution forwarded to Registrar-General—Notice of winding-up resolution—Publication in Government Gazette—Companies Act 1890 (No. 1074), secs. 54, 118.]—It was proved that a resolution for the voluntary winding-up of a company was recorded in writing, and signed by the chairman of the meeting of shareholders at which the resolution was passed, and that a copy was sent to the Registrar-General and recorded by him, and that a copy was published in the *Government Gazette*. *Held*, that there was *prima facie* evidence that all that took place at the meeting was done lawfully, and therefore, if a quorum was requisite at such meeting, that there was such a quorum present. *McLean Brothers & Rigg Ltd.* v. *Grice*, 4 C.L.R., 835; 13 A.L.R., 77. H.C., *Griffith*, *C.J.*, *Barton* and *O'Connor*, *JJ.* (1907).

Presumption arising from ordinary course of business—Legality of subsequent act dependent upon performance of prior act—Performance of prior act presumed from doing of subsequent Act—Proceedings of corporation—Resolution passed at meeting of shareholders—Presumption that quorum present at meeting.]—Where an act is done which can be done legally only after the performance of some prior act, proof of the latter carries with it a presumption of the due performance of the prior act. This presumption applies to the proceedings of corporations, and, therefore, proof of the passing of a resolution for the voluntary winding-up of a company is *prima facie* evidence that, if a quorum was necessary at the meeting at which the resolution was passed, such quorum was present. *McLean Brothers & Rigg Ltd.* v. *Grice* 4,

C.L.R., 835; 13 A.L.R., 77. H.C., *Griffith*, *C.J.*, *Barton* and *O'Connor*, *JJ.*(1907.)

Companies Act 1890 (No. 1074), sec. 54—Printed copy of resolution of shareholders forwarded to Registrar-General—Presumption against fraud—Validity of resolution, prima facie evidence of.]—By reason of the presumption against fraud in the carrying out of duties to be performed under an Act of Parliament, a certified copy of a printed copy of a resolution for the voluntary winding-up of a company forwarded to the Registrar-General by the company is *prima facie* evidence of a valid resolution. *McLean Brothers & Rigg Ltd.* v. *Grice*, 4 C.L.R., 835; 13 A.L.R., 77. H.C., *Griffith*, *C.J.*, *Barton* and *O'Connor*, *JJ.* (1907).

(5) As to Other Matters.

Parent and child—Purchase by parent in name of child—Presumption of advancement, when rebutted—Retention of life interest by parent—Real property, rule applicable to.]—See ADVANCEMENT, cols. 3, 4. *Stuckey* v. *Trustees, Executors and Agency Co. Ltd.*, (1910) V.L.R., 55; 31 A.L.T., 157; 16 A.L.R., 65.

Fiduciary relation—Undue influence, presumption of—Whether principle confined to voluntary transactions.]—See FRAUD. *Union Bank of Australia Ltd.* v. *Whitelaw*, (1906) V.L.R., 711; 28 A.L.T., 17; 12 A.L.R., 393.

Licensed carriage—Negligence of driver—Liability of owner—By-law 78 of the City of Melbourne—Regulation prohibiting owner from entrusting licensed carriage to any person except as his servant—Prima facie presumption of relation of master and servant.]—Although every owner licensed under by-law 78 of the City of Melbourne, which provides that no owner of a licensed carriage shall entrust it to any person as driver except as his servant, is presumed to have obeyed the by-law, the presumption is not irrebuttable, and therefore the fact that a person other than the owner is driving such carriage is not conclusive evidence that such person is the servant of the owner. *Clutterbuck* v. *Curry*, (1885) 11 V.L.R., 810, followed. *Gates* v. *Bill*, (1902) 2 K.B., 38, distinguished. *Mc-*

Kinnon v. *Gange*, (1910) V.L.R., 32 ; 31 A.L.T., 112 ; 15 A.L.R., 640. F.C., *Madden*, *C.J.*, *Hood* and *Cussen, JJ.*

Secret Commissions Prohibition Act 1905 (No. 1974), sec. 2—Corruptly giving valuable consideration to agent—Secret giving, presumption as to corruptness arising from.]—The fact that a secret commission has been given raises the presumption that it was given "corruptly" within the meaning of sec. 2 of the *Secret Commissions Prohibition Act* 1905. *Rex* v. *Scott*, (1907) V.L.R., 471 ; 29 A.L.T., 60 ; 13 A.L.R., 143. *Cussen, J.*

(d) Foreign Law.

Evidence—Foreign law—Rendition of fugitive offender—Fugitive Offenders Act 1881 (44 & 45 Vict. c. 69), secs. 5, 29.]—In proceedings before a Magistrate under the *Fugitive Offenders Act* 1881 to have a fugitive returned to Natal, the law of Natal relating to the alleged offence may be proved by the certificate of the Attorney-General of Natal, and by the depositions of a Natal lawyer taken in Natal. *McKelvey* v. *Meagher* 4 C.L.R., 265 ; 12 A.L.R., 483. High Court, *Griffith*, *C.J.*, *Barton* and *O'Connor, JJ.* (1906).

(e) Unsworn Statements.

Criminal law—Unsworn statement of prisoner—Evidentiary nature of—Evidence Act 1890 (No. 1088), sec. 52—Crimes Act 1891 (No. 1231), sec. 38.]—When a prisoner makes a statement of facts under sec. 52 of the *Evidence Act* 1890 the jury should be directed to the statement as *prima facie* a possible version of the facts, and to consider it with the sworn evidence, giving it such weight as it appears to be entitled to in comparison with the facts established by evidence. *Peacock* v. *The King*, (1911) 13 C.L.R., 619 ; 17 A.L.R., 566. High Court, *Griffith, C.J.*, *Barton* and *O'Connor, JJ.*

Crimes Act 1891 (No. 1231), sec. 38—Statement by accused person not on oath—Proper time to announce intention to make such statement.]—*See* CRIMINAL LAW, col. 352. *Rex* v. *Kellow*, (1912) V.L.R., 162 ; 33 A.L.T., 203 ; 18 A.L.R., 170.

Juryman, alleged misconduct of—Evidence on oath to prove misconduct—Denial of juryman not on oath accepted by Judge—Denial in nature of plea of not guilty—No objection raised—Waiver.]—*See* JURY. *David Syme & Co.* v. *Swinburne*, 10 C.L.R., 43 ; 16 A.L.R., 93.

Certiorari to Judge of a County Court—Evidence—Conflict of evidence as to proceedings in County Court—Unsworn statement of Judge, whether admissible.]—*See* COUNTY COURT, cols. 329, 330. *Macartney* v. *A. Macrow & Sons Proprietary Ltd.*, (1911) V.L.R., 393 ; 33 A.L.T., 64 ; 17 A.L.R., 397.

(f) Stage of Proceedings at which Evidence May be Received.

(1) Appeal.

Appeal to High Court—Fresh evidence, jurisdiction of Court to receive—Evidence that original judgment based on perjured testimony.]—On an appeal from the Supreme Court the High Court has no jurisdiction to receive further evidence. *Held*, therefore, that leave to read affidavits for the purpose of showing that the evidence on which an original judgment had been obtained was perjured should be refused. *Ronald* v. *Harper*, (1910) 11 C.L.R., 63 ; 16 A.L.R., 415. High Court, *Griffith*, *C.J.*, *Barton* and *O'Connor, JJ.*

Order LVIII., r. 4—Appeal—Fresh evidence—Discretion to receive.]—*Semble* (per *Hodges* and *Cussen, JJ.*).—The rules laid down in *Ward* v. *Hearne*, (1884) 10 V.L.R. (L.), 163 ; 6 A.L.T., 49, and *Ashley* v. *Ashley*, 24 V.L.R., 220 ; 4 A.L.R., 154, though sound and to be followed in most cases, may not apply in cases where the rights of others than the immediate parties are concerned, *e.g.*, in cases of trustees, guardians of infants, committees of lunatics, and where the action of the person tendering fresh evidence is really brought in the interests of the public at large. *The King* v. *Watt* ; *Ex parte Slade*, (1912) V.L.R., 225 ; 33 A.L.T., 222 ; 18 A.L.R., 158. F.C., *Madden, C.J.*, *Hodges* and *Cussen, JJ.*

Order LVIII., r. 4—Appeal from order granting mandamus—"Judgment after trial

or hearing of cause or matter on the merits "
—Discretion to receive further evidence.]—
An appeal from an order granting a mandamus
is not an appeal from " a judgment after
trial or hearing of a cause or matter on the
merits " within Order LVIII., r. 4 of the
Rules of the Supreme Court 1906, and the
Court has full discretion to receive further
evidence. *The King* v. *Watt*; *Ex parte
Slade*, (1912) V.L.R., 225 ; 33 A.L.T., 222 ;
18 A.L.R., 158: F.C. *Madden, C.J., Hodges*
and *Cussen, JJ.*

**Appeal—Evidence, admissibility of—Appli-
cation for new trial on ground of misconduct
of juryman—Evidence as to such misconduct given before primary Judge —
Affidavit as to such evidence.]**—During the
trial of an action by a Judge and jury one of
the jurymen was charged with misconduct
in making a certain statement to a clerk
of the defendant's solicitor. After hearing
the clerk's sworn testimony as to what had
occurred and the denial of the juryman not
on oath, the Judge accepted the denial of
the juryman and directed the case to proceed
On defendant's application to the State Full
Court for a new trial, an affidavit was tendered setting out the evidence of their solicitor's clerk as given before the primary
Judge. The Full Court (*Hood, J.*, dissenting) rejected the affidavit. On appeal to the
High Court, *Held, per O'Connor, J.*—The
affidavit should have been admitted, but (per
Isaacs, J.,) it was rightly rejected. *David
Syme & Co.* v. *Swinburne*, 10 C.L.R., 43 ;
16 A.L.R., 93 (1909).

(2) In Other Cases.

**Habeas corpus—Truth of return, whether
it must be verified.]**—The truth of the return
to a writ of *Habeas Corpus* need not be verified by affidavit. *Ah Sheung* v. *Lindberg*,
(1906) V.L.R., 323 ; 27 A.L.T., 189 ; *sub
nom. Rex* v. *Ah Sheung*, 12 A.L.R., 190.
Cussen, J. (1906).

**Arbitration—Discovery of fresh evidence
since publication of award—Remitting award
to arbitrator for reconsideration—Jurisdiction.]**—The Court has jurisdiction to remit an
award to the arbitrator for reconsideration

on the ground of the discovery of fresh evidence, notwithstanding that such evidence
might by due diligence have been discovered
and produced at the former inquiry by the
party in whose favour it is. *Re Keighley,
Maxsted & Co.*, (1893) 1 Q.B., 405, and
Sprague v. *Allen*, 15 T.L.R., 150, followed.
In re Bennett Brothers, (1910) V.L.R., 51 ;
31 A.L.T., 148 ; 16 A.L.R., 30. *Madden,
C.J.*

**Pure food—Adulteration—Division of article
taken into parts—Request to justices to send
part to Board—Request made after close of
evidence—Whether too late—Pure Food Act
1905 (No. 2010), sec. 23.]**—*See* HEALTH.
Gunner v. *Payne*, (1910) V.L.R., 45 ; 31
A.L.T., 138 ; 16 A.L.R., 29.

(*g*) *Statutory Requirements of Written
Evidence.*

(1) Statute of Frauds.

(*a*) Memorandum, Sufficiency of.

**Instruments Act 1890 (No. 1103), secs. 208,
209—Statute of Frauds (29 Car. II. c. 3)—
Contract for sale of land—Signature to note
or memorandum—Signature by amanuensis in
presence and by direction of party to be
charged, whether sufficient.]**—To satisfy
the requirements of secs. 208 and 209 of
the *Instruments Act* 1890, there must be a
personal signature by the hand of the party
to be charged, or a signature by an agent
authorised in writing by the party to be
charged, and the signature by an amanuensis,
in the presence by the direction and with the
name of the party to be charged, cannot be
regarded as a signature by that party with
his own hand, and is therefore insufficient.
Thomson v. *McInnis*, (1911) 12 C.L.R.,
562 ; 17 A.L.R., 354. H.C., *Griffith, C.J.,
Barton* and *O'Connor, JJ.*

**Sale of goods—Memorandum of agreement,
whether necessary—Contract itself in writing
—Sale of Goods Act 1896 (No. 1422), sec. 9.]**—
A signed and sent to B a letter offering to
sell him goods of the value of £10 and upwards on conditions therein specified. B,
by a subsequent letter, accepted A's offer.
Held, that the provisions of sec. 9 (1) of the
Sale of Goods Act 1896 requiring a note or

memorandum of the contract did not preclude B from enforcing the agreement to sell. *Patterson* v. *Dolman*, (1908) V.L.R., 354; 29 A.L.T., 256; 14 A.L.R., 240. F.C., *a' Beckett, Hodges* and *Cussen, JJ.*

Instruments Act 1890 (No. 1103), sec. 208 —Memorandum of contract contained in several documents—Agreement to act as manager of company—Agreement implied from Articles of Association and conduct of parties.]—Article 55 of the P company's Articles of Association was to the following effect :—" B.G. shall be the first managing director of the P company and shall hold such office for the term of ten years from August 1st, 1900. B.G. shall be entitled as such managing director to receive out of the funds of the company during his tenure of office the sum of £500 per annum payable by weekly instalments. The remuneration of B.G. after the expiration of the said term of ten years from August 1st 1900 or any other managing director appointed in his stead shall be fixed by the directors." For a period of over four years B.G. acted as managing director of the P company, without any objection by any director or officer or member of the company, and during all that period from August 1st, 1900, was paid for his services at the rate mentioned in the Articles of Association. B.G. signed a consent to act and in the directors' report was returned as managing director. On February 15th, 1905, B.G. wrote a letter to the secretary of the P company in the following terms :—" Take notice that I claim by virtue of clause 55 of the Articles of Association of the above company and every other right enabling me so to do to be retained in my position as managing director of the P company for the period of ten years from August 1st, 1900, at the remuneration of £500 as therein provided and that any sale of the company's business assets and goodwill to the D company must be subject to my claim or its equivalent in money." On the next day the secretary wrote in reply as follows :—" In reply to your letter of the 15th which was submitted to my board of directors at their meeting held to-day I am instructed to inform you that the contemplated sale of this company's assets to the D company will carry with it the obligation to carry out the contract with you so far as regards the salary of £500 per annum for the balance of the term of ten years from August 1st, 1900." The minutes of the P company showed that the secretary was instructed by the board of directors to write the above letter, and that a copy of that letter was submitted to the board on March 2nd and again approved. In an action by B.G. against the P company for breach of contract to employ him, *Held*, that there was sufficient evidence that a contract was in fact made between the P company and B.G. to employ him for the time and on the terms stated in Article 55 of the Articles of Association, and that a memorandum of such contract sufficient to comply with the *Statute of Frauds* (*Instruments Act* 1890, sec. 208) was contained in the various documents referred to. *Glass* v. *Pioneer Rubber Works of Australia Ltd.*, (1906) V.L.R., 754; 28 A.L.T., 64; 12 A.L.R., 529. F.C., *a' Beckett, A. C.J., Hodges* and *Chomley, JJ.*

Statute of Frauds—Conveyancing Act 1904 (No. 1953), sec. 75—Charge—Parol declaration.]—An equitable charge under sec. 75 of the *Conveyancing Act* 1904 may be created by parol. *In re Smith*; *Smith* v. *Smith*, (1909) V.L.R., 91; 30 A.L.T., 214; 15 A.L.R., 25. *Hood, J.*

(b) Parol Evidence.

Instruments Act 1890 (No. 1103), sec. 208— Sale of land—Note or memorandum—Several documents—Parol evidence, when admissible to connect—Reference to document—Reference to transaction in which document may or may not have been written.]—Where the memorandum of a contract is sought to be constituted from several documents, the reference in the document signed by the party to be charged must be to some other document the identity of which may be proved by parol evidence, and not merely to some transaction in the course of which another document may or may not have been written. *Held*, therefore, that the words " purchase money " in a receipt given by the vendor of land for a sum of money " being a deposit and first part purchase money " could not refer to another document and that parol evidence was not admissible. *Thomson* v. *Mc Innes*, (1911) 12 C.L.R., 562 ; 17 A.L.R., 354. H.C., *Griffith, C.J., Barton* and *O'Connor, JJ.*

Written contract—Parol evidence to identify subject matter, admissibility of—Latent ambiguity—Language apt to express a specific article of a class or any article of that class—Statute of Frauds.]—Where a written contract for the sale of a particular chattel is couched in general terms equally apt to express the sale of any article of a certain class or the sale of a specific article of that class, parol evidence is admissible to show that a specific article was contracted for and to ascertain and identify that specific article. *Bank of New Zealand* v. *Simpson*, (1900) A.C., 182, followed. *Smith* v. *Jeffryes*, 15 M. & W., 561, and *Wilkie* v. *Hunt*, 1 W.W. & a'B. (L.), 66, distinguished. *Bruton* v. *Farm and Dairy Machinery Co. Proprietary Ltd.*, (1910) V.L.R., 196 ; 31 A.L.T., 200 ; 16 A.L.R., 241. F.C., *Madden, C.J., a'Beckett* and *Hood, JJ.*

Instruments Act 1890 (No. 1103), sec. 208—Parol lease for less than three years—Lessee in possession of premises under existing tenancy.]—An agreement to lease for less than three years premises of which the lessee is already in possession under an existing tenancy, may be proved by parol, and is not affected by the *Statute of Frauds.* The existing tenancy is surrendered by operation of law and the possession of the lessee is referable to the new tenancy. *Knott* v. *Mc Kendrick*, 28 A.L.T. (Supplement), 4 ; 12 A.L.R. (C.N.), 23. *Judge Box* (1906).

(2) Statute of Limitations.

Statute of Limitations—Simple contract debt—Acknowledgment—Letter from debtor's solicitor expressing debtor's inability to pay—Promise as to payment by debtor's wife.]— *See* LIMITATIONS (STATUTES OF). *Holden* v. *Lawes Wittewronge*, (1912) V.L.R., 82 ; 33 A.L.T., 153 ; 18 A.L.R., 28.

(3) Under Mines Act.

Mines Act 1897 (No. 1514), sec. 75—Mining on private property—Compensation—Agreement with owner—Necessity for writing—Waiver.]—*Semble.*—Sec. 75 (2) of the *Mines Act* 1897 which provides that no agreement between the applicant for a mining lease on private property and the owner thereof as to compensation shall have any force or validity unless it is in writing signed by the parties thereto is for the benefit of the owner and may be waived by him. *Armstrong* v. *The Duke of Wellington G.M. Co. No Liability*, (1906) V.L.R., 145 ; 27 A.L.T., 146 ; 12 A.L.R., 67. *Madden, C.J.*

V.—IMPROPER ADMISSION OR REJECTION OF EVIDENCE, EFFECT OF.

Justices Act 1890 (No. 1105), secs. 141—Order to review conviction—Improper admission of evidence—Whether duty of Court either to set aside conviction or remit for rehearing.]—Where, on the return of an order to review a conviction, the Court is satisfied that on the evidence properly admitted the defendant clearly should have been convicted, the Court is not bound to set the conviction aside or to remit the case because some written or oral statement, possibly having some effect on the Justices' decision, has been wrongfully admitted as evidence. *Macmanamny* v. *King*, (1907) V.L.R., 535 ; 28 A.L.T., 250 ; 13 A.L.R., 258. F.C., *a'Beckett, Hood* and *Cussen, JJ.*

Justices Act 1890 (No. 1105), sec. 141—Order to review conviction—Evidence improperly admitted—Whether Court bound either to set aside conviction or remit case for re-hearing.]—On the return of an order to review, even in a criminal matter, the Court is not bound to set aside a conviction or remit the case for re-hearing because some written or oral statement, possibly having some effect on the Justices' decision, has been wrongly admitted in evidence, if, in the opinion of the Court, on the evidence properly admitted, the defendant clearly should have been convicted. *Reg.* v. *Gibson*, 18 Q.B.D., 537, considered. *Knox* v. *Thomas Bible*; *Knox* v. *J. L. Bible*, (1907) V.L.R., 485 ;

29 A.L.T., 23 ; 13 A.L.R., 352. *Cussen, J.*
[Leave to appeal to High Court refused, 4
C.L.R., 1462].

**Order to review—Evidence properly rejected
on the ground upon which it was tendered—
Admissibility of evidence on another ground—
Whether to be relied on upon order to review.]**
—Where evidence is tendered before Justices
on a ground on which it is not admissible,
and it is rejected by them, their order will
not be reviewed on the ground that such
evidence was admissible on a ground other
than that on which it was tendered. *Sanderson* v. *Nicholson*, 27 A.L.T., 215 ; (1906)
V.L.R., 371 ; 12 A.L.R., 208, not followed.
Honeybone v. *Glass*, (1908) V.L.R., 466 ;
30 A.L.T., 54 ; 14 A.L.R., 345. *Madden,
C.J.*

**Criminal law—New trial, when to be
granted after quashing conviction—Circumstances to be considered in exercise of discretion—Failure to warn jury against convicting on uncorroborated evidence of accomplice.—Evidence improperly admitted and
afterwards withdrawn from jury—Crimes Act
1890 (No. 1079), sec. 482.]**—*See* Criminal
Law. *Peacock* v. *The King*, (1911) 13
C.L.R., 619 ; 17 A.L.R., 566.

VI.—Documentary Evidence.

(a) *Execution and Revocation.*

**Will — Execution — Evidence — State-
ments made by testator after execution.]**—
Statements made by a person after the alleged
execution of a will by him are not admissible
as evidence of such execution. *Atkinson* v.
Morris, (1897) P., 40, followed. *Gair* v.
Bowers ; *Falconar* v. *Bowers* ; *Gair* v.
Falconar, (1909) 9 C.L.R., 510 ; 15 A.L.R.,
494. H.C., *Griffith, C.J., O'Connor, Isaacs*
and *Higgins, JJ.*

**Will—Revocation by subsequent will—
Subsequent will not produced.]**—The revocation of a will which has been duly executed
will not be established by the execution of
a subsequent will which is not produced,
unless the latter is clearly proved to have
contained an express revocation of the
earlier will or dispositions inconsistent with
those in the earlier will. *Cutts* v. *Gilbert*,

9 Moo. P.C.C., 131. *Gair* v. *Bowers* ; *Falconar*
v. *Bowers* ; *Gair* v. *Falconar*, (1909) 9 C.L.R.,
510 ; 15 A.L.R., 494. H.C., *Griffith, C.J.,
O'Connor, Isaacs* and *Higgins, JJ.*

(b) *Extrinsic Evidence ; Secondary Evidence.*

**Patent—Provisional specification—Evidence
to explain, admissibility of.]**—*Per Griffith,
C.J.* :—If a provisional specification is ambiguous in the sense that the language is apt
to describe two different things, evidence is
admissible to show of which the applicant is
actually speaking. *Per O'Connor, Isaacs*
and *Higgins, JJ.* :—On an opposition to an
application for a patent, the construction
of a provisional specification is to be determined by a consideration of what meaning
is conveyed by its words alone aided by
such evidence as will enable those words to
be understood, but the state of mind of the
applicant at the time he lodges his provisional
specification is irrelevant for the purposes
of its construction. *Dunlop* v. *Cooper*,
(1908) 7 C.L.R., 146 ; 14 A.L.R., 652.

**Will—Interpretation— Extrinsic evidence,
admissibility of—Facts known to testator at
time of making will.]**—For the purpose of
ascertaining the object of a testator's bounty,
the Court has a right to ascertain all the facts
known to the testator at the time he made
his will ; and such evidence is always admissible to explain what the testator has written
whether an ambiguity is raised by the will
or not. *Charter* v. *Charter*, L.R. 7 H.L.,
364, applied ; *Re Ely, Tottenham* v. *Ely*, 65
L.T., 452, and *In re Whorwood, Ogle* v. *Lord
Sherborne*, 34 Ch. D., 446, distinguished.
In re Loughlin ; *Acheson* v. *O'Meara*, (1906)
V.L.R., 597 ; 28 A.L.T., 28 ; 12 A.L.R., 411.
Hood, J.

**Gift of " the following twelve properties "—
Eleven properties only enumerated—Accidental omission, whether Court may supply—
Ambiguity.]**—Testator by his will devised
to his daughter " the following twelve
properties," and then enumerated not twelve
properties but eleven. Evidence was given
that in the draft will prepared under the
testator's instructions a twelfth property
had been included in the list of properties

given to the testator's daughter, but that it had been accidentally omitted therefrom in the will as executed. The twelfth property was nowhere mentioned in the will. *Held*, that no words in the will required interpretation, and the wrong enumeration of twelve could not be corrected by adding to the properties specified another property. *Harter* v. *Harter*, L.R. 3 P. & D., 11, applied. *In re Green*; *Crowson* v. *Wild*, (1907) V.L.R., 284; 28 A.L.T., 206; 13 A.L.R., 121. *a' Beckett, J*, (1907).

Will—Ambiguity—Parol evidence, admissibility of—Language ordinarily used by testatrix in referring to certain of her property—Intention of testatrix expressed in conversation.]—The only land which testatrix had was a block of 145 acres in the parish of Waaia, divided into three paddocks, containing 45, 38½ and 61½ acres respectively. By her will testatrix devised " unto W. 40 acres of land situated in the parish of Waaia being part of . . . 140 land . . and to my grandchildren the remaining one hundred acres." The question before the Court being what was meant by the devise to W. of " 40 acres," *Held*, that evidence that testatrix used to speak of the 38½ acre paddock as " the forty acre block " or " the forty acre paddock " was admissible, but that evidence that testatrix when she asked W. to draw up her will, told him she wished him to have the 38½ acre paddock, and that the testatrix intended the words used in the will to describe that paddock, was inadmissible. *In re Leaf*; *Donaldson* v. *Leaf*, (1907) V.L.R., 278; 29 A.L.T., 54; 13 A.L.R., 148. *a' Beckett, J.*

Evidence — Legacy — Ademption — Gifts made for same purpose as legacy—Statements by donor made subsequently to gifts as to intention in making gifts.]—Where a pecuniary legacy was given by a will for particular purposes, and the testatrix subsequently during her lifetime made gifts of money towards the same purposes, statements made by her subsequently to the gifts are admissible to negative any intention that the gifts should reduce or supersede the legacy. *In re Leggatt*; *Griffith* v. *Calder*, (1908) V.L.R.,

385; 30 A.L.T., 34; 14 A.L.R., 314. *a' Beckett, J.*

Written contract—Parol evidence to identify subject-matter, admissibility of—Latent ambiguity—Language apt to express a specific article of a class or any article of that class.]—*See* STATUTORY REQUIREMENTS OF WRITTEN EVIDENCE. *Bruton* v. *Farm and Dairy Machinery Co. Proprietary Ltd.*, (1910) V.L.R., 196; 31 A.L.T., 200; 16 A.L.R., 241.

Police Offences Act 1890 (No. 1126), sec. 57—Gaming—Search warrant, on what materials issued—" Complaint on oath," meaning of—Oral evidence to supplement written information, admissibility of.]—The complaint on oath required by sec. 57 of the *Police Offences Act* 1890 must be in writing. *Semble*, where the information on which a warrant is issued does not set out all the matters specified by the section, oral evidence sufficiently specifying these matters is inadmissible. *Montague* v. *Ah Shen*, (1907) V.L.R., 458; 28 A.L.T., 248; 13 A.L.R., 261. F.C., *Madden, C.J., a' Beckett* and *Hood, JJ.*

Secondary evidence of document.—Notice to produce, whether necessary—Thistle Act 1890 (No. 1145), sec. 4—Notice calling upon defendant to destroy thistles—Offence constituted by disobedience to notice.]—In proceedings under sec. 4 of the *Thistle Act* 1890 for not effectually destroying thistles after written notice, secondary evidence of such notice is admissible, although notice to produce it has not been given. *Sanderson* v. *Nicholson*, (1906) V.L.R., 371; 27 A.L.T., 215; 12 A.L.R., 208. *a' Beckett, A.-C.J.*

(c) *Public and Official Documents.*

(1) Crown Grant; Certificate of Title.

Crown grant—Evidence as to the land to which it relates—Long and unchallenged occupancy.]—In the absence of survey marks there can be no better indication of the land to which a Crown grant relates than long and unchallenged occupation. *National Trustees Executors &c. Co. of Australasia Ltd.* v. *Hassett and the Registrar of Titles*, (1907)

V.L.R., 404; 28 A.L.T., 232; 13 A.L.R.; 208. *Cussen, J.*

Transfer of Land Act 1890 (No. 1149), secs. 69, 74—Certificate of title, how far conclusive —Same land included in two certificates— Subsequent certificate, when it may be conclusive.]—Although, where the same piece of land is included in two certificates of title, it is the prior certificate which usually has the conclusive effect mentioned in sec. 69, yet, where there has been a wrong description of boundaries, or where there are rights acquired by adverse possession, the prior certificate may not be conclusive in whole or in part, and the subsequent certificate may then have the conclusive effect. *National Trustees Executors &c. Co. of Australasia Ltd, v. Hassett and the Registrar of Titles*, (1907) V.L.R., 404; 28 A.L.T., 232; 13 A.L.R., 208. *Cussen, J.*

(2) Court Records; Public Registers.

Evidence—Public document—Suitor's cash book (Rule 10, Rules under the Justices Act 1890)—Entries made by Clerk of Petty Sessions not in official capacity—Maintenance order—Direction to pay to clerk—Entries of payments—Marriage Act 1890 (No. 1166), sec. 51.]—Entries in a book (whether the suitor's cash book or not) kept by the Clerk of Petty Sessions for the time being, and purporting to record certain payments made to such Clerk under a maintenance order, are not admissible, in proceedings for disobedience of such order under sec. 51 of the *Marriage Act* 1890, to prove non-payment of the balance. It is not a part of the Clerk's official duty to receive such payments, and so far as such entries are concerned the book is not a public document or public book. *Cohen v. MacDonough (or O'Donough)*, (1906) V.L.R., 521; 28 A.L.T., 97; 12 A.L.R., 447. *Cussen, J.*

Marriage Act 1890 (No. 1166), sec. 43— Maintenance order—Payments to be made to Clerk of Petty Sessions—Failure to comply with order, evidence of—Suitors' cash book, how it may be used.]—Default in compliance with a maintenance order directing payments to be made to the Clerk of Petty Sessions may be proved by the statement of that officer; and, though the Solicitor's Cash Book kept by him, being the book in which it would have been his duty to record payment, if made, is not admissible to prove default, it may be looked at by him to refresh his memory by showing that no payment was recorded. *Shee v. Larkin*, (1907) V.L.R., 295; 28 A.L.T., 188; 13 A.L.R., 97. *a'Beckett, J.*

Trade mark—Effect of registration—Presence on register for five years, how far conclusive.]—The presence on the register of a trade mark makes it *prima facie* good for five years. After that period, it becomes conclusive evidence that it is such a trade mark, provided it is possible for it to be a trade mark at all. *In re Trade Marks Act 1890 (No. 2); Lysaght Ltd. v. Reid Bros. & Russell Proprietary Ltd.*, (1907) V.L.R., 432; 28 A.L.T., 223; 13 A.L.R., 241. F.C., *Madden, C.J., a'Beckett* and *Hood, JJ.*

(3) Official Certificates.

Commonwealth Conciliation and Arbitration Act 1904 (No. 13 of 1904), sec. 57—Registrar's certificate of registration of organization—Whether conclusive evidence of validity of registration.]—A certificate of the Registrar of the Commonwealth Court of Conciliation and Arbitration of the registration of an organization given under sec. 57 of the *Commonwealth Conciliation and Arbitration Act* 1904 is not conclusive evidence of the validity of such registration. *Federated Engine-Drivers and Firemen's Association of Australasia v. Broken Hill Proprietary Co. Ltd.*, (1911) 12 C.L.R., 398; 17 A.L.R., 285. *Griffith, C.J., Barton, O'Connor, Isaacs* and *Higgins, JJ.*

Commonwealth Conciliation and Arbitration Act 1904 (No. 13 of 1904), sec. 21—Evidence—Registrar's certificate as to existence and extent of dispute—Whether evidence of existence of dispute.]—A certificate given by the Registrar under sec. 21 of the *Commonwealth Conciliation and Arbitration Act* 1904 that a dispute relating to industrial matters is an industrial dispute extending beyond the limits of one State is not evidence of the existence of an industrial dispute within the meaning of the Act. *Federated Engine-Drivers and Firemen's Association of Australasia* v. *Broken Hill Proprietary Co. Ltd.,* (1911) 12 C.L.R., 398; 17 A.L.R., 285. *Griffith, C.J., Barton, O'Connor, Isaacs* and *Higgins, JJ.*

Friendly Societies Act 1890 (No. 1094), secs. 11, 13 (v.)—Rules of Society—Acknowledgment of registration issued by Registrar—How far conclusive as to validity of rules.]—An acknowledgment of registry of an amendment of a rule issued by the Registrar under sec. 13 (v.) of the *Friendly Societies Act* 1890 is only conclusive that the things which might lawfully be done have been done, and has not the effect of declaring that a thing which could not be lawfully done has been lawfully done. *Shillinglaw* v. *Carroll,* 3 C.L.R., 1099; 12 A.L.R., 347. H.C., *Griffith, C.J., Barton* and *O'Connor, JJ.* (1906).

Evidence—Date of birth—Certificates of death and burial.]—Certificates of death and of burial containing the age of a deceased person are *prima facie* evidence of the date of birth. *In re Osmand; Bennett* v. *Booty,* (1908) V.L.R., 67; 29 A.L.T., 168; 13 A.L.R., 728. F.C., *a' Beckett, A.-C.J., Hodges* and *Hood, JJ.* (1908), affirming *Cussen, J.* (1906) V.L.R., 455; 27 A.L.T., 218; 12 A.L.R., 256.

Local Government Act 1903 (No. 1893), secs. 324, 341, 342, 343, 704—Recovery of rates—Evidence of ownership of land—Certificate of Registrar-General that a certain person appears from memorial of registration to be owner—Effect of such certificate where such person is in fact dead.]—*Per Hood, J.:*—Section 704 of the *Local Government Act* 1903 is merely an evidence section, and the provision making the certificate of the Registrar-General *prima facie* evidence of ownership does not enable a plaintiff to get over the difficulty of suing a dead man. *In re the Transfer of Land Act; Ex parte Anderson,* (1911) V.L.R., 397; 33 A.L.T., 78; 17 A.L.R., 399. (1911).

Vermin Destruction Act 1890 (No. 1153), sec. 26—Costs incurred by Inspector in destroying vermin—Certificate of amount, how far conclusive.]—The certificate of the Inspector under sec. 26 of the *Vermin Destruction Act* 1890 does not preclude evidence to show that the charges were not reasonably incurred. *McCallum* v. *Purvis,* (1906) V.L.R., 578; 28 A.L.T., 31; 12 A.L.R., 329. *Hood, J.* (1906).

(d) *Judgments and Warrants.*

Res judicata—Judgment—Finding of fact, whether conclusive in other proceedings against another party—Finding of fact as to status—Prohibited immigrant—Immigration Restriction Act 1901 (No. 17).]—One, Ah Sheung, was charged, upon the information of C., an officer of Customs, with being a prohibited immigrant, and he set up the defence that he was a naturalised subject of the King in Victoria. C. admitted that there was a naturalised subject of the King in Victoria named Ah Sheung, but disputed the identity of the accused with that person. In support of this defence, a judgment of the Supreme Court—in proceedings by way of writ of *habeas corpus* issued at the instance of Ah Sheung, and directed to the master of the ship by which Ah Sheung came to the Commonwealth, who claimed to detain Ah Sheung as a prohibited immigrant, and under the authority of the *Immigration Restriction Act* 1901—was tendered and admitted in evidence by which it appeared that the Court had found as a fact that Ah Sheung was identical with the Ah Sheung who was admittedly a naturalised subject of the King in Victoria. *Held,* that the judgment was not admissible in evidence upon the question of fact of the identity of Ah Sheung. *Christie* v. *Ah Sheung,* (1906) 3 C.L.R., 998; 12 A.L.R., 432. H.C., *Griffith, C.J., Barton* and *O'Connor, JJ.*

Habeas Corpus—Return to writ—Legal justification for restraint disclosed—Evidence, admissibility of—Conviction or warrant of Superior Court—Conviction or warrant of inferior Court—No judgment of Court—Procedure.]—*See* HABEAS CORPUS. *Ah Sheung* v. *Lindberg,* (1906) V.L.R., 323; 27 A.L.T., 189; *sub nom., Rex* v. *Ah Sheung,* 12 A.L.R., 190.

Return of writ of habeas corpus—Whether Court bound by recitals in warrant—Evidence to show want of jurisdiction.]—*See* HABEAS CORPUS. *Ex parte Dunn* ; *Ex parte Aspinall*, (1906) V.L.R., 493 ; 28 A.L.T., 3 ; 12 A.L.R., 358.

VII.—WITNESSES.

(a) Competency and Compellability.

Evidence—Wife, whether competent witness against husband—Wife desertion—Neglect to comply with order for maintenance—Marriage Act 1901 (No. 1737), secs. 3, 4—Crimes Act 1891 (No. 1231), sec. 34.]—The prisoner's wife is a competent witness against him on an indictment for wife desertion under sec. 3 (1) (a) of the *Marriage Act* 1901, but not in an indictment for wilfully neglecting to comply with an order for maintenance under sec. 4 of that Act. *Rex* v. *Jacono*, (1911) V.L.R., 326 ; 33 A.L.T., 28 ; 17 A.L.R., 340. F.C., *Madden, C.J., Hodges* and *Hood, JJ.*

Companies Act 1890 (No. 1074), sec. 109—Practice—Winding up—Examination of persons capable of giving information concerning the trade dealings of the company—Jurisdiction.]—The Court has no power to summon before it under section 109 of the *Companies Act* 1890 a person claiming to be a creditor of a debtor of a company which is being compulsorily wound up by the Court where it is not shown that such person knows anything of the trade dealings estate or effects of the company. *In re City of Melbourne Bank*, (1910) V.L.R., 282 ; 32 A.L.T., 20 ; 16 A.L.R., 283. *Hodges, J.* (1910).

Insolvency Act 1890 (No. 1102), sec. 149—Insolvency Act 1897 (No. 1513), sec. 91—Insolvency Rules 1898 Appendix of Forms (No. 64)—Contempt of Court—Certificate—Compulsory appearance—Refusal of insolvent to be sworn—Refusal to give answers tending to render him liable to imprisonment—Power of committal—Form of notice of motion to insolvent.]—*Semble*, by virtue of section 91 of the *Insolvency Act* 1897 the Insolvency Court has power to compel an insolvent who has been required to appear before it under section 149 of the *Insolvency Act* 1890 to be sworn and give evidence although such evidence might tend to render him liable to imprisonment. *In re Aarons*, 6 V.L.R. (1), 56 ; 2 A.L.T., 51, distinguished. The notice required under section 149 of the *Insolvency Act* 1890 requiring the insolvent to attend before the Court to have the question of the grant or refusal of his certificate dealt with, should direct attention to the fact that the insolvent may be punished or otherwise dealt with as if the certificate had been applied for by him. *In re Hickman*, 31 A.L.T. (Supplement), 10 ; 15 A.L.R. (C.N.), 21. *Judge Moule* (1909).

Questions asked by Comptroller-General of Customs—Duty to answer—Prosecution pending—Person interrogated not charged—Corporation—Australian Industries Preservation Act 1906-1909 (No. 9 of 1906—No. 26 of 1909), sec. 15B.]—*See* AUSTRALIAN INDUSTRIES PRESERVATION ACT, cols. 68, 69. *Melbourne Steamship Co.* v. *Moorehead*, (1912) 15 C.L.R., 333 ; 18 A.L.R., 533.

(b) Privilege.

Evidence Act 1890 (No. 1088), sec. 55—Evidence of physician or surgeon—Privilege—" Information acquired," what is.]—Section 55 of the *Evidence Act* 1890 provides that :—" No physician or surgeon shall without the consent of his patient divulge in any civil suit or proceeding (unless the sanity of the patient be the matter in dispute) any information which he may have acquired in attending the patient and which was necessary to enable him to prescribe or act for the patient." *Held*, that the prohibition in that section extends to anything which comes to the knowledge of the physician or surgeon with regard to the health or physical condition of the patient, as well as anything said by the patient to him. while the relationship of medical adviser and patient continues, and which is necessary for the purpose stated. *Warnecke* v. *Equitable Life Assurance Society*, (1906) V.L.R., 482 ; 27 A.L.T., 236 ; 12 A.L.R., 254, approved. *National Mutual Life Association of Australasia Ltd.* v. *Godrich*, 10 C.L.R., 1 ; 16 A.L.R., 110. *Griffith, C.J., Barton. O'Connor, Isaacs* and *Higgins, JJ.* (1909).

Evidence Act 1890 (No. 1088), sec. 55—
Evidence of physician or surgeon—Privilege
—" Information necessary to enable him to
prescribe or act for the patient "—Information acquired after prescription or at or after
operation.]—Held, (per Barton, O'Connor,
Isaacs and Higgins, JJ.) that the prohibition in section 55 of the Evidence Act 1890
against the disclosure of information acquired
by a physician or surgeon is not limited to
information acquired before a prescription is
given or an operation undertaken, but extends at least to all information acquired
until the professional attendance on the
patient is at an end, provided the information
is material to proper treatment. Held, per
Griffith, C.J., that it does not extend to mere
physical facts ascertainable by observation
only, irrespective of confidential communications, ascertained by such observations after
the necessity for treatment is at an end.
National Mutual Life Association of Australasia Ltd. v. Godrich, 10 C.L.R., 1 ; 16
A.L.R., 110 (1909).

Evidence Act 1890 (No. 1088), sec. 55—
Evidence of physician or surgeon—Information
acquired in attending a patient—Privilege—
Death of patient, effect of—Personal representative of patient, power of.]—The operation of section 55 of the Evidence Act 1890
is not limited to the lifetime of the patient.
Quaere, whether the executor of a deceased
patient can consent to the divulgation of the
information acquired by a physician or surgeon in attending the patient. National
Mutual Life Association of Australasia Ltd.
v. Godrich, 10 C.L.R., 1 ; 16 A.L.R., 110.
H.C., Griffith, C.J., Barton, O'Connor,
Isaacs and Higgins, JJ. (1909).

Evidence Act 1890 (No. 1088), sec. 55—
Evidence of physician or surgeon—Information acquired in attending a patient outside
Victoria—Whether privileged from disclosure
within Victoria.]—Section 55 of the Evidence
Act which prohibits the disclosure of information acquired by a physician or surgeon
in attending a patient is applicable in every
case where the evidence is offered in Victoria
notwithstanding that the events or facts
sought to be proved occurred elsewhere.

National Mutual Life Association of Aus-
tralasia Ltd. v. Godrich, 10 C.L.R., 1 ; 16
A.L.R., 110. H.C., Griffith, C.J., Barton,
O'Connor, Isaacs and Higgins, JJ. (1909).

Evidence Act 1890 (No. 1088), sec. 55—
Evidence of physician or surgeon—Information acquired in attending a patient—Inadvertent disclosure of—Whether Court should
ignore.]—Quaere, per Higgins, J., whether
section 55 of the Evidence Act 1890 makes
it incumbent on the Court to ignore the evidence of a physician or surgeon which,
through inadvertence or otherwise, divulges
information acquired by him in attending a
patient. National Mutual Life Association
of Australasia Ltd. v. Godrich, 10 C.L.R.,
1 ; 16 A.L.R., 110.

Evidence Act 1890 (No. 1088), sec. 55—
Privilege—Information acquired by medical
adviser attending patient—Prohibition against
disclosure, extent of.]—Section 55 of the
Evidence Act 1890 provides that no physician
or surgeon shall without the consent of his
patient divulge in any civil action or proceeding (unless the sanity of his patient be
the matter in dispute) any information which
he may have acquired in attending the
patient and which was necessary to enable
him to prescribe or act for the patient.
Held, that the prohibition against divulging
information is not confined to communications made to the physician or surgeon by
the patient, but extends to any information
which he has acquired as the result of observation or examination of the patient. Warnecke v. Equitable Life Assurance Society
of the United States, (1906) V.L.R., 482 ;
27 A.L.T., 236 ; 12 A.L.R., 254, F.C.,
a'Beckett, A.C.J., Hodges and Chomley, JJ.
(1906).

Foreign Statute—Adoption in Victoria—
Principle of interpretation—Foreign decisions.]
—Section 55 of the Evidence Act 1890 having
been taken from a Statute of the State of
New York, which had been judicially inter-
preted by the Courts of that State before
its adoption in Victoria, the Parliament of
Victoria is to be regarded as having legis-
lated with reference to such interpretation.
Warnecke v. Equitable Life Assurance Society

of the United States, (1906) V.L.R., 482;
27 A.L.T., 236; 12 A.L.R., 254. F.C.,
a'Beckett, A.C.J., Hodges and Chomley, JJ.
(1906).

**Subpoena duces tecum—Order XXXVII., rr.
7, 8—Refusal of Presbytery clerk of Presbyterian Church of Victoria to produce documents
in civil action—Ecclesiastical privilege.]—**
Where the Clerk of a Presbytery or Court
of the Presbyterian Church of Victoria, being
served with a subpoena duces tecum to produce at the hearing of a civil action certain
documents relevant to the issue, which were
in his possession as Clerk to the Presbytery,
refused to produce them, on the ground that
he had taken an oath to the Presbytery not
to hand over any document in his possession
as clerk, without the Presbytery's authority,
the Court ordered him to be imprisoned
until he should purge his contempt and
adjourned the hearing of the case. Semble,
that if, on the application for release of the
clerk, the parties had asked for the expenses
occasioned by the clerk's conduct, he would
not have purged his offence until he had
paid such expenses. Ronald v. Harper, 15
A.L.R. (C.N.), 5. Hodges, J. (1909).

(c) Attendance ; Expenses.

**Order XXXVII.—Subpoena—Service beyond State—Application for leave—Affidavit
in support—Service and Execution of Process
Act 1901 (No. 11 of 1901), sec. 16 (1).]—**
Leave to serve a subpoena upon a person
in any other State or part of the Commonwealth will not be granted under sec. 16 (1)
of the Service and Execution of Process Act
1901, where the affidavit filed in support
of the application for such leave does not
show what facts the witness is likely to
prove. Trapp, Couche & Co. v. H.
McKenzie Ltd., 30 A.L.T., 200 ; 15 A.L.R.,
179. Hood, J. (1909).

**Evidence Act 1890 (No. 1088), sec. 12—
Royal Commission—Summons to witness,
form of.]—**A summons to a witness under
sec. 12 of the Evidence Act 1890 to attend
to give evidence before a Royal Commission
should state on its face that it is the Commission who desire the witness to attend,

and who consider his evidence necessary,
and that the Commission summon him to
attend, and it should be signed by the
Chairman. Barry v. Cullen, (1906) V.L.R.,
393; 27 A.L.T., 227 ; 12 A.L.R., 235.
a'Beckett, A.C.J.

**Evidence Act 1890 (No. 1088), sec. 12—
Royal Commission—Informal summons to
witness—Attendance of witness in obedience
to—Refusal to be sworn, whether justifiable.]**
—A summons to a witness to attend before
a Royal Commission to give evidence stated
that in the judgment of the Chairman, the
evidence of the witness was material to the
matter of the inquiry, and that the Chairman therefore summoned the witness to
attend before the Commission and be examined touching the matter of the inquiry.
The summons was signed by the Chairman.
The Commission had, in fact, resolved that
the evidence of the witness was material,
and that he should be called. The witness
attended but refused to be sworn, without,
however, taking objection to the form of
the summons. Held, that the summons,
though defective in form, was in fact the
summons of the Commission, and that the
witness being in attendance on such summons,
was not justified in refusing to be sworn.
Barry v. Cullen, (1906) V.L.R., 393; 27
A.L.T., 227 ; 12 A.L.R., 235. a'Beckett,
A.C.J. (1906).

**Imprisonment of Fraudulent Debtors Act
1890 (No. 1100), Part III.—Court of Petty
Sessions—Jurisdiction—Judgment debtor served with summons to debtor—Whether he
may be also served with summons to witness—
Non-attendance as witness, power to fine
upon—Justices Act 1890 (No. 1105), secs. 20
(2), 36 (4).]—**See DEBTORS ACT, col. 383.
Caldecott v. Cunningham, (1908) V.L.R., 38 ;
29 A.L.T., 94 ; 13 A.L.R., 639.

**Imprisonment of Fraudulent Debtors Act
1890 (No. 1100), Part III.—Proceedings upon
summons to debtor—Adjournment—Whether
witness bound to attend without issue or
service of further summons—Justices Act
1890 (No. 1105), sec. 78 (4).]—**See DEBTORS
ACT. Caldecott v. Cunningham, (1908)
V.L.R., 38 ; 29 A.L.T., 94 ; 13 A.L.R., 639.

Landlord and Tenant Act 1890 (No. 1108), secs. 92, 93—Justices Act 1890 (No. 1105), secs. 4, 29—Recovery of possession—Justices —Jurisdiction to issue summons to witness —Notice of intention to apply, service of— " Complaint."]—See LANDLORD AND TENANT. *Lesser* v. *Knight*, 29 A.L.T., 111 ; 13 A.L.R., 708.

Justices Act 1890 (No. 1105), secs. 20, 36, 78 (4)—Witness who has been paid his expenses failing to attend—Adjournment— Whether witness entitled to expenses of attending adjourned hearing.]—See JUSTICES OF THE PEACE. *Caldecott* v. *Cunningham*, (1908) V.L.R., 38 ; 29 A.L.T., 94 ; 13 A.L.R., 639.

Costs—Witness—Permanent residence at place of trial—Temporary residence at another place—Scale applicable—Allowance for attendance at trial—Time occupied in travelling —Travelling expenses.]—See COSTS, cols. 274, 275. *Jarrett* v. *Strempel*, (1911) V.L.R., 179 ; 32 A.L.T., 160 ; 17 A.L.R., 141.

(d) Oath, Administration of.

Justices—Oath of witness—Who to administer—Clerk of Petty Sessions—Subordinate clerk—Justices Act 1890 (No. 1105), sec. 77 (7)—Evidence Act 1890 (No. 1088), sec. 62.]— In proceedings before Justices in Petty Sessions the oath may be administered to witnesses by any Justice or by the Clerk of Petty Sessions, or by any person so directed by the Justices. The giving of the oath in all such cases is the act of the Court. *Rex* v. *Shuttleworth*, (1909) V.L.R., 431 ; 31 A.L.T., 50 ; 15 A.L.R., 492. F.C., *Madden, C.J., a' Beckett, Hodges, Hood* and *Cussen, JJ.*

Justices Act 1890 (No. 1105), secs. 41, 64, 77 (7)—Administration of oath—Acting Clerk of Petty Sessions—Perjury.]—A witness sworn by an acting Clerk of Petty Sessions may be guilty of perjury. *Reg.* v. *Barber*, 3 A.L.R. (C.N.), 21, approved. *Rex* v. *Turnbull*, (1907) V.L.R., 11 ; 28 A.L.T., 103 ; 12 A.L.R., 351. *Cussen, J.*

Justices Act 1890 (No. 1105), sec. 77 (7)— Administration of oath—Clerk of Petty Sessions, who is.]—*Quaere*, whether under sec. 77 (7) of the *Justices Act* 1890, a person who

de facto acts as a clerk of Petty Sessions may not lawfully administer the oath to a witness. *Rex* v. *Turnbull*, (1907) V.L.R., 11 ; 28 A.L.T., 103 ; 12 A.L.R., 551. *Cussen, J.*

(e) Ordering out of Court.

Justices Act 1890 (No. 1105), sec. 77 (11)— Ordering witnesses out of Court at request of party—Discretion of Justices—Counsel and solicitor of opposite party subpoenaed as witnesses—Permission to remain in Court, effect of.]—The provisions of sec. 77 (11) of the *Justices Act* 1890 do not necessarily make it improper for Justices to permit the counsel and solicitor appearing for a party to remain in Court, although the opposite party has subpoenaed them as witnesses, and has requested that all witnesses be ordered out of Court. Even if it were an error to permit them to remain, the proceedings would not thereby be invalidated, if it were evident that the request for their removal was made for the purpose of obstruction, and that the denial of the request in no way resulted in a denial of justice or prevented a proper hearing of the case. *Barry* v. *Cullen*, (1906) V.L.R., 393 ; 27 A.L.T., 227 ; 12 A.L.R., 235. *a' Beckett, A.-C.J.* (1906).

(f) Examination.

Witness—Whether Judge may call—Request by jury—Further proceedings.]—A Judge for the better ascertainment of the truth has a discretion, whether in a civil or a criminal case, to call a fresh witness, particularly where the jury requests it, and this is so in a trial before a jury, even when the jury has retired to consider its verdict. The Judge also has a discretion, after hearing the evidence of such fresh witness, and having regard to all the circumstances of the case, to say what further proceedings (if any) should be taken, e.g., he may permit counsel to cross-examine, or to again address the jury, or may allow further evidence to be called. *Rex* v. *Collins*, (1907) V.L.R., 292 ; 28 A.L.T., 222 ; 13 A.L.R., 184. *Cussen, J.*

Insolvency Act 1890 (No. 1102), sec. 135— Insolvency Act 1897 (No. 1513), sec. 111— Examination of insolvent and witnesses— Whether creditor may conduct examination.]

—A creditor has not the right to examine any person other than the insolvent brought before the Court under sec. 135 of the *Insolvency Act* 1890, and the Court will not under ordinary circumstances allow him to examine any such other person. *In re Foller*, 31 A.L.T. (Supplement) 15 ; 16 A.L.R. (C.N.), 1. *Judge Moule* (1910).

County Court—Evidence—Action for trial before Judge and jury—Examination of witnesses before trial—Jurisdiction.]—*See* COUNTY COURT, col. 309. *Ferris* v. *Litchfield*, 28 A.L.T. (Supplement), 14 ; 13 A.L.R. (C.N.), 10.

Crimes Act 1891 (No. 1231), sec. 34 (3)— Witness on own behalf—Cross-examination as to credit, when admitted—Evidence as to good character in the particular class of transactions in issue—Prosecution under Health Acts.]—At the hearing of an information under the *Health Acts* for selling adulterated food, the defendant in giving evidence, said :—" I always take every precaution." *Held,* that this statement was evidence of good character as applied to the trade in question, and that cross-examination directed to impeaching it was permissible under sec. 34 (3) of the *Crimes Act* 1891. *Gunner* v. *Payne,* (1910) V.L.R., 45 ; 31 A.L.T., 138 ; 16 A.L.R., 29. *Madden, C.J.*

Lotteries Gaming and Betting Act 1906 (No. 2055), sec. 38—Application for declaration that premises are a common gaming house—Affidavit of police officer showing reasonable grounds for suspecting—Whether police officer may be cross-examined thereon.] *See* GAMING AND WAGERING. *In re Lotteries Gaming and Betting Act* 1906 ; *In re Shanghai Club* ; *In re Ah Pow* ; *Ex parte Gleeson.* (1907) V.L.R., 463 ; 29 A.L.T., 31 ; 13 A.L.R., 360.

Lotteries Gaming and Betting Act 1906 (No. 2055), sec. 38—Application for declaration that premises are a common gaming house— Affidavits in reply to affidavits of party opposing, admissibility of—Cross-examination of deponents.]—*See* GAMING and WAGERING. *In re Lotteries Gaming and Betting Act* 1906 ; *In re Shanghai Club* ; *In re Ah Pow* ;

Ex parte Gleeson, (1907) V.L.R., 463 ; 29 A.L.T., 31 ; 13 A.L.R., 360.

(g) Corroboration.

Criminal law—Evidence of accomplice— Warning by Judge to jury against convicting on uncorroborated evidence—Whether Judge under positive duty to give warning—Omission to give warning, effect of—Quashing conviction—Entry on record that party ought not to have been convicted—Corroboration, sufficiency of—Crimes Act 1890 (No. 1079), sec. 482.]—*Per Griffith, C.J.*—It is now settled law in England that if the Judge omits to give the jury the usual warning as to convicting upon the evidence of an accomplice, and such evidence is not in fact corroborated, the conviction will be quashed. *Quære,* whether this is a new rule established under the *Criminal Appeal Act* 1907 (7 Edw. VII. c. 22), or a modern statement of the common law introduced into Australia. *Per Barton, J.* :—(1) When the evidence of the accomplice is not substantially corroborated, the duty of the Judge to warn the jury against acting upon it has not yet become a positive rule of law, although it is a matter of settled practice ; (2) In England, if there is an absence of substantial corroboration, and the Judge has failed to warn the jury according to the usual practice, the Court will treat the conviction as a " miscarriage of justice " within the meaning of the *Criminal Appeal Act,* sec. 41 (1) and set it aside ; *quaere,* whether in such a case in Victoria there should be an entry on the record that " the party ought not to have been convicted " under sec. 482 of the *Crimes Act* 1890 ; (3) The corroboration will be deemed sufficient if it is substantial, and is upon a material part of the case, and it need not amount to independent evidence implicating the prisoner. *Per O'Connor, J.* :—The omission to give warning, where the evidence of the accomplice is not in fact corroborated, is not an error in law entitling the prisoner to have the conviction quashed under the *Crimes Act* 1890. *Peacock* v. *The King,* (1911) 13 C.L.R., 619 ; 17 A.L.R., 566.

Crimes Act 1891 (No. 1231), sec. 33—Evidence Act 1890 (No. 1088), sec. 50—Unsworn

evidence of child of tender years—Corroboration—Indecent assault.]—In all cases of the nature provided for in sec. 33 (1) of the *Crimes Act* 1891, the testimony admitted by virtue of that section must notwithstanding sec. 50 of the *Evidence Act* 1890, be corroborated by some other material evidence in support thereof implicating the accused. Such implication of the accused ought to be by evidence of some direct kind, which would show that he more probably than any other person, was the man who committed the offence charged. *Per a' Beckett, J.* :—A Judge or Justice may in such cases, if the provisions of sec. 33 (2) of the *Crimes Act* 1891 are fulfilled, disregard the requirements of sec. 50 of the *Evidence Act* 1890. *Rex* v. *O'Brien,* (1912) V.L.R., 133 ; 33 A.L.T., 177 ; 18 A.L.R., 38. F.C., *Madden, C.J., a' Beckett* and *Hodges, JJ.*

Criminal law—Murder—Evidence, sufficiency of—Circumstantial evidence—Proof of fact of death—Proof that prisoner caused death—Reasonable hypothesis consistent with innocence—Direction to jury—Accomplice, evidence of—Corroboration of part of his evidence, sufficiency of.]—*See* Criminal Law. *Peacock* v. *The King,* (1911) 13 C.L.R., 619 ; 17 A.L.R., 566.

VIII.—Evidence out of Court.

(a) *Commission.*

Evidence Act 1890 (No. 1088), secs. 4, 10—Commission for examination of witness out of Victoria—Whether commission may issue in case of witness whose attendance can be enforced—Service and Execution of Process Act 1901 (No. 11), sec. 16.]—A commission will not be granted under sec. 4 of the *Evidence Act* 1890 to examine a witness whose attendance at the trial can be enforced under the provisions of the *Service and Execution of Process Act* 1901. *Willis* v. *Trequair,* (1906) 3 C.L.R., 912 ; 12 A.L.R., 507, principles of, applied. *National Mutual Life Association of Australasia Ltd.* v. *Australian Widows' Fund &c. Society Ltd.,* (1910) V.L.R., 411 ; 32 A.L.T., 51 ; 16 A.L.R., 460. *Hood, J.*

Marriage Act 1890 (No. 1166), sec. 114—Divorce—Evidence de bene esse—Application for commission—Citation not served.]—In a suit for dissolution of marriage, an examination *de bene esse* may be ordered prior to the service of the citation. *Vallentine* v. *Vallentine,* (1901) P., 283, followed. *Mackay* v. *Mackay,* (1910) V.L.R., 50 ; 31 A.L.T., 138 ; 16 A.L.R., 29. *Madden, C.J.*

Commission to examine witnesses—Costs reserved until trial—Judgment for general costs of action—No mention at hearing of costs of commission—Jurisdiction to amend—Order XXVIII., r. 11—" Accidental slip or omission " in judgment, correction of after appeal—Special circumstances—Complicated issues and lengthy trial.]—*See* Practice and Pleading, Order XXVIII. *Melbourne Harbour Trust Commissioners* v. *Cuming Smith & Co. Proprietary Ltd.,* (1906) V.L.R., 192 ; 27 A.L.T., 186 ; 12 A.L.R., 142.

(b) *Affidavits.*

Probate—Order nisi—Affidavit of attesting witness made on application for probate, whether it can be used on hearing of an order nisi.]—*Per Griffith, C.J.* :—*Quaere,* whether the affidavit of an attesting witness filed in support of an application for probate can be used on the hearing of an order *nisi* to remove a caveat lodged against the application *Gair* v. *Bowers* ; *Falconar* v. *Bowers* ; *Gair* v. *Falconar,* (1909) 9 C.L.R., 510 ; 15 A.L.R., 494. H.C., *Griffith, C.J., O'Connor, Isaacs* and *Higgins, JJ.*

Habeas corpus—Evidence—Proof by affidavit—Oral evidence.]—So far as evidence is admissible in *habeas corpus* proceedings, it may, at the discretion of the Court, be received by way of affidavit, or an issue may be directed before a jury when oral evidence might be given. *Ah Sheung* v. *Lindberg,* (1906) V.L.R., 323 ; 27 A.L.T., 189 ; *sub nom.,* *Rex* v. *Ah Sheung,* 12 A.L.R., 190. *Cussen, J.* (1906).

Service of copy of maintenance order—Proof of, by affidavit—Proceedings for disobedience of order—Marriage Act 1890 (No. 1166), sec. 51—Justices Act 1890 (No. 1105), sec. 74—Service of copy order, whether neces-

sary.]—A proceeding under sec. 51 of the *Marriage Act* 1890 for disobedience of a maintenance order is a proceeding within the jurisdiction of a Court of Petty Sessions, and service of a copy of the maintenance order may, under sec. 74 of the *Justices Act* 1890, be proved by the affidavit of the person who has served the same. *Semble.*—It is not necessary to serve the defendant with a copy of such order before proceeding against him under sec. 51 of the *Marriage Act* 1890. *Cohen* v. *MacDonough* (or *O'Donough*), (1906) V.L.R., 521 ; 28 A.L.T., 97 ; 12 A.L.R., 447. *Cussen, J.*

Husband and wife—Divorce—Service, proof of—Affidavit of service by process server—Death of process server before hearing—Proof by affidavit.]—Where the person, to whom a copy of the citation and a sealed copy of the petition had been handed for service on the respondent, had made an affidavit (afterwards filed in the office of the Prothonotary in compliance with the Divorce Rules) stating that he had served the documents on the respondent within the jurisdiction and that he knew and was well acquainted with the respondent, and knew him to be the husband of the petitioner, and the deponent had died before the hearing of the petition, the Court accepted the affidavit as proof of service, there being no suspicion of any fraud or collusion. *Jewell* v. *Jewell*, 2 W. & W. (I. E. & M.), 136, distinguished. *Constable* v. *Constable*, 1 W.W. & A'B. (I. E. & M.), 88, and *Ridge* v. *Ridge*, 22 A.L.T., 44 ; 6 A.L.R., 149, applied *Maddock* v. *Maddock*, (1911) V.L.R., 127 ; 32 A.L.T., 124 ; 17 A.L.R. 66. *Hood, J.*

Supreme Court Act 1890 (No. 1142), secs. 185, 186—Order XXXVIII., r. 3 (Rules of 1906)—Charging stock and shares—Charging order, whether final or interlocutory—Affidavit of information and belief, admissibility of.]—*See* PRACTICE AND PLEADING. *Manson* v. *Ponninghaus*, (1911) V.L.R., 239 ; 33 A.L.T., 1 ; 17 A.L.R., 238.

Order XXXVIII. (Rules of 1906)—Affidavit filed but not used—Whether a part of the proceedings.]—*See* PRACTICE AND PLEADING. *Manson* v. *Ponninghaus*, (1911) V.L.R., 239 ;

33 A.L.T., 1 ; 17 A.L.R., 238. *Madden, C.J.* (1911).

Order XXXVIII., r. 3 (Rules of 1906)—Affidavit as to belief—Grounds of belief not stated—Admissibility.]—*See* PRACTICE AND PLEADING. *Manson* v. *Ponninghaus*, (1911) V.L.R., 239 ; 33 A.L.T., 1 ; 17 A.L.R., 238.

Petition by company for winding up of another company—Affidavit supporting petition—Companies Act 1890 (No. 1074), secs. 252, 253—Mines Act 1890 (No. 1120), sec. 180.]—*See* MINING. *Re Mount Lyell Consols Mining Corporation No Liability* (*No.* 2), 30 A.L.T. (Supplement), 17 ; 14 A.L.R. (C.N.), 41.

Order to review—Affidavits of justices—Duty of justices as to—Facts to which Justices may properly depose.]—*See* JUSTICES OF THE PEACE. *Larkin* v. *Penfold*, (1906) V.L.R., 535 ; 28 A.L.T., 42 : 12 A.L.R., 337.

Order to review—Affidavits in reply, when they may be used.]—*See* JUSTICES OF THE PEACE. *Larkin* v. *Penfold*, (1906) V.L.R., 535 ; 28 A.L.T., 42 ; 12 A.L.R., 337.

Order to review—Practice—Order nisi and affidavit in support—How brought to the knowledge of Justices—Subsequent affidavits, suggested practice as to.]—*See* JUSTICES OF THE PEACE. *Larkin* v. *Penfold*, (1906) V.L.R., 535 ; 28 A.L.T., 42 ; 12 A.L.R., 337.

Instruments Act 1890 (No. 1103), secs. 133, 144—Declarations and Affidavits Act 1890 (No. 1191), sec. 6—Bill of sale—Registration—Affidavit verifying bill—Affidavit of renewal—Such affidavits to be made before Commissioners for taking Affidavits and Declarations—Affidavits — Commissioners of Supreme Court—Restriction of authority.]—*See* BILL OF SALE.—*Wrigglesworth* v. *Collis* ; *Spencer* (*claimant*), 33 A.L.T. (Supplement), 13 ; 18 A.L.R. (C.N.), 6.

Lotteries Gaming and Betting Act 1906 (No. 2055), sec. 38—Application for declaration that premises are a common gaming house —Affidavit of police officer showing reasonable grounds for suspecting — Suspicion, whether in mind of police officer or Court—Prima facie case, how established—Prima

17

facie case, how answered.]—*See* GAMING AND WAGERING. *In re Lotteries Gaming and Betting Act* 1906 ; *In re Shanghai Club* ; *In re Ah Pow* ; *Ex parte Gleeson*, (1907) V.L.R., 463 ; 29 A.L.T., 31 ; 13 A.L.R., 360.

Lotteries Gaming and Betting Act 1906 (No. 2055), sec. 38—Application for declaration that premises are a common gaming house—Affidavits in reply to affidavits of party opposing—Cross-examination of deponents.]—*See* GAMING AND WAGERING. *In re Lotteries Gaming and Betting Act* 1906 ; *In re Shanghai Club* ; *In re Ah Pow* ; *Ex parte Gleeson*, (1907) V.L.R., 463 ; 29 A.L.T., 31 ; 13 A.L.R., 360.

Interpleader summons—Affidavit in support—County Court Rules 1891, r. 230.]—*See* COUNTY COURT. *Looker* v. *Mercer*, 28 A.L.T. (Supplement), 15 ; 13 A.L.R. (C.N.), 13.

EXCISE TARIFF.

The Constitution (63 & 64 Vict. c. 12), secs. 51 (ii.), 99—Taxation, power of Commonwealth with respect to—Discrimination between States or parts of States—Preference to one State over another State—Excise Tariff 1906 (No. 16 of 1906), whether ultra vires.]—*See* COMMONWEALTH OF AUSTRALIA CONSTITUTION, cols. 116, 117. *The King* v. *Barger* ; *The Commonwealth* v. *McKay*, (1908) 6 C.L.R., 41 ; 14 A.L.R., 374.

The Constitution (63 & 64 Vict. c. 12), sec. 51—Legislative powers of Commonwealth—Validity of Act, principles to be observed in determining question of—Form of Act—Substance of Act—Direct and indirect effect—Motive and object of legislation—Interference with domestic affairs of State—Taxation—Excise Tariff 1906 (No. 16 of 1906).]—*See* COMMONWEALTH OF AUSTRALIA CONSTITUTION, cols. 115, 116. *The King* v. *Barger* ; *The Commonwealth* v. *McKay*, (1908) 6 C.L.R., 41 ; 14 A.L.R., 374.

The Constitution (63 & 64 Vict. c. 12), sec. 51 (ii.)—Legislative powers of the Commonwealth — Taxation — Regulative legislation, what is—Excise Tariff 1906 (No. 16 of 1906), whether a taxing or a regulative Act.]—*See* COMMONWEALTH OF AUSTRALIA CONSTITUTION, cols. 117, 118.]—*The King* v. *Barger* ; *The Commonwealth* v. *McKay*, (1908) 6 C.L.R., 41 ; 14 A.L.R., 374.

The Constitution (63 & 64 Vict. c. 12), sec. 55—Laws imposing taxation—To deal only with imposition of taxation—Excise Tariff 1906 (No. 16 of 1906), whether it deals with matters other than excise duty.]—*See* COMMONWEALTH OF AUSTRALIA CONSTITUTION, col. 118. *The King* v. *Barger* ; *The Commonwealth* v. *McKay*, (1908) 6 C.L.R., 41 ; 14 A.L.R., 374.

EXECUTION.

I.—FIERI FACIAS AND LIKE PROCESS IN INFERIOR COURTS.

Conveyancing Act 1904 (No. 1953), sec. 4 (6)—Auction Sales Act (No. 1065), secs. 3, 29—Sale of land by Sheriff under fi. fa.—Whether a " sale by auction "—Sheriff's costs of perusal of conveyance—Stipulation in contract of sale for payment by purchaser, legality of.]—A sale of land by auction conducted by the Sheriff under a writ of *fi. fa.* is, notwithstanding the provisions of the *Auction Sales Act* 1890 excusing the Sheriff from the responsibilities imposed by that Act, a sale by auction within the meaning of sec. 4 (6) of the *Conveyancing Act* 1904, and a clause in the contract of sale charging the purchaser with the payment of the Sheriff's costs of perusal of the conveyance is accordingly illegal. *Re Rogers and Rodd's Contract*, (1907) V.L.R., 511 ; 29 A.L.T., 13 ; 13 A.L.R., 312. *Madden, C.J.*

Order XLII., r. 23 (a) (Rules of 1906)—Justices Act 1890 (No. 1105), sec. 115—Leave to issue execution—Judgment in Court of Petty Sessions—Lapse of over six years—Date of judgment, what is.]—Under Order XLII., r. 23 (*a*) leave may be granted to issue a writ of *fieri facias* on a certificate of a judgment, obtained in a Court of Petty Sessions and filed in the Supreme Court under sec. 115 of the *Justices Act* 1890, where six years have elapsed since the judgment. The six years should in such a case be counted as starting from the original order in the Court of Petty Sessions. *Trent Brewery* v. *Lehane* 21 V.L.R., 283; 1 A.L.R., 89, followed. *Sack* v. *Wolstencroft*, 29 A.L.T., 85; 13 A.L.R., 588. *Cussen, J.* (1907).

Judgment—Execution—Rate of interest—Supreme Court Act 1890 (No. 1142), secs. 4, 177—Order XLI., r. 4*, Order XLII., r. 16 (Rules of 1884).]—By virtue of sec. 177 of the *Supreme Court Act* 1890, a judgment of the Supreme Court carries interest at the rate of 8 per cent. per annum. Order XLI., r. 4*, and Order XLII., r. 16 (Rules of 1884) so far as they purport to provide that such a judgment shall carry interest at the rate of 6 per cent. per annum are *ultra vires*. *In re Whitelaw*, (1906) V.L.R., 265; 27 A.L.T., 187; 12 A.L.R., 143. *Hood, J.* (1906).

County Court—Execution of judgment, difficulty in or about—Attendance and examination of judgment debtor—Rule 323 (Rules of 1891).]—Where a judgment debtor had in his possession at the time of the trial of the action goods which could not be found when the warrant of execution upon the judgment was attempted to be enforced, *Held*, that under rule 323 of *The County Court Rules* 1891, the Judge had power to order the attendance and examination of the judgment debtor. *Tye & Co. Proprietary Ltd.* v. *Presland*, 28 A.L.T. (Supplement), 3; 12 A.L.R. (C.N.), 17. *Judge Eagleson* (1906).

County Court Act 1890 (No. 1078), sec. 104—County Court judgment—Loss of certificate of judgment—Issue of duplicate certificate.]—See COUNTY COURT. *Ireland* v. *Floate*, 28 A.L.T. (Supplement), 16; 13 A.L.R. (C.N.), 13.

Justices Act 1890 (No. 1105), secs. 94, 102—Civil debt—Order for payment—Warrant of distress—Whether defendant entitled to be heard before issue—Jurisdiction of Justice.]—Where a Court of Petty Sessions has made an order for payment of a civil debt and in default distress, a Justice may thereafter, on the *ex parte* application of the plaintiff, issue a warrant of distress. *Warr* v. *Templeton*, 3 V.R. (L.), 56, discussed. *Cross* v. *Daffy*, (1910) V.L.R., 316; 32 A.L.T., 10; 16 A.L.R., 279. F.C., *Madden, C.J., Hodges* and *Cussen, JJ.*

Justices—Order for payment of money made in Petty Sessions—Death of party in whose favour order was made—Right of executors to enter suggestion of death on record of Court—Justices Act 1890 (No. 1105).]—See JUSTICES OF THE PEACE. *Goodman* v. *Jonas*, (1909) V.L.R., 307: 31 A.L.T., 16; 15 A.L.R., 308.

Insolvency Act 1890 (No. 1102), sec. 37 (viii.)—Act of insolvency—Failure to satisfy judgment—Duty of officer charged with execution—Whether bound to demand the precise sum remaining unpaid.]—See INSOLVENCY. *Hamilton* v. *Warne*, 4 C.L.R., 1293; 13 A.L.R., 420.

II.—CHARGING ORDER.

Supreme Court Act 1890 (No. 1142), secs. 185, 186—Order XXXVIII., r. 3 (Rules of 1906)—Charging stock and shares—Charging order, whether final or interlocutory—Affidavit of information and belief, admissibility of.]—An order charging shares under sec. 185 of the *Supreme Court Act* 1890 is a final as distinguished from an interlocutory order; consequently an affidavit of information and belief is inadmissible in an application for a charging order *nisi*. *Manson* v. *Ponninghaus*, (1911) V.L.R., 239; 33 A.L.T., 1; 17 A.L.R., 238. *Madden, C.J.* (1911).

III.—ATTACHMENT OF DEBTS.

Attachment of debts—Money ordered to be paid by Court of General Sessions—Attachment by Court of Petty Sessions—Jurisdiction.]—*See*

JUSTICES OF THE PEACE. *Brown* v. *Gunn*; *McKay, Garnishee,* (1913) V.L.R., 60; 34 A.L.T., 115; 18 A.L.R. (C.N.), 21.

Justices Act 1890 (No. 1105), secs. 117, 119, 128, 141—Attachment of debt—Judgment debt—Order of General Sessions—Garnishee order—Petty Sessions—Effect of—Jurisdiction—Order to review—" Person aggrieved."]—*See* JUSTICES OF THE PEACE. *Brown* v. *Gunn*; *McKay, Garnishee,* (1912) V.L.R., 463; 34 A.L.T., 113; 18 A.L.R., 462.

Attachment of debts—Garnishee order—Judgment debtor trustee of moneys attached—Appearance of judgment debtor before Justices to protect fund—Justices Act 1890 (No. 1105), sec. 117.]—A judgment debtor, who is a trustee of moneys sought to be attached by a garnishee order *nisi* for payment of a judgment debt due by him personally, has a right, and is under a duty, to appear before the Justices on the garnishee proceedings to show that the moneys are trust moneys and ought not therefore be attached. *Roberts* v. *Death,* 8 Q.B.D., 319, followed. *Regina* v. *Justices of Heywood,* 21 V.L.R., 654; 17 A.L.T., 238; 2 A.L.R., 135, distinguished. *Richards* v. *Jager,* (1909) V.L.R., 140; 30 A.L.T., 163; 15 A.L.R., 119. *Madden, C.J.*

Attachment of debts—Action for unlawfully attaching trust funds.]—No action will lie for unlawfully causing moneys standing to the credit of a trust account in the name of the plaintiff to be attached for his personal debt. *Jager* v. *Richards,* (1909) V.L.R., 181; 30 A.L.R., 199; 15 A.L.R., 123. *Cussen, J.*

County Court—Attachment of debts—Service of garnishee order nisi—Notice of order directed to be sent by telegram to garnishee to be followed by personal service upon him of a copy of such order—Order nisi made returnable before a Judge of a County Court sitting in place other than where judgment obtained—County Court Act 1890 (No. 1078), secs. 108, 109.]—*Greenwood* v. *Cormack, Blakeley Garnishee,* 28 A.L.T. (Supplement), 5; 12 A.L.R. (C.N.), 24. *Judge Eagleson* (1906).

IV.—ATTACHMENT OF THE PERSON.

Order XLII., rr. 3, 6, 7, 17 (Rules of 1884)—Order XLIV., r. 2 (Rules of 1884)—Attachment—Disobedience of order to pay costs—Imprisonment of Fraudulent Debtors Act 1890 (No. 1100)—Whether power to attach for disobedience affected by.]—Notwithstanding the provisions of the *Imprisonment of Fraudulent Debtors. Act* 1890 the Court has power to issue a writ of attachment for disobedience of its order to pay costs. *Re Sandilands; Ex parte Browne,* 4 V.L.R. (L.), 318, followed. *Pope* v. *Peacock,* (1906) V.L.R., 667; 28 A.L.T., 63; 12 A.L.R., 440. *Hodges, J.*

Order XLII., rr. 3, 17 (Rules of 1884)—Order XLIV., r. 2—Order for payment of money—Execution under fi. fa.—Attachment for disobedience—Election of remedy, whether creditor bound by.]—A writ of attachment for disobedience of an order of the Court for payment of a sum of money may issue, although a writ of *fi. fa.* to enforce such payment has been issued previously. *In re Ball,* L.R. 8 C.P., 104, explained. *Pope* v. *Peacock,* (1906) V.L.R., 667; 28 A.L.T., 63; 12 A.L.R., 440. *Hodges, J.*

Insolvency Act 1890 (No. 1102), secs. 76, 113—Execution of process or judgment, stay of—Debt due by insolvent to creditor—Trust moneys which are or ought to be in hands of trustee—Trustee ordered to pay moneys into Court—Disobedience of order—Attachment.]—Secs. 76 and 113 of the *Insolvency Act* 1890 are both directed to process for the enforcement of the payment of money as a debt due by the insolvent to a creditor. The insolvency of a person, who in the position of a trustee has not accounted for money he once had and still ought to have, and who has been ordered to pay the money into Court, does not operate as a stay upon process of attachment against him for non-compliance with the order for payment into Court. *Peterson* v. *M'Lennan,* (1907) V.L.R., 94; 28 A.L.T., 135; 12 A.L.R., 577. *Cussen, J.*

Insolvency Act 1890 (No. 1102), secs. 76, 113—Stay of execution—Whether limited to process in execution of judgment for payment of money.]—*Semble.*—In secs. 76 and 113 of the *Insolvency Act* 1890, the meaning of the word " process " should be limited to process issuing after judgment ordering money to be paid by one party to another. *Peterson* v. *M'Lennan*, (1907) V.L.R., 94 ; 28 A.L.T., 135 ; 12 A.L.R., 577. *Cussen, J.*

Order LII., r. 11—Order LXVII. r. 9— Writ of attachment—Sheriff, refusal of to execute—Execution, how enforced—Whether mandamus may issue.]—Where the Sheriff refuses to execute a writ of attachment he should be called upon to return the writ or bring in the body within a given time, and on his non-compliance application should be made under Order LII., r. 11, for his committal. A writ of mandamus will not issue, there being an alternative remedy. *Peterson* v. *M'Lennan*, (1907) V.L.R., 94 ; 28 A.L.T., 135 ; 12 A.L.R., 577. *Cussen, J.*

Attachment of person—Sheriff, duty of— Writ of attachment regular on its face.]— *Quaere*, whether under a writ of attachment the Sheriff is not bound, in every case in which the writ of attachment is regular on its face, to attach the person named in the writ, leaving it to the Court to say whether he ought to be discharged. *Peterson* v. *M'Lennan*, (1907) V.L.R., 94 ; 28 A.L.T., 135 ; 12 A.L.R., 577. *Cussen, J.*

The County Court Rules 1891, rr. 333, 334, 335, 343—Judgment that defendant deliver a certain chattel to plaintiff—Warrant of delivery under rule 343 returned unsatisfied— Warrant of attachment, issue of—Jurisdiction.]—*See* COUNTY COURT. *Macrow & Sons Co. Proprietary Ltd.* v. *Davidson*, 27 A.L.T. (Supplement), 11 ; 12 A.L.R. (C.N.), 9.

V.—IMPRISONMENT OF FRAUDULENT DEBTORS ACT 1890.

See also, DEBTORS ACT.

Imprisonment of Fraudulent Debtors Act 1890 (No. 1100), Part III.—Court of Petty Sessions—Proceedings upon summons to debtor, nature of—Whether a mere method of enforcing judgment.]—*See* DEBTORS ACT. *Caldecott* v. *Cunningham*, (1908) V.L.R., 38 ; 29 A.L.T., 94 ; 13 A.L.R., 639.

VI.—INTERPLEADER.

Interpleader—Grounds of claim, statement of—Alternative and inconsistent grounds— Rule 236 (County Court Rules of 1891).]—*See* COUNTY COURT, cols. 311, 312. *Moorhead* v. *Chauncey, Hays (claimant)*, 28 A.L.T. (Supplement), 7 ; 12 A.L.R. (C.N.), 27.

County Court Rules 1891, r. 236—Interpleader—Particulars of claim—Grounds of claim—Defective particulars—Amendment.]— *See* COUNTY COURT, col. 312. *Rogers* v. *Metters* ; *Metters (claimant)*, 34 A.L.T. (Supplement), 4 ; 18 A.L.R. (C.N.), 21.

Interpleader—Grounds of claim—Order giving leave to amend—Whether necessary to draw up.]—*See* COUNTY COURT, col. 312. *Moorhead* v. *Chauncey, Hays (claimant)*, 28 A.L.T. (Supplement), 7 ; 12 A.L.R. (C.N.), 27.

Justices Act 1890 (No. 1105), sec. 98, Schedule II., Form 55—Interpleader summons —Withdrawal of claim—Jurisdiction of Justices to adjudicate.]—*See* JUSTICES OF THE PEACE *Watson* v. *Barby* ; *O'Connor, claimant*, (1910) V.L.R., 134.

VII.—STAY OF PROCEEDINGS ; EXECUTION OF JUDGMENT OF APPELLATE COURT.

Practice—Appeal to High Court from Supreme Court—Special leave—Stay by Supreme Court of proceedings under judgment—Conditions—Order LVIII., r. 16.]—It is only in very exceptional circumstances that the High Court will grant special leave to appeal from an order made by a Judge of the Supreme Court in the exercise of his discretion staying proceedings under a judgment of the Supreme Court subject to conditions. *Howard Smith & Co. Ltd.* v. *Varawa*, (1910) 10 C.L.R., 607. H.C., *Griffith, C.J., O'Connor, Isaacs* and *Higgins, JJ.*

Order LVIII., r. 16 (Rules of 1906)—Stay of proceedings pending appeal—Application for stay—Whether Full Court may entertain.] —An application for a stay of proceedings pending an appeal to the Full Court may under Order LVIII., r. 16 be made to the Full Court. *O'Sullivan* v. *Morton*, (1911) V.L.R., 235 ; 32 A.L.T., 172 ; 17 A.L.R., 140.

F.C., *Madden, C.J., Hodges* and *Hood, JJ.* (1911).

Practice—Money paid into Court under Order XIV., r. 6—Defendant successful at trial—Order for payment out of money to defendant—Appeal to High Court—" Execution of the judgment appealed from "—Stay of execution—High Court Appeal Rules 1903, r. 19.]—The defendant obtained leave to defend under Order XIV., r, 6 upon payment into Court of £500. Subsequently on 17th October 1906 judgment in the action was given for the defendant, and an order was made that he be at liberty after the expiration of fourteen days to take out of Court the said sum of £500. On the 29th October 1906 the plaintiff duly instituted an appeal against the judgment to the High Court. *Held*, that the order for payment out of the money was not " execution of the judgment appealed from " within the meaning of rule 19 of Sec III of the *High Court Appeal Rules* 1903, and that in any case the due institution of the appeal against the judgment did not operate as a stay of such order. *Christie* v. *Robinson*, (1907) V.L.R., 118. *Hodges, J.*

Judiciary Act 1903 (No. 6), sec. 37—Appeal to High Court from Supreme Court—Cause remitted to Supreme Court for execution of judgment of High Court—Duty of Supreme Court—Staying proceedings.]—When the High Court on the hearing of an appeal from the Supreme Court has remitted the case to the Supreme Court for the execution of the judgment of the High Court pursuant to sec. 37 of the *Judiciary Act* 1903 the Supreme Court is authorized to make any order for the purpose of executing the judgment of the High Court but not to make an order which has the effect of preventing or obstructing the execution of that order. Where, therefore, a cause was remitted to the Supreme Court for an inquiry as to damages an order by the Supreme Court staying proceedings as to the inquiry was on appeal to the High Court discharged. *Peacock* v. *Osborne*, (1907) 4 C,L.R., 1564 ; 13 A.L.R., 565. H.C., *Griffith, C.J., Barton, O'Connor, Isaacs* and *Higgins, JJ.*

Judgment of High Court on appeal from Supreme Court—Judgment remitted to Supreme Court—Stay of proceedings, jurisdiction of Supreme Court to order.]—On an appeal from the Supreme Court to the High Court, the High Court, in allowing the appeal ordered the judgment appealed from to be discharged, and that in lieu thereof there should be substituted a declaration that the plaintiffs were entitled to recover a sum to be thereafter ascertained, and further ordered that the cause " be remitted to the Supreme Court to do therein what is right in pursuance of the judgment." Leave to appeal to the Privy Council from the judgment of the High Court having been obtained by the defendants, and a stay of proceedings having been granted by the High Court and subsequently renewed, an application to the Supreme Court to proceed with the inquiry directed by the High Court was made by the plaintiff. *Held* that an order made by the Supreme Court, that the matter should be deferred until the decision of the Privy Council should be made known, was a stay of proceedings, and therefore was an order which the Supreme Court had no authority to make. *Peacock* v. *D. M. Osborne & Co.*, 4 C.L.R., 1564 ; 13 A.L.R., 565, applied. *Bayne* v. *Blake*, (1908) 5 C.L.R., 497 ; 14 A L R., 103. H.C., *Griffith, C.J., Barton* and *O'Connor, JJ.*

Judgment of High Court on appeal from Supreme Court—Duty of Supreme Court to execute—Judiciary Act 1903 (No. 6 of 1903), sec. 37, whether ultra vires—The Constitution, sec. 51 (xxxix.)—Commonwealth of Australia Constitution Act (63 & 64 Vict. c. 12), sec. v.]—Sec. 37 of the *Judiciary Act* 1903 in so far as it authorizes the High Court in the exercise of its appellate jurisdiction to remit a cause to the Supreme Court for the execution of the judgment of the High Court, and imposes upon the Supreme Court the duty of executing the judgment of the High Court in the same manner as if that judgment were the judgment of the Supreme Court is a valid exercise by Parliament of the power conferred by sec. 51 (xxxix.) of the Constitution. *Bayne* v. *Blake*, 5 C.L.R.,

497; 14 A.L.R., 103. H.C., *Griffith, C.J.,* *Barton* and *O'Connor, JJ.* (1908).

Judgment of High Court on appeal from Supreme Court—Judgment remitted to Supreme Court for execution—Officer of Supreme Court—Whether subject to control of High Court.]—The High Court may directly order an officer of the Supreme Court to obey a judgment of the High Court. *Bayne* v. *Blake,* (1908) 5 C.L.R., 497; 14 A.L.R., 103. H.C., *Griffith, C.J., Barton* and *O'Connor, JJ.*

Practice—Order of the Privy Council on an appeal from the High Court made an order of the High Court.]—*See Cock* v. *Smith,* 13 C.L.R., 129; 18 A.L.R., 139. *Griffith, C.J.*

EXECUTORS AND ADMINISTRATORS.

I.—PROBATE AND LETTERS OF ADMINISTRATION.

(a) *Testamentary Documents.*

Draft will—Clauses omitted from engrossed will in error—Omission unknown to testator—Probate of both documents.]—A testator duly executed a draft will appointing certain persons as executors, but being in some doubt as to whether he should change his executors, he left that question open for further consideration. He afterwards instructed his solicitor to change the executors. An engrossment was then made which the solicitor told the testator was to the same effect as the draft will already executed, with the exception of the alterations in the executorship which the testator had directed. Acting upon that statement the testator duly executed the engrossment without reading it. After the testator's death it was discovered that certain important clauses contained in the draft will had been omitted from the engrossed will. *Held,* that, as the omitted clauses were omitted without the testator's knowledge or consent and purely in error, and as the true intention of the testator was expressed by reading the draft will and the engrossed will together, both documents should be admitted to probate.

In re Porter, 28 A.L.T., 92 ; 12 A.L.R.,
496. *Chomley, J.* (1906).

**Probate—Of what documents—Will dealing
with whole of testator's property—Codicil
dealing with English property only and appoint
ing separate executor therefor—Whether
documents independent or interdependent.]—**
Testator made a will in Melbourne disposing
of the whole of his property, and appointing
A. as executor thereof. Subsequently he
executed in England a testamentary paper
commencing with the words "This is a
codicil to the will made in Melbourne." By
this testamentary paper the testator, after
reciting certain provisions of the will including the bequest of a legacy to his son B.,
appointed B. to be the sole executor of his
" said will " so far as it related to his property
in the United Kingdom, and devised and
bequeathed to B. all his property in the
United Kingdom upon trust, after payment
thereout of debts due to persons in the
United Kingdom, and the expenses incurred
by B. in the administration of testator's
estate in the United Kingdom or wherever
situated, to appropriate to himself the said
legacy " in my said will " specified. *Held*,
that the two documents were not independent
but interdependent, and that probate of
both should be granted, the Melbourne will
by itself not being entitled to probate. *In
the Will of Butler*, 32 A.L.T., 8 ; 16 A.L.R.,
283. *Hodges, J.* (1910).

**Wills Act 1890 (No. 1159), secs. 3, 18—
Testamentary disposition, what amounts to—
Letter declaring intention to revoke legacies
executed in same manner as a will.]—**By
instructions to his solicitor for a will executed
in conformity with the requirements for the
execution of a valid will, testator directed
certain legacies to be given to G. and Y.
respectively. But by letter of the same date,
similarly executed and addressed to the
same solicitor the testator expressed his
desire that G. and Y. should receive the sums
which he had directed to be given to them
as legacies, and requested the solicitor to pay
to them out of certain moneys due to him,
such sums, and " if they should receive
the amounts prior to my death such legacies

as I have directed must be revoked by a
codicil to my will if same is executed by me."
No formal will was drawn up, and the sums
mentioned were paid to G. and Y. in the
testator's life time. *Held*, that the letter
came within sec. 18 of the *Wills Act* 1890,—
and operated as a conditional revocation
of the legacies, and that, the condition having
been fulfilled, the letter must be annexed
to the grant of administration. The Court
directed that the grant should not be operative until G. and Y. had been served with
notice of the Court's intention to annex
the letter to the grant. *In the Will and
Estate of Johnston, deceased*, (1912) V.L.R.,
55 ; 33 A.L.T., 151 ; 18 A.L.R., 7. *Cussen,
J.*

(b) *Execution of Will.*

**Will—Signature of testator and witnesses
in margin—Validity—Wills Act 1890 (No.
1159), secs. 7, 8.]—**The various dispositions
and the attestation clause of what purported
to be the last will of M. took up almost
the whole of one side of a sheet of paper with
the exception of a margin so that very little
room was left at the bottom for the signatures
of M. and the witnesses. Accordingly, the
signature of M. was written lengthwise in
the margin opposite and at right angles
only to the earlier dispositions. The signatures of the witnesses were written lengthwise in the margin at right angles to the
attestation clause, and the last provision.
Held, that the document should be admitted
to probate. *In re Mathew*, (1906) V.L.R.,
531 ; 28 A.L.T., 7 ; 12 A.L.R., 417.
a' Beckett, A.-C.J.

**Wills Act 1890 (No. 1159), secs. 7, 8—Will—
Execution—Foot or end of will—Will written
on first, third and second pages—Testator's
signature on second page.]—**A will was written
on a sheet of paper which was doubled so as
to make four pages. The will commenced
on the first page, and was continued on the
third page at the foot of which was a blank
space. On the second page were the concluding six words of the will, the signature
of the testator, the attestation clause, and
the signature of witnesses. There were no
new beneficial interests created by the words

on the second page which simply created part of the machinery for carrying into effect the trusts contained in the will. *Held*, that the will was signed at the foot or end thereof within the meaning of the *Wills Act* 1890. *In the Goods of Wotton*, L.R. 3 P. & D., 159, followed. *In re Hall*, (1910) V.L.R., 14; 31 A.L.T., 132; 16 A.L.R., 15. *a'Beckett, J.*

Will—Execution—Wills Act 1890 (No. 1159), sec. 7—Witnesses "shall attest and shall subscribe the will," meaning of.]— Sec. 7 of the *Wills Act* 1890 requires that the two witnesses in whose presence the testator has signed or acknowledged a document as his will shall thereafter subscribe the will. A signed document as his will in the presence of B., who signed the document as attesting witness. A crossed out his signature and again signed the document in the presence of B. and C. C. signed his name as attesting witness to the second signature of A., but B. did not again sign. *Held*, that the requirement of sec. 7 had not been complied with. *In re Burr*, (1912) V.L.R., 246; 33 A.L.T., 237; 18 A.L.R., 212.

(c) Testamentary Capacity; Undue Influence

Will—Testamentary capacity—Delusions.] —Delusions are only material to the question of testamentary capacity if they are connected with the dispositions made by the will. *Tipper v. Moore*, (1911) 13 C.L.R., 248; 18 A.L.R., 341. H.C., *Griffith, C.J., Barton* and *O'Connor, JJ.*

Will—Revocation—Mental capacity.]—The revocation of a will requires the same degree of mental capacity as the making of a will. *In re Richards*, (1911) V.L.R., 284; 33 A L.T., 38. *a'Beckett, J.*

"Undue influence," what is.]—"Undue influence" is the improper use of the ascendancy acquired by one person over another for the benefit of the ascendant person himself or someone else, so that the acts of the person influenced are not, in the fullest sense of the word, his free voluntary acts. *Union Bank of Australia Ltd. v. Whitelaw*, (1906) V.L.R., 711; 28 A.L.T., 17; 12 A.L.R., 393. *Hodges, J.*

(d) Persons Entitled to Grant.

See, also, *post (e) Delegation of Right to Grant.*

Administration, grant of—Discretion of Court—Effect of English practice.]—The Court has a very large discretion in the grant of administration, and although it will have regard to the rules of preference laid down by English Courts, it does not consider itself as rigidly bound by them. *In re Hoarey*, (1906) V.L.R., 437; 28 A.L.T., 93; 12 A.L.R., 450. *Cussen, J.*

Administration, right to—Next-of-kin of deceased woman—Executor of deceased's widower.]—The Court has a discretion as to whether it will grant administration *de bonis non* to the next-of-kin of a deceased woman or to the executor of her widower. *In re Hoarey*, (1906) V.L.R., 437; 28 A.L.T., 93; 12 A.L.R., 450. *Cussen, J.*

Administration cum testamento annexo— Right of corporation aggregate, a beneficiary, to administer—Grant to syndic of corporation aggregate.]—A corporation aggregate, not specially authorised by Act of Parliament, even though a beneficiary cannot be appointed administrator *cum testamento annexo*, nor can it lawfully authorise a trustee company, or, *semble*, any other syndic to apply for such a grant. *In re Basse*, (1909) V.L.R., 313; 31 A.L.T., 17; 15 A.L.R., 302. *Madden, C.J.*

Probate, to whom granted—Several testamentary documents—Revocation by subsequent document of appointment of executor in previous document.]—Testator left three testamentary documents which were entitled to be admitted to probate. By the first of these documents T. was appointed an executor, and by the second his appointment was revoked. He was not re-appointed. *Held*, that, upon the filing of a renunciation of probate by T., probate should be granted to the persons other than T. named in the three documents. *In the Will of Porter*, 28 A.L.T., 92; 12 A.L.R., 496. *Chomley, J.* (1906).

Administration, grant of—Discretion of Court, matters affecting exercise of—Application by party who has parted with his interest

—**Party with major interest.**]—The E. company became surety to the administration bond given by A., the widower and administrator of the estate of B., and, under an agreement which practically vested the administration of the estate in it, managed and advanced moneys to the estate. The only persons besides A. interested in the estate were X., Y., and Z., the next-of-kin of B. X., Y. and Z., had each released his interest in B.'s estate, and X. and Y. had been paid, but there was a balance remaining due to Z. Upon the death of A. the E. company under the authority of X. applied for administration *de bonis non* of the estate of B. The N. company, to which probate of the will of A. had been granted, lodged a caveat and applied for administration *de bonis non* as executor of such will. Both the applications were advertised within a week of the death of A., the advertisement of the E. company being prior in date. *Held*, that administration should be granted to the N. company, it undertaking to pay to Z. the balance due to him under the release. *In re Hoarey*, (1906) V.L.R., 437; 28 A.L.T., 93; 12 A.L.R., 450. *Cussen, J.*

Administration and Probate—Practice—Administration—Joint grant of administration when made.]—The Court may and should grant joint administration of an estate, if it be shown that there are special circumstances which render such a course convenient or beneficial to the estate. *In re McMurchy*, (1909) V.L.R., 359; 31 A.L.T., 2; 15 A.L.R., 328. *Madden, C.J.*

Will—Executor predeceasing testator—No beneficiary within jurisdiction entitled to apply for administration c.t.a. — Beneficiaries outside the jurisdiction not notified of their rights—Power of Court to take goods of deceased into its own hands.]—In a fit case, the Court may take the goods of a deceased person, who has no executor or administrator, into its own hands, and perform all necessary acts in connection with such goods until the will of those interested is ascertained. Where a testator had died leaving a will appointing an executor who had predeceased him, and the only beneficiaries

in the jurisdiction being corporations aggregate, were held unable to apply or to authorise any syndic to apply for administration c.t.a., and the remaining beneficiaries were in Germany, and had not been notified of their rights to apply by attorney for administration c.t.a., the goods of the testator were ordered to be handed over to the Master-in-Equity to abide the order of the Court. *In re Basse*, (1909) V.L.R., 313; 31 A.L.T., 17; 15 A.L.R., 302. *Madden, C.J.*

(e) *Delegation of Right to Grant.*

Administration and Probate Act 1907 (No. 2120), sec. 7—Authority to trustee company to apply for probate—Revocation—Form of authority—Form of application.]—An authority given to a trustee company under sec. 70 of the *Administration and Probate Act 1907* is irrevocable. An authority thus given does not create the relation of principal and agent, but is a complete delegation by the executor of his rights and powers as executor. No formal application to the Court or Registrar is necessary under the section. Form of authority considered. *In the Will of Synot*, (1912) V.L.R., 99; 33 A.L.T., 182; 18 A.L.R., 82. *Hood, J.*

Practice—Grant of administration—Trustee company authorised by next-of-kin to obtain administration — Complicated transactions between next-of-kin and intestate—Discretion of Court to refuse application of trustee company.]—Where a person claiming as one of the next-of-kin to be entitled to administration of the estate of an intestate has authorised a trustee company to apply for and obtain a grant of letters of administration to itself, and the appointment of the company as such administrator is contested, the Court may in the exercise of its discretion refuse to appoint such company where one of its duties as such administrator would be carefully to examine and scrutinize transactions between such next-of-kin and the deceased. *In re Forbes*, (1909) V.L.R., 485; 31 A.L.T., 95; 15 A.L.R., 627. *Hodges, J.*

Executors — Renunciation — Appointment of a trustee company—Power of sole remaining executor—The Union Trustees Executors

and Administrators Company Act (**No. 839**), **sec. 3.**]—Where several executors are appointed by a will, and one or more of them renounces probate, the remaining executor or executors may under sec. 3 of the *Union Trustees Executors and Administrators Company Act* authorise the company to apply for administration with the will annexed. *In the Will of Gilbert*, 27 A.L.T., 241; 12 A.L.R., 528. *a'Beckett, J.* (1906).

"**Equity Trustees Executors and Agency Company Limited Act**" (**No. 978**), **sec. 9—Appointment of company, under, effect of.**]—*Quaere*, whether under sec. 9 of the *Equity Trustees Executors and Agency Company Limited Act* (No. 978) an executor administrator or trustee can permanently appoint the company to act in his stead. *In re Hoarey*, (1906) V.L.R., 437; 28 A.L.T., 93; 12 A.L.R., 450. *Cussen, J.*

Intestacy—Next-of-kin entitled to administration—Resident abroad—Authority to trustee company to attain administration—Form of grant to company—The Perpetual Executors and Trustees Association Act (No. 840), sec. 4.]—Sec. 4 of the *Perpetual Executors and Trustees Association Act* (No. 840) provides as follows:—" Any person entitled to obtain administration to the estate of any intestate as his next of kin may instead of himself applying for administration, authorise the company to apply for administration to such estate and administration to the estate of the intestate may be granted to the said company upon its application when so authorised." *Held*, that a person residing abroad may be a " person entitled " within the meaning of the section. *In the Estate of Morris*, (1909) V.L.R., 425; 31 A.L.T., 61; 15 A.L.R., 446. F.C., *a'Beckett, Hodges* and *Hood, JJ.*

National Trustees Executors and Agency Company of Australasia Limited Act (No. 938), sec. 10—Appointment with consent of Court of Company to perform administrator's duties—Title of administrator not perfected — Letters of administration not issued.]—A person to whom administration has been granted, but to whom the letters of administration have not been issued, cannot under sec. 10 of the Act No. 938 appoint the National Trustees Executors and Agency Company of Australasia Ltd. to perform and discharge his acts and duties as administrator. *In the Will of James*, 13 V.L.R., 154, followed. *In re Moriarty*, (1907) V.L.R., 315; 29 A.L.T., 65; 13 A.L.R., 307. *a'Beckett, J.*

Administration, application for grant of—Advertisement of intention to apply—Person named in advertisement not entitled to grant—Authority of person not named in advertisement, effect of.]—The foundation of every application for administration is the advertisement; if, therefore, the advertisement states that the applicant, a trustee company, is applying on the authority of one of the next-of-kin and such one of the next-of-kin is not himself entitled to a grant, and the application is opposed, the applicant is not entitled to rely on the support of other of the next-of-kin as being in any sense equivalent to prior authority from him. *Re Maynard*, 12 V.L.R., 313, followed. *In re Hoarey*, (1906) V.L.R., 437; 28 A.L.T., 93; 12 A.L.R., 450. *Cussen, J.*

Administration, application for grant of—Power of attorney, interpretation of—Whether attorney under power authorised to support application—General words, effect of on special powers.]—A power of attorney authorised D. to apply for and obtain letters of administration to take steps to compel a proper administration and, if he thought fit, to adjust, settle, and compromise the appointor's claim as one of the next-of-kin, etc., and generally to act as the appointor's attorney in relation to the premises and on his behalf to execute and do all instruments, acts, and things as fully and effectually in all respects as the appointor could himself do if personally present. *Held*, that D. was not authorised to support a claim to administration *de bonis non* by another of the next-of-kin. *In re Hoarey*, (1906) V.L.R., 437; 28 A.L.T., 93; 12 A.L.R., 450. *Cussen, J.*

(f) Certain Limited Grants.

Administration ad litem—Application under peculiar circumstances — Proposed action

under Wrongs Act for benefit of widow and children of deceased—Time for bringing action about to expire—Poverty of widow, the applicant for administration—Wrongs Act 1890 (No. 1160), secs. 14, 15, 16.]—Sec. 16 of the *Wrongs Act* 1890 requiring that an action in respect of the death of a person caused by negligence must be brought within twelve months of his death, the facts that, unless administration is granted immediately, the twelve months will have expired, and that the applicant, the widow of the intestate, has been prevented by poverty from applying earlier, are sufficient reasons for granting administration *ad litem. Greenway* v. *McKay,* (1911) 12 C.L.R., 310 ; 17 A.L.R., 350. H.C., *Griffith, C.J., Barton* and *O'Connor, JJ.*

Probate—Grant limited as to performance of particular duties—Executors appointed by will—Executors of will and another person appointed executors of codicil—Limitation of grant to carry out purpose of codicil.]—Where a testator by her will appointed two persons executors and trustees thereof, and by a codicil, which merely increased legacies given by the will, and made one additional bequest, appointed the same two persons together with her husband as executors of the codicil, *Held,* that the husband was executor of the codicil merely, and that the grant of probate of the will and codicil should be to the three persons named in the codicil, but limited as to the husband to carrying out the purposes of the codicil. *In re Graham,* (1910) V.L.R., 16 ; 31 A.L.T., 130 ; 16 A.L.R., 15. *a' Beckett, J.*

Administration—Will disposing of real estate out of the jurisdiction—Real and personal estate within the jurisdiction undisposed of—Intestacy as to estate within the jurisdiction—Grant of letters of administration—Form.]—Where a deceased person whose will disposed only of his real estate in Tasmania, probate of which had been obtained in Tasmania by the executor appointed by the will, had also left real and personal estate in Victoria, the Supreme Court of Victoria granted letters of administration to the widow of the deceased, and directed

that he be therein described as "intestate in respect of his real and personal estate in Victoria." *In re Trethewie,* (1913) V.L.R. 26 ; 34 A.L.T., 136 ; 18 A.L.R., 560. *Cussen, J.*

(g) *Delay in Making Application, Effect of.*

Probate—Stale will—Making title.]—*Semble.*—The Court may grant probate of a stale will in order to make title. *In re Smith,* (1907) V.L.R., 717 ; 29 A.L.T., 89 ; 13 A.L.R., 615. *Cussen, J.*

Administration—Death of intestate in 1864 —Intestate entitled to estate in land in remainder after life estate and to no other property—Death of life tenant in 1905—Application for administration after death of life tenant.]—G. died intestate in 1864 leaving no property except a vested interest in certain real estate in remainder expectant upon the death of a tenant for life The tenant for life died in 1905. *Held,* that administration of G.'s estate should be granted to G.'s next-of-kin. *Re Norton,* 3 V.L.R., (I. P. & M.), 58 ; and *Re Cropley,* 4 V.L.R., (I. P. & M.), 61, distinguished. *In re Ghillmetei,* (1907) V L R , 657 ; 29 A.L.T., 81 ; 13 A.L.R., 519. *Hood, J.*

Practice—Delay—Administration with will annexed—Death of testator in 1870—Executrix dying without proving in 1907—Application after death of executrix.]—A testator died in the year 1870 leaving a will by which he gave his widow a life interest in all his estate, and appointed her executrix. The widow died in the year 1907 without having proved the will. On application after the widow's death for administration with the will annexed, *Held,* that the application should be granted notwithstanding the delay. *In re Smith,* (1907) V.L.R., 717 ; 29 A.L.T., 89 ; 13 A.L.R., 615. *Cussen, J.*

Practice—Administration de bonis non— Death of executor—Executorial duties all performed—Real property—Legal estate outstanding—Trusts declared in respect of real property—Unadministered estate, what is.]— Where the executor to whom probate of a will has been granted, has died after having performed all the executorial duties, the

Court will not grant administration *de bonis non*. The mere fact that there is real property which belonged to the testator and vested in his executor and trustee, on whose death the legal estate is outstanding, and with regard to which the testator declared trusts that give rights to persons in succession, does not constitute such property unadministered estate in the proper sense of the term. *In re Graham*, (1910) V.L.R., 466; 32 A.L.T., 68; 16 A.L.R., 512. *a' Beckett, J.*

Administration de bonis non c.t.a. when granted — Unadministered estate — Executor registered as proprietor of land under Transfer of Land Act 1890 (No. 1149).]—Administration *de bonis non* c.t.a. will be granted only where there is something left to be administered after the death of the executor. The executrix and executor of a deceased person, who were entitled respectively to a life estate and an estate in fee in remainder in a piece of land, procured themselves to be registered under the *Transfer of Land Act* 1890 as proprietors of such piece of land, but without any notification on the register that they were registered as executors. They afterwards died. *Held*, that there was nothing left unadministered in the estate in respect of such land. *In re Graham*, (1910) V.L.R., 466; 32 A.L.T., 68; 16 A.L.R., 512, followed. *In re Martin*, (1912) V.L.R., 206; 34 A.L.T., 1; 18 A.L.R., 216. *Hodges, J.*

Administration de bonis non c.t.a. when granted—Unadministered estate—Real estate—Executorial duties—Executor not registered as proprietor under Transfer of Land Act 1890—Administration and Probate Act 1890. (No. 1060), sec. 8.]—Where a testator has left land, of which he was registered proprietor, it is the duty of his executor to procure himself to be registered as proprietor of the land as executor, and until that is done his executorial duties are not completed. Where an administrator with the will annexed, having administered the personal estate, died without becoming registered proprietor of the land as administrator of the real estate of the testator, administration *de bonis non* c.t.a. of the estate of the original testator was granted to his daughter.

In re Allan, (1912) V.L.R., 286; 34 A.L.T., 2; 18 A.L.R., 217. *Madden, C.J.*

(h) Bonds and Sureties.

Administration bond—Duration of sureties liability—Title of beneficiaries to the residue—Completion of the administration.]—In a suit in 1904 by the plaintiffs upon an administration bond executed in 1886 and conditioned for the due administration by their eldest sister of the estate of their mother, who had died intestate in 1885, the defendants, as sureties thereto, so far as any misconduct on the part of administratrix might be proved, pleaded a deed of indemnity duly executed in their favour by herself and the plaintiffs, otherwise that the losses complained of did not result from the misconduct as alleged, but from the acts and conduct of the three sisters after the estate had been fully and properly administered, and whilst they were absolutely entitled to and in actual enjoyment of the property derived from the intestate. *Held*, on the evidence, overruling the High Court—(1) that there had been no misconduct by the administratrix and no loss of assets in the course of administration. (2) that the deed of indemnity was fully and properly explained to the plaintiffs, to whom the defendants did not stand in any fiduciary relation, that they perfectly understood it, and that no independent advice could have made the matter clearer; (3) that after the payment of the intestate's debts the three sisters were entitled to the residue of the estate in equal undivided shares, had consented so to enjoy it, and were jointly responsible for the mode in which it had been dealt with and lost. *Cooper v. Cooper*, L.R. 7 H.L., 53, followed. *Bayne v. Blake* (1908) A.C., 371; 14 A.L.R., 317. Privy Council.

Administration bond—Sureties—Deed of indemnity by beneficiaries, validity of.]—Where as a condition to becoming sureties to an administration bond, the sureties, prior to the execution of the bond, demand and obtain from the beneficiaries an indemnity against any liability under the bond, such indemnity is not *ipso facto* illegal. *Semble, per Griffith, C.J.* and *Barton, J.*—

If the circumstances are such that, if the indemnity were disclosed to the Court, the grant of administration might be refused, and that a stipulation that the indemnity should be concealed from the Court ought to be inferred, such a stipulation will violate the indemnity. *Bayne* v. *Blake*, 4 C.L.R., 1 ; 12 A.L.R., 454.

Administration and Probate Act 1890 (No. 1060), secs. 15, 16—Administration bond—Jurisdiction to dispense with, whether Court has.]—The Court has no jurisdiction to dispense with the administration bond required by sec. 15 of the *Administration and Probate Act* 1890. *In re Snelling*, 24 V.L.R., 753 ; 20 A.L.T., 256 ; 5 A.L.R., 102, not followed. *In re Allen*, (1908) V.L.R., 20 ; 29 A.L.T., 164 ; 14 A.L.R., 28. *Cussen, J.*

Sureties to administration bond—Evidence in support of application to dispense with—Consent of beneficiary—Necessity for proving beneficiary fully aware of his rights and of the risk he runs—Administration and Probate Act 1890 (No. 1060), sec. 16.]— *In re Storey*, 28 V.L.R., 336 ; 24 A.L.T., 80 ; 8 A.L.R., 210, followed, announcement *per Hood, J.*, after consulting the other Judges. 34 A.L.T., 86 ; 18 A.L.R. (C.N.), 20.

Administrator—Transfer of assets to sureties to administration bond to be administered by them—Breach of trust—Recovery of control of assets by administrator.]—An administrator transferred certain land which formed the only asset in the estate to certain persons, who had become sureties for his due administration, for sale and distribution of the net proceeds arising therefrom among the beneficiaries entitled thereto. Upon action brought by the administrator against the sureties claiming a declaration that the trustees had no power to sell the land, an injunction restraining them from so doing, a re-transfer of the land, and other consequential relief. *Held*, that the administrator had been guilty of a breach of trust in transferring the land, and that he was entitled to the relief sought. *Ackerly* v. *Palmer*, (1910) V.L.R., 339 ; 32 A.L.T., 23 ; 16 A.L.R., 326. *Cussen, J.*

(i) *Proof in Solemn Form, Whether Necessary.*

Probate—Practice—Valid will executed by testator—Later document purporting to be a will—Application for probate of valid will—Affidavits showing invalidity of later document—Consent of beneficiaries under later document—No intention to apply for probate of later document—Proof in solemn form, whether necessary.]—Upon their application for probate of a will appointing them executors, the applicants disclosed in their affidavit the fact that the testator had executed a later document purporting to be a will which they believed to be invalid on the ground of testator's want of testamentary capacity at the time of the making thereof, and they produced conclusive extrinsic evidence of such incapacity ; all the beneficiaries interested in upholding the later document consented to the grant of the application, and the executors named in such document had no intention of seeking probate thereof. *Held*, that probate should be granted without further proceedings. *In re Munro*, (1911) V.L.R., 20 ; 32 A.L.T., 107 ; 16 A.L.R., 603. *a'Beckett, J.*

Application for probate of document purporting to be a will—Caveat—Order nisi—Testamentary incapacity—Proof of by propounders—Evidence on affidavit—Summary hearing.]—After an order *nisi* had been granted calling upon a caveator to show cause why probate should not be granted to certain documents, the applicants for probate obtained evidence of the invalidity of such documents owing to want of testamentary capacity on the part of the alleged testator, and on the return day of the order *nisi* applied for leave to bring such evidence before the Court on affidavit. *Held*, that, upon service of notice upon the beneficiaries such evidence might be given on affidavit. *Held*, further (upon consideration of the evidence so given) that the order *nisi* should be discharged, and that the costs of all parties should be paid out of the estate. *In re Sabelberg*, (1911) V.L.R., 157 ; 32 A.L.T., 182 ; 17 A.L.R., 142. *Hodges, J.*

Will and codicils—Subsequent document purporting to be last will believed by executor

to have been executed when testatrix not of sound mental capacity—Same executor in will and codicils and in subsequent document— Application for probate of will and codicils notwithstanding the existence of subsequent document—Order nisi calling on beneficiaries under subsequent document to show cause why probate of will and codicils should not be granted—Form of order nisi.]— *In re Suter*, 12 A.L.R. (C.N.), 1. *Holroyd, J.* (1906).

(j) Caveat, Who may Lodge.

Administration and Probate Act 1890 (No. 1060), sec. 18—Will—Caveat, who may lodge — Infant — Next friend — Appointment of guardian as—Form of caveat where both next friend and infant interested in estate.]— A caveat against the granting of probate to a will may be lodged by an infant by his next friend, and a guardian of the infant need not in all cases be specially appointed for that purpose. Where the caveator and the infant are both interested in the estate, and therefore entitled to lodge a caveat, the caveat should state distinctly whether it is lodged by the caveator on his own behalf or by him as next friend on behalf of the infant. *In the Will of Adcock*, 26 A.L.T., 127; 10 A.L.R., 268, approved and applied. *In re Simeon*, (1910) V.L.R., 335; 32 A.L.T., 25; 16 A.L.R., 362. *a'Beckett, J.*

(k) Evidence; Discovery of Documents.

Probate—Order nisi—Affidavit of attesting witness made on application for probate— Whether it can be used on hearing of an order nisi.]—*Per Griffith, C.J.—Quaere*, whether the affidavit of an attesting witness filed in support of an application for probate can be used on the hearing of an order *nisi* to remove a caveat lodged against the application. *Gair v. Bowers; Falconar v. Bowers; Gair v. Falconar*, (1909) 9 C.L.R., 510; 15 A.L.R., 494. H.C., *Griffith, C.J., O'Connor, Isaacs* and *Higgins, JJ.*

Will Execution — Evidence — Will not produced—Presumption of due execution.]— The *prima facie* presumption that a will with a regular attestation clause has been duly executed, even when the attesting witnesses deny or cannot remember the due execution, does not apply to a document which is not produced after the testator's death, and as to which the fact of the signature of the deceased is not established *aliunde*. A testator instructed his solicitor to prepare a will, which was duly engrossed and left with the testator for execution, and he was instructed as to the proper mode of execution. The document was not found at the testator's death, about 18 years afterwards, and an application was made for probate of a draft of it, which was supported by an affidavit of one of the alleged witnesses (the other being then dead) who swore to facts which if believed would have proved beyond doubt that the will was duly executed by the testator shortly after he received the engrossment. On the hearing of an order *nisi* for probate, that affidavit was put in evidence, but the deponent being examined *viva voce* swore that he did not know that the document he signed was a will except from what the other witness had told him some time after ; that he did not see the testator sign ; that he did not see the testator's signature upon the will ; and did not know whether the other witness signed or not. *Held*, that, it appearing that the statements in the affidavits were made on information and belief, there was no evidence that the will was duly executed, and that therefore probate should not be granted of the draft. *Gair v. Bowers; Falconar v. Bowers; Gair v. Falconar*, (1909) 9 C.L.R., 510; 15 A.L.R., 494. H.C., *Griffith, C.J., O'Connor, Isaacs* and *Higgins, JJ.*

Will — Execution — Evidence — Statements made by testator after execution.]—Statements made by a person after the alleged execution of a will by him are not admissible as evidence of such execution. *Atkinson v. Morris*, (1897) P., 40, followed. *Gair v. Bowers; Falconar v. Bowers; Gair v. Falconar*, (1909) 9 C.L.R., 510; 15 A.L.R., 494. H.C., *Griffith, C.J., O'Connor, Isaacs* and *Higgins, JJ.*

Practice — Probate — Discovery — Testamentary scripts—English practice, whether applicable—Supreme Court Act 1890 (No. 1142), secs. 20, 21.]—In proceedings to show cause why a caveat against the grant of probate should not be removed, the Court may order the discovery of testamentary scripts. *Semble*, the terms of secs. 20 and 21 of the *Supreme Court Act* 1890 are wide enough to introduce the English practice where no other provision has been made. *In re Carew*, 25 A.L.T., 117 ; 9 A.L.R., 266, followed. *In re Cotter*, (1907) V.L.R., 78 ; 28 A.L.T., 106 ; 12 A.L.R., 550. *Cussen, J.*

Discovery of documents—Probate—Caveat —Testamentary incapacity and undue influence alleged—Discovery by caveator, how limited—Rules of Supreme Court 1906 (Probate), rule 32.]—In a case in which testamentary incapacity and undue influence were alleged by a caveator opposing the grant of probate, the Court refused to order discovery by the caveator generally, but directed him to make discovery of all documents or letters signed by or in the handwriting of the testator, and of all letters or documents addressed to him. *Re Baker*, (1907) V.L.R., 234 ; 28 A.L.T., 189 ; 13 A.L.R., 121. *a' Beckett, J.* (1907).

(*l*) *Parties.*

Administration cum testamento annexo— Application by beneficiary—Right of Curator of Intestate Estates to appear on such application.]—The Curator of Intestate Estates has no right to appear on an application to the Court by a beneficiary under a will for a grant of administration *cum testamento annexo*. *In re Basse*, (1909) V.L.R., 313 ; 31 A.L.T., 17 ; 15 A.L.R., 302. *Madden, C.J.*

(*m*) *Citations ; Notices ; Advertisements.*

Administration cum testamento annexo— Application by beneficiary—Notice to beneficiary with prior right.]—Wherever a party has a prior right to administer, the Court requires that he should be cited or consent, before it will grant administration to any other person. *In re Basse*, (1909) V.L.R., 313 ; 31 A.L.T., 17 ; 15 A.L.R., 302. *Madden, C.J.*

Administration ad litem—Notice of intention to apply, necessity for—Application under peculiar **circumstances—Administration and Probate Act 1890 (No. 1060), sec. 14,— Probate and Administration Rules 1906, rr. 4, 15.]**—The Supreme Court having jurisdiction under the *Administration and Probate Act* 1890 to grant administration *ad litem* may do so under r. 15 of the *Probate and Administration Rules* 1906, without the previous publication of the notice of intention to apply required by r. 4. *Greenway* v. *McKay*, (1911) 12 C.L.R., 310 : 17 A.L.R., 350. H.C., *Griffith, C.J., Barton* and *O'Connor, JJ.*

Administration and Probate Act 1911 (No. 2342), secs. 3, 4—Executors—Claims against testator's estate—Notice of—Contemplated proceedings for revocation of probate—Notice to claimant—Application by executor for order to bar or disregard claim.]—The claims referred to in sec. 3 of the *Administration and Probate Act* 1911 are the ordinary claims which are made against an estate of a deceased person, or against an executor or administrator as representing the estate. That section does not apply to the case of an executor having notice that a person contemplates taking proceedings to revoke the probate granted to such executor, and consequently the executor cannot make an application to the Court or a Judge under sec. 4 in regard thereto. *In re Timm*, (1912) V.L.R., 460 ; 34 A.L.T., 97 ; 18 A.L.R., 496. *Cussen, J.*

Probate and Administration Rules 1906, r. 4 —Practice—Advertisement of intention to apply for probate—Number of codicils must be mentioned in advertisement.]—The advertisement required by rule 4 of the *Probate Rules* 1906, must specify the exact number of testamentary papers of which it is the intention of the applicant to seek probate. *In re Blake*, (1912) V.L.R., 59 ; 33 A.L.T., 155 ; 18 A.L.R., 7. *Cussen, J.*

(*n*) *Discharge or Removal of Executor or Administrator.*

Administration and Probate Act 1907 (No. 2120), sec. 5—Executors—Discharge of one co-executor—Appointment of administrator in his place—Discharge by Judge.]—Sec. 5

of the *Administration and Probate Act* 1907 applies to the case of co-executors, and under that section a Judge of the Supreme Court has a discretion to order the discharge of one of two or more co-executors without appointing any person as administrator in his place. *In re Coverdale*, (1909) V.L.R., 248; 30 A.L.T., 199; 15 A.L.R., 233. *Cussen, J.*

Administration and Probate Act 1907 (No. 2120), sec. 5—Administration—Executor of executor—Right to renounce as to original testator's estate.]—Sec. 5 (1) of the *Administration and Probate Act* 1907 does not authorise the Court to discharge the executor of an executor from his duties in relation to the first testator's estate while leaving him executor with respect to his own testator's estate. *In re Keys*, (1909) V.L.R., 325; 31 A.L.T., 1; 15 A.L.R., 304. *Madden, C.J.*

Administration and Probate Act 1907 (No. 2120), sec. 5 (1), (2)—Executor, removal of—Summons, parties to—Application to Judge to indicate parties to be served.]—No directions will be given under sec. 5 (2) of the *Administration and Probate Act* 1907 as to the persons upon whom a summons under sec. 5 (1) for the removal of an executor or administrator should be served until after the issue of such summons. *In re Mitchell* (1910) V.L.R., 44; 31 A.L.T., 113; 15 A.L.R., 643. *a' Beckett, J.*

Administration and Probate Act 1907 (No. 2120), sec. 5—Executors—Discharge of one co-executor —Vesting order.] — *Semble.* — On the discharge of one of several executors, an order is not necessary to vest the property in the continuing executors. *In re Coverdale*, (1909) V.L.R., 248; 30 A.L.T., 199; 15 A.L.R., 233. *Cussen, J.*

(o) *Revocation of Grant.*

Administration ad litem—Revocation — Whether defendant in proposed action may apply for.]—*Semble.*—The Supreme Court having granted administration *ad litem* has no jurisdiction to revoke that grant on the motion of the defendant in the proposed action. *Greenway* v. *McKay*, (1911) 12

C.L.R., 310; 17 A.L.R., 350. H.C., *Griffith, C.J.*, *Barton* and *O'Connor, JJ.*

Revocation of grant of administration—Practice—Consent of administrator.]—An application for the revocation of a grant of administration may, if consented to by the administrator, be made on motion. *In re Sutherland*, (1910) V.L.R., 118; 31 A.L.T., 150; 16 A.L.R., 63. *Cussen, J.*

(p) *Appeal.*

Appeal to High Court—Appealable amount —Order nisi for probate—Interest of caveator less than £300—Judiciary Act 1903 (No. 6 of 1903), sec. 35.]—*See* APPEAL, col. 24. *Tipper* v. *Moore*, (1911) 13 C.L.R., 248; 18 A.L.R., 341.

(q) *Costs.*

Will—Caveat—Withdrawal of caveat—Motion for probate—Costs against caveator.]—Where a caveat against a grant of probate to the executors has been withdrawn prior to the motion for probate occasioned by the lodging of such caveat, the Court has no power to award costs against the caveator. *In re Downey*, 5 V.L.R. (I. P. & M.), 72, distinguished. *In re Johnson*, (1909) V.L.R., 324; 31 A.L.T., 2; 15 A.L.R., 304. *Madden, C.J.*

Caveat — Costs — Administration and Probate Act 1890 (No. 1060), sec. 21.]—In cases of contested wills, costs should follow the event unless there are adequate reasons for an order of a different character. Where the testator by his conduct, habits or mode of life has given the opponent of the will reasonable grounds for questioning his testamentary capacity, the costs of the opponent, although he is unsuccessful, should be paid out of the estate. Where that is not so, but the opponent after due inquiry entertains a *bona fide* belief in the existence of a state of things, which, if it did exist, would justify the litigation, the unsuccessful party must bear his own costs. *In re Millar*, (1908) V.L.R., 682; 30 A.L.T., 106; 14 A.L.R., 564. *Hood, J.*

Probate — Practice — Costs — Order nisi to revoke probate—Costs of unsuccessful pro-

pounder of will—Reasonable belief in validity of will.]—An executor who has obtained probate of an instrument which he reasonably and *bona fide* believes to be a valid will, but probate of which is afterwards revoked on the ground of want of testamentary capacity, should be allowed out of the estate his costs as between solicitor and client both of propounding the will and of opposing the application for revocation of probate. *Twist* v. *Tye*, (1902) P., 92, considered. *In re Keane*, (1909) V.L.R., 231; 30 A.L.T., 216; 15 A.L.R., 198. *Hodges, J.*

Will—Party supporting invalid revocation— Costs.]—*Semble.*—The costs of a party supporting an apparently valid, but really invalid revocation of a will by destruction, are governed by the same considerations as govern the costs of an executor propounding an apparently valid but really invalid will. *In re Richards*, (1911) V.L.R., 284; 33 A.L.T., 38. *a'Beckett, J.*

Order LXV., r. 28 (Rules of 1906)—Whether applicable to probate matters—Appeal from Taxing Officer's decision on item " Instructions for Brief "—Discretion of Judge.]— *Quaere*, whether Order LXV., r. 28, applies to probate matters or to any proceedings other than actions. *Re Duke's Will*, (1907) V.L.R., 632; 29 A.L.T., 50; 13 A.L.R., 477. *Cussen, J.*

Costs—Taxation—Attendance on Registrar of Probates—What should be allowed for.]— *Quaere*, whether an allowance of 10s. for attendance on the Registrar of Probates should not have been 6s. 8d. *In re Duke's Will*, (1907) V.L.R., 632; 29 A.L.T., 50; 13 A.L.R., 477. *Cussen, J.* (1907).

Costs—Taxation—Appendix N.—Drawing pleadings and other documents—Accounts, statements, &c., for Judge's Chambers— Statement for duty.]—A statement for duty is not included under the item in Appendix N. " Accounts, statements and other documents for the Judge's Chambers, when required, and fair copy to leave." *In re Duke's Will*, (1907) V.L.R., 632; 29 A.L.T., 50; 13 A.L.R., 477. *Cussen, J.*

II.—DUTIES OF REPRESENTATIVES.

(a) Payment of Debts.

(1) Generally.

Will—Land subject to an equitable charge —Charge created by parol—Charge in favor of devisee—Conveyancing Act 1904 (No. 1953), sec. 75—Parol evidence, admissibility of to establish charge.]—The words " land charged with the payment of money by way of mortgage or other equitable charge " in sec. 75 of the *Conveyancing Act* 1904 include a charge in favor of a devisee. A charge under this section may be created by parol. When any person in a fiduciary position, including an agent, has invested trust money in the purchase of land, the beneficial owner may have a charge on the property for the amount of the trust money, and trust money may be followed into land on parol evidence. *In re Smith*; *Smith* v. *Smith*, (1909) V.L.R., 91; 30 A.L.T., 214; 15 A.L.R., 25. *Hood, J.*

Solicitor to trustee of deceased person's estate—Lien for costs.]—A solicitor to the trustee of the estate of a deceased person is not a solicitor to the estate and therefore does not acquire a lien over the trust property for his costs. *In re Nolan* (*No.* 2), 30 A.L.T. (Supplement), 1; 14 A.L.R. (C.N.), 25. *Judge Moule* (1908).

Insolvency Act 1890 (No. 1102), secs. 4, 59, 61, 70 (iii.), 150—Insolvent continuing to carry on business—Knowledge and acquiescence of trustee—Debts incurred after insolvency—Rights of subsequent creditors — Death of insolvent—Interest of executrix in property acquired after insolvency.]—*See* INSOLVENCY. *In re Poole*, 31 A.L.T. (Supplement), 13; 15 A.L.R. (C.N.), 25. *Judge Moule* (1909).

(2) Calls on Shares.

Trusts Act 1901 (No. 1769), sec. 2—Shares not fully paid up held by testator at death— Distribution of assets of estate by executor— Whether necessary to reserve portion for payment of calls—Transfer of shares for nominal consideration to avoid liability—Whether executor liable — Companies Act 1896 (No. 1482), sec. 168 (2).]—Sec. 2 of the *Trusts Act*

1901 is a special enabling section for the benefit of executors, and is intended to apply to every case falling naturally within the words, so that in certain cases it may, so far as an executor's personal liability is concerned, cut down the effect which, standing alone, sec. 168 (2) of the *Companies Act* 1896 would have. *In re Blackwood; Power v. Melbourne Flour Milling Co. Proprietary Ltd.*, (1908) V.L.R., 517; 30 A.L.T., 14; 14 A.L.R., 368. *Cussen, J.*

Companies Act 1896 (No. 1482), sec. 168 (2)—Transfer of shares for nominal consideration in order to avoid liability—Shares of deceased testator—Liability of executor.]—Sec. 168 (2) of the *Companies Act* 1896 applies to a transfer made by an executor of shares in a company belonging to the estate of his testator. *In re Blackwood; Power v. Melbourne Flour Milling Co. Proprietary Ltd.*, (1908) V.L.R., 517; 30 A.L.T., 14; 14 A.L.R., 368. *Cussen, J.*

Transfer of shares by executor—Registration delayed—Distribution of assets of testator's estate—Facts insufficient to justify determination on originating summons.]—Where the question to be determined on an originating summons was whether, having regard to certain facts, the executor of a will could safely and properly, and should he, hand over the remaining assets in the testator's estate to the sole beneficiary under the will without making any provisions for any liability for calls made after a certain date on shares not fully paid up in an incorporated company, of which shares the testator was the registered holder, and which the executor had previously to such date transferred in order to free the estate from contingen liability for a nominal consideration to the executor and for a consideration to be paid to the transferee upon the transfer being registered which transfer was not registered till subsequently to such date : *Held* that no order or declaration which would justify the executor on the facts as they then stood in distributing the assets could be made. *In re Blackwood; Power v. Melbourne Flour Milling Co. Proprietary Ltd.*, (1908) V.L.R., 517; 30 A.L.T., 14; 14 A.L.R., 368. *Cussen, J.*

Calls on shares in no-liability company—Power in will to postpone sale of personal property—Retention of shares by trustees—Whether liable for calls paid by them.]—*See* TRUSTS AND TRUSTEES. *Grunden v. Nissen*, (1911) V.L.R., 267; 33 A.L.T., 11; 17 A.L.R., 260.

(b) Legacies, Interest and Accretions, and Other Matters Incidental Thereto.

Will and codicil—Interest on legacies—From what time payable—Rate of interest.]—Certain legatees under a will were given interest on their legacies at the rate of 5 per cent. per annum from the death of the testator. The greater part of the estate in the hands of the trustees was returning 5 per cent. per annum. *Held* that the general legacies under a codicil carried interest at the rate of 5 per cent. per annum from a year after the testator's death. *In re Stroud; Bell v. Stroud*, (1908) V.L.R., 33; 29 A.L.T., 104; 13 A.L.R., 645. *Cussen, J.*

Legacy—Interest—Date from which payable —Death of testator presumed—Lapse of considerable time between presumed date of death and grant of probate—Infants—Maintenance clause—Executor's year.]—Testator was a passenger by the s.s. "Waratah" which left Durban on or about 27th July 1909 and was never afterwards heard of. Probate to testator's will was granted in September 1910, the Court presuming that he died on 27th July 1909. *Held* that interest on legacies to infants, for whose maintenance during infancy provision was made in the will, should run from the presumed date of testator's death, and on other legacies from one year after that date. *In re Black; Black v. Melbourne Hospital*, (1911) V.L.R., 280; 33 A.L.T., 2; 17 A.L.R., 240. F.C. *Madden, C.J., Hodges* and *Hood, JJ.*

Interest on legacies—Rate of—Order LV., r. 64 (Rules of 1906).]—Upon an originating summons enquiring as to the rate of interest to be paid on certain legacies, *Held*, that the rate should be such as the executors might expect to get upon investments of the estate, and that, accordingly, interest on the legacies should be at the rate of 4 per cent. per annum. *National Trustees Executors &c. Co.* v. *McCracken*, 19 A.L.T., 175; 4 A.L.R., 31, discussed. *In re Black*; *Black* v. *Melbourne Hospital*, (1911) V.L.R., 280; 33 A.L.T., 2; 17 A.L.R., 240. F.C. *Madden, C.J., Hodges* and *Hood, JJ.*

Will and codicil—Interest directed to be paid on legacies to legatees under will—No general direction—Further legacies under codicil without direction as to interest.]—*See* WILL. *In re Stroud*; *Bell* v. *Stroud*, (1908) V.L.R., 33; 29 A.L.T., 104; 13 A.L.R., 645.

Gift of residuary personal property— Whether it carries intermediate income— Intention of testator.]—*See* WILL. *In re Watson*; *Cain* v. *Watson*, (1910) V.L.R., 256; 31 A.L.T., 212; 16 A.L.R., 76.

Will—Construction—Contingent legacies— Interim interest, whether infant contingent legatees entitled to—Trusts Act 1896 (No. 1421), sec. 18.]—*See* WILL. *In re Thompson*; *Brahe* v. *Mason*, (1910) V.L.R., 251; 31 A.L.T., 210; 16 A.L.R., 215.

Tenant for life and remainderman—Dividends declared by company, whether capital or income.]—*See* WILL. *In re Longley*; *Reid* v. *Silke*, (1906) V.L.R., 641; 28 A.L.T. 82; 12 A.L.R., 499.

Will—Construction—Shares in company owned by testator—Bequest to life tenant of dividends and to remainderman absolutely— Bonus declared by company on shares— New shares issued and offered to shareholders —Bonus applicable in payment therefor— Whether bonus capital or income.]—*See* TENANT FOR LIFE AND REMAINDERMAN. *In re Smith* : *Edwards* v. *Smith*, 29 A.L.T., 173; 14 A.L.R., 22.

Ademption—Pecuniary legacy to be applied in uncontrolled discretion of trustees to several purposes—Subsequent gift by testatrix towards one of such purposes which was only imperfectly accomplished at death—Statements as to her intention made by testatrix subsequently to gifts.]—*See* WILL. *In re Leggatt*; *Griffith* v. *Calder*, (1908) V.L.R., 385; 30 A.L.T., 34; 14 A.L.R., 314.

Will and codicil—Gift of residue by will— Gift by codicil of property forming part of residue—Lapse of gift by codicil—Whether lapsed gift falls into residue.]—*See* WILL. *In re Stead*; *McArthur* v. *Stead*, (1908) V.L.R., 10; 29 A.L.T., 155; 13 A.L.R., 683.

(c) *Probate Duty.*

Administration and Probate Act 1903 (No. 1815), sec. 13—Duty—General power of appointment—By will only—Property subject to power, whether dutiable.]—*See* DUTIES ON THE ESTATES OF DECEASED PERSONS, cols. 414, 415. *Webb* v. *McCracken*, 3 C.L.R., 1018; 12 A.L.R., 313.

Administration and Probate Duties Act 1907 (No. 2089), sec. 3—Exemption from duty—Public charitable bequest or settlement —Institution for the promotion of science and art, what is.]—*See* DUTIES ON THE ESTATES OF DECEASED PERSONS, col. 415. *Edgar* v. *Greenwood*, (1910) V.L.R., 137; 31 A.L.T., 132; 16 A.L.R., 6.

Settlement, duty on—Trusts or dispositions to take effect after the death of the settlor— Trust to come into operation on death of survivor of settlor or his wife — Death of settlor before his wife—Administration and Probate Act 1890 (No. 1060), sec. 112—Administration and Probate Act 1903 (No. 1815), sec. 8.]—*See* DUTIES ON THE ESTATES OF DECEASED PERSONS, cols. 415, 416. *In re Rosenthal*; *Rosenthal* v *Rosenthal*, (1910) 11 C.L.R., 87; 16 A.L.R., 455.

Administration and Probate Act 1890 (No. 1060), sec. 112—Settlements exempted from duty—Administration and Probate Act 1903 (No. 1815), secs. 8 and 9—Repeal of exemptions—Retrospective.]—*See* DUTIES ON THE ESTATES OF DECEASED PERSONS, col. 416. *Whiting* v. *McGinnis*, (1909) V.L.R., 250; 30 A.L.T., 207; 15 A.L.R., 203.

Administration and Probate Act 1890 (No. 1060), sec. 112—Administration and Probate Act 1903 (No. 1815), secs. 8 and 9—Settlement Duty—Trusts and dispositions to take effect after death—Repeal of exemptions—Retrospective effect of.]—A settlement upon trust for the settlor's wife for life and after her death upon trust for the settlor for life and after her death upon trust for the children of the marriage must, even where the settlor predeceases his wife, be registered under section 112 of the *Administration and Probate Act* 1890, and is liable to duty on the value of the whole property comprised in the settlement. *Whiting* v. *McGinnis*, (1909) V.L.R., 250 ; 30 A.L.T., 207 ; 15 A.L.R., 203. F.C. *Madden, C.J., Hodges, J. (a' Beckett, J.,* doubting). Approved by High Court in *Rosenthal* v. *Rosenthal* (1910) 11 C.L.R., 87 ; 16 A.L.R., 455.

Administration and Probate Act 1903 (No. 1815), sec. 11—Probate duty—Liability for—Gift purporting to act as immediate gift inter vivos—Donor continuing in possession under lease at full rental from donee—Whether bona fide possession and enjoyment immediately assumed and retained to exclusion of donor or of any benefit to him by contract or otherwise.]—*See* DUTIES ON THE ESTATES OF DECEASED PERSONS, cols. 416, 417. *Lang* v. *Webb*, (1911) 13 C.L.R., 503 ; 18 A.L.R., 49.

Administration and Probate Act 1890 (No. 1060), sec. 112—Settlement containing trusts which may take effect either before or after setlor's death—Property transferred in lifetime of settlor—Whether duty payable in respect thereof.]—*See* DUTIES ON THE ESTATES OF DECEASED PERSONS, col. 417. *In re Rosenthal* ; *Rosenthal* v. *Rosenthal*, (1911) V.L.R., 55 ; 32 A.L.T., 46 ; 16 A.L.R., 399.

Will — Probate duty—Voluntary transfer by testator during lifetime—Duty chargeable on property transferred, how to be paid—Administration and Probate Act 1903 (No. 1815), sec. 11.]—*See* DUTIES ON THE ESTATES OF DECEASED PERSONS, cols. 417, 418. *In re Draper* ; *Graham* v. *Draper*, (1910) V.L.R., 376 ; 32 A.L.T., 34 ; 16 A.L.R., 370.

Administration and Probate Act 1907 (No. 2120), sec. 3—Administration and Probate Act 1903 (No. 1815), sec. 11—Probate duty on property voluntarily transferred in lifetime of deceased—Whether payable out of residue.]—*See* DUTIES ON THE ESTATES OF DECEASED PERSONS, col. 418. *In re Draper* ;

Graham v. *Draper*, (1910) V.L.R., 376 ; 32 A.L.T., 34 ; 16 A.L.R., 370.

Will—Construction—Direction to pay funeral testamentary expenses and debts—Probate duty in respect of property transferred by testator in his lifetime—Administration and Probate Act 1903 (No. 1815), sec. 11.]—*See* DUTIES ON THE ESTATES OF DECEASED PERSONS, col. 418. *In re Draper* ; *Graham* v. *Draper*, (1910) V.L.R., 376 ; 32 A.L.T., 34 ; 16 A.L.R., 370.

Probate duty, how payment to be apportioned—Direction that each beneficiary shall pay duty payable in regard to his interest—Tenants for life and remainderman.]—*See* DUTIES ON THE ESTATES OF DECEASED PERSONS, cols. 418, 419. *In re Buckhurst* ; *Equity Trustees Executors and Agency Co.* v. *Buckhurst*, (1907) V.L.R., 252 ; 28 A.L.T., 190 ; 13 A.L.R., 74.

Administration and Probate Act 1907 (No. 2120), sec. 3—Administration and Probate Act 1890 (No. 1060), sec. 103—Probate duty —Apportionment—Tenant for life and remainderman—Whether legislation retrospective.]—*See* DUTIES ON THE ESTATES OF DECEASED PERSONS, col. 419. *In re Staughton* ; *Oliver* v. *Staughton*, (1910) V.L.R., 415 ; 32 A.L.T., 63 ; 16 A.L.R., 443.

Probate duty—Apportionment—Tenant for life and remainderman—Mistake of law—Agreement between executors and tenant for life as to apportionment of duty based on wrong principle—Duty of executors.]—*See* DUTIES ON THE ESTATES OF DECEASED PERSONS, cols. 419, 420. *In re Staughton* ; *Oliver* v. *Staughton*, (1910) V.L.R., 415 ; 32 A.L.T., 63 ; 16 A.L.R., 443.

Will and codicil—General direction in will exempting legacies from probate duty—Further legacies given in codicil without reference to exemption from probate duty.]—*See* WILL. *In re Stroud* ; *Bell* v. *Stroud*, (1903) V.L.R., 33 ; 29 A.L.T., 104 ; 13 A.L.R., 645.

Probate duty — Testamentary expenses — Estate for life devised subject to payment thereof—Tenant for life, refusal of payment by—No income from realty available—Pay-

ment by trustees of probate duty and testamentary expenses out of personalty bequeathed to other beneficiaries—Mortgage of real estate to recoup such beneficiaries—Whether a breach of trust.]—*See* TRUSTS AND TRUSTEES. *Croui* v. *Beissel*, (1909) V.L.R., 207 ; 30 A.L.T., 185 ; 15 A.L.R., 143.

Administration and Probate Act 1890 (No. 1060), sec. 100, 112, 116—Administration and Probate Act 1903 (No. 1815), secs. 9 (2), 15 (2)—Second Schedule—" Total value of the property "—Settlement—Rate at which duty payable—Whether based on value of all the settled property.]—*See* DUTIES ON THE ESTATES OF DECEASED PERSONS, cols. 420, 421. *Edgar* v. *Greenwood*, (1910) V.L.R., 137 ; 31 A.L.T., 132 ; 16 A.L.R., 6.

Function imposed upon tribunal by legislature—No machinery provided—Power of Court—Ascertainment of amount of duty payable—Administration and Probate Act 1903 (No. 1815), secs. 9 (2), 15 (2)—Second Schedule.]—*See* DUTIES ON THE ESTATES OF DECEASED PERSONS, col. 421. *Edgar* v. *Greenwood*, (1910) V.L.R., 137 ; 31 A.L.T., 132 ; 16 A.L.R., 6.

Administration and Probate Act 1890 (No. 1060), sec. 99—Probate duty—Procedure on assessment — Valuation of assets — Summons by Master, when it may be issued.]—*See* DUTIES ON THE ESTATES OF DECEASED PERSONS, col. 421. *Brookes* v. *The King*, (1911) V.L.R., 371 ; 33 A.L.T., 91 ; 17 A.L.R., 402.

Administration and Probate Act 1890 (No. 1060), sec. 98—Case stated—Right to begin.] —*See* DUTIES ON THE ESTATES OF DECEASED PERSONS, col. 421. *In re McCracken*, 27 A.L.T., 233 ; 12 A.L.R., 303.

(d) *Distribution.*

(1) Generally.

Administration and Probate Act 1890 (No. 1060), Part III. — Foreign Probates and Letters of Administration—Sealing foreign letters of administration—Distribution of estate, whether the same as if original letters granted in Victoria.]—Where letters of administration are granted under Part III. of the *Administration and Probate Act* 1890 the estate should be distributed in the same way as if original letters of administration had been granted in Victoria. *Permezel* v. *Hollingworth*, (1905) V.L.R., 321 ; 26 A.L.T., 213 ; 11 A.L.R., 217, followed. *In re Ralston* ; *Perpetual Executors and Trustees Association* v. *Ralston*, (1906) V.L.R., 689 ; 28 A.L.T., 45 ; 12 A.L.R., 365. *Cussen, J.*

Trusts Act 1890 (No. 1150), sec. 60—Petition for advice—Jurisdiction—Small estate—Further inquiries as to next of kin—Expense of inquiries nearly equal to value of estate.]— On a petition for advice under section 60 of the *Trusts Act* 1890 a Judge has jurisdiction to advise whether certain alleged facts should be further investigated and whether certain inquiries should he made ; and where an intestate estate consisted of a small sum of money and the expense of making further inquiries as to the next of kin would have amounted to nearly the whole of such sum, the administrator was advised that it was not necessary to make any further inquiries. *In re Cave-Brown-Cave*, (1906) V.L.R., 283 ; 27 A.L.T., 183 ; 12 A.L.R., 167. *Cussen, J.* (1906).

Trusts Act 1890 (No. 1150), sec. 60—Petition for advice—Distribution of intestate estate on footing of death of certain persons before intestate—Value of interests involved.]—On a petition by the administrator of an intestate estate for advice whether the estate might be distributed on the footing that two persons had pre-deceased the intestate, each of whom, if he survived the intestate, would be entitled to the sum of £718 as one of the next-of-kin, *Held*, that, having regard to the value of the interests involved, no advice should be given. *In the matter of O'Grady*, 26 V.L.R., 171 ; 6 A.L.R., 162, followed ; *In the matter of Cave-Brown-Cave*, (1906) V.L.R., 283 ; 27 A.L.T., 183 ; 12 A.L.R., 167, explained. *In re Cavin*, (1906) V.L.R., 517 ; 28 A.L.T., 39 ; 12 A.L.R., 333. *Cussen, J.*

Will—Gift to daughter with remainder to her children—Gift over upon default of children — Forfeiture of daughter's share — Daughter childless and past child-bearing—When share distributable.]—*See* WILL. *In re Lyons*; *Grant* v. *Trustees Executors &c. Co. Ltd.*, (1908) V.L.R., 190; 29 A.L.T., 202; 14 A.L.R., 147.

(2) Share of Widow.

Married Women's Property Act 1890 (No. 1116), sec. 25—Intestate's Estate Act 1896 (No. 1419)—Married woman—Intestacy— Estate less than £1,000—No issue— Rights of husband and next-of-kin.]—The *Intestates' Estate Act* 1896, which provides that the widow of a man who dies intestate without issue leaving an estate of the net value of not more than £1,000 shall be entitled to the whole of such estate and if the net value exceed £1,000 that she shall be entitled to £1,000 of it and to a charge over the whole estate for such sum, is not a law which makes an alteration of the law as to the manner and proportions in which the estate real and personal as to which a married man dies intestate is distributable between his widow and his children or next-of-kin within the meaning of section 25 of the *Married Women's Property Act* 1890. *Quaere,* whether that section incorporates future alterations of the law as to distribution. *Held,* therefore, that the estate of a married woman, who died intestate without issue, leaving her surviving her husband and next-of-kin, the value of the estate not exceedong £1,000, was distributable one-half to the husband and one-half to the next of kin. *In re Jamieson*; *Jamieson* v. *Christensen*, 4 C.L.R., 1489; 13 A.L.R., 566 H.C. *Griffith, C.J., Barton, O'Connor* and *Higgins, JJ.* (1907).

Intestates' Estate Act 1896 (No. 1419)— Death intestate leaving a widow and no issue —Provision of one thousand pounds for widow —Domicile of deceased, whether widow's rights affected by—Movable and immovable estate.]—If a deceased who died intestate leaving a widow and no issue was domiciled in Victoria the *Intestates' Estate Act* 1896 applies both to his movable and immovable Victorian estate, but if he was not so domiciled it applies to his immovable Victorian estate only. *In re Ralston*; *Perpetual Executors and Trustees Association of Australia Ltd.* v. *Ralston*, (1906) V.L.R., 689; 28 A.L.T., 45; 12 A.L.R., 365; *Cussen, J.*

Intestates' Estate Act 1896 (No. 1419)— Provision of one thousand pounds for widow —Deceased intestate domiciled abroad—Immovable estate alone available to provide for widow—Apportionment of debts between movable and immovable estate.]—Where an intestate dies domiciled abroad possessed of movable and immovable estate in Victoria, in order to determine the amount of the immovable estate available for payment of the provision for the widow under the *Intestates' Estate Act* 1896, the debts and testamentary expenses should be deducted from the value of the immovable estate on the basis of the proportion which the value of the immovable estate bears to the value of the movable estate. *Quaere,* in such a case what debts are to be deducted from the Victorian estate. *In re Ralston*; *Perpetual Executors and Trustees Association of Australia Ltd.* v. *Ralston*, (1906) V.L.R., 689; 28 A.L.T., 45; 12 A.L.R., 365. *Cussen, J.*

Movables—Debts secured on land—No allegation of want of solvency on part of debtor.]—Debts secured on land where there is no allegation of want of solvency on the part of the debtor are movables. *In re Ralston*; *Perpetual Executors and Trustees Association of Australia Ltd.* v. *Ralston*, (1906) V.L.R., 689; 28 A.L.T., 45; 12 A.L.R., 365. *Cussen, J.*

III.—POWERS RIGHTS AND LIABILITIES OF REPRESENTATIVE.

(a) *Sale* ; *Charge* ; *Conveyance or Transfer of Land* ; *Appointment.*

Administrator—Real estate—Power of sale for purposes of distribution after debts paid —Consent of next-of-kin.]—The debts of an intestate having been paid, the administrator is entitled to sell real estate of the intestate for the purpose of distribution without the consent of the next-of-kin or beneficiaries. *Blake* v. *Bayne*, (1908) A.C., 371; 14 A.L.R., 317, explained; *Cooper* v. *Cooper*, L.R. 7 H.L., 53, followed. *In re Transfer of Land Act*; *Ex parte Equity Trustees Executors &c. Co. Ltd. and O'Halloran*, (1911) V.L.R., 197; 32 A.L.T., 183; 17 A.L.R., 154. F.C. *Madden, C.J., a'Beckett* and *Hood, JJ.*

Executors, money lent to—Absence of inquiry as to purposes for which money wanted—Misapplication by executors—Securities for loan—Contract to give security.]—The doctrine that the mere absence of inquiry by a lender as to purposes for which the executors want money will not invalidate the security given for money which the executors misapply does not apply to a case where a person has merely a contract by the executors to give security the giving of which would injure the beneficiaries who ask the Court to prevent the executors from giving it. *Crout v. Beissel,* (1909) V.L.R., 207; 30 A.L.T., 185; 15 A.L.R., 143. *a' Beckett, J.*

Will—Interpretation—Life estate—Gift over in event of life tenant leaving no children—Intestacy—Power of sale.]—*See* WILL. *Altson v. Equity Trustees &c. Co. Ltd.,* (1912) 14 C.L.R., 341; 18 A.L.R., 316.

Direction for sale—" With all convenient speed "—Duty of trustee—Whether sale may be postponed.]—*See* WILL. *In re Watson; Cain v. Watson,* (1910) V.L.R., 256; 31 A.L.T., 212; 16 A.L.R., 76.

Transfer of Land Act 1890 (No. 1149), secs. 186, 194, 209—Administrator—Sale of land more than twenty years after death of intestate—Registration of transfer—Registrar of Titles, powers of.]—Where a transfer by an administrator of land of his intestate was lodged for registration twenty-five years after the death of the intestate. *Held,* that the Registrar of Titles was not entitled to require the administrator to justify the sale by adducing evidence that debts of the intestate remained unpaid or that the sale was authorized by the next-of-kin or other persons beneficially entitled to the land. *In re Transfer of Land Act; Ex parte Equity Trustees Executors &c. Co. Ltd. and O'Halloran,* (1911) V.L.R., 197; 32 A.L.T., 183; 17 A.L.R., 154. F.C. *Madden, C.J., a' Beckett* and *Hood, JJ.* (1911).

Transfer of Land Act 1890 (No. 1149), secs. 89, 91—Transfer of land, registration of—Transfer by administrator as such to himself in his own right—Whether an instrument fit for registration.]—The Registrar of Titles has no power to refuse to register a transfer upon the mere ground that it is a transfer by an executor or administrator as such to himself in his own right. *Ex parte Wisewould,* 16 V.L.R., 149; 11 A.L.T., 182, approved. *In re Transfer of Land Act; Ex parte Danaher,* (1911) V.L.R., 214; 32 A.L.T., 190; 17 A.L.R., 160. F.C. *Madden, C.J,* and *a' Beckett, J.* (*Hood, J.* dissenting).

Transfer of Land Act 1890 (No. 1149), Part IV.—Gift to person standing in fiduciary relation—Transfer by administrator as such to himself in his own right—Assignment by next-of-kin of their interests to administrator—Whether Commissioner entitled to call for proof that next-of-kin had independent legal advice and understood nature of transaction.]—*See* TRANSFER OF LAND. *In re Transfer of Land Act; Ex parte Danaher,* (1911) V.L.R., 214; 32 A.L.T., 190; 17 A.L.R., 160.

Vendor and purchaser—Title—Executor of an administrator—Conveyance by—Administration and Probate Act 1890 (No. 1060), sec. 6.]—*See* VENDOR AND PURCHASER. *In re Thomas and McKenzie's Contract,* (1912) V.L.R., 1; 33 A.L.T., 141; 17 A.L.R., 451.

Will—Interpretation—" Any balance to be left as my executor may direct "—Power of appointment — Trust — Uncertainty. — *See* WILL. *In the Will of Lewis; Gollan v. Pyle,* 29 A.L.T., 36; 13 A.L.R., 431.

(b) Management of Estate.

Joint executors carrying on business of testator—Partnership—Insolvency — Partnership Act 1891 (No. 1222), sec. 5—Registration of Firms Act 1892 (No. 1256), sec. 4]—Several executors carrying on the business of their testator pursuant to the terms of his will in the firm name are not necessarily partners, notwithstanding section 5 of the *Partnership Act* 1891, even though the executors have registered themselves as a firm under the *Registration of Firms Act* 1892. *In re Whitelaw; Savage v. The Union Bank of Australia Ltd; Whitelaw v. The Same,* (1906) 3 C.L.R., 1170; 12 A.L.R., 285; H.C. *Griffith, C.J., Barton* and *O'Connor, JJ.* (1906)

Will—Construction—" Upkeep and maintenance and carrying on of " house " as a home and residence "—What expenses included therein—Household expenses—Repairs —Rates and taxes—Outgoings.]—See WILL. *In re Stroud*; *Bell* v. *Stroud*, (1908) V.L.R., 33; 29 A.L.T., 104; 13 A.L.R., 645.

Direction as to investment of trust funds in certain named securities—Power to invest in securities authorized by Trusts Acts— Trusts Act 1890 (No. 1150), secs. 88, 90— Trusts Act 1896 (No. 1421), sec. 22—Trusts Act 1906 (No. 2022), sec. 4.]—See WILL. *In re Meagher*; *Trustees Executors and Agency Co. Ltd.* v. *Meagher*, (1910) V.L.R., 407; 32 A.L.T., 69; 16 A.L.R., 551

(c) Erection of Tombstone.

Tombstone over testator's grave—How far executors may spend money in erection of.] —Executors may, without express authority, erect a tombstone over the grave of the testator at a cost regulated by the amount usually expended on tombstones of persons dying in the same condition of life and by the amount available for funeral expenses. *Grunden* v. *Nissen*, (1911) V.L.R., 267; 33 A.L.T., 11; 17 A.L.R., 260. F.C. *Madden, C.J., Hodges* and *Hood, JJ.*

(d) Commission.

Executors administrators and trustees— Commission—Jurisdiction of Supreme Court to grant—Whether limited to applications in a summary way—Administration action— Future commission—Supreme Court Act 1890 (No. 1142), sec. 21—Administration and Probate Act 1890 (No. 1060), sec. 26.]—The Supreme Court has, under section 21 of the *Supreme Court Act* 1890 (section 16 of 15 Vict. No. 10) jurisdiction to grant commission both past and future to executors, administrators and trustees for their pains and trouble, and this jurisdiction is not limited in its exercise by the provisions of section 26 of the *Administration and Probate Act* 1890 empowering the Court to grant commission in a summary way to executors administrators and trustees on passing their accounts; an order granting such commission may be made in an administration action.

Nissen v. *Grunden*, (1912) 14 C.L.R., 297; 18 A.L.R., 254. H.C. *Griffith, C.J., Barton* and *Isaacs, JJ.*

Administration and Probate Act 1890 (No. 1060), sec. 26—Commission—Retainer out of estate without order of Court—Breach of trust.]—It is a breach of trust for executors to retain commission out of an estate without obtaining an order of the Court. *Crout* v. *Beissel*, (1909) V.L.R., 207; 30 A.L.T., 185; 15 A.L.R., 143. *a' Beckett, J.*

Commission—Whether executor may safely help himself.]—Executors and trustees may not safely help themselves to commission. *Crout* v. *Beissel*, (1909) V.L.R., 211; 30 A.L.T., 185; 16 A.L.R., 636, followed. *Grunden* v. *Nissen*, (1911) V.L.R., 97; 32 A.L.T., 117; 16 A.L.R., 636. *a' Beckett, J.* (1910).

Administration and Probate Act 1890 (No. 1060), sec. 26—Remuneration of executors and trustees—Legacy given as remuneration for pains and trouble—Allowance of commission.]—A testator by his will gave to each of his executors and trustees, either original or by substitution, who should act " £200 per annum for his trouble therein until my youngest child shall attain the age of twenty-one years . . ." The trusts were not completed until after the youngest child attained the age of twenty-one years. *Held*, that the trustees should be allowed commission for the period after the youngest child attained the age of twenty-one years, but should not be allowed any commission for the period before that event, even though the remuneration received in respect of the latter period might be inadequate. *Per Madden, C.J.* Although the Court has, under section 26 of the *Administration and Probate Act* 1890, jurisdiction wherever it thinks it just and reasonable to allow commission to executors and trustees under a will, the Court will not allow commission where the testator has in clear and distinct terms measured the amount of the remuneration to be received by them. *Per a' Beckett, J.* Where a legacy is given to executors expressly as remuneration, and there are no exceptional circumstances to justify the

Court in exercising its powers under section 26, the mere inadequacy of the remuneration provided by the testator is no ground for giving more than the testator intended to give. *Per Hodges, J.*—There may be cases where the Court may allow commission, although the testator has made provision for what the executor is to get. *Re Howell,* (1906) V.L.R., 223 ; 27 A.L.T., 172 ; 12 A.L.R., 92, overruled ; *Re Fellows,* 5 V.L.R. (I. P. & M.), 82 ; 1 A.L.T., 53, followed ; *Re Millin,* 2 V.L.R. (I. P. & M.), 58, 86, explained. *In re Winter* ; *Winter- Irving* v. *Winter,* (1907) V.L.R., 546 ; 29 A.L.T., 4 ; 13 A.L.R., 298. F.C. *Madden, C.J., a' Beckett, Hodges* and *Hood, JJ.*

Executor's commission—Commission given to executors by will as remuneration—Further remuneration—Administration and Probate Act 1890 (No. 1060), sec. 26.]—Although by a will the executors are given a definite commission as remuneration, the Court, if it thinks that such commission is inadequate, ought, in the exercise of its jusridiction under section 26 of the *Administration and Probate Act* 1890, to allow them an additional sum by way of commission, taking into account in estimating such additional sum the amount of the commission given by the will. *Re Millin,* 2 V.L.R. (I. P. & M.), 58, 86 and *Re Lee,* 28 V.L.R., 510 ; 22 A.L.T., 117 ; 6 A.L.R., 235, approved. *In re Howell,* (1906) V.L.R., 223 ; 27 A.L.T., 172 ; 12 A.L.R., 29. F.C. *Holroyd, A.-C.J., a' Beckett,* and *Hodges JJ.* (1906).

Administration and Probate Act 1890 (No. 1060), sec. 26—Remuneration of executors administrators and trustees—Agreement as to amount of, effect of.]—An executor or administrator may by agreeing as to the amount of his remuneration with the person proposing to appoint him disentitle himself to further or other remuneration under section 26 of the *Administration and Probate Act* 1890. *Cattanach* v. *Macpherson,* (1908) V.L.R., 390 ; 29 A.L.T., 259 ; 14 A.L.R., 214. *Madden, C.J.*

Executor—Commission—Probate in Scotland and Victoria—Victorian executors also attorneys of trustees of will in Scotland—

Agreement as to commission—Costs of executor passing accounts—Administration and Probate Act 1890 (No. 1060), sec. 26.]—A testator who died domiciled in Scotland by his will appointed certain persons executors and trustees thereof in Scotland and devised and bequeathed to them all his property, including his property in Australia, on certain trusts. Probate of this will was sealed in Victoria on the application of persons duly authorized by power of attorney on that behalf. The Scotch trustees of the testator's will from time to time by powers of attorney appointed these persons to be their attorneys (*inter alia*) to get in the Victorian assets and remit the moneys representing same to Scotland, and authorized them to deduct their expenses and reasonable " gratification " for their services. The attorneys got in outstanding Victorian assets, and for a period of eleven years remitted so much of the moneys representing the same to Scotland as was required from time to time by the Scotch trustees, deducting therefrom as the reasonable " gratification " for their services 5 per cent. on the income got in by them and in one exceptional case 5 per cent. on the corpus. This last-mentioned deduction was challenged by the Scotch trustees, but, after explanation, was subsequently allowed by them. The plaintiff, one of such attorneys as aforesaid, being dissatisfied with his remuneration, and failing to induce the Scotch trustees to increase it, instituted this action claiming (*inter alia*) (1) to be discharged from the office of trustee of the testator's will in Victoria. (2) The appointment of another trustee in his place ; (3) an order that he be at liberty to pass his accounts and be allowed commission. *Held,* that though an executor in Victoria of the trustee's will the plaintiff was not a trustee of such will, and was not in the circumstances entitled to any further commission, and that though entitled to pass his accounts, he should, in the circumstances, do so at his own cost. *Permezel* v. *Hollingsworth,* (1905) V.L.R., 321 ; 26 A.L.T., 213 ; 11 A.L.R., 217, distinguished. *Cattanach* v. *Macpherson,* (1908) V.L.R., 390 ; 29 A.L.T., 259 ; 14 A.L.R., 214. *Madden, C.J.*

Administration and Probate Act 1890 (No. 1060), sec. 26—Commission—Payment of, how calculated.]—Where lands and houses forming part of the estate are to remain unconverted under the management of executors until transferred to the beneficiaries ultimately entitled, the value of these lands and houses is not to be estimated as part of the amount upon which they are entitled to commission. *Crout v. Biessel,* (1909) V.L.R., 207; 30 A.L.T., 185; 15 A.L.R., 143. *a`Beckett, J.*

Trustee—Commission on corpus—Trusts not fully completed—Part only of trust estate sold—Administration and Probate Act 1890 (No. 1060), sec. 26.]—The Court may allow a trustee commission on corpus the proceeds of the sale of real estate before the same is disposed of in accordance with the trusts. *In re Johnson* ; *Perpetual Executors and Trustees Association &c. Ltd. v. Johnson,* (1911) V.L.R., 263; 32 A.L.T., 179; 17 A.L.R., 187. *a'Beckett, J.*

Administration and Probate Act 1890 (No. 1060), sec. 26—Trustees of will—Commission —Individual trustee and trustee company— Prospective order for allowance of commission and passing accounts—Existing accounts passed by Judge.]—Where a trustee company and an individual were executors and trustees under a will, and, upon an order made under an originating summons, the individual trustee had been allowed upon passing accounts commission upon corpus and income up to the date of that order and he subsequently under leave reserved in that order, made application for an order allowing him commission on corpus and income received since the date of the previous order on passing the accounts relating thereto, and also for a prospective order with respect to commission on future receipts of corpus and income, and the passing of accounts half-yearly in the future, *Held,* that the application should be granted, and that the accounts then before His Honor should be passed by him, instead of being sent to be dealt with by the Chief Clerk. *Sharp v. Hobson,* (1911) V.L.R., 321; 33 A.L.T., 18; 17 A.L.R., 274. *a'Beckett, J.*

Trustees—Passing accounts—Commission— Originating summons for sole purpose of passing accounts and obtaining commission.] —Trustees seeking leave by originating summons to pass their accounts and obtain commission out of the testator's estate, on passing their accounts may be allowed their costs out of the estate, even though no other questions are asked by the summons. Accounts passed and commission fixed by Judge without reference to Chief Clerk. *In re Foulkes* ; *Ford v. Foulkes,* (1909) V.L.R., 76; 30 A.L.T., 108; 14 A.L.R., 729. *Madden, C.J.*

Executors—Commission—Order for upon passing accounts—Originating summons— Administration and Probate Act 1890 (No. 1060), sec. 26.]—An application for leave to pass accounts and to be allowed commission may be made by executors and trustees upon originating summons. *Re Foulkes,* (1909) V.L.R., 76; 30 A.L.T., 108; 14 A.L.R., 729, followed. *Re Garrett* ; *Smith v. Garrett,* (1910) V.L.R., 287; 31 A.L.T., 203; 16 A.L.R., 215. *Cussen, J.* (1910).

(e) *Indemnity.*

Insolvency Act 1890 (No. 1102), sec. 37— " Secured debt " what is—Business of testator carried on by executors under provisions of will—Debt properly incurred — Right of executors to indemnity out of assets of estate —Petitioning creditor having security over property used in business—Whether such security must be given up or valued.]—Each of several executors carrying on the business of their testator pursuant to the terms of the will has a right of indemnity against the assets of the testator, including a lien over those assets, for liabilities properly incurred and any security held by a creditor which interferes with that right is a security the giving up of which will go to augment the estate of each executor, and therefore a creditor in respect of a debt so incurred, who has a security over property used in such business, must offer to give up or value that security when petitioniug to sequestrate the estate of one of the executors. *In re Whitelaw* ; *Savage v. The Union Bank of*

Australia Ltd. ; *Whitelaw* v. *The Same*, 3 C.L.R., 1170 ; 12 A.L.R., 285. H.C. *Griffith, C.J., Barton* and *O'Connor, JJ.* (1906).

Insolvency Act 1890 (No. 1102), sec. 123 (iii.)—Insolvency Act 1897 (No. 1513), sec. 113—Sequestration of estate of deceased person—Testamentary expenses incurred by the representative of a deceased person in or about the debtor's estate—Right of trustee to reimbursement as a preferential debt.]— The representative of a deceased person's estate is upon sequestration thereof entitled to payment of the amount of costs incurred by him in the administration of the estate as a preferential debt under section 123 (iii.) of the *Insolvency Act* 1890. *In re Nolan deceased* (*No.* 2), 30 A.L.T. (Supplement), 1 ; 14 A.L.R. (C.N.) 25. *Judge Moule* (1908).

(f) Passing Accounts.

Costs — Trustees — Passing accounts and allowance of commission—Order for in action —Trustees' costs of obtaining commission— Whether chargeable against estate—Administration and Probate Act 1890 (No. 1060), sec. 26.]—Where, under an order in an action, trustees are authorized to pass their accounts and apply for commission, they are entitled to charge the estate with the costs incurred by them in relation to commission, as well as in regard to passing their accounts. *Abbot* v. *Morris*, 24 A.L.T., 228 ; 9 A.L.R., 96, not followed on this point. *Macartney* v. *Kesterson*, (1907) V.L.R., 226 ; 28 A.L.T., 170 ; 13 A.L.R., 14. *Hodges, J.*

Executor or trustee passing accounts— Costs—Whether payable out of estate.]— Although ordinarily an executor or trustee is entitled to have his costs of passing his accounts and obtaining his discharge paid out of the estate, yet if in so doing he seeks to cast an unnecessary burden on the estate, he must abide those costs himself. *Cattanach* v. *Macpherson*, (1908) V.L.R., 390 ; 29 A.L.T., 259 ; 14 A.L.R., 214. *Madden, C.J.*

Administration and Probate Act 1890 (No. 1060), sec. 26—Practice—Executors and trustees—Passing accounts before Chief Clerk— Costs of executors and trustees—Objection to allowance thereof—Time to take.]—Where beneficiaries desire to object that executors and trustees should not be allowed their costs of the proceedings before the Chief Clerk for the passing of accounts and allowance of commission, they should ask the Chief Clerk to certify specially upon the matter, and then raise the question upon further consideration before the Judge on the certificate. *In re Dingwall* ; *Ross* v. *Ross*, 34 A.L.T., 137 ; 18 A.L.R., 584. *a'Beckett, J.* (1912).

Appendix O*, Rules of Supreme Court 1884 — Trustees — Passing accounts — Accounts agreed upon between parties—Fees chargeable.]—See COSTS, col. 280. *In re Winter* ; *Winter-Irving* v. *Winter*, (1908) V.L.R., 74 ; 29 A.L.T., 144 ; 13 A.L.R., 701.

(g) Legal Proceedings.

(1) Parties.

Order XVI. (Rules of 1906)—Parties— Administrator—Assets transferred by administrator in breach of trust—Action by administrator to recover—Whether beneficiaries necessary parties.]—An administrator in breach of trust transferred the assets of the estate to the sureties of the administration bond to be administered by them. In an action by the administrator against the sureties claiming a declaration that they had no power to sell the assets, an injunction, a re-transfer of the assets and other consequential relief, *Held*, that the beneficiaries were not necessary parties. *Ackerley* v. *Palmer*, (1910) V.L.R., 339 ; 32 A.L.T., 23 ; 16 A.L.R., 326. *Cussen, J.*

Practice—Joinder of parties—Administration action—Trustee sued as representative —Refusal of trustee to appeal—Judgment not yet drawn up—Joinder of cestui que trustent —Order XVI., r. 8 (Rules of 1906).]—See APPEAL, cols. 26, 27. *Connolly* v. *Macartney,* (1908) 7 C.L.R., 48 ; 14 A.L.R., 558.

" Actio personalis moritur cum persona " —Action for personal injuries—Judgment for plaintiff—Death of plaintiff pending appeal— Survival of action to executor—Executor added as respondent to appeal.]—See MAXIMS.

Farrands v. *Melbourne, The Mayor, &c. of the City of,* (1909) V.L.R., 531.

Local Government Act 1903 (No. 1893), secs. 341, 342—County Court Rules 1891, r. 103—Rates—Charge on land—Proceedings to enforce—Death of owner—Parties—Executor of executor—Order for sale—Title.]— *See* LOCAL GOVERNMENT. *Moorabbin, Shire of* v. *Soldi,* (1912) V.L.R., 389 ; 34 A.L.T., 93 ; 18 A.L.R., 493.

County Court Act 1890 (No. 1078), sec. 62— County Court Rules 1891, rr. 197, 200—Action against defendants as executors and as beneficiaries—Payment into Court by executors—Acceptance in satisfaction of claim against executors—Survival of claim against beneficiaries.]—*See* COUNTY COURT, cols. 306, 307. *Smart* v. *Buchanan,* 31 A.L.T. (Supplement), 8 ; 15 A.L.R. (C.N.), 25. *Judge Chomley.*

(2) Other Matters of Practice.

Evidence Act 1890 (No. 1088), sec. 55— Evidence of physician or surgeon—Information acquired in attending a patient—Privilege —Death of patient, effect of—Personal representative of patient, power of.]—The operation of sec. 55 of the *Evidence Act* 1890 is not limited to the lifetime of the patient. *Quaere,* whether the executor of a deceased patient can consent to the divulgation to the information acquired by a physician or surgeon in attending the patient. *National Mutual Life Association of Australasia Ltd.* v. *Godrich,* 10 C.L.R., 1 ; 16 A.L.R., 110. H.C., *Griffith, C.J., Barton, O'Connor, Isaacs* and *Higgins, JJ.* (1909).

Order II., r. 3 (Rules of 1906)—Administration action—Writ of summons—Form of heading.]—In an action claiming the administration of an estate it is not necessary that the writ of summons should be headed " In the Matter of the Estate of A.B. Deceased." *Eyre* v. *Cox,* 24 W.R., 317, not followed. *Cameron* v. *Cameron,* (1906) V.L.R., 13 ; 28 A.L.T., 169 ; 13 A.L.R., 10. *a' Beckett, J.*

Costs—Originating summons — Litigation arising out of plaintiff's mistake as executor.] —*See* COSTS, col. 264. *Perpetual Executors and Trustees Association* v. *Simpson,* 27 A.L.T., 179 ; 12 A.L.R., 95.

EXECUTORY TRUST.

See TRUSTS AND TRUSTEES.

EXTRADITION.

See FUGITIVE OFFENDERS, SERVICE AND EXECUTION OF PROCESS ACT.

FACTORIES AND SHOPS ACT.

I.—FACTORY, WHAT IS.

Factories and Shops Act 1905 (No. 1975), secs. 5, 14 (3)—" Factory or workroom "— " Preparing or manufacturing articles for sale "—Sorting, weighing and packing goods.] Defendant occupied premises in which four persons were employed by him in sorting, weighing and packing into cartons and boxes, nails manufactured by him in a factory close by. *Held,* that these persons were employed in preparing articles for sale within the meaning of sec. 5 of the *Factories and*

Shops Act 1905, and that therefore the premises were a "factory or workroom" within the meaning of that section. *Alderson* v. *Gold*, (1909) V.L.R., 219; 30 A.L.T., 189; 15 A.L.R., 180. *a'Beckett, J.* (But see *Henry Bull & Co. Ltd.* v. *Holden*, (1912) 13 C.L.R., 569, reversing decision of N.S.W. Supreme Court in *Holden* v. *Henry Bull & Co. Ltd.*, 11 S.R. (N.S.W.), 564.

II.—Shops; Closing Hours and Conditions of Employment.

Factories and Shops Act 1905 (No. 1975), sec. 134—Suspension of provisions as to closing—Who may revoke.]—It is not essential to the validity of a revocation of a suspension of the provisions of sub-sec. 1 of sec. 134 of the *Factories and Shops Act* 1905 that it should be signed by the same person as signed the suspension. It is sufficient if it is signed by or by the authority of the Minister for the time being. *Billingham* v. *Gaff*, (1907) V.L.R., 691; 29 A.L.T., 159; 13 A.L.R., 474. *Hodges, J.*

Licensing Act 1890 (No. 1111), secs. 5, 10, 11, 128—Factories and Shops Act 1890 (No. 1091), secs. 3, 46—Sale of liquor during prohibited hours—Grocer's licence—Licensee—Selling liquor only—"Shop"—Sale after hours—Hotels, whether affected by law relating to closing of shops.]—The premises on which the holder of a grocer's licence sells nothing but liquor are a "shop" within the meaning of section 46 of the *Factories and Shops Act* 1890, and of section 11 of the *Licensing Act* 1890; and the sale of liquor there, after the hour at which shops are by sec. 46 of the *Factories and Shops Act* 1890 required to be closed, is a sale otherwise than during the hours authorized by the licence and an offence under section 128 of the *Licensing Act* 1890, notwithstanding that the grocer's licence, pursuant to the Second Schedule of the last-mentioned Act, purported to authorize the sale of liquor at the time the sale was made. *Per Cussen, J.*—Holders of victuallers' licenses are not affected by the law relating to the closing of shops. *Mackinnon* v. *Hannay*, (1906) V.L.R., 604; 28 A.L.T., 33; 12 A.L.R., 381. F.C. *Hood, Cussen* and *Chomley, JJ.*

Factories and Shops Act 1905 (No. 1975), sec. 149—Sitting accommodation for employees—Sufficiency of—Seats provided for customers—Employees at liberty to use.]—The sitting accommodation required by section 149 of the *Factories and Shops Act* 1905 to be provided for the employees in a shop must be reserved for them and must be always available. The section is not complied with if the seats provided, though of the requisite number, are aviable for customers in the first instance. *Trainor* v. *Younger*, 28 A.L.T., 171; 13 A.L.R., 50. *Hood, J.* (1907).

III.—Weekly Half-Holiday.

Factories and Shops Act 1905 (No. 1975), sec. 134—Factories and Shops Act 1905 (No. 2) (No. 2008), sec. 22—Weekly half-holiday —Two businesses in same shop—One business of the kind specified in the Fourth Schedule —Whether shop must be closed for purposes of latter business.]—A person who carries on in the same shop two businesses, one of which is and the other of which is not of the kind specified in the Fourth Schedule to the *Factories and Shops Act* 1905, must, on the weekly half-holiday he has chosen or is deemed to have chosen, close his shop for all purposes and not merely for the purposes of the business not of the kind specified in the Fourth Schedule. *Billingham* v. *Gaff*, (1907) V.L.R., 691; 29 A.L.T., 159; 13 A.L.R., 474. *Hodges, J.*

Factories and Shops Act 1905 (No. 1975), sec. 144—Factories and Shops Act 1905 (No. 2) (No. 2008), sec. 27—Carters and Carriers —Limitation of hours—Weekly half-holiday —Employee of General Carrier.]—An employee of a general carrier was engaged as a carter during a certain week in carrying goods to different places, including for one day a factory. During that week he did not have a half-holiday. *Held*, that section 144 of the *Factories and Shops Act* 1905 (No. 1957) and section 27 of the *Factories and Shops Act* 1905 (*No. 2*) (No. 2008) and the Regulations thereunder did not apply to such employe, and that, therefore, the carrier was not liable to a penalty for not permitting such employe to have a half-holiday during the week in question. *Duncan v. Skinner,* (1908) V.L.R., 534 ; 30 A.L.T., 25 ; 14 A.L.R., 434. *Cussen, J.*

Factories and Shops Act 1905 (No. 1975), sec. 134—Factories and Shops Act 1905 (No. 2) (No. 2008), secs. 22, 24—Weekly half-holiday—Whether time of closing on Wednesday 1 o'clock or 6 o'clock—Choice of shopkeeper, burden of proof of.]—By the conjoint operation of sections 22 and 24 of the *Factories and Shops Act* 1905 (No. 2), 1 o'clock on Wednesday is to be deemed to be the closing time for shops (other than Fourth Schedule shops), except those in respect of which the shopkeeper may have chosen 6 o'clock as the closing time on that day, and in a prosecution for keeping his shop open after 1 o'clock on that day the onus is on the shopkeeper to show that he has made that choice. *Billingham v. Gaff,* (1907) V.L.R., 691 ; 29 A.L.T., 159 ; 13 A.L.R., 474. *Hodges, J.*

IV.—LIMITATION OF WORKING HOURS.

Factory—Restriction of hours of labour—"Work," meaning of—Factories and Shops Act 1905 (No. 1975), secs. 5, 42.]—Section 42 of the *Factories and Shops Act* 1905 provides that " in any factory or workroom where any Chinese person is at any time employed . . . no person shall work for himself or for hire or reward, either directly or indirectly, or shall employ or authorize or permit any person whomsoever to work on any day before half-past seven o'clock in the morning or after five o'clock in the evening." By section 5 of the Act " any office building or place in which . . . . one or more Chinese person are or is employed directly or indirectly in working in any handicraft " is a " factory " and that term " handicraft " includes " any work whatsoever done in any laundry . . . and whether or not done in preparing or manufacturing articles for trade or sale." *Held,* that the word " work " in section 42 means " work at factory work," and therefore that the section does not apply to a Chinese ironing his own shirt during the prohibited hours in a Chinese laundry. *Ingham v. Hie Lee,* (1912) 15 C.L.R., 267 ; 18 A.L.R., 453. H.C. *Griffith, C.J.* and *Barton, J.*

Factories and shops—Carters and drivers—Carting during prohibited hours—Empties carted back to stable—Carting goods " from outside a city "—Factories and Shops Act 1907 (No. 2137), sec. 40—Factories and Shops Act 1909 (No. 2184), sec. 12—Factories and Shops Act 1910 (No. 2305), sec. 38.]—Section 40 of the *Factories and Shops Act* 1907 as amended by section 38 of the *Factories and Shops Act* 1910 provides that :—" No person shall cart or deliver . . . any goods wares and merchandise or materials whatsoever before half-past seven o'clock in the morning or after half-past seven o'clock in the evening " on certain days. Section 12 of the *Factories and Shops Act* 1909 provides that :—" Nothing in section 40 of the *Factories and Shops Act* 1907 shall be taken to prevent any person who has carted any . . . goods . . . from outside a city town or borough completing his journey in such city town or borough after the hours stated in this section to the extent only of taking the horse or other animal cart and goods into a yard but such goods shall not be unloaded until the next day." A carter employed by a contracting carrier having delivered at a hotel in the City of Prahran barrels of beer which he had carted from a brewery, placed on his lorry certain empty barrels and crates to be returned to the brewery and proceeded to his employer's stables in the City of Richmond where he did not arrive until after half-past seven o'clock in the evening, his intention being to deliver the barrels and crates at the brewery the next day. He was prosecuted on an information charging him with having unlawfully carted goods after half-past seven o'clock in the evening in the City of Richmond. *Held,* that the carter should have been convicted of the offence with which he was charged. *Pemberton v. Banfield,* (1912) 15 C.L.R., 323 ; 18 A.L.R., 486. H.C. *Griffith, C.J., Barton* and *Isaacs, JJ.*

V.—Determinations of Court of Industrial Appeals and of Special Boards.

(a) *Principles to be Applied in Arriving at.*

Factories and Shops Act 1905 (No 1975), Parts IX. and X.—Special Boards—Court of Industrial Appeals—Minimum wage, determination of—Matters to be taken into consideration.]—The intention of the Legislature in the provisions of the *Factories and Shops Acts* relating to the fixing of wages is that, while the interests of the workers are to be primarily attended to, regard must be had to all concerned, and that the decisions must be arrived at without any feelings of sympathy or benevolence towards either employers or employees. *In re the Starch Board*, 13 A.L.R., 558. *Hood, J.* (1907).

Factories and Shops Act 1905 (No. 1975), sec. 75—" Lowest prices or rates which may be paid to persons employed in factories "—Provisions not confined to protected industry.]—The mere fact that an industry does not participate in the protective policy of Australia does not exempt it from the provisions of the Factories and Shops Acts. *In re the Fellmongers' Board*, 15 A.L.R., 225. *a' Beckett, J.* (1909).

Factories and Shops Act 1905 (No. 1975), Part IX.—Minimum wage, determination of—Consideration of the merits of each particular case—Whether every adult male entitled as of right to at least £2 a week.]—A fixed minimum wage for all employees cannot be laid down. Each trade must be dealt with on its own merits. There is no foundation for the contention that every adult male is entitled as of right to at least £2 a week. *In re the Starch Board*, 13 A.L.R., 558. *Hood, J.* (1907).

Factories and Shops Act 1905 (No. 1975), secs. 83, 122—Reference of determination to Court of Industrial Appeals—Average prices paid by reputable employers insufficient to afford a reasonable limit—Principles upon which Board should act—Whether determination may prejudice the progress &c. of the trade.]—In dealing with a determination of a Special Board upon a reference under sec. 83 (c) of the *Factories and Shops Act* 1905 (No. 1975), the provisions of sec. 122, though strictly speaking applicable to appeals only, afford a guide to the Court. *In re the Starch Board*, 13 A.L.R., 558. *Hood, J.* (1907).

Wages Boards—Factories and Shops Acts—Alterations of industrial conditions—Principles upon which they should be made.]—It is not the intention of the Factories and Shops Acts that alterations of any sort should be made in industrial conditions without satisfactory proof of the existence of some evil, or that changes should be made out of mere benevolence, or upon conjecture founded mainly upon hearsay and rumour. *In re the Bread Board*, 13 A.L.R., 589. *Hood, J.* (1907).

Minimum wage, how to be determined—Alteration of—Matters to be considered—Circumstances of a temporary or fluctuating nature.]—The circumstances to be taken into consideration in fixing a minimum wage must be of a permanent character. The current wage should not be altered for some mere passing temporary or fluctuating cause, *e.g.*, a temporary fluctuation in the cost of living or in the nature of the work. No change should be made in the determination of the Board or of the Court unless on some ground which may reasonably be considered as permanent, or at least likely to last for some considerable time. *In re the Bread Board*, 13 A.L.R., 589. *Hood, J.* (1907).

Minimum wage, how to be determined—Comparison with rates of wages paid in other trades in Victoria and in other States.]—Wages should not be increased in a particular trade where they compare favourably with the wages paid in all other trades in Victoria, and with those paid in the same trade in other States. *In re the Bread Board*, 13 A.L.R., 589. *Hood, J.* (1907).

Factories and Shops Act 1905 (No. 1975), sec. 75—" Lowest prices or rates," what are—Principles of determination.]—The determination of a Special Board as to a particular industry should be arrived at by comparing the hours of labour and rates of pay generally prevailing in cognate industries, *i.e.*, industries resembling in their general characteristics the industry under consideration.

Neither the Boards nor the Court should resort to a new standard on a more liberal scale than that which has already prevailed, if to do so would cause an industrial upheaval. *In re the Fellmongers' Board*, 15 A.L.R., 225. *a' Beckett, J.* (1909).

Minimum wage, what is—Matters to be considered in determining—Factories and Shops Act 1905 (No. 1975), sec. 75—Court of Industrial Appeals.]—It is the duty of Wages Boards in fixing a minimum wage under section 75 of the *Factories and Shops Act* 1905 (No. 1975), and of the Court of Industrial Appeals, in reviewing their decisions, not to fix the very lowest amount reasonably consistent with existence, but to take the current wage, and ascertain what evil exists under that wage, considering the various surrounding circumstances, and then to fix a fair amount. *In re the Bread Board*, 13 A.L.R., 589 (1907).

Factories and Shops Act 1905 (No. 1975), sec. 75—" Lowest prices or rates," what are —Mode of ascertaining.]—The principles laid down by *Hood, J.*, in *Re the Artificial Manure Board*, (1905) V.L.R., 19; 26 A.L.T., 87; 10 A.L.R., 230, as to how the Court of Industrial Appeals and the Special Boards should arrive at their determinations, adopted. *In re the Fellmongers' Board*, 15 A.L.R., 225. *'a' Beckett, J.* (1909).

Factories and Shops Act 1905 (No. 1975), sec. 122—" Living wage," personal, not family wage.]—The term " living wage " as used in sec. 122 of the Act 1975 refers to the personal living wage and not to the family living wage, *i.e.*, such a wage as will support a man and his wife and family in frugal comfort. *In re the Fellmonger's Board*, 15 A.L.R., 225. *a' Beckett, J.* (1909).

Factories Act 1905 (No. 1975), sec. 122— " Living wage "—How to be estimated.]— A " living wage," which includes the case of a healthy bachelor without a soul dependent on him and also that of a married man with seven children, cannot be fixed with any pretension to accuracy. All that can be done is to adopt some general rough estimate. *In re the Starch Board*, 13 A.L.R., 558. *Hood, J.* (1907).

Factories and Shops Act 1905 (No. 1975), sec. 122 — Court of Industrial Appeals — Whether determination may prejudice the progress maintenance of or scope of employment in trade concerned—What to be considered.]—In considering whether a determination may prejudice the progress, &c. of the trade concerned, the danger of injury to the trade as a whole, with the consequent contraction in the scope of employment, is the chief factor to be kept in mind. *In re the Starch Board*, 13 A.L.R., 558. *Hood, J.* (1907)

Factories and Shops Act 1905 (No. 1975), Parts IX. and X.—Minimum wage, determination of—Matters to be taken into consideration—Competition amongst employers— State of trade.]—If the employers choose to cut prices in order to crush one another, the burden of such competition must not be thrown upon the employes. But even in such a case some consideration must be given to the state of trade in fixing the rates of wages of employes. *In re the Starch Board*, 13 A.L.R., 558. *Hood, J.* (1907).

Wages board—Lowest prices or rates, how to be determined—Ability of individual worker.]—Wages rates will not be fixed on the ability of the individual worker. *In re Boilermakers' Board*, 18 A.L.R., 399. *Hood, J.* (1912).

Wages Boards—Minimum wage, how to be determined—Cost of living, general increase in.]—For observations as to raising wages on account of a general increased cost of living, see *In re the Bread Board*, 13 A.L.R., 589. *Hood, J.* (1907).

Factories and Shops Acts—Minimum wage —Matters to be considered in determining.]— Observations as to the fixing of a minimum wage having regard to the skill or want of skill required in the work performed, to the questions whether it is heavy or light, healthy or unhealthy, regular or intermittent, to the necessity for special clothing while the workmen are engaged in it, and to the wages payable in other trades. *See In re the Ice Board*, 16 A.L.R., 46. *Hodges, J.* (1909).

Wages Board—Lowest prices or rates, how to be determined—Classification of work with regard to skill, onerousness, &c.—Nature. kind and class of work and mode and manner in which it is to be done.]—Where, by the determination of a Special Board, a rate of wage was prescribed—(a) for labourers assisting in manufacturing work (except a specified class of them), and (b) for labourers employed in that specified class, and for all other labourers not provided for in the determination, the Court directed that the employes included in the two groups should be classified according to the nature of the work to be done, and that the rate of wages should be fixed according to the degree of skill and of onerousness, or risk to health, in each class. *In re Boilermakers' Board*, 18 A.L.R., 399. *Hood, J.* (1912).

Wages Board—Lowest prices or rates— Current rate of wages—Agreement between employers and employes as evidence of.]— Where an agreement has been made between representatives of the employers and employes, the rates of pay mentioned in it will be taken as fixing the current rate of wage in the trade or industry at the time, irrespective of other evidence. *In re Boilermakers' Board*, 18 A.L.R., 399. *Hood, J.* (1912).

Factories and Shops Act 1905—Maximum hours.]—Forty-eight hours as a rule should be the maximum hours of work in all industries, unless the special exigencies of an industry require a longer period to be worked for the minimum rate of pay. *In re the Fellmongers' Board*, 15 A.L.R., 225. *a' Beckett, J.* (1909).

(b) Appeals, Nature and Scope of; Practice.

Court of Industrial Appeals—Purpose of its existence—Principles governing its determination—Absence of absolute discretion.]— The Court of Industrial Appeals exists for the purpose of correcting mistakes made by Special Boards in making determinations as to the lowest rates of pay and maximum hours of work in the various industries for which such Boards are appointed. The Court and the Board should be governed by the same principles in arriving at a determination, and the Court, on the hearing of an appeal, has not an absolute discretion in the matter without regard to prevailing usage or rates of pay. *In re the Fellmongers' Board*, 15 A.L.R., 225. *a' Beckett, J.* (1909).

Court of Industrial Appeals— Appeal, whether in the nature of a re-hearing—Factories and Shops Act 1905 (No. 1975), sec. 122.]—An appeal from a determination of a Wages Board to the Court of Industrial Appeals is an appeal by way of re-hearing on any evidence procurable, and the Court is not limited to dealing with the determination on the materials which were before the Board. *In re the Bread Board*, 13 A.L.R., 589. *Hood, J.* (1907).

Factories and Shops Act 1905 (No. 1975), sec. 122—Court of Industrial Appeals—Factories and Shops Act 1907 (No. 2137), sec. 33— Appeal, nature of—Re-hearing—Whether Court confined to materials before Wages Board.]—An appeal to the Court of Industrial Appeals from the determination of a Wages Board is in the nature of a re-hearing, and the Court is not confined to a consideration of the materials which were before the Board in coming to a conclusion as to what should be the minimum wage in the process, trade or business for which the Board was appointed. *In re the Ice Board*, 16 A.L.R., 46. *Hodges, J.* (1909).

Factories and Shops Act 1905 (No. 1975), sec. 122—Determination alleged to prejudice progress, maintenance of or scope of employment in industry—Appeal to Court of Industrial Appeals—In respect of what matters it may be brought.]—*Quaere*, whether parties who desire to show that the rate of wages fixed by a Special Board may have the effect of prejudicing the progress, maintenance of, or scope of employment in the trade or industry affected are not bound to appeal against the whole determination, and not merely against particular items therein. *In re Boilermakers' Board*, 18 A.L.R., 399. *Hood, J.* (1912).

**Wages Board—Determination of lowest price or rate—Matters affecting—Cost of living—Evidence as to.]—Observations on the evidence required to warrant an increase on the current wage by reason of increased cost of living. *In re Boilermakers' Board,* 18 A.L.R., 399. *Hood, J.* (1912).

Court of Industrial Appeals—Evidence on hearing of appeal.]—For observations as to the evidence to be given on the hearing of industrial appeals, see *In re the Bread Board,* 13 A.L.R., 589. *Hood, J.* (1907).

(c) Failure to Observe Provisions of, What is.
(1) Wages.

Factories and Shops Act 1905 (No. 1975), sec. 119 (1)—Employing person at lower rate than rate determined by Special Board— Mens rea, whether a necessary element of offence—Employer, liability of, for act of agent.]—The defendant was convicted under sec. 119 (1) of the *Factories and Shops Act* 1905, of employing a person at a lower rate of pay than the rate determined by the Saddlery Board. The evidence showed that the employe was engaged by the defendant's foreman at a lower rate than the rate so determined, that the defendant paid the employe at the rate at which he was engaged, and that the defendant was a member of the Saddlery Board which made the determination. *Held,* that there was evidence of every element of the offence created by the section, and that the defendant was rightly convicted. *Semble.*—He would not have been liable if he had shown that he honestly and reasonably believed in the existence of facts which would make his conduct innocent. *Semble,* also, he would not have been liable for the act of his foreman if he had *bona fide* given the foreman instructions to employ men only in accordance with the determination of the Board. *Reg.* v. *Tolson,* 23 Q.B.D., 168, applied. *Billingham* v. *Oaten,* (1911) V.L.R., 44 ; 32 A.L.T., 170 ; 17 A.L.R., 36. *Hodges, J.*

(2) Apprentices and Improvers.

Factories and Shops Act 1903 (No. 1857), sec. 7—Factories and Shops Act 1900 (No. 1654), secs. 4, 15, 22—Indentures of apprenticeship binding employer to instruct, what are—

Agreement to employ an " apprentice " in connection with employer's business—No clause binding employer to instruct—Nature of business not described.]—By an agreement in writing not under seal made between an employer and a person described in the agreement as an apprentice, the employer agreed to employ the apprentice and the apprentice agreed to work for the employer in connection with his business for the term of six years. There was no clause in the agreement binding the employer to instruct the apprentice, nor did the agreement say anything as to the nature of the employer's business. *Held,* that the apprentice did not come within the exception provided by sec. 7 of the *Factories and Shops Act* 1903, and that he was therefore an improver and entitled to be paid the wages fixed for improvers by the determination of the Special Board of the employer's trade. *Hines* v. *Phillips,* (1906) V.L.R., 417 ; 28 A.L.T., 1 ; 12 A.L.R., 249. *a'Beckett, A.-C.J.* (1906).

Factories and Shops Act 1900 (No. 1654), secs. 4, 15—Factories and Shops Act 1903 (No. 1857), sec. 7—" Improver," who is— Apprentice under indentures or agreement not binding employer to instruct for not less than three years.]—The construction to be put upon the word " apprentice " in sec. 15 of the *Factories and Shops Act* 1900 is governed by sec. 7 of the *Factories and Shops Act* 1903 which provides that all apprentices except those bound in the manner described in sec. 7 shall be deemed to be improvers. *Hines* v. *Phillips,* (1906) V.L.R., 417 ; 28 A.L.T., 1 ; 12 A.L.R., 249. *a'Beckett, A.-C.J.* (1906).

Indentures of apprenticeship, what are— Writing not under seal—Factories and Shops Act 1903 (No. 1857), sec. 7.]—The term " indentures of apprenticeship " has no specific legal significance and will include a writing not under seal. *Quaere,* whether such term in sec. 7 of the *Factories and Shops Act* 1903 is limited to agreements under seal. *Hines* v. *Phillips,* (1906) V.L.R., 417 ; 28 A.L.T., 1 ; 12 A.L.R., 249. *a'Beckett, A.-C.J.* (1906).

(d) *Effect of Awards of Commonwealth Court of Conciliation and Arbitration.*

Factories and Shops Acts—Determination of Special Board—Commonwealth Court of Conciliation and Arbitration—Award of—Inconsistency with determination—Commonwealth of Australia Constitution Act (62 & 63 Vict. c. 12), cl. v., sec. 51 (xxxv.).]—The Commonwealth Court of Conciliation and Arbitration has no power to make an enforceable award, which is inconsistent with a determination of a Wages Board empowered by a State Statute to fix a minimum rate of wages. *The Federated Sawmill, Timberyard and General Woodworkers Employes Association of Australasia v. James Moore & Sons Proprietary Ltd.,* (1909) 8 C.L.R., 465 ; ·15 A.L.R., 374. *Griffith, C.J., O'Connor, J. (Isaacs and Higgins, JJ., dissentientous).*

Conciliation and Arbitration—Commonwealth Court—Jurisdiction—Award inconsistent with determination of Wages Board—The Constitution, sec. 51 (xxxv.).]—*See* COMMONWEALTH OF AUSTRALIA CONSTITUTION, col. 136. *Australian Boot Trade Employes Federation v. Whybrow,* 10 C.L.R., 266 ; 16 A.L.R., 185.

Factories and Shops Act 1909 (No. 2241), sec. 39—No person compellable to pay more than the minimum wage unless he contract so to do—Jurisdiction of Commonwealth Court of Conciliation and Arbitration—How far affected by State legislation.]—*See* COMMONWEALTH OF AUSTRALIA CONSTITUTION, cols. 136, 137. *Australian Boot Trade Employes Federation v. Whybrow,* 10 C.L.R., 266 ; 16 A.L.R., 185.

VI.—LEGAL PROCEEDINGS.
(a) Parties.

See, also, *ante* V. *(b).*

Factories and Shops Act 1905 (No. 1975), secs. 42, 162 (c), (d)—Factories and Shops Act 1905 (No. 2), (No. 2008), sec. 9—Conviction against firm in firm name—Rules under the Justices Act 1890, rr. 18, 20—Information, form of.]—In proceedings against a firm for an offence under sec. 42 of the Act No.

1975, the conviction ought to be against the individual members of the firm, and a conviction in the firm name is bad. *Quaere,* whether, in such proceedings, the information should be against the individuals, and not against the firm. *Bishop* v. *Chung Brothers,* 4 C.L.R., 1262 ; 13 A.L.R., 412. H.C., *Griffith, C.J., Barton* and *Isaacs, JJ., Higgins, J.,* dissenting (1907). [*See,* Act No. 2137, sec. 39].

(b) Evidence.

Factories and Shops Act 1905 (No. 1975), sec. 134—Keeping shop open when it should be closed—Whether necessary to prove a sale of goods.]—In order to establish an offence under sec. 134 of the *Factories and Shops Act* 1905, it is not necessary to prove that a sale of goods has taken place. *Billingham* v. *Gaff,* (1907) V.L.R., 691 ; 29 A.L.T., 159 ; 13 A.L.R., 474. *Hodges, J.* (1907).

Factories and Shops Act 1905 (No. 1975), sec. 134—Closing of shop—Carrying on business of a kind necessitating closing of shop—Evidence of the carrying on of such business before and after the day stated in information—Admissibility of.]—In support of a charge that a particular business was carried on in a shop on a particular day, evidence is admissible of sales of goods pertaining to such business shortly before and after such day. *Billingham* v. *Gaff,* (1907) V.L.R., 691 ; 29 A.L.T., 159 ; 13 A.L.R., 474. *Hodges, J.* (1907).

FAIR COMMENT.

See DEFAMATION.

FALSE PRETENCES.

Criminal law—Jurisdiction—False pretences made in Tasmania—Attempt to obtain money in Victoria—Crimes Act 1890 (No. 1079), sec. 165.]—*See* CRIMINAL LAW. *Rex* v. *Waugh,* (1909) V.L.R., 379 ; 31 A.L.T., 37 ; 15 A.L.R., 366.

FEDERAL LAW.

See CUSTOMS ; COMMONWEALTH OF AUSTRALIA CONSTITUTION.

FEES.

See COSTS.

FIERI FACIAS.

See EXECUTION.

FIRM.

Factories and Shops Act 1905 (No. 1975), sec. 162—Factories and Shops Act 1905 (No. 2) (No. 2008), sec. 9—Conviction against firm in firm name—Rules under Justices Act 1890, rr. 18, 20—Information, form of.]—*See* CONVICTION, col. 244. *Bishop* v. *Chung Brothers*, 4 C.L.R., 1262 ; 13 A.L.R., 412.

FISHERIES ACT.

Fisheries Act 1890 (No. 1093), secs. 3, 15—Fishing in inland waters—" Fixed engine "—Line and hook attached to stick driven into bank.]—A fishing line and hook attached to a stick driven into a river bank are not a " fixed engine " within the meaning of sec. 15 of the *Fisheries Act* 1890. *Myers* v. *Hooke*, (1912) V.L.R., 191 ; 33 A.L.T., 214 ; 18 A.L.R., 176. F.C., *Madden*, *C.J.*, *a' Beckett* and *Hood*, *JJ.* [See the section substituted by the *Fisheries Act* 1912 (No. 2391), sec. 5].

FIXTURES.

Fixture, nature of—Purpose with which chattel attached to freehold—Attachment for better enjoyment of freehold—Evidence, admissibility of.]—*See* LANDLORD AND TENANT. *Love* v. *Bloomfield*, (1906) V.L.R., 723 ; 28 A.L.T., 52 ; 12 A.L.R., 383.

Fixtures—Tenant's right to remove, how affected by taking new lease.]—*See* LANDLORD AND TENANT. *Love* v. *Bloomfield*, (1906) V.L.R., 723 ; 28 A.L.T., 52 ; 12 A.L.R., 383.

FOREIGN COMPANY.

See COMPANY.

FOREIGN LAW.

See INTER-STATE AND INTER-NATIONAL LAW.

FOREIGN PROBATE.

See EXECUTORS AND ADMINISTRATORS.

FORGERY.

See CRIMINAL LAW.

FORMS.

See COUNTY COURT, PRACTICE AND PLEADING.

FRAUD AND MISREPRESENTATION.

See also INSOLVENCY.

Undue influence—Parent and child—Trustee and cestui que trust—Whether transaction may be set aside against third party—Ordinary business transaction—Beneficiary surety for trustees—Independent advice.]—The trustees of a will who were carrying on the business of the testator in trust to divide the profits of the business between the beneficiaries named in the will were pressed by their bank to reduce their indebtedness to the bank by means of the sale of some of the goods of the business. The trustees objected to do so, and asked for further advances for the purposes of the business, and on their suggestion it was arranged that their account should be guaranteed by the beneficiaries, and that then the bank should allow the trustees more accommodation. The trustees accordingly procured and handed to the bank guarantees signed by the beneficiaries, and further advances were made. One of the trustees was the mother and another of the trustees was the elder brother of the beneficiaries. The bank manager, with whom the arrangement was made, was aware of facts from which, had he adverted to them, he must have inferred that some of the beneficiaries were not much over 21 years of age. The bank had nothing to do with the procuring of the guarantees. *Held*, that, even if as between the trustees and the beneficiaries, the guarantees were of no avail until the trustees proved that the beneficiaries had had independent advice, it was not necessary for the bank to give such proof before it could enforce the guarantees against the beneficiaries. *Semble.*—It would have been otherwise if the bank had procured the guarantees from the beneficiaries, or had been in any way mixed up in the obtaining of them, or if the guarantees had been simply to secure a past debt, and not to procure future advances, or if the beneficiaries had had no direct interest in the business. *Union Bank of Australia Ltd.* v. *Whitelaw*, (1906) V.L.R., 711; 28 A.L.T., 17; 12 A.L.R., 393. *Hodges, J.*

" Undue influence," what is.]—" Undue influence " is the improper use of the ascend-

ancy acquired by one person over another for the benefit of the ascendant person himself or someone else, so that the acts of the person influenced are not, in the fullest sense of the word, his free voluntary acts. *Union Bank of Australia Ltd.* v. *Whitelaw*, (1906) V.L.R., 711; 28 A.L.T., 17; 12 A.L.R., 393. *Hodges, J.*

" Undue concealment "—Business carried on by trustees in breach of trust—Moneys advanced to trustees upon guarantee of beneficiaries—Ordinary business transaction—Whether creditor under duty to inform himself and beneficiaries as to conduct of trustees.]—The trustees of a will who were in fact carrying on the business of their testator in breach of trust were pressed by their banker to reduce their indebtedness to the bank by means of the sale of some of the goods of the business. The trustees objected to this, and it was arranged on their suggestion that they should get their account guaranteed by the beneficiaries who, under the will, were interested in the business, and that then the bank would make further advances. The trustees accordingly procured and handed to the bank guarantees signed by the beneficiaries, and further advances were made. The banker had through balance-sheets and a copy of the will the means of knowing, but had not applied his mind to and did not in fact know of the breach of trust. The only matter with which he concerned himself was to see the bank protected, and it never occurred to him to question the legality of the acts of the trustees. The bank took no part in the procuring of the guarantees. An action to enforce the guarantees was resisted on the ground of " undue concealment." *Held*, that there was no duty imposed on the bank to search after the persons who proposed to become surety, and to inform them of the conduct or behaviour of the persons for whom they proposed to become surety, such conduct being outside the dealing between the creditor and the principal debtor, and that there was no " undue concealment." *Union Bank of Australia Ltd.* v. *Whitelaw*, (1906) V.L.R., 711; 28 A.L.T., 17; 12 A.L.R., 393. *Hodges, J.*

Fiduciary relation—Undue influence, presumption of—Whether principle confined to voluntary dealings.]—*Per Hodges, J.*—" I think that the principle enunciated in *Huguenin* v. *Baseley*, 14 Ves., 273, has gone beyond purely voluntary transactions, but I can find no case where it has been applied to an ordinary business transaction such as this, where the person suing (*i.e.*, a bank which had made advances) has had nothing to do with the procuring of the guarantee, and where the surety (the person alleged to have been subject to undue influence) has had a direct personal pecuniary interest in the business which is being conducted by means of the account guaranteed, and has for years derived all the benefits that accrued from the account." *Union Bank of Australia Ltd.* v. *Whitelaw*, (1906) V.L.R., 711; 28 A.L.T., 17; 12 A.L.R., 393.

Insolvency—Fraudulent preference—" With a view to prefer "—Disposition advantageous to particular creditor—Disposition made to carry out supposed legal obligation—Intention—Motive—Insolvency Act 1890 (No. 1102), sec. 73—Insolvency Act 1897 (No. 1513), sec. 116.]—In order that a disposition of property made by a debtor in insolvent circumstances to one of his creditors may be a fraudulent preference within the meaning of sec. 73 of the *Insolvency Act* 1890, the giving of a preference must be the substantial object which the debtor desires to achieve. The motive or reason which induces that desire is irrelevant. Defendant, a cattle salesman, sold for a principal cattle to A, a dealer, advancing the purchase money himself and taking A's promissory notes therefor. As part of the transaction it was verbally agreed that A would re-sell the cattle through defendant, who might repay himself the advance out of purchase money. A, having come into insolvent circumstances, instructed his solicitor to call a meeting of his creditors. Two days afterwards, when requested by other creditors to allow them to take some of the cattle in payment of their debts, he refused, stating that to do so would be unfair to the other creditors. Eight days afterwards, and within a month of his insolvency, and before the notes became due, A, at the request of the defendant and believing that he was fulfilling his obligation to defendant, and that it would be wrong to do otherwise, sold the cattle through the defendant, who received the purchase money and applied it in discharge of A's liability to him. In an action by trustee in insolvency of A, *Held* (*Isaacs, J.,* dissenting), that A. had made a fraudulent preference in favour of the defendant, and that the trustee was entitled to recover the amount received by the defendant as purchase money for the cattle. *Muntz* v. *Smail*, 8 C.L.R., 262; 15 A.L.R., 162. H.C., *Griffith, C.J., Barton, O'Connor* and *Isaacs, JJ.* (1909).

Illegal contract—Transfer of land to defeat creditors—No proof that creditors defeated—Resulting trust.]—*See* TRUSTS AND TRUSTEES. *Payne* v. *McDonald*, (1908) 6 C.L.R., 208; 14 A.L.R., 366.

Transfer of Land Act 1890 (No. 1149), sec. 140—Mortgage by trustee in breach of trust—Actual notice of breach—Absence of fraud or dishonesty—Mortgage not lodged for registration till after issue of writ.]—*See* TRANSFER OF LAND ACT. *Crout* v. *Beissel*, (1909) V.L.R., 207; 30 A.L.T., 185; 15 A.L.R., 143.

Partnership—Contract with individual who afterwards takes another into partnership—Election to hold firm liable on contract—Solicitors—Liability for fraud of co-partner.]—*See* PARTNERS AND PARTNERSHIP. *Reid* v. *Silberberg*, (1906) V.L.R., 126.

Companies Act 1896 (No. 1482), sec. 133 (1)—Company—Winding up—Public examination of promoters, directors and others—Application for order—Materials—Fraud.]—*See* COMPANY, col. 161. *In re Rubber Inventions Co. Ltd.*, (1908) V.L.R., 414; 30 A.L.T., 41; 14 A.L.R., 350.

Companies Act 1890 (No. 1074), sec. 54—Printed copy of resolution of shareholders forwarded to Registrar-General—Presumption against fraud—Validity of resolution, prima facie evidence of.]—*See* EVIDENCE, col. 484. *McLean Brothers & Rigy Ltd.* v. *Grice*, 4 C.L.R., 835; 13 A.L.R., 77.

FRIENDLY SOCIETY.

Friendly Society—Domestic tribunal—Disqualification of Judge—Personal interest—Nemo debet esse judex in propria sua causa.]—Where the rules of a Friendly Society formed under the *Friendly Societies Act* 1890 provide for the constitution of a judicial tribunal to adjudicate upon charges against members, in order to exclude the principle that a man must not be a Judge in his own cause, an intention to exclude it must appear in the rules either expressly or by necessary implication. *Dickason* v. *Edwards*, 10 C.L.R., 243; 16 A.L.R., 149. H.C., *Griffith, C.J., O'Connor* and *Isaacs, JJ.* (1910).

Friendly Society — Domestic tribunal — Officer acting as Judge in his own case.]—By the direction of the District Executor of a Friendly Society, of which Executive the District Chief Ranger was a member, a member was charged with conduct calculated to bring disgrace on the Society. The conduct complained of consisted of personal abuse of the District Chief Ranger and other officers of the Society. The District Chief Ranger presided at the tribunal which heard the charge, but took no active part in the proceedings. The member was found guilty and was *de facto* expelled from the Society. *Held*, that the whole proceedings were invalid by reason of the presence of the District Chief Ranger on the tribunal, that the expulsion was ineffectual, and that the member was entitled to a declaration that he was still a member of the Society. *Dickason* v. *Edwards*, 10 C.L.R., 243; 16 A.L.R., 149. H.C., *Griffith, C.J., O'Connor* and *Isaacs, JJ.* (1910).

Friendly Society—Domestic tribunal—Rules, interpretation of—Whether officer disqualified from acting as Judge—Personal interest—Nemo debet esse judex in propria sua causa.]—By a rule of a Friendly Society constituted under the *Friendly Societies Act* 1890 it was provided that the District Chief Ranger, who was the head of the Society, " shall preside at " certain meetings, including the meetings of a certain judicial tribunal constituted by the rules. *Held*, that this rule did not require or permit the District Chief Ranger to preside, even formally, on the judicial tribunal on the hearing of a charge against a member in which the District Chief Ranger was in the position of a person complaining of an offence against him personally. *Held* (*per Griffith, C.J., and Isaacs, J.*), that notwithstanding the absence of express provisions in the rules, the tribunal had inherent power to appoint a Chairman *pro hac vice* in the absence of the District Chief Ranger. *Dickason* v. *Edwards*, 10 C.L.R., 243; 16 A.L.R., 149. H.C., *Griffith, C.J., O'Connor* and *Isaacs, JJ.* (1910).

Friendly Society—Trial of member by domestic tribunal—Member found guilty—Whether Court may review finding—Interpretation of rules of Society.]—A rule of a Friendly Society provided that—" Should any member be adjudged . . . by a Judicial Committee . . . guilty of any . . . conduct calculated to bring disgrace on the Order, he shall be expelled." A member adjudged guilty under this rule objected that the conduct with which he was charged was incapable of coming within the rule. *Held*, that the Court might review the matter for the purpose of determining this objection. *Per Griffith, C.J. and O'Connor, J.* The only ground upon which the Court can interfere is that no reasonable man could come to the conclusion that the facts proved amounted to the offence charged. *Per Isaacs, J.*—The Court has only to see whether the finding was arrived at in accordance with the rules, without any departure from the principles of natural justice and *bona fide*, and if those conditions be complied with, the Court will not interfere so long as it finds it impossible to designate the finding as one at which no reasonable man could honestly arrive. *Dickason* v. *Edwards*, 10 C.L.R., 243; 16 A.L.R., 149 (1910).

Society—Orange Lodge—Charge against member—Notice of charge—Compliance with rule requiring—Whether a condition precedent—Domestic tribunal, right of appeal to—Failure to so appeal—Effect on right of action.] The plaintiff was a member of a Lodge of the

Loyal Orange Institution of Victoria. One of the Lodge rules (No. 10) provided that ten days before the hearing by the Lodge of a charge made against a member, the charge should be furnished him in writing, and rule No. 14 provided that—" Any member guilty of an offence of an aggravated character against religion or morality or of habitual drunkenness, or violating a resolution of the Grand Lodge shall be liable to expulsion." The plaintiff was notified in writing of a charge against him " of conduct unbecoming an Orangeman under rule No. 14," and was, on the hearing, in spite of his protest, suspended from membership. *Held,* that compliance with rule No. 10 was a condition precedent to the jurisdiction of the Lodge, and that the notice required by that rule must limit the point in dispute so as to bind the accuser, and give definite information to the accused. The notice given had not that effect, and the plaintiff was entitled to a declaration that his suspension was unlawful, and to damages for the temporary loss of membership privileges. *Held* further, that, as the notice was not merely vague, but radically wrong, the plaintiff's right of action was not affected by a rule empowering him to appeal to the Grand Lodge. *Carbines* v. *Pittock,* (1908) V.L.R., 292 ; 29 A.L.T., 282 ; 14 A.L.R., 248. *Hood, J.*

Friendly Societies Act 1890 (No. 1094), secs. 5, 11, 13—Medical Act 1890 (No. 1118), secs. 93, 97—Friendly Society—Rule providing for sale of medicines to " purchasing members " Ultra vires—Unlawfully carrying on business as chemist and druggist—Sales to the public.] —The objects of a Friendly Society were, according to its rules, " to raise a fund by voluntary subscriptions of the members to supply medicines and other articles required for relief in sickness or other ailment, medical advice and attendance to members, their wives children and kindred as hereinafter provided." By rule 7 it was provided that— " In addition to the membership provided for in the Rules and Regulations of this Institution there shall also be a restricted form of membership which shall entitle the persons requiring the same to purchase

medicines . . . at a scale of charges to be adopted by the Institution . . . Such members shall be known as " Purchasing Members " and shall acquire no interest whatever in the funds of the Institution, nor shall they acquire any of the rights and privileges of the other members, nor any other rights or privileges whatsoever save only the right of purchase from the Dispensary of the Institution at the prices as aforesaid. Any person may become a ' Purchasing Member ' on payment of the sum of sixpence to the Dispenser . . . and may continue such membership by the payment of an annual subscription of sixpence." *Held,* that rule 7 was outside the powers conferred by sec. 5 of the *Friendly Societies Act* 1890, and therefore that sales of medicines to such " Purchasing Members " were a violation of sec. 97 of the *Medical Act* 1890. *Shillinglaw* v. *Carroll,* 3 C.L.R., 1099 ; 12 A.L.R., 347. *Griffith, C.J., Barton* and *O'Connor, JJ.* (1906).

Friendly Societies Act 1890 (No. 1094), secs. 11, 13 (v.)—Rules of Society—Acknowledgment of registration issued by Registrar—How far conclusive as to validity of rules.]—An acknowledgment of registry of an amendment of a rule issued by the Registrar under sec. 13 (v.) of the *Friendly Societies Act* 1890 is only conclusive that the things which might lawfully be done have been done, and has not the effect of declaring that a thing which could not be lawfully done has been lawfully done. *Shillinglaw* v. *Carroll,* 3 C.L.R , 1099 ; 12 A.L.R., 347. *Griffith, C.J., Barton* and *O'Connor, JJ.* (1906).

Friendly Societies Act 1890 (No. 1094), sec 16 (iii.), (vi.)—Property of Society, legal proceedings concerning—Owners, who to be named as—Trustees.]—Sec. 16 (vi.) of the *Friendly Societies Act* 1890, which provides that in legal proceedings all property of a Friendly Society shall be stated to be the property of the trustees in their proper names as trustees for the Society, does not apply unless the property in question has actually become the property of the trustees. *Rex* v. *Watson,* (1908) V.L.R., 103 ; 29 A.L.T.,

146 ; 13 A.L.R., 724. F.C., *Madden, C.J., Hodges* and *Hood, JJ.* (1907).

Criminal law—Larceny—Property, in whom to be laid—Trustees of Friendly Society—Friendly Societies Act 1890 (No. 1094), sec. 16 (vi.).]—*Per Hood, J.*—Quaere, whether a prosecution for theft is a " proceeding concerning property " within the meaning of sec. 16 (vi.) of the *Friendly Societies Act* 1890, which provides that in such a proceeding the property of a Friendly Society shall be stated to be the property of the trustees in their proper names as trustees for the Society. *Rex* v. *Watson,* 13 A.L.R., at p. 725.

Larceny—Money of Friendly Society—Money in possession of treasurer—Felonious taking by trustee—In whom property should be laid—Friendly Societies Act 1890 (No. 1094), sec. 16 (iii.), (vi.).]—The treasurer of a Friendly Society received on behalf of the Society moneys which, under the rules of the Society, it was his duty within twenty-four hours to pay into a bank to the credit of the trustees. By the rules the trustees were to hold all property of the Society which came into their possession in trust for the Society. The treasurer placed the moneys in a safe and, within twenty-four hours of their being received by the treasurer, one of the trustees broke into the safe, abstracted the moneys, and applied them to his own use. The trustee was charged on presentment with larceny of the moneys of the Treasurer and found guilty. *Held,* that, as the moneys had not within the rules of the Society come into the possession of the trustees, but were at the time of the asportation in the lawful possession of the treasurer, they were rightly laid in the presentment as the moneys of the treasurer, and the trustee was rightly convicted. *Rex* v. *Watson,* (1908) V.L.R., 103 ; 29 A.L.T., 146 ; 13 A.L.R., 724. F.C., *Madden, C.J., Hodges* and *Hood, JJ.* (1907).

Embezzlement — Secretary of Friendly Society—Moneys of trustees—No relation of master and servant.]—*See* CRIMINAL LAW, col. 336. *Rex* v. *M'Auslan,* (1907) V.L.R., 710 ; 29 A.L.T., 83 ; 13 A.L.R., 609.

Friendly Society, Secretary of—Trustees—No relation of agency—Fraudulent conversion by agent—Larceny—Crimes Act 1896 (No. 1478), sec. 2.]—*See* CRIMINAL LAW, col. 340. *Rex* v. *Buckle,* 31 A.L.T., 43 ; 15 A.L.R., 372.

FUGITIVE OFFENDERS.

I.—UNDER FUGITIVE OFFENDERS ACT 1881.

Fugitive Offenders Act 1881 (44 & 45 Vict. c. 69)—Commonwealth of Australia Constitution Act (63 & 64 Vict. c. 12)—Authority of State of Victoria with regard to fugitive offenders—How far affected by establishment of Commonwealth.]—Unless the Commonwealth Parliament has power under the Constitution to make laws under sec. 32 of the *Fugitive Offenders Act* 1881 or to deal with the surrender of fugitive offenders between the Commonwealth and other parts of the British dominions, the establishment of the Commonwealth has had no effect whatever upon the position and authority of the State of Victoria with regard to that Act. *McKelvey* v. *Meagher,* 4 C.L.R., 265 ; 12 A.L.R., 483. H.C., *Griffith, C.J., Barton* and *O'Connor, JJ.* (1906).

Commonwealth of Australia Constitution Act (63 & 64 Vict. c. 12)—The Constitution, sec. 51 (xxxix.)—External affairs—Surrender of fugitive offenders—Power of the Commonwealth Parliament with regard to.]—*Semble.*—Sec. 51 (xxix.) of the Constitution empowers the Parliament of the Commonwealth to make laws with respect to the surrender of fugitive offenders between the Commonwealth and other parts of the British dominions. *McKelvey* v. *Meagher,* 4 C.L.R., 265 ; 12 A.L.R., 483. H.C., *Griffith, C.J., Barton* and *O'Connor, JJ.* (1906).

Rendition of fugitive offenders—Law of Victoria—Effect of establishment of the Commonwealth—Commonwealth of Australia Con-

stitution Act (63 & 64 Vict. c. 12)—The Constitution, secs. 108, 109—Fugitive Offenders Act 1881 (44 & 45 Vict. c. 69).]—The *Fugitive Offenders Act* 1881 was a law in force in Victoria at the time of the establishment of the Commonwealth within the meaning of sec. 108 of the Constitution, and, the Parliament of the Commonwealth not having exercised the powers (if any) which it possesses to make provision in that behalf, the law of Victoria remains exactly the same as it was, and the powers of the Governor, the Judges and the Magistrates of Victoria under the *Fugitive Offenders Act* 1881 are exactly as they were before the establishment of the Commonwealth. *McKelvey* v. *Meagher*, 4 C.L.R., 265 ; 12 A.L.R., 483. H.C., *Griffith, C.J., Barton* and *O'Connor, JJ.* (1906).

Subordinate legislature—Power in criminal matters, territorial limits of — " Quitting Natal," whether legislature may make it a criminal offence—Fugitive Offenders Act 1881 (44 & 45 Vict. c. 69), secs. 2, 9—Offences to which Act applies—Criminality dependent upon event happening after " quitting Natal."] Sec. 76 of Law No. 47 of the Colony of Natal provides :—" If any person who is adjudged insolvent or has his affairs liquidated by arrangement after the presentation of an insolvency petition by or against him or the commencement of the liquidation or within four months before such presentation or commencement quits Natal and takes with him . . any part of his property to the amount of £20 or upwards which ought by law to be divided amongst his creditors he shall (unless the jury is satisfied that he had no intent to defraud) be guilty of an offence punishable with imprisonment for a time not exceeding two years with or without hard labour." In proceedings under the *Fugitive Offenders Act* 1881 for the rendition of a fugitive accused of the crime of contravening the above law, it appeared that the fugitive had not been adjudged insolvent until after he had left Natal. *Held*, that the Law was not *ultra vires* of the legislature of Natal. *Held*, also, that the acts which the Law of Natal made an offence had been completed so far as they rested with the fugitive, if he,

being a person whose financial position was such and who within Natal had done or suffered such an act as rendered him liable to be adjudged insolvent, had left Natal taking with him property to the said amount divisible amongst his creditors, and that the fact that he had not actually been adjudged insolvent was not material. *McKelvey* v. *Meagher*, 4 C.L.R., 265 ; 12 A.L.R., 483. H.C., *Griffith, C.J., Barton* and *O'Connor, JJ.* (1906).

Fugitive Offenders Act 1881 (44 & 45 Vict. c. 69)—" Judge of a superior Court "— " Magistrate."]—A State Judge or Magistrate having authority in any portion of the Commonwealth is a " Judge of a superior Court " or a " Magistrate " for the purposes of the *Fugitive Offenders Act* 1881. *McKelvey* v. *Meagher*, 4 C.L.R., 265 ; 12 A.L.R., 483. H.C., *Griffith, C.J., Barton* and *O'Connor, JJ.* (1906).

Fugitive Offenders Act 1881 (44 & 45 Vict. c. 69), secs. 3, 5, 9—Warrant for apprehension of fugitive—Statement of offence charged, sufficiency of.]—An endorsed warrant sufficiently mentions, within the meaning of sec. 5 of the *Fugitive Offenders Act* 1881, the offence with which the fugitive is charged, if the charge be substantially sufficient according to the law of the State where the warrant was issued. *McKelvey* v. *Meagher*, 4 C.L.R., 265 ; 12 A.L.R., 483. H.C., *Griffith, C.J., Barton* and *O'Connor, JJ.* (1906).

Fugitive Offenders Act 1881 (44 & 45 Vict. c. 69), sec. 5—Endorsed warrant—Statement of offence, sufficiency of.]—An endorsed warrant alleged that the accused had committed " the crime of contravening sec. 76 of Law 47, 1887 (Natal)." The certificate of the Attorney-General of Natal stated " that the crime of contravention of sec. 76 of the Insolvency Law No. 47 of 1887 . . . is punishable in Natal," &c. *Held*, that the warrant was sufficient to give a Magistrate in Victoria jurisdiction to commit the defendant to prison to await his return to Natal. *McKelvey* v. *Meagher*, 4 C.L.R., 265 ; 12 A.L.R., 483. H.C., *Griffith, C.J., Barton* and *O'Connor, JJ.* (1906).

Evidence—Foreign law—Rendition of fugitive offender—Fugitive Offenders Act 1881 (44 & 45 Vict. c. 69), secs. 5, 29.]—In proceedings before a Magistrate under the *Fugitive Offenders Act* 1881 to have a fugitive returned to Natal, the law of Natal relating to the alleged offence may be proved by the certificate of the Attorney-General of Natal, and by the depositions of a Natal lawyer taken in Natal. *McKelvey* v. *Meagher*, 4 C.L.R., 265 ; 12 A.L.R., 483. H.C., *Griffith, C.J., Barton* and *O'Connor, JJ.* (1906).

Evidence—Foreign law—Fugitive Offenders Act 1881 (44 & 45 Vict. c. 69)—Law of other country, whether a question of fact—How Magistrate may be satisfied as to.]—*Semble.*— The law of another part of the dominions is, for the purposes of the *Fugitive Offenders Act* 1881, not a matter of fact required to be legally proved, but is a matter as to which a Magistrate may satisfy himself by any available means. *McKelvey* v. *Meagher*, 4 C.L.R., 265 ; 12 A.L.R., 483. H.C., *Griffith, C.J., Barton* and *O'Connor, JJ.* (1906).

Justices Act 1890 (No. 1105), sec. 141— Fugitive Offenders Act 1881 (44 & 45 Vict. c. 69)—Order of Victorian Magistrate exercising powers conferred by Imperial Act— Whether it may be dealt with by order to review.]—The order of a Victorian Magistrate made in the exercise of powers conferred by the *Fugitive Offenders Act* 1881 is not subject to the provisions of the *Justices Act* 1890 relating to order to review. *O'Donnell* v. *McKelvey*, (1906) V.L.R., 207 ; 27 A.L.T., 164 ; 12 A.L.R., 39. F.C., *a'Beckett, Hodges* and *Hood, JJ.*

Fugitive Offenders Act 1881 (44 & 45 Vict. c. 69), secs. 5, 6—Fugitive committed to prison to await return—Legality of detention affirmed by Supreme Court—Bail, whether Court may grant.]—A decision of the Full Court on the return of a writ of *habeas corpus* affirming the legality of the detention of a fugitive offender committed to prison to await his return is a final decision within the meaning of sec. 6 of the *Fugitive Offenders Act* 1881, and the Court has no jurisdiction to grant bail. *Re McKelvey*, (1906) V.L.R., 304 ; 12 A.L.R.,

168. F.C., *Holroyd, A.-C.J., a'Beckett* and *Hodges, JJ.* (1906).

Fugitive Offenders Act 1881 (44 & 45 Vict. c. 69), secs. 5, 6—Fugitive committed to prison to await return—Legality of detention affirmed by Supreme Court—Appeal to High Court— Bail.]—Where the legality of the detention of a fugitive offender committed to prison to await his return had been affirmed by the Supreme Court, and the fugitive had obtained leave to appeal to the High Court, the Supreme Court liberated the fugitive upon giving bail to surrender himself when required by the Governor under the *Fugitive Offenders Act* 1881. *Re McKelvey*, (1906) V.L.R., 304 ; 12 A.L.R., 209. F.C., *a'Beckett, A.-C.J., Hodges* and *Hood, JJ.* (1906).

II.—UNDER SERVICE AND EXECUTION OF PROCESS ACT.

Service and Execution of Process Act 1901 (No. 11), sec. 18—Person arrested on warrant issued in another State—Duty of Justice of Peace before whom such person is brought.]— *See* SERVICE AND EXECUTION OF PROCESS ACT. *O'Donnell* v. *Heslop*; *The King* v. *Cresswell, Ex parte Heslop*, (1910) V.L.R., 162 ; 31 A.L.T., 173 ; 16 A.L.R., 168.

Service and Execution of Process Act 1901 (No. 11), sec. 18 (4)—Person arrested on warrant issued in another State—Return of such person to such other State, whether unjust or oppressive—Dispute as to facts alleged in defence—Bona fide assurance of dispute by prosecutor.]—*See* SERVICE AND EXECUTION OF PROCESS ACT. *O'Donnell* v. *Heslop*; *The King* v. *Cresswell, Ex parte Heslop*, (1910) V.L.R., 162 ; 31 A.L.T., 173 ; 16 A.L.R., 168.

Service and Execution of Process Act 1901 (No. 11), sec. 18 (4)—Application to Judge— Jurisdiction—Whether original or appellate.] *See* SERVICE AND EXECUTION OF PROCESS ACT. *O'Donnell* v. *Heslop*; *The King* v. *Cresswell, Ex parte Heslop*, (1910) V.L.R., 162 ; 31 A.L.T., 173 ; 16 A.L.R., 168.

Service and Execution of Process Act 1901 (No. 11 of 1901), sec. 18—Warrant endorsed

for execution in another State—Apprehension of accused on unsustainable charge—Exercise of discretion by Justice—Jurisdiction of Judge —Review of Justice's discretion by Judge.]— *See* SERVICE AND EXECUTION OF PROCESS ACT. *In re George*, (1909) V.L.R., 15; 30 A.L.T., 141; 15 A.L.R., 27.

Service and Execution of Process Act 1901 (No. 11), sec. 18 (4)—Practice—Application to Judge for discharge of prisoner, how made.] *See* SERVICE AND EXECUTION OF PROCESS ACT. *O'Donnell* v. *Heslop; The King* v. *Cresswell, Ex parte Heslop*, (1910) V.L.R., 162; 31 A.L.T., 173; 16 A.L.R., 168.

Service and Execution of Process Act 1901 (No. 11), sec. 18 (4)—Warrant—Execution— Application for discharge of person apprehended—Procedure—Form of order.]—Upon an application under sec. 18 (4) of the *Service and Execution of Process Act* 1901 for the discharge of a person who is held under a warrant issued in another State on which a Justice of the Peace in Victoria has made an indorsement authorizing the execution thereof within Victoria, the order should in the first instance be in the nature of an order *nisi* calling upon the informant to show cause on a subsequent day why the order applied for should not be made. *In re George*, (1908) V.L.R., 734; 30 A.L.T., 113; 14 A.L.R., 699. *a'Beckett, J.* (1908).

Service and Execution of Process Act 1901 (No. 11), sec. 18—Person charged with offence in another State—Execution of warrant in Victoria — Power to discharge accused— Whether it may be exercised after his admission to bail to appear and answer the charge.] *See* SERVICE AND EXECUTION OF PROCESS ACT. *O'Donnell* v. *Heslop; The King* v. *Cresswell, Ex parte Heslop*, (1910) V.L.R., 162; 31 A.L.T., 173; 16 A.L.R., 168.

Service and Execution of Process Act 1901 (No. 11 of 1901), sec. 18—Execution of warrant issued in another State—Order of Justice of Peace directing return of accused—Review of order by Judge—Costs,, jurisdiction to award.]—*See* SERVICE AND EXECUTION OF PROCESS ACT. *In re George*, (1909) V.L.R., 15; 30 A.L.T., 141; 15 A.L.R., 27.

GAME ACT.

Game Act 1890 (No. 1095), sec. 15—Wilful trespass on land in search or pursuit of game— Crossing land—Intention to go to a place and there search for or pursue game.]—A person is not trespassing in search or pursuit of game when he crosses another man's land with the intention of going to some place, on which, when he reaches it, he intends to search for game, or on which he intends to pursue game. *Moffatt* v. *Hassett*, (1907) V.L.R., 515; 29 A.L.T., 87; 13 A.L.R., 266. *Hodges, J.* (1907).

Game Act 1890 (No. 1095), sec. 15—Wilful trespass on land in search or pursuit of game— "Wilful," meaning of—Crossing land to reach other land and there search for game.]— The defendant entered and crossed the complainant's land to reach a lake, situated on Crown land, where he intended to shoot wild ducks. The defendant knew he was going on and intended to go on the complainant's land. *Held*, that, although he wilfully trespassed on complainant's land, the defendant was not then in search or pursuit of game, and therefore could not be convicted under sec. 15 of the *Game Act* 1890. *Moffatt* v. *Hassett*, (1907) V.L.R., 515; 29 A.L.T., 87; 13 A.L.R., 266. *Hodges, J.* (1907).

Game Act 1890 (No. 1095), sec. 15—Wilful trespass on land in search or pursuit of game— Whether complainant must show that defendant was not on Crown land—Mens rea— Honest belief of defendant.]—In a complaint under sec. 15 of the *Game Act* 1890 it lies upon the complainant to show that the defendant was not on Crown land. If the defendant, although in fact on complainant's land, honestly believed he was on Crown land, the trespass was not wilful. *Moffatt* v. *Hassett*, (1907) V.L.R., 515; 29 A.L.T., 87; 13 A.L.R., 266. *Hodges, J.* (1907).

GAMING AND WAGERING.

I.—OFFENCES.

(a) Against By-laws of Racing Club.

By-law—Validity—Unreasonableness and uncertainty—Regulation of " bookmaking " on public racecourse—Victoria Racing Club Act 1871 (No. 398), secs. 7-20.]—Certain land was by Statute vested in an officer of a racing club to be held only for the purpose of its being maintained and used for a public racecourse, and the committee of the club was empowered by such Statute to make by-laws for regulating the admission of persons to the land, the expulsion of persons from the land, the rates and charges to be paid for admission, and for the general management of the racecourse. Purporting to act under this power the Committee made a by-law forbidding any person to carry on upon any part of the land the vocation of a bookmaker unless he was approved of by the committee and paid to the committee in advance such registration fee as the committee should from time to time determine, and unless he complied with such directions as might from time to time be given by or on behalf of the committee. A person offending against the by-law incurred a penalty of £5, and was liable to be removed from the land. *Held*, that, in the method prescribed for fixing the fees, and in its requirements as to the approval of the committee and as to compliance with directions, the by-law was unreasonable and uncertain, and was therefore invalid. *Col-*

man v. *Miller*, (1906) V.L.R., 622 ; 28 A.L.T., 35 ; 12 A.L.R., 386. F.C., *Hodges, Hood* and *Chomley, JJ.*

" Bookmaking " on racecourse—How far lawful—By-law regulating " bookmaking "— Validity of.]—*Per Hood, J.*—Provided that in doing so he violates no Statute law nor interferes unduly with others, any person lawfully on a racecourse may make wagers either privately with his friends or publicly as a business. Public betting as business may become a nuisance or an annoyance, and by-laws designed to prevent this should be supported if possible, but, like all by-laws interfering with private rights, they must be reasonable and certain. *Colman* v. *Miller*, (1906) V.L.R., 622 ; 28 A.L.T., 35 ; 12 A.L.R., 386.

(b) User of Place for Gaming; Common Gaming Houses.

Police Offences Act 1890 (No. 1126), secs. 49, 51—" Business," assisting in conducting —Club incorporated as company—Shareholders in company members of Club—Totalisator—Whether conducted as a business— Percentage of stakes retained—Burden of proof—Moneys received as consideration for an assurance to pay moneys on contingencies relating to horse races.]—Certain premises were leased from the owners by an institution known as the Metropolitan Club. The Club was incorporated under the *Companies Act* 1890 with an alleged capital of £700 divided into 7,000 shares of 2s. each. Membership was acquired by payment of the latter sum, whereupon a scrip certificate (signed by two of the defendants) was issued to the incoming member as the holder of a share. All the defendants were members. The most important business of the club was wagering on horse races through the totalisator, in which all the defendants assisted, but some of the defendants laid the odds also, and some of the members were in the habit of betting with one another. The club premises consisted principally of a club-room fitted with counters behind which each of the defendants stood from time to time receiving moneys invested on the totalisator. Of the moneys so received, 90 per cent. was handed over to the backers of the winning horses and 10 per cent. retained. Black-boards were hung upon the walls of the club-room for the purpose of recording wagers made through the totalisator, and certain wagers made between members and certain of the defendants. A balance-sheet which was published disclosed *inter alia* a receipt described as " Commission &c. £515 9s. 9d." and a disbursement described as " Salary and wages and directors' fees £366 7s. 6d." The results of races received through the telephone were published on blackboards in the club-room. On the above facts the Court of General Sessions affirmed the conviction of the defendants of the offence of assisting in conducting the business of a room which was used for the purpose of money being received by persons conducting the business thereof as a consideration for an assurance to pay moneys in contingencies relating to horse-races contrary to the provisions of sec. 51 of the *Police Offences Act* 1890. Upon case stated for the determination of the Supreme Court, *Held*, that the reasonable inference from the conduct of the defendants was that they were carrying on a business for their own profit ; that the facts did not sustain the defence that the defendants carried on the gaming, not as a business in the ordinary way for profit, but for the social gratification of the members, and obtained no profit or advantage out of the 10 per cent. retained other than they might obtain as members of the Club ; that the moneys invested in the totalisator were received by the defendants as the consideration for an assurance as alleged ; and that the defendants were rightly convicted. *O'Donnell* v. *Solomon*, (1906) V.L.R., 425 ; 27 A.L.T., 237 ; 12 A.L.R., 283. F.C., *a' Beckett, A.-C.J., Hodges* and *Chomley, JJ.* (1906).

Police Offences Act 1890 (No. 1126), secs. 49, 51—" Assisting " in conducting a common gaming house—Principal or person other than employe.]—*Semble*.—The offence of " assisting " in conducting the business of a common gaming house may be committed by a person who himself actually conducts

the business and does not act under the control or orders of some other person. *Rogerson* v. *Phillips and O'Hagan*, (1906) V.L.R., 272 ; 27 A.L.T., 166 ; 12 A.L.R., 147. *a' Beckett, J.* (1906).

Gaming—Contrivance for gaming—Poker machine—Unlawful gaming—Room used for the purpose of unlawful gaming being carried on therein—Police Offences Act 1890 (No. 1126), secs. 62, 64—Lotteries Gaming and Betting Act 1906 (No. 2055), sec. 31.]—The committee of a club registered under the Licensing Acts caused to be placed upon a counter in one of the club-rooms a machine called a " poker machine ") which was used. by many members of the club in this way :— A coin (3d.) was placed in a slot and a lever pressed and by means of certain mechanism in the machine a hand of five playing cards was exposed to view in the front face of the machine. According to the value of the hand of cards thus shown which was determined by the rules of the game called poker, the playing member either lost his coin or became entitled to a greater or less number of tokens stamped with different face values. For these tokens he could obtain from the club, drinks, cigars, chocolates, etc. It was shown that for every £100 invested in the machine about £76 was returned to the players, the club retaining the balance. *Held*, that this machine was a contrivance for gaming within sec. 31 of the *Lotteries Gaming and Betting Act* 1906, that the use of it by members was unlawful gaming within the meaning of sec. 62 of the *Police Offences Act* 1890, and that the members of the club could be properly convicted under that section of having used a room for the purpose of unlawful gaming being carried on therein. *O'Donnell* v. *Dodd*, (1910) V.L.R., 482 ; 32 A.L.T., 87 ; 16 A.L.R., 539. F.C., *Madden, C.J., Hodges* and *Hood, JJ.*

Police Offences Act 1890 (No. 1126), secs. 49, 50, 51, 52, 62—Lotteries Gaming and Betting Act 1906 (No. 2055), sec. 12—Gaming houses, &c.—Place used for the purpose of unlawful gaming being carried on therein—" Place "—" User "]—In order to convict a person charged with unlawfully assisting in conducting the business of a place used for the purpose of unlawful gaming being carried on therein, contrary to section 62 of the *Police Offences Act* 1890, it is essential to show that the area of operations was in some special and peculiar way or in some degree under the control and ordering of the defendant as a proprietor or of someone who managed it for him or assisted him in his business, and that that area was used by the defendant as principal or as assistant for the purpose of unlawful gaming being carried on by persons resorting thereto. A defendant charged under sec. 62 of the *Police Offences Act* 1890 assisted in conducting the business of unlawful gaming on an excavated portion of the land of a public park to which the public generally had resort; neither the defendant nor those associated with him in such business claimed or had any right to prevent any of the public from going on any portion of such land, nor did they attempt to exercise any dominion or control over it, nor did they use any specialized part of such portion of land as their particular stand or place of conducting the said business. *Held*, that the defendant was not guilty of an offence within sec. 62 of the Act. *Prior* v. *Sherwood*, 3 C.L.R., 1054, and *Powell* v. *The Kempton Park Racecourse Co. Ltd.*, (1899) A.C., 143, as to "user." followed. *McCann* v. *Morgan*, (1912) V.L.R., 303; 34 A.L.T., 43; 18 A.L.R., 334. *Madden, C.J.*

Lotteries Gaming and Betting Act 1906 (No. 2055), secs. 5 (2), 10, 15, 17—Place used as a common gaming house, meaning of— User of place in such a way that it is by Statute deemed and taken to be a common gaming house—Whether limited in sec. 17 to user as a betting house.]—The phrase "used as a common gaming house" in sec. 17 of the *Lotteries Gaming and Betting Act* 1906 means "used as a common gaming house within the meaning of that expression in this Act" or "used in the way in which a house that by reason of such user is deemed to be a common gaming house is used." That phrase is not confined to the cases mentioned in sec. 15. *Macmanamny* v. *King*, (1907)

V.L.R., 535; 28 A.L.T., 250; 13 A.L.R., 258. F.C., *a'Beckett, Hood* and *Cussen, JJ.*

(c) Printing or Publishing Advertisements, Notices, &c.

Lotteries Gaming and Betting Act 1906 (No. 2055), sec. 22—Information as to the betting on intended horse race—Publication in newspaper—Betting odds offered in betting market.]—The defendant was the registered printer of a newspaper in which it was stated that there was a betting market on two intended horse races, that in that market the layers of odds were offering certain prices, and that those prices were at the time of publication the current prices. *Held*, that information was given by the newspaper as to the "betting" on intended horse races, and that the defendant was, accordingly, rightly convicted of an offence under sec. 22 of the *Lotteries Gaming and Betting Act* 1906. *O'Donnell* v. *Smart*, (1907) V.L.R., 439; 28 A.L.T., 245; 13 A.L.R., 255. *Cussen, J.* (1907).

Lotteries Gaming and Betting Act 1906 (No. 2055), sec. 22—" Information or advice " as to the betting on intended horse race, meaning of.]—The "information or advice" referred to in sec. 22 of the *Lotteries Gaming and Betting Act* 1906 is not confined to information or advice given by someone in the position of a turf commission agent or tipster, and such as would be given for reward and would be directly intended to induce the public or some member of the public to enter into betting transactions. But, *quaere*, whether it must not be of such a nature that it might possibly induce some person to bet. *O'Donnell* v. *Smart*, (1907) V.L.R., 439; 28 A.L.T., 245; 13 A.L.R., 255. *Cussen, J.* (1907).

Lotteries Gaming and Betting Act 1906 (No. 2055), sec. 22—Information as to intended horse-race—" The betting," meaning of.]—The phrase " the betting " in sec. 22 does not refer only to the bets actually made. *O'Donnell* v. *Smart*, (1907) V.L.R., 439; 28 A.L.T., 245; 13 A.L..R, 255. *Cussen, J.* (1907).

Licensing Act 1906 (No. 2068), sec. 98—Licensed premises, posting information relating to betting upon—Past betting on past horse-race.]—The posting up on licensed premises of information relating to past betting on a past horse race is not of itself an offence within sec. 98 of the *Licensing Act* 1907. *Ryan* v. *Foran*, (1910) V.L.R., 422; 32 A.L.T., 66; 16 A.L.R., 459. *Hood, J.*

(d) *Lotteries.*

Lottery, law relating to—4 Geo. IV. c. 60, sec. 41—Penalty for sale of ticket—Exception where lottery authorised by Act of Parliament—Lottery got up in Tasmania—Lottery authorised by Act of Parliament of Tasmania—Sale of ticket in Victoria.]—A lottery carried on in Tasmania is in Victoria a lottery within the meaning of 4 Geo. IV., c. 60, and the sale in Victoria of a ticket in such lottery is contrary to such Act. The exception of the sale of tickets authorised by Act of Parliament in sec. 41 of such Act has no efficacy as an authorization of the sale in Victoria of tickets in a lottery legally carried on in Tasmania by virtue of Tasmanian legislation. Act of Parliament in such exception to sec. 41 means Act of the Imperial Parliament. *The Attorney-General* v. *Moses*, (1907) V.L.R., 130; 28 A.L.T., 125; 12 A.L.R., 606. F.C., *a'Beckett, A.-C.J., Hodges* and *Chomley, JJ.*

Lottery, law relating to—Imperial Statutes, whether impliedly repealed by Victorian legislation—6 Geo. II., c. 35; 4 Geo. IV., c. 60—Police Offences Act 1890 (No. 1126), sec. 37.]—There has been no implied repeal by Victorian legislation of the Statutes 6 Geo. II. c. 35, and 4 Geo. IV., c. 60. *The Attorney-General* v. *Moses*, (1907) V.L.R., 130; 28 A.L.T., 125; 12 A.L.R., 606. F.C., *a'Beckett, A.-C.J., Hodges* and *Chomley, JJ.*

6 Geo. II., c. 35—" Foreign " lottery, what is—Lottery got up in Tasmania.]—A lottery got up in Tasmania is not in Victoria a " foreign " lottery or a pretended " foreign " lottery within the meaning of the Act, 6 Geo. II., c. 35. *The Attorney-General* v. *Moses*, (1907) V.L.R., 130; 28 A.L.T., 125; 12 A.L.R., 606. F.C., *a'Beckett, A.-C.J., Hodges* and *Chomley, JJ.*

Lottery, law relating to—Foreign lottery—Imperial Statutes, whether in force in Victoria—6 Geo. II., c. 35; 4 Geo. IV., c. 60; 9 Geo. IV., c. 83, sec. 24.]—The Statutes 6 Geo. II., c. 35 and 4 Geo. IV., c. 60, are, by virtue of 9 Geo. IV., c. 83, in force in Victoria for the purposes of an action for the recovery of the penalties thereunder in the name of the Attorney-General. *The Attorney-General* v. *Moses*, (1907) V.L.R., 130; 28 A.L.T., 125; 12 A.L.R., 606. F.C., *a'Beckett, A.-C.J., Hodges* and *Chomley, JJ.*

II.—DECLARATION THAT HOUSE IS A COMMON GAMING HOUSE.

Lotteries Gaming and Betting Act 1906 (No. 2055), sec. 38 (1), (2)—Declaration that premises are a common gaming house—Whether " may " means " shall "—Discretion of Court.]—The Court has a discretion whether it will make a declaration under sec. 38 (1) of the *Lotteries Gaming and Betting Act* 1906. *In re The Lotteries Gaming and Betting Act* 1906; *Ex parte Gleeson*, (1907) V.L.R., 368; 28 A.L.T., 228; 13 A.L.R., 146. *Cussen, J.*

Lotteries Gaming and Betting Act 1906 (No. 2055), sec. 38—Application for declaration that premises are a common gaming house—Owner or occupier whether entitled to be heard.]—Upon an application under sec. 38 of the *Lotteries Gaming and Betting Act* 1906 for a declaration that certain premises are a common gaming house the owner or occupier is entitled to be heard in opposition. *In re Lotteries Gaming and Betting Act* 1906; *In re Shanghai Club*; *In re Ah Pow*; *Ex parte Gleeson*, (1907) V.L.R., 463; 29 A.L.T., 31; 13 A.L.R., 360. F.C., *a'Beckett, Hood* and *Cussen, JJ.*

Lotteries Gaming and Betting Act 1906 (No. 2055), sec. 38 (1), (2)—Application for declaration that premises are common gaming house—Who may be heard—Owner or occupier.]—On the hearing of an application for a declaration under sec. 38 (1) of the *Lotteries Gaming and Betting Act* 1906 the owner or occupier of the premises in respect of which the declaration is sought (or one of them) is entitled to be heard and to bring before the

20

Court anything which would influence the Court in exercising its discretion. *In re Lotteries Gaming and Betting Act* 1906; *Ex parte Gleeson*, (1907) V.L.R., 368; 28 A.L.T., 228; 13 A.L.R., 146. *Cussen, J.*

Lotteries Gaming and Betting Act 1906 (No. 2055), sec. 38—Application for declaration that premises are a common gaming house—Affidavit of police officer showing reasonable grounds for suspecting—Suspicion, whether in mind of police officer or Court—Prima facie case, how established—Prima facie case, how answered.]—In an application under sec. 38 of the *Lotteries Gaming and Betting Act* 1906 for a declaration that certain premises are a common gaming house, the suspicion, for which reasonable grounds must be shown by the affidavit of an officer of police, is a suspicion in the mind of that officer. A *prima facie* case for the exercise of the Court's jurisdiction is established if the affidavit of such an officer alleges, that he suspects the premises are being used as a common gaming house, and shows reasonable grounds for his suspicions. The owner or occupier may answer such a *prima facie* case by showing that the suspicion is unfounded altogether, and by showing that the premises have not at all material times been used as a gaming house. *In re Lotteries Gaming and Betting Act* 1906; *In re Shanghai Club*; *In re Ah Pow*; *Ex parte Gleeson*, (1907) V.L.R., 463; 29 A.L.T., 31; 13 A.L.R., 360. F.C., *a' Beckett, Hood* and *Cussen, JJ.*

Lotteries Gaming and Betting Act 1906 (No. 2055), sec. 38—Application for declaration that premises are a common gaming house—Affidavit of police officer showing reasonable grounds for suspecting—Whether police officer may be cross-examined thereon.]—In proceedings under sec. 38 of the *Lotteries Gaming and Betting Act* 1906, the officer of police, who makes the affidavit showing reasonable grounds for suspecting that the premises in question are used as a common gaming house, cannot be cross-examined on such affidavit. *In re Lotteries Gaming and Betting Act* 1906; *In re Shanghai Club*; *In re Ah Pow*; *Ex parte Gleeson*, (1907)

V.L.R., 463; 29 A.L.T., 31; 13 A.L.R., 360. F.C., *a' Beckett, Hood* and *Cussen, JJ.*

Lotteries Gaming and Betting Act 1906 (No. 2055), sec. 38—Application for declaration that premises are a common gaming house—Affidavits in reply to affidavits of party opposing, admissibility of — Cross-examination of deponents.]—In an application under sec. 38 of the *Lotteries Gaming and Betting Act* 1906 for a declaration that certain premises are a common gaming house, the applicant may file affidavits in reply to those of the party opposing, and both classes of deponents are subject to cross-examination. *In re Lotteries Gaming and Betting Act* 1906; *In re Shanghai Club*; *In re Ah Pow*; *Ex parte Gleeson*, (1907) V.L.R., 463; 29 A.L.T., 31; 13 A.L.R., 360. F.C., *a' Beckett, Hood* and *Cussen, JJ.*

III.—PROCEDURE.

(a) Information; Complaint; Warrant.

Police Offences Act 1890 (No. 1126), secs. 49, 51—Gaming—Information under two sections.]—The defendants were charged with assisting in conducting the business of a room used for the purpose of moneys being received by persons conducting the business thereof as the consideration for an assurance to pay moneys on contingencies relating to horse-races. *Held*, that secs. 49 and 51 of the *Police Offences Act* are to be read together and that the information disclosed an offence. *Rogerson* v. *Phillips and O'Hagan*, (1906) V.L.R., 272; 27 A.L.T., 166; 12 A.L.R., 147. *a' Beckett, J.*

Police Offences Act 1890 (No. 1126), sec. 51—Occupier of house permitting same to be used for betting—No allegation in information of person by whom house was used.]—An information charging that the defendant " being the occupier of a certain shop at D. did unlawfully, knowingly and wilfully permit the same to be used for the purpose of betting with persons resorting thereto " discloses no offence under sec. 51 of the *Police Offences Act* 1890. It would disclose an offence if after the words " for the purpose of " followed the words " one T. B. a person using the same." *Knox* v. *Thomas Bible* ; *Knox* v. *J. L. Bible*, (1907) V.L.R., 485 ; 29 A.L.T., 23 ; 13 A.L.R., 352. *Cussen, J.* [Special leave to appeal refused, (1907) 4 C.L.R., 1462].

Gaming—Search warrant—On what materials issued—" Complaint on oath," meaning of—Oral evidence to supplement written information, admissibility of—Police Offences Act (No. 1126), sec. 57, Second Schedule—Lotteries Gaming and Betting Act (No. 2055), sec. 50 — Justices Act 1890 (No. 1105), secs. 4, 18, 19 (2) — Licensing Act 1906 (No. 2068), sec. 23.]— The complaint on oath required by sec. 57 of the *Police Offences Act* 1890 must be in writing. *Semble.*—Where the information on which a warrant is issued does not set out all the matters specified in the section, oral evidence sufficiently specifying those matters is inadmissible. *Montague* v. *Ah Shen*, (1907) V.L.R., 458 ; 28 A.L.T., 248 ; 13 A.L.R., 261. F.C., *Madden, C.J., a' Beckett* and *Hood, JJ.*

Police Offences Act 1890 (No. 1126), sec. 57—Gaming—Search warrant issued on insufficient materials, validity of.]—A warrant issued under sec. 57 of the *Police Offences Act* 1890 upon an information which does not comply with the requirements of the section by setting out the various matters therein specified is bad. *Montague* v. *Ah Shen*, (1907) V.L.R., 458 ; 28 A.L.T., 248 ; 13 A.L.R., 261. F.C., *Madden, C.J., a' Beckett* and *Hood, JJ.*

(b) Evidence.

See also, *ante*, II. DECLARATION THAT HOUSE IS A COMMON GAMING HOUSE.

Lotteries Gaming and Betting Act 1906 (No. 2055), secs. 10, 17—Evidence—Use as a common gaming house—Acts of persons other than defendant—Acts prior to the date of the alleged offence.]—To establish the fact that on the date named in the information, a house was used as a common gaming house, the informant may give evidence of the acts showing such user of persons other than the defendant, and of acts showing such user previous to the date so named, and also of

facts from which a continuance of that user might fairly be inferred. *Macmanamny* v. *King*, (1907) V.L.R., 535 ; 28 A.L.T., 250. 13 A.L.R., 258. F.C. *a' Beckett, Hood* and *Cussen, JJ.*

Police Offences Act 1890 (No. 1126), secs 49, 51—Use of room for purpose of betting—User, sufficiency of evidence to prove—Repeated acts, whether necessary to show—Character of use, proof of by admission, express or implied.]—In order to prove an offence under secs. 49 and 51 of the *Police Offences Act* 1890 (which relate to the use of premises for betting) it is not absolutely necessary to show a user extending over more than one day, or to show that the acts were many times repeated. If there is nothing else, there cannot be user without repeated acts ; but a defendant may either by express or implied admission show the character of his use of the place in connection with a single act or with a few acts. Accordingly where but few bets were shown to have been made, but a systematic course of conduct was proved, the evidence was held to be sufficient. *Knox* v. *Thomas Bible* ; *Knox* v. *J. L. Bible*, (1907) V.L.R., 485 ; 29 A.L.T., 23 ; 13 A.L.R., 352. *Cussen, J.* [Special leave to appeal refused, (1907) 4 C.L.R., 1462].

Police Offences Act 1890 (No. 1126), sec. 51—Assisting in conducting gaming house—Relationship with person assisted and character in which assistance given—How far necessary to prove.]—Upon an information for assisting in conducting the business of a house, &c., in contravention of sec. 51 of the *Police Offences Act* 1890, it is not necessary to show the precise relationship between the defendant and the person whom he assisted, or the precise character in which the defendant gave the assistance. *Knox* v. *Thomas Bible* ; *Knox* v. *J. L. Bible*, (1907) V.L.R., 485 ; 29 A.L.T., 23 ; 13 A.L.R., 352. *Cussen, J.* (1907). [Special leave to appeal refused, (1907) 4 C.L.R., 1462].

Lotteries Gaming and Betting Act 1906 (No. 2055), secs. 10, 17—House opened kept or used for purpose of illegal lottery—Method

of drawing of lottery, whether necessary to prove.]—In order to show that a house is kept or used for the purpose of an illegal or proposed illegal lottery, it is not necessary to show the precise method of the drawing of the lottery. *Macmanamny* v. *King*, (1907) V.L.R., 535; 28 A.L.T., 250; 13 A.L.R., 258. F.C., *a'Beckett, Hood* and *Cussen, JJ.*

Lotteries Gaming and Betting Act 1906 (No. 2055), sec. 61—Evidence of certain fact made prima facie evidence of commission of offence—Procedural provision—Whether applicable to offences committed before passing of Act.]—*Quaere*, whether sec. 61 of the *Lotteries Gaming and Betting Act* 1906 being procedural would not apply to offences committed before that Act. *Knox* v. *Thomas Bible*; *Knox* v. *J. L. Bible*, (1907) V.L.R., 485; 29 A.L.T., 23; 13 A.L.R., 352. *Cussen, J.* [Special leave to appeal refused, (1907) 4 C.L.R., 1462].

Police Offences Act 1890 (No. 1126), sec. 64—Scope of section—Prima facie evidence that place is a common gaming house.]—Sec. 64 applies only where the charge is one of keeping a common gaming house. *O'Donnell* v. *Dodd*, (1910) V.L.R., 482; 32 A.L.T., 87; 16 A.L.R., 539. *Madden, C.J., Hodges* and *Hood, JJ.*

(c) *Conviction; Punishment.*

Police Offences Act 1890 (No. 1126), sec. 51—Street Betting Suppression Act 1896 (No. 1436), sec. 7—Using house for betting purposes—" First offence," " second offence," meaning of.]—*Semble.*—The words " first offence " in sec. 7 of the *Street Betting Suppression Act* 1896 include all offences up to the time of the first conviction, and probably all offences where it is not proved that there has been a prior conviction. *Semble.*—" A second offence " means any offence where it is proved that the act was done after a prior conviction. *Knox* v. *Thomas Bible*; *Knox* v. *J. L. Bible*, (1907) V.L.R., 485; 29 A.L.T., 23; 13 A.L.R., 352. *Cussen, J.* [Special leave to appeal refused, (1907) 4 C.L.R , 1462].

Police Offences Act 1890 (No. 1126), sec. 51—Assisting in conducting business of house used for betting—Two charges of assisting during consecutive periods—Continuous offence—Whether one offence or two.]—Where a defendant was convicted and fined for an offence under sec. 51 of the *Police Offences Act* 1890 of assisting between the 26th October and the 2nd November 1906 in conducting the business of a certain house, &c., and was on the same day charged before the same Court with having committed the same offence between the 3rd and 6th November 1906, *Held*, that the Justices were not bound to assume that the two offences were one continuous offence, and in the absence of evidence to that effect, might rightly convict of the second offence. *Crepps* v. *Durden*, 1 S.L.C. (9th ed.), p. 692, distinguished. *Knox* v. *Thomas Bible*; *Knox* v. *J. L. Bible*, (1907) V.L.R., 485; 29 A.L.T., 23; 13 A.L.R., 352. *Cussen, J.* [Special leave to appeal refused, (1907) 4 C.L.R., 1462].

Police Offences Act 1890 (No. 1126), secs. 49, 51, 89—Street Betting Suppression Act 1896 (No. 1436), sec. 7—Assisting in conducting a common gaming house—First offence, punishment for—Imprisonment in default of payment of fine—Term of imprisonment in default greater than maximum term provided for offence—Jurisdiction.]—Although sec. 51 of the *Police Offences Act* 1890 as amended by the *Street Betting Suppression Act* 1896 provides that for a first offence the punishment shall be either a fine or imprisonment for a term not exceeding three months, the justices, in imposing a fine, have jurisdiction under sec. 89 of the *Police Offences Act* 1890 to impose a period of six months imprisonment in default of payment of the fine. *Macmanamny* v. *McCulloch* (or *McMahon*), 18 A.L.T., 164; 3 A.L.R., 14, approved. *Rogerson* v. *Phillips and O'Hagan* (1906) V.L.R., 272; 27 A.L.T., 166; 12 A.L.R., 147. *a'Beckett, J.*

Police Offences Act 1890 (No. 1126), secs. 49, 51, 89—Fine in default imprisonment—No time fixed for payment of fine.]—Where Justices do not in their order name a time for payment of a fine, the fine is to be treated as having been ordered to be paid immediately. *Rogerson* v. *Phillips and O'Hagan*, (1906) V.L.R., 272; 27 A.L.T., 166; 12 A.L.R., 147. *a'Beckett, J.*

GAOL.

Leave to appeal to High Court—Applicant in prison—Appearance in person—Whether High Court has jurisdiction to order that it be allowed.]—*See* CRIMINAL LAW, col. 365. *Horwitz* v. *Connor*, (1908) 6 C.L.R., 38; 14 A.L.R., 342.

Crimes Act 1890 (No. 1079), sec. 540—Regulations providing for mitigation of sentence as incentive to good conduct—Habeas corpus by prisoner alleging entitled to liberty under regulations.]—*See* CRIMINAL LAW, col. 368. *Horwitz* v. *Connor*, (1908) 6 C.L.R., 38; 14 A.L.R., 342.

GARNISHEE.

See also, ATTACHMENT.

Attachment of debts—Garnishee order—Judgment debtor—Trustee of moneys attached—Appearance of judgment debtor before Justices to protect fund—Justices Act 1890 (No. 1105), sec. 117.]—A judgment debtor who is a trustee of moneys sought to be attached by a garnishee order *nisi* for payment of a judgment debt due by him personally has a right, and is under a duty, to appear on the garnishee proceedings to show that the moneys and ought not therefore be attached. *Roberts* v. *Death*, 8 Q.B.D., 319, followed. *R.* v. *Justices of Heywood*, 21 V.L.R., 654; 17 A.L.T., 238, distinguished. *Richards* v. *Jager*, (1909) V.L.R., 140; 30 A.L.T., 163; 15 A.L.R., 119. *Madden, C.J.*

Action for unlawfully attaching trust funds—Dismissal as frivolous and vexatious—Rules of the Supreme Court 1906, Order XIVa.]—No action will lie for unlawfully causing moneys standing to the credit of a trust account in the name of the plaintiff

to be attached for his personal debt. *Jager* v. *Richards*, (1909) V.L.R., 181; 30 A.L.T., 199; 15 A.L.R., 123. *Cussen, J.*

GAZETTE.

See EVIDENCE.

GENERAL SESSIONS.

I.—APPEAL.

(a) *Jurisdiction.*

Marriage Act 1890 (No. 1166), secs. 51, 52—Maintenance order—Disobedience by husband—Proceedings to enforce—Dismissal by Justices—Appeal to general Sessions.]—No appeal or application under sec. 52 of the *Justices Act* 1890 lies in respect of an order of Justices dismissing proceedings by a wife against her husband under sec. 51 for disobedience of a maintenance order. *Bloxham* v. *Bloxham*, 33 A.L.T. (Supplement), 11; 18 A.L.R. (C.N.), 1. *Judge Wasley* (1912).

Appeal to General Sessions—Increase of fine to facilitate, propriety of—Justices Act 1890 (No. 1105), secs. 59 (1), 127.]—*See* JUSTICES OF THE PEACE. *Kane* v. *Dureau*, (1911) V.L.R., 293; 33 A.L.T., 15; 17 A.L.R., 277.

(b) *Practice.*

(1) Notice of Appeal, Form and Service of.

Marriage Act 1890 (No. 1166), sec. 52—Justices Act 1890 (No. 1105), sec. 131—Main-

tenance appeals—Notice of intention to appeal
—Statement of grounds of appeal—Filing
notices.]—A notice of intention to appeal
against an order for maintenance made by
Justices under Part IV. of the *Marriage Act*
1890 is invalid, unless it states the grounds of
appeal. The appellant should file a copy
of his notice of intention to appeal before or at
the time that he applies to have the appeal
set down for trial. *Gavey* v. *Gavey*, 31
A.L.T. (Supplement), 6 ; 15 A.L.R. (C.N.),
17. *Judge Eagleson* (1909).

**Marriage Act 1890 (No. 1166), sec. 52—
Marriage Act 1900 (No. 1684), sec. 7—Practice
—Applications to quash, etc.—Orders under
the Marriage Acts—Service of notices.]**—The
Chairmen of the Courts of General Sessions
have, by order dated the 8th November,
1909, directed that notices of all applications
to quash, alter or vary orders under the
Marriage Act 1890, sec. 52, and the *Marriage
Act* 1900 must be served personally. *In re
Applications to quash, &c.*, 31 A.L.T.,
(Supplement), 10 ; 15 A.L.R. (C.N.), 25.
(1909).

(2) Recognizances.

**Justices Act 1890 (No. 1105), secs. 128,
132—Notice of appeal—Security for appearance of appellant—Recognizance entered into
before notice of appeal given—Invalidity of
recognizance—Refusal to hear appeal.]**—
Where the recognizance required of an
appellant by sec. 128 (5) of the *Justices Act*
1890 has been entered into before notice of
appeal has been given by him in accordance
with sec. 128 (2), the recognizance is invalid
and the Court of General Sessions should
strike out the appeal. *Dungey* v. *Dunlevie*,
31 A.L.T. (Supplement), 3 ; 15 A.L.R.
(C.N.), 13. *Judge Chomley* (1909).

**General Sessions—Notice of appeal—Recog-
nisances, when it must be entered into—
Recognisance entered into after service of
notice on Clerk of Petty Sessions but before
service on respondent—Justices Act 1890 (No.
1105), sec. 128.]**—In appeals from Petty
Sessions to General Sessions, the recognisance,
required to be entered into under sec. 128
of the *Justices Act* 1890 must be entered

into " after " service of the requisite notices
of appeal provided by that section. Accordingly, where a notice of appeal under that
section had been given to a Clerk of Petty
Sessions and a recognisance then entered
into, and subsequently a similar notice had
been served on the respondent. *Held*, that
as section 128 had not been complied with,
the Court could not hear the appeal. *Dungey* v. *Dunlevie*, 31 A.L.T. (Supplement), 3 ;
15 A.L.R. (C.N.), 13, followed. *Ormond* v.
Joske, 16 A.L.R. (C.N.), 1. *Judge Chomley*
(1910).

**Justices Act 1890 (No. 1105), sec. 128 (5)—
Appeal—Recognisance—Notice of appeal—
Time for entering into recognisance.]**—The
recognisance required to be entered into by
an appellant under sec. 128 (5) of the
Justices Act 1890 may be entered into on the
day on which the notice of appeal is given.
Martin v. *Rowden*, 32 A.L.T. (Supplement), 8 ;
16 A.L.R. (C.N.), 10. *Judge Box* (1910).

(3) Amendment.

**Appeal from Court of Petty Sessions—
Conviction—Amendment, powers of—Justices Act 1890 (No. 1105), secs. 133, 185.]**—
On an appeal to a Court of General Sessions
from a conviction by a Court of Petty Sessions
the former Court has, under the *Justices Act*
1890, power to make all proper amendments
although the written information is defective.
Lin Wan Quai v. *Christie*, (1906) 3 C.L.R.,
1125 ; 12 A.L.R., 429. H.C. *Griffith, C.J.,
Barton* and *O'Connor, JJ.*

**General Sessions—Appeal against conviction
—Information—Whether Court may amend—
Justices Act 1890 (No. 1105), secs. 73 (4),
128 (7), 133.]**—At the hearing of an appeal
against a conviction the Court of General
Sessions has power to amend the information
upon which the appellant was convicted.
Delaney v. *Napthine*, 32 A.L.T. (Supplement),
10 ; 16 A.L.R. (C.N.), 19. *Judge Moule*
(1910).

(4) Enforcement of Orders.

**Attachment of debts—Money ordered to be
paid by Court of General Sessions—Attachment
by Court of Petty Sessions—Jurisdiction.]**—

See JUSTICES OF THE PEACE. *Brown* v. *Gunn*; *McKay, Garnishee*, 34 A.L.T., 115; 18 A.L.R. (C.N.), 21.

Justices Act 1890 (No. 1105), secs. 117, 119, 124 (12), 141—Attachment of debt—Judgment debt—Order of General Sessions—Garnishee order—Petty Sessions—Effect of—Jurisdiction —Order to review—" Person aggreived."]— *See* JUSTICES OF THE PEACE. *Brown* v. *Gunn*; *McKay Garnishee*, (1912) V.L.R., 463; 34 A.L.T., 113; 18 A.L.R., 463.

II.—CONTEMPT OF COURT.

Court of General Sessions—Contempt of Court—Extent of powers of Court of General Sessions—Justices Act 1890 (No. 1105), sec. 184.]—The Court of General Sessions has no power to punish for contempt of Court except in the cases specified and to the extent limited in the *Justices Act* 1890. *Ex parte Dunn*; *Ex parte Aspinall*, (1906) V.L.R., 493 28 A.L.T., 3; 12 A.L.R., 358. *Cussen, J.* (1906).

General Sessions—Attempt to influence a juryman—Contempt of Court—Power of Supreme Court to punish.]—*Semble*, An attempt to influence a juror in the Court of General Sessions is a contempt punishable by the Supreme Court *brevi manu*. *Ex parte Dunn*; *Ex parte Aspinall*, (1906) V.L.R., 493; 28 A.L.T., 3; 12 A.L.R., 358. *Cussen, J.*

III.—CASE STATED.

Justices Act 1890 (No. 1105), sec. 139 — General Sessions—Special case, contents of— What should be stated.]—In stating a case for the determination of the Supreme Court under section 139 of the *Justices Act* 1890, the Court of General Sessions must set out all the facts. *Russell* v. *Sheehan*, (1911) V.L.R., 81; 32 A.L.T., 181; 17 A.L.R., 83. *Hood, J.*

Justices Act 1890 (No. 1105), sec. 139— General Sessions—Invalidity of recognisance —Refusal to hear an appeal—Power to state a case.]—Where an appeal has been struck out on the ground that the recognizance is invalid, the Court of General Sessions, not having " heard and determined " the appeal, has no power to state a case with regard thereto under section 139 of the *Justices Act* 1890. *Dungey* v. *Dunlevie*, 31 A.L.T. (Supplement), 3; 15 A.L.R. (C.N.), 13. *Judge Chomley* (1909).

IV.—CERTIORARI.

Certiorari—Court of General Sessions— Person committed for contempt by warrant of Chairman—No jurisdiction—Whether act judicial or administrative—Party aggrieved— Whether entitled ex debito justitiæ.]—The Chairman of General Sessions by warrant under his hand committed a woman for a contempt, and on the return of a writ of *habeas corpus* the woman was discharged on the ground that there was no jurisdiction to commit her. In proceedings for a writ of *certiorari, Held,* that, the Court of General Sessions having assumed to exercise jurisdiction over a person thought to be subject thereto, there was a judicial act controllable by *certiorari,* and that the woman was a party aggrieved and would on proper materials be entitled to the issue of the writ *ex debito justitiæ*. *Ex parte Dunn*; *Ex parte Aspinall*, (1906) V.L.R., 584; 28 A.L.T., 72; 12 A.L.R., 418. *Cussen, J.*

Certiorari—Court of General Sessions— Notice of proceedings to Chairman and Justices, necessity for—13 Geo. II., c. 18, sec. 5 —9 Geo. IV., c. 83—Supreme Court Act 1890 (No. 1142), secs. 25, 31.]—Even assuming that section 5 of the Act 13 Geo. II., c. 18, is not in force with regard to Courts of General Sessions by virtue of 9 Geo. IV., c. 83, the same result as if it were in force is brought about by secs. 25 and 31 of the *Supreme Court Act* 1890 or one of them, and consequently in proceedings to remove any criminal matter from a Court of General Sessions by way of *certiorari* it is necessary to show that the notice required by sec. 5 has been duly given. The notice must be given before the application even though an order *nisi* only is granted in the first instance. *Ex parte Dunn*; *Ex parte Aspinall*, (1906) V.L.R., 584; 28 A.L.T., 72; 12 A.L.R., 418. *Cussen, J.*

Certiorari—13 Geo. II., c. 18— Whether
Act in force in Victoria as regards Justices
and Courts of General Sessions.]—So far as
relates to Justices, the Act 13 Geo. II., c. 18,
is in force in Victoria. *Quaere*, whether the
Act is not also in force in regard to Courts
of General Sessions, notwithstanding the fact
that when 9 Geo. IV., c. 83 was passed there
were no Courts of Quarter or General Sessions in New South Wales. *Quan Yick* v.
Hinds, (1905) 2 C.L.R., 345 ; 11 A.L.R., 223,
considered. *Ex parte Dunn* ; *Ex parte
Aspinall*, (1906) V.L.R., 584 ; 28 A.L.T., 72 ;
12 A.L.R., 418. *Cussen, J.*

GIFT.

See also WILL.

Transfer of Land Act 1890 (No. 1149), Part
IV.—Gift to person standing in fiduciary
relation to donor—Transfer by administrator as such to himself in his own right—Assignment by next-of-kin of their interests to
administrator—Whether Commissioner entitled to call for proof that next-of-kin had
independent legal advice and understood
nature of transaction.]—*See* TRANSFER OF
LAND ACT. *In re Transfer of Land Act* ;
Ex parte Danaher, (1911) V.L.R., 214 ;
32 A.L.T., 190 ; 17 A.L.R., 160.

GOODS BARGAINED AND SOLD ;
GOODS SOLD AND DELIVERED.

See CONTRACT OR AGREEMENT ;
MEDICAL MAN.

GROCER.

See also, FACTORIES AND SHOPS ACT.

Grocer's licence—Grant of new licence—
Local option poll, whether necessary—Licensing Act 1890 (No. 1111), sec. 38—Licensing
Act 1906 (No. 2068), sec. 51.]—*See* LICENSING.
Anderson v. *Mooney*, (1907) V.L.R., 623 ;
29 A.L.T., 42 ; 13 A.L.R., 471.

GUARANTEE OR INDEMNITY.

Insolvency Act 1890 (No. 1102), sec. 37—
" Secured debt," what is—Business of testator carried on by executors under provisions
of will—Debt properly incurred—Right of
executors to indemnity out of assets of estate—
—Petitioning creditor having security over
property used in business—Whether such
security must be given up or valued.]—*See*
EXECUTORS AND ADMINISTRATORS. *In re
Whitelaw* ; *Savage* v. *The Union Bank of
Australia Ltd* ; *Whitelaw* v. *The Same*, 3
C.L.R., 1170 ; 12 A.L.R., 285.

Undue influence—Parent and child—Trustee and cestui trust—Whether transaction may
be set aside against third party—Ordinary business transaction—Beneficiary surety for trustees—Independent advice.]—*See* FRAUD AND
MISREPRESENTATION. *Union Bank of Australia Ltd.* v. *Whitelaw*, (1906) V.L.R., 711 ;
28 A.L.T., 17 ; 12 A.L.R., 393.

" Undue concealment "—Business carried
on by trustees in breach of trust—Moneys
advanced to trustees upon guarantee of beneficiaries—Ordinary business transaction —
Whether creditor under duty to inform himself
and beneficiaries as to conduct of trustees.]—
See FRAUD AND MISREPRESENTATION. *Union
Bank of Australia Ltd.* v. *Whitelaw*, (1906)
V.L.R., 711 ; 28 A.L.T., 17 ; 12 A.L.R., 393.

Insolvency—Costs of examination summons
—Trustee indemnified against by creditor—
Whether trustee entitled to be paid by insolvent or out of estate—Insolvency Act 1897
(No. 1513), sec. 111.]—Although a trustee
holds an indemnity from a creditor against
the costs of an examination summons, he is
entitled (unless the Court otherwise order)
to have them paid by the insolvent or out of
the insolvent estate. *In re Ostberg*, 33
A.L.T. (Supplement), 10 ; 17 A.L.R. (C.N.),
28. *Judge Moule* (1911).

GUARDIAN AND WARD.

Custody of infant—Procedure — Habeas
corpus—Who may apply by—Application
to Court for appointment of guardian, where

necessary.]—*See* INFANT. *The King* v. *Waters,* (1912) V.L.R., 372 ; 34 A.L.T., 48 ; 18 A.L.R., 304.

HABEAS CORPUS.

See also, FUGITIVE OFFENDERS.

Custody of infant—Procedure—Habeas corpus—Who may apply by—Application to Court for appointment of guardian, when necessary.]—No-one can take out a writ of *habeas corpus* for the custody of an infant child except a person who has an absolute legal right to that custody. If the custody of an infant child is sought by a person who has only a discretionary right, so far as the Court is concerned, to the custody of the child, the proper course is for him to proceed in a Court of Equity to have himself appointed guardian. Where an infant child is detained by a person who is acting as its guardian in fact, and is as such maintaining the child, and it is suggested that this is a wrongful detention, the only persons who can take out a writ of *habeas corpus* for the recovery of the child are, where the child is a legitimate child, its father, and after his death the mother of the child or the testamentary guardian appointed by the father, and after the death of both parents, if no guardian has been appointed by the father, the testamentary guardian appointed by the mother ; and, where the child is an illegitimate child, its mother, and after her death the testamentary guardian appointed by her. Blood relationship to an infant child, except in the case of its father and mother, confers no right to the guardianship of such child ; but the Court, in looking at the child's own benefit and interests (by which it will be guided), will always have special regard to the blood relations. Any person may, at his or her own proper cost, come into a Court of Equity, and inform the Court that somebody acting *de facto* as guardian is detaining a child against its interests, and the Court will inquire into that matter, and direct what is for the benefit of the child. *The King* v. *Waters,* (1912) V.L.R., 372 ; 34 A.L.T., 48 ; 18 A.L.R., 304. *Madden, C.J.* (1912).

Supreme Court—Jurisdiction—Habeas corpus—Applicant held under restraint under authority of Commonwealth—Immigration Restriction Amendment Act 1905 (No. 17), sec. 14 (13b)—Judiciary Act 1903 (No. 6) Part VI.]—The Supreme Court has jurisdiction by way of *habeas corpus* to inquire into the validity of the restraint by the respondent of the applicant, although the respondent exercised such restraint under the authority or colour of authority, of the Commonwealth. *Ah Sheung* v. *Lindberg,* (1906) V.L.R., 323 ; 27 A.L.T., 189 ; *sub nom., Rex* v. *Ah Sheung,* 12 A.L.R., 190. *Cussen, J.* (1906).

Habeas corpus—Return to writ—No legal justification for restraint disclosed—Procedure.]—If the return to a writ of *habeas corpus* shows no legal justification for the restraint, there is no necessity for any evidence or any further proceeding by way of demurrer or otherwise, and, unless the return is amended, the Court is bound at once to make an order for discharge. *Ah Sheung* v. *Lindberg,* (1906) V.L.R., 323 ; 27 A.L.T., 189 ; *sub nom., Rex* v. *Ah Sheung,* 12 A.L.R., 190. *Cussen, J.* (1906).

Return of writ of habeas corpus—Whether Court bound by recitals in warrant—Evidence to show want of jurisdiction.]—*Semble.*—On the return of a writ of *habeas corpus,* the Court is not bound by the recitals in the warrant of commitment, but may receive affidavits for the purpose of seeing whether jurisdiction ever attached. *Ex parte Dunn ; Ex parte Aspinall,* (1906) V.L.R., 493 ; 28 A.L.T., 3 ; 12 A.L.R., 358. *Cussen, J.*

Habeas corpus—Evidence—Proof by affidavit—Oral evidence.]—So far as evidence is admissible in *habeas corpus* proceedings, it may, at the discretion of the Court, be received by way of affidavit, or an issue may be directed before a jury when oral evidence might be given. *Ah Sheung* v. *Lindberg,* (1906) V.L.R., 323 ; 27 A.L.T., 189 ; *sub nom., Rex* v. *Ah Sheung,* 12 A.L.R., 190. *Cussen, J.* (1906).

Habeas corpus—Return to writ—Legal justification for restraint disclosed—Evidence, admissibility of—Conviction or warrant of

superior Court—Conviction or warrant of inferior Court—No judgment of Court—Procedure.]—If the return to a writ of *habeas corpus* shows on the face of it a legal justification for the restraint, the question whether evidence will be permitted to any, and what extent, depends upon the circumstances under which the restraint is imposed. (*a*) It is not permissible on *habeas corpus* proceedings to controvert a record or to attack a conviction of a superior Court on which a warrant is based. Such record or conviction must be got rid of, if possible, by proceedings by way of appeal or error; (*b*) It is not permissible to contradict the truth of recitals and statements in warrants, convictions or orders of inferior Courts or tribunals, if the matters therein stated are amongst those which the Court or tribunal could properly have decided; (*c*) But it is permissible to show that there was no such warrant or order of, or a total absence of jurisdiction in, the inferior Courts, and this may be shown by proof that the defendant is, by reason of his status or of some special privilege, not subject to their jurisdiction; (*d*) Where there is not a judgment of any Court, or an order made under the provisions of any Statute, the truth of the return can be generally challenged or additional matter brought forward. *Ah Sheung* v. *Lindberg*, (1906) V.L.R., 323; 27 A.L.T., 189; *sub nom.*, *Rex* v. *Ah Sheung*, 12 A.L.R., 190. *Cussen, J.* (1906).

Habeas corpus—Truth of return, whether it must be verified.]—The truth of the return to a writ of *habeas corpus* need not be verified by affidavit. *Ah Sheung* v. *Lindberg*, (1906) V.L.R., 323; 27 A.L.T., 189; *sub nom.*, *Rex* v. *Ah Sheung*, 12 A.L.R., 190. *Cussen, J.* (1906).

Appeal—Order on habeas corpus—Jurisdiction of High Court.]—The High Court has jurisdiction to entertain an appeal from an order of a Judge of the Supreme Court directing the discharge of a person from custody on *habeas corpus*. *Attorney-General for the Commonwealth* v. *Ah Sheung*, (1907) 4 C.L.R., 949; 12 A.L.R., 432. H.C., *Griffith, C.J., Barton* and *O'Connor, JJ.*

Leave to appeal to High Court—Applicant in prison—Appearance in person—Whether High Court has jurisdiction to order that it be allowed.] — *See* CRIMINAL LAW, col. 26. *Horwitz* v. *Connor*, (1908) 6 C.L.R., 38; 14 A.L.R., 342.

Immigration Restriction Acts 1901-1905—Habeas corpus—Return, sufficiency of—Allegations of law—Allegation of fact of failure to pass the dictation test—No facts alleged to show that person detained was subject to the Acts.]—*See* IMMIGRATION RESTRICTION ACTS. *Ah Sheung* v. *Lindberg*, (1906) V.L.R., 323; 27 A.L.T., 189; *sub nom.*, *Rex* v. *Ah Sheung*, 12 A.L.R., 190.

HARBOR TRUST.

See MELBOURNE HARBOR TRUST.

HEALTH (PUBLIC).

I.—PURE FOOD.

Pure Food Act 1905 (No. 2010), sec. 41 (2)—Cleanliness and freedom from contamination of articles of food—Regulation, validity of—Reasonableness—Certainty.]—Sec. 41 (2) of the *Pure Food Act* 1905 empowers the Board of Public Health to make regulations for carrying out the provisions of the Act and for securing the cleanliness, freedom from contamination and adulteration of any article of food. Purporting to act (*inter alia*) under this provision the Board made regulations "for securing the cleanliness and freedom from contamination of certain articles of food to wit . . . fruit and other articles of food to which flies are attracted and which are ordinarily consumed in the condition in which they are purchased." One of these regulations provided that "No person shall transport through the street for sale any of the abovenamed articles of food unless the same is, as far as practicable, protected from dust and flies." *Held,* that such regulation was not *ultra vires* the Board, that it was reasonable, was certain, and what was demanded by the circumstances. *Robertson* v. *Abadee*, (1907) V.L.R., 235; 28 A.L.T., 184; 13 A.L.R., 137. F.C., *Madden, C.J., Hood* and *Cussen, JJ.*

Public health—Pure Food Act 1905 (No. 2010), sec. 41 (2)—Regulations of 28th June, 1907—Transport of milk—Secure closing of milk-cans — Method of Closing — Departmental approval—Delivery by producer personally.]—A regulation provided that every person who consigns or sends milk in a wholesale quantity to a milk vendor for retail sale shall prior to despatch cause the cans or other receptacles by which it is conveyed, to be securely closed by means of a leaden seal or a lock or by other means unless such milk be delivered personally by the producer or owner thereof to the retail vendor. *Held,* that the method of securely closing referred to in the regulation should be a closing of a kind which would ensure the ascertainment of tampering, if any tampering occurred. The fact that the Department is satisfied with the method of closing adopted has nothing to do with the interpretation of the regulation. *Mitchell* v. *Crawshaw,* (1903) 1 K.B., 701. *O'Connor* v. *Anderson,* (1909) V.L.R., 1; 30 A.L.T., 145; 15 A.L.R., 22. *Madden, C.J.*

Pure Food Act 1905 (No. 2010), secs. 35, 36—Article of food—Keeping for sale an adulterated article of food—Several offences alleged on one day—Conviction for one offence.]—A person cannot, under sec. 35 of the *Pure Food Act* 1905, be convicted of more than one offence of keeping for sale adulterated milk on the same day on the same premises, although the milk is kept in different vessels and in different parts of the premises. *O'Connor* v. *Bini,* (1908) V.L.R., 567; 30 A.L.T., 74; 14 A.L.R., 537. *Hodges, J.*

"Second offence," what is—Pure Food Act 1905 (No. 2010), sec. 36.]—*See* CRIMINAL LAW, cols. 367, 368. *O'Connor* v. *Bini,* (1908) V.L.R., 567; 30 A.L.T., 74; 14 A.L.R., 537.

Pure Food Act 1905 (No. 2010), secs. 3, 35 —Sale for human consumption or use—Sale for analysis.]—*Quaere,* whether sec. 35 of the *Pure Food Act* 1905 refers to a sale for analysis. *Rider* v. *Dunn,* (1908) V.L.R., 377; 29 A.L.T., 279; 14 A.L.R., 245. *Cussen, J.*

Pure Food Act 1905 (No. 2010), sec. 23— Sale of adulterated article of food—Article taken for analysis—Justices requested at hearing to send part for analysis—No part in existence—Compliance with request, whether condition precedent to conviction.]—Where on the hearing of an information under the Health Acts the defendant requests that part of the article taken for analysis should be sent to the Board of Public Health under sec. 23 of the *Pure Food Act* 1905, the Justices must comply with the request before they can convict the defendant. If compliance with the request is impossible by reason of none of the parts of the article taken being in existence the defendant should be discharged. *Suckling* v. *Parker,* (1906) 1 K.B., 527, distinguished. *Gunner* v. *Payne,* (1908) V.L.R., 363; 29 A.L.T., 264; 14 A.L.R., 243. *Cussen, J.*

Pure food — Adulteration — Division of article taken into parts—Request to Justices to send part to Board—Request made after close of evidence—Whether too late—Pure Food Act 1905 (No. 2010), sec. 23.]—Upon the hearing of an information for selling adulterated food, the Justices are not bound under sec. 23 of the *Pure Food Act* 1905, to send to the Board a part of the article taken for anlaysis, unless the request that this shall be done is made before the close of the evidence. *Gunner* v. *Payne,* (1910) V.L.R., 45; 31 A.L.T., 138; 16 A.L.R., 29. *Madden, C.J.*

Pure Food Act 1890 (No. 2010), secs. 32, 33 and 35—Sale of article of food which is adulterated—Purchase with warranty—What amounts to—When a complete defence— Health Act 1890 (No. 1098), secs. 43, 47, 49, 71.]—Sec. 71 of the *Health Act* 1890 does not apply to a prosecution under sec. 35 of the *Pure Food Act* 1905. It applies only where the purchaser has demanded a commodity of a certain nature and quality, and an article of that nature, substance and quality has not been supplied to him. But in such a proceeding proof by the defendant that he complied with the requirements of sec. 71 of the *Health Act* 1890 by purchasing the article with a written warranty that the same was of the nature, substance and quality demanded by him, and having no reason to believe it to be otherwise, is evidence from which the Justices may find under sec. 32 of the *Pure Food Act* 1905 that the defendant has taken all reasonable precautions against committing an offence against the Health Acts. *O'Connor* v. *McKimmie*, (1909) V.L.R., 166; 30 A.L.T., 179; 15 A.L.R., 118. F.C., *Madden, C.J., Hodges* and *Hood, JJ.*

Health Act 1890 (No. 1098), sec. 71—Warranty that article same in nature, substance and quality as that demanded by prosecutor.]— A warranty sufficient to satisfy sec. 71 of the *Health Act* 1890 must be such as amounts to a contract binding both parties. *O'Connor* v. *McKimmie*, (1909) V.L.R., 166; 30 A.L.T., 179; 15 A.L.R., 118. F.C., *Madden, C.J., Hodges* and *Hood, JJ.*

Health Act 1890 (No. 1098), sec. 71—Warranty incomplete and indefinite.]—A producer gave to a retail vendor a document addressed to him and signed by the producer in the following form :—" A renewal guarantee re milk.—I do hereby guarantee to supply you with milk under the same conditions as the executrix and executors of the late A. were doing. And guarantee the milk to be pure and all that is required by the Pure Food and Health Acts.'' Afterwards the producer supplied milk to retail vendor. *Held*, that in the circumstances the document did not amount to a " written warranty " of the nature, substance, and quality of the milk demanded within the meaning of sec. 71 of the *Health Act* 1890. *O'Connor* v. *McKimmie*, (1909) V.L.R., 166; 30 A.L.T., 179; 15 A.L.R., 118. F.C., *Madden, C.J., Hodges* and *Hood, JJ.*

Pure Food Act 1905 (No. 2010), secs. 32, 35 and 36 — Adulterated article of food — Sale by servant — Reasonable precautions by master against committing an offence.]— Where a sale is effected contrary to the pro-

visions of sec. 32 of the *Pure Food Act* 1905 the person selling is not guilty of an offence if he proves, so far as he personally is concerned, the exculpatory facts referred to in that section. *O'Connor* v. *Jenner*, (1909) V.L.R., 468; 31 A.L.T., 71; 15 A.L.R., 519. F.C., *Madden, C.J., Hodges* and *Cussen, JJ.*

Pure Food Act 1905 (No. 2010), sec. 32— Proof of reasonable precautions against committing offence—Whether necessary where special exculpatory provisions exist—Health Act 1890 (No. 1098), sec. 71.]—Where there are special provisions in the Health Acts, as in sec. 71 of the *Health Act* 1890, exculpating a defendant on proof of certain facts, sec. 32 of the *Pure Food Act* 1905 does not apply. *Rider* v. *Dunn*, (1908) V.L.R., 377; 29 A.L.T., 279; 14 A.L.R., 245. *Cussen, J.*

Health Act 1890 (No. 1098), secs. 43, 71— Article purchased as same in nature, substance and quality as demanded by prosecutor —Written warranty—Exculpatory provisions, when available—Pure Food Act 1905 (No. 2010), sec. 35.]—*Semble.*—Sec. 71 of the *Health Act* 1890 refers to all cases of a sale of an article differing from that demanded by the purchaser. *Kelly* v. *Lonsdale*, (1906) 2 K.B., 486, distinguished. *Rider* v. *Dunn*, (1908) V.L.R., 377; 29 A.L.T., 279; 14 A.L.R., 245. *Cussen, J.*

Pure Food Act 1905 (No. 2010), sec. 32 (1) (a)—Sale of adulterated article of food— Reasonable precautions against committing an offence, what are—Health Act 1890 (No. 1098), sec. 71.]—Where a person charged with selling an adulterated article of food proves that he took a written warranty specially supplied to him with the article by a reputable vendor, and had no reason to suspect anything wrong with the same, and sold it in the same state as he received it, *prima facie*, he has taken all reasonable precautions against committing an offence against the Health Acts within the meaning of sec. 32 (1) (a) of the *Pure Food Act* 1905, but in every case it is a question of fact for the magistrates to decide whether reasonable precautions have been taken. *Rider* v.

Dunn, (1908) V.L.R., 377; 29 A.L.T., 279; 14 A.L.R., 245. *Cussen, J.*

Health Act 1890 (No. 1098), secs. 53, 54—Unwholesome food—Prosecution for having such food under control for purpose of sale for human consumption—Prima facie case proved by informant—Burden of proof that food not intended for sale—Effect of statements made by defendant elicited on cross examination of informant's witnesses.]—Sec. 53 of the *Health Act* 1890 makes it an offence for any person to have (amongst other articles) unwholesome fish in his possession for the purpose of sale for human consumption and sec. 54 of that Act provides that if it appears that such articles are of a kind usually used as food for human consumption the proof that such articles were not intended for sale for human consumption shall be on the party contending that they were not so intended. *Held*, that an admission elicited in cross-examination of the informant's witnesses that statements were made by the defendant and his employee to the informant that the fish in question were not intended for sale for human consumption could not discharge the onus cast on the defendant. *Mellis* v. *Jenkins*, (1910) V.L.R., 380; 32 A.L.T., 36; 16 A.L.R., 430. *a' Beckett, J.*

Crimes Act 1891 (No. 1231), sec. 34 (3)—Witness on own behalf—Cross-examination as to credit, when admitted—Evidence as to good character in the particular class of transactions in issue— Prosecution under Health Acts.] — *See* EVIDENCE, col. 509. *Gunner* v. *Payne*, (1910) V.L.R., 45; 31 A.L..T, 138; 16 A.L.R., 29.

II.—VACCINATION.

Vaccination—Duty of parent to have child vaccinated—No public vaccinator — Notice specifying when and where public vaccinator will attend—Parent attending with child at time and place specified—Health Act 1890 (No. 1098), secs. 191, 204—Eighteenth Schedule.]—The *Health Act* 1890 makes it a duty on the parent to cause his child to be vaccinated, and the provisions for the appointment of public vaccinators are merely means for facilitating the performance of that duty

by the parent. Accordingly, it is no answer to a charge of neglecting to cause a child to be vaccinated that there was no public vaccinator for the district in which the child resided during the time within which it should have been vaccinated, and that the parent had the child once at the place, at which and at a time when as stated by the notice served on the parent, the public vaccinator would attend, but found no public vaccinator in attendance. *Thornton* v. *Kelly*, (1910) V.L.R., 156; 31 A.L.T., 197; 16 A.L.R., 142 (1910).

Health Act 1890 (No. 1098), Part IX., Eighteenth Schedule—Vaccination—Notice of the requirement of vaccination—Notification of place of attendance of public vaccinator for the district—" District " meaning of—Place of attendance outside district of Registrar of Births and Deaths causing notice to be given.] The word " district " throughout Part IX. of the *Health Act* 1890 means vaccination district; and consequently the fact that the place set out in the notice prescribed by sec. 204, at which the public vaccinator of the district would attend, is not in the district of the Registrar of Births is no defence to the information above referred to. *O'Malley* v. *Russell*, (1908) V.L.R., 545; 30 A.L.T., 39; 14 A.L.R., 462. *Cussen, J.* (1908).

Information—Allegation as to date of offence incorrect—Health Act 1890 (No. 1098), Part IX.—Vaccination—Justices Act 1890 (No. 1105), sec. 73 (3).]—In an information against a father for not having his child vaccinated as required by Part IX. of the *Health Act* 1890, the offence was alleged as upon the date of the information. It appeared in evidence that the child was not vaccinated within six months from its birth. *Held*, that the allegation as to the date of the offence was immaterial. *O'Malley* v. *Russell*, (1908) V.L.R., 545; 30 A.L.T., 39; 14 A.L.R., 462. *Cussen, J.* (1908).

Information, sufficiency of—Charge against father for not having child vaccinated—Allegation that vaccination notice given by Registrar of the district in which father resided—Who may properly give such notice—Health Act 1890 (No. 1098), Part IX.]—An information against a father for not having his child vaccinated as required by Part IX. of the *Health Act* 1890 alleged that the notice in writing of the requirement of vaccination, prescribed by sec. 204 of the Act, had been given to the defendant by the Registrar of the district in which the defendant was resident. *Held*, on an objection that the allegation should have been that it was given by the Registrar of the district in which the child was resident, that this was an immaterial allegation. The Registrar of the district in which the registration of the birth of the child is effected is a proper person to give the notice above referred to. *O'Malley* v. *Russell*, (1908) V.L.R., 545; 30 A.L.T., 39; 14 A.L.R., 462. *Cussen, J.* (1908).

III.—NUISANCES; OFFENSIVE TRADES.

Health Act 1890 (No. 1098), secs. 216, 222—Nuisance—Common nuisance—Chimney sending forth smoke—Defence — Fireplace or furnace constructed to consume smoke as far as possible.]—On a prosecution under sec. 222 of the *Health Act* 1890 charging that by the sufferance of the defendants a nuisance within the meaning of sec. 216 of the Act arose, viz., a chimney (not being the chimney of a private dwelling-house) sending forth smoke in such quantity as to be a nuisance it is not a defence that the fireplace or furnace connected with such chimney is constructed in such manner as to consume as far as practicable, having regard to the nature of the manufacture or trade, all smoke arising therefrom, and that such fireplace or furnace has for that purpose been carefully attended to by the person having the charge thereof. The word "nuisance" in the phrase "sending forth smoke in such quantity as to be a nuisance" in sec. 216 (7) means a common nuisance. *McKell* v. *Rider*, (1908) 5 C.L.R., 480; 14 A.L.R., 145. H.C., *Griffith, C.J., O'Connor* and *Higgins, JJ.*

By-law, validity of—Power to make by-laws as to the position and construction of privies, &c., generally—Retrospective operation of by-law—Health Act 1890 (No. 1098), secs. 32, 35.]—By sec. 35 of the *Health Act* 1890, municipalities are authorized to make by-laws (*inter alia*) for "The regulation of

noxious or offensive trades businesses or manufactories whether established before or after the passing of this Act in order to prevent or diminish the noxious or offensive effects thereof, and to prevent nuisance or injury to health arising therefrom; the position and manner of construction of privies earth-closets and cesspools or urinals" . . . And generally for the abatement and prevention of nuisances not hereinbefore specified and for securing the healthfulness of the district and of its inhabitants." *Held*, that a Council was thereby authorized to make by-laws as to the position and manner of construction of privies, &c., generally, and not merely of privies, &c., connected with noxious or offensive trades, businesses or manufactories, and that the power was not confined to privies, &c., to be erected in the future, but extended to these in existence when the Act was passed. *Charlton, President, &c., of Shire of* v. *Ruse*, (1912) 14 C.L.R., 220; 18 A.L.R., 207. H.C., *Griffith, C.J., Barton* and *Isaacs, JJ.*

By-law, validity of—By-law regulating privies, &c., generally—Penalty not following the words of the by-law—Penalty not imposed on person responsible for existence of thing prohibited—Health Act 1890 (No. 1098), secs. 32, 35.]—A by-law made under the *Health Act* 1890 provided that no privy, &c., should "be constructed, built, formed or be allowed to remain" within a certain distance of any kitchen, &c., and that "if the owner or occupant of any land uses or permits to be used any privy, &c." in breach of the foregoing provisions, he should be subject to a certain penalty. *Held*, that the by-law was valid. *Charlton, President, &c., of Shire of* v. *Ruse*, (1912) 14 C.L.R., 220; 18 A.L.R., 207. H.C., *Griffith, C.J., Barton* and *Isaacs, JJ.*

Health Act 1890 (No. 1098), sec. 226—Noxious trades—Nuisance—Fumes causing bad smell widely diffused and continuous.]—On the hearing of a complaint under sec. 226 of the *Health Act* 1890, it appeared that the defendant company so carried on its business as to cause offensive fumes creating a bad smell widely diffused, not merely offending persons in close proximity to its source, but invading the neighbourhood and lasting for several hours. *Held*, that there was sufficient evidence to justify a finding that the smell was of such a pervading, continuous, and offensive character as to amount to a nuisance within the meaning of the section. *Bullows* v. *Kitchen & Sons Ltd.*, (1910) V.L.R., 130 ; 31 A.L.T., 172 ; 16 A.L.R., 147. *a' Beckett, J.*

Health Act 1890 (No. 1098), sec. 226— Noxious trades—Nuisance—Negligent use by employees of means sufficient to prevent nuisance if properly used—Nuisance arising from accident.]—In a prosecution under sec. 226 of the *Health Act* 1890, if the Justices are satisfied that a nuisance was in fact created, it is immaterial whether the nuisance arose from the insufficiency of the means provided for preventing it, or from the negligent use by employes of means sufficient, if properly used, to have prevented the nuisance. But a nuisance caused by an accident not arising from negligence would not justify a conviction under the section. *Bullows* v. *Kitchen & Sons Ltd.*, (1910) V.L.R., 130 ; 31 A.L.T., 172 ; 16 A.L.R., 147. *a' Beckett, J.*

Health Act 1890 (No. 1098), sec. 226— Noxious trades—Nuisance—Escape of bad smell on two occasions owing to negligence of employes—Sudden or exceptional matter— —Evidence, sufficiency of.]—Evidence that on two occasions separated by an interval of two days a bad smell escaped from defendant's premises, owing to the negligent use by defendant's employes of apparatus which if properly used would have prevented the smell, may be sufficient to support a finding that the escape of the bad smell was not a sudden or exceptional matter, but was incidental to the carrying on of the defendant's business and a nuisance within the meaning of sec. 226 of the *Health Act* 1890. *Bullows* v. *Kitchen & Sons Ltd.*, (1910) V.L.R., 130 ; 31 A.L.T., 172 ; 16 A.L.R., 147. *a' Beckett, J.*

Noxious trade establishment—Refusal of council to register—Appeal to Board of Health —Right of appellant to be heard and to know what he had to answer—Audi alteram, partem

—Health Act 1890 (No. 1098), sec. 225.]— An appeal under sec. 225 of the *Health Act* 1890 to the Board of Public Health from the refusal by a council to register premises as a noxious trade establishment is in the nature of a judicial inquiry. The appellant is therefore entitled to an opportunity of presenting his case before the Board and of knowing what is alleged in opposition to his application. *The King* v. *Prahran, Mayor &c., of ; Ex parte Morris*, (1910) V.L.R., 460 ; 32 A.L.T., 92 ; 16 A.L.R., 507. *Hood, J.*

Health Act 1890 (No. 1098), sec. 225— Appeal—Mandamus to Board of Public Health to hear—Appellants not given an opportunity of being heard.]—Mandamus directed to the Board of Public Health commanding it to hear and determine an appeal under sec. 225 of the *Health Act* 1890 where the Board had given a decision upon appeal adverse to the appellants without giving them an opportunity of being heard. *The King* v. *Prahran, Mayor, &c., of ; Ex parte Morris*, (1910) V.L.R., 460 ; 32 A.L.T., 92 ; 16 A.L.R., 507. *Hood, J.*

Parties—Board of Public Health—How Board may be sued.]—*Per Hood, J.*— "Whether the name 'Board of Health' is a short and convenient way of describing the individual members, or whether the Board be considered as a statutory entity, having large powers, in either event the Board can, in my opinion, be sued under that name." *The King* v. *Prahran, Mayor, &c. of ; Ex parte Morris*, (1910) V.L.R., 460 ; 32 A.L.T. 92 ; 16 A.L.R., 507.

HIGH COURT OF AUSTRALIA.

See also APPEAL.

High Court—Practice—Declaratory judgment—Abstract question of law in decision of which rights of parties are not involved— —Whether High Court will decide—Rules of High Court 1903, Part I. Order III., r. 1— Order XXV., r. 5 (Rules of Supreme Court 1906)—Trade Marks Act 1905 (No. 20), Part VII., constitutionality of.]—Notwithstanding the provisions of Part I. Order III., r. 1 of the Rules of the High Court 1903, the High Court will not entertain abstract questions of law or give an opinion as to the power of the Commonwealth to enact certain legislation where the opinion cannot be followed up by an effective order. Therefore where, an action having been brought in the High Court to restrain the registration of a trade mark under Part VII. of the *Trade Marks Act* 1905, the application for registration was withdrawn before the action came on for hearing, on a reference to the Full Court of the question whether the Parliament had power to enact Part VII. of that Act the Court refused to entertain the question, and ordered the case to be struck out. *Bruce* v. *Commonwealth Trade Marks Label Association*, (1907) 4 C.L.R., 1569; 13 A.L.R., 582. H.C., *Griffith,* C.J., *Barton, O'Connor, Isaacs* and *Higgins, JJ.*

High Court—Practice—Prohibition —Rule nisi for enlarged to enable error to be corrected.]—*See* Prohibition. *The King and the Commonwealth Court of Conciliation and Arbitration and the President thereof and the Boot Trade Employes Federation, Ex parte Whybrow & Co.*, (1910) 11 C.L.R., 1; 16 A.L.R., 373.

High Court—Practice—Motion for prohibition to restrain Commonwealth Court of Conciliation and Arbitration—Finding by President that dispute existed, whether High Court bound by—The Commonwealth Constitution, sec. 51 (xxxv.).]—*See* Prohibition. *The King and the Commonwealth Court of Court of Conciliation and Arbitration and the President thereof and the Boot Trade Employes Federation; Ex parte Whybrow & Co.*, (1910) 11 C.L.R., 1; 16 A.L.R., 373.

High Court Practice—Appeal—Cross appeal —Rules of the High Court 1903, Part II., Sec. III., r. 13.]—*See* Appeal, col. 26. *Wilson* v. *Moss*, 8 C.L.R., 146; 15 A.L.R., 131. H.C. (1909).

HIGHWAY.

See also, Local Government.

Melbourne and Metropolitan Board of Works Act 1890 (No. 1197), secs. 79, 81, 87, 88— Highway — Obstruction — Sewer constructed under highway—Shaft opening on surface of highway—Covering of shaft—Duty to keep in repair—Neglect of duty.]—*See* Melbourne and Metropolitan Board of Works. *Frenchman* v. *Melbourne and Metropolitan Board of Works*, (1911) V.L.R., 363; 33 A.L.T., 30; 17 A.L.R., 333.

Highway—Obstruction—Standing or loitering in street and not moving on when requested—Collecting a crowd—Interference; with traffic—By-law—Police Offences Act 1890 (No. 1126), sec. 6.]—*See* Police Offences Acts. *Haywood* v. *Mumford*, (1908) 7 C.L.R., 133; 14 A.L.R., 555.

Street—Primary object of—Reasonable user —Prayer meeting.]—*Per Hood, J.*—The primary object of a street is the free passage of the public, who are entitled to use it *eundo et redeundo*, and for a short time *morando*. To hold a prayer meeting in a street is not a reasonable user of it. *Mumford* v. *Haywood*, (1908) V.L.R., 308; 29 A.L.T., 247; 14 A.L.R., 206.

HIRER.

See INSOLVENCY.

HORSE.

See also Cattle.

Crimes Act 1890 (No. 1079), sec. 74—Using another person's cattle without his consent— Unlawful user by person in lawful possession.] *See* Criminal Law, col. 344. *Wimble* v. *Foulsham*, (1908) V.L.R., 98; 29 A.L.T., 158; 13 A.L.R., 727.

HUSBAND AND WIFE.

I.—MARRIAGE.

Husband and wife—Maintenance—Former marriage—Husband not heard of for more than seven years—Presumption—Validity of second marriage—Proof of invalidity—Onus —Marriage Act 1890 (No. 1166), sec. 46.]— Upon the hearing, under sec. 46 of the *Marriage Act* 1890, of a complaint by a woman that she had been left by her husband, the defendant, without means of support, evidence was given that she had, previously to her marriage with the defendant, been married to a man who had disappeared about fifteen years ago, and of whom she had not heard since his disappearance ; that after the lapse of seven years from his disappear-

ance she had obtained a decree *nisi* for dissolution of her marriage with him on the ground of desertion, which decree had not been made absolute ; and that she was subsequently married to the defendant, who was then aware of her previous marriage and of the divorce proceedings. *Held*, that the evidence raised the presumption of the first husband's death before the second marriage, and that, even if it did not, the second marriage should not have been treated by the Justices as bad until it was proved to be so. *Held*, further, that where in such proceedings the complainant proves a marriage with the defendant, which would be valid but for a first husband's existence, the onus of proving the invalidity of such marriage is on the defendant, who denies its validity. *Ousley* v. *Ousley*, (1912) V.L.R., 32 ; 33 A.L.T., 155 ; 18 A.L.R., 5. *a'Beckett, J.*

Evidence—Legitimacy, presumption as to— Father and mother living together as man and wife—European woman and Chinese man.]— See EVIDENCE. *Potter* v. *Minahan*, (1908) 7 C.L.R., 277 ; 14 A.L.R., 635.

Child born in wedlock—Presumption of legitimacy.]—See EVIDENCE. *In re Osmand ; Bennett* v. *Booty*, (1908) V.L.R., 67 ; 29 A.L.T., 168 ; 13 A.L.R., 728. F.C., *a'Beckett, Hodges* and *Hood, JJ.* (1908), affirming *Cussen, J.*, (1906) V.L.R., 455 ; 27 A.L.T., 218 ; 12 A.L.R., 256.

II.—JUDICIAL SEPARATION AND DIVORCE.

(a) *Domicil and Jurisdiction.*

Dissolution of marriage — Jurisdiction— Domicile—Submission to jurisdiction by respondent, effect of.]—Domicile is the sole test of jurisdiction to grant a decree of dissolution of marriage. On a petition for dissolution of marriage, jurisdiction not otherwise possessed by the Court, cannot be conferred by an entry of appearance or submission to the jurisdiction by the respondent. *Le Mesurier* v. *Le Mesurier*, (1895) A.C., 517, followed. *Callwell* v. *Callwell*, 3 Sw. & Tr., 259, considered. *Ho-a-mie* v. *Ho-a-mie*, 6 V.L.R. (I. P. & M.), 113 ; *Firkins* v. *Firkins*, 23 A.L.T., 122 ; 4 A.L.R., 74,

and *Crook* v. *Crook*, 23 A.L.T., 123; 8
A.L.R., 2, over-ruled. *Forster* v. *Forster*,
(1907) V.L.R., 159; 28 A.L.T., 144; 13
A.L.R., 33. F.C., *a' Beckett*, *A.-C.J.*,
Hodges, Hood, Cussen and *Chomley, JJ.*

**Marriage Act 1890 (No. 1166), secs. 74,
75, 76—" Any wife," " any husband,"
meaning of—Domicile—Wife domiciled in
Victoria at time of desertion.**]—In the *Marriage Act* 1890 general words such as " any
wife," " any husband," are to be construed
as " any wife (any husbnad) domiciled in
Victoria at the time of the institution of
the suit "—and perhaps in the case of a
wife, as meaning also " any wife who has
been deserted by her husband and who at
the time of the desertion was domiciled. in
Victoria." *Forster* v. *Forster*, (1907) V.L.R.,
159; 28 A.L.T., 144; 13 A.L.R., 33. F.C.,
a' Beckett, *A.-C.J.*, *Hodges, Hood, Cussen*
and *Chomley, JJ.*

**Marriage Act 1890 (No. 1166), sec. 74—
Divorce—Wife deserted in Victoria when
domiciled there—Husband subsequently becoming domiciled elsewhere—Jurisdiction of
Court on cross petition by husband.**]—Apart
from special enactment, such as that enabling
a wife deserted in Victoria to petition for
dissolution of marriage, the Court has no
jurisdiction to dissolve a marriage unless the
husband is at the time of the institution
of the proceedings, domiciled in Victoria.
Accordingly, where a wife so deserted,
petitions against a husband domiciled elsewhere than in Victoria, the Court has no
jurisdiction to entertain a cross-petition
by him for dissolution of the marriage.
Bailey v. *Bailey*, (1909) V.L.R., 299; 30
A.L.T., 217; 15 A.L.R., 237. *Cussen, J.*

Domicile of origin—Change of, what constitutes.]—In order that a man may lose his
domicile of origin and acquire a new domicile,
he must voluntarily change his residence
to another country with the intention of
residing there permanently or indefinitely
and *sine animo revertendi*. *Forster* v. *Forster*,
(1907) V.L.R., 159; 28 A.L.T., 144; 13
A.L.R., 33. F.C., *Hood, Cussen* and *Chomley, JJ.*

**Domicile—Dissolution of marriage—Victoria the domicile of origin of both parties—
Victorian marriage—Change of domicile and
subsequent desertion—Jurisdiction of Victorian
Court.**]—Both of the parties to a suit by the
wife for dissolution of marriage on the ground
of desertion had their domicile of origin in
Victoria, the marriage took place in Victoria,
and the matrimonial home was for several
years after the marriage in Victoria. The
parties subsequently went to reside in South
Australia, where the husband deserted the
petitioner. The desertion took place after
the husband had acquired a South Australian
domicile. *Held*, that, though the wife had
not resorted to Victoria merely for the purpose of petitioning under sec. 74 of the *Marriage Act* 1890, the Victorian Court had no
jurisdiction to entertain the petition. *Forster*
v. *Forster*, (1907) V.L.R., 159; 28 A.L.T.,
144; 13 A.L.R., 33. F.C., *Hood, Cussen*
and *Chomley, JJ.*

**Domicil—Commonwealth Public servant—
Voluntary removal from domicil of choice to
take up similar duties in the same department
in another State—Whether he acquires new
domicil of choice.**]—H, whose domicil of
origin is outside the Commonwealth had, in
February 1907, a Victorian domicil of choice.
In that month and year he was an officer in
the Commonwealth Customs Department,
residing and performing all his duties in
Melbourne. He then answered a departmental call for applications from Victorian
officers willing to go to Adelaide on temporary
work in connection with a reorganization
of the Customs Department there. He was
chosen and went to Adelaide. There existed
reasons which made it probable that he was
not sorry to leave Victoria. Soon after he
was in Adelaide he applied for and was
appointed to the position there corresponding
to that which he had previously occupied in
Melbourne. The evidence showed that he
intended to remain in South Australia indefinitely, though if he could get promotion,
he would go to any of the other States.
Held, that H was domiciled in South Australia. *Semble.*—If H had gone to South
Australia under orders or if his work in South
Australia had been of the temporary character

which at first it was, the decision would have been different. Case of soldier or sailor distinguished. *Bailey* v. *Bailey*, (1909) V.L.R., 299; 30 A.L.T., 217; 15 A.L.R., 237. *Cussen, J.*

Domicile, change of—Evidence — Statements of intention, weight to be attached to—Contrary inference from conduct and Acts.]— For a case in which, upon a question of change of domicile, statements of intention made by the person, whose domicile was in issue, were not allowed to countervail the inference drawn from his conduct and acts, *see Forster* v. *Forster*, (1907) V.L.R., 159; 28 A.L.T., 144; 13 A.L.R., 33. F.C., *Hood, Cussen* and *Chomley, JJ.*

(b) Grounds for.

(1) Desertion.

Desertion, commencement of—Intention to abandon matrimonial relationship—Separation under pressure of eternal circumstances, effect of.]—Desertion commences when one of the spouses, without the consent of the other, terminates an existing matrimonial relationship, with the intention of forsaking that other, and permanently or indefinitely abandoning such relationship. An existing matrimonial relationship is not ended so long as both spouses *bona fide* recognise it as subsisting. It is not ended by a separation brought about by the pressure of external circumstances such as an absence on professional or business pursuits, or in search of health, or it may be even of pleasure. *Tulk* v. *Tulk*; *Hoffmeyer* v. *Hoffmeyer*, (1907) V.L.R., 64; 28 A.L.T., 165; 13 A.L.R., 45. *Cussen, J.*

Desertion—Wife compelled to leave husband—Lazy husband refusing to support wife —Wife unwilling to work for support of husband.]—A husband is guilty of desertion if he behaves in such a way that his wife cannot reasonably be expected to live with him, and is compelled to leave him for her own safety and welfare, whether physical, mental or moral. But where a wife leaves her husband, because he refuses to work to support her and she is unwilling to work to support him, the husband is not guilty of desertion.

Hutchinson v. *Hutchinson*, (1908) V.L.R., V.L.R., 411; 30 A.L.T., 23; 14 A.L.R., 274. *Hood, J.*

Constructive desertion—Conduct amounting to.]—In determining whether there has been a desertion, the fact that the parties are living under one roof is not necessarily conclusive, nor need the offending spouse be the one who has left the common home. Desertion occurs where one of the parties by his or her conduct intentionally drives the other away. *Tulk* v. *Tulk*; *Hoffmeyer* v. *Hoffmeyer*, (1907) V.L.R., 64; 28 A.L.T., 165; 13 A.L.R., 45. *Cussen, J.*

Divorce—Desertion—Deed of separation, when no bar to decree for dissolution—Abandonment of petitioner by respondent not attributable to deed.]—A deed of separation will be no bar to a decree of dissolution of marriage on the ground of desertion, where the respondent has set the deed at nought in such a way that it would be absurd to attribute the abandonment of the petitioner by the respondent to any permission given by the deed. *Jordan* v. *Jordan*, (1906) V.L.R., 414; 27 A.L.T., 229; 12 A.L.R., 252. *a' Beckett, J.* (1906).

Divorce—Desertion—Deed of separation, effect of as licence to live apart—Failure to perform obligations under deed—Revocation of licence.]—Non-performance of a husband's obligations under a deed of separation does not *ipso facto* deprive it of its effect as a licence to live apart, which puts an end to desertion. But the deed is not necessarily a permanent bar against a decree for dissolution of marriage on the ground of desertion. If the husband continued to make default, the licence might be effectually revoked by the wife and desertion would then commence. *Mackenzie* v. *Mackenzie*, (1906) V.L.R., 416; 27 A.L.T., 241; 12 A.L.R., 252. *a' Beckett, A.-C.J.* (1906).

Divorce—Desertion—Deed of separation, how far a bar to divorce—Default in observance of covenants.]—In December 1902 a husband deserted his wife and child. In December, 1903, a deed of separation was executed in which the husband and wife mutually agreed to live apart and covenanted not to molest one another. The husband covenanted that the wife should have the custody of the child, and that he would pay a certain weekly sum for the maintenance of the child. The husband paid nothing at all under the deed. In a suit by the wife for dissolution of marriage on the ground of desertion commencing in December, 1902, *Held*, that, notwithstanding the non-performance by the husband of his obligations under the deed, it was a good answer to the desertion. *Crabb* v. *Crabb*, L.R. 1 P. & D., 601, followed. *Jordan* v. *Jordan*, (1906) V.L.R., 414; 27 A.L.T., 229; 12 A.L.R., 252. *a' Beckett, A.-C.J.* (1906).

Separation by mutual consent—Subsequent desertion, commencement of.]—In the case of a separation by mutual consent, or by the adverse act of one of the parties, which separation is intended to be permanent or indefinite, there cannot be desertion until after the matrimonial relationship is re-established, and, *semble*, in the case of separation by adverse act a conditional intention of possible resumption makes no difference. *Tulk* v. *Tulk*; *Hoffmeyer* v. *Hoffmeyer*, (1907) V.L.R., 64; 28 A.L.T., 165; 13 A.L.T., 45. *Cussen, J.*

Desertion without just cause or excuse—Separation by mutual consent—Offer to resume matrimonial relations—Refusal of offer—Marriage Act 1890 (No. 1166), sec. 74.]—Where there has been a separation by mutual consent, of husband and wife who have lived together as such, which separation is intended to be permanent or indefinite, there can be no hesitation till the matrimonial relationship is re-established. Desertion where husband and wife have lived together as such, can only commence where one of the parties has actively and wilfully brought to an end the existing state of co-habitation. Where the state of co-habition has otherwise ceased, a refusal to re-establish it is not desertion on the part of the refusing spouse. *Bailey* v. *Bailey*, (1909) V.L.R., 299; 30 A.L.T., 217; 15 A.L.R., 237. *Cussen, J.*

Desertion, termination of—Offer by deserting spouse to re-establish matrimonial rela- tionship—Refusal of offer, effect of—Consent by deserted spouse to continuance of separation.]—Desertion once commenced continues until either the matrimonial relationship is re-established, or until the deserting spouse, by a sincere and *bona fide* offer to re-establish it, has manifested a change in his or her intention, or until the deserted spouse consents to the separation, or otherwise indicates that he or she is not desirous of re-establishing the matrimonial relationship. Consent to the continuance of desertion will not be inferred from a refusal to live with a husband or wife whose conduct at the time of the refusal is such as to justify it. *Tulk* v. *Tulk*; *Hoffmeyer* v. *Hoffmeyer*, (1907) V.L.R., 64; 28 A.L.T., 165; 13 A.L.R., 45. *Cussen, J.*

Marriage Act 1890 (No. 1166), sec. 74 (a)—Divorce—Desertion—Insanity arising after desertion—Whether statutory period continues to run.]—Two years after a husband had deserted his wife he became insane and remained insane up to the time of the presentation of a petition by his wife for dissolution of marriage on the ground of desertion for three years and upwards. *Held*, that the insanity did not prevent the statutory period of three years from continuing to run. *Laing* v. *Laing*, (1911) V.L.R., 37; 32 A.L.T., 144; 16 A.L.R., 601. *a' Beckett, J.*

Marriage Act 1890 (No. 1166), sec. 74 (a)—Desertion for statutory period—Subsequent offer by offending spouse to re-establish matrimonial relationship—Refusal of offer, effect of.]—Where desertion has existed for the statutory period, and the matrimonial offence is complete, it is not put an end to by the refusal of an offer by the offending spouse to re-establish the matrimonial relationship. *Tulk* v. *Tulk*; *Hoffmeyer* v. *Hoffmeyer*, (1907) V.L.R., 64; 28 A.L.T., 165; 13 A.L.R., 45. *Cussen, J.*

Marriage Act 1890 (No. 1166), sec. 74.—Divorce—Desertion.]—Appeal from order dismissing petition based on desertion dismissed on ground that the evidence that desertion had continued for a period of three years and upwards was not satisfactory. *Stewart*

v. *Stewart*, (1907) 4 C.L.R., 920. H.C., *Griffith, C.J., Barton, O'Connor, Isaacs* and *Higgins, JJ.*

(2) Adultery.

Adultery — Evidence — Communication of a venereal disease—Surrounding circumstances, whether they may be considered.]—Upon a petition by the wife for a dissolution of marriage on the ground of a repeated act of adultery, the only evidence of the husband's adultery was that the wife had been twice infected with a venereal disease. When cured, the wife refused to allow her husband to cohabit with her, on the ground of his misconduct, and he submitted to her refusal and continued to support her. The husband never unequivocally denied the adultery, either verbally or in the written correspondence carried on between the parties after separation. The husband was personally served with the petition, but did not defend the suit. The wife's conduct was free from suspicion. *Held*, that, although the existence of a venereal disease might not of itself be evidence of adultery, the surrounding circumstances should be looked at, and were sufficient to warrant the conclusion that the husband had been guilty of a repeated act of adultery. *Collett* v. *Collett*, 1 Curt. Eccl. Rep., 678, considered. *Isles* v. *Isles*, (1906) V.L.R., 86 ; 12 A.L.R. (C.N.), 26. *a'Beckett, J.*

Divorce—Adultery, evidence of—Admissions—Registration by husband of birth of illegitimate child—Certified copy of entry in Register of Births—Admission therein of paternity.]—On the hearing of a petition by a wife for dissolution of marriage on the ground of a repeated act of adultery by her husband, the only evidence tendered in support of such ground was a certified copy of an entry in the Register of Births in Brisbane, showing that the husband had registered the birth of an illegitimate child of which he therein described himself as the father. *Held*, that the Court might act upon the admission of adultery contained in such entry, as set out in the certified copy thereof, there being no reasonable doubt of the identity of the husband with the person

who registered the birth, and no circumstances of suspicion. *Wright* v. *Wright*, (1911) V.L.R., 28 ; 32 A.L.T., 114 ; 16 A.L.R., 602. *a'Beckett, J.*

(3) Repeated Assaults, &c.

Marriage Act 1890 (No. 1166), sec. 74 (d)—Divorce, grounds of—Repeatedly assaulting and cruelly beating petitioner within previous year—Acts constituting the offence.]—The Court will not grant a decree for dissolution on the ground that the respondent during one year previously has repeatedly assaulted and cruelly beaten the petitioner, unless grave acts of assault and cruel violence are proved. *Worland* v. *Worland*, (1910) V.L.R., 374 ; 32 A.L.T., 27 ; 16 A.L.R., 352. *a'Beckett, J.*

Divorce, grounds of—Repeated assaults and cruel beatings—Nature of acts constituting such offence—Period during which such acts must continue—Marriage Act 1890 (No. 1166), sec. 74 (d).]—The acts, which entitle a petitioner to a decree for dissolution of marriage on the ground that the respondent has repeatedly during one year previous to the presentation of the petition assaulted and cruelly beaten the petitioner, must be acts of physical cruelty. *Semble.*—It is not necessary for such acts to continue throughout the whole period of one year previous to the presentation of the petition. *Ruddell* v. *Ruddell*, (1911) V.L.R., 330 ; 33 A.L.T., 38 ; 17 A.L.R., 401. *Hodges, J.*

Marriage Act 1890 (No. 1166), sec. 74 (d)—Divorce—Ground of petition—Repeated assaults and cruel beatings within previous year—Naure of assaults and beatings.]—Where a wife petitions for dissolution of marriage on the ground that the respondent has repeatedly within the year previous to the presentation of the petition assaulted and cruelly beaten her, and she proves a series of assaults by him upon her within that period, it is not necessary for her to prove a series of serious bodily injuries resulting to her from such assaults in order to give her a claim for relief. *Hocking* v. *Hocking*, 32 A.L.T., 134 ; 17 A.L.R., 13. *a'Beckett, J.* (1911).

Divorce—Repeated cruel beatings charged in petition—No misconduct charged in answer —Justification—Evidence of improprieties on part of petitioner, admissibility of—Beatings not result of altercations as to alleged improprieties.]—Upon the hearing of a petition by the wife for dissolution of marriage on the ground that the respondent had repeatedly within a year previous to the presentation of the petition assaulted and cruelly beaten her, the Court refused to receive certain evidence tendered on behalf of the respondent to show laxity of conduct on the part of the petitioner, as no misconduct was charged in the answer, and the alleged improprieties would have afforded no excuse or justification for beatings on occasions when no inpropriety occurred, and on which no altercation as to alleged impropriety had arisen. *Hocking* v. *Hocking*, 32 A.L.T., 134; 17 A.L.R., 13. *a'Beckett, J.* (1911).

(4) Frequent Convictions.

Marriage Act 1890 (No. 1166), sec. 74 (c)— " Frequent " convictions for crime—Test of frequency—Criminal tendency—Evidence of, what is.]—*Per Cussen, J.*—" The word ' frequent ' is a relative word, and in order to understand it in reference to any particular set of circumstances, some test must be applied. I find it very difficult to say what is the right test to apply under sec. 74 (c) . . . On the whole I find no other test than that of a criminal tendency as expressed by *Hodges, J.*, in *Richards* v. *Richards*, 17 V.L.R., 758; 13 A.L.T., 133, and by *a'Beckett, J.*, in his judgment in this case, and I need only add that this tendency must be shown by convictions, and not by evidence of criminal tendency given at the hearing." *Kemp* v. *Kemp*, (1907) V.L.R., 718; 29 A.L.T., 92; 13 A.L.R., 615.

Marriage Act 1890 (No. 1166), sec. 74 (c)— Dissolution of marriage—" Frequent convictions for crime "—Two convictions—Second conviction more than two years after release from prison on first conviction.]—A marriage took place in 1899. In August, 1902, the husband was convicted of forgery and sentenced to two years imprisonment. In March, 1907, he was convicted of conspiracy and sentenced to two years and six months imprisonment. In June 1907 the wife presented a petition for divorce on the ground that the respondent had within five years undergone frequent convictions for crime and been sentenced in the aggregate to imprisonment for three years and upwards, and had left the petitioner habitually without means of support. At the hearing the above convictions were proved. *Held*, that the convictions proved were not " frequent " within the meaning of sec. 74 (c) of the *Marriage Act* 1890. *Kemp* v. *Kemp*, (1907) V.L.R., 718; 29 A.L.T., 92; 13 A.L.R., 615. F.C., *Madden, C.J., a'Beckett* and *Cussen, JJ.*

(5) Discretionary Bars.

Marriage Act 1890 (No. 1166), sec. 86— Discretionary bars—Adultery of petitioner— Discretion of Court, how exercised.]—In the exercise of its discretion under sec. 86 of the *Marriage Act* 1890 to refuse to pronounce a decree if it find that the petitioner has been guilty of adultery, the Court should endeavour to promote virtue and morality, and to discourage vice and immorality. *Aldred* v. *Aldred*, (1908) V.L.R., 58; 29 A.L.T., 107; 13 A.L.R., 635. F.C., *Madden, C.J., Hood* and *Cussen, JJ.*

Marriage Act 1890 (No. 1166), sec. 86— Adultery of petitioner—Discretion of Court, how exercised—Deserted wife left in poverty.] —Mere desertion by a husband leaving his wife in poverty with two children to support is not a sufficient excuse for the wife's adultery, so as to justify the Court in exercising in her favour its discretion under sec. 86 of the *Marriage Act* 1890, on her petition for dissolution of the marriage. *Aldred* v. *Aldred*, (1908) V.L.R., 58; 29 A.L.T., 107; 13 A.L.R., 635. F.C., *Madden, C.J., Hood* and *Cussen, JJ.*

Divorce—Marriage Act 1890 (No. 1166), secs. 74 (a), 86—Petitioner guilty of adultery— Discretionary bar, nature of.]—In exercising the discretion vested in the Court by sec. 86 of the *Marriage Act* 1890, the Court must have regard not only to the rights and liabilities of the matrimonial person wronged and of the wrong-doer respectively *inter se*, but also to the interests of society and public morality, and a decree of dissolution of marriage will not be granted ordinarily or generally to a petitioner who has been guilty of matrimonial infidelity. *McRae* v. *McRae*, (1906) V.L.R., 778 ; 28 A.L.T., 90 ; 12 A.L.R., 479. *Hodges, J.*

Marraige Act 1890 (No. 1166), sec. 86—Discretionary bars—Petitioner guilty of adultery—Discretion of Court, how exercised.]— The power of the Court to pronounce a decree in favor of a petitioner found guilty of adultery is not limited to those cases in which the petitioner's misconduct was directly due to the conduct of the respondent. The Court will look at the special circumstances of each case in order to determine whether, having regard to the rights and liabilities of the parties and the interests of public morality, the divorce ought to be granted. *Wyke* v. *Wyke*, (1904) P., 149, disapproved ; *Evans* v. *Evans and Elford*, (1906) P., 125, followed. *Mulder* v. *Mulder*, (1906) V.L.R., 388 ; 27 A.L.T., 216 ; 12 A.L.R., 210. *a'Beckett, J.*

Marriage Act 1890 (No. 1166), sec. 86—Discretionary bars—Adultery—Petitioner living in adultery at time of presentation of petition and of hearing.]—Petition of deserted wife, who at the date of the petition, and up to the trial was living in adultery, dismissed. *Per Hood, J.—Semble*, the fact that at the hearing the petitioner is living in adultery is in itself an insuperable bar to relief. *Aldred* v. *Aldred*, (1908) V.L.R., 58 ; 29 A.L.T., 107 ; 13 A.L.R., 635. F.C., *Madden, C.J., Hood* and *Cussen, JJ.*

Divorce—Petition by husband on ground of respondent's adultery—Adultery of petitioner, whether a bar to decree—Discretion of Court—Marriage Act 1890 (No. 1166), sec. 86.]— Where a husband, who petitioned for dissolution of marriage on the ground of his wife's adultery, had himself committed adultery, but his misconduct had not conduced to that of the wife, the Court in the exercise of its discretion under sec. 86 of the *Marriage Act* 1890, granted the petition—

the Court taking into consideration (*inter alia*) the fact that if it refused him relief, it would probably conduce to irregular relations injurious to society. *Harvey* v. *Harvey* ; *Thomas, Co-respondent*, (1911) V.L.R., 345 ; 33 A.L.T., 53 ; 17 A.L.R., 368. *a'Beckett, J.*

Marriage Act 1890 (No. 1166), secs. 74, 86—Divorce— Desertion — Delay in presenting petition—Discretionary bar—Excuse—Want of means—Wife with young children to support.]—A wife, who presented a petition for dissolution of marriage on the ground of desertion sixteen years after the desertion commenced and thirteen years after the cause of divorce accrued, excused herself for the delay on the ground that she had had no means to take proceedings earlier, and that she thought her husband might some day or other return. She had young children, and to find means of support for them she had to keep lodgers. *Held*, that the delay was not unreasonable, and that therefore the discretionary power of the Court to refuse to pronounce a decree of dissolution where there has been unreasonable delay should not be exercised against the petitioner. *Hutchinson* v. *Hutchinson*, (1907) V.L.R., 211 ; 28 A.L.T., 182 ; 13 A.L.R., 96. *Hood, J.*

6. Suppression of Facts.

Divorce—Suppression of facts by petitioner, effect of.]—Petitioners in divorce proceedings should make a full and clear disclosure of all important facts relating to the matrimonial life, and the suppression of any material fact is a fraud upon the Court, which may be punished by the refusal of the petition. *Evans* v. *Evans and Eldred*, (1906) P., 125, approved. *McRae* v. *McRae*, (1906) V.L.R., 778 ; 28 A.L.T., 90 ; 12 A.L.R., 479. *Hodges, J.*

(7) Condonation.

Marriage Act 1890 (No. 1166), sec. 83—Divorce—Petition by wife—Condonation after presentation of petition—Subsequent misconduct of respondent—Revival of petition.]—After the presentation and before the hearing of a petition by a wife against her husband for dissolution of marriage on the ground that the respondent had been an habitual drunkard and had left her without means of support for three years and upward, the petitioner and respondent resumed cohabitation on the express understanding that, if the respondent should be guilty of further acts of drunkenness or failure to support, the petitioner would go on with the petition. The respondent having been guilty of such further misconduct the petitioner proceeded with the suit and proved the misconduct alleged in the petition. *Held,* that the further misconduct of the respondent placed the petitioner in the position she occupied when she presented the petition and entitled her to have the prayer of that petition granted. *Moore v. Moore,* (1892) P., 382, applied. *Strong v. Strong,* (1910) V.L.R., 122; 31 A.L.T., 156; 16 A.L.R., 62. *Hodges, J.* (1910).

(c) *Practice.*

(1) Service of Citation and Petition.

Husband and wife—Divorce—Service on respondent—Evidence in proof of—Nature of.]—In undefended divorce suits the Court has to be satisfied by the best evidence reasonably procurable that service on the respondent has been duly effected. *Maddock v. Maddock,* (1911) V.L.R., 127; 32 A.L.T., 124; 17 A.L.R., 66. *Hood, J.*

Husband and wife—Divorce—Service, proof of—Affidavit of service by process server—Death of process server before hearing—Proof by affidavit.]—Where the person, to whom a copy of the citation and a sealed copy of the petition had been handed for service on the respondent, had made an affidavit (afterwards filed in the office of the Prothonotary in compliance with the Divorce Rules) stating that he had served the documents on the respondent within the jurisdiction and that he knew and was well acquainted with the respondent and knew him to be the husband of the petitioner, and the deponent had died before the hearing of the petition, the Court accepted the affidavit as proof of service, there being no suspicion of any fraud or collusion. *Jewell v. Jewell,* 2 W. & W. (I. E. & M.), 136, distinguished. *Constable v. Constable,* 1 W.W. & A'B. (I. E & M.), 88,

and *Ridge v. Ridge,* 26 V.L.R., 220; 22 A.L.T. 44; 6 A.L.R., 149, applied. *Maddock v. Maddock,* (1911) V.L.R., 127; 32 A.L.T., 124; 17 A.L.R., 66. *Hood, J.*

Practice—Petition and citation—Enlargement of time for service—Application after time limited for service—Divorce Rules 1906, rr. 7, 126, 128—Rules of the Supreme Court 1906, Order LXIV., r. 7; Order LXX., r. 1.]—A Judge in Chambers has power to enlarge the time for service of a copy citation and petition in a divorce suit, though the application for such enlargement of time is not made until after the time limited by the *Divorce Rules* 1906 for such service. *Lyons v. Lyons,* (1909) V.L.R., 89; 30 A.L.T., 142; 15 A.L.R., 39. *a'Beckett, J.*

Divorce—Practice—Petition by wife—Answer charging adultery and praying for divorce—Joining and citing alleged adulterer—Marriage Act 1890 (No. 1166), sec. 110.]—Where the respondent files an answer to a petition by his wife for dissolution of marriage in which he alleges adultery on her part with a person named in such answer, and prays for a dissolution of the marriage on the ground of such adultery, he may cause to be issued a citation directed to that person, and joining him in the suit as the party cited and serve the same and the answer to the petition upon him without serving him with a copy of the petition. *Bailey v. Bailey,* (1909) V.L.R., 138; 30 A.L.T., 150; 15 A.L.R., 38. *Hodges, J.*

(2) Joining Co-respondent.

Divorce—Practice—Husband petitioner—Adultery of wife—Adulterer's identity unknown at the time of filing petition—Identity subsequently ascertained—Absence of evidence against alleged adulterer—Whether petitioner may be excused from making alleged adulterer a co-respondent—Marriage Act 1890 (No. 1166), sec. 78—Divorce Rules 1907, r. 5.]—Where a husband has adopted in his petition a charge, by whomsoever originally made, of adultery with his wife against any person, and the identity of that person is or becomes known to the petitioner, it is necessary to show some exceptional circumstances to induce the Court to excuse the petitioner from making such person a co-respondent. The mere fact that at the time of the application to be excused the petitioner has not evidence against such person is not an exceptional circumstance sufficient to justify the granting of the application. *Saunders* v. *Saunders*, (1897) P., at p. 104, principle laid down by *Rigby, L.J.*, adopted. *Richards* v. *Richards*, (1911) V.L.R., 42; 32 A.L.T., 101; 16 A.L.R., 579. *Cussen, J.*

(3) Discovery; Interrogatories; Evidence *de bene esse.*

Divorce—Practice—Petition on ground of adultery—Discovery of documents and interrogatories directed to fact of adultery—Divorce Rules 1906, rr. 26, 126.]—In a suit for dissolution of marriage on the ground of adultery neither the respondent nor the co-respondent can be compelled to answer interrogatories as to the fact of adultery, or to make discovery of documents relating to that fact. *Davis* v. *Davis*; *Hattrick, Co-respondent*, (1912) V.L.R., 12; 33 A.L.T., 109; 17 A.L.R., 552. F.C., *Hodges, Hood* and *Cussen, JJ.* (1911).

Divorce—Discovery and interrogatories—Adultery—Objection that discovery of documents or answering interrogatories may tend to criminate—How objection properly raised.] The proper way of raising the objection, that compliance with an order for discovery and interrogatories obtained against a co-respondent would disclose or tend to disclose adultery on his part, and would or might criminate him, is upon oath in his affidavit of documents and his answers to interrogatories. *Davis* v. *Davis and Hattrick*, (1912) V.L.R., 23; 33 A.L.T., 108; 17 A.L.R., 607. *Hood, J.*

Husband and wife—Divorce—Practice—Discovery—Jurisdiction to order ex parte—Divorce Rules 1906, rr. 126, 128—Rules of the Supreme Court 1906, Order XXXI., rr. 1, 1a, 12.]—In a divorce suit an order for discovery and interrogatories may be made *ex parte*. *Rees* v. *Dunbar*, 14 V.L.R., 645; 10 A.L.T., 147, followed. *Davis* v. *Davis and Hattrick*, (1912) V.L.R., 23; 33 A.L.T., 108; 17 A.L.R., 607. *Hood, J.* (1911).

Marriage Act 1890 (No. 1166), sec. 114—Divorce—Evidence de bene esse—Application for commission—Citation not served.]—In a suit for dissolution of marriage an examination *de bene esse* may be ordered prior to the service of the citation. *Vallentine* v. *Vallentine*, (1901) P., 283, followed. *Mackay* v. *Mackay*, (1910) V.L.R., 50; 31 A.L.T., 138; 16 A.L.R., 29. *Madden, C.J.*

(4) Particulars.

Divorce—Particulars—Inability of petitioner to supply better particulars—When better particulars may be dispensed with.]—Upon a summons for further and better particulars under a petition for dissolution of marriage, the petitioner swore that he was unable to give better particulars than those already given. *Held*, that, if the petitioner's proctor would file an affidavit, stating that after interviewing his witnesses he was unable to furnish better particulars, the summons would be dismissed. *Watt* v. *Watt*, 29 A.L.T., 198; 14 A.L.R., 43. *Cussen, J.* (1908).

(5) Summons, Service of.

No appearance by respondent—Service of summons by filing—Divorce Rules 1907, rr. 36, 38, 39, 59—Marriage Act 1890 (No. 1166), sec. 111.]—Where the husband respondent has not appeared in the suit, a summons to obtain an order that he pay into Court the sum fixed by the taxing officer for his wife's costs may be served by filing with the Prothonotary. *Farrer* v. *Farrer*, (1907) V.L.R., 382; 28 A.L.T., 221; 13 A.L.R., 236. *Cussen, J.*

(6) Other Points.

Marriage Act 1890 (No. 1166), sec. 126—Supreme Court Act 1890 (No. 1142), sec. 90—Evidence—Affidavits sworn outside Victoria—Judicial notice of signature.]—*See* EVIDENCE *Davis* v. *Davis and Hattrick*, (1912) V.L.R., 427; 34 A.L.T., 66; 18 A.L.R., 398.

Insolvency Act 1890 (No. 1102), sec. 96—Certificate of discharge—Effect of—Order or judgment in matrimonial cause—Insolvent, as co-respondent ordered to pay damages—Certificate subject to condition—Statutory

dividend.]—*See* INSOLVENCY. *In re Ware*, 34 A.L.T. (Supplement), 1 ; 18 A.L.R. (C.N.), 5.

(d) *Costs.*

(1) Generally.

Marriage Act 1890 (No. 1166), sec. 111——Petition by husband—No substance in wife's case— Counter-charges without reasonable basis—Wife's costs, how to be borne.]—In a suit for dissolution of marriage a wife will not be allowed her costs unless her case has substance and the costs have been reasonably incurred ; and if charges are presented which have no reasonable basis, the costs are treated as costs which are incurred at the risk of those who have incurred them. *Kay* v. *Kay*, (1904) P., 382, at p. 397, followed and applied. *Garrick* v. *Garrick* ; *Sutton, co-respondent*, (1908) V.L.R., 420 ; 30 A.L.T., 21 ; 14 A.L.R., 312. *Hood, J.*

Marriage Act 1890 (No. 1166), sec. 111—Wife's costs, how to be borne—Petition by husband on ground of adultery—Wife's denial withdrawn — Unfounded counter-charges against husband.]—In answer to a husband's petition for dissolution of marriage on the ground of his wife's adultery, the wife pleaded a denial of the adultery, and set up counter-charges of cruelty, connivance, and misconduct. The denial of the adultery was withdrawn shortly before the hearing of the petition, and the Court found that in face of the facts the counter-charges ought never to have been made, and certainly ought never to have been carried into Court. *Held*, that the wife's costs be not allowed, and that the £20 paid into Court by the petitioner under sec. 111 of the *Marriage Act* 1890 be returned to him or his proctor. *Garrick* v. *Garrick* ; *Sutton, co-respondent*, (1908) V.L.R., 420 ; 30 A.L.T., 21 ; 14 A.L.R., 312. *Hood, J.*

(2) Under Sec. 111 of the *Marriage Act* 1890.

Marriage Act 1890 (No. 1166), secs. 111—Divorce—Money for investigation of wife's case—" Merits of her case "—" Demerits of husband's case."]—A wife who is respondent in a suit for dissolution of marriage on the ground of adultery, is not entitled under sec. 111 of the *Marriage Act* 1890 to an order for the payment into Court by her husband, the petitioner, of a sum of money merely for the purpose of enabling her to have investigated by her proctor a countercharge of adultery which she intends to make against him in the suit. *Rackham* v. *Rackham* ; *Stokes, co-respondent*, (1913) V.L.R., 120 ; 34 A.L.T., 141 ; 18 A.L.R., 581. *Hodges, J.*

Marriage Act 1890 (No. 1166), sec. 111—Wife's costs— Sum fixed by taxing master on proctor's certificate—Order to pay sum so fixed into Court—Jurisdiction—No preliminary order as to investigation of merits of case.]—Where the wife's proctor, no order having been obtained with reference to having the merits of her case investigated, filed a certificate that she had a good cause of action on the merits, and the Taxing Master thereupon fixed the sum which was to be paid into Court, an order was made that the husband should forthwith pay such sum into Court. *Zanoni* v. *Zanoni*, 24 V.L.R., 940 ; 5 A.L.R., 206, and *Rickerby* v. *Rickerby*, 25 A.L.T., 95 ; 10 A.L.R., 30, followed. *Farrer* v. *Farrer*, (1907) V.L.R., 382 ; 28 A.L.T., 221 ; 13 A.L.R., 236. *Cussen, J.*

Marriage Act 1890 (No. 1166), secs. 111, 118—Divorce—Wife's costs—No order for Preliminary Investigation costs—Suit by husband in Forma Pauperis—Payment into Court of wife's costs—Jurisdiction to order.]—Under sec. 111 of the *Marriage Act* 1890 an order may be made for payment into Court by a husband of the sum fixed by the Taxing Master as the amount of the wife's costs, although no order has been obtained for payment by him of money to enable her to have her case investigated. Under that section a husband who has been granted leave under sec. 118 to sue in *forma pauperis* may be ordered to pay into Court the sum so fixed. *Howard* v. *Howard*, (1913) V.L.R., 46 ; 34 A.L.T., 116 ; 18 A.L.R., 528. *a' Beckett, J.*

Divorce—Practice—Application for investigation money—Time for making—Answer already filed by wife respondent—Marriage Act 1890 (No. 1166), sec. 111.]—An order, that the husband, petitioner, shall pay into

Court a sum of money for the investigation of the respondent's case, may be made after the respondent has filed her answer; but the application should be made promptly, and before any further steps are taken. *Goodman* v. *Goodman*, (1906) V.L.R., 671; 28 A.L.T., 122; 12 A.L.R., 548. *Hodges, J.*

Marriage Act 1890 (No. 1166), sec. 111— Costs of preliminary investigation—Application after investigation made—Whether too late.]—An application by the respondent for the costs of having the merits of her case investigated is too late if made after the work of investigation has been done. *Wilson* v. *Wilson*, 17 A.L.T., 154; and *Vogt* v. *Vogt*, 25 V.L.R., 283; 21 A.L.T., 109; 5 A.L.R. (C.N.), 77, followed. *Kidd* v. *Kidd*, (1908) V.L.R., 409; 30 A.L.T., 29; 14 A.L.R., 274. *Hood, J.*

Marriage Act 1890 (No. 1166), sec. 111— Costs of investigating case of wife—Time for making application—Petition by wife—Respondent's answer filed—Case already investigated.]—An application, in a suit in which the wife is petitioner, for an order under sec. 111 of the *Marriage Act* 1890 for payment into Court of a sum of money sufficient to enable her to have the merits of her case investigated, is not too late, although made after the respondent has filed his answer. But no order will be made, if, prior to such application, an investigation of the merits of the petitioner's case has been made by her proctor. *Ruddell* v. *Ruddell*, (1911) V.L.R., 277; 33 A.L.T., 10; 17 A.L.R., 276. *Cussen, J.* (1911).

Marriage Act 1890 (No. 1166), sec. 111— Wife respondent not appearing at trial—Order that £20 paid into Court be paid out to wife's proctor.]—Where, under sec. 111 of the *Marriage Act* 1890, the sum of £20 had been paid into Court, but the wife respondent did not appear at the trial, the money was ordered to be paid out to the wife's proctor on account of his costs for preparing her defence. *Montgomery* v. *Montgomery and Andrews*, 12 A.L.R. (C.N.), 1. *Madden, C.J.* (1906).

Marriage Act 1890 (No. 1166), sec. 111— Order for payment into Court of wife's costs—

Failure to obey order—Stay of proceedings— Jurisdiction.]—Whether an order will be made staying all proceedings in a suit for dissolution of marriage until the husband who is petitioner therein shall have paid into Court the sum fixed by the Taxing Master under sec. 111 for the wife's costs is a matter of discretion. Where proceedings in a suit by a husband against his wife for dissolution of marriage had been stayed until payment into Court of the respondent's costs under sec. 111, and the petitioner subsequently instituted in *forma pauperis* another suit on the same ground, the petitioner was ordered in the latter suit to pay into Court the sum of £20 for the respondent's costs, but, in view of the circumstances of the case, the hearing of this suit was not to be stayed pending payment into Court under this order or by reason of the order made in the previous suit. *Howard* v. *Howard*, (1913) V.L.R., 46; 34 A.L.T., 116; 18 A.L.R., 528. *a' Beckett, J.*

(e) *Alimony and Allowance to Wife.*

Divorce—Alimony pendente lite—Deed of separation containing covenant by wife not to require payment for her maintenance and support—Petition by wife for dissolution of marriage.]—A covenant by a wife in a deed of separation that she will not require or by any means whatsoever endeavour to compel her husband to pay any money for her maintenance and support is a bar to her claim for alimony *pendente lite* in a suit by her for dissolution of marriage. *Brooker* v. *Brooker*, (1910) V.L.R., 488; 32 A.L.T., 108; 16 A.L.R., 580. *Cussen, J.*

Marriage Act 1890 (No. 1166), sec. 87— Alimony pendente lite, amount of—Separation deed providing for payment of weekly sum to wife.]—Where the petitioner and his wife had at the commencement of a suit for dissolution of marriage been living apart under a deed of separation, an order was made, on her application for alimony *pendente lite* under sec. 87 of the *Marriage Act* 1890, fixing the amount of such alimony at the amount of the weekly sum agreed by him to be paid for her maintenance under the deed. *Rackham* v. *Rackham*; *Stokes, co-*

respondent, (1913) V.L.R., 120 ; 34 A.L.T., 141 ; 18 A.L.R., 581. *Hodges, J.*

Judicial separation—Suit for—Deed of separation—Covenants—Dum casta clause—Maintenance clause—Duration of allowance to wife.]—Although the Court has a discretion with regard to the insertion of a *dum casta* clause in deeds of separation between husband and wife, such a clause should be inserted as a matter of course in all cases. *Wood* v. *Wood*, (1891) P., 272, distinguished. Where a deed of separation is agreed to be executed in proceedings for judicial separation sought by a wife the husband's covenant to pay an allowance to her should be limited in such deed to the joint lives of the husband and wife. *Woods* v. *Woods*, (1913) V.L.R., 39 ; 34 A.L.T., 104 ; 18 A.L.R., 460. *a'Beckett, J.*

Marriage Act 1890 (No. 1166), sec. 88—Divorce and Matrimonial Rules 1906, r. 86—Permanent alimony—Application to vary amount.]—Where the Court in granting a decree of dissolution of marriage has made an order on the husband for payment of permanent alimony to the wife, an application by the husband for the reduction of the amount of such alimony will not be granted unless he shows that, after making all proper allowances for the living expenses of himself and his family and for the cost of carrying on his business, he is unable to obey the order. *Naylor* v. *Naylor*, (1912) V.L.R., 430 ; 34 A.L.T., 122 ; 18 A.L.R., 459. *Hood, J.*

Divorce—Practice—Alimony—No claim for alimony in petition—Service of summons for alimony after decree nisi—Retainer of respondent's proctor.]—After a decree *nisi* for dissolution of marriage has been granted on the petition of a wife, which contains no claim for alimony, the proctor who was retained by the respondent to defend the suit has no authority by virtue of such retainer, to accept service of a summons asking for an order that the respondent pay alimony to the petitioner. *Richardson* v. *Richardson*, (1909) V.L.R., 448 ; 31 A.L.T., 66 ; 15 A.L.R., 515. *Hood, J.*

III.—PROPERTY, RIGHTS RELATING TO.
(a) Generally.

Husband and wife—Agency—Destitute wife—Sale of husband's goods to purchase necessaries—Wife's authority.]—Where a wife has been left by her husband without the necessaries of life and without means of support, she is not at liberty to sell his goods for the purpose of providing herself with necessaries ; and therefore she cannot give a good title to goods of her husband sold by her under such circumstances and for such purpose. *Moreno* v. *Slinn*, (1910) V.L.R., 457 ; 32 A.L.T., 66 ; 16 A.L.R., 503. *Madden, C.J.*

Married Women's Property Act 1890 (No. 1116), sec. 13—Insolvency Act 1890 (No. 1102), sec. 70 (v.)—Insolvent's property divisible among creditors—Gift by husband to wife—" Reputed owner."]—Where a husband and wife, living together, have been, prior to and at the date of the sequestration of his estate, in joint possession of goods which had been given by him to her, he is not deemed to be the " reputed owner " of such goods within the meaning of sec. 70 (v.) of the *Insolvency Act* 1890, if he has not been in possession of them in such a manner that he might have been able to obtain false or delusive credit. *In re Mitchell,* 31 A.L.T. (Supplement), 7 ; 15 A.L.R. (C.N.), 18. *Judge Moule* (1909).

Husband and wife—Marriage settlement—Restraint on anticipation—Second marriage—Revival of restraint.]—*See* MARRIED WOMAN; *Trustees Executors and Agency Co. Ltd.* v. *Webster*, (1907) V.L.R., 318 ; 28 A.L.T., 225 ; 13 A.L.R., 188.

Will — Construction — Gift — Limitation—Condition subsequent—Wife living apart from husband.]—*See* WILL. *In re Anderson* ; *Longstaff* v. *Anderson*, (1908) V.L.R., 593 ; 30 A.L.T., 30 ; 14 A.L.R., 412.

Evidence—Burden of proof—Husband and wife living in same house—Wife tenant of the house—Possession of goods in the house—Possession prima facie evidence of title.]—*See* EVIDENCE. *McKenzie* v. *Balchin* ; *Mc-*

Kenzie, Claimant, (1908) V.L.R., 324; 29 A.L.T., 246; 14 A.L.R., 238.

(b) *Interest of Survivor in Estate of Deceased Spouse.*

(1) Upon Intestacy.

Married Women's Property Act 1890 (No. 1116), sec. 25—Intestates' Estate Act 1896 (No. 1419)—Married woman—Intestacy—Estate less than £1,000—No issue—Rights of husband and next-of-kin.]—The *Intestate Estates' Act* 1896, which provides that the widow of a man who dies intestate, without issue, leaving an estate of the net value of not more than £1,000 shall be entitled to the whole of such estate and if the net value exceed £1,000 that she shall be entitled to £1,000 of it and to a charge over the whole estate for such sum, is not a law which makes an alteration of the law as to the manner and proportions in which the estate real and personal as to which a married man dies intestate is distributable between his widow and his children or next-of-kin within the meaning of sec. 25 of the *Married Women's Property Act* 1890. *Quaere,* whether that section incorporates future alterations of the law as to distribution. *Held,* therefore, that the estate of a married woman, who died intestate without issue, leaving her surviving her husband and next-of-kin, the value of the estate not exceeding £1,000, was distributable one-half to the husband and one half to the next of kin. *In re Jamieson ; Jamieson v. Christensen,* 4 C.L.R., 1489; 13 A.L.R., 566. H.C., *Griffith, C.J., Barton, O'Connor* and *Higgins, JJ.* (1907).

(2) Under *Widows and Young Children Maintenance Act.*

Widows and Young Children Maintenance Act 1906 (No. 2074), secs. 3, 9—Widow's maintenance—Application for further provision—Widow's interest under testator's will—Limit on amount of provision.]—Where a testator has by his will given to his widow more than the income or interest on such portion of his estate as she would have been entitled to had he died intestate, the Court has no power under the *Widows and Young Children Maintenance Act* 1906 to order any further provision to be made for her out of the estate in or towards her maintenance and support. *In re Maslin,* (1908) V.L.R., 641; 30 A.L.T., 70; 14 A.L.R., 499. *Hodges, J.*

Widows and Young Children Maintenance Act 1906 (No. 2074)—Purpose of Act—Capricious and unreasonable testamentary dispositions.]—See WIDOWS AND YOUNG CHILDREN MAINTENANCE ACT. *In re McGoun,* (1910) V.L.R., 153; 31 A.L.T., 193; 16 A.L.R., 141.

Widows and Young Children Maintenance Act 1906 (No. 2074), sec. 3—Disposition of property by will—Widow and children left without sufficient means for maintenance—Provision for maintenance by order of Court—Discretion, how exercised.]—See WIDOWS AND YOUNG CHILDREN MAINTENANCE ACT. *In re Read,* (1910) V.L.R., 68; 31 A.L.T., 154; 16 A.L.R., 60.

Widows and Young Children Maintenance Act 1906 (No. 2074), sec. 3—Disposition of property by will—Provision for widow and children—Sufficient means for their maintenance and support, what are.]—See WIDOWS AND YOUNG CHILDREN MAINTENANCE ACT. *In re Read,* (1910) V.L.R., 68; 31 A.L.T., 154; 16 A.L.R., 60.

Widows and Young Children Maintenance Act 1906 (No. 2074), secs. 3, 9—Insufficient provision by testator for maintenance of widow—Application by widow for further allowance—Limit of amount of provision Court may allow.]—See WIDOWS AND YOUNG CHILDREN MAINTENANCE ACT. *In re Bennett,* (1909) V.L.R., 205; 30 A.L.T., 181; 15 A.L.R., 141.

Widows and Young Children Maintenance Act 1906 (No. 2074), secs. 3, 8, 9 (5)—Maintenance—Application by widow—Husband and wife separated—Misconduct of wife—Widow left destitute.]—See WIDOWS AND YOUNG CHILDREN MAINTENANCE ACT. *In re McGoun,* (1910) V.L.R., 153; 31 A.L.T., 193; 16 A.L.R., 141.

Widows and Young Children Maintenance Act 1906 (No. 2047), secs. 3, 7, 8 (2)—Maintenance—Application by widow—Order mak-

ing provision for widow assignable—Small estate.]—*See* WIDOWS AND YOUNG CHILDREN MAINTENANCE ACT. *In re Mailes,* (1908) V.L.R., 269 ; 29 A.L.T., 263 ; 14 A.L.R., 181.

IV.—MAINTENANCE ; CONFINEMENT EXPENSES.

See also, MAINTENANCE AND MAINTENANCE ORDERS.

Maintenance of destitute and deserted wives—" Desertion "—" Leaving without means of support "—Wife compelled by husband's conduct to leave matrimonial home—Marriage Act 1890 (No. 1166), secs. 42, 43.]— Where a wife has been forced by her husband's violence or by his threats of violence to leave his house and for the safety of her life to live elsewhere, if he does not provide her with maintenance and she is in fact without means of support, he " leaves her without means of support " within the meaning of sec. 42 of the *Marriage Act* 1890. " Desertion " in Part IV. of the Act means going away from his wife or children, or where he does not go away from them, leaving them without means of support. *Regina* v. *Collins, Ex parte Collins,* 7 V.L.R. (L.), 74 ; 2 A.L.T., 118, followed ; *Chantler* v. *Chantler,* 4 C.L.R., 585 ; 13 A.L.R., 540, discussed. *Ross* v. *Ross,* (1909) V.L.R., 318 ; 30 A.L.T., 220 ; 15 A.L.R., 305. *Madden, C.J.*

Marriage Act 1890 (No. 1166), secs. 42, 43—Maintenance of deserted wives—Leaving wife without means of support—Wife leaving husband of her own accord.]— Where a woman of her own accord and without legal justification, has left her husband, she cannot afterwards summon him for leaving her without means of support unless she has in the meantime, by a sincere and *bona fide* offer to return to him, put an end to the position which she herself has created. *Male* v. *Male,* (1912) V.L.R., 455 ; 34 A.L.T., 123 ; 18 A.L.R., 582. *Cussen, J.*

Marriage Act 1890 (No. 1166), secs. 42, 43—Wife compelled by husband's conduct to leave matrimonial home—Husband and wife residing in different bailiwicks—Order made against husband in bailiwick where wife resides—Jurisdiction of Justices.—*See* MAINTENANCE AND MAINTENANCE ORDERS. *Ross* v. *Ross,* (1909) V.L.R., 318 ; 30 A.L.T., 220 ; 15 A.L.R., 305.

V.—CUSTODY OF CHILDREN.

Marriage Act 1900 (No. 1684), secs. 4, 5—Confinement expenses—Wife voluntarily leaving husband, whether entitled to.]— Although a wife has voluntarily left her husband, an order may be made against him for payment of her confinement expenses upon her application therefor under the *Marriage Act* 1900. *Ruddell* v. *Ruddell,* (1912) V.L.R., 221 ; 34 A.L.T., 4 ; 18 A.L.R., 200. *Hodges, J.*

Infant, custody of—Infant a girl of three years of age in custody of mother—Mother a fit person—Right of father—Welfare of child—Marriage Act 1890 (No. 1166), secs. 31, 33.] *See* INFANT. *Moule* v. *Moule,* (1911) 13 C.L.R., 267 ; 17 A.L.R., 446.

Infant, custody of—Right to custody, how determined—Welfare of child, importance of—Marriage Act 1890 (No. 1166), secs. 31, 33.]— *See* INFANT. *Moule* v. *Moule,* (1911) 13 C.L.R., 267 ; 17 A.L.R., 446.

VI.—CRIMINAL LIABILITY OF HUSBAND.

Marriage Act 1901 (No. 1737), sec. 3—Criminal law—Desertion of wife—Leaving her without adequate means of support—Meaning of " adequate."—*See* CRIMINAL LAW, cols. 345, 346. *Rex* v. *Mackie,* (1908) V.L.R., 689 ; 30 A.L.T., 60 ; 14 A.L.R., 488.

Evidence—Wife, whether competent witness against husband—Wife desertion—Neglect to comply with order for maintenance—Marriage Act 1901 (No. 1737), secs. 3, 4—Crimes Act 1891 (No. 1231), sec. 34.]— The prisoner's wife is a competent witness against him on an indictment for wife desertion under sec. 3 (1) (*a*) of the *Marriage Act* 1901, but not on an indictment for wilfully neglecting to comply with an order for maintenance under section 4 of that Act. *Rex* v. *Jacano,* (1911) V.L.R., 326 ; 33 A.L.T., 28 ; 17 A.L.R., 340. F.C., *Madden, C.J., Hodges* and *Hood, JJ.* (1911).

ILLEGITIMACY.

See EVIDENCE; MAINTENANCE AND MAINTENANCE ORDERS.

IMMIGRATION RESTRICTION ACTS.

Prohibited immigrant—Infant—Domicile of father in Australia—Immigration Restriction Act 1905 (No. 17 of 1905), sec. 4—Immigration Restriction Act 1901 (No. 17 of 1901), sec. 3.] The fact that the father of an infant, born out of Australia, and who has never been in Australia, is domiciled in Australia is irrelevant to the question whether such infant on coming to Australia is a prohibited immigrant within the meaning of the Immigration Restriction Acts 1901-1905. *Ah Yin* v. *Christie,* 4 C.L.R., 1428; 13 A.L.R., 372. H.C., *Griffith, C.J., Barton, Isaacs* and *Higgins, JJ.* (1907).

Immigration Restriction Act 1901 (No. 17 of 1901)—Prohibited immigrant—Application of Act to Australian citizen—Commonwealth Constitution, sec. 51.]—*Semble.*—There is no Australian nationality, as distinguished from British nationality, so as to limit the power of the Commonwealth under sec. 51 of the constitution to exclude persons from Australia. *Quaere,* whether the power of the Parliament under sec. 51 to deal with "immigration" extends to the case of Australians absent from Australia on a visit *animo revertendi. Attorney-General for Commonwealth* v. *Ah Sheung,* (1907) 4 C.L.R., 949. H.C. *Griffith, C.J., Barton* and *O'Connor, JJ.*

The Constitution (63 & 64 Vict. c. 12), sec. 51 (xxvii.)—"Immigrant," meaning of—Member of Australian community returning from abroad.]—A person whose permanent home is Australia and who, therefore, is a member of the Australian community, is not, on arriving in Australia from abroad, an immigrant in respect of whose entry the Parliament of the Commonwealth can legislate under the power conferred by sec. 51 (xxvii.) of the Constitution to make laws with respect to immigration, and, therefore, such a person is not an immigrant within the meaning of the Immigration Restriction Acts 1901-1905. *Potter* v. *Minahan,* (1908) 7 C.L.R., 277; 14 A.L.R., 635. H.C., *Griffith, C.J., Barton, O'Connor, Isaacs* and *Higgins, JJ.*

Immigration Restriction Acts 1901-1905 Original home in State of Victoria—Residence in China for many years—Whether original Victorian home abandoned.]—*Held,* on the evidence (*per Griffith, C.J., Barton* and *O'Connor, Isaacs* and *Higgins, JJ.,* dissenting), that the illegitimate son of a Victorian woman who had his original home in Victoria, but at the age of five was taken by his father, a Chinese, to China, where he remained for 26 years, had never abandoned that home, and, therefore, on his return to Australia was not an immigrant within the Immigration Restriction Acts 1901-1905. *Potter* v. *Minahan,* (1908) 7 C.L.R., 277; 14 A.L.R., 635.

Immigration Restriction Acts 1901-1905— "Immigrant," meaning of—Naturalised subject domiciled in Victoria—Return to Victoria from China.]—A Chinese came to Victoria in 1881, and obtained in 1883 letters of naturalisation under the *Aliens Statute* 1865, and thereupon became and continued to be a domiciled Victorian subject of the reigning sovereign. Prior to 1901 he made two visits to China, and on each occasion returned to Victoria, and was admitted without objection, and was in Victoria at the date of Federation. In 1901 he again went to China and remained there until early in 1906. At the end of March, 1906, he returned to Victoria in the steamship *Tsinan,* when the Commonwealth authorities required him to submit to the dictation. He failed to pass and was detained by the Captain of the *Tsinan.* Upon a return to a writ of *habeas corpus* directed to the Captain. *Held,* that the applicant was not an "immigrant" within the meaning of the *Immigration Restriction Acts* 1901-1905. *Chia Gee* v. *Martin,* 3 C.L.R., 649; 12 A.L.R., 425, discussed and distinguished. *Ah Sheung* v. *Lindberg,* (1906) V.L.R., 323; 27 A.L.T., 189; *sub-nom., Rex* v. *Ah Sheung,* 12 A.L.R., 190. *Cussen, J.* (1906).

Immigration Restriction Acts 1901-1905—Habeas corpus—Return, sufficiency of—Allegations of law—Allegation of fact of failure to pass dictation test—No facts alleged to show that person detained was subject to the Acts.]—To a writ of *habeas corpus*, commanding Charles Lindberg, Captain of the steamship *Tsinan*, then at the River Yarra in the State of Victoria, to have the body of one Ah Sheung before a Judge of the Supreme Court, together with the cause of his being taken and detained, the said Charles Lindberg made the following return :—" The said Ah Sheung was a prohibited immigrant within the meaning of the Immigration Restriction Acts 1901-1905, inasmuch as he was and is a person who on the 28th day of March, 1906, failed to pass the dictation test, within the meaning of and as required by the said Acts, and, as master of the steamship *Tsinan*, I was liable to a penalty of one hundred pounds if the said Ah Sheung, being a prohibited immigrant, entered the Commonwealth, contrary to the said Acts, and I was authorised and required by the said Acts to prevent and did prevent the said Ah Sheung as such prohibited immigrant, from entering the Commonweaith from the said vessel." *Held*, that the return was bad, inasmuch as it failed to allege facts showing that Ah Sheung was a person to whom the Acts applied. *Ah Sheung* v. *Lindberg*, (1906) V.L.R., 323 ; 27 A.L.T., 189 ; *sub nom.*, *Rex* v. *Ah Sheung*, 12 A.L.R., 190. *Cussen, J.* (1906).

Immigration Restriction Acts 1901-1905—" Immigrants " and " prohibited immigrants," who are—Whether administrative officers of the Commonwealth may determine such questions.]—For a discussion of the question whether the officers administering the Immigration Restriction Acts are the final arbiters as to who are, and who are not, " immigrants " or " prohibited immigrants," *see Ah Sheung* v. *Lindberg*, (1906) V.L.R., 323 ; 27 A.L.T., 189 ; *sub nom.*, *Rex* v. *Ah Sheung*, 12 A.L.R., 190. *Cussen, J.* (1906).

Immigration Restriction Act 1901 (No. 17 of 1901), secs. 3 (a), (k), 5 (1), (2), 7—" Evading " an officer—Member of crew deserting ship and not present at muster before ship permitted to clear out.]—A member of the crew of a vessel not being a public vessel of any Government who in a port of the Commonwealth deserts that vessel and is absent from a muster of the crew made under sec. 3 (*k*) of the *Immigration Restriction Act* 1901 is an immigrant who has evaded an officer within the meaning of sec. 5 of that Act. *Lin Wan Quai* v. *Christie*, (1906) 3 C.L.R., 1125 ; 12 A.L.R., 429. H.C., *Griffith, C.J.*, *Barton* and *O'Connor, JJ.*

Immigration Restriction Act 1901 (No. 17 of 1901), sec. 3—Immigration Restriction Act 1905 (No. 17 of 1905), secs. 4, 8—Dictation test, how to be applied.]—An officer of Customs intending to put the dictation test to the defendant as provided by sec. 3 (*a*) of the *Immigration Restriction Act* 1901 (as amended by sec. 4 of the *Immigration Restriction Act* 1905) told him he would read the passage slowly and then if the defendant said he could write it, he, the officer, would read it again slowly. The officer then read the passage slowly, the defendant said he could not write it, the passage was not read again, and the officer told the defendant he was a prohibited immigrant. *Held* (by *O'Connor, Isaacs* and *Higgins, JJ.*), that the dictation test was not properly put so as to make the defendant a prohibited immigrant *Potter* v. *Minehan*, (1908) 7 C.L.R., 277 ; 14 A.L.R., 635.

Supreme Court—Jurisdiction—Habeas corpus—Applicant held under restraint under authority of Commonwealth—Immigration Restriction Amendment Act 1905 (No. 17), sec. 14 (13b)—Judiciary Act 1903 (No. 6), Part VI.]—The Supreme Court has jurisdiction by way of *habeas corpus* to inquire into the validity of the restraint by the respondent of the applicant, although the respondent exercised such restraint under the authority, or color of authority, of the Commonwealth. *Ah Sheung* v. *Lindberg*, (1996) V.L.R., 323 ; 27 A.L.T., 189 ; *sub nom.*, *Rex* v. *Ah Sheung*, 12 A.L.R., 190. *Cussen, J.* (1906).

Res judicata—Judgment—Finding of fact, whether conclusive in other proceedings against another party—Finding of fact as to

status—Prohibited immigrant—Immigration Restriction Act 1901 (No. 17).]—One Ah Sheung was charged, upon the information of C., an officer of Customs, with being a prohibited immigrant, and he set up the defence that he was a naturalised subject of the King in Victoria. C. admitted that there was a naturalised subject of the King in Victoria named Ah Sheung, but disputed the identity of the accused with that person. In support of the defence a judgment of the Supreme Court—in proceedings by way of writ of *habeas corpus* issued at the instance of Ah Sheung and directed to the master of the ship by which Ah Sheung came to the Commonwealth, who had claimed to detain Ah Sheung as a prohibited immigrant, and under the authority of the *Immigration Restriction Act*—was tendered and admitted in evidence by which it appeared that the Court had found as a fact that Ah Sheung was identical with the Ah Sheung who was admittedly a naturalised subject of the King in Victoria. *Held*, that the judgment was not admissible in evidence upon the question of fact of the identity of Ah Sheung. *Christie* v. *Ah Sheung*, (1906) 3 C.L.R., 998 ; 12 A.L.R., 432. H.C., *Griffith, C.J., Barton* and *O'Connor, JJ.*

IMPERIAL LAW.

See GAMING AND WAGERING ; SUN-DAY.

IMPOUNDING.

See POUNDS AND IMPOUNDING.

IMPRISONMENT OF FRAUDULENT DEBTORS ACT.

See DEBTORS ACT.

INCOME.

See TENANT FOR LIFE AND RE-MAINDERMAN ; TRUSTS AND TRUSTEES ; WILL.

INCOME TAX ACTS.

I.—TAXABLE INCOME, WHAT IS.

(a) *Generally.*

Income tax—Profits of company, what are —Assets taken over for realization—Valuation of assets—Decrease in value—Reduction of capital—Surplus above valuation on realization—Income Tax Act 1903 (No. 1819), sec. 9.] The A. company was formed for the purpose of carrying on the business of banking and also to take over, for a certain price paid in cash shares and deposit receipts, and realize the assets of another company consisting of debts owing to it and real estate held as security therefor. The amount of the price paid was the total amount of the debts so owing. The capital of the A. company was in 1905 reduced pursuant to the *Companies Act* 1896 by a sum representing the difference between the price paid for the assets and their estimated value in 1904. Subsequently to the reduction of the capital certain of the assets were realized, some of them for sums less than the values placed on them in 1904, others for greater sums, but all for sums less than the amount of the debts for which they were securities, with the result that in each of the years 1905, 1906 and 1907 the total amount obtained by realization was greater than the total valuation in 1904 of the properties realized. By certain of the original articles of association provision was made for keeping an account of the realization of these assets, for charging against the sum realized the price paid for the assets, and for placing to the credit of the reserve fund any sum realized beyond that price. On the reduction of capital these articles were replaced by an article providing that all surpluses over the paid up capital so reduced which might arise on realization should be carried to the credit of the reserve fund. Another of the

22

original articles provided that the reserve fund might be encroached upon for the purpose of equalizing dividends. *Held*, that the surpluses of realization in 1905, 1906, and 1907 were not "profits" within the meaning of section 9 of the *Income Tax Act* 1903 and were not chargeable with income tax. *Webb* v. *Australian Deposit and Mortgage Bank Ltd.*, (1910) 11 C.L.R., 223; 16 A.L.R., 446. H.C. *Griffith*, *C.J.*, *O'Connor*, *Isaacs* and *Higgins*, *JJ.*

Income Tax—Company formed to realize assets—Profits of company—Income Tax Act 1903 (No. 1819), sec. 9 (1).]—The respondents were a company formed in 1903 to take over, nurse, develop and realize the assets of three other companies, which had taken over and partially realized and distributed the respective assets of three Australian banks in liquidation. Payment was made for the assets by the allotment to the three companies of debenture stock and paid up shares in the respondent company, the amounts allotted being in accordance with the values of the assets in the books of the three companies. The respondents from time to time sold a large part of the assets, including assets in Victoria, at prices which showed a surplus over the purchase prices. By October 1909 they had paid off or bought in the market partly below the face value), the whole of the debenture stock; in May 1910 they paid a bonus of 6d. per share to the shareholders, and in August 1910 they distributed debenture stock at the rate of 3s. 4d. per share. The articles of association provided that no dividends should be paid except out of profits. The *Income Tax Act* 1903, section 9 (1) provides that "so far as regards any company liable to pay tax, the income thereof chargeable with tax shall . . . be the profits earned in or derived from Victoria by such Company during the year immediately preceding the year of assessment. *Held*, that the surplus realized by the respondents over the purchase prices paid for the assets sold, after making all just deductions, was profit taxable as income in the following year; (2) that the respondents were entitled to hold in suspense part of the surplus

realized to meet possible losses on other assets, and that under the circumstances the profit was earned, for the purposes of the Act, when distributed to the shareholders; (3) that the amount of the bonus and the pecuniary value of the debenture stock distributed, so far as they were earned in or derived from Victoria, were taxable as profits under the above Act. *Commissioner of Taxes* v. *Melbourne Trust Ltd.*, (1914) A.C., 1001.

Income Tax Act 1903 (No. 1819), sec. 9—Company—Registered in Victoria—Purchase and sale of land in New South Wales on behalf of company to be formed—Transactions of company in Victoria—Profit, whether earned in Victoria—Re-sales of land by promoter of Company—Contracts taken over by company—Purchase moneys payable by instalments—Taxation on sums not yet received.]—On the 15th April 1903, M. by a contract made in Victoria purchased from W. on behalf of a projected company an estate situated in New South Wales. M. made payments of the purchase money and before the 20th April 1904 subdivided the estate and re-sold a great portion of it in lots. The purchase moneys on the re-sales was payable by instalments extending over several years. On the 20th April 1904 the Company was incorporated in Victoria with its registered office in Melbourne. On the 21st April 1904 M. by deed assigned to the Company all his rights and obligations as purchaser from W. On the 1st July 1904 M. by deed assigned to the company all his rights and obligations as vendor of the lots sold by him. In both deeds it was recited that M. had acted as trustee for the Company then in course of formation. The company sold the balance of the estate in lots upon similar terms as to payment of the purchase money by instalments. With one exception all the contracts relating to the re-sales, whether made by M. or the Company, were entered into in New South Wales. The purchase moneys in connection with the re-sales were mostly paid at the estate, but sometimes by cheque posted to the Company in Melbourne, and in every case were banked in the Company's account which was kept at Melbourne. The sole business of the company was the purchase and re-sale of the estate. The only meeting of shareholders took place in Melbourne. The deeds of 21st April 1904 and 1st July 1904 were both executed in Melbourne. There were no regular meetings of the directors, but any consultations between them took place in Melbourne. The difference between the price at which the company bought the estate and that obtained for it on re-sale gave a net profit of £19,000. *Held*, (1) that this sum was taxable as income earned by the company in Victoria ; (2) that the fact, that all the moneys due to the Company in respect of re-sales had not been paid, was immaterial. *In re Income Tax Acts ; Ex parte Quat Quatta Co.*, (1907) V.L.R., 54 ; 28 A.L.T., 100 ; 12 A.L.R., 526. F.C. *a' Beckett*, A.C.J., *Hodges* and *Chomley*, JJ.

Income Tax Act 1895 (No. 1374), sec. 9 (1), (14)—" **Dividends or profits or part of capital credited to any member or shareholder of any company** "—**Mining company**—**Proceeds of sale of land**—**Dividends payable out of profits only**—" **Outgoings,** " **what may be deducted.**]—The taxpayer was a shareholder in a company formed in the year 1881 registered under the *Mining Companies Act* 1871. The objects of the company were as follows : —To purchase a certain freehold estate in Victoria ; to purchase lease or acquire lands in Victoria together with mining and other rights benefits and advantages appertaining thereto ; the letting and selling of such lands ; the granting of licences and leases of any of such lands for mining purposes ; and the carrying on of the business of a mining company. The articles of association prohibited the company from paying dividends except out of profits. The nominal capital of the company was £200,000 in 10,000 shares of £20 each but the sum of £10,000 only was subscribed and this sum was paid as part of the purchase money of the said estate. The company made very large profits out of which £20,000 the balance of the purchase money for the said estate was paid and dividends amounting to over £300,000 were up to December 1901 distributed among the

shareholders. In 1901 the Company sold portion of the said estate for £43,175, and the cash payment made by the purchasers, viz., £8,653 was distributed by way of dividends to the shareholders the tax-payers share being £3,375. *Held*, that the said sum of £3,375 was by virtue of section 9 (14) of the *Income Tax Act* 1895 part of the income of the tax-payer. *Held*, also, that the tax-payer having received back by way of dividends all the capital contributed by him towards the purchase of his capital interest in the Company, including the land in question, nothing was to be deducted under section 9 (1) of the Act. *In re Income Tax Acts*, 28 V.L.R., 203 ; 24 A.L.T., 38 ; 8 A.L.R., 157, approved. *In re Income Tax Acts ; The Seven Hills Estate Company's Case*, (1906) V.L.R., 225 ; 27 A.L.T., 175 ; 12 A.L.R., 188. F.C. *Holroyd*, A.C.J., *a' Beckett* and *Hodges*, JJ. (1906).

Income Tax Act 1903 (No. 1819), sec. 9 (1) —" **Profits** " **of company, what are**—**Mutual benefit association incorporated as a company** —**Profits from club established for benefit of members and other persons**—**Subscriptions by members to benefit funds**—**Interest on investment of benefit funds**—**Income Tax Act 1895 (No. 1374), secs. 2, 7 (e)**—**Companies Act 1890 (No. 1074), sec. 181.**]—The tax-payer was an association registered under the *Companies Act* 1890 whose main object was the promotion of the welfare of persons carrying on a certain specified business, which was achieved by the establishment of an ordinary club to which persons other than members of the association (called club members) might belong, and also by the establishment of certain benefit funds participation in which was confined to members of the association and their families. By the rules of the association its clear net profits for each financial year were to be paid into the benefit funds, and in addition a fixed part of the subscriptions of the members of the association was to be paid into such funds. *Held*, that income tax was payable on the whole of the profits of the tax-payer ; that not only should the profits of the club be included, but that in estimating the profits the entrance fees and subscriptions of the members of the association, and all moneys received by the tax-payer by way of interest from the investment of the capital of its benefit funds should also be taken into consideration. *In re Income Tax Acts*, (1907) V.L.R., 185 ; 28 A.L.T., 168 ; 13 A.L.R., 31. F.C. *Hood, Cussen* and *Chomley, JJ.*

Income Tax Act 1903 (No. 1819), sec. 9—Companies Act 1896 (No. 1482), sec. 88—Profits of company—Reduction of capital—Receipts in excess of amount of reduced capital—Whether such receipts may be capital.]—The fact of the reduction of the capital of a company, pursuant to section 88 of the *Companies Act* 1896, is not by itself decisive of the question of what are the profits of the company for the purposes of the *Income Tax Acts*. Receipts beyond the honestly estimated value of assets representing the reduced amount of capital may for such purposes be capital moneys and not profits. *Webb* v. *Australian Deposit and Mortgage Bank Ltd.*, (1910) 11 C.L.R., 223 ; 16 A.L.R., 446. H.C. *Griffith, C.J., O'Connor, Isaacs* and *Higgins, JJ.*

Company — Income tax — " Profits " of company, what are—Income Tax Act 1903 (No. 1819), sec. 9.]—Sec. 9 of the *Income Tax Act* 1903 has not the effect of rendering taxable as income profits of a company which would not be income in the ordinary sense of that term. *Webb* v. *Australian Deposit and Mortgage Bank Ltd.*, (1910) 11 C.L.R., 223 ; 16 A.L.R., 446. H.C., *Griffith, C.J., O'Connor, Isaacs* and *Higgins, JJ.*

Income Tax Act 1903 (No. 1819), sec. 9 (1), (2)—Whether tax payable by trading company only—" Profits," meaning of—Income Tax Act 1895 (No. 1374), secs. 2, 7 (e).]—The use of the word " profits " in sec. 9 (1) of the *Income Tax Act* 1903 does not confine the payment of income tax to trading companies only. *Quaere*, whether the profits referred to in the section are those from which dividends might legally be payable. *In re Income Tax Acts*, (1907) V.L.R., 185 ; 28 A.L.T., 168 ; 13 A.L.R., 31. F.C., *Hood, Cussen* and *Chomley, JJ.*

Income Tax Act 1903 (No. 1819), sec. 11 (1)—Companies Act 1890 (No. 1074), sec. 334—Income of life assurance company—Premiums in respect of " insurances or assurances "—Consideration for annuities.] — Annuities granted by a company carrying on the business of life assurance are within the term " insurances or assurances " in sec. 11 (1) of the *Income Tax Act* 1903, and the considerations received by the company for them are premiums in respect of insurances or assurances and form part of the amount which under that section is the basis for ascertaining the taxable amount of the income of the company. *In re Income Tax Acts* ; *In re Australian Mutual Provident Society*, (1913) V.L.R., 42 ; 34 A.L.T., 118 ; 18 A.L.R., 524. F.C., *a' Beckett, Hodges* and *Cussen, JJ.*

(b) *Salaries of Federal Officers.*

Commonwealth of Australia Constitution Act (63 & 64 Vict. c. 12)—Interference by State with legislative or executive authority of Commonwealth—Implied prohibition—Income Tax Acts, validity of.]—*Per Griffith, C.J., Barton* and *O'Connor, JJ.*—The Income Tax Acts in so far as they purport to tax the emoluments of Federal officers are inoperative and void. *Per Isaacs J.*— These Acts do not infringe the doctrine of non-interference inasmuch as they cannot by any fair and reasonable intendment be read as impairing the usefulness or efficiency of the officers concerned to serve the Federal Government. *Per Isaacs and Higgins, JJ.* It is not an improper interference with a Federal agent for a State to collect from him a tax upon his income, on the same scale as from other citizens of the State, even though his salary as a Federal agent has to be included in his return. *Baxter* v. *Commissioners of Taxation* ; *Flint* v. *Webb*, 4 C.L.R., 1087, 1178 ; 13 A.L.R., 313 (1907).

Commonwealth of Australia Constitution (63 & 64 Vict. c. 12)—Income of Federal officer—Whether liable to income tax imposed by State—Power of State Legislature—Whether restricted by Commonwealth Constitution.]—*Held*, that the respondent, an officer of the Commonwealth resident in

Victoria and receiving his official salary in that State, is liable to be assessed in respect thereof for income tax imposed by an Act of the Victorian Legislature. No restriction on the power of the Victorian Legislature in favor of such officer is expressly enacted by the Commonwealth *Constitution Act*, nor can one be implied on any recognised principle of interpretation applicable thereto. *Webb* v. *Outtrim*, (1907) A.C., 81 ; 13 A.L.R., (C.N.), 1. Privy Council.

Practice—Special leave to appeal to Privy Council from judgment of High Court—State income tax—Liability of Commonwealth officers.]—*See* APPEAL. cols. 12, 13. *Webb* v. *Crouch* ; *Same* v. *Flint*, (1908) A.C., 214.

II—EXEMPTIONS AND DEDUCTIONS.

Income tax—Assessment—Deduction—Outgoings incurred in production of income—Disbursements or expenses wholly and exclusively laid out or expended for purposes of trade—Commonwealth Land Tax—Income Tax Act 1895 (No. 1374), sec. 9.]—Sec. 9 of the *Income Tax Act* 1895 provides that— " (1) All losses and outgoings actually incurred in Victoria by any taxpayer in production of income . . . shall be deducted from the gross amount of such taxpayer's income. (2) In estimating the balance of the income liable to tax no sum shall be deducted therefrom for . . . (g) Any disbursements or expenses whatever not being money wholly or exclusively laid out or expended for the purposes of such trade." *Held*, that land tax under the Land Tax Acts of the Commonwealth by a person who carries on the business of a grazier, in respect of land in Victoria on which he carries on that business, is an " outgoing actually incurred by " him " in production of income," and is also a " disbursement " of " money wholly and exclusively laid out or expended for the purposes of such trade " within the meaning of sec. 9 ; and therefore that, for the purpose of assessing the income tax payable by him, he is entitled to deduct the sum paid for such land tax from his gross income. In assessing such income tax, no distinction can be drawn between land for the purpose of carrying on

the business of grazing thereon, and land already in possession which is applied to that purpose. *Moffatt* v. *Webb*, (1913) 16 C.L.R., 120 ; 19 A.L.R., 190. H.C., *Griffith*, *C.J.*, *Barton*, *Isaacs* and *Duffy, JJ.*

Income Tax Act 1903 (No. 1819), secs. 5, 9 —Taxation of company—Deductions, authority for making—Income Tax Act 1895 (No. 1374), sec. 9—Income Tax Act 1896 (No. 1467), sec. 6.]—The profits of a company chargeable with income tax under sec. 9 of the *Income Tax Act* 1903 are to be ascertained without any reference to sec. 9 of the *Income Tax Act* 1895 and sec. 6 of the *Income Tax Act* 1896, the latter Acts not applying to companies other than foreign companies. *Re Income Tax Acts*, (1907) V.L.R., 327 ; 28 A.L.T., 196 ; 13 A.L.R., 154. F.C., *Madden, C.J.*, *Hodges* and *Hood, JJ.*

Income tax—Deductions—Company formed for one venture—Profits from venture—Deduction of promotion expenses.]—Law costs and preliminary expenses incurred in the promotion of a company formed for one venture may, in assessing income, be deducted from the gross profits of the venture. *In re Income Tax Acts* ; *Ex parte Quat Quatta Co.*, (1907) V.L.R., 54 ; 28 A.L.T., 100 ; 12 A.L.R., 526. F.C., *a'Beckett*, *A.-C.J.*, *Hodges* and *Chomley, JJ.*

Income Tax Act 1903 (No. 1819), secs. 5, 9— Taxation of company—Deductions—Depreciation of machinery.]—A company chargeable with income tax under the *Income Tax Act* 1903 may, on account of depreciation of machinery, deduct a fair and reasonable sum, having regard to the lifetime of the machinery and the knowledge of experts. The amount so deducted may be challenged by the Commissioner. *Re Income Tax Acts* (*Hydraulic Company's Case*), (1905) V.L.R., 185 ; 26 A.L.T., 177 ; 11 A.L.R., 65, commented on. *Re Income Tax Acts*, (1907) V.L.R., 327 ; 28 A.L.T., 196 ; 13 A.L.R., 154. F.C., *Madden, C.J.*, *Hodges* and *Hood, JJ.*

Income Tax Act 1903 (No. 1819), secs. 5, 9 —Taxation of company—Interest on borrowed

capital—Interest on bills given for purchase of stock in trade.]—A company chargeable with income tax under the *Income Tax Act 1903* is entitled, in calculating its profits, to deduct interest paid upon capital borrowed for the purpose of carrying on its business and also on overdue bills given by it for the purchase of goods used in its business. *Re Income Tax Acts,* (1907) V.L.R., 327; 28 A.L.T., 196; 13 A.L.R., 154. F.C., *Madden, C.J., Hodges* and *Hood, JJ.*

Income Tax Act 1895 (No. 1374), secs. 2, 5, 9 (1)—Profit on Victorian station property—Loss on New South Wales station property—Whether such loss a proper deduction—Income derived from property within Victoria—Losses and outgoings incurred in Victoria.]—The taxpayer carried on a station property in Victoria and a separate station property in New South Wales. The working of the Victorian property resulted in a profit, but there was a loss incurred in respect of the New South Wales property. *Held,* that the taxpayer was not entitled to deduct from the income of the Victorian property the loss incurred in respect of that in New South Wales. *Re Income Tax Acts,* (1907) V.L.R., 358; 28 A.L.T., 215; 13 A.L.R., 151. F.C., *Madden, C.J., Hood* and *Cussen, JJ.*

Income Tax Act 1895 (No. 1374), sec. 9 (1), (14)—" Dividends or profits or part of capital credited to any member or shareholder of any company "—Mining company—Proceeds of sale of land—Dividends payable out of profits only—" Outgoings," what may be deducted.] *See, ante,* TAXABLE INCOME, WHAT IS. *Generally. In re Income Tax Acts; The Seven Hills Estate Company's Case,* (1906) V.L.R., 225; 27 A.L.T., 175; 12 A.L.R., 188.

III.—RATE OF TAX; BY WHOM TAX PAYABLE.

Income tax—Income derived from trust estate—Trade carried on by trustees—Income tax from personal exertion or income the produce of property—Income Tax Act 1895 (No. 1374), secs. 2, 8, 9, 12—Income Tax Act 1896 (No. 1467), secs. 4, 12.]—Where a business is carried on by trustees under trusts which, although for the benefit of the beneficiaries, do not constitute them the owners of the business, and the beneficiaries are entitled to the income of the trust estate, the beneficiaries and not the trustees are the taxpayers in respect of the incomes of the beneficiaries, and the trustees are not taxpayers at all except so far as they are answerable under sec. 12 of the *Income Tax Act 1895* for income tax payable by the beneficiaries or except so far as they may be liable under sec. 12 (1) (*d*) of the *Income Tax Act 1896.* A testator gave the whole of his real and personal estate to six trustees, who included his five sons, upon trusts for conversion, with full power of postponement and management, but the power of conversion was not to be exercised as to a newspaper business, which had been carried on by the testator until the death of the last survivor of the sons. After giving certain legacies and annuities payable in one case out of the general income of the estate and in another out of the profits from the newspaper business, and directing certain sums to be set aside for specific purposes, he directed that subject to these trusts, the trustees should hold his residuary real and personal estate including the newspaper business upon trust until the death of the last survivor of the sons, to divide the income into five equal shares and to pay one share to each of his five sons during his life or until attempted alienation, and on further trusts which would not terminate until the death of the last survivor of the sons. He gave to the trustees the fullest powers of carrying on and managing the newspaper business, and expressed his desire that that business should remain " in the possession of his five sons and the survivors and survivor till the death of the last survivor." A large part of the fund annually distributable by the trustees among the five sons consisted of profits from carrying on the newspaper business. *Held* (*Isaacs, J., dissentiente*) that each of the five sons was chargeable primarily with income tax in respect of the income derived by him from the trust estate and that the whole of that income was taxable as income the produce of property. *Quaere, per Griffith, C.J.,* whether the case would be different if the beneficiary could be and had been put in actual possession for his exclusive benefit of any part of the estate. *Webb* v. *Syme* 10 C.L.R., 482; 17 A.L.R., 18. H.C., (1911). [This decision was overruled by the Privy Council in *Syme* v. *Commissioner of Taxes*, (1914) A.C., 1013.]

Income Tax Act 1896 (No. 1467), sec. 12 (d)—Income derived by trustee—No other person presently entitled in actual receipt and liable as taxpayer in respect thereof—Beneficiaries contingently entitled—Whether tax payable on whole amount or on each interest separately—Income Tax Act 1895 (No. 1374), sec. 2—Person liable in representative capacity.]—Where income has been received by a trustee in trust for beneficiaries who are not presently ascertainable, *e.g.*, where their relative interests are contingent, the income is to be treated as belonging to the beneficiaries as a class, and the trustee should be assessed *in globo* on the total income received by him, and not on the separate income of each particular beneficiary. *Rathbone* v. *The Public Trustee*, 24 L.R., N.Z., 801, and *In re Income Tax Act* 1902 Queensland S.R. (1904) 57, distinguished. *Re Income Tax Acts*, (1907) V.L.R., 358; 28 A.L.T., 215; 13 A.L.R., 151. F.C., *Madden, C.J., Hood* and *Cussen, JJ.*

Income Tax—Scheme of Income Tax Acts—Income Tax Act 1895 (No. 1374), secs. 2, 8, 9 and 12—Income Tax Act 1896 (No. 1467), secs. 4, 12.]—The obligation imposed by the Income Tax Acts is one imposed on individuals *qua* individuals and the scheme of those Acts is to tax the actual, and not the formal, recipient of the income in respect of the income which actually comes into his hands. *Webb* v. *Syme*, 10 C.L.R., 482; 17 A.L.R., 18. H.C., *Griffith, C.J., Barton* and *O'Connor, JJ.* (*Isaacs, J.*, dissenting) (1911).

IV.—Legal Proceedings.

Commonwealth of Australia Constitution (63 & 64 Vict. c. 12)—Power of Victorian Legislation (18 & 19 Vict. c. 55)—Income tax —Right of appeal from Supreme Court to Privy Council—Whether Commonwealth Parliament may take away.]—*Held*, that a petition of the Commonwealth for dismissal on the ground of incompetency of an appeal from an order of the Supreme Court of Victoria relating to the assessment of an officer of the Commonwealth, resident in Victoria and receiving his official salary in that State, for income tax in respect of such salary, the income being imposed by an Act of the Victorian Legislature, should be dismissed. The Constitution Act does not authorize the Commonwealth Parliament to take away the right of appeal to the Privy Council existing in such case. *Webb* v. *Outtrim*, (1907) A.C., 81; 13 A.L.R. (C.N.), 1. Privy Council.

Commonwealth of Australia Constitution Act (63 & 64 Vict. c. 12)—The Constitution, secs. 73, 74, 76, 77—Question as to limits inter se of Constitutional powers of Commonwealth and State, what is—Question raised by defence whether State tax on Federal salary an interference with powers of the Commonwealth—Exercise of Federal jurisdiction by Court of Petty Sessions—Appeal to High Court, competency of—Judiciary Act 1903 (No. 6 of 1903), sec. 39.]—*See* APPEAL, cols. 19, 20. *Baxter* v. *Commissioners of Taxation*; *Flint* v. *Webb*, 4 C.L.R., 1087, 1178; 13 A.L.R., 313.

Income Tax Act 1895 (No. 1374), sec. 27— Special case for opinion of Supreme Court— Number of counsel who may be heard.]—As a general rule one counsel only will be heard on the argument of a special case. *Re Income Tax Acts*, (1907) V.L.R., 358. F.C.

INDECENT ASSAULT.

See CRIMINAL LAW.

INDEMNITY.

See CONTRACT OR AGREEMENT; EXECUTORS AND ADMINISTRATORS; GUARANTEE; INSOLVENCY.

INDETERMINATE SENTENCES ACT 1907.

See CRIMINAL LAW.

INFANT.

INFANT.

I.—Capacity ; Domicil.

Infant—Intended marriage—Goods supplied—Necessaries.]—An infant about to marry may make himself liable for things reasonably required for the marriage, or for the joint establishment after marriage. *Quiggan Bros.* v. *Baker*, (1906) V.L.R., 259 ; 27 A.L.T., 174 ; 12 A.L.R., 168. *a'Beckett, J.* (1906).

Prohibited immigrant—Infant—Domicile of father in Australia—Immigration Restriction Act 1905 (No. 17 of 1905), sec. 4—Immigration Restriction Act 1901 (No. 17 of 1901), sec. 3.]—*See* Immigration Restriction Acts. *Ah Yin* v. *Christie*, 4 C.L.R., 1428 ; 13 A.L.R., 372.

Local Government Act 1903 (No. 1893), secs. 119, 120, 143, 149—Election of councillors—Infant's name inscribed on roll—Voting by infant—Validity of election.]—*See* Local Government. *In re Hollins ; Ex parte Daly*, (1912) V.L.R., 87 ; 33 A.L.T., 157 ; 18 A.L.R., 43.

Local Government Act 1903 (No. 1893), secs. 120, 143—Council election—Persons whose names are on the roll—Infant—"Every person," meaning of.]—*See* Local Government. *In re Hollins ; Ex parte Daly*, (1912) V.L.R., 87 ; 33 A.L.T., 157 ; 18 A.L.R., 43.

II.—Custody ; Ward of Court, Control of.

Infant — Custody of — Father's rights—Child in custody of others—Abdication—Welfare of child—Burden of proof.]—The father of a child five months old, her mother being dead, gave her into the custody of her maternal grandparents and left her in their custody until she was nine years old. In the opinion of the majority of the Court the father had by certain acts indicated his intention to abandon his right to the custody of the child in favour of her grandparents, but he had not otherwise disentitled himself to his natural right to the custody of the child. Shortly after the death of the child's mother, the father married again and had by his second wife four other children. The grandparents were desirable guardians of the child and she was happy with them. In proceedings by the father to recover the custody of the child. *Held* (*Higgins, J.*, dissenting), that under the circumstances it would be injurious to her welfare to make such a change of custody and that the Court should refuse to order her to be handed over to her father. *Per Griffith, C.J.*—Where a child has long been out of the father's custody the father's natural right is only one of many circumstances to be taken into consideration. It throws the burden of proof on the other side, but it cannot be regarded as raising anything more than a rebuttable presumption which may be rebutted in the same way as any other such presumption. *Per O'Connor, J.*—The happiness of a child's daily life is a serious and important matter in the consideration of its welfare. *Per Higgins, J.*—In such a case the proper form of question for the Court to ask itself is not " Which residence would be the better for the infant on the materials before the Court ? " but " What proof is there that to permit the father to have his child would involve any serious injury to the child ? " *Reg.* v. *Gyngall*, (1893) 2 Q.B., 232 and *In re Agar-Ellis*, 10 Ch. D., 49, considered and applied. *Goldsmith* v. *Sands*, 4 C.L.R., 1648 ; 13 A.L.R., 601 ; H.C. (1907).

Infant, custody of—Right to custody, how determined—Welfare of the child, importance of—Marriage Act 1890 (No. 1166), secs. 31, 33.]—On a question of who should have the custody of a child the dominant matter is the welfare of the child. *Moule* v. *Moule*, (1911) 13 C.L.R., 267 ; 17 A.L.R., 446. H.C. *Griffith, C.J., Barton* and *O'Connor, JJ.*

Infant, custody of—Infant a girl of three years of age in custody of mother—Mother a fit person—Right of father—Welfare of child—Marriage Act 1890 (No. 1166), secs. 31, 33.] —A husband and wife had lived apart for over a year, and the only child of the marriage, a girl of three years of age, had always lived with her mother. There was no evidence to show that the mother was not a fit person to have the custody of the child. On a writ of *habeas corpus* issued by the father to obtain from his wife the custody of the child. *Held*, that it was for the welfare of the child that she should remain with her mother. *Goldsmith* v. *Sands*, 4 C.L.R., 1648; 13 A.L.R., 601, applied. *Moule* v. *Moule*, (1911) 13 C.L.R., 267; 17 A.L.R., 446; H.C. *Griffith, C.J., Barton* and *O'Connor, JJ.*

Infant—Custody—Rights of father—Benefit of infant—Power of Court.]—Though the Court is satisfied that the health and happiness of children are more likely to be promoted by leaving them in their present custody, yet, if their father insists on his right to do what he pleases for his children, he is entitled to have his own way, so long as no serious injury is to be apprehended which would justify the Court's interference. *R.* v. *Gyngall*, (1893) 2 Q.B., 232, explained. *The King* v. *Lennie*; *The King* v. *Mackenzie*, 29 A.L.T., 56; 13 A.L.R., 505. *a'Beckett, J.* (1907).

Custody of infant—Father outside jurisdiction—Order which cannot be enforced—Whether Court will make.]—The Court, even though it has jurisdiction, will not make an order which it cannot enforce. Accordingly, where the father of an infant was out of the jurisdiction, the Court refused to make an order affecting either directly or indirectly his right to the custody of the infant. *Knipe* v. *Alcock*, (1907) V.L.R., 611; 29 A.L.T., 98; 13 A.L.R., 433. *Madden, C.J.*

Custody of infant—Procedure—Habeas corpus—Who may apply by—Application to Court for appointment of guardian, where necessary.]—No one can take out a writ of *habeas corpus* for the custody of an infant child except a person who has an absolute legal right to that custody. If the custody of an infant child is sought by a person who has only a discretionary right, so far as the Court is concerned, to the custody of the child, the proper course is for him to proceed in a Court of Equity to have himself appointed guardian. Where an infant child is detained by a person who is acting as its guardian in fact, and is as such maintaining the child, and it is suggested that this is a wrongful detention, the only persons who can take out a writ of *habeas corpus* for the recovery of the custody of the child are, where the child is a legitimate child, its father, and after his death the mother of the child or the testamentary guardian appointed by the father, and after the death of both parents, if no guardian has been appointed by the father, the testamentary guardian appointed by the mother; and, where the child is an illegitimate child, its mother, and after her death the testamentary guardian appointed by her. Blood relationship to an infant child, except in the case of its father and mother, confers no right to the guardianship of such child; but the Court, in looking at the child's own benefit and interests (by which it will be guided), will always have special regard to the blood relations. Any person may, at his or her own proper cost, come into a Court of Equity, and inform the Court that somebody acting *de facto* as guardian is detaining a child against its interests, and the Court will inquire into that matter, and direct what is for the benefit of the child. *The King* v. *Waters*, (1912) V.L.R., 372; 34 A.L.T., 48; 18 A.L.R., 304. *Madden, C.J.* (1912).

Infant—When a ward of Court.]—An infant does not become a ward of Court unless whether as plaintiff or defendant, he is party to a suit in relation to his estate or person and for his benefit, or for the administration of property in which he is interested, or unless a petition to make him a ward of Court has been presented by someone acting as his next friend. *Knipe* v. *Alcock*, (1907) V.L.R., 611; 29 A.L.T., 98; 13 A.L.R., 433. *Madden, C.J.*

Order XXX. (Rules of 1906)—Summons for directions—Claim for appointment of guardian of infant—Infant not a party—Whether a ward of the Court—Order for examination of witnesses as to infant's whereabouts—Whether order may be made.]—The plaintiff and her infant daughter were beneficiaries under the will of plaintiff's father, of which the defendants were trustees. The plaintiff by her action claimed against the defendants as trustees of the will administration accounts and the appointment of a guardian of the infant. Neither the infant nor her father, in whose custody she was alleged to be, was a party to the action. *Held*, that the infant was not a ward of the Court, and that on a summons for directions no order could be made for the examination of witnesses as to the whereabouts of the infant. *Knipe* v. *Alcock*, (1907) V.L.R., 611; 29 A.L.T., 98; 13 A.L.R., 433. *Madden, C.J.*

III.—MAINTENANCE AND EDUCATION.

See also, MAINTENANCE AND MAINTENANCE ORDERS; WIDOWS AND YOUNG CHILDREN MAINTENANCE ACT.

Trusts Act 1896 (No. 1421), sec. 19—Infant—Maintenance and education—Trust fund—Breaking into corpus—Advancement.]—The Court will direct the application of the corpus of a trust fund to the education of an infant beneficiary when satisfied that it is for the infant's benefit. *In re English*, (1909) V.L.R., 430; 31 A.L.T., 74; 15 A.L.R., 517. *Hood, J.*

Trust—Corpus in trust for infant—Breaking into in order to provide University fees—Trusts Act 1896 (No. 1421), sec. 19.]—*See* TRUSTS AND TRUSTEES. *Re Keam (or Kean)*, (1911) V.L.R., 165; 32 A.L.T., 159; 17 A.L.R., 130.

Infant—Maintenance by breaking into corpus—Heading of papers, form of.]—In applications respecting the maintenance of infants by breaking into corpus and otherwise, the heading of the papers should be simply :—" In the matter of A an infant." *Re Smith*, 12 A.L.R. (C.N.), 5. *a'Beckett, J.* (1906).

Will—Construction—Maintenance of infants out of income—Whether to be treated as a common fund or separate shares—Income directed to form part of the capital of the share when it arose.]—*See* WILL. *In re Munro; National Trustees Executors &c. Co. of Australasia Ltd.* v. *Dunbar*, (1910) V.L.R., 395; 32 A.L.T., 41; 16 A.L.R., 363.

Will — Construction — Perpetuities, rule against—Remoteness—Trust for maintenance and education—Validity.]—*See* WILL. *In re Stevens; Trustees, Executors and Agency Co. Ltd.* v. *Teague*, (1912) V.L.R., 194; 33 A.L.T., 233; 18 A.L.R., 195.

IV.—PROPERTY ; POWER OF SALE ; CONTINGENT INTERESTS.

Settled Estates and Settled Lands Act 1909 (No. 2235), secs. 51, 124, 127—Sale of settled land—Infant being person with powers of tenant for life—Appointment of persons to exercise such powers.]—Where under a will an infant took such an interest in land that, by virtue of sec. 124 of the *Settled Estates and Settled Lands Act* 1909, she had the powers of a tenant for life, the Court appointed the executors of the will to exercise the powers of sale under the Act. *In re Cheke or Akhurst; Cheke* v. *Hamilton*, (1910) V.L.R., 310; 32 A.L.T., 5; 16 A.L.R., 246. *Hodges, J.*

Settled Estates and Settled Lands Act 1909 (No. 2235), secs. 127, 128—Contract of sale—' Purchase in name of infants—Settled estate—Tenant for life—Settlement—Appointment of trustees—Trustees to exercise powers of infant tenants for life.]—*See* SETTLED ESTATES AND SETTLED LANDS ACT. *In re Weir*, (1912) V.L.R., 77; 33 A.L.T., 162; 18 A.L.R., 26.

Will—Construction—Contingent legacies—Interim interest, whether infant contingent legatees entitled to—Trusts Act 1896 (No. 1421), sec. 18.]—*See* WILL. *In re Thompson; Brahe* v. *Mason*, (1910) V.L.R., 251; 31 A.L.T., 210; 16 A.L.R., 215.

**Will—Construction—Trust to hold for infants until they shall have attained 21—Interest of infants.]—*See* WILL. *In re Vickers*; *Vickers* v. *Vickers*, (1912) V.L.R., 385; 34 A.L.T., 133; 18 A.L.R., 521.

V.—LEGAL PROCEEDINGS BY AND AGAINST.

Infant complainant in Court of Petty Sessions—Claim for wages—Order to review obtained by infant—Next friend, whether infant must proceed by—Justices Act 1890 (No. 1105), sec. 72—Rules of Supreme Court 1884, Order XVI., r. 16.]—An infant complainant in a Court of Petty Sessions cannot obtain an order *nisi* to review a dismissal of his complaint, except through a next friend, even in cases where he may proceed in the Court below without a next friend. *Cash* v. *Cash*, 22 V.L.R., 110; 17 A.L.T., 326; 2 A.L.R., 153, approved. *Hines* v. *Phillips*, (1906) V.L.R., 417; 28 A.L.T., 1; 12 A.L.R., 249. *a'Beckett, A.-C.J.*

Order to review — Infant respondent—Guardian ad litem—Practice.]—Where an infant is the party called upon by an order to review to support the order of Justices a guardian *ad litem* for the infant will be appointed on the return of the order *nisi*. *Brown* v. *Gunn*; *McKay, Garnishee*, (1913) V.L.R., 60; 34 A.L.T., 115; 18 A.L.R. (C.N.), 21. *Cussen, J.* (1912).

County Court Act 1890 (No. 1078), sec. 60—County Court Rules 1891, r. 107—Infant, by — Appointment of next friend.] — *See* COUNTY COURT, col. 305. *Thompson* v. *Peach*, 28 A.L.T. (Supplement), 10; 13 A.L.R. (C.N.), 5.

County Court Act 1890 (No. 1078), secs. 81, 148—Infant, whether interrogatories may be administered to—Rules of Supreme Court 1906, Order XXXI., r. 29.]—*See* COUNTY COURT, col. 307. *Brock* v. *Victorian Railways Commissioners*, 29 A.L.T. (Supplement), 3; 13 A.L.R. (C.N.), 21.

Administration and Probate Act 1890 (No. 1060), sec. 18—Will—Caveat, who may lodge — Infant — Next friend — Appointment of guardian as—Form of caveat where both next friend and infant interested in estate.]—A caveat against the granting of probate to a will may be lodged by an infant by his next friend, and a guardian of the infant need not in all cases be specially appointed for that purpose. Where the caveator and the infant are both interested in the estate, and therefore entitled to lodge a caveat, the caveat should state distinctly whether it is lodged by the caveator on his own behalf or by him as next friend on behalf of the infant. *In the Will of Adcock*, 26 A.L.T., 127; 10 A.L.R., 268, approved and applied. *In re Simeon*, (1910) V.L.R., 335; 32 A.L.T., 25; 16 A.L.R., 362. *a'Beckett, J.*

INFORMATION.

I.—WHO MAY LAY.

Local Government Act 1903 (No. 1893), Part XXXVIII., secs. 693, 694, 695, 696, 697 (c)—Breach of municipal building regulations—Who may lay information and prosecute—Officer of Council—Information and proceedings in name of officer.]—Under Part XXXVIII. of the *Local Government Act* 1903, secs. 694, 695, a municipal council may order a prosecution in the name of the council or corporation, or it may authorise an officer to undertake a prosecution—which would include the laying of the information—in his own name. *Steane* v. *Whitchell*, (1906) V.L.R., 704; 28 A.L.T., 60; 12 A.L.R., 390. F.C., *Hood, Cussen* and *Chomley, JJ.*

Information, who may lay.]—For a full discussion of the principles which determine the right to lay an information, *see Steane* v. *Whitchell*, (1906) V.L.R., 704; 28 A.L.T., 60; 12 A.L.R., 390. F.C., *Hood, Cussen,* and *Chomley JJ.*

Local Government Act 1903 (No. 1893), Part XXXVIII.—Breach of building regulations—Prosecution by municipal officer—Authority to prosecute, sufficiency of.]—S., who was the building surveyor of the town of Northcote was authorised by the municipality by a document under the seal of the

municipality in the following terms :—
" Mr. S., surveyor and building surveyor of
the town of Northcote, is hereby authorised
to take proceedings against any person
offending against the building regulations of
the town of Northcote." *Held*, that S. was
authorised to prosecute thereunder in his
own name. *Steane* v. *Whitchell*, (1906)
V.L.R., 704; 28 A.L.T., 60; 12 A.L.R.,
390. F.C., *Hood, Cussen* and *Chomley JJ.*

**Information, who may lay—Tramways Act
1890 (No. 1148), sec. 5, Second Schedule, Part
II., clause 17—Tramway fare, penalty for
avoiding payment of—Delegation of authority
of municipal council—Whether delegate may
enforce penalty.]**—A municipal council, by
agreement under seal, delegated to a company,
under sec. 5 of the *Tramways Act* 1890,
the authority conferred by the Order in
Council authorizing the municipal council
as the promotor to construct a certain tramway, and neither the Order in Council nor
the agreement contained anything as to rights
or powers to impose or enforce penalties.
Held, that the company could not sue for
penalties for offences under clause 17, of the
Second Schedule of that Act. *Cochrane* v.
Tuthill, (1908) V.L.R., 549; 30 A.L.T., 50;
14 A.L.R., 453. *Madden, C.J.*

II.—FORM ; MATERIAL FACTS.

**Factories and Shops Act 1905 (No. 1975),
sec. 162 (c), (d)—Proceedings against firm—
Form of information—Rules under the Justices Act 1890, rr. 18, 20.]**—*Quaere*, whether
in proceedings against a firm for an offence
under the Act No. 1975 the information
should be against the individual members
of the firm, and not against the firm. *Bishop*
v. *Chung Brothers*, 4 C.L.R., 1262; 13
A.L.R., 412. H.C. (1906).

**Police Offences Act 1890 (No. 1126), secs.
49, 51—Gaming—Information under two
sections.]**—The defendants were charged
with assisting in conducting the business of a
room used for the purpose of moneys being
received by persons conducting the business
thereof as the consideration for an assurance
to pay moneys on contingencies relating to
horse-races. *Held*, that secs. 49 and 51 of

the *Police Offences Act* 1890 are to be read
together and that the information disclosed
an offence. *Rogerson* v. *Phillips and O'Hagan*,
(1906) V.L.R., 272; 27 A.L.T., 166; 12
A.L.R., 147. *a'Beckett, J.* (1906).

**Information—Allegation as to date of
offence incorrect—Health Act 1890 (No.
1098), Part IX.—Vaccination—Justices Act
1890 (No. 1105), sec. 73 (3).]**—In an information against a father for not having his child
vaccinated as required by Part IX. of the
Health Act 1890, the offence was alleged as
upon the date of information. It appeared
in evidence that the child was not vaccinated
within six months from its birth. *Held*,
that the allegation as to the date of the
offence was immaterial. *O'Malley* v. *Russell*,
(1908) V.L.R., 545; 30 A.L.T., 39; 14
A.L.R., 462. *Cussen, J.*

**Information, sufficiency of—Charge against
father for not having child vaccinated—Allegation that vaccination notice given by Registrar
of district in which father resided—Who may
properly give such notice—Health Act 1890
(No. 1098), Part IX.]**—An information against
a father for not having his child vaccinated
as required by Part IX. of the *Health Act*
1890 alleged that the notice in writing of
the requirement of vaccination, prescribed
by sec. 204 of the Act, had been given to the
defendant by the Registrar of the district
in which the defendant was resident. *Held*,
on an objection that the allegation should
have been that it was given by the Registrar
of the district in which the child was resident,
that this was an immaterial allegation. The
Registrar of the district in which the registration of the birth of the child is effected is a
proper person to give the notice above referred
to. *O'Malley* v. *Russell*, (1908) V.L.R., 545;
30 A.L.T., 39; 14 A.L.R., 462. *Cussen, J.*

**Police Offences Act 1890 (No. 1126), sec. 40
—Information, sufficiency of—Allegation of
facts set out in sub-sec. VI.—No allegation
that defendant was an idle and disorderly
person.]**—An information under sec. 40 (VI.)
of the *Police Offences Act* 1890 alleged that
the defendant was found by night armed with
a bludgeon and being thereto required did
not give a good account of his means of sup-

port and assign a valid and satisfactory reason for being so armed, but did not allege that he was an idle and disorderly person because he was so found by night. *Held*, that the information was defective. *Hickling* v. *Skerritt*, (1912) V.L.R., 322; 34 A.L.T., 72; 18 A.L.R., 329. *Madden, C.J.*

Police Offences Act 1890 (No. 1128), sec. 51—Occupier of house permitting same to be used for betting—No allegation in information of person by whom house used.]—*See* GAMING AND WAGERING. *Knox* v. *Thomas Bible*; *Knox* v. *J. L. Bible*, (1907) V.L.R., 485; 29 A.L.T., 23; 13 A.L.R., 352.

III.—AMENDMENT.

Information—Defect in—Amendment—Discretion of Justices—Justices Act 1890 (No. 1105), sec. 187.]—The provisions of sec. 187 of the *Justices Act* 1890 are not mandatory but give a discretionary power to Courts of Petty Sessions or Justices which ought ordinarily to be exercised, but not where the effect of the proposed amendment will be to raise a new case for the defendant to answer. *Reg.* v. *Templeton*; *Ex parte England*, (1877) 3 V.L.R. (L.), 305, followed. *Burvett* v. *Moody*, (1909) V.L.R., 126; 30 A.L.T., 160; 15 A.L.R., 91. *Madden, C.J.*

Justices Act 1890 (No. 1105), sec. 141—Information disclosing no offence—Conviction thereon—Amendment on return of order to review—Powers of Court—Defendant never charged with an offence.]—Where the defendant has been convicted upon an information which discloses no offence, the Court should not on the return of an order to review (at all events without hearing or giving an opportunity to call fresh evidence) amend the information and the conviction based upon it where the proposed amendment would raise a new allegation of fact, notwithstanding that the testimony given would go to show than an offence was in fact committed. *Knox* v. *Thomas Bible*; *Knox* v. *J. L. Bible*, (1907) V.L.R., 485; 29 A.L.T., 23; 13 A.L.R., 352. *Cussen, J.*

Justices Act 1890 (No. 1105), sec. 141—Return of order to review conviction—Amend- ment of information and conviction—Altering offence charged in information to a different offence.**]—*Quaere*, whether the Court has power on the return of an order to review to alter an information charging one offence, and, if necessary, a conviction based on it, so as to make it refer to another offence. *Knox* v. *Thomas Bible*; *Knox* v. *J. L. Bible*, (1907) V.L.R., 485; 29 A.L.T., 23; 13 A.L.R., 252. *Cussen, J.*

General Sessions—Appeal against conviction — Information — Whether Court may amend—Justices Act 1890 (No. 1105), secs. 73 (4), 128 (7), 133.]—At the hearing of an appeal against a conviction the Court of General Sessions has power to amend the information upon which the appellant was convicted. *Delaney* v. *Napthine*, 32 A.L.T. (Supplement), 10; 16 A.L.R. (C.N.), 19. *Judge Moule* (1910).

INJUNCTION.

Trade mark—Innocent use of and not as a trade mark.]—Where a person has innocently applied to his goods a word which is the registered trade mark of another, not as a trade mark, but merely as a distinguishing or-shipping mark, and on learning of the trade mark has, before action, offered to remove the mark from his goods, and not again to apply it, an injunction will not be granted at the instance of the owner of the trade mark. *Austral Canning Co. Proprietary Ltd.* v. *Austral Grain and Produce Proprietary Ltd.*, 34 A.L.T., 37; 18 A.L.R., 354; *a'Beckett, J.* (1912).

Trade name—Similarity of names—Mining companies—Names taken from locality of mining operations—Injunction.]—*See* TRADE MARKS AND TRADE NAMES. *Mount Balfour Copper Mines No Liability* v. *Mount Balfour Mines No Liability*, (1909) V.L.R., 542; 31 A.L.T., 122; 15 A.L.R., 556.

Company—Management of internal affairs —Injunction—When Court will interfere by.] —*See* COMPANY, col. 149. *Oliver* v. *North Nuggety Ajax Co. No Liability*, (1912) V.L.R., 416; 34 A.L.T., 58; 18 A.L.R., 309.

Nuisance—Church bell—Early morning toll —Injunction—Material interference with ordinary comfort of existence.]—*See* Nuisance. *Haddon* v. *Lynch*, (1911) V.L.R., 230 ; 33 A.L.T., 4 ; 17 A.L.R., 185.

County Court Act 1890 (No. 1078), sec. 45 —Costs—Amount recovered not exceeding ten pounds—Injunction a material part of the action—Professional costs.]—*See* County Court, cols. 319, 320. *Harrison San Miguel Proprietary Ltd.* v. *Alfred Lawrence & Co.*, (1912) V.L.R., 367 ; 34 A.L.T., 88 ; 18 A.L.R., 394.

Order LXV., r. 12—Costs—Action of tort— Judgment for damages under £50 and injunction—Supreme Court costs—" Sum recovered "—Impossibility of valuing injunction.]—*See* Costs, cols. 261, 262. *Harrison San Miguel Proprietary Ltd.* v. *Alfred Lawrence & Co.*, (1912) V.L.R., 367 ; 34 A.L.T., 88 ; 18 A.L.R., 394.

INSOLVENCY.

I.—Sequestration.

(a) *Who Subject to Insolvency Law.*

Who may be made insolvent—Person domiciled and resident abroad—Debts contracted in Victoria.]—A person domiciled and resident out of Victoria may be made insolvent in respect of debts incurred within Victoria. *In re Whitelaw*, (1906) V.L.R., 265 ; 27 A.L.T., 187 ; 12 A.L.R., 143. *Hood, J.*

(b) *Discretion as to Sequestration Generally.*

Insolvency—Order nisi for sequestration based on judgment for costs of prior action— Appeal pending before High Court from prior judgment—Adjournment of insolvency proceedings.]—After notice of appeal to the High Court from a judgment dismissing an action with costs, the defendants in the action, having in a subsequent action recovered judgment for the costs, presented a petition for sequestration of the plaintiff's estate, the acts of insolvency being failure to comply with a debtor's summons founded on the judgment and to satisfy a writ of *fi. fa.* issued upon it. It was not suggested that the debtor had any estate, or that the judgment creditor would obtain any advantage from the sequestration other than putting difficulties in the way of prosecuting the appeal. *Held*, that an order for sequestration ought not to have been made, but that the petition should have been adjourned until after the hearing of the appeal or dismissed. *Bayne* v. *Baillieu* (*or Blake*), (1907) 5 C.L.R., 64; 13 A.L.R., 503. H.C., *Griffith, C.J., Barton* and *O'Connor, JJ.*

Insolvency — Sequestration of estate — Debtor without assets—Whether a ground for refusing sequestration.]—The mere fact that there are no reasons for suspecting that a debtor has any assets is not a ground for refusing to make a debtor insolvent. *Bayne* v. *Blake*, (1909) 9 C.L.R., 360. H.C., *Griffith, C.J., Barton* and *O'Connor, JJ.*

Sequestration — Petition — Chief Clerk, whether bound to accept petition where no assets.]—The Chief Clerk is not bound to accept the surrender of an estate which does not exist, and when the affidavit shows distinctly that there are no assets he may refuse to make an order for sequestration. *In re Law*, 16 A.L.R. (C.N.), 13. *Judge Moule* (1910).

(c) *Petition by Attorney.*

Insolvency Act 1890 (No. 1102), sec. 37— Compulsory sequestration—Petitioning creditor—Power of attorney—Authority of attorney to present petition.]—A power of attorney (*inter alia*) authorized the attorney " to bring . . . any action, suit or other proceeding for recovering or compelling payment of any sum of money due to the donor." *Held*, that the attorney was authorized to present and prosecute a petition for the sequestration of the estate of a debtor of his principal. *In re Anderson*, (1909) V.L.R., 465; 31 A.L.T., 72; 15 A.L.R., 518. *Cussen, J.*

(d) *The Petitioning Creditor's Debt.*

Insolvency Act 1890 (No. 1102), sec. 37— " Secured debt," what is—Business of testator carried on by executors under provisions of will — Debt properly incurred — Right of executors to indemnity out of assets of estate— Petitioning creditor having security over property used in business—Whether such security must be given up or valued.]—Each of several executors carrying on the business of their testator pursuant to the terms of the will has a right of indemnity against the assets of the testator, including a lien over those assets, for liabilities properly incurred, and any security held by a creditor which interferes with that right is a security, the giving up of which will go to augment the estate of each executor, and therefore a creditor in respect of a debt so incurred, who has a security over property used in such business, must offer to give up or value that security when petitioning to sequestrate the estate of one of the executors. *In re Whitelaw*; *Savage* v. *The Union Bank of Australia Ltd.*; *Whitelaw* v. *The Same*, 3 C.L.R., 1170; 12 A.L.R., 285. H.C., *Griffith, C.J., Barton* and *O'Connor, JJ.* (1906).

Insolvency — Partners — Sequestration of estate of one partner—Security over joint estate—Petition for sequestration—Offer to give up or value security whether necessary— Insolvency Act 1890 (No. 1102), secs. 37, 41 —Insolvency Act 1897 (No. 1513), sec. 109.] A creditor petitioning for the sequestration of the estate of one of several partners must, under section 37 of the *Insolvency Act* 1890, in his petition offer to give up or value any security which he, the creditor, may hold over the joint estate. The rule that a creditor need not give up his security applies only after sequestration in the administration of the joint and separate estates. *In re Stevenson*, 19 V.L.R., 660; 15 A.L.T., 119, overruled. *In re Whitelaw*; *Savage* v. *The Union Bank of Australia Ltd.*; *Whitelaw* v. *The Same*, 3 C.L.R., 1170; 12 A.L.R., 285. H.C. *Griffith, C.J., Barton* and *O'Connor, JJ.* (1906).

Insolvency Act 1890 (No. 1102), sec. 37— Insolvency Act 1897 (No. 1513), sec. 106 (2) —Sequestration—Petitioning creditor's debt— Current promissory note.]—Section 37 of the *Insolvency Act* 1890 as amended by section 106 (2) of the *Insolvency Act* 1897 provides, in reference to a petition for the sequestration of a debtor's estate, that " the debt of the petitioning creditor must be a liquidated sum due at law or in equity, payable either immediately or at some future time." *Held*, that a debt in respect of a current promissory note made by the debtor and of which the creditor was the holder at the date of the petition was a good petitioning creditor's debt. *David* v. *Malouf*, (1908) 5 C.L.R., 749 ; 14 A.L.R., 297. H.C. *Griffith, C.J., Barton, O'Connor, Isaacs* and *Higgins, JJ.*

Insolvency — Sequestration — Petitioning creditor's debt—Merger—Judgment debt.]—In an action brought by a plaintiff against a defendant, the defendant counter-claimed for a judgment debt owing by the plaintiff to him, and obtained judgment on that counter-claim. *Held*, that the earlier judgment debt was not merged in the later judgment debt so as to prevent it from being a good petitioning creditor's debt upon which the defendant might have the plaintiffs' estate sequestrated. *Quaere (per Griffith, C.J.)* whether there is a merger of a debt in a judgment for the purpose of a petitioning creditor's debt in insolvency proceedings. *Bayne* v. *Blake*, (1909) 9 C.L.R., 360. H.C. *Griffith, C.J., Barton* and *O'Connor, JJ.*

(e) *Acts of Insolvency.*

Insolvency—Act of insolvency—Deed of assignment for benefit of creditors generally—Creditor acquiescing in deed—Delay, effect of—Estoppel—Insolvency Act 1890 (No. 1102), sec. 37 (1).]—Mere delay in presenting a petition for sequestration for the space of four months after the petitioning creditor has knowledge that his debtor has executed a deed of assignment for the benefit of his creditors generally, does not prevent him relying on it as an act of insolvency. *In re Carr*, (1902) 85 L.T., 552, distinguished. *In re Camp*, (1910) V.L.R., 42 ; 31 A.L.T., 126 ; 15 A.L.R., 642. *a'Beckett, J.*

Insolvency Act 1890 (No. 1102), sec. 37 (1) —Act of insolvency—Assignment for benefit of creditors generally—No objection raised by creditor—Whether estopped from treating assignment as act of insolvency.]—A creditor knowing of and not objecting to the execution by the debtor of a deed of assignment for the benefit of creditors may treat the execution of the deed of assignment as an act of insolvency, unless he has done something or lain by in such a manner that it would be unfair to other creditors or to the debtor to permit him to do so. *In re Stray*, L.R. 2 Ch., 374, commented on ; *In re Carr*, 85 L.T., 552, followed. *In re Knights ; Ex parte Purcell*, (1910) V.L.R., 188 ; 31 A.L.T., 178 ; 16 A.L.R., 184. *a'Beckett, J.*

Insolvency Act 1890 (No. 1102), sec. 37 (1) — Act of insolvency — Meeting of creditors — Assignment for benefit of creditors — Assent by petitioning creditors—Objection to subsequent resolution that assets be sold for a certain sum—Estoppel.]—At a meeting of creditors a resolution was carried in the presence and with the assent of the petitioner, that the debtor's estate should be assigned for the benefit of his creditors and a deed of assignment was thereupon executed. Immediately afterwards a motion was carried that the debtor's assets should be sold for a sum which would give a dividend of 7s. in the pound. The petitioner spoke strongly against the motion. After a delay, which was satisfactorily explained, he presented a petition for the sequestration of the debtor's estate, relying on the execution of the deed as an act of insolvency. *Held*, that it was not necessary for the petitioner, in order to preserve his rights, expressly to recall the assent he had given to the assignment *simpliciter*, and that therefore he was not estopped from relying on the execution of the deed as an act of insolvency. *In re Knights ; Ex parte Purcell*, (1910) V.L.R., 188 ; 31 A.L.T., 178 ; 16 A.L.R., 184. *a'Beckett, J.*

Insolvency Act 1890 (No. 1102), sec. 37 (viii.)—Act of insolvency—Failure to satisfy judgment—Demand for more than is owing whether a good demand.]—Where after judgment has been obtained against a debtor he pays part of the amount due, a subsequent demand for the whole amount of the judgment is not a good demand on the debtor to satisfy the judgment so as to constitute an act of insolvency within the meaning of section 37 (viii.) of the *Insolvency Act* 1890. *Hamilton* v. *Warne*, 4 C.L.R., 1293 ; 13 A.L.R., 420 (1907).

Insolvency Act 1890 (No. 1102), sec. 37 (viii.)—Act of insolvency—Failure to satisfy judgment—Duty of officer charged with execution—Whether bound to demand the precise sum remaining unpaid.]—*Per Griffith, C.J., Barton* and *Isaacs, JJ.*—In calling upon the debtor to satisfy the judgment it is the duty of the officer charged with the execution to demand the precise sum remaining unpaid or otherwise unsatisfied under the judgment. *Per Higgins, J.*—*Semble,* the officer need only ask the debtor to "satisfy the judgment," and the debtor must, at his peril, tender the amount which is in fact adequate to satisfy it. *Hamilton* v. *Warne,* 4 C.L.R., 1293 ; 13 A.L.R., 420. (1907).

Insolvency Act 1890 (No. 1102), sec. 37 (viii.)—Creditor's petition—Act of insolvency —Execution on a judgment attained in " any Court "—County Court judgment.] — The words " any Court " in section 37 (viii.) of the *Insolvency Act* 1890 include a County Court. *In re Anderson,* (1909) V.L.R., 465 ; 31 A.L.T., 72 ; 15 A.L.R., 518. *Cussen, J.*

(f) The Order Nisi ; The Notice of Intention to Oppose.

Order nisi—Amendment—Unsatisfied execution—Omission of statement that person making the demand was the officer charged with execution—Insolvency Act 1890 (No. 1102), secs. 31, 37—Insolvency Act 1897 (No. 1513), sec. 10 (2).]—Where an order *nisi* for sequestration on the ground of an unsatisfied execution omits to state that the person who made the demand was an officer or person charged with execution of the judgment, the Court will amend. *Re Field,* 21 V.L.R., 278 ; 16 A.L.T., 162 ; 1 A.L.R., 26, followed. *In re Hamilton,* 28 A.L.T., 124 ; 12 A.L.R., 523. *Hood, J.* (1906).

Insolvency Act 1890 (No. 1102), secs. 37 (viii.), 43, 45—Petition for sequestration— Notice of intention to oppose—Failure to satisfy judgment—Notice that respondent disputes the act of insolvency—Whether he may show that greater sum demanded than owing —" Special defence."]—*Per Isaacs* and *Higgins, JJ.* (and *Semble, per Griffith, C.J* and *Barton, J.*)—A notice of intention to oppose

a petition for sequestration stating that the respondent disputes the act of insolvency alleged, *i.e.* that execution issued on a judgment had been returned unsatisfied in whole and that the debtor had failed to satisfy the judgment when called upon to do so by the officer charged with the execution, will entitle the respondent to show that the demand of the officer was for a larger sum than was due, and, therefore, to give evidence that before the issue of execution he had paid part of the judgment debt. *Per Griffith, C.J., Semble,* " Special defence " is something in the nature of a plea in confession and avoidance. *Hamilton* v. *Warne,* 4 C.L.R., 1293 ; 13 A.L.R., 420. (1907).

(g) Annulment of Sequestration.

Application to annul sequestration—Sequestration based on judgment for costs ordered to be paid in prior action—Judgment in prior action set aside on appeal—Judgment for costs in subsequent action still standing.]— After notice of appeal to the High Court from a judgment dismissing an action with costs, the defendants in the action, having in a subsequent action recovered judgment for the costs, presented a petition for sequestration of the plaintiff's estate, the acts of insolvency being failure to comply with a debtor's summons founded on the judgment and to satisfy a writ of *fi. fa.* issued thereon. It was not suggested that the debtor had any estate, or that the judgment creditor would obtain any advantage from the sequestration other than putting difficulties in the way of prosecuting the appeal. An order absolute sequestrating the estate was made, the prior judgment having on appeal to the High Court been discharged, an application was made to the Supreme Court to annul the sequestration. *Held,* that the application should have been granted notwithstanding that the judgment for the costs was still standing. *Bayne* v. *Baillieu,* (1907) 5 C.L.R., 64 ; 13 A.L.R., 503. H.C., *Griffith, C.J., Barton* and *O'Connor, JJ.*

(h) Effect of Sequestration upon Other Proceedings against Insolvent.

Insolvency Act 1890 (No. 1102), secs. 76, 113—Execution of process or judgment, stay

23

of—Debt due by insolvent to creditor—Trust moneys which are or ought to be in hands of trustee—Trustee ordered to pay moneys into Court—Disobedience of order—Attachment.] —Sections 76 and 113 of the *Insolvency Act* 1890 are both directed to process for the enforcement of the payment of money as a debt due by the insolvent to a creditor. The insolvency of a person, who in the position of a trustee has not accounted for money he once had and still ought to have, and who has been ordered to pay such money into Court, does not operate as a stay upon process of attachment against him for non-compliance with the order for payment into Court. *Peterson* v. *M'Lennan*, (1907) V.L.R., 94 ; 28 A.L.T., 135 ; 12 A.L.R., 577. *Cussen, J.*

Insolvency Act 1890 (No. 1102), secs. 76, 113—Stay of execution—Whether limited to process in execution of judgment for payment of money.]—*Semble*, In sections 76 and 113 of the *Insolvency Act* 1890 the meaning of the word " process " should be limited to process issuing after judgment ordering money to be paid by one party to another. *Peterson* v. *M'Lennan*, (1907) V.L.R., 94 ; 28 A.L.T., 135 ; 12 A.L.R., 577. *Cussen, J.*

Imprisonment of Fraudulent Debtors Act 1890 (No. 1100), sec. 16—Sequestration of judgment debtor's estate—Liability contracted by fraud.]—Where a judgment debtor's estate had been sequestrated, a judgment summons under Part II. of the *Imprisonment of Fraudulent Debtors Act* 1890 was dismissed, although the ground alleged was that he had contracted the liability which was the subject of the judgment by fraud. *Davies* v. *Burley*, 29 A.L.T. (Supplement), 18 ; 13 A.L.R. (C.N.), 34. *Judge Box* (1907).

Insolvency Act 1890 (No. 1102)—Imprisonment of Fraudulent Debtors Act 1890 (No. 1100)—Insolvency—Effect of upon existing order on fraud summons—Payments made thereunder after insolvency.] — *Quaere* : Whether, once a person's estate is sequestrated, he should continue to make payments under an existing order made under the *Imprisonment of Fraudulent Debtors Act*

1890. *In re Watt*, 33 A.L.T. (Supplement), 1 ; 17 A.L.R. (C.N.), 13. *Judge Moule* (1911).

Satisfaction after insolvency of orders made on judgment summonses.]—For comments on the state of the law which permits orders made upon judgment summonses just prior to the insolvency of judgment debtors to be satisfied in full after insolvency, see *In re Summers*, 32 A.L.T. (Supplement), 1 ; 16 A.L.R. (C.N.), 15. *Judge Moule* (1910).

II.—PROPERTY DIVISIBLE AMONGST CREDITORS.

(a) Reputed Ownership.

Insolvency Act 1890 (No. 1102), sec. 70 (v.) —Married Woman's Property Act 1890 (No. 1116), sec. 13—Insolvent's property divisible amongst creditors—Gift by husband to wife —" Reputed owner."]—Where a husband and wife, living together have been prior to and at the date of the sequestration of his estate in joint possession of goods which had been given by him to her, he is not deemed to be the " reputed owner " of such goods within the meaning of section 70 (v.) of the *Insolvency Act* 1890 if he has not been in possession of them in such a manner that he might have been able to obtain false or delusive credit. *In re Mitchell*, 31 A.L.T. (Supplement), 7 ; 15 A.L.R. (C.N.), 18. *Judge Moule* (1909).

(b) After Acquired Property and Like Matters.

Insolvency Act 1890 (No. 1102), secs. 4, 59, 61, 63, 70 (iii.), 150—Insolvency Act 1897 (No. 1513), sec. 5—Insolvent continuing to carry on business—Knowledge and acquiescence of trustee—Debts incurred after insolvency—Rights of subsequent creditors—Death of insolvent—Interest of executor in property acquired after insolvency.]—An uncertificated insolvent carried on business after his insolvency with the knowledge and acquiescence of the then trustee of his estate, and continued to carry on the business after such trustee's death till his own death, during which period there was no trustee of his insolvent estate and in doing so acquired property and incurred debts ; on a new trustee being subsequently appointed he attached such property claiming the same as part of the insolvent estate. *Held*, that such property, which was insufficient to meet the above-mentioned debts, did not vest in the new trustee, but that it vested in the executrix of the insolvent for the purpose of the payment of such debts. *Tucker* v. *Hernaman*, 1 Sm. & G., 394; 4 DeG. M. & G., 395, followed. *In re Poole*, 31 A.L.T. (Supplement), 13; 15 A.L.R. (C.N.), 25. *Judge Moule* (1909).

Composition with creditors—Debtor's duty to disclose assets—Non-disclosure of valueless assets of a deceased person—Assets subsequently becoming valuable—Rights of creditors and next of kin.]—In inducing his creditors to accept a composition and to release him from all liability in respect of the debts due by him to them, a debtor should disclose everything which would affect the judgment of a rational creditor governing himself by the principles and calculations on which creditors do in practice act. Certain shares in building societies that were part of the estate of a deceased person, which was insolvent, were not disclosed to the creditors of such estate on their agreeing by deed to accept a composition (which they did accept) and on payment thereof to discharge his estate (which they did discharge) from all liability in respect of his debts. Such shares were valueless at that time, but some considerable time subsequently became valuable. *Held*, that the creditors were not entitled to the proceeds of the sale of such shares, as against the next of kin of the deceased, because the creditors' judgment would not, under the circumstances of the case, have been affected by the disclosure of the shares. *In re Warren; National Trustees Executors and Agency Co. of Australasia Ltd.* v. *Daniel White & Co. Ltd.*, (1909) V.L.R., 6; 30 A.L.T., 129; 14 A.L.R., 683. *Cussen, J.*

Company—Liquidation—Surplus after discharge of liabilities—Distribution—Shareholder with fully paid up and contributing shares—Sequestration of estate—Composition with creditors—Release, effect of.]—*See* COMPANY, col. 164. *In re Metropolitan Bank Ltd.*, (1912) V.L.R., 449; 34 A.L.T., 138; 18 A.L.R., 463.

(c) *Fraudulent Preference.*

Fraudulent preference—" With a view to prefer "—Insolvency Act 1890 (No. 1102), sec. 73—Insolvency Act 1897 (No. 1513), sec. 116.]—*Per Griffith, C.J., Barton* and *O'Connor, JJ.*—In order that a disposition of property made by a debtor in insolvent circumstances to one of his creditors may be a fraudulent preference within the meaning of sec. 73 of the *Insolvency Act* 1890, the giving of the preference must be the substantial object which the debtor desires to achieve. The motive or reason which induces the desire is irrelevant. *Muntz* v. *Smail*, (1909) 8 C.L.R., 262; 15 A.L.R., 162.

Fraudulent preference—" With a view to prefer "—Disposition made to carry out a legal obligation—Insolvency Act 1890 (No. 1102), sec. 73—Insolvency Act 1897 (No. 1513), sec. 116.]—The defendant, a cattle salesman, on behalf of a principal sold cattle to A. advancing the purchase money himself and receiving from A. a promissory note for the amount of the advance, and also entering into a verbal agreement with A. that A. would re-sell the cattle through the defendant, who might repay himself the amount of the advance out of the purchase money. A. having come into insolvent circumstances instructed his solicitor to call a meeting of his creditors. Two days afterwards, being requested by other creditors to allow them to take some of the cattle in payment of their debts, he refused to do so on the ground that it would not be fair to the other creditors. Eight days afterwards and within a month of his insolvency, and before the promissory note became due A., at the request of the defendant and believing that he was thereby fulfilling his obligation to the defendant, and that it would be wrong to do otherwise, sold his cattle through the defendant who received the purchase money and applied it in discharge of A.'s liability to him. In an action by the trustee in insolvency of A. against the defendant, *Held* (per *Griffith, C.J., Barton* and *O'Connor, JJ., Isaacs, J.* dissenting), that A. had made a fraudulent preference in favour of the defendant, and that the trustee was entitled to recover the amount received by the defendant as purchase money of the cattle. *Muntz* v. *Smail*, (1909) 8 C.L.R., 262 ; 15 A.L.R., 162.

Insolvency—Fraudulent preference—Purchaser in good faith and for valuable consideration—" Payment made "—Insolvency Act 1890 (No. 1102), sec. 37 (1), 71, 73, 74.]—A. being indebted to B., a stock and station agent, put property into the hands of B. for sale, in pursuance of an antecedent agreement, the intent being that B. should retain out of the moneys received from the sale the amount of the debt owing to him by A. B. sold the property and appropriated the proceeds to the amount of the debt. At no time before the sale did B. know that A. was in financial difficulties. *Held*, that the transaction was not a fraudulent preference, as the agent, having no knowledge of A.'s insolvent circumstances, was a " payee in good faith and for valuable consideration." *Held, per* a' *Beckett* and *Hood, JJ.* (sed contra per *Madden, C.J.*), that the transaction amounts to a " payment made " within sec. 73 of the *Insolvency Act* 1890. *Muntz* v. *Smail*, 8 C.L.R., 262 ; 15 A.L.R., 162, discussed. *In re McConnell* ; *Macfarlane* v. *McDonald*, (1912) V.L.R., 102 ; 33 A.L.T., 195 ; 18 A.L.R., 90. F.C., *Madden, C.J.*, a' *Beckett* and *Hood, JJ.*

Fraudulent preference—Transfer with intent to defeat or delay creditors—Desire to protect sureties—Banker and customer—Payments made in the ordinary course of banking business—Insolvency Act 1890 (No. 1102), secs. 37 (ii.), 73.]—M., an hotelkeeper, bought an hotel, and in order to carry on the business obtained an overdraft from a Bank which was guaranteed by two sureties to the extent of £450. He was not successful in the business and with the intention, made known by him to the Bank, of protecting the sureties but with the belief, also made known by him to the Bank, that he was still solvent he sold the hotel and business which were substantially all his assets. The overdraft at this time amounted to £576. The purchase money consisted of £350 in cash and three promissory notes of £200 each. One

of the notes was by M.'s desire and with the consent of the Bank discounted and after payment of £140, the amount due to one of M's creditors, the balance of the proceeds together with the £350 was paid into M.'s account in the ordinary way and the remaining two notes were lodged with the Bank for collection. Cheques drawn on M.'s account for small amounts were paid and another of the notes was discounted and after payment of £57, the amount due to another of M.'s creditors, the balance of the proceeds was paid into M.'s account. The Bank discounted the remaining note paid the proceeds into M.'s account, thereby extinguishing the overdraft, and released the sureties. Within three months from the payment of the purchase money into the Bank M.'s estate was compulsorily sequestrated. The debts remaining unpaid amounted to £335 and the assets were practically nothing. *Held*, that the payment to the Bank was neither a fraudulent preference nor a transfer made with intent to defeat or delay creditors. *Re Mills*, 58 L.T., 871, followed. *M'Donald* v. *Bank of Victoria*, (1906) V.L.R., 199 ; 27 A.L.T., 177 ; 12 A.L.R., 120. a' *Beckett, J.* (1906).

Insolvency—Fraudulent preference—View of giving preference—Insolvency Act 1890 (No. 1102), sec. 73.]—A. was indebted to B. and other creditors, the total amount of his liabilities being, as he knew, such that if all his creditors had demanded payment at once, he would have been unable to pay them in full. From his relation, however, with them and his knowledge of them, he never anticipated they would so act. Not contemplating the possibility of insolvency, and without a view of giving a preference, A. assigned to B. by means of an H. order his right to have returned to him his Savings Bank pass-book, showing that there was a certain sum in the Bank to his credit, and a withdrawal order, duly signed, by means of which that sum could be withdrawn from the Bank, both of which had been deposited by him with the Commonwealth as security for the completion of a contract. Notice of the assignment was given to the Commonwealth by B. The H. order authorized the

Commonwealth to hand over the pass-book and withdrawal order to B. Within three months from the date of the assignment A. became insolvent. *Held*, that the asignment was not a fraudulent preference within sec. 73 of the *Insolvency Act* 1890. *Cox* v. *Smail*, (1912) V.L.R., 274 ; 18 A.L.R., 299. *Cussen, J.*

Insolvency Act 1890 (No. 1102), sec. 73—View of giving a preference—Statement of insolvent as to state of mind.]—Sec. 73 of the *Insolvency Act* 1890 was meant as a plain guide for ordinary people, and if a debtor is intelligent, honest, and desirous of telling the truth, his statement as to his state of mind in doing any act should be treated at least as of great weight. *Cox* v. *Smail*, (1912) V.L.R., 274 ; 18 A.L.R., 299. *Cussen, J.*

Insolvency Act 1890 (No. 1102), sec. 73—View of giving a preference—State of mind of debtor—What matters may be evidentiary of.]—For a discussion of matters of an evidentiary character which may lead to a conclusion with respect to the state of mind of an insolvent, *see Cox* v. *Smail*, (1912) V.L.R., 274 ; 18 A.L.R., 299. *Cussen, J.*

Insolvency Act 1890 (No. 1102), sec. 73—Fraudulent preference—Insolvent builder—Architect's certificate—Payment thereon to creditor of builder.]—A building contractor, shortly prior to filing his schedule, handed to a timber merchant, to whom he owed money, an architect's certificate for a progress payment in respect of the erection of a certain building, and the building owner subsequently duly made such payment to the timber merchant. *Held*, that the timber merchant should pay the money received by him upon such certificate to the trustee of the contractor's insolvent estate, as the circumstances showed the transaction to amount to a fraudulent preference. *Semble.*—An architect's certificate for a progress payment is " property " within the meaning of the Insolvency Acts. *In re Black*, 33 A.L.T. (Supplement), 3 ; 17 A.L.R. (C.N.), 19. *Judge Moule* (1911).

Insolvency Act 1890 (No. 1102), sec. 73—Fraudulent preference—Payee in good faith.]—

For a case in which it was held on the facts that the insolvent by indorsing a promissory note made in his favour and handing such note to a creditor intended to and did in fact prefer such creditor, and that the creditor had not received the note in " good faith," *see In re Black*, 33 A.L.T. (Supplement), 5 ; 17 A.L.R. (C.N.), 17. *Judge Moule* (1911).

" Fraudulent preference," meaning of—Motive of insolvent—Insolvency Act 1890 (No. 1102), secs. 73, 141 (xiii.).]—*See, post*, OFFENCES. *Re Cohen*, (1908) V.L.R., 171 ; 29 A.L.T., 187 ; 14 A.L.R., 74.

Fraudulent preference—Burden of proof—Nature of offence—Motive of insolvent—Knowledge of insolvent as to his insolvent condition—Insolvency Act 1890 (No. 1102), secs. 73, 141 (xiii.)—Insolvency Act 1897 (No. 1513), sec. 116.]—*See, post*, OFFENCES. *Re Cohen*, (1908) V.L.R., 171 ; 29 A.L.T., 187 ; 14 A.L.R., 74.

Insolvency Act 1890 (No. 1102), secs. 73, 141 (xiii.)—Insolvency Act 1897 (No. 1513), sec. 116—Fraudulent preference—Pressure of creditor, effect of—Insolvent's hope of saving his business.]—*See, post*, OFFENCES. *Re Cohen*, (1908) V.L.R., 171 ; 29 A.L.T., 187 ; 14 A.L.R., 74.

(d) Voluntary Settlements.

Settlement by widow on children—Non-registration—Validity of settlement—Insolvency Act 1897 (No. 1513), sec. 100.]—A settlement by a widow upon her children does not come within sec. 100 of the *Insolvency Act* 1897 and therefore need not be registered under that section in order to make it valid and to protect it in the event of the insolvency of the settlor. *Lorimer* v. *Smail*, (1911) 12 C.L.R., 504 ; 17 A.L.R., 441. H.C., *Griffith, C.J., Barton* and *O'Connor, JJ.*

Illegal contract—Transfer of land to defeat creditors—No proof that creditors defeated—Resulting trust.]—*See* TRUSTS AND TRUSTEES. *Payne* v. *McDonald*, (1908) 6 C.L.R., 208 ; 14 A.L.R., 366.

III.—DEBTS AND CLAIMS AGAINST THE
ESTATE.

(a) Proof by Secured Creditor.

**Insolvency Rules 1898, r. 270—Voting by
secured creditor—Omission to value security—
Whether omission arose from " inadvertence."**—Where a creditor deliberately, although on mistaken grounds, omits to value
his security, such omission is not an omission
which has arisen from " inadvertence "
within the meaning of rule 270 of the *Insolvency Rules* of 1898. *In re McGee*, 28
A.L.T. (Supplement), 12 ; 13 A.L.R. (C.N.),
7. *Judge Molesworth* (1907)..

(b) Preferential Debts.

**Preferential claims—Wages—Small sum in
hand—Whether to be expended in payment of
preferential claims or in costs of examination
summons—Insolvency Act 1890 (No. 1102),
secs. 40, 115, 123—Insolvency Act 1897 (No.
1513), sec. 111.**]—For a case in which, the
trustee having only a small sum in hand,
the question was considered whether he
should expend such sum in payment of the
preferential claims of employes or in an
examination of the insolvent, *see, In re
Wilson*, 16 A.L.R. (C.N.), 17. *Judge Moule*
(1910).

**Mines Act 1897 (No. 1514), sec. 168—
Insolvency Act 1890 (No. 1102), sec. 115—
Insolvency Act 1897 (No. 1513), sec. 79—
Companies Act 1890 (No. 1074), secs. 250, 303
—Mining Company—Assignment for benefit
of creditors—Workmen's wages—Payment—
Priority.**]—The trustee under a deed of assignment for the benefit of creditors, made by a
no-liability mining company, paid in priority
to other debts those due to workmen who had
been in the company's employment within two
months of the date of the cessation of its
work, but were not in such employment at
that date. *Held*, that such payments had
been validly made under sec. 168 of the *Mines
Act* 1897. *In re Old Jubilee Gold Mines
No Liability*, 34 A.L.T. (Supplement), 2 ;
18 A.L.R. (C.N.), 21. *Judge Moule* (1912).

**Insolvency Act 1890 (No. 1102), sec. 115—
Preferential debts—Municipal rates due at
date of sequestration of estate of occupier—**
Payment by landlord and owner with
acquiescence and concurrence of trustee—
Repayment in full in priority to all other
debts ordered.]—*See In re Pater* ; *In re
Robertson*, 30 A.L.T. (Supplement), 9 ; 14
A.L.R. (C.N.), 37. *Judge Moule* (1908).

**Insolvency Act 1890 (No. 1102), sec. 123
(iii.)—Insolvency Act 1897 (No. 1513), sec.
113—Sequestration of estate of deceased
person—Testamentary expenses incurred by
the representative of a deceased person in or
about the debtor's estate—Right of trustee to
reimbursement as a preferential debt.**]—The
representative of a deceased person's estate
is upon sequestration thereof entitled to
payment of the amount of costs incurred
by him in the administration of the estate
as a preferential debt under sec. 123 (iii.)
of the *Insolvency Act* 1890. *In re Nolan,
deceased* (*No. 2*), 30 A.L.T. (Supplement), 1 ;
14 A.L.R. (C.N.), 25. *Judge Moule* (1908).

**Taxed costs incurred in an action—A
preferential debt—Insolvency Act 1890 (No.
1102), secs. 77, 115, 123 (3).**]—" Taxed costs
incurred in an action " within the meaning of
sec. 77 of the *Insolvency Act* 1890 are notwithstanding sec. 115 " preferential debts "
within the meaning of sec. 123 (3) and to be
paid in preference to other ordinary debts.
In re Nolan (*No. 1*), 29 A.L.T. (Supplement),
31 ; 14 A.L.R. (C.N.), 21. *Judge Moule*
(1908).

**" Taxed costs incurred in action "—Party
and party costs—Costs of warrant of execution
to satisfy a judgment of the County Court—
Party and party costs—Sequestration—Effect
of on warrant of execution—Expenses of
execution prior to sequestration—Insolvency
Act 1890 (No. 1102), sec. 77—County Court
Rules 1891, r. 441.**]— The term " taxed
costs " in sec. 77 of the *Insolvency Act*
1890 refers to costs taxed in the ordinary
way between party and party and does not
include costs of execution of a County Court
judgment other than the costs of issuing the
warrant of execution (including the bailiff's
fee for executing the warrant). *In re Long
& Co.*, 20 Q.B.D., 316, applied. *In re
Nolan, deceased* (*No. 1*), 30 A.L.T. (Supple-

INSOLVENCY.

ment), 1; 14 A.L.R. (C.N.), 21. *Judge Moule* (1908).

(c) *Costs of Preparing Insolvent's Schedule and Deeds of Assignment.*

Insolvency Act 1890 (No. 1102), sec. 41— Insolvency Rules 1898, rr. 166, 167, 168, 169, 288—Appendix to Rules, Part 2, Scale of Solicitor's costs — "Instructions for Schedule" — Sequestration of partnership estate—Separate schedules, whether solicitor entitled to charge in respect of.]—In the case of the sequestration of a partnership estate, where the schedule of the firm has been filed, a solicitor is not entitled, in addition to the allowance of the item "instructions for schedule" in respect of the partnership schedule, to charge for "instructions for schedule" in respect of the individual members of the partnership. *In re Day and Sloan*, 32 A.L.T. (Supplement), 3; 16 A.L.R. (C.N.), 9. *Judge Moule* (1910).

Insolvency Act 1897 (No. 1513), Part VI.— Insolvency Rules 1898—Deeds of assignment— Solicitor's costs—Trustees' commission.]— Solicitors' costs and trustees' charges for commission in connection with deeds of assignment are not governed by the *Insolvency Rules* 1898. *In re Power*, 26 A.L.T. (Supplement), 10; 11 A.L.R. (C.N.), 37, disapproved and not followed. *In re Alderman*, 28 A.L.T. (Supplement), 13; 13 A.L.R. (C.N.), 6. *Judge Molesworth* (1907).

Insolvency Act 1897 (No. 1513), Part VI.— Deed of assignment—Costs of preparation —Taxation—Scale of costs—Rules of Supreme Court 1906, Appendix N., Conveyancing.]— The costs of preparing a deed of assignment should be taxed under the Conveyancing Scale in Appendix N. to the *Rules of the Supreme Court* 1906. *In re Hipper and Butcher*, 28 A.L.T. (Supplement), 17; 13 A.L.R. (C.N.), 9. *Judge Molesworth* (1907).

Insolvency—Deed of assignment—Printed form—Costs of preparing—Engrossing.]— Where a deed of assignment was on a printed form, *Held*, that the solicitor should be allowed a fair charge for "engrossing" the deed, which was fixed at 3d. per folio, and that the allowance should not be restricted

to that part of the deed which was in writing. *In re Hipper and Butcher*, 28 A.L.T. (Supplement), 17; 13 A.L.R. (C.N.), 9. *Judge Molesworth* (1907).

Costs — Taxation — Allocatur — Objection thereto by Chief Official Accountant.]— Insolvency Rules 1898, r. 151.]—The taxing officer's decision as to an item in a solicitor's bill of costs cannot be questioned by the Official Accountant in exercise of his powers under rule 151 of the *Insolvency Rules* 1898. *Re Schutze*, 29 A.L.T., (Supplement), 20; 14 A.L.R. (C.N.), 5. *Judge Moule* (1908).

(d) *Costs of Trustee; Auctioneer's Charges.*

See, also, post IV., *Examination of Insolvent and Witnesses.*

Costs—Certificate application — Trustee's report—Offences charged in report—Costs of employing solicitor to frame &c. such charges—Insolvency Act 1897 (No. 1513), secs. 27 (1), 91 (4)—Insolvency Rules 1898, r. 297.] —Where there are legal difficulties as to the form of the charges to be laid against the insolvent for offences under the insolvency law in the report required to be filed by the trustee under sec. 91 of the *Insolvency Act* 1897, the trustee will be allowed his costs of instructing a solicitor to frame such charges and of the drawing, copying and engrossing by the solicitor of so much of the report as relates to such charges. *In re Early*, 32 A.L.T. (Supplement), 9; 17 A.L.R. (C.N.), 9. *Judge Moule* (1911).

Costs of examination summons—Trustee indemnified against by creditor—Whether trustee entitled to be paid by insolvent or out of estate—Insolvency Act 1897 (No. 1513), sec. 111.]—Although a trustee holds an indemnity from a creditor against the costs of an examination summons, he is entitled (unless the Court otherwise orders) to have them paid by the insolvent or out of the insolvent estate. *In re Ostberg*, 33 A.L.T. (Supplement), 10; 17 A.L.R. (C.N.), 28. *Judge Moule* (1911).

Insolvency Act 1897 (No. 1513), Part VI.— Deed of assignment—Costs of trustee—Costs of taxation—Insolvency Rules 1898, r. 152.]— Rule 152 of the *Insolvency Rules* 1898 does not apply to the costs of taxation of a bill of costs of a solicitor acting for a trustee of an estate assigned by deed. *In re Hipper and Butcher*, 28 A.L.T. (Supplement), 17 ; 13 A.L.R. (C.N.), 9. *Judge Molesworth* (1907).

Insolvency Act 1890 (No. 1102), secs. 12, 153, 154—Insolvency Act 1897 (No. 1513), sec. 27 (3)—Insolvency Act 1903 (No. 1836), sec. 10—Insolvency Rules 1898—Schedule of Fees and Costs — Rules of Supreme Court 1906, Order LXV., r. 27 (35)—Costs—Trustee's solicitor—Deed of assignment—Charge for drawing bill of costs and copy for Chief Clerk—Allowance on taxation.]—Owing to the repeal by sec. 10 of the *Insolvency Act* 1903 of the provision in sec. 27 (3) of the *Insolvency Act* 1897 prohibiting the allowance of any costs " for preparing or taxing " bills of costs, a solicitor acting for the trustee under a deed of assignment, which provides for the payment by the trustee of all costs, charges and expenses out of the assigned estate, is entitled on the taxation of his bill of costs by the Chief Clerk to charge against the estate for drawing the bill of costs for taxation and a copy for the Chief Clerk. *In re Nichols and Skelton*, 32 A.L.T. (Supplement), 10 ; 17 A.L.R. (C.N.), 2. *Judge Moule* (1911).

Insolvency—Surcharges—Auctioneer's fees —Commission allowed to auctioneer on advertising charges—Out of pocket expenses—Appendix of Forms to Insolvency Rules 1898, Part 4.]—Where an auctioneer engaged in the sale of property of an insolvent estate incurs expenses in advertising the sale in the newspapers and pays the proprietors of the newspapers their account, less a certain commission, he is not entitled to charge the estate with the full amount, *i.e.*, without deducting the commission. *In re McBain*, 32 A.L.T. (Supplement), 2 ; 16 A.L.R. (C.N.), 9. *Judge Moule* (1910).

IV.—Examination of Insolvent and Witnesses.

Insolvency Act 1890 (No. 1102), sec. 135—Insolvency Act 1897 (No. 1513), sec. 111—Application by summons to examine insolvent—Refusal by trustee to make such application—Trustee's right to indemnity by creditors.]—A trustee, when requested in writing by one-fourth of the creditors in number and value who have proved on the insolvent estate must take all proceedings necessary to summon the insolvent or any witness for examination under sec. 135 of the *Insolvency Act* 1890 and is not entitled to demand as a condition precedent thereto an indemnity for costs from the creditors so requesting. *Semble.*—Where the Court upon the application of a creditor directs an examination, it may order an indemnity to be given. *In re Cooper*, 30 A.L.T. (Supplement), 13 ; 14 A.L.R. (C.N.), 43. *Judge Moule* (1908).

Insolvency—Examination of insolvent—Examination of other witnesses—Limit of—Power of creditors to examine—Power of Court to conduct examination through creditor's counsel.]—There is no power given to a creditor to examine any one but the insolvent, and the duty of examining other persons is thrown upon the Court. *Semble.*—The Court may on the examination of an insolvent conduct the examination of persons other than the insolvent by the creditor's counsel. *In re Cooper*, 30 A.L.T. (Supplement), 13 ; 14 A.L.R. (C.N.), 43. *Judge Moule* (1908).

Insolvency Act 1890 (No. 1102), sec. 135—Insolvency Act 1897 (No. 1513), sec. 111—Examination of insolvent and witnesses—Whether creditor may conduct examination.]—A creditor has not the right to examine any person other than the insolvent brought before the Court under sec. 135 of the *Insolvency Act* 1890, and the Court will not under ordinary circumstances allow him to examine any such other person. *In re Foller*, 31 A.L.T. (Supplement), 15 ; 16 A.L.R. (C.N.), 1. *Judge Moule* (1910).

Insolvent — Examination at instance of trustee—Examination at instance of creditor — Choice of solicitor — Insolvency Act 1890 (No. 1102), sec. 135.]—Where a trustee desires to hold an examination of an insolvent and assumes the responsibility thereof, he is free to choose his own solicitor, but where a creditor instigates such an examination and desires to carry it on, he is not bound to employ the solicitor nominated by the trustee. *In re Mackay*, 3 A.J.R., 10, discussed and distinguished. *In re Cooper*, 30 A.L.T. (Supplement), 13; 14 A.L.R. (C.N.), 43. *Judge Moule* (1908).

Insolvency—Examination—Application by creditors for direction that trustee summon before Court insolvent or witnesses—Trustee's indemnity against costs.]—*Semble.*—Where the Court upon the application of a creditor directs an examination it may order an indemnity to be given to the trustee for his costs. *In re Cooper*, 30 A.L.T. (Supplement), 13; 14 A.L.R. (C.N.), 43. *Judge Moule* (1908).

V.—ASSIGNEES AND TRUSTEES.

(a) *Appointment.*

Insolvency Act 1897 (No. 1513), sec. 19—Appointment of trustee—Solicitation.]—" I feel however satisfied that if a person uses *means* (and it is not possible to define specifically what the " means " may or may not include) to induce a creditor to vote for him, or makes suggestions why a creditor should vote for him rather than for another possible trustee, the Court may be able to hold that ' solicitation ' has been used. It is always a question of degree. The means used or the suggestions made may or may not satisfy the Court as proof of solicitation." *In re Fitzpatrick Brothers*, 29 A.L.T. (Supplement), 15; 14 A.L.R. (C.N.), 3. *Judge Moule* (1908).

(b) *Duties and Powers.*

Insolvency—Statutory duty of trustee—Obligation to perform even though pecuniary loss involved—Acts Interpretation Act 1890 (No. 1058), sec. 17.]—A trustee is bound to perform the statutory duties pertaining to his office, though the performance of such duties may involve him in a pecuniary loss. *In re Cooper*, 30 A.L.T. (Supplement), 13; 14 A.L.R. (C.N.), 43. *Judge Moule* (1908).

Trustees — Statutory duties — Whether trustee may delegate.]—A trustee must perform all the ordinary statutory duties himself. He cannot delegate these duties so as to cast an extra burden on the estate. *In re Early*, 32 A.L.T. (Supplement), 9; 17 A.L.R. (C.N.), 9. *Judge Moule* (1911).

Trustees in insolvency—Duty to Court—Disclosure of offences and frauds.]—*Semble.*—It is the duty of a trustee, as an officer of the Court, to bring all offences and suspected frauds under the notice of the Court. *In re McConnell*, 29 A.L.T. (Supplement), 26; 14 A.L.R. (C.N.), 19. *Judge Moule* (1908).

Insolvency Act 1897 (No. 1513), secs. 40, 41, 42—Trustee—Duty of trustee—Investigation and report.]—" Although secs. 40 and 41 of the Act of 1897 do not in express language refer to a ' report ' by the trustee in the earlier stages of the proceedings as to the conduct of the insolvent, I nevertheless think that the intention of the Legislature was to have a full report of the whole matter at the earliest possible stage of the proceedings." *In re Barker and Smail*, 14 A.L.R. (C.N.), 1. *Judge Moule* (1908).

Insolvency Act 1897 (No. 1513), secs. 40, 41 — Trustee — Duty of trustee — Investigation and report—Insufficiency of report—Costs and expenses.]—" I shall in the future require all trustees to make the fullest reports in connection with the insolvency in the first instance, and then if I am forced afterwards, through the insufficiency of such report, to direct further investigation and report under sec. 41 (2), I shall take every care to see that the extra costs and expenses are borne by the trustees themselves." *Re Barker and Smail*, 14 A.L.R. (C.N.), 1. *Judge Moule* (1908).

Insolvency — Imprisonment of Fraudulent Debtors Act 1890 (No. 1100)—Order on fraud summons in force—Duty of trustee in insolvency.]—Whenever trustees in insolvency know that orders under the *Imprisonment of Fraudulent Debtors Act* are outstanding and in full force, they should warn insolvents that they are not to use their money (that is the money of the trustees) to discharge such orders. *In re Watts*, 33 A.L.T. (Supplement), 1; 17 A.L.R. (C.N.), 13. *Judge Moule* (1911).

Insolvency—Deed of assignment—Solicitor's costs—Trustee's duties.]—Bills of costs are not rendered to trustees as a matter of form merely, but in order that the trustees may have the necessary opportunity of duly protecting the interests of the creditors whom they represent. *In re Hipper and Butcher*, 50 A.L.T. (Supplement), 18; 15 A.L.R. (C.N.), 1. *Judge Moule* (1909).

Insolvency—Money paid to trustee under mistake of law—Whether trustee may avail himself of such mistake in resisting demand.]—Where a trustee of an insolvent estate has been paid money under a mistake of law, the Insolvency Court will not allow him to avail himself of that mistake in resisting a demand for the repayment thereof. *In re Black*, 33 A.L.T. (Supplement), 5; 17 A.L.R. (C.N.), 17. *Judge Moule* (1911).

(c) Remuneration.

Insolvency Act 1897 (No. 1513), Part VI.——Deed of assignment—Trustee's commission, agreement as to by creditors—Whether Official Accountant may question the amount agreed on.]—Where the creditors under a deed of assignment had agreed to the amount of remuneration to be retained by the trustee, *Held*, that the Official Accountant had no right, in auditing the trustees' accounts, to object to such amount being charged therein. *In re Alderman*, 28 A.L.T. (Supplement), 13; 13 A.L.R. (C.N.), 6. *Judge Molesworth* (1907).

Insolvency Act 1890 (No. 1102), sec. 53—Insolvency Act 1897 (No. 1513), sec. 65—Committee of inspection—Remuneration.]—A committee of inspection cannot derive any profit or advantage out of any transaction unless the prior consent of the Court or the creditors has been obtained, nor receive any payment " out of the estate " under sec. 65 of the *Insolvency Act* 1897 for services rendered except the amount voted at the date of its appointment. *In re Finn*, 30 A.L.T. (Supplement), 6; 14 A.L.R. (C.N.), 30. *Judge Moule* (1908).

Insolvency Act 1903 (No. 1836), sec. 4—Insolvency Rules 1898, r. 154—Assignee carrying on insolvent's business—Remuneration of assignee.]—The assignee in an insolvent estate (being empowered so to do) carried out certain contracts which had been part performed by the insolvent, and by careful supervision substantially benefitted the es-tate. *Held*, that the Court of Insolvency had no power to grant any remuneration to the assignee for his services beyond the sum mentioned in sec. 4 (ii.) of the *Insolvency Act* 1903. *In re Best*, 9 A.L.T., 32, approved. *In re McConnell*, 29 A.L.T. (Supplement), 8; 13 A.L.R. (C.N.), 32. *Judge Moule* (1907).

Insolvency Act 1897 (No. 1513), sec. 20—Insolvency Act 1903 (No. 1836), sec. 9—Remuneration of trustees—Commission, upon what amount calculated—" Net amount realized and available for payment "—Whether assignee's remuneration should be deducted.]—In calculating the trustee's commission or percentage under sec. 20 of the *Insolvency Act* 1897 (as amended by sec. 9 of the *Insolvency Act* 1903), the assignee's remuneration paid by the trustee under sec. 4 of the *Insolvency Act* 1903 ought not to be deducted in order to ascertain " the net amount realized and available for payment and application under sec. 123 of the *Insolvency Act* 1890," *i.e.*, the amount upon which the trustee's commission or percentage is payable. *In re Mitchell*, 28 A.L.T. (Supplement), 12; 13 A.L.R. (C.N.), 8. *Judge Molesworth* (1907).

Trustee's commission, how calculated—" Net amount realized and available for payment and application "—" Expenses of realization "—Insolvency Act 1890 (No. 1102), sec. 123—Insolvency Act 1897 (No. 1513), sec. 20—Insolvency Act 1903 (No. 1836), sec. 9.]—In fixing the amount of the commission to be allowed to a trustee by virtue of sec. 20 of the *Insolvency Act* 1897 as amended by sec. 9 of the *Insolvency Act* 1903, the expenses of realization which are to be deducted from the amount realized and available for application under sec. 123 of the *Insolvency Act* 1890 are the costs of the actual realization, and not expenses that lead up to or are merely incidental to the cost of the realization itself. *In re O'Neill*, (1905) V.L.R., 64; 26 A.L.T., 108 discussed. *In re Nolan*, 33 A.L.T. (Supplement). 2; 17 A.L.R. (C.N.), 14. *Judge Moule* (1911)

Trustee's commission—Upon what moneys chargeable—Moneys recovered in action and expended in costs of action.]—A trustee is empowered to charge commission on moneys recovered in an action against a debtor to the estate, and paid to the trustee's solicitor on account of the costs of such action. *Re Cohen*, 27 A.L.T. (Supplement), 12 ; 12 A.L.R. (C.N.), 7. *Judge Molesworth* (1906).

Insolvency Act 1897 (No. 1513), Part VI.— Deed of assignment—Goods hired by the assignors under letting and hiring agreements —Sale by trustee under arrangement with owner—Trustees commission on amount due to owner.]—Under an arrangement with the " owner " of certain goods which had been let to the " hirers " by the former under agreements of letting and hiring, the trustee of the estate of the hirers (who had assigned their estate for the benefit of creditors) sold such goods and realized by the sale more than sufficient to pay the amount due to the owner for such goods. *Held*, that the trustee was not entitled to claim any commission upon the amount to be paid to the owner, although the deed of assignment provided that the trustee was to be entitled to commission upon all moneys that should come to his hands. *In re A. V. and L. L. Coles*, 30 A.L.T. (Supplement), 22 ; 15 A.L.R. (C.N.), 1. *Judge Moule* (1909).

Insolvency Rules 1898, r. 151—Trustee's commission—Trustee under deed of assignment—Surcharge by Official Accountant.]— *See Re Schutze*, 29 A.L.T. (Supplement), 20 ; 14 A.L.R. (C.N.), 5. *Judge Moule* (1908).

(d) Control by Court.

Insolvency Act 1890 (No. 1102), sec. 135— Insolvency Act 1897 (No. 1513), sec. 32 (1)— Insolvency Rules 1898, r. 367 (2)—Ineffectual examination summons—Disappearance of one of insolvent's books—" Receipt " for books lodged with assignee—Punishment for non-compliance with rules—Costs against assignee.] Where the examination of an insolvent under sec. 135 of the *Insolvency Act* 1890 upon a matter well grounded on facts as they appeared to the trustee was rendered nugatory, because one of the books relating to the insolvent's business had disappeared, and the Court was unable to ascertain whether it had or had not been lodged by the insolvent

with the assignee, who had failed to comply with the provisions of rule 367 (2) of the *Insolvency Rules* 1898, the Court held that it had power under sec. 32 (1) of the *Insolvency Act* 1897 to order and ordered the assignee to pay the taxed costs of the trustee in the examination summons, including therein such costs as might have been incurred in the investigation of the facts connected with the disappearance of the book. *In re Leber* ; *In re Shackell*, 29 A.L.T. (Supplement), 9 ; 13 A.L.R. (C.N.), 35. *Judge Moule* (1907).

Insolvency Act 1890 (No. 1102), sec. 99— Insolvency Act 1897 (No. 1513), sec. 69— Lodging of orders of Court—Misuse of order of Court.]—*See Re Sharpe*, 29 A.L.T. (Supplement), 12 ; 14 A.L.R. (C.N.), 1. *Judge Moule* (1908).

Trustee in insolvency—Misuse of order of Court—False and misleading reports of trustee—Non-compliance with sec. 43 of the Insolvency Act 1897—Cancellation of registration—Insolvency Act 1897, secs. 30, 32 (1), 35, 115.]—*See In re Greaves* ; *Mitchell, Trustee*, 29 A.L.T. (Supplement), 23 ; 14 A.L.R. (C.N.), 11.

VI.—Certificate of Discharge.

(a) Generally.

Insolvency Act 1890 (No. 1102), sec. 139— Certificate of discharge—Delay in applying therefor.]—A certificate of discharge should not be refused unless some offence on the part of the insolvent is disclosed. Nine years' delay in applying, though a dangerous circumstance, is not in itself a ground for the refusal of a certificate of discharge. *In re Wood*, 29 A.L.T. (Supplement), 21 ; 14 A.L.R. (C.N.), 9. *Judge Moule* (1908).

Certificate of discharge—Second insolvency —Discharge not obtained in former insolvency The Court of Insolvency will not deal with an application for a discharge from a second insolvency until the insolvent has purged himself of his former insolvency. *In re Binko*, 2 Morr., 45, followed. *In re McConnell*, 29 A.L.T. (Supplement), 26 ; 14 A.L.R. (C.N.), 19. *Judge Moule* (1908).

(b) Statutory Conditions ; Dispensation ;
Special Reasons, &c.

Insolvency Act 1890 (No. 1102), sec. 139—Conditions as to certificate of discharge—" Insolvent estate," meaning of.]—The words " insolvent estate " in sec. 139 of the *Insolvency Act 1890* mean the estate which was vested in the assignee by operation of law, and not the estate which has been left after payment of costs occasioned by examinations, &c. *In re Wood*, 29 A.L.T. (Supplement), 21 ; 14 A.L.R. (C.N.), 9. *Judge Moule* (1908).

Insolvency Act 1890 (No. 1102), secs. 138, 139—Dispensation with condition that estate shall pay seven shillings in the pound—Circumstances justifying refusal of dispensation.]—The mere fact that an insolvent was never in a position to pay seven shillings in the pound to his creditors is not sufficient to cause the Court to refuse to dispense with the payment of the statutory dividend. *In re Ross, an Insolvent*, 31 A.L.T. (Supplement), 3 ; 15 A.L.R. (C.N.), 13. *Judge Moule* (1909).

Insolvency Act 1897 (No. 1513), sec. 92—Certificate of discharge—Insolvent found guilty of an offence—" Special reasons " for not refusing certificate, what does not constitute.]—Where an insolvent, by serving his sentence, had expiated the crime of embezzlement committed in the course of his trading, his subsequent good conduct was held not to constitute " special reasons " within the meaning of sec. 92 of the *Insolvency Act* 1897, although six years had elapsed since his insolvency. *In re Solomons*, 10 Man., 369, discussed and followed. *In Re Moulton*, 30 A.L.T. (Supplement), 4 ; 14 A.L.R.(C.N.), 29. *Judge Moule* (1908).

Insolvency Act 1890 (No. 1102), sec. 96—Certificate of discharge—Effect of—Order or judgment in matrimonial cause—Insolvent, as co-respondent, ordered to pay Damages—Certificate subject to condition—Statutory dividend.]—Where an insolvent as co-respondent in a divorce suit has been ordered to pay damages to the petitioner therein, the Court has power, under sec. 96 of the *Insolvency Act* 1897, to grant him a certificate of discharge subject to the payment by him

to such petitioner of 7s. in the pound on the amount of such damages. *In re Ware*, 34 A.L.T. (Supplement), 1 ; 18 A.L.R. (C.N.), 5. *Judge Moule* (1912).

Costs of trustee, what are—Costs of examination summons—Insolvency Act 1897 (No. 1513), sec. 93—Insolvency Act 1903 (No. 1836), sec. 16.]—The trustee's costs of an examination summons are " costs, charges, expenses, &c." of the trustee within the meaning of sec. 93 of the *Insolvency Act* 1897 as amended by sec. 16 of the *Insolvency Act* 1903. *In re Ostberg*, 33 A.L.T. (Supplement), 10 ; 17 A.L.R. (C.N.), 28. *Judge Moule* (1911).

(c) Practice.

Insolvency Act 1890 (No. 1102), sec. 149—Insolvency Act 1897 (No. 1513), sec. 91—Insolvency Rules 1898, Appendix of Forms, No. 64—Contempt of Court—Certificate—Compulsory appearance—Refusal of insolvent to be sworn—Power of committal—Form of notice of motion to insolvent.]—*Semble.*—By virtue of sec. 91 of the *Insolvency Act* 1897, the Insolvency Court has power to compel an insolvent who has been required to appear before it under sec. 149 of the *Insolvency Act* 1890 to be sworn and give evidence, although such evidence might tend to render him liable to imprisonment. *In re Aarons*, 6 V.L.R. (I.), 56 ; 2 A.L.T., 51, distinguished. The notice required under sec. 149 of the *Insolvency Act* 1890 requiring the insolvent to attend before the Court to have the question of the grant or refusal of his certificate dealt with, should direct attention to the fact that the insolvent may be punished or otherwise dealt with as if the certificate had been applied for by him. *In re Hickman*, 31 A.L.T. (Supplement), 10 ; 15 A.L.R. (C.N.), 21. *Judge Moule* (1909).

Insolvency Act 1890 (No. 1102), secs. 142, 149—Insolvency Act 1897 (No. 1513), sec. 41 Insolvency Rules 1898, r. 308—Certificate of discharge—Compulsory application—Power of trustee—Procedure—Costs.]—A trustee of an insolvent estate may apply to the Court to require an insolvent to come up for a certificate of discharge. The trustee's report should be as full as possible and should specify the particular charges or offences of which the trustee thinks the insolvent has been guilty. A copy of such report should be served upon the insolvent a reasonable time before the hearing and will be treated as notice to the insolvent of such charges and offences. The trustee is entitled to an order that the insolvent pay his costs of the application. *In re McConnell*, 29 A.L.T. (Supplement), 26; 14 A.L.R. (C.N.), 19. *Judge Moule* (1908).

Insolvency Act 1890 (No. 1102), sec. 56—Insolvency Act 1897 (No. 1513), secs. 40, 91 (4)—Insolvency Rules, 1898, rr. 297, 373—Certificate of discharge, application for—Absence of Official Assignee's report—Jurisdiction of Court to call upon Official Accountant to furnish report.]—Where at the time an insolvent applies for his certificate of discharge the Official Assignee has not furnished a report as required by sec. 91 (4) of the *Insolvency Act* 1897 and rule 297 of the *Insolvency Rules* 1898, the Court has power under rule 373 to call upon the Official Accountant to furnish a report in the absence of the Official assignee. *In re Summers*, 32 A.L.T. (Supplement), 1; 16 A.L.R. (C.N.), 15. *Judge Moule* (1910).

Certificate of discharge—Trustee's costs, dispute as to—Practice—Application for Judge's signature to certificate—Insolvency Act 1890 (No. 1102), sec. 145—Insolvency Act 1897 (No. 1513), sec. 93—Insolvency Act 1903 (No. 1836), sec. 16.]—Where there is a question in dispute between an insolvent and the trustee of his estate, as to whether the latter has been paid all the costs, charges, expenses and allowances, and remuneration required to be paid under sec. 93 of the *Insolvency Act* 1897 as amended by sec. 16 of the *Insolvency Act* 1903 before the insolvent is entitled to an absolute grant of a certificate of discharge, such question may be raised by the insolvent making, on notice to the trustee, an application to the Judge to sign such certificate under sec. 145 of the *Insolvency Act* 1890. *In re Ostberg*, 33 A.L.T. (Supplement), 10; 17 A.L.R. (C.N.), 28. *Judge Moule* (1911).

Insolvency Act 1890 (No. 1102), secs. 138, 139—Insolvency Rules 1898, Appendix of Forms, Form No. 67—Grant of certificate of discharge and suspension of issue thereof until payment of statutory dividend—Whether Court may make such order where statutory dividend not paid.]—*Per Judge Moule.*—"The form of order that has generally been made is one which grants the certificate, but suspends its issue or operation until the statutory condition of the payment of 7s. in the £ has been complied with. This ordinary form of order would now appear to be wrong, as the provisions of sec. 139 appear to be clear that no certificate can be granted, and the Court has no power to grant and suspend the certificate unless it is satisfied . . . that the failure to pay the 7s. in the £ arose from circumstances for which the insolvent could not, in the opinion of the Court, be justly held responsible . . . The form No. 67 in the Appendix of Forms *Insolvency Rules* 1898 is wrong according to the decision of *In re Caulfield*, 27 V.L.R., 588; 23 A.L.T., 133; 7 A.L.R. (C.N.), 94." *In re Cohen*, 13 A.L.R. (C.N.), 33. (1907).

VII.—OFFENCES.

Insolvency Act 1890 (No. 1102), secs. 141, 145—Offences under Insolvency Acts—Habits of gambling—Extravagance or vice.]—The words "becoming insolvent" in sub-sec. (v.) of sec. 141 of the *Insolvency Act* 1890 are used in the same sense as the words "become insolvent" in sec. 145 of that Act and refer to the order actually making the person insolvent. *In re O'Hanlon*, 30 A.L.T. (Supplement), 8; 14 A.L.R. (C.N.), 33. *Judge Moule* (1908).

Insolvency Act 1890 (No. 1102), sec. 141 (12)—Offence of "unlawfully" expending or appropriating certain property—Actual dishonesty, necessary to constitute.]—To constitute the offence under sec. 141 (12) of the *Insolvency Act* 1890 of "unlawfully" expending for his own benefit or appropriating to his own use any property of which he has had the charge or disposition as a trustee or agent, factor or broker only and not in any other capacity there must have been actual dishonesty (and not merely culpable negligence) or the part of the insolvent. *In re Martin*, 2 A.L.T., 48, discussed. *In re Scott,*

4 A.J.R., 50, distinguished. *In re Ross*,
31 A.L.T. (Supplement), 3; 15 A.L.R. (C.N.),
13. *Judge Moule* (1909).

**Insolvency Act 1890 (No. 1102), sec. 141
(xii.)—Trustee, agent or broker—Unlawful
appropriation of property held as agent—
Principal's goods sold by agent on commission
—Relationship of debtor and creditor—Insolvency of agent—Whether agent liable for
offence.]**—Where, in the case of goods sold
by an agent on behalf of his principal, the
principal has treated the relationship between
them as that of debtor and creditor, the
principal cannot on the insolvency of the
agent charge him with an offence under
sec. 141 (xii.) of the *Insolvency Act* 1890.
In re James, 32 A.L.T. (Supplement), 12;
17 A.L.R. (C.N.), 5. *Judge Moule* (1911).

**" Fraudulent preference " meaning of —
Motive of insolvent—Insolvency Act 1890 (No.
1102), secs. 73, 141 (xiii.).]**—The term
" fraudulent preference " in sec. 141 (xiii.)
of the *Insolvency Act* 1890 means a transaction covered by sec. 73. For the purposes
of these sections the term " fraudulent "
means no more than that the dominant
motive was to prefer the creditor. *Re Cohen*,
(1908) V.L.R., 171; 29 A.L.T., 187; 14
A.L.R., 74. F.C., *a' Beckett, Hodges* and
Cussen, JJ.

**Fraudulent preference—Burden of proof—
Nature of offence—Motive of insolvent—
Knowledge of insolvent as to his insolvent
condition—Insolvency Act 1890 (No. 1102),
secs. 73, 141 (xiii.)—Insolvency Act 1897 (No.
1513), sec. 116.]**—Where an insolvent is
charged with having given a creditor a
fraudulent preference under sec. 141 (xiii.)
of the *Insolvency Act* 1890 the onus of proof
is upon the party alleging the offence; and
he must prove that the insolvent's dominant
motive was to prefer the creditor. The fact
that the debtor knew he was insolvent and
that the payment would give a preference is
not necessarily sufficient to establish the
charge. *Re Cohen*, (1908) V.L.R., 171;
29 A.L.T., 187; 14 A.L.R., 74. F.C.,
a' Beckett, Hodges and *Cussen, JJ.* (1908).

**Insolvency Act 1890 (No. 1102), secs. 73,
141 (xiii.)—Insolvency Act 1897 (No. 1513),**
sec. 116—Fraudulent preference—Pressure of
creditor, effect of—Insolvent's hope of saving
his business.]—C., a manufacturer in involved
circumstances, owed £1,400 to S. and Co.,
a firm of warehousemen, without whose
support he could not continue in business.
S. and Co. notified him that unless he got his
wife to guarantee the debt to the extent of
£1,000 and unless he, in addition, undertook
to pay off £10 weekly, they would not trade
further with him. C., hoping thus to save
his business and believing this to be his
only chance of so doing, complied with the
demand, and thus conferred upon S. and Co.
a considerable advantage. Some of the
weekly instalments were paid within three
months of the sequestration of C.'s estate.
Held (per Hodges and *Cussen, JJ., a' Beckett,
J.,* dissenting), that the payments did not
amount to a fraudulent preference. *Re
Cohen*, (1908) V.L.R., 171; 29 A.L.T., 187;
14 A.L.R., 74. F.C. (1908).

VIII.—ABUSE OF PROCESS.

**Abuse of process—Insolvency proceedings
to stifle litigation—Action by non-trader—
No actual damage.** *Quaere,* whether proceedings in insolvency taken to stifle litigation between the parties amount to an
abuse of process of the Court in respect of
which an action will lie. *Quaere,* also,
whether such an action, if it will lie at all,
will lie by a non-trader without proof of
actual damage. *Bayne* v. *Baillieu; Bayne*
v. *Riggall,* (1908) 6 C.L.R., 382; 14 A.L.R.,
426. H.C., *Griffith, C.J., Barton* and *O'Connor, JJ.*

**Abuse of process of Court—Petition in
insolvency during pendency of action between
parties—Good petitioning creditor's debt.]**—
In an action to recover damages for personal
injuries the defendant counterclaimed for a
judgment debt owing to him by the plaintiff.
Judgment was given for the defendant on the
claim and on the counter-claim, and the
plaintiff gave notice of appeal to the High
Court from the judgment. The defendant
then took proceedings, based on the original
judgment debt, to have the plaintiff's estate
sequestrated. *Held,* that such proceedings
were not an abuse of the process of the Court.

Bayne v. *Blake*, (1909) 9 C.L.R., 360. H.C., *Griffith, C.J., Barton* and *O'Connor, JJ.*

Abuse of process of Court—Insolvency proceedings to stifle litigation—Action for damages in respect of—Special damage, whether necessary to prove.]—Assuming that the taking of proceedings in insolvency for the purpose of stifling litigation between the parties amounts to an abuse of the process of the Court in respect of which an action will lie (as to which *quaere*) a necessary ingredient in the cause of action is that damage has thereby resulted. *Held*, therefore, that the action must fail where the litigation attempted to be stifled was in respect of a claim which was afterwards determined to be untenable. *Bayne* v. *Blake*, (1909) 9 C.L.R., 347; 15 A.L.R., 486. H.C., *Griffith, C.J., Barton* and *O'Connor, JJ.*

Malicious use of process of Court of Insolvency—Action claiming damages in respect of —Good petitioning creditors debt and available act of insolvency—Whether an answer to claim.]—A claim for fraudulently falsely and maliciously and without reasonable or probable cause, putting in motion the process of the Insolvency Court, is answered by proof that at the time the proceedings were taken there was a good petitioning creditor's debt and an available act of insolvency. *Bayne* v. *Blake*, (1909) 9 C.L.R., 347; 15 A.L.R., 486. H.C., *Griffith, C.J., Barton* and *O'Connor, JJ.*

Order XIV. (A) (Rules of 1906)—Frivolous or vexatious action, what is—Order for arrest of witness in insolvency proceedings—Purpose of order not to discover assets but to hamper appeal to High Court—Action for damages in respect of such order—Conspiracy to oppress —No actual damage.—*See* PRACTICE and PLEADING. *Bayne* v. *Baillieu*; *Bayne* v. *Riggall*, (1908) 6 C.L.R., 382; 14 A.L.R., 426.

INSTRUMENTS ACT.

I.—BILLS AND NOTES.

Promissory note—Liability of indorser— Order in time of indorsement—Indorsement by payee—Holder in due course—Estoppel— Instruments Act 1890 (No. 1103), secs. 21, 38, 55, 56, 57, 90.]—*See* BILLS OF EXCHANGE AND PROMISSORY NOTES, cols. 76, 77. *Ferrier* v. *Stewart*, (1912) 15 C.L.R., 32; 18 A.L.R., 262.

Promissory note—Material alteration, what is—Place of payment, what is—Instruments Act 1890 (No. 1103), sec. 65 (2).]—A promissory note when made contained nothing indicating the place of payment other than the printed words " Payable at " followed by a blank. After delivery and without the authority or assent of the maker the blank, was filled in with the words and figures " 15 Queen's Bridge Street, Melbourne." In proceedings against the maker for money due on the note, *Held*, that it had been materially altered and was accordingly avoided as against the maker. *Semble*, that it was an alteration of the "place of payment" within the meaning of sec. 65 (2) of the *Instruments Act* 1890. *Sims* v. *Anderson*, (1908) V.L.R., 348; 29 A.L.T., 241; 14 A.L.R., 210. *Cussen, J.* (1908).

Negotiable instrument—Material alteration, nature of—Instruments Act 1890 (No. 1103), sec. 65—Enumeration of material alterations, whether exhaustive.]—The enumeration of material alterations in sec. 65 of the *Instruments Act* 1890 is not exhaustive. An alteration is a material alteration if it makes the instrument operate differently. *Sims* v. *Anderson*, (1908) V.L.R., 348; 29 A.L.T., 241; 14 A.L.R., 210. *Cussen, J.* (1908).

Banker and customer—Cheques drawn with spaces afterwards fraudulently filled up— Liability of Bank—Duty of customer—Negligence. *See* BANKER AND CUSTOMER, col. 70. *Colonial Bank of Australasia* v. *Marshall*, (1906) A.C., 559.

Money lender—Re-opening transaction— Promissory note—" Agreement or security " —Money Lenders Act 1906 (No. 2061), sec. 4.]—An action upon a promissory note is an " action to enforce an agreement or security " within the meaning of sec. 4 of the *Money Lenders Act* 1906. *Wilson* v. *Moss*, 8 C.L.R., 146; 15 A.L.R., 131. H.C., *Griffith*, *C.J.*, *Barton*, *O'Connor* and *Isaacs*, *JJ.* 1909.

Instruments Act 1890 (No. 1103), secs. 92, 93—" Resides," meaning of in sec. 93.]—A writ under the Act may be served on a person temporarily resident in Victoria, who is permanently domiciled and resident in another State. *Philips* v. *Cooper*, (1906) V.L.R., 31; 12 A.L.R. (C.N.), 5. *a'Beckett*, *J.* (1906).

Bill of exchange—Action upon under Instruments Act 1890 — Writ—Service out of jurisdiction—Indorsement by Prothonotary— Necessity for Judge's order for such indorsement—Instruments Act 1890 (No. 1103), sec. 92—Service and Execution of Process Act 1901 (No. 11 of 1901), secs. 5, 8.]—*Sternberg* v. *Egan*, 18 A.L.R. (C.N.), 20. *Hood*, *J.* (1912).

Stamps Act 1890 (No. 1140), sec. 81, Third Schedule—Stamps Act 1892 (No. 1274), Schedule—" Promissory note " — Mortgage debenture charging property and providing means for enforcing security.]—*See* STAMPS ACTS. *In re Stamps Acts*, (1906) V.L.R., 364; 27 A.L.T., 204; 12 A.L.R., 186.

Insolvency Act 1890 (No. 1102), sec. 37— Insolvency Act 1897 (No. 1513), sec. 106 (2)— Sequestration—Petitioning creditor's debt— Current promissory note.]—*See* INSOLVENCY. *David* v. *Malof*, (1908) 5 C.L.R., 749; 14 A.L.R., 297.

II.—BILLS OF SALE AND STOCK MORTGAGES.

Bill of sale given by way of security—Consideration—Statement of in notice of intention to file, whether sufficient—Instruments Act 1890 (No. 1103), secs. 134, 135, Schedule V.]— *See* BILLS OF SALE, col. 74. *O'Connor* v. *Quinn*, (1911) 12 C.L.R., 239; 17 A.L.R., 345.

Instruments Act 1890 (No. 1103), secs. 134, 135, Schedule V.—Notice of intention to file— Statement of consideration, whether sufficient —Past debt.—See* BILLS OF SALE, cols. 74, 75. *O'Connor* v. *Quinn*, (1911) 12 C.L.R., 239; 17 A.L.R., 345.

Instruments Act 1890 (No. 1103), secs. 133, 144—Declarations and Affidavits Act 1890 (No. 1191), sec. 6—Bill of sale—Registration—Affidavit verifying bill—Affidavit of renewal—Such affidavits to be made before Commissioners for taking declarations and affidavits—Affidavits—Commissioners of the Supreme Court—Restriction of authority.]— *See* BILLS OF SALE. col. 75. *Wrigglesworth* v. *Collis*; *Spencer, claimant*, 33 A.L.T. (Supplement), 13; 18 A.L.R. (C.N.), 6.

Instruments Act 1890 (No. 1103), sec. 142 —Bill of sale—Removal of caveat—Summons, form of.]—*See* BILLS OF SALE, cols. 75, 76. *In re Coburn*, 28 A.L.T. (Supplement), 3; 12 A.L.R. (C.N.), 17.

Instruments Act 1890 (No. 1103), sec. 142— Bill of sale—Caveat—Tender of amount due to caveator—Refusal to accept—Removal of caveat—Jurisdiction of Judge to order.]—, *See* BILLS OF SALE, col. 76. *In re Coburn*, 28 A.L.T. (Supplement), 3; 12 A.L.R. (C.N.), 17.

Bill of sale—Given and registered in New South Wales over goods in New South Wales— Goods subsequently brought to Victoria— Bill of sale valid in Victoria.]—*Taylor* v. *Lovegrove*; *Original Mont de Piete, claimant*, 18 A.L.R. (C.N.), 22. *Hodges*, *J.* (1912).

Instruments Act 1890 (No. 1103), sec. 169, 170, 171—Stock mortgage—" Other chattels " meaning of.]—The words " other chattels on any station in Victoria " in secs. 169, 170, and 171 of the *Instruments Act* 1890 include all other chattels whatever may be their nature and whatever may be the purpose for which they are used on such station. *Anderson* v. *Carter*, (1894) 20 V.L.R., 246; 16 A.L.T., 49, distinguished. *The International Harvester Co. of America* v. *Rowe*, (1909) V.L.R., 244; 30 A.L.T., 201; 15 A.L.R., 212. F.C., *Madden*, *C.J.*, *a'Beckett* and *Hood*, *JJ.* [But see *Stock Mortgages Act* 1910 (No. 2252)].

III.—STATUTE OF FRAUDS.

Instruments Act 1890 (No. 1103), secs. 208, 209—Statute of Frauds (29 Car. II. c. 3)— Contract or sale of land—Signature to note

or memorandum—Signature by amanuensis in presence and by direction of party to be charged.]—*See* CONTRACT OR AGREEMENT, col. 194. *Thomson* v. *Mc Innes*, (1911) 12 C.L.R., 562 ; 17 A.L.R., 354.

Sale of goods—Memorandum of agreement, whether necessary—Contract itself in writing —Sale of Goods Act 1896 (No. 1422), sec. 9.] *See* CONTRACT OR AGREEMENT, col. 194. *Patterson* v. *Dolman*, (1908) V.L.R., 354 ; 29 A.L.T., 256 ; 14 A.L.R., 240.

Instruments Act 1890 (No. 1103), sec. 208— Memorandum of contract contained in several documents—Agreement to act as manager of company—Agreement implied from Articles of Association and conduct of parties.]—*See* CONTRACT OR AGREEMENT, cols. 194, 195, 196. *Glass* v. *Pioneer Rubber Works of Australia Ltd.*, (1906) V.L.R., 754 ; 28 A.L.T., 64 ; 12 A.L.R., 529.

Instruments Act 1890 (No. 1103), sec. 208— Sale of land—Note or memorandum—Several documents—Parol evidence, whether admissible to connect—Reference to document— Reference to transaction in which document may or may not have been written.]—*See* CONTRACT OR AGREEMENT, col. 196. *Thomson* v. *Mc Innes*, (1911) 12 C.L.R., 562 ; 17 A.L.R., 354.

Written contract—Parol evidence to identify subject matter, admissibility of—Latent ambiguity—Language apt to express a specific article of a class or any article of that class— Statute of Frauds.]—*See* CONTRACT OR AGREEMENT, cols. 196, 197. *Bruton* v. *Farm and Dairy Machinery Co. Proprietary Ltd.*, (1910) V.L.R., 196 ; 31 A.L.T., 200 ; 16 A.L.R., 241.

Instruments Act 1890 (No. 1103), sec. 208— Parol lease for less than three years—Lessee in possession of premises under existing tenancy.]—*See* CONTRACT OR AGREEMENT, col. 197. *Knott* v. *McKendrick*, 28 A.L.T. (Supplement), 4 ; 12 A.L.R. (C.N.), 23.

INSURANCE.

Insurance — Re-insurance — Construction of policy—Statements basis of contract—Settlement of claim by re-insured—Liability of re-insurers.]—By a policy dated 2nd January, 1908, the respondents insured the life of M. for £5,000 with profits, the policy providing that certain written statements made by M. as to his health, should be the basis of the contract, and that the policy would be void if they were untrue. By a proposal form of the same date the respondents applied to the appellant's to re-insure M's life for £5,000. This proposal contained a provision that in accepting the risk the appellants did so on the same terms and conditions as those on which the policy had been granted by the respondents " by whom, in the event of claim, the settlement will be made." The appellants on 28th January, 1908, issued a policy of re-insurance for £5,000, but limited to the amount which the respondents should pay irrespective of any bonus. The policy recited that the written statement of M. was the basis of the contract, also that the appellants had agreed to accept the respondent's proposal. M. died in May, 1909, and a claim was made against the respondents by his executrix. The appellants informed the respondents that they had reason to believe that some of the statements made by M. were untrue, and warned them that they would not acquiesce in a settlement. The respondents, however, paid £5,000 in settlement of the claim, and sued the appellants upon the policy of re-insurance. The jury found that certain of M.'s statements were untrue, and that he had been guilty of concealment and misrepresentation, but that the respondents, in settling the claim, had acted reasonably and *bona fide. Held*, that, assuming that the provision in the proposal form that a settlement should be effected by the respondents was incorporated in the policy of re-insurance, that provision could not alter the express terms of the policy, which warranted the truth of M.'s statements, and that, the jury having found those statements to be false, the appellants were not liable. *Australian Widows' Fund Life Assurance Society Ltd* v. *National Mutual Life Association of Australasia Ltd.*, (1914) A.C., 634. P.C.

Contract—When contracting party bound to disclose all material facts known to him—

Innocent failure to disclose material fact, effect of—Life insurance.]—When the circumstances show that confidence is reposed in one party to a contract by the other, the former is bound to disclose all material facts which he knows, unless the latter knows those facts or is presumed to know them, or takes on himself knowledge, or waives information about them, and if this disclosure is not made, whether from design, accident, inadvertence or mistake, the contract is voidable at the option of the party misled. This rule applies as well to contracts of life assurance as to those of marine insurance. *Hambrough* v. *Mutual Life &c. of New York*, 72 L.T., 140, disapproved. *Dalgety & Co. Ltd.* v. *Australian Mutual Provident Society*, (1908) V.L.R., 481; 30 A.L.T., 4; 14 A.L.R., 299. *Cussen, J.* (1908).

Contract—Life assurance—Statements by party proposing to insure to be basis of contract—Whether a warranty.]—The statement in a proposal for life assurance that " the proponent agrees that answers or statements shall be the basis of the contract " does not amount to a warranty. *Dalgety & Co. Ltd.* v. *Australian Mutual Provident Society*, (1908) V.L.R., 481; 30 A.L.T., 4; 14 A.L.R., 299. *Cussen, J.* (1908).

Representation made during negotiation for contract—Whether deemed to be a continuing representation until altered—Life insurance.] —A representation once made in the course of negotiations for a contract, *prima facie* continues in force until it is withdrawn or altered, and such a representation is construed to mean that the facts represented are then true, and, when made by a proponent for life assurance, that no other material facts are then known to him. *Dalgety & Co. Ltd.* v. *Australian Mutual Provident Society*, (1908) V.L.R., 481; 30 A.L.T., 4; 14 A.L.R., 299. *Cussen, J.* (1908).

Contract — Insurance — Innocent non-disclosure of material facts discovered before completion of contract.]—H., having made a proposal for assurance on his life with a company, received from the company a notice stating that the proposal was accepted and that a policy would issue on payment of the premium, and that the company reserved the right of cancelling the notice " should anything to the prejudice of the life transpire in the meantime." On the next day from certain circumstances that then happened H. knew and believed that a growth on his neck was possibly malignant, and that his medical advisers suspected it of being so. H. without fraud made no disclosure of this matter to the company, and three days afterwards the premium was ˙paid. *Held*, that the contract was revocable at the option of the company. *Dalgety & Co. Ltd.* v. *Australian Mutual Provident Society*, (1908) V.L.R., 481; 30 A.L.T., 4; 14 A.L.R., 299. *Cussen, J.* (1908).

Life assurance—Transfer of policy—Right to policy moneys.]—A policy of life assurance was taken out by A. on his own life and was transferred to B. to secure the money invested by B. in a partnership business of which A. was the manager. The partnership was afterwards dissolved and B's share in the partnership assets was paid to him. Until the dissolution of the partnership the premiums on the policy were paid by B. and thereafter until A.'s death they were paid by A. *Held*, on the evidence that B. was entitled to the policy moneys. *Caulfield* v. *Caulfield*, (1908) 6 C.L.R., 202. H.C., *Griffith, C.J., Barton* and *O'Connor, JJ.*

Contract of life assurance—Parties—Policy for benefit of assured only—Refusal of executors of will of assured to sue on policy—Action by beneficiaries under will of insured—Cause of action.]—Where a person takes out a policy of assurance on his own life for his own benefit, and dies while the policy is still in force, leaving a will disposing of all his property, the beneficiaries under the will have no right either at law or in equity to enforce payment by the insurer of the moneys due under the policy, even though the executors refuse to sue and are made parties to the action. *Miller* v. *National Mutual Life Association of Australasia Ltd.*, (1909) V.L.R., 193; 30 A.L.T., 193; 15 A.L.R., 141. *Hodges, J.*

Tenant for life and remainderman—Fire premiums paid prior to the Trusts Act 1896

(No. 1421)—Whether chargeable to income or corpus.]—*See* TRUSTS AND TRUSTEES. *Holmes v. Holmes*, 28 A.L.T., 22 ; 12 A.L.R., 409.

Tenant for life and remainderman—Income, what is—Shares in insurance company—Dividends paid out of fund accumulated as security for life assurance liabilities—Dividends paid out of contingency fund to provide against depreciation of securities.]—*See* WILL. *In re Longley* ; *Reid* v. *Silke*, (1906) V.L.R., 641 ; 28 A.L.T., 82 ; 12 A.L.R., 499.

Insurance of trust property—Premiums whether payable out of income or corpus—Trusts Act 1896 (No. 1421), sec. 28.]—*See* TRUSTS AND TRUSTEES. *In re Tong* ; *Tong* v. *Trustees, Executors and Agency Co. Ltd.*, (1907) V.L.R., 338 ; 28 A.L.T., 200 ; 13 A.L.R., 119.

County Court—Action on insurance policy—Arbitration a condition precedent to right of action—Stay of proceedings—Adjournment—Jurisdiction—County Court Act 1890 (No. 1078), sec. 71.]—*See* COUNTY COURT. *Borrett* v. *Norwich and London Accident Insurance Association*, 29 A.L.T. (Supplement), 1 ; 13 A.L.R. (C.N.), 22. *Judge Chomley* (1907).

Companies Act 1890 (No. 1074), sec. 335—Purpose of this section—Protection of funds of life assurance branch of company carrying on other business besides life assurance.]—Sec. 335 of the *Companies Act* 1890 was intended to protect the funds of the life assurance branch of a company, carrying on life assurance and also other business, from claims arising in connection with such other business, and the section applies only to a company which is carrying on life assurance business as well as other business. *In re Longley* ; *Reid* v. *Silke*, (1906) V.L.R., 641 ; 28 A.L.T., 82 ; 12 A.L.R., 499. *Cussen, J.*

Income Tax Act 1903 (No. 1819), sec. 11 (1)—Companies Act 1890 (No. 1074), sec. 334 —Income of life assurance company—Premiums in respect of insurance or assurance — Consideration for annuities.] — *See* COMPANY, cols. 155, 156. *In re Income Tax Acts* ; *In re Australian Mutual Provident Society*, (1913) V.L.R., 42 ; 34 A.L.T., 118 ; 18 A.L.R., 524.

INTEREST.

Money lender—Re-opening transaction—Excessive interest—Res ipsa loquitur—Money Lenders Act 1906 (No. 2061), sec. 4.]—Where the rate of interest charged by a money lender upon a loan is, either originally or in the result, larger than in the opinion of the Court is fair and reasonable under the circumstances, it is excessive within the meaning of sec. 4 of the Act, and the rate of interest may in itself be evidence that it is excessive. *Wilson* v. *Moss*, 8 C.L.R., 146 ; 15 A.L.R., 131. H.C., *Griffith, C.J., Barton, O'Connor* and *Isaacs, JJ.* (1909).

Judgment—Execution—Rate of interest—Supreme Court Act 1890 (No. 1142), secs. 4, 177—Order XLI., r. 4*, Order XLII., r. 16 (Rules of 1884).]—*See* PRACTICE AND PLEADING. *In re Whitelaw*, (1906) V.L.R., 265 ; 27 A.L.T., 187 ; 12 A.L.R., 143.

Company—Liquidation—Voluntary liquidation—Surplus after discharge of liabilities—Distribution—Rights of " A " and " B " contributories—Interest on unpaid calls.]—*See* COMPANY, cols. 163, 164. *In re Metropolitan Bank Ltd.*, (1912) V.L.R., 449 ; 34 A.L.T., 138 ; 18 A.L.R., 463.

Will and codicil—Interest directed to be paid on legacies to legatees under will—No general direction—Further legacies under codicil without direction as to interest.]—*See* WILL. *In re Stroud* ; *Bell* v. *Stroud*, (1908) V.L.R., 33 ; 29 A.L.T., 104 ; 13 A.L.R., 645.

Will—Construction—Contingent legacies—Interim interest, whether infant contingent legatees entitled to—Trusts Act 1896 (No. 1421), sec. 18.]—*See* WILL. *In re Thompson* ; *Brahe* v. *Mason*, (1910) V.L.R., 251 ; 31 A.L.T., 210 ; 16 A.L.R., 215.

Legacy—Interest—Date from which payable —Death of testator presumed—Lapse of considerable time between presumed date of death and grant of probate—Infants—Maintenance clause—Executor's year.]—*See* EXECUTORS AND ADMINISTRATORS, col. 550. *In re Black* ; *Black* v. *Melbourne Hospital*, (1911) V.L.R., 280 ; 33 A.L.T., 2 ; 17 A.L.R., 240.

Will and codicil—Interest on legacies—From what time payable—Rate of interest.]—*See* EXECUTORS AND ADMINISTRATORS, col. 550. *In re Stroud*; *Bell* v. *Stroud*, (1908) V.L.R., 33; 29 A.L.T., 104; 13 A.L.R., 645.

Interest on legacies—Rate of—Order LV., r. 64 (Rules of 1906).]—*See* EXECUTORS AND ADMINISTRATORS, cols. 550, 551. *In re Black*; *Black* v. *Melbourne Hospital*, (1911) V.L.R., 280; 33 A.L.T., 2; 17 A.L.R., 240.

Tenant for life and remainderman—Trust funds invested upon mortgage—Proceeds of sale of mortgaged property insufficient to pay principal and interest due—Apportionment of proceeds—Rate of interest.]—*See* TENANT FOR LIFE AND REMAINDERMAN. *Holmes* v. *Holmes*, 28 A.L.T., 22; 12 A.L.R., 409.

Life tenant and remainderman—Investment on mortgage—Apportionment of proceeds of realization—Interest on cost of sewerage—Rate of interest upon mortgage.]—*See* TENANT FOR LIFE AND REMAINDERMAN. *Macartney* v. *Macartney*, 33 A.L.T., 183; 18 A.L.R., 1.

Will—Tenant for life and remainderman—Capital and income—Payment of annuities—Apportionment—Rate of interest.]—*See* TENANT FOR LIFE AND REMAINDERMAN. *Cock* v. *Aitken*, (1911) 13 C.L.R., 461; 18 A.L.R., 337.

INTERNATIONAL LAW.

See INTERSTATE AND INTERNATIONAL LAW.

INTERPLEADER.

County Court Rules 1891, r. 230—Action for commission—Claim by third party—Interpleader by defendant—Claims arising out of same subject matter—Whether claims for one and same debt.]—The plaintiff, an estate agent, sued the defendant for commission alleged to be due to him on the sale of a house of the defendant. Another estate agent claimed from the defendant commission in respect of the same sale of the same house. *Held*, that the defendant was not entitled to relief by way of interpleader. *Greatorex* v. *Schackle*, (1895) 2 Q.B., 249, followed. *Looker* v. *Mercer*, 28 A.L.T. (Supplement), 15; 13 A.L.R. (C.N.), 13. *Judge Eagleson* (1907).

Interpleader summons—Affidavit in support—Rules of County Court 1891, r. 230.]—An interpleader summons under rule 230 of the County Court Rules 1891 should be supported by an affidavit. *Looker* v. *Mercer*, 28 A.L.T. (Supplement), 15; 13 A.L.R. (C.N.), 13. *Judge Eagleson* (1907).

Interpleader—Grounds of claim, statement of—Alternative and inconsistent grounds—Rule 236 (Rules of 1891).]—*See* COUNTY COURT, col. 311. *Moorhead* v. *Chauncey, Hays* (*claimant*), 28 A.L.T. (Supplement), 7; 12 A.L.R. (C.N.), 27.

County Court Rules 1891, r. 236—Interpleader—Particulars of claim—Grounds of claim—Defective particulars—Amendment.]—*See* COUNTY COURT, col. 312. *Rogers* v. *Metters*; *Metters, claimants*, 34 A.L.T. (Supplement), 4; 18 A.L.R. (C.N.), 21.

Interpleader—Grounds of claim—Order giving leave to amend—Whether necessary to draw up.]—*See* COUNTY COURT, col. 312. *Moorhead* v. *Chauncey, Hays claimant*, 28 A.L.T. (Supplement), 7; 12 A.L.R. (C.N.), 27.

Justices Act 1890 (No. 1105), sec. 98, Schedule II., Form 55—Interpleader summons—Withdrawal of claim—Jurisdiction of Justices to adjudicate.]—*See* JUSTICES OF THE PEACE. *Watson* v. *Barby*; *O'Connor, claimant*, (1910) V.L.R., 134.

INTERPRETATION.

See also, STATUTES.

Interpretation of Statute—Punctuation, effect of.]—The punctuation of Statutes does not control the sense if the meaning is otherwise reasonably clear. *Charlton, President &c. of* v. *Ruse*, (1912) 14 C.L.R., 220; 18 A.L.R., 207. H.C., *Griffith, C.J., Barton* and *Isaacs, JJ.*

Statute—Interpretation—Adoption of Statute which has been judicially interpreted—**Foreign Statutes interpreted by foreign Courts.**]—The doctrine that, where the Legislature adopts in identical language an English Statute which has been interpreted by the English Courts, they are to be taken to have accepted that interpretation, is not applicable to the case of a Statute enacted in Victoria in 1857 and based (but not in identical language) upon a New York Statute, some of the terms of which had been the subject of judicial decision in the State of New York. *National Mutual Life Association of Australasia Ltd.* v. *Godrich*, 10 C.L.R., 1 ; 16 A.L.R., 110. *Griffith, C.J.* and *Barton, J.* (1909).

Foreign Statute—Adoption in Victoria— Principle of interpretation—Foreign decisions.] —Sec. 55 of the *Evidence Act* 1890 having been taken from a Statute of the State of New York, which had been judicially interpreted by the Courts of that State before its adoption in Victoria, the Parliament is to be regarded as having legislated with reference to such interpretations. *Warnecke* v. *Equitable Life Assurance Society of the United States*, (1906) V.L.R., 482 ; 27 A.L.T., 236 ; 12 A.L.R., 254. F.C., *a'Beckett, A.-C.J., Hodges* and *Chomley*, JJ.

Patents Act 1903 (No. 21 of 1903)—Forms of expression taken from English Patent Acts —In what sense used by Commonwealth Parliament.]—*See* PATENT. *National Phonograph Co. of Australia Ltd.* v. *Menck*, 7 C.L.R., at p. 529 ; 15 A.L.R., at p. 13.

Statutes — Construction — Ambiguity.]— Where the language of an enactment is susceptible of two constructions, regard must be had to the general object and purpose of the Act, and, if the act done is not within the general purview of the Statute, regard may be had to the consequences of either construction. If one construction will do manifest injustice and the other avoid it, the latter construction should be adopted. *Ingham* v. *Hie Lee*, (1912) 15 C.L.R., 267 ; 18 A.L.R., 453. H.C., *Griffith, C.J.* and *Barton, J.*

Conveyancing Act 1904 (No. 1953), sec. 4 (6), (9)—Interpretation—Repugnant clauses

—Insertion of words to give effect to clear intention of Statute.]—Sub-sec. 9 of sec. 4 of the *Conveyancing Act* 1904 should be read as though it contained some words excluding sub-sec. 6 from its operation. *Re Stewart and Park's Contract*, (1907) V.L.R., 31 ; 28 A.L.T., 133 ; 12 A.L.R., 553. *Hood, J.*

Power of attorney—Interpretation—General words, effect of on special powers.]—General words in a power of attorney are restricted to what is necessary for the proper execution of the special powers contained therein, and are construed as enlarging such special powers only when necessary for the accomplishment of the purpose for which authority is given. *In re Hoarey*, (1906) V.L.R., 437 ; 28 A.L.T., 93 ; 12 A.L.R., 450. *Cussen, J.*

Lottery, law relating to—Imperial Statutes, whether impliedly repealed by Victorian legislation—6 Geo. II., c. 35 ; 4 Geo. IV., c. 60— Police Offences Act 1890 (No. 1126), sec. 37.]— *See* GAMING AND WAGERING. *The Attorney-General* v. *Moses*, (1907) V.L.R., 130 ; 28 A.L.T., 125 ; 12 A.L.R., 606.

Lottery, law relating to—Foreign lottery— Imperial Statutes, whether in force in Victoria —6 Geo. II., c. 35 ; 4 Geo. IV. c. 60—9 Geo. IV., c. 83, sec. 24.]—*See* GAMING AND WAGERING. *The Attorney-General* v. *Moses*, (1907) V.L.R., 130 ; 28 A.L.T., 125 ; 12 A.L.R., 606.

INTERROGATORIES.

See DISCOVERY, PRACTICE AND PLEADING.

INTERSTATE AND INTERNATIONAL LAW.

I.—DOMICIL ; NATIONALITY.

See also, post, III. SUCCESSION.

Marriage Act 1890 (No. 1166), secs. 74, 75, 76—" Any wife," " any husband," meaning of—**Domicile**—Wife domiciled in Victoria at time of desertion.]—*See* HUSBAND AND WIFE. *Forster* v. *Forster,* (1907) V.L.R., 159 ; 28 A.L.T., 144 ; 13 A.L.R., 33.

Domicil—Dissolution of marriage—Victoria the domicil of both parties—Victorian marriage — Change of domicil and subsequent desertion—Jurisdiction of Victorian Court.]—*See* HUSBAND AND WIFE. *Forster* v. *Forster,* (1907) V.L.R., 159 ; 28 A.L.T., 144 ; 13 A.L.R., 33.

Domicil of origin—Change of, what constitutes.]—*See* HUSBAND AND WIFE. *Forster* v. *Forster,* (1907) V.L.R., 159 ; 28 A.L.T., 144 ; 13 A.L.R., 33.

Domicil, change of—Evidence—Statements of intention, weight to be attached to—Contrary inference from conduct and acts.]—*See* HUSBAND AND WIFE. *Forster* v. *Forster,* (1907) V.L.R., 159 ; 28 A.L.T., 144 ; 13 A.L.R., 33.

Dissolution of marriage—Jurisdiction—Domicil—Submission to jurisdiction by respondent, effect of.]—*See* HUSBAND AND WIFE. *Forster* v. *Forster,* (1907) V.L.R., 159 ; 28 A.L.T., 144 ; 13 A.L.R., 33.

Marriage Act 1890 (No. 1166), sec. 74—Desertion—Wife deserted in Victoria when domiciled there—Husband subsequently becoming domiciled elsewhere—Jurisdiction of Court on cross petition by husband—Commonwealth officer transferred from Victoria to another State.]—*See* HUSBAND AND WIFE. *Bailey* v. *Bailey,* (1909) V.L.R., 299 ; 30 A.L.T., 217 ; 15 A.L.R., 237. *Cussen, J.*

Immigration Restriction Acts 1901-1905—Original home in State of Victoria—Residence in China for many years—Whether original Victorian home abandoned.]—*See* IMMIGRATION RESTRICTION ACTS. *Potter* v. *Minahan,* (1908) 7 C.L.R., 277 ; 14 A.L.R., 635.

Prohibited immigrant—Infant—Domicil—of father in Australia—Immigration Restriction Act 1905 (No. 17 of 1905), sec. 4—Immigration Restriction Act 1901 (No. 17 of 1901), sec. 3.]—*See* IMMIGRATION RESTRICTION ACTS. *Ah Yin* v. *Christie,* 4 C.L.R., 1428 ; 13 A.L.R., 372.

The Constitution (63 & 64 Vict. c. 12), sec. 51 (xxvii.)—" Immigrant," meaning of—Member of Australian community returning from abroad.]—*See* IMMIGRATION RESTRICTION ACTS. *Potter* v. *Minahan,* (1908) 7 C.L.R., 277 ; 14 A.L.R., 635.

Immigration Restriction Acts 1901-1905—" Immigrant," meaning of—Naturalised subject domiciled in Victoria—Return to Victoria from China.]—*See* IMMIGRATION RESTRICTION ACTS. *Ah Sheung* v. *Lindberg,* (1906) V.L.R., 323 ; 27 A.L.T., 189 ; *sub nom., Rex* v. *Ah Sheung,* 12 A.L.R., 190.

Who may be made insolvent—Person domiciled and resident abroad—Debts contracted in Victoria.]—*See* INSOLVENCY. *In re Whitelaw,* (1906) V.L.R., 265 ; 27 A.L.T., 187 ; 12 A.L.R., 143.

Companies Act 1890 (No. 1074), sec. 76—Companies Act 1896 (No. 1482), secs. 1, 2, 70—Company—Incorporated outside Victoria—Registered in Victoria as a foreign company—Winding up—Jurisdiction.]—*See* COMPANY, col. 159. *In re the Egerton and Gordon Consolidated Gold Mines Co. No Liability,* (1908) V.L.R., 22 ; 29 A.L.T., 165 ; 14 A.L.R., 7.

The Aliens Statute 1865 (No. 256)—Letters of naturalisation issued under, effect of.]—For a discussion on the extra-territorial effect of naturalisation under a Victorian law, see *Ah Sheung* v. *Lindberg,* (1906) V.L.R., 323 ; 27 A.L.T., 189 ; *sub nom., Rex* v. *Ah Sheung,* 12 A.L.R., 190. *Cussen, J.* (1906).

Immigration Restriction Act 1901 (No. 17 of 1901)—Prohibited immigrant—Application of Act to Australian citizen—Commonwealth Constitution, sec. 51.]—*See* IMMIGRATION RESTRICTION ACTS. *Attorney-General of the Commonwealth* v. *Ah Sheung*, (1907) 4 C.L.R., 949.

Licensing—British subject—Licensing Act 1890 (No. 1111), sec. 177—Aliens Act 1890 (No. 1063), sec. 6—Naturalization Act 1903 (No. 11 of 1903), secs. 9, 10.]—*See* LICENSING. *In re Hall*, 18 A.L.R. (C.N.), 20.

II.—MOVABLES ; IMMOVABLES ; LOCUS OF ACTS.

Bill of sale—Given and registered in New South Wales over goods in New South Wales—Goods subsequently brought to Victoria—Bill of sale valid in Victoria.]—*Taylor* v. *Lovegrove ; Original Mont de Piete Ltd.*, 18 A.L.R. (C.N.), 22. *Hodges, J.* (1912).

Movables—Debts secured on land—No allegation of want of solvency on part of debtor.]—Debts secured on land where there is no allegation of want of solvency on the part of the debtor are movables. *In re Ralston ; Perpetual Executors and Trustees Association of Australia Ltd.* v. *Ralston*, (1906) V.L.R., 689 ; 28 A.L.T., 45 ; 12 A.L.R., 365. *Cussen, J.*

Intestate Estates Act 1896 (No. 1419)—Death intestate leaving a widow and no issue—Provision of one thousand pounds for widow—Domicil of deceased, whether widow's rights affected by—Movable and immovable estate.]—*See, post*, III. SUCCESSION. *In re Ralston ; Perpetual Executors and Trustees Association of Australia Ltd.* v. *Ralston*, (1906) V.L.R., 689 ; 28 A.L.T., 45 ; 12 A.L.R., 365.

Intestate Estates Act 1896 (No. 1419)—Provision of one thousand pounds for widow—Deceased intestate domiciled abroad—Immovable estate alone available to provide for widow—Apportionment of debts between movable and immovable estate.]—*See, post*, III. SUCCESSION. *In re Ralston ; Perpetual Executors and Trustees Association of Australia Ltd.* v. *Ralston*, (1906) V.L.R., 689 ; 28 A.L.T., 45 ; 12 A.L.R., 365.

Income Tax Act 1903 (No. 1819), sec. 9—Company—Registered in Victoria—Purchase and sale of land in New South Wales on behalf of Company to be formed—Transactions of Company in Victoria—Re-sales of land by promoter of Company—Contracts taken over by Company—Purchase moneys payable by instalments—Tax on sums not yet received.]—*See* INCOME TAX ACTS. *In re Income Tax Acts ; Ex parte Quat Quatta Co.*, (1907) V.L.R., 54 ; 28 A.L.T., 100 ; 12 A.L.R., 526.

III.—SUCCESSION.

See also, EXECUTORS AND ADMINISTRATORS.

Intestates' Estates Act 1896 (No. 1419)—Death intestate leaving a widow and no issue—Provision of thousand pounds for widow—Domicil of deceased, whether widow's rights affected by—Movable and immovable estate.]—If a deceased intestate who died leaving a widow and no issue was domiciled in Victoria the *Intestates' Estates Act* 1896 applies both to his movable and immovable Victorian estate, but if he was not so domiciled it applies to his immovable Victorian estate only. *In re Ralston ; Perpetual Executors and Trustees Association of Australia Ltd.* v. *Ralston*, (1906) V.L.R., 689 ; 28 A.L.T., 45 ; 12 A.L.R., 365. *Cussen, J.*

Intestates' Estates Act 1896 (No. 1419)—Provision of one thousand pounds for widow—Deceased intestate domiciled abroad—Immovable estate alone available to provide for widow—Apportionment of debts between movable and immovable estate.]—Where an intestate dies domiciled abroad possessed of movable and immovable estate in Victoria, in order to determine the amount of the immovable estate available for payment of the provision for the widow under the *Intestates' Estate Act* 1896, the debts and testamentary expenses should be deducted from the value of the immovable estate on the basis of the proportion which the value of the immovable estate bears to the value of the movable estate. *Quaere*, in such a case what debts are to be deducted from the Victorian estate. *In re Ralston ; Perpetual Executors and Trustees Association of Australia Ltd.* v. *Ralston*, (1906) V.L.R., 689 ; 28 A.L.T., 45 ; 12 A.L.R., 365. *Cussen, J.*

Administration and Probate Act 1890 (No. 1060), Part III.—Foreign probate and letters of administration—Sealing foreign letters of administration — Distribution of estate, whether the same as if original letters granted in Victoria.]—*See* EXECUTORS AND ADMINIS-TRATORS, cols. 555, 556. *In re Ralston*; *Perpetual Executors and Trustees Association of Australia Ltd.* v. *Ralston*, (1906) V.L.R., 689 ; 28 A.L.T., 45 ; 12 A.L.R., 365.

IV.—CONTRACTS.

(a) Generally.

Supreme Court Act 1890 (No. 1142), sec. 85 — Where cause of action arises—Agent out-side jurisdiction—Goods improperly sold by agent—Action by principal for money had and received—Place of payment—Rule that debtor must seek out creditor.]—If an agent abroad acting for a principal within the jurisdiction deals with goods in a manner not authorised by the principal and receives the proceeds thereof and the principal, waiving the tort, sues for money had and received, the cause of action does not arise within the jurisdic-tion. The rule that the debtor must seek out his creditor particularly applies to cases where the question depends upon an excuse alleged for non-payment of money within the jurisdiction. *Gosman* v. *Ockerby*, (1908) V.L.R., 298 ; 29 A.L.T., 266 ; 14 A.L.R., 186. *Cussen, J.*

Locus solutionis — Variation thereof — Course of dealing.]—The place of perform-ance of a contract may be varied by a course of dealing between the parties thereto. *Kelsey* v. *Caselberg*, (1909) V.L.R., 347 ; 31 A.L.T., 31 ; 15 A.L.R., 362. *Madden, C.J.*

Principal and agent—Agent for foreign shipping company—Sale of passenger's ticket —Failure by principal to carry passenger on terms mentioned in ticket—Liability of agent —No undertaking by agent that passenger should be so carried.]—*See* CONTRACT OR AGREEMENT, col. 214. *Cheong* v. *Lohmann*, (1907) V.L.R., 571 ; 28 A.L.T., 252 ; 13 A.L.R., 269.

Principal and Agent—Agent contracting on behalf of disclosed foreign principal—Whether agent personally liable on contract.]—*See* PRINCIPAL AND AGENT. *Cheong* v. *Lohmann*, (1907) V.L.R., 571 ; 28 A.L.T., 252 ; 13 A.L.R., 269.

(b) Jurisdiction.

Supreme Court Act 1890 (No. 1142), sec. 85—Writ for service outside jurisdiction—Breach outside jurisdiction—Substantial per-formance within jurisdiction—" A cause of action which arose within the jurisdiction." *See* PRACTICE AND PLEADING. *Kelsey* v. *Caselberg*, (1909) V.L.R., 347 ; 31 A.L.T., 31 ; 15 A.L.R., 362.

Supreme Court Act 1890 (No. 1142), sec. 85 —Foreign procedure — Contract made in Queensland—Part performance by plaintiff in Victoria—Breach by defendant in Queensland.] *See* PRACTICE AND PLEADING. *J. E. Lindley & Co.* v. *Pratt*, (1911) V.L.R., 444 ; 33 A.L.T., 50 ; 17 A.L.R., 404.

Supreme Court Act 1890 (No. 1142), sec. 85—Foreign procedure—Cause of action aris-ing within the jurisdiction, what is.]—*See* PRACTICE AND PLEADING. *J. E. Lindley & Co.* v. *Pratt*, (1911) V.L.R., 444 ; 33 A.L.T., 50 ; 17 A.L.R., 404.

Supreme Court Act 1890 (No. 1142), sec. 85 — Writ containing several causes of action—Some within sec. 85, some outside that section—Application to set aside—Plain-tiff put on terms—Election to strike out causes of action improperly joined—Undertaking to confine trial to causes of action properly joined—Costs.]—*See* PRACTICE AND PLEAD-ING. *Gosman* v. *Ockerby*, (1908) V.L.R., 298 ; 29 A.L.T., 266 ; 14 A.L.R., 186.

Contract—Sale of goods to be shipped abroad—C.i.f.e. contract—Place of delivery—County Court practice—Jurisdiction—Part of cause of action arising out of jurisdiction.]—*See* CONTRACT OR AGREEMENT, cols. 225, 226. *H. Beecham & Co.* v. *R. W. Cameron & Co.*, (1910) V.L.R., 19 ; 31 A.L.T., 100 ; 15 A.L.R., 598.

County Court—Jurisdiction—Contract for sale of goods—Breach in Victoria—Cause of action—Quantum of damages—County Court Act 1890 (No. 1078), sec. 5.]—*See* COUNTY.

COURT, cols. 299, 300. *Railton* v. *Fleming*, (1912) V.L.R., 113; 33 A.L.T., 180; 18 A.L.R., 24.

V.—TORTS.

Malicious arrest—Arrest under process of foreign Court—Termination of proceedings in favour of plaintiff before action brought—Setting aside of order to hold to bail and writ of ca. re.—Reasonable and probable cause.]— *See* MALICIOUS PROSECUTION. *Varawa* v. *Howard Smith Co. Ltd.*, (1911) 13 C.L.R., 35; 17 A.L.R., 499.

VI.—LUNACY.

Lunacy—Lunatic so found by inquisition in England—Lunatic's estate in Victoria—Filing inquisition of record in Victoria—Appointment of committee in Victoria—Order for sale of lunatic's estate—Time and extent of order—Lunacy Act 1890 (No. 1113), secs. 130, 206, Lunacy Rules 1906, rr. 10, 64.]— *See* LUNATIC. *In re A.B., a lunatic*, (1909) V.L.R., 100; 30 A.L.T., 158; 15 A.L.R., 85.

VII.—CRIMINAL MATTERS.

(a) Offences.

Attempt—False pretences made in Tasmania—Attempt to obtain money in Victoria—Crimes Act 1890 (No. 1079), sec. 165.]—An act done in Victoria forming part of a series of acts which, if uninterrupted would result in the obtaining of money in Victoria as a consequence of false representations made out of Victoria is an attempt to obtain money by false pretences which the Victorian Courts have jurisdiction to try. W. wrote and posted a letter in Victoria addressed to C. in Tasmania, and the letter contained false representations, by means of which W. hoped to induce C. to send money to him in Victoria. *Held*, that the Victorian Courts had jurisdiction to convict W. of attempting to obtain money by false pretences. *R.* v. *Burdett*, 4 B. & A., 95; *R.* v. *Hensler*, 11 Cox., 570; and *R.* v. *Ellis*, (1899) 1 Q.B., 230, discussed. *Rex* v. *Waugh*, (1909) V.L.R., 379; 31 A.L.T., 37; 15 A.L.R., 366. F.C., *Madden, Hodges and Cussen, JJ.*

Subordinate legislation—Power in criminal matters, territorial limits of — " Quitting

Natal," whether legislature may make it a criminal offence—Fugitive Offenders Act 1881 (44 & 45 Vict. c. 69), secs. 2, 9—Offences to which Act applies—Criminality dependent upon event happening after " Quitting Natal."]** *See* CRIMINAL LAW. cols. 369, 370. *McKelvey* v. *Meagher*, 4 C.L.R., 265; 12 A.L.R., 483.

Conspiracy—Jurisdiction of Court—Agreement made outside overt acts within.]— *See* CRIMINAL LAW, col. 333. *R.* v. *Kellow*, (1912) V.L.R., 162; 33 A.L.T., 203; 18 A.L.R., 170. *Cussen, J.*

(b) Fugitive Offenders.

Fugitive Offenders Act 1881 (44 & 45 Vict. c. 69)—Commonwealth of Australia Constitution Act (63 & 64 Vict. c. 12)—Authority of State of Victoria with regard to fugitive offenders—How far effected by establishment of Commonwealth.]— *See* COMMONWEALTH OF AUSTRALIA CONSTITUTION, col. 136. *McKelvey* v. *Meagher*, 4 C.L.R., 265; 12 A.L.R., 483.

Rendition of fugitive offenders—Law of Victoria—Effect of establishment of the Commonwealth — Commonwealth of Australia Constitution Act (63 & 64 Vict. c. 12)—The Constitution, secs. 108, 109—Fugitive Offenders Act 1881 (44 & 45 Vict. c. 69.]— *See* COMMONWEALTH OF AUSTRALIA CONSTITUTION, cols. 135, 136. *McKelvey* v. *Meagher*, 4 C.L.R., 265; 12 A.L.R., 483.

Commonwealth of Australia Constitution Act (63 & 64 Vict. c. 12)—The Constitution, sec. 51 (xxix.)—External affairs—Surrender of fugitive offenders—Power of Commonwealth Parliament with regard to.]— *See* COMMONWEALTH OF AUSTRALIA CONSTITUTION, col. 121. *McKelvey* v. *Meagher*, 4 C.L.R., 265; 12 A.L.R., 483.

Fugitive Offenders Act 1881 (44 & 45 Vict. c. 69)—" Judge of a superior Court "—" Magistrate."]— *See* FUGITIVE OFFENDERS, col. 598. *McKelvey* v. *Meagher*, 4 C.L.R., 265; 12 A.L.R., 483.

Fugitive Offenders Act 1881 (44 & 45 Vict. c. 69), secs. 3, 5, 9—Warrant for apprehension of fugitive—Statement of offence charged, sufficiency of.]— *See* FUGITIVE OFFENDERS, col. 598. *McKelvey* v. *Meagher*, 4 C.L.R., 265 ; 12 A.L.R., 483.

Fugitive Offenders Act 1881 (44 & 45 Vict. c. 69), sec. 5—Endorsed warrant—Statement of offence, sufficiency of.]—*See* FUGITIVE OFFENDERS, col. 598. *McKelvey* v. *Meagher*, 4 C.L.R., 265 ; 12 A.L.R., 483.

Justices Act 1890 (No. 1105), sec. 141— Fugitive Offenders Act 1881 (44 & 45 Vict. c. 69)—Order by Victorian Magistrate exercising powers conferred by Imperial Act— Whether it may be dealt with by order to review.]—*See* FUGITIVE OFFENDERS, col. 599. *O'Donnell* v. *McKelvey*, (1906) V.L.R., 207 ; 27 A.L.T., 164 ; 12 A.L.R., 39.

Fugitive Offenders Act 1881 (44 & 45 Vict. c. 69), secs. 5, 6—Fugitive committed to prison to await return—Legality of detention affirmed by Supreme Court—Bail, whether Court may grant.]—*See* FUGITIVE OFFENDERS, cols. 599, 600. *Re McKelvey*, (1906) V.L.R., 304 ; 12 A.L.R., 168.

Fugitive Offenders Act 1881 (44 & 45 Vict. c. 69), secs. 5, 6—Fugitive committed to prison to await return—Legality of detention affirmed by Supreme Court—Appeal to High Court—Bail.]—*See* FUGITIVE OFFENDERS, col. 600. *Re McKelvey*, (1906) V.L.R., 304 ; 12 A.L.R., 209.

Service and Execution of Process Act 1901 (No. 11), sec. 18—Person arrested on warrant issued in another State—Duty of Justice of Peace before whom such person is brought.]— *See* SERVICE AND EXECUTION OF PROCESS ACT. *O'Donnell* v. *Heslop*; *The King* v. *Cresswell, ex parte Heslop*, (1910) V.L.R., 162 ; 31 A.L.T., 173 ; 16 A.L.R., 168.

Service and Execution of Process Act 1901 (No. 11), sec. 18—Warrant endorsed for execution in another State—Apprehension of accused on unsustainable charge—Exercise of discretion by Justice—Jurisdiction of Judge —Review of Justice's discretion by Judge.]— *See* SERVICE AND EXECUTION OF PROCESS ACT. *In re George*, (1909) V.L.R., 15 ; 30 A.L.T., 141 ; 15 A.L.R., 27.

Service and Execution of Process Act 1901 (No. 11), sec. 18 (4)—Application to Judge—

Jurisdiction—Whether original or appellate.] —*See* SERVICE AND EXECUTION OF PROCESS ACT. *O'Donnell* v. *Heslop* ; *The King* v. *Cresswell, Ex parte Heslop*, (1910) V.L.R., 162 ; 31 A.L.T., 173 ; 16 A.L.R., 168.

Service and Execution of Process Act 1901 (No. 11), sec. 18—Person charged with offence in another State—Execution of warrant in Victoria — Power to discharge accused— Whether it may be exercised after his admission to bail to appear and answer the charge.] —*See* SERVICE AND EXECUTION OF PROCESS ACT. *O'Donnell* v. *Heslop* ; *The King* v. *Cresswell, Ex parte Heslop*, (1910) V.L.R., 162 ; 31 A.L.T., 173 ; 16 A.L.R., 168.

Service and Execution of Process Act 1901 (No. 11), sec. 18 (4)—Person arrested on warrant issued in another State—Return of such person to such other State, whether unjust or oppressive—Dispute as to facts alleged in defence—Bona fide assurance of dispute by prosecutor.]—*See* SERVICE AND EXECUTION OF PROCESS ACT. *O'Donnell* v. *Heslop* ; *The King* v. *Cresswell, Ex parte Heslop*, (1910) V.L.R., 162 ; 31 A.L.T., 173 ; 16 A.L.R., 168.

Service and Execution of Process Act 1901 (No. 11), sec. 18 (4)—Practice—Application to Judge for discharge of prisoner, how made.]— *See* SERVICE AND EXECUTION OF PROCESS ACT. *O'Donnell* v. *Heslop* ; *The King* v. *Cresswell, Ex parte Heslop*, (1910) V.L.R., 162 ; 31 A.L.T., 173 ; 16 A.L.R., 168.

Service and Execution of Process Act 1901 (No. 11), sec. 18 (4)—Warrant—Execution— Application for discharge of person apprehended—Procedure—Form of order.]—*See* FUGITIVE OFFENDERS. *In re George*, (1908) V.L.R., 734 ; 30 A.L.T., 113 ; 14 A.L.R., 699.

Service and Execution of Process Act 1901 (No. 11), sec. 18—Execution of warrant issued in another State—Order of Justice of Peace directing return of accused—Review of order by Judge—Costs, jurisdiction to award.]—*See* SERVICE AND EXECUTION OF PROCESS ACT. *In re George*, (1909) V.L.R., 15 ; 30 A.L.T., 141 ; 15 A.L.R., 27.

VIII.—Procedure.

(a) Service; Leave to Proceed.

Service and Execution of Process Act 1901 (No. 11 of 1901), sec. 16 (1)—Subpoena—Application for leave to serve beyond State—Affidavit in support.]—*See* Service and Execution of Process Act 1901. *Trapp, Couche & Co.* v. *Mc Kenzie Ltd.*, 30 A.L.T., 200; 15 A.L.R., 179.

Bill of exchange—Action upon under Instruments Act 1890—Writ—Service out of jurisdiction—Indorsement by Prothonotary—Necessity for Judge's order for such indorsement—Instruments Act 1890 (No. 1103), sec. 92—Service and Execution of Process Act 1901 (No. 11 of 1901), secs. 5, 8.]—*Sternberg* v. *Egan*, 18 A.L.R. (C.N.), 20. *Hood, J.* (1912).

Service and Execution of Process Act 1901 (No. 11), sec. 10—Writ of summons served in another State—Security for costs—Discretion.]—*See* Service and Execution of Process Act. *Smith* v. *Chisholm*, (1908) V.L.R., 579; 30 A.L.T., 48; 14 A.L.R., 471.

Service and Execution of Process Act 1901 (No. 11), sec. 11—Writ—Service in another State—No appearance entered—Application for leave to proceed—Affidavit of service—Particulars.]—*See* Service and Execution of Process Act. *Jarrett* v. *Brown*, (1908) V.L.R., 478; 30 A.L.T., 17; 14 A.L.R., 349.

(b) Evidence.

Evidence—Foreign law—Rendition of fugitive offender—Fugitive Offenders Act 1881 (44 & 45 Vict. c. 69), secs. 5, 29.]—In proceedings before a Magistrate under the *Fugitive Offenders Act* 1881 to have a fugitive returned to Natal, the law of Natal relating to the alleged offence may be proved by the certificate of the Attorney-General of Natal and by the depositions of a Natal lawyer taken in Natal. *McKelvey* v. *Meagher*, 4 C.L.R., 265; 12 A.L.R., 483. H.C., *Griffith, C.J., Barton* and *O'Connor, JJ.* (1906).

Evidence—Foreign law—Fugitive Offenders Act 1881 (44 & 45 Vict. c. 69)—Law of other country, whether a question of fact—How Magistrate may be satisfied as to.]—*Semble.*—The law of another part of the Dominions is, for the purposes of the *Fugitive Offenders Act* 1881, not a matter of fact required to be legally proved, but is a matter as to which a Magistrate may satisfy himself by any available means. *McKelvey* v. *Meagher*, 4 C.L.R., 265; 12 A.L.R., 483.

Evidence Act 1890 (No. 1088), sec. 55—Evidence of physician or surgeon—Information acquired in attending a patient outside Victoria—Whether privileged from disclosure within Victoria.]—Sec. 55 of the *Evidence Act* 1890, which prohibits the disclosure of information acquired by a physician or surgeon in attending a patient, is applicable in every case where the evidence is offered in Victoria notwithstanding that the events or facts sought to be proved occurred elsewhere. *National Mutual Life Association of Australasia Ltd.* v. *Godrich*, 10 C.L.R., 1; 16 A.L.R., 110. H.C., *Griffith, C.J., Barton, O'Connor, Isaacs,* and *Higgins, JJ.* (1909).

Service and Execution of Process Act 1901 (No. 11), sec. 16—Evidence Act 1890 (No. 1088), secs. 4, 10—Commission for examination of witness out of Victoria—Whether Commission may issue in case of witness whose attendance can be enforced.]—*See* Evidence, col. 511. *National Mutual Life Association of Australasia Ltd.* v. *Australian Widow's Fund, &c. Society Ltd.*, (1910) V.L.R., 411; 32 A.L.T., 51; 16 A.L.R., 460.

(c) Stay of Proceedings.

Practice—Staying proceedings—Cause of action arising out of jurisdiction.]—Where an action was brought within the jurisdiction of the Supreme Court in respect of a cause of action which arose out of the jurisdiction, *Held,* that a stay was properly refused, the injustice which would be occasioned to the plaintiffs by a stay being as great as that which would be occasioned to the defendants by allowing the action to proceed. *Logan* v. *Bank of Scotland (No. 2)*, (1906) 1 K.B., 141; and *Egbert* v. *Short*, (1907) 2 Ch., 205, considered and applied. *Maritime Insurance Co. Ltd.* v. *Geelong Harbour Trust Commissioners,*

(1908) 6 C.L.R., 194 ; 14 A.L.R., 424. H.C,
Griffith, C.J., Barton, O'Connor and *Higgins,
JJ.*

INTESTATES' ESTATES ACT.

See also, INTERSTATE AND INTERNATIONAL
LAW III.—SUCCESSION.

**Married Women's Property Act 1890 (No.
1116), sec. 25—Intestates' Estates Act 1896
(No. 1419)— Married woman — Intestacy —
Estate less than £1,000—No issue—Rights of
husband and next of kin.**]—*See* HUSBAND AND
WIFE. *In re Jamieson* ; *Jamieson* v. *Christensen,* 4 C.L.R., 1489 ; 13 A.L.R., 566.

IRRIGATION.

See MILDURA IRRIGATION TRUSTS ACT.

JUDGMENT.

**Judgment—Reason for decision—Statement
by Judge thereof, whether obligatory.**]—A
Judge is not bound to give reasons for his
decision nor to state which evidence he
believes or disbelieves. *Swinburne* v. *David
Syme & Co.,* (1909) V.L.R., 550 ; 31 A.L.T.,
81 ; 15 A.L.R., 579. *Madden, C.J., a'Beckett* and *Hood, JJ.*

JUDGMENT SUMMONS.

See DEBTORS ACT.

JUDICIAL NOTICE.

See EVIDENCE.

JUDICIARY ACT.

**Judiciary Act 1903 (No. 6), sec. 37—Appeal
to High Court from Supreme Court—Cause
remitted to Supreme Court for execution of
judgment of High Court—Duty of Supreme
Court—Stay of proceedings.**]—*See* APPEAL,
cols. 30, 31. *Peacock* v. *Osborne,* (1907) 4
C.L.R., 1564 ; 13 A.L.R., 565.

**Judiciary Act 1903 (Commonwealth) (No.
6 of 1903), sec. 39—Federal jurisdiction of
State Courts—Validity of grant of—Right of
appeal to High Court—Prerogative right of
appeal to Privy Council, whether affected—
Commonwealth of Australia Constitution Act
63 & 64 Vict. c. 12—The Constitution, secs.
71, 77—Colonial Laws Validity Act 28 and
29 Vict. c. 63.**]—*Per Griffith, C.J., Barton,
O'Connor* and *Isaacs, JJ.* Even if section
39 (2) (*a*) of the *Judiciary Act* 1903 purports
to take away the prerogative right of appeal
to the Privy Council, and the section is to
that extent *ultra vires* and inoperative, its
failure in that respect does not affect the
validity of the grant of federal jurisdiction
to State Courts contained in the rest of the
section and the consequent right of appeal
to the High Court. *Sed Quaere,* whether
sub-section (2) (*a*) should be construed as
affecting the prerogative. *Baxter* v. *Commissioners of Taxation* ; *Flint* v. *Webb,* 4
C.L.R., 1087, 1178 ; 13 A.L.R., 313. (1907).

**Commonwealth of Australia Constitution
Act 63 & 64 Vict. c. 12—The Constitution,
sections 73, 74, 76, 77—Question as to limits
inter se of Constitutional powers of Commonwealth and State, what is—Question raised by
defence whether State tax on federal salary
an interference with powers of Commonwealth
—Exercise of federal jurisdiction by Court of
Petty Sessions—Appeal to High Court, competency of—Judiciary Act 1903 (No. 6 of 1903),
sec. 39.**]—*See* APPEAL, cols. 19, 20. *Baxter* v.
Commissioners of Taxation ; *Flint* v. *Webb,* 4
C.L.R., 1087 1178 ; 13 A.L.R., 313.

**Federal jurisdiction—Exercise of, what is—
Two questions decided, one federal and the
other not—Each decision sufficient to sustain
judgment—Court of Petty Sessions—Appeal
to High Court, whether it lies—Judiciary Act
1903 (No. 6), sec. 39 (2) (d)—Commonwealth
of Australia Constitution Act, 63 & 64 Vict. c.
12, The Constitution, sec. 77.**]—*See* APPEAL,
col. 20. *Miller* v. *Haweis,* (1907) 5 C.L.R.,
89 ; 13 A.L.R., 583.

**Court of Petty Sessions—Federal jurisdic-
tion—Exercise of, what is—Commonwealth
of Australia Constitution Act secs. 31, 76—
Constitution Act Amendment Act 1890 No.**

1075), sec. 282—Judiciary Act 1903 (No. 6), sec. 39 (2) (d)—Question decided involving interpretation of section 31 of Constitution—Other question decided involving interpretation of Commonwealth Electoral Act 1902 (No. 19)—Appeal to High Court, whether it lies.] —*See* APPEAL, cols. 20, 21. *Miller* v. *Haweis*, (1907) 5 C.L.R., 89 ; 13 A.L.R., 583.

Judiciary Act 1903 (No. 6), secs. 56, 64— Action against Commonwealth— Right to discovery from Commonwealth.] — *See* DISCOVERY, cols. 402, 403. *Commonwealth* v. *Miller*, 10 C.L.R., 742 ; 16 A.L.R., 424.

Judiciary Act 1903 (No. 6 of 1903), sec. 69 (3)—Indictable offences against the Commonwealth—Committal for trial—Appointment of counsel for defence—Application—Materials in support—" Interests of justice."]—*See* CRIMINAL LAW, col. 360. *Rex* v. *Forrest*, (1012) V.L.R., 466 ; 34 A.L.T., 95 ; 18 A.L.R., 495.

Judiciary Act 1903 (No. 6 of 1903), sec. 69 (3)—Legal assistance for defence of prisoner —Whether solicitor as well as counsel may be provided.]—*See* CRIMINAL LAW, cols. 360, 361. *Rex* v. *Forrest*, (1912) V.L.R., 466 ; 34 A.L.T., 95 ; 18 A.L.R., 495.

Evidence — Larceny — Recent possession —Offences against the Commonwealth— Judiciary Act 1903 (No. 6), sec. 80.]—*See* CRIMINAL LAW, cols. 355, 356. *Rex* v. *Forrest*, (1912) V.L.R 466 ; 34 A.L.T., 95 ; 18 A.L.R., 495.

JURY.

I.—POWERS AND DUTIES OF JUDGE AND JURY.

See also, post, III.—NEW TRIAL.

Supreme Court Act 1890 (No. 1142), sec. 58—Charge to jury—Duty of judge—Issues and evidence applicable thereto — Order XXXIX. (Rules of 1906).]—It is the duty of the Judge in his charge to the jury to state the issues to be determined and the evidence applicable to these issues. *Holford and Wife* v. *Melbourne Tramway and Omnibus Co.*, (1909) V.L.R., 497 ; 29 A.L.T., 112 ; 13 A.L.R., 667. F.C. *Madden, C.J., a' Beckett* and *Cussen, JJ.*

Evidence—Admissible but such that no reasonable man could form a conclusion— Direction to acquit.]—*Per Cussen, J.*—" I am of opinion that if at the end the evidence is such that the Court thinks no reasonable man could form a conclusion on it the Court would be bound to direct a jury to acquit the prisoner." *R.* v. *Parker*, (1912) V.L.R., 152 ; 33 A.L.T., 215 ; 18 A.L.R., 150. F.C. *Madden, C.J., Hodges* and *Cussen, JJ.*

Trial by jury—Discharge of jury—Withdrawal of discharge—Juries Act 1895 (No. 1391), sec. 4 (2).]—Section 4 of the *Juries Act* 1895 provides that the party who asks for a jury shall pay the jury fees to the Sheriff each day before the Court sits, that if he does not the other party may pay them, and that if the other party does not pay them, the jury is to be discharged, and the trial is to proceed before a Judge. The defendants having withdrawn from the case did not on a subsequent day pay the jury fees. Counsel for the plaintiff expressed the willingness of the plaintiff to pay the fees if the Judge should think it fairest to do so, but the Judge, being under the erroneous belief that the result of non-payment of the fees would be that the trial would come to an end, expressed no opinion as to the payment of the fees by the plaintiff, and plaintiff's counsel said that the plaintiff would not pay them. Thereupon the Judge announced to the Jury that they were discharged and said that the trial was at an end. Counsel for the plaintiff immediately drew the Judge's attention to the provision of section 4, and the Judge said that he would prefer the case to be tried with a jury rather than by himself. Counsel for the plaintiff then said that the plaintiff would pay the jury fees. The jury had not left the box and the case proceeded to a determination before them. *Held* (*Isaacs, J.*, dissenting) that the jury had not been effectually discharged, and that the trial properly proceeded. *David Syme & Co.* v. *Swinburne*, (1909) 10 C.L.R., 43 ; 16 A.L.R., 93. H.C. *Griffith, C.J., Barton, O'Connor, Isaacs* and *Higgins, JJ.*

Trial by jury—Right and discretion of Judge to discharge jury—Appeal from exercise of Judge's discretion to discharge jury.]—The presiding Judge has a discretion to discharge the jury in circumstances of evident necessity or need of very high degree. Such discretion being a judicial discretion, is in civil cases appealable, but the Court of Appeal will interfere only in cases where the Judge has gone wrong in principle or an obvious injustice has been done. *Swinburne* v. *David Syme & Co.*, (1909) V.L.R., 550 ; 31 A.L.T., 81 ; 15 A.L.R., 579. F.C. *Madden, C.J., a'Beckett* and *Hood, JJ.*

Trial by jury—Reduction of number of jurors—Consent of parties.]—The Judge in a civil trial by jury may, at any stage of the proceedings, with the consent of both parties, reduce the original number of jurors. *Swinburne* v. *David Syme & Co.*, (1909) V.L.R., 550 ; 31 A.L.T., 81 ; 15 A.L.R., 579. F.C. *Madden, C.J., a'Beckett* and *Hood, JJ.*

Witness—Whether Judge may call—Request by jury—Further proceedings.]—*See* CRIMINAL LAW, col. 364. *Rex* v. *Collins*, (1907) V.L.R., 292 ; 28 A.L.T., 222 ; 13 A.L.R., 184.

Local Government Act 1903 (No. 1893), secs. 708, 710—Action in respect of injury sustained by reason of accident on highway —Notice of accident not given in time— Whether sufficient reason shown why person injured unable to give notice—By whom such question to be determined—Jury.]—*See* LOCAL GOVERNMENT. *Leeder* v. *Ballarat East,*

Mayor &c. of, (1908) V.L.R., 214 ; 29 A.L.T., 192 ; 14 A.L.R., 124.

II.—TRIAL BY JURY, RIGHT TO.

Order XXXVI., rr. 3, 4, 5, 6 (Rules of 1884) —Trial by jury—Equity case—Claim put in form cognisable in a Court of common law.]— The plaintiff's claim was for damages for breach by the defendants of their covenant with him, in a mortgage deed made to secure the payment of a debt due by him to them, that they would not realise on the security thereby given until they had realised on the security of a prior mortgage given by the plaintiff to them to secure the same debt. *Held*, that the case was one " heretofore within the cognisance of the Court in its Equitable jurisdiction " within the meaning of Order XXXVI., r. 3, and therefore must be tried by a Judge without a jury unless the Court or a Judge otherwise ordered. *Hay* v. *Dalgety & Co. Ltd.*, 4 C.L.R., Pt. I., 913 ; 13 A.L.R., 125. H.C., *Griffith, C.J., Barton, O'Connor* and *Higgins, JJ.* (1907).

Order XXXVI., r. 5 (Rules of 1884)—Trial by jury—" Prolonged examination of documents or accounts."]—*Per Griffith, C.J.* and *O'Connor, J.*—The words " prolonged examination of documents or accounts " in Order XXXVI., r. 5, refer to an examination by a jury. *Hay* v. *Dalgety & Co. Ltd.*, 4 C.L.R., Pt. I., 913 ; 13 A.L.R., 125.

Order XXXVI., rr. 4, 6 (Rules of 1884)— Right to jury—Negligence in navigating ship— Collision.]—An action to recover damages for negligence in the navigation of the defendant's ship whereby it collided with that of the plaintiff is within Order XXXVI., r. 6 of the *Rules of the Supreme Court* 1884, and either party is entitled to have it tried with a jury. *Union Steamship &c. Co.* v. *The Melbourne Harbour Trust Commissioners*, (1907) V.L.R., 204 ; 29 A.L.T., 63 ; 13 A.L.R., 136. *Hood, J.*

Rules of Supreme Court 1906—Order XXXVI., r. 6—Money Lenders Act 1906 (No. 2061), sec. 4—Action by money-lender on promissory note—Intended defence and counterclaim that interest excessive or bargain harsh and unconscionable—Mode of trial—

Right to jury.]—Where the defendant in an action brought by a money-lender for the recovery of principal and interest due on a promissory note given in respect of a loan to the defendant, intends to rely upon the provisions of sec. 4 of the *Money Lenders Act* 1906, he is, under Order XXXV., r. 6, of the *Rules of the Supreme Court* 1906, entitled as of right to a trial of the action with a jury. *Moss* v. *Jenkins,* (1909) V.L.R., 275; 30 A.L.T., 206; 15 A.L.R., 240. *Cussen, J.*

Order XXXVI., rr. 3, 6 (Rules of 1906)— Practice—Trial by jury—Common law claim —Defence of release by deed—Reply that release obtained by fraud or undue influence— Cause or matter previously within equitable jurisdiction—Certain issues directed to be tried by jury.]—One of the defences pleaded to a claim for money lent was a release by deed, and to that defence the plaintiff replied that the deed had been obtained by fraud or undue influence. *Held,* that the action was a cause or matter which would, within the meaning of rule 3, have been within the cognizance of the Court in its Equitable jurisdiction previously to the commencement of the *Judicature Act* 1883, and that the plaintiff was not entitled as of right to the trial of the action by a jury. But order made for the trial by jury of the issues (1) whether the deed was procured by fraud, (2) whether it was procured by undue influence. *Lind* v. *Lind,* (1910) V.L.R., 302; 32 A.L.T., 2; 16 A.L.R., 265. *Hodges, J.*

Order XXXVI., rr. 3, 6 (Rules of 1884)— Order XVIII (a), r. 6 (Rules of 1904)—Trial by jury—Writ endorsed for trial without jury— Amendment of endorsement—Memorandum of close of the pleadings filed—Case listed for trial without jury.]—In a cause within r. 6 of Order XXXVI. (Rules of 1884) the mode of trial endorsed on the writ was " before a Judge without a jury." The order on directions gave the plaintiff leave to amend the endorsement by striking out the mode of trial, and to apply thereafter for a jury. After the pleadings had been closed, the memorandum filed, and the case set down by the plaintiff for trial before a Judge without a jury and placed in the list of trials

to be commenced on the 15th June, the plaintiff on the 12th June applied, under the order on directions, for a jury. *Held,* that, having regard to the circumstances and to the terms of the order on directions, the plaintiff was not entitled to a jury. *Brisbane* v. *Stewart,* (1906) V.L.R., 608; 28 A.L.T., 110; 12 A.L.R., 549. F.C., *Hodges, Hood* and *Chomley, JJ.* (1906).

Order XVIII. (a), r. 6 (Rules of 1904)—Writ endorsed for trial without a jury—Right of plaintiff to jury—Order XXXVI., r. 6 (Rules of 1884).]—*Per Hood, J.*—The plaintiff in an action within Order XXXVI., r. 6, who states in his writ that the mode of trial is before a Judge without a jury, is not entitled to a jury as of right. *Brisbane* v. *Stewart,* (1906) V.L.R., 608; 28 A.L.T., 110; 12 A.L.R., 549.

Order XXXVI., r. 6 (Rules of 1884)—Application for jury—Memorandum of close of pleadings filed—Order XXIII., r. 5 (Rules of 1884).]—*Per Hood, J.*—The case of *Butters* v. *Durham G. M. Co.,* 11 V.L.R., 375; 7 A.L.T., 30, settled the practice in regard to ordering a trial by jury under Order XXXVI., r. 6, where the memorandum of the close of the pleadings has been filed, and that practice should be followed. *Brisbane* v. *Stewart,* (1906) V.L.R., 608; 28 A.L.T., 110; 12 A.L.R., 549.

Order XXXVI., r. 2—Action of libel—Right to jury.]—Order XXXVI., r. 2, gives to the plaintiff in the actions therein specified the right to have his case tried by a jury where he indorses his writ to the effect that he desires to have the case so tried. The words at the commencement of rule 2 " Subject to any order to be made on a summons for directions " apply to the case where neither party has notified in accordance with the rule his desire for a trial by a Judge with a jury. jury. *North* v. *Jamieson,* (1908) V.L.R., 533; 30 A.L.T., 47; 14 A.L.R., 410. *Madden, C.J.*

County Court Act 1890 (No. 1078), sec. 89 —Jury, right of party to trial by—Whether limited to cases where claim is for liquidated amount.]—Under sec. 89 of the *County*

Court Act 1890 the right of either party to have the case tried by a jury is not limited to actions other than those for the recovery of unliquidated damages, but extends to all actions in which the amount claimed exceeds twenty pounds. *The King* v. *Beecham,* (1910) V.L.R., 204; 31 A.L.T., 183; 16 A.L.R., 173, applied. *Annear* v. *Inskip,* (1910) V.L.R., 235; 31 A.L.T., 220; 16 A.L.R., 276. F.C., *Madden, C.J., a' Beckett* and *Hood, JJ.*

County Court Act 1890 (No. 1078), sec. 89 —Jury, right to trial by—Common law claim for liquidated amount—Claim for declaration that plaintiff entitled to that amount— Whether action equitable.]—In an action in the County Court, by the particulars of demand, it was alleged that the parties agreed that the plaintiff should prepare building plans for a competition to be sent in in the name of the defendant, on condition that the plaintiff should receive one quarter of the prize or reward which the plans might win; that the plans were prepared and sent in and won the prize or reward which was the amount of the architect's commission estimated by the plaintiff at £720; and that the defendant refused to pay the plaintiff one quarter or any proportion of the commission or to return the plans. The plaintiff claimed a declaration that he was entitled to one quarter of the prize or reward, viz., £180, or alternatively return of the plans or damages £180; and he also claimed an injunction restraining the defendant from using the plans. *Held,* that the particulars of demand set out no circumstances to which a Court of Equity attaches its jurisdiction, and that the claim for a declaration did not in itself make the claim an equitable one, and that the plaintiff was entitled under sec. 89 of the *County Court Act* 1890 to have the action tried by a jury. *Biggs* v. *Kelly,* 24 V.L.R., 402; 20 A.L.T., 105; 4 A.L.R., 153, 228; *Barker* v. *Henty,* 29 V.L.R., 293; 25 A.L.T., 34; 9 A.L.R., 160 and *Porteous* v. *Lindley,* 28 V.L.R., 606; 24 A.L.T., 139; 9 A.L.R., 25, distinguished. *Annear* v. *Inskip,* (1910) V.L.R., 235; 31 A.L.T., 220; 16 A.L.R., 276. F.C., *Madden, C.J., a' Beckett* and *Hood, JJ.*

III.—NEW TRIAL.

(a) Misdirection and Other Errors of Judge.

Order XXXIX., r. 6 (Rules of 1906)—New trial—Misdirection — Substantial wrong or miscarriage.]—Wherever it is reasonable to conclude that substantial mischief did or in all probability may have come from a misdirection a new trial will be granted. *Holford* v. *Melbourne Tramway and Omnibus Co.,* (1909) V.L.R., 497; 29 A.L.T., 112; 13 A.L.R., 667. F.C., *Madden, C.J., a' Beckett* and *Cussen, JJ.*

Order XXXIX. (Rules of 1906)—Supreme Court Act 1890 (No. 1142), sec. 58—New trial—Misdirection as to law—No objection taken at the trial—Relevancy of evidence, misdirection as to.]—*See* PRACTICE AND PLEADING. *Holford* v. *Melbourne Tramway and Omnibus Co.,* (1909) V.L.R., 497; 29 A.L.T., 112; 13 A.L.R., 667.

New trial—Trial by jury—Observations made by Judge in summing up—Whether directions to jury — Order XXXIX.]— *See* PRACTICE AND PLEADING. *Ronald* v. *Harper,* (1910) 11 C.L.R., 63; 16 A.L.R., 415.

Criminal law—New trial—When to be granted after quashing of conviction—Circumstances to be considered in exercise of discretion—Failure to warn jury against convicting on uncorroborated evidence of accomplice—Evidence improperly admitted and afterwards withdrawn from jury—Crimes Act 1890 (No. 1079), sec. 482.]—*See* CRIMINAL LAW, cols. 366, 367. *Peacock* v. *The King,* (1911) 13 C.L.R., 619; 17 A.L.R., 566.

Order XXXIX., r. 6 (Rules of 1906)—Improper rejection of evidence—Substantial wrong or miscarriage.]—*See* PRACTICE AND PLEADING. *National Mutual Life Association of Australasia Ltd.* v. *Godrich,* 10 C.L.R., 1; 16 A.L.R., 110.

(b) Default or Misconduct of Parties as Jurors.

Juryman, alleged misconduct of—Evidence on oath to prove misconduct—Denial by juryman not on oath accepted by Judge—Denial in nature of plea of not guilty—No objection raised—Waiver.]—During the hearing of a trial before a jury counsel for the plaintiff informed the Court, in the presence of the jury, that he had been told by counsel for the defendants that a conversation had taken place between one of the jurymen and a clerk of the defendant's solicitor. At the instance of the Judge, the clerk was sworn, and deposed to a certain conversation having taken place between him and a particular juryman. The defendants' counsel thereupon applied for the discharge of the jury. Before dealing with the application the Judge then told the juryman he might make a statement if he desired, and the juryman, not upon oath, admitted that a conversation had taken place, but denied the substantial portions of it. The Judge then ordered the trial to proceed. He afterwards gave his reasons, stating that he did not believe the evidence of the clerk. *Held*, upon the evidence (*Isaacs, J.* dissenting), that the Judge had not acted upon unsworn evidence, the statement of the juryman being in the nature of a plea of not guilty. *Held*, further (*Isaacs, J.*, dissenting), that even if the Judge had admitted the unsworn statement as evidence, the defendants, not having at the time objected, had waived the objection, and could not rely upon the admission of that evidence as ground for a new trial. *David Syme & Co. v. Swinburne*, 10 C.L.R., 43 ; 16 A.L.R., 93 ; H.C., *Griffith, C.J., Barton, O'Connor* and *Higgins, JJ.* (1909).

New trial—Misconduct of juryman—Conversation between juryman and party—Whether course of justice substantially affected.]—A conversation between a juryman and one of the parties or his representatives is not of itself ground for a new trial unless there is reasonable ground for believing that the course of justice has been, or was likely to be, substantially affected. *David Syme & Co. v. Swinburne*, 10 C.L.R., 43 ; 16 A.L.R., 93. H.C., *Griffith, C.J., Barton, O'Connor, Isaacs* and *Higgins, JJ.* (1909).

New trial—Communications between interested party and jury—Possibility that verdict affected—Reasonable suspicion of unfair trial.]—A new trial will be ordered where it is shown that communications have taken place between members of the jury and interested parties, which might have influenced the verdict and might have caused reasonable people to doubt whether there had been a fair trial. *Trewartha v. Confidence Extended Co.*, (1906) V.L.R., 285 ; 28 A.L.T., 8 ; 12 A.L.R., 332. F.C., *Holroyd, A.-C.J., Hood* and *Cussen, JJ.* (1906).

Trial by jury—Counsel's right in addressing the jury—Partisans observations by counsel for one party—New trial.]—Where counsel for one party in summing up to the jury has made observations on the trial which, though partisan, would find their natural corrective in the speech of counsel on the other side, the fact that the latter, having thrown up his brief, is absent, does not make such observations a good ground for a new trial. *Swinburne v. David Syme & Co.*, (1909) V.L.R., 550 ; 31 A.L.T., 81 ; 15 A.L.R., 579. *Madden, C.J., a'Beckett* and *Hood, JJ.*

New trial—Order XXXIX.—Several issues—Wrong finding by jury on one issue.]—A wrong finding by a jury on one issue does not necessarily vitiate their findings on other issues. *Ronald v. Harper*, (1910) 11 C.L.R., 63 ; 16 A.L.R., 415. H.C., *Griffith, C.J., Barton* and *O'Connor, JJ.*

New trial—Trial by jury—Libel—Fair comment—Excessive damages.]—*See* PRACTICE AND PLEADING. *David Syme & Co. v. Swinburne*, (1909) 10 C.L.R., 43 ; 16 A.L.R., 93.

(c) *Limitation of Issues at the Re-hearing.*

County Court Act 1890 (No. 1078), secs. 96, 133, 148—Order XXXIX., r. 7 (Rules of 1906)—County Court—New trial—Whether issues to be tried may be limited—Full Court, power of on appeal.]—*See* APPEAL, col. 39. *Holford v. Melbourne Tramway and Omnibus Co.*, (1909) V.L.R., 497 ; 29 A.L.T., 112 ; 13 A.L.R., 667.

New trial—Limitation of issues to be tried—Verdict finding negligence and amount of damages—New trial as to issue of negligence only—County Court—Appeal to Full Court—County Court Act 1890 (No. 1078), secs. 96, 133, 148—Order XXXIX. (Rules of 1906), r.

7.]—*See* APPEAL, cols. 39, 40. *Holford* v. *Melbourne Tramway and Omnibus Co.,* (1909) V.L.R., 497 ; 29 A.L.T., 112 ; 13 A.L.R., 667.

IV.—VENUE.

Crimes Act 1890 (No. 1079), sec. 406—Venue—Application to change—Trial on criminal charge—Disagreement of jury—Remand of prisoner—Publication of statements by jurymen in favour of acquittal—Venue of second trial changed to another place—"Expedient to the ends of justice."]—*See* CRIMINAL LAW, col. 361. *Rex* v. *Long*, (1911) V.L.R., 30 ; 32 A.L.T., 130 ; 17 A.L.R., 68.

V.—SPECIAL JURY.

Juries Act 1890 (No. 1104), sec. 39—Jury—Criminal cases—Trial by special jury—Discretion of Court.]—The power conferred upon the Court by sec. 39 of the *Juries Act* 1890 to order that a criminal inquest shall be tried by a special jury is discretionary. *Rex* v. *Milburn*, (1908) V.L.R., 591 ; 30 A.L.T., 59 ; 14 A.L.R., 474. *Hodges, J.*

VI.—OFFENCES ; CORRUPTLY INFLUENCING JURORS.

Embracery—Juryman sworn to act—Attempt to induce him to give false verdict if he should be impanelled.]—*Quaere*, whether an attempt to induce a person sworn to act as a juryman to give a false verdict should he be impanelled is embracery. *Ex parte Dunn* ; *Ex parte Aspinall*, (1906) V.L.R., 493 ; 28 A.L.T., 3 ; 12 A.L.R., 358. *Cussen, J.*

Contempt of Court—Attempt to influence juryman—Juryman not yet empanelled for trial of accused person in whose favour attempt is made.]—*See* CRIMINAL LAW, col. 334. *Ex parte Dunn* ; *Ex parte Aspinall*, (1906) V.L.R., 493 ; 28 A.L.T., 3 ; 12 A.L.R., 358.

General Sessions—Attempt to influence a juryman—Contempt of Court—Power of Supreme Court to punish.]—*See* CONTEMPT. col. 186. *Ex parte Dunn* ; *Ex parte Aspinall*, (1906) V.L.R., 493 ; 28 A.L.T., 3 ; 12 A.L.R., 358.

VII.—COSTS ; JURY FEES.

Order LXV., r. 1—Costs—Trial by jury—Wrongful dismissal—One farthing damages—"Good cause."]—*See* COSTS, cols. 258, 259. *Galsworthy* v. *Reid*, 32 A.L.T., 189 ; 17 A.L.R., 144.

Order LXV., r. 1 (Rules of 1906)—Costs—Trial by jury—"Event," meaning of—Several causes of action—Taxation.]—*See* COSTS, col. 259. *O'Sullivan* v. *Morton*, (1911) V.L.R., 249 ; 32 A.L.T., 198 ; 17 A.L.R., 201.

Order XXIII., r. 5 (a)—Order XXXVI., r. 7 (c)—Jury fees—Action—Order for trial with jury—Memorandum of close of pleadings—Statement therein of number of jurors—Payment of jury fees on entering the case for trial.]—*See* PRACTICE AND PLEADING. *Moss* v. *Donnelly*, (1909) V.L.R., 443 ; 31 A.L.T., 49 ; 15 A.L.R., 516.

County Court—Costs—Items not included in Schedule of Scale of Costs—Jury fees and expenses—View—Travelling and other expenses—Juries Act 1890 (No. 1104), sec. 77, Tenth Schedule.]—By virtue of sec. 77 of the *Juries Act* 1890 and the Tenth Schedule thereto, jury fees and travelling and other expenses paid by one of the parties to an action tried with a jury, in respect to a view by the jury, are allowable on the taxation of his costs under an order giving him the costs of the action. *Reid* v. *Panton*, 32 A.L.T. (Supplement), 7 ; 16 A.L.R. (C.N.), 13. *Judge Eagleson* (1910).

JUSTICES OF THE PEACE.

I.—BIAS.

Justice of the Peace—Interest disqualifying—Present on the bench although taking no part in the proceedings.]—During the hearing of an information laid by the Harbor Master of the port of Melbourne charging the defendant with a breach of the regulations made by the Melbourne Harbor Trust Commissioners, one of the Commissioners who was a Justice of the Peace was present on the Bench. He regularly attended as a Justice at that Court, and had been adjudicating in the previous case. When the case was called on he informed his colleagues that he was a Commissioner, and that therefore he would take no part in the proceedings, and in fact did not do so, but no public announcement was made, and he retained his seat while the case was being dealt with, and then took part in the next business that was called on. Neither of the parties was at the time aware that he was one of the Melbourne Harbour Trust Commissioners. The defendant was convicted. *Held*, that the defendant might reasonably suspect he had not been fairly treated, and that therefore the conviction must be quashed. *Vincent* v. *Curran*, (1909) V.L.R., 370 ; 31 A.L.T., 24 ; 15 A.L.R.,359. *Hodges, J.*

II.—JURISDICTION GENERALLY.

(a) *Causes and Matters.*

Landlord and Tenant Act 1890 (No. 1108), secs. 81, 83—Distress for rent—Proceeds of sale—Overplus in hands of landlord's agent—Claim by tenant against landlord—Money had and received—Jurisdiction of Court of Petty Sessions.]—Where, after the payment of charges and rent out of the moneys arising from the sale of a tenant's goods under a distress for rent, there is an overplus remaining, which has not been paid to the tenant as provided by sec. 81 of the *Landlord and Tenant Act* 1890, he may proceed against the landlord in a Court of Petty Sessions upon a complaint for money had and received. Although such overplus is retained, not by the landlord personally, but by the bailiff or licensed auctioneer employed by him, a claim for money had and received will lie against the landlord. The tenant's remedy is not restricted to that provided by sec. 83 of the *Landlord and Tenant Act* 1890. *Rhodes* v. *Parrott*, (1912) V.L.R., 333 ; 34 A.L.T., 90 ; 18 A.L.R., 353. *a' Beckett, J.*

Police Regulation Act 1890 (No. 1127), sec. 58—Disputed property in possession of police——" Goods "—Money found on prisoners when arrested—Order as to disposal of such money—Jurisdiction of Justices.]—The word " goods " in sec. 58 of the *Police Regulation Act* 1890 includes money. Consequently, Justices have jurisdiction to make an order under that section for the disposal of money found on prisoners when arrested. *McKenna* v. *Dent and Williamson*, (1912) V.L.R., 150 ; 33 A.L.T., 202 ; 18 A.L.R., 148. *a' Beckett, J.*

Custody of child—Jurisdiction of Justices to determine—Marriage Act 1890 (No. 1166), secs. 42, 43.]—Justices have no power under sec. 43 of the *Marriage Act* 1890 to deal with the question of the custody of an illegitimate child at the hearing of a complaint under sec. 43 by or with the authority of the mother of the child against the father. *Fisher* v. *Clark*, 2 A.L.R. (C.N.), 321, considered. *Russ* v. *Carr*, (1909) V.L.R., 78; 30 A.L.T., 131; 15 A.L.R., 24. *Hodges, J.*

Rendition of fugitive offenders—Law of Victoria—Effect of establishment of the Commonwealth—Commonwealth of Australia Constitution Act (63 & 64 Vict. c. 12)—The Constitution, secs. 108, 109—Fugitive Offenders Act 1881 (44 & 45 Vict. c. 69).]—See FUGITIVE OFFENDERS, cols. 596, 597. *McKelvey* v. *Meagher*, 4 C.L.R., 265; 12 A.L.R., 483.

(b) *Limitations as to Amount, Locality and Questions of Title.*

Justices Act 1890 (No. 1105), secs. 59 (3), 70—Claim for detention of goods—Dividing cause of action for purpose of making two or more complaints.]—A complaint for detention of goods under sec. 59 (3) of the *Justices Act* 1890 is not a " cause of action " within the meaning of sec. 70 of that Act, and a complainant may therefore make a separate complaint for each article detained. *Mulder* v. *Adami*, (1907) V.L.R., 206; 28 A.L.T., 178; 13 A.L.R., 69. *Hood, J.*

Justices—Local jurisdiction—Objection that offence committed outside jurisdiction—How Justices may satisfy themselves on the question—Whether formal evidence necessary—Effect of erroneous conclusion—Justices Act 1890 (No. 1105), sec. 73 (3).]—Where on the hearing of an information before a Court of Petty Sessions an objection is taken that the offence was committed at a place outside the local jurisdiction of the Court, it is not necessary that formal evidence should be called to show that such place is within such jurisdiction, and the Court, if otherwise satisfied of that fact, should proceed with the hearing. The decision of the Court may be nullified if it is afterwards shown that the Court was wrong in concluding that it was

acting within its jurisdiction. *Carberry* v. *Cook*, 3 C.L.R., 995; 12 A.L.R., 265, applied. *Webb* v. *Rooney*, 21 V.L.R., 355; 17 A.L.T., 103; 1 A.L.R., 83, discussed. *Le Cocq* v. *McErvale*, (1908) V.L.R., 69; 29 A.L.T., 134; 13 A.L.R., 699. F.C., *a'Beckett* and *Cussen, JJ. (Madden, C.J.,* doubting).

Justices—Local limits of jurisdiction, how to be ascertained—Judicial notice.]—Where the local limits of a Court of Petty Sessions are described in a public Statute, the Court may take judicial notice of the area enclosed in those limits, and that the place described in an information is within or without those limits. *Le Cocq* v. *McErvale*, (1908) V.L.R., 69; 29 A.L.T., 134; 13 A.L.R., 699. F.C., *per a'Beckett* and *Cussen, JJ.*

Marriage Act 1890 (No. 1166), secs. 42 and 43—Wife compelled by husband's conduct to leave the matrimonial home—Husband and wife residing in different bailiwicks—Order made against husband in bailiwick where wife resides—Jurisdiction of Justices.]—See MAINTENANCE AND MAINTENANCE ORDERS. *Ross* v. *Ross*, (1909) V.L.R., 318; 30 A.L.T., 220; 15 A.L.R., 305. *Madden, C.J.*

Crimes Act 1890 (No. 1079), sec. 194—Maliciously destroying fence—Question of title—Jurisdiction of Justices—Justices Act 1890 (No. 1105), sec. 69.]—The jurisdiction of Justices under sec. 194 of the *Crimes Act* 1890 is ousted by a *bona fide* claim by the defendant that the land whereon the fence stood belongs to him solely, although the Justices may think that he is in fact only jointly interested in the same with some other person. *McLaren* v. *Bradley*, (1908) V.L.R., 318; 29 A.L.T., 239; 14 A.L.R., 252. *a'Beckett, J.*

(c) *Conditions Precedent.*

Marriage Act 1890 (No. 1166), secs. 43, 51—Maintenance order—Necessity for service of order before proceedings to enforce.]—Before proceedings are taken under sec. 51 of the *Marriage Act* 1890 a copy of the maintenance order must have been served on the defendant. *Cohen* v. *MacDonough*, (1906) V.L.R., 521; 28 A.L.T., 97; 12 A.L.R., 447, dictum of *Cussen, J.,* disapproved. *Cohen* v.

MacDonough, (1907) V.L.R., 7; 28 A.L.T., 119; 12 A.L.R., 566.   F.C., *Hodges*, *Hood* and *Chomley*, JJ.

Marriage Act 1890 (No. 1166), secs. 43, 51— Maintenance order—Whether necessary to serve copy before proceedings to enforce.]— *Semble.*—It is not necessary to serve a copy of a maintenance order before proceeding to enforce the same under section 51 of the *Marriage Act* 1890. *Cohen* v. *MacDonough* (or *O'Donough*), (1906) V.L.R., 521; 28 A.L.T., 97; 12 A.L.R., 447. *Cussen, J.*

Marriage Act 1890 (No. 1166), sec. 43— Justices Act 1904 (No. 1959), sec. 20—Order for maintenance—Defendant to find surety " forthwith " — Immediate committal to prison—Service of copy order whether condition precedent to issue of warrant of committal.]—*See* MAINTENANCE AND MAINTENANCE ORDERS. *Adams* v. *Rogers*, (1907) V.L.R., 245; 28 A.L.T., 180; 13 A.L.R., 71.

(d) Consent of Parties.

Justices Act 1890 (No. 1105), sec. 89 (1) (2) —Order for costs alone—Agreement between parties that Justices shall fix the costs—Order made as Justices and not as arbitrators.]— The complainant laid a complaint against the defendant for detention of a bird. Before the return day the defendant delivered the bird to the complainant, and it was agreed between the parties that they should leave the amount of costs to be fixed by the Justices. The Justices made an order for 2 guineas costs, in default distress, but made no other order of any kind. *Held*, that although the Justices might have fixed the costs as arbitrators, they had no right to do it as Justices, and that the order was bad. *O'Sullivan* v. *Humphris*, (1906) V.L.R.; 563; 28 A.L.T., 13; 12 A.L.R., 328. *Cussen, J.* (1906).

(e) By Whom Exercisable.

Marriage Act 1890 (No. 1166), secs. 42, 43— Maintenance order—Summons to appear before Court of Petty Sessions—Order in fact made by two Justices—Jurisdiction of Justices —Justices Act 1896 (No. 1458), sec. 4.]— Defendant was summoned to appear before a Court of Petty Sessions to show cause why he should not support his illegitimate child. At the time and place referred to in the summons, an order for maintenance was made by two Justices. *Held*, that the Justices had jurisdiction to make the order. *Shee* v. *Larkin*, (1907) V.L.R., 295; 28 A.L.T., 188; 13 A.L.R., 97. *a'Beckett, J.*

Fugitive Offenders Act 1881 (44 & 45 Vict. c. 69)—" Judge of a superior Court—" Magistrate."]—*See* FUGITIVE OFFENDERS, col. 598. *McKelvey* v. *Meagher*, 4 C.L.R., 265; 12 A.L.R., 483.

III.—PROCEDURE BEFORE JUSTICES.
(a) Parties.

Factories and Shops Act 1905 (No. 1975), secs. 42, 162 (c), (d)—Factories and Shops Act 1905 (No. 2), (No. 2008), sec. 9—Proceedings against firm—Parties.]— *Quaere*, whether in proceedings against a firm for an offence under the Act No. 1975 the information should not be against the firm but against the individual members thereof. *Bishop* v. *Chung Brothers*, 4 C.L.R., 1262; 13 A.L.R., 412. H.C. [*See* the Act No. 2137), sec. 39].

Practice—Complaint by one person on behalf of himself and other persons having the same interest—Jurisdiction.]— One of several persons having the same interest cannot in a Court of Petty Sessions sue on behalf of himself and the rest of such persons. *Hill* v. *Hill*, 19 V.L.R., 187; 14 A.L.T., 269, distinguished. *Buttle* v. *Hart*, (1906) V.L.R., 195; 27 A.L.T., 184; 12 A.L.R. (C.N.), 5. *Hood, J.* (1906).

Justices—Order for payment of money made in Petty Sessions—Death of party in whose favour order made—Whether executors may enter suggestion of death on record of Court —Justices Act 1890 (No. 1105).]— Justices, whether sitting as a Court of Petty Sessions or not, have no power to grant leave to the executors of the will of a deceased person, in whose favour an unsatisfied order for payment of money exists, to file a suggestion of the death of the deceased or to have execution under such order. *Hill* v. *Hill*, 19 V.L.R., 187; 14 A.L.T., 269, distinguished. *Goodman* v. *Jonas*, (1909) V.L.R., 308; 31 A.L.T., 16; 15 A.L.R., 308. *Cussen, J.*

(b) Information ; Complaint ; Warrant ; Summons.

Police Offences Act 1890 (No. 1126), secs. 49, 51—Gaming—Information under two sections.]—*See* GAMING AND WAGERING. *Rogerson* v. *Phillips and O'Hagan,* (1906) V.L.R., 272 ; 27 A.L. I., 166 ; 12 A.L.R., 147.

Factories and Shops Act 1905 (No. 1975), sec. 162 (c) (d)—Proceedings against firm— Form of information—Rules under Justices Act 1890, rr. 18, 20.]—*See* INFORMATION. *Bishop* v. *Chung Brothers,* 4 C.L.R., 1262 : 13 A.L.R., 412.

Police Offences Act 1890 (No. 1126), sec. 51—Occupier of house permitting same to be used for betting—No allegation in information of person by whom house was used.]—*See* GAMING AND WAGERING. *Knox* v. *Thomas Bible ; Knox* v. *J. L. Bible,* (1907) V.L.R., 485 ; 29 A.L.T., 23 ; 13 A.L.R., 352.

Information—Allegation as to date of offence incorrect—Health Act 1890 (No. 1098), Part IX.—Vaccination—Justices Act 1890 (No. 1105), sec. 73 (3).]—*See* INFORMATION. *O'Malley* v. *Russell,* (1908) V.L.R., 545 ; 30 A.L.T., 39 ; 14 A.L.R., 462.

Information, sufficiency of—Charge against father for not having child vaccinated—Allegation that vaccination notice given by Registrar of District in which father resided—Who may properly give such notice—Health Act 1890 (No. 1098), Part IX.]—*See* INFORMATION. *O'Malley* v. *Russell,* (1908) V.L.R., 545 ; 30 A.L.T., 39 ; 14 A.L.R., 462.

Police Offences Act 1890 (No. 1126), sec. 40 (vi.)—Information, sufficiency of—Allegation of facts set out in sub-section vi.—No allegation that defendant was an idle and disorderly person.]—*See* INFORMATION. *Hickling* v. *Skerritt,* (1912) V.L.R., 322 ; 34 A.L.T. 72 ; 18 A.L.R., 329.

Landlord and Tenant Act 1890 (No. 1108), sec. 92—Eighth Schedule—Ninth Schedule— Notice of intention to apply to justices to recover possession—Complaint — Immaterial matters contained in, effect of.]—*See* LANDLORD AND TENANT. *Equity Trustees Execu-*

tors and Agency Co. Ltd. v. *Harston,* (1908) V.L.R., 23 ; 29 A.L.T., 131 ; 13 A.L.R., 686.

Fugitive Offenders Act 1881 (44 & 45 Vict. c. 69) secs. 3, 5, 9—Warrant for apprehension of fugitive—Statement of offence charged, sufficiency of.]—*See* FUGITIVE OFFENDERS, col. 598. *McKelvey* v. *Meagher,* 4 C.L.R., 265 ; 12 A.L.R., 483.

Fugitive Offenders Act 1881 (44 & 45 Vict. c. 69), sec. 5—Endorsed warrant—Statement of offence, sufficiency of.]—*See* FUGITIVE OFFENDERS, col. 598. *McKelvey* v. *Meagher,* 4 C.L.R., 265 ; 12 A.L.R., 483.

Police Offences Act 1890 (No. 1126), sec. 57 —Gaming—Search warrant issued on insufficient material, validity of.]—*See* POLICE OFFENCES ACTS. *Montague* v. *Ah Shen,* (1907) V.L.R., 458 ; 28 A.L.T., 248 ; 13 A.L.R., 261.

Gaming — Search warrant — On what materials issued—" Complaint on oath," meaning of—Oral evidence to supplement written information, admissibility of—Police Offences Act 1890 (No. 1126), sec. 57, 2nd Schedule—Lotteries Gaming and Betting Act 1906 (No. 2055), sec. 50—Justices Act 1890 (No. 1105), secs. 4, 18, 19 (2), 2nd Schedule— Licensing Act 1906 (No. 2068), sec. 23.]—*See* POLICE OFFENCES ACTS. *Montague* v. *Ah Shen,* (1907) V.L.R., 458 ; 28 A.L.T., 248 ; 13 A.L.R., 261.

Information, who may lay.]—For a discussion of the principles which determine the right to lay an information, *see Steane* v. *Whitchell,* (1906) V.L.R., 704 ; 28 A.L.T 60 ; 12 A.L.R., 390. F.C. *Hood, Cussen* and *Chomley, JJ.*

Local Government Act 1903 (No. 1893), Part XXXVIII.—Breach of building regulations—Prosecution by municipal officer— Authority to prosecute, sufficiency of.]—*See* INFORMATION. *Steane* v. *Whitchell,* (1906) V.L.R., 704 ; 28 A.L.T., 60 ; 12 A.L.R., 390.

Local Government Act 1903 (No. 1893), Part XXXVIII., secs. 693, 694, 695, 696, 697 (c)—Breach of municipal building regulations—Who may lay information and prosecute—Officer of Council—Information and

proceedings in name of officer.]—*See* INFOR-
MATION. *Steane* v. *Whitchell*, (1906) V.L.R.,
704 ; 28 A.L.T., 60 ; 12 A.L.R., 390.

**Information, who may lay—Tramways Act
1890 (No. 1148), sec. 5, Second Schedule,
Part II., Clause 17—Tramway fare, penalty
for avoiding payment of—Delegation of
authority of municipal council—Whether delegate may enforce penalty.]—*See* INFORMA-
TION. *Cochrane* v. *Tuthill*, (1908) V.L.R.,
549 ; 30 A.L.T., 50 ; 14 A.L.R., 453.

**Justices Act 1890 (No. 1105), sec. 187—
Information—Defect in amendment—Discre-
tion of justices.]—*See* INFORMATION, col. 697.
Burvett v. *Moody*, (1909) V.L.R., 126 ; 30
A.L.T., 160 ; 15 A.L.R., 91.

**Justices Act 1890 (No. 1105), sec. 141—
Information disclosing no offence—Conviction
thereon—Amendment on return of order to
review—Power of Court—Defendant never
charged with offence.]—*See* INFORMATION.
Knox v. *Thomas Buble* ; *Knox* v. *J. L.
Bible*, (1907) V.L.R., 485 ; 29 A.L.T., 23 ;
13 A.L.R., 352.

**General Sessions—Appeal against convic-
tion — Information — Whether Court may
amend—Justices Act 1890 (No. 1105), secs.
73 (4), 128 (7), 133.]—*See* INFORMATION.
Delaney v. *Napthine*, 32 A.L.T. (Supplement),
10 ; 16 A.L.R. (C.N.), 19.

**Police Offences Act 1890 (No. 1126), sec.
40 (1)—" Duly summoned," meaning of.]—
In section 40 (1) of the *Police Offences Act*
1890 the expression " duly summoned "
means reasonably notified by a justice to
appear before him ; it does not refer to a
summons under the *Justices Act* 1890. *Wilson*
v. *Travers*, (1906) V.L.R., 734 ; 28 A.L.T.,
56 ; 12 A.L.R., 413. F.C. *a' Beckett*, *A.C.J.*,
Cussen and *Chomley*, *JJ.* (*See Police Offences Act* 1912, sec. 70.)

**Police Offences Act 1890 (No. 1126), sec.
40 (1)—" Brought before any justice in pursuance of the provisions of this Part."]—*See*
POLICE OFFENCES ACTS. *Wilson* v. *Travers*,
(1906) V.L.R., 734 ; 28 A.L.T., 56 ; 12
A.L.R., 413.

**Police Offences Act 1890 (No. 1126), sec.
40 (1)—" Required," meaning of.]— *See*
POLICE OFFENCES ACTS. *Wilson* v. *Travers*,
(1906) V.L.R., 734 ; 28 A.L.T., 56 ; 12
A.L.R., 413.

(c) Default Summonses.

**Justices Act 1904 (No. 1959), sec. 17—
Default summons—Subsequent ordinary summons for same cause of action—Jurisdiction.]
—Justices have no jurisdiction to issue an
ordinary summons under the *Justices Act*
1890 while a default summons for the same
claim, issued and served under section 17
of the *Justices Act* 1904, is pending. *Wilson*
v. *Cole*, (1911) V.L.R., 423 ; 33 A.L.T., 82 ;
17 A.L.R., 435. *Madden*, *C.J.* (1911).

**Justices Act 1890 (No. 1105), sec. 59—
Justices Act 1904 (No. 1959), sec. 17, Third
Schedule—Medical Act 1890 (No. 1118), sec.
12—Default summons—Claim for medical
services—Work and labour done—Goods sold
and delivered.]—The procedure by way of
" default summons " under the *Justices Act*
1904, section 17 is applicable to a claim " for
medical services " under the *Medical Act*
1890, section 12. *Iredell* v. *Skinner*, (1909)
V.L.R., 108 ; 30 A.L.T., 154 ; 15 A.L.R., 41.
F.C. *Madden*, *C.J.*, *Hood* and *Cussen*, *JJ.*
(*Cussen*, *J.* expressing some doubt).

**Justices Act 1904 (No. 1959), sec. 17, Third
Schedule—Medical Act 1890 (No. 1118), sec.
12—Default summons—Claim for medical
services—Evidence—Necessity for proof of
registration of medical practitioner.]—Where
defendant gives no notice of his intention to
defend a default summons in which the claim
is for medical services, proof of complainant's
registration under the *Medical Act* is not
necessary. *Iredell* v. *Skinner*, (1909) V.L.R.,
108 ; 30 A.L.T., 154 ; 15 A.L.R., 41. F.C.
Madden, *C.J.*, *Hood* and *Cussen*, *JJ.*, *Cussen*,
J. expressing some doubt.

**Justices Act 1890 (No. 1105), secs. 77 (10),
89 (4), 141—Justices Act 1904 (No. 1959), sec.
17 (3) (4)—Default summons—Notice of intention to defend not served in time—Non-
appearance of complainant at hearing—
Summons dismissed—Remedy, form of—

Order to review.]—The complainant took out and served a default summons under section 17 of the *Justices Act* 1904, but did not receive in due time a notice of intention to defend under that section, and did not attend on the return day, when, on the application of the defendant, the case was dismissed. *Held*, that the proper procedure to set aside the order dismissing the case was by order to review, and that section 89 (4) of the *Justices Act* 1890 did not apply. *Clarke* v. *Inverarity*, (1907) V.L.R., 589; 29 A.L.T., 86; 13 A.L.R., 387. *Madden, C.J.* (1907).

(d) Service.

Justices—Service of summons—Summons left at last place of abode—Defendant absent in England—Justices Act 1890 (No. 1105), sec. 23 (1).]—Where the defendant's last place of abode is within Victoria, service of a summons under the *Justices Act* 1890 by leaving the summons at such place of abode in the manner prescribed by section 23 (1) of the *Justices Act* 1890 is good service, although the defendant is out of the jurisdiction at the time. *Reg.* v. *Webb*, (1896) 1 Q.B., 487, followed. *Rces* v. *Downer*, (1910) V.L.R., 5; 31 A.L.T., 97; 15 A.L.R., 630. *Hodges, J.*

Justices Act 1890 (No. 1105), sec. 23 (1)—Service of summons—Service on person other than defendant—Defendant unaware of service—Hearing case in his absence.]—Where justices have reason to believe that, although the statutory requirements for service of a summons have been complied with, the defendant is unaware of such service, they should not proceed with the hearing in his absence. *Hunter* v. *Stewart*, (1907) V.L.R., 619; 29 A.L.T., 39; 13 A.L.R., 440. *a'Beckett, J.*

Service of copy of maintenance order—Proof of, by affidavit—Proceedings for disobedience of order—Marriage Act 1890 (No. 1166), sec. 51—Justices Act 1890 (No. 1105), sec. 74.]—A proceeding under section 51 of the *Marriage Act* 1890 to enforce a maintenance order is a proceeding within the jurisdiction of a Court of Petty Sessions, and service of a copy of the maintenance order may, under section 74 of the *Justices Act* 1890, be proved by the affidavit of the person who has served the same. *Cohen* v. *MacDonough* (or *O'Donough*), (1906) V.L.R., 521; 28 A.L.T., 97; 12 A.L.R., 447. *Cussen, J.*

Justices—Service of summons—Summons left at last place of abode—Defendant absent in England—Objection to service taken before Justices—Summons dismissed on other grounds —Order to renew—Renewal of objection— Justices Act 1890 No. 1105), secs. 23 (1), 146.] —*See, post*, ORDER TO REVIEW. *Rees* v. *Downer*, (1910) V.L.R., 5; 31 A.L.T., 97; 15 A.L.R., 630.

(e) Mode of Trial Where Several Accused Persons or Several Charges.

Informations heard together—Same defendant—Conviction, validity of.]—Two informations against the same defendant for different offences were heard together. He was convicted of both offences. He was not prejudiced by the evidence in both matters being taken at the same time. *Held*, that the convictions were valid. *Joske* v. *Lubrano*, (1906) V.L.R., 407; 28 A.L.T., 40; 12 A.L.R., 311. *a'Beckett, A.C.J.* (1906).

Criminal or quasi-criminal cases—Practice —Several persons charged with similar offences —Consent to be tried together and to be absent from Court—Several persons tried separately —Agreement to be bound by evidence taken in one case, effect of.]—For observations as to the effect in criminal or *quasi* criminal cases of the consent by several persons charged with similar offences to be tried together and to be absent from the Court during the whole or part of the proceedings and also as to the effect, where persons charged with similar offences are tried separately, of an agreement to be bound by the evidence taken in the case of one of such persons and by the view taken by the Court of that evidence, *see Larkin* v. *Penfold*, (1906) V.L.R., 535; 28 A.L.T., 42; 12 A.L.R., 337. *Cussen, J.* (1906).

(f) Adjournment.

Adjournment—Application by defendant for —No opportunity for preparing defence—Duty of justices—Licensing—Prohibition order— Licensing Act 1890 (No. 1111), sec. 125.]—

Defendant was served between 9 and 10 o'clock in the morning with notice that an application would be made to the Court sitting at 11 o'clock the same morning for an order against him under section 125 of the *Licensing Act* 1890. Defendant appeared at 11 o'clock and asked for an adjournment to obtain legal assistance, but an adjournment was refused, and the order sought made against him. *Held*, that the order must be set aside as there was no reasonable opportunity allowed to the defendant to make his defence and prepare and bring his evidence to Court. *Strange* v. *Strange*, (1908) V.L.R., 187 ; 29 A.L.T., 177 ; 14 A.L.R., 42. *Hodges, J.* (1908).

Justices—Court of Petty Sessions—Conviction—Sentence—Remand for sentence after determination of guilt of accused—Justices Act 1890 (No. 1105), sec. 78.]—Where Justices sitting in Petty Sessions are satisfied that the person charged before them is guilty of the alleged offence, but, in the absence of evidence as to prior convictions, are unable at once to fix the quantum of punishment, they may remand the prisoner, and at a future date, after hearing evidence as to prior convictions, formally record the conviction and pass sentence. *Quaere*, whether a Court of Petty Sessions has any jurisdiction to adjourn a case after pronouncing judgment. *Mc Innes* v. *King* ; *De la Rue* v. *Everett*, (1909) V.L.R., 368 ; 31 A.L.T., 27 ; 15 A.L.R., 356. *Hodges, J.*

(g) Witnesses.

Imprisonment of Fraudulent Debtors Act 1890 (No. 1100), Part III.—Court of Petty Sessions — Jurisdiction — Judgment debtor served with summons to debtor—Whether he may be also served with summons to witness —Non-attendance as witness, power to fine upon—Justices Act 1890 (No. 1105), secs. 20 (2), 36 (4).]—A judgment debtor served with a summons to debtor issued under Part III. of the *Imprisonment of Fraudulent Debtors Act* 1890 may also be served with a summons to witness, and, if he neglects or refuses to obey the latter summons, he may be fined for non-attendance as a witness under section 36 (4) of the *Justices Act* 1890. *Caldecott* v.

Cunningham, (1908) V.L.R., 38 ; 29 A.L.T., 94 ; 13 A.L.R., 639. F.C. *Hodges, Hood* and *Cussen, JJ.* (1907).

Justices Act 1890 (No. 1105), secs. 4, 29—Landlord and Tenant Act 1890 (No. 1108), secs. 92, 93—Recovery of possession—Justices—Jurisdiction to issue summons to witness—Notice of intention to apply, service of—" Complaint."]—Upon the service of a notice of intention to apply to Justices to recover possession under the *Landlord and Tenant Act* 1890 there is a " complaint " within the meaning of the *Justices Act* 1890, and the justices have jurisdiction to issue a summons to witness. *Lesser* v. *Knight*, 29 A.L.T., 111 ; 13 A.L.R., 708. *Madden, C.J.* (1907).

Justices—Court of Petty Sessions—Oath of witness—Who to administer—Clerk of Petty Sessions—Subordinate clerk — Justices Act 1890 (No. 1105), sec. 77 (7).]—Evidence Act 1890 (No. 1088), sec. 62.]—In proceedings before Justices in Petty Sessions, the oath may be administered to witnesses by any Justice, or by the Clerk of Petty Sessions, or by any person so directed by the Justices. The giving of the oath in all such cases is the act of the Court. *Rex* v. *Shuttleworth*, (1909) V.L.R., 431 ; 31 A.L.T., 50 ; 15 A.L.R., 492. F.C. *Madden, C.J., a'Beckett, Hodges, Hood* and *Cussen, JJ.*

Justices Act 1890 (No. 1105), secs. 41, 64, 77 (7)—Administration of oath—Acting clerk of Petty Sessions—Perjury.]—A witness sworn by an acting clerk of Petty Sessions may be guilty of perjury. *Reg.* v. *Barber*, 3 A.L.R. (C.N.), 21, approved. *Rex* v. *Turnbull*, (1907) V.L.R., 11 ; 28 A.L.T., 103 ; 12 A.L.R., 551. *Cussen, J.*

Justices Act 1890 (No. 1105), sec. 77 (7)—Administration of oath—Clerk of Petty Sessions, who is.]—*Quaere*, whether under section 77 (7) of the *Justices Act* 1890 a person who *de facto* acts as a clerk of Petty Sessions may not lawfully administer the oath to a witness. *Rex* v. *Turnbull*, (1907) V.L.R., 11 ; 28 A.L.T., 103 ; 12 A.L.R., 551. *Cussen, J.*

Imprisonment of Fraudulent Debtors Act 1890 (No. 1100), Part III.—Proceedings upon

summons to debtor—Adjournment—Whether witness bound to attend without issue or service of further summons—Justices Act 1890 (No. 1105), sec. 78 (4).]—Sub-section 4 of section 78 of the *Justices Act* 1890 applies to all adjournments by justices, *e.g.*, to the adjournment of proceedings upon a summons to debtor issued under the *Imprisonment of Fraudulent Debtors Act* 1890. *Caldecott v. Cunningham,* (1908) V.L.R., 38 ; 29 A.L.T., 94 ; 13 A.L.R., 639. F.C. *Hodges, Hood* and *Cussen, JJ.* (1907).

Justices Act 1890 (No. 1105), secs. 20, 36, 78 (4)—Witness who has been paid his expenses failing to attend—Adjournment—Whether witness entitled to expenses of attending adjourned hearing.]—Where a person, who has been served with a summons to witness and been paid his expenses as a witness, does not attend at the time and place appointed by the summons, and the hearing is adjourned, he is not entitled to further expenses to attend the adjourned hearing. *Caldecott v. Cunningham,* (1908) V.L.R., 38 ; 29 A.L.T., 94 ; 13 A.L.R., 639. F.C. *Hodges, Hood* and *Cussen, JJ.* (1907).

Justices Act 1890 (No. 1105), sec. 77 (11)—Ordering witnesses out of Court at request of party—Discretion of justices—Counsel and solicitor of opposite party subpoenaed as witnesses—Permission to remain in Court, effect of.]—The provisions of section 77 (11) of the *Justices Act* 1890 do not necessarily make it improper for justices to permit the counsel and solicitor appearing for a party to remain in Court, although the opposite party has subpoenaed them as witnesses and has requested that all witnesses be ordered out of Court. Even if it were an error to permit them to remain the proceedings would not be thereby invalidated, if it were evident that the request for their removal was made for the purpose of obstruction, and that the denial of the request in no way resulted in a denial of justice or prevented a proper hearing of the case. *Barry v. Cullen,* (1906) V.L.R., 393 ; 27 A.L.T., 227 ; 12 A.L.R., 235. *a'Beckett, A.C.J.* (1906).

(*h*) *Evidence ; Interrogation of Prisoner by Justices.*

Court of Petty Sessions—Jurisdiction—Discretion as to sentence—Evidence of character—Prior convictions.]—Where, on the hearing of an information before a Court of Petty Sessions, the justices have convicted the defendant, they have jurisdiction to receive evidence on oath as to the character of the defendant, and particularly of prior convictions, in order to assist them in the exercise of their discretion as to the amount of punishment they will award. *O'Donnell v. Perkins ; Tognini v. Hargreaves,* (1908) V.L.R., 537 ; 30 A.L.T., 45 ; 14 A.L.R., 435. F.C. *a'Beckett, Hood* and *Cussen, JJ.* (1908).

Evidence—Information in possession of Magistrates but not in evidence before them—Whether magistrates may act upon—Licensing—Prohibition order—Licensing Act 1890 (No. 1111), sec. 125.]—In making a prohibition order under section 125 of the *Licensing Act* 1890 the magistrates acted on certain special and peculiar information with regard to the defendant possessed by one of their number, who had communicated it to them but not to the defendant. *Held,* that a magistrate possessing such information was not at liberty to use it himself, or to influence his fellow magistrates by it in coming to a determination on the matter before them. *Strange v. Strange,* (1908) V.L.R., 187 ; 29 A.L.T., 177 ; 14 A.L.R., 42. *Hodges, J.*

Evidence—Public document—Suitors' cash book (Rule 10, Rules under the Justices Act 1890)—Entries made by Clerk of Petty Sessions not in official capacity—Maintenance order—Direction to pay to Clerk—Entries of payments—Marriage Act 1890 (No. 1166), sec. 51.] — *See* EVIDENCE, col. 497. *Cohen v. MacDonough* (or *O'Donough*), (1906) V.L.R., 521 ; 28 A.L.T., 97 ; 12 A.L.R., 447.

Evidence—Foreign law—Fugitive Offenders Act 1881 (44 & 45 Vict. c. 69)—Law of other country, whether a question of fact—How magistrate may be satisfied as to.]—*See* FUGITIVE OFFENDERS, col. 599. *McKelvey v. Meagher,* 4 C.L.R., 265 ; 12 A.L.R., 483.

Evidence—Foreign law—Rendition of fugitive offender—Fugitive Offenders Act 1881 (44 & 45 Vict. c. 69), secs. 5, 29.]—See EVIDENCE, col. 485. *McKelvey* v. *Meagher*, 4 C.L.R., 265 ; 12 A.L.R., 483.

Police Offences Act 1907 (No. 2093), sec. 8 (a), (b)—Vagrancy—Evidence of bad character, when it must be tendered—Evidence as to general character, what is—Evidence to rebut.]—See POLICE OFFENCES ACTS. *Hickling* v. *Skerritt*, (1912) V.L.R., 322 ; 34 A.L.T., 72 ; 18 A.L.R., 329.

Police Offences Act 1890 (No. 1126), sec. 40 (1)—Account of means of support—Whether justices may be required to call upon accused to give.]—See POLICE OFFENCES ACTS. *Wilson* v. *Travers*, (1906) V.L.R., 734 ; 28 A.L.T., 56 ; 12 A.L.R., 413. [*See Police Offences Act* 1912, section 70.]

(i) *Adjudication, Duty of Justices as to.*

Justices Act 1890 (No. 1105), sec. 59 (3)—Obligation of justices to exercise their functions—Special cases excepted—Refusal to make an "order," effect of.] — The *Justices Act* 1890 imposes upon justices the obligation of pronouncing a decision one way or the other in all cases except those which are the subject of special exceptions. A complaint for detention of goods under section 59 (3) is not a special exception. *McMahon* v. *Johnston*, (1909) V.L.R., 376 ; 31 A.L.T., 36 ; 15 A.L.R., 371. *a' Beckett, J.*

Uncontradicted evidence—Decision of Justices against—Duty to give reasons.]—Justices are not at liberty, by disregarding uncontradicted evidence before them, to determine a question of fact against such evidence, unless they at the same time give some definite reason justifying their decision. *Richards* v. *Jager*, (1909) V.L.R., 140 ; 30 A.L.T., 163 ; 15 A.L.R., 119. *Madden, C.J.*

(j) *Reserving Decision.*

Two charges against one defendant—Reserving decision in first case pending hearing of second charge.]—For observations as to the propriety of Justices reserving their decision upon one information until they have heard the evidence upon a second information against the same defendant, where such evidence might influence their decision upon the first information, see *Hunter* v. *Stewart*, (1907) V.L.R., 619 ; 29 A.L.T., 39 ; 13 A.L.R., 440. *a' Beckett, J.*

(k) *Practice under Service and Execution of Process Act.*

See also, PART IV.—CONTROL OF SUPERIOR COURTS. (c) *Under Service and Execution of Process Act.*

Service and Execution of Process Act 1901 (No. 11 of 1901), sec. 18—Warrant endorsed for execution in another State—Apprehension of accused on unsustainable charge.]—Where in the case of a person who has been apprehended in Victoria under the provisions of sec. 18 of the *Service and Execution of Process Act* 1901, in consequence of the issue in another State of a warrant for his apprehension upon a charge of having committed an offence within such other State, it appears to the Justice of the Peace before whom he is brought, that, if the accused were put on trial upon the charge alleged against him, he ought on the undisputed facts to be acquitted, the Justice ought to discharge him. *In re George*, (1909) V.L.R., 15 ; 30 A.L.T., 141 ; 15 A.L.R., 27. *a' Beckett, J.*

Service and Execution of Process Act 1901 (No. 11), sec. 18 (4)—Person arrested on warrant issued in another State—Return of such person to such other State, whether unjust or oppressive—Dispute as to facts alleged in defence—Bona fide assurance of dispute by prosecutor.]—See SERVICE AND EXECUTION OF PROCESS ACT. *O'Donnell* v. *Heslop* ; *The King* v. *Cresswell, Ex parte Heslop*; (1910) V.L.R., 162 ; 31 A.L.T., 173 ; 16 A.L.R., 168.

(l) *Convictions ; Orders.*

Justices Act 1890 (No. 1105), secs. 4, 59 (3)—Complaint for detention of goods—Refusal to make order—Dismissal—Second complaint for some cause of action—Estoppel.]—Where on a complaint for detention of goods under sec. 59 (3) of the *Justices Act* 1890 the Justices not being satisfied that the complainant has proved his case, refuse to make any order, such a refusal is in such circumstances in effect a dismissal and an adjudication in favour of the defendant, and such adjudication is a defence to a subsequent complaint against the defendant in respect of the same cause of complaint. *McMahon* v. *Johnson*, (1909) V.L.R., 376; 31 A.L.T., 36; 15 A.L.R., 371. *a' Beckett, J.*

Factories and Shops Act 1905 (No. 1975), secs. 42, 162 (c), (d)—Factories and Shops Act 1905 (No. 2), (No. 2008), sec. 9—Conviction against firm in firm name—Rules under Justices Act 1890, rr. 18, 20.]—In proceedings against a firm for an offence under the Act No. 1975 the conviction ought to be against the individual members of the firm, and a conviction in the firm name is bad. *Bishop* v. *Chung Brothers*, 4 C.L.R., 1262; 13 A.L.R., 412. H.C., *Griffith, C.J., Barton* and *Isaacs, JJ., Higgins, J.*, dissenting. (1906). [*See,* the Act No. 2137, sec. 39.]

Police Offences Act 1890 (No. 1126), secs. 49, 51, 89—Fine in default imprisonment—No time fixed for payment of fine.]—Where Justices do not in their order name a time for payment of a fine, the fine is to be treated as having been ordered to be paid immediately. *Rogerson* v. *Phillips and O'Hagan*, (1906) V.L.R., 272; 27 A.L.T., 166; 12 A.L.R., 147. *a' Beckett, J.* (1906).

Marriage Act 1890 (No. 1166), sec. 43—Maintenance order—Direction to pay to Clerk of Petty Sessions at particular place—Whether Clerk a " person."]—By a maintenance order under sec. 43 of the *Marriage Act* 1890, the defendant was directed to pay a weekly sum to " the Clerk of Petty Sessions at Fitzroy." *Held*, that such direction did not invalidate the order; but, *quaere*, whether " the Clerk of Petty Sessions at Fitzroy " is a " person " within the meaning of sec. 43. *Cohen* v. *MacDonough (or O'Donough)*, (1906) V.L.R., 521; 28 A.L.T., 97; 12 A.L.R., 447. *Cussen, J.*

Marriage Act 1890 (No. 1166), sec. 42, 43, 51—Order for maintenance of child—Disobedience of Order—Jurisdiction of Justices to order the arrears of maintenance to be paid by instalments.]—Under sec. 51 of the *Marriage Act* 1890, Justices have jurisdiction to order the defendant to pay by instalments, arrears of maintenance. *Lobley* v. *Lobley*, (1909) V.L.R., 383; 31 A.L.T., 46; 15 A.L.R., 443. F.C., *Madden, C.J., Hodges* and *Cussen, JJ.*

Marriage Act 1890 (No. 1166), sec. 51—Discretion of Justices—Dismissal of complaint—Giving defendant time to pay.]—*See* MAINTENANCE AND MAINTENANCE ORDERS. *Aarons* v. *Aarons*, (1907) V.L.R., 21; 28 A.L.T., 117; 12 A.L.R., 567.

Marriage Act 1890 (No. 1166), s. 43—" In such manner " as Justices think fit—Order directing payment to clerk of Petty Sessions at particular place, validity of.]—*See* MAINTENANCE AND MAINTENANCE ORDERS. *Aarons* v. *Aarons*, (1907) V.L.R., 21; 28 A.L.T., 117; 12 A.L.R., 567.

Marriage Act 1890 (No. 1166), sec. 43—Justices Act 1904 (No. 1959), sec. 20—Order for maintenance—Defendant to find surety " forthwith "—Immediate committal to prison—Service of copy order whether condition precedent to issue of warrant of committal.]—*See* MAINTENANCE AND MAINTENANCE ORDERS. *Adams* v. *Rogers*, (1907) V.L.R., 245; 28 A.L.T., 180; 13 A.L.R., 71.

Marriage Act 1890 (No. 1166), secs. 42, 43—Maintenance order—Surety directed—Person to whom security to be given, whether necessary to specify—Justices Act 1890 (No. 1105), sec. 108.]—*See* MAINTENANCE AND MAINTENANCE ORDERS. *Shee* v. *Larkin*, (1907) V.L.R., 295; 28 A.L.T., 188; 13 A.L.R., 97.

Marriage Act 1890 (No. 1166), secs. 42, 43—Maintenance order — Surety directed — To whom security to be given—Payments to be made to Clerk of Petty Sessions.]—*See* MAINTENANCE AND MAINTENANCE ORDERS. *Shee* v. *Larkin*, (1907) V.L.R., 295; 28 A.L.T., 188; 13 A.L.R., 97.

Marriage Act 1890 (No. 1166), secs. 42, 43—Order for maintenance of child—Subsequent return of child to father—Order still valid.]—*See* MAINTENANCE AND MAINTENANCE

ORDERS. *Lobley* v. *Lobley*, (1909) V.L.R., 383 ; 31 A.L.T., 46 ; 15 A.L.R., 443.

Maintenance order made by Court of Petty Sessions—Money due thereunder—Action in Supreme Court to recover—Marriage Act 1890 (No. 1166), secs. 43, 51—Justices Act 1890 (No. 1105), secs. 115, 131—Justices Act 1896 (No. 1458), sec. 4.]—No action will lie in the Supreme Court for the recovery of money due under a maintenance order made by a Court of Petty Sessions under sec. 43 of the *Marriage Act* 1890. *Falconer* v. *Falconer*, (1910) V.L.R., 489 ; 32 A.L.T. 100 ; 16 A.L.R., 578. *Cussen, J.*

Order of Court of Petty Sessions—Whether it may be sued upon in another Court.]—*Semble.*—Upon the death of a complainant, who has obtained an order in a Court of Petty Sessions for the payment of a sum of money, his executor may sue on the order of the Court of Petty Sessions in the County Court and possibly in the Supreme Court. *Goodman* v. *Jonas*, (1909) V.L.R., 308 ; 31 A.L.T., 16 ; 15 A.L.R., 308. *Cussen, J.*

(m) Execution ; Interpleader ; Attachment of Debts.

Imprisonment of Fraudulent Debtors Act 1890 (No. 1100), Part III.—Court of Petty Sessions—Proceedings upon summons to debtor, nature of—Whether a mere method of enforcing judgment.]—The procedure upon a summons to debtor issued under sec. 22 of the *Imprisonment of Fraudulent Debtors Act* 1890 is nothing more than a stringent or severe method of bringing pressure to bear upon the debtor to pay his debt. *Caldecott* v. *Cunningham*, (1908) V.L.R., 38 ; 29 A.L.T., 94 ; 13 A.L.R., 639. F.C., *Hodges, Hood* and *Cussen, JJ.*

Justices Act 1890 (No. 1105), secs. 94, 102—Civil debt—Order for payment—Warrant of distress—Whether defendant entitled to be heard before issue—Jurisdiction of Justice.]—Where a Court of Petty Sessions has made an order for payment of a civil debt and in default distress, a Justice may thereafter, on the *ex parte* application of the plaintiff, issue a warrant of distress. *Warr* v. *Temple-*

ton, 3 V.R. (L.), 56 ; 3 A.J.R., 37, discussed. *Cross* v. *Daffy*, (1910) V.L.R., 316 ; 32 A.L.T., 10 ; 16 A.L.R., 279. F.C., *Madden, C.J., Hodges* and *Cussen, JJ.*

Marriage Act 1890 (No. 1166), sec. 43—Maintenance order — Surety directed — Liability of surety, when it arises—Declaration of forfeiture, whether necessary.]—*See* MAINTENANCE AND MAINTENANCE ORDERS. *Shee* v. *Larkin*, (1907) V.L.R., 295 ; 28 A.L.T., 188 ; 13 A.L.R., 97.

Order XLII., r. 23 (a) (Rules of 1906)—Justices Act 1890 (No. 1105), sec. 115—Leave to issue execution—Judgment in Court of Petty Sessions—Lapse of over six years—Date of judgment, what is.]—Under Order XLII., r. 23 (a) leave may be granted to issue a writ of *fieri facias* on a certificate of a judgment, obtained in a Court of Petty Sessions and filed in the Supreme Court under sec. 115 of the *Justices Act* 1890, where six years have elapsed since the judgment. The six years should in such a case be counted as starting from the original order in the Court of Petty Sessions. *Trent Brewery* v. *Lehane*, 21 V.L.R., 283 ; 1 A.L.R., 89, followed. *Sack* v. *Wolstencroft*, 29 A.L.T., 85 ; 13 A.L.R., 588. *Cussen, J.* (1907).

Local Government Act 1903 (No. 1893), secs. 324 to 328, 340 to 343—Rates, interest and costs, how far a charge upon land—Costs of removing an order from Petty Sessions to Supreme Court.]—*See* LOCAL GOVERNMENT. *Mayor, &c., of Malvern* v. *Johnson*, 28 A.L.T. (Supplement), 7 ; 12 A.L.R. (C.N.), 28.

Justices Act 1890 (No. 1105), sec. 98, Schedule II., Form 55—Interpleader summons —Withdrawal of claim—Jurisdiction of Justices to adjudicate.]—On the hearing of a summons under sec. 98 of the *Justices Act* 1890 the Justices may adjudicate on the claim although it is withdrawn and the judgment debt has been satisfied. *Watson* v. *Barby* ; *O'Connor, claimant*, (1910) V.L.R., 134. *a'Beckett, J.*

Attachment of debts—Money ordered to be paid by Court of General Sessions—Attachment by Court of Petty Sessions—Jurisdiction.]

Where a Court of General Sessions has ordered a sum of money to be paid, a Court of Petty Sessions cannot make an order of attachment by way of garnishee proceedings in aid of the judgment creditor. *Brown* v. *Gunn*; *McKay, Garnishee,* (1913) V.L.R., 60; 34 A.L.T., 115; 18 A.L.R. (C.N.), 21. *Cussen, J.* (1912).

Attachment of debts—Garnishee order—Judgment debtor trustee of moneys attached—Appearance of judgment debtor before Justices to protect fund—Justices Act 1890 (No. 1105), sec. 117.]—A judgment debtor who is a trustee of moneys sought to be attached by a garnishee order *nisi* for payment of a judgment debt due by him personally, has a right and is under a duty, to appear before the justices on the garnishee proceedings to show that the moneys are trust moneys and ought not therefore be attached. *Roberts* v. *Death,* 8 Q.B.D., 319, followed. *Regina* v. *Justices of Heywood,* 21 V.L.R., 654; 17 A.L.T., 238; 2 A.L.R., 135, distinguished. *Richards* v. *Jager,* (1909) V.L.R., 140; 30 A.L.T., 163; 15 A.L.R., 119. *Madden, C.J.*

(n) Contempt of Court.

Justices Act 1890 (No. 1105), sec. 198—Contempt of Court—Misbehaviour not witnessed by Court itself—Formal adjournment of Court before occurrence of misbehaviour, effect of.]—A Court of Petty Sessions has jurisdiction under section 198 of the *Justices Act* 1890 to punish a person who wilfully misbehaves himself in the Court-room whilst the Court is sitting, although the Court has not itself witnessed the misbehaviour. *Semble* : Justices who have been sitting as a Court of Petty Sessions have no jurisdiction under section 198 to punish a person for misbehaviour that takes place in the Court-room after the Court has been formally adjourned. *Westcott* v. *Lord,* (1911) V.L.R., 452; 33 A.L.T., 54; 17 A.L.R., 433. *Madden, C.J.*

Justices Act 1890 (No. 1105), sec. 198—Contempt of Court—Wilful misbehaviour in a Court of Petty Sessions—Insulting language to a witness after case decided.]—If a person calls a witness a " champion liar " in a Court of Petty Sessions, after the case in which the witness gave evidence has been decided, but before the Court has concluded its business, such person wilfully misbehaves himself within the meaning of section 198 of the *Justices Act* 1890. *Westcott* v. *Lord,* (1911) V.L.R., 452; 33 A.L.T., 54; 17 A.L.R., 433. *Madden, C.J.*

(o) Trifling Offence.

Justices Act 1890 (No. 1105), sec. 191—Information—Assault—Offence of a trifling nature—Discretion of justices.]—An offence of a trifling nature within the meaning of section 191 of the *Justices Act* 1890 may be an offence of a trifling nature in itself, or when serious where the facts of the particular case reduce the gravity of it, but in the latter event the mitigating circumstances ought to be very marked. In a prosecution for an unlawful assault, the evidence showed that the informant had been seriously assaulted by the defendant, whose only excuse was revenge either for an injury or for an insult. The justices dismissed the information. *Held,* that the dismissal was not justifiable under section 191 of the *Justices Act* 1890. *Williams* v. *May,* (1908) V.L.R., 605; 30 A.L.T., 89; 14 A.L.R., 504. *Hood, J.*

(p) Fines and Penalties.

Appeal to General Sessions—Increase of fine to facilitate, propriety of—Justices Act 1890 (No. 1105), secs. 59 (1), 127.]—Justices ought not to increase the amount of a fine at the request of the defendant in order to enable him to appeal to the Court of General Sessions under section 127 of the *Justices Act* 1890. *Kane* v. *Dureau,* (1911) V.L.R., 293; 33 A.L.T., 15; 17 A.L.R., 277. *Cussen, J.*

Police Offences Act 1890 (No. 1126), secs. 49, 51, 89—Street Betting Suppression Act 1896 (No. 1436), sec. 7—Assisting in conducting a common gaming house—First offence, punishment for—Imprisonment in default of payment of fine—Term of imprisonment in default greater than maximum term provided for offence—Jurisdiction.]—*See* GAMING AND WAGERING. *Rogerson* v. *Phillips and*

O'Hagan, (1906) V.L.R., 272; 27 A.L.T., 166; 12 A.L.R., 147.

"Second offence," what is—Pure Food Act 1905 (No. 2010), sec. 36.]—*See* CRIMINAL LAW, cols. 367, 368. *O'Connor* v. *Bini*, (1908) V.L.R., 567; 30 A.L.T., 74; 14 A.L.R., 537.

Marriage Act 1890 (No. 1166), secs. 43, 51 —Maintenance order — Imprisonment for breach—Whether jurisdiction to imprison for a second breach.]—*See* MAINTENANCE AND MAINTENANCE ORDERS. *Aarons* v. *Aarons*, (1907) V.L.R., 21; 28 A.L.T., 117; 12 A.L.R., 567.

IV.—CONTROL OF SUPERIOR COURTS.

(a) *Order to Review.*

(1) Where Review Lies.

Justices Act 1890 (No. 1105), sec. 141— Fugitive Offenders Act 1881 (44 & 45 Vict. c. 69)—Order by Victorian magistrate exercising powers conferred by Imperial Act—Whether it may be dealt with by order to review.]— The order of a Victorian Magistrate made in the exercise of powers conferred by the *Fugitive Offenders Act* 1881 is not subject to the provisions of the *Justices Act* 1890 relating to orders to review. *O'Donnell* v. *McKelvie*, (1906) V.L.R., 207; 27 A.L.T., 164; 12 A.L.R., 39. F.C., *a'Beckett, Hodges* and *Hood, JJ.*

Justices Act 1890 (No. 1105), sec. 141— Jurisdiction of Supreme Court—Order remanding prisoner—Whether it may be dealt with by order to review.]—An order of a Justice remanding an alleged offender is not an "order" within the meaning of sec. 141 of the *Justices Act* 1890. *Kennedy* v. *Purser*, 23 V.L.R., 530; 19 A.L.T., 192; 4 A.L.R., 54; followed. *O'Donnell* v. *McKelvie*, (1906) V.L.R., 207; 27 A.L.T., 164; 12 A.L.R., 39. F.C., *a'Beckett, Hodges* and *Hood, JJ.*

Justices Act 1890 (No. 1105), sec. 141— Order to review—Order which may be reviewed, what is—Order remanding accused to custody—Remand not for convenience of hearing but for another purpose—Neglected Children's Act 1890 (No. 1121), secs. 18, 19—

Children's Court Act 1906 (No. 2058).]— Where a person, arrested and brought before a Children's Court nominally charged with being a neglected child, is remanded to custody not for the purpose of enabling the charge to be proceeded with but really, as appears on the face of the proceedings, for another purpose, *e.g.*, in order to detain accused as a witness, the order remanding the accused is an order within sec. 141 of the *Justices Act* 1890 and is reviewable. *Mc-Sweeney* v. *Haggar*, (1911) V.L.R., 130; 32 A.L.T., 194; 17 A.L.R., 70. *Hood, J.*

Appeal from Court of Petty Sessions exercising Federal jurisdiction—Order to review— No appeal under State law—Rules of High Court 1911, Part II., sec. IV., r. 1—Justices Act 1904 (No. 1959), sec. 21.]—An appeal to the High Court from a decision of a Court of Petty Sessions exercising Federal jurisdiction in the case of a civil debt recoverable summarily when the sum involved does not exceed £5 may under the *Rules of the High Court*, Part II., Sec. IV., r. 1, be brought by way of order to review notwithstanding that by sec. 21 of the *Justices Act* 1904 in such a case the granting of an order to review is prohibited. *Prentice* v. *Amalgamated Mining Employees Association of Victoria and Tasmania*, (1912) 15 C.L.R., 235; 18 A.L.R., 343. H.C., *Griffith, C.J., Barton* and *Isaacs, JJ.*

Justices Act 1890 (No. 1105), sec. 141—Justices Act 1904 (No. 1959), sec. 21—Sum in respect to which applicant aggrieved not exceeding five pounds—Important public matter of law, etc.—When question to be determined.]—The question, whether in view of the provisions of sec. 21 of the *Justices Act* 1904 an order to review may be granted, should be determined on the application for the order *nisi*, and not upon the return. *O'Sullivan* v. *Humphris*, (1906) V.L.R., 563; 28 A.L.T., 13; 12 A.L.R., 328. *Cussen, J.* (1906).

Justices Act 1904 (No. 1959), sec. 21—Order to review—Order for amount not exceeding Five pounds—Whether order nisi may be granted—When question to be decided—

Objection to grant of order, how taken.]—
The question, whether in view of the provisions of sec. 21 of the *Justices Act* 1904
an order to review may be granted, should be
determined on the application for the order
nisi. But an order *nisi* wrongly granted
as being obnoxious to sec. 21 may be set aside
on summons. It is too late to take such an
objection on the return of the order *nisi*.
Bevan v. *Moore*, 24 V.L.R., 792 ; 20 A.L.T.,
238 ; 5 A.L.R., 100, explained. *McCallum*
v. *Purvis*, (1906) V.L.R., 578 ; 28 A.L.T., 31 ;
12 A.L.R., 329. *Hood, J.* (1906).

**Court of Petty Sessions—Federal jurisdic-
tion—Exercise of, what is—Commonwealth of
Australia Constitution, secs. 31, 76—Constitution Act Amendment Act 1890 (No. 1075), sec.
282—Judiciary Act 1903 (No. 6), sec. 39 (2)
(d)—Question decided involving interpretation
of sec. 31 of Constitution—Other question
decided involving interpretation of Commonwealth Electoral Act 1902 (No. 19)—Appeal
to High Court, whether it lies.]**—On a complaint for work and labour done at an election
for the House of Representatives of the
Commonwealth Parliament, the defence being
that sec. 282 of the *Constitution Act Amendment Act* 1890 was a bar to the complaint,
the Court of Petty Sessions held that sec. 282
was a " law relating to elections " and by
virtue of sec. 31 of the Commonwealth Constitution applied to elections for the House of
Representatives until Parliament otherwise
provided, but also held that Parliament had
otherwise provided by passing the *Commonwealth Electoral Act* 1902 and had thereby
repealed sec. 282, and the Court therefore
gave judgment for the complainant. *Held*,
that in determining the second point the
Court of Petty Sessions had not exercised
Federal jurisdiction, and therefore that no
appeal lay to the High Court from the judgment of the Court of Petty Sessions. *Miller*
v. *Haweis*, (1907) 5 C.L.R., 89 ; 13 A.L.R.,
583. H.C., *Griffith, C.J., Barton, O'Connor,
Isaacs* and *Higgins, JJ.*

**Court of Petty Sessions—Federal jurisdic-
tion—Exercise of, what is—Two questions
decided, one Federal and the other not—Each
sufficient to sustain judgment—Appeal to**
**High Court, whether it lies—Judiciary Act
1903 (No. 6), sec. 39 (2) (d).]**—A Court of
Petty Sessions exercises Federal jurisdiction
within the meaning of sec. 39 (2) (d) of the
Judiciary Act 1903, if it be necessary in the
particular case for the Court to decide any
question arising under the Commonwealth
Constitution or involving its interpretation.
If, however, whether that question be
answered rightly or wrongly, the Court
answers another question not arising under
the Commonwealth Constitution or involving
its interpretation, and the Court's answer to
such other question enables it to decide the
case, the Court does not exercise Federal
jurisdiction, and therefore no appeal lies to
the High Court. *Miller* v. *Haweis*, (1907) 5
C.L.R., 89 ; 13 A.L.R., 583. H.C., *Griffith, C.J.,
Barton, O'Connor, Isaacs* and *Higgins, JJ.*

**Commonwealth of Australia Constitution
Act (63 & 64 Vict. c. 12)—The Constitution,
secs. 73, 74, 76, 77—Question as to limits
inter se of Constitutional powers of Commonwealth and State, what is—Question
rasied by defence whether State tax on Federal
salary an interference with powers of Commonwealth—Exercise of Federal jurisdiction by
Court of Petty Sessions—Appeal to High
Court, competency of—Judiciary Act 1903
(Commonwealth) (No. 6 of 1903), sec. 39.]**—
See APPEAL, cols. 19, 20. *Baxter* v. *Commissioners of Taxation* ; *Flint* v. *Webb*, 4
C.L.R., 1087, 1178 ; 13 A.L.R., 313.

(2) Parties ; Person Aggrieved.

**Infant complainant in Court of Petty Ses-
sions—Claim for wages—Order to review
obtained by infant—Next friend, whether
infant must proceed by—Justices Act 1890
(No. 1105), sec. 72—Rules of Supreme Court
1884, Order XVI. r. 16.]**—An infant complainant in a Court of Petty Sessions cannot
obtain an order *nisi* to review a dismissal
of his complaint, except through a next
friend, even in cases where he may proceed
in the Court below without a next friend.
Cash v. *Cash*, 22 V.L.R., 110 ; 17 A.L.T., 326 ;
2 A.L.R., 153, approved. *Hines* v. *Phillips*,
(1906) V.L.R., 417 ; 28 A.L.T., 1 ; 12
A.L.R., 249. *a'Beckett, A.-C.J.* (1906).

Order to review — Infant respondent— Guardian ad litem—Practice.]—Where an infant is the party called upon by an order to review to support the order of Justices a guardian *ad litem* for the infant will be appointed on the return of the order *nisi*. *Brown* v. *Gunn*; *McKay, Garnishee,* (1913) V.L.R., 60; 34 A.L.T., 115; 18 A.L.R. (C.N.), 21. *Cussen, J.* (1912).

Justices Act 1890 (No. 1105), secs. 117, 119, 124, 128 (12), 141—Attachment of debt— Judgment debt—Order of General Sessions— Garnishee order—Petty Sessions Order — Effect thereof—Jurisdiction—Order to Review —" Person aggrieved."]—Where, on the return of an order *nisi* for the attachment of a debt which shows on its face that the judgment debt arose upon an order of a Court of General Sessions, a Court of Petty Sessions makes an order for payment to the judgment creditor by the alleged garnishee of the debt due by him to the judgment debtor, the Supreme Court will not, at the instance of the judgment debtor, review the last mentioned order on the ground of its having been made without jurisdiction, as he is not a " person aggrieved " within the meaning of sec. 141 of the *Justices Act* 1890. *Brown* v. *Gunn; McKay, Garnishee (No.* 1), (1912) V.L.R., 463; 34 A.L.T., 113; 18 A.L.R., 462. *Cussen, J.*

(3) Affidavits of Justices.

Order to review—Affidavit of Justices— Duty of Justices as to filing—Facts to which Justices may properly depose.]—Where an order *nisi* to review has been granted, the Justices, if they think they can help the Court or the administration of justice by filing an affidavit as provided by the *Justices Act* 1890, should do so without waiting to be asked. In their affidavit the Justices should confine themselves to the grounds of their decision, and the material facts affecting it. *Larkin* v. *Penfold,* (1906) V.L.R., 535; 28 A.L.T., 42; 12 A.L.R., 337. *Cussen, J.*

Order to review—Practice—Order nisi and affidavit in support—How brought to the knowledge of Justices—Subsequent affidavits, suggested practice as to.]—*Per Cussen, J.*—

" In the absence of any rules under sec. 153 of the Act, and having regard to the fact that it is not usual to call upon Justices to show cause, a practice has grown up of inserting in orders *nisi* a direction that a copy of the order and of the affidavit should be left with the Clerk of the Court . . . I think it would be well to carry the practice a little further, and either to provide in the order *nisi*, or by an intimation from the Court, that either of the parties is to be at liberty to send by prepaid letter to the Clerk of the Court copies of any of the subsequent affidavits." *Larkin* v. *Penfold,* (1906) V.L.R., 535; 28 A.L.T., 42; 12 A.L.R., 337.

(4) Grounds for Review ; Practice on Return of Order *Nisi*.

Order to review—Party to begin argument.] —The Court called upon counsel moving the order *nisi* absolute to begin the argument, but reserved to him his right of reply. *Graham* v. *Lucas,* (1907) V.L.R., 478; 29 A.L.T., 10; 13 A.L.R., 262. F.C., *a' Beckett, Hood* and *Cussen, JJ.*

Order to review—Affidavits in reply, when they may be used.]—On the return of an order *nisi* to review, each party may use an affidavit or affidavits in reply to the affidavits of the opposite party upon any new matter arising out of such affidavits. *Larkin* v. *Penfold,* (1906) V.L.R., 535; 28 A.L.T., 42; 12 A.L.R., 337. *Cussen, J.*

Justices Act 1890 (No. 1105), sec. 144— Order to review—Grounds, addition to.]— *Semble.*—*Per Madden, C.J.*—On the return of an order to review a decision of a Court of Petty Sessions, the Court cannot add a new ground to the order *nisi*. *Lobley* v. *Lobley,* (1909) V.L.R., 383; 31 A.L.T., 46; 15 A.L.R., 443. F.C., *Madden, C.J., Hodges* and *Cussen, JJ.*

Thistle Act 1890 (No. 1145), sec. 4—Thistle Act 1893 (No. 1337)—Notice to destroy thistles—Foundation of offence—Insufficient notice—Objection first taken in order nisi to review.]—As the giving of the notice under sec. 4 of the *Thistles Act* 1890 is the foundation of the offence, an objection that no

26

sufficient notice was given to the defendant as required by sec. 4 of the *Thistle Act* 1890 may be taken for the first time in an order *nisi* to review the conviction of the defendant under that section. *Murphy* v. *Shiells*, (1908) V.L.R., 513; 30 A.L.T., 20; 14 A.L.R., 410. *Cussen, J.*

Order to review—Evidence properly rejected on the ground upon which it was tendered—Admissibility of evidence on another ground—Whether to be relied on upon order to review.] —Where evidence is tendered before Justices on a ground on which it is not admissible and it is rejected by them, their order will not be reviewed on the ground that such evidence was admissible on a ground other than that on which it was tendered. *Sanderson* v. *Nicholson*, (1906) V.L.R., 371; 27 A.L.T., 215; 12 A.L.R., 208, not followed. *Honeybone* v. *Glass*, (1908) V.L.R., 466; 30 A.L.T., 54; 14 A.L.R., 345. *Madden, C.J.*

Justices—Service of summons—Summons left at last place of abode—Defendant absent in England—Objection to service taken before Justices—Summons dismissed on other ground — Order to review—Renewal of objection—Justices Act 1890 (No. 1105), secs. 23 (1), 146.]—Where the objection was unsuccessfully taken before the Justices that the summons was not properly served, but the information was dismissed on other grounds, it is open to the defendant again to take the objection upon the return of an order *nisi* to review obtained by the informant. *Rees* v. *Downer*, (1910) V.L.R., 5; 31 A.L.T., 97; 15 A.L.R., 630. *Hodges, J.*

Justices Act 1890 (No. 1105), sec. 70—Dividing cause of action in order to make two complaints—When objection should be taken.] —An objection that a complainant has divided his cause of action must be taken at the hearing, and if not then taken cannot be entertained subsequently. *Mulder* v. *Adami*, (1907) V.L.R., 206; 28 A.L.T., 178; 13 A.L.R., 69. *Hood, J.*

Amendment—Order to review—Conviction under Police Offences Act 1890 (No. 1126), sec. 40 (vi.)—No material disadvantage to defendant—Justices Act 1890 (No. 1105), sec. 147.]—For an instance in which upon the return of an order *nisi* to review a conviction under sec. 40 (vi.) of the *Police Offences Act* 1890, the Court was prepared to make an amendment in the conviction whereby the defendant would suffer no substantial disadvantage, *see Hickling* v. *Skerritt*, (1912) V.L.R., 322; 34 A.L.T., 72; 18 A.L.R., 329. *Madden, C.J.*

Justices Act 1890 (No. 1105), sec. 141—Information disclosing no offence—Conviction thereon—Amendment on return of order to review—Powers of Court—Defendant never charged with an offence.]—Where a conviction has been based on an information which discloses no offence, the Court upon order to review should not, at all events without giving an opportunity to call fresh evidence, amend the information so as to raise a new allegation of fact, notwithstanding that the testimony given would go to show that an offence was in fact committed. *Quaere*, whether the Court may alter an information and conviction for one offence, so as to make them refer to another offence. *Knox* v. *Thomas Bible*; *Knox* v. *J. L. Bible*, (1907) V.L.R., 485; 29 A.L.T., 23; 13 A.L.R., 352. *Cussen, J.* Leave to appeal refused by High Court, 4 C.L.R., 1462.

Order to review—Conflict of evidence as to what took place before Justices—Acceptance of version supporting decision of Justices.]— Where there is a conflict of evidence as to what took place before the Justices, the practice is to accept the version which supports the Justices' decision, *i.e.*, their decision on any matter incidentally arising during the hearing or their ultimate decision, as the case may be. *Larkin* v. *Penfold*, (1906) V.L.R., 535; 28 A.L.T., 42; 12 A.L.R. 337. *Cussen, J.* (1906).

Justices Act 1890 (No. 1105), secs. 141—Order to review conviction—Improper admission of evidence—Whether duty of Court either to set aside conviction or remit for rehearing.]—Where, on the return of an order to review a conviction, the Court is satisfied that on the evidence properly admitted the defendant clearly should have been convicted, the Court is not bound to set the conviction aside or to remit the case because some written or oral statement possibly having some effect on the Justices' decision, has been wrongly admitted as evidence. *Knox* v. *Thomas Bible,* (1907) V.L.R., 485; 29 A.L.T., 23; 13 A.L.R., 352, approved. *Macmanamny* v. *King,* (1907) V.L.R., 535; 28 A.L.T., 250; 13 A.L.R., 258. F.C., *a' Beckett, Hood* and *Cussen, JJ.*

Justices Act 1890 (No. 1105), sec. 141— Order to review conviction—Evidence improperly admitted—Whether Court bound either to set aside conviction or remit case for re-hearing.]—On the return of an order to review, even in a criminal matter, the Court is not bound to set aside a conviction or remit the case for re-hearing because some written or oral statement, possibly having some effect on the Justices' decision, has been wrongly admitted, if, in the opinion of the Court, on the evidence properly admitted, the defendant clearly should have been convicted. *Reg.* v. *Gibson,* 18 Q.B.D., 537, considered. *Knox* v. *Thomas Bible*; *Knox* v. *J. L. Bible,* (1907) V.L.R., 485; 29 A.L.T., 23; 13 A.L.R., 352. *Cussen, J.*

Justices Act 1890 (No. 1105), sec. 146— Remitting case for re-hearing—Conviction against firm in firm name—Liability of individual members of firm.]—An order to review the conviction of a firm under the firm name for an offence under sec. 42 of the *Factories and Shops Act* 1905 was made absolute by the Supreme Court. *Held, per Griffith, C.J., Barton* and *Isaacs, JJ.,* that the case should have been remitted to the Justices to convict the persons proved to be members of the firm. *Bishop* v. *Chung Brothers,* 4 C.L.R., 1262; 13 A.L.R., 412 (1907).

(5) Costs.

Costs—Taxation—Appeal from Court of Petty Sessions to High Court—Order to review —Limitation of amount of costs—Justices Act 1890 (No. 1105), sec. 148—Rules of the High Court 1903, Part L, Order XLVI., r. 14; Part II., Sec. IV., r. 1; Rules of the High Court of 12th October 1903, r. 3.]—Order XLVI., r. 14 of Part I., of the *Rules of the High Court* 1903 which prescribes the scale for taxation of costs, does not refer to any maximum amount of costs to be allowed, and, therefore, the provision in sec. 148 of the *Justices Act* 1890, which limits the total amount of costs that can be allowed in the Supreme Court upon an order to review a decision of a Court of Petty Sessions to £20, does not apply to the costs of an appeal by way of order to review from a Court of Petty Sessions exercising Federal jurisdiction to the High Court. *Lyons* v. *Smart,* (1908) 6 C.L.R., 285; 14 A.L.R., 619. H.C., *Griffith, C.J., Barton, O'Connor, Isaacs* and *Higgins, JJ.*

(b) *Mandamus and Certiorari.*

Police Offences Act 1890 (No. 1126), sec. 40 (1)—Idle and disorderly person—No visible lawful means of support—Inquiry into means of support—Nature of act, whether administrative or judicial.]—The act of inquiry into means of support under sec. 40 (1) of the *Police Offences Act* 1890 is of an administrative or extra-judicial character, and is not a judicial act whose performance can be compelled by *mandamus* or controlled by *certiorari. Wilson* v. *Travers,* (1906) V.L.R., 734; 28 A.L.T., 56; 12 A.L.R., 413. F.C., *a' Beckett, A.-C.J., Cussen* and *Chomley, JJ.*

Certiorari—13 Geo. II., c. 18—Whether Act in force as regards Justices.]—So far as relates to Justices, the Act 13 Geo. II., c. 18, is in force in Victoria. *Ex parte Dunn*; *Ex parte Aspinall,* (1906) V.L.R., 584; 28 A.L.T., 72; 12 A.L.R., 418. *Cussen, J.*

(c) *Under the Service and Execution of Process Act.*

Service and Execution of Process Act 1901 (No. 11 of 1901), sec. 18—Exercise of discretion by Justices—Review by Supreme Court.] —A Judge of the Supreme Court has jurisdiction under sec. 18 (4) of the *Service and Execution of Process Act* 1901 to discharge the accused person absolutely, although a Justice of the Peace has previously finally dealt with the matter and has made an order under sec. 18 (3). *In re George*, (1909) V.L.R., 15; 30 A.L.T., 141; 15 A.L.R., 27. *a'Beckett, J.*

Service and Execution of Process Act 1901 (No. 11), sec. 18 (4)—Application to Judge— Jurisdiction—Whether original or appellate.] —*See* SERVICE AND EXECUTION OF PROCESS ACT. *O'Donnell* v. *Heslop*; *The King* v. *Cresswell, Ex parte Heslop*, (1910) V.L.R., 162; 31 A.L.T., 173; 16 A.L.R, 168.

Service and Execution of Process Act 1901 (No. 11), sec. 18 (4)—Practice—Application to Judge for discharge of prisoner, how made.] *See* SERVICE AND EXECUTION OF PROCESS ACT *O'Donnell* v. *Heslop*; *The King* v. *Cresswell, Ex parte Heslop*, (1910) V.L.R., 162; 31 A.L.T., 173; 16 A.L.R., 168.

Service and Execution of Process Act 1901 (No. 11), sec. 18 (4)—Warrant—Execution— Application for discharge of person apprehended—Procedure—Form of order.]—*See* FUGITIVE OFFENDERS ACT, col. 601. *In re George*, (1908) V.L.R., 734; 30 A.L.T., 113; 14 A.L.R., 699.

Service and Execution of Process Act 1901 (No. 11), sec. 18—Person charged with offence in another State—Execution of warrant in Victoria — Power to discharge accused — Whether it may be exercised after his admission to bail to appear and answer the charge.] *See* SERVICE AND EXECUTION OF PROCESS ACT. *O'Donnell* v. *Heslop*; *The King* v. *Cresswell, Ex parte Heslop*, (1910) V.L.R., 162; 31 A.L.T., 173; 16 A.L.R., 168.

Service and Execution of Process Act 1901 (No. 11 of 1901), sec. 18—Execution of warrant issued in another State—Order of Justice of Peace directing return of accused—Review of order by Judge—Costs, jurisdiction to award.]—*See* COSTS, cols. 250, 251. *In re George*, (1909) V.L.R., 15; 20 A.L.T., 141; 15 A.L.R., 27.

(d) Appeal to General Sessions.

See GENERAL SESSIONS, col. 618 *et seq.*

LAND.

See also, EASEMENTS, LAND ACTS, REAL PROPERTY ACT.

Fixture, nature of—Purpose with which chattel attached to freehold—Attachment for better enjoyment of freehold — Evidence, admissibility of.]—*See* LANDLORD AND TENANT. *Love* v. *Bloomfield*, (1906) V.L.R., 723; 28 A.L.T., 52; 12 A.L.R., 383.

Fixtures—Tenant's right to remove, how affected by taking new lease.]—*See* LANDLORD AND TENANT. *Love* v. *Bloomfield*, (1906) V.L.R., 723; 28 A.L.T., 52; 12 A.L.R., 383.

Crown grant—Evidence of land to which it relates—Long and unchallenged occupancy.]— *See* CROWN GRANT, cols. 373, 374. *National Trustees Executors &c. Co. of Australasia Ltd.* v. *Hassett and the Registrar of Titles*, (1907) V.L.R., 404; 28 A.L.T., 232; 13 A.L.R., 208.

Processes of nature—Natural user of land— Injury arising from combined effect of.]— Injury arising from the combined effect of the processes of nature and the natural user of land does not give rise to an actionable wrong. *Glenelg, Shire of* v. *Grills*; *Matheson* v. *Grills*, (1907) V.L.R., 673; 29 A.L.T., 67; 13 A.L.R., 550. F.C., *a'Beckett, Hood* and *Cussen, JJ.*

Water—Natural user of land—Dividing fence and hedge—Bed of creek filled up by processes of nature—Consequent overflow of water of creek—Water deflected by fence and hedge on to land of another.]—*See* WATER. *Glenelg, Shire of* v. *Grills*; *Matheson* v. *Grills*, (1907) V.L.R., 673; 29 A.L.T., 67; 13 A.L.R., 550.

Trespass to land—Entry by person entitled to possession—Trespass committed before entry but after right to enter arose—Reference back of actual entry to time when right arose—Right of action for trespass.]—*See* POSSESSION. *Ebbels* v. *Rewell*, (1908) V.L.R., 261; 29 A.L.T., 252; 14 A.L.R., 121.

Trespass to land—Possession—Two persons on land each asserting land to be his— Right of person with title.]—*See* POSSESSION. *Ebbels* v. *Rewell*, (1908) V.L.R., 261; 29 A.L.T., 252; 14 A.L.R., 121.

LAND ACTS.

Settlement of Lands Act 1893 (No. 1311), secs. 5, 10—Lease by Board of Land and Works —Relief against forfeiture for non-payment of rent—Crown, relief against—Supreme Court Act 1890 (No. 1142), sec. 202.]—With regard to relief from forfeiture for non-payment of rent, the Crown and its tenants stand to one another in the same position as do ordinary landlords and tenants. Therefore, a lessee from the Board of Land and Works under the *Settlement of Lands Act* 1893, who has made default in payment of his rent, but has tendered the full amount due, is entitled to relief against forfeiture. *Kickham* v. *The Queen*, 8 V.L.R. (E.), 1, 6 ; 3 A.L.T., 86, followed. *The King* v. *Dale*, (1906) V.L.R., 662 ; 28 A.L.T., 140 ; 12 A.L.R. 549. *a' Beckett, J.*

Local Government Act 1903 (No. 1893), sec. 265—Land Act 1901 (No. 1749), sec. 160 —Rates—Occupier, who is—Crown land, unauthorised residence upon for a considerable period—Unauthorised occupation of Crown land an offence.]—*See* Local Government. *Poowong, Shire of* v. *Gillen*, (1907) V.L.R., 37 ; 28 A.L.T., 123 ; 12 A.L.R., 522.

Licence to cut race—Land alienated from the Crown in fee simple on or after 29th December 1884, what is—Lease acquired from Crown before 1884—Crown grant issued after 1884—Mines Act 1890 (No. 1120), sec. 64— Mines Act 1897 (No. 1514), sec. 44—Land Act 1869 (No. 360), secs. 19, 20.]—*See* Mining. *Hegarty* v. *Ellis*, (1908) 6 C.L.R., 264 ; 14 A.L.R , 445.

Vendor and purchaser—Sale of land—Grazing area leases—Condition as to conversion into agricultural and grazing allotment leases —Production of title within specified time— Vendors' readiness to produce, whether a compliance with provision for production— Duty of purchaser—Areas reduced in agricultural and grazing allotment leases—Right of rescission—Land Act 1901 (No. 1749).]—*See* Vendor and Purchaser. *In re Hoban and Cox's Contract*, (1911) V.L.R., 49 ; 32 A.L.T., 97 ; 16 A.L.R., 576. Affirmed by High Court, 12 C.L.R., 256 ; 17 A.L.R., 195.

LANDLORD AND TENANT.

I.—Creation of Tenancy ; Covenants ; Evidence.

Landlord and tenant—Evidence of tenancy —Promise to pay rent and request for time to pay.]—A. had been in possession of land as a monthly tenant, but there was no evidence as to who was then the owner. Subsequently B. became the owner, and A. continued in possession, and, on rent being demanded from her, promised B. to pay it and asked for time. *Held*, that there was evidence of a tenancy between A. and B. *Bayne* v. *Love*, (1909) 7 C.L.R., 748. H.C., *Griffith, C.J., Barton, O'Connor* and *Isaacs, JJ.*

Landlord and tenant—Agreement void for uncertainty—Weekly tenancy with additional provision attempting to create a tenancy for uncertain period—Occupation and payment of rent by tenant, effect of—Tenancy from year to year.]—A tenancy agreement provided that the tenant, who was a State School teacher stationed at H., should take the premises " at the weekly rent of ten shillings payable weekly, such tenancy to commence on . . . and not cease (except as hereinafter provided) until one week's notice in writing shall have been given . . . and such tenancy is to continue during the time the said tenant is stationed at H." The tenant occupied the premises for several years during which the rent was paid, but not always regularly or in weekly sums. The tenant being still stationed at H. a weeks' notice to quit was given. *Held*, that, as portion of the agreement as to the duration of the tenancy was void for uncertainty, the whole agreement was inoperative, but that on the facts a tenancy from year to year should be implied. *Morison* v. *Edmiston*, (1907) V.L.R., 191; 28 A.L.T., 148; 12 A.L.R., 613. *Chomley, J.*

Instruments Act 1890 (No. 1103), sec. 208 —Parol lease for less than three years—Lessee in possession of premises under existing tenancy—Surrender by operation of law.]— An agreement to lease for less than three years premises of which the lessee is already in possession under an existing tenancy may be proved by parol, and is not affected by the *Statute of Frauds*. The existing tenancy is surrendered by operation of law and the possession of the lessee is referable to the new tenancy. *Knott* v. *McKendrick*, 28 A.L.T. (Supplement), 4; 12 A.L.R. (C.N.), 23. *Judge Box* (1906).

Real Property Act 1890 (No. 1136), secs. 18, 23—Adverse possession—Period of limitation, commencement of—New tenancy at will, what will create—Request for transfer of land.]—*See* LIMITATIONS (STATUTES OF). *Wilson* v. *Equity Trustees Executors &c. Co. Ltd.*, (1911) V.L.R., 481; 33 A.L.T., 89; 17 A.L.R., 523.

Real Property Act 1890 (No. 1136), sec. 23 —Adverse possession—Statutory period, when time begins to run—Tenancy at will—Creation of new tenancy—Permission of owner, acknowledgment by tenant that he holds by.]—*See* LIMITATIONS (STATUTES OF). *Wilson* v. *Equity Trustees Executors &c. Co. Ltd.*, (1911) V.L.R., 481; 33 A.L.T., 89; 17 A.L.R., 523.

Mining on private property—Crown lease to mine—Interpretation—Whether lessee entitled to possession of surface of land.]—A Crown lease to mine on private property contained a grant and demise unto the lessee his executors administrators and assigns of " all those mines of gold and silver in and under that piece of land " which was described and delineated in a plan and also

covenants by the lessee not to use or occupy or permit to be used or occupied the said land " for other than mining purposes or for pasturage or as garden ground for the persons employed in or about the said mine," and not to transfer underlet or part with " the possession of the said land mine and premises " without the consent of the Governor-in-Council. *Held*, that under the lease the lessee's assignee, to whom the lease had been duly transferred, was entitled to possession of the surface of the whole of the land covered by the lease. *Ebbells* v. *Rewell*, (1908) V.L.R., 261; 29 A.L.T., 252; 14 A.L.R., 121. *Hodges, J.* (1908).

Mining on private property—Agreement between applicant for lease and owner—Purchase money or compensation, how to be ascertained—Future payments, nature of— Agreement to pay per centage of value of gold to be won, legality of—Mines Act 1897 (No. 1514), secs. 29, 73-79, 98, 112—Mines Act 1904 (No. 1961), sec. 37.]—*See* MINES AND MINING. *Armstrong* v. *The Duke of Wellington G. M. Co. N. L.*, 3 C.L.R., 1028; 12 A.L.R., 316.

Mining on private property—Agreement as to amount of purchase money or compensation —Obligations running with the land—Transfer of application for mining lease—Whether transferree bound by agreement—Mines Act 1897 (No. 1514), secs. 29, 73-79, 98, 112.]—*See* MINES AND MINING. *Armstrong* v. *Duke of Wellington G. M. Co. N. L.*, 3 C.L.R., 1028; 12 A.L.R., 316.

II.—FIXTURES.

Fixture, nature of—Purpose with which chattel attached to freehold—Attachment for better enjoyment of freehold—Evidence as to purpose, admissibility of.]—In considering the question whether or not a chattel is a fixture the purpose with which it was attached to the freehold must be looked at. It is a fixture if the chattel was attached not for enjoyment of the chattel itself but for the better enjoyment of the freehold. In order to determine such purpose the nature of the chattel itself and the degree and the object of the annexation can alone be looked at, and no regard can be paid to any written or verbal expressions of intention on the part of the tenant. *Love* v. *Bloomfield*, (1906) V.L.R., 723 ; 28 A.L.T., 52 ; 12 A.L.R., 383. *Hood, J.*

Fixtures—Tenant's right to remove, how affected by taking new lease.]—A tenant who takes a new lease loses his right to remove fixtures unless there be some reservation of that right in the new agreement. *Love* v. *Bloomfield*, (1906) V.L.R., 723 ; 28 A.L.T., 52 ; 12 A.L.R., 383. *Hood, J.*

III.—DISTRESS FOR RENT.

Landlord and Tenant Act 1890 (No. 1108), secs. 86, 87 and 88—Distress—Privilege from distress—" Lodger "—Protection of lodger's goods—Distress by superior landlord—Immediate tenant residing elsewhere.]—A person may be a " lodger " in the house of another who does not reside there, but resides in another place altogether, provided the owner or tenant has some dominion over the house. *Freeman* v. *Wells*, (1909) V.L.R., 361 ; 31 A.L.T., 13 ; 15 A.L.R., 325. *Madden C.J.* And see *Landlord and Tenant Act 1909 (No. 2211).*]

Landlord and Tenant Act 1890 (No. 1108), secs. 81, 83—Distress for rent—Proceeds of sale—Overplus in hands of landlord's agent—Claim by tenant against landlord—Complaint for money had and received—Jurisdiction of Court of Petty Sessions.]—Where, after payment of charges and rent out of the moneys arising from the sale of a tenant's goods under a distress for rent, there is an overplus remaining, which has not been paid to the tenant as provided by section 81 of the *Landlord and Tenant Act* 1890, he may proceed against the landlord in a Court of Petty Sessions upon a complaint for money had and received. Although such overplus is retained, not by the landlord personally, but by the bailiff or licensed auctioneer employed by him, a claim for money had and received will lie against the landlord. The tenant's remedy is not restricted to that provided by section 83 of the *Landlord and Tenant Act* 1890. *Rhodes* v. *Parrott*, (1912)

V.L.R., 333 ; 34 A.L.T., 90 ; 18 A.L.R., 353. *a' Beckett, J.*

IV.—ASSIGNMENT.

Assignment of lease—Covenant against assignment—Consent of lessor not to be withheld where proposed assignee reputable and solvent—Lessee declared trustee of third party—Assignment to third party.]—In an action in which the Court declared that a lease entered into by the defendant had been obtained by him as trustee for the plaintiff, it appeared that the lease contained a covenant against assigning without the lessor's consent, such consent not to be withheld in the case of a reputable and solvent transferee. *Held*, that though the plaintiff fulfilled these conditions a transfer to him should not be directed in the lessor's absence. *Prebble* v. *Reeves*, (1909) V.L.R., 436 ; 31 A.L.T., 64 ; 15 A.L.R., 408. *a' Beckett, J.*

Lessor and lessee—Breach of covenant by lessee—Subsequent assignment of lease—Liability of assignee.]—Where a lessee failed to observe a covenant that he his executors administrators and permitted assigns would paint the leased premises in the third year of the term, and afterwards assigned. *Held*, that the assignee was not liable in damages to the lessor for the breach. *The Churchwardens of St. Saviour's, Southwark* v. *Smith*, 1 Wm. Bl., 351 and *Grescot* v. *Green*, I Salk. 198, followed. *Renshaw* v. *Maher*, (1907) V.L.R., 520 ; 29 A.L.T., 237 ; 13 A.L.R., 265. *Madden, C.J.*

V.—RELIEF AGAINST FORFEITURE.

Relief against forfeiture for non-payment of rent—Crown, relief against—Settlement of Lands Act 1893 (No. 1311), secs. 5, 10—Lease by Board of Land and Works—Supreme Court Act 1890 (No. 1142), sec. 202.]—With regard to relief from forfeiture for non-payment of rent, the Crown and its tenants stand to one another in the same position as do ordinary landlords and tenants. Therefore, a lessee from the Board of Land and Works under the *Settlement of Lands Act* 1893, who has made default in payment of his rent, but has tendered the full amount due, is entitled to relief against forfeiture. *Kickham v. The Queen*, 8 V.L.R. (E.), 1, 6 ; 3 A.L.T., 86; followed. *The King v. Dale*, (1906) V.L.R., 662 ; 28 A.L.T., 140 ; 12 A.L.R., 549. *a' Beckett, J.*

VI.—DETERMINATION OF TENANCY.

(a) Notice to Quit ; Condition of Re-entry.

Notice to quit—Monthly tenancy—Length of notice.]—One month before one of the monthly periods of a monthly tenancy the landlord gave to the tenant a notice in writing demanding payment of rent then alleged to be due, and, in default of payment, that the tenant should immediately quit, and stating that in the event of the tenant not paying the sum demanded, the tenancy would be determined at the end of the particular monthly period. A. paid no rent. *Held*, that the tenancy was properly determined. *Bayne v. Love*, (1909) 7 C.L.R., 748. H.C. *Griffith, C.J., Barton, O' Connor and Isaacs, JJ.*

Landlord and Tenant Act 1890 (No. 1108), secs. 92, 93—Notice to quit—Second notice, effect of—Offer of new tenancy—Non-acceptance—Whether second notice a waiver of the first.]—A second notice to quit requiring the tenant to vacate at a time later than the expiry of the first notice operates merely as an offer of a new tenancy, and not as a waiver of the first notice in a case where the facts are inconsistent with the acceptance of such new tenancy by the tenant. *Green v. Summers*, 29 A.L.T., 245 ; 14 A.L.R., 218. *Hodges, J.* (1908).

Lease—Power to re-enter and determine tenancy on non-payment of rent—Necessity for demand of rent made upon the land not dispensed with—Termination of tenancy—Whether demand of rent essential.]—A lease gave the lessor power to re-enter and determine the tenancy when rent had been due and unpaid for more than fourteen days but did not provide that no demand of rent should be necessary to the exercise of the power. *Held*, that the tenancy could not be determined under such power unless the common law requirements as to demand of rent on the land had been fulfilled. *Sand-*

hurst and Northern District &c. Agency Co. Ltd. v. Canavan, (1908) V.L.R., 373 ; 30 A.L.T., 1 ; 14 A.L.R., 250. *a' Beckett, J.*

(b) Surrender.

Surrender of tenancy by operation of law—Acceptance of fresh lease.]—For a case in which the acceptance of a fresh lease was held to amount to a surrender by operation of law of an existing tenancy, *see Knott v. McKendrick*, 28 A.L.T. (Supplement), 4 ; 12 A.L.R. (C.N.), 23. *Judge Box* (1906).

Mining on private property—Agreement as to amount of purchase money or compensation—Surrender of lease from Crown and acceptance of new lease—Effect of on rights of owner under the agreement—Mines Act 1897 (No. 1514), secs. 29, 75—Mines Act 1904 (No. 1961), sec. 37.]—See MINES AND MINING. *Armstrong v. Duke of Wellington G. M. Co. N. L.*, 3 C.L.R., 1028 ; 12 A.L.R., 316.

(c) Recovery of Possession.

See also, ante,(a) Notice to Quit ; Condition of Re-entry.

Landlord and Tenant Act 1890 (No. 1108), sec. 92—Eighth Schedule—Notice of intention to apply to justices to recover possession—Signature of notice—Sufficiency of—Application by corporation—Name of corporation signed by agent authorised so to do.]—Where a tenant holds over a tenement owned by a corporation a notice of the latter's intention to apply to recover possession of the property following the form in the Eighth Schedule of the *Landlord and Tenant Act* 1890 may be validly given by the manager authorised so to do signing the name of the corporation and his own name as manager and agent. *Jackson v. Napper*, 35 Ch. D., 162, at p. 172, passage in, cited and approved. *Reg v. Moore; Ex parte Myers*, 10 V.L.R. (L.), 322 ; 6 A.L.T., 151, followed. *Equity Trustees Executors and Agency Co. Ltd. v. Harston*, (1908) V.L.R. 23 ; 29 A.L.T., 131 ; 13 A.L.R., 686. *Cussen, J.*

Landlord and Tenant Act 1890 (No. 1108), sec. 92—Eighth Schedule—Notice of owner's intention to apply to justices to recover posses-

sion—Statement that tenement held over and detained from purchaser—Legal estate still in vendor—Whether equitable owner might himself obtain warrant.]—A notice of the owner's intention to apply to recover possession of property following the form in the Eighth Schedule is not invalidated by alleging that the property is held over and detained from a third person by whom the property has been purchased since the tenancy began. *Quaere*, whether such a purchaser could apart from the original owner obtain a warrant of possession under the Act. *Equity Trustees Exors. and Agency Co. Ltd. v. Harston*, (1908) V.L.R., 23 ; 29 A.L.T., 131 ; 13 A.L.R., 686. *Cussen, J.*

Landlord and Tenant Act 1890 (No. 1108), sec. 92—Eighth Schedule—Ninth Schedule—Notice of intention to apply to justices to recover possession — Complaint — Immaterial matters contained in, effect of.]—A notice in the form in the Eighth Schedule to the *Landlord and Tenant Act* 1890 and a complaint in the form in the Ninth Schedule to the Act signed by the legal owner of the property held over are not invalidated by being signed also by a purchaser of the property who has not yet acquired the legal estate. *Kennedy v. Miller*, 4 W.W. & a'B., (L.), 255, followed. *Equity Trustees Exors. and Agency Co. Ltd. v. Harston*, (1908) V.L.R., 23 ; 29 A.L.T., 131 ; 13 A.L.R., 686. *Cussen, J.*

Landlord and Tenant Act 1890 (No. 1108), secs. 92, 93—Justices Act 1890 (No. 1105), secs. 4, 29—Recovery of possession—Justices —Jurisdiction to issue summons to witness— Notice of intention to apply, service of— " Complaint."]—Upon the service of a notice of intention to apply to justices to recover possession under the *Landlord and Tenant Act* 1890 there is a " complaint " within the meaning of the *Justices Act* 1890 and the justices have jurisdiction to issue a summons to witness. *Lesser v. Knight*, 29 A.L.T., 111 ; 13 A.L.R., 708. *Madden, C.J.* (1907).

VII.—Trespass and Damage to Premises.

Lease—Constructive trust—Exclusion of person beneficially interest—Trespass.]—A.

obtained a lease under such circumstances as to constitute him constructively a trustee of the lease for B. After A. had entered into possession of the premises under the lease he excluded B. therefrom. *Held*, that B. had no action for trespass against A. *Prebble v. Reeves*, (1910) V.L.R., 88 ; 31 A.L.T., 114 ; 15 A.L.R., 631. *Madden, C.J., Hood* and *Cussen, JJ.*

Crown lease to mine on private property— Slums lying on land—Whether owner of freehold can confer right to possession for purpose of working slums for gold.]—During the currency of a Crown lease to mine on private property the owner of the freehold agreed to allow a person other than the lessee to extract gold from heaps of slum lying on the surface. *Held*, that, whether the slums remained chattels or not, the owner of the freehold had no right to give such person leave to interfere with the possession of the land for the purpose of winning gold on the surface or anywhere else. *Ebbels v. Rewell*, (1908) V.L.R., 261 ; 29 A.L.T., 252 ; 14 A.L.R., 121. *Hodges, J.* (1908).

Trespass to land—Entry by person entitled to possession—Trespass committed before entry but after right to enter arose—Reference back of actual entry to time when right arose— Right of action for trespass.]—*See* Trespass. *Ebbels v. Rewell*, (1908) V.L.R., 261 ; 29 A.L.T., 252 ; 14 A.L.R., 121.

Trespass to land—Possession—Two persons on land each asserting land to be his—Right of person with title.]—*See* Possession. *Ebbels v. Rewell*, (1908) V.L.R., 261 ; 29 A.L.T., 252 ; 14 A.L.R., 121.

Negligence—Malicious act of third party— Reasonable precautions—Overflow of water from lavatory in upper floor.]—In an action for damages to property located on the second floor of a building leased to the defendant, through a continuous overflow of water from a lavatory basin on the top floor caused by the water tap having been turned on full and the waste pipe plugged, the jury found that " this was the malicious act of some person." *Held*, (1) that the defendant was not responsible unless either he instigated the act or the jury found that he ought reasonably to have prevented it; (2) that his having on his premises a proper and reasonable supply of water was an ordinary and proper use of his house, and that although he was bound to exercise all reasonable care he was not responsible for damage not due to his own default, whether caused by inevitable accident or the wrongful act of third persons. *Rylands* v. *Fletcher*, L.R. 3 H.L., 330, distinguished. *Rickards* v. *Lothian*, (1913) A.C., 263.

VIII.—OTHER POINTS.

Master and servant—Business—Attempted sale of as a going concern—Servant assisting—Lease of premises procured by servant for himself—Fiduciary relation—Whether servant trustee of lease for master—Covenant against assignment—Transfer of lease, whether master entitled to.]—*See* TRUSTS AND TRUSTEES. *Prebble* v. *Reeves*, (1910) V.L.R., 88; 31 A.L.T., 114; 15 A.L.R., 631.

Insolvency Act 1890 (No. 1102), sec. 115—Preferential debts—Municipal rates due at date of sequestration of estate of occupier—Payment by landlord and owner with acquiescence and concurrence of trustee—Repayment in full in priority to all other debts ordered.]—*See* In re *Pater*; *In re Robertson*, 30 A.L.T. (Supplement), 9; 14 A.L.R. (C.N.), 37. *Judge Moule* (1908).

LANDS COMPENSATION ACT.

See WATER.

LAND TAX.

Land Tax Assessment Act 1910 (No. 22 of 1910), sec. 11—Several parcels of land—Number of deductions of £5,000 to be allowed.]—Under sec. 11 (2) (*b*) of the *Land Tax Assessment Act* 1910, a taxpayer who owns several parcels of land is not entitled to a deduction of £5,000 from the value of each parcel, but to one deduction of £5,000 from the sum of the values of the several parcels. *Bailey* v. *Federal Commissioner of Land Tax*, (1911) 13 C.L.R., 302. H.C., *Griffith*, *C.J.*, *Barton* and *O'Connor*, *JJ.*

Land Tax Assessment Act 1910 (No. 22 of 1910), secs. 11, 33, 35, 38, 43—Deductions—Owner of several parcels of land—One of several joint owners—Secondary taxpayer—Deductions to prevent double taxation.]—Where one of several joint owners is also the owner in severalty of other land, the amount described in sec. 38 as "the tax payable in respect of his interests in the land," and from which that section directs an amount to be deducted to prevent double taxation, which amount is to be ascertained in the mode prescribed by sec. 43, is the whole amount payable by him as a secondary taxpayer in respect of that land, and not a part of that amount proportional to the value of his joint interest as compared with the value of the land owner by him in severalty. *Bailey* v. *Federal Commissioner of Land Tax*, (1911) 13 C.L.R., 302. H.C., *Griffith*, *C.J.*, *Barton* and *O'Connor*, *JJ.*

Vendor and purchaser—Contract of sale—Provision for apportionment of Federal land tax—Validity—Interpretation—Land Tax Assessment Act 1910 (No. 22 of 1910), secs. 37, 63.]—*See* VENDOR AND PURCHASER. *Patterson* v. *Farrell*, (1912) 14 C.L.R., 348; 18 A.L.R., 237.

Income tax—Assessment—Deduction—Outgoings incurred in production of income—Disbursements or expenses wholly and exclusively laid out or expended for purposes of trade—Commonwealth land tax—Income Tax Act 1895 (No. 1374), sec. 9.]—*See* INCOME TAX ACTS. *Moffatt* v. *Webb*, (1913) 16 C.L.R., 120; 19 A.L.R., 190.

LARCENY.

See CRIMINAL LAW.

LEGACY.

See WILL.

LEGAL PRACTITIONERS RECIPROCITY ACT.

See SOLICITOR.

Legal Practitioners Reciprocity Act 1903 (No. 1887), sec. 2—Rules for the Admission of Barristers and Solicitors, 16th February, 1905, r. 11—Rules of the Supreme Court of New South Wales, 19th December, 1904, r. 484—Admission of New South Wales practitioner still practising in New South Wales.]—*See* SOLICITOR. *In re Tietyens*, (1906) V.L.R. 354 ; 27 A.L.T., 206 ; 12 A.L.R. (C.N.), 9.

LEGITIMACY.

Evidence—Legitimacy, presumption as to—Father and mother living together as man and wife—European woman and Chinese man.]—*See* EVIDENCE, col. 481. *Potter* v. *Minahan*, (1908) 7 C.L.R., 277 ; 14 A.L.R., 635.

LESSOR AND LESSEE.

See LANDLORD AND TENANT.

LIBEL.

See DEFAMATION.

LICENCE.

See also, CARRIAGES ACT, BUTCHERS AND ABATTOIRS ACT.

Railways—Damages by sparks—Fire on land between railway fences—Occupation by licensee—Reservation of control by Railways Commissioners — Negligence — Omission to burn off grass.]—*See* RAILWAYS. *Victorian Railways Commissioners* v. *Campbell*, 4 C.L.R., 1446 ; 13 A.L.R., 403.

Melbourne Harbor Trust Act 1890 (No. 1119), sec. 142 (xix.)—Carter plying for hire without licence from Harbour Trust Commissioners—Regulation in prohibition thereof, how far valid—Licence from City of Melbourne.]—*See* MELBOURNE HARBOUR TRUST. *Vincent* v. *Curran*, (1909) V.L.R., 370 ; 31 A.L.T., 24 ; 15 A.L.R., 359.

LICENSING.

I. LICENCES.

(a) *Who may be Licensee.*

Licensing—British subject—Licensing Act 1890 (No. 1111), sec. 177—Aliens Act 1890 (No. 1063), sec. 6—Naturalization Act 1903 (No. 11 of 1903), secs. 9, 10.]—An alien woman married to a natural-born or naturalised subject of His Majesty is capable of holding a licence under sec. 177 of the *Licensing Act* 1890. *In re Hall,* 18 A.L.R. (C.N.), 20. *Judge Moule* (1912).

Licensing Act 1906 (No. 2068), sec. 53—Prohibition against licence being granted or held by woman under 25 years of age—Whether applicable to existing licences.]—*Per Hood, J.* (*Cussen, J.,* doubting).—Sec. 53 of the *Licensing Act* 1906 does not affect licences existing at the date of the Act, but merely prohibits the future grant of any licence to a woman, unless she is 25 years of age. *Graham* v. *Lucas,* (1907) V.L.R., 478 ; 29 A.L.T., 10 ; 13 A.L.R., 262.

(b) Grant ; Renewal ; Transfer.

Licensed victuallers—Permit to sell liquors after hours—Licensed premises in the neighbourhood and place from which railway trains depart—Licensing Act 1890 (No. 1111), sec. 7.]—The holder of a victualler's licence for the premises known as the Vienna Cafe, situated in Collins Street, Melbourne, within nine minutes walking distance of the Flinders Street Railway Station, applied for a special permit under sec. 7 of the *Licensing Act* 1890 to sell liquor after 11.30 at night. There were many other licensed premises nearer to the Station than the Vienna Cafe, but none of them had such a permit. *Held,* that the Licensing Court might, properly find, that the Vienna Cafe was in the neighbourhood of the Flinders Street Railway Station, within the meaning of the section. *Lucas* v. *Mooney,* (1909) 9 C.L.R., 231 ; 15 A.L.R., 490. *Griffith, C.J., O'Connor* and *Higgins, JJ.*

Licensed premises—Permit to sell liquor after hours—Licensed premises in the neighbourhood of places at which railway trains arrive or from which they depart—Licensing Act 1890 (No. 1111), sec. 7.]—The meaning of " in the neighbourhood " is " conveniently available for use by persons desiring to go to a railway station." *Lucas* v. *Mooney,* (1909) 9 C.L.R., 230 ; 15 A.L.R., 490. H.C., *Griffith, C.J., O'Connor* and *Higgins, JJ.*

Licensed victuallers—Permit to sell liquor after hours—Permit necessary for public convenience—" Public," class of — Theatregoers having supper with liquor until past 11.30 p.m.—Licensing Act 1890 (No. 1111), sec. 7.]—The licensed premises in respect of which a special permit was sought under sec. 7 of the *Licensing Act* 1890 were used by theatre-goers who were in the habit of supping there till after 11.30 p.m., and afterwards returning to their homes by trains which left the railway station up to midnight These persons desired liquor with their suppers. *Held,* that upon these facts the Licensing Court might determine that a special permit to sell liquor in the premises in question after 11.30 p.m. was necessary for the public convenience. *Lucas* v. *Mooney,* (1909) 9 C.L.R., 231 ; 15 A.L.R., 490. H.C., *Griffith, C.J., O'Connor* and *Higgins, JJ.*

Grocer's licence—Grant of new licence—Local option poll, whether necessary—Licensing Act 1890 (No. 1111), sec. 38—Licensing Act 1906 (No. 2068), sec. 51.]—Inasmuch as sec. 38 of the *Licensing Act* 1890 is repealed by sec. 51 of the *Licensing Act* 1906, there is, since the coming into operation of the latter Act, no necessity to take a local option poll before granting a new grocer's licence in any licensing district. *Mooney* v. *Anderson,* (1907) V.L.R., 623 ; 29 A.L.T., 42 ; 13 A.L.R., 471. F.C., *Madden, C.J., Hodges* and *Hood, JJ.*

Licensing Act 1890 (No. 1111), secs. 92, 93—Application for licence—Petition by objecting ratepayers—Determination as to " the neighbourhood "—Vagueness.]—In dealing with a petition from ratepayers objecting to the granting of an application for an Australian wine licence for premises situated at Werribee, the Licensing Court made a determination under sec. 93 of the *Licensing Act* 1890 " that the neighbourhood for the purposes of the application of this licence was the township of Werribee and the surrounding districts for such reasonable distances as the inhabitants thereof regularly visited Werribee for business or any other reason." *Held,* that this determination was too vague.

Taylor v. *Sinn*, (1910) V.L.R., 125 ; 31 A.L.T. 161 ; 16 A.L.R., 127. *Hood, J.*

Employment by licensee of another person to manage his business—Whether contrary to Licensing Acts.]—There is nothing in the Licensing Acts which makes it improper for a licensee to employ another person to manage his business. *Ex parte Mellington*, 32 A.L.T., 6 ; 16 A.L.R., 247. *Hodges, J.* (1910)

Wine and Spirit Merchant's Licence—Power of Treasurer—Refusal to grant—Mandamus—Customs and Excise Duties Act 1890 (No. 1032), ss. 155, 156.]—*See, post,* IV.—MANDAMUS ; PROHIBITION ; SPECIAL CASE. *The King* v. *Watt* ; *Ex parte Slade*, (1912) V.L.R., 225 ; 33 A.L.T., 222 ; 18 A.L.R., 159.

(c) Licensing Court, Jurisdiction and Practice.

Licensing Act 1890 (No. 1111), sec. 85—Licensing Act 1906 (No. 2068), secs. 65, 66—Annual Sittings of Licensing Court—Extension thereof by Order-in-Council—Application for grocer's licence—Adjournment to day beyond extended sittings—Adjournment to procure attendance of the necessary number of Magistrates—Applicant not at fault—Jurisdiction.]—The ordinary term for the sittings of a Licensing Court was the month of December, 1906, but by Order-in-Council the time for holding the Court was extended to February 28th, 1907. On February 25th, 1907, an application for a grocer's licence was properly made to the Magistrate then sitting. The application was opposed and the Court adjourned the hearing till March 13th, in order to obtain the full Bench of Magistrates necessary to hear an opposed application, and at the adjourned hearing the application was granted. *Held*, that under the provisions of the Licensing Acts and also upon general principles the adjournment was lawful and that the Court had jurisdiction to deal with the application at the adjourned hearing. *R.* v. *Justices of the County of London and the London County Council*, (1893) 2 Q.B., 476, followed. *Mooney* v. *Anderson*, (1907) V.L.R., 623 ; 29 A.L.T., 42 ; 13 A.L.R., 471. F.C., *Madden, C.J., Hodges* and *Hood, JJ.*

Licensing Act 1890 (No. 1111), secs. 58, 62, 85—Appeal to Supreme Court against determination of Licensing Court—Matter remitted for re-hearing—Time for holding annual sitting of Licensing Court expired.]—*Semble.*—Notwithstanding that the time for holding the annual sitting of the Licensing Court has expired, that Court can re-hear an application for a licence which, upon the hearing of a case stated, has been remitted by the Supreme Court for re-hearing by the Licensing Court. *Taylor* v. *Sinn*, (1910) V.L.R., 125 ; 31 A.L.T., 161 ; 16 A.L.R., 127. *Hood, J.*

Licensed Premises Act 1894 (No. 1364), sec. 2—Licensing Act 1890 (No. 1111), sec. 115—Application by owner for renewal of licence—When it may be made—Lapse of six months since death of licensee.]—The mere fact that a period of six months has elapsed since the death of the previous licensee is no answer to an application by the owner of the licensed premises for a renewal of the licence under sec. 2 (2) of the *Licensed Premises Act* 1894 *Ex parte Hunter Brothers*, (1911) V.L.R., 138 ; 32 A.L.T., 143 ; 17 A.L.R., 92. *Hodges J.*

Licensed victualler—Permit to sell liquor after hours—Evidence of effect of previous permits on good order of district—Admissibility of—Licensing Act 1890 (No. 1111), sec. 7.]—Upon an application for a special permit with regard to certain premises under sec. 7 of the *Licensing Act* 1890, evidence as to the effect upon the good order of the city and the drinking habits of the public which followed from prior grants of special permits under such section in respect of other premises, is not admissible. *Mooney* v. *Lucas*, (1909) V.L.R., 333 ; 15 A.L.R., 296 ; *sub nom., In re Lucas* ; *Ex parte Mooney*, 31 A.L.T., 3. F.C., *a' Beckett, Hodges* and *Hood, JJ.*

Licensing Act 1890 (No. 1111), secs. 92, 93—Application for licence—Petition by objecting ratepayers—Determination as to what is to be deemed " the neighbourhood "—Pronouncement in open Court.]—Where a petition from ratepayers objecting to the granting of an application for a licence is before the

Licensing Court, the determination of such Court under sec. 93 of the *Licensing Act* 1890 as to what is to be deemed " the neighbourhood " of the house proposed to be licensed must be pronounced in open Court. *Taylor v. Sinn*, (1910) V.L.R., 125 ; 31 A.L.T., 161 ; 16 A.L.R., 127. *Hood, J.*

Licensing Act 1906 (No. 2068), sec. 68—Application for licence—Report of Inspector upon applicant's character and suitability—Right of applicant to see and answer report—Audi alteram partem.]—*Semble.*—Where the Inspector of Licensing Districts makes a report to the Licensing Court under sec. 68 of the *Licensing Act* 1906 as to the character and suitability of an applicant for a victualler's licence or Australian wine licence or for a transfer thereof to himself, and as to the genuineness and value of the testimonials furnished by the applicant, the Court should give the applicant an opportunity of seeing and answering such report if it seriously affects his character. *Ex parte Mellington,* 32 A.L.T., 6 ; 16 A.L.R., 247. *Hodges, J.* (1910).

Licensing Act 1890 (No. 1111), sec. 55—Licensing Court—Evidence, how to be taken—Evidence not on oath, whether Court may receive.]—A Licensing Court has no authority to determine questions on materials not proved before it on the oath of a witness or by documents which prove themselves. *Ex parte Hunter Brothers,* (1911) V.L.R., 138 ; 32 A.L.T., 143 ; 17 A.L.R., 92. *Hodges, J.*

(d) *Licences Reduction Board.*

(1) Reduction of Number of Licences.

Licences Reduction Board—Determination as to what premises to be de-licensed—Convictions to be considered, nature of—" Permitting or suffering drunkenness on the premises "—Suffering drunken persons to be on licensed premises—Licensing Act 1906 (No. 2068), sec. 44 (a)—Licensing Act 1890 (No. 1111), sec. 121.]—A conviction under sec. 121 of the *Licensing Act* 1890 of a licensee for suffering drunken persons to be upon his licensed premises is a conviction for " permitting or suffering drunkenness on the premises "

within the meaning of sec. 44 (*a*) (V.) of the *Licensing Act* 1906. *The King v. The Licences Reduction Board ; Ex parte Carlton Brewery Ltd.,* (1908) V.L.R., 79 ; 29 A.L.T., 148 ; 14 A.L.R., 7. F.C., *Madden, C.J., a'Beckett* and *Cussen, JJ.* (1907).

Licences Reduction Board—Determination as to what premises to be delicensed—Convictions to be considered, nature of—" Selling or allowing or suffering to be sold any liquor to persons apparently under the age of 18 years "—Selling to person under 16 years of age liquor in unsealed vessel—Licensing Act 1906 (No. 2068), sec. 44 (a) (i.)—Licensing Act 1904 (No. 1929), sec. 6.]—A conviction under sec. 6 of the *Licensing Act* 1904 of a licensee for selling in his licensed premises to a person under the age of 16 years for consumption by some person off the licensed premises, liquor in an unsealed vessel, is not a conviction for " selling or allowing or suffering to be sold any liquor to persons apparently under the age of eighteen years " within the meaning of sec. 44 (*a*) (I.) of the *Licensing Act* 1906. *The King v. The Licences Reduction Board ; Ex parte Carlton Brewery Ltd.,* (1908) V.L.R., 79 ; 29 A.L.T., 148 ; 14 A.L.R., 7. F.C., *Madden, C.J., a'Beckett* and *Cussen, JJ.* (1907).

(2) Compensation.

Licensing Act 1890 (No. 1111), secs. 31-44—Licensed premises part of testator's estate—Compensation for deprivation of licence—Tenant for life and remainderman—Apportionment.]—A testator was the owner of and held a licensed victualler's licence in respect of certain premises. He left all his real and personal estate to his widow with remainder over. The premises were let and the licence transferred to the lessee. Subsequently under the provisions of Part II. of the *Licensing Act* 1890 the number of licences in the Licensing District in which such premises were situated, was reduced, and the premises were deprived of their licence and the compensation due to the owner and occupier was assessed under sec. 44. *Held,* that the compensation due to the owner formed part of the corpus of the estate. *McKee v. Bal-*

larat *Trustees, Executors, &c., Co. Ltd.,* (1910) V.L.R., 358; 32 A.L.T., 22; 16 A.L.R., 323. *Cussen, J.*

Licensing Act 1906 (No. 2068), secs. 42 (1), 45 (1)—Licences Reduction Board—Forfeited licence — Third offence — Owner's agent authorized to carry on business—Renewal of licence—Deprivation of licence by Licences Reduction Board—Compensation—Meaning of licence " forfeited "—Licensing Act 1885 (No. 857), sec. 54—Licensing Act 1890 (No. 1111), secs. 3, 5, 7, 44, 74, 101, 134, 154, 170, 181.]— The forfeiture of a licence referred to in sec. 42 (1) of the *Licensing Act* 1906 means that class of forfeiture which has the effect of completely extinguishing the licence as distinguished from a forfeiture subsequently to which a renewal of the old licence may be granted. M. was in August, 1907, the licensee of a hotel and was then convicted of a third offence under sec. 134 of the *Licensing Act* 1890. She consequently forfeited her licence. An agent of the owners of the hotel was subsequently authorized to carry on the business on the premises, and in the following December a renewal of the licence for those premises was granted to him. The Licences Reduction Board, having determined that the premises should be deprived of their licence, also determined that, the hotel being premises the licence of which had been forfeited by virtue of sec. 42 (1) of the *Licensing Act* 1906, such deprivation was not the subject of compensation. *Held,* that though the decision of the Board was correct in determining that premises could be deprived of their licence, though no compensation might be payable in respect of them, they were wrong in determining that the licence of these premises had been forfeited within the meaning of sec. 42 (1); and, *Held,* consequently, that compensation was payable. The decision of the Licences Reduction Board that premises shall be deprived of their licence confers no immunity on the licensee from the obligation attaching to licences in general or from the consequences of their breach. *Per a' Beckett, J.,* compensation assessed for deprivation by the Board would not be payable if the premises were deprived of a licence from some

other cause. *The King* v. *Licences Reduction Board* ; *Ex parte Martin and Godfrey,* (1908) V.L.R., 721 ; 30 A.L.T., 133 ; 14 A.L.R., 675. F.C., *a' Beckett, Hodges* and *Cussen, JJ.*

(3) Lost Licence and Compensation Fees.

Licences Act 1906 (No. 2068), secs. 110, 112 Reduction of licences—Apportionment of Lost Licence and compensation fees between incoming and outgoing licensees—Determination by Licences Reduction Board.]—In apportioning the compensation fees under sec. 110 and lost licence fees under sec. 112 of the *Licensing Act* 1906, the former will be treated on the basis of being payable in advance, the latter as not so payable. *In re Lost Licence and Compensation Fees,* 33 A.L.T. (Supplement), 12 ; 18 A.L.R. (C.N.), 1.

(4) Practice.

Licences Reduction Board—Procedure on deprivation of victualler's licences—Right of owners and occupiers of licensed premises, if interested, to be heard—Licensing Act 1890 (No. 1111), sec. 32—Licensing Act 1906 (No. 2068)—Licensing Act 1907 (No. 2103), sec. 7.] —Where an owner or occupier of licensed premises is summoned to show cause why such premises should not be deprived of a licence, the Licences Reduction Board should hear the owners and occupiers of other premises, if their interests are in direct antagonism to those of the person whose case the Board is considering. *The King* v. *The Licences Reduction Board* ; *Ex parte Miller,* (1909) V.L.R., 327 ; 30 A.L.T., 223 ; 15 A.L.R., 282. F.C., *a' Beckett, Hodges* and *Hood, JJ.*

Licences Reduction Board—Determination to de-licence premises—Procedure—Convenience of public and requirements of locality— Whether relative merits of all licensed premises must be considered—Licensing Act 1906 (No. 2068), secs. 44, 50—Licensing Act 1890 (No. 1111), secs. 32, 33, 34, 66.]—The Licences Reduction Board may make a determination to close licensed premises in a licensing district to which paragraphs (a) and (b) of sec. 44 apply, without hearing summonses with respect to all the other licensed premises in the district, so long as the Board in coming to a determination has considered the convenience of the public and the requirements of the several localities in the district. *The King* v. *The Licences Reduction Board* ; *Ex parte Carlton Brewery Ltd.*, (1908) V.L.R., 79 ; 29 A.L.T., 148 ; 14 A.L.R., 7. F.C., *Madden, C.J., a' Beckett* and *Cussen, JJ.* (1907).

Licensing Act 1906 (No. 2068), sec. 45—Licences Reduction Board — Jurisdiction—Fixing maximum valuation of licensed premises in district—Whether condition precedent to determining which premises shall be delicensed.]—Under the *Licensing Act* 1906 the Licences Reduction Board, before proceeding to determine which licensed premises should be deprived of their licences, need not fix the maximum valuation of all licensed premises in the licensing district. *The King* v. *The Licences Reduction Board* ; *Ex parte Carlton Brewery Ltd.*, (1908) V.L.R., 79 ; 29 A.L.T., 148 ; 14 A.L.R., 7. F.C., *Madden, C.J., a' Beckett* and *Cussen, JJ.*

Licences Reduction Board—Power of Board to review its own decision considered.]—*See Yan Yean Hotel*, 16 A.L.R. (C.N.), 11.

II.—Prohibition Orders.

Adjournment—Application by defendant for —No opportunity for preparing defence—Duty of Justices—Prohibition order—Licensing Act 1890 (No. 1111), sec. 125.]—*See* Justices of the Peace. *Strange* v. *Strange*, (1908) V.L.R., 187 ; 29 A.L.T., 177 ; 14 A.L.R., 42.

Evidence—Information in possession of Magistrates but not in evidence before them—Whether Magistrates may act upon—Prohibition order—Licensing Act (No. 1111), sec. 125.]—*See* Justices of the Peace. *Strange* v. *Strange*, (1908) V.L.R., 187 ; 29 A.L.T., 177 ; 14 A.L.R., 42.

III.—Offences.

(a) Selling Liquor without a Licence.

Licensing Act 1890 (No. 1111), secs. 3, 4, 182—Selling liquor without a licence—" Liquor," meaning of.]—" Liquor " within the meaning of sec. 182 of the *Licensing Act* 1890 means a liquid which is commonly known and is adapted for use as a drink or beverage for human consumption, or which is reasonably capable of being used as a substitute for such a beverage, or of being converted into such a beverage, and does not include every liquid which on analysis may be found to contain any appreciable quantity of alcohol. *Gleeson* v. *Hobson*, (1907) V.L.R., 148 ; 28 A.L.T., 151 ; 13 A.L.R., 10. *Cussen, J.*

Licensing Act 1890 (No. 1111), sec. 182—Selling liquor without a licence—Ignorance of the nature of the liquid, whether a defence—Mens rea.]—*Quaere*, whether in a prosecution under sec. 182 of the *Licensing Act* 1890 the ignorance of the seller of the fact that the liquid sold was " liquor " within the meaning of the Act, is a defence. *Gleeson* v. *Hobson*, (1907) V.L.R., 148 ; 28 A.L.T., 151 ; 13 A.L.R., 10. *Cussen, J.*

Licensing Act 1890 (No. 1111), sec. 182—" Liquor," what is—What facts to be considered.]—In deciding the question of fact whether a liquid is " liquor " within the meaning of sec. 182 of the *Licensing Act* 1890, it is material to consider the uses to which the compound is usually put, the purposes for which it is usually bought, and its usual effect upon the system. *Gleeson* v. *Hobson*, (1907) V.L.R., 148 ; 28 A.L.T., 151 ; 13 A.L.R., 10. *Cussen, J.*

Licensing Act (No. 1111), sec. 182—Selling liquor without a licence—Proprietary medicine, whether liquor—Presence of alcohol, effect of.]—Whether or not a proprietary medicine is " liquor " within the meaning of the *Licensing Act* 1890 is a question of fact. Even should such a liquid contain a large percentage of alcohol, the Court would or might be warranted in finding that it is not " liquor " within the Act, if the alcohol is essential to its use as a medicine, or is necessary for extraction, or as a preservative or vehicle, or if the other ingredients are as compared with the contained alcohol of such potency or of such a disagreeable character that the use of the liquid as a beverage would ordinarily result in danger to life or health, or in nausea and sickness, or if the alcohol is so compounded as to be counteracted by the other ingredients, and loses its distinctive character, so that it would not reasonably be used or separated for use as a beverage. *Gleeson* v. *Hobson*, (1907) V.L.R., 148 ; 28 A.L.T., 151 ; 13 A.L.R., 10. *Cussen, J.*

Licensing—Restaurant—Sale by unlicensed persons—Liquor supplied to customer at meal —Order and money for liquor received and liquor brought by waitress—Licensing Act 1890 (No. 1111), sec. 182.]—A waitress in a restaurant or unlicensed premises who gets an order from a customer for liquor, receives the payment therefor and being supplied with the liquor brings it to the customer, is not a person selling liquor within the meaning of sec. 182 of the *Licensing Act* 1890. *Ex parte Wylie* ; *Ex parte Butler*, (1882) 4 A.L.T., 41, explained and distinguished. *Mooney* v. *Still*, (1909) V.L.R., 227 ; 30 A.L.T., 191 ; 15 A.L.R., 197. *Hood, J.*

Licensing Act 1890 (No. 1111), sec. 182— Sale of intoxicating liquor without a licence— Waitress at unlicensed restaurant serving customer with liquor.]—A customer in a restaurant in respect to which no licence had been granted asked a waitress for a bottle of champagne with his supper. The waitress asked for the money, and was handed a sovereign. The champagne was then obtained by another servant from licensed premises near by, of which the restaurant proprietor was the licensee. The waitress handed the customer five shillings change, and brought and poured out the champagne. *Held*, that the waitress was not a person selling liquor within the meaning of sec. 182 of the *Licensing Act* 1890 (*No.* 1111). *Mooney* v. *Still*, (1909) V.L.R., 227 ; 30 A.L.T., 191 ; 15 A.L.R., 197, followed. Observations of Lord Alverstone, C.J., in *Pasquier* v. *Neale*, (1902) 2 K..B, 287, distinguished. *Mooney* v. *McKeand*, (1909) V.L.R., 294 ; 30 A.L.T., 225 ; 15 A.L.R., 280. F.C., *a' Beckett, Hodges* and *Hood, JJ.*

(b) Sunday Trading ; Trading During Prohibited Hours.

Licensing Act 1890 (No. 1111), sec. 134— Interpretation—Whether sales, &c., to lodgers excepted.]—Sec. 134 of the *Licensing Act* 1890, which commences " Every licensed person on whose licensed premises any sale or barter of or **traffic** in liquor takes place or on which any liquor is drunk on Sunday except by lodgers, &c.," should be read—" Every licensed person on whose licensed premises any sale or barter of or traffic in liquor takes place except sales, &c., to lodgers, &c., and the words " by lodgers in such house, &c." should be applied to the last part of the clause only. *Cahill* v. *Millett*, (1907) V.L.R., 605 ; 29 A.L.T., 16 ; 13 A.L.R., 375. *Hodges J.*

Licensing Act 1890 (No. 1111), sec. 134— Licensing Act (1906) (No. 2068), sec. 81—Traffic in Liquor on Sunday—Sale, &c., to lodger— Liquor taken outside licensed premises.]—It is not an offence under sec. 134 of the *Licensing Act* 1890 for a licensed person within the meaning of that Act to supply liquor on a Sunday to a lodger who, to the knowledge of the licensee, intends to take it and drink it outside the licensed premises, and who does in fact take it outside such premises. Sec. 1 of the *Licensing Act* 1906 does not refer back to sec. 134 of the *Licensing Act* 1890. *Biggs* v. *Powell*, (1908) V.L.R., 404 ; 30 A.L.T., 2 ; 14 A.L.R., 311. *Hood, J.*

Licensing Act 1890 (No. 1111), secs. 5, 10, 11, 128—Factories and Shops Act 1890 (No. 1091), secs, 3, 46—Sale of liquor during prohibited hours—Grocer's licence — Licensee selling liquor only—" Shop "—Sale after hours—Holders of victuallers' licences, whether affected by law relating to closing of shops.]—The premises on which the holder of a grocer's licence sells nothing but liquor are a " shop " within the meaning of sec. 46 of the *Factories and Shops Act* 1890, and of sec. 11 of the *Licensing Act* 1890 ; and the sale of liquor there, after the hour at which shops are by sec. 46 of the *Factories and Shops Act* 1890 required to be closed, is a sale otherwise than during the hours authorized by the licence, and an offence under sec. 128 of the *Licensing Act* 1890, notwithstanding that the grocer's licence, pursuant to the Second Schedule of the last-mentioned Act, purported to authorize the sale of liquor at the time the sale was made. *Per Cussen, J.*—Holders of victuallers' licences are not affected by the law relating to the closing of shops. *Mackinnon* v. *Hannay*, (1906) V.L.R., 604; 28 A.L.T., 33; 12 A.L.R., 381. F.C., *Hood, Cussen* and *Chomley, JJ.*

(c) *Bringing on Premises Liquor not Authorised by Licence.*

Licensing Act 1906 (No. 2068), secs. 31, 32 —Licensing Act 1890 (No. 1111), secs. 5, 12 —" Australian " wine licence—" Colonial " wine licence—Rights and obligations of licensee —Liquor purchased for customer — Permitting liquor other than wine, &c., to be brought on premises.]—The effect of sec. 31 (1) of the *Licensing Act* 1906 is to change the name of a Colonial wine licence to an Australian wine licence. Sec. 32 imposes the same restrictions upon the holders of all such licences, whether they were originally granted as Colonial wine licences or as Australian wine licences. *Held,* therefore, that a person who, before the *Licensing Act* 1906 came into force, obtained pursuant to the *Licensing Act* 1890 a renewal of his Colonial wine licence, and who in 1907 permitted stout bought on behalf of a customer to be brought on his licensed premises, was properly convicted of an offence under sec. 32 (1) of the *Licensing Act* 1906, which forbids the bringing of liquor other than Australian wine on premises for which an Australian wine licence is in force. *Lucas* v. *Graham*, (1907) 5 C.L.R., 188. H.C., *Griffith, C.J., Barton, O'Connor, Isaacs* and *Higgins, JJ.*

Licensing Act 1906 (No. 2068), sec. 32 (1) —Australian wine licence—Prohibition against bringing on licensed premises liquor not made from Australian fruit—Whether limited to liquor brought by licensee for purpose of sale.]—Section 32 (1) of the *Licensing Act* 1906 provides that—" The holder of an Australian wine licence shall not keep nor bring

or permit to be brought any liquor other than wine cider or perry the produce of fruit grown in any Australian State on the premises specified in such licence." *Held,* that the prohibition against bringing on the premises liquor other than wine, &c. is not limited to liquor other than wine &c. brought on such premises for the purpose of sale by the licensee or which is the property of the licensee. *Lucas* v. *Graham*, 5 C.L.R., 188. H.C. *Griffith, C.J., Barton, O'Connor, Isaacs* and *Higgins, JJ.* (1907).

Licensing Act 1906 (No. 2068), sec. 32 (1) (2)—Holder of Australian wine licence— Permitting liquor other than wine cider or perry to be brought on licensed premises— Liquor purchased for customer.]—It is a contravention of section 32 (1) of the *Licensing Act* 1906 for the holder of an Australian wine licence to permit to be brought any liquor other than wine, cider or perry, the produce of fruit grown in any Australian State, on the premises specified in such licence, although such liquor has been sent out for and purchased on behalf of certain of his customers whose property such liquor became at the moment of purchase. *Graves* v. *Panam*, (1905) V.L.R., 297; 26 A.L.T., 232; 11 A.L.R., 180, discussed. *Graham* v. *Matoorekos*, (1907) V.L.R , 270; 28 A.L.T., 173; 13 A.L.R., 113. F.C. *Madden, C.J., Hood* and *Cussen, JJ.*

Licensing Act 1906 (No. 2068), sec. 32 (1) —Holder of Australian wine licence—Permitting liquor other than wine, cider or perry to be brought on licensed premises—Penalty for such offence.]—Section 102 of the *Licensing Act* 1906 provides the penalties for a contravention of section 32 (1) of that Act. *Graham* v. *Matoorekos*, (1907) V.L.R., 270; 28 A.L.T., 173; 13 A.L.R., 113. F.C. *Madden, C.J., Hood* and *Cussen, JJ.*

Licensing Act 1906 (No. 2068), sec. 31— Whether Act applies to Colonial wine licences.] —*Quaere (per Madden, C.J.* and *Cussen, J.)* whether the *Licensing Act* 1906 applies to Colonial wine licences. *Graham* v. *Matoorekos* (1907) V.L.R , 270; 28 A.L.T., 173; 13 A.L.R., 113.

(d) Where Persons Found on Premises During Prohibited Hours.

Licensed premises—Presence thereon " in contravention of " provisions of the Act—Purpose of presence—Licensing Act 1906 (No. 2068), sec. 76.]—The words " in contravention of the provisions of this Act " in section 76 (2) of the *Licensing Act* 1906 mean " in prosecution of a purpose inconsistent with observance of the provisions of this Act." Therefore, where a person went into an hotel on a Sunday (when the sale of liquor is prohibited) with the object of obtaining liquor, but was unsuccessful, his presence there was in contravention of the provisions of the Act, and he was properly convicted of having been found on licensed premises at a time when such premises should not be open for the sale of liquor to the public. *Charles* v. *Grierson*, (1908) 7 C.L.R., 18; 14 A.L.R., 615. H.C. *Griffith, C.J., Barton* and *Isaacs, JJ.* (*O'Connor, J.* dissenting).

Licensing Act 1906 (No. 2068), sec. 76 (2) —Licensing Act 1890 (No. 1111), sec. 134— Being found on licensed premises when they should not open for sale of liquor to public— Sunday, whether a time when premises should not be so open.]—Section 76 (2) of the *Licensing Act* 1906 imposes a penalty upon any person found on licensed premises at any time when such premises should not be open for the sale of liquor to the public, unless he satisfies the Court that he was a *bona fide* lodger, boarder, traveller, inmate or servant, or that his presence on the premises was not in contravention of the provisions of the Act. *Held*, that inasmuch as section 134 of the *Licensing Act* 1890 prohibits the sale of liquor on licensed premises on Sunday that day is a time when such premises should not be open for the sale of liquor to the public within the meaning of section 76 (2) of the *Licensing Act* 1906. *McGee* v. *Wolfenden*, (1907) V.L.R., 195; 28 A.L.T., 163: 13 A.L.R., 51, distinguished. *Biggs* v. *Lamley*, (1907) V.L.R., 300; 28 A.L.T., 202; 13 A.L.R., 144. F.C. *Madden, C.J Hodges* and *Hood, JJ.*

Licensing Act 1906 (No. 2068), sec. 91— " Hours during which the sale of liquor to the public is prohibited "—Whether the whole of Sunday included—Persons found on licensed premises within such hours.]—The expression " the hours during which the sale of liquor to the public is prohibited " in section 91 of the *Licensing Act* 1906 does not refer to the whole of Sunday, but is confined to the hours outside those specified in the licence as hours within which liquor may be sold. *M'Gee* v. *Wolfenden*, (1907) V.L.R., 195; 28 A.L.T., 163; 13 A.L.R., 51. *Hood, J.* [Special leave to appeal to the High Court refused, (1907) 4 C.L.R., 946.]

(e) Drunken Persons ; Supplying with Liquor ; Presence on Premises.

Licensing Act 1890 (No. 1111), sec. 124— Licensing Act 1906 (No. 2068), sec. 73— Licensee, liability for act of servant—Supplying liquor to person in state of intoxication— Supply by servant in the absence without knowledge and contrary to instructions of licensee.]—Under section 124 of the *Licensing Act* 1890, which provides that " no licensed person shall . . . in his licensed premises . . . supply any liquor to a person in a state of intoxication," the licensee is guilty of an offence where one of his barmen, acting within the scope of his employment, supplies liquor on the licensed premises to a drunken person, even though the liquor is supplied in the absence of the licensee, without his knowledge, and in disobedience to his express instructions. *Commissioners of Police* v. *Cartman*, (1896) 1 Q.B., 655, followed. *Davies* v. *Young*, (1910) V.L.R., 369; 32 A.L.T., 39; 16 A.L.R., 368. *a'Beckett, J.*

Licensing Act 1890 (No. 1111), sec. 124— Supplying liquor to person in state of intoxixation—Knowledge of intoxicated state of person supplied—Whether a necessary ingredient of offence.]—Knowledge that the person supplied is intoxicated is not a necessary ingredient in the offence of supplying on licensed premises liquor to a person in a state of intoxication. *Cundy* v. *Le Cocq*, 13 Q.B.D., 207, followed. *Davies* v. *Young*, (1910) V.L.R., 369; 32 A.L.T., 39; 16 A.L.R., 368. *a'Beckett, J.* (1910).

Licensing Act 1890 (No. 1111), sec. 121—Drunken Person on licensed premises—Liability of licensee—Reasonable excuse.]—Section 121 of the *Licensing Act* 1890, which makes it an offence for a licensed victualler to suffer or permit a drunken person to be in or upon any part of his licensed premises, does not mean that whenever a drunken man is on such premises, the licensee is bound forthwith under all circumstances to put the man out or get him put out. Where the circumstances are such as to render it necessary for the protection of a man who comes into an hotel drunk to permit him to remain there, and the licensee sends speedily for the police, the licensee does not commit an offence under that section. *Canty* v. *Buttrose*, (1912) V.L.R., 363; 34 A.L.T., 91; 18 A.L.R., 370. *Hodges, J.*

Licensing Act 1890 (No. 1111), sec. 153—"Found drunk on any licensed victualler's premises"—Lodger found drunk on licensed premises closed according to law.]—A lodger at an hotel, who is found drunk on the premises when they are and ought by law to be closed, is not found drunk on a licensed victualler's premises within the meaning of section 153 of the *Licensing Act* 1890. *Lester* v. *Torrens*, 2 Q.B.D., 403, followed. Dictum of *Lord Alverstone* in *Thompson* v. *McKenzie*, (1908) 1 K.B., at p. 908, approved. *McKinnon* v. *Colborne*, (1911) V L R, 486; 33 A L T, 117; 17 A.L.R., 524. *Hood, J.*

(f) Delaying Admittance of Police Officer.

Licensing Act 1890 (No. 1111), sec. 148—Licensing Act 1906 (No. 2068), sec. 93—Demand of entrance into licensed premises by member of police force—Wilfully delaying admittance.]—If a duly qualified member of the police, after demanding entrance and being refused admittance into an hotel, persists in his demand and if admittance continues to be refused to him for such time as to show that wilful delay is intended, it is an offence under section 148 of the *Licensing Act* 1890 (as substituted by section 93 of the *Licensing Act* 1906). *Thomas* v. *Ivey*, 13 A.L.T., 190, distinguished.

Riely v. *Biggs*, 28 A.L.T. (Supplement), 11; 13 A.L.R. (C.N.), 5. *Judge Chomley* (1907).

(g) Publishing Information Relating to Betting.

Licensing Act 1906 (No. 2068), sec. 98—Licensed premises—Posting up of information relating to betting—Past betting on past horse race.]—The posting up on licensed premises of information relating to past betting on a past horse-race is not of itself an offence within section 98 of the *Licensing Act* 1906. *Ryan* v. *Foran*, (1910) V.L.R., 422; 32 A.L.T., 66; 16 A.L.R., 459. *Hood, J.*

(h) Evidence.

Licensing Act 1890 (No. 1111), secs. 134, 135—Licensing Act 1906 (No. 2068), sec. 78 (2)—Unlawful sale of liquor—Prima facie evidence of sale of liquor—Presence of two or more persons on licensed premises—Onus of proof as to lodgers, &c.]—Where in a prosecution for a breach of section 134 of the *Licensing Act* 1890 the informant relies on section 78 (2) of the *Licensing Act* 1906, which makes the presence of two or more persons on licensed premises *prima facie* evidence of a sale of liquor having taken place, the onus is on the informant to prove that the person shown to have been on the licensed premises of the defendant did not come within the excepted classes mentioned in section 78 (2). *Semble*, evidence that such persons resided in the locality of the licensed premises will *prima facie* discharge that onus. *Biggs* v. *Cunningham*, (1907) V.L.R., 344; 29 A.L.T., 14; 13 A.L.R., 244. *Cussen, J.*

Licensing Act 1890 (No. 1111), secs. 134, 135—Licensing Act 1906 (No. 2068), sec. 78 (2)—Unlawful sale of liquor—Evidence—Presence on licensed premises of two or more persons—Onus of proof as to bona fide lodgers, &c.]—Where on an information against a licensed person for selling liquor on a Sunday, the informant does not prove that any individual was supplied with liquor, but relies upon section 78 (2) of the *Licensing Act* 1906, he must prove not only the presence on the licensed premises of two or more persons, but also that such persons were persons other than *bona fide* lodgers weekly or other boarders travellers inmates or servants. The provisions as to burden of proof contained in the first part of section 135 of the *Licensing Act* 1890 applies only where the prosecution proves that some individual was supplied with liquor. *Cahill* v. *Millett*, (1907) V.L.R., 605; 29 A.L.T., 16; 13 A.L.R., 375. *Hodges, J.*

IV.—MANDAMUS; PROHIBITION; SPECIAL CASE.

Wine and spirit merchant's licence—Power of treasurer—Refusal to grant—Mandamus—Customs and Excise Duties Act 1890 (No. 1082), secs. 155, 156.]—The instructions in section 156 of the *Customs and Excise Duties Act* 1890 to the Treasurer to issue a licence to any person who, complies with the provisions of sections 155 and 156, and is not subject to any disqualification therein mentioned, is mandatory, and will be enforced by mandamus. Where the ostensible applicant had no intention of carrying on business on his own behalf and was merely applying as "dummy" for another person, who was subject to a disqualification, and the Treasurer refused to issue a licence the Court refused to issue a mandamus to compel him to do so. *The King* v. *Watt*; *Ex parte Slade*, (1912) V.L.R., 225; 33 A.L.T., 222; 18 A.L.R., 158. F.C. *Madden, C.J., Hodges* and *Cussen, JJ.* [Note section 156 (*supra*) is repealed by the *Spirit Merchants' Licences Act* 1912 (No. 2376).]

Licenses Reduction Board—Prohibition—Class constituted by those premises against which two convictions are recorded—Decision that premises fall within such class—Licensing Act 1906 (No. 2068), sec. 44.]—Prohibition will lie in respect of an erroneous determination by the Licences Reduction Board that licensed premises are within paragraph (*a*) or paragraph (*b*) of section 44 of the *Licensing Act* 1906. *The King* v. *The Licenses Reduction Board*; *Ex parte Carlton Brewery Ltd.*, (1908) V.L.R., 79; 29 A.L.T., 148; 14 A.L.R., 7. F.C. *Madden, C.J., a'Beckett* and *Cussen, JJ.* (1907).

Licences Reduction Board—Procedure on deprivation of victualler's licences—Mistaken refusal to hear owners and occupiers of other licensed premises who are interested—Erroneous belief in absence of jurisdiction to hear them — Prohibition—Costs.]—Notwithstanding the existence of a fund under the control of the Licences Reduction Board out of which the costs of all parties in *The King* v. *Licences Reduction Board*; *Ex parte Martin and Godfrey*, (1908) V.L.R., 721; 30 A.L.T., 133; 14 A.L.R., 675, had been ordered to be paid, where the error of the Board was in holding that they had no power to permit the relator to intervene, the order *nisi* for a writ of prohibition was made absolute without costs. *The King* v. *Licences Reduction Board*; *Ex parte Miller*, (1909) V.L.R., 327; 30 A.L.T., 223; 15 A.L.R., 282. F.C. *Hodges* and *Hood, JJ.* (*a'Beckett, J.*, dissentiente).

Licensing Act 1890 (No. 1111), sec. 58—Special case—Right to begin.]—Upon a Special Case stated by a Licensing Court under section 58 of the *Licensing Act* 1890 the party who began proceedings in the Court below should begin. *In re Crown Hotel*; *Ex parte Waxman*, 28 V.L.R., 710; 24 A.L.T., 234; 9 A.L.R., 108, not followed. *Mooney* v. *Lucas*, (1909) V.L.R., 333; 15 A.L.R., 296. *Sub nomine, In re Lucas*; *Ex parte Mooney*, 31 A.L.T., 3. F.C. *Hodges* and *Hood, JJ.* (*a'Beckett, J.*, dissentiente).

LIEN.

See COSTS.

LIFE ASSURANCE.

See INSURANCE.

LIFE TENANT.

See TENANT FOR LIFE AND REMAINDERMAN; TRUSTS AND TRUSTEES; WILL.

LIMITATIONS (STATUTES OF).

I.—Simple Contract Debts; Calls upon Shares.

Statute of Limitations—Simple Contract debt—Acknowledgment—Letter from debtor's solicitors expressing debtor's inability to pay—Promise as to payment by debtor's wife.]— On an application for judgment in an action for the recovery of a simple contract debt, which the defendant opposed on the ground that the debt was barred by the *Statute of Limitations*, the plaintiff relied upon two letters, which, according to him, were written by the defendant's solicitors. In the first letter, after stating that the defendant had no means whatever, the writers expressed their opinion that, if the plaintiff delayed the matter for a few weeks, they might be able to persuade the defendant's wife to pay the plaintiff's account, and in the second, after explaining why the defendant's wife had been unable to settle the account as promised, they stated that if the plaintiff would wait for a certain further time, within which the wife would be likely to receive the balance of her usual quarter's income, the whole amount of the income would be paid, and they asked plaintiff to send them the exact amount of the account as it had been mislaid. *Held,* that such letters did not contain such an acknowledgment of the debt that a promise by or on behalf of the defendant to pay it should be inferred therefrom, and that therefore the *Statute of Limitations* was not prevented from running. *Quaere,* whether a mere general statement that solicitors are acting for a client in connection with a certain claim, and nothing more, is sufficient evidence that such solicitors are agents of the debtor to make an acknowledgement. *Holden v. Lawes Wittewronge,* (1912) V.L.R., 82; 33 A.L.T., 153; 18 A.L.R., 28. *Cussen J.*

Company — Calls — Shares forfeited — Continuance of liability in respect of calls made before forfeiture and interest—Statute of Limitations, 21 Jac., 1, c. 16.]— The Articles of Association of a company provided that " any member whose shares have been forfeited shall notwithstanding be liable to pay and shall forthwith pay to the company all calls, instalments, interest . and expenses owing upon or in respect of such shares at the time of forfeiture until payment at the rate of ten per cent. per annum." The defendant had been owner of the shares in the company, but his shares in 1900 had been forfeited for non-payment of calls. The claim in the action was for the unpaid calls and interest thereon. *Held,* that this claim arose upon a contract other than a specialty and that, there being no express provision in the Act making the obligation to pay moneys which may arise on the forfeiture of shares a specialty debt, the *Statute of Limitations,* 21 Jac., 1, afforded a good defence to this action. *Cork and Bandon Railway* v. *Goode,* (1853) 13 C.B., 826, distinguished. *James Gillespie & Co. Ltd.* v. *Reid,* (1905) V.L.R., 101; 26 A.L.T., 154; 11 A.L.R., 12, considered. *The Land Mortgage Bank of Victoria Limited* v. *Reid,* (1909) V.L.R., 284; 31 A.L.T., 9; 15 A.L.R., 234. *Cussen, J.* But *see Goldsmith* v. *The Colonial Finance, Mortgage, Investment and Guarantee Corporation Ltd.,* 8 C.L.R., 241; 15 A.L.R., 431.

Real Property Act 1907 (No. 2086), secs. 3, 4—Arrears of interest—Statute of Limitations.]— *Cussen, J.* : " The wording of those sections seems to make it perfectly clear that the legislature is placing the same limitations on the recovery of interest whether payable in respect of money charged on land or not I do not think you can recover more than six years' interest " *The Land Mortgage Bank of Victoria Ltd.* v. *Reid,* (1909) V.L.R., 284, at p. 286.

II.—Land ; Charges upon Land.

(a) Where no Statutory Bar.

Real Property Act 1890 (No. 1136), sec. 47 —Rates—Charge upon land—Statutes of Limitations—Local Government Act 1903 (No. 1893), secs. 2, 341—Local Government Act 1891 (No. 1243), sec. 64—Local Government Act 1890 (No. 1112), sec. 235.]—The *Real Property Act* 1890 (No. 1136, sec. 47) is no bar to the enforcement of a charge under section 341 of the *Local Government Act* 1903. *Mayor, &c. of Richmond* v. *The Federal Building Society*, (1909) V.L.R., 413 ; 31 A.L.T., 52 ; 15 A.L.R., 439. F.C. *Madden, C.J., Hodges* and *Cussen, J.J.*

(b) When Time Begins to Run.

Real Property Act 1890 (No. 1136), sec. 23 —Adverse possession—Statutory period, when time begins to run—Tenancy at will—Creation of new tenancy—Permission of owner, acknowledgment by tenant that he holds by.]—In the case of a tenant at will the statutory period of limitation is given a fresh start by the creation of a new tenancy, but a new tenancy will not be implied unless there is at least a definite acknowledgment by the tenant that he holds by permission of the owner. *Wilson* v. *Equity Trustees Executors &c. Co. Ltd.*, (1911) V.L.R., 481 ; 33 A.L.T., 89 ; 17 A.L.R., 523. *a'Beckett, J.*

Real Property Act 1890 (No. 1136), secs. 18, 23—Adverse possession—Period of limitation, commencement of—New tenancy at will, what will create—Request for transfer of land.]—W., who had gone into possession of certain land as tenant at will, after he had been in possession eight or nine years asked the owner of the land for the title deeds, and on being told that he could have them if he paid for them, W. said he was willing to pay, but nothing further was done. On another occasion about the same time W. asked the owner to transfer the land to him and the owner said " You will mortgage it if I do, and I will not have any land mortgaged." *Held*, that no new tenancy had been created. *Wilson* v. *Equity Trustees Executors &c. Co. Ltd.*, (1911) V.L.R., 481 ; 33 A.L.T., 89 ; 17 A.L.R., 523. *a'Beckett, J.*

(c) Adverse Possession, Nature of.

Possession—Land of two owners within one fence—Presumption of possession—Possession follows title—Equivocal acts of possession— Intention.]—There is no presumption of law or fact that when land of more than one owner is enclosed in one common fence, the whole of the land is in the view of the law in the possession of the person who happens to be using the land. In the case of unoccupied land the possession follows the title, that is, the person who has the title is to be deemed to have possession of the land unless the contrary is shown. That applies as much to land within a fence as to land outside it. When possession or dispossession has to be inferred from equivocal acts, the intention with which they are done is all important. *Clement* v. *Jones*, 8 C.L.R., 133 ; 15 A.L.R., 158. H.C., *Griffith, C.J., O'Connor* and *Isaacs, JJ.* (1909).

Adverse possession, title by—Land under operation of Transfer of Land Act 1890 (No. 1149)—Land of several owners—Enclosed by common fence—Common use—Presumption of possession—Equivocal acts of possession— Transfer of Land Act 1904 (No. 1931), secs. 10, 11—Real Property Act 1890 (No. 1136), Part II.—Intention.]—Where two pieces of land belonging to two different owners are enclosed in one ring fence, the presumption is that the possession of each of the pieces remains in the respective owners, and this presumption is not rebutted by the fact that the whole of the land is used by only one of the owners, unless other facts show that the intention of the owner using the land is to exclude the other owner from possession. A. bought of another person in the year 1875 a grazing paddock containing about 2,000 acres which was surrounded by one ring fence, but within this fence and not fenced off from the rest of the paddock was a block of 80 acres, of which B. was the owner. From the time of the purchase and for more than 15 years afterwards A. used the whole of the paddock for grazing his cattle. During this period B. on several occasions cut firewood on his own block and carried it away, and on one occasion B. renewed the survey marks on the boundaries of his block. In an action by A. against B. after the expiration of fifteen years for a declaration under the *Transfer of Land Act* 1904 that by possession adverse to or in derogation of the title of B., A. had acquired a title to an estate in fee simple in possession of the 80 acre block. *Held*, that A. was not entitled to such declaration, inasmuch as on the evidence any exclusive possession by A. of the 80 acre block and any intention on his part to assert exclusive possession of it were negatived. *Clement* v. *Jones*, 8 C.L.R., 133; 15 A.L.R., 158. H.C., *Griffiths, C.J., O'Connor* and *Isaacs, JJ.* (1909).

Possession—Adverse possession—Land of two owners within one fence—Re-entry of registered proprietor—Cutting firewood—Renewal of survey marks on boundaries—Effect of.]—Where land of A. and land of B. were enclosed within one fence and the whole of tho land so enclosed had been used by A. for grazing cattle for a period of fifteen years during which time B. entered his land only for the cutting of firewood or the renewal of survey marks on boundaries. *Held*, that the taking of firewood was evidence that B. was using the land in such a way as would only be justified by actual possession, and, *semble*, the renewal of the survey marks would have been sufficient to establish a resumption of possession. *Clement* v. *Jones*, 8 C.L.R., 133; 15 A.L.R., 158. H.C., *Griffith, C.J., O'Connor* and *Isaacs, JJ.* (1909).

Death of registered proprietor intestate—Next of kin unknown—Possession of widow.]—Where the registered proprietor of land had died intestate, and no administration was taken out, and it was not known whether he left any next of kin, and his widow had continued in possession of the land from his death, her possession was deemed adverse although she had purported to hold the land by virtue of the Crown grants in her possession. *Lambourn* v. *Hosken*, (1912) V.L.R., 394; 34 A.L.T., 101; 18 A.L.R., 371. *a' Beckett, J.*

(d) Disabilities.

Adverse possession—Registered proprietor dead before commencement of adverse possession—No administration of his estate—Next of kin unknown—Duration of adverse possession.]—*See, post,* III. PROCEEDINGS TO ESTABLISH TITLE UNDER TRANSFER OF LAND ACT. *Lambourn* v. *Hosken*, (1912) V.L.R., 394; 34 A.L.T., 101; 18 A.L.R., 371

(e) Barring of One of Remedies of Mortgagee, Effect of.

Mortgagor and mortgagee—Recovery of money secured by mortgage barred by determination of period of limitation—Mortgagee in possession—Power of sale, whether exercise of also barred—Real Property Act 1890 (No. 1136), secs. 18, 43, 47—Transfer of Land Act 1890 (No. 1149), secs. 114, 116.]—A mortgagee's power of sale under the *Transfer of Land Act* 1890, where he has entered into possession of the mortgaged land and is in receipt of the rents and profits thereof, is not affected by reason only that his right to recover by suit or action the money secured by the mortgage is barred by sec. 47 of the *Real Property Act* 1890. *Ex parte The Australian Deposit and Mortgage Bank Ltd.,* (1907) V.L.R., 348; 28 A.L.T., 192; 13 A.L.R., 132. F.C., *Madden, C.J., Hodges* and *Hood, JJ*

Real Property Act 1890 (No. 1136), sec. 47—"Other proceeding," meaning of—Mortgagee's power of sale.]—The "other proceeding" mentioned in sec 47 of the *Real Property Act* 1890 is *ejusdem generis* with "action or suit" and does not include the exercise of a mortgagee's power of sale *Ex parte The Australian Deposit and Mortgage Bank Ltd.,* (1907) V.L.R., 348; 28 A.L.T., 192; 13 A.L.R., 132. F.C., *Madden C.J., Hodges* and *Hood, JJ.*

Mortgagor and mortgagee—Real Property Act 1890 (No. 1136), secs. 18, 43, 47—Exercise of power of sale—Whether barred by expiration of period of limitation.]—Sec. 43 of the *Real Property Act* 1890 is to be read with sec. 18, and not with sec. 47. *Ex parte The Australian Deposit and Mortgage Bank Ltd.,*

(1907) V.L.R., 348 ; 28 A.L.T., 192 ; 13 A.L.R., 132. F.C., *Madden, C.J., Hodges* and *Hood, JJ.*

III.—Proceedings to Establish Title under Transfer of Land Act 1904.

Transfer of Land Act 1904 (No. 1931), sec. 10—Adverse possession—Registered proprietor dead before commencement of adverse possession—No administration of his estate— Next of kin unknown—Duration of adverse possession.]—The provisions of sec. 10 of the *Transfer of Land Act* 1904 were not intended to alter the conditions necessary to the acquisition of a title by adverse possession to land. Consequently, where the registered proprietor has died intestate, and no administration of his estate has been granted, and it is not known whether he left any next of kin a title cannot be acquired under sec. 10 of the *Transfer of Land Act* 1904 by adverse possession commencing after the death of the registered proprietor, until such possession has continued for thirty years. *Lambourn* v. *Hosken*, (1912) V.L.R., 394 ; 34 A.L.T., 101 ; 18 A.L.R., 371. *a'Beckett, J.*

Transfer of Land Act 1904 (No. 1931), secs. 10, 11—Land alienated after 1st October, 1862 —Crown grant not registered—Adverse possession.]—The *Transfer of Land Act* 1904, sec. 10, applies only where the adverse possession is in derogation of the estate of a deceased proprietor. It does not apply where there has never been a registered proprietor of the land. *Burns* v. *The Registrar of Titles*, (1912) V.L.R., 29 ; 18 A.L.R., 47. *Cussen, J.*

Transfer of Land Act 1904 (No. 1931), sec. 10—Title by adverse possession against registered proprietor — Declaratory judgment sought—Action brought too soon—Liberty to apply at future date.]—Where an action under sec. 10 of the *Transfer of Land Act* 1904 had been brought too soon, no declaration as to title was made, but on the evidence it was declared that the plaintiff and those through whom he claimed had since the death of the registered proprietor been in undisturbed possession of the land adversely to the right-

ful owners thereof, and the plaintiff was given liberty to apply at any time to obtain the declaration sought in the action. *Lambourn* v. *Hosken*, (1912) V.L.R., 394 ; 34 A.L.T., 101 ; 18 A.L.R., 371. *a'Beckett, J.*

Transfer of Land Act 1904 (No. 1931), sec. 10—Supreme Court Rules 1906, Chapter VIII., rule 2—Adverse possession, title by—Vesting order—Registered proprietor deceased—Practice.]—In proceedings to establish title by adverse possession under the *Transfer of Land Act* 1904, sec. 10, where the person, who was registered proprietor, and whose name remains on the register, is dead, the plaintiff is not bound to adopt the procedure prescribed by the Supreme Court Rules, Chapter VIII. *Marriott* v. *Hosken*, (1911) V.L.R., 54 ; 32 A.L.T., 115 ; 16 A.L.R., 604. *a'Beckett, J.*

Transfer of Land Act 1904 (No. 1931), sec. 10—Rules of Supreme Court 1906, Chapter VIII., r. 2—Adverse possession against registered proprietor—Procedure—Registered proprietor deceased.]—The rules in Chapter VIII. of the *Rules of the Supreme Court* 1906, other than rule 2, apply to a case where the registered proprietor is dead. *Marriott* v. *Hosken*, (1911) V.L.R., 54 ; 32 A.L.T., 115 ; 16 A.L.R., 604, explained. *Lambourn* v. *Hosken*, (1912) V.L.R., 394 ; 34 A.L.T., 101 ; 18 A.L.R., 371. *a'Beckett, J.*

LIQUIDATION.

See COMPANY.

LIQUIDATOR.

See COMPANY.

LOCAL GOVERNMENT.

See also, HEALTH (PUBLIC).

I.—ELECTION OF COUNCILLORS ; OUSTER FROM OFFICE.

Local Government Act 1903 (No. 1893), secs. 120, 143—Council election—Persons whose names are on roll—Infant—" Every person," meaning of.]—The words " every person " in section 120 of the *Local Government Act* 1903 include persons under age. Although section 143 qualifies section 120 to a certain extent, it does not restrict the meaning of those words so that they shall be read to mean " every person of full age." *In re Hollins* ; *Ex parte Daly*, (1912) V.L.R., 87 ; 33 A.L.T., 157 ; 18 A.L.R., 43. *Cussen, J.*

Local Government Act 1903 (No. 1893), secs. 119, 120, 143, 149—Election of councillors—Infant's name inscribed on roll—Voting by infant—Validity of election.]—At an ordinary election of councillors for a municipality certain persons whose names were on the printed voters' list, but who were on the 10th June preceding the election under the age of twenty-one, voted for the successful candidate, and thus gave him majority of votes. *Held*, that the election was not thereby invalidated. *In re Hollins* ; *Ex parte Daly*, (1912) V.L.R., 87 ; 33 A.L.T. 157 ; 18 A.L.R., 43. *Cussen, J.*

Local Government Act 1903 (No. 1893), Part III., Part IV., sec. 155—Election of councillor—Ouster from office—Voter's roll—Conclusiveness of—Infant voters—Whether election invalidated.]—The Court cannot, on an application to oust a councillor of a municipality under the *Local Government Act* 1903, go behind the printed voters' roll, although such roll contains the names of persons under twenty-one which could not be allowed to remain there if objection were duly made to a Revision Court, and although such infants vote at an election at which such councillor is declared elected and vote in his favour. *In re Hollins* ; *Ex parte Daly*, (1912) V.L.R., 87 ; 18 A.L.T., 157 ; 33 A.L.R., 43. *Cussen, J.*

II.—PROCEEDINGS OF COUNCIL.

Local Government Act 1903 (No. 1893), secs. 179, Thirteenth Schedule, Part XI., r. 29—Voting—Show of hands—Mandatory or directory provision.] — A municipal by-law (adopting the terms of *Local Government Act* 1903, Thirteenth Schedule, Part XI., r. 29) provided that " The Council shall vote by show of hands, and any councillor present and not voting not being disabled by law from so doing shall be guilty of an offence : " *Held*, that the words " shall vote by show of hands " are directory and not mandatory. *Semble* : The by-law applies only when a formal division is called for. *Honeybone* v. *Glass*, (1908) V.L.R., 466 ; 30 A.L.T., 54 ; 14 A.L.R., 345. *Madden, C.J.*

III.—BY-LAWS.

Local Government Act 1903 (No. 1893), sec. 197—By-law—Validity—Power to regulate or control—Power to prohibit.]—By section 197 (21) of the *Local Government Act* 1903 power is conferred upon municipalities to make by-laws for " regulating or controlling quarrying or blasting operations." *Held*, that a by-law prohibiting within a particular part of a municipality the blasting of rock, &c. " in or within 100 yards from any public or private street or within a distance of 200 yards from any occupied or unoccupied dwelling within the said part " was not within the power conferred and was invalid. *Slattery* v. *Naylor*, 13 App. Cas., 446, distinguished ; *Municipal Corporation of the City of Toronto* v *Virgo*, (1896) App. Cas., 88, followed. *Co-operative Brick Co. Proprietary Ltd.* v. *Hawthorn, Mayor, &c. of City of*, (1909) 9 C.L.R., 301 ; 15 A.L.R., 479. H.C. *Griffith, C.J., Barton* and *O'Connor, JJ.*

Local government—By-law—Public highway—Traction engine—Power to regulate—Restrictions on construction and user—Local Government Act 1903 (No. 1893), secs. 197, 594.]—A municipality made a by-law prohibiting the use on a public highway of any traction engine having on its wheels any bars, spikes, grips, or other projections, but providing that this prohibition should not apply to (*a*) any traction engine used only for hauling agricultural machinery if the projections on the driving wheels conformed to certain specified conditions ; (*b*) any traction engine the driving wheels of which were cylindrical and smooth soled and had no other projections than those specified, provided that in this last case the owner of the traction engine had previously obtained the written permission of an officer of the Council to use it on specified roads and that it was used on those roads, and that the owner had agreed in writing to pay the cost of any damage that might be done to any road bridge or culvert by the engine or any vehicle drawn by it. The by-law further provided that no person should use in any public highway any traction engine unless there were carried on the engine, or on some vehicle drawn by it four wooden planks of specified dimensions upon which the engine should cross over any bridge or culvert. *Held*, that the by-law was valid and was authorized by sections 197 and 594 of the *Local Government Act President, &c. of the Shire of Tungamah* v.

Merrett, (1912) 15 C.L.R., 407 ; 18 A.L.R., 511. H.C *Griffith, C.J., Barton* and *Isaacs, JJ.*

Local government — By-law — Validity — Traction engine—Vehicle—Local Government Act 1903 (No. 1893), sec. 197 (29).]—A traction engine is a " vehicle " within the meaning of section 197 (29) of the *Local Government Act* 1903. *Ahern* v. *Cathcart*, (1909) V.L.R., 132 ; 30 A.L.T., 156 ; 15 A.L.R., 67, overruled. *President, &c. of the Shire of Tungamah* v. *Merrett*, (1912) 15 C.L.R., 407 ; 18 A.L.R., 511. H.C. *Griffith, C.J., Barton, J.* (*Isaacs, J.*, dubitante).

Local Government Act 1903 (No. 1893), secs. 203, 213, 222, 609, 610, 613, 635 — By-law, validity of—Licensing yards for sale of cattle—Prohibition of use of unlicensed premises — Penalty — Wilfulness — Limiting locality of licensed yards—Differentiation between kinds of cattle.]—Under section 635 (*c*) of the *Local Government Act* 1903, which authorizes a municipal council to make by-laws for licensing yards and premises for the sale of cattle, a council has no power to prohibit the use of unlicensed yards and premises for the sale of cattle. So *held* by *a'Beckett* and *Cussen, JJ.* (*Hood, J.* dissenting). Section 222 of the *Local Government Act* 1903 authorizes the imposition by a by-law of a penalty for a " wilful act or default contrary thereto." *Held*, by *a'Beckett* and *Cussen, JJ.* (*Hood, J.* dissenting), that a by-law imposing a penalty on " every person offending against or committing any breach of " the by-law was invalid. A municipal council may by a by-law made under section 635 (*c*) define a particular area of the municipality within which alone yards and premises will be licensed for the sale of cattle. *Per a'Beckett* and *Hood, JJ.*, a municipal council may by such a by-law differentiate between different kinds of cattle. *In re City of Bendigo ; Ex parte Edwards*, (1908) V.L.R., 609 ; 30 A.L.T., 63 ; 14 A.L.R., 475.

By-law, regulation made under—By-law made under Act subsequently repealed—Provision that by-law continue in force notwithstanding repeal—Regulation purporting to be

made under repealing Act—Clear intention to exercise a power—Effect of mis-recital of authority—Local Government Act 1874 (No. 506), Sch. XIII., Part V., sec. 1—Local Government Act 1890 (No. 1112), sec. 2, Sch. XIII., Part V., sec. 1—Local Government Act 1903 (No. 1893), sec. 2.] — Prior to the *Local Government Act* 1890 a municipality passed a by-law adopting section 1 of Part V. of the Thirteenth Schedule of the *Local Government Act* 1874. Subsequently to the passing of the *Local Government Act* 1890, such by-law not having been repealed, the municipality purported under it to make a regulation which recited that it was made "under section 1 of Part V. of the Thirteenth Schedule of the *Local Government Act* 1890" in force in the municipality "by virtue of the by-law" mentioned. *Held,* that the recital was justified by section 2 of the *Local Government Act* 1890 and that the regulation was valid. *Held,* further, that even if the by-law had not been justified the regulation would have been valid inasmuch as a clear intention was expressed to exercise the power which the municipality had under the *Local Government Act* 1890 and the above-mentioned by-law. *Ex parte Swan; In re the Mayor, &c. of the City of Hawthorn,* (1907) V.L.R., 16; 28 A.L.T., 113; 12 A.L.R., 611. *Cussen, J.*

Local Government Act 1903 (No. 1893), sec. 197 (29)—" Vehicle "—Traction engine.]—A traction engine is not a vehicle within the meaning of the *Local Government Act* 1903 (No. 1893) sec. 197 (29). *Per Cussen, J.*—"The object of a vehicle is to carry persons or things, while the object of a traction engine when it is moving from place to place is to haul loads. It happens occasionally that a traction engine moves from place to place without doing any haulage, but neither this nor the fact that ancillary to its main purpose it carries a driver and fuel should, I think, lead to its being called a vehicle or carriage." *Ahern* v. *Cathcart,* (1909) V.L.R., 132; 30 A.L.T., 156; 15 A.L.R., 67. F.C. *a'Beckett, Hood* and *Cussen, JJ.* (1909).

See, supra, President &c., of the Shire of Tungamah v. *Merrett.*

By-law, validity of—Power to make by-laws as to the position and construction of privies, &c., generally—Retrospective operation of by-law—Health Act 1890 (No. 1098), secs. 32, 35.]—*See* HEALTH (PUBLIC). *Charlton, President &c. of Shire of* v. *Ruse,* (1912) 14 C.L.R., 220; 18 A.L.R., 207.

By-law, validity of—By-law regulating privies, &c. generally—Penalty not following the words of the by-law—Penalty not imposed on person responsible for existence of thing prohibited—Health Act 1890 (No. 1098), secs. 32, 35.]—*See* HEALTH (PUBLIC). *Charlton, President &c. of Shire of* v. *Ruse,* (1912) 14 C.L.R., 220; 18 A.L.R., 207.

Highway—Obstruction—Standing or loitering in street and not moving on when requested—Collecting a crowd—Interference with traffic—By-law— Police Offences Act 1890 (No. 1126), sec. 6.]—*See* POLICE OFFENCES ACTS. *Haywood* v. *Mumford,* (1908) 7 C.L.R., 133; 14 A.L.R., 555.

Local government—Registration of place of amusement—Discretion of municipal council —Mandamus—Local Government Act 1903 (No. 1893), sec. 197; Thirteenth Schedule, Part VI.]—A municipal council had adopted Part VI. of the Thirteenth Schedule to the *Local Government Act* 1903, which requires the occupier of any ground in which public amusements are conducted, to register the ground each year, imposes a penalty upon the causing or permitting of any public amusement on an unregistered ground, and provides that the Council on the application of the occupier may, if they see fit, cause any ground to be registered and grant a certificate of registration thereof. *Held,* that mandamus would lie to compel the council to exercise their discretion as to granting or refusing an application for registration. *Held,* also, that in exercising their discretion the council might properly take into consideration the fact that the ground sought to be registered adjoined a public house, of which the applicant was licensee; that the applicant intended to use the ground for the purpose of making money for himself, and that the ground, if licensed, would enter into competition with a public recreation ground of which some of the councillors were trustees and on which the council had spent money of the municipality. *Per Higgins, J.*—No duty is imposed on the councillors to " hear and determine " in the judicial sense ; and, *Semble*, if the councillors took grounds into consideration which ought not to have been taken, mandamus to hear and determine is not the appropriate remedy. The councillors are in a position analogous to that of trustees. *Randall* v. *The Council of the Town of Northcote*, 11 C.L.R., 100 ; 16 A.L.R., 249. H.C., *Griffith, C.J., O'Connor, Isaacs* and *Higgins, JJ.* (1910).

Local government — By-law — Validity— Evidence Act 1890 (No. 1088), sec. 48—Local Government Act 1903 (No. 1893), sec. 232.]— The right to apply to quash a by-law of a municipality under sec. 48 of the *Evidence Act* 1890 has not been impliedly repealed by sec. 232 of the *Local Government Act* 1903. *Merrett and Whiteman* v. *President &c. of Shire of Tungamah*, (1912) V.L.R., 248 ; 34 A.L.T., 35 ; 18 A.L.R., 214. F.C., *a'Beckett, Hood* and *Cussen, JJ.*

IV.—Rates.

(a) Rateable Property.

Local government—Rates—Land " beneficially occupied in any manner whatsoever "—Wharves vested in Melbourne Harbour Trust Commissioners—Preferential right of occupancy granted by Commissioner—Melbourne and Geelong Corporation Acts Amendment Act 1863 (27 Vict. No. 178), secs. 42, 43— Melbourne Harbour Trust Act 1890 (No. 1119), secs. 62, 85.]—Sec. 42 of the *Melbourne and Geelong Corporation Acts Amendment Act* 1863 gives authority to the council of the City of Melbourne to make an assessment of " all lands beneficially occupied in any manner whatsoever " within the limits of the city, and sec. 43 gives the council upon the assessment so made to make rates. On lands vested in the Melbourne Harbour Trust Commissioners, and exempted from rating unless occupied for private purposes, were erected wharves, and sheds were built on the

wharves. Pursuant to authority given them by the *Melbourne Harbour Trust Act* 1890, by an instrument under seal, therein called a lease, the Commissioners granted to the respondents " full and free privilege and liberty (subject to the provisions herein contained) to use and enjoy for the term mentioned in the Schedule " a certain berth at a wharf " for the purpose of discharging passengers and cargo from and receiving passengers and cargo on board the steamers or vessels which may for the time being belong to the lessee together with the use of any shed which for the time being may be opposite to the said berth and used in connection therewith such use and enjoyment as aforesaid to be at all times subject to all the regulations of the Commissioners." It was also provided by the instrument that the respondents might not transfer the rights and privileges given to them without the prior consent of the Commissioners ; that the Harbor Master should be at liberty to use or permit the use of the berth or part of it for the accommodation of other vessels when the berth was unoccupied and not actually required by the respondents for the purposes above mentioned and might order the removal of the respondents' ships from the berth in the same manner as in the case of any other ship lying at the wharves ; that the business of the respondents should be conducted at the berth and shed the subject matter of the " lease " ; and that the respondents would not be entitled to accommodation at the public berths without the written consent of the Harbor Master. *Held*, that the wharf and shed referred to in the instrument were not " beneficially occupied in any manner whatsoever " by the respondents, and therefore that the respondents were not liable to be rated by the council in respect of them. *Rochdale Canal Co.* v. *Brewster*, (1894) 2 Q.B., 852, followed. *Mayor &c. of City of Melbourne* v. *Howard Smith Co. Ltd.*, (1911) 13 C.L.R., 253 ; 17 A.L.R., 437. H.C., *Griffith, C.J., Barton* and *O'Connor, JJ.*

Local Government Act 1903 (No. 1893), sec. 249 (1)—Rates—Rateable property —" Land

the property of His Majesty used for public purposes "—Teacher's residence attached to State School.]—Where land the property of His Majesty is occupied in any substantial degree for the advantage of the occupier, although it may be occupied for the benefit of the public also, it does not fall within the exemption in sec. 249 (1) of the *Local Government Act* 1903, and is not an occupation for public purposes." So *held* by *Madden, C.J.* and *Hood, J.* (*a' Beckett, J., dissentiente*). *Held*, therefore, that that portion of a State School building which was occupied by a State School teacher was rateable. Sec. 246 of the *Local Government Act* 1890 and sec. 249 (1) of the *Local Government Act* 1903 compared. *The President &c. of the Shire of Ferntree Gully* v. *Johnston*, (1909) V.L R., 113; 30 A.L.T., 194; 15 A.L.R., 62. F.C.

Local Government Act 1903 (No. 1893), sec. 265—Rates—Occupier, who is—Crown land, unauthorized residence upon for a considerable period—Unauthorized occupation of Crown land an offence—Land Act 1901 (No. 1749), sec. 160.]—Without title or authority G. lived upon and used Crown land continuously for a period of six years. *Held*, that G. was liable to be rated as an " occupier," and that it was immaterial that his unauthorized occupation of the land rendered him liable to a penalty under sec. 160 of the *Land Act* 1901. *Wimmera, Shire of* v. *Brimacombe*, 23 V.L.R., 217; 19 A.L.T., 12; 3 A.L.R., 146, explained. *Poowong, Shire of* v. *Gillen*, (1907) V.L.R., 37; 28 A.L.T., 123; 12 A.L.R., 522. *Hood, J.*

Local Government Act 1903 (No. 1893), sec. 249—Rates—Exemption from rating—Land used exclusively for Mechanics' Institutes—Hall let for public entertainments—Rent applied to purposes of Institute.]—The exemption from rateability of " land used exclusively for Mechanics' Institutes " in sec. 249 of the *Local Government Act* 1903 refers to land used exclusively for buildings known as Mechanics' Institutes, and not to land used exclusively for the purposes of Associations known as Mechanics' Institutes. The fact that a hall in such a building owned by such an Association is from time to time let for

public entertainments, public meetings, &c., the rent being applied to the purposes of the Association, does not deprive the land of its exemption from rateability. *Geelong Mechanics' Institute Incorporated* v. *Geelong, Mayor, &c. of*, (1907) V.L R, 580; 29 A.L.T., 33; 13 A.L.R., 377. *a' Beckett, J.*

(b) *Payment of Rates; Enforcement of Charge upon Land.*

Rates—Payment without protest after due notice and demand—Rates not lawfully demandable—Money had and received.]—Money paid, without protest and after due notice and demand, for municipal rates not lawfully demandable is not recoverable as money had and received. *Geelong Mechanics' Institute Incorporated* v. *Geelong, Mayor &c. of*, (1907) V.L.R., 580; 29 A.L.T., 33; 13 A.L.R., 377. *a' Beckett, J.*

Insolvency Act 1890 (No. 1102), sec. 115—Preferential debts—Municipal rates due at date of sequestration of estate of occupier—Payment by landlord and owner with acquiescence and concurrence of trustee—Repayment in full in priority to all other debts ordered.]—*See In re Pater; In re Robertson*, 30 A.L.T. (Supp.), 9; 14 A.L.R. (C.N.), 37. *Judge Moule* (1908).

Local Government Act 1903 (No. 1893), secs. 324, 341, 342, 343, 704—Recovery of rates—Evidence of ownership of land—Certificate of Registrar-General that a certain person appears from a memorial of registration to be owner—Effect of such certificate where such person is in fact dead.]—*Per Hood, J.*—Sec. 704 of the *Local Government Act* 1903 is merely an evidence section, and the provision making the certificate of the Registrar-General *prima facie* evidence of ownership does not enable a plaintiff to get over the difficulty of suing a dead man. *In re the Transfer of Land Act; Ex parte Anderson*, (1911) V.L.R., 397. 33 A.L.T., 78; 17 A.L.R. 399.

Local Government Act 1903 (No. 1893), secs. 2, 341—Local Government Act 1891 (No. 1243), sec. 64—Local Government Act 1890 (No. 1112), sec. 235—Real Property Act 1890

(No. 1136), sec. 47—Rates—Charge upon land—Statutes of Limitation.]—The *Statute of Limitation* (No. 1136), sec. 47, is no bar to the enforcement of a charge under sec. 341 of the *Local Government Act* 1903. *Mayor, &c. of Richmond* v. *The Federal Building Society*, (1909) V.L.R., 413; 31 A.L.T., 52; 15 A.L.R., 439. F.C., *Madden, C.J., Hodges* and *Cussen, JJ.*

Local Government Act 1903 (No. 1893), secs. 341, 342—County Court Rules 1891, r. 103—Rates—Charge on land—Proceedings to enforce—Death of owner—Parties—Executor of executor—Order for sale—Title.]—The purchaser of land at a sale made pursuant to an order in an action under sec. 342 of the *Local Government Act* 1903 (No. 1893) wherein the executor of the executor of the registered proprietor of the land is defendant will acquire a good title to the land. *Moorabbin Shire* v. *Soldi*, (1912) V.L.R., 389; 34 A.L.T., 93; 18 A.L.R., 493. F.C., *a' Beckett, Hodges* and *Cussen, JJ.*

Local Government Act 1903 (No. 1893), secs. 324 to 328, 340 to 343—Rates, interest and costs, how far a charge upon land—Costs of removing an order from Petty Sessions to Supreme Court.]—The statutory charge over lands for payment of municipal rates, interest and costs, includes the costs of removing an order for rates, interest and costs, obtained in a Court of Petty Sessions, into the Supreme Court and of issuing execution thereon. *Mayor &c. of Malvern* v. *Johnson*, 28 A.L.T. (Supplement), 7; 12 A.L.R. (C.N.), 28. *Judge Box* (1906).

Local Government Act 1903 (No. 1893), secs. 324 to 328, 340 to 343—Rates—Enforcement of charge upon land—County Court practice—Special defence, notice of—County Court Act 1890 (No. 1078), sec. 66.]—Sec. 66 of the *County Court Act* 1890 requiring notice of special defences applies to actions for enforcing charges upon land for rates. *Mayor &c. of Malvern* v. *Johnson*, 28 A.L.T. (Supplement), 7; 12 A.L.R. (C.N.), 28. *Judge Box* (1906).

Action to enforce charge upon land for rates—County Court—Scale of costs, how determined—Value of land.]—In actions to enforce by sale a charge for municipal rates over land, the value of the land and not the amount of the charge, fixes the scale upon which costs should be taxed. *Mayor &c. of Malvern* v. *Johnson*, 28 A.L.T. (Supplement), 7; 12 A.L.R. (C.N.), 28. *Judge Box* (1906).

Application to bring land under the Transfer of Land Act—Sale of land for non-payment of rates under decree of County Court—Dead owner made defendant—Order for substituted service—Commissioner of Titles acting upon records in the office—Refusal to issue certificate—Local Government Act 1903 (No. 1893), secs. 324, 341, 342, 343, 704.]—*See* TRANSFER OF LAND ACT. *In re Transfer of Land Act; Ex parte Anderson*, (1911) V.L.R., 397; 33 A.L.T., 78; 17 A.L.R., 399.

Will—Construction—" Upkeep and maintenance and carrying on of " house " as a home and residence "—What expenses included therein—Household expenses—Repairs—Rates and taxes—Outgoings.]—*See* WILL. *In re Stroud; Bell* v. *Stroud*, (1908) V.L.R., 33; 29 A.L.T., 104; 13 A.L.R., 645.

V.—BORROWING POWERS.

Local Government Act 1903 (No. 1893), secs. 345, 354, 372—Borrowing powers of council—Provision that plans &c. be prepared before borrowing—Whether mandatory.]—The provisions of sec. 354, requiring the council of a municipality before proceeding to borrow for permanent works and undertakings to cause to be prepared plans and specifications, and an estimate of the cost and a statement showing the proposed expenditure of the money, are mandatory as between the council and its ratepayers. A council proceeding to borrow without complying with such provisions will be restrained by injunction at the suit of the Attorney-General. *The Attorney-General (ex rel. Bate)* v. *Camberwell, Mayor &c. of*, (1907) V.L.R., 448; 28 A.L.T., 242; 13 A.L.R., 237. *Cussen, J.*

Municipality—Borrowing money for permanent works—Plans and specifications, sufficiency of—Local Government Act 1903 (No. 1893), sec. 354.]—*Semble.*—The plans and specifications prepared under sec. 354 of the *Local Government Act* 1903 should be of a kind reasonably intelligible to an ordinary ratepayer. *Attorney-General (ex rel. Dodd)* v. *Ararat, Mayor &c. of Borough of*, (1911) V.L.R., 489; 33 A.L.T., 99; 17 A.L.R., 474. *Madden, C.J.*

Local Government Act 1903 (No. 1893), secs. 354, 355—Borrowing powers of council for permanent works—Plans and specifications to be prepared before borrowing—Nature and extent of information to be supplied.]—The plans and specifications required by sec. 354 of the *Local Government Act* 1903, though preliminary in nature, must disclose sufficient information to enable an approximate estimate to be made, and to afford to the ratepayers an opportunity of judging in a general way, whether the proposed works will be of such a character that it is desirable that moneys shall be borrowed for their construction. *Semble.*—If the site of the proposed works is sufficiently indicated, the municipality is entitled to rely on any information or knowledge that can be gained by an inspection of the locality in which the works are to be constructed. *The Attorney-General (ex rel. Bate)* v. *Camberwell, Mayor &c. of*, (1907) V.L.R., 448; 28 A.L.T., 242; 13 A.L.R., 237. *Cussen, J.*

Local Government Act 1903 (No. 1893), secs. 354, 355—Particulars to be supplied before proceeding to borrow money for permanent works.]—In the schedule of works referred to in the statement showing the proposed expenditure of money to be borrowed there appeared the item—" Tar-paving footpaths various streets.' There was no plan of the footpaths to be paved, nor any specifications as to width and depths or the nature of the material to be used. *Held*, not to be a compliance with the provisions of sec 354 of the *Local Government Act* 1903. *The Attorney-General (ex rel Bate)* v *Camberwell, Mayor &c of*, (1907) V L R, 448; 28 A.L.T., 242; 13 A.L.R., 237. *Cussen, J.*

VI.—CONTRACTS.

Local Government Act 1903 (No. 1893), secs. 455, 456—Contract—Consideration—Tender — Deposit — Forfeiture —Withdrawal of tender before acceptance—Mode of making contract—Burden of proof.]—In response to an advertisement by a municipal council for tenders for certain work the plaintiff made a tender in which he stated :—" I herewith make a preliminary deposit of £50 . . . such sum to be absolutely forfeited to the council as liquidated damages and not by way of penalty in the event of withdrawing cancelling or rescinding this tender or failing to enter into a properly executed contract for the performance of the work within 48 hours after being called upon so to do." The plaintiff deposited £50 with the tender accordingly. Before acceptance of the tender the plaintiff withdrew it. In an action by the plaintiff against the municipality to recover the £50. *Held*, that there was a binding contract under which the council could retain the £50 in the event of the plaintiff withdrawing his tender before acceptance ; that the promise of the council to consider the tender was a sufficient consideration to support the contract, notwithstanding sec. 456 of the *Local Government Act* 1903 ; and that the burden of proving that the contract was not made in the manner prescribed by sec. 455 of that Act was upon the plaintiff. *Stafford* v. *City of South Melbourne*, (1908) V.L.R., 584; 30 A.L.T., 43; 14 A.L.R., 464. F.C., *a'Beckett, Hood* and *Cussen, JJ.*

VII.—STREETS, ROADS, DRAINS, &c.

(a) *Laying out, Making and Repairing.*

Local Government Act 1903 (No. 1893), sec. 526 (1)—Street—" Set Out " on private property—Meaning of " Set out "—Adjoining Owner—Liability of.]—In sec. 526 (1) (a) of the *Local Government Act* 1903, the words " set out " on private property, in reference to a street, contemplate something being done on the land itself, of a like kind to " forming," that will indicate that it is a street. The setting out should be done on the ground itself by some overt act observable for some reasonable time and indicating to those who desire to know it where the street is. The mere altering, with the approval of the Commissioner of Titles, of an original plan of subdivision lodged with the Office of Titles, is not a sufficient " setting out " within the meaning of the section. *Metropolitan Bank Ltd.* v. *Town of Camberwell*, (1909) V.L.R., 82 ; 30 A.L.T., 151 ; 15 A.L.R., 43. F.C., *Madden, C.J., Hood* and *Cussen, JJ.*

Street, laying out of—Certificate of municipal council that land can be " sufficiently drained "—Land subject to river flooding—Local Government Act 1903 (No. 1893), secs. 514, 522, 523, 524, 525.]—In determining whether land can be " sufficiently drained " for the purposes of a certificate under the *Local Government Act* 1903, secs. 522 and 523, a municipal council has to consider whether the proposed street will interfere with the drainage of the lands abutting thereon, and will itself be capable of being drained. It is immaterial that the land is subject to river flooding, unless the laying out of the road will in itself diminish the facilities for the escape of the flood water. *Hagelthorn* v. *Mayor, &c. of Kew*, (1911) V.L.R., 242 ; 32 A.L.T., 196 ; 17 A.L.R., 165. F.C., *Madden, C.J., Hodges* and *Hood, JJ.*

Street, laying out of—Refusal by municipal council of certificate that land can be " sufficiently drained "—Notice of intention to appeal—Time—Local Government Act 1903 (No. 1893), secs. 517, 523.]—When an application for a certificate under sec. 523 of the *Local Government Act* 1903 has been refused, and a second application is entertained by the council and, after consideration, refused, the time for giving notice of intention to appeal under sec. 517 of the Act runs from the last refusal. *Hagelthorn* v. *Mayor &c. of Kew*, (1911) V.L.R., 242 ; 32 A.L.T., 196 ; 17 A.L.R., 165. F.C., *Madden, C.J., Hodges* and *Hood, JJ.*

Local Government Act 1903 (No. 1893), sec. 492—Stopping certain kind of traffic on road—Procedure to be adopted.]—A municipal council made an order forbidding a certain kind of traffic on a certain road. Notice of the order was published in a newspaper and posted on the road. *Held*, that the proper procedure had been adopted. *Ahern* v. *Sharp*, (1907) V.L.R., 42 ; 28 A.L.T., 107 ; 12 A.L.R., 498. *Chomley, J.*

Local Government Act 1903 (No. 1893), sec. 492—Road—Temporary closing—When order for closing may be made.]—A municipal council has power under sec. 492 of the Act No. 1893 to stop traffic on a road for the purpose of executing works which make the road temporarily dangerous or unusable ; but that section does not confer a power to make an order closing a road merely for the purpose of preventing the injury resulting from ordinary user. *Ahern* v. *Sharp*, (1907) V.L.R., 42 ; 28 A.L.T., 107 ; 12 A.L.R., 498. *Chomley, J.*

(b) *Accidents, Liability in Respect of.*

Nuisance—Drain on highway constructed by municipal authority.]—A drain constructed on a highway for the purpose of draining the highway is not in itself an indictable nuisance. *Benalla, President, &c. of* v. *Cherry*, (1911) 12 C.L.R., 642 ; 17 A.L.R., 537. H.C., *Griffith, C.J., Barton* and *O'Connor, JJ.*

Highway—Open drain lawfully constructed for purpose of draining highway—Liability of municipal authority, nature and extent of.]—The duty of a municipal authority which has lawfully constructed an open drain on a highway for the purpose of draining it, is only to guard against injuries which may be reasonably anticipated as likely to arise from its condition and that duty is towards persons and owners of animals using the highway for the ordinary purposes of a highway. *Benalla, President &c. of* v. *Cherry*, (1911) 12 C.L.R., 642 ; 17 A.L.R., 537. H.C., *Griffith, C.J., Barton* and *O'Connor, JJ.*

Highway—Open drain lawfully constructed by municipal authority—Liability of municipal authority—Damages, whether too remote—Wandering horse entering drain at shallow part and walking along drain to deep part—Horse unable to extricate itself.]—In a portion of a street which was a *cul de sac* and was not much used for traffic, the municipal authority constructed an open drain with sloping sides, which was about four feet deep at the deepest part where an underground pipe discharged into it the drainage from another part of the road, and ran out to a shallow depression at the other end. The drain was fifteen inches wide at the bottom and at the deepest part was about five feet wide at the top. The plaintiff's horse, having escaped from a paddock, wandered to this street, entered the drain at its shallow end, walked up it to the deepest part, and, not being able to get any further or to turn round and return by the way it came, injured itself in its efforts to extricate itself, and died soon after being extricated. The deepest part of the drain was protected to a certain extent by fences, but the lower end was not fenced across. In an action by the plaintiff against the municipal authority to recover damages, *Held*, that the municipal authority was not shown to have been guilty of any breach of duty, and that even if it were the injury complained of did not arise in consequence of such breach. *Benalla, President &c. of* v. *Cherry*, (1911) 12 C.L.R., 642 ; 17 A.L.R., 537. H.C., *Griffith, C.J., Barton* and *O'Connor, JJ.*

Melbourne and Metropolitan Board of Works Act 1890 (No. 1197), secs. 79, 81, 85, 87, 88—Highway—Obstruction—Sewer constructed under highway—Shaft opening on surface of highway—Covering of shaft—Duty to keep in repair—Neglect of duty.]—*See* MELBOURNE AND METROPOLITAN BOARD OF WORKS. *Frencham* v. *Melbourne and Metropolitan Board of Works*, (1911) V.L.R., 363 ; 33 A.L.T., 30 ; 17 A.L.R., 333.

VIII.—MARKETS.

Markets—City of Melbourne—Transfer of functions, powers, &c., of Commissioners to Council—Penalty for selling marketable commodities elsewhere than in markets—3 Vict. No. 19 (N.S.W.), sec. 23—Markets Act 1890 (No. 1115), sec. 25—6 Vict. No. 7 (N.S.W.), secs. 71, 72.]—3 Vict. No. 19 (substantially re-enacted by the *Markets Act* 1890) after providing for the appointment of Commissioners of markets by sec. 23 (sec. 25 of the *Markets Act* 1890) authorized the Commissioners to establish in certain towns markets, which should be the only places in those towns where certain goods should be sold, and enacted that any person who should sell any of those goods elsewhere than in the market places so established (except in his dwelling-house or shop), should on conviction before a justice be liable to a penalty. 6 Vict. No. 7, which established the corporation of the town of Melbourne and the council thereof, by sec. 71 conferred on the council "the same powers authorities duties and immunities in respect of markets". as by 3 Vict. No. 19 were given to the Commissioners, and by sec. 72 transferred to the council, from and after the election of the first mayor, "all the functions duties and responsibilities" at that time performed by or belonging to the Commissioners under 3 Vict. No. 19, and provided that all the functions of the Commissioners should thereupon cease and determine. The Council having established markets in the city of Melbourne, *Held*, that a person who sold marketable goods elsewhere in the city than in those markets were liable to a penalty under sec. 25 of the *Markets Act* 1890. *Weedon* v. *Davidson*, (1907) 4 C.L.R., 895 ; 13 A.L.R., 87. H.C., *Griffith, C.J., Barton, O'Connor* and *Higgins, JJ.*

Markets Act 1890 (No. 1115), sec. 25—Place fixed for holding of market for sale of corn, butchers' meat, poultry, &c.—Sale of such articles in a private place not being a place fixed for holding a market or a dwelling-house or shop — Whether an offence—"Shop," meaning of—Disturbance of market, ordinary remedies for—Whether excluded by section.] — *See* MARKETS. *Richardson* v. *Austin*, (1911) 12 C.L.R., 463 ; 17 A.L.R., 324.

IX.—POUNDS.

Pounds Act 1890 (No. 1129), secs. 4 to 9, 18 to 22, 28—Duties imposed by Act on poundkeeper—Liability of municipality—Master and servant.]—*See* POUNDS AND IMPOUNDING. *Ryan* v. *Swan Hill, President, &c. of*, 28 A.L.T. (Supplement), 17 ; 13 A.L.R. (C.N.), 17. *Judge Eagleson* (1907).

Impounded horse—Escape owing to insecure condition of pound fence—Retaking of horse—Authority of municipality.]—*See* POUNDS AND IMPOUNDING. *Ryan* v. *Swan Hill, President, &c. of*, 28 A.L.T. (Supplement), 17 ; 13 A.L.R. (C.N.), 17.

Pounds Act 1890 (No. 1129), secs. 21, 22—Sale by poundkeeper—Provisions of act duly observed—Title of purchaser.]—*See* POUNDS AND IMPOUNDING. *Doig* v. *Keating*, (1908) V.L.R., 118 ; 29 A.L.T., 171 ; 14 A.L.R., 20.

Pounds Act 1890 (No. 1129), secs. 21, 22—Sale by poundkeeper—Failure to observe provisions of Act—Title of purchaser.]—*See* POUNDS AND IMPOUNDING. *Doig* v. *Keating*, (1908) V.L.R., 118 ; 29 A.L.T., 171 ; 14 A.L.R., 20.

Pounds Act 1890 (No. 1129), sec. 9—Trespassing cattle—Trespass rates—" Substantial fence," whether creek may be.]—*See* POUNDS AND IMPOUNDING. *Helding* v. *Davis*, (1911) V.L.R., 74 ; 32 A.L.T., 188 ; 17 A.L.R., 72.

Pounds Act 1890 (No. 1129), sec. 9—Third Schedule—Right to charge sustenance fees—Liability of poundkeeper to return sustenance fees wrongly demanded and paid.]—*See* POUNDS AND IMPOUNDING. *Martin* v. *Turner*, 31 A.L.T. (Supplement), 9 ; 15 A.L.R. (C.N.), 17.

X.—ELECTRICITY, SUPPLY OF.

Electric Light and Power Act 1896 (No. 1413), secs. 38, 39—Electric Light and Power Act 1901 (No. 1775), sec. 3—Construction—Powers of undertakers to vary rates of charge.]—*See* ELECTRIC LIGHT AND POWER ACT, cols. 428, 429. *Attorney-General for Victoria* v. *Melbourne, Mayor &c. of*, (1907) A.C , 469; 5 C.L.R., 257.

Local Government Act 1903 (No. 1893), repealing effect of—Electric Light and Power Act 1896 (No. 1413) ; Electric Light and Power Act 1900 (No. 1694).]—*See* ELECTRIC LIGHT AND POWER ACT, col. 429. *Attorney-General (ex rel. Dodd)* v. *Ararat, Mayor, &c. of Borough of*, (1911) V.L.R., 489 ; 33 A.L.T., 99 ; 17 A.L.R., 474.

Municipality, powers of—Supply of electricity for public or private purposes within municipal district—Whether municipality entitled as of right to Order-in-Council authorising—Electric Light and Power Act 1896 (No. 1413), secs. 8, 9, 10, 11, 13, 16, 17, 18.]—*See* ELECTRIC LIGHT AND POWER ACT, col. 429. *Attorney-General (ex rel. Dodd)* v. *Ararat, Mayor, &c. of Borough of*, (1911) V.L.R., 489 ; 33 A.L.T., 99 ; 17 A.L.R., 474.

Municipality, powers of—Supply of electricity, Order-in-Council authorising—Borrowing money for the purpose of erecting works——Order-in-Council, whether a condition precedent to publication of notice of intention to borrow—Electric Light and Power Act 1896 (No. 1413), secs. 5, 10—Local Government Act 1903 (No. 1893), sec. 355).]—*See* ELECTRIC LIGHT AND POWER ACT, col. 429. *Attorney-General (ex rel Dodd)* v. *Ararat, Mayor &c. of Borough of*, (1911) V.L.R., 489 ; 33 A.L.T., 99 ; 17 A.L.R., 474.

Municipality, powers of—Supply of electricity for light, heat and power—Power to borrow money to construct necessary works—Electric Light and Power Act 1896 (No. 1413), secs. 5, 10, 16, 17 ; Electric Light and Power Act 1900 (No. 1694), secs. 2, 3—Local Government Act 1890 (No. 1112), secs. 304, 311 ; Local Government Act 1891 (No. 1243), sec. 77 (xi.) ; Local Government Act 1903 (No. 1893), secs. 345, 346, 347 (6), 595.]—*See* ELECTRIC LIGHT AND POWER ACT, cols. 429, 430. *Attorney-General (ex rel. Dodd)* v. *Ararat, Mayor, &c. of Borough of*, (1911) V.L.R., 489 ; 33 A.L.T., 99 ; 17 A.L.R., 474.

XI.—TRAMWAYS.

Tramways Act 1890 (No. 1148), Second Schedule, Part II., clause 17—" Avoiding " payment of fare—Refusal to pay full fare—Honest belief that full fare not payable—Mens rea.]—Tickets sold by a tramway company—to which the powers of the municipal council had been delegated under the *Tramways Act* 1890—entitled a passenger to travel at a cheaper rate than the ordinary cash fare, subject to the condition that such tickets were not available on holidays. On being asked by one of the company's conductors for his fare, a passenger tendered one of such tickets, but the conductor refused it and demanded the ordinary cash fare on the ground that the day was a holiday (it being in fact a half-holiday); the passenger honestly believing a ticket to be a valid discharge of the full fare, completed his journey, and left the tram without paying. *Held*, that the passenger " avoided " payment of his fare within the meaning of the *Tramways Act* 1890, Second Schedule, Part II., clause 17. *Cochrane* v. *Tuthill*, (1908) V.L.R., 549; 30 A.L.T., 50; 14 A.L.R., 453. *Madden, C.J.*

Tramways Act 1890 (No. 1148)—Tramway tickets sold subject to condition that they shall not be available on holidays—Whether available on half-holidays.]—Tickets sold by a tramway company entitled a passenger to travel at a cheaper rate than the ordinary cash fare, but indorsed on the tickets was a condition that they were not to be available on holidays. *Held*, that such condition applied to half-holidays. *Cochrane* v. *Tuthill*, (1908) V.L.R., 549; 30 A.L.T., 50; 14 A.L.R., 453. *Madden, C.J.*

XII.—LEGAL PROCEEDINGS.

See also, *ante*, III. BY-LAWS; VII. STREETS, ROADS, DRAINS, &c. (*b*) *Accidents. Liability in Respect of.*

(a) Information, Who May Lay.

Local Government Act 1903 (No. 1893), Part XXXVIII., secs. 693, 694, 695, 696, 697 (c)—Breach of municipal building regulations—Who may lay information and prosecute—Officer of council—Information and proceedings in name of officer.]—Under Part XXXVIII. of the *Local Government Act* 1903, secs. 694, 695, a municipal council may order a prosecution in the name of the council or corporation, or it may authorise an officer to undertake a prosecution—which would include the laying of the information—in his own name. *Steane* v. *Whitchell*, (1906) V.L.R., 704; 28 A.L.T., 60; 12 A.L.R., 390. F.C., *Hood, Cussen* and *Chomley, JJ.*

Local Government Act 1903 (No. 1893), Part XXXVIII.—Breach of building regulations—Prosecution by municipal officer—Authority to prosecute, sufficiency of.]—S., who was the building surveyor to the town of Northcote, was authorized by the municipality by a document under the seal of the municipality in the following terms :—" Mr. S., surveyor and building surveyor of the Town of Northcote, is hereby authorised to take proceedings against any person offending against the building regulations of the Town of Northcote." *Held*, that S. was authorised to prosecute thereunder in his own name. *Steane* v. *Whitchell*, (1906) V.L.R., 704; 28 A.L.T., 60; 12 A.L.R., 390. F.C., *Hood, Cussen* and *Chomley, JJ.*

Information, who may lay—Tramways Act 1890 (No. 1148), sec. 5, Second Schedule, Part II., clause 17—Tramway fare, penalty for avoiding payment of—Delegation of authority of municipal council—Whether delegate may enforce penalty.]—A municipal council, by agreement under seal, delegated to a company, under sec. 5 of the *Tramways Act* 1890, the authority conferred by the Order in Council authorizing the municipal council as the promoter to construct a certain tramway, and neither the Order-in-Council nor the agreement contained anything as to rights or powers to impose or enforce penalties. *Held*, that the company could not sue for penalties for offences under clause 17, of the Second Schedule of that Act. *Cochrane* v. *Tuthill*, (1908) V.L.R., 549; 30 A.L.T., 50; 14 A.L.R., 453. *Madden, C.J.*

(b) Notice of Accident on Highway, &c.

Local Government Act 1903 (No. 1893), sec. 708—Notice of injury—Sufficiency—Place at which the accident took place—" Bridge "—" Approach."]—Plaintiff wrote to the defendant municipality calling attention to the bad state of the " approach " to a certain " culvert " and stating that in the " approach " to such " culvert " there was a dangerous hole which had caused his horse to fall and suffer injury. The " culvert " was a wooden bridge 135 feet in length built

on piles and passing over a creek 63 feet wide
and having at each end a short inclined
macadamised roadway leading up to it. The
evidence at the trial showed that the hole in
question was in the wooden decking of the
bridge or culvert at a spot about 5 feet
from the macadamised roadway at one end,
and not in that part of the structure which
actually spanned the stream. *Held*, that the
notice of injury did not comply with section
708 (1) of the *Local Government Act* 1903 in
that it did not state " the place at which "
the accident took place. *Daniel* v. *Benalla,
President, &c. of Shire of,* (1906) V.L.R.,
101 ; 27 A.L.T., 141 ; 12 A.L.R., 16. *Madden, C.J., Holroyd* and *Hodges, JJ.*

**Local Government Act 1903 (No. 1893),
secs. 708, 710—Non-compliance with conditions of section 708—Whether application
for stay of action imperative.**]—In order that
a municipality may take advantage of the
plaintiff's non-compliance with the conditions
of section 708 it is not imperative that
application should be made under section
710 for a stay of the action. If no such
application has been made the municipality
may raise the defence of non-compliance at
the trial of the action *Daniel* v *Benalla,
President, &c of Shire of,* (1906) V L R , 101
Madden, C J , Holroyd and *Hodges, J J*

**Local Government Act 1903 (No. 1893),
sec. 708—Notice of accident, failure to give—
" Sufficient reason why the person injured
. . . . was unable to give such notice "—
Evidence to show, nature of—Ignorance of
the law.**]—Where the notice required by
section 708 of the *Local Government Act* 1903
has not been given within the prescribed
time by a person who seeks to recover
damages from a municipality for injuries
sustained by reason of an accident on a
highway, he shows " sufficient reason why
the person injured　　　　was unable to
give such notice " if he shows that under the
circumstances there were preventing causes
which afforded sufficient reason for omitting
to give the notice although it might have been
possible for him to have given it *Per
Hodges, J*—A mental and bodily condition
which makes it dangerous or even substantially injurious for the person injured to
give the notice, or which makes him oblivious
of business matters altogether, or which
makes him really unfit to give the notice,
may render him " unable " within the meaning of the Statute *Per Cussen, J*—A
plaintiff may show sufficient reason why the
person injured was unable to give the notice
required although it could not be said absolutely that in the circumstances and at all
times he could not possibly have given the
notice or have caused it to be given *Quaere*,
whether ignorance of the necessity for giving
the notice would be a sufficient reason for
inability to give it. *Leeder* v *Ballarat East,
Mayor, &c of,* (1908) V L R , 214 ; 29
A L T , 192 ; 14 A.L.R., 124. F.C. *a' Beckett,
Hodges* and *Cussen, JJ.*

**Local Government Act 1903 (No. 1893),
secs. 708, 710—Action in respect of injury
sustained by reason of accident on highway—
Notice of accident not given in time—Whether
sufficient reason shown why person injured
unable to give notice—By whom such question to be determined—Jury.**]—Where an
action against a municipality for damages in
respect of injury sustained by the plaintiff
by reason of an accident upon a highway is
tried by a jury, and the notice required by
section 708 of the *Local Government Act*
1903 has not been given in time and an
application under section 710 to stay proceedings has been previously refused, the
question whether the plaintiff can show
some sufficient reason why he was unable
to give such notice is for the jury. *Leeder*
v. *Ballarat East, Mayor, &c. of,* (1908)
V.L.R., 214 ; 29 A.L.T., 192 ; 14 A.L.R.,
124. F.C *a' Beckett, Hodges* and *Cussen, JJ.*

**Local Government Act 1903 (No. 1893),
secs. 708, 710—Notice of action against
municipality—Failure to comply with conditions—Stay of action—Judge in Chamber
—Jurisdiction.**]—A Judge in Chambers has
under section 710 of the *Local Government
Act* 1903 a discretion, where the facts relating to the injury its nature and extent and
the consequent suffering are in dispute, to
say that he will not stay the action at that
juncture. In such a case it is for the Judge

who presides at the trial, after hearing the evidence, to say whether so far as section 708 (1) is concerned the plaintiff has shown sufficient reason why he was unable to give the notice required by that sub-section. *Leeder* v. *Ballarat East, Mayor, &c. of,* 29 A.L.T. (Supplement), 6; 13 A.L.R. (C.N.), 25. *Judge Eagleson* (1907).

Local Government Act 1903 (No. 1893), secs. 708, 710—Accident upon highway, &c. —Notice before action, when necessary.]— The notice before action required by section 708 of the *Local Government Act* 1903 need not be given where the cause of action arose out of an accident occasioned by a negligent act of a servant of the municipality which had no connection with any defect in a highway, street, road, &c. *Gordon* v. *Ballarat, Mayor, &c. of,* 29 A.L.T. (Supplement), 4; 13 A.L.R. (C.N.), 19. *Judge Johnston* (1907).

XIII.—FEDERAL CONTROL.

Instrumentality of State Government, what is—Municipal corporation engaging in trading enterprise.]—*See* COMMONWEALTH OF AUSTRALIA CONSTITUTION, col. 139. *Federated Engine Drivers and Firemen's Association of Australasia* v. *Broken Hill Proprietary Co. Ltd.,* (1911) 12 C.L.R., 398; 17 A.L.R., 285.

LORD'S DAY.

See SUNDAY.

LOTTERY.

See GAMING AND WAGERING; LOTTERIES GAMING AND BETTING ACT.

LOTTERIES GAMING AND BETTING ACT.

Lotteries Gaming and Betting Act 1906 (No. 2055), sec. 38 (1) (2)—Declaration that premises are a common gaming house— Whether " may " means " shall "—Discretion of Court.]—The Court has a discretion whether it will make a declaration under section 38 (1) of the *Lotteries Gaming and Betting Act* 1906. *In re the Lotteries Gaming and Betting Act* 1906; *Ex parte Gleeson,* (1907) V.L.R., 368; 28 A.L.T., 228; 13 A.L.R., 146. *Cussen, J.*

Lotteries Gaming and Betting Act 1906 (No. 2055), sec. 38—Application for declaration that premises are a common gaming house —Owner or occupier, whether entitled to be heard.]—Upon an application under section 38 of the *Lotteries Gaming and Betting Act* 1906 for a declaration that certain premises are a common gaming house the owner or occupier is entitled to be heard in opposition. *In re Lotteries Gaming and Betting Act* 1906 *In re Shanghai Club; In re Ah Pow; Ex parte Gleeson,* (1907) V.L.R., 463; 29 A.L.T., 31; 13 A.L.R., 360. F.C. *a'Beckett, Hood* and *Cussen, JJ.*

Lotteries Gaming and Betting Act 1906 (No. 2055), sec. 38 (1), (2)—Application for declaration that premises are common gaming house—Who may be heard—Owner or occupier.]—On the hearing of an application for a declaration under section 38 (1) of the *Lotteries Gaming and Betting Act* 1906 the owner or occupier of the premises in respect of which the declaration is sought (or one of them) is entitled to be heard and to bring before the Court anything which would influence the Court in exercising its discretion. *In re the Lotteries Gaming and Betting Act* 1906; *Ex parte Gleeson,* (1907) V.L.R., 368; 28 A.L.T., 228; 13 A.L.R., 146. *Cussen, J.*

Lotteries Gaming and Betting Act 1906 (No. 2055), sec. 38—Application for declaration that premises are a common gaming house—Affidavit of police officer showing reasonable grounds for suspecting—Suspicion, whether in mind of police officer or Court—

Prima facie case, how established—Prima facie case, how answered.]—In an application under section 38 of the *Lotteries Gaming and Betting Act* 1906 for a declaration that certain premises are a common gaming house the suspicion, for which the affidavit of an officer of police must show reasonable grounds, is a suspicion in the mind of that officer. A *prima facie* case for the exercise of the Court's jurisdiction is established if the affidavit of such an officer alleges, that he suspects the premises are being used as a common gaming house, and shows reasonable grounds for his suspicion. The owner or occupier may answer such a *prima facie* case by showing that the suspicion is unfounded altogether, and by showing that the premises have not at all material times been used as a gaming house. *In re Lotteries Gaming and Betting Act* 1906; *In re Shanghai Club*; *In re Ah Pow*; *Ex parte parte Gleeson*, (1907) V.L.R., 463; 29 A.L.T., 31; 13 A.L.R., 360. F.C. *a'Beckett, Hood* and *Cussen, JJ.*

Lotteries Gaming and Betting Act 1906 (No. 2055), sec. 38—Application for declaration that premises are a common gaming house—Affidavit of police officer showing reasonable grounds for suspecting—Whether police officer may be cross-examined thereon.]—In proceedings under sec. 38 of the *Lotteries Gaming and Betting Act* 1906, the officer of police, who makes the affidavit showing reasonable grounds for suspecting that the premises in question are used as a common gaming house, cannot be cross-examined on such affidavit. *In re Lotteries Gaming and Betting Act* 1906; *In re Shanghai Club*; *In re Ah Pow*; *Ex parte Gleeson*, (1907) V.L.R., 463; 29 A.L.T., 31; 13 A.L.R., 360. F.C., *a'Beckett, Hood* and *Cussen, JJ.*

Lotteries Gaming and Betting Act 1906 (No. 2055), sec. 38—Application for declaration that premises are a common gaming house—Affidavits in reply to affidavits of party opposing, admissibility of—Cross-examination of deponents.]—In an application under sec. 38 of the *Lotteries Gaming and Betting Act* 1906 for a declaration that certain premises are a common gaming house, the applicant may file affidavits in reply to those of the party opposing, and both classes of deponents are subject to cross-examination. *In re Lotteries Gaming and Betting Act* 1906; *In re Shanghai Club*; *In re Ah Pow*; *Ex parte Gleeson*, (1907) V.L.R., 463; 29 A.L.T., 31; 13 A.L.R., 360. F.C., *a'Beckett, Hood* and *Cussen, JJ.*

Lotteries Gaming and Betting Act 1906 (No. 2055), sec. 61—Evidence of certain fact made prima facie evidence of commission of offence—Procedural provision—Whether applicable to offences committed before passing of Act.]—*Quaere*, whether sec. 61 of the *Lotteries Gaming and Betting Act* 1906 being procedural would not apply to offences committed before that Act. *Knox v. Thomas Bible*; *Knox v. J. L. Bible*, (1907) V.L.R., 485; 29 A.L.T., 23; 13 A.L.R., 352. *Cussen, J.*

Lotteries Gaming and Betting Act 1906 (No. 2055), secs. 5 (2), 10, 15, 17—Place used as a common gaming house, meaning of—User of place in such a way that it is by Statute deemed and taken to be a common gaming house—Whether limited in sec. 17 to user as a betting house.]—*See* GAMING AND WAGERING, cols. 607, 608. *Macmanamny v. King*, (1907) V.L.R., 535; 28 A.L.T., 250; 13 A.L.R., 258.

Gaming—Contrivance for gaming—Poker machine—Unlawful gaming—Room used for the purpose of unlawful gaming being carried on therein—Police Offences Act 1890 (No. 1126), secs. 62, 64—Lotteries, Gaming and Betting Act 1906 (No. 2055), sec. 31.]—*See* GAMING AND WAGERING, col. 606. *O'Donnell v. Dodd*, (1910) V.L.R., 482; 32 A.L.T., 87; 16 A.L.R., 539.

Police Offences Act 1890 (No. 1126), secs. 49, 50, 51, 52, 62—Lotteries Gaming and Betting Act 1906 (No. 2055), sec. 12—Gaming houses, &c.—Place used for the purpose of unlawful gaming being carried on therein—" Place " — " User."]—*See* GAMING AND WAGERING, cols. 606, 607. *McCann v. Morgan*, (1912) V.L.R., 303; 34 A.L.T., 43; 18 A.L.R., 334.

Lotteries Gaming and Betting Act 1906 (No. 2055), secs. 10, 17—Use as a common gaming house—Acts of persons other than defendant—Acts prior to the date of the alleged offence.]—See GAMING AND WAGERING, cols 614, 615. *Macmanamny v. King*, (1907) V.L.R., 535 ; 28 A.L.T., 250 ; 13 A.L.R., 258.

Lotteries Gaming and Betting Act 1906 (No. 2055), secs. 10, 17—House opened, kept or used for purpose of illegal lottery—Method of drawing of lottery, whether necessary to show.]—See GAMING AND WAGERING, cols. 614, 615. *Macmanamny v. King*, (1907) V.L.R., 535 ; 28 A.L.T., 250 ; 13 A.L.R., 258.

Lotteries Gaming and Betting Act 1906 (No. 2055), sec. 22—" Information or advice " as to betting on intended horse race, meaning of.]—See GAMING AND WAGERING, col. 608. *O'Donnell* v. *Smart*, (1907) V.L.R., 439 ; 28 A.L.T., 245 ; 13 A.L.R., 255.

Lotteries Gaming and Betting Act 1906 (No. 2055), sec. 22—Information as to intended horse race—" The betting," meaning of.]—See GAMING AND WAGERING, col. 608. *O'Donnell* v. *Smart*, (1907) V.L.R., 439 ; 28 A.L.T., 245 ; 13 A.L.R., 255.

Lotteries Gaming and Betting Act 1906 (No. 2055), sec. 22—Information as to betting on intended horse race—Publication in newspaper —Betting odds offered in betting market.]—See GAMING AND WAGERING, col. 608. *O'Donnell* v. *Smart*, (1907) V.L.R., 439 ; 28 A.L.T., 245 ; 13 A.L.R., 255.

LUNATIC.

Lunacy Act 1890 (No. 1113), secs. 130, 206 —Lunatic so found by inquisition in England —Lunatic's estate in Victoria—Filing inquisition of record in Victoria—Appointment of Committee in Victoria—Order for sale of Lunatic's estate—Time and extent of order —Discretion of committee— Bringing land under Act—Transfer of Land Act 1890 (No. 1149), sec. 21.]—Under secs. 130 and 206 of the *Lunacy Act* 1890 the Supreme Court of Victoria has power, for the purpose of carry-

ing out an order of the English Court in Lunacy, to order the sale of the real estate in Victoria of a lunatic resident in England and so found there, and to give all necessary directions. Such an order will not be made on an application to file the English inquisition under sec. 130, but should be made the subject of a subsequent application, after reference to the Mater-in-Lunacy. *Semble.*—There is jurisdiction under sec. 130 of the *Lunacy Act* 1890 to direct a sale of land, and to authorise a committee to bring land under the *Transfer of Land Act* and the power to be exercised under the Statute certainly enables the Court to entrust the whole discretion as to the sale and the mode of carrying it out, and so on to the committee. *In re A.B., a Lunatic*, (1909) V.L.R., 100 ; 30 A.L.T., 158 ; 15 A.L.R., 85. *a'Beckett, J.*

Two trustees—One incapable—Appointment of new trustee by other trustee—Estate including land under the Transfer of Land Act— Vesting order—Trusts Act 1890 (No. 1150), sec. 4—Trusts Act 1896 (No. 1421), sec. 7— Transfer of Land Act 1890 (No. 1149), sec. 188.]—See TRUSTS AND TRUSTEES. *Re Hope*, (1910) V.L.R., 492 ; 32 A.L.T., 71 ; 16 A.L.R., 581.

Marriage Act 1890 (No. 1166), sec. 74 (a)— Divorce—Desertion—Insanity arising after desertion—Whether statutory period continues to run.]—See HUSBAND AND WIFE, col. 648. *Laing* v. *Laing*, (1911) V.L.R., 37 ; 32 A.L.T., 144 ; 16 A.L.R., 601.

MAINTENANCE AND MAINTENANCE ORDERS.

See also, HUSBAND AND WIFE, TRUSTS AND TRUSTEES, WIDOWS AND YOUNG CHILDREN MAINTENANCE ACT.

I.—JURISDICTION.

(a) Generally.

Marriage Act 1890 (No. 1166), secs. 42, 43—Maintenance order—Summons to appear before Court of Petty Sessions—Order in fact made by two Justices—Jurisdiction of Justices—Justices Act 1896 (No. 1458), sec. 4.]—Defendant was summoned to appear before a Court of Petty Sessions to show cause why he should not support his illegitimate child. At the time and place referred to in the summons an order for maintenance was made by two Justices. *Held,* that the Justices had jurisdiction to make the order. *Shee* v. *Larkin,* (1907) V.L.R., 295; 28 A.L.T., 188; 13 A.L.R., 97. *a' Beckett, J.*

Marriage Act 1890 (No. 1166), sec. 43—Custody of child, right to—Whether Justices have jurisdiction to determine.]—Justices have no power under sec. 43 of the *Marriage Act* 1890 to deal with the question of the custody of an illegitimate child at the hearing of a complaint laid under sec. 42 by or with the authority of the mother of the child against the father. *Fisher* v. *Clack,* 2 A.L.R. (C.N.), 321, considered. *Russ* v. *Carr,* (1909) V.L.R., 78; 30 A.L.T., 131; 15 A.L.R., 24. *Hodges, J.*

Marriage Act 1890 (No. 1166), secs. 42, 43—Wife compelled by husband's conduct to leave the matrimonial home—Husband and wife residing in different bailiwicks—Order made against husband in bailiwick where wife resides—Jurisdiction of Justices.]—A complaint made under sec. 42 of the *Marriage Act* 1890 by a wife against her husband was heard and determined by Justices of the Peace in and for the Central Bailiwick at a Court of Petty Sessions held in such Bailiwick, and the Justices had evidence before them that the husband had unlawfully compelled his wife to leave his residence, which was at a place in the Northern Bailiwick, and to live at her sister's house, which was at a place within the Central Bailiwick, and had, prior

to her departure promised to provide for her maintenance at her sister's, and that she was in fact without means of support and that he was able to maintain her. *Held,* that such Justices had jurisdiction to make an order against the husband under sec. 43 of the *Marriage Act* 1890 for the maintenance of his wife. *Ross* v. *Ross,* (1909) V.L.R., 318; 30 A.L.T., 220; 15 A.L.R., 305. *Madden, C.J.*

(b) Conditions of Jurisdiction.

Maintenance of destitute and deserted wives " Desertion "—" Leaving without means of support "—Wife compelled by husband's conduct to leave the matrimonial home—Marriage Act 1890 (No. 1166), secs. 42, 43.]—Where a wife has been forced by her husband's violence or by his threats of violence to leave his house, and for the safety of her life to live elsewhere, if he does not provide her with maintenance and she is in fact without means of support, he " leaves her without means of support " within the meaning of sec. 42 of the *Marriage Act* 1890. Desertion, in Part IV. of the Act, means " goes away from his wife and children," or " leaves them, where he does not go away, without means of support." *Regina* v. *Collins; Ex parte Collins,* 7 V.L.R. (L.), 74; 2 A.L.T., 118, followed. *Chantler* v. *Chantler,* 4 C.L.R., 585; 13 A.L.R., 540, discussed. *Ross* v. *Ross,* (1909) V.L.R., 318; 30 A.L.T., 220; 15 A.L.R., 305. *Madden, C.J.*

Marriage Act 1890 (No. 1166), secs. 42, 43—Maintenance of deserted wives—Leaving wife without means of support—Wife leaving husband of her own accord.]—Where a woman, of her own accord and without legal justification, has left her husband, she cannot afterwards summon him for leaving her without means of support unless she has in the meantime, by a sincere and *bona fide* offer to return to him, put an end to the position which she herself has created. *Male* v. *Male,* (1912) V.L.R., 455; 34 A.L.T., 123; 18 A.L.R., 582. *Cussen, J.*

Marriage Act 1890 (No. 1166), secs. 42, 43—Illegitimate child without adequate means of support—Offer by father to provide home

for child—Agreement by mother to support child.]—Justices have no power under sec. 43 of the *Marriage Act* 1890 to dismiss a complaint against the father of an illegitimate child for leaving it without adequate means of support merely by reason of the fact that the father *bona fide* offers to take it and is able and willing to support it if it is handed over to him, and of the fact that the mother has by deed agreed with the father to support it herself without any assistance from him. *Russ* v. *Carr*, (1909) V.L.R., 78 ; 30 A.L.T., 131 ; 15 A.L.R., 24. *Hodges, J.*

Marriage Act 1900 (No. 1684), secs. 4, 5—Confinement expenses—Wife vountarily leaving husband, whether entitled to.]—*See* HUSBAND AND WIFE, col. 668. *Ruddell* v. *Ruddell*, (1912) V.L.R., 221 ; 34 A.L.T., 4 ; 18 A.L.R., 200.

II.—ORDERS.

(a) *Nature and Effect of* ; *Res Judicata.*

Marriage Act 1890 (No. 1166), secs. 42, 43—Order for maintenance of child—Subsequent return of child to father—Order still valid.]—An order made against a father under sec. 43 of the *Marriage Act* 1890, is not extinguished by the fact that the child subsequently lives with the father and is maintained by him. *Robert* v. *Roberts*, (1903) 29 V.L.R., 158 ; 25 A.L.T., 54 ; 10 A.L.R., 20, distinguished, and (by *Cussen, J.*), doubted. *Lobley* v. *Lobley*, (1909) V.L.R., 383 ; 31 A.L.T., 46 ; 15 A.L.R., 443. F.C., *Madden, C.J., Hodges* and *Cussen, JJ.*

Marriage Act 1890 (No. 1166), secs. 42, 43—Illegitimate child without adequate means of support—Dismissal of previous complaint—Res judicata.]—*Semble,*—The mere fact that a complaint against a father for leaving his child without adequate means of support, has been dismissed does not entitle the defendant to plead *res judicata* to a similar complaint subsequently laid against him. *Russ* v. *Carr*, 30 A.L.T., 131. *Hodges, J.* (1908).

Maintenance order made by Court of Petty Sessions—Money due thereunder—Action in Supreme Court to recover—Marriage Act 1890 (No. 1166), secs. 43, 51—Justices Act 1890 (No. 1105), secs. 115, 131—Justices Act 1896 (No. 1458), sec. 4.]—No action will lie in the Supreme Court for the recovery of money due under a maintenance order made by a court of Petty Sessions under sec. 43 of the *Marriage Act* 1890. *Falconer* v. *Falconer*, (1910) V.L.R., 489 ; 32 A.L.T., 100 ; 16 A.L.R., 578. *Cussen, J.*

(b) *Form and Interpretation.*

Marriage Act 1890 (No. 1166), sec. 43—Maintenance order—Direction to pay to Clerk of Petty Sessions at particular place—Whether Clerk is a " person."]—By a maintenance order under sec. 43 of the *Marriage Act* 1890 the defendant was directed to pay a weekly sum to " the Clerk of Petty Sessions at Fitzroy." *Held*, that such direction did not invalidate the order ; but, *quaere*, whether " the Clerk of Petty Sessions at Fitzroy " is a " person " within the meaning of sec. 43. *Cohen* v. *MacDonough (or O'Donough*), (1906) V.L.R., 521 ; 28 A.L.T., 97 ; 12 A.L.R., 447. *Cussen, J.*

Marriage Act 1890 (No. 1166), sec. 43—" In such manner " as the Justices think fit—Order directing payment to Clerk of Petty Sessions at particular place, validity of.]—An order for maintenance under sec. 43 of the *Marriage Act* 1890 directing payment to " the Clerk of Petty Sessions, North Melbourne," is an order directing payment " in such manner " . . . as the Justices think fit, and is therefore valid. *Aarons* v. *Aarons*, (1907) V.L.R., 21 ; 28 A.L.T., 117 ; 12 A.L.R., 567. F.C., *Hodges, Hood* and *Chomley, JJ.*

Marriage Act 1890 (No. 1166), sec. 43—Justices Act 1904 (No. 1959), sec. 20—Order for maintenance—Defendant to find surety " forthwith " — Immediate committal to prison—Service of copy order, whether condition precedent to issue of warrant of committal.]—By an order under sec. 43 of the *Marriage Act* 1890 the defendant was ordered to pay a weekly sum for the maintenance of his illegitimate child. The order also required him " to find forthwith one good and sufficient surety " and directed that " in default of finding such surety " he be committed to gaol until such order be complied with. As the defendant did not comply with the order by finding a surety he was detained in Court, whence he was removed to gaol under the warrant of one of the Justices. *Held*, that the word " forthwith " in sec. 20 of the *Justices Act* 1904 means " at once " without the lapse of any interval of time ; that there was jurisdiction to make the order, and to issue the warrant ; and that it was not necessary to serve a copy of the order upon the defendant before issuing the warrant. *Foley* v. *Monaghan*, 14 A.L.T., 240, and *R.* v. *M'Cormick*, 4 V.L.R. (L.), 36, discussed. *Adams* v. *Rogers*, (1907) V.L.R., 245 ; 28 A.L.T., 180 ; 13 A.L.R., 71. *Hood, J.*

Marriage Act 1890 (No. 1166), secs. 42, 43— Maintenance order—Surety directed—Person to whom security to be given, whether necessary to specify—Justices Act 1890 (No. 1105), sec. 108.]—An order for maintenance directing the defendant to find a surety need not specify the person to whom security is to be given. *Shee* v. *Larkin*, (1907) V.L.R., 295 ; 28 A.L.T., 188 ; 13 A.L.R., 97. *a' Beckett, J.*

Marriage Act 1890 (No. 1166), secs. 42, 43— Maintenance order — Surety directed — To whom security to be given—Payments to be made to Clerk of Petty Sessions.]—Where an order for maintenance, which requires a surety to be found, directs the periodical payments to be made to the Clerk of Petty Sessions, it may be inferred that he is the person to whom security is to be given. *Shee* v. *Larkin*, (1907) V.L.R., 295 ; 28 A.L.T., 188 ; 13 A.L.R., 97. *a' Beckett, J.*

(c) *Sureties.*

See also, *ante* (b) *Form and Interpretation.*

Marriage Act 1890 (No. 1166), sec. 43— Maintenance order—Surety directed—Variation of order on appeal—Character of order not changed by variation—Whether surety discharged.]—An order for maintenance was varied on appeal by directing that the periodical payments should commence from a date later than that fixed by the order appealed from for such commencement.

Default was made subsequent to the date fixed on appeal. *Held*, that as the original order remained in force, subject to a variation which in no way changed its character, the surety was not discharged by such variation. *Shee* v. *Larkin*, (1907) V.L.R., 295 ; 28 A.L.T., 188 ; 13 A.L.R., 97. *a' Beckett, J.*

Marriage Act 1890 (No. 1166), sec. 43— Maintenance order—Surety directed—Liability of surety, when it arises—Declaration of forfeiture, whether necessary.]—A surety under sec. 43 of the *Marriage Act* 1890 becomes liable immediately upon the defendant making default, and there is no necessity for a declaration of forfeiture. *Shee* v. *Larkin*, (1907) V.L.R., 295 ; 28 A.L.T., 188 ; 13 A.L.R., 97. *a' Beckett, J.*

(d) *Enforcement.*

See also, *post*, III. EVIDENCE.

Marriage Act 1890 (No. 1166), secs. 43, 51— Maintenance order—Necessity for service of order before proceedings to enforce.]—Before proceedings are taken under sec. 51 of the *Marriage Act* 1890 a copy of the maintenance order must have been served on the defendant. *Cohen* v. *MacDonough*, (1906) V.L.R., 521 ; 28 A.L.T., 97 ; 12 A.L.R., 447, dictum of *Cussen, J.*, disapproved. *Cohen* v. *MacDonough*, (1907) V.L.R., 7 ; 28 A.L.T., 119 ; 12 A.L.R., 566. F.C., *Hodges, Hood* and *Chomley, JJ.*

Marriage Act 1890 (No. 1166), sec. 51— Service of copy order for maintenance, whether necessary.] — *Semble*.—It is not necessary to serve a person against whom an order for maintenance has been made with a copy of such order before proceeding against him under sec. 51 of the *Marriage Act* 1890. *Cohen* v. *MacDonough* (or *O'Donough*), (1906) V.L.R., 521 ; 28 A.L.T., 97 ; 12 A.L.R., 447. *Cussen, J.*

Marriage Act 1890 (No. 1166), secs. 43, 51— Maintenance order—Imprisonment for breach —Whether jurisdiction to imprison for a second breach.]—The fact that a person has been committed to prison for one breach of a maintenance order made against him, will not free him from liability to be committed to prison for another breach of such order. *Aarons* v. *Aarons*, (1907) V.L.R., 21 ; 28 A.L.T., 117 ; 12 A.L.R., 567. F.C., *Hodges, Hood* and *Chomley, JJ.*

Marriage Act 1890 (No. 1166), secs. 43, 51—Maintenance order—Enforcement of—Defendant in prison for previous breach of order—Whether he may be guilty of disobedience to order—No evidence of want of means.]— The mere fact, without proof of want of means, that the defendant is in prison under commitment for disobedience of a maintenance order, is no answer to a complaint for subsequent disobedience of the order. *Aarons* v. *Aarons*, (1907) V.L.R., 21 ; 28 A.L.T., 117 ; 12 A.L.R., 567. F.C., *Hodges, Hood* and *Chomley, JJ.*

Marriage Act 1890 (No. 1166), sec. 51—Discretion of Justices—Dismissal of complaint—Giving defendant time to pay.]— Under sec. 51 of the *Marriage Act* 1890 the Justices have a discretion, if the allegation is not proved, to dismiss the complaint. They also have a discretion to give the defendant time to pay, if they are satisfied that through no fault of his own he is unable to pay the amount he was ordered to pay. *Aarons* v. *Aarons*, (1907) V.L.R., 21 ; 28 A.L.T., 117 ; 12 A.L.R., 567. F.C., *Hodges, Hood* and *Chomley, JJ.*

Marriage Act 1890 (No. 1166), sec. 51—Order for maintenance—Disobedience of order—Arrears of maintenance—Payment by instalments—Jurisdiction.]— Under sec. 51 of the *Marriage Act* 1890, Justices have jurisdiction to order the defendant to pay by instalments, arrears of maintenance. *Lobley* v. *Lobley*, (1909) V.L.R., 383 ; 31 A.L.T., 46 ; 15 A.L.R., 443. F.C., *Madden, C.J., Hodges* and *Cussen, JJ.*

III.—EVIDENCE.

Evidence—Public document—Suitors' Cash Book (Rule 10, Rules under the Justices Act 1890)—Entries made by Clerk of Petty Sessions not in official capacity—Maintenance order—Direction to pay to clerk—Entries of payments—Marriage Act 1890 (No. 1166), sec. 51.]— Entries in a book (whether the Suitors' Cash Book or not) kept by the Clerk of Petty Sessions for the time being and purporting to record certain payments made to such clerk under a maintenance order, are not admissible, in proceedings under sec. 51 of the *Marriage Act* 1890, to prove non-payment of the balance. It is not part of the clerk's official duty to receive such payments, and so far as such entries are concerned the book is not a public document or public book. *Cohen* v. *MacDonough* (or *O'Donough*), (1906) V.L.R., 521 ; 28 A.L.T., 97 ; 12 A.L.R., 447. *Cussen, J.*

Marriage Act 1890 (No. 1166), sec. 43—Maintenance order—Payments to be made to Clerk of Petty Sessions—Failure to comply with order, evidence of—Suitors' Cash Book, how it may be used.]— Default in compliance with a maintenance order directing payments to be made to the Clerk of Petty Sessions may be proved by the statement of that officer and, though the Suitors' Cash Book kept by him, being the book in which it would have been his duty to record payment, if made, is not admissible to prove default, it may be looked at by him to refresh his memory by showing that no payment was recorded. *Shee* v. *Larkin*, (1907) V.L.R., 295 ; 28 A.L.T., 188 ; 13 A.L.R., 97. *a' Beckett, J.*

Service of copy of maintenance order—Proof of, by affidavit—Proceedings for disobedience of order—Marriage Act 1890 (No. 1166), sec. 51—Justices Act 1890 (No. 1105), sec. 74.]— A proceeding under sec. 51 of the *Marriage Act* 1890 for disobedience of a maintenance order is a proceeding within the jurisdiction of a Court of Petty Sessions, and service of a copy of the maintenance order may, under sec. 74 of the *Justices Act* 1890, be proved by the affidavit of the person who has served the same. *Cohen* v. *MacDonough* (or *O'Donough*), (1906) V.L.R., 521 ; 28 A.L.T., 97 ; 12 A.L.R., 447. *Cussen, J.*

Husband and wife—Maintenance—Former marriage—Husband not heard of for seven years—Presumption—Validity of second marriage—Proof of invalidity—Onus—Marriage Act 1890 (No. 1166), sec. 46.]—*See* HUSBAND AND WIFE, cols. 641, 642. *Ousley* v. *Ousley.*

(1912) V.L.R., 32 ; 33 A.L.T., 155 ; 18 A.L.R., 5.

Marriage Act 1901 (No. 1737), sec. 4—Wilful neglect to comply with order for maintenance of wife—Evidence—Whether wife competent witness against husband—Crimes Act 1891 (No. 1231), sec. 34.]—On an indictment of a husband under sec. 4 of the *Marriage Act* 1901 for wilfully neglecting to comply with an order for the maintenance of his wife, his wife is not a competent witness against him. But she is a competent witness against him upon an indictment for wife desertion under sec. 3 (1) (*a*). *Rex* v. *Jacono*, (1911) V.L.R., 326 ; 33 A.L.T., 28 ; 17 A.L.R., 340. *Madden, C.J., Hodges* and *Hood, JJ.* (1911).

IV.—APPEALS.

Marriage Act 1890 (No. 1166), secs. 51, 52—Maintenance order—Disobedience by husband—Proceedings to enforce—Dismissal by Justices—Appeal to General Sessions.]—No appeal or application under sec. 52 of the *Justices Act* 1890 lies in respect of an order of Justices dismissing proceedings by a wife against her husband under sec. 51 for disobedience of a maintenance order. *Bloxham* v. *Bloxham*, 33 A.L.T. (Supplement), 11 ; 18 A.L.R. (C.N.), 1. *Judge Wasley.*

Marriage Act 1890 (No. 1166), sec. 52—Marriage Act 1900 (No. 1684), sec. 7—Practice—Applications to quash, etc.—Orders under the Marriage Acts—Service of notices.]—The Chairman of the Courts of General Sessions have by order dated the 8th November, 1909, directed that notices of all applications to quash, alter or vary orders under the *Marriage Act* 1890, sec. 52, and the *Marriage Act* 1900, must be served personally. *In re Applications to Quash, &c.,* 31 A.L.T. (Supplement), 10 ; 15 A.L.R. (C.N.), 25 (1909).

Marriage Act 1890 (No. 1166), sec. 52—Justices Act 1890 (No. 1105), sec. 131—Maintenance appeals—Notice of intention to appeal—Statement of grounds of appeal—Filing notices.]—A notice of intention to appeal against an order for maintenance made by Justices under Part IV. of the *Marriage Act* 1890 is invalid unless it States the grounds of appeal. The appellant should file a copy of his notice of intention to appeal before or at the time that he applies to have the appeal set down for trial. *Gavey* v. *Gavey,* 31 A.L.T. (Supplement), 6 ; 15 A.L.R. (C.N.), 17. *Judge Eagleson* (1909).

MALICE.

See DEFAMATION.

MALICIOUS ACTS.

Negligence—Proximate cause of damage the malicious act of third party—Liability in respect of.]—*See* NEGLIGENCE. *Rickards* v. *Lothian,* (1913) A.C., 263 ; 19 A.L.R., 105.

Negligence—Overflow of water from lavatory in upper floor—Malicious act of third party—Liability in respect of.]—*See* NEGLIGENCE. *Rickards* v. *Lothian,* (1913) A.C., 263 ; 19 A.L.R., 105.

Action, cause of—Inducing employer to discharge employee from his employment—Interference—Lawful justification or excuse—Intention to injure—Malice—Self-interest—Trades Union Secretary.]—*See* EMPLOYER AND EMPLOYEE, cols, 450, 451. *Bond* v. *Morris,* (1912) V.L.R., 351 ; 34 A.L.T., 52 ; 18 A.L.R., 348.

Malicious use of process of Court of Insolvency—Action claiming damages in respect of—Good petitioning creditor's debt and available act of insolvency—Whether an answer to claim.]—*See* INSOLVENCY, col. 733. *Bayne* v. *Blake,* (1909) 9 C.L.R., 347 ; 15 A.L.R., 486.

MALICIOUS ARREST.

See MALICIOUS PROSECUTION.

MALICIOUS PROSECUTION.

Malicious arrest—Arrest under process of foreign Court—Termination of proceedings in favour of plaintiff before action brought——Setting aside of order to hold to bail and writ of ca. re—Reasonable and probable cause.]—H.S. Co. brought an action against V. in the Supreme Court of New South Wales claiming damages for breach of contract, and in that action obtained an order for a writ of ca. re., under which V. was arrested and held to bail. Prior to obtaining the order H.S. Co. had submitted to their solicitors a statement of the facts and the documents, which were alleged to constitute the contract, and consisted mainly of cablegrams, and on the solicitors' advice the affidavits in support of the order were sworn, and the application made. Before the trial of that action, which was eventually determined in favour of V., he commenced an action against H.S. Co. in the Supreme Court of Victoria claiming damages for malicious arrest under the ca. re. *Held*, that the judgment entered for H.S. Co. should be affirmed, because (*per Griffith, C.J.* and *O'Connor, J.*), V. had failed to establish the absence of reasonable and probable cause for asserting the claim in the New South Wales action and malice on the part of H.S. Co., and (*per Isaacs, J.*), because V. had commenced his action prematurely. *Semble* (*per Griffith, C.J.*,) that neither the fact that the previous action in the Supreme Court of New South Wales was not determined when V. brought his action, nor the existence of the order to hold to bail nor of the writ of *capias* was a bar to the bringing of V.'s action in the Supreme Court of Victoria. *Per Isaacs, J.*—No action is maintainable for the malicious use of legal process in a suit instituted in any Court of competent jurisdiction, whether local or foreign, until that suit, in so far as it relates to the matter complained of, has terminated in the plaintiff's favour, where such termination is legally possible. *Varawa* v. *Howard Smith Co. Ltd.*, (1911) 13 C.L.R., 35 ; 17 A.L.R., 499.

Malicious arrest—Abuse of process of Court.] The distinction between an action for malicious arrest, and an action founded on an abuse of the process of the Court considered. *Varawa* v. *Howard Smith Co. Ltd.*, (1911) 13 C.L.R., 35 ; 17 A.L.R., 499. H.C., *Griffith, C.J.*, *O'Connor* and *Isaacs, JJ.*

Order XIV. (a) (Rules of 1906)—Frivolous or vexatious action, what is—Order for arrest of witness in insolvency proceedings—Purpose of order not to discover assets but to hamper appeal to High Court—Action for damages in respect of such order—Conspiracy to oppress—No actual damage.]—*See* PRACTICE AND PLEADING. *Bayne* v. *Baillieu* ; *Bayne* v. *Riggall*, (1908) 6 C.L.R., 382.

Abuse of process—Insolvency proceedings to stifle litigation—Action by non-trader—No actual damage.]—*See* ABUSE OF PROCESS, cols. 1, 2. *Bayne* v. *Baillieu* ; *Bayne* v. *Riggall*, (1908) 6 C.L.R., 382 ; 14 A.L.R., 426.

MANDAMUS.

Discretion of Governor in Council—Prisoner under sentence—Remission of sentence—Mandamus.]—Mandamus will not lie to the Governor in Council of the State, and no Court has jurisdiction to review his discretion in the exercise of the prerogative of mercy *Horwitz* v. *Connor*, (1908) 6 C.L.R., 38 ; 14 A.L.R., 342. H.C., *Griffith, C.J.*, *Barton, O'Connor, Isaacs* and *Higgins, JJ.*

Mandamus—Local Government—Discretion of Council—Exercise of—Local Government Act 1903 (No. 1893), sec. 197, Thirteenth Schedule, Part VI.]—A municipal council had adopted Part VI. of the Thirteenth Schedule to the *Local Government Act* 1903 which requires the occupier of any ground in which public amusements are conducted to register the ground each year, imposes a penalty upon the causing or permitting of any public amusement on an unregistered ground, and provides that the Council on the application of the occupier may, if they see fit, cause any ground to be registered and grant a certificate of registration thereof. *Held*, that mandamus would lie to compel the council to exercise their discretion as to granting or refusing an application of registration. *Per*

Higgins, J.—No duty is imposed on the Councillors to " hear and determine " in the judicial sense ; and, *Semble*, if the councillors took grounds into consideration which ought not to have been taken, mandamus to hear and determine is not the appropriate remedy. The councillors are in a position analogous to that of trustees. *Randall* v. *The Council of the Town of Northcote*, 11 C.L.R., 100 ; 16 A.L.R., 249. H.C., *Griffith, C.J., O'Connor, Isaacs* and *Higgins, JJ.* (1910).

Mandamus—Remedy by appeal available— Discretion of Court, matters to be considered in exercise of—Comparative advantage of applying one remedy rather than the other— County Court—Case struck out for want of jurisdiction—Jurisdiction to entertain defendant's application for costs, declined by Judge.] A Judge of County Courts, having ordered a a case to be struck out for want of jurisdiction, refused to consider the defendant's application for costs on the ground that he had no jurisdiction to do so. *Held*, per *a'Beckett* and *Cussen, JJ.* (*Madden, C.J.*, dissenting), that, notwithstanding the existence of the remedy by appeal, the Court should exercise its discretion in favour of granting a writ of mandamus ordering the Judge to consider the question of costs, as in all the circumstances that remedy was more appropriate, less expensive, and more desirable from a judicial point of view than the remedy by way of appeal. *The King v. Beecham, Ex parte Cameron*, (1910) V.L.R., 204 ; 31 A.L.T., 183 ; 16 A.L.R., 173.

Wine and spirit merchant's licence—Power of Treasurer—Refusal to grant—Mandamus— Customs and Excise Duties Act 1890 (No. 1082), secs. 155, 156.]—The instructions in sec. 156 of the *Customs and Excise Duties Act* 1890 to the Treasurer to issue a licence to any person who complies with the provisions of secs. 155 and 156, and is not subject to any disqualification therein mentioned, is mandatory, and will be enforced by mandamus Where the ostensible applicant had no intention of carrying on the business on his own behalf, and was merely applying as " dummy " for another person, who was subject to a dis-

qualification, and the Treasurer refused to issue a licence, the Court refused to issue a mandamus to compel him to do so. *The King* v. *Watt, Ex parte Slade*, (1912) V.L.R., 225 ; 33 A.L.T., 222 ; 18 A.L.R., 158. F.C., *Madden, C.J., Hodges* and *Cussen, JJ.*

Mandamus—Minister of Crown—Disobedience — Public Statute—Criminal contempt— Attachment—Privilege.]—Disobedience to a public Statute for disobedience to which no other penalty is provided by the Legislature, is an indictable misdemeanour ; therefore contempt in refusing to obey a writ of mandamus ordering compliance with the Statute is of a criminal or quasi-criminal nature, and *Semble*, there is no privilege in a Minister of the Crown or in any one else from attachment for such contempt. *The King* v. *Watt , Ex parte Slade*, (1912) V.L.R., 225 ; 33 A.L.T., 222 ; 18 A.L.R., 158. F.C., *Madden, C.J., Hodges* and *Cussen, JJ.*

Mandamus—Disobedience of public Statute —Appeal from mandamus—Civil or mixed matters—Supreme Court Act 1890 (No. 1142), sec. 37.]—A proceeding by mandamus granted on the application of a private person ordering the Treasurer to comply with the mandatory provisions of a public Statute imposing a duty upon him is a civil or mixed matter " within the meaning of sec. 37 of the *Supreme Court Act* 1890, although the refusal to so comply may be an indictable misdemeanour. There may therefore be an appeal to the Full Court from the order of a single Judge granting such mandamus. *The King* v. *Watt ; Ex parte Slade*, (1912) V.L.R., 225 ; 33 A.L.T., 222 ; 18 A.L.R., 158. F.C., *Madden, C.J., Hodges* and *Cussen, JJ.*

Order LII., r. 11—Order LXVII.* r. 9— Writ of attachment—Sheriff, refusal of to execute—Execution, how enforced—Whether mandamus will issue.]—Where the Sheriff refuses to execute a writ of attachment, he should be called upon to return the writ or bring in the body within a given time, and on his non-compliance, application should be made under Order LII., r. 11, for his committal. A writ of mandamus will not issue there being an alternative remedy. *Peterson*

v. *M'Lennan*, (1907) V.L.R., 94 ; 28 A.L.T., 135 ; 12 A.L.R., 577. *Cussen, J.*

Health Act 1890 (No. 1098), sec. 225—Appeal—Mandamus to Board of Public Health to hear—Appellants not given an opportunity of being heard.]—*See* HEALTH (PUBLIC). col. 638. *The King* v. *Prahran, Mayor &c. of; Ex parte Morris*, (1910) V.L.R., 460 ; 32 A.L.T., 92 ; 16 A.L.R., 507.

Mortgage—Registration—Improper refusal to register—Mandamus, whether mortgagee has a remedy by—Existence of another remedy—Transfer of Land Act 1890 (No. 1149), sec. 209.]—*See* TRANSFER OF LAND ACT. *Perpetual Executors and Trustees Association &c. Ltd.* v. *Hosken*, (1912) 14 C.L.R., 286 ; 18 A.L.R., 201.

MARKET.

Markets Act 1890 (No. 1115), sec. 25—Place fixed for holding of market for sale of corn, butchers' meat, poultry, &c.—Sale of such articles in a private place not being a place fixed for holding of market or a dwelling-house or shop—Whether an offence—" Shop," meaning of—Disturbance of market, ordinary remedies for—Whether excluded by section.] Sec. 25 of the *Markets Act* 1890 provides that the Commissioners of markets " may fix the places within such town or portion of a town for the holding of markets, and may there erect and build or cause to be erected and built market houses with shambles stalls and other convenient buildings. And the said market places shall be the only places within the said town or portion of a town where any market for the sale of corn (except corn or grain sold by sample) butchers' meat poultry eggs fresh butter vegetables or other provisions shall for the future be held and kept. And if any person sell or expose to sale any of the said articles or other provisions usually sold in markets in any of the streets lanes entries or other public passages or places other than the places which may be so appointed by the Commissioners as aforesaid except in his dwelling house or shop, every such person shall on conviction

thereof for every such offence forfeit and pay the sum of five pounds." *Held*, that in the phrase " other public passages or places " the word " public " qualifies " places " as well as passages, and therefore that a sale or exposure for sale in a private place was not an offence against the section. *Held*, also, on the evidence that the place in question was a shop within the meaning of the section. *Held*, also, that the section does not exclude the ordinary remedies for disturbance of market. *Weedon* v. *Davidson*, 4 C.L.R., 895 ; 13 A.L.R., 87, explained. *Richardson* v. *Austin*, (1911) 12 C.L.R., 463 ; 17 A.L.R., 324. H.C., *Griffith, C.J.*, Barton and *O'Connor, JJ.*

Markets—City of Melbourne—Transfers of functions powers, &c. of Commissioners to Council—Penalty for selling marketable commodities elsewhere than in markets—3 Vict. No. 19 (N.S.W.), sec. 23—Markets Act 1890 (No. 1115), sec. 25—6 Vict. No. 7 (N.S.W.), secs. 71, 72.]—3 Vict. No. 19 (substantially re-enacted by the *Markets Act* 1890) after providing for the appointment of Commissioners of markets, by sec. 23 (sec. 25 of the *Markets Act* 1890) authorized the Commissioners to establish in certain towns, markets which should be the only places in those towns where certain goods should be sold, and enacted that any person who should sell any of those goods elsewhere than in the market places so established (except in his dwelling-house or shop), should on conviction before a Justice be liable to a penalty. 6 Vict. No. 7, which established the corporation of the Town of Melbourne and the Council thereof, by sec. 71 conferred on the Council " the same powers, authorities duties and immunities in respect of markets " as by 3 Vict. No. 19 were given to the Commissioners, and by sec. 72 transferred to the Council, from and after the election of the first Mayor, " all the functions duties and responsibilities " at that time performed by or belonging to the Commissioners under 3 Vict. No. 19, and provided that all the functions of the Commissioners should thereupon cease and determine. The Council having established markets in the City of Melbourne, *Held*, that a person who sold marketable goods elsewhere in the City than in those markets was liable to penalty under sec. 25 of the *Markets Act* 1890. *Weedon* v. *Davidson*, (1907) 4 C.L.R., 895; 13 A.L.R., 87. H.C. *Griffith*, *C.J.*, *Barton*, *O'Connor* and *Higgins*, *JJ*.

MARRIAGE; MARRIAGE ACTS.

See also, HUSBAND AND WIFE, MAINTENANCE AND MAINTENANCE ORDERS.

Marriage Act 1909 (No. 2192), secs. 2, 3 —Permission by Justice of celebration of marriage without notice — Counter-feiting signature of Justice—Intention of counterfeiter to gain advantage—Forgery.]—A permission by a Justice of the Peace under sec. 2 of the *Marriage Act* 1909 for a marriage being celebrated without notice is a document of a public nature, and may be the subject of forgery without proof of an intent to defraud. *The King* v. *Elton*, (1910) V.L.R., 1; 31 A.L.T., 98; 15 A.L.R., 596. F.C., *Madden*, *C.J.*, *Hood* and *Cussen*, *JJ*.

Infant—Intended marriage—Goods supplied — Necessaries.]—*See* INFANT, col. 687. *Quiggan* v. *Baker*, (1906) V.L.R., 259; 27 A.L.T., 174; 12 A.L.R., 168.

MARRIED WOMAN.

See also, HUSBAND AND WIFE.

Husband and wife—Marriage settlement— Restraint on anticipation—Second marriage— Revival of restraint.]—By an ante-nuptial settlement certain property of the intended wife was assigned to trustees upon trust to pay the income thereof to her for her sole and separate use independently of the intended husband (who was mentioned by name), and of his debts, control, and engagements, with a restraint upon anticipation, and after the death of the settlor to stand possessed of the trust funds and income in trust for other persons. The marriage took place, and upon the death of the husband mentioned in the settlement, the settlor married again. *Held*, that the restraint on anticipation was not confined to the life of the husband named in the settlement, but revived on the second marriage. *Stroud* v. *Edwards*, 77 L.T. N.S., 280, followed; *Re Gaffee*, 1 Mac. & G., 541, discussed. *Trustees Executors and Agency Co. Ltd.* v. *Webster*, (1907) V.L.R., 318; 28 A.L.T., 225; 13 A.L.R., 188. *Cussen*, *J*.

Declaration that woman past child-bearing.]—Declaration made that a woman in her fifty-sixth year was past child-bearing, where on her statements and their own observations, two medical practitioners stated that they were satisfied that the woman would never bear a child. *In re Lyons*; *Grant* v. *Trustees Executors &c. Co. Ltd.*, (1908) V.L.R., 190; 29 A.L.T., 202; 14 A.L.R., 147. *a'Beckett*, *J*.

Declaration that woman is past child-bearing —Circumstances in which Court will make.]— The circumstances in which the Court will declare a woman to be past child-bearing considered, and a declaration refused in the case of a woman in her forty-sixth year, though two medical practitioners stated that in their opinion it was beyond all reasonable probability that the woman would bear a child. *In re Lees*; *Lees* v. *National Trustees Co.*, (1908) V.L.R., 211; 30 A.L.T., 26; 14 A.L.R., 147. *a'Beckett*, *J*.

Married Women's Property Act 1890 (No. 1116), sec. 25—Intestates' Estates Act 1896 (No. 1419)—Married woman—Intestacy—Estate less than £1,000—No issue—Rights of husband and next of kin.]—*See* HUSBAND AND WIFE. *In re Jamieson*; *Jamieson* v. *Christensen*, 4 C.L.R., 1489; 13 A.L.R., 566.

MASTER AND SERVANT.

See EMPLOYER AND EMPLOYEE FACTORIES AND SHOPS ACTS.

MAXIMS.

Action personalis moritur cum persona—Action for personal injuries—Judgment for plaintiff—Death of plaintiff pending appeal—Survival of action to executor—Executor added as respondent to appeal.]—The plaintiff succeeded in an action in the County Court for damages for personal injuries, and judgment was entered for her. The defendant moved for a new trial which was refused, and then appealed from such refusal. Before the appeal came on for hearing the plaintiff died. *Held,* that the maxim *actio personalis moritur cum persona* did not apply, and that the plaintiff's rights under the judgment survived to her executor, who was added as a party. *Farrands* v. *Melbourne, The Mayor, &c. of City of,* (1909) V.L.R., 531. F.C., *Madden, C.J., Hodges* and *Cussen, JJ.*

Audi alteram partem.]—For a discussion of this maxim, *See In re Lotteries Gaming and Betting Act* 1906 ; *Ex parte Gleeson,* (1907) V.L.R., 368 ; 28 A.L.T., 228 ; 13 A.L.R., 146. *Cussen, J.*

Mines Act 1907 (No. 2127), secs. 9, 14—Sludge abatement—Order of Sludge Abatement Board—Order made without notice to party to be affected thereby— Whether order valid—Audi alteram partem.]—*See* MINING. *Bremner* v. *New Normanby Quartz Mining Co. N. L.,* (1910) V.L.R., 72 ; 31 A.L.T., 140 ; 16 A.L.R., 25.

Audi alteram partem—Licensing Act 1906 (No. 2068), sec. 68—Application for licence—Report of inspector upon applicant's character and suitability—Right of applicant to see and answer report.]—*See* LICENSING. *Ex parte Mellington,* 32 A.L.T., 6 ; 16 A.L.R., 247.

Audi alteram partem—Justices Act 1890 (No. 1105), secs. 94, 102—Civil debt—Order for payment—Warrant of distress—Whether defendant entitled to be heard before issue—Jurisdiction of justice.]—*See* JUSTICES. *Cross* v. *Daffy,* (1910) V.L.R., 316 ; 32 A.L.T., 10 ; 16 A.L.R., 279.

Audi alteram partem—Health Act 1890 (No. 1098), sec. 225—Noxious trade estab-lishment—Refusal of Council to register—Appeal to Board of Health—Right of appellant to be heard and to know what he has to answer.]**—*See* HEALTH (PUBLIC). *The King* v. *Prahran, Mayor &c. of* ; *Ex parte Morris,* (1910) V.L.R., 460 ; 32 A.L.T., 92 ; 16 A.L.R., 507.

Falsa demonstratio non nocet—Construction of will—Gift to a class—Misstatement of number of persons constituting class—Gift to " the child " of a niece—How gift construed.]—*See* WILL. *In re McNicol*; *Heron* v. *McNicol,* (1909) V.L.R., 311 ; 30 A.L.T., 220 ; 15 A.L.R., 308.

Nemo debet bis vexari pro una et eadem causa—Autrefois acquit—Arrest by two constables—Dismissal of charge of assaulting one constable in the execution of his duty—Whether an answer to charge of assaulting other constable in execution of his duty.]—*See* CRIMINAL LAW, cols. 363, 364. *McLiney* v. *Minster,* (1911) V.L.R., 347 ; 33 A.L.T., 33 ; 17 A.L.R., 336.

Nemo debet esse judex in propria sua causa—Extent of this rule—Nature of interest that disqualifies—Principles on which rules appointing domestic tribunals interpreted—Friendly Society.]—The rule of natural justice that no man shall be judge in his own cause applies to domestic tribunals created under the rules of Friendly Societies, unless it is expressly or by necessary implication excluded. The interest which disqualifies a man from acting must be substantial and not merely nominal. *Per O'Connor, J.*—In interpreting rules giving jurisdiction to any tribunal there must always be read into the rules the underlying statement that the proceedings of the tribunal shall be carried on in accordance with the fundamental principles of natural justice, and these principles apply unless they are expressly or impliedly excluded. *Dickason* v. *Edwards,* (1910) 10 C.L.R., 243 ; 16 A.L.R., 149. H.C. *Griffith, C.J., O'Connor* and *Isaacs, JJ.*

Omnia praesumuntur rite esse acta—Public office—Person acting in discharge of—Presumption of due appointment.]—A public officer who is proved to have acted as such is presumed to have been validly appointed, and the burden of proving the invalidity of his appointment lies on the persons alleging it. *Rex* v. *Turnbull*, (1907) V.L.R., 11 28 A.L.T., 103 ; 12 A.L.R., 551. *Cussen, J.*

Omnia praesumuntur rite esse acta—Presumption afforded by the records of transactions required by law to be kept—Proceedings at meeting of shareholders of company, validity of—Printed copy of resolution forwarded to Registrar-General—Notice of winding-up resolution—Publication in Government Gazette—Companies Act 1890 (No. 1074), secs. 54, 118.]—*See* EVIDENCE, col. 483. *McLean Brothers & Rigg Ltd.* v. *Grice*, 4 C.L.R., 835 ; 13 A.L.R., 77.

Omnia praesumuntur rite esse acta—Will—Execution of, evidence as to—Contradictory evidence of attesting witness.]—*See* EVIDENCE, cols. 482, 483. *Gair* v. *Bowers* ; *Falconar* v. *Bowers* ; *Gair* v. *Falconar*, (1909) 9 C.L.R., 510 ; 15 A.L.R., 494.

Quando lex aliquid concedit concedere videtur et illud sine quo res ipsa valere non protest.]—For the application of this doctrine in the interpretation of the Federal Constitution, *see Baxter* v. *Commissioners of Taxation* ; *Flint* v. *Webb*, 4 C.L.R., 1087, 1178 ; 13 A.L.R., 313 (1907).

MECHANICS INSTITUTE.

See LOCAL GOVERNMENT.

MEDICAL MAN ; MEDICAL ACT.

Medical Act 1890 (No. 1118), sec. 12—Justices Act 1890 (No. 1105), sec. 59—Justices Act 1904 (No. 1957), sec. 17, Third Schedule—Default summons—Claim for medical services—" Work and labour done "—" Goods sold and delivered "—" Work and labour done and materials for the same provided "—Evidence—Necessity for medical practitioner to prove registration.]—The procedure by way of " default summons " under *Justices Act* 1904, sec. 17, is applicable to a claim for " medical services " under the *Medical Act* 1890. The phrase " for medical services rendered " is equivalent to " work and labour done " or " goods sold and delivered " or " work and labour done and materials supplied." *Iredell* v. *Skinner*, (1909) V.L.R., 108 ; 30 A.L.T., 154 ; 15 A.L.R., 41. F.C., *Madden, C.J., Hood* and *Cussen, JJ.* (*Cussen, J.,* with doubt).

Medical Act 1890 (No. 1118), sec. 12—Justices Act 1890 (No. 1105), sec. 59—Justices Act 1904 (No. 1959), sec. 17, Third Schedule—Default summons—Evidence—Proof of registration of medical man, whether necessary.]—Where a defendant has given no notice of intention to defend a default summons in respect of a claim for medical services, proof by the complainant that he is duly registered under the *Medical Act* 1890 is unnecessary. *Iredell* v. *Skinner*, (1909) V.L.R., 108 ; 30 A.L.T., 154 ; 15 A.L.R., 41. F.C., *Madden, C.J., Hood* and *Cussen, JJ.* (*Cussen, J.,* expressing some doubt).

Friendly Societies Act 1890 (No. 1094), secs. 5, 11, 13—Medical Act 1890 (No. 1118), secs. 93, 97—Friendly Society—Rule providing for sale of medicines to " Purchasing Members "—Ultra vires—Unlawfully carrying on business as chemist and druggist—Sales to the public.]—*See* FRIENDLY SOCIETY, cols. 593, 594. *Shillinglaw* v. *Carroll*, 3 C.L.R., 1099 ; 12 A.L.R., 347.

Evidence Act 1890 (No. 1088), sec. 55—Evidence of physician or surgeon—Privilege—" Information acquired," what is.]—*See* EVIDENCE, col. 502. *National Mutual Life Association of Australasia Ltd.* v. *Godrich*, 10 C.L.R., 1 ; 16 A.L.R., 110.

Evidence Act 1890 (No. 1088), sec. 55—Evidence of physician or surgeon—Privilege—" Information necessary to enable him to prescribe or act for the patient "—Information acquired after prescription or at or after operation.]—*See* EVIDENCE, col. 503. *National Mutual Life Association of Australasia Ltd.* v. *Godrich*, 10 C.L.R., 1 ; 16 A.L.R., 110.

Evidence Act 1890 (No. 1088), sec. 55—Evidence of physician or surgeon—Information acquired in attending a patient outside Victoria—Whether privileged from disclosure within Victoria.]—See EVIDENCE, cols. 503, 504. *National Mutual Life Association of Australasia Ltd.* v. *Godrich*, 10 C.L.R., 1; 16 A.L.R., 110.

Evidence Act 1890 (No. 1088), sec. 55—Evidence of physician or surgeon—Information acquired in attending a patient—Privilege—Death of patient, effect of—Personal representative of patient, power of.]—See EVIDENCE, col. 503. *National Mutual Life Association of Australasia Ltd.* v. *Godrich*, 10 C.L.R., 1; 16 A.L.R., 110.

Evidence Act 1890 (No. 1088), sec. 55—Evidence of physician or surgeon—Information acquired in attending a patient—Inadvertent disclosure of—Whether Court should ignore.]—See EVIDENCE, col. 504. *National Mutual Life Association of Australasia Ltd.* v. *Godrich*, 10 C.L.R., 1; 16 A.L.R., 110.

Evidence Act 1890 (No. 1088), sec. 55—Privilege—Information acquired by medical adviser attending patient—Prohibition against disclosure, extent of.]—See EVIDENCE, col. 504. *Warnecke* v. *Equitable Life Assurance Society of the United States*, (1906) V.L.R., 482; 27 A.L.T., 236; 12 A.L.R., 254.

MELBOURNE.

See also, ELECTRIC LIGHT AND POWER ACTS.

Markets—City of Melbourne—Transfer of functions, powers, etc. of the Commissioners to Council—Penalty for selling marketable commodities elsewhere then in markets—3 Vict. No. 19 (N.S.W.), s. 23—Markets Act 1890 (No. 1115), sec. 25—6 Vict. No. 7 (N.S.W.) secs. 71, 72.]—See MARKET. *Weedon* v. *Davidson*, (1907) 4 C.L.R., 895; 13 A.L.R., 87.

Carriages Act 1890 (No. 1070), secs. 3, 4 [Licensed Carriages Statute 1864 (No. 217), secs.

3, 4]—By-law, validity of—City of Melbourne By-laws No. 78, sec. 8—Hackney carriage—Vehicle plying for hire, licensing of.]—*See* CARRIAGES ACT, cols. 92, 93. *Montgomery* v. *Gerber*, (1907) V.L.R., 428; 28 A.L.T., 230; 13 A.L.R., 219.

Licensed carriage—Negligence of driver—Liability of owner—By-law No. 78 of City of Melbourne—Regulation prohibiting owner from entrusting licensed carriage to any person except as his servant—Prima facie presumption of relation of master and servant.]—*See* CARRIAGES ACT, col. 93. *McKinnon* v. *Gange*, (1910) V.L.R., 32; 31 A.L.T., 112; 15 A.L.R., 640.

Local Government—Rates—Land " beneficially occupied in any manner whatsoever "—Wharves vested in Melbourne Harbor Trust Commissioners—Preferential right of occupancy granted by Commissioners—Melbourne and Geelong Corporation Acts Amendment Act 1863 (27 Vict. No. 178), secs. 42, 43—Melbourne Harbour Trust Act 1890 (No. 1119), secs. 62, 85.]—*See* LOCAL GOVERNMENT. *Mayor &c. of City of Melbourne* v. *Howard Smith Co. Ltd.*, (1911) 13 C.L.R., 253; 17 A.L.R., 437.

MELBOURNE AND METROPOLITAN BOARD OF WORKS.

Melbourne and Metropolitan Board of Works Act 1890 (No. 1197), secs. 79, 81, 85, 87, 88—Highway—Obstruction—Sewer constructed under highway—Shaft opening on surface of highway—Covering of shaft—Duty to keep in repair—Neglect of duty.]—By the *Melbourne and Metropolitan Board of Works Act* 1890 the Board was authorized to enter upon certain highways and to construct under them sewers and works connected therewith, and was given power to repair and maintain such sewers and works. The Board accordingly constructed a sewer under a highway with a shaft leading from the sewer to the surface of the highway. The opening was closed with an iron grid which formed part of the surface of the highway. *Held,* that the Board was under a duty to keep the grid in repair, and was liable to any person who, whilst using the highway, was injured owing to the neglect of that duty. *Chapman* v. *Fylde Waterworks Co.,* (1894) 2 Q.B., 599, followed. *Frencham* v. *Melbourne and Metropolitan Board of Works,* (1911) V.L.R., 363; 33 A.L.T., 30; 17 A.L.R., 333. F.C., *Madden, C.J., Hood* and *Cussen, JJ.*

MELBOURNE HARBOUR TRUST.

Melbourne Harbor Trust Act 1890 (No. 1119), sec. 142 (xix.)—Carter plying for hire without licence from Harbor Trust Commissioners—Regulation in prohibition thereof, how far valid—Licence from City of Melbourne.]—By sec. 142 (xix.) of the *Melbourne Harbour Trust Act* 1890, the Melbourne Harbour Trust Commissioners are empowered to make regulations " for prohibiting persons from acting as porters, carters, draymen and cabmen within the Port without previously obtaining a licence to that effect." *Semble.*—The Commissioners cannot under this sub-section make a regulation requiring all such persons to obtain licences from them, but they can require all such persons to hold licences either from some other body authorized by law to grant licences for those purposes within the Port, or else from them. *Vincent* v. *Curran,* (1909) V.L.R., 370; 31 A.L.T., 24; 15 A.L.R., 359. *Hodges, J.*

Local government—Rates—Land " beneficially occupied in any manner whatsoever "—Wharves vested in Melbourne Harbor Trust Commissioners—Preferential right of occupancy granted by Commissioners—Melbourne and Geelong Corporation Acts Amendment Act 1863 (27 Vict. No. 178), secs. 42, 43—Melbourne Harbor Trust Act 1890 (No. 1119), secs. 62, 85.]—*See* LOCAL GOVERNMENT *Mayor &c. of City of Melbourne* v. *Howard Smith Co. Ltd.,* (1911) 13 C.L.R., 253; 17 A.L.R., 437.

MENS REA.

Mens rea—Meaning of—Definition of offence created by Statute—How to be ascertained.]—*Mens rea* means no more than that the definition of all or nearly all crimes contains not only an outward and visible element, but a mental element, varying according to the different nature of different crimes. If in a section creating an offence the language is not clear as to what is the outward and visible element and what the mental element that is to enter into the offence and impose responsibility, the rest of the Statute should be examined, and the subject matter with which it deals and the character of the punishment for the offence should be considered. *Moffatt* v. *Hassett,* (1907) V.L.R., 515; 29 A.L.T., 87; 13 A.L.R., 266, *Hodges, J.* (1907).

Game Act 1890 (No. 1095), sec. 15—Wilful trespass on land—Mens rea—Honest belief.]—If A, although in fact on B's land, honestly believes that he is on Crown land, he is not guilty of wilful trespass on B.'s land. *Moffatt* v. *Hassett,* (1907) V.L.R., 515; 29 V.L.R., 87; 13 A.L.R., 266. *Hodges, J.* (1907).

Corporation—Liability for criminal offence—Mens rea.]—*See* CRIMINAL LAW., col. 346. *Rex* v. *Kellow,* (1912) V.L.R., 162; 33 A.L.T., 203; 18 A.L.R., 170.

Butchers and Abattoirs Act 1890 (No. 1069), s. 26—Slaughtering cattle without licence—Mens rea.]—*See* CRIMINAL LAW, col. 346. *Dugdale* v. *Charles Dight; Same* v. *West; Same* v. *George Dight,* (1906) V.L.R., 783; 28 A.L.T., 186; 13 A.L.R., 15.

Mens rea—Selling liquor without licence—Ignorance of nature of liquor sold, whether a defence—Licensing Act 1890 (No. 1111), sec. 182.]—*See* CRIMINAL LAW, col. 347. *Gleeson* v. *Hobson,* (1907) V.L.R., 148; 28 A.L.T., 151; 13 A.L.R., 10.

Licensing Act 1890 (No. 1111), sec. 124—Supplying liquor to person in state of intoxication—Knowledge of intoxicated state of person supplied—Whether a necessary ingredient of

offence.]—*See* LICENSING. *Davies* v. *Young*, (1910) V.L.R., 369 ; 32 A.L.T., 39 ; 16 A.L.R., 368.

Licensing Act 1890 (No. 1111), sec. 124—Licensing Act 1906 (No. 2068), sec. 73—Licensee, liability for act of servant—Supplying liquor to person in state of intoxication—Supply by servant in absence without knowedge and contrary to instructions of licensee.]—*See* LICENSING. *Davies* v. *Young*, (1910) V.L.R., 369 ; 32 A.L.T., 39 ; 16 A.L.R., 368.

Factories and Shops Act 1905 (No. 1975), sec. 119 (1)—Employing person at lower rate than rate determined by Special Board—Mens rea, whether a necessary element of offence—Employer, liability of for act of agent.]—*See* FACTORIES AND SHOPS ACT, col. 581. *Billingham* v. *Oaten*, (1911) V.L.R., 44 ; 32 A.L.T., 170 ; 17 A.L.R., 36.

Tramways Act 1890 (No. 1148), Second Schedule, Part II., clause 17—" Avoiding " payment of fare—Refusal to pay full fare—Honest belief that full fare not payable—Mens rea.]—*See* LOCAL GOVERNMENT. *Cochrane* v. *Tuthill*, (1908) V.L.R., 549 ; 30 A.L.T., 50 ; 14 A.L.R., 453.

MERGER.

Insolvency—Sequestration—Petitioning creditors' debt—Merger—Judgment debt.]—*See* INSOLVENCY, col. 703. *Bayne* v. *Blake*, (1909) 9 C.L.R., 360.

MILDURA IRRIGATION TRUSTS ACT.

Mildura Irrigation Trusts Act 1895 (No. 1409), sec. 69—Regulation—Use of water for irrigation of land without authority of Trust—Regulation imposing penalty upon person without reference to his connection with forbidden act—Power to make such a regulation.]—A regulation which purports to impose a penalty on a person without reference to his connection with an act that is forbidden by the regulation as framed, and might impose liability upon a person even though he has done his best to prevent a breach of the regulation, is invalid, unless the power of making such a regulation is exercised by Parliament, or under some enactment of Parliament whereby this exceptional power is given to a subordinate body either expressly or by necessary implication. Purporting to act under sec. 69 of the *Mildura Irrigation Trusts Act* 1895, which authorized an Irrigation Trust, *inter alia*, to make regulations for the prevention and remedying of the waste or undue consumption of water, and generally for duly administering and carrying out the provisions of the Act, the Trust made a regulation that, " If water shall be used for the irrigation of any land without the authority of the Trust, the owner or occupier of such land shall be liable in a penalty not exceeding £50." *Held*, that such regulation was *ultra vires*. *Brown* v. *Burrow*, 30 A.L.T., 102 ; 14 A.L.R., 460. *Cussen, J.* (1908).

MINING.

I.—MINING ON PRIVATE PROPERTY.

Mining—Mining lease—Consolidated lease of Crown lands and private lands—Authority to grant—Right of holder of lease to take other private lands—Mines Act 1897 (No.

1514), secs. 29, 67, 91.]—A consolidated lease comprising Crown land and private land granted under sec. 29 is a lease granted pursuant to Part I., so far as relates to the Crown land comprised in it, and pursuant to Part II., so far as relates to the private land comprised in it, and therefore, the holder of such a consolidated lease is entitled, under sec. 91, to take for mining purposes private land within the boundaries of or adjoining or abutting on the private land comprised in the consolidated lease. *Liddell* v. *Lansell*, (1912) 14 C.L.R., 668 ; 18 A.L.R., 297. H.C., *Griffith*, *C.J.*, *Barton* and *Isaacs*, JJ.

Licence to cut race—Land alienated from the Crown in fee simple on or after 29th December, 1884, what is—Lease acquired from Crown before 1884—Crown grant issued after 1884—Mines Act 1890 (No. 1120), sec. 64—Mines Act 1897 (No. 1514), sec. 44—Land Act 1869 (No. 360), secs. 19, 20.]—The expression " any land alienated from the Crown in fee simple on or after the 29th day of December 1884 " in sec. 64 of the *Mines Act* 1890 as amended by sec. 44 of the *Mines Act* 1897 includes land in respect of which a licence and a subsequent lease from the Crown had been issued under sec. 19 of the *Land Act* 1869 before the 29th of December 1884, and a Crown grant pursuant to such licence and lease had been issued after that date, and therefore a licence under those sections of the Mines Acts to construct a water race over such land might be lawfully granted by the Crown. *Hegarty* v. *Ellis*, (1908) 6 C.L.R., 264 ; 14 A.L.R., 445. H.C., *Barton*, *Isaacs* and *Higgins*, JJ.

Mines—Mineral lease—" Mineral," what is—" Bluestone "—Mines Act 1897 (No. 1514), sec. 67.]—" Bluestone " is a mineral within the definition of minerals in sec. 67 of the *Mines Act* 1897. *Cairns* v. *O'Hanlon*, 17 A.L.R. (C.N.), 6. *Judge Moule* (1911).

Mining on private property—Agreement as to amount of purchase money or compensation—Obligations running with the land—Transfer of application for mining lease—Whether transferee bound by agreement—Mines Act 1897 (No. 1514), secs. 29, 73-79, 98, 112.]—An agreement in writing made under sec. 75 of the *Mines Act* 1897 by the applicant for a lease with the owner for the payment of purchase money or compensation so far as it is to be performed in the future runs with the land apart from the operation of the Act, but it is also by the operation of the Act incorporated with the covenants of the lease itself, for the benefit of the owner and runs with the land both in favour of an assignee of the freehold and against an assignee of the lease, and where the applicant has, pursuant to sec. 112 of the Act, transferred his interest in the application the agreement is binding on the transferee. *Armstrong* v. *Duke of Wellington G. M. Co.*, *No Liability*, 3 C.L.R., 1028 ; 12 A.L.R., 316. H.C., *Griffith*, *C.J.*, *Barton* and *O'Connor*, JJ. (1906).

Mining on private property—Agreement between applicant for lease and owner—Purchase money or compensation, how to be ascertained—Future payments, nature of—Agreement to pay percentage of value of gold to be won, legality of—Mines Act 1897 (No. 1514), secs. 29, 73-79, 98, 112—Mines Act 1904 (No. 1961), sec. 37.]—An applicant for a gold mining lease on private land may under sec. 75 of the *Mines Act* 1897, agree with the owner of such land for the payment of any sum to be ascertained in any way mutually agreed upon for purchase money or compensation, and when the payment is to be made by way of future instalments, it is in the nature of rent. Such payment may be estimated by way of a percentage of the value of the gold that may thereafter be won from the mine. *Armstrong* v. *The Duke of Wellington G. M. Co. No. Liability*, 3 C.L.R., 1028 ; 12 A.L.R., 316. H.C., *Griffith*, *C.J.*, *Barton* and *O'Connor*, JJ. (1906).

Mining on private property—Agreement as to amount of purchase money or compensation—Surrender of lease from Crown and acceptance of new lease—Effect of on rights of owner under the agreement—Mines Act 1897 (No. 1514), secs. 29, 75—Mines Act 1904 (No. 1961), sec. 37.]—The rights of the owner under an agreement as to the amount of purchase money or compensation made pursuant to sec. 75 of the *Mines Act* 1897 will not be prejudiced by a surrender of the lease and the acceptance of a new lease from the Crown. *London &c. Discount Co.* v. *Drake*, 6 C.B. N.S., 798, followed. *Armstrong* v. *Duke of Wellington G. M. Co., No Liability,* 3 C.L.R., 1028 ; 12 A.L.R., 316. H.C., *Griffith, C.J.,* Barton and *O'Connor, JJ.* (1906).

Mines Act 1897 (No. 1514), sec. 75—Mining on private property—Compensation—Agreement with owner—Necessity for writing—Waiver.]—*Semble.*—Sec. 75 (2) of the *Mines Act* 1897, which provides that no agreement between the applicant for a mining lease on private property and the owner thereof as to compensation shall have any force or validity unless it is in writing signed by the parties thereto is for the benefit of the owner, and may be waived by him. *Armstrong* v. *The Duke of Wellington G. M. Co., No Liability,* (1906) V.L.R., 145 ; 27 A.L.T., 146 ; 12 A.L.R., 67. *Madden, C.J.*

Crown lease to mine on private property—Slums lying on land—Whether owner of freehold can confer right to possession for purpose of working slums for gold.]—During the currency of a Crown lease to mine on private property, the owner of the freehold agreed to allow a person other than the lessee to extract gold from heaps of slums lying on the land. *Held,* that, whether the slums remained chattels or not, the owner of the freehold had no right to give such person leave to interfere with the possession of the land for the purpose of winning gold on the surface or anywhere else. *Ebbels* v. *Rewell,* (1908) V.L.R., 261 ; 29 A.L.T., 252 ; 14 A.L.R., 121. *Hodges, J.*

Mining on private property—Crown lease to mine—Interpretation—Whether lessee entitled to possession of surface of land.]—A Crown lease to mine on private property contained a grant and demise unto the lessee his executors, administrators and assigns of " all those mines of gold and silver in and under that piece of land," which was described and delineated in a plan, and also covenants by the lessee not to use or occupy or permit to be used or occupied the said land " for other than mining purposes or for pasturage or as garden ground for the persons employed in or about the said mine " and not to transfer, underlet or part with " the possession of the said land mine and premises " without the consent of the Governor-in-Council. *Held,* that under the lease the lessee's assignee, to whom the lease had been duly transferred, was entitled to possession of the surface of the whole of the land covered by the lease. *Ebbels* v. *Rewell,* (1908) V.L.R., 261 ; 29 A.L.T., 252 ; 14 A.L.R., 121. *Holroyd, J.*

II.—CLAIMS, &c.

See also, ante, I.—MINING ON PRIVATE PROPERTY.

Actual legal possession—Disturbance of, how far permissible—Rights of true owner, how to be asserted—Person in possession of ground as a claim under prima facie title—Claim registered—Failure to observe mining by-laws.] — The principle established by *Critchley* v. *Graham,* 2 W. & W. (L.), 211 that a party in actual possession of ground as a claim, under a pretty strong *prima facie* title, is only to be disturbed by legal proceedings, applies even as against a person who claims under a registered title, and who may, in fact, be really entitled to possession, and even where the party in possession has failed to observe the by-laws. A person in possession of a quartz prospecting area and on the register in respect thereof, and who has put and has his posts thereon in a correct position, and can show that registration and manifest possession to anyone, has a pretty strong *prima facie* title. *Antony* v. *Dillon,* 15 V.L.R., 240, discussed. *Bell* v. *Clarke,* (1906) V.L.R., 567 ; 28 A.L.T., 24 ; 12 A.L.R., 308. *Cussen, J.*

Claim, title to—Claim marked out before miner's right obtained—Claim registered after miner's right obtained—Mines Act 1890 (No. 1120), secs. 4, 5—District by-laws.]—Where a quartz mining area is marked out by a person prior but registered subsequently to his obtaining a miner's right, *Quaere,* whether his previous marking out does not enure for the benefit of his subsequent registration. *Bell* v. *Clarke*, (1906) V.L.R., 567; 28 A.L.T., 24; 12 A.L.R., 308. *Cussen, J.*

By-laws—Maryborough mining district—Prospector discovering payable gold—Prospector's claim, extent of—" Other alluvial gold workings," what are—Abandoned gold workings.]—The by-laws of the Maryborough Mining district provided that the dimensions of a prospecting claim should depend upon its distance from any "other alluvial gold workings." *Held*, that workings which had been abandoned came within the meaning of the expression "other alluvial gold workings," and that it was immaterial whether such workings had been worked in conformity with the by-laws and the Mines Acts or not. *Semble.*—In order to constitute a " gold working " it is necessary that gold should have been found. *Pelletier* v. *Porter*, (1907) V.L.R., 213; 28 A.L.T., 211; 13 A.L.R., 68. *a' Beckett, J.*

Land excepted from occupation—Application by holder of miner's right—Right to mine thereon—Order in Council excepting land—Invalid order—Registrar, whether bound to obey—Mines Act 1890 (No. 1120), sec. 203—Mines Act 1897 (No. 1514), sec. 113.]—It is the duty of the Registrar of Mines to register a proper application to mine upon property under a miner's right, although such property has been, by Order-in-Council " excepted from occupation," if it is shown that such Order is invalid. The Registrar, although a ministerial officer, should not obey an invalid Order-in-Council. *In re Graham* 33 A.L.T. (Supplement), 8; 17 A.L.R. (C.N.), 21. *Judge Moule* (1911).

Mines Act 1890 (No. 1120), sec. 5—Claim Registration—Application as to land to a limited depth—Invalidity.]—The holder of a miner's right cannot obtain the registration of a claim limited to the surface of the land and a definite depth from the surface where no by-law exists prescribing a limitation as to depth. *Lansell* v. *Liddell*, 34 A.L.T. (Supplement), 3 18 A.L.R. (C.N.), 9. *Judge Moule* (1912).

III.—SLUDGE ABATEMENT.

Mines Act 1907 (No. 2127), sec. 9—Sludge Abatement Board — Order, cumulative or alternative—Validity of order.]—Sec. 9 o the *Mines Act* 1907 (No. 2127), empowers the Sludge Abatemeut Board to either order a person carrying on mining operations to refrain from doing or continuing any act or operation causing pollution to a watercourse etc., or to order him to make such provision or take such steps as the Board directs to prevent the continuance of pollution ; but it does not empower the Board to order him to refrain from doing or continuing any such act or operation, and also to make such provision or take such steps to prevent the continuance of pollution. *Semble.*—Sec. 9 of the *Mines Act* 1907 (No. 2127), only gives the Board power to order a person to refrain from doing or continuing any specific act or operation, or to order him to make any specific provision or to take any specific steps. *Bremner* v. *Victoria United Co., No Liability* ; *Goodenough* v. *Same*, (1909) V.L.R., 95 ; 30 A.L.T., 147 ; 15 A.L.R., 36. *Hodges, J.*

Sludge Abatement Board—Extent of powers —Mines Act 1909 (No. 2127), sec. 9.]—For observations as to the powers of the Sludge Abatement Board being limited to the prohibition of specific acts, *see Bremner* v. *Victoria United Co., No Liability* ; *Goodenough* v. *Same*, (1909) V.L.R., 95 ; 30 A.L.T., 147 ; 15 A.L.R., 36. *Hodges, J.*

Mines Act 1907 (No. 2127), secs. 9, 14—Sludge Abatement—Order of Sludge Abatement Board—Order made without notice to party to be affected thereby—Whether order valid—Audi alteram partem.]—Purporting to act under sec. 9 of the *Mines Act* 1907 the Sludge Abatement Board made an order requiring a mining company to make certain provisions and take certain steps to prevent the continuance of pollution or injury caused by its mining operations. This order was made by the Board without previous notice to the company. The company was duly served with the order and for a time made attempts to carry it out. Subsequently tho company was proceeded against under sec. 14 of the Act for disobedience of the order of the Board. At the hearing the company objected that the order of the Board was bad inasmuch as it was made without previous notice to the company and without giving the company an opportunity of being heard in the matter. The company was convicted. *Held*, that notice should have been given to the company before the Board made the order, which was therefore invalid, and that the conviction was accordingly bad. *Cooper v. Wandsworth District Board of Works*, 14 C.B. (N.S.), 180, followed. *Vestry of Saint James and Saint John v. Feary*, 24 Q.B.D., 703, and *Attorney-General v. Hooper*, (1893) 3 Ch., 483, distinguished. *Bremner v. New Normanby Quartz Mining Co., No Liability*, (1910) V.L.R., 72; 31 A.L.T., 140; 16 A.L.R., 25. *a'Beckett, J.*

IV.—The Conduct of Mining Operations and Rules to be Observed in.

Mines Act 1904 (No. 1961), sec. 45 (36) (37) —General rules to be observed in mines— Parts of machinery to be kept in fit condition —Temporary platform used for convenience in cleaning tank—Dangerous parts of machinery to be fenced—Machinery not in itself dangerous—Danger arising from height above the ground and not from the nature of machinery itself.]—A tank used for supplying water to a battery at the defendant's mine rested on a permanent scaffolding, which stood at the height of 25 feet on poppet legs. It was necessary that the tank should be cleaned out at intervals of several years. Rungs fastened to the poppet legs formed a permanent ladder to the top. Except the cross beams of the scaffolding there was nothing to afford a footing for a person employed in cleaning out the tank, nor was there any fencing of any kind. The plaintiff, an employee of the defendant at the mine and another employee, having been ordered to clean out the tank ascended the ladder and placed laths across the cross-beams of the scaffolding so as to form a temporary platform. The platform was formed to provide a place on which to deposit the dirt taken out

of the tank, so as to prevent it from falling on the pump which supplied the tank with water. The laths projected beyond the cross-beams, and were not nailed or fastened in any way. The plaintiff stepped on the projecting end of one of the laths which tipped up and so caused him to fall to the ground and suffer damage. *Held*, that the temporary platform did not fall within sec. 45 (36) as part of the " machinery " used for any mining purpose and required to be kept in a fit state and condition ; and that neither the cross-beams nor the temporary platform nor the tank were within the meaning of sec. 45 (37) " dangerous or exposed parts of the machinery " which had to be kept securely and safely fenced, the machinery contemplated by sub-sec. (37) being machinery which is in itself dangerous to those who come in contact with it. *Eames v Birthday Tunnel G. M. Co.*, (1906) V.L.R., 293 ; 27 A.L.T., 164 ; 12 A.L.R., 37. F.C., *a'Beckett, Hodges* and *Hood, JJ.*

Mines Act 1904 (No. 1961), sec. 45 (8)— Entrance between the bottom of working shaft and poppet head pulley wheels and all elevated platforms—Quaere, whether the word " entrance " includes surface entrance—" Poppet head " and " pulley wheels," discussion upon meaning of.]—*Fitches v. Campigli*, 12 A.L.R., (C.N.), 26. *Cussen, J.* (1906).

V.—Mining Companies.

(a) *Registration ; Management and Administration.*

Mining company—Trade name—Similarity of name—Name taken from locality of mining operations—Companies Act 1890 (No. 1074), sec. 21.]—The name of a mining company called after the locality in which it is carrying on mining operations may be sufficiently distinctive to be entitled to protection. *Quaere*, whether in sec. 21 of the *Companies Act* 1890, the words " no company " may not be read as meaning " no association " so as to extend to companies formed under Part II. of the Act, *i.e.*, for mining purposes, the prohibition against the registration of a company under a name identical with that by which a subsisting company is registered or so nearly resembling the same as in the opinion of the Registrar-General to be calculated to deceive." *Mount Balfour Copper Mines, No Liability v. Mount Balfour Mines No Liability,* (1909) V.L.R., 542; 31 A.L.T., 122; 15 A.L.R., 556. *Cussen, J.*

Transfer of Land Act 1890 (No. 1149), sec. 59—Companies Act 1890 (No. 1074), sec. 235—Mortgage by mining company—Registration, sufficiency of—Land under general law.] —Where a mining company gives a mortgage over land under the *Transfer of Land Act,* registration of the instrument under that Act is the only registration necessary in order to comply with the requirements of sec. 235 of the *Companies Act* 1890 The provision requiring registration with the Registrar-General applies only to land under the general law. *In re Transfer of Land Act; Ex parte Coronation Syndicate Gold Mining Co., No Liability,* (1911) V.L.R., 78; 32 A.L.T., 129; 17 A.L.R., 39. *F.C., a' Beckett, Hodges* and *Hood, JJ.*

Mining company—No liability company—Sale of assets by majority of shareholders—Payment to be taken in part by shares in another company in another State—Companies Act 1890 (No. 1074), Part II.]—A Victorian No Liability mining company has no authority to sell its assets by resolution of a majority of its shareholders, and take payment in part by shares in a Limited liability company to be formed in another State. *Ellison v. Ivanhoe Gold Mining Co., No Liability,* 23 V.L.R., 224; 19 A.L.T., 104; 3 A.L.R., 209, distinguished. *Manning v. Tewksbury Freehold Gold Dredging Co., No Liability,* (1908) V.L.R., 50; 29 A.L.T., 78; 13 A.L.R., 547. *Hood, J.*

(b) *Winding-up.*

(1) The Petition and Practice Relating thereto.

Petition by company to wind up another company—Sealing and verification of same—Sufficiency thereof—Companies Act 1890 (No. 1074), sec. 253.]—" In my opinion, the words ' if presented by a company ' in sec. 253 of the *Companies Act* 1890 refer to the Company proposed to be wound up and not to a company which is presenting the petition either as a creditor or shareholder." *Re The Mount Lyell Consols Mining Corporation, No Liability (No. 2),* 30 A.L.T. (Supplement), 17; 14 A.L.R. (C.N.), 41. *Judge Chomley* (1908).

Petition by company to wind up another company—Sealing and verification of same—Sufficiency thereof—Companies Act 1890 (No. 1074), secs. 252 and 253.]—A petition for winding up a mining company, under Part II. of the *Companies Act* 1890, presented by another company, is sufficiently verified if signed by the attorney of the petitioning company in that company's name and supported by an affidavit of a person who can depose to the facts set out in it. *Re The Mount Lyell Consols Mining Corporation, No Liability (No. 2),* 30 A.L.T. (Supplement), 17; 14 A.L.R. (C.N.), 41. *Judge Chomley* (1908).

Petition by company for winding up of another company—Affidavit supporting petition—Companies Act (No. 1074), secs. 252, 253—Mines Act 1890 (No. 1120), sec. 180.] It is not necessary that the person deposing to the facts set out in a petition for winding up a company should swear of his own knowledge to such facts. *Re The Mount Lyell Consols Mining Corporation, No Liability (No. 2),* 30 A.L.T. (Supplement), 17; 14 A.L.R. (C.N.), 41. *Judge Chomley* (1908).

Petition for winding up of company—Day fixed by Judge for hearing—No direction that notice be served—Companies Act (No. 1074), secs. 252, 253.]—A copy of the petition for the winding up of a company need not be served with the notice of intention to present a petition. *Re The Mount Lyell Consols Mining Corporation, No Liability (No. 2),* 30 A.L.T. (Supplement), 17; 14 A.L.R. (C.N.), 41. *Judge Chomley* (1908).

Petition for winding up of company—Day fixed by Judge for hearing—No direction that notice be served—Companies Act (No. 1074), secs. 252, 253 — Mines Act 1890 (No. 1120), sec. 180.]—Where a Judge of the Court of Mines, having before him the petitioner for the winding up of a company, and the representatives of the Company, fixes a day for the hearing of the petition, he need not order service of notice of such hearing to be made on any party. *Re the Mount Lyell Consols Mining Corporation, No Liability* (*No.* 2), 30 A.L.T. (Supplement), 17; 14 A.L.R. (C.N.), 41. *Judge Chomley* (1908).

Petition to wind up company—Notice of intention to present—Proof of—Companies Act 1890 (No. 1074), secs. 252, 253—Mines Act 1890 (No. 1120), sec. 180.]—Upon the presentation of a petition for winding up of a mining company, the Judge of the Court of Mines ordered that the petition be heard on a day fixed by him. No proof of notice of intention to present was then given, but on the day fixed for the hearing, it was proved by oral evidence that the notice was given. *Held*, that such proof was sufficient. *Re The Mount Lyell Consols Mining Corporation, No Liability,* (*No.* 2), 30 A.L.T. (Supplement), 17; 14 A.L.R. (C.N.), 41. *Judge Chomley* (1908).

Court of Mines—Petition to wind up mining company—Practice — Security for costs — Mines Act 1890 (No. 1120), sec. 180.]—Under sec. 180 of the *Mines Act* 1890, a Court of Mines has jurisdiction to deal with an application that a petitioner resident out of the jurisdiction of the Court should be required to give security for costs before proceeding with the petition. The usual practice is that security for costs is ordered to be given where the petitioner resides out of the jurisdiction of the Court, and the respondent would, if successful, have great difficulty in recovering the costs incurred by the presentation of a petition. The exception is where the petitioner is clearly a creditor of the respondent company to such an amount as to sufficiently secure all probable costs occasioned by the presentation of the petition to wind up. *Re The Mount Lyell Consols Mining Corporation, No Liability* (*No.* 2), 30 A.L.T. (Supplement), 17; 14 A.L.R. (C.N.), 40. *Judge Chomley* (1908).

Notice of intention to present a petition for the winding up of a mining company—

Service of notice—Petition not presented—Power of Court to award costs—Companies Act 1890 (No. 1074), sec. 252—Mines Act 1890 (No. 1120), secs. 179.]—Courts of Mines have jurisdiction to award costs where notice of intention to present a petition on a certain day for the winding up of a mining company has been given, although no such petition is presented. *Re The Mount Lyell Consols Mining Corporation, No Liability* (*No.* 1), 30 A.L.T. (Supplement), 13; 14 A.L.R. (C.N.), 40. *Judge Eagleson* (1908).

(2) Debts; Expenses of Administration; Priorities.

Mines Act 1897 (No. 1514), sec. 168—Mines Act 1904 (No. 1961), sec. 64—Mining company—Winding up—Assets insufficient to satisfy liabilities—Miners' wages—" Costs of administration or otherwise "—Priority of payment.]—Where a no liability mining company is being wound up, the miners are only entitled to priority of payment in respect of wages (not exceeding £50 in any individual case) for services rendered to the company during two months immediately before the commencement of the winding up, and that priority is subject to the " costs of administration or otherwise." in the winding up, as provided by the *Mines Act* 1897, sec. 168 (3). The phrase " costs of administration or otherwise " in that section means something similar to " costs of winding up." Sec. 64 (1) of the *Mines Act* 1904, relates merely to a case where a judgment creditor seizes property of a mining company which is not being wound up or has not ceased work within the meaning of sec. 168 (2) of the *Mines Act* 1897 *In re Egerton and Gordon Consolidated Gold Mines, No Liability,* (1908) V L R, 526; 30 A.L.T., 27; 14 A.L.R., 372. *Madden, C.J.*

Mines Act 1897 (No. 1514), sec. 168—Insolvency Act 1890 (No. 1102), sec. 115—Insolvency Act 1897 (No. 1513), sec. 79—Companies Act 1890 (No. 1074), secs. 250, 303—Mining Company—Assignment for benefit of creditors—Workmen's wages—Payment—Priority.]—The trustee under a deed of assignment for the benefit of creditors, made by a no liability mining company, paid in priority to other debts those due to workmen who had been in the company's employment within two months of the date of the cessation of its work, but were not in such employment at that date. *Held*, that such payments had been validly made under sec. 168 of the *Mines Act* 1897. *In re Old Jubilee Gold Mines, No Liability*, 34 A.L.T. (Supplement), 2; 18 A.L.R. (C.N.), 21. *Judge Moule* (1912).

Court of mines—Company in liquidation— Delivery up of company's property to the liquidator—Costs—Solicitor's lien—Companies Act 1890 (No. 1074), sec. 274.]—An order made under sec. 274 of the *Companies Act* 1890 for delivery up to the liquidator of any books, documents or property belonging or relating to the company in the possession of a solicitor, deprives the solicitor of his lien thereon for costs ; and the order for delivery cannot be made conditionally on the payment of or the undertaking by the liquidator to pay the soliitor's costs. *Re Mount Murphy Wolfram Co., No Liability*, 29 A.L.T. (Supplement), 19; 14 A.L.R. (C.N.), 6. *Judge Box* (1908).

(3) Distribution of Surplus Assets.

Winding-up mining company— Unclaimed dividends in liquidator's hands — Payment into Court—Costs.]—Order made for payment into Court of the amount of unclaimed dividends in the hands of the liquidator of a mining company in the course of winding-up under Part II. of the *Companies Act* 1890 after deducting therefrom the costs of the liquidator. *In re The Lyell Tharsis Mining Co., No Liability*, 29 A.L.T. (Supplement), 5 ; 13 A.L.R. (C.N.), 27. *Judge Eagleson* (1907).

Companies Act 1890 (No. 1074), Part II.— Mining companies—Company in liquidation— Proposed plan of distribution of surplus—Distribution between holders of paid up and contributing shares—Power of shareholders to make and to amend rules—Amendment providing, that all holders of shares whether paid up or contributing, entitled to share in surplus in proportion to the number of shares held, declared to be valid and not unfair to or

in breach of the contract with certain of the holders of paid up shares who were original vendors to the company and had taken the purchase money partly in cash and partly in paid up shares.]—*In re Quartz Hill Gold Mining Company, No Liability*, 27 A.L.T. (Supplement), 13 ; 12 A.L.R. (C.N.), 11. *Judge Eagleson* (1906).

MISREPRESENTATION.

See CONTRACT, FRAUD AND MISREPRESENTATION.

MISTAKE.

Trusts Act 1896 (No. 1421), sec. 11—Trustee —Power to compromise—Agreement between trustee and tenant for life—Compromise as to future liability of tenant for life for repairs— Disadvantage of the estate—Mistake of law, effect of.]—*See* TRUSTS AND TRUSTEES. *In re Tong* ; *Tong* v. *Trustees Executors &c. Co. Ltd.*, (1910) V.L.R., 110 ; 31 A.L.T., 169 ; 16 A.L.R., 87.

Probate duty—Apportionment—Tenant for life and remainderman—Mistake of law— Agreement between executors and tenant for life as to apportionment of duty based on wrong principle—Duty of executors.]—*See* DUTIES ON THE ESTATES OF DECEASED PERSONS, cols. 419, 420. *In re Staughton* ; *Oliver* v. *Staughton*, (1910) V.L.R., 415 ; 32 A.L.T., 63 ; 16 A.L.R., 443.

Insolvency—Money paid to trustee under mistake of law—Whether trustee may avail himself of such mistake in resisting demand.]— *See* INSOLVENCY, col. 723. *In re Black*, 33 A.L.T. (Supplement), 5 ; 17 A.L.R. (C.N.), 17.

Mistake—Money paid under mistake of fact —Effect of payer's neglect or misconduct— Conditions precedent to right to recover such money.]—*See* MONEY PAID TO THE USE OF ANOTHER. *Morton & Son* v. *Smith*, 34 A.L.T., 79 ; 18 A.L.R., 322.

Company—Mortgage over uncalled capital—Indenture containing recitals—Insertion by mistake—Rectification—Companies Act 1896 (No. 1482), sec. 53.]—*See* COMPANY, col. 153. *Caulfield, Elsternwick and Malvern Tramway Co.* v. *The Royal Bank of Australia Ltd.*, 33 A.L.T., 14 ; 17 A.L.R., 91.

Will—Division of residue into forty-three parts—Gift of forty-two parts—Allotment of parts to specified beneficiaries—One part unallotted—Mistake—Intestacy as to unallotted part.]—*See* WILL. *Trustees Executors and Agency Co. Ltd.* v. *Sutherland*, (1909) V.L.R., 223 ; 30 A.L.T., 182 ; 15 A.L.R., 179. *Hood, J.*

Order XXXVI.—Trial—Order made by Judge in error—Whether it may be corrected.]—*See* PRACTICE AND PLEADING. *David Syme & Co.* v. *Swinburne*, 10 C.L.R., 43 ; 16 A.L.R., 93.

Juries Act 1895 (No. 1391), sec. 4 (2)—Discharge of jury—Withdrawal of discharge.]—*See* JURY, cols. 762, 763. *David Syme & Co.* v. *Swinburne*, 10 C.L.R., 43 ; 16 A.L.R., 93.

MONEY HAD AND RECEIVED.

Supreme Court Act 1890 (No. 1142), sec. 85—Where cause of action arises—Agent outside jurisdiction—Goods improperly sold by agent—Action by principal for money had and received—Place of payment—Rule that debtor must seek out creditor.]—If an agent abroad acting for a principal within the jurisdiction deals with goods in a manner not authorized by the principal and receives the proceeds thereof and the principal, waiving the tort, sues for money had and received, the cause of action does not arise within the jurisdiction. The rule that the debtor must seek out his creditor particularly applies to cases where the question depends upon an excuse alleged for non-payment of money within a jurisdiction. *Gosman* v. *Ockerby*, (1908) V.L.R., 298 ; 29 A.L.T., 266 ; 14 A.L.R., 186. *Cussen, J.*

Customs Act 1901 (No. 6), sec. 167—Customs Tariff 1908 (No. 7), sec. 7—Duties collected under proposed Tariff—Proposed Tariff different from Tariff enacted—Payment without protest—Recovery back of money paid—Money exacted colore officii—Deposit of amount demanded under section 167 of the Customs Act 1901—Whether the only remedy —" Dispute," what is.]—*See* CUSTOMS, col. 375. *Sargood Bros.* v. *The Commonwealth*, (1910) 11 C.L.R., 258 ; 16 A.L.R., 483.

Rates—Payment without protest after due notice and demand—Rates not lawfully demandable—Money had and received.]—*See* LOCAL GOVERNMENT. *Geelong Mechanics' Institute Incorporated* v. *Geelong, Mayor &c. of*, (1907) V.L.R., 580 ; 29 A.L.T., 33 ; 13 A.L.R., 377.

Vendor and purchaser—Deposit paid to agent of vendor—Rescission of contract—Recovery of deposit from vendor—Stakeholder —Money had and received.]—*See* VENDOR AND PURCHASER. *Christie* v. *Robinson*, (1907) 4 C.L.R., 1338 ; 13 A.L.R., 288.

Deposit receipt, security by way of—Contract to supply goods to Crown—Security for due performance of contract—Deposit receipt in name of servant of the Crown procured by contractor and delivered to such servant—Contractor's account with bank overdrawn — Contract duly performed — Whether amount of deposit receipt a debt due by Crown to contractor—Money had and received—Set-off of bank's claim against contractor, whether justifiable.]—*See* BANKER AND CUSTOMER, cols. 70, 71. *The King* v. *Brown*, (1912) 14 C.L.R., 17 ; 18 A.L.R., 111.

Landlord and Tenant Act 1890 (No. 1108), secs. 81, 83—Distress for rent—Proceeds of sale—Overplus in hands of landlord's agent—Claim by tenant against landlord—Money had and received—Jurisdiction of Court of Petty Sessions.]—*See* LANDLORD AND TENANT. *Rhodes* v. *Parrott*, (1912) V.L.R., 333 ; 34 A.L.T., 90 ; 18 A.L.R., 353.

MONEY LENDERS ACT.

Money lenders—Excessive interest—Reopening transaction—" The Court may re-open the transaction ''—**Money Lenders Act 1906 (No. 2061), sec. 4.**]—The authority given to a Court to re-open a money lending transaction is discretionary. *Wilson* v. *Moss*, 8 C.L.R., 146 ; 15 A.L.R., 131. H.C. *Griffith, C.J., Barton, O'Connor* and *Isaacs, JJ.* (1909).

Money lenders—Re-opening transactions— Excessive interest — Retrospective effect— Money Lenders Act 1906 (No. 2061), sec. 4.] —The transactions which may be re-opened under section 4 may include dealings between the parties prior to the commencement of the Act if the Court is of opinion that they form part of a transaction of which the making or giving of an agreement or security after the passing of the Act is another part. *Wilson* v. *Moss*, 8 C.L.R., 146 ; 15 A.L.R., 131. H.C. *Griffith, C.J., Barton, O'Connor* and *Isaacs, JJ.* (1909).

Money lenders—Re-opening transaction— Excessive interest, what is—Res ipsa loquitur —Money Lenders Act 1906 (No. 2061), sec. 4.] —Where the rate of interest charged by a money lender upon a loan is, either originally or in the result, larger than in the opinion of the Court is fair and reasonable under the circumstances, it is excessive within the meaning of section 4 of the Act and the rate of interest may in itself be evidence that it is excessive. *Wilson* v. *Moss*, 8 C.L.R., 146 ; 15 A.L.R., 131. H.C. *Griffith, C.J., Barton, O'Connor* and *Isaacs, JJ.* (1909).

Money lender—Re-opening transaction— "Agreement or security "—Money Lenders Act 1906 (No. 2061), sec. 4.]—An action upon a promissory note is an action to enforce an agreement or security within the meaning of section 4. *Wilson* v. *Moss*, 8 C.L.R., 146 ; 15 A.L.R., 131. H.C. *Griffith, C.J., Barton, O'Connor* and *Isaacs, JJ.* (1909).

Money lender—Re-opening transaction— Excessive interest—Action to enforce agreement or security—Promissory note—Retrospective effect—Money Lenders Act 1906 (No. 2061), sec. 4.]—A money lender lent to an officer in the Victorian Public Service with a salary of £350 a year, a sum of £50 and took from the borrower a promissory note for £55 10s. payable in three months and indorsed by a third person. At the end of the three months the borrower paid £5 10s., and gave a fresh promissory note for £55 10s. This was repeated every three months until June 1904, when the borrower paid off £20 in addition to the £5 10s. then due and gave a promissory note for £33 10s. payable in three months. Thereafter at the end of each three months the borrower paid £3 10s. and gave a fresh promissory note for £33 10s. This continued until, in January 1907, after the commencement of the *Money Lenders Act* 1906, the borrower gave a promissory note for £33 10s. The money lender having brought an action in the County Court upon the last promissory note. *Held,* that from the original loan of £50 to the giving of the promissory note sued on this was one transaction. *Held,* also, that the rate of interest was excessive. *Held,* further, that any rate above £35 per cent. per annum would have been unreasonable, and that as, even assuming a rate as high as 35 per cent. to be a reasonable rate, the payments which were in fact made before the commencement of the Act would have amounted to more than the total sum of the original debt and interest at that rate, judgment should have been given for the defendant on the promissory note. *Wilson* v. *Moss,* 8 C.L.R., 146 ; 15 A.L.R., 131. H.C. *Griffith, C.J., Barton, O'Connor* and *Isaacs, JJ.* (1909).

Money Lenders Act 1906 (No. 2061), sec. 4 —Action on promissory note—Loan by money lender—Intended defence and counterclaim that interest excessive or bargain harsh and unconscionable—Mode of trial—Right to a jury.]—Where the defendant in an action brought by a money lender for the recovery of principal and interest due on a promissory note given in respect of a loan to the defendant intends to rely upon the provisions of section 4 of the *Money Lenders Act* 1906, he is, under Order XXXVI., r. 6, of the *Rules of the Supreme Court* 1906, entitled as of right to a trial of the action with a jury. *Moss* v. *Jenkins,* (1909) V.L.R., 275 ; 30 A.L.T, 206 ; 15 A.L.R., 240. *Cussen, J.*

MONEY PAID TO THE USE OF ANOTHER.

Mistake—Money paid under mistake of fact—Effect of payer's neglect or misconduct—Conditions precedent to right to recover such money.]—A person who has paid money under a mistake of fact is not entitled to recover it back where he has by neglect or misconduct placed the defendant in a worse position than if he had not been paid. In order to entitle a person to recover back money paid under a mistake of fact, the mistake must be as to a fact which, if true, could make the person paying liable to pay the money. Such mistake must be a mistake between the person paying and the person receiving the money. *Morton & Son v. Smith*, 34 A.L.T., 79 ; 18 A.L.R., 322. *Madden, C.J.* (1912).

MORTGAGOR AND MORTGAGEE.

See also, BILLS OF SALE, cols. 74 *et seq.*

I.—REGISTRATION.

Mortgage—Registration—Covenant by persons not parties guaranteeing repayment of principal—Mortgage otherwise in statutory form—Whether Registrar bound to register—Transfer of Land Act 1890 (No. 1149), secs. 113, 240.]—The Registrar of Titles is not justified in refusing to register a mortgage, otherwise in the ordinary statutory form, of land under the *Transfer of Land Act* 1890 on the ground that there is added to it a covenant by persons not parties to the mortgage guaranteeing repayment of the mortgage money. *Perpetual Executors and Trustees Association &c. Ltd. v. Hosken*, (1912) 14 C.L.R., 286 ; 18 A.L.R., 201 ; H.C. *Griffith, C.J., Barton* and *Isaacs, JJ.*

Mortgage — Registration — Contributing mortgage—Money advanced by mortgagees in unequal shares—Tenancy in common—Transfer of Land Act 1890 (No. 1149), secs. 57, 65, 113, 229, 240.]—By an instrument of mortgage a mortgagor mortgaged land under the *Transfer of Land Act* 1890 to two mortgagees. The instrument, after setting out the usual covenants, contained a number of provisos. At the end of the first proviso, which related to the postponement of the time of payment of the principal in the event of punctual payment of interest and due performance of the covenants, was a clause stating that "it is hereby agreed" that the principal sum "belongs to" the two mortgagees in unequal specified proportions. The Registrar of Titles refused to register the instrument. *Held*, that the mortgage was a mortgage to the mortgagees as several owners, that there was nothing in the Act prohibiting the registration of such a mortgage, and, therefore that the Registrar should have registered it. *Drake v. Templeton*, (1913) 16 C.L.R., 153 ; 19 A.L.R., 93. H.C. *Griffith, C.J., Barton, Isaacs* and *Duffy, JJ.*

Mortgage—Registration—Improper refusal to register—Mandamus, whether mortgagee has a remedy by—Existence of another remedy—Transfer of Land Act 1890 (No. 1149), sec. 209.]—Where the Registrar improperly refuses to register a mortgage the mortgagee has a remedy by *mandamus* to compel registration, notwithstanding that right is specifically given by the *Transfer of Land Act* 1890, section 209 to the owner or proprietor of the land to summon the Registrar to substantiate the grounds of his refusal before the Supreme Court. *Perpetual Executors and Trustees Association &c. Ltd. v. Hosken*, (1912) 14 C.L.R., 286 ; 18 A.L.R., 201. H.C. *Griffith, C.J., Barton* and *Isaacs, JJ.*

**Transfer of Land Act 1890 (No. 1149), sec. 59—Companies Act 1890 (No. 1074), sec. 235—Mortgage by mining company—Registration, sufficiency of—Land under the general law.]—*See* COMPANY, col. 153. *In re Transfer of Land Act*; *Ex parte Coronation Syndicate Gold Mining Co. No Liability*, (1911) V.L.R., 78; 32 A.L.T., 129; 17 A.L.R., 39.

II.—EQUITABLE ASSIGNMENT; GETTING IN LEGAL ESTATE.

Mortgage — Equitable security — Amount secured repaid by a stranger—Preservation of incumbrance.]—Where a mortgage is paid off by a stranger to the mortgagor and no re-conveyance is executed the mortgage may, in certain circumstances, be presumed to be kept alive in favour of the person paying off. *Butler* v. *Rice*, (1910) 2 Ch., 277, applied. The registered proprietors of certain land by deed gave X. an equitable mortgage over the land to secure repayment of moneys advanced and to be advanced by him, and in such deed covenanted to execute a legal mortgage on demand. Subsequently X., who desired to be paid off, arranged with Y. to advance the amount of such moneys and to take as security therefor a legal mortgage of such land to be executed by the registered proprietors. Y. paid the amount of such moneys to X., obtained his receipt therefor, but no assignment of his security. One of the registered proprietors, who was aware of the transaction with Y. afterwards refused to execute a legal mortgage in Y.'s favour. In a partition action, the parties to which were the registered proprietors of the above-mentioned land, Y. claimed to be an incumbrancer. *Held*, that Y. was to be deemed an equitable assignee of X.'s security and was entitled to be declared an incumbrancer. *Cuddigan* v *Poole*, 33 A.L.T., 210; 18 A.L.R., 120. *a'Beckett, J.* (1912).

Equitable incumbrance—Legal estate got in —Pendente lite.]—A legal estate may be got in by an equitable incumbrancer and may be used against persons having equitable interests although it has been got in *pendente lite*. *Crout* v. *Beissel*, (1909) V.L.R., 207; 30 A.L.T., 185; 15 A.L.R., 143. *a' Beckett, J.*

Unregistered Mortgage—Equitable incumbrance—Registration pendente lite—Transfer of Land Act 1890 (No. 1149), sec. 140.]—

Where at the date of the issue of a writ in an action for breaches of trust, one of which consists in the giving of a mortgage of trust realty to a mortgagee who has actual notice of the breach, the mortgage is unregistered, there being nothing which the Court would call fraud or which was in fact dishonest on the part of any of the persons concerned, the mortgage if registered under the *Transfer of Land Act pendente lite* will be valid. *Crout* v. *Beissel*, (1909) V.L.R., 207; 30 A.L.T., 185; 15 A.L.R., 143. *a' Beckett, J.*

III.—COVENANT TO PAY, ENFORCEMENT OF.

See also, post, IV.—FORECLOSURE.

Foreclosure—Action on covenant to pay— Alterations to premises by mortgagee—Whether an answer to action.]—The right of a mortgagee after foreclosure to bring an action on the covenant in the mortgage to pay principal and interest will not be defeated by the fact that the plaintiff has made alterations in the mortgaged premises unless the alterations are of such a character as to prejudice the right to redeem. *Robertson* v. *Fink*, (1906) V.L.R., 554; 28 A.L.T., 27; 12 A.L.R., 355. *Chomley, J.*

IV.—FORECLOSURE.

Transfer of Land Act 1890 (No. 1149), secs. 74, 89, 95, 121, 124, 129, 130, 230—Mortgage — Foreclosure — Whether after foreclosure mortgagee may sue on the covenant to pay— Extinguishment of mortgage debt.]—On foreclosure under sections 129 and 130 of the *Transfer of Land Act* 1890 the title of the mortgagee, when, pursuant to section 130, he is registered as proprietor of the mortgaged land, is, in the absence of fraud, absolute and unimpeachable, and, by reason of the provision in section 130 that the mortgagee shall be deemed a transferree of the mortgaged land, and of the other provisions in the Act defining the obligations incurred by a transferree of mortgaged land with respect to the mortgage debt, the mortgage debt is extinguished, and, therefore, no action will lie subsequently by the mortgagee upon the covenant in the mortgage to repay the mortgage debt. *In re Premier Permanent Build-*

ing Land and Investment Association; *Ex parte Lyell*, 25 V.L.R., 77; 21 A.L.T., 67; 5 A.L.R., 209, overruled. *Fink* v. *Robertson*, 4 C.L.R., 864; 13 A.L.R., 157. H.C. *Griffith, C.J.*, *Barton* and *O'Connor, JJ.*, *Higgins, J.* dissenting. (1907).

Mortgage—Reversionary interest under will—Foreclosure, remedy by.]—The mortgagee of a reversionary interest of unascertained value under a will is entitled, on default being made, to an order for foreclosure, if the parties intended that in such an event the mortgagee should have the right to immediately resort to his security. The jurisdiction to make such an order should be cautiously exercised. *In re Mallett*; *Colonial Mutual &c. Society Ltd.* v. *Mallett*, (1907) V.L.R., 655; 29 A.L.T., 74; 13 A L.R., 545. *a' Beckett, J.*

Rules of High Court 1911 (Consolidated), Part 1, Order XIV.—Practice—Action for account of mortgage and foreclosure—Summary order.]—Where a writ has been indorsed with a claim for an account of the money owing on a mortgage and for foreclosure, the plaintiff is not entitled on an application under the *Rules of the High Court* 1911, Part I., Order XIV. to an order for foreclosure. *Dalgety & Co. Ltd.* v. *Brown*, 24 V.L.R., 161; 20 A.L.T., 45; 4 A.L.R., 170, commented on. *Riggall* v. *Muirhead*, (1911) 13 C.L.R., 436. *Higgins, J.*

Practice—Foreclosure action—Default of appearance—Equitable mortgage — Allegation of amount due in statement of claim—Claim for accounts—Declaration that account be deemed to have been taken and settled at the amount alleged—No reference to Chief Clerk.]—In an action for foreclosure of an equitable mortgage of land under the *Transfer of Land Act* 1890 the amount due under the mortgage at the issue of the writ was stated in the statement of claim. There was a claim for accounts if and so far as necessary. On motion for judgment in default of appearance it was ordered and declared that the account sought for in the statement of claim should be deemed to have been taken and settled by the Court at the

amount therein alleged without reference to the Chief Clerk. *Beath* v. *Armstrong*, 16 A.L.R., 581. *Cussen, J.* (1910).

V.—SALE, POWER OF; APPORTIONMENT OF PROCEEDS.

Mortgage—Sale by mortgagee—Duty of mortgagee to have regard to interests of mortgagor—Auction sale—Advertisements, sufficiency of.]—A mortgagee in exercising the power of sale conferred upon him by the mortgage, not being at liberty to disregard the interests of the mortgagor, is bound, before selling, either by auction or privately, to ascertain the value of the mortgaged property, and, if the sale is by auction, so far as the circumstances will permit, to give notice of the sale of such a nature, both as to particulars given and as to the places in which, and the modes by which, it is given, as is likely to bring the property to the notice of likely buyers, and so to induce such competition as will be likely to secure a fair price. The omission from such a notice of such statements as are plainly and obviously necessary in order to enable the particular land to be identified by those invited to buy it, renders the mortgagee liable for any loss occasioned by such omission. *Kennedy* v. *De Trafford*, (1897) A.C., 180, and *Barns* v. *Queensland National Bank*, 3 C.L.R., 925, followed. *Pendlebury* v. *Colonial Mutual &c. Society Ltd.*, (1912) 13 C.L.R., 676; 18 A.L.R., 124. H.C. *Griffith, C.J.*, *Barton* and *Isaacs, JJ.*

Mortgagor and mortgagee—Sale by mortgagee—Disregard of interest of mortgagor—Liability of mortgagee—Account on basis of wilful default.]—*Held*, on the evidence, that a mortgagee, who had sold the mortgaged land by auction, had entirely disregarded the interests of the mortgagor, and *Held*, further, that the mortgagee was responsible to the same extent as a party who is liable for wilful default, and that he was therefore liable to account to the mortgagor for the amount which would have been realised on a sale of the property conducted without such wilful default. *Pendlebury* v. *Colonial Mutual &c. Society Ltd.*, (1912) 13 C.L.R., 676; 18

A.L.R., 124. H.C., *Griffith, C.J., Barton* and *Isaacs, JJ.*

Mortgagor and mortgagee—Recovery of money secured by mortgagee barred by determination of period of limitation—Mortgagee in possession—Power of sale, whether exercise of also barred—Real Property Act 1890 (No. 1136), secs. 18, 43, 47—Transfer of Land Act 1890 (No. 1149), secs. 114, 116.]—A mortgagee's power of sale under the *Transfer of Land Act* 1890, where he has entered into possession of the mortgaged land, and is in receipt of the rents and profits thereof, is not affected by reason only that his right to recover by action or suit the money secured by the mortgage is barred by sec. 47 of the *Real Property Act* 1890. *In re The Australian Deposit and Mortgage Bank Ltd.*, (1907) V.L.R., 348; 28 A.L.T., 192; 13 A.L.R., 132. F.C., *Madden, C.J., Hodges* and *Hood, JJ.*

Real Property Act 1890 (No. 1136), sec. 47—" Other proceeding," meaning of—Mortgagee's power of sale.]—The " other proceeding " mentioned in sec. 47 of the *Real Property Act* 1890 is *ejusdem generis* with " action or suit " and does not include the exercise of a mortgagee's power of sale. *In re The Australian Deposit and Mortgage Bank Ltd.*, (1907) V.L.R., 348; 28 A.L.T., 192; 13 A.L.R., 132. F.C., *Madden, C.J., Hodges* and *Hood. JJ.*

Mortgagor and mortgagee—Real Property Act 1890 (No. 1136), secs. 18, 43, 47—Exercise of power of sale—Whether barred by expiration of period of limitation.]—Section 43 of the *Real Property Act* 1890 is to be read with section 18 and not with section 47. *Ex parte The Australian Deposit and Mortgage Bank Ltd.*, (1907) V.L.R., 348; 28 A.L.T., 192; 13 A.L.R., 132. F.C. *Madden, C.J., Hodges* and *Hood, JJ.*

Tenant for life and remainderman—Apportionment, basis of—Mortgage effected by testator—Trustee authorized to invest on similar securities—Proceeds of sale of mortgaged property insufficient to pay principal and interest.]—*See* TENANT FOR LIFE AND REMAINDERMAN.

Holmes v. *Holmes*, 28 A.L.T., 22 ; 12 A.L.R., 409.

Tenant for life and remainderman—Trust funds invested upon mortgage—Proceeds of sale of mortgaged property insufficient to pay principal and interest due—Apportionment of proceeds—Rate of interest.]—*See* TENANT FOR LIFE AND REMAINDERMAN. *Holmes* v. *Holmes*, 28 A.L.T., 22 ; 12 A.L.R., 409.

Trustee and cestui que trust—Tenant for life and remainderman—Investment on mortgage—Apportionment of proceeds of realization—Interest on cost of sewerage—Rate of interest upon mortgage—Commission on proceeds of realization.]—*See* TRUSTS AND TRUSTEES. *Macartney* v. *Macartney*, 33 A.L.T., 183 ; 18 A.L.R., 1.

VI.—OTHER MATTERS.

Life assurance—Equitable mortgage of policy—Evidence—Pleading—Amendment to raise new case.]—In an action against the widow, who was also the executrix of A., to enforce an equitable mortgage of a policy of life assurance which had been effected by A. on his own life, and legally transferred to the defendant, and then deposited by A. with the plaintiffs as security for his indebtedness to them, the pleadings raised a case of mortgage of the policy by the defendant acting through A. as her agent. The Court of first instance found that her authority to A. to make the mortgage was not proved. On appeal to the High Court, *Held*, that the finding was supported by the evidence, and that the plaintiffs should not be allowed to amend their pleadings so as to raise a case of a mortgage by A., anterior to, and having priority over the transfer to the defendant. *Trengrouse & Co.* v. *Story*, (1908) 6 C.L.R., 10 ; 14 A.L.R., 420. H.C. *Griffith, C.J., O'Connor* and *Higgins, JJ.*

Contract — Interpretation — Agreement to deposit time payment agreements as security —Depositor allowed to collect debts due— Deposit of additional time payment agreements equal in value to those discharged by payment—Equitable assignment—Book Debts Act 1896 (No. 1424), secs. 2, 3—Non-registra-

tion.]—*See* Contract or Agreement, cols. 203, 204. *In re Jones*, (1906) V.L.R., 432 ; 27 A.L.T., 230 ; 12 A.L.R., 279.

Instruments Act 1890 (No. 1103), secs. 169, 170, 171—Stock mortgage—" Other chattels," meaning of.]—*See* Instruments Acts, col. 736. *International Harvester Co. of America* v. *Rowe*, (1909) V.L.R., 244 ; 30 A.L.T., 201 ; 15 A.L.R., 212.

Company — Mortgage — Over uncalled capital—Indenture containing recitals—Insertion by mistake—Rectification—Companies Act 1896 (No. 1482), sec. 53.]—*See* Company, col. 153. *Caulfield, Elsternwick and Malvern Tramway Co.* v. *The Royal Bank of Australia Ltd.*, 33 A.L.T., 14 ; 17 A.L.R., 91.

Stamps Act 1890 (No. 1140), sec. 81, Third Schedule—Stamps Act 1892 (No. 1274), Schedule — " Promissory note " — Mortgage debenture charging property and providing means for enforcement of security.]—*See* Stamps Acts. *In re Stamps Acts*, (1906) V.L.R., 364 ; 27 A.L.T., 204 ; 12 A.L.R., 186.

Trustee—Bringing land under transfer of Land Act 1890—Mortgage of trust estate to pay costs of—Breach of trust.]—*See* Trusts and Trustees. *Crout* v. *Beissel*, (1909) V.L.R., 207 ; 30 A.L.T., 185 ; 15 A.L.R., 143.

Trusts Act 1890 (No. 1150), sec. 17—Trustee dying without next of kin—Vesting order subject to mortgage.]—*See* Trusts and Trustees. *In re Vance* ; *Ex parte Carr*, (1906) V.L.R., 664 ; 28 A.L.T., 62 ; 12 A.L.R., 439.

MOTIVE.

Motive—Intention—Fraudulent preference with a view to prefer—Disposition made to carry out legal obligation.]—*See* Insolvency, cols. 710, 711. *Muntz* v. *Smail*, 8 A.L.R., 262 ; 15 A.L.R., 162.

MOTOR CAR ACT.

Motor Car Act 1909 (No. 2237), sec. 10—Reckless driving—" Recklessly," meaning of.]—The offence of " recklessly " driving a motor car within the meaning of section 10 (1) of the *Motor Car Act* 1909 does not necessarily involve high speed or circumstances amounting to gross negligence. Indifference to consequences in such circumstances that substantial harm may happen to another person using the road is the essential element of the offence. *Kane* v. *Dureau*, (1911) V.L.R., 293 ; 33 A.L.T., 15 ; 17 A.L.R., 277. *Cussen, J.*

Motor Car Act 1909 (No. 2237), sec. 14—Obligation of motor car driver to supply information, nature of.]—Section 14 of the *Motor Car Act* 1909 is mandatory in its nature, and in the case of an accident casts a positive obligation on the driver of the motor car to give all the information required by such section, although no request for such information has been made by any of the persons to whom the section directs it to be given. *Hyde* v. *O'Reilly*, 16 A.L.R. (C.N.), 12. *Judge Box* (1910).

Motor car—Rule of the road—" Driving on the wrong side of the road without justifiable cause "—Motor car and tram car proceeding in same direction—Duty of motor car to pass on off side—" Vehicle "—Validity of regulation—Motor Car Act 1909 (No. 2237), sec. 15—Motor Car Regulations, reg. 2 (3)—Police Offences Act 1890 (No. 1126), sec. 17 (1) (a)—Police Offences Act 1891 (No. 1241), sec. 5.]—*See* Police Offences Acts. *Gillin* v. *Malmgren*, (1912) V.L.R., 26 ; 33 A.L.T., 118 ; 17 A.L.R., 564.

MURDER.

See CRIMINAL LAW.

NATAL.

See FUGITIVE OFFENDERS.

NATURALIZATION.

The Aliens Statute 1865 (No. 256)—Letters of naturalization issued under, effect of.]—For a discussion on the extra-territorial effect of naturalization under a Victorian law, *see Ah Sheung* v. *Lindberg*, (1906) V.L.R., 323 ; 27 A.L.T., 189 ; *sub nom. Rex* v. *Ah Sheung*, 12 A.L.R., 190. *Cussen, J.* (1906).

Immigration Restriction Acts 1901-1905— " Immigrant," meaning of—Naturalized subject domiciled in Victoria—Return to Victoria from China.]—*See* IMMIGRATION RESTRICTION ACTS, col. 670. *Ah Sheung* v. *Lindberg*, (1906) V.L.R., 323 ; 27 A.L.T., 189 ; *sub nom. Rex* v. *Ah Sheung*, 12 A.L.R., 190.

Licensing—British subject—Licensing Act 1890 (No. 1111), sec. 177—Aliens Act 1890 (No. 1063), sec. 6—Naturalization Act 1903 (No. 11 of 1903), secs. 9, 10.]—*See* LICENSING. cols. 822, 823. *In re Hall*, 18 A.L.R. (C.N.), 20.

NEGLECTED CHILDREN'S ACT.

Justices Act 1890 (No. 1105), sec. 141— Order to review—Order which may be reviewed what is—Order remanding accused to custody —Remand not for convenience of hearing but for another purpose—Neglected Children's Act 1890 (No. 1121), secs. 18, 19—Children's Court Act 1906 (No. 2058).]—*See* JUSTICES OF THE PEACE, cols. 797, 798. *McSweeney* v. *Haggar*, (1911) V.L.R., 130 ; 32 A.L.T., 194 ; 17 A.L.R., 70.

NEGLIGENCE.

I.—GENERALLY.

Negligence—Proximate cause of damage the malicious act of third party—Liability in respect of.]—To sustain an action for negligence it must be shown that the negligence found by the jury is the proximate cause of the damage. Where the proximate cause is the malicious act of a third party against which precautions would have been inoperative, the defendant is not liable in the absence of a finding either that he instigated it or that he ought to have foreseen and provided against it. *Rickards* v. *Lothian*, (1913) A.C., 263 ; 19 A.L.R., 105 Privy Council.

Processes of nature—Natural user of land —Injury arising from combined effect of.]— Injury arising from the combined effect of the processes of nature and the natural user of property does not give rise to an actionable wrong. *Glenelg, Shire of* v. *Grills* ; *Matheson* v. *Grills*, (1907) V.L.R., 673 ; 29 A.L.T., 67 ; 13 A.L.R., 550. F.C. *a' Beckett, Hood* and *Cussen, JJ.*

II.—BURDEN OF PROOF.

Negligence—Evidence equally consistent with negligence of either party—Whether case to be left to jury.]—In an action for negligence where the evidence called for the plaintiff is equally consistent with the wrong complained of having been caused by the negligence of the plaintiff and with its having been caused by the negligence of the defendant, the case should not be left to the jury. *Fraser* v. *Victorian Railways Commissioners*, (1909) 8 C.L.R., 54 ; 15 A.L.R., 93. H.C.

Negligence — Railway Crossing—Accident due to negligence of plaintiff or defendant— Evidence consistent with either view.]—In an action in the County Court by the representative of a man, who had been killed by a train at a railway crossing, against the Victorian Railways Commissioners alleging that the death of the deceased had been caused by the negligence of the defendants, at the close of the plaintiff's case the plaintiff was non-suited. *Held*, that the evidence being equally consistent with the death of the deceased having been caused by the omission

of the engine driver to sound a whistle, and
with its having been caused by the negligence
of the deceased in that he did not look, or
if he did look, voluntarily undertook the
risk of crossing, the plaintiff was properly
non-suited. *Wakelin* v. *London and South
Western Railway Co.*, 12 App. Cas., 41,
applied. *Dublin. Wicklow and Wexford Railway Co.* v. *Slattery*, 3 App. Cas., 1155;
Smith v. *South Eastern Railway Co.*, (1896)
1 Q.B., 178, and *Toronto Railway Co.* v.
King, (1908) A.C., 260, distinguished.
Fraser v. *The Victorian Railways Commissioners*, (1909) 8 C.L.R., 54; 15 A.L.R., 93.
H.C., *Griffith, C.J., Barton* and *O'Connor,
JJ.* (*Isaacs, J.*, dissenting).

III.—WATER; FIRE.

**Negligence—Overflow of water from lava-
tory in upper floor—Malicious act of third
party—Liability in respect of.**]—In an action
for damages to property located on the
second floor of a building leased to the
plaintiff by the defendant, through a continuous overflow of water from a lavatory
basin on the top floor caused by the water-
tap having been turned on full and the waste
pipe plugged, the jury found that " this was
the malicious act of some person." *Held*,
(1) that the defendant was not responsible
unless either he instigated the act or the jury
had found that he ought reasonably to have
prevented it; (2) that his having on his
premises a proper and reasonable supply
of water was an ordinary and proper use of
his house, and that although he was bound
to exercise all reasonable care he was not
responsible for damage not due to his own
default, whether caused by inevitable accident or the wrongful acts of third parties.
Rylands v. *Fletcher*, L.R. 3 H.L., 330,
distinguished. *Rickards* v. *Lothian*, (1913)
A.C., 263; 19 A.L.R., 105. Privy Council.

**Water—Natural user of land—Dividing
fence and hedge—Bed of creek filled up by
processes of nature—Consequent overflow of
water of creek—Water deflected by hedge
and fence on to land of another.**]—A. and B.
were adjoining owners, A.'s land forming the
northern boundary of B.'s land. A creek

ran in a southerly direction through A.'s
and B.'s land. A post and rail fence had
been erected along B.'s northern boundary
and a hedge grown. The fence and hedge
did not in any way obstruct the bed of the
creek. Many years after the erection of the
fence, and the growth of the hedge the creek
silted up and, as a result, in times of flood,
the water overflowed its banks at a point
in A.'s land and flowed southerly till it came
to the hedge and fence on B.'s northern
boundary, and there in course of time a
bank of silt was formed which prevented the
water flowing on to B.'s land, and diverted its
flow in a westerly direction on to the road
of the plaintiff Shire and the land of the
plaintiff Matheson. The plaintiffs brought
an action for damages and for an injunction
for the removal of the hedge and fence.
Held (*per a'Beckett* and *Cussen, JJ., Hood,
J.*, dissenting on the facts), that the erection
of the fence and the growth of the hedge
in the first place was a natural user of the
land and that the subsequent deflection by
the hedge and fence of flood water on to the
plaintiffs' land did not give the plaintiffs a
right of action. *Glenelg, Shire of* v. *Grills;
Matheson* v. *Grills*, (1907) V.L.R., 673; 29
A.L.T., 67; 13 A.L.R., 550.

**Railway—Water—Railway embankment—
Flood water blocked—Diversion of water—
Damage to adjoining land—Board of land
and Works—Constructing authority—Exercise of statutory powers—Subsequent vesting
in Railways Commissioners—Negligence—
Railways Act 1891 (No. 1250), secs. 4, 5.**]—
The *Railways Act* 1891, sec. 4, provides that
the Board of Land and Works shall construct
and complete all lines of railway which Parliament may hereafter authorise to be constructed. Sec. 5 provides that when a
railway line is completed it is to be transferred to the Victorian Railways Commissioners, and when transferred shall vest in
them and shall be supervised and maintained
by them and all further powers duty authority or responsibility of the Board in regard
to such line shall cease the settlement of
past contracts alone excepted. The Board
under statutory authority constructed a rail-

way line in a district subject to occasional floods from the River Murray. The line when completed was duly transferred to and vested in the Commissioners, in pursuance of the above-mentioned Act. The plaintiff suffered damage by reason of flood waters from the Murray being obstructed by the railway embankment, and thus diverted on to his land. The diversion of the flood waters and the consequent damage could not have been avoided except by a radical alteration in the construction of the line. *Held*, in an action against the Commissioners for damages for the flooding, that the defendants were not liable. *Bourchier v. Victorian Railways Commissioners*, (1910) V.L.R., 385 ; 32 A.L.T., 48 ; 16 A.L.R., 396. F.C., *a' Beckett, Hodges* and *Cussen, JJ.* (1910).

Railways—Damages by sparks—Fire on land between railway fences—Occupation by licence—Reservation of control by Railways Commissioners—Negligence—Omission to burn off grass.]—By an agreement with the Victorian Railways Commissioners A. was allowed permission to use certain land between the Commissioners' railway fences for grazing purposes at reasonable times and under the control of the officer of the Commissioners in charge of the section of the railway line in which such land was situated, and A. agreed to take every precaution to prevent the spreading of fire on the land, and also to allow the Commissioners by their officers or servants to enter upon the land and burn off the grass should they consider it necessary. *Held*, that the agreement did not relieve the Commissioners from the liability which, according to *Dennis v. Victorian Railways Commissioners*, 28 V.L.R., 576 ; 24 A.L.T., 196 ; 9 A.L.R., 69, attaches to them for damages arising from their negligent omission to burn or clear off grass naturally growing within their railway fences with the result that sparks from a railway engine set fire to such grass, and the fire spread to adjoining land. *Victorian Railways Commissioners v. Campbell*, 4 C.L.R., 1446 ; 13 A.L.R., 403. H.C., *Griffith, C.J., Barton, Isaacs* and *Higgins, JJ.* (1907).

IV.—HIGHWAYS ; RAILWAYS.

See also, ante, III.—WATER ; FIRE.

Highway—Open drain lawfully constructed by municipal authority—Liability of municipal authority—Damages, whether too remote—Wandering horse entering drain at shallow part and walking along drain to deep part—Horse unable to extricate itself.]—In a portion of a street which was a *cul de sac* and was not much used for traffic the municipal authority constructed an open drain with sloping sides which was about four feet deep at the deepest part where an underground pipe discharged into it the drainage from another part of the road, and ran out to a shallow depression at the other end. The drain was fifteen inches wide at the bottom, and at the deepest part was about five feet wide at the top. The plaintiff's horse, having escaped from a paddock, wandered to this street, entered the drain at its shallow end, walked up it to the deepest part, and, not being able to get any further or to turn round and return by the way it came, injured itself in its efforts to extricate itself, and died soon after being extricated. The deepest part of the drain was protected to a certain extent by fences, but the lower end was not fenced across. In an action by the plaintiff against the municipal authority to recover damages. *Held*, that the municipal authority was not shown to have been guilty of any breach of duty, and that even if it were the injury did not arise in consequence of that breach. *Benalla, President, &c. of v. Cherry*, (1911) 12 C.L.R., 642 ; 17 A.L.R., 537. H.C., *Griffith, C.J., Barton* and *O'Connor, JJ.*

Highway—Open drain lawfully constructed for purpose of draining highway—Liability of municipal authority, nature and extent of.] The duty of a municipal authority which has lawfully constructed an open drain on a highway for the purpose of draining it is only to guard against injuries which may be reasonably anticipated as likely to arise from its condition and that duty is towards persons and owners of animals using the highway for the ordinary purposes of a highway. *Benalla, President, &c. of v. Cherry*, (1911)

12 C.L.R., 642; 17 A.L.R., 537. H.C.,
Griffith, C.J., Barton and *O'Connor, JJ.*

Melbourne and Metropolitan Board of Works Act 1890 (No. 1197), secs. 79, 81, 85, 87, 88—Highway—Obstruction—Sewer constructed under highway—Shaft opening on surface of highway—Covering of shaft—Duty to keep in repair—Neglect of duty.]—By the *Melbourne and Metroploitan Board of Works Act* 1890 the Board was authorized to enter upon certain highways, and to construct under them sewers and works connected therewith, and was given power to repair and maintain such sewers and works. The Board accordingly constructed a sewer under a highway with a shaft leading from the sewer to the surface of the highway. The opening was closed with an iron grid which formed part of the surface of the highway. *Held,* that the Board was under a duty to keep the grid in repair, and was liable to any person who, whilst using the highway, was injured owing to that neglect of duty. *Chapman v. Fylde Waterworks Co.,* (1894) 2 Q.B., 599, followed. *Frencham v. Melbourne and Metropolitan Board of Works,* (1911) V.L.R., 363; 33 A.L.T., 30; 17 A.L.R., 333. F.C., *Madden, C.J., Hood* and *Cussen, JJ.*

Negligence — Railway — Level crossing—Duty of persons crossing and of owners of railway respectively.]—Where a railway crosses a road at a level crossing without gates and an approaching train is visible from all material positions to persons about to pass over the crossing, it is the duty of the owners of the railway to take reasonable precautions to prevent such persons from being injured by trains. It is equally the duty of such persons to look for approaching trains, and they are not excused from looking by the omission of precautions on the part of the owners of the railway. *Fraser v. Victorian Railways Commissioners,* (1909) 8 C.L.R., 54; 15 A.L.R., 93. H.C.

V.—MINES.

Mines Act 1904 (No. 1961), sec. 45 (36), (37)—General rules to be observed in mines—Parts of machinery to be kept in fit condition— Temporary platform used for convenience in cleaning tank—Dangerous parts of machinery to be fenced—Machinery not in itself dangerous—Danger arising from height above the ground and not from the nature of machinery itself.]—A tank used for supplying water to a battery at the defendant's mine rested on a permanent scaffolding which stood at the height of 25 feet on poppet legs. It was necessary that the tank should be cleaned out at intervals of several years. Rungs fastened to the poppet legs formed a permanent ladder to the top. Except the cross-beams of the scaffolding there was nothing to afford a footing for a person employed in cleaning out the tank, nor was there any fencing of any kind. The plaintiff, an employee of the defendant at the mine, and another employee, having been ordered to clean out the tank, ascended the ladder and placed laths across the cross-beams of the scaffolding so as to form a temporary platform. The platform was formed to provide a place on which to deposit the dirt taken out of the tank, so as to prevent it from falling on the pump which supplied the tank with water. The laths projected beyond the cross-beams, and were not nailed or fastened in any way. The plaintiff stepped on the projecting end of one of the laths which tipped up and so caused him to fall to the ground and suffer damage. *Held,* that the temporary platform did not fall within sec. 45 (36) as part of the "machinery" used for any mining purpose and required to be kept in a fit state and condition; and that neither the cross-beams nor the temporary platform nor the tank were within the meaning of sec. 45 (37) "dangerous or exposed parts of the machinery" which had to be kept securely and safely fenced, the machinery contemplated by sub-sec. 37 being machinery which is in itself dangerous to those who come in contact with it. *Eames v. Birthday Tunnel G. M. Co.,* (1906) V.L.R., 293; 27 A.L.T., 164; 12 A.L.R., 37. F.C., *a'Beckett, Hodges* and *Hood, JJ.*

VI.—ANIMALS.

Agister— Negligence — Liability — Horse placed among horned cattle—Horse injured by

bull—Scienter.]—An agister for reward of a horse, who had put the horse in a paddock where there were a bull and cows, was held liable in damages for injuries caused by the bull to the horse, though the agister did not know the bull was of a mischievous disposition. *Sanderson* v. *Dunn*, 32 A.L.T. (Supplement), 14 ; 17 A.L.R. (C.N.), 9. *Judge Box* (1911).

VII.—EMPLOYER AND EMPLOYEE.

Negligence—Employer and employee—Evidence—Employers and Employees Act 1890 (No. 1087), sec. 38.]—Sec. 38 of the *Employers and Employees Act* 1890 provides that where personal injury is caused to a workman (*inter alia*) :—" (2) by reason of the negligence of any person in the service of the employer who has any superintendence entrusted to him whilst in the exercise of such superintendence ; or (3) by reason of the negligence of any person in the service of the employer to whose orders or directions the workman at the time of the injury was bound to conform and did conform, where such injury resulted from his having so conformed ; or (4) by reason of the act or omission of any person in the service of the employer done or made . . . in obedience to particular instructions given by any person delegated with the authority of the employer in that behalf " the workman or his representative " shall have the same right of compensation and remedies against the employer as if the workman had not been a workman of or not in the service of the employer nor engaged in his work." In an action under that section by the representative of a man who was killed by the explosion of a charge during blasting operations at a quarry. *Held*, on the evidence, *per Griffith, C.J.* and *Barton, J.* (*Isaacs, J.*, dissenting), that the plaintiff was properly nonsuited. *Footscray Quarries Proprietary Ltd.* v. *Nicholls*, (1912) 14 C.L.R., 321.

VIII.—BANKER AND CUSTOMER.

Banker and customer—Cheques drawn with spaces afterwards fraudulently filled up—Liability of Bank—Duty of customer—Negligence.]—The mere fact that a cheque is drawn with spaces which can be utilised for the purpose of fraudulent alteration, is not by itself any violation of duty by the customer to his banker. Five cheques were drawn on the defendant bank by the two plaintiffs and defendant M. to the debit of their joint account. After they were signed by the plaintiffs M. enhanced their apparent amounts by adding words and figures in the blank spaces to the left of those originally written. In a suit to recover the balance of account, the bank claimed to debit it with the enhanced amounts of the cheques, and the jury found that the bank could not, by the exercise of ordinary care and caution, have avoided paying the cheques as altered, and that the cheques were drawn by the plaintiffs in neglect of their duty to the bank. *Held*, that there was no evidence of negligence on the part of the respondents proper to be left to the jury. *Scholfield* v. *Londesborough*, (1896) A.C., 514, followed. *Colonial Bank of Australasia* v. *Marshall*, (1906) A.C., 559. Privy Council.

IX.—LEGAL PROCEEDINGS.

(a) *Notice of Accident ; Conditions of Right of Action.*

Local Government Act 1903 (No. 1893), sec. 708—Notice of injury—Sufficiency—Place at which the accident took place—" Bridge "—" Approach."]—Plaintiff wrote to the defendant municipality calling attention to the bad state of the " approach " to a certain " culvert," and stating that in the " approach " to such " culvert " there was a dangerous hole which had caused his horse to fall and suffer injury. The " culvert " was a wooden bridge 135 feet in length, built on piles and passing over a creek 63 feet wide and having at each end a short inclined macadamised roadway leading up to it. The evidence at the trial showed that the hole in question was in the wooden decking of the bridge or culvert at a spot about 5 feet from the macadamised roadway at one end, and not in that part of the structure which actually spanned the stream. *Held*, that the notice of injury did not comply with sec. 708 (1) of the *Local Government Act* 1903 in that it did not state " the place at which " the accident took place. *Daniel* v. *Benalla, President, &c. of Shire of,* (1906) V.L.R., 101 ; 27 A.L.T., 141 ; 12 A.L.R., 16. F.C., *Madden, C.J., Holroyd* and *Hodges, JJ.*

Local Government Act 1903 (No. 1893), sec. 708—Notice of accident, failure to give— " Sufficient reason why the person injured . . . was unable to give such notice "— Evidence to show, nature of—Ignorance of the law.]—Where the notice required by sec. 708 of the *Local Government Act* 1903 has not been given within the prescribed time by a person who seeks to recover damages from a municipality for injuries sustained by reason of an accident on a highway, he shows " sufficient reason why the person injured . . . was unable to give such notice " if he shows that under the circumstances there were preventing causes which afforded sufficient reason for omitting to give the notice although it might have been possible for him to have given it. *Per Hodges, J.*—A mental and bodily condition which makes it dangerous or even substantially injurious for the person injured to give the notice, or which makes him oblivious of business matters altogether, or which makes him really unfit to give the notice, may render him " unable " within the meaning of the Statute. *Per Cussen, J.*—A plaintiff may show sufficient reason why the person injured was unable to give the notice required, although it could not be said absolutely that in the circumstances and at all times he could not possibly have given the notice or caused it to be given. *Quaere,* whether ignorance of the necessity for giving the notice would be a sufficient reason for inability to give it. *Leeder* v. *Ballarat East, Mayor, &c., of,* (1908) V.L.R., 214 ; 29 A.L.T., 192 ; 14 A.L.R., 124. F.C., *a' Beckett, Hodges* and *Cussen, JJ.* (1908).

Local Government Act 1903 (No. 1893), secs. 708, 710—Non-compliance with conditions of sec. 708—Whether application for stay of action imperative.]—In order that a municipality may take advantage of the plaintiff's non-compliance with the conditions of sec. 708 it is not imperative that application should be made under sec. 710 for a stay of the action. If no such application has been made the municipality may raise the defence of non-compliance at the trial of the action. *Daniel* v. *Benalla, President, &c. of Shire of,* (1906) V.L.R., 101. *Madden, C.J., Holroyd* and *Hodges, JJ.*

Local Government Act 1903 (No. 1893), secs. 708, 710—Action in respect of injury sustained by reason of accident on highway— Notice of accident not given in time—Whether sufficient reason shown why person injured unable to give notice—By whom such question to be determined—Jury.]—Where an action against a municipality for damages in respect of injury sustained by the plaintiff by reason of an accident upon a highway is tried by a jury, and the notice of action required by sec. 708 of the *Local Government Act* 1903 has not been given in time and an application under sec. 710 to stay proceedings has been previously refused, the question whether the plaintiff can show some sufficient reason why he was unable to give such notice is for the jury. *Leeder* v. *Ballarat East, Mayor, &c. of,* (1908) V.L.R., 214 ; 29 A.L.T., 192 ; 14 A.L.R., 124. F.C., *a' Beckett, Hodges* and *Cussen, JJ.* (1908).

Local Government Act 1903 (No. 1893), secs. 708, 710—Notice of action against municipality—Failure to comply with conditions— Stay of action—Judge in Chambers—Jurisdiction.]—A Judge in Chambers has, under sec. 710 of the *Local Government Act* 1903 a discretion, where the facts as to the injury its nature and extent and the consequent suffering are in dispute, to say that he will not stay the action at that juncture. In such a case, it is for the Judge who presides at the trial, after hearing the evidence, to say whether so far as sec. 708 (1) is concerned the plaintiff has shown sufficient reason why he was unable to give the notice required by that sub-section. *Leeder* v. *Ballarat East, Mayor, &c., of,* 29 A.L.T. (Supplement), 6 ; 13 A.L.R. (C.N.), 25. *Judge Eagleson* (1907).

Local Government Act 1903 (No. 1893), secs. 708, 710—Accident upon highway, &c.—

Notice before action, when necessary.]— The notice before action required by sec. 708 of the *Local Government Act* 1903 need not be given where the cause of action arose out of an accident occasioned by a negligent act of a servant of the municipality which had no connection with any defect in a highway, street, road, etc. *Gordon* v. *Ballarat, Mayor, &c., of*, 29 A.L.T. (Supplement), 4 ; 13 A.L.R. (C.N.), 19. *Judge Johnson* (1907).

(b) Death of Party or Person Injured.

" **Actio personalis moritur cum persona "— Action for personal injuries—Judgment for plaintiff—Death of plaintiff pending appeal— Survival of action to executor—Executor added as respondent to appeal.]—**The plaintiff succeeded in an action in the County Court for damages for personal injuries, and judgment was entered for her. The defendant moved for a new trial which was refused, and then appealed from such refusal. Before the appeal came on for hearing the plaintiff died. *Held*, that the maxim " actio personalis moritur cum persona " did not apply, and that the plaintiff's rights under the judgment survived to her executor, who was added as a party. *Farrands* v. *Melbourne, The Mayor &c. of the City of*, (1909) V.L.R., 531. F.C., *Madden, C.J., Hodges* and *Cussen, JJ.*

Administration ad litem—Application under peculiar circumstances—Proposed action under Wrongs Act for benefit of widow and children of deceased—Time for bringing action about to expire—Poverty of widow, the applicant for administration—Wrongs Act 1890 (No. 1160), secs. 14, 15, 16.]—*See* Executors and Administrators, cols. 534, 535. *Greenway* v. *McKay*, (1911) 12 C.L.R., 310 ; 17 A.L.R., 350.

(c) Evidence.

Negligence—Evidence—Railway — Regulation of owners of railway requiring whistle to be sounded—Omission to sound.]—A regulation issued by the owners of the railway directing their engine-drivers to sound a whistle when approaching a level crossing without gates, is evidence that the sounding of the whistle is a reasonable precaution to be taken in such circumstances, and the omission to sound a whistle is evidence of negligence. *Fraser* v. *Victorian Railways Commissioners*, (1909) 8 C.L.R., 54 ; 15 A.L.R., 93. H.C.

Motor Car Act 1909 (No. 2237), sec. 14— Obligation of motor car driver to supply information, nature of.]—*See* Motor Car Act. *Hyde* v. *O' Rielly*, 16 A.L.R. (C.N.), 12.

(d) Other Matters.

Negligence—General damages—No sufficient evidence of particular item of damage— New trial motion—Exercise of discretion to grant a new trial—" Substantial wrong or miscarriage "—Rules of Supreme Court 1906 —Order XXXIX., r. 6.]—Subsequently to injuries caused to a woman by the negligence of the defendants, she had a miscarriage, and that was left to the jury as a matter in respect of which they might award her damages. The jury gave a general verdict in her favor. After notice of appeal, and pending appeal, the woman died. The Court, being of opinion that it was at least doubtful whether there was evidence fit to be submitted to a jury that the miscarriage was the result of the accident. *Held* (*Hodges, J.*, dissenting), that under the circumstances, as there had been no substantial wrong or miscarriage, neither a new trial nor a new assessment of damages should be ordered. *Farrands* v. *Mayor &c. of Melbourne*, (1909) V.L.R., 531 ; 31 A.L.T., 78 ; 15 A.L.R., 520. F.C., *Madden, C.J., Hodges* and *Cussen, JJ.*

Order XXXVI., rr. 4, 6 (Rules of 1884)— Right to jury—Negligence in navigating ship —Collision.]—*See* Jury, col. 764. *Union Steamship &c. Co.* v. *The Melbourne Harbour Trust Commissioners*, (1907) V.L.R., 204 ; 29 A.L.T., 63 ; 13 A.L.R., 136.

NEW TRIAL.

See also, Practice and Pleading.

New trial—Several issues—Wrong finding by jury on one issue.]—A wrong finding by a jury on one issue does not necessarily vitiate their finding on other issues. *Ronald* v. *Harper*, (1910) 11 C.L.R., 63 ; 16 A.L.R., 415. H.C., *Griffith, C.J., Barton* and *O'Connor, JJ.*

Trial by jury—Alleged misconduct of juryman—Evidence—Unsworn statement by juryman—No objection—New trial.]—*See* JURY. cols. 768, 769. *David Syme & Co.* v. *Swinburne*, (1909) 10 C.L.R., 43 ; 16 A.L.R., 93.

Order XXXIX.—New trial—Misconduct of juryman—Conversation between juryman and party—Whether course of justice substantially affected.] — *See* PRACTICE AND PLEADING. *David Syme & Co.* v. *Swinburne*, 10 C.L.R., 43 ; 16 A.L.R., 93

Order XXXIX.— New trial — Communications between interested party and jury—Possibility that verdict affected—Reasonable suspicion of unfairness.] — *See* PRACTICE AND PLEADING. *Trewartha* v. *Confidence Extended Co.*, (1906) V.L.R., 285 ; 28 A.L.T., 8 ; 12 A.L.R., 332.

New trial—Trial by jury—Libel—Fair comment—Excessive damages.]—*See* PRACTICE AND PLEADING. *David Syme & Co.* v. *Swinburne*, (1909) 10 C.L.R., 43 ; 16 A.L.R., 93. H.C.

Order XXXIX.—New trial — Appeal — Evidence, admissibility of—Application for new trial on ground of misconduct of juryman—Evidence as to such misconduct given before primary Judge—Affidavit as to such evidence.] —*See* APPEAL, cols. 38, 39. *David Syme & Co.* v. *Swinburne*, 10 C.L.R., 43 ; 16 A.L.R., 93.

Trial by jury—Counsel's right in addressing the jury—Partisan observations by counsel for one party—New trial.]—*See* JURY, col. 770. *Swinburne* v. *David Syme & Co.*, (1909) V.L.R., 550 ; 31 A.L.T., 81 ; 15 A.L.R., 579. *Madden, C.J., a' Beckett* and *Hood, JJ.*

Order XXXIX.—New trial—Misconduct of counsel.] — *See* PRACTICE AND PLEADING. *David Syme & Co.* v. *Swinburne*, 10 C.L.R., 43 ; 16 A.L.R., 93.

New trial—Trial by jury—Observations made by Judge in summing up—Whether

directions to jury—Order XXXIX.]—*See* PRACTICE AND PLEADING. *Ronald* v. *Harper*, (1910) 11 C.L.R., 63 ; 16 A.L.R., 415.

Order XXXIX.—Supreme Court Act 1890 (No. 1142), sec. 58—Charge to jury—Duty of Judge—Issues and evidence applicable thereto.] —*See* PRACTICE AND PLEADING. *Holford and Wife* v. *Melbourne Tramway and Omnibus Co.*, (1909) V.L.R., 497 ; 29 A.L.T., 112 ; 13 A.L.R., 667

Criminal law—New trial, when to be granted after quashing of conviction—Circumstances to be considered in exercise of discretion—Failure to warn jury against convicting on uncorroborated evidence of accomplice—Evidence improperly admitted and afterwards withdrawn from jury—Crimes Act 1890 (No. 1079), sec. 482.]—*See* CRIMINAL LAW, cols. 366, 367. *Peacock* v. *The King*, (1911) 13 C.L.R., 619 ; 17 A.L.R., 566.

Order XXXIX., r. 6—Improper rejection of evidence—Substantial wrong or miscarriage.] —*See* PRACTICE AND PLEADING. *National Mutual Life Association of Australasia Ltd.* v. *Godrich*, 10 C.L.R., 1 ; 16 A.L.R., 110.

Order XXXIX. r. 6—New trial—Misdirection —Substantial wrong or miscarriage.]—*See* PRACTICE AND PLEADING. *Holford and Wife* v. *Melbourne Tramway and Omnibus Co.*, (1909) V.L.R., 497 ; 29 A.L.T., 112 ; 13 A.L.R., 667.

Order XXXIX. — Supreme Court Act 1890 (No. 1142), sec. 58—New trial—Misdirection as to law — No objection taken at trial — Relevancy of evidence, misdirection as to.]— *See* PRACTICE AND PLEADING. *Holford and Wife* v. *Melbourne Tramway and Omnibus Co.*, (1909) V.L.R., 497 ; 29 A.L.T., 112 ; 13 A.L.R., 667.

Order to review—Evidence properly rejected on the ground upon which it was tendered—Admissibility of evidence on another ground—Whether to be relied on upon order to review,] —*See* EVIDENCE col. 493. *Honeybone* v. *Glass*, (1908) V.L.R., 466 ; 30 A.L.T., 54 ; 14 A.L.R., 345.

County Court—New trial—Notice of application served out of time—Refusal of

Judge to enlarge time—Jurisdiction of Court of Appeal to enlarge—Misdirection—No objection taken at trial—Jurisdiction of Judge to grant new trial—Refusal of Judge to grant new trial—Whether High Court will grant new trial—Infinitesimal hope of success if new trial granted—County Court Act 1890 (No. 1078), sec. 96—County Court Rules, 188, 424.]—*See* COUNTY COURT, cols. 316, 317. *Armstrong* v. *Great Southern Gold Mining Co., No Liability,* (1911) 12 C.L.R., 382; 17 A.L.R., 377.

County Court Act 1890 (No. 1078), secs. 96, 133, 148—Order XXXIX. r. 7—County Court —New trial—Whether issues to be tried may be limited.]—*See* COUNTY COURT, col. 317. *Holford and Wife* v. *Melbourne Tramway and Omnibus Co.,* (1909) V.L.R., 497; 29 A.L.T., 112; 13 A.L.R., 667.

New trial—Exercise of discretion to grant new trial.]—*See* COUNTY COURT, cols. 317, 318. *Farrands* v. *Mayor, &c., of Melbourne,* (1909) V.L.R., 531; 31 A.L.T., 78; 15 A.L.R., 520.

County Court—New trial—Service of notice of application — Time — " Clear days "— County Court Rules 1891, r. 188, Interpretation clause.]—*See* COUNTY COURT, col. 317. *Armstrong* v. *Great Southern Gold Mining Co., No Liability,* (1911) 12 C.L.R., 382; 17 A.L.R., 377.

NOTARY PUBLIC.

See EVIDENCE, cols. 478, 482.

NOTICE.

Notice to produce, whether necessary— Secondary evidence of documents — Thistle Act 1890 (No. 1145), sec. 4—Notice calling upon defendant to destroy thistles—Offence constituted by disobedience to notice.]—*See* EVIDENCE, col. 496. *Sanderson* v. *Nicholson,* (1906) V.L.R., 371; 27 A.L.T., 215; 12 A.L.R., 208.

Certiorari—Court of General Sessions— Notice of proceedings to Chairman and Jus-

tices, necessity for—13 Geo. II., c. 18, sec. 5— 9 Geo. IV., c. 83—Supreme Court Act 1890 (No. 1142), secs. 25, 31.]—*See* CERTIORARI, col. 96. *Ex parte Dunn*; *Ex parte Aspinall,* (1906) V.L.R., 584; 28 A.L.T., 72; 12 A.L.R., 418.

County Court—New trial—Notice of application served out of time—Refusal of Judge to enlarge time—Jurisdiction of Court of Appeal to enlarge.]—*See* COUNTY COURT, cols. 316, 317. *Armstrong* v. *Great Southern Gold Mining Co., No Liability,* (1911) 12 C.L.R., 382; 17 A.L.R., 377.

County Court—New trial—Service of notice of application — Time — " Clear days "— County Court Rules 1891, r. 188, interpretation clause.]—*See* COUNTY COURT, ccl. 317. *Armstrong* v. *Great Southern Gold Mining Co., No Liability,* (1911) 12 C.L.R., 382; 17 A.L.R., 377

Appeal—Dismissal on ground that it is incompetent—No notice of objection before hearing—Costs.]—*See* APPEAL, col. 32. *Jenkins* v. *Lanfranchi,* 10 C.L.R., 595; 16 A.L.R., 275.

Marriage Act 1890 (No. 1166), secs. 43, 51— Maintenance order—Necessity for service of order before proceedings to enforce.]—*See* MAINTENANCE AND MAINTENANCE ORDERS. *Cohen* v *MacDonough,* (1907) V.L.R., 7; 28 A.L.T., 119; 12 A.L.R., 566.

Marriage Act 1890 (No. 1166), sec. 51— Service of copy order for maintenance, whether necessary.]—*See* MAINTENANCE AND MAINTENANCE ORDERS. *Cohen* v. *MacDonough* (or *O'Donough*), (1906) V.L.R., 521; 28 A.L.T., 97; 12 A.L.R., 447.

Marriage Act 1890 (No. 1166), sec. 43— Justices Act 1904 (No. 1959), sec. 20—Order for maintenance—Defendant to find surety " forthwith "—Immediate committal to prison — Service of copy order, whether condition precedent to issue of warrant of committal.]— *See* MAINTENANCE AND MAINTENANCE ORDERS *Adams* v. *Rogers,* (1907) V.L.R., 245; 28 A.L.T., 180; 13 A.L.R., 71.

Marriage Act 1890 (No. 1166), sec. 52— Justices Act 1890 (No. 1105), sec. 131—Maintenance appeal—Notice of intention to appeal—Statement of grounds of appeal—Filing notices.]—*See* GENERAL SESSIONS, cols. 618, 619. *Gavey* v. *Gavey*, 31 A.L.T. (Supplement), 6 ; 15 A.L.R. (C.N.), 17.

Marriage Act 1890 (No. 1166), sec. 52—Marriage Act 1900 (No. 1684), sec. 7—Practice Applications to quash, &c.—Order under the Marriage Acts—Service of notices.]— *See* MAINTENANCE AND MAINTENANCE ORDERS. *In re Applications to Quash*, 31 A.L.T. (Supplement), 10 ; 15 A.L.R. (C.N.), 25. (1909).

General Sessions—Notice of appeal—Recognizance, when it must be entered into—Recognizance entered into after service of notice on Clerk of Petty Sessions but before service on respondent—Justices Act 1890 (No. 1105), sec. 128.]—*See* GENERAL SESSIONS, cols. 619, 620. *Ormond* v *Joske*, 16 A.L.R. (C.N.), 1.

Justices Act 1890 (No. 1105), sec. 128 (5)—Appeal—Recognizance—Notice of appeal—Time for entering into recognizance.]—*See* GENERAL SESSIONS, col. 620. *Martin* v. *Rowden*, 32 A.L.T. (Supplement), 8 ; 16 A.L.R. (C.N.), 10.

Administration ad litem—Notice of intention to apply, necessity for—Application under peculiar circumstances—Administration and Probate Act 1890 (No. 1060), secs. 14, 110—Probate and Administration Rules 1906, rr. 4, 15.]—*See* EXECUTORS AND ADMINISTRATORS, cols. 543, 544. *Greenway* v. *McKay*, (1911) 12 C.L.R., 310 ; 17 A.L.R., 350.

Notice under section 149 of Insolvency Act 1890—Form of.]—*See* INSOLVENCY col. 728. *In re Hickman*, 31 A.L.T. (Supplement), 10 ; 15 A.L.R. (C.N.), 21.

Society—Orange lodge — Charge against member—Notice of charge—Compliance with rule requiring—Whether a condition precedent—Domestic tribunal, right of appeal to—Failure to so appeal—Effect on right of action.]—*See* FRIENDLY SOCIETY, cols. 592, 593. *Carbines* v. *Pittock*, (1908) V.L.R., 292 ; 29 A.L.T., 282 ; 14 A.L.R., 248.

Mines Act 1907 (No. 2127), secs. 9, 14—Sludge abatement—Order of Sludge Abate-

ment Board—Order made without notice to party to be affected thereby—Whether order valid—Audi alteram partem.]—*See* MINING. *Bremner* v. *New Normanby Quartz Mining Co. No Liability*, (1910) V.L.R., 72 ; 31 A.L.T., 140 ; 16 A.L.R., 25.

Vermin Destruction Act 1890 (No. 1153), sec. 20—Service of notice by registered letter, effect of—Notice never received by addressee.]—*See* VERMIN. *McCallum* v. *Purvis*, (1906) V.L.R., 578 ; 28 A.L.T., 31 ; 12 A.L.R., 329.

Vermin Destruction Act 1890 (No. 1153), sec. 20—Service of notice by registered letter—Addressee's name misspelt—Name on letter sounding the same as addressee's name.]—*See* VERMIN. *McCallum* v. *Purvis*, (1906) V.L.R., 578 ; 28 A.L.T., 31 ; 12 A.L.R., 329.

Local Government Act 1903 (No. 1893), sec. 708—Notice of injury—Sufficiency—Place at which the accident took place—" Bridge " — " Approach."] — *See* LOCAL GOVERNMENT. *Daniel* v. *Benalla, President &c of Shire of*, (1906) V.L.R., 101 ; 27 A.L.T., 141 ; 12 A.L.R., 16.

Local Government Act 1903 (No. 1893), secs. 708, 710—Non-compliance with conditions of section 708—Whether application for stay of action imperative.]—*See* LOCAL GOVERNMENT. *Daniel* v. *Benalla, President &c. of*, (1906) V.L.R., 101.

Local Government Act 1903 (No. 1893), sec. 708—Notice of accident, failure to give—" Sufficient reason why the person injured . . . was unable to give such notice "—Evidence to show, nature of—Ignorance of the law.]—*See* LOCAL GOVERNMENT. *Leeder* v. *Ballarat East, Mayor &c. of*, (1908) V.L.R., 214 ; 29 A L T., 192 ; 14 A.L.R., 124.

Local Government Act 1903 (No. 1893), secs. 708, 710—Action in respect of injury sustained by reason of accident on highway—Notice of accident not given in time—Whether sufficient reason shown why person injured unable to give notice—By whom such question to be determined—Jury.]—*See* LOCAL GOVERNMENT. *Leeder* v. *Ballarat East, Mayor &c. of*, (1908) V.L.R., 214 ; 29 A.L.T., 192 ; 14 A.L.R., 124.

Local Government Act 1903 (No. 1893), secs. 708, 710—Accident upon highway, &c.—Notice before action, when necessary.]—*See* LOCAL GOVERNMENT. *Gordon* v. *Ballarat, Mayor &c. of,* 29 A.L.T. (Supplement), 4 ; 13 A.L.R. (C.N.), 19.

Local Government Act 1903 (No. 1893), secs. 708, 710—Notice of action against municipality—Failure to comply with conditions—Stay of action—Judge in chambers—Jurisdiction.]—*See* LOCAL GOVERNMENT. *Leeder* v. *Ballaret East, Mayor &c. of,* 29 A.L.T. (Supplement), 6 ; 13 A.L.R. (C.N.), 25.

Health Act 1890 (No. 1098), Part IX., Eighteenth Schedule—Notice of requirement of vaccination—Notification of place of attendance of public vaccinator for the district —" District," meaning of—Place of attendance outside district of registrar of births and deaths causing notice to be given.]—*See* HEALTH (PUBLIC) col. 634. *O'Malley* v. *Russell,* (1908) V.L.R., 545 ; 30 A.L.T., 39 ; 14 A.L.R., 462.

Information, sufficiency of—Charge against father for not having child vaccinated—Allegation that vaccination notice given by Registrar of district in which father resided—Who may properly give such notice—Health Act 1890 (No. 1098), Part IX.]—*See* HEALTH (PUBLIC) cols. 634, 635. *O'Malley* v. *Russell,* (1908) V.L.R., 545 ; 30 A.L.T., 39 ; 14 A.L.R., 462.

Thistle Act 1890 (No. 1145), sec. 4—Notice to destroy thistles—Sufficiency of.]—*See* THISTLE ACTS. *Murphy* v. *Shiells,* (1908) V.L.R., 513 ; 30 A.L.T., 20 ; 14 A.L.R., 410.

Thistle Act 1890 (No. 1145), sec. 4—Thistle Act 1893 (No. 1337)—Notice to destroy thistles—Foundation of offence—Insufficient notice—Objection first taken in order nisi to review.]—*See* JUSTICES OF THE PEACE, cols. 802, 803. *Murphy* v. *Shiells,* (1908) V.L.R., 513 ; 30 A.L.T., 20 ; 14 A.L.R., 410.

Order III., r. 6—Order XIV.—" Debt or liquidated demand "—Assignment of debt—No written notice of assignment—Supreme Court Act 1890 (No. 1142), sec. 63 (6).]—*See*

PRACTICE AND PLEADING. *Caddy* v. *Beattie,* (1908) V.L.R., 17 ; 29 A.L.T., 165 ; 13 A.L.R., 643.

Assignment of debt—No written notice of assignment — Proceedings by assignee — Parties.]—*See* ASSIGNMENT, col. 59. *Caddy* v. *Beattie,* (1908) V.L.R., 17 ; 29 A.L.T., 165 ; 13 A.L.R., 643.

Notice to quit—Monthly tenancy—Length of notice.]—*See* LANDLORD AND TENANT, col. 815. *Bayne* v. *Love,* (1909) 7 C.L.R., 748.

Landlord and Tenant Act 1890 (No. 1108), secs. 92, 93—Notice to quit—Second notice, effect of—Offer of new tenancy—Non-acceptance—Whether second notice a waiver of the first.]—*See* LANDLORD AND TENANT. col. 815. *Green* v. *Summers,* 29 A.L.T., 245 ; 14 A.L.R., 218.

NUISANCE.

Nuisance—Church bell—Early morning toll —Injunction—Material interference with ordinary comfort of existence.]—The ringing of a church bell in the early morning hours of Sunday and public holidays in such a manner as to disturb persons residing in the neighbourhood may be a legal nuisance ; whether it is so or not is a question of fact depending among other things on the degree of disturbance caused. *Haddon* v. *Lynch,* (1911) V.L.R., 230 ; 33 A.L.T., 4 ; 17 A.L.R., 185. F.C., *Madden, C.J., Hodges* and *Hood, JJ.*

Nuisance—Drain on highway constructed by municipal authority.]—A drain constructed by a municipal authority on a highway for the purpose of draining the highway is not in itself an indictable nuisance. *Benalla, President, &c. of* v. *Cherry,* (1911) 12 C.L.R., 642 ; 17 A.L.R., 537. *Griffith, C.J., Barton* and *O'Connor, JJ.*

Nuisance—Chimney sending forth smoke— Whether a defence that as far as practicable all smoke is consumed—Health Act 1890 (No. 1098), sec. 216 (7)—Second proviso of section, effect of.]—*See* HEALTH (PUBLIC), col. 635.

M' Kell v. *Rider*, 5 C.L.R., 480 ; 14 A.L.R., 145.

Health Act 1890 (No. 1098), sec. 226—Noxious trades—Nuisance—Fumes causing bad smell widely diffused and continuous.]—*See* HEALTH (PUBLIC) cols. 636, 637. *Bullows* v. *Kitchen & Sons Ltd.*, (1910) V.L.R., 130 ; 31 A.L.T., 172 ; 16 A.L.R., 147.

Health Act 1890 (No. 1098), sec. 226—Noxious trades—Nuisance—Negligent use by employees of means sufficient to prevent nuisance if properly used—Nuisance arising from accident.]—*See* HEALTH (PUBLIC). col. 637. *Bullows* v. *Kitchen & Sons Ltd.*, (1910) V.L.R., 130 ; 31 A.L.T., 172 ; 16 A.L.R., 147.

Health Act 1890 (No. 1098), sec. 226—Noxious trades—Nuisance—Escape of bad smell on two occasions owing to negligence of employees—Sudden or exceptional matter—Evidence, sufficiency of.]—*See* HEALTH (PUBLIC), col. 637. *Bullows* v. *Kitchen & Sons Ltd.*, (1910) V.L.R., 130 ; 31 A.L.T., 172 ; 16 A.L.R., 147.

OBSCENITY.

See POLICE OFFENCES ACTS.

OPIUM SMOKING PROHIBITION ACT.

Opium Smoking Prohibition Act 1905 (No. 2003), sec. 10—" Privy " to offending against Act, meaning of.]—A person found in a room used for opium smoking, in which are a man smoking opium and all the appliances and appurtenances of an opium den and the door of which is locked, may properly be convicted under section 10 of the *Opium Smoking Prohibition Act* 1905 of being " privy " to offending against one of the provisions of the Act. *Stapleton* v. *Davis* ; *Stapleton* v. *Bell*, (1908) V.L.R., 114 ; 29 A.L.T., 162 ; 14 A.L.R., 26. *Hodges, J.* (1907).

Opium Smoking Prohibition Act 1905 (No. 2003), sec. 10—Conviction of principal of-fender of smoking opium—**Whether evidence against person charged with being " privy " to offending.]**—D. was charged with being " privy " to offending against a provision of the *Opium Smoking Prohibition Act* 1905. The evidence showed that D. was found locked in a small room in which J., another man, was smoking opium. *Held*, that the fact that J. had been convicted of smoking opium at the time and place in question was not evidence against D. *Stapleton* v. *Davis* ; *Stapleton* v. *Bell*, (1908) V.L.R., 114 ; 29 A.L.T., 162 ; 14 A.L.R., 26. *Hodges, J.* (1907).

ORDER TO REVIEW.

See JUSTICES OF THE PEACE.

PARENT.

See ADVANCEMENT ; CHILDREN, INFANT ; MAINTENANCE AND MAINTENANCE ORDERS.

PARTICULARS.

See DEFAMATION ; PRACTICE AND PLEADING, AND THE HEADINGS RELATING TO THE VARIOUS COURTS.

PARTIES.

Contract of life assurance—Parties—Policy for benefit of assured only—Refusal of executors of will of assured to sue on policy—Action by beneficiaries under will of insured—Cause of action.]—Where a person takes out a policy of assurance on his own life for his own benefit, and dies while the policy is still in force, leaving a will disposing of all his property, the beneficiaries under the will have no right either at law or in equity to enforce payment by the insurer, even though the executors refuse to sue and are made parties to the action. *Miller* v.

National Mutual Life Association of Australasia Ltd., (1909) V.L.R., 193 ; 30 A.L.T., 193 ; 15 A.L.R., 141. *Hodges, J.*

Order XVI. — Parties — Administrator — Assets transferred by administrator in breach of trust — Acting by administrator to recover —Whether beneficiaries necessary parties.]— *See* PRACTICE AND PLEADING. *Ackerly v. Palmer*, (1910) V.L.R., 339 ; 32 A.L.T., 23 ; 16 A.L.R., 326.

Order XVI., r. 8—Practice — Joinder of parties—Administration action—Trustee sued as representative—Refusal of trustee to appeal —Judgment not yet drawn up—Joinder of cestui que trustent.]—See APPEAL, cols. 26, 27. *Connolly v. Macartney*, (1908) 7 C.L.R., 48 ; 14 A.L.R., 558.

Administration ad litem—Revocation — Whether defendant in proposed action may apply for.]—See EXECUTORS AND ADMINISTRATORS, cols. 545, 546. *Greenway v. McKay*, (1911) 12 C.L.R., 310 ; 17 A.L.R., 350.

Local Government Act 1903 (No. 1893), secs. 341, 342—County Court Rules 1891, r. 103—Rates—Charge on land—Proceedings to enforce—Death of owner—Parties—Executor of executor—Order for sale—Title.]—See LOCAL GOVERNMENT col. 861. *Moorabbin, Shire of v. Soldi*, (1912) V.L.R., 389 ; 34 A.L.T., 93 ; 18 A.L.R., 493.

County Court Act 1890 (No. 1078), sec. 62 —County Court Rules 1891, rr. 197, 200— Payment into Court—Action against defendants as executors and as beneficiaries—Payment into Court by executors—Acceptance in satisfaction of claim against executors—Survival of claim against beneficiaries.]—See COUNTY COURT, cols. 306, 307. *Smart v. Buchanan*, 31 A.L.T. (Supplement), 8 ; 15 A.L.R. (C.N.), 25.

Parties—Board of Public Health—How Board may be sued.]—See HEALTH (PUBLIC). col. 638. *The King v. Prahran, Mayor &c. of ; Ex parte Morris*, (1910) V.L.R., 460 ; 32 A.L.T., 92 ; 16 A.L.R., 507.

Company—Name struck off Register— Motion to restore—Parties—Registrar-General

—Companies Act 1896 (No. 1482), Div. VIII.— Defunct companies.]—See COMPANY, cols. 141, 142. *In re Great Southern Land Investment Co. Ltd.*, (1910) V.L.R., 150 ; 31 A.L.T., 129 ; 16 A.L.R., 14.

Will—Charity, gift of—Compromise, jurisdiction of Court to sanction—Attorney-General, consent of.]—See CHARITY, col. 99. *In re Buckhurst ; Melbourne Hospital v. Equity Trustees Executors &c. Co. Ltd.*, (1911) V.L.R., 61 ; 32 A.L.T., 165 ; 17 A.L.R., 63.

Order XVI.—Parties—Friendly Societies Act 1890 (No. 1094), sec. 16 (iii.) (vi.)— Property of society, legal proceedings concerning—Owner, who to be named as—Trustees.] —See CRIMINAL LAW, col. 339. *Rex v. Watson*, (1908) V.L.R., 103 ; 29 A.L.T., 146 ; 13 A.L.R., 724.

Assignment of debt—No written notice of assignment — Proceedings by assignee — Parties.]—See ASSIGNMENT, ccl. 59. *Caddy v. Beattie*, (1908) V.L.R., 17 ; 29 A.L.T., 165 ; 13 A.L.R., 643.

" Actio personalis moritur cum persona "— Action for personal injuries—Judgment for plaintiff—Death of plaintiff pending appeal— Survival of action to executor—Executor added as respondent to appeal.]—See MAXIMS. *Farrands v. Melbourne, The Mayor, &c. of the City of*, (1909) V.L.R., 531.

Parties to contract—Sale of patented articles to jobbers and dealers—Consideration —Breach of contract.]—See PATENT. *National Phonograph Co. of Australia Ltd. v. Menck*, 7 C.L.R., 481 ; 15 A.L.R., 1 ; S.C. L.R. (1911) A.C., 336 (P.C.) ; 17 A.L.R., 94.

Order XVI., r. 6—Joinder of parties—Persons liable as co-contractors—Co-contractor out of jurisdiction—Joinder of as defendant— Discretion of Court.]—See PRACTICE AND PLEADING. *Sands & McDougall Ltd. v. Whitelaw*, (1908) V.L.R., 131 ; 29 A.L.T., 199 ; 14 A.L.R., 79.

Order XIV., r. 1—Order XVI., r. 6—Fina judgment—Joint debt—Joint contractor not joined as defendant—Objection for want of parties, how to be taken.]—See PRACTICE AND

PLEADING. *Sands & McDougall Ltd.,* v. *Whitelaw,* (1908) V.L.R., 131; 29 A.L.T., 199; 14 A.L.R., 79.

Order XVIII., r. 6—Order XVI., r. 1—Joinder of parties—Joinder of causes of action—Slander actions—Joint and separate claims—Arising out of the same transaction or series of transactions—" The same publication or series of publications."]—*See* PRACTICE AND PLEADING. *Smith* v. *Foley,* (1912) V.L.R., 314; 34 A.L.T., 75; 18 A.L.R., 333.

Order XVI., r. 32 (b)—Representative order—Parties within the jurisdiction to represent parties outside.]—*See* PRACTICE AND PLEADING. *In re Foulkes; Ford* v. *Foulkes,* 30 A.L.T., 108; 14 A.L.R., 729.

Order XVI., rr. 11, 13—Order IX., r. 2—Amendment of writ by adding plaintiff—Service of amended writ, whether necessary—Discretion of Court.]—*See* PRACTICE AND PLEADING. *Coulson* v. *Butler,* (1907) V.L.R., 201; 28 A.L.T., 210; 13 A.L.R., 67.

Order XVI., r. 48—Third party procedure—Claim for contribution or indemnity—Claim in respect of one of plaintiff's claims.]—*See* PRACTICE AND PLEADING. *Edwards* v. *Edwards,* (1913) V.L.R., 30; 34 A.L.T., 103; 18 A.L.R., 580.

Order XVI., r. 48—Order XXVIII., rr. 1, 12—Amendment—Third party notice—Substitution of name of firm for name of individual members thereof.]—*See* PRACTICE AND PLEADING. *Richard Hornsby & Sons Ltd.* v *King,* (1910) V.L.R., 326; 32 A.L.T., 21; 16 A.L.R., 303.

Administration and Probate Act 1890 (No. 1060), sec. 18—Will—Caveat, who may lodge—Infant, next friend of—Appointment of guardian as—Form of caveat where both infant and next friend interested in estate.]—*See* INFANT, cols. 693, 694. *In re Simeon,* (1910) V.L.R., 335; 32 A.L.T., 25; 16 A.L.R., 362.

Infant complainant in Court of Petty Sessions—Claim for wages—Order to review obtained by infant—Next friend, whether infant must proceed by—Justices Act 1890 (No. 1105), sec. 72—Rules of Supreme Court 1884, Order XVI., r. 16.]—*See* INFANT, col.

693. *Hines* v. *Phillips,* (1906) V.L.R., 417; 28 A.L.T., 1; 12 A.L.R., 249.

Order to review—Infant respondent—Guardian ad litem—Practice.]—*See* INFANT, col. 693. *Brown* v. *Gunn; McKay, Garnishee,* (1913) V.L.R., 60; 34 A.L.T., 115; 18 A.L.R., (C.N.), 21.

County Court Act 1890 (No. 1078), sec. 60—County Court Rules 1891, r. 107—Infant, action by—Appointment of next friend.]—*See* COUNTY COURT, col, 305. *Thompson* v. *Peach,* 28 A.L.T. (Supplement), 10; 13 A.L.R. (C.N.), 5.

Factories and Shops Act 1905 (No. 1975), secs. 42, 162 (c) (d)—Factories and Shops Act 1905 (No. 2) (No. 2008), sec. 9—Proceedings against firm—Parties.]—*See* JUSTICES OF THE PEACE, col. 778. *Bishop* v. *Chung Brothers,* 4 C.L.R., 1262; 13 A.L.R., 412.

Practice—Complaint by one person on behalf of himself and other persons having the same interest—Jurisdiction.]—*See* JUSTICES OF THE PEACE, col. 778. *Buttle* v. *Hart,* (1906) V.L.R., 195; 27 A.L.T., 184; 12 A.L.R. (C.N.), 5.

Justices—Order for payment of money made in Petty Sessions—Death of party in whose favour order made—Whether executors may enter suggestion of death on record of Court—Justices Act 1890 (No. 1105).]—*See* JUSTICES OF THE PEACE, col. 778. *Goodman* v. *Jonas,* (1909) V.L.R., 307; 31 A.L.T., 16; 15 A.L.R., 308.

PARTNERS AND PARTNERSHIP.

Insolvency — Partnership — Joint executors carrying on business of testator—Partnership Act 1891 (No. 1222), sec. 5—Registration of Firms Act 1892 (No. 1256), sec. 4.]—Several executors carrying on the business of their testator pursuant to the terms of the will in the firm name are not necessarily partners, notwithstanding section 5 of the *Partnership Act* 1891, even though the executors have registered themselves as a firm under the *Registration of Firms Act* 1892. *In re Whitelaw; Savage* v. *Union Bank of Australia*

Ltd.; *Whitelaw* v. *The same*, (1906) 3 C.L.R., 1170; 12 A.L.R., 285. H.C. *Griffith, C.J., Barton* and *O'Connor, JJ.* (1906).

Partnership, formation of—Contract made before partnership in existence.]—In an action by the plaintiffs to recover damages for breach of contract from the three defendants, who, it was alleged, were partners, and as such had entered into a joint adventure with the plaintiffs. *Held*, on the evidence, that the existence of the partnership was not established and that, even if the partnership existed, it had not been formed at the time when the contract was alleged to have been made. *Lang* v. *Morrison & Co. Ltd.*, (1911) 13 C.L.R., 1; 17 A.L.R., 530. H.C. *Griffith, C.J., Barton* and *O'Connor, JJ.*

Partnership agreement — Construction — Share payable on death of partner—Whether at his absolute disposal or in trust for widow and children.]—By a deed of partnership between the members of a firm of solicitors it was provided that in the event of the death or retirement of any of the partners, the future profits of the business should be liable to the payment to his widow, child or children, or some one or other of them as he might by writing under his hand direct or to himself (as the case might be) of the sum of £2,500. *Held*, that in the event of the death of a partner a trust was created in favour of the widow and children or such of them as he should have appointed. *England* v. *Bayles*, (1906) V.L.R., 94; 27 A.L.T., 181; 12 A.L.R., 122. *Madden, C.J.*

Partnership—Contract with individual who afterwards takes another into partnership—Election to hold firm liable on contract—Solicitors—Liability for fraud of co-partner.]—Plaintiff, having agreed to purchase a piece of land, instructed B. to act as his solicitor, and do what was necessary for completing the purchase. While the business was pending, B. took the defendant into partnership, one of the terms of the partnership agreement being that all outstanding costs owing to B. should become part of the assets of the firm. Plaintiff knew of the partnership, and while the business was still pending,

received a bill of costs from and in the name of the firm, paid part of the bill—amounting to £4 10s.—to defendant at the firm offices by cheque payable to the firm or bearer, and was given a receipt by defendant in the firm name. Shortly afterwards plaintiff called at the offices of the firm, and asked for B. who was out. He waited until B. returned, and then paid him a cheque for £105 representing the balance of the purchase money which was outstanding on mortgage, and a cheque for one guinea for costs of the release. Both the latter cheques were payable to B. or bearer. The cheques for £4 10s. and one guinea were each paid into the firm's business account, but the £105 was paid by B. into his private account and misappropriated by him. The work in respect of which the costs were paid was never in fact done either by B. or by the firm. B.'s estate was subsequently sequestrated. *Held*, that the plaintiff had not elected to continue to employ B. alone, but had treated the firm as his solicitors, and the defendant had treated him as a client of the firm and was liable for B.'s fraud. *Held*, also, that defendant was liable to refund the amounts paid for costs. *British Homes Assurance Corporation* v. *Paterson*, (1902) 2 Ch., 404, distinguished. *Reid* v. *Silberberg*, (1906) V.L.R., 126. *a'Beckett, J.*

Partnership—Contract with individual who afterwards takes another into partnership—Liability of firm in respect of contract.]—Where A. has a contract with B. and B. takes C. into partnership, A. may elect to abide by his contract with B. alone, or may accept the liability of the partnership. The mere fact that he prefers, in connection with his contract, to see and consult the partner who had previously acted for him, does not prove an election not to deal with the firm. *Reid* v. *Silberberg*, (1906) V.L.R., 126. *a'Beckett, J.*

Partnership—Dissolution—At will or for single venture — Unequal contribution of capital—Repayment—Partnership Act 1891 (No. 1222), secs. 28, 30, 36, 39, 48.]—A. and B. made a verbal contract whereby they agreed to enter into partnership in the business of buying racehorses in Australia, shipping them to South Africa, and there selling them, that A. should provide £800 as capital for the business and that the profits should be equally divided between A. and B. A. provided the £800 and racehorses were bought and raced in Australia, but none were sent to South Africa. A. gave notice of dissolution of the partnership. In an action by A. for winding up the partnership, he claimed a declaration that the £800 should be paid to him out of the assets of the partnership in priority to any payment to B. in respect of the profits. Judgment was given declaring that the partnership was dissolved, and that A. was entitled to be allowed the whole of the £800, and ordering that, in taking the accounts, the sum of £800 should be allowed to A. as capital of the partnership business. *Held*, that there was evidence to justify a finding that there was an implied agreement that the £800 should be repaid to A. before there was any division of the profits. *Held*, also (*Higgins, J.*, dissenting), that there was evidence to justify a finding that the adventure to South Africa was abandoned, and therefore that the partnership became one for an indefinite term and was determined by the notice. *Kelly* v. *Tucker*, (1907) 5 C.L.R., 1. H.C., *Griffith, C.J., Barton, Isaacs* and *Higgins, JJ.*

Insolvency—Partners—Sequestration of estate of one partner—Security over joint estate—Petition for sequestration—Offer to give up or value security, whether necessary—Insolvency Act 1890 (No. 1102), secs. 37, 41—Insolvency Act 1897 (No. 1513), sec. 109.]— A creditor petitioning for the sequestration of the estate of one of several partners must, under sec. 37 of the *Insolvency Act* 1890, in his petition offer to give up or value any security which he, the creditor, may hold over the joint estate. The rule that a creditor need not give up his security applies only after sequestration in the administration of the joint and separate estates. *In re Stevenson*, 19 V.L.R., 660 ; 15 A.L.T., 119, over-ruled. *In re Whitelaw* ; *Savage* v. *The Union Bank of Australia Ltd.* ; *Whitelaw* v. *The Same*, 3 C.L.R., 1170 ; 12 A.L.R.,

285. H.C., *Griffith, C.J., Barton* and *O'Connor, JJ.* (1906).

Insolvency Act 1890 (No. 1102), sec. 41—Insolvency Rules 1898, rr. 166, 167, 168, 169, 288—Appendix to Rules, Part 2, Scale of Solicitor's Costs—" Instructions for Schedule "—Sequestration of partnership estate—Estates of partners—Separate schedules, whether solicitor entitled to charge in respect of.]— In the case of the sequestration of a partnership estate, where the schedule of the firm has been filed, a solicitor is not entitled, in addition to the allowance of the item " instructions for schedule " in respect of the partnership schedule, to charge for " instructions for schedule " in respect of the individual members of the partnership. *In re Day and Sloan*, 32 A.L.T. (Supplement), 3 ; 16 A.L.R. (C.N.), 9. *Judge Moule* (1910).

Factories and Shops Act 1905 (No. 1975), sec. 162 (c), (d)—Conviction against firm in firm name — Rules under the Justices Act 1890, rr. 18, 20—Information, form of.]— *See* Justices of the Peace, col. 791. *Bishop* v. *Chung Brothers*, 4 C.L.R., 1262 ; 13 A.L.R., 412.

Taxation—Solicitor and client—Firm of solicitors carrying on business in Melbourne and country town—Correspondence between Melbourne and country office—Close copies for country office—Whether costs may be allowed.]— *See* Costs, col. 271. *In re Lamrock, Brown and Hall's Costs*, (1908) V.L.R., 238 ; 29 A.L.T., 214 ; 14 A.L.R., 81.

———

PATENT.

I. SUBJECT-MATTER.

Patent—Combination—Rotary disc plough.] —A patent was granted in Victoria for rotary disc ploughs, and the specification contained several claims, each of them being for a combination. In an action by the patentee for an infringement, *Held*, on the evidence, that each of the claims was new, was good subject matter for a patent, and was useful, and that the patent was valid. *International Harvester Co. of America v. Peacock*, (1908) 6 C.L.R., 287. Privy Council.

Patent—Discovery of new principle—Invention of mode of carrying it into effect—Failure to state all the cases in which the principle will operate—Inability to state—Protection.]—If a person has discovered a new principle, and invented a mode of carrying it into effect, he may obtain a patent for that principle, coupled with the mode of carrying it into effect, and he is thereby protected against persons carrying the principle into effect by other modes. *Chamberlain & Hookham Ltd. v. Mayor, &c. of Bradford*, 20 R.P.C., 673, followed. Such a patent is not invalidated because the patentee does not state, and is unable to state, all the cases in which the principle will operate. *Minerals Separation Ltd. v. Potter's Sulphide Ore Treatment Ltd*; *Potter's Sulphide Ore Treatment Ltd. v. Minerals Separation Ltd.*, (1909) 8 C.L.R., 779; 15 A.L.R., 332. H.C., *Griffith, C.J.* and *O'Connor, J.* [Leave to appeal refused by Privy Council, *see* 15 A.L.R., *addenda et corrigenda*].

Patent—Subject matter—" New manner of manufacture " — Patent for process, whether distinguishable from other patents.]—The phrase " new manner of manufacture " includes any invention consisting of a newly discovered principle or idea carried into effect by some practical mode, new or old. No distinction is to be drawn between patents for processes and other patents. *Gillies v. Hartnett Patent Milking Machine Co. Ltd.*, 31 A.L.T., 164; 16 A.L.R., 88. *Hood, J.* (1910).

Patent — Combination.]—Observations on the requirements and validity of a claim for a combination, *see, Broken Hill South Silver &c. Co. v. N. Guthridge Ltd.*, (1909) 8 C.L.R., 187. H.C, *Isaacs, J.*

Patent—Revocation—Want of novelty—Anticipation.]—An invention, entitled " improvements in shaking table ore concentrators " for which letters patent were granted by the Commonwealth, *Held*, on the evidence, to be not novel and to have been anticipated, and that the letters patent should be revoked. *Broken Hill South Silver &c. Co. v. N. Guthridge Ltd.*, (1909) 8 C.L.R., 187. H.C., *Isaacs, J.*

Patent—Prior publication, what constitutes —Written document, interpretation—Duty of Court—Evidence, admissibility of, to explain terms of art and state of knowledge amongst persons familiar with subject matter.]—The validity of a patent for improvements in ore concentrators was challenged on the ground of prior publication, founded upon a description in an engineering journal of the invention the subject matter of the patent. It was alleged by the patentees that the description so published was unintelligible. *Held*, that the question was whether the description was sufficient to convey to men of science and employers of labour information which would enable them, without any exercise of inventive ingenuity, to understand the invention and give a workman specific directions for the making of the machine; that subject to proof of the state of common knowledge among persons familiar with the subject matter, and to proof of the meaning of technical terms used in the document alleged to be a prior publication, the interpretation of that document was for the Court, and that, applying these tests, the document contained a clear and intelligible description of the invention, and that consequently prior publication was proved. *Betts v. Menzies*, 10 H.L.C., 117, and *Anglo-American Brush Electric Light Corporation v. King, Brown & Co.*, (1892) A.C., 367, applied. *N. Guthridge Ltd. v. Wilfley Ore Concentrator Syndicate Ltd.*, 3 C.L.R., 583; 12 A L R, 398. H.C., *Griffith, C.J., Barton* and *O'Connor, JJ.* (1906). [Leave to appeal refused by Privy Council, 12 A.L.R. (C.N.), 21.

Patent—Validity—Want of novelty—Prior sale to public, effect of—Prior user—User

without knowledge of the nature of the process
—Statute of Monopolies, 21 Jac. I. c. 3, sec.
6.]—A patent was obtained in Victoria for
" an improved hood for incandescent gas
burners," the specification for which described
the mode of manufacture of the hood, and the
claim therein was for a hood prepared as
described. The Court having found that
hoods manufactured according to the specification had been publicly sold in Victoria
prior to the patent, and that the hood was
of such a composition and construction that
any person conversant with the subject and
applying the common knowledge at the time
of the sale could have reproduced it. *Held,*
that the patent was invalid on the ground
that, where a patent is obtained for a process
of manufacture, and there has been a prior
public sale of the product of that manufacture,
if the product is such that any person conversant with the subject and applying the
common knowledge at the time of the sale
could have brought about the same result,
the patent is invalidated. *Quaere, per
Higgins, J.,* whether prior user of a subsequently patented article by others than the
patentees, even without proof of actual or
potential knowledge by the public of the
process by which the article is to be reproduced, would not invalidate the patent.
Cullen v. *Welsbach Light Co. of Australasia
Ltd.,* 4 C.L.R., 990; 13 A.L.R., 194. H.C.,
Griffith, C.J., Barton, O'Connor and *Higgins,
JJ.* (1907).

**Application for patent—Opposition—Want
of novelty—Prior publication—Substantial
identity—Want of inventiveness—Patents Act
1903 (No. 21 of 1903), sec. 56 (e).]**—The word
" novel " in sec. 56 (*e*) of the *Patents Act*
1903 is to be read in the sense in which it
has always been used in patent law and
(*Higgins, J.,* dissenting) the objection permitted by that sub-section includes an objection that the alleged invention is substantially
identical as to the degree of inventiveness
with a process or " manner of manufacture "
already known to the public, in other words,
that the difference is not sufficient to differentiate that which has gone before from that
which is claimed. An application for letters

patent for an alleged invention for cleaning
the two edges of the matrices of linotype
machines by means of two pairs of brushes
in two particular places, was opposed on the
ground of want of novelty. The objection
was based on a known invention for cleaning
one edge of the matrices by means of a
brush which might be placed at any part of
the course of the matrices. *Held* (*Higgins,
J.,* dissenting), that the alleged invention
the subject of the application was substantially identical with that already known and
was therefore not novel, and that the application should be refused. *Per Higgins, J.—*
The alleged invention achieved substantially
additional results by substantially additional
means, and as the objection of want of
novelty does not allow the opponent to raise
the question of want of sufficient inventiveness, the application should be allowed.
Morgan & Co. v. *Windover & Co.,* 7 R.P.C.,
131; *In re Todd's Application,* 9 R.P.C.,
487; *Harwood* v. *Great Northern Railway
Co.,* 11 H.L.C., 654, applied. *The Linotype
Co. Ltd.* v. *Mounsey,* (1909) 9 C.L.R., 194;
15 A.L.R., 310.

**Patents Act 1890 (No. 1123), sec. 56—
Foreign invention patented out of Victoria—
Grant within a year of patent for Victoria—
Absolute identity of patents, whether essential.]**—Section 56 of the *Patents Act* 1890
operates to protect a patent the specification
of which contains several claims, one of
which is identical with one of several claims in
a specification for a prior patent granted out
of Victoria, and is not limited to cases where
there is absolute identity between the invention sought to be patented and that in respect
of which a patent has been granted out of
Victoria. *International Harvester Co. of
America* v. *Peacock,* (1908) 6 C.L.R., 287.
Privy Council.

**Patent—Want of novelty—Anticipation—
Result of subsequent discovery and mode of
producing such result not disclosed by prior
publications.]**—In order to facilitate the
transit of milk through the milk passage
into the receiver of a pneumatic milking
machine by admitting atmospheric pressure
behind the milk A. made a small air inlet

either in the milk passage or preferably at the top of the teat-cup, and obtained letters patent for this improvement. Prior to A.'s patent there had been publication of two inventions showing the admission of air behind the milk, in one case as part of the mechanism to produce the pulsations in the teat-cup which induced the milk to flow, and in the other case for the purpose of keeping the teat moist and warm ; but in neither case was the admission of air designed to achieve the result produced by A.'s device, nor did it produce that result. *Held*, that there was no anticipation of A.'s patent. *Gillies* v. *Hartnett Patent Milking Machine Co. Ltd.*, 31 A.L.T., 164 ; 16 A.L.R., 88. *Hood, J.* (1910).

Patent—Subject matter—Whether any invention involved in patent—How question tested.]—The question whether or not any invention is involved in a patent, consisting in the practical application of a principle, cannot be tested by treating the principle as well-known and then seeing how the inventor has applied it. The principle cannot be thus separated from the mode of carrying it out. If the inventor has suggested some mechanical mode, however simple and well-known, of carrying out the idea which he has discovered, he is entitled to a patent. *Neilson* v. *Harford*, 1 Web. Pat. Cas., 295, distinguished. *Gillies* v. *Hartnett Patent Milking Machine Co. Ltd.*, 31 A.L.T., 164 ; 16 A.L.R., 88. *Hood, J.* (1910).

II.—APPLICATION ; GRANT.

(a) Specifications.

Patent — Combination — Specification, contents of.]—Where a patent is sought for a combination of several parts, it is not necessary in the specification to distinguish between those parts which are old and those which are new. *International Harvester Co. of America* v. *Peacock*, (1908) 6 C.L.R., 287. Privy Council.

Patents Act 1903 (No. 21 of 1903), sec. 36—Application for patent for combination of subordinate processes—Application also for patent for subordinate process—Claim, necessity for clear statement of.]—Where a patent is sought for a combination of subordinate processes, and also for some of these subordinate processes themselves, the applicant must make it plain that he intends to claim protection not only for the combination but also for those subordinate processes. *Clark* v. *Adie*, 2 App. Cas., 315, applied. *Moore* v. *Phillips*, 4 C.L.R., 1411 ; 13 A.L.R., 424. H.C., *Griffith, C.J., Barton, Isaacs* and *Higgins, JJ.* (1907).

Patents Act 1903 (No. 21 of 1903) (Commonwealth), sec. 36—Specification, interpretation of—Statement of the invention claimed, necessity for.]—Although in construing a claim the whole specification must be taken into account, yet the applicant for a patent is not entitled to protection for anything which is not claimed. *Moore* v. *Phillips*, 4 C.L.R., 1411 ; 13 A.L.R., 424. H.C., *Griffith, C.J., Barton, Isaacs* and *Higgins, JJ.* (1907).

Patents Act 1903 (No. 21 of 1903), sec. 56—Opposition—Whether invention obtained by applicant from opponent—Whether invention described in complete specification other than that described in provisional specification.]—The respondents lodged an application for a patent for an " improved earth scoop " and at a later hour on the same day the appellant lodged an application for " improvements in methods and machinery for excavating." The appellant opposed the respondents' application on the grounds that the respondents obtained their invention from him, and that their complete specification described an invention other than that described in their provisional specification. The respondents opposed the appellant's application on the ground that the appellant obtained his invention from them. The complete specification in both cases described the same machine. The Commissioner of Patents dismissed the opposition of the appellant and upheld the opposition of the respondents. On appeal to the High Court, *Held (per Griffith, C.J., O'Connor, Isaacs* and *Higgins, JJ.)*, on the evidence, that the respondents did not obtain their invention from the appellant, and that the appellant did not obtain his invention from the respondent. *Held,* further, on the evidence (*Isaacs, J.,* dissenting), that the complete specification of the respondents described an invention other than that described in their provisional specification, and, therefore, that the appellant's application, which was not open to that objection, should have been granted, and that of the respondents refused. *Dunlop* v. *Cooper,* (1908) 7 C.L.R., 146; 14 A.L.R., 652.

Patent—Provisional specification—Evidence to explain, admissibility of.]—*Per Griffith, C.J.*—If a provisional specification is ambiguous in the sense that the language is apt to describe two different things, evidence is admissible to show that of which the applicant was actually speaking. *Per O'Connor, Isaacs* and *Higgins, JJ.*—On an opposition to an application for a patent, the construction of a provisional specification is to be determined by a consideration of what meaning is conveyed by its words alone, aided by such evidence as will enable those words to be understood, but the state of mind of the applicant at the time he lodges his provisional specification is irrelevant for the purposes of its construction. *Dunlop* v. *Cooper,* (1908) 7 C.L.R., 146; 14 A.L.R., 652.

Patents Act 1903 (No. 21 of 1903), sec. 56—Provisional specification—Description of invention not yet conceived by applicant.]—*Per Griffith, C.J.*—A provisional specification must describe an invention of which the applicant is in actual possession at the time of his application, and, although his words may convey to others the idea of an invention of which he has not himself conceived the idea, yet, if in fact he has not then conceived the idea, he is not in possession of the invention. *Dunlop* v. *Cooper,* (1908) 7 C.L.R., 146; 14 A.L.R., 652.

Patents Act 1903 (No. 21 of 1903), sec. 56—Grounds of opposition to grant of patent—Invention not fairly described in provisional specification.]—*Per Isaacs, J.*—The fact that an invention is not fairly described in a provisional specification is not admissible under sec. 56 of the *Patents Act* 1903 as an objection to an application for a patent. *Dunlop* v. *Cooper,* (1908) 7 C.L.R., 146; 14 A.L.R., 652.

Patent — Specification, sufficiency of — " Small " hole for admission of air—Competent and willing workmen able to make machine from specification.]—The specifications of a patent for an improvement to a pneumatic milking machine stated that the inventor, in order to facilitate the travel of the milk to the receiver, had found it advantageous to introduce a small quantity of air into the milk passage, and for this purpose made, in the milk passage, a hole the size of which was not specified otherwise than by describing it as " small." The milk was drawn from the cow's teat by the intermittent creation of a vacuum, and a competent and willing workman would know that the making of a hole in the place indicated would, if it admitted so much air as to destroy the vacuum, interfere with the working of the machine. *Held,* that the specification of the hole as " small " would enable such a workman to make an efficient machine, and was therefore sufficient. *Gillies* v. *Hartnett Patent Milking Machine Co. Ltd.,* 31 A.L.T., 164; 16 A.L.R., 88. *Hood, J.* (1910).

Patents Act 1903 (No. 21 of 1903), secs. 36, 56, 78—Application—Invention already in possession of public—Description in specification of State patent—Amendment so as to include claim for invention otherwise disclosed in specification.]—An application for letters patent for a method of treating ores, including iron oxide ores, was opposed by the holder of a patent granted in one of the States for a method of treating iron oxide ores. The Court having found on the evidence that the applicant's invention, as described in his specification and claim, had, so far as it applied to iron oxide ores, been described in the specification of the opponent's patent. *Held,* that the applicant's invention was " otherwise in the possession of the public " within the meaning of sec. 56 (*f*) of the *Patents Act* 1903, and that a patent should not be granted to him, unless he should within a limited time amend his specification so as to claim any new invention that might be disclosed in his specification. *Deeley* v. *Perkes*, 13 R.P.C., 581, followed on question of amendment. *Moore* v. *Phillips*, 4 C.L.R., 1411 ; 13 A.L.R., 424. H.C., *Griffith*, *C.J.*, *Barton*, *Isaacs* and *O'Connor*, *JJ.* (1907).

Patents Act 1903 (No. 21 of 1903), sec. 71—Specification—Amendment — " Disclaimer, correction or explanation."]—An amendment of a specification is a " disclaimer " within sec. 71 of the *Patents Act* 1903, if it is a renunciation of some claim actually or apparently made or supposed to be made by the original specification. *Ralston* v. *Smith*, 11 H.L.C., 223, followed. An amendment of a specification is an " explanation " within that section if, without giving any additional information to the class of persons to whom the specification is addressed, it gives information not possessed by other persons not so familiar with the subject. *Minerals Separation Ltd.* v. *Potters' Sulphide Ore Treatment Ltd.* ; *Potter's Sulphide Ore Treatment Ltd.* v. *Minerals Separation Ltd.*, (1909) 8 C.L.R., 779 ; 15 A.L.R., 332. H.C., *Griffith*, *C.J.*, and *O'Connor*, *J.*

(b) Grounds of Opposition.

Patents Act 1903 (No. 21 of 1903), sec. 56—Opposition to grant of patent—What objections may be relied upon.]—*Per Higgins*, *J.*—On an opposition to an application for a patent the Court is not entitled to consider objections not included in sec. 56 of the *Patents Act* 1903. *Dunlop* v. *Cooper*, (1908) 7 C.L.R., 146 ; 14 A.L.R., 652.

Application for patent—Want of novelty—Opposition— Prior publication — Substantial identity—Want of inventiveness—Patents Act 1903 (No. 21 of 1903), sec. 56 (2).]—*See, ante,* I.—SUBJECT-MATTER. *The Linotype Co. Ltd.* v. *Mounsey*, (1909) 9 C.L.R., 194 ; 15 A.L.R., 310.

Patents Act 1903 (No. 21 of 1903), sec. 56—Opposition—Whether invention obtained by applicant from opponent—Whether invention described in complete specification other than that described in provisional specification.]—*See, ante, (a)* SPECIFICATIONS. *Dunlop* v. *Cooper*, (1908) 7 C.L.R., 146 ; 14 A.L.R., 652.

Patents Act 1903 (No. 21 of 1903), sec. 56—Grounds of opposition to grant of patent—Invention not fairly described in provisional specification.]—*See, ante, (a)* SPECIFICATIONS. *Dunlop* v. *Cooper*, (1908) 7 C.L.R., 146 ; 14 A.L.R., 652.

Patents Act 1903 (No. 21 of 1903), secs. 36, 56, 78—Application—Invention already in possession of public—Description in specification of State patent—Amendment so as to include claim for invention otherwise disclosed in specification.]—*See, ante, (a)* SPECIFICATIONS. *Moore* v. *Phillips*, 4 C.L.R., 1411 ; 13 A.L.R., 424.

(c) Appeal.

Patent, application for—Opposition—State Patents Act—Transfer of administration to Commonwealth pending proceedings—Appeal to State Supreme Court — Jurisdiction — Patents Act 1890 (No. 1123), sec. 33—Patents Act (No. 21 of 1903).]—At the date of the proclamation by the Governor-General under sec. 18 of the Federal *Patents Act* 1903 transferring the administration of the State *Patents Act* 1890 to the Commonwealth, the hearing of an opposed application for a patent was pending before the Commissioner of Patents. After that date the hearing was continued and concluded by the same officer acting as a Deputy Commissioner of Patents appointed under the *Patents Act* 1903, and he refused the application. The applicant then appealed to the Crown Solicitor of the Commonwealth as a Federal Law Officer, and he granted the patent. From that decision the opponent appealed to the Supreme Court of Victoria under sec 33 of the *Patents Act* 1890 *Held*, that the State *Patents Act* 1890 having ceased to be administered by the State by reason of sec. 19 (a) of the *Patents Act* 1903, the Supreme Court had no jurisdiction to entertain the appeal *In re McLeod's Patent* ; *Burton* v. *McLeod*, (1906) V.L.R., 488 ; 12 A.L.R., 335. *a'Beckett*, *J.* (1906).

Patents Act 1903 (No. 21 of 1903), sec. 58—Appeal from decision of Commissioner of Patents — Directions as to procedure — The Patents Regulations 1904, r. 80—Appeal book.]—In a pending appeal from a decision of the Commissioner of Patents, a Justice of the High Court, upon an application under rule 80 of *The Patents Regulations* 1904, directed that the appeal should be set down for hearing at the then current sittings of the Court, and that it be heard before the Full Court, but not until ten days after the delivery of the appeal book. His Honor also gave directions as to the preparation and printing of the appeal book. *Moore v. Phillips*, 13 A.L.R., 66. *Isaacs, J.* (1907).

Patent—Application for—Law Officer's decision—Appeal, setting down—Whether order by Judge necessary—Patents Act 1890 (No. 1123), sec. 33.]—When notice has been given of an appeal to the Supreme Court from a decision of the Law Officer, under sec. 33 of the *Patents Act* 1890, an order from a Judge is not necessary before the appeal can be set down by the Prothonotary in the list for hearing before a Judge. *In re McLeod's Patent*; *Burton v. McLeod*, (1906) V.L.R., 387; 28 A.L.T., 1; 12 A.L.R., 307. *a'Beckett, A.-C.J.* (1906).

Patents Act 1903 (No. 21 of 1903), secs. 14, 58, 111—Appeal against decision of Commissioner of Patents—Costs of opposition to grant of patent before Commissioner.]—The costs of a successful appellant's opposition before the Commissioner were allowed on the lower Supreme Court scale. *Moore v. Phillips*, 4 C.L.R., 1411; 13 A.L.R., 424. *H.C., Griffith, C.J., Barton, Isaacs and Higgins, JJ.* (1907).

Patent—Appeal from Commissioner—Right of Commissioner when unsuccessful to his costs—Patents Act 1903 (No. 21 of 1903), sec. 111.]—Where the Commissioner of Patents is represented upon the hearing of an appeal from his decision, and the appeal succeeds, the costs of the Commissioner are in the discretion of the Court, and ordinarily, the successful appellant will not be ordered to pay them. *Re McKay's Application*, (1909) V.L.R., 423; 31 A.L.T., 63; 15 A.L.R., 445. *a'Beckett, Hodges and Hood, JJ.*

Patent—Practice—Application to Court for indulgence—Attendance of Commissioner of Patents—Costs.]—Where an applicant for a patent applies to the High Court or an indulgence on notice to the Commissioner of Patents it is the duty of the Commissioner to attend the hearing and the applicant, whether he is or is not successful, must pay the costs of the Commissioner. *In re Stanley's Application*, (1908) 5 C.L.R., 508; 14 A.L.R., 238. *Isaacs, J.*

III.—PRIVILEGE OF PATENTEE; INFRINGEMENT.

Patented article—Sales of patented articles to jobbers and dealers—Infringement by dealer of patentee's rights—Rights of patentee—Condition imposed upon dealer—Patents Act 1903 (No. 21 of 1903), sec. 62.]—It is open to a licensee by virtue of his statutory monopoly to make a sale *sub modo*, or accompanied by restrictive conditions which would not apply in the case of ordinary chattels; the imposition of these conditions in the case of a sale is not presumed, but, on the contrary, a sale having occurred the presumption is that the full right of ownership was meant to be vested in the purchaser; while the owner's rights in a patented chattel will be limited if there is brought home to him the knowledge of conditions imposed by the patentee or those representing the patentee upon him at the time of sale *National Phonograph Co. of Australia Ltd. v. Menck*, (1911) A.C., 336 (P.C.).

Patents Act 1903 (No. 21 of 1903), sec. 62—" Vend the invention."]—The meaning of "invention" as the object of the verb "vend" cannot be limited to the idea itself but extends to the product of the invention. Dictum of *Griffith, C.J.*, approved on appeal. *National Phonograph Co. of Australia Ltd. v. Menck*, 7 C.L.R., 481, at p. 512; 15 A.L.R., 1, at p. 6. On appeal, (1911) A.C., 336 (P.C.) at p. 348; 17 A.L.R., 94, at p. 97.

Patents Act 1903 (No. 21 of 1903), First Schedule—Form of Patent.]—*Per Griffith, C.J.*—"It appears that the letters patent issued in England under the *Statute of Monopolies* purported to grant the patentee the sole right "to make use exercise and vend the invention," and to forbid any other person

" to make use or put in practice the said invention." The form of letters patent in use in Australia does not contain the prohibitory clause, but follows the words of sec. 62, taken from the English Act of 1883, which itself, no doubt, derived them from the form of letters patent then in use. In both cases the substance of the privilege is, as already said, a right to forbid the use of the invention by others." *National Phonograph Co. of Australia Ltd.* v. *Menck*, 7 C.L.R., 481, at p. 510 ; 15 A.L.R., 1, at p. 6.

Patents Act 1903 (No. 21 of 1903)—Forms of expression adopted from English Patent Acts— In what sense used by Commonwealth Parliament.]—*Per O'Connor, J.*—" In the absence of expressions to the contrary, it will be taken that the Commonwealth Legislature, in adopting the forms of expression used in the English Acts from the *Statute of Monopolies* downwards, has used them in the sense which the English Courts have always attached to them." *National Phonograph Co. of Australia Ltd.* v. *Menck*, 7 C.L.R., 481, at p. 529 ; 15 A.L.R., 1, at p. 13.

Patents Act 1903 (No. 21 of 1903) sec. 62— Schedule—Statute of Monopolies.]—*Per Higgins, J.*—" The words of sec. 62 and of the grants of patents, in England as well as here, seem to be loose and ill-chosen, and, apparently have to be interpreted by reference to the *Statute of Monopolies* and decisions thereunder." *National Phonograph Co. of Australia Ltd.* v. *Menck*, 7 C.L.R., 481, at p. 543 ; 15 A.L.R., 1, at p. 18.

Burden of proof—Want of novelty by reason of prior sales—Identity of articles so sold with articles made in accordance with patent— Identity proved by circumstantial evidence— Facts within exclusive knowledge of other party, failure to prove.]—In an action for infringement of a patent for an improved hood for incandescent gas burners, the defendant raised the defence of want of novelty by reason of sales by the inventor to the public prior to the grant of the patent. The evidence for the defence to establish the identity of hoods sold prior to the grant of the patent with hoods manufactured in

accordance therewith did not include any chemical analysis of the hoods, but consisted of the testimony of a salesman engaged in the trade who had sold on, behalf cf the plaintiff's agent, many hoods before the grant of the patent and who since the grant had been for a long time engaged in the sale of hoods which were undoubtedly manufactured in accordance with the patent, and who said there was not so far as he could see any difference in the shape of the hoods or in the brilliancy of the light they gave, or the quantity of the light they diffused. *Held*, that the natural inference from the evidence was that hoods made in accordance with plaintiff's patent were in use before the grant thereof ; and that therefore, in the absence of evidence by the plaintiff that the hoods supplied before the grant of the patent were of a different kind and made according to a different specification, the defence of want of novelty had been sustained. *Cullen* v. *Welsbach Light Co. of Australasia Ltd.*, 4 C.L.R., 990 ; 13 A.L.R., 194. H.C. *Griffith, C.J., Barton, O'Connor and Higgins, JJ.* (1907).

Patent — Infringement — Use of another though similar mode of carrying principle of patent into practical effect.]—A. was the maker of a pneumatic milking apparatus, consisting of a metal teat-cup having a flexible bag within it, so arranged that, by means of a pipe from an air pump communicating with the space between the outer surface of the bag and inside of the cup, a vacuum was created intermittently causing the bag to cling closely to the teat and then relapse. This action combined with the suction induced the milk to flow. In order to facilitate the transit of the milk to the receiver A. made a small air inlet either in the milk passage or preferably at the top of the teat-cup thus admitting atmospheric pressure behind the milk, and for this improvement he obtained letters patent. B. a rival trader made and sold machines in which air was introduced behind the milk by means of a groove in the sides or flap of a rubber cap fitting over the top of a teat-cup identical in construction with that used by A.

Held, an infringement of A.'s patent. *Gillies v. Hartnett Patent Milking Machine Co. Ltd.*, 31 A.L.T., 164 ; 16 A.L.R., 88. *Hood, J.* (1910).

Patents Act 1890 (No. 1123), sec. 50—Costs—Defendant's particulars of objections—Certificate of reasonableness.]—For a case in which, for the purposes of taxation of costs under the special circumstances of the case, a certificate was granted that the particulars of the defendant under section 50 of the *Patents Act* 1890 were reasonable, *see Potter* v. *Broken Hill Proprietary Co. Ltd.*, 13 A.L.R. (C.N.), 3. *a' Beckett, J.* (1907).

PAWNBROKERS ACT.

Pawnbrokers Act 1890 (No. 1124), secs. 17, 39—Pledge, loan upon—Interest chargeable—Loan beyond £10.]—Where a sum greater than ten pounds has been lent by a pawnbroker upon a pledge, he is entitled, under section 17 of the *Pawnbrokers Act* 1890, to demand and receive of and from the person applying or offering to redeem the goods pledged interest at the following rates :— Up to and including ten pounds of the sum lent, interest at the rate of one shilling and fourpence per month for each pound, and for the balance of the sum lent interest at a rate not exceeding fifty per centum per annum. *Vanderspan* v. *Visbord*, (1907) V.L.R., 591 ; 29 A.L.T., 38 ; 13 A.L.R., 386. *Madden, C.J.*

PAYMENT.

Supreme Court Act 1890 (No. 1142), sec. 85—Where cause of action arises—Agent outside jurisdiction—Goods improperly sold by agent—Action by principal for money had and received—Place of payment—Rule that debtor must seek out creditor.]—*See* CONTRACT, col. 216. *Gosman* v. *Ockerby*, (1908) V.L.R., 298 ; 29 A.L.T., 266 ; 14 A.L.R., 186.

PERPETUITY.

See also, WILL.

Settlement, construction of—Life estate to A.—Remainder to children of A.—Gift over of share of child dying without issue—Rule against perpetuities—Gift void by—Subsequent limitation, whether also void—Gift over in default of grandchildren—Whether it includes gift over in default of children.]—By a settlement land was granted to the grantee to uses to the use of A. the wife of B. for her life, after her decease to the use of the child or children of A. and B. as A. should appoint, in default of appointment " To the use of all and every the said children and child their his and her heirs and assigns and . if more than one in equal shares as tenants in common. And if any one or more of the said children shall die without issue, then to the use of the other or others of the said children their heirs and assigns, and if more than one in equal shares. And in default of such issue to the right heirs of the said A. for ever." A. died never having had a child. *Held*, that the words " in default of issue " contemplated the failure of the grandchildren who were to take the ultimate fee, and that the rule against perpetuities invalidating the gift over to the grandchildren invalidated also the gift over to the right heirs of A. *Held*, also, that the gift over in the event of the default of grandchildren could not be split up so as to make the gift over take effect in the event, which had happened, but was not specially and separately provided for, of A. dying without ever having had a child. *In re Bence*, (1891) 3 Ch., 242, followed. *Milligan* v. *Shaw*, (1907) V.L.R., 668 ; 29 A.L.T., 75 ; 13 A.L.R., 545. *a' Beckett, J.*

PENSION.

See ASSIGNMENT, col. 56.

PERJURY.

See CRIMINAL LAW, cols. 341, 342.

PLEDGE.

See PAWNBROKERS ACT.

POISONS ACT.

Poisons Act 1890 (No. 1125), secs. 4, 11—Sale of poison by unqualified person—Sale by assistant—Offence by master.]—The combined effect of secs. 4 and 11 of the *Poisons Act* 1890 is to make a sale of poison in contravention of the former section by an assistant on behalf of his master an offence by the master. *Shillinglaw* v. *Redmond*, (1908) V.L.R., 427; 30 A.L.T., 37; 14 A.L.R., 343. *Madden, C.J.*

POLICE AND POLICE REGULATION ACT.

Police Regulation Act 1890 (No. 1127), sec. 58—" Goods " meaning of.]—The word " goods " in sec. 58 of the *Police Regulation Act* 1890 includes money. *McKenna* v. *Dent and Williamson*, (1912) V.L.R., 150; 33 A.L.T., 202; 18 A.L.R., 148. *a' Beckett, J.*

Pension—Whether assignable—Liability of pensioner to be recalled to duty—Police Regulation Act 1890 (No. 1127), secs. 20, 24.] —A pension granted to a police officer under Part III. of the *Police Regulation Act* 1890 is not assignable, inasmuch as under sec. 24 it is subject to the condition that the officer shall remain in the service of the Government to the extent that, though he is for the time being not employed, he may be recalled to his duties and be actively employed. *Crouch* v. *Victorian Railways Commissioners*, (1907) V.L.R,, 80; 28 A.L.T., 141; 12 A.L.R., 574, followed. *In re Hilliard; Ex parte Tinkler*, (1907) V.L.R., 375; 28 A.L.T., 204; 13 A.L.R., 138. F.C., *Madden, C.J., Hodges* and *Hood, JJ.*

POLICE OFFENCES ACTS.

I.—HIGHWAYS; VEHICLES.

Highway—Obstruction—Standing or loitering in street and not moving on when requested—Collecting a crowd—Interference with traffic—By-law—Police Offences Act 1890 (No. 1126), sec. 6.]—The term " obstruction " as used in sec. 6 of the *Police Offences Act* 1890 includes any continuous physical occupation of portion of a street which appreciably diminishes the space available for passing and re-passing, or which renders such passing and repassing less commodious, whether or not any person is in fact affected thereby, and the lawfulness or unlawfulness of the obstruction, considered apart from the Act, is immaterial. The two defendants, at about half-past six on a summer's evening, stood in the carriage-way of a street of Sale playing a drum and a concertina and singing, and thereby collected a crowd of about 80 persons, and they refused to move on when requested to do so by a police officer. The Magistrate found that there was no actual interference with the traffic, and that the defendants were not making an unreasonable use of the street, but that their acts brought together a crowd which was likely to cause an obstruction to the street. *Held*, that the defendants were properly convicted under a by-law made under sec. 6 of the *Police Offences Act* 1890, which provided that any person obstructing any carriage-way, etc., within the municipality by standing or loitering therein or thereon, should, upon being requested so to do by a member of the police force, discontinue such standing or loitering, and that any person committing a wilful breach of that by-law should be guilty of an offence against the section. *Haywood* v. *Mumford*, (1908) 7 C.L.R., 133; 14 A.L.R., 555. H.C., *Griffith, C.J., Barton, O'Connor* and *Higgins, JJ.*

Street, purpose of—Reasonable user.]— *Per Hood, J.—*The primary object of a street is the free passage of the public who are entitled to use it *eundo et redeundo,* and for a short time *morando.* To hold a prayer meeting in a street is not a reasonable user of it. *Mumford* v. *Haywood,* (1908) V.L.R., 308; 29 A.L.T., 247; 14 A.L.R., 206.

Motor car—Rule of the road—" Driving on wrong side of the road without justifiable cause "—Motor car and tram car proceeding in same direction—Duty of motor car to pass on off side—" Vehicle "—Validity of regulation—Motor Car Act 1909 (No. 2237), sec. 15 —Motor Car Regulations 1910, reg. 2 (3)— Police Offences Act 1890 (No. 1126), sec. 17 (1) (a)—Police Offences Act 1891 (No. 1241) sec. 5.]—Regulation 2 (3) of the Motor Car Regulations 1910 provides that " every person driving or in charge of a motor car when used on any road, street, lane, highway, or other public place, shall . . . when passing any vehicle " &c. " proceeding in the same direction, keep the motor car on the right or off side of the same." *Held,* that a cable tram car is a " vehicle " within the meaning of that regulation, and that such regulation is not *ultra vires* sec. 15 of the *Motor Car Act* 1909. *Held,* therefore, that a motor car driver, obeying the direction of such regulation in passing a cable tram car, which is proceeding practically along the middle of the road in the same direction as the motor car, is not guilty of the offence under sec. 17 (1) (*a*) of the *Police Offences Act* 1890 (as amended by sec. 5 of the *Police Offences Act* 1891) of " driving on the wrong side of the road without justifiable cause." *Gillin* v. *Malmgren,* (1912) V.L.R., 26; 33 A.L.T, 118; 17 A.L.R., 564. *a'Beckett, J.*

Motor Car Act 1909 (No. 2237), sec. 10— Reckless driving—" Recklessly," meaning of.]—*See* MOTOR CAR ACT. *Kane* v. *Dureau,* (1911) V.L.R., 293; 33 A.L.T., 15; 17 A.L.R., 277.

II.—INSULTING AND RIOTOUS BEHAVIOUR.

Police Offences Act 1890 (No. 1126), secs. 26, 27—Insulting behaviour—" Divine service," what is—Address—Musical performance—Opening and closing with hymn and prayer.]—At a meeting held at the Gaiety Theatre, Melbourne, on Sunday afternoon, an address was delivered on the subject of " Melbourne's Sins and Follies." During the half-hour preceding the delivery of the address music was played by an orchestra and songs were sung. Limelight views were also shown. The meeting was opened and closed with a hymn and prayer, and during the meeting several hymns were sung. *Held,* that, the primary objects of the meeting being the address and the musical and other attractions, the proceedings were not converted into " divine service " within the meaning of the *Police Offences Act* 1890 by the addition of prayers and hymns. *Goodson* v. *M'Namara,* (1907) V.L.R., 89; 28 A.L.T., 115; 12 A.L.R., 547. *Hood, J.*

Police Offences Act 1891 (No. 1241), sec. 7, sub-sec. 1 (a)—Behaving in a riotous manner, what necessary to constitute.]—A person cannot be convicted of behaving in a riotous manner within the meaning of the *Police Offences Act* 1891, sec. 7, sub-sec. 1 (*a*) unless his behaviour has been such as is calculated to alarm the public. *Scott* v. *Howard and Parkinson,* (1912) V.L.R., 189; 33 A.L.T., 221; 18 A.L.R., 157. (*See Police Offences Act* 1912 (No. 2422), sec. 25).

III.—VAGRANCY.

Police Offences Act 1890 (No. 1126), sec. 40 (1)—No visible lawful means or insufficient lawful means of support—Elements of offence, what are.]—In order to prove an offence under sec. 40 (1) of the *Police Offences Act* 1890 it must be shown not only that the person charged " has no visible lawful means of support " or " insufficient lawful means of support," but that he has been required by a Justice to give a good account of his means and has failed to do so, or that he has been duly summoned by a Justice to appear before him and has either failed to attend, or, attending, has failed to give such good account. *Wilson* v. *Benson*, (1905) V.L.R., 229; 26 A.L.T., 144; 11 A.L.R., 85, approved. *Wilson* v. *Travers*, (1906) V.L.R., 734; 28 A.L.T., 56; 12 A.L.R., 413. F.C., *a'Beckett*, *A.-C.J.*, *Cussen* and *Chomley*, *JJ.* See *Police Offences Act* 1907 (No. 2093), secs. 3, 4].

Police Offences Act 1890 (No. 1126), sec. 40 (1)—Account of means of support—Whether Justices may be required to call upon accused to give.]—Where a person has been arrested and brought before Justices sitting as a Court of Petty Sessions upon a warrant issued upon an information stating that he is " a person having insufficient lawful means of support," the Justices cannot be required by the informant to require the accused to give an account of his means of support under sec. 40 (1) of the *Police Offences Act* 1890. *Wilson* v. *Travers*, (1906) V.L.R., 734; 28 A.L.T., 56; 12 A.L.R., 413. F.C., *a'Beckett*, *A.-C.J.*, *Cussen* and *Chomley*, *JJ.*

Police Offences Act 1890 (No. 1126), sec. 40 (1)—" Visible means of support."]—In sec. 40 (1) of the *Police Offences Act* 1890 the expression " visible means of support " does not mean merely that which can be seen at a glance, but extends to what is visible to the bodily or mental eye of an attentive observer after reasonable opportunity and inquiry. *Wilson* v. *Travers*, (1906) V.L.R., 734; 28 A.L.T., 56; 12 A.L.R., 413. F.C., *a'Beckett*, *A.-C.J.*, *Cussen* and *Chomley*, *JJ.*

Police Offences Act 1890 (No. 1126), sec. 40 (1)—" Required," meaning of.]—In sec. 40 (1) of the *Police Offences Act* 1890 the word " required " refers primarily to the case where the investigating Justice is willing to go and does go to or meets the person into whose means of support an inquiry is to be made. *Wilson* v. *Travers*, (1906) V.L.R., 734; 28 A.L.T., 56; 12 A.L.R., 413. F.C., *a'Beckett*, *A.-C.J.*, *Cussen* and *Chomley*, *JJ.*

Police Offences Act 1890 (No. 1126), sec. 40 (1)—" Duly summoned," meaning of.]—In sec. 40 (1) of the *Police Offences Act* 1890 the expression " duly summoned " means reasonably notified by a Justice to appear before him ; it does not refer to a summons under the *Justices Act* 1890. *Wilson* v. *Travers*, (1906) V.L.R., 734; 28 A.L.T., 56; 12 A.L.R., 413. F.C., *a'Beckett*, *A.-C.J.* *Cussen* and *Chomley*, *JJ.*

Police Offences Act 1890 (No. 1126), sec. 40 (1)—" Brought before any Justice in pursuance of the provisions of this Part."]—*Quaere* as to the meaning of the words " brought before any Justice in pursuance of the provisions of this Part." *Wilson* v. *Travers*, (1906) V.L.R., 734; 28 A.L.T., 56; 12 A.L.R., 413. F.C., *a'Beckett*, *A.-C.J.*, *Cussen* and *Chomley*, *JJ.*

Police Offences Act 1890 (No. 1126), sec. 40 (1)—Idle and disorderly person—No visible lawful means of support—Inquiry into means of support—Nature of act, whether administrative or judicial.]—The act of inquiry into means of support under sec. 40 (1) of the *Police Offences Act* 1890 is of an administrative or extra-judicial character, and is not a judicial act whose performance can be compelled by mandamus or controlled by *certiorari*. *Wilson* v. *Travers*, (1906) V.L.R., 734; 28 A.L.T., 56; 12 A.L.R., 413. F.C., *a'Beckett*, *A.-C.J.*, *Cussen* and *Chomley*, *JJ.*

Police Offences Act 1907 (No. 2093), sec. 4 Lawful means of support—Prostitution.]—The practice of prostitution is not a " lawful means of support " within the meaning of sec. 4 of the *Police Offences Act* 1907. *Reg.* v. *Sayers*, 4 W.W. & a'B. (L.), 46, applied. *Porter* v. *Martin*, (1910) V.L.R., 38; 31 A.L.T., 105; 16 A.L.R., 12. *a'Beckett*, *J.*

Police Offences Act 1890 (No. 1126), sec. 40 —Vagrancy—Lawful means of support—Savings from prostitution.]—A prostitute cannot be convicted of being an idle and disorderly person on the ground that she has insufficient lawful means of support, if, as the result of savings by her from her earnings as a prostitute, she possesses money and other property sufficient for her support. *Green*

v. *Jones*, (1910) V.L.R., 284; 31 A.L.T., 203; 16 A.L.R., 304. *Cussen, J.*

Police Offences Act 1907 (No. 2093), sec. 4 —No lawful means of support—Production by accused of some money or property honestly earned, effect of.]—The production or possession by the accused of some money or property honestly obtained is not in itself an answer to a charge that the accused has no lawful means of support or has insufficient lawful means of support. *Porter* v. *Martin* (1910) V.L.R., 38; 31 A.L.T., 105; 16, A.L.R., 12. *a' Beckett, J.*

Police Offences Act 1907 (No. 2093), sec. 4 —Money or property " honestly " obtained— Prostitution.]—*Quaere*, whether money obtained by prostitution is money honestly obtained within the meaning of sec. 4 of the *Police Offences Act* 1907. *Porter* v. *Martin*, (1910) V.L.R., 38; 31 A.L.T., 105; 16 A.L.R., 12. *a' Beckett, J.*

Police Offences Act 1907 (No. 2093), sec. 4 —Savings from earnings as a prostitute— Whether property " honestly obtained."]— Moneys saved by a prostitute out of her earnings as such on property purchased therewith is not money or property that has been dishonestly obtained. *Green* v. *Jones*, (1910) V.L.R., 284; 31 A.L.T., 203; 16 A.L.R., 304. *Cussen, J.*

Police Offences Act 1907 (No. 2093), sec. 8 (a), (b)—Vagrancy—Evidence of bad character, when it must be tendered—Evidence as to general character, what is—Evidence to rebut.]—The defendant was charged under sec. 40 (VI.) of the *Police Offences Act* 1890 with being an idle and disorderly person. He gave evidence in his defence and described the nature of his employment and added that he was living respectably and earning an honest living. *Held*, that the latter statements did not amount to evidence as to general character such as to permit the informant to give evidence in rebuttal under the *Police Offences Act* 1907 (No. 2093), sec. 8 (*b*). *Held*, also, that the evidence permitted by sec. 8 (*a*) of the *Police Offences Act* 1907 as to the defendant's bad character cannot be given after the informant has closed

his case, unless the defendant has in his defence given evidence as to his general character. *Hickling* v. *Skerritt*, (1912) V.L.R., 322; 34 A.L.T., 72; 18 A.L.R., 329. *Madden, C.J.*

Police Offences Act 1890 (No. 1126), sec. 40 (iv.)—Police Offences Act 1907 (No. 2093), sec. 5 (4)—Idle and disorderly person—Occupier of house frequented by persons having no visible lawful means of support—House frequented by prostitutes—Proof that prostitutes have visible means of support—Whether a defence.]—Where on the hearing of a charge of being the occupier of a house frequented by persons having no visible lawful means of support, the complainant proves that the defendant's house is frequented by certain prostitutes, proof by the defendant that such prostitutes had in fact visible lawful means of support, will not be a defence. *Reg.* v. *Sayers*, 4 W.W. & A'B. (L.), 46, followed. *Jones* v. *Roxby*, 32 A.L.T. (Supplement), 8; 16 A.L.R. (C.N.), 18. *Judge Moule* (1910).

Police Offences Act 1890 (No. 1126), sec. 40 (vi.)—Information, sufficiency of—Allegation of facts set out in sub-sec. vi.—No allegation that defendant was an idle and disorderly person.]—An information under sec. 40 (VI.) of the *Police Offences Act* 1890 alleged that the defendant was found by night armed with a bludgeon, and being thereto required, did not give a good account of his means of support and assign a valid and satisfactory reason for being so armed, but did not allege that he was an idle and disorderly person because he was so found by night. *Held*, that the information was defective. *Hickling* v. *Skerritt*, (1912) V.L.R., 322; 34 A.L.T., 72; 18 A.L.R., 329. *Madden, C.J.*

Police Offences Act 1890 (No. 1126), sec. 41 (iv.)—Obscene book—Wilfully exposing to view in a public place—Distributing books which on examination are found to contain obscene matter.]—To establish the offence under sec. 41 (IV.) of the *Police Offences Act* 1890 of wilfully exposing to view in any public place any obscene book, &c., it must be shown that the obscene matter was exhibited in such a way that it could be seen by any one passing by who cared to look. The mere distribution among the public of books, which may on examination be found to contain obscene matter, is not an offence within sec. 41 (IV.). *Porter* v. *Taylor*, (1907) V.L.R., 112; 28 A.L.T., 150; 12 A.L.R., 614.

Police Offences Act 1890 (No. 1126), sec. 41 (xii.)—" Place of public resort "—Charge for admission.]—A place may be a place of public resort though a charge is made for admission thereto. *Howard* v. *Murphy*; *Sainsbury* v. *Palmer*, 28 A.L.T. (Supplement), 10; 13 A.L.R. (C.N.), 3. *Judge Johnston* (1906).

IV.—LIVING ON PROSTITUTION.

Police Offences Act 1907 (No. 2093), sec. 5 (4)—" Brothel," meaning of—Keeper of brothel—Evidence.]—Where a person is prosecuted under sec. 5 (4) of the *Police Offences Act* 1907 for keeping a brothel, and it is proved that he was in charge or had control of a place resorted to by persons of both sexes for the purpose of prostitution, it is not necessary to prove that the defendant actually received payment for allowing the place to be so used. *Appleby* v. *Reddan*, (1912) V.L.R., 270; 34 A.L.T., 28; 18 A.L.R., 326. *Hood, J.*

V.—PROPERTY SUSPECTED OF BEING STOLEN.

Police Offences Act 1907 (No. 2093), sec. 10—Property suspected of being stolen—Unexplained possession—Actual, not constructive possession meant.]—The persons liable to punishment under sec. 10 of the *Police Offences Act* 1907 for having in their possession any personal property suspected of being stolen are only those who are found in actual physical control of the property. The section does not apply to mere constructive possession of such property. *Tatchell* v *Lovett*, (1908) V.L.R., 645; 30 A.L.T., 88; 14 A.L.R., 540. *Hood, J.*

Police Offences Act 1907 (No. 2093), sec. 10—Property suspected of being stolen—Unexplained possession—Suspicion and possession, whether necessarily contemporaneous.]—

A person cannot be convicted under sec. 10 of the *Police Offences Act* 1907 for " having in his possession personal property suspected of being stolen " unless such property was at the time he was in possession of it, suspected of being stolen. *Brown* v. *Schiffman*, (1911) V.L.R., 133; 32 A.L.T., 115; 16 A.L.R., 633. *Hodges, J.*

Police Offences Act 1907 (No. 2093), sec. 10—Unexplained possession of stolen property——Property suspected of being stolen—Basis of suspicion.]—A person cannot be apprehended or convicted under sec. 10 of the *Police Offences Act* 1907 for having in his possession any personal property suspected of being stolen where at the time of his arrest the constable or other person apprehending him had no knowledge or information that a larceny of property similar to the property in question had been committed. *McCarthy* v. *Williams*, 30 A.L.T. (Supplement), 23; 15 A.L.R. (C.N.), 3. *Judge Box* (1909). [Section 10 of the *Police Offences Act* 1907 is reproduced in sec. 40 of the *Police Offences Act* 1912 (No. 2422).

VI.—OPIUM SMOKING.

Opium smoking Prohibition Act 1905 (No. 2003), sec. 10—" Privy " to offending against Act, meaning of.]—*See* OPIUM SMOKING PROHIBITION *Stapleton* v. *Davis*; *Stapleton* v. *Bell*, (1908) V.L.R., 114; 29 A.L.T., 162; 14 A.L.R., 26.

Opium Smoking Prohibition Act 1905 (No. 2003), sec. 10—Conviction of principal offender of smoking opium—Whether evidence against person charged with being " privy " to offending.]—*See* OPIUM SMOKING PROHIBITION. *Stapleton* v. *Davis*; *Stapleton* v. *Bell*, (1908) V.L.R., 114; 29 A.L.T., 162; 14 A.L.R., 26.

VII.—GAMING.

(a) *Various Offences.*

Police Offences Act 1890 (No. 1126), secs. 49, 50, 51, 52, 62—Lotteries Gaming and Betting Act 1906 (No. 2055), sec. 12—Gaming houses, &c.—Place used for the purpose of unlawful gaming being carried on therein—

"Place"—"User."]—In order to convict a person charged with unlawfully assisting in conducting the business of a place used for the purpose of unlawful gaming being carried on therein, contrary to section 62 of the *Police Offences Act* 1890, it is essential to show that the area of operations was in some special and peculiar way or in some degree under the control and ordering of the defendant as a proprietor or of someone who managed it for him or assisted him in his business, and that that area was used by the defendant as principal or as assistant for the purpose of unlawful gaming being carried on by persons resorting thereto. A defendant charged under section 62 of the *Police Offences Act* 1890 assisted in conducting the business of unlawful gaming on an excavated portion of the land of a public park to which the public generally had resort; neither the defendant nor those associated with him in such business claimed or had any right to prevent any of the public from going on any portion of such land, nor did they attempt to exercise any dominion or control over it, nor did they use any specialized part of such portion of land as their particular stand or place of conducting the said business. *Held*, that the defendant was not guilty of an offence within section 62 of the Act. *Prior* v. *Sherwood*, 3 C.L.R., 1054; 12 A.L R., 510; and *Powell* v. *The Kempton Park Racecourse Co. Ltd.*, (1899) A.C., 143, as to "user," followed. *McCann* v. *Morgan*, (1912) V.L.R., 303; 34 A.L.T., 43; 18 A.L.R., 334. *Madden, C J*

Police Offences Act 1890 (No. 1126), secs. 49, 51—"Assisting" in conducting a common gaming house—Principal or person other than employee.]—*Semble*, The offence of "assisting" in conducting the business of a common gaming house may be committed by a person who himself actually conducts the business and does not act under the control or orders of some other person. *Rogerson* v *Phillips and O'Hagan*, (1906) V L.R., 272; 27 A L T., 166; 12 A.L.R., 147. *a'Beckett, J.* (1906).

Police Offences Act 1890 (No. 1126), secs. 49, 51—"Business," assisting in conducting —Club incorporated as a company—Share-holders in company members of club—Totalisator—Whether conducted as a business—Percentage of stakes retained—Burden of proof—Moneys received as consideration for an assurance to pay moneys on contingencies relating to horse-races.]—*See* GAMING AND WAGERING, cols. 604, 605. *O'Donnell* v. *Solomon*, (1906) V.L.R., 425; 27 A.L.T., 237; 12 A.L.R., 283. F.C. *a'Beckett, A.C.J., Hodges* and *Chomley, JJ.* (1906).

Gaming—Contrivance for gaming—Poker machine—Unlawful gaming—Room used for purpose of unlawful gaming being carried on therein—Police Offences Act 1890 (No. 1126), secs. 62, 64—Lotteries Gaming and Betting Act 1906 (No. 2055), sec. 31.]—*See* GAMING AND WAGERING, col 606 *O'Donnell* v *Dodd*, (1910) V L R , 482; 32 A.L.T., 87; 16 A.L.R., 539.

Lotteries Gaming and Betting Act 1906 (No. 2055), secs. 5 (2), 10, 15, 17—Place used as a common gaming house, meaning of— User of place in such a way that it is by Statute deemed and taken to be a common gaming house—Whether limited in section 17 to user as a betting house.]—*See* GAMING AND WAGERING, cols. 607, 608. *Macmanamny* v. *King*, (1907) V.L.R., 535; 28 A.L.T., 250; 13 A.L.R., 258.

Lotteries Gaming and Betting Act 1906 (No. 2055), sec. 22—Information as to betting on intended horse race—Publication in newspaper—Betting odds offered in betting market.] *See* GAMING AND WAGERING, col. 608. *O'Donnell* v. *Smart*, (1907) V.L.R., 439; 28 A.L.T., 245; 13 A.L.R., 255.

Lotteries Gaming and Betting Act 1906 (No. 2055), sec. 22—"Information or advice" as to the betting on intended horse race, meaning of.]—*See* GAMING AND WAGERING, col. 608. *O'Donnell* v. *Smart*, (1907) V.L.R., 439; 28 A.L.T., 245; 13 A.L.R., 255.

Lotteries Gaming and Betting Act 1906 (No. 2055), sec. 22—Information as to intended horse race—"The betting," meaning of.]—*See* GAMING AND WAGERING, col. 608. *O'Donnell* v. *Smart*, (1907) V.L.R., 439; 28 A.L.T., 245; 13 A.L.R., 255.

Lottery, law relating to—Imperial Statutes, Whether impliedly repealed by Victorian legislation—6 Geo. II., c. 35 ; 4 Geo. IV., c. 60—Police Offences Act 1890 (No. 1126), sec. 37.]—There has been no implied repeal by Victorian legislation of the Statutes 6 Geo. II., c 35 and 4 Geo. IV., c. 60. *The Attorney-General* v. *Moses,* (1907) V.L.R., 130 ; 28 A.L.T., 125 ; 12 A.L.R., 606. F.C. *a' Beckett, A.C.J., Hodges* and *Chomley, JJ.*

Lottery, law relating to—4 Geo. IV., c. 60, sec. 41—Penalty for sale of ticket—Exception where lottery authorized by Act of Parliament —Lottery got up in Tasmania—Lottery authorized by Act of Parliament of Tasmania —Sale of ticket in Victoria.]—*See* GAMING AND WAGERING, col. 609. *The Attorney-General* v. *Moses,* (1907) V.L.R., 130 ; 28 A.L.T., 125 ; 12 A.L.R., 606.

6 Geo. II., c. 35—" Foreign " lottery, what is—Lottery got up in Tasmania.]—*See* GAMING AND WAGERING, col. 609. *The Attorney-General* v. *Moses,* (1907) V.L.R., 130 ; 28 A.L.T., 125 ; 12 A.L.R., 606.

Lottery, law relating to—Foreign lottery— Imperial Statutes, whether in force in Victoria—6 Geo. II., c. 35 ; 4 Geo. IV., c. 60— 9 Geo. IV., c. 83.]—*See* GAMING AND WAGERING col. 610. *The Attorney-General* v. *Moses,* (1907) V.L.R., 130 ; 28 A.L.T., 125 ; 12 A.L.R., 606.

(b) Declaration that House is a Common Gaming House.

Lotteries Gaming and Betting Act 1906 (No. 2055), sec. 38 (1), (2)—Declaration that premises are a common gaming house— Whether " may " means " shall "—Discretion of Court.]—*See* GAMING AND WAGERING, col. 610. *In re The Lotteries Gaming and Betting Act* 1906 ; *Ex parte Gleeson,* (1907) V.L.R., 368 ; 28 A.L.T., 228 ; 13 A.L.R., 146.

Lotteries Gaming and Betting Act 1906 (No. 2055), sec. 38—Application for declaration that premises are a common gaming house—Owner or occupier whether entitled

to be heard.]—*See* GAMING AND WAGERING, col. 610. *In re Lotteries Gaming and Betting Act* 1906 ; *In re Shanghai Club* ; *In re Ah Pow* ; *Ex parte Gleeson,* (1907) V.L.R., 463 ; 29 A.L.T., 31 ; 13 A.L.R., 360.

Lotteries Gaming and Betting Act 1906 (No. 2055), sec. 38 (1), (2)—Application for declaration that premises are common gaming house—Who may be heard—Owner or occupier.]—*See* GAMING AND WAGERING, cols. 610, 611. *In re Lotteries Gaming and Betting Act* 1906 ; *Ex parte Gleeson,* (1907) V.L.R., 368 ; 28 A.L.T., 228 ; 13 A.L.R., 146.

Lotteries Gaming and Betting Act 1906 (No. 2055), sec. 38—Application for declaration that premises are a common gaming house—Affidavit of police officer showing reasonable grounds for suspecting—Suspicion, whether in mind of police officer or Court— Prima facie case, how established—Prima facie case, how answered.]—*See* GAMING AND WAGERING, col. 611. *In re Lotteries Gaming and Betting Act* 1906 ; *In re Shanghai Club* ; *In re Ah Pow* ; *Ex parte Gleeson,* (1907) V.L.R., 463 ; 29 A.L.T., 31 ; 13 A.L.R., 360.

Lotteries Gaming and Betting Act 1906 (No. 2055), sec. 38—Application for declaration that premises are a common gaming house —Affidavit of police officer showing reasonable grounds for suspecting—Whether police officer may be cross-examined thereon.]— *See* GAMING AND WAGERING, cols. 611, 612. *In re Lotteries Gaming and Betting Act* 1906 ; *In re Shanghai Club* ; *In re Ah Pow* ; *Ex parte Gleeson,* (1907) V.L.R., 463 ; 29 A.L.T., 31 ; 13 A.L.R., 360.

Lotteries Gaming and Betting Act 1906 (No. 2055), sec. 38—Application for declaration that premises are a common gaming house—Affidavits in reply to affidavits of party opposing, admissibility of — Cross-examination of deponents.]—*See* GAMING AND WAGERING, cols. 611, 612. *In re Lotteries Gaming and Betting Act* 1906 ; *In re Shanghai Club* ; *In re Ah Pow* ; *Ex parte Gleeson,* (1907) V.L.R., 463 ; 29 A.L.T., 31 ; 13 A.L.R., 360.

(c) Practice and Procedure.

Police Offences Act 1890 (No. 1126), secs. 49, 51—Gaming—Information under two sections.]—The defendants were charged with assisting in conducting the business of a room used for the purpose of moneys being received by persons conducting the business thereof as the consideration for an assurance to pay moneys on contingencies relating to horse-races. *Held*, that sections 49 and 51 of the *Police Offences Act* 1890 are to be read together and that the information disclosed an offence. *Rogerson v. Phillips and O'Hagan*, (1906) V.L.R., 272; 27 A.L.T., 166; 12 A.L.R., 147. *a'Beckett, J.* (1906).

Police Offences Act 1890 (No. 1126), sec. 51—Occupier of house permitting same to be used for betting—No allegation in information of person by whom house was used.]—An information charging that the defendant " being the occupier of a certain shop at D. did unlawfully knowingly and wilfully permit the same to be used for the purpose of betting with persons resorting thereto " discloses no offence under section 51 of the *Police Offences Act* 1890. It would disclose an offence if after the words " for the purpose of " followed the words " one T.B. a person using the same." *Knox* v. *Thomas Bible*; *Knox* v. *J. L. Bible*, (1907) V.L.R., 485; 29 A.L.T., 23; 13 A.L.R., 352. *Cussen, J.* [Special leave to appeal refused, (1907) 4 C.L.R., 1462.]

Gaming—Search warrant—On what materials issued—" Complaint on oath," meaning of—Oral evidence to supplement written information, admissibility of—Police Offences Act 1890 (No. 1126), sec. 57, 2nd Schedule—Lotteries Gaming and Betting Act 1906 (No. 2055), sec. 50—Justices Act 1890 (No. 1105), secs. 4, 18, 19 (2), 2nd Schedule—Licensing Act 1906 (No. 2068), sec. 23.]—The complaint on oath required by section 57 of the *Police Offences Act* 1890 must be in writing. *Semble*, where the information on which a warrant is issued does not set out all the matters specified by the section, oral evidence sufficiently specifying those matters is inadmissible. *Montague* v. *Ah Shen*, (1907) V.L.R,

458; 28 A.L.T., 248; 13 A.L.R., 261. F.C. *Madden, C.J., a'Beckett* and *Hood, JJ.*

Police Offences Act 1890 (No. 1126), sec. 57—Gaming—Search warrant issued on insufficient materials, validity of.]—A warrant issued under section 57 of the *Police Offences Act* 1890 upon an information which does not comply with the requirements of the section by setting out the various matters therein specified is bad. *Montague* v. *Ah Shen*, (1907) V.L.R., 458; 28 A.L.T., 248; 13 A.L.R., 261. F.C. *Madden, C.J., a'Beckett* and *Hood, JJ.*

Police Offences Act 1890 (No. 1126), secs. 49, 51—Use of room for purpose of betting—User, sufficiency of evidence to prove—Repeated acts, whether necessary to show—Character of use, proof of by admission express or implied.]—In order to prove an offence under sections 49 and 51 of the *Police Offences Act* 1890, it is not absolutely necessary to show a user extending over more than one day, or to show that the acts were many times repeated. If there is nothing else, there cannot be user without repeated acts ; but a defendant may either by express or implied admission show the character of his use of the place in connection with a single act or with a few acts. Accordingly, where but few bets were shown to have been made, but a systematic course of conduct was proved, the evidence was held to be sufficient. *Knox* v. *Thomas Bible*; *Knox* v. *J. L. Bible*, (1907) V.L.R., 485; 29 A.L.T., 23; 13 A.L.R., 352 *Cussen, J.* (1907). [Special leave to appeal refused, 4 C.L.R., 1462.]

Lotteries Gaming and Betting Act 1906 (No. 2055), secs. 10, 17—Evidence—Use as a common gaming house—Acts of persons other than defendants—Acts prior to the date of the alleged offence.]—*See* GAMING AND WAGERING, cols. 613, 614. *Macmanamny* v. *King*, (1907) V.L.R., 535; 28 A.L.T., 250; 13 A.L.R., 258.

Police Offences Act 1890 (No. 1126), sec. 51—Assisting in conducting gaming house—Relationship with person assisted and character in which assistance given—How far necessary to prove.]—Upon an information for assisting in conducting the business of a house, &c. in contravention of section 51 of the *Police Offences Act* 1890, it is not necessary to show the precise relationship between the defendant and the person whom he assisted, or the precise character in which the defendant gave the assistance. *Knox* v. *Thomas Bible*; *Knox* v. *J. L. Bible*, (1907) V.L.R., 485; 29 A.L.T., 23; 13 A.L.R., 352. *Cussen, J.* (1907). [Special leave to appeal refused, (1907) 4 C.L.R., 1462.]

Lotteries Gaming and Betting Act 1906 (No. 2055), secs. 10, 17—House opened kept or used for purpose of illegal lottery—Method of drawing lottery, whether necessary to prove.]—*See* GAMING AND WAGERING, cols. 614, 615. *Macmanamny* v. *King*, (1907) V.L.R., 535; 28 A.L.T., 250; 13 A.L.R., 258.

Lotteries Gaming and Betting Act 1906 (No. 2055), sec. 61—Evidence of certain fact made prima facie evidence of commission of offence—Procedural provision—Whether applicable to offences committed before passing of Act.]—*See* GAMING AND WAGERING, col. 615. *Knox* v. *Thomas Bible*; *Knox* v. *J. L. Bible*, (1907) V.L.R., 485; 29 A.L.T., 23; 13 A.L.R., 352.

Police Offences Act 1890 (No. 1126), sec. 64—Scope of section—Prima facie evidence that place is a common gaming house.]—Section 64 applies only where the charge is one of keeping a common gaming house. *O'Donnell* v. *Dodd*, (1910) V.L.R., 482; 32 A.L.T., 87; 16 A.L.R., 539. *Madden, C.J., Hodges* and *Hood, JJ.*

Police Offences Act 1890 (No. 1126), sec. 51—Street Betting Suppression Act 1896 (No. 1436), sec. 7—Using house for betting purposes—" First offence," " second offence," meaning of.]—*Semble*, the words "first offence" in section 7 of the *Street Betting Suppression Act* 1896 include all offences up to the time of the first conviction and probably all offences where it is not proved that there has been a prior conviction. *Semble*, " a second offence " means any offence where it is proved that the act was done after a prior conviction for a former offence. *Knox* v *Thomas Bible*; *Knox* v.

J. L. Bible, (1907) V.L.R., 485; 29 A.L.T., 23; 13 A.L.R., 352. *Cussen, J.* [Special leave to appeal refused, (1907) 4 C.L.R., 1462.]

Police Offences Act 1890 (No. 1126), sec. 51—Assisting in conducting business of house used for betting—Two charges of assisting during consecutive periods—Continuous offence—Whether one offence or two.]—Where a defendant was convicted and fined for an offence under section 51 of the *Police Offences Act* 1890 of assisting between the 26th October and the 2nd November 1906 in conducting the business of a certain house, &c and was on the same day charged before the same Court with having committed the same offence between the 3rd and 6th November 1906. *Held*, that the justices were not bound to assume that the two offences were one continuous offence, and in the absence of evidence to that effect might rightly convict of the second offence. *Crepps* v. *Durden*, 1 S.L.C. (9th ed.), 692, distinguished. *Knox* v. *Thomas Bible*; *Knox* v. *J. L. Bible*, (1907) V L R , 485; 29 A L T , 23; 13 A L R., 352. *Cussen, J.* (1907). [Special leave to appeal refused, (1907) 4 C.L.R., 1462.]

Police Offences Act 1890 (No. 1126), secs. 49, 51, 89—Street Betting Suppression Act 1896 (No. 1436), sec. 7—Assisting in conducting a common gaming house—First offence, punishment for—Imprisonment in default of payment of fine—Term of imprisonment in default greater than maximum term provided for offence—Jurisdiction.]—Although section 51 of the *Police Offences Act* 1890 as amended by the *Street Betting Suppression Act* 1896 provides that for a first offence the punishment shall be either a fine or imprisonment for a term not exceeding three months, the justices, in imposing a fine, have jurisdiction under section 89 of the *Police Offences Act* 1890 to impose a period of six months' imprisonment in default of payment of the fine. *Macmanamny* v. *McCulloch (or McMahon)*, 18 A.L.T., 164; 3 A.L.R., 14, approved. *Rogerson* v. *Phillips and O'Hagan*, (1906) V.L.R., 272; 27 A.L.T., 166; 12 A.L.R., 147. *a'Beckett, J.*, (1906).

VIII.—ARREST; PUNISHMENT.

Arrest—Person found offending by layman —Arrest by layman—Delivery to constable— Duty of constable—Police Offences Act 1890 (No. 1126), sec. 82.]—Under sec. 82 of the *Police Offences Act* 1890, a constable is under a duty to take into custody a person tendered to him by a layman who has arrested such person and alleges that he has found him offending against the provisions of Part I., II., or III., of the Act unless (*per Madden, C.J.*), the circumstances are such as to make the charge plainly or probably absurd, ridiculous or unreasonable. *McLiney* v. *Minster,* (1911) V.L.R., 347; 33 A.L.T., 33; 17 A.L.R., 336. F.C., *Madden, C.J., Hood* and *Cussen, JJ.*

Police Offences Act 1890 (No. 1126), sec. 82 —Apprehension of person found offending— Apprehension, what amounts to—Whether actual manual arrest necessary.]—*Semble.*— There may be constructive apprehension under sec. 82 of the *Police Offences Act* 1890 without any manual arrest. *Reg.* v. *Huxley and Walsh,* 8 V.L.R. (L.), 15; 3 A.L.T., 96, followed. *McLiney* v. *Minster,* (1911) V.L.R., 347; 33 A.L.T., 33; 17 A.L.R., 336. F.C., *Madden, C.J., Hood* and *Cussen, JJ.*

Police Offences Act 1890 (No. 1126), sec. 94—Person unlawfully arrested by constable —Whether justified in resisting arrest.]—A person unlawfully arrested by a constable is justified in resisting and endeavouring to escape from such constable provided he does not use undue violence in so doing. *McLiney* v. *Minster,* (1911) V.L.R., 347; 33 A.L.T., 33; 17 A.L.R., 336. F.C., *Madden, C.J., Hood* and *Cussen, JJ.*

Autrefois acquit—Arrest by two constables —Dismissal of charge of assaulting one constable in execution of his duty—Whether an answer to charge of assaulting other constable in execution of his duty.]—The dismissal of a charge of assaulting constable A. in the execution of his duty is no bar to a charge of assaulting constable B. in the execution of his duty, even though the two charges arise out of the same set of facts and the evidence on both is substantially the same. *McLiney* v. *Minster,* (1911) V.L.R., 347; 33 A.L.T., 33; 17 A.L.R., 336. F.C., *Madden, C.J., Hood* and *Cussen, JJ.*

Police Offences Act 1890 (No. 1126), secs. 49, 51, 89—Fine in default imprisonment— No time fixed for payment of fine.]—Where Justices do not in their order name a time for payment of a fine, the fine is to be treated as having been ordered to be paid immediately *Rogerson* v. *Phillips and O'Hagan,* (1906) V.L.R., 272; 27 A.L.T., 166; 12 A.L.R., 147. *a'Beckett, J.* (1906).

PORTIONS.

See WILL.

POSSESSION

See also, LIMITATIONS (STATUTES OF).

Trespass to land—Entry by person entitled to possession—Trespass committed before entry but after the right to enter arose—Reference back of actual entry to time when right arose—Right of action for trespass.]—For an instance of the application of the rule that the entry upon land by a person having the right to enter has reference to the time at which such right arose, and entitles such person to bring an action for a trespass committed before his actual entry provided that the trespass was subsequent to the right to enter, *see Ebbels* v. *Rewell,* (1908) V.L.R., 261; 29 A.L.T., 252; 14 A.L.R., 121. *Hodges, J.*

Trespass to land—Possession—Two persons on land each asserting land to be his—Right of person with title.]—For an instance of the application of the rule that, where two persons are on land each asserting that the land is his and each doing some act in assertion of his right of possession, the one who has the title is in actual possession and has a right of action against the other for trespass, *see Ebbels* v. *Rewell,* (1908) V.L.R., 261; 29 A.L.T., 252; 14 A.L.R., 121. *Hodges, J.*

Evidence—Burden of proof—Husband and wife living in same house—Wife tenant of house—Possession of goods in house—Possession prima facie evidence of title.]—Under an execution for a judgment debt against a husband goods were seized in a house of which his wife was the tenant, and in which she lived with her husband. On an interpleader issue in which the wife claimed the goods, *Held*, that the fact of the goods being on property of which the wife was tenant was *prima facie* evidence that she was in possession of the goods ; that a *prima facie* title to the goods was to be inferred from her possession of them ; and, therefore, that the burden of showing that the goods were the property of the husband was upon the judgment creditor. *McKenzie* v. *Balchin* ; *McKenzie, Claimant*, (1908) V.L.R., 324 ; 29 A.L.T., 246 ; 14 A.L.R., 238. F.C., *a'Beckett, Hodges* and *Cussen, JJ.*

Actual legal possession—Disturbance of, how far permissible—Rights of true owner, how to be asserted—Person in possession of ground as a claim under prima facie title—Claim registered—Failure to observe by-laws.]—*See* Mining, col. 912. *Bell* v. *Clarke*, (1906) V.L.R., 567 ; 28 A.L.T., 24 ; 12 A.L.R., 308.

Crimes Act 1890 (No. 1079), sec. 307—Receiving property knowing the same to have been feloniously stolen—Stolen articles deposited in a certain place by pre-existing arrangement—No knowledge by accused that particular goods stolen or deposited—No act of dominion.]—*See* Criminal Law, cols. 342, 343. *Rex* v. *Merriman*, (1907) V.L.R., 1 ; 28 A.L.T., 108 ; 12 A.L R , 571.

Police Offences Act 1907 (No. 2093), sec. 10—Property suspected of being stolen—Unexplained possession—Actual, not constructive, possession meant.]—*See* Police Offences Acts, col. 993. *Tatchell* v. *Lovett*, (1908) V.L.R., 645 ; 30 A.L.T., 88 ; 14 A.L.R., 540.

POST AND TELEGRAPH ACTS.

Post and Telegraph Act 1901 (No. 12) (C.), secs. 80, 97 (r.)—Telephone Regulations 126A (Statutory Rules 1908, No. 87)—Telephone system—Lists of subscribers—Whether Postmaster-General has exclusive right to publish—Publication by private persons—Regulation, whether ultra vires.]—Sec. 97 (r.) of the *Post and Telegraph Act* 1901 provides that the Governor-General may make regulations for—"All other matters and things which may be necessary for carrying out this Act or for the efficient administration thereof." *Held*, that this did not authorise the making of a regulation imposing a penalty upon any person who, without the authority of the Postmaster-General, printed, published or circulated any list of subscribers connected with any telephone exchange. *Commonwealth* v. *Progress Advertising and Press Agency Co. Proprietary Ltd.*, (1910) 10 C.L.R., 457 ; 16 A.L.R., 305. H.C., *Griffith*, C.J., *O'Connor, Isaacs* and *Higgins, JJ.*

POUNDS AND IMPOUNDING.

Pounds Act 1890 (No. 1129), secs. 21, 22—Sale by poundkeeper—Failure to observe provisions of the Act—Title of purchaser.]—The authority of a poundkeeper to sell impounded animals does not arise until the provisions of secs. 21 and 22 of the *Pounds Act* 1890 as to the time of selling, and as to the giving notice of sale have been complied with. *Held*, therefore, that where an impounded animal was sold within 21 days of the publishing of a notice of intention to sell and that notice misdescribed the animal which was subsequently sold, such sale did not, as against the original owner, confer a good title on the purchaser. *Palmer* v. *Bourke*, 28 V.L.R., 275 ; 24 A.L.T., 11 ; 8 A.L.R., 151, distinguished. *Doig* v. *Keating*, (1908) V.L.R., 118 ; 29 A,L.T., 171 ; 14 A.L.R., 20 F.C., *a'Beckett, Hodges* and *Cussen, JJ*

Pounds Act 1890 (No. 1129), secs. 21, 22—Sale by poundkeeper—Provisions of Act duly observed—Title of purchaser.]—A sale by a poundkeeper where all the provisions of secs 21 and 22 of the *Pounds Act* 1890 have been complied with, confers a good title on the purchaser as against the original owner *Doig* v *Keating*, (1908) V L R , 118 ; 29 A L T , 171 ; 14 A.L.R., 20. F.C., *a' Beckett, Hodges* and *Cussen, JJ.*

Pounds Act 1890 (No. 1129), sec. 9—Trespassing cattle—Trespass rates—" Substantial fence," whether creek may be.]—A creek may be a " substantial fence " within the meaning of sec. 9 of the *Pounds Act* 1890. *Helding* v. *Davis*, (1911) V.L.R., 74 ; 32 A.L.T., 188 ; 17 A.L.R., 72. *Hood, J.*

Impounded horse—Escape owing to insecure condition of pound fence—Retaking of horse—Authority of municipality.]—Where the plaintiff's horse escaped in August from the defendant municipality's pound, owing to the insecure condition of the fence of such pound, and was retaken from the plaintiff's place in the following October by persons acting as defendants' servants and under their express instructions, and was afterwards sold by the poundkeeper and the plaintiff was consequently deprived of his horse, *Held*, that the defendants were liable for the damage sustained by the plaintiff. *Ryan* v. *Swan Hill, President &c. .of,* 28 A.L.T. (Sup.), 17 ; 13 A.L.R. (C.N.), 17. *Judge Eagleson* (1907).

Pounds Act 1890 (No. 1129), secs. 4 to 9, 18 to 22, 28—Duties imposed by Act on poundkeeper—Liability of municipality—Master and servant.]—When performing the duties imposed on him by the *Pounds Act* 1890, a poundkeeper duly appointed by a municipality is acting as a public officer, and not as a servant of the municipality, and consequently the municipality is not liable for his acts in discharging such duties. *Ryan* v. *Swan Hill, President &c. of,* 28 A.L.T. (Supplement), 17 ; 13 A.L.R. (C.N.), 17. *Judge Eagleson* (1907).

Pounds Act 1890 (No. 1129), secs. 6, 9—Third Schedule—Right to charge sustenance fees—Liability of poundkeeper to return sustenance fees wrongly demanded and paid.]—A poundkeeper cannot legally demand sustenance fees for cattle impounded, unless the animals were sustained in the pound during the time they were impounded. *Martin* v. *Turner*, 31 A.L.T. (Supplement), 9 ; 15 A.L.R. (C.N.), 17. *Judge Moule* (1909).

POWERS.

See also STAMPS ACTS.

Will—Interpretation—" Any balance to be left as my executor may direct "—Power of appointment — Trust — Uncertainty.]—*See* WILL. *In re Lewis* ; *Gollan* v. *Pyle*, 29 A.L.T., 36 ; 13 A.L.R., 431.

Rule against perpetuities—Power of appointment—Possibility of exercising power in breach of rule against perpetuities—Power to select so as to make valid appointment.]—*See* WILL. *In re Hobson* ; *Hobson* v. *Sharp*, (1907) V.L.R., 724 ; 29 A.L.T., 125 ; 13 A.L.R., 703.

Rule against perpetuities—Power of appointment void for remoteness—Limitations over in default of appointment, whether valid.]—*See* WILL. *In re Hobson* ; *Hobson* v. *Sharp*, (1907) V.L.R., 724 ; 29 A.L.T., 125 ; 13 A.L.R., 703.

Will—Power of appointment of certain land to testator's children—Appointment to testator's sons—Legacies to daughters out of his own estate—If such estate insufficient to pay legacies payment to extent of deficiency charged on land—Validity of charge.]—*See* WILL. *In re Connell* ; *National Trustees, Executors &c. Co. of Australasia Ltd.* v. *Connell*, (1910) V.L.R., 471 ; 32 A.L.T., 83 ; 16 A.L.R., 504.

Administration and Probate Act 1903 (No. 1815), sec. 13—Duty—General power of appointment—By will only—Property subject to power, whether dutiable.]—*See* DUTIES ON ESTATES OF DECEASED PERSONS, cols. 414. 415. *In re McCracken* ; *Webb* v. *McCracken*, 3 C.L.R., 1018 ; 12 A.L.R., 313.

Stamps Act 1892 (No. 1274), secs. 4, 28—Schedule, Part VIII.—Settlement, meaning of—Special power of appointment created by instrument executed prior to passing of Act—Power exercised after passing of Act—Fee simple appointed to certain of objects of power.]—*See* STAMPS ACTS. *Davidson* v. *Armytage*, 4 C.L.R., 205 ; 12 A.L.R., 538.

POWER OF ATTORNEY.

See also, INSOLVENCY.

Power of attorney—Interpretation—General words, effect of on special powers.]—General words in a power of attorney are restricted to what is necessary for the proper exercise of the special powers contained therein, and are construed as enlarging such special powers only when necessary for the accomplishment of the purpose for which authority is given. *In re Hoarey,* (1906) V.L.R., 437; 28 A.L.T., 93; 12 A.L.R., 450. *Cussen, J.*

Administration, application for grant of—Power of attorney, interpretation of—Whether attorney under power authorized to support application—General words, effect of on special powers.]—A power of attorney authorized D. to apply for and obtain letters of administration, to take steps to compel a proper administration and, if he thought fit, to adjust, settle, and compromise the appointor's claim as one of the next-of-kin &c., and generally to act as the appointor's attorney in relation to the premises and on his behalf to execute and do all instruments, acts, and things as fully and effectually in all respects as the appointor could himself do if personally present. *Held,* that D. was not authorized to support a claim to administration *de bonis non* by another of the next-of-kin. *In re Hoarey,* (1906) V.L.R., 437; 28 A.L.T., 93; 12 A.L.R., 450. *Cussen, J.*

PRACTICE AND PLEADING.

———

A.—UNDER THE SUPREME COURT ACT 1890 (No. 1142).

(1) SECS. 20 AND 21—PROBATE JURISDICTION; ALLOWANCE OF COMMISSION TO PERSONS ADMINISTERING ASSETS OF ESTATES.

Supreme Court Act 1890 (No. 1142), sec. 21—Administration and Probate Act 1890 (No. 1060), sec. 26—Executors administrators and trustees—Commission—Jurisdiction of Supreme Court to grant—Whether limited to applications in a summary way—Future commission.]—*See* EXECUTORS AND ADMINISTRATORS, cols. 561 *et seq. Nissen* v. *Grunden,* (1912) 14 C.L.R., 297; 18 A.L.R., 245.

Supreme Court Act 1890 (No. 1142), secs. 20, 21—Practice — Probate — Discovery — Testamentary scripts — English practice, whether applicable.]—See DISCOVERY, cols. 408, 409. *In re Cotter*, (1907) V.L.R., 78 ; 28 A.L.T., 106 ; 12 A.L.R., 550.

(2) SECS. 25 AND 31—CRIMINAL PROCEDURE ; ENGLISH PRACTICE.

Supreme Court Act 1890 (No. 1142), sec. 25—Criminal causes and matters—Proceedings by way of certiorari in case of criminal contempt.]—A proceeding by way of *certiorari* in a case of criminal contempt is itself a criminal cause or matter in the broad sense of that phrase, and, *Semble*, in a criminal cause or matter within the meaning of section 25 of the *Supreme Court Act* 1890. *Ex parte Dunn* ; *Ex parte Aspinall*, (1906) V.L.R., 584 ; 28 A.L.T., 72 ; 12 A.L.R., 418. *Cussen, J.*

Certiorari—Court of General Sessions—Notice of proceedings to chairman and justices, necessity for—13 Geo. II., c. 18, sec. 5 —9 Geo. IV., c. 83—Supreme Court Act 1890 (No. 1142), secs. 25, 31.]—See CERTIORARI, col. 96. *Ex parte Dunn* ; *Ex parte Aspinall*, (1906) V.L.R., 584 ; 28 A.L.T., 72 ; 12 A.L.R., 418.

(3) SEC. 37.—CIVIL OR MIXED MATTERS, APPEAL IN.

Supreme Court Act 1890 (No. 1142), sec. 37—" Civil or mixed matter "—Appeal from mandamus.]—A proceedng by mandamus granted on the application of a private person ordering the treasurer to comply with the mandatory provisions of a public Statute imposing a duty upon him is a " civil or mixed matter " within the meaning of section 37 of the *Supreme Court Act* 1890 although the refusal to so comply may be an indictable misdemeanour. There may therefore be an appeal to the Full Court from the order of a Judge granting such a mandamus. *The King* v. *Watt* ; *Ex parte Slade*, (1912) V.L.R., 225 ; 33 A.L.T., 222 ; 18 A.L.R., 158. F.C. *Madden, C.J., Hodges* and *Cussen, JJ.*

(4) SEC. 58—DIRECTION TO JURY, DUTY OF JUDGE AS TO.

See also, *post*, Order XXXIX., NEW TRIAL, &c.

Supreme Court Act 1890 (No. 1142), sec. 58—Charge to jury—Duty of Judge—Issues and evidence applicable thereto — Order XXXIX.]—It is the duty of the Judge in his charge to the jury to state the issues to be determined and the evidence applicable to those issues *Holford and Wife* v *Melbourne Tramway and Omnibus Co.*, (1909) V.L.R., 497 ; 29 A.L.T., 112 ; 13 A.L.R., 667. F.C.. *Madden, C.J., a' Beckett* and *Cussen, JJ.*

Supreme Court Act 1890 (No. 1142), sec. 58—Order XXXIX.—New trial—Misdirection as to law—No objection taken at the trial —Relevancy of evidence, misdirection as to.] —See post, ORDER XXXIX. *Holford and Wife* v. *Melbourne Tramway and Omnibus Co*, (1909) V.L.R., 497 ; 29 A.L.T., 112 ; 13 A.L.R., 667

(5) SEC. 60—ORDERS NOT SUBJECT TO APPEAL.

Supreme Court Act 1890 (No. 1142), sec. 60—Appeal—Costs—Order directing trustees to pay costs.]—An appeal lies from an order directing a trustee to pay costs in an action for administration, because it is a settled rule that such an order cannot be made unless the occasion of the suit has arisen from something in the nature of the trustee's own misconduct It is also settled that the question, whether a trustee has been guilty of such misconduct as to justify the Court in ordering him to pay costs, is appealable. *Amos* v. *Fraser*, 4 C.L.R., 78 ; 12 A.L.R., 481. H.C. *Griffith, C.J., Barton* and *O' Connor, JJ.* (1906).

(6) SEC. 62 (5)—STAY OF PROCEEDINGS.

See also, *post*, ORDER XIV. (A.)—SUMMARY JUDGMENT BY DEFENDANT.

Practice—Staying proceedings—Cause of action arising out of jurisdiction.]—Where an action was brought within the jurisdiction of the Supreme Court in respect of a cause of action which arose out of the jurisdiction. *Held,* that a stay was properly refused, the injustice which would be occasioned to the plaintiffs by a stay being as great as that which would be occasioned to the defendants by allowing the action to proceed. *Logan* v. *Bank of Scotland (No. 2),* (1906) 1 K.B., 141 ; and *Egbert* v. *Short,* (1907) 2 Ch., 205, considered and applied. *Maritime Insurance Co. Ltd.* v. *Geelong Harbor Trust Commissioners,* (1908) 6 C.L.R., 194 ; 14 A.L.R., 424. H.C. *Griffith, C.J., Barton, O'Connor* and *Higgins, JJ.*

Supreme Court Act 1890 (No. 1142), sec. 62 (5) —Frivolous and vexatious proceedings, stay of —Order XIVA.]—Where an action is instituted for unlawfully causing moneys standing to the credit of a trust account in the name of the plaintiff to be attached for his personal debt, such action may be stayed or dismissed both under the inherent jurisdiction of the Supreme Court and under Order XIVA. of the *Supreme Court Rules* 1906. *Jager* v. *Richards,* (1909) V.L.R., 181 ; 30 A.L.T., 199 ; 15 A.L.R., 123. *Cussen, J.*

Supreme Court Act 1890 (No. 1142), sec. 62 (5)—Stay of proceedings—Appeal to High Court from Supreme Court—Cause remitted to Supreme Court for execution of judgment of High Court—Duty of Supreme Court—Judiciary Act 1903 (No. 6), sec. 37.]—*See* APPEAL, cols. 30, 31. *Peacock* v. *Osborne,* (1907) 4 C.L.R., 1564 ; 13 A.L.R., 565.

Judgment of High Court on appeal from Supreme Court—Judgment remitted to Supreme Court—Stay of proceedings, jurisdiction of Supreme Court to order.]—*See* APPEAL. cols. 31, 32. *Bayne* v. *Blake,* (1908) 5 C.L.R., 497 ; 14 A.L.R., 103.

Practice—Appeal to High Court from Supreme Court—Stay of Supreme Court proceedings under judgment—Conditions—Order LVIII., r. 16.]—*See* APPEAL, cols. 25, 26. *Howard Smith & Co. Ltd.* v. *Varawa,* (1910) 10 C.L.R., 607.

Practice—Money paid into Court under Order XIV., r. 6—Defendant successful at trial—Order for payment out of money to defendant—Appeal to High Court—" Execution of judgment appealed from "—Stay of execution—High Court Appeal Rules 1903, sec. III., r. 19.]—*See* APPEAL, col. 27. *Christie* v. *Robinson,* (1907) V.L.R., 118.

(7) SEC. 63 (6)—ASSIGNMENT OF DEBTS AND CHOSES IN ACTION.

Supreme Court Act 1890 (No. 1142), sec. 63 (6)—Chose in action consisting of a right against the Crown—Assignment—Petition of right by assignee—Crown Remedies and Liability Act 1890 (No. 1080), sec. 20.]—A chose in action consisting of a right against the Crown can be assigned so as to entitle the assignee to present a petition of right under the *Crown Remedies and Liability Act* 1890, section 20, in respect of it. *The King* v. *Brown,* (1912) 14 C.L.R., 17 ; 18 A.L.R., 111. H.C. *Griffith, C.J., Barton* and *Isaacs JJ.*

Supreme Court Act 1890 (No. 1142), sec. 63 (6)—Order III., r. 6—Order XIV.—Debt or liquidated demand—Assignment of debt— No written notice of assignment.]—*Quaere,* whether in the case of an assignment of a debt the assignee's claim is for a " debt or liquidated demand " within the meaning of Order III., r. 6, unless the assignment is a legal assignment completed by written notice under the *Supreme Court Act* 1890, section 63 (6). *Caddy* v. *Beattie,* (1908) V.L.R., 17 ; 29 A.L.T., 165 ; 13 A.L.R., 643. *Cussen, J.*

Supreme Court Act 1890 (No. 1142), sec. 63 (6)—Assignment of debt—No written notice of assignment—Proceedings by assignee —Parties.]—For a discussion of the question whether, in proceedings by the assignee of a debt, it is necessary that the assignor should be before the Court, where the assignment is not a legal assignment. *See Caddy* v. *Beattie,* (1908) V.L.R., 17 ; 29 A.L.T., 165 ; 13 A.L.R., 643. *Cussen, J.* (1907).

Contract — Interpretation — Agreement to deposit time payment agreements as security —Depositor allowed to collect debts due— Deposit of additional time payment agreements equal in value to those discharged by payment —Equitable assignment—Book Debts Act

1896 (No. 1424), secs. 2, 3—Non-registration.]
—See ASSIGNMENT, col. 57. *In re Jones*,
(1906) V.L.R., 432 ; 27 A.L.T., 230 ; 12
A.L.R., 279.

Book debt — Assignment — Future debt —
Money to become payable by agent to principal
on sale of goods—Book Debts Act 1896 (No.
1424), secs. 2, 3.]—See ASSIGNMENT, cols.
57, 58. *Shackell* v. *Howe, Thornton and
Palmer*, (1909) 8 C.L.R., 170 ; 15 A.L.R., 176.

Equitable assignment of future fund—
Registration—Book Debts Act 1896 (No.
1424), sec. 2—Instruments Act 1890 (No.
1103), Part VI.]—See ASSIGNMENT, col. 58.
Muntz v. *Smail*, (1909) 8 C.L.R., 262 ; 15
A.L.R., 162.

Supreme Court Act 1890 (No. 1142), sec.
63 (6)—Assignment—Deposit of Savings Bank
pass book and order for payment out of
money in Bank—Debt due in connection with
business carried on by assignor—Book Debts
Act 1896 (No. 1424), sec. 2 (a).]—See ASSIGN-
MENT, cols. 58, 59. *Cox* v. *Smail*, (1912)
V.L.R., 274 ; 18 A.L.R., 299.

(8) SEC. 63 (8)—MANDAMUS ; INJUNCTION.

Discretion of Governor in Council—Prisoner
under sentence—Remission of sentence—
Mandamus.]—See MANDAMUS, col. 892. *Horwitz* v. *Connor*, 6 C.L.R., 38 ; 14 A.L.R., 342.

Mandamus—Local Government—Discretion
of Council—Exercise of—Local Government
Act 1903 (No. 1893), sec. 197, Thirteenth
Schedule, Part VI.]—See MANDAMUS, cols.
892, 893. *Randall* v. *The Council of the
Town of Northcote*, 11 C.L.R., 100 ; 16
A.L.R., 249.

Supreme Court Act 1890 (No. 1142), sec.
63 (8)—Mandamus—Remedy by appeal available—Discretion of Court, matters to be considered in exercise of—Comparative advantage of applying one remedy rather than
another—County Court—Case struck out for
want of jurisdiction—Jurisdiction to entertain defendant's application for costs declined
by Judge.]—See MANDAMUS, col. 893. *The
King* v. *Beecham* ; *Ex parte Cameron*, (1910)
V.L.R., 204 ; 31 A.L.T., 183 ; 16 A.L.R., 173.

Wine and spirit merchant's licence—
Power of Treasurer—Refusal to grant—
Mandamus—Customs and Excise Duties Act
1890 (No. 1082), secs. 155, 156.]—See MAN-
DAMUS, cols. 893, 894. *The King* v. *Watt* ;
Ex parte Slade, (1912) V.L.R., 225 ; 33
A.L.T., 222 ; 18 A.L.R., 158.

Mandamus—Minister of Crown—Disobedience—Public Statute—Criminal contempt—
Attachment — Privilege.]—See MANDAMUS,
col. 894. *The King* v. *Watt* ; *Ex parte Slade*,
(1912) V.L.R., 225 ; 33 A.L.T., 222 ; 18
A.L.R., 158.

Mandamus—Disobedience of public Statute
—Appeal from mandamus—Civil or mixed
matters—Supreme Court Act 1890 (No. 1142),
sec. 37.]—See MANDAMUS, col. 894. *The
King* v. *Watt* ; *Ex parte Slade*, (1912)
V.L.R., 225 ; 33 A.L.T., 222 ; 18 A.L.R.,
158.

Order LII., r. 11—Order LXVIIA., r. 9—
Writ of attachment—Sheriff, refusal of to
execute—Execution, how enforced—Whether
mandamus will issue.]—See, *post*, ORDER
LII. *Peterson* v. *M'Lennan*, (1907) V.L.R.,
94 ; 28 A.L.T., 135 ; 12 A.L.R., 577.

Health Act 1890 (No. 1098), sec. 225—
Appeal—Mandamus to Board of Public Health
to hear—Appellants not given an opportunity
of being heard.]—See HEALTH (PUBLIC), col.
638. *The King* v. *Prahran, Mayor, &c. of* ;
Ex parte Morris, (1910) V.L.R., 460 ; 32
A.L.T., 92 ; 16 A.L.R., 507.

Mortgage—Registration—Improper refusal
to register—Mandamus, whether mortgagee
has a remedy by—Existence of another remedy
—Transfer of Land Act 1890 (No. 1149), sec.
209.]—See TRANSFER OF LAND ACT. *Perpetual Executors and Trustees Association
&c. Ltd.* v. *Hosken*, 14 C.L.R., 286 ; 18
A.L.R., 201.

Supreme Court Act 1890 (No. 1142), sec.
63 (8)—Nuisance—Church bell—Early morning toll—Injunction—Material interference
with ordinary comfort of existence.]—See
NUISANCE. *Haddon* v. *Lynch*, (1911) V.L.R.,
230 ; 33 A.L.T., 4 ; 17 A.L.R., 185.

Trade mark—Innocent use of and not as a trade mark.]—*See* INJUNCTION, col. 698. *Austral Canning Co. Proprietary Ltd.* v. *Austral Grain and Produce Proprietary Ltd.*, 34 A.L.T., 37; 18 A.L.R., 354.

Trade name—Similarity of names—Mining companies—Names taken from locality of mining operations—Injunction.]—*See* TRADE MARKS AND TRADE NAMES. *Mount Balfour Copper Mines No Liability* v. *Mount Balfour Mines No Liability*, (1909) V.L.R., 542; 31 A.L.T., 122; 15 A.L.R., 556.

Company—Management of internal affairs—Injunction—When Court will interfere by.]—*See* COMPANY, col. 149. *Oliver* v. *North Nuggetty Ajax Co. No Liability*, (1912) V.L.R., 416; 34 A.L.T., 58; 18 A.L.R., 309.

County Court Act 1890 (No. 1078), sec. 45—Costs—Amount recovered not exceeding ten pounds—Injunction a material part of the action—Professional costs.]—*See* COUNTY COURT, cols. 319, 320. *Harrison San Miguel Proprietary Ltd.* v. *Alfred Lawrence & Co.* (1912) V.L.R., 367; 34 A.L.T., 88; 18 A.L.R., 394.

Order LXV., r. 12—Costs—Action of tort—Judgment for damages under £50 and injunction—Supreme Court costs—"Sum recovered"—Impossibility of valuing injunction.]—*See* COSTS, cols. 261, 262. *Harrison San Miguel Proprietary Ltd.* v. *Alfred Lawrence & Co.*, (1912) V.L.R., 367; 34 A.L.T., 88; 18 A.L.R., 394.

(9) SEC. 63 (11)—CONFLICT BETWEEN EQUITY. AND COMMON LAW RULES.

Supreme Court Act 1890 (No. 1142), sec. 63 (11)—Rules of practice—Equitable rules in conflict with those of common law.]—*Quaere*, Whether, since the *Judicature Act* 1883, the chancery practice is to prevail where there is a difference between the practice at law and in equity. *Powell* v. *Wilson and Mackinnon*, (1908) V.L.R., 574; 30 A.L.T 84; 14 A.L.R., 458. *Hodges, J.*

(10) SEC. 85—FOREIGN PROCEDURE.

See also, SERVICE AND EXECUTION OF PROCESS ACT.

Supreme Court Act 1890 (No. 1142), sec. 85—Where cause of action arises—Agent outside jurisdiction—Goods improperly sold by agent—Action by principal for money had and received—Place of payment—Rule that debtor must seek out creditor.]—If an agent abroad acting for a principal within the jurisdiction deals with goods in a manner not authorised by the principal and receives the proceeds thereof and the principal, waiving the tort, sues for money had and received, the cause of action does not arise within the jurisdiction. The rule that the debtor must seek out his creditor particularly applies to cases where the question depends upon an excuse alleged for the non-payment of money within a jurisdiction. *Gosman* v. *Ockerby*, (1908) V.L.R., 298; 29 A.L.T., 266; 14 A.L.R., 186. *Cussen, J.*

Supreme Court Act 1890 (No. 1142), sec. 85—Writ containing several causes of action—Some within section 85 other outside that section—Application to set aside—Plaintiff put on terms—Election to strike out causes of action improperly joined—Undertaking to confine trial to causes of action properly joined—Costs.]—Where a writ contained several causes of action, some within and others outside section 85 of the *Supreme Court Act* 1890, upon application by the defendant (before entering an appearance) that the writ, and service, and all subsequent proceedings be set aside, the Judge announced that if the plaintiff elected to strike out the causes of action outside section 85 and undertook to confine himself at the trial to the causes of action within that section no order would be made except that he pay the defendant £8 8s. costs, but that if he did not so elect and undertake an order would be made in terms of the application with costs to be taxed. *Gosman* v. *Ockerby*, (1908) V.L.R., 298; 29 A.L.T., 266; 14 A.L.R., 186. *Cussen, J.* (1908).

Supreme Court Act 1890 (No. 1142), sec. 85—Writ for service outside jurisdiction—

Contract made outside the jurisdiction—
Breach outside the jurisdiction—Substantial
performance within the jurisdiction—" A
cause of action which arose within the jurisdiction."]—Where a contract made outside
Victoria has been substantially performed
within Victoria there is " a cause of action
which arose within the jurisdiction " within
the meaning of section 85 of the *Supreme
Court Act* 1890, even though the breach
sued on took place out of Victoria. The
principle laid down in *Wilson* v. *Threlkeld*,
3 W.W. & a'B. (L.), 158, applied. *Cussen* v.
MacPherson, 6 A.L.T., 205, followed. The
decision in *Sirdar Gurdyal Singh* v. *Rajah
of Faridkote*, (1894) A.C., 670, distinguished.
Kelsey v. *Caselberg*, (1909) V.L.R., 347 ; 31
A.L.T., 31 ; 15 A.L.R., 362. *Madden, C. J.*

**Supreme Court Act 1890 (No. 1142), sec.
85—Foreign procedure—Cause of action arising within the jurisdiction, what is.]**—The
expression " a cause of action which arose
within the jurisdiction " in section 85 of the
Supreme Court Act 1890 means the whole
cause of action. *J. E. Lindley & Co.* v.
Pratt, (1911) V.L.R., 444 ; 33 A.L.T., 50 ;
17 A.L.R., 404. *Hodges, J.*

**Supreme Court Act 1890 (No. 1142), sec.
85—Foreign procedure—Contract made in
Queensland—Part performance by plaintiff in
Victoria—Breach by defendant in Queensland.]**
—The defendant, a merchant in Brisbane,
made a contract in Brisbane with the plaintiffs, merchants in Melbourne, for the purchase of goods to be delivered f.o.b. in Melbourne and paid for in Brisbane. The goods
when landed in Brisbane were not according
to sample and the defendant refused to pay
for them. In an action for the price of the
goods, *Held*, that the cause of action did
not arise within the jurisdiction, and that
service of the writ under section 85 of the
Supreme Court Act 1890 should be set aside.
J. E. Lindley & Co. v. *Pratt*, (1911) V.L.R.,
444 ; 33 A.L.T., 50 ; 17 A.L.R., 404.
Hodges, J. (1911).

**Supreme Court Act 1890 (No. 1142), sec.
85—Writ for service out of jurisdiction—
Application of Supreme Court Rules—Rules**
of Supreme Court 1906—Order IX.]—The
provisions of Order IX. of the Rules of the
Supreme Court 1906 do not apply to an
action commenced under section 85 of the
Supreme Court Act 1890 against a person
resident out of the jurisdiction. *Moubray*
v. *Riordan*, 15 V.L.R., 354 ; 11 A.L.T.,
19, followed. *Kelsey* v. *Caselberg*, (1909)
V.L.R., 347 ; 31 A.L.T., 31 ; 15 A.L.R., 362.
Madden, C.J.

**Service and Execution of Process Act 1901
(No. 11), sec. 11—Writ—Service in another
State—No appearance entered—Application
for leave to proceed—Affidavit of service—
Particulars.]**—*See* SERVICE AND EXECUTION
OF PROCESS ACT. *Jarrett* v. *Brown*, (1908)
V.L.R., 478 ; 30 A.L.T., 17 ; 14 A.L.R., 349.

(11) SEC. 90—AFFIDAVITS.

**Marriage Act 1890 (No. 1166), sec. 126—
Supreme Court Act 1890 (No. 1142), sec. 90
—Evidence—Affidavits sworn outside Victoria—Notary Public—Judicial notice of signature.]**—Where an affidavit purports to be
sworn out of Victoria, but within the King's
dominions, before a person who therein subscribes his name and describes himself as a
notary public, the Court assumes that he is
acting within his jurisdiction as such and
takes judicial notice of the signature. *Howard*
v. *Jones*, 14 A.L.T., 106 ; 18 V.L.R., 578,
distinguished *Davis* v *Davis*, *Hattrick,
Co-respondent*, (1912) V L R , 427 ; 34
A L T , 66 ; 18 A L R , 398. *Hood, J.*

**Supreme Court Act 1890 (No. 1142), sec.
90—Order XXXVIII., r. 6 (Rules of 1906)—
Judicial notice—Certificate of notary public
authenticating signature of party to document
—Signature of notary, whether sufficient.]**—
See EVIDENCE, col. 478. *In re Sutherland*,
(1910) V.L.R., 118 ; 31 A.L.T., 150 ; 16
A.L.R., 63.

(12) SECS 91, 110, 141, 152 AND 160—FOR-
EIGN ATTACHMENT ; ARREST AND BAIL ;
ARBITRATION

**Supreme Court Act 1890 (No. 1142), sec.
91—Foreign attachment—Affidavit to be
filed.]**—The conditions prescribed by section

91 of the *Supreme Court Act* 1890 as precedent to the issue of a writ of foreign attachment, must be strictly complied with The affidavit must set forth facts from which the Court can judge whether or not the cause of action arose wholly within Victoria and what the nature and character of the action is. It is not sufficient that the affidavit should state generally the cause of action and that it arose in Victoria If made on information and belief the affidavit must set out the source of the deponent's knowledge and the facts on which it is based. *Henderson* v. *Ward*, (1912) V.L.R., 289; 34 A.L.T., 13; 18 A.L.R., 218 *Madden, C.J.*

Supreme Court Act 1890 (No. 1142), sec. 110—Arrest and bail—Order to hold to bail, effect of.]—*Per Griffith, C.J.*—"I think, therefore, that the only effect of an order to hold to bail is to enable the plaintiff, at his option, to issue a writ of *capias*, which is then his act and not the act of the Court, in the same sense as the issue of a writ of execution on a judgment is said to be the act of the party, and not the act of the Court." *Varawa* v. *Howard Smith Co. Ltd.*, (1911) 13 C.L.R., at p. 53; 17 A.L.R., at pp. 504-5.

Arbitration—Agreement to submit to—Intention to make, how to be ascertained.]—*See* ARBITRATION, col. 45. *Briscoe & Co. Ltd.* v. *The Victorian Railways Commissioners*, (1907) V.L.R., 523; 29 A.L.T., 17; 13 A.L.R., 308.

Contract for sale of goods—Condition that goods may be rejected if not to satisfaction of purchaser's storekeeper—Condition that disputes shall be determined by storekeeper—Arbitration clause not providing for or implying a judicial inquiry.]—*See* ARBITRATION, cols. 45, 47. *Briscoe & Co. Ltd.* v. *The Victorian Railways Commissioners*, (1907) V.L.R., 523; 29 A.L.T., 17; 13 A.L.R., 308.

Arbitration—Building contract—Extension of time fixed for completion—Determination of contract by employer during currency of further time allowed for completion—Arbitration provision, whether applicable—Stay of action—Supreme Court Act 1890 (No. 1142),

sec. 152.]—*See* ARBITRATION, cols. 47, 48, 49. *Burton* v. *Bairnsdale, President, &c. of Shire of*, (1908) 7 C.L.R., 76; 14 A.L.R., 529.

Arbitration — Submission — Revocation — Incorporation of laws of Victoria—Bankruptcy of one of the parties to the agreement for reference—Leave to revoke submission—Supreme Court Act 1890 (No. 1142), secs. 141, 160.]—*See* ARBITRATION, col. 49. *Re Freeman and Kempster*, (1909) V.L.R., 394; 31 A.L.T., 42; 15 A.L.R., 444.

Arbitration—Award, validity of—Uncertainty—Refusal to hear evidence—Specific performance of agreement ordered—Lease, time of commencement—Covenant not to alter will.]—*See* ARBITRATION. cols. 49, 50. *Jopling* v. *Jopling*, 8 C.L.R., 33.

Arbitration—Publication of award—Amendment of award—Power of arbitrator—Remission of award by Court.]—*See* ARBITRATION, cols. 50, 51. *In re Bennett Brothers*, (1910) V.L.R., 51; 31 A.L.T., 148; 16 A.L.R., 30.

Arbitration—Discovery of fresh evidence since publication of award—Remitting award to arbitrator for reconsideration—Jurisdiction.]—*See* ARBITRATION, col. 51. *In re Bennett Brothers*, (1910) V.L.R., 51; 31 A.L.T., 148; 16 A.L.R., 30.

(13) SECS. 177, 185, 186, AND 202—INTEREST ON JUDGMENT; CHARGING STOCKS AND SHARES; RELIEF AGAINST FORFEITURE.

Order XLI., r. 4*, Order XLII., r. 16 (Rules of 1884)—Supreme Court Act 1890 (No. 1142), secs. 4, 177—Judgment—Execution—Rate of interest.]—By virtue of section 177 of the *Supreme Court Act* 1890 a judgment of the Supreme Court carries interest at the rate of 8 per cent. per annum. Order XLI., r. 4* and Order XLII., r. 16 (Rules of 1884) so far as they purport to provide that such a judgment shall carry interest at the rate of 6 per cent. per annum are *ultra vires*. *In re Whitelaw*, (1906) V.L.R., 265; 27 A.L.T., 187; 12 A.L.R., 143. *Hood, J.*

Supreme Court Act 1890 (No. 1142), secs. 185, 186—Order XXXVIII., r. 3—Charging Stock and Shares—Charging order, whether

final or interlocutory—Affidavit of information and belief, admissibility of.]—An order charging shares under sec. 185 of the *Supreme Court Act* 1890 is a final as distinguished from an interlocutory order; consequently, an affidavit of information and belief is inadmissible in an application for a charging order nisi. *Manson* v. *Ponninghaus*, (1911) V.L.R., 239; 33 A.L.T., 1; 17 A.L.R., 238. *Madden, C.J.* (1911).

Supreme Court Act 1890 (No. 1142), sec. 202—Relief against forfeiture for non-payment of rent—Crown, relief against—Settlement of Lands Act 1893 (No. 1311), secs. 5, 10—Lease by Board of Land and Works.]— *See* LANDLORD AND TENANT, cols 814, 815. *The King* v. *Dale*, (1906) V.L.R., 662; 28 A.L.T., 140; 12 A.L.R., 549.

.(14) SEC. 231 AND THE ORDER-IN-COUNCIL OF 9TH JUNE, 1860—APPEAL TO PRIVY COUNCIL.

Commonwealth of Australia Constitution (63 & 64 Vict. c. 12)—Power of Victorian Legislature (18 & 19 Vict. c. 55)—Income tax—Right of appeal from Supreme Court to Privy Council—Whether Commonwealth Parliament may take away.]—*Held*, that a petition by the Commonwealth for the dismissal on the ground of incompetency of an appeal from an order of the Supreme Court of Victoria relating to the assessment of an officer of the Commonwealth, resident in Victoria and receiving his official salary in that State, for income tax in respect of such salary, the income tax being imposed by an Act of the Victorian Legislature, should be dismissed. The Constitution Act does not authorise the Commonwealth Parliament to take away the right of appeal to the Privy Council existing in such case. *Webb* v. *Outtrim*, (1907) A.C., 81; 13 A.L.R. (C.N.), 1. (Privy Council).

Judiciary Act 1903 (No. 6 of 1903), sec. 39—Federal jurisdiction of State Courts—Validity of grant of—Right of appeal to High Court—Prerogative right of appeal to Privy Council, whether affected—Commonwealth of Australia Constitution Act (63 & 64 Vict. c. 12—The Constitution, secs. 71, 77—Colonial Laws Validity Act (28 & 29 Vict. c. 63.]—*Per Griffith, C.J., Barton, O'Connor* and *Isaacs, JJ.* : Even if sec. 39 (2) (*a*) of the *Judiciary Act* 1903 purports to take away the prerogative right of appeal to the Privy Council, and the section is to that extent *ultra vires* and inoperative, its failure in that respect does not affect the validity of the grant of federal jurisdiction to State Courts contained in the rest of the section and the consequent right of appeal to the High Court. *Sed Quaere*, whether sub-sec. (2) (*a*) should be construed as affecting the prerogative. *Baxter* v. *Commissioners of Taxation*; *Flint* v. *Webb*, 4 C.L.R., 1087, 1178; 13 A.L.R., 313 (1907).

Appeal—Supreme Court Act 1890 (No. 1142) sec. 231—Whether ultra vires the Parliament of Victoria.]—The Full Court of the State refused to go into the question whether sec. 231 of the *Supreme Court Act* 1890 is *ultra vires* the Parliament of Victoria—the validity of that section having been assumed in a long series of decisions. *In re* "*Maizo*" and "*Maizena*" *Trade Marks*; *Robert Harper & Co.* v. *National Starch Co.*, (1906) V.L.R., 246; 27 A.L.T., 168; 12 A.L.R., 164. F.C., *Holroyd, A.-C.J., a'Beckett* and *Hodges, JJ.* (1906).

Privy Council—Supreme Court Act 1890 (No. 1142), sec. 231—Appealable amount—" Matter in issue," what is—Assumption that contention of unsuccessful party was correct —Res judicata—Uncontradicted affidavits.]— An application by R. for the registration as a trade mark of a pictorial label containing the word " Maizo " was opposed by N. on the ground that the word " Maizo " so resembled N.'s trade mark and trade name " Maizena " as to be likely to deceive and to create confusion in trade by causing R.'s goods to be passed off and mistaken for N.'s goods; N. did not dispute that the word " Maizo " as used in the label could not deceive, but he contended that upon the true construction of sec. 17 of the *Trade Marks Act* 1890 (No. 2) registration should be refused if the word " Maizo " might by any means or in any connection be used so as to deceive. The

Court decided against this contention and granted the application. On motion for leave to appeal to the Privy Council, *Held*, that in order to determine what was the matter in issue within the meaning of sec. 231 of the *Supreme Court Act* 1890 not only must the decision be assumed to be erroneous but that the said contention of N. must be assumed to be correct ; and that, on the uncontradicted affidavit of N. " that the average sales of maizena in Victoria amounted to about £8,000 per annum " and " that the matter in issue—namely whether R.'s trade mark should be registered and whether the opposition should be allowed—amounts to more than the sum of £1,000 " leave to appeal should be granted. *In re "Maizo" and "Maizena" Trade Marks*; *Robert Harper & Co. v. National Starch Co.*, (1906) V.L.R., 246 ; 27 A.L.T., 168 ; 12 A.L.R., 164. F.C., *Holroyd, A.-C.J., a'Beckett* and *Hodges, JJ.* (1906).

Order-in-Council 9th June 1860—Supreme Court Act 1890 (No. 1142), sec. 231—Appealable amount—Judgment respecting property of value of £500—Trade mark.]—On motion by L. to expunge a trade mark of M., and a cross motion by M. to expunge or limit a trade mark of L., the Court dismissed the motion of L., and on M.'s motion limited the trade mark of L. to the class of goods in respect of which alone it was then being used by L. L. applied for leave to appeal to the Privy Council under the Order in Council of 9th June 1860. *Held*, that the fact that L.'s trade mark was worth over £500 did not entitle L. to have leave to appeal. Where the circumstances are such as to preclude the Court from forming, not a guess, but a reasonable conclusion as to the amount at stake, leave should not be given to appeal. *Amos v. Fraser*, 4 C.L.R., 78 ; 12 A.L.R., 481, considered. *Lever Bros. Ltd. v. G. Mowling & Son*, 30 A.L.T, 144 ; 15 A.L.R., 40. *a'Beckett, J.* (1908).

(15) SECS. 261 AND 262.—CONVEYANCING BY UNQUALIFIED PERSON ; AGREEMENT AS TO SOLICITOR'S REMUNERATION.

Supreme Court Act 1890 (No. 1142), sec. 261—Conveyancing by unqualified persons— " **Conveyance or other deed or instrument in writing relating to real estate** "**—Agreement between father and son for transfer of land after father's death in consideration of son's support.**]—Sec. 261 of the *Supreme Court Act* 1890 in prohibiting unqualified persons from drawing or preparing for any fee, gain or reward " any conveyance or other deed or instrument in writing relating to real estate " is confined in its operation to something akin in its nature to what is commonly known as conveyancing. A document which is really in its essence an agreement between father and son that, in consideration of the son's supporting the father during the latter's lifetime certain land owned by the father is to be transferred to the son after the father's death, does not come within the section. *In re Wayth*, 5 V.L.R. (L.), 389 ; 1 A.L.T., 97, followed. *In re Simpson and Fricke*; *Ex parte Robinson*, (1910) V.L.R., 177 ; 31 A.L.T., 163 ; 16 A.L.R., 125. *Hood, J.*

Supreme Court Act 1890 (No. 1142), sec. 262—Solicitor—Client—Costs—Agreement as to solicitor's remuneration—Agreement to pay lump sum for work wholly past.]—Sec. 262 of the *Supreme Court Act* 1890 does not relate to agreements between solicitor and client as to the amount of the solicitor's professional remuneration for work wholly past. Such agreements are governed by the rules of common law and equity. *Bear v. Waxman*, (1912) V.L.R., 293 ; 34 A.L.T., 6 ; 18 A.L.R., 269. F.C., *Madden, C.J., Hood* and *Cussen, JJ.*

B.—UNDER THE RULES OF THE SUPREME COURT.

(NOTE.—Unless it is otherwise stated the Rules referred to are the *Rules of the Supreme Court* 1906).

(1) ORDER II.—WRIT OF SUMMONS.

Order II., r. 3—Administration action—Writ of summons—Form of heading.]—In an action claiming the administration of an estate it is not necessary that the writ of summons should be headed " In the Matter of the Estate of A. B. Deceased." *Eyre v. Cox*, 24 W.R., 317, not followed. *Cameron v. Cameron*, (1906) V.L.R., 13 ; 28 A.L.T., 169 ; 13 A.L.R., 10. *a'Beckett, J.* (1905).

Order II., r. 6—Practice under the Instruments Act 1890 (No. 1103).]—A writ under the Act may be issued and served on a defendant who is only temporarily in Victoria on a visit from another State, where he has his permanent residence. *Philips* v. *Cooper*, (1906) V.L.R., 31; 12 A.L.R. (C.N.), 5.

Order II., rr. 5, 6—Bill of exchange—Action under Instruments Act 1890 — Writ Service out of jurisdiction—Indorsement by Prothonotary—Necessity for Judge's order for such indorsement—Instruments Act 1890 No. 1103), sec. 92—Service and Execution of Process Act 1901 (No. 11 of 1901), secs. 5, 8.]—*Sternberg* v. *Egan*, 18 A.L.R. (C.N.), 20. *Hood, J.* (1912).

(2) ORDER III.—INDORSEMENTS OF CLAIM.

See also, post, ORDER XIV.

Order III.—Statement of claim, indorsement on writ ordered to be taken as—Indorsement, how construed.]—*See post,* ORDER XIX. *National Trustees Executors &c. Co. of Australasia Ltd.* v. *Hassett and the Registrar of Titles*, (1907) V.L.R., 404; 28 A.L.T., 232; 13 A.L.R., 208.

Order III., r. 6—Order XIV.—" Debt or liquidated demand "—Assignment of debt—No written notice of assignment—Supreme Court Act 1890 (No. 1142), sec. 63 (6).]—*Quaere*, whether in the case of an assignment of a debt the assignee's claim is for a " debt or liquidated demand " within the meaning of Order III., r. 6, unless the assignment is a legal assignment completed by written notice under the *Supreme Court Act* 1890, sec. 63 (6). *Caddy* v. *Beattie*, (1908) V.L.R., 17; 29 A.L.T., 165; 13 A.L.R., 643. *Cussen, J.* (1907).

(3) ORDER IX.—SERVICE OF WRIT OF SUMMONS.

See also, SERVICE AND EXECUTION OF PROCESS ACT.

Order IX., r. 2—Order XVI., rr. 11, 13—Amendment of writ by adding plaintiff—Service of amended writ, whether necessary—Discretion of Court.]—A writ amended by adding a plaintiff need not necessarily be served upon the defendant ; but the Court has a discretion, and should it think that an injustice might be done if the writ as amended were not served personally on the defendant, it can impose the condition that the writ shall be so served. *Coulson* v. *Butler*, (1907) V.L.R., 201; 28 A.L.T., 210; 13 A.L.R., 67. *Hood, J.*

Order IX.—Writ for service out of jurisdiction—Application of rules—Supreme Court Act 1890 (No. 1142), sec. 85.]—The provisions of Order IX. of the *Rules of the Supreme Court* 1906, do not apply to an action commenced under sec. 85 of the *Supreme Court Act* 1890 against a person resident out of the jurisdiction. *Moubray* v. *Riordan*, (1889) 15 V.L.R., 354; 11 A.L.T., 19, followed. *Kelsey* v. *Caselberg*, (1909) V.L.R., 347; 31 A.L.T., 31; 15 A.L.R., 362. *Madden, C.J.*

Instruments Act 1890 (No. 1103), secs. 92, 93—" Resides," meaning of in sec. 93—A writ under the Act may be served on a person temporarily resident in Victoria, who is permanently domiciled and resident in another State.]—*Philips* v. *Cooper*, (1906) V.L.R., 31; 12 A.L.R. (C.N.), 5.

(4) ORDER XIV.—LEAVE TO SIGN JUDGMENT OR DEFEND WHERE WRIT SPECIALLY INDORSED.

Order XIV., r. 2—Application for final judgment—When to be made—What constitutes making of application—Issue and service of summons.]—An application for final judgment under Order XIV., is made within the time limited by rule 2 of that Order, if the summons in support is served on the party against whom the application is made within five days after appearance, although it may not be returnable until such five days have expired. *Colonial Bank of Australia Ltd.* v. *Nicholl*, (1907) V.L.R., 402; 28 A.L.T., 222; 13 A.L.R., 297. *Hodges, J.*

Order XIV., r. 2—Leave to enter final judgment—Time for making application.]—Under Order XIV., r. 2, it is not necessary that the application should be heard by the

Judge within five days after appearance. It is sufficient if the summons is taken out within that time. *Colonial Bank of Australia Ltd.* v. *Nicholl*, (1907) V.L.R., 402 ; 28 A.L.T., 222 ; 13 A.L.R., 297, followed. *Australian Widows' Fund &c. Society Ltd.* v. *Story*, (1907) V.L.R., 594 ; 29 A.L.T., 110 ; 13 A.L.R., 588. *a'Beckett, J.*

Order XIV., rr. 1, 2—" Application shall be made within five days after appearance," meaning of—Affidavit when to be sworn.]— *Per a'Beckett, Hood* and *Cussen, JJ.*—An application is made within five days after appearance within the meaning of Order XIV., r. 2, of the *Rules of the Supreme Court* 1906, if the summons therein referred to is issued within that time. It is not necessary that the affidavit therein referred to should be in existence at the date of the issue of the summons. *Per Hood, J.*— The word " made " in rule 2 should be read as " commenced." *Martin* v. *Greig*, (1912) V.L.R., 254 ; 34 A.L.T., 5 ; 18 A.L.R., 213. F.C.

Order XIV.—Application for final judgment —Affidavit verifying cause of action, sufficiency of—Condition precedent.]—In an action upon a guarantee by the defendant to pay certain moneys upon receiving the written request of the plaintiff so to do, an application for final judgment under Order XIV was made. *Held,* that it was not necessary that the affidavit verifying the cause of action should contain an allegation that the written request for payment had been made. *May* v. *Chidley*, (1894) 1 Q.B., 451, followed. *Colonial Bank of Australia Ltd.* v. *Nicholl*, (1907) V.L.R., 402 ; 13 A.L.R., 297. *Hodges J.* (1907).

Order XIV., r. 1—Order III., r. 6—Application for liberty to enter final judgment— Affidavit in support—What must be shown— Deponent's knowledge of the facts.]—In the affidavit in support of a summons for final judgment under Order XIV., r. 1, it must be shown, either expressly or by necessary implication, that the deponent can swear positively to the facts verifying the cause of action. *Caddy* v. *Beattie*, (1908) V.L.R., 17 ; 29 A.L.T., 165 ; 13 A.L.R., 643. *Cussen, J.* (1907).

Order XIV., r. 1—Order III., r. 6—Application for liberty to enter final judgment— Affidavit of plaintiff in support—Refusal of plaintiff to submit himself for cross-examination.]—*Semble,* the fact that the plaintiff is not willing to submit himself for cross-examination on his affidavit in support of an application for liberty to enter final judgment is sufficient ground for refusing the application. *Caddy* v. *Beattie*, (1908) V.L.R., 17 ; 29 A.L.T., 165 ; 13 A.L.R., 643. *Cussen, J.* (1907).

Order XIV., r. 1—Summary judgment— Practice—Leave to defend, when to be granted.]—In an action for money lent, and on account stated, the plaintiff and defendant both alleged that the money lent was advanced by the plaintiff to a partnership of which they were the members, and that a settlement of accounts had taken place between them. The plaintiff's solicitor deposed to a conversation in which the defendant promised to repay the money, but this was denied by the defendant. On application for summary judgment leave was given to sign final judgment. *Held,* on appeal, that the application should have been refused. *Sinclair* v. *Sinclair*, (1909) 8 C.L.R., 184. H.C., *Griffith, C.J., Isaacs* and *Higgins, JJ.*

Order XVI., r. 6—Order XIV., r. 1—Final judgment—Joint debt—Joint contractor not joined as defendant—Objection for want of parties, how to be taken.]—The plaintiff brought an action against one only of two joint contractors, and the defendant took no steps to have the co-contractor joined, but objected on the return of a summons for final judgment that the co-contractor should be joined. *Held,* that this was not a defence to the action and that leave should be given to sign final judgment against the defendant. *Held,* also, that the defendant's proper course would have been to have proceeded by summons to have the co-contractor joined. *Sands & McDougall Ltd.* v. *Whitelaw*, (1908) V.L.R., 131 ; 29 A.L.T., 199 ; 14 A.L.R., 79. *Cussen, J.*

Rules of High Court 1911 (Consolidated) Part I., Order XIV.—Practice—Action for account of mortgage and foreclosure—Summary order.]—Where a writ has been indorsed with a claim for an account of the money owing on a mortgage and for a foreclosure, the plaintiff is not entitled in an application under the Rules of the High Court 1911, Part I., Order XIV., to an order for foreclosure. *Dalgety & Co. Ltd.* v. *Brown,* 24 V.L.R., 161; 20 A.L.T., 45; 4 A.L.R., 170, commented on. *Riggall* v. *Muirhead,* (1911) 13 C.L.R., 436. *Higgins, J.*

Order XIV.—Order III., r. 6—" Debt or liquidated demand "—Assignment of debt— No written notice of assignment—Supreme Court Act 1890 (No. 1142), sec. 63 (6).]—*See ante,* ORDER III. *Caddy* v. *Beattie,* (1908) V.L.R., 17; 29 A.L.T., 165; 13 A.L.R., 643.

Order XIV., r. 8—Costs—Application for liberty to enter final judgment dismissed— Order made as on summons for directions.]— No general rule will be laid down as to the costs of an application for liberty to enter final judgment where the application is dismissed, and the matter is treated as a summons for directions. *International Harvester Co. of America Ltd.* v. *Mullavey,* (1906) V.L.R., 659; 28 A.L.T., 51; 12 A.L.R., 380. *Hodges, J.* (1906).

Order XIV., rr. 1, 8—Dismissal of summons for final judgment—Directions given after dismissal—Costs.]—Where a plaintiff takes out a summons under Order XIV., rule 1, on which he ought to know he cannot succeed, he should on the dismissal of such summons be ordered to pay the costs of the application for final judgment. Where a summons under Order XIV., rule 1, which is taken out *bona fide* by the plaintiff, is dismissed on the strength of an affidavit filed by the defendant which may or may not, in reality, have anything substantial in it, and the Judge then gives directions under Order XIV., rule 8, the ordinary costs allowed on a summons for directions, should be increased by one guinea, and the whole amount made costs in the cause. The practice indicated in *The International Harvester Co. of America*

Ltd. v. *Mullavey,* (1906) V.L.R., 659; 28 A.L.T., 51; 12 A.L.R., 380, approved. *Colonial Bank of Australasia Ltd.* v. *Martin,* (1912) V.L.R., 383; 34 A.L.T., 47; 18 A.L.R., 325. *Madden, C.J.*

(5) ORDER XIV. (A)—SUMMARY JUDGMENT BY DEFENDANT.

Order XIV. (a)—Frivolous or vexatious action, what is—Order for arrest of witness in insolvency proceedings—Purpose of order not to discover assets but to hamper appeal to High Court—Action for damages in respect of such order—Conspiracy to oppress—No actual damage.]—A., having been made insolvent on the petition of R., in respect of the costs of an action by A. and B. against R., the assignee in insolvency of A., acting at the request of R., and on his indemnity, applied to the Court of Insolvency for a warrant for the apprehension of B. on the ground of her neglect to attend on summons as a witness in certain proceedings in insolvency. The warrant was ordered to issue, but no more was done upon it. The insolvency of A. was subsequently annulled, but the order for the issue of the warrant was left standing. In an action by B. against the assignee and R. for damages in respect of the order for the warrant, any actual damage being negatived, *Held,* that summary judgment for the assignee under Order XIV. (A) was properly given, even assuming that the order for the warrant was obtained not *bona fide* for the purpose of discovering assets of A., but for the indirect purpose of hampering an appeal to the High Court in the original action of A. and B. against R. *Bayne* v. *Baillieu or Blake; Bayne* v. *Riggall,* (1908) 6 C.L.R., 382; 14 A.L.R., 426. H.C., *Griffith, C.J., Barton* and *O'Connor, JJ.*

Order XIV. (a)—Frivolous or vexatious action, what is—Abuse of process—Action raising important and difficult question of law on sufficient material—Proceedings in insolvency to stifle litigation—Whether action will lie at suit of non-trader—No actual damage.]—An action which, being brought upon sufficient materials, seeks to raise and put in train for decision an important and difficult question of law, is not frivolous or vexatious or an abuse of the process of the, Court, so as to justify the Court in giving summary judgment under Order XIV. (A) or in staying the action. *Quaere*, whether proceedings in insolvency taken to stifle litigation between the parties amount to an abuse of the process of the Court in respect of which an action will lie. *Quaere*, also, whether such an action, if it will lie at all, will lie by a non-trader without proof of actual damage. *Bayne* v. *Baillieu or Blake* ; *Bayne* v. *Riggall*, (1908) 6 C.L.R., 382 ; 14 A.L.R., 426. H.C., *Griffith, C.J., Barton* and *O'Connor, JJ.*

Order XIV. (a)—Stay of action—Inherent jurisdiction—Abuse of process—Action frivolous or vexatious—Summary judgment.]— One of the conditions of a contract between a Shire Council and a contractor for building a bridge provided that the contractor should complete the whole of the works on a certain day. Another condition provided that if the contractor should, in the opinion of the engineer, fail to make such progress with the works as the engineer should deem sufficient to ensure their completion within the specified time, and should fail or neglect to rectify such cause of complaint for seven days after being thereunto required in writing by the engineer, it should be lawful for the Council to determine the contract. A third condition provided, should " any doubt dispute or difference arise or happen touching or concerning the said works . . . or in relation to the exercise of any of the powers of the Council or the engineer under this contract or any claim made by the contractor in consequence thereof or in any way arising therefrom or in relation to any impediment prevention or obstruction to or in the carrying on of the works of this contract or any part thereof (or any extras additions enlargements deviations or alterations thereon or thereof) by the Council or the engineer . . . or any claim made by the contractor in consequence thereof or in any way arising therefrom or touching or concerning the meaning or intention of this contract or of the specifications or conditions or any other part thereof . . . or respecting any other

matter or thing not hereinbefore left to the decision or determination of the engineer " every such doubt dispute and difference should from time to time be referred to and settled and decided by the engineer. Subsequently the Council agreed to extend the time for completion and, by an indenture between the parties, the condition for completion on a certain day was rescinded and a new condition was substituted identical in terms except that a new date for completion was inserted. The Council, after the original date for completion and before the new date, purported to determine the contract in pursuance of the conditions in that behalf. An action was brought by the contractor claiming (*inter alia*) damages for breach of contract, for wrongful prevention of due and complete performance, and for wrongful determination of the contract, and upon a *quantum meruit* for work and labour done. The Supreme Court, on a motion by the Council to enter summary judgment for them or for a stay, gave judgment for the Council. *Held*, that the circumstances were not such that the Court should, under Order XIV. (A) of the *Rules of the Supreme Court* 1906, have given judgment for the Council or, under its inherent jurisdiction have stayed the action as being an abuse of the process of the Court. *Burton* v. *Bairnsdale, President &c. of Shire of*, (1908) 7 C.L.R., 76 ; 14 A.L.R., 529. H.C., *Barton, O'Connor, Isaacs* and *Higgins, JJ.*

Order XIV. (a), r. 1—Summary judgment by defendant—Action frivolous or vexatious—Action arising out of matters already litigated—Hopelessness of re-opening matters.]—The plaintiffs having brought an action against the defendants in respect of matters which had already been litigated between the plaintiffs and some of the defendants when the plaintiffs were defeated, and the Court being of opinion, in view of all the probabilities and of the judicial history of the case, that any attempt to re-open the matters would be hopeless, *Held*, that summary judgment for the defendants had been properly given. *Bayne* v. *Blake*, (1909) 9 C.L.R., 366. *Griffith, C.J., Barton* and *O'Connor, JJ.*

Order XIV. (a)—Supreme Court Act 1890 (No. 1142), sec. 62 (5)—Action for unlawfully attaching trust funds—Dismissal as frivolous and vexatious.]—No action will lie for unlawfully causing moneys standing to the credit of a trust account in the name of the plaintiff to be attached for his personal debt. Such an action may be stayed or dismissed both under Order XIV. (A) of the *Supreme Court Rules* 1906 or under the inherent jurisdiction of the Supreme Court. *Jager* v. *Richards*, (1909) V.L.R., 181 ; 30 A.L.T., 199 ; 15 A.L.R., 123. *Cussen, J.*

(6) ORDER XVI.—PARTIES.

Order XVI., r. 1—Order XVIII., r. 6—Joinder of parties—Joinder of causes of action—Slander actions—Joint and separate claims—Arising out of " the same transaction or series of transactions "—" The same publication or series of publications."]—The joint and separate claims allowed under Order XVIII., rule 6, to be joined against the same defendant, must, by virtue of Order XVI., rule 1, be such claims as arise out of the same transaction or series of transactions. The words " arising out of the same transaction or series of transactions " in Order XVI., rule 1, must in relation to actions of libel or slander, be read as meaning " arising out of the same publication or series of publications." *Smith* v. *Foley*, (1912) V.L.R., 314 ; 34 A.L.T., 75 ; 18 A.L.R., 333. *Madden, C.J.* (1912).

Order XVI., r. 6—Order XIV., r. 1—Final judgment—Joint debt — Joint contractor not joined as defendant—Objection for want of parties, how to be taken.]—The plaintiff brought an action against one only of two joint contractors, and the defendant took no steps to have the co-contractor joined, but objected on the return of a summons for final judgment that the co-contractor should be joined. *Held*, that this was not a defence to the action and that leave should be given to sign final judgment against the defendant. *Held*, also, that the defendant's proper course would have been to have proceeded by summons to have the co-contractor joined. *Sands & McDougall*

Ltd. v. *Whitelaw*, (1908) V.L.R., 131 ; 29 A.L.T., 199 ; 14 A.L.R., 79. *Cussen, J.*

Order XVI., r. 6—Joinder of parties—Persons liable as co-contractors—Co-contractor out of jurisdiction—Joinder of as defendant—Discretion of Court.]—*Semble.*—Even where a co-contractor is out of the jurisdiction, the Court has a discretion, where the circumstances are exceptional, to refuse to order such co-contractor to be joined as a defendant. *Sands & McDougall Ltd.* v. *Whitelaw*, (1908) V.L.R., 131 ; 29 A.L.T., 199 ; 14 A.L.R., 79. *Cussen, J.*

Order XVI., r. 8—Practice—Joinder of parties—Administration action—Trustee sued as representative—Refusal of trustee to appeal—Judgment not yet drawn up—Joinder of cestui que trustent.]—Where a trustee is sued as a representative of his *cestui que trustent*, and a judgment adverse to them is given from which the trustee refuses to appeal, the *cestui que trustent* before the judgment is drawn up, are entitled *ex debito justitiae* to be added as parties so that they may appeal. *Connolly* v. *Macartney*, (1908) 7 C.L.R., 48 ; 14 A.L.R., 558. H.C., *Griffith, C.J., Barton, O'Connor* and *Isaacs, JJ.*

Order XVI., rr. 11, 13—Order IX., r. 2—Amendment of writ by adding plaintiff—Service of amended writ, whether necessary—Discretion of Court.]—A writ amended by adding a plaintiff need not necessarily be served upon the defendant ; but the Court has a discretion, and should it think that an injustice might be done if the writ as amended were not served personally on the defendant, it can impose the condition that the writ shall be so served. *Coulson* v. *Butler*, (1907) V.L.R., 201 ; 28 A.L.T., 210 ; 13 A.L.R., 67. *Hood, J.*

Order XVI., r. 32 (b)—Representative order—Parties within jurisdiction to represent parties outside.]—Where three out of five beneficiaries resided out of the jurisdiction, order made that the two beneficiaries within the jurisdiction should represent themselves and all other beneficiaries. *In re Foulkes* ; *Ford* v. *Foulkes*, 30 A.L.T , 108 ; 14 A L R , 729 *Madden, C J.* (1907).

Order XVI., r. 48—Order XXVIII., rr. 1, 12—Amendment—Third party notice—Substitution of name of firm for names of individual members thereof.]—The Court or a Judge has power to allow a defendant to amend a third party notice so as to substitute the name of a firm for the names of individuals, the members of such firm, against whom such notice has been issued. *Richard Hornsby & Sons Ltd.* v. *King*, (1910) V.L.R., 326; 32 A.L.T., 21; 16 A.L.R., 303. *Hodges, J.*

Order XVI., r. 48—Third party procedure—Claim for contribution or indemnity—Claim in respect of one of plaintiff's claims.]—Order XVI., rule 48, is not restricted to cases in which the defendant claims to be entitled to contribution or indemnity in respect of the whole of the plaintiff's claims in the action. *Speller* v. *Bristol Steam Navigation Co.*, 13 Q.B.D., 96, distinguished. *Edwards* v. *Edwards*, (1913) V.L.R., 30; 34 A.L.T., 103; 18 A.L.R., 580. *Hodges, J.*

Order XVI.—Parties—Administrator—Assets transferred by administrator in breach of trust—Action by administrator to recover—Whether beneficiaries necessary parties.]—An administrator in breach of trust transferred the assets of the estate to the sureties to the administration bond to be administered by them. In an action by the administrator against the sureties claiming a declaration that they had no power to sell the assets, an injunction, a re-transfer of the assets and other consequential relief, *Held*, that the beneficiaries were not necessary parties. *Ackerly* v. *Palmer*, (1910) V.L.R., 339; 32 A.L.T., 23; 16 A.L.R., 326. *Cussen, J.*

Order XVI.—Assignment of debt—No written notice of assignment—Proceedings by assignee—Parties.]—See ASSIGNMENT, col. 59. *Caddy* v. *Beattie*, (1908) V.L.R., 17; 29 A.L.T., 165; 13 A.L.R., 643.

Order XVI., r. 16—Infant complainant in Court of Petty Sessions—Claim for wages—Order to review obtained by infant—Next friend, whether infant must proceed by—Justices Act 1890 (No. 1105), sec. 72.]—See INFANT, col. 693. *Hines* v. *Phillips*, (1906) V.L.R., 417; 28 A.L.T., 1; 12 A.L.R., 249.

Order XVI.—Parties—Board of Public Health—How Board may be sued.]—*Per Hood, J.*—" Whether the name ' Board of Health ' is a short and convenient way of describing the individual members, or whether the Board be considered as a statutory entity, having large powers, in either event, the Board can, in my opinion, be sued under that name." *The King* v. *Prahran, Mayor &c. of ; Ex parte Morris*, (1910) V.L.R., 460; 32 A.L.T., 92; 16 A.L.R., 507.

Order XVI.—Company—Name struck off Register—Motion to restore name—Parties—Registrar-General—Companies Act 1896 (No. 1482), Div. VIII.—Defunct companies.]—See COMPANY, cols 141, 142. *In re Great Southern Land Investment Co. Ltd.*, (1910) V.L.R., 150; 31 A.L.T., 129; 16 A.L.R., 14.

Order XVI.—Parties—Friendly Societies Act 1890 (No. 1094), sec. 16 (iii.), (vi.)—Property of Society, legal proceedings concerning—Owners, who to be named as—Trustees.]—See CRIMINAL LAW, col. 339. *Rex* v. *Watson*, (1908) V.L.R., 103; 29 A.L.T., 146; 13 A.L.R., 724.

(7) ORDER XVII.—CHANGE OF PARTIES BY DEATH, &c.

Action for personal injuries—Judgment for plaintiff—Appeal from refusal of new trial—Death of plaintiff pending appeal—Survival of action to executor—Executor added as respondent to appeal.]—The plaintiff had succeeded in the County Court in an action for damages for personal injuries and judgment was entered for her. The defendant moved for a new trial which was refused, and then appealed from such refusal. Before the appeal came on for hearing the plaintiff died. *Held*, that the maxim *actio personalis moritur cum persona* did not apply, and that the rights under the judgment survived to her executor who was added as a party respondent to the appeal. *Farrands* v. *Mayor &c. of Melbourne*, (1909) V.L.R., 531; 31 A.L.T., 78; 15 A.L.R., 520. F.C., *Madden, C.J., Hodges* and *Cussen, JJ.*

(8) ORDER XVIII.—JOINDER OF CAUSES OF ACTION.

Order XVIII., r. 6—Order XVI., r. 1—Joinder of parties—Joinder of causes of action—Slander actions—Joint and separate claims—Arising out of " the same transaction or series of transactions "—" The same publication or series of publications."]—*See, ante,* ORDER XVI. *Smith* v. *Foley,* (1912) V.L.R., 314; 34 A.L.T., 75; 18 A.L.R., 333.

(9) ORDER XVIII. (A) (RULES OF 1904).— TRIAL WITHOUT PLEADINGS, &c.

Order XVIII. (a), r. 6 —Writ endorsed for trial without a jury—Right of plaintiff to jury—Order XXXVI., r. 6 (Rules of 1884).]— *Per Hood, J.*—The plaintiff in an action within Order XXXVI., r. 6, who states in his writ that the mode of trial is before a Judge without a jury, is not entitled to a jury as of right. *Brisbane* v. *Stewart,* (1906) V.L.R., 608; 28 A.L.T., 110; 12 A.L.R., 549.

Order XVIII. (a), r. 6—Order XXXVI., rr. 3, 6 (Rules of 1884)— Trial by jury —Writ endorsed for trial without a jury Amendment of endorsement — Memorandum of close of pleading filed—Case listed for trial without a jury.]—In a cause within r. 6 of Order XXXVI. (Rules of 1884) the mode of trial endorsed on the writ was " before a Judge without a jury." The order on directions gave the plaintiff leave to amend the endorsement by striking out the mode of trial and to apply thereafter for a jury. After the pleadings had been closed, the memorandum filed, and the case set down by the plaintiff for trial before a Judge without a jury and placed in the list of trials to be commenced on the 15th June, the plaintiff on the 12th June applied under the order on directions, for a jury. *Held,* that, having regard to the circumstances and to the terms of the order on directions, the plaintiff was not entitled to a jury. *Brisbane* v. *Stewart,* (1906) V.L.R., 608; 28 A.L.T., 110; 12 A.L.R., 549. F.C., *Hodges, Hood* and *Chomley, JJ.* (1906).

(10) ORDER XIX.—PLEADING GENERALLY.

Order XIX., r. 3—Set-off or counterclaim——Claim sounding in damages—Extent of right of set-off—Whether affected by rule 3.]— Rule 3 of Order XIX. does not create any new right, but merely enables the defendant to plead any right to set-off, which he may otherwise possess. *Held,* accordingly, that the defendant was not entitled to raise as a set-off a claim for damages which he could not have so raised before the *Judicature Act,* but that his proper course was to raise it by way of counterclaim. *Smail* v. *Zimmerman,* (1907) V.L.R., 702; 29 A.L.T., 63; 13 A.L.R., 587. *Hood, J.* (1907).

Order XIX. — Defamation — Libel — Defence—Justification—Fair comment—Particulars of meaning of expressions used in defence—Particulars of facts relied on— Relevant facts not mentioned in the libel— Particulars and right to prove.]—In his defence to an action for libel in respect of an article published in his newspaper the defendant pleaded that " in so far as such words consist of statements of fact they are true in substance and in fact, and in so far as such words consist of comment they are fair and *bona fide* comment on matters of public interest " ; and he gave particulars of facts intended to be relied on in support of that plea. *Held,* that the defendant must state the sense in which he used the expressions " true in substance and in fact " and " comment " and must give particulars of all facts he intended to rely upon in support of the plea ; that the plaintiff was not entitled to particulars stating definitely which portions of the matter complained of were statements of fact and which were comment ; that the defendant on giving particulars of all the facts on which he intended to rely in support of the allegations in such plea might say, that as regards statements in the publication complained of which may be found to be defamatory statements of fact, the defence is to be given the same effect as an ordinary plea that the matters complained of are true in substance and in fact, and that as regards statements in such publication which may be found to be defamatory comments, the defence is relied on as warranting the proof of any additional relevant facts forming a basis for such comment ; and that the defendant being entitled to prove relevant facts, whether mentioned in the alleged libel or not, particulars of all facts relied upon must be given. *Clarke* v. *Norton*, (1910) V.L.R., 494 ; 32 A.L.T., 109 ; 16 A.L.R., 544. *Cussen, J.*

Order XIX.—Defamation—Justification— Fair comment—Particulars of defence properly given—Undertaking given by plaintiff on suggestion of Judge—Particulars struck out—Jurisdiction.]—Plaintiff sued defendant for libel in respect of the whole of an article published by the defendant and reflecting on the plaintiff. The defendant pleaded justification and fair comment, and under his defence gave certain particulars, which as the statement of claim and defence stood, were unobjectionable, but might have prolonged the trial greatly. On summons to strike out these particulars the Judge in Chambers ordered that upon the plaintiff giving an undertaking to make certain admissions, and not to rely on the parts of the article to which the particulars related, the particulars should be struck out, and upon such undertaking being given they were struck out accordingly. *Held*, that the Judge had no power to strike out particulars on such terms, and that the proper course was for the plaintiff to amend his statement of claim *Clarke* v *Norton*, (1911) V.L.R., 83 ; 32 A.L.T., 126 ; 17 A.L.R., 59. F.C., *Madden,* ˙ *C.J.,* a'*Beckett* and *Hood, JJ.* [Leave to appeal refused, (1910) 12 C.L.R., 13].

Order XIX.—Statement of claim, indorsement on writ ordered to be taken as—Indorsement, how construed.]—Where upon a summons for directions, the defendant not asking for a further statement of claim or for particulars and the plaintiff not asking for leave to deliver any further statement of claim, an order is made that the indorsement on the writ shall be taken as the statement of claim, the plaintiff is entitled to construe the allegations in the indorsement as widely as possible and to ask for any relief fairly arising out of

those allegations, but is not entitled to rely on any allegation that is not in fact made. *National Trustees Executors &c. Co. of Australasia Ltd.* v. *Hassett and the Registrar of Titles,* (1907) V.L.R , 404 ; 28 A.L.T., 232 ; 13 A.L.R., 208. *Cussen, J.*

Order XIX., r. 16—Pleading—Departure— New ground of claim—Allegation of fact inconsistent with previous pleading—Defence alleging agreement of release from plaintiff's claim—Reply alleging such agreement made by mutual mistake.]—To a claim for money due under an agreement the defendant pleaded an indenture releasing him from all claims by the plaintiff. In his reply the plaintiff pleaded that such indenture was made by mutual mistake, and that the defendant should not be allowed to set up the release as a defence, and that no effect should be given to it as a defence. No claim was made for rectification of the indenture. *Held*, that the reply did not raise any new ground of claim or contain any allegation of fact inconsistent with the previous pleadings of the plaintiff, and that an application to strike it out should be dismissed. *Hiscock* v. *Salmon*, (1910) V.L.R., 63 ; 31 A.L.T., 145 ; 16 A.L.R., 48. *Hodges, J.*

Order XIX.—Allegation by plaintiff that he is seised of land in fee—Denial by defence— Certificate of title produced by plaintiff in support of allegation—Whether defendant may show certificate not conclusive owing to land being included by wrong description of boundaries.]—Where the plaintiff alleges that he is seised in fee of certain land and uses a certificate of title to prove it, it is open to the defendant, who has simply denied the allegation in his defence, to show that the certificate is not conclusive owing to the land in question being included therein by a wrong description of boundaries. *National Trustees Executors &c. of Australasia Ltd.* v. *Hassett and the Regisrtar of Titles,* (1907) V.L.R., 404 ; 28 A.L.T., 232 ; 13 A.L.R., 208. *Cussen, J.*

Order XIX.—Defamation—Justification, no plea of—Evidence of truth, admissibility of.]— If justification is not pleaded, the words complained of are admitted to be false, and evidence as to their truth cannot be given. *Peatling* v. *Watson*, (1909) V.L.R., 198 ; 30 A.L.T., 176 ; 15 A.L.R., 150. F.C., *Madden, C.J., Hodges* and *Hood, JJ.*

Order XIX., r. 27—Order XXXVI., r. 37—Pleading—Tendency to embarrass—Libel——Defence—Matters in mitigation of damages.] In an action for libel a defendant may not in his defence, allege matters merely in mitigation of damages. *Wood* v. *Earl of Durham*, 21 Q.B.D., 501 ; *Heffernen* v. *Hayes*, 25 V.L.R., 156 ; 21 A.L.T., 118 ; 5 A.L.R., 269, followed. *Millington* v. *Loring*, 6 Q.B.D., 190, not followed. *Wilson* v. *Dun's Gazette Ltd.*, (1912) V.L.R., 342 ; 34 A.L.T., 77 ; 18 A.L.R., 327. *Madden, C.J.* (1912).

Wrongs Act 1890 (No. 1160), sec. 5—Order XXII., r. 1—Practice—Libel Action against newspaper proprietor — Defence — Payment into Court with denial of liability—Defence under Wrongs Act and payment into Court thereunder.]—In an action against a proprietor of a newspaper for the recovery of damages for libel, the defendant pleaded in one paragraph of his defence payment into Court of £10 with a denial of liability, and in another paragraph thereof, whilst denying the meanings ascribed by the plaintiff to the words complained of, he pleaded a defence and a payment into Court as under sec. 5 of the *Wrongs Act* 1890. Only one sum of £10 was paid into Court by the defendant. *Held*, that the words denying the innuendoes should be struck out of the latter paragraph, and a second sum of £10 should be brought into Court as under that paragraph. *Kiel* v. *Clark*, (1908) V.L.R., 627 ; 30 A.L.T., 86 ; 14 A.L.R., 500. *Madden, C.J.* (1908).

Order XIX., r. 27—Pleading—Tendency to embarrass—Libel contained in public newspaper—Allegation of apology and absence of malice and gross negligence—No payment into Court—Wrongs Act 1890 (No. 1160), sec. 5.]— In an action for libel against a newspaper, a defence stating the defendant's intention to rely on sec. 5 of the *Wrongs Act* 1890, and alleging the absence of malice and gross negligence, and the publication of an apology,

is embarrassing and will be struck out, where no money is paid into Court by the defendant. *Wilson* v. *Dun's Gazette Ltd.*, (1912) V.L.R., 342 ; 34 A.L.T., 77 ; 18 A.L.R., 327. *Madden, C.J.* (1912).

Order XVI., r. 1—Order XVIII., r. 5—Joinder of parties—Joinder of causes of action—Slander actions—Joint and separate claims—Arising out of " the same transaction or series of transactions "—" The same publication or series of publications."]—*See ante*, ORDER XVI. *Smith* v. *Foley*, (1912) V.L.R., 314 ; 34 A.L.T., 75 ; 18 A.L.R., 333.

Order XIX.—Pleading — Defamation — Matter of public interest—" True in substance and in fact "—" Comment "—Meaning of, whether ambiguous.]—*See* DEFAMATION, col. 395. *Clarke* v. *Norton*, (1910) V.L.R., 494 ; 32 A.L.T., 109 ; 16 A.L.R., 544.

Libel—Publication of copy of record kept by Registrar-General—Mistake in record owing to agent of plaintiff—Whether a defence.]—*See* DEFAMATION, cols. 393, 394. *Wilson* v. *Dun's Gazette Ltd.*, (1912) V.L.R., 342 ; 34 A.L.T., 77 ; 18 A.L.R., 327.

Order XIX.—Pleadings—Reply—Right to deliver—Order on summons for directions for pleading—English practice.]—*See post*, ORDER XXIII. *Johnson* v. *Fergie*, 31 A.L.T., 81 ; 15 A.L.R., 560.

Appeal—Pleadings—Amendment to meet new case.]—*See* APPEAL, col. 28. *Trengrouse & Co.* v. *Story*, (1908) 6 C.L.R., 10 ; 14 A.L.R., 420.

(11) ORDER XX.—STATEMENT OF CLAIM.

Order XX.—Statement of claim, indorsement on writ ordered to be taken as—Indorsement, how construed.]—*See ante*, ORDER XIX. *National Trustees Executors &c. Co. of Australasia Ltd.* v. *Hassett and the Registrar of Titles*, (1907) V.L.R., 404 ; 28 A.L.T., 232 ; 13 A.L.R., 208.

(12) ORDER XXII.—PAYMENT INTO AND OUT OF COURT AND TENDER.

Order XXII.—Action tried in County Court —Appeal to Full Court—Re-trial ordered in

Supreme Court—Payment into Court.]—When the Full Court on appeal from the County Court has directed the cause to be reheard before a Judge of the Supreme Court, and has ordered that the costs of the first trial shall abide the result of the re-hearing, leave will not be given to the defendant to pay money into Court. Order XXII. does not apply to such a case. *Fitzgerald* v. *Murray*, (1907) V.L.R., 715 ; 29 A.L.T., 158 ; 13 A.L.R., 645. *Cussen, J.*

Wrongs Act 1890 (No. 1160), sec. 5—Order XXII., r. 1—Practice—Libel action against newspaper proprietor — Defence — Payment into Court with denial of liability—Defence under Wrongs Act and payment into Court thereunder.]—*See, ante,* ORDER XIX. *Kiel* v. *Clark*, (1908) V.L.R., 627 ; 30 A.L.T., 86 ; 14 A.L.R , 500

Order XIX., r. 27—Pleading—Tendency to embarrass—Libel contained in public newspaper—Allegation of apology and absence of malice and gross negligence—No payment into Court—Wrongs Act 1890 (No. 1160), sec. 5.]—*See, ante,* ORDER XIX *Wilson* v *Dun's Gazette Ltd.*, (1912) V L R., 342 ; 34 A.L.T., 77 ; 18 A.L.R., 327.

Order XXII., rr. 6, 7—Payment into Court—Time for refusal or acceptance of money paid in.]—Rules 6 and 7 of Order XXII., read together, mean that the plaintiff has eight days within which to say whether he will refuse or accept the money paid into Court by the defendant under the Order. *Tye & Co. Proprietary Ltd.* v. *Kino*, (1907) V.L.R., 544 ; 29 A.L.T., 45 ; 13 A.L R., 436. *Madden, C.J.*

Order XXII.—Payment into Court—Payment in of full amount recoverable—Subsequent summons by plaintiff.]—Where the plaintiff, by accepting the amount paid into Court would have obtained all he could have got by going to trial, no order was made on an interlocutory summons taken out by him. *Tye & Co. Proprietary Ltd.* v. *Kino*, (1907) V.L.R., 544 ; 29 A.L.T., 45 ; 13 A.L.R., 436. *Madden, C.J.* (1907).

Order XXII.—Practice—Money paid into Court under Order XIV., r. 6—Defendant successful at trial—Order for payment out of money to defendant—Appeal to High Court —" Execution of the judgment appealed from "—Stay of execution—High Court Appeal Rules, Section IV., r. 19.]—*See* APPEAL, col. 27. *Christie* v. *Robinson*, (1907) V.L.R., 118.

(13) ORDER XXIII.—REPLY AND SUBSEQUENT PLEADINGS.

Order XXIII., r. 1—Order XXX., r. 2—Reply—Right to deliver—Order on summons for directions for pleading—English practice.]—If an order directing pleadings is made upon a summons for directions, that order includes an order to deliver a reply. The English practice to the contrary, as laid down by a rule of the Masters of the King's Bench Division—1909 *Annual Practice*, Vol. I., p. 330—is not followed in Victoria. *Johnson* v. *Fergie*, 31 A.L.T., 81 ; 15 A.L.R., 560. (1909) *Cussen, J.*

Order XXIII. r. 5 (a)—Order XXXVI. r. 7 (c)—Jury fees—Action—Order for trial with jury—Memorandum of close of pleadings—Statement therein of number of jurors—Payment of jury fees on entering the case for trial.]—Where, on the application of the defendant upon the summons for directions, an order has been made for the trial of an action with a jury, the plaintiff must, under Order XXIII., r. 5 (a), state in the memorandum of the close of pleadings the number of jurors with whom the issues are to be tried and pay the jury fees payable on entering the case for trial. Order XXXVI., r. 7 (c) does not apply to such a case. *Moss* v. *Donnelly* (1909) V.L.R., 443 ; 31 A.L.T., 49 ; 15, A.L.R., 516. *a' Beckett, J.*

Order XXIII., r. 5* ; Order XXXVI., r. 6 (Rules of 1884)—Application for jury—Memorandum of close of pleadings filed.]—*See* ORDER XXXVI. *Brisbane* v. *Stewart*, (1906) V.L.R., 608 ; 28 A.L.T., 110 ; 12 A.L.R., 549.

(14) ORDER XXIV.—MATTERS ARISING PENDING THE ACTION.

Order XXIV., r. 1—Writ issued in an action for breach of trust—Trust realty mortgaged in

breach of trust, of which mortgagee has notice —Mortgage unregistered when action commenced—Declaration of invalidity sought— Mortgage registered under Transfer of Land Act 1890, pendente lite—Absence of fraud— Transfer of Land Act 1890 (No. 1149), sec. 140.]—Where at the date of issue of a writ in an action for breaches of trust, one of which was the giving of a mortgage over trust realty to a mortgagee, who had actual notice of the breach, the mortgage is unregistered, there being nothing which the Court would call fraud or which was in fact dishonest on the part of any of the persons concerned, the mortgage, if registered under the *Transfer of Land Act, pendente lite*, is valid, and such registration may be pleaded by the mortgagee as a defence to a claim for a declaration of its invalidity. *Crout* v. *Beissel*, (1909) V.L.R., 207; 30 A.L.T., 185; 15 A.L.R., 143. *a' Beckett, J.*

(15) ORDER XXV.—PROCEEDINGS IN LIEU OF DEMURRER.

Order XXV., r. 5—Declaratory judgment— When pronounced.]—*Per Hodges, J.*—A plaintiff is entitled, under Order XXV., r. 5, to a declaratory judgment in all cases in which immediate relief might be given. *Colman* v. *Miller*, (1906) V.L.R., 622; 28 A.L.T., 35; 12 A.L.R., 386.

Order XXV., r. 5—Declaratory judgment— Action for wrongful dismissal—Claim for declaration that plaintiff relieved from covenant—No dispute—Anticipatory declaration as to rights in an event not likely to arise.]— In an action for wrongful dismissal it appeared that the agreement under which the plaintiff had served contained a covenant by him that for whatever reason the agreement should be determined, he would not within five years take service or set up in business within a certain area. The statement of claim asked for a declaration that the plaintiff was discharged from this obligation. *Held*, that, although the plaintiff was discharged from the covenant by his wrongful dismissal, the Court should not make a declaration to that effect, the defendant having made no threat, nor

indicated any intention of enforcing the covenant. *Galsworthy* v. *Reid*, 32 A.L.T., 189; 17 A.L.R., 144. *a' Beckett, J.* (1911).

Order XXV., r. 5—Declaratory judgment— High Court—Practice—Abstract question of law in decision of which rights of parties are not involved—Whether High Court will decide—Rules of High Court 1903, Part I., Order III., r. 1—Trade Marks Act 1905 (No. 20), Part VII., constitutionality of.]—*See* HIGH COURT OF AUSTRALIA, cols. 638, 639. *Bruce* v. *Commonwealth Trade Marks Label Association*, (1907) 4 C.L.R., 1569; 13 A.L.R., 582.

(16) ORDER XXVIII.—AMENDMENT.

Order XXVIII.—Amendment—Order made by Judge in error—Whether it may be corrected.]—An order made by a Judge under a misapprehension may be corrected by him before it has been acted upon or made a record. *R.* v. *Vodden*, Dears. 229, and *R.* v. *Parkin*, 1 Mood. C.C., 45, approved. *David Syme & Co.* v. *Swinburne*, 10 C.L.R., 43; 16 A.L.R., 93. H.C., *Griffith, C.J., Barton, O'Connor* and *Higgins, JJ.* (1909).

Order XXVIII., r. 11—" Accidental slip or omission " in judgment, correction of after appeal—Special circumstances—Jurisdiction to amend—Commission to examine witnesses —Costs reserved—Judgment for general costs of action—No mention at hearing of costs of commission—Complicated issues and lengthy trial.]—By an order in an action made on the 17th March, 1902, directing that a commission should issue for the examination of witnesses, the costs of the commission were reserved until the trial of the action. The case came on for trial about two years later. The issues were of a very complicated and technical nature, and after a hearing lasting for several weeks judgment was on March 14th, 1904, given for the plaintiff with costs, but at the trial no reference was made to the costs of the commission. The judgment was duly entered up. After the defendant had unsuccessfully appealed to the State Full Court and then to the High Court the plaintiff applied on motion for an order that the judgment of March 14th, 1904, should be rectified by providing that the costs of the commission should be paid by the defendant. *Held*, that the Court had jurisdiction to make such order; that the omission to ask for such costs at the trial was an "accidental slip or omission" within the meaning of Order XXVIII., r. 11; and that the complicated nature of the case and the length of hearing were special circumstances sufficient to excuse the failure to bring the matter before the Court at the trial. *Melbourne Harbour Trust Commissioners* v. *Cuming Smith & Co. Proprietary Ltd.*, (1906) V.L.R., 192; 27 A.L.T., 186; 12 A.L.R., 142. *Hood, J.* (1906).

Order XXVIII., rr. 1, 12—Order XVI., r. 48—Amendment—Third party notice—Substitution of name of firm for names of individual members thereof.]—The Court or a Judge has power to allow a defendant to amend a third party notice so as to substitute the name of a firm for the names of individuals the members of such firm, against whom such notice has been issued. *Richard Hornsby & Sons Ltd.* v. *King*, (1910) V.L.R., 326; 32 A.L.T., 21; 16 A.L.R., 303. *Hodges, J.*

Order LV., r. 3—Originating summons—Amendment of summons—Adding new question after judgment.]—Where an order in its nature final had been made on an originating summons, the Court refused to amend the summons by adding a new question, the answering of which would involve the correctness of the order already made. *In re McPherson*; *Willan* v. *Union Trustee Co. of Australia Ltd.*, (1909) V.L.R., 103; 30 A.L.T., 162; 14 A.L.R., 734. *Madden, C.J.* (1908).

Order XVI., rr. 11, 13—Order IX., r. 2—Amendment of writ by adding plaintiff—Service of amended writ, whether necessary—Discretion of Court.]—*See, ante*, ORDER XVI. *Coulson* v. *Butler*, (1907) V.L.R., 201; 28 A.L.T., 210; 13 A.L.R., 67.

(17) ORDER XXX.—SUMMONS FOR DIRECTIONS.

Order XXX.—Order LXIV., r. 4—Time—Issue of summons in vacation.]—The issue of a summons for directions is not a "proceeding carried on in the Court" within the meaning of Order LXIV., r. 4, and a summons for directions may therefore be taken out in vacation. *Williams* v. *Ahern*, (1911) V.L.R., 77; 32 A.L.T., 181; 17 A.L.R., 38. *Hood, J.*

Order XXX., rr. 1 (a), 8 (a)—Order LXIV., r. 7—Summons for directions—Expiration of time for taking out—Enlargement of time.]—Under Order LXIV., r. 7, a Judge may enlarge the time fixed by Order XXX. for taking a summons for directions, notwithstanding the provisions of Order XXX., r. 8 (a) with respect to pleadings. *Varley Bros.* v. *Woolley*, (1908) V.L.R., 231; 29 A.L.T., 200; 14 A.L.R., 153. *Madden, C.J.*

Order XXX.—Summons for directions—Claim for appointment of guardian of infant—Infant not a party—Order for examination of witnesses as to infant's whereabouts—Whether order may be made.]—The plaintiff and her infant daughter were beneficiaries under the will of plaintiff's father, of which the defendants were the trustees. The plaintiff by her action claimed against the defendants as trustees of the will administration accounts and the appointment of a guardian of the infant. Neither the infant nor her father, in whose custody she was alleged to be, was a party to the action. *Held*, that the infant was not a ward of the Court, and that on a summons for directions no order could be made for the examination of witnesses as to the whereabouts of the infant. *Knipe* v. *Alcock*, (1907) V.L.R., 611; 29 A.L.T., 98; 13 A.L.R., 433. *Madden, C.J.* (1907).

Order XXX., r. 2—Railways Act 1896 (No. 1439), sec. 21—Practice—Summons for directions—Action against Railways Commissioner for losses caused by sparks from railway engine—Order on summons—Arbitration.]—The only order which can be made upon a summons for directions in an action brought against the Victorian Railways Commissioners for losses caused by sparks from railway engines is an order referring the action to arbitration under sec. 21 of the *Railways Act*

1896. *Roach* v. *Victorian Railways Commissioners*, (1910) V.L.R., 314 ; 32 A.L.T., 10 ; 16 A.L.R., 302. *Hodges, J.* (1910).

Order XXX., r. 2—Summons for directions —Order directing pleadings—Reply—Right to deliver without further order—English practice.]—If an order directing pleadings is made upon a summons for directions, that order includes an order to deliver a reply. The English practice to the contrary as laid down by a rule of the Masters of the King's Bench Division—1909 *Annual Practice*, Vol. I., p. 330—is not followed in Victoria. *Johnson* v. *Fergie*, 31 A.L.T., 81 ; 15 A.L.R., 560. (1909) *Cussen, J.*

Order XXXI., r. 3 (a)—Order XXXII.— Order XXXIV.—Order XXXVI., r. 11 (a)— Summons for directions—Interrogatories— Notices to admit—Costs—Certificate for counsel.]—" In future the costs of summonses for directions will not be allowed, nor will a certificate for counsel be granted, as a matter of course. Attention is drawn to the fact that under Order XXXIV. and under Order XXXVI., r. 11 (*a*), the expense of summonses for directions and of pleadings may be avoided in appropriate cases. Whenever a summons for directions is taken out it is expected that the parties will attend prepared to explain the matters in dispute so as to obtain mutual concessions, and narrow the issues in conflict and thereby save costs. Attention is also called to the fact that in granting an order for interrogatories *ex parte*, weight will be given to the presence or absence of notices to admit under Order XXXII. and a like consideration may affect the allowance of costs of interrogatories if opposed at the trial under Order XXXI., r. 3 (*a*)." *In re Summonses for Directions and Interrogatories ; Statement on behalf of the Judges of the Supreme Court*, (1909) V.L.R., 393 ; 31 A.L.T., 49 ; 15 A.L.R. (C.N.), 17. *Hood, J.* (1909).

Order XXX.—Order XIV., rr. 1, 8—Dismissal of summons for final judgment— Directions given after dismissal—Costs.]— *See, ante,* ORDER XIV. *Colonial Bank of Australasia Ltd.* v. *Martin*, (1912) V.L.R., 383 ; 34 A.L.T., 47 ; 18 A.L.R., 325.

(18) ORDER XXXI.—DISCOVERY AND INSPECTION.

Order XXXI., rr. 1, 5, 12—Judiciary Act 1903 (Commonwealth) (No. 6), secs. 56, 64— Judicature Act—Commonwealth party to action—Discovery—Right to, from Commonwealth.]—In an action to which the Commonwealth is a party, by the joint effect of the *Judicature Act* and secs. 56 and 64 of the *Judiciary Act* 1903, discovery can be obtained from the Commonwealth by the opposite party. *Commonwealth* v. *Miller*, 10 C.L.R., 742 ; 16 A.L.R., 424. H.C., *Griffith, C.J., Barton, O'Connor, Isaacs* and *Higgins, JJ.* (1910).

Order XXXI.—Action against Commonwealth—Right to discovery from Commonwealth—Judiciary Act 1903 (Commonwealth) (No. 6), secs. 56, 64.]—The " rights " referred to in sec. 64 of the *Judiciary Act* 1903 include the " right to discovery." *Commonwealth* v. *Miller*, 10 C.L.R., 742 ; 16 A.L.R., 424. H.C. *Griffith, C.J., Barton, O'Connor, Isaacs* and *Higgins, JJ.* (1910).

Order XXXI.—Interrogatories—What questions may be asked.]—*See* DISCOVERY, col. 403. *Powell* v. *Wilson and Mackinnon*, (1908) V.L.R., 574 ; 30 A.L.T., 84 ; 14 A.L.R., 458.

Interrogatories — Practice — Libel — Interrogatories as to fresh cause of action.]—In an action for libel in which the plaintiff alleges specific instances of publication of libel, he is not allowed to interrogate the defendant for the purpose of finding out whether there have been other instances of publication of which he is unaware. *Mutual Life &c. Co. Ltd.* v. *National Mutual Fire Association of Australia Ltd.*, (1909) V.L.R., 445 ; 31 A.L.T., 60 ; 15 A.L.R., 476. *Hood, J.*

Order XXXI.—Libel—Intention of defendant in using words complained of—Interrogatories as to, whether permissible.]—*See* DISCOVERY, cols. 403, 404. *Powell* v. *Wilson and Mackinnon*, (1908) V.L.R., 574 ; 30 A.L.T., 84 ; 14 A.L.R., 458.

Divorce—Practice—Petition on ground of adultery—Discovery of documents and in-

terrogatories directed to adultery—Divorce Rules 1906, rr. 26, 126.]—*See* DISCOVERY, col. 404. *Davis* v. *Davis* ; *Hattrick, co-respondent*, (1912) V.L.R., 12 ; 33 A.L.T., 109 ; 17 A.L.R., 552.

Interrogatories — Privilege — Communications between solicitor and client—Abuse of process—Allegation of fraud.]—*See* DISCOVERY, col. 404. *Varawa* v. *Howard Smith & Co. Ltd.*, (1910) 10 C.L.R., 382 ; 16 A.L.R., 526.

Order XXXI., r. 10—Sufficiency of answer to interrogatories—Assumption that allegations in pleadings are true—Whether such assumption extends to matters not alleged in pleadings.]—*Semble, per Cussen, J.*—The assumption for the purposes of discovery that an allegation in a pleading is true cannot be extended to warrant the assumption that everything which, though not pleaded, a party suggests would go to prove an allegation in his pleading, is also true. *Varawa* v. *Howard Smith & Sons*, (1910) V.L.R., 289 ; 31 A.L.T., 179 ; 16 A.L.R., 137.

Order XXXI., r. 11—Interrogatories — Action for libel—Further and better answers to interrogatories—Contents of written document — Criminal presentment.]— *See* DISCOVERY, col. 405. *Powell* v. *Wilson and Mackinnon*, (1908) V.L.R., 574 ; 30 A.L.T., 84 ; 14 A.L.R., 458.

Divorce—Discovery and interrogatories— Adultery—Objection that discovery of documents or answering interrogatories may tend to criminate—How objection properly raised.] —*See* DISCOVERY, col. 405. *Davis* v. *Davis and Hattrick*, (1912) V.L.R., 23 ; 33 A.L.T., 108 ; 17 A.L.R., 607.

Husband and wife—Divorce—Practice— Discovery—Jurisdiction to order ex parte— Divorce Rules 1906, rr. 126, 128—Order XXXI., rr. 1, 1 (a), 12.]—*See* DISCOVERY, cols. 405, 406. *Davis* v. *Davis and Hattrick*, (1912) V.L.R., 23 ; 33 A.L.T., 108 ; 17 A.L.R., 607.

Order XXXI., r. 3* (Rules of 1900) — Interrogatories — Costs — No application as to at trial — Application for after trial.]— Where a party had omitted to apply at the trial for the costs of interrogatories, an order was made allowing such costs after the lapse of two years from the trial, no special circumstances being shown why the order should not be made. *General Finance &c. Co.* v. *National Trustees &c. Co.*, 12 A.L.R. (C.N.), 1. *a' Beckett, J.* (1906).

Order XXXI., r. 3 (a)—Order XXXII.— Interrogatories—Notices to admit—Costs.]— "Attention is called to the fact that in granting an order for interrogatories *ex parte*, weight will be given to the presence or absence of notices to admit under Order XXXII., and a like consideration may affect the allowance of costs of interrogatories, if opposed at the trial under Order XXXI., rule 3A." *In re Summonses for Directions and Interrogatories ; Statement on behalf of the Judges of the Supreme Court*, (1909) V.L.R., 393 ; 31 A.L.T., 49 ; 15 A.L.R. (C.N.), 17. *Hood, J.* (1909).

Order XXXI.—Probate—Practice—Discovery —Testamentary scripts — English practice, whether applicable—Supreme Court Act 1890 (No. 1142), secs. 20, 21.]—*See* DISCOVERY, cols. 407, 408. *In re Cotter*, (1907) V.L.R., 78 ; 28 A.L.T., 106 ; 12 A.L.R., 550.

Rules of Supreme Court 1906 (Probate), r. 32—Discovery of documents—Probate— Caveat—Testamentary incapacity and undue influence alleged—Discovery by caveator, how limited.]—*See* DISCOVERY, col. 408. *Re Baker*, (1907) V.L.R., 234 ; 28 A.L.T., 189 ; 13 A.L.R., 121. *a' Beckett, J.* (1907).

Order XXXI., r. 12 (Rules of 1906) — Discovery of documents — Privilege — Documents brought into existence prior to and not for purposes of litigation — Possession by solicitor for purposes of litigation.]— Documents brought into existence before and not for the purposes of litigation are not privileged from inspection merely because possession of them has been obtained by a party or his solicitor for the purposes of the litigation. *O'Sullivan* v. *Morton*, (1911) V.L.R., 70 ; 32 A.L.T., 104 ; 17 A.L.R., 12. F.C., *Madden, C.J., a' Beckett* and *Hodges, JJ.*

Order XXXI., r. 12—Discovery—Documents —Professional privilege.]—The petitioners in their affidavit of documents objected to produce certain documents on the ground that they were communications between various branches of their business for the purpose of submitting matters to their solicitors, or for the purpose of obtaining advice. *Held*, that as the documents were not alleged to be for the purpose of being submitted to the solicitors they were not privileged from inspection. *Brown* v. *The King*, (1911) V.L.R., 159; 32 A.L.T., 150; 17 A.L.R., 131. *Hodges, J.* (1911).

Order XXXI., r. 15—Discovery and inspection—Privilege—Shorthand report of proceedings in Court—Transcript obtained for purpose of subsequent litigation.]—An action for libel was threatened to be brought against the proprietors of a newspaper in respect of a report published in the newspaper of proceedings in a Court of Petty Sessions. The defendants obtained a transcript of a shorthand note of such proceedings for the purpose of enabling their solicitor to advise them in relation to the threatened libel action. The action was brought and possession of the transcript was disclosed by the defendants in an affidavit of documents, but they refused to produce it for inspection on the ground of privilege. *Held*, that the transcript was not privilged from inspection. *Chadwick* v. *Bowman*, 16 Q.B.D., 561, followed. *Shaw* v. *David Syme & Co.*, (1912) V.L.R., 336; 34 A.L.T., 68; 18 A.L.R., 345. F.C., *Madden, C.J., Hodges* and *Hood, JJ.* (1912).

Order XXXII., r. 2—Order XXXI., r. 12— Summons for directions—Action by beneficiary against executrix for accounts and administration—Discovery of documents before statement of claim.]—A testator had by his will given a life interest in his estate to the defendant, his widow, who was also executrix, with remainder in fee to the plaintiff, his daughter. At testator's death the plaintiff was a child of tender years, and after his death the defendant, as life tenant and executrix, had enjoyed and managed the estate. In an action in which the plaintiff sought declarations that certain real and personal property belonged to the estate and should be vested in trustees, the removal of the defendant and the appointment of a new trustee, and all necessary accounts and inquiries, *Held*, on summons for directions, in which plaintiff asked for general discovery before delivery of the statement of claim, that discovery before such delivery should be limited to documents relating to the estate of the testator. *Boulton* v. *Robinson*, 32 A.L.T., 35; 16 A.L.R., 367. *a'Beckett, J.* (1910).

(19) Order XXXIV.—Special Case.

Administration and Probate Act 1890 (No. 1060), sec. 98—Case stated—Right to begin.] —On a case stated by the Master-in-Equity under sec. 98 of the *Administration and Probate Act* 1890, the Crown should begin. *In re McCracken*, 27 A.L.T., 233; 12 A.L.R., 303. F.C., *a'Beckett, A.-C.J., Hodges* and *Hood, JJ.* (1906).

Order XXXIV.—Special case—Number of counsel who may be heard.]—As a general rule one counsel only will be heard on the argument of a special case. *Re Income Tax Acts*, (1907) V.L.R., 358. F.C.

Special case—Right to begin—Stamps Act 1890 (No. 1140), sec. 71.]—*See* STAMPS ACTS. *Armytage* v. *Collector of Imposts*, (1906) V.L.R., 504; 28 A.L.T., 9; 12 A.L.R., 305.

(20) Order XXXVI.—Trial.

Order XXXVI., rr. 3, 4, 5, 6—Trial by jury— Equity case—Claim put in form cognisable in a Court of common law.]—The plaintiff's claim was for damages for breach by the defendants of their covenant with him, in a mortgage deed made to secure the payment of a debt due by him to them, that they would not realise on the security thereby given until they had realised on the security of a prior mortgage given by plaintiff to them to secure the same debt. *Held*, that the case was one " heretofore within the cognizance of the Court in its equitable jurisdiction " within the meaning of Order XXXVI., r. 3, and therefore must be tried by a Judge without a jury unless the Court or a Judge otherwise ordered. *Hay* v. *Dalgety & Co. Ltd.*, 4 C.L.R., 913 ; 13 A.L.R., 125. H.C., *Griffith, C.J., Barton, O'Connor* and *Higgins, JJ.* (1907).

Order XXXVI., r. 5 (Rules of 1884)—Trial by jury—"Prolonged examination of documents or accounts."]—*Per Griffith, C.J.,* and *O'Connor. J.*—The words " prolonged examination of documents or accounts " in Order XXXVI., r. 5. refer to an examination by a jury. *Hay* v. *Dalgety & Co. Ltd.*, 4 C.L.R., 913 ; 13 A.L.R., 125 (1907).

Order XVIII. (a), r. 6 (Rules of 1904)—Trial by jury—Writ endorsed for trial without jury—Amendment of endorsement—Memorandum of close of pleadings filed—Case listed for trial without jury.]—In a cause within r. 6 of Order XXXVI. (Rules of 1884) the mode of trial endorsed on the writ was " before a Judge without a jury." The order on directions gave the plaintiff leave to amend the endorsement by striking out the mode of trial, and to apply thereafter for a jury. After the pleadings had been closed, the memorandum filed, and the case set down by the plaintiff for trial before a Judge without a jury, and placed in the list of trials to be commenced on the 15th June, the plaintiff, on the 12th June, applied, under the order on directions, for a jury. *Held,* that, having regard to the circumstances and to the terms of the order on directions, the plaintiff was not entitled to a jury. *Brisbane* v. *Stewart*, (1906) V.L.R., 608 ; 28 A.L.T., 110 ; 12 A.L.R., 549. F.C., *Hodges, Hood* and *Chomley, JJ.* (1906).

Order XXXVI., r. 6 (Rules of 1884)—Order XVIII. (a), r. 6 (Rules of 1904)—Writ endorsed for trial without a jury—Right of plaintiff to jury.]—*Per Hood, J.*—The plaintiff in an action within Order XXXVI., r. 6, who states in his writ that the mode of trial is before a Judge without a jury, is not entitled to a jury as of right. *Brisbane* v. *Stewart*, (1906) V.L.R., 608 ; 28 A.L.T., 110 ; 12 A.L.R., 549.

Order XXXVI., r. 6 (Rules of 1884)—Application for jury—Memorandum of close of pleadings filed—Order XXIII., r. 5*.]—The case of *Butters* v. *Durham G. M. Co.*, 11 V.LR., 375 ; 7 A.L.T., 30, settled the practice in regard to ordering a trial by jury under Order XXXVI., r. 6, where the memorandum of the close of the pleadings has been filed, and that practice should be followed. *Brisbane* v. *Stewart* (1906) V.L.R., 608 ; 28 A.L.T., 110 ; 12 A.L.R., 549. *Hood, J.*

Order XXXVI., rr. 4, 6—Right to jury—Negligence in navigating ship—Collision.]—An action to recover damages for negligence in the navigation of the defendant's ship whereby it collided with that of the plaintiff is within Order XXXVI., r. 6 of the *Rules of the Supreme Court* 1884, and either party is entitled to have it tried with a jury. *Union Steamship &c. Co.* v. *The Melbourne Harbour Trust Commissioners*, (1907) V.L.R., 204 ; 29 A.L.T., 63 ; 13 A.L.R., 136. *Hood, J.*

Order XXXVI., r. 2—Action of libel—Right to jury.]—Order XXXVI., r. 2, gives to the plaintiff in the actions therein specified the right to have his case tried by a jury where he indorses his writ to the effect that he desires to have the case so tried. The words at the commencement of r. 2 (" Subject to any order to be made on a summons for directions ") apply to the case where neither party has notified in accordance with the rule his desire for a trial by a Judge with a jury. *North* v. *Jamieson*, (1908) V.L.R., 533 ; 30 A.L.T., 47 ; 14 A.L.R., 410. *Madden, C.J.*

Order XXXVI., r. 6—Money Lenders Act 1906 (No. 2061), sec. 4—Action by money-lender on promissory note—Intended defence and counterclaim that interest excessive or bargain harsh and unconscionable—Mode of trial—Right to jury.]—Where the defendant in an action brought by a money-lender for the recovery of principal and interest due on a promissory note given in respect of a loan to the defendant intends to rely upon the provisions of sec. 4 of the *Money Lenders Act* 1906, he is, under Order XXXV., r. 6, of the *Rules of the Supreme Court* 1906, entitled as of right to a trial of the action with a jury. *Moss* v. *Jenkins*, (1909) V.L.R., 275 ; 30 A.L.T., 206 ; 15 A.L.R., 240. *Cussen, J.*

Order XXXVI., rr. 3, 6—Practice—Trial with jury — Common law claim — Defence of release by deed — Reply that release obtained by fraud or undue influence—Cause or matter previously within equitable jurisdiction — Certain issues directed to be tried by jury.]—One of the defences pleaded to a claim for money lent was a release by deed, and to that defence the plaintiff replied that the deed had been obtained by fraud or undue influence. *Held*, that the action was a cause or matter which would, within the meaning of r. 3, have been within the cognizance of the Court in its equitable jurisdiction previously to the commencement of the *Judicature Act* 1883, and that the plaintiff was not entitled as of right to the trial of the action by a jury. But order made for the trial by jury of the issues (1) whether the deed was procured by fraud ; (2) whether it was procured by undue influence. *Lind* v. *Lind*, (1910) V.L.R., 302 ; 32 A.L.T., 2 ; 16 A.L.R., 265. *Hodges, J.*

Order XXIII., r. 5 (a)—Order XXXVI., r. 7 (c)—Jury fees—Action—Order for trial with jury—Memorandum of close of pleadings—Statement therein of number of jurors—Payment of jury fees on entering the case for trial.]—Where, on the application of the defendant, upon the summons for directions, an order has been made for the trial of an action with a jury, the plaintiff must, under Order XXIII., r. 5 (a), state in the memorandum of the close of pleading the number of jurors by whom the issues are to be tried and pay the jury fees payable on entering the case for trial. Order XXXVI. r. 7 (c) does not apply to such a case. *Moss* v. *Donnelly*, (1909) V.L.R., 443 ; 31 A.L.T., 49 ; 15 A.L.R., 516. *a' Beckett, J.*

Order XXXVI., r. 11—Entering case for trial —Circuit Court—" Sittings that shall be holden next after the time of entering."]—Where Melbourne is not the place of trial the Deputy Prothonotary should, under Order XXXVI., r. 11, set the cause down for hearing at the next sittings of a Circuit Court, although twenty-one days will not expire before the day fixed for the first sit-

tings of that Court. *Doyle* v. *Ferne*, 25 V.L.R., 291 ; 5 A.L.R. (C.N.), 93. followed. *Harney* v. *Huntley, President, &c., of Shire of*, (1910) V.L.R., 455 ; 32 A.L.T., 82 ; 16 A.L.R., 582. *Hood, J.*

Order XXXVI., r. 37—Order XIX., r. 27— Pleading—Tendency to embarrass—Libel— Defence—Matters in mitigation of damages.] —*See, ante,* ORDER XIX. *Wilson* v. *Dun's Gazette, Ltd.*, (1912) V.L.R., 342 ; 34 A.L.T., 77 ; 18 A.L.R., 327.

Trial by jury—Right and discretion of Judge to discharge jury—Appeal from exercise of Judge's discretion to discharge jury.]—The presiding Judge has a discretion to discharge the jury in circumstances of evident necessity or need of very high degree. Such discretion being a judicial discretion, is in civil cases appealable, but the Court of Appeal will interfere only in cases where the Judge has gone wrong in principle or an obvious injustice has been done. *Swinburne* v. *David Syme & Co.*, (1909) V.L.R.. 550 ; 31 A.L.T., 81 ; 15 A.L.R., 579. F.C., *Madden, C.J., a' Beckett* and *Hood, JJ.*

Trial by jury—Reduction of number of jurors—Consent of parties.]—The Judge in a civil trial by jury may, at any stage of the proceedings, with the consent of both parties reduce the original number of jurors. *Swinburne* v. *David Syme & Co.*, (1909) V.L.R., 550 ; 31 A.L.T., 81 ; 15 A.L.R., 579. F.C., *Madden, C.J., a' Beckett* and *Hood, JJ.*

Order XXXVI.—Trial—Order made by Judge in error—Whether it may be corrected.] —An order made by a Judge under a misapprehension may be corrected by him before it has been acted upon or made a record. *R.* v. *Vodden*, Dears., 229 and *R.* v. *Parkin*, 1 Mood. C.C., 45, approved. *David Syme & Co.* v. *Swinburne*, 10 C.L.R., 43 ; 16 A.L.R., 93. H.C. *Griffith, C.J., Barton, O' Connor* and *Higgins, JJ.* (1909).

Order XXXVI.—Trial—Juries Act 1895 (No. 1391), sec. 4 (2)—Discharge of jury—With-drawal of discharge.]—*See* JURY. cols. 762, 763. *David Syme & Co.* v. *Swinburne*, 10 C.L.R., 43 ; 16 A.L.R., 93.

Order XXXVI.—Trial—Juryman, alleged misconduct of—Evidence on oath to prove misconduct—Denial by juryman not on oath accepted by Judge—Denial in nature of plea of not guilty—No objection raised—Waiver.] —See JURY, cols. 768, 769. *David Syme & Co.* v. *Swinburne*, 10 C.L.R., 43 ; 16 A.L.R., 93.

(21) ORDER XXXVII.—EVIDENCE.

Order XXXVII.—Subpoena—Service beyond State—Application for leave—Affidavit in support—Service and Execution of Process Act 1901 (No. 11 of 1901), sec. 16 (1).]—Leave to serve a subpoena upon a person in any other State or part of the Commonwealth will not be granted under sec. 16 (1) of the *Service and Execution of Process Act* 1901 where the affidavit filed in support of the application for such leave does not show what facts the witness is likely to prove. *Trapp, Couche & Co.* v. *H. McKenzie Ltd.*, 30 A.L.T., 200 ; 15 A.L.R., 179. *Hood, J.* (1909).

Evidence Act 1890 (No. 1088), secs. 4, 10—Commission for examination of witnesses outside Victoria—Whether commission may issue in case of witness whose attendance can be enforced—Service and Execution of Process Act 1901 (No. 11), sec. 16.]—See EVIDENCE, col. 511. *National Mutual Life Association of Australasia Ltd.* v. *Australian Widows' Fund &c. Society Ltd.*, (1910) V.L.R., 411 ; 32 A.L.T., 51 ; 16 A.L.R., 460.

Marriage Act 1890 (No. 1166), sec. 114—Divorce—Evidence de bene esse—Application for commission—Citation not served.]—See EVIDENCE, col. 512. *Mackay* v. *Mackay*, (1910) V.L.R., 50 ; 31 A.L.T., 138 ; 16 A.L.R., 29.

Commission to examine witness—Costs reserved until trial—Judgment for general costs of action—No mention at hearing of costs of commission—Jurisdiction to amend—Order XXVIII., r. 11—" Accidental slip or omission " in judgment, correction of after appeal—Special circumstances—Complicated issues and lengthy trial.]—See, ante, ORDER XXVIII. *Melbourne Harbour Trust Commissioners* v.

Cuming Smith & Co. Proprietary Ltd., (1906) V.L.R., 192 ; 27 A.L.T., 186 ; 12 A.L.R., 142.

Order XXXVII.—Subpoena duces tecum—Contempt of Court—Ecclesiastical privilege—Presbyterian Church of Victoria—Refusal of Presbytery Clerk to produce documents in civil action.]—See CONTEMPT, cols. 186, 187. *Ronald* v. *Harper*, 15 A.L.R. (C.N.), 5.

(22) ORDER XXXVIII.—AFFIDAVITS AND DEPOSITIONS.

See, also, EVIDENCE, cols. 511 et seq.

Order XXXVIII., r. 3—Supreme Court Act 1890 (No. 1142), secs. 185, 186—Charging stock and shares—Charging order, whether final or interlocutory—Affidavit of information and belief, admissibility of.]—An order charging shares under sec. 185 of the *Supreme Court Act* 1890 is a final as distinguished from an interlocutory order ; consequently, an affidavit of information and belief is inadmissible in an application for a charging order *nisi*. *Manson* v. *Ponnnighaus*, (1911) V.L.R., 239 ; 33 A.L.T., 1 ; 17 A.L.R., 238. *Madden, C.J.* (1911).

Order XXXVIII., r. 3—Affidavit as to belief —Grounds of belief not stated—Admissibility.] An affidavit made on information and belief in an interlocutory matter is not admissible unless it sets out the source of deponent's information and belief. *Manson* v. *Poninghaus*, (1911) V.L.R., 239 ; 33 A.L.T., 1 ; 17 A.L.R., 238. *Madden, C.J.* (1911).

Order XXXVIII., r. 6—Supreme Court Act 1890 (No. 1142), sec. 90—Judicial notice—Certificate of notary public authenticating signature of party to document—Signature of notary, whether sufficient.]—The Court will take judicial notice of the certificate of a notary public in the United Kingdom authenticating the signature of a party to a document, and in such a case the signature of the notary to the certificate is sufficient without his official notarial seal. *In re Sutherland*, (1910) V.L.R., 118 ; 31 A.L.T., 150 ; 16 A.L.R., 63. *Cussen, J.*

Order XXXVIII., r. 6—Evidence—Affidavits sworn outside Victoria—Notary public—Judicial notice of signature.]—Where an affidavit purports to be sworn out of Victoria, but within the King's dominions, before a person who therein subscribes his name and describes himself as a notary public, the Court assumes that he is acting within his jurisdiction as such and takes judicial notice of his signature. *Howard* v. *Jones*, 18 V.L.R., 578 ; 14 A.L.T., 106, distinguished. *Davis* v. *Davis and Hattrick*, (1912) V.L.R., 427 ; 34 A.L.T., 66 ; 18 A.L.R., 398. *Hood, J.*

Instruments Act 1890 (No. 1103), secs. 133, 144—Declarations and Affidavits Act 1890 (No. 1191), sec. 6—Bill of sale—Registration—Affidavit verifying bill—Affidavit of renewal—Such affidavits to be made before Commissioners for taking affidavits and declarations—Affidavits—Commissioners of Supreme Court Restriction of authority.]—*See* BILL OF SALE, col. 75. *Wrigglesworth* v. *Collis* ; *Spencer, Claimant*, 33 A.L.T. (Supplement), 13 ; 18 A.L.R. (C.N.), 6.

Order XXXVIII.—Affidavit filed but not used—Whether a part of the proceedings.]—The mere filing of an answering affidavit by one of the parties does not make it part of the proceedings. *Manson* v. *Ponninghaus*, (1911) V.L.R., 239 ; 33 A.L.T., 1 ; 17 A.L.R., 238. *Madden, C.J.*

(23) ORDER XXXIX.—NEW TRIAL, ETC.

Order XXXIX.—Supreme Court Act 1890 (No. 1142), sec. 58—New trial—Misdirection as to law—No objection taken at the trial—Relevancy of evidence, misdirection as to.]—An error in law in the direction of a Judge to the jury is a ground for granting a new trial although no objection was taken at the trial. But a new trial will not be ordered, if the Court is of opinion that the verdict must inevitably have been the same if there had been no misdirection or can with sufficient accuracy measure and allow for the effect produced by it. A misdirection as to the relevancy of the evidence going to the issues to be tried is a misdirection in law. *Holford* v. *Melbourne Tramway and Omnibus Co.*, (1909) V.L.R., 497 ; 29 A.L.T., 112 ; 13 A.L.R., 667. F.C., *Madden, C.J., a' Beckett and Cussen, JJ.*

Order XXXIX., r. 6—New trial—Misdirection—Substantial wrong or miscarriage.]—Wherever it is reasonable to conclude that substantial mischief did or in all probability may have come from a misdirection a new trial will be granted. *Holford* v. *Melbourne Tramway and Omnibus Co.*, (1909) V.L.R., 497 ; 29 A.L.T., 112 ; 13 A.L.R., 667. F.C., *Madden, C.J., a' Beckett and Cussen, JJ.*

Order XXXIX., r. 6—Improper rejection of evidence—Substantial wrong or miscarriage.] For observations upon refusal of a new trial for improper rejection of evidence, where no substantial wrong or miscarriage has thereby been occasioned in the trial, *see*, *National Mutual Life Association of Australasia Ltd.* v. *Godrich*, 10 C.L.R., 1 ; 16 A.L.R., 110. H.C. (1909).

New trial—Negligence—General damages—No sufficient evidence of particular items of damage—New trial motion—Exercise of discretion to grant a new trial—" Substantial wrong or miscarriage "—Order XXXIX., r. 6.]—Subsequently to injuries caused to a woman by the negligence of the defendants, she had a miscarriage, and that was left to the jury as a matter in respect of which they might award her damages. The jury gave a verdict in her favor. After notice of appeal and pending appeal the woman died. The Court being of opinion that it was at least doubtful whether there was evidence fit to be submitted to a jury that the miscarriage was the result of the accident, *Held* (*Hodges, J.*), dissenting, that under the circumstances, as there had been no substantial wrong or miscarriage, neither a new trial nor a new assessment of damages should be ordered. *Farrands* v. *Mayor &c. of Melbourne*, (1909) V.L.R., 531 ; 31 A.L.T., 78 ; 15 A.L.R., 520. F.C., *Madden, C.J., Hodges and Cussen, JJ.*

New trial—Order XXXIX.—Trial by jury—Observations made by Judge in his summing up Whether directions to the jury.]—Whether observations made by the Judge in the course of his summing up are directions to the jury is a question of fact depending upon all the circumstances of the case. *Ronald* v. *Harper*, (1910) 11 C.L.R., 63 ; 16 A.L.R., 415. H.C., *Griffith, C.J., O' Connor and Barton, JJ.*

Order XXXIX.—Supreme Court Act 1890 (No. 1142), sec. 58—Charge to jury—Duty of Judge—Issues and evidence applicable thereto.]—It is the duty of the Judge in his charge to the jury to state the issues to be determined, and the evidence applicable to these issues. *Holford* v. *Melbourne Tramway and Omnibus Co.*, (1909) V.L.R., 497; 29 A.L.T., 112; 13 A.L.R., 667. F.C., *Madden, C.J., a' Beckett* and *Cussen, JJ.*

Order XXXIX.—New trial—Misconduct of counsel.]—Misconduct of counsel, where such conduct has taken place in Court, is not a ground for granting a new trial. *David Syme & Co.*, v. *Swinburne*, 10 C.L.R., 43; 16 A.L.R., 93. H.C., *Griffith, C.J., Barton, O' Connor* and *Higgins, JJ.* (1909).

Trial by jury—Counsel's right in addressing the jury—Partisan observations by counsel for one party—New trial.]—Where counsel for one party in summing up to the jury has made observations on the trial, which though partisan, would find their natural corrective in the speech of counsel on the other side, the fact that the latter, having thrown up his brief, is absent, does not make such observations a good ground for a new trial. *Swinburne* v. *David Syme & Co.*, (1909) V.L.R. 550; 31 A.L.T., 81; 15 A.L.R., 579. *Madden, C.J., a' Beckett* and *Hood, JJ.*

Order XXXIX.—New trial—Misconduct of juryman—Conversation between juryman and party—Whether course of justice substantially affected.]—A conversation between a juryman and one of the parties or his representatives is not of itself ground for a new trial unless there is reasonable ground for believing that the course of justice has been, or was likely to be, substantially affected. *David Syme & Co.* v. *Swinburne*, 10 C.L.R., 43; 16 A.L.R., 93. H.C., *Griffith, C.J., Barton, O' Connor, Isaacs* and *Higgins, JJ.* (1909).

Order XXXIX.—New trial—Communications between interested party and jury—Possibility that verdict affected—Reasonable suspicion of unfairness.]—A new trial will be ordered where it is shown that communications have taken place between members of the jury and interested parties, which might have influenced the verdict, and might have caused reasonable people to doubt whether there had been a fair trial. *Trewartha* v. *Confidence Extended Co.*, (1906) V.L.R., 285; 28 A.L.T., 8; 12 A.L.R., 332. F.C., *Holroyd, A.-C.J., Hood* and *Cussen, JJ.* (1906).

Trial by jury—Alleged misconduct of juryman—Evidence—Unsworn statement by juryman—No objection—New trial.]—During the hearing of a trial before a jury, counsel for the plaintiff informed the Court in the presence of the jury, that he had been told by counsel for the defendants that a conversation had taken place between one of the jurymen and a clerk of the defendants' solicitor. At the instance of the Judge, the clerk was sworn, and deposed to a certain conversation having taken place between him and a particular juryman. The defendants' counsel thereupon applied for a discharge of the jury. Before dealing with the application, the Judge told the juryman that he might make a statement if he so desired, and the juryman, not on oath, admitted that a conversation had taken place, but denied the substantial portion of it. The Judge then ordered the trial to proceed. He afterwards gave his reasons, saying that he did not believe the evidence of the clerk. *Held*, on the evidence (*Isaacs, J.*, dissenting), that the Judge had not acted upon unsworn evidence, the statement of the juryman being only in the nature of a plea of not guilty. *Held*, further (*Isaacs, J.*, dissenting), that even if the Judge had admitted the unsworn statement as evidence, the defendants, not having at the time objected, had waived the objection, and could not rely upon the admission of that evidence as a ground for a new trial *David Syme & Co* v. *Swinburne*, (1909) 10 C.L.R., 43; 16 A.L.R., 93. H.C., *Griffith, C.J., Barton, O' Connor, Isaacs* and *Higgins, JJ.*

Order XXXIX.—New trial—Jury—Wrong finding upon one issue—Effect on findings upon other issues.]—A wrong finding by a jury on one issue does not necessarily vitiate their findings on other issues. *Ronald* v. *Harper*, (1910) 11 C.L.R., 63; 16 A.L.R.,

415. H.C., *Griffith, C.J., Barton* and *O'Connor, JJ.*

New trial—Trial by jury—Libel—Fair comment—Excessive damages.]—In an action for libel brought by a Minister of the Crown against newspaper proprietors, based on statements made in an article in the newspaper which were capable of being interpreted as alleging that the plaintiff dishonestly wasted public money on his own favorites and was a person of habitual mendacity whose presence in Parliament was a disgrace, the defence was fair comment, and the jury gave a verdict for the plaintiff of £3,250. *Held,* that in the circumstances of the case, the damages were not excessive. *David Syme & Co.* v. *Swinburne,* (1909) 10 C.L.R., 43 ; 16 A.L.R., 93. H.C., *Griffith, C.J., Barton, O'Connor, Isaacs* and *Higgins, JJ.*

Order XXXIX.—New trial—Appeal— Evidence, admissibility of—Application for new trial on ground of misconduct of juryman— Evidence as to such misconduct given before primary Judge—Affidavit as to such evidence.] —*See* APPEAL, cols. 38, 39. *David Syme & Co.* v. *Swinburne,* 10 C.L.R., 43 ; 16 A.L.R., 93.

Order XXXIX., r. 7—County Court Act 1890 (No. 1078), secs. 96, 133, 148—County Court—New trial—Whether issues to be tried may be limited—Full Court, power of on appeal.]—In the case of an action in a County Court involving the determination of several issues the Full Court on appeal (and, *semble,* the County Court on an application for a new trial) may order a new trial on some only of the issues tried in the case to the exclusion of others. *Holford* v. *Melbourne Tramway and Omnibus Co.,* (1909) V.L.R., 497 ; 29 A.L.T., 112 ; 13 A.L.R., 667. F.C., *Madden, C.J., a' Beckett* and *Cussen, JJ.*

Order XXXIX., r. 7 — New trial — Limitation of issues to be tried—Verdict finding negligence and amount of damages— New trial as to issue of negligence only— County Court—Appeal to Full Court—County Court Act 1890 (No. 1078), ss. 96, 133, 148.] —In an action for damages for negligence tried in a County Court, the jury having found for the plaintiffs and awarded them damages and a new trial having been refused by the Judge of the County Court, on appeal to the Full Court a new trial before a Judge of the Supreme Court of the question of negligence or no negligence was ordered, leaving the finding as to the amount of damages standing. *Holford and Wife* v. *Melbourne Tramway and Omnibus Co.,* (1909) V.L.R., 497 ; 29 A.L.T., 112 ; 13 A.L.R., 667. F.C. *Madden, C.J., a' Beckett* and *Cussen, JJ.*

(24) ORDER XLI.—ENTRY OF JUDGMENT.

Judgment — Execution — Rate of interest —Supreme Court Act 1890 (No. 1142), secs. 4, 177—Order XLI., r. 4*, Order XLII., r. 16 (Rules of 1884).]—By virtue of section 177 of the *Supreme Court Act* 1890 a judgment of the Supreme Court carries interest at the rate of 8 per cent. per annum. Order XLI. r. 4* and Order XLII. r. 16 (Rules of 1884) so far as they purport to provide that such a judgment shall carry interest at the rate of 6 per cent. per annum are *ultra vires. In re Whitelaw,* (1906) V.L.R., 265 ; 27 A.L.T., 187 ; 12 A.L.R., 143. *Hood, J.*

Order XVI., r. 8—Practice—Joinder of parties—Administration action—Trustee sued as representative—Refusal of trustee to appeal —Judgment not yet drawn up—Joinder of cestui que trustent.]—*See ante,* ORDER XVI. *Connolly* v. *Macartney,* (1908) 7 C.L.R., 48 ; 14 A.L.R., 558.

(25) ORDER XLII.—EXECUTION.

Order XLII., rr. 3, 6, 7, 17 (Rules of 1884) —Order XLIV., r. 2 (Rules of 1884)—Attachment—Disobedience of order to pay costs— Imprisonment of Fraudulent Debtors Act 1890 (No. 1100)—Whether power to attach for disobedience affected by.]—Notwithstanding the provisions of the *Imprisonment of Fraudulent Debtors Act* 1890 the Court has power to issue a writ of attachment for disobedience of its order to pay costs. *Re Sandilands ; Ex parte Browne,* 4 V.L.R. (L.), 318, followed. *Pope* v. *Peacock,* (1906) V.L.R., 667 ; 28 A.L.T., 63 ; 12 A.L.R., 440. *Hodges, J.*

Order XLII., rr. 3, 17 (Rules of 1884)—Order XLIV., r. 2 (Rules of 1884) - Order for payment of money—Execution under fi. fa.—Attachment for disobedience — Election of remedy, whether creditor bound by.]—A writ of attachment for disobedience of an order of the Court for payment of a sum of money may issue, although a writ of *fi. fa.* to enforce such payment has been issued previously. *In re Ball*, L.R. 8 C.P., 104, explained. *Pope* v. *Peacock*, (1906) V.L.R., 667; 28 A.L.T., 63; 12 A.L.R., 440. *Hodges, J.*

Order XLII., r. 16 – Order XLII., r. 4* (Rules of 1884)—Supreme Court Act 1890 (No. 1142), secs. 4, 177—Judgment—Execution —Rate of interest.]—By virtue of section 177 of the *Supreme Court Act* 1890 a judgment of the Supreme Court carries interest at the rate of 8 per cent. per annum. Order XLI., r. 4* and Order XLII., r. 16 (Rules of 1884), so far as they purport to provide that such a judgment shall carry interest at the rate of 6 per cent. per annum are *ultra vires*. *In re Whitelaw*, (1906) V.L.R., 265; 27 A.L.T., 187; 12 A.L.R., 143. *Hood, J.*

Order XLII., r. 23 (a)—Justices Act 1890 (No. 1105), sec. 115—Leave to issue execution— Judgment in Court of Petty Sessions—Lapse of over six years—Date of judgment, what is.]— Under Order XLII., r. 23 (*a*) leave may be granted to issue a writ of *fieri facias* on a certificate of a judgment, obtained in a Court of Petty Sessions and filed in the Supreme Court under section 115 of the *Justices Act* 1890, where six years have elapsed since the judgment. The six years should in such a case be counted as starting from the original order in the Court of Petty Sessions. *Trent Brewery* v. *Lehane*, 21 V.L.R., 283; 1 A.L.R., 89, followed. *Sack* v. *Wolstencroft*, 29 A.L.T., 85; 13 A.L.R., 588. *Cussen, J.* (1907).

Order XLII.—Insolvency Act 1890 (No. 1102), secs. 76, 113—Stay of execution— Whether limited to process in execution of judgment for payment of money.]—*See* INSOLVENCY, col. 707. *Peterson* v. *McLennan*, (1907) V.L.R., 94; 28 A.L.T., 135; 12 A.L.R., 577.

Order XLII.—Insolvency Act 1890 (No. 1102), secs. 76, 113—Execution of process or judgment, stay of—Debt due by insolvent to creditor—Trust moneys which are or ought to be in hands of trustee—Trustee ordered to pay moneys into Court—Disobedience of order—Attachment.]—*See* INSOLVENCY, cols. 706, 707. *Peterson* v. *McLennan*, (1907) V.L.R., 94; 28 A.L.T., 135; 12 A.L.R., 577.

Judgment of High Court on appeal from Supreme Court—Judgment remitted to Supreme Court for execution—Officer of Supreme Court—Whether subject to control of High Court.]—The High Court may directly order an officer of the Supreme Court to obey a judgment of the High Court. *Bayne* v. *Blake*, (1908) 5 C.L.R., 497; 14 A.L.R., 103. H.C. *Griffith, C.J., Barton* and *O'Connor, JJ.*

Judgment of High Court on appeal from Supreme Court—Duty of Supreme Court to execute—Judiciary Act 1903 (No. 6 of 1903), sec. 37, whether ultra vires—The Constitution, sec. 51 (xxxix.) Commonwealth of Australia Constitution Act (63 & 64 Vict. c. 12), sec. V.] —*See* APPEAL, col. 30. *Bayne* v. *Blake*, (1908) 5 C.L.R., 497; 14 A.L.R., 103.

(26) ORDER XLIV.—ATTACHMENT.

See also, CONTEMPT, cols. 183 *et seq.*

Order XLIV., r. 2 (Rules of 1884)—Order XLII., rr. 3, 6, 7, 17 (Rules of 1884)—Attachment—Disobedience of order to pay costs— Imprisonment of Fraudulent Debtors Act 1890 (No. 1100)—Whether power to attach for disobedience affected by.]— Notwithstanding the provisions of the *Imprisonment of Fraudulent Debtors Act* 1890 the Court has power to issue a writ of attachment for disobedience of its order to pay costs. *Re Sandilands; Ex parte Browne*, 4 V.L.R. (L.), 318, followed. *Pope* v. *Peacock*, (1906) V.L.R., 667; 28 A.L.T., 63; 12 A.L.R., 440. *Hodges, J.*

Order XLIV., r. 2 (Rules of 1884)—Order XLII., rr. 3, 17—Order for payment of money —Execution under fi. fa.—Attachment for disobedience—Election remedy, whether creditor bound by.]—A writ of attachment for disobedience of an order of the Court for payment of a sum of money may issue, although a writ of *fi. fa.* to enforce such payment has been issued previously. *In re Ball,* L.R. 8 C.P., 104 explained. *Pope v. Peacock,* (1906) V.L.R., 667; 28 A.L.T., 63; 12 A.L.R., 440. *Hodges, J.*

Attachment—Contempt of Court—Mandamus—Statutory public duty—Minister of the Crown.]—*See* ATTACHMENT, col. 63. *The King v. Watt; Ex parte Slade,* (1912) V.L.R., 225; 33 A.L.T., 222; 18 A.L.R., 158.

Order XLIV.—Insolvency Act 1890 (No. 1102), secs. 76, 113—Execution of process or judgment, stay of—Debt due by insolvent to creditor—Trust moneys which are or ought to be in hands of trustee—Trustee ordered to pay moneys into Court—Disobedience of order —Attachment.]—*See* ATTACHMENT, col. 64. *Peterson v. McLennan,* (1907) V.L.R., 94; 28 A.L.T., 135; 12 A.L.R., 577.

Contempt of Court—Ecclesiastical privilege —Presbyterian Church of Victoria—Refusal of Presbytery Clerk to produce documents in civil action.]—*See* CONTEMPT, cols. 186, 187. *Ronald v. Harper,* 15 A.L.R. (C.N.), 5.

Contempt of Court—Nature of offence— Publications of statements concerning a Judge of the High Court.]—*See* CONTEMPT, col. 186. *Rex v. Nicholls,* (1911) 12 C.L.R., 280; 17 A.L.R., 309.

Order XLIV.—Order LII., r. 11—Order LXVII.A.— Writ of attachment—Sheriff, refusal of to execute—Execution ,how enforced —Whether mandamus may issue.]—*See* ATTACHMENT, col. 64. *Peterson v. McLennan,* (1907) V.L.R., 94; 28 A.L.T., 135; 12 A.L.R., 577.

Order XLIV.—Attachment of person— Sheriff, duty of—Writ of attachment regular on its face.]—*See* ATTACHMENT, cols. 64, 65. *Peterson v. McLennan,* (1907) V.L.R., 94; 28 A.L.T., 135; 12 A.L.R., 577.

Contempt of Court—Pending criminal trial —Petition to Attorney-General in relation to —Whether a contempt.]—*See* ATTACHMENT, col. 66. *In re Mann; In re King,* (1911) V.L.R., 171; 32 A.L.T., 156; 16 A.L.R., 598.

(27) ORDER XLVI.—CHARGING ORDERS AND STOP ORDERS.

Order XLVI.—Supreme Court Act 1890 (No. 1142), secs. 185, 186—Order XXXVIII., r. 3 —Charging stock and shares—Charging order, whether final or interlocutory—Affidavit of information and belief, admissibility of.]—*See ante,* ORDER XXXVIII. *Manson v. Ponninghaus,* (1911) V.L.R., 239; 33 A.L.T., 1; 17 A.L.R., 238.

(28) ORDER L.—INTERLOCUTORY ORDERS AS TO MANDAMUS INJUNCTIONS OR INTERIM PRESERVATION OF PROPERTY.

See also, NUISANCE; TRADE MARKS AND TRADE NAMES.

Order L.—Company—Management of internal affairs—Injunction—When Court will interfere by.]—*See* COMPANY, col. 149. *Oliver v. North Nuggetty Ajax Co. No Liability,* (1912) V.L.R., 416; 34 A.L.T., 58; 18 A.L.R., 309.

(29) ORDER LI.—SALES BY THE COURT.

Order LI.—Practice—Originating summons —Payment of costs out of estate—Order for sale of settled properties.]—*See* COSTS, cols 266. *In re Lees; Lees v. National Trustees Co.,* (1908) V.L.R., 211; 30 A.L.T., 26; 14 A.L.R., 147.

Lunacy Act 1890 (No. 1113), secs. 130, 206—Lunacy Rules 1906, rr. 10, 64—Lunatic as found by inquisition in England—Lunatic's estate in Victoria—Filing inquisition of record in Victoria—Appointment of committee in Victoria—Order for sale of lunatic's estate— Time and extent of order—Discretion of committee—Bringing land under Transfer of Land Act.]—*See* LUNATIC. *In re A.B. v Lunatic,* (1909) V.L.R., 100; 30 A.L.T., 158; 15 A.L.R., 85.

(30) ORDER LII.—MOTIONS AND OTHER APPLICATIONS.

Order LII., r. 11—Order LXVII.A*, r. 9— Writ of attachment—Sheriff, refusal of to execute—Execution, how enforced—Whether mandamus may issue.]—Where the sheriff refuses to execute a writ of attachment he should be called upon to return the writ or bring in the body within a given time, and on his non-compliance application should be made under Order LII., r. 11 for his committal. A writ of mandamus will not issue, there being an alternative remedy. *Peterson v. McLennan*, (1907) V.L.R., 94; 28 A.L.T., 135; 12 A.L.R., 577. *Cussen, J.*

(31) ORDER LIII.—CERTIORARI; MANDA-MUS; PROHIBITION; HABEAS CORPUS.

(a) *Certiorari*.

Certiorari—Court of General Sessions—Person committed for contempt by warrant of Chairman—No jurisdiction—Whether act judicial or administrative—Party aggrieved—Whether entitled ex debito justitiae.]—*See* CERTIORARI, col. 95. *Ex parte Dunn*; *Ex parte Aspinall*, (1906) V.L.R., 584; 28 A.L.T., 72; 12 A.L.R., 418.

Supreme Court Act 1890 (No. 1142), sec. 25—Criminal causes and matters—Proceedings by way of certiorari in case of criminal contempt.]—*See* CERTIORARI, cols. 95, 96. *Ex parte Dunn*; *Ex parte Aspinall*, (1906) V.L.R., 584; 28 A.L.T., 72; 12 A.L.R., 418.

Certiorari—13 Geo. II. c. 18—Whether Act in force in Victoria as regards Justices and Courts of General Sessions.]—*See* CERTIORARI, col. 96. *Ex parte Dunn*; *Ex parte Aspinall*, (1906) V.L.R., 584; 28 A.L.T., 72; 12 A.L.R., 418.

Certiorari—Court of General Sessions—Notice of proceedings to Chairman and Justices, necessity for—13 Geo. II. c. 18, sec. 5—9 Geo. IV. c. 83—Supreme Court Act 1890 (No. 1142), secs. 25, 31.]—*See* CERTIORARI, col. 96. *Ex parte Dunn*; *Ex aparte Aspinall*, (1906) V.L.R., 584; 28 A.L.T., 72; 12 A.L.R., 418.

Certiorari to Judge of a County Court—Evidence—Conflict of evidence as to proceedings in County Court—Unsworn statement of Judge, whether admissible.]—*See* CERTIORARI, col. 96. *Macartney v. A. Macrow & Sons Proprietary Ltd.*, (1911) V.L.R., 393; 33 A.L.T., 64; 17 A.L.R., 397.

(b) *Mandamus*.

Discretion of Governor in Council—Prisoner under sentence—Remission of sentence—Mandamus.]—*Horwitz v. Connor*, (1908) 6 C.L.R., 38; 14 A.L.R., 342.

Mandamus—Local Government—Discretion of Council—Exercise of—Local Government Act 1903 (No. 1893), sec. 197, Thirteenth Schedule, Part VI.]—*Randall v. The Council of the Town of Northcote*, 11 C.L.R., 100; 16 A.L.R., 249.

Mandamus—Remedy by appeal available—Discretion of Court, matters to be considered in exercise of—Comparative advantage of applying one remedy rather than the other—County Court—Case struck out for want of jurisdiction—Jurisdiction to entertain defendant's application for costs declined by Judge.] *The King v. Beecham*; *Ex parte Cameron*, (1910) V.L.R., 204; 31 A.L.T., 183; 16 A.L.R., 173.

Wine and spirit merchant's licence—Power of Treasurer—Refusal to grant—Mandamus—Customs and Excise Duties Act 1890 (No. 1082), secs. 155, 156.]—*The King v. Watt, Ex parte Slade*, (1912) V.L.R., 225; 33 A.L.T., 222; 18 A.L.R., 158.

Mandamus—Minister of Crown—Disobedience—Public Statute—Criminal contempt—Attachment—Privilege.]—*The King v. Watt Ex parte Slade*, (1912) V.L.R., 225; 33 A.L.T., 222; 18 A.L.R., 158.

Mandamus—Disobedience of public Statute—Appeal from mandamus—Civil or mixed matters—Supreme Court Act 1890 (No. 1142), sec. 37.]—*The King v. Watt, Ex parte Slade*, (1912) V.L.R., 225; 33 A.L.T., 222; 18 A.L.R., 158.

Order LII., r. 11—Order LXVII.A, r. 9—Writ of attachment—Sheriff, refusal of to execute—Execution, how enforced—Whether mandamus will issue.]—Where the sheriff refuses to execute a writ of attachment, he should be called upon to return the writ or bring in the body within a given time, and on his non-compliance, application should be made under Order LII., r. 11, for his committal. A writ of mandamus will not issue, there being an alternative remedy. *Peterson v. McLennan*, (1907) V.L.R., 94 ; 28 A.L.T., 135 ; 12 A.L.R., 577. *Cussen, J.*

Health Act 1890 (No. 1098), sec. 225—Appeal—Mandamus to Board of Public Health to hear—Appellants not given an opportunity of being heard.]—*See* HEALTH (PUBLIC). *The King v. Prahran, Mayor, &c. of ; Ex parte Morris*, (1910) V.L.R., 460 ; 32 A.L.T., 92 ; 16 A.L.R., 507.

Mortgage—Registration—Improper refusal to register—Mandamus, whether mortgagee has a remedy by—Existence of another remedy—Transfer of Land Act 1890 (No. 1149), sec. 209.]—*See* TRANSFER OF LAND ACT. *Perpetual Executors and Trustees Association &c. Ltd. v. Hosken*, (1912) 14 C.L.R., 286 ; 18 A.L.R., 201.

(c) *Prohibition.*

See also, APPEAL ; CONSTITUTIONAL LAW.

Order LIII.—Licences Reduction Board—Prohibition — Class constituted by those premises against which two convictions are recorded—Decision that premises fall within that class—Licensing Act 1906 (No. 2068), sec. 44.]—*See* LICENSING. *The King v. The Licences Reduction Board ; Ex parte Carlton Brewery Ltd.*, (1908) V.L.R., 79 ; 29 A.L.T., 148 ; 14 A.L.R., 7.

(d) *Habeas Corpus.*

Custody of infant—Procedure—Habeas Corpus—Who may apply by—Application to Court for appointment of guardian, when necessary.]—*See* HABEAS CORPUS, col. 625. *The King v. Waters*, (1912) V.L.R., 372 ; 34 A.L.T., 48 ; 18 A.L.R , 304.

Supreme Court—Jurisdiction—Habeas Corpus—Applicant held under restraint under authority of Commonwealth—Immigration Restriction Amendment Act 1905 (No. 17), sec. 14 (13B)—Judiciary Act 1903 (No. 6), Part VI.]—*See* HABEAS CORPUS, col. 626. *Ah Sheung v. Lindberg*, (1906) V.L.R., 323 ; 27 A.L.T., 189 ; *sub. nom., Rex v. Ah Sheung*, 12 A.L.R., 190.

Habeas Corpus—Return to writ—No legal justification for restraint disclosed—Procedure.]

See HABEAS CORPUS, col. 626. *Ah Sheung v. Lindberg*, (1906) V.L.R., 323 ; 27 A.L.T., 189 ; *Sub. nom., Rex v. Ah Sheung*, 12 A.L.R., 190.

Return of writ of habeas corpus—Whether Court bound by recitals in warrant—Evidence to show want of jurisdiction.]—*See* HABEAS CORPUS, col. 626. *Ex parte Dunn ; Ex parte Aspinall*, (1906) V.L.R., 493 ; 28 A.L.T., 3 ; 12 A.L.R., 358.

Habeas corpus—Evidence—Proof by affidavit—Oral evidence.]—*See* HABEAS CORPUS, col. 626. *Ah Sheung v. Lindberg*, (1906) V.L.R., 323 ; 27 A.L.T., 189 ; *Sub nom., Rex v. Ah Sheung*, 12 A.L.R., 190.

Habeas corpus—Return to writ—Legal justification for restraint disclosed—Evidence, admissibility of—Conviction or warrant of superior Court—Conviction or warrant of inferior Court—No judgment of Court—Procedure.]—*See* HABEAS CORPUS, cols. 626, 627. *Ah Sheung v. Lindberg*, (1906) V.L.R., 323 ; 27 A.L.T., 189 ; *Sub nom. Rex v. Ah Sheung*, 12 A.L.R., 190.

Habeas corpus—Truth of return, whether it must be verified.]—*See* HABEAS CORPUS, col. 627. *Ah Sheung v. Lindberg*, (1906) V.L.R., 323 ; 27 A.L.T., 189 ; *Sub nom. Rex v. Ah Sheung*, 12 A.L.R., 190.

Appeal—High Court, jurisdiction of to entertain—Order of Judge of Supreme Court on habeas corpus.]—*See* HABEAS CORPUS, col. 627. *Attorney-General for the Commonwealth v. Ah Sheung*, 4 C.L.R., 949 ; 12 A.L.R., 432.

Leave to appeal to High Court—Applicant in prison—Appearance in person—Whether High Court has jurisdiction to order that it shall be allowed.]—*See* CRIMINAL LAW, col. 26. *Horwitz v. O'Connor*, 6 C.L.R., 38 ; 14 A.L.R., 342.

Immigration Restriction Acts 1901-1905—Habeas corpus—Return, sufficiency of—Allegations of law—Allegation of fact of failure to pass dictation test—No facts alleged to show that person detained was subject to the Acts.]—*See* IMMIGRATION RESTRICTION ACTS, col. 671. *Ah Sheung v. Lindberg*,

(1906) V.L.R., 323 ; 27 A.L.T., 189 ; *Sub nom. Rex* v. *Ah Sheung*, 12 A.L.R., 190.

(32) ORDER LIV.—APPLICATIONS AND PROCEEDINGS AT CHAMBERS.

Order LIV.—Order in Chambers—Whether appeal lies from to High Court.]—An appeal lies to the High Court from an order in Chambers of a Judge of the Supreme Court staying proceedings in a cause remitted to the Supreme Court for the execution of the judgment of the High Court pronounced on appeal from the Supreme Court. *Peacock* v. *Osborne*, (1907) 4 C.L.R., 1564 ; 13 A.L.R., 565. H.C. *Griffith, C.J., Barton, O'Connor, Isaacs* and *Higgins, JJ.*

(33) ORDER LV.—CHAMBERS IN MATTERS WITHIN THE COGNIZANCE OF THE COURT IN ITS EQUITABLE JURISDICTION PREVIOUSLY TO THE COMMENCEMENT OF THE JUDICATURE ACT 1883.

Order LV. — Executors — Commission — Order for upon passing accounts—Originating summons—Administration and Probate Act 1890 (No. 1060), sec. 26.]—An application for leave to pass accounts and to be allowed commission may be made by executors and trustees upon originating summons. *Re Foulkes*, (1909) V.L.R., 76 ; 30 A.L.T., 108 ; 14 A.L.R., 729, followed. *Re Garrett, Smith* v. *Garrett*, (1910) V.L.R., 287 ; 31 A.L.T., 203 ; 16 A.L.R., 215. *Cussen, J.*

Order LV.—Probate duty, liability for—Question as to between Master-in-Equity and trustee—Whether it can be dealt with upon originating summons.]—*Quaere,* Whether a question between the Master-in-Equity and the trustees of a settlement within section 112 of the *Administration and Probate Act* 1890 and the *Administration and Probate Act* 1903 as to whether any and what duty is payable in respect of property at any time comprised in such settlement can be dealt with on originating summons. *In re Rosenthal* ; *Rosenthal* v. *Rosenthal*, (1911) V.L.R., 55 ; 32 A.L.T., 46 ; 16 A.L.R., 399. *Hodges, J.*

Transfer of shares by executor—Registration delayed—Distribution of assets of testator's estate—Facts insufficient to justify determination on originating summons.]—Where the question to be determined on an originating summons was whether, having regard to certain facts, the executor of a will could safely and properly hand over the remaining assets in the testator's estate to the sole beneficiary under the will without making any provisions for any liability for calls made after a certain date on shares not fully paid up in an incorporated company of which shares the testator was the registered holder, and which the executor, in order to free the estate from contingent liability, had previously to such date transferred for a nominal consideration to the executor and for a consideration to be paid to the transferee upon the transfer being registered, which transfer was not registered till subsequently to such date. *Held,* that no order could be made which would justify the executor, on the facts as they then stood, in distributing the assets. *In re Blackwood* ; *Power* v. *Melbourne Flour Milling Co. Proprietary Ltd.*, (1908) V.L.R., 517 ; 30 A.L.T., 14 ; 14 A.L.R., 368. *Cussen, J.* (1908).

Order LV., rr. 3, 7—Originating summons—Final judgment—Liberty to apply.]—Liberty to apply is impliedly reserved only when the judgment or order is not in its nature final. *In re McPherson* ; *Willan* v. *Union Trustee Co. of Australia Ltd.*, (1909) V.L.R., 103 ; 30 A.L.T., 162 ; 14 A.L.R., 734. *Madden, C.J.*

Order LV., rr. 3, 7—Final order on originating summons—Adding question after judgment—Amendment.]—Where an order made on an originating summons is of a final nature, the Court will not, years after the judgment has been given, allow the summons to be amended in order to raise a question not previously raised. *In re McPherson* ; *Willan* v. *Union Trustee Co. of Australia Ltd.*, (1909) V.L.R., 103 ; 30 A.L.T., 162 ; 14 A.L.R., 734. *Madden, C.J.*

Order LV.—Trustees—Passing accounts and allowance of commission—Costs of trustee—Summons for sole purpose of obtaining leave to pass accounts and commission.]—Trustees seeking leave by originating summons to pass their accounts and obtain commission out of the testator's estate on passing accounts, may be allowed their costs out of the estate, even though no other questions are asked by the summons. *In re Foulkes* ; *Ford* v. *Foulkes*, (1909) V.L.R., 726 ; 30 A.L.T., 108 ; 14 A.L.R., 729. *Madden, C.J.* (1908).

Order LV.—Practice—Originating summons —Payment of costs out of estate—Order for sale of settled properties.]—An originating summons was taken out asking for certain declarations affecting several properties settled by the will of the testator, and seeking the sale of such properties. The sale was refused on the ground on which it was asked for, but there being no part of the testator's estate other than the properties in question out of which the costs of the summons could properly be taken, the Court in the circumstances directed a sale of the whole of the properties for the payment of the costs, though the sale of some only of such properties would have been sufficient for the purpose. *In re Lees* ; *Lees* v. *National Trustees Co.,* (1908) V.L.R., 211 ; 30 A.L.T., 26 ; 14 A.L.R., 147. *a'Beckett, J.*

Order LV.—Originating summons—King's counsel appearing with junior—Certificate for counsel.]—On an originating summons in which King's counsel appeared with a junior, the Judge, upon an application that he should certify for one counsel only, left the matter to the discretion of the taxing officer. *In re Jamieson* ; *Christensen* v. *Jamieson,* (1907) V.L.R., 103 ; 28 A.L.T., 138 ; 12 A.L.R., 570. *Cussen, J.* (1906).

Practice—Foreclosure action—Default of appearance—Equitable mortgage—Allegation of amount due in statement of claim—Claim for accounts—Declaration that account be deemed to have been taken and settled at the amount alleged—No reference to Chief Clerk.] In an action for foreclosure of an equitable mortgage of land under the *Transfer of Land Act* 1890 the amount due under the mortgage at the issue of the writ was stated in the statement of claim. There was a claim for accounts if and so far as necessary. On

motion for judgment in default of appearance it was ordered and declared that the account sought for in the statement of claim should be deemed to have been taken and settled by the Court at the amount therein alleged without reference to the Chief Clerk. *Beath* v. *Armstrong,* 16 A.L.R., 581. *Cussen, J.* (1910).

Order LV.—High Court, jurisdiction of— Case remitted to Supreme Court on appeal to High Court—Accounts and inquiries directed by High Court—Determination of questions arising on taking of accounts.]—On appeal from the Supreme Court the High Court remitted the cause to the Supreme Court with a declaration of rights and an order for accounts and inquiries. *Held,* that the High Court had no jurisdiction to determine questions arising on the taking of the accounts by the Chief Clerk of the Supreme Court as to the extent of the accounts and inquiries actually directed. *Cock* v. *Smith,* (1910) 12 C.L.R., 11 ; 17 A.L.R., 467. *Griffith, C.J.*

Administration and Probate Act 1890 (No. 1060), sec. 26—Practice—Executors and trustees—Passing accounts before Chief Clerk— Costs of executors and trustees—Objection to allowance thereof—Time to time.]—*See* Costs. cols. 265, 266. *In re Dingwall* ; *Ross* v. *Ross,* 34 A.L.T., 137 ; 18 A.L.R., 584.—

Order LV., r. 64—Interest on legacies— Rate of.]—Upon an originating summons enquiring as to the rate of interest to be paid on certain legacies, *Held,* that the rate should be such as the executors might expect to get upon investments of the estate, and that, accordingly, interest on the legacies should be at the rate of 4 per cent. per annum. *National Trustees Executors &c. Co.* v. *McCracken,* 19 A.L.T., 175 ; 4 A.L.R., 31, discussed. *In re Black* ; *Black* v. *Melbourne Hospital,* (1911) V.L.R., 280 ; 33 A.L.T., 2 ; 17 A.L.R., 240. F.C., *Madden, C.J., Hodges* and *Hood, JJ.* (1911).

Order LV., r. 74—Originating summons— Order settled by Chief Clerk—Passing and entering.]—*See Perpetual Executors and Trustees' Association* v. *McLean,* 15 A.L.R. (C.N.), 13. *Hood, J.* (1909).

Taxation—Appendix N.—Drawing pleadings and other documents—Accounts, statements, &c. for Judge's Chambers—Statement for duty.]—*See* Costs, col. 270. *In re Duke's Will*, (1907) V.L.R., 632; 29 A.L.T., 50; 13 A.L.R., 477.

4) ORDER LVIII.—APPEALS TO THE FULL COURT.

See also, APPEAL, cols. 33 *et seq.*

Order LVIII. — Appeal — Judgment of Supreme Court — Notice of appeal to High Court—Subsequent notice of appeal to Full Court — Jurisdiction — High Court Procedure Rules 1903, Part II., Sec. IV., r. 19.]— The pendency of an appeal to the High Court does not deprive the State Full Court of jurisdiction to hear an appeal to it in respect of the same matter. *O'Sullivan* v. *Morton*, (1911) V.L.R., 235; 32 A.L.T., 172; 17 A.L.R., 140. F.C., *Madden, C.J., Hodges* and *Hood, JJ.* (1911).

Appeal—Reference—Reference as to law applicable on findings of fact—Right to appeal notwithstanding reference.]—*See* APPEAL, col. 34. *Glass* v. *Pioneer Rubber Works of Australia Ltd.*, (1906) V.L.R., 754; 28 A.L.T., 64; 12 A L.R., 529.

Supreme Court Act 1890 (No. 1142), sec. 37 —" Civil or mixed matter "—Appeal from mandamus.]—*See* APPEAL, col. 35. *The King* v. *Watt* ; *Ex parte Slade*, (1912) V.L.R., 225; 33 A.L.T., 222; 18 A.L.R., 158.

Practice—Overruling previous Full Court decision—Summoning Full Bench.]—The Full Court will not summon a Full Bench to consider a previous decision of the Full Court unless it doubts the correctness of that decision. *McKinnon* v. *Gange*, (1910) V.L.R., 32; 31 A.L.T., 112; 15 A.L.R., 640. *Madden, C.J., Hood* and *Cussen, JJ.*

Order LVIII., r. 6—Appeal to Full Court— Cross appeal, notice of—Practice.]—*Semble,* where a judgment deals with two causes of action, and an appeal in respect to one only of such causes of action is brought, the respondent cannot raise an appeal in respect of the other cause of action without having given notice. *Prebble* v. *Reeves*, (1910)

V.L.R., 88 ; 31 A.L.T., 114; 15 A.L.R., 631. F.C., *Madden, C.J., Hood* and *Cussen, JJ.*

Order LVIII., r. 4—Appeal from order granting mandamus—" Judgment after trial or hearing of a cause or matter on the merits "—Discretion to receive further evidence.]— An appeal from an order granting a mandamus is not an appeal from a "judgment after trial or hearing of a cause or matter on the merits " within Order LVIII., r. 4, of the *Rules of the Supreme Court* 1906, and the Court has full discretion to receive further evidence. *The King* v. *Watt*; *Ex parte Slade*, (1912) V.L.R., 225; 33 A.L.T., 222; 18 A.L.R., 158. F.C., *Madden, C.J., Hodges* and *Cussen, JJ.*

Order LVIII., r. 4—Appeal—Fresh evidence —Discretion to receive.]—*Semble (per Hodges* and *Cussen, JJ.*), the rules laid down in *Ward* v. *Hearne*, (1884) 10 V.L.R. (L.), 163; 6 A.L.T., 49, and *Ashley* v. *Ashley*, 24 V.L.R., 220; 4 A.L.R., 154, though sound, and to be followed in most cases, may not apply in cases where the rights of others than the immediate parties are concerned, *e.g.*, in cases of trustees, guardians of infants, committees of lunatics, and where the action of the party tendering fresh evidence is really brought in the interests of the public at large. *The King* v. *Watt*; *Ex parte Slade*, (1912) V.L.R., 225; 33 A.L.T., 222; 18 A.L.R., 158. F.C., *Madden, C.J., Hodges* and *Cussen, JJ.*

Appeal—Evidence, admissibility of—Application for new trial on ground of misconduct of juryman—Evidence as to such misconduct given before primary Judge—Affidavit as to such evidence.]—*See* APPEAL, cols. 38, 39. *David Syme & Co.* v. *Swinburne*, 10 C.L.R., 43 ; 16 A.L.R., 93.

Order LVIII., r. 16—Stay of proceedings pending appeal—Application for stay— Whether Full Court may entertain.]—An application for a stay of proceedings pending an appeal to the Full Court may under Order LVIII., r. 16, be made to the Full Court. *O'Sullivan* v. *Morton*, (1911) V.L.R., 235; 32 A.L.T., 172; 17 A.L.R., 140. F.C., *Madden, C.J., Hodges* and *Hood, JJ.* (1911).

Order LVIII., r. 16—Practice—Appeal to High Court from Supreme Court—Stay by Supreme Court of proceedings under judgment —Conditions.]—*See* APPEAL, cols. 25, 26. *Howard Smith & Co. Ltd.* v. *Varawa*, (1910) 10 C.L.R., 607.

(35) ORDER LVIIIA.—CROWN CASES RESERVED.

Crimes Act 1890 (No. 1079), secs. 481, 482 —Crown cases reserved—Question of difficulty in point of law—Arising " on the trial," meaning of—Whether case may be stated after termination of sittings.]—*See* APPEAL, cols. 35, 36. *Rex* v. *Turnbull*, (1907) V.L.R., 11 ; 28 A.L.T., 103 ; 12 A.L.R., 551.

Criminal law—Practice—Crown case reserved—Right to begin—Crimes Act 1890 (No. 1079), sec. 481.]—*See* APPEAL, cols. 37, 38. *Rex* v. *Shuttleworth*, (1909) V.L.R., 431 ; 31 A.L.T., 50 ; 15 A.L.R., 492.

(36) ORDER LVIIIB.—APPEALS TO PRIVY COUNCIL.

See APPEAL, cols. 14 *et seq.*

(37) ORDER LIX.—APPEALS FROM INFERIOR JURISDICTIONS.

See APPEAL, cols. 33 *et seq.*

(38) ORDER LXII.—SETTLING AND PASSING JUDGMENTS AND ORDERS IN MATTERS WITHIN THE COGNIZANCE OF THE COURT IN ITS EQUITABLE JURISDICTION PREVIOUSLY TO THE JUDICATURE ACT 1883.

Order LV., r. 3—Originating summons— Liberty to apply—Amendment of summons— Adding new question after judgment.]—Liberty to apply is not impliedly reserved in a judgment or order which is in its nature final. Where an order in its nature final had been made on an originating summons the Court refused to amend the summons by adding a new question the answering of which would involve the correctness of the order already made. *In re McPherson* ; *Willan* v. *Union Trustee Co. of Australia Ltd.*, (1909) V.L.R., 103; 30 A.L.T., 162; 14 A.L.R., 734. *Madden, C.J.* (1908).

(39) ORDER LXIV.—TIME.

Order LXIV., r. 4— Time — Summons for directions—Issue in vacation.]--The issue of a summons for directions is not a proceeding carried on in the Court within the meaning of Order LXIV., r. 4, and a summons for directions may, therefore, be taken out in vacation. *Williams* v. *Ahern*, (1911) V.L.R., 77 ; 32 A.L.T., 181 ; 17 A.L.R., 38. *Hood, J.*

Order LXIV., r. 7—Order XXX., rr. 1 (a), 8 (a)—Summons for directions—Expiration of time for taking out—Enlargement of time.] Under Order LXIV., r. 7, a Judge may enlarge the time fixed by Order XXX. for taking out a summons for directions notwithstanding the provisions of Order XXX., r. 8 (a) with respect to pleadings. *Varley Bros.* v. *Woolley*, (1908) V.L.R., 231 ; 29 A.L.T., 200 ; 14 A.L.R., 153. *Madden, C.J.*, (1908).

(40) ORDER LXV.—COSTS.

I. Jurisdiction to Hear Appeals as to Costs—*See* COSTS, col. 249 *et seq.*

II. In Divorce Proceedings—*See* COSTS, cols. 254 *et seq.*

III. Bills of Costs—*See* COSTS, cols. 267 *et seq.*

IV. Taxation—*See* COSTS, cols. 268 *et seq.*

V. Security for Costs—*See* COSTS, cols. 291 *et seq.*

VI. Agreement for Remuneration of Solicitors—*See* COSTS, col. 292.

VII. Recovery of Costs—*See* COSTS, cols. 293 *et seq.*

COL.

A. JURISDICTION.

Service and Execution of Process Act 1901 (No. 11 of 1901), sec. 18—Execution of warrant issued in another State—Order of Justice of Peace directing return of accused—Review of order by Judge—Costs, jurisdiction to award.]—Upon review of the decision of a justice of the peace ordering an accused person to be returned to the State in which the warrant for his apprehension was issued a Judge has no jurisdiction to award costs. *In re George,* (1909) V.L.R., 15 ; 30 A.L.T., 141 ; 15 A.L.R., 27. *a' Beckett, J.*

Costs — Probate — Will — Caveat — Withdrawal before motion—Costs against caveator.]—Where a caveat against a grant of probate has been withdrawn prior to the motion for probate occasioned by the lodging of such caveat, the Court has no power to award costs against the caveator. *In re Downey,* 5 V.L.R. (I.P. & M.), 72, distinguished. *In re Johnson,* (1909) V.L.R., 324 ; 31 A.L.T., 2 ; 15 A.L.R., 304. *Madden, C.J.*

B. DISCRETION.

(1) *Public Officers.*

Licenses Reduction Board—Procedure on deprivation of victualler's licenses—Mistaken refusal to hear owners and occupiers of the licensed premises who are interested—Erroneous belief in absence of jurisdiction to hear them—Prohibition—Costs.] —Notwithstanding the existence of a fund under the control of the Licences Reduction Board out of which the costs of all parties in *The King* v. *Licences Reduction Board ; Ex parte Martin and Godfrey,* (1908) V.L.R., 721 ; 30 A.L.T., 133 ; 14 A.L.R., 675, had been ordered to be paid, where the error of the Board was in holding that they had no power to permit the relator to intervene, the order *nisi* for a writ of prohibition was made absolute, without costs. *The King* v. *Licences Reduction Board ; Ex parte Miller,* (1909) V.L.R., 327 ; 30

A.L.T., 223 ; 15 A.L.R., 282. F.C., *Hodges,* and *Hood, JJ.* (*a' Beckett, J.,* dissenting).

Patent—Appeal from Commissioner—Right of Commissioner when unsuccessful to his costs—Patents Act 1903 (No. 21 of 1903), sec. 111.]—Where the Commissioner of Patents is represented upon the hearing of an appeal from his decision and the appeal succeeds, the costs of the Commissioner are in the discretion of the Court, and ordinarily the successful appellant will not be ordered to pay them. *Re McKay's Application,* (1909) V.L.R., 423 ; 31 A.L.T., 63 ; 15 A.L.R., 445. *a' Beckett, Hodges* and *Hood, JJ.*

(2) *Where Trial by Jury.*

Order LXV., r. 1—Costs—Trial by a jury—Wrongful dismissal—One farthing damages—"Good cause."]—In an action for wrongful dismissal, the jury awarded the plaintiff a farthing damages. The Judge was of opinion that the verdict was attributable to disapproval of the plaintiff's conduct and disbelief of his denials on the part of some at least of the jury, and His Honor also disapproved of such conduct, and disbelieved such denials. *Held,* that there was " good cause " for depriving the plaintiff of his costs. *Galsworthy* v. *Reid,* 32 A.L.T., 189 ; 17 A.L.R., 144. *a' Beckett, J.* (1911).

Order LXV., r. 1— Costs—Trial by Jury —" Event " meaning of—Several causes of action—Taxation.]—Where in an action for several causes of action tried before a jury the plaintiff succeeds on some causes of action, and fails on others, the result of each cause of action is an " event " within the meaning of Order LXV., r. 1, and, unless there is good cause shown, judgment should be given for the plaintiff for the amount recovered by him with costs on the causes of action on which he succeeded, and for the defendant for the costs of the causes of action on which he has succeeded, and the costs of each cause of action should be taxed as if it were a separate action. *O'Sullivan* v. *Morton,* (1911) V.L.R., 249 ; 32 A.L.T., 198 ; 17 A.L.R., 201. F.C., *Madden, C.J., Hodges* and *Hood, JJ.* (1911). [Leave to appeal refused, (1911) 12 C.L.R., 390.]

(3) Defendants in Same Interest or Joining in Defence.

Order LXV.—Costs of two parties appearing in same interest.]—For observations on the allowance of costs to two parties appearing in the same interest, see *In re Hobson ; Hobson v. Sharp,* (1907) V.L.R., 724 ; 29 A.L.T., 125 ; 13 A.L.R., 703. *Cussen, J.*

Costs — Two defendants joining in one defence—One succeeding, the other failing — Order that each abide his own costs.]—*See Crout v. Beissel,* (1909) V.L.R., 207 ; 30 A.L.T., 185 ; 15 A.L.R., 143. *a'Beckett, J.*

(4) Set-off.

Order LXV., r. 14—Several causes of action—Set-off of costs recovered by defendant against damages and costs recovered by plaintiff—Complication of evidence and argument on several causes of action.]—Where in an action for several causes of action which crossed one another in evidence and argument, the plaintiff obtained judgment for damages on one cause of action with the costs thereof, and the defendant obtained judgment for costs on the other causes of action, *Held*, that the costs of the defendant in respect of the causes of action on which he succeeded should be set off against the damages and costs in respect of the cause of action on which the plaintiff succeeded. *O'Sullivan v. Morton,* (1911) V.L.R , 249 ; 32 A.L.T., 198 ; 17 A.L.R., 201. F.C., *Madden, C.J., Hodges* and *Hood, JJ.* (1911). [Leave to appeal refused, (1911) 12 C.L.R., 390].

(5) Special Scales of Costs.

Patents Act 1903 (No. 21 of 1903), secs. 14, 58, 111—Appeal against decision of Commissioner of Patents—Costs of opposition to grant of patent before Commissioner.]—The costs of a successful appellant's opposition before the Commissioner were allowed on the lower Supreme Court scale. *Moore and Hesketh v. Phillips,* 4 C.L.R., 1411 ; 13 A.L.R., 424. H.C., *Griffith, C.J., Barton, Isaacs* and *Higgins, JJ.* (1907).

Taxation—Scale of costs—Action for recovery of land—No monetary claim—Order LXV., r. 29 (a), Appendix N. (Rules of 1904), whether applicable.]—Order LXV., r. 29 (a) (Rules of 1904) applies only to cases where a plaintiff is seeking to recover a sum of money which does not exceed £500, and does not apply to an action for the recovery of land. *Griffin v. Millane,* (1907) V.L.R., 46 ; 28 A.L.T., 97 ; 12 A.L.R., 494. *Hood, J.* (1906).

Order LXV., r. 29 (a)—Special scale of costs in Appendix N.—Application that costs be taxed on ordinary scale—When application to be made—Discretion of Judge.]—An application by a successful party that his costs may be allowed on the ordinary scale, notwithstanding that the notice under Order LXV., r. 29 (a) has been given, should be made at the conclusion of the trial to the Judge who tries the action. Such an application will not be granted unless definite special reasons are shown why the scale of costs in Appendix N. should be departed from. *Bloomfield v. Dunlop Tyre Co. Ltd.,* 28 V.L.R., 72 ; 23 A.L.T., 227 ; 8 A.L.R., 103, followed. *Chomley v. Watson,* (1907) V.L.R., 502 ; 29 A.L.T., 46 ; 13 A.L.R., 380. *Madden, C.J.* (1907).

Order LXV., r. 29 (a)—Costs—Special scale in Appendix N.—Notice of intention to proceed under, given by defendant on entry of appearance—Judgment for plaintiff—Application by plaintiff that the Judge should " otherwise order " as to scale of costs—When such application should be made.]—When either party to an action has given notice under Order LXV., r. 29 (a) that he intends to proceed under the special scale of costs in Appendix N., an application by the other party for an order that the costs of the action shall not be taxed under that scale must be made at the trial and before judgment. *Leviston v. Douglas,* (1912) V.L.R., 318 ; 34 A.L.T., 15 ; 18 A.L.R., 309. *Hodges, J.*

Order LXV., r. 12—Costs—Action of tort —Judgment for damages under £50 and injunction—Supreme Court costs—" Sum recovered "—Impossibility of valuing injunction.]—Order LXV., r. 12, of the *Rules of the Supreme Court* 1906, does not apply to an action where the plaintiff, in addition to damages, obtains judgment for an injunction which is a substantial part of his action. The principle determined in *Doherty* v. *Thompson*, 94 L.T., 626, and *Keates* v. *Woodward*, (1902) 1 K.B., 532, followed. An injunction is not, nor can its value be estimated so as to make it a " sum recovered " *Harrison San Miguel Proprietary Ltd.* v. *Alfred Lawrence & Co.*, (1912) V.L.R., 367; 34 A.L.T., 88; 18 A.L.R., 394. *Madden, C.J.*

(6) *Omission to Deal with Costs at Hearing.*

Order XXXI., r. 3* (Rules of 1900)—Interrogatories—Costs—No application as to at trial—Application for after trial.]—Where a party had omitted to apply at the trial for the costs of interrogatories, an order was made allowing such costs after the lapse of two years from the trial, no special circumstances being shown why the order should not be made. *General Finance &c. Co.* v. *National Trustees &c. Co.*, 12 A.L.R (C.N.), 1. *a'Beckett, J.* (1906).

Commission to examine witnesses—Costs reserved until trial—Judgment for general costs of action—No mention at hearing of costs of commission—Jurisdiction to amend —Order XXVIII., r. 11—" Accidental slip or omission " in judgment, correction of after appeal—Special circumstances—Complicated issues and lengthy trial.]—*See* Order XXVIII. *Melbourne Harbour Trust Commissioners* v. *Cuming Smith & Co. Proprietary Ltd.*, (1906) V.L.R., 192; 27 A.L.T., 186; 12 A.L.R., 142.

(7) *Application for Final Judgment.*

Order XIV., r. 8 (Rules of 1900)—Costs—Application for liberty to enter final judgment dismissed — Order made as on summons for directions.]—No general rule will be laid down as to the costs of an application for liberty to enter final judgment where the application is dismissed and the matter is treated as a summons for directions. *International Harvester Co. of America Ltd.* v. *Mullavey*, (1906) V.L.R., 659; 28 A.L.T., 51; 12 A.L.R., 380 *Hodges, J.*

Order XIV., rr. 1, 8—Dismissal of summons for final judgment—Directions given after dismissal — Costs.] — *See ante*, Order XIV. *Colonial Bank of Australasia Ltd.* v. *Martin*, (1912) V.L.R., 383; 34 A.L.T., 47; 18 A.L.R., 325.

(8) *Contested Wills.*

Will — Probate — Caveat — Costs — Administration and Probate Act 1890 (No. 1060), sec. 21.]—In cases of contested wills, costs should follow the event unless there are adequate reasons for an order of a different character. Where the testator by his conduct, habits or mode of life has given the opponent of the will reasonable grounds for questioning his testamentary capacity, the costs of the opponent, although he is unsuccessful, should be paid out of the estate. Where that is not so, but the opponent after due inquiry entertains a *bona fide* belief in the existence of a state of things, which, if it did exist, would justify the litigation, the unsuccessful party must bear his own costs. *In re Miller*, (1908) V.L.R., 682; 30 A.L.T., 106; 14 A.L.R., 564. *Hood, J.*

Will — Probate — Practice — Costs — Order nisi to revoke probate—Costs of unsuccessful propounder of will—Reasonable belief in validity of will.]—An executor who has obtained probate of an instrument which he reasonably and *bona fide* believes to be a valid will, but which is afterwards revoked on the ground of want of testamentary capacity, should be allowed out of the estate his costs, as between solicitor and client, both of propounding the will and of opposing the application for revocation of probate. *Twist* v. *Tye*, (1902) P., 92, considered. *In re Keane*, (1909) V.L.R., 231; 30 A.L.T., 216; 15 A.L.R., 198. *Hodges, J.*

Will—Party supporting invalid revocation—Costs.]—*Semble*, the costs of a party supporting an apparently valid but really invalid revocation of a will by destruction, are governed by the same considerations as govern the costs of an executor propounding an apparently valid but really invalid will, *In re Richards*, (1911) V.L.R., 284; 33 A.L.T., 38. *a'Beckett, J.*

(9) *Administration of Estates*; *Interpretation of Wills*, &c.

Costs—Originating summons — Litigation arising out of plaintiff's mistake as executor.]—Plaintiff, executor of a will, ordered to bear his own costs cf an originating summons, the main purpose of which was to adjust a difference between the plaintiff and a beneficiary arising out of a mistake made by the plaintiff as executor. *Perpetual Executors and Trustees Association* v. *Simpson*, 27 A.L.T., 179; 12 A.L.R., 95. *a'Beckett, J.* (1905).

Will—Construction—Validity of Trusts—Originating summons—Costs.]—" The cases to which counsel referred on the question of costs show that at all events since 1908 it has been the practice in cases like the present to grant costs out of the estate as between solicitor and client to all parties, and as there are here no circumstances to justify a departure from that practice I accordingly make that order. The costs are to be paid one half out of the accumulation within the twenty-one years and the other half out of the accumulations since." *In re Stevens; The Trustees Executors &c. Co. Ltd.* v. *Teague*, (1912) V.L.R., 194; 33 A.L.T., 233; 18 A.L.R., 195. *Hood, J.*

Costs — Trustees — Unsuccessful appeal.]—The costs of trustees, unsuccessful appellants, were in the special circumstances allowed out of the estate. *In re Rosenthal; Rosenthal* v. *Rosenthal,* (1910) 11 C.L.R., 87; 16 A.L.R., 455. H.C., *Griffith, C.J.,* and *Isaacs, J.* (*Higgins, J.,* dissenting).

Costs — Originating summons — King's counsel appearing with junior—Certificate for counsel.]—On an originating summons in which King's Counsel appeared with a junior, the Judge, upon an application that he should certify for one counsel only, left the matter to the discretion of the Taxing Officer. *In re Jamieson; Christensen* v. *Jamieson*, (1907) V.L.R., 103; 28 A.L.T., 138; 12 A.L.R., 570. *Cussen, J.*

Costs—Trustees—Passing accounts and allowance of commission—Order for in action—Trustees' costs of obtaining commission—Whether chargeable against estate—Adminis- tration and Probate Act 1890 (No. 1060), sec. 26.]—Where, under an order in an action, trustees are authorised to pass their accounts and apply for commission, they are entitled to charge the estate with the costs incurred by them in relation to commission, as well as in regard to passing their accounts. *Abbott* v. *Morris*, 24 A.L.T., 228; 9 A.L.R., 96, not followed on this point. *Macartney* v. *Kesterson*, (1907) V.L.R., 226; 28 A.L.T., 170; 13 A.L.R., 14. *Hodges, J.*

Trustees—Passing accounts and allowance of commission—Costs of trustee—Summons for sole purpose of obtaining leave to pass accounts and commission.]—Trustees seeking leave by originating summons to pass their accounts and obtain commission out of the testator's estate on passing accounts, may be allowed their costs out of the estate, even though no other questions are asked by the summons. *In re Foulkes; Ford* v. *Foulkes*, 30 A.L.T., 108; 14 A.L.R., 729. *Madden, C.J.* (1908).

Executor or trustee passing accounts—Costs—Whether payable out of estate.]—Although ordinarily an executor or trustee is entitled to have his costs of passing his accounts and obtaining his discharge paid out of the estate, yet, if in so doing he seeks to cast an unnecessary burden on the estate, he must abide those costs himself. *Cattanach* v. *Macpherson*, (1908) V.L.R., 390; 29 A.L.T., 259; 14 A.L.R., 214. *Madden, C.J.*

Administration and Probate Act 1890 (No. 1060), sec. 26—Practice—Executors and trustees—Passing accounts before Chief Clerk—Costs of executors and trustees—Objection to allowance thereof—Time to take.]—Where beneficiaries desire to object that executors and trustees should not be allowed their costs of the proceedings before the Chief Clerk for the passing of accounts and allowance of commission, they should ask the Chief Clerk to certify specially upon the matter, and then raise the question upon further consideration before the Judge on the certificate. *In re Dingwall; Ross* v. *Ross*, 34 A.L.T., 137; 18 A.L.R., 584. *a'Beckett, J.* (1912).

Trustees—Corpus and income interested—Mathemetical adjustment of the burden of costs impossible—Burden divided equally.]—See *Macartney* v. *Macartney*, (1909) V.L.R., 183; 30 A.L.T., 172; 15 A.L.R., 139 *Hodges, J*

Practice—Originating Summons—Payment of costs out of estate—Order for sale of settled properties.]—An originating summons was taken out asking for certain directions affecting several properties settled by the will of the testator and seeking the sale of such properties The sale was refused on the ground on which it was asked for, but there being no part of the testator's estate other than the properties in question out of which the costs of the summons could properly be taken the Court in the circumstances directed a sale of the whole of the properties for the payment of the costs, though the sale of some only of such properties would have been sufficient for the purpose *In re Lees*; *Lees* v. *National Trustees Co.*, (1908) V.L.R., 211; 30 A.L.T., 26; 14 A.L.R., 147. *a' Beckett, J.*

(10) *Conveyancing.*

Vendor and purchaser—Apparent flaw on title—Costs of proving existence of facts negativing existence of flaw.]—The costs of proving facts negativing the existence of what, on the face of the documents, appeared to be a flaw in the title, were ordered to be paid by the vendor. *In re Kenna and Ritchie's Contract*, (1907) V.L.R., 386; 28 A.L.T., 218; 13 A.L.R., 191. *a' Beckett, J.*

(11) *In Patent Matters.*

Patents Act 1890 (No. 1123), sec. 50—Costs—Defendant's particulars of objections—Certificate of reasonableness.]—For a case in which, for the purposes of taxation of costs under the special circumstances of the case, a certificate was granted that the particulars of the defendant under sec. 50 of the *Patents Act* 1890 were reasonable, see *Potter* v. *Broken Hill Proprietary Co. Ltd.*, 13 A.L.R. (C.N.), 3. *a' Beckett, J.* (1907)

(12) *Other Cases.*

Costs—Attorney-General necessary party—Attorney-General not joined until after pro- ceedings instituted—Special order as to costs.]—The Attorney-General having been held to be a necessary party, and having accordingly been joined as a party to proceedings after they had been instituted against a municipal council, a special order was made as to costs. *Attorney-General (ex rel. Dodd)* v. *Ararat, Mayor, &c., of Borough of*, (1911) V.L.R., 489; 33 A.L.T., 99; 17 A.L.R., 474. *Madden, C.J.*

(41) ORDER LXVIIA.—SHERIFF'S RULES.

Order LXVIIa.—Attachment of person—Sheriff, duty of—Writ of attachment regular on its face.]—See ATTACHMENT, cols. 64, 65. *Peterson* v. *McLennan*, (1907) V.L.R., 94; 28 A.L.T., 135; 12 A.L.R., 577.

Order LXVII.* r. 9—Order LII., r. 11—Writ of attachment—Sheriff, refusal of to execute—Execution, how enforced—Whether mandamus may issue.]—See, *ante*, ORDER LII. *Peterson* v. *McLennan*, (1907) V.L.R., 94; 28 A.L.T., 135; 12 A.L.R., 577.

Conveyancing Act 1904 (No. 1953), sec. 4 (6)—Auction Sales Act (No. 1065), secs. 3, 29—Sale of land by Sheriff under fi. fa.—Whether a " sale by auction "—Sheriff's costs of perusal of conveyance—Stipulation in contract of sale for payment by purchaser, legality of.]—See EXECUTION, col. 516. *Re Rogers and Rodd's Contract*, (1907) V.L.R., 511; 29 A.L.T., 13; 13 A.L.R., 312.

(42) ORDER LXXIII.*—COURT FEES AND PERCENTAGES.

Rules of the Supreme Court 1884, Order LXXIII.—Appendix O.—Court fees and percentages—Attendance of officer on production of document.]—The fee of £1 provided by Appendix O. must be paid whenever, at the request of the solicitor, a document from the Prothonotary's Office is produced in Court by an officer. *Daniel* v. *McNamara*, 17 A.L.R. (C.N.), 9. *Madden, C.J.* (1911).

Appendix O.*, Rules of Supreme Court 1884 — Trustees — Passing accounts — Accounts agreed upon between parties—Fees chargeable.]—Where trustees are ordered by the

Court to pass their accounts before the Chief Clerk, the fees prescribed for " taking accounts " by Appendix O.* to the *Rules of the Supreme Court* 1884 are chargeable, although the parties agree among themselves not to dispute the accounts presented by the trustees and the Chief Clerk accordingly accepts them as proper accounts. There is also chargeable 10s. per hour for each hour occupied by the Chief Clerk in inquiring as to the commission to be allowed the trustees. *Re Hutchinson*, 32 W.R., 392, approved and applied. *In re Winter*; *Winter-Irving* v. *Winter*, (1908) V.L.R., 74 ; 29 A.L.T., 144 ; 13 A.L.R., 701. F.C., *Madden, C.J., a' Beckett* and *Cussen, JJ.* (1907).

C.—MISCELLANEOUS.

Maintenance order made by Court of Petty Sessions—Money due thereunder—Action in Supreme Court to recover—Marriage Act 1890 (No. 1166), secs. 43, 51—Justices Act 1890 (No. 1105), secs. 115, 131—Justices Act 1896 (No. 1458), sec. 4.]—No action will lie in the Supreme Court for the recovery of money due under a maintenance order made by a Court of Petty Sessions under sec. 43 of the *Marriage Act* 1890. *Falconer* v. *Falconer*, (1910) V.L.R., 489 ; 32 A.L.T., 100 ; 16 A.L.R., 578. *Cussen, J.*

Function imposed upon tribunal by Legislature—No machinery provided—Power of Court—Ascertainment of amount of duty payable—Administration and Probate Act 1903 (No. 1815), secs. 9 (2), 15 (2)—Second Schedule.]—*See* DUTIES ON THE ESTATES OF DECEASED PERSONS, col. 421. *Edgar* v. *Greenwood*, (1910) V.L.R., 137 ; 31 A.L.T., 132 ; 16 A.L.R., 6.

Custody of infant—Father outside jurisdiction — Order which cannot be enforced — Whether Court will make.]—*See* INFANT, col. 689. *Knipe* v. *Alcock*, (1907) V.L.R., 611 ; 29 A.L.T., 98 ; 13 A.L.R., 433.

General Sessions—Attempt to influence a juryman—Contempt of Court—Power of Supreme Court to punish.]—*Semble.*—An attempt to influence a juror in the Court of General Sessions is a contempt punishable by the Supreme Court *brevi menu*. *Ex parte*

Dunn ; *Ex parte Aspinall*, (1906) V.L.R., 493 ; 28 A.L.T., 3 ; 12 A.L.R., 358. *Cussen, J.*

Fugitive Offenders Act 1881 (44 & 45 Vict. c. 69), secs. 5, 6—Fugitive committed to prison to await return—Legality of detention affirmed by Supreme Court—Bail, whether Court may grant.]—*See* FUGITIVE OFFENDERS, col. 599. *Re McKelvey*, (1906) V.L.R., 304 ; 12 A.L.R., 168.

Fugitive Offenders Act 1881 (44 & 45 Vict. c. 69), secs. 5, 6—Fugitive committed to prison to await return — Legality of detention affirmed by Supreme Court—Appeal to High Court—Bail.]—*See* FUGITIVE OFFENDERS, col. 600. *Re McKelvey*, (1906) V.L.R., 304 ; 12 A.L.R., 209.

Order of Court made in error—Withdrawal.] —An order of a Court may be withdrawn before it is drawn up or acted upon. *David Syme & Co.* v. *Swinburne*, (1909) 10 C.L.R., 43 ; 16 A.L.R., 93. H.C., *Griffith, C.J., Barton, O'Connor, Isaacs* and *Higgins, JJ.*

Order—Reasons for decision—Statement by Judge thereof, whether obligatory.]—A Judge is not bound to give reasons for his decision nor to state which evidence he believes or disbelieves. *Swinburne* v. *David Syme & Co.*, (1909) V.L.R., 550 ; 31 A.L.T., 81 ; 15 A.L.R., 579. *Madden, C.J., a' Beckett* and *Hood, JJ.*

PRE-MATERNITY ORDERS.

See HUSBAND AND WIFE.

PRESBYTERIAN CHURCH OF VICTORIA.

Contempt of Court—Ecclesiastical privilege —Presbyterian Church of Victoria—Refusal of Presbytery Clerk to produce documents in civil action.]—*See* CONTEMPT, cols. 186, 187. *Ronald* v. *Harper*, 15 A.L.R. (C.N.), 5

PRESCRIPTION.

See EASEMENTS, cols. 422 *et seq.*

PRESUMPTIONS.

See EVIDENCE, cols. 481 *et seq.*

PRINCIPAL AND AGENT.

I.—AUTHORITY OF AGENT.

Husband and wife—Agency—Destitute wife —Sale of husband's goods to purchase necessaries—Wife's authority.]—Where a wife has been left by her husband without the necessaries of life and without means of support, she is not at liberty to sell his goods for the purpose of providing herself with necessaries. *Moreno v. Slinn* (1910) V.L.R., 457; 32 A.L.T., 66; 16 A.L.R., 503. *Madden, C.J.*

Principal and agent—Sale of land—Deposit payable to agent on named day—Authority of agent to receive deposit after due date—Payment to agent by way of promissory note— Payment to agent by way of set-off—Cancellation of contract by principal after receipt of deposit by agent—Commission, right of agent to—" Total amount realised "—Right of agent to deduct commission from moneys of principal coming to his hands.]—The defendant was A.'s agent to find a purchaser for his land at £3,200 at a commission of 2½ per centum " on the total amount realised." The defendant induced the plaintiff, who to his knowledge was worth only £550 and had little available cash, to buy the land, and on 13th September, 1907, a contract was signed by the plaintiff and A., the conditions of which provided that the purchaser should, on the 1st October, 1907, pay to the vendor's agent a deposit of £100 and that time should be of the essence of the contract; and on the same day the plaintiff gave the defendant a cheque dated 28th September, for £100.

On the 23rd September, plaintiff informed defendant of his inability to meet the cheque, and paid him £5 on account of the deposit. The cheque for £100 was dishonored, and A., being informed of this, wrote to defendant on 12th October, that he " hoped plaintiff had attended to same by this time." On 3rd December the plaintiff agreed to sell his horses to the defendant for £85, and to give him a promissory note for £10 (the balance of the deposit) due in February 1909, with interest added, the defendant undertaking to " fix up the deposit " with A. On 4th December, defendant wrote to A. enclosing a cheque for £18 12s. purporting to be the deposit, less £81 8s. deducted by the defendant as his commission on the sale. On 5th December, before the receipt of the promissory note, and before the receipt of this letter by A., his solicitor, acting on instructions given by A. some days previously, had written a letter intimating that the contract had been cancelled on account of non-payment of the deposit, and subsequently the cheque for £18 12s. was returned to the defendant. *Held*, by the Full Court, affirming the decision of *a'Beckett, J.*, that there had been no payment of the deposit as required by the conditions, and that the plaintiff was entitled to recover the £85 and the promissory note from the defendant. *Held*, by the Full Court, that an agent has no authority to receive payment on behalf of his principal by way of a promissory note. *Held*, by *a'Beckett, J.*, that, even apart from the express provision as to time being of the essence of the contract, A. would have been entitled to decline to receive the deposit on the 4th December; that it was unnecessary for A. expressly to revoke the authority to receive the deposit contained in the old conditions; and that it required some new authority, or a recognition of the old authority as still subsisting, to make payment to or receipt by the defendant on the 4th December payment to or receipt by A. *Quaere, per a'Beckett, J.*, whether the defendant had earned his commission as against A. and whether, if he had earned it, he would have been entitled to deduct it from money of A.'s coming to his hands. *Walder v. Cutts,*

(1909) V.L.R., 261; 31 A.L.T., 19; 15 A.L.R., 352. F.C., *Hodges, Hood* and *Cussen, JJ.*

Contract—Agency—Order to supply goods —Condition for cancellation—Authority of agent.]—The plaintiff employed an agent to obtain signed orders on a printed form for certain machines. On the form was printed in special black type immediately above the place for the signatures the following statement :—" No conditions representations or promise are authorized and shall not be binding except such as are printed or written hereon." Another provision was that the order was not to be binding on the plaintiff until ratified by him. The defendant signed an order and at the same time the plaintiff's agent signed and handed to the defendant a document stating that the defendant might cancel the order before a certain date if he did not have a fair average crop to his satisfaction. The plaintiff, without knowing of the arrangements for cancellation, ratified the order. The Full Court of the State decided that the defendant might nevertheless cancel the order before the date mentioned. The amount claimed was £23 10s. *Held*, that the case was not one for special leave to appeal *House* v. *Whitlock*, (1911) 13 C.L.R., 334. H.C., *Griffith, C.J., Barton* and *O'Connor, JJ.*

Statute of Limitations—Acknowledgement —Solicitor acting in connection with claim— Whether debtor's agent to make an acknowledgment.] — *Quiere.* — Whether a mere general statement that solicitors are acting for a client in connection with a certain claim, and nothing more, is sufficient evidence that such solicitors are agents of the debtor to make an acknowledgment of debt. *Holden* v. *Lawes Wittewronge*, (1912) V.L.R., 82; 33 A.L.T., 153: 18 A.L.R., 28. *Cussen, J*

Principal and agent—Landlord and Tenant Act 1890 (No. 1108), sec. 92—Eighth Schedule —Notice of intention to apply to Justices to recover possession — Signature of notice, sufficiency of—Application by corporation— Name of corporation signed by agent authorised so to do.]—Where a tenant holds over a tenement owned by a corporation, a notice of the latter's intention to apply to recover possession of the property following the form in the Eighth Schedule of the *Landlord and Tenant Act* 1890 may be validly given by the manager authorized so to do signing the name of the corporation and his own name as manager and agent. *Jackson* v. *Napper*, 35 Ch. D., 162, at p. 172, passage in, recited and approved. *Reg.* v. *Moore, Ex parte Myers*, 10 V.L.R. (L.), 322; 6 A.L.T., 151, followed. *Equity Trustees Executors and Agency Co. Ltd.* v. *Harston*, (1908) V.L.R., 23; 29 A.L.T., 131; 13 A.L.R., 686. *Cussen, J.*

Insolvency Act 1890 (No. 1102), sec. 37— Compulsory sequestration—Petitioning creditor—Power of attorney—Authority of attorney to present petition.]—*See* INSOLVENCY, col. 701. *In re Anderson*, (1909) V.L.R., 465; 31 A.L.T., 72; 15 A.L.R., 518.

II.—Relations between Principal and Agent.

Principal and agent—Contract of agency— Agent to procure purchaser—Right to commission—Statement by vendor that he is ready to sell for a certain sum " net."]—The respondents who were cork and general merchants, and as such had had previous dealings with the appellant, a brewer, wrote to the appellant as follows :—" The writer is under the impression that he heard somewhere that you were inclined to sell your business. If such is the case we should be glad to hear from you stating what amount you require for same and any particulars that are likely to help us to make a sale. We have an inquiry for a small brewery and shall be glad to hear from you on the subject." The appellant wrote in reply :—" In reference to sale of brewery, I want £2,500 net for the business. If I can't get that I don't sell. The only reason for selling I am getting too old, if I was 20 years younger I would not think of selling. Any further particulars you can have by applying." The respondents brought the business under the notice of S. who subsequently purchased it directly from the appellant for £2,500. *Held*, that the letters did not establish a contract between the appellant and respondents that the appellant would employ the respondents as his agents to introduce a purchaser on a promise by the appellant that, if the respondents did so, he would pay them commission ; and, therefore, that the respondents were not entitled to recover commission on the sale. *Dolphin* v. *Harrison, San Miguel Proprietary Ltd.*, (1911) 13 C.L.R., 271 ; 17 A.L.R., 444. H.C., *Griffith, C.J., Barton* and *O' Connor, JJ.*

Estate agent—Contract to " introduce a buyer "—" Effect a sale."]—The defendant by writing authorised the plaintiffs, who were estate agents, to sell a property for " £550 or offer," and also to accept a deposit and sign contracts of sale on his behalf, and agreed " to pay their usual commission if they effect a sale or introduce a buyer." The plaintiffs obtained an offer of £450 from P. and communicated it to the defendant, without disclosing who made it. The offer was declined, and whilst the plaintiffs were endeavouring to induce P. to offer £500, he bought the property for that amount through another agent. *Held* (*per Hodges* and *Hood, JJ., Madden, C.J.*, doubting), that the plaintiffs had not " introduced a buyer " within the meaning of the contract. *Semble* (*per Hodges, J.*), that in such contract the words " effect a sale " meant " sign a valid contract." *Looker & Son* v. *Doveton*, (1911) V.L.R., 23 ; 32 A.L.T., 95 ; 16 A.L.R., 592. F.C. (1910).

Supreme Court Act 1890 (No. 1142), sec. 85—Where cause of action arises—Agent outside jurisdiction—Goods improperly sold by agent—Action by principal for money had and received—Place of payment—Rule that debtor must seek out creditor.]—If an agent abroad acting for a principal within the jurisdiction deals with goods in a manner not authorised by the principal and receives the proceeds thereof and the principal, waiving the tort, sues for money had and received, the cause of action does not arise within the jurisdiction. The rule that the debtor must seek out his creditor particularly applies to cases where the question depends upon an excuse alleged for non-payment of money within a jurisdiction. *Gosman* v. *Ockerby*, (1908) V.L.R., 298 ; 29 A.L.T., 266 ; 14 A.L.R., 186. *Cussen, J.*

Principal and agent—Commission—Sale of property—Property for sale at a fixed price in hands of two agents—Offer by one of agents to a probable purchaser at price fixed refused—No communication as to such negotiation by agent to principal—Sale of property to same person subsequently by other agent for less sum after conferring with principal—Whether first agent may claim commission.]—The defendant, the owner of a certain house property, placed it in hands of two separate agents for sale at £675. W. called upon the complainant, one of the agents, and inspected the property, which he desired to buy, but for which he would not give £675 ; the complainant, without communicating with the defendant to see if he would take less, informed W. that this was the lowest price for the property. W. then went to B., the other agent, told him about his having seen the house and the complainant, and of his intention not to go back to the complainant or to give £675 for the property. Thereupon B. communicated with the defendant, who agreed to reduce the price to £640 clear of commission, and B. then sold the property to W. for £650. *Held*, that the complainant was not entitled to recover commission on such a sale, as it had not been effected through his agency—that he had done more than introduce the property to the purchaser, and had not done his duty to the defendant by neglecting to communicate with him in regard to the interview with the purchaser. *Overton* v. *Phillips*, (1912) V.L.R., 143 ; 33 A.L.T., 188 ; 18 A.L.R., 95. *Hood, J.*

Principal and agent—Sale of land—Deposit payable to agent on named day—Authority of agent to receive deposit after due date—Payment to agent by way of promissory note—Payment to agent by way of set-off—Cancellation of contract by principal after receipt of deposit by agent—Commission, right of agent to—" Total amount realised "—Right of agent to deduct commission from moneys of principal coming to his hands.]—*See, ante,* I. AUTHORITY OF AGENT. *Walder* v. *Cutts,*

(1909) V.L.R., 261; 31 A.L.T., 19; 15 A.L.R., 352.

Future debt—Money to become payable by agent to principal on sale of goods—" On account of or in connection with . . . business "—Book Debts Act 1896 (No. 1424), secs. 2, 3.]—Money which will become payable by an agent to his principal, a trader, as purchase money on the sale of goods of the principal consigned to the agent for sale, constitutes a debt to become due by the agent to the principal, but not a debt " on account of or in connection with the business " of the principal, within the meaning of the *Book Debts Act* 1896, and is therefore not a " book debt " within the meaning of the Act. An order by the principal to the agent to pay the proceeds of the sale to a third person does not require to be registered under sec. 3 of the Act. *Shackell* v. *Howe, Thornton & Palmer,* 8 C.L.R., 170; 15 A.L.R., 176. H.C., *Griffith, C.J., Isaacs* and *O'Connor, JJ.*

Master and servant—Business—Attempted sale of as a going concern—Servant assisting —Lease of premises procured by servant for himself—Fiduciary relation—Whether servant a trustee of lease for master—Covenant against assignment — Transfer of lease, whether master entitled to.]—*See* TRUSTS AND TRUSTEES. *Prebble* v. *Reeves,* (1910) V.L.R., 88; 31 A.L.T., 114; 15 A.L.R., 408.

Conveyancing Act 1904 (No. 1953), sec. 75 —Equitable charge upon land, how created— Investment of trust money by agent in purchase of land—Parol evidence.]—*See* TRUSTS AND TRUSTEES. *In re Smith; Smith* v. *Smith,* (1909) V.L.R., 91; 30 A.L.T., 214; 15 A.L.R., 25.

County Court Rules 1891, r. 230—Action for commission—Claim of third party— Interpleader by defendant—Claims arising out of same subject matter—Whether claims for one and the same debt.]—*See* COUNTY COURT, col. 311. *Looker* v. *Mercer,* 28 A.L.T. (Supplement), 15; 13 A.L.R. (C.N.), 13.

III.—RELATIONS BETWEEN PRINCIPAL AND THIRD PARTIES.

Vendor and purchaser—Deposit paid to agent of vendor—Rescission of contract—

Recovery of deposit from vendor—Stakeholder —Money had and received.]—By the conditions of a contract in writing for the sale of land and stock it was provided that a deposit of £500 should be paid by the purchasers to A. " as agent for the vendor." By another condition it was provided that as soon as the purchasers had accepted title " the deposit shall be paid over to the vendor." The £500 was paid by the purchasers to A., and was never paid by him to the vendor. Subsequently in writing the contract was " cancelled by mutual consent " of the vendor and purchasers, title never having been accepted. *Held,* (per *Griffith* C.J., *O'Connor* and *Higgins* JJ., *Isaacs* J. dissenting) that the purchasers were entitled to recover the £500 from the vendor. *Christie* v. *Robinson,* (1907) 4 C.L.R., 1338; 13 A.L.R., 288.

Vendor and purchaser—Deposit received by agent after expiration of authority—Contract cancelled by vendor—Action for return of deposit—Whether principal or agent liable.] Where the agent of the vendor of certain land, after his authority under the contract to do so had expired, received a deposit from the purchaser, and the vendor cancelled the contract. *Held,* that the purchaser's right of action to recover the deposit was against the agent and not against the vendor. *Walder* v. *Cutts,* (1909) V.L.R., 261; 31 A.L.T., 19; 15 A.L.R., 352.

Instruments Act 1890 (No. 1103), ss. 208, 209—Statute of Frauds (29 Car. II. c. 3)— Contract for sale of land—Signature to note or memorandum—Signature by amanuensis in presence and by direction of party to be charged, whether sufficient.]—To satisfy the requirements of sections 208 and 209 of the *Instruments Act* 1890, there must be a personal signature by the hand of the party to be charged, or a signature by an agent authorized in writing by the party to be charged, and the signature by an amanuensis, in the presence by the direction and with the name of the party to be charged, cannot be regarded as a signature by that party with his own hand, and is therefore insufficient. *Thomson* v. *McInnes,* (1911) 12 C.L.R.,

562; 17 A.L.R., 354. H.C. *Griffith*, *C.J.*, *Barton* and *O'Connor*, *JJ.*

Landlord and Tenant Act 1890 (No. 1108), secs. 81, 83—Distress for rent—Proceeds of sale—Overplus in hands of landlord's agent —Claim by tenant against landlord—Money had and received—Jurisdiction of Court of Petty Sessions.]—*See* LANDLORD AND TENANT. cols. 813, 814. *Rhodes* v. *Parrott*, (1912) V.L.R., 333; 34 A.L.T., 90; 18 A.L.R., 353.

IV.—RELATIONS BETWEEN AGENT AND THIRD PARTIES.

Principal and agent—Breach of warranty of authority, nature of action for—Breach of duty as agent.]—An action for breach of warranty of authority lies only where a person having in fact no authority purports to bring his supposed principal into legal relations with the plaintiff. If an agent alleges that he has concluded a contract on behalf of his principal with a third party, and he has not in fact done so, the principal's cause of action is for breach of duty by the agent, and not for breach of warranty of authority. *Gosman* v. *Ockerby*, (1908) V.L.R., 298; 29 A.L.T., 266; 14 A.L.R., 186. *Cussen*, *J.*

Principal and agent—Agent for foreign shipping company—Sale of passenger's ticket —Failure by principal to carry passenger on terms mentioned in ticket—Liability of agent —No undertaking by agent that passenger should be so carried.]—In an action for breach of contract the Court found on the evidence that the plaintiff approached the defendant's firm as a medium through which to obtain contracts for the carriage of passengers by the N.D.L. a shipping company incorporated and having its head office in Germany, the contracts to be represented by tickets to be used in ordinary way; that the defendant's firm agreed to provide the contracts and did so as to certain tickets actually issued; that the defendants' firm never undertook that the passengers should be carried by the route or on the terms mentioned in the tickets; and that the plaintiff looked to the N.D.L. as alone bound to provide the passages. *Held*, that the defendant was not liable to the plaintiff for the failure

by the N.D.L. to carry the passengers. *Cheong* v. *Lohmann*, (1907) V.L.R., 571; 28 A.L.T., 252; 13 A.L.R., 269. *a'Beckett*, *J.*

Principal and agent—Agent contracting on behalf of disclosed foreign principal—Whether agent personally liable on contract.]—In determining whether an agent contracting on behalf of a disclosed foreign principal is personally liable on the contract, the Court will take into consideration the character of the transaction in which the parties are engaged and the subject matter of the contract resulting from their negotiations. *Cheong* v. *Lohmann*, (1907) V.L.R., 571; 28 A.L.T., 252; 13 A.L.R., 269. *a'Beckett*, *J.*

Agent—Disclosed principal—Liability of agent—Question of fact.]—An agent who contracts personally though on behalf of his principal is personally liable and may be sued in his own name on the contract whether the principal is named therein or is known to the other contracting party or not. Whether an agent who discloses his principal contracts personally is a question of intention to be decided on the facts, where there is nothing in the language employed in making the contract which expressly declares the intention. *Cooper* v. *Fisken*, 33 A.L.T., 231; 18 A.L.R., 155 *a'Beckett*, *J.* (1912).

Vendor and purchaser—Deposit paid to agent of vendor—Rescission of contract— Recovery of deposit from vendor—Stakeholder —Money had and received.]—*See*, *ante*, III.—RELATIONS BETWEEN PRINCIPAL AND THIRD PARTIES. *Christie* v. *Robinson*, (1907) 4 C.L.R., 1338; 13 A.L.R., 288.

Vendor and purchaser—Deposit received by agent after expiration of authority—Contract cancelled by vendor—Action for return of deposit—Whether principal or agent liable.] *See*, *ante*, III.—RELATIONS BETWEEN PRINCIPAL AND THIRD PARTIES. *Walder* v. *Cutts*, (1909) V.L.R., 261; 31 A.L.T., 19; 15 A.L.R., 352.

V.—OFFENCES, LIABILITY WITH REGARD TO.

Larceny—Fraudulent conversion by agent —Secretary of Friendly Society—Trustees—

No relation of agency—Crimes Act 1890 Amendment Act 1896 (No. 1478), sec. 2.]— *See* CRIMINAL LAW, col. 340. *Rex* v. *Buckle,* 31 A.L.T., 43 ; 15 A.L.R., 372.

Secret Commissions Prohibition Act 1905 (No. 1974), secs. 2, 14—Giving money to agent without principal's knowledge—Burden of proof.]—*See* CRIMINAL LAW, col. 243. *Rex* v. *Stevenson,* (1907) V.L.R., 475 ; 29 A.L.T., 62 ; 13 A.L.R., 383.

Secret Commissions Prohibition Act 1905 (No. 1974), sec. 2—" Corruptly," meaning of.]—*See* CRIMINAL LAW, cols. 343, 344. *Rex* v. *Stevenson,* (1907) V.L.R., 475 ; 29 A.L.T., 62 : 13 A.L.R., 383.

Secret Commissions Prohibition Act 1905 (No. 1974), sec. 2—Corruptly giving valuable consideration to agent—Secret giving, presumption as to corruptness arising from.]— *See* CRIMINAL LAW, col. 344. *Rex* v. *Scott,* (1907) V.L.R., 471 ; 29 A.L.T., 60 ; 13 A.L.R., 143.

Secret Commissions Prohibition Act 1905 (No. 1974), sec. 2—Giving of valuable consideration to agent—Tendency to influence agent to show favour.]—*See* CRIMINAL LAW, col. 344. *Rex* v. *Scott,* (1907) V.L.R., 471 ; 29 A.L.T., 60 ; 13 A.L.R., 143.

Poisons Act 1890 (No. 1125), secs. 4, 11— Sale of poisons by unqualified person—Sale by assistant—Offence by master.]—*See* POISONS ACT. *Shillinglaw* v. *Redmond,* (1908) V.L.R., 427 ; 30 A.L.T., 37 ; 14 A.L.R., 343.

Factories and Shops Act 1905 (No. 1975), sec. 119 (1)—Employing person at lower rate than rate determined by Special Board— Mens rea, whether a necessary element of offence—Employer, liability of for act of agent.]—*See* FACTORIES AND SHOPS ACT, col. 581. *Billingham* v. *Oaten,* (1911) V.L.R., 44 ; 32 A.L.T., 170 ; 17 A.L.R., 36.

Pure Food Act 1905 (No. 2010), secs. 32, 35, 36—Adulterated article of food, sale of—Sale by servant—Reasonable precautions by master against committing offence.]—*See* HEALTH (PUBLIC). *O'Connor* v. *Jenner,* (1909) V.L.R. 468 ; 31 A.L.T., 71 ; 15 A.L.R., 519.

Licensing Act 1890 (No. 1111), sec. 124— Licensing Act 1906 (No. 2068), sec. 78—Licensee, liability for act of servant—Supplying liquor to person in state of intoxication— Supply by servant in absence without the knowledge and contrary to instructions of licensee.] —*See* LICENSING, col. 838. *Davies* v. *Young,* (1910) V.L.R., 369 ; 32 A.L.T., 39 ; 16 A.L.R., 368.

Agent—Liability of candidate for acts of.] —*See* COMMONWEALTH ELECTORAL ACTS, col. 112. *Crouch* v. *Ozanne,* (1910) 12 C.L.R., 539.

Insolvency Act 1890 (No. 1102), sec. 141 (xii.)—Trustee agent or broker—Unlawful appropriation of property held as agent— principal's goods sold by agent on commission—Relationship of debtor and creditor— Insolvency of agent—Whether agent liable for offence.]—*See* INSOLVENCY, col. 731. *In re James,* 32 A.L.T. (Supplement), 12 ; 17 A.L.R. (C.N.), 5.

PRINCIPAL AND SURETY.

See also, EXECUTORS AND ADMINISTRATORS, cols. 538 *et seq.*

Undue influence—Parent and child—Trustee and cestui que trust—Whether transaction may be set aside against a third party—Ordinary business transaction—Beneficiary surety for trustees — Independent advice.] — *See* FRAUD AND MISREPRESENTATION, col. 587. *Union Bank of Australia Ltd.* v. *Whitelaw* (1906) V.L.R., 711 ; 28 A.L.T., 17 ; 12 A.L.R., 393.

" Undue concealment "—Business carried by trustees in breach of trust—Moneys advanced to trustees on guarantee of beneficiaries—Ordinary business transaction— Whether creditor under duty to inform himself and beneficiaries as to conduct of trustees.] —*See* FRAUD AND MISREPRESENTATION, col. 588. *Union Bank of Australia Ltd.* v. *Whitelaw,* (1906) V.L.R., 711 ; 28 A.L.T., 17 ; 12 A.L.R., 393.

Fraudulent preference—Transfer with intent to defeat or delay creditors—Desire to protect sureties—Banker and customer—Payments made in the ordinary course of banking business—Insolvency Act 1890 (No. 1102), secs. 37 (ii.), 73.]—*See* INSOLVENCY, cols. 711, 712. *McDonald* v. *Bank of Victoria*, (1906) V.L.R., 199; 27 A.L.T., 177: 12 A.L.R., 120.

Marriage Act 1890 (No. 1166), sec. 43—Maintenance order—Surety directed—Variation of order on appeal—Character of order not changed by variation—Whether surety discharged.]—*See* MAINTENANCE AND MAINTENANCE ORDERS, cols. 885, 886. *Shee* v. *Larkin*, (1907) V.L.R., 295; 28 A.L.T., 188: 13 A.L.R., 97.

Marriage Act 1890 (No. 1166), sec. 43—Maintenance order—Surety directed — Liability of surety, when it arises—Declaration of forfeiture, whether necessary.]—*See* MAINTENANCE AND MAINTENANCE ORDERS, col. 886. *Shee* v. *Larkin*, (1907) V.L.R., 295; 28 A.L.T., 188; 13 A.L.R., 97.

Order for maintenance—Defendant to find surety " forthwith "—Immediate committal to prison—Service of order, whether a condition precedent to issue of warrant of committal—Marriage Act 1890 (No. 1166), sec. 43—Justices Act 1904 (No. 1959), sec. 20.]—*See* MAINTENANCE AND MAINTENANCE ORDERS cols. 884, 885. *Adams* v. *Rogers*, (1907) V.L.R., 245; 28 A.L.T., 180; 13 A.L.R., 71.

Marriage Act 1890 (No. 1166), secs. 42, 43—Maintenance order—Surety directed—Person to whom security to be given, whether necessary to specify—Justices Act 1890 (No. 1105), sec. 108.]—*See* MAINTENANCE AND MAINTENANCE ORDERS, col. 885. *Shee* v. *Larkin*, (1907) V.L.R., 295; 28 A.L.T., 188; 13 A.L.R., 97.

Marriage Act 1890 (No. 1166), secs. 42, 43—Maintenance order—Surety directed—To whom surety to be given—Payments to be made to clerk of Petty Sessions.]—*See* MAINTENANCE AND MAINTENANCE ORDERS, col. 885. *Shee* v. *Larkin*, (1907) V.L.R., 295; 28 A.L.T., 188; 13 A.L.R., 97.

PRISONER.

Leave to appeal to High Court—Applicant in prison—Appearance in person—Whether High Court has jurisdiction to order that it be allowed.]—*See* CRIMINAL LAW, col. 365. *Horwitz* v. *Connor*, (1908) 6 C.L.R., 38; 14 A.L.R., 342.

Crimes Act 1890 (No. 1079), sec. 540—Regulations providing for mitigation of sentence as incentive to good conduct—Habeas corpus by prisoner alleging entitled to liberty under regulations.]—*See* CRIMINAL LAW, col. 368. *Horwitz* v. *Connor*, (1908) 6 C.L.R., 38; 14 A.L.R., 342.

PRIVY.

See OPIUM SMOKING PROHIBITION ACT.

PRIVILEGE.

See DEFAMATION, cols. 390 *et seq.*

PRIVY COUNCIL.

See APPEAL.

PROBATE.

See EXECUTORS AND ADMINISTRATORS.

PROBALE DUTY.

See DUTIES ON THE ESTATES OF DECEASED PERSONS.

PROHIBITION.

Commonwealth of Australia Constitution Act (63 & 64 Vict.), c. 12—The Constitution, secs. 71, 73, 75 (v.)—Commonwealth Conciliation and Arbitration Act 1904 (No. 13 of

1904), sec. 31—Judiciary Act 1903 (No. 6 of 1903), secs. 30, 33 (b), 38—Prohibition—Jurisdiction of High Court to issue to Commonwealth Court of Conciliation and Arbitration—Whether prohibition original or appellate jurisdiction.]—See APPEAL, col. 17. *The King and the Commonwealth Court of Conciliation and Arbitration and the President thereof and the Boot Trade Employees Federation; Ex parte Whybrow & Co.*, (1910) 11 C.L.R., 1; 16 A.L.R., 373.

Prohibition—Rule nisi enlarged to enable error to be corrected—High Court Practice.] —A rule *nisi* for prohibition having been granted to set aside an award of the Commonwealth Court of Conciliation and Arbitration, the invalid portion of the award being severable, the rule *nisi* was enlarged so as to enable the award to be amended. *The King and the Commonwealth Court of Conciliation and Arbitration and the President thereof and the Boot Trade Employees Federation; Ex parte Whybrow & Co.*, (1910) 11 C.L.R., 1; 16 A.L.R., 373. H.C. *Griffith, C.J., Barton, O'Connor* and *Isaacs, JJ.*

High Court—Practice—Motion for prohibition to restrain Commonwealth Court of Conciliation and Arbitration—Finding by President that dispute existed, whether High Court bound by—The Commonwealth Constitution, sec. 51 (xxxv.).]—Upon motion for a prohibition restraining the Commonwealth Court of Conciliation and Arbitration the High Court is not bound by the finding of the President that there was a dispute. *The King and the Commonwealth Court of Conciliation and Arbitration and the President thereof and the Boot Trade Employees Federation; Ex parte Whybrow & Co.*, (1910) 11 C.L.R., 1; 16 A.L.R., 373. H.C. *Griffith, C.J., Barton, O'Connor* and *Isaacs, JJ.*

Licences Reduction Board—Prohibition—Class constituted by those premises against which two convictions are recorded—Decision that premises fall within that class—Licensing Act 1906 (No. 2068), sec. 44.]—See LICENSING, col. 841. *The King v. The Licences Reduction Board; Ex parte Carlton Brewery Limited.*, (1908) V.L.R., 79; 29 A.L.T., 148; 14 A.L.R., 7.

PUBLIC SERVICE.

Officer of department transferred to Commonwealth—Whether Commonwealth Parliament may reduce salary—" Existing rights"—Public Service Act 1900 (No. 1721), sec. 19—Commonwealth Constitution, sec. 84.]—Section 19 of the *Public Service Act* 1900 was merely a temporary provision to fix the status of the officers therein referred to when they should be transferred with their departments to the Commonwealth. That section therefore does not, notwithstanding section 84 of the Constitution, restrict the power of the Commonwealth Parliament to reduce the salaries of officers of Victorian Government departments transferred with those departments to the Commonwealth. *Cousins v. The Commonwealth*, 3 C.L.R., 529; 12 A.L.R., 175. H.C. *Griffith, C.J., Barton* and *O'Connor, JJ.* (1906).

Commonwealth Public Service Act 1902 (No. 5 of 1902), secs. 8, 51, 60, 80—Officer of department transferred to Commonwealth—Whether salary altered—" Existing rights"—Commonwealth Constitution, sec. 84.]—The provisions of the Commonwealth *Public Service Act* 1902 purporting to affect the salaries of officers in the public service of the Commonwealth apply to officers transferred with their departments from the several States to the Commonwealth as well as to other officers in that service, even if the effect in particular cases is to reduce the salaries those officers were entitled to receive when such departments were so transferred. *Cousins v. The Commonwealth*, 3 C.L.R., 529; 12 A.L.R., 175. H.C. *Griffith, C.J., Barton* and *O'Connor, JJ.* (1906).

Commonwealth Public Service Act 1902 (No. 5 of 1902), sec. 78 (1)—Salary not appropriated by Parliament—Whether public servant entitled to.]—Officers of the Commonwealth Public Service are, by reason of section 78 (1) of the Act of 1902, not entitled to sue for salary not appropriated by Parliament. *Cousins v. The Commonwealth*, 3 C.L.R., 529; 12 A.L.R., 175. H.C. *Griffith, C.J., Barton* and *O'Connor, JJ.* (1906).

Commonwealth Public Service—Transferred department—Officer transferred from State to Commonwealth—Salary—Officer of corresponding position—" Any Australian Colony "—Meaning of in Public Service Act 1900 (No. 1721), sec. 19.]—The words " any Australian Colony " in section 19 of the *Public Service Act* 1900 do not include the Colony of Victoria. *Curley* v. *The Commonwealth*, 8 C.L.R., 178 ; 15 A.L.R., 192 H.C. *Griffith, C.J., Barton* and *O'Connor, JJ.* (1909).

Public Service Act 1900 (No. 1721), sec. 19—Post and Telegraph Department—Transfer to Commonwealth—" Any Australian Colony."]—The words " any Australian Colony " in section 19 of the *Public Service Act* 1900 do not include the Colony of Victoria. *Curley* v. *The King*, (1906) V.L.R., 633 ; 28 A.L.T., 12 ; 12 A.L.R., 555. F.C. *Hodges, Hood* and *Chomley, JJ.* (1906).

Public Service Act 1900 (No. 1721), sec. 19 —Post and Telegraph Department—Transfer to Commonwealth—" Officer of corresponding position "]—The position of a mail-cart driver in the Post and Telegraph Department of South Australia, whose duty is to collect letters from pillar boxes, and while so doing to drive the mail-cart, is not a " corresponding position " within the meaning of section 19 of the *Public Service Act* 1900 to that occupied by a porter in the service of the Department in Victoria, whose duty is to collect letters from pillar-boxes, but not to drive the mail-cart. *Curley* v. *The King*, (1906) V.L.R., 633 ; 28 A.L.T., 12 ; 12 A.L.R., 555. F.C. *Hodges* and *Hood, JJ.* (*Chomley, J.* dissenting). (1906).

Public Service Act 1900 (No. 1721), secs. 8, 19—Departments of Trade and Customs, Defence and Post and Telegraph—Salaries of officers until taken over by Commonwealth —" Corresponding position in any Australian Colony "—Effect of subsequent appointment on officer's rights.]—In 1886 the petitioner, who was then a letter-carrier in the Post and Telegraph Department of the Public Service of Victoria, was " transferred to the position of sorter temporarily without promotion " and thereafter always discharged the duties of a sorter. On 28th February 1901 upon the recommendation of the Public Service Board of Victoria which purported to be made (*inter alia*) under section 8 of the *Public Service Act* 1900, the petitioner, who was described as a letter carrier, was " promoted to fill a new appointment on the staff of sorters, such appointment to take effect as from the 27th December 1900," which was the date of the passing of the said Act. *Held*, that the operation of section 19 of the Act could not be affected by the subsequent appointment aforesaid of the petitioner on 28th February 1901, and that the petitioner was entitled under the section for the period between the 27th December 1900 and the 28th February 1901, when the said Department was taken over by the Commonwealth, to a salary at a rate equal to the highest rate of salary payable on the said 27th December 1900 to a letter carrier (but not to a sorter) in a corresponding position in another Australian Colony—namely, at the rate of £150 per annum. *Cain* v. *The King*, (1907) V.L.R., 259. *Hodges, J.*

Commonwealth Public Service Act 1902 (No. 5 of 1902), sec. 46—Public servant— Dismissal—Procedure—Admission of offence charged—Power to dismiss without inquiry by board—Withdrawal of admission.]—When an officer of the Commonwealth Public Service is suspended and, being furnished with a copy of a charge made against him, admits the charge in writing, the charge is admitted within the meaning of section 46 (5) of the *Commonwealth Public Service Act* 1902, and, thereupon, on the recommendation of the Chief Officer, the consequences prescribed by the sub-section as to punishment follow as of course, and without any further proceedings. An admission of the charge once made cannot be withdrawn as of right, but only by permission as an act of grace. *Bridges* v. *The Commonwealth*, 4 C.L.R., 1195 ; 13 A.L.R., 362. H.C. *Griffith, C.J., Barton* and *O'Connor, JJ.* (*Higgins, J.* dissenting). (1907).

Commonwealth Public Service Act 1902 (No. 5 of 1902), sec. 46—Tenure of office of public servant—Conditions of the exercise of the power to dismiss—Civil servant dismissed

without observance of conditions—**Whether entitled to declaration that he is still in the Service—Wrongful dismissal, remedy for.**]—There is no right to dismiss an officer at will otherwise than in accordance with the procedure prescribed by the Commonwealth *Public Service Act* 1902. The power of dismissal under section 46 of that Act must be exercised strictly, and suspension from duty of an officer on the charges for which he is subsequently dismissed is a condition precedent to his rightful dismissal; but although the power has been wrongfully exercised, if he has been in fact put out of the service, he is not entitled to a declaration that he remains in the Service. He has the same remedy as any other servant wrongfully dismissed. *Williamson* v. *The Commonwealth*, (1907) 5 C.L.R., 174; 14 A.L.R., 1. *Higgins, J.*

Commonwealth Public Service Act 1902 (No. 5 of 1902), sec. 46—Public servant—Dismissal—Procedure prescribed by Act, failure to observe—Effect of—Suspension—Dismissal based on charge on which public servant not suspended.]—On the 30th January 1907 an officer of the Public Service of the Commonwealth was suspended from duty in reference to a shortage which had been discovered in his accounts. He was prosecuted criminally in connection with that shortage, was tried and was acquitted. Afterwards on 2nd May the officer was charged under the *Commonwealth Public Service Act* 1902 by the Chief Officer with three offences, one being in connection with the shortage in his accounts, and was required to admit, deny, or explain these charges, but the original suspension had not been removed, nor was the officer suspended on the later charges. The officer, having denied these charges, was on 7th May further suspended, and, after proceedings which were in accordance with section 46, the Governor-in-Council " approved " of his dismissal, and the Government excluded him from the Department, and would not allow him to perform his duties. *Held*, that the officer was wrongfully dismissed and was entitled to recover damages from the Commonwealth for such wrongful dismissal. *Williamson* v.

The Commonwealth, (1907) 5 C.L.R., 174; 14 A.L.R., 1. *Higgins, J.*

Wrongful dismissal of public servant—Damages—Liability to be dismissed rightfully—Whether an element in determining amount of damages—Commonwealth Public Service Act 1902 (No. 5 of 1902), sec. 46.]—Where a public servant has been dismissed without the observance of the conditions precedent to rightful dismissal prescribed by the *Commonwealth Public Service Act* 1902, the Court, in assessing damages for such wrongful dismissal, will take into consideration the fact that the public servant was liable to be dismissed rightfully under the process prescribed by the Act. *Williamson* v. *The Commonwealth*, (1907) 5 C.L.R., 174; 14 A.L.R., 1. *Higgins, J.*

Commonwealth Public Service Act 1902 (No. 5 of 1902), sec. 78—Public servant—Wrongful dismissal—Claim for damages—Money not voted by Parliament—Whether a defence.]—Section 78 of the *Commonwealth Public Service Act* 1902 is not an answer to a claim for damages for wrongful dismissal from the Commonwealth Public Service. *Williamson* v. *The Commonwealth*, (1907) 5 C.L.R., 174; 14 A.L.R., 1. *Higgins, J.*

Commonwealth Public Servant—Voluntary removal from domicil of choice to take up similar duties in the same department in another State—Whether he acquires new domicil of choice.]—*See* DOMICIL, cols. 412, 413. *Bailey* v. *Bailey*, (1909) V.L.R., 299; 30 A.L.T., 217; 15 A.L.R., 237.

Public Service—Pension or superannuation allowance, right to—Date of appointment—Pensions Abolition Act 1881 (No. 710), secs. 1, 2—Public Service Act 1883 (No. 773), sec. 99—Public Service Act 1890 (No. 1133), sec. 107—Public Service Act 1893 (No. 1324), sec. 22.]—The petitioner was first employed in a department of the public service in 1874 as a supernumerary officer but was not appointed by the Governor-in-Council. In 1880 his services were dispensed with, and he was paid compensation for the loss of his employment not under the authority of any Act On 24th December 1881 the Act No. 710 was passed. On 1st May 1883 the petitioner was again employed in the public service, and on 20th February 1884 he was appointed by the Governor-in-Council and was duly classified under the *Public Service Act* 1883. The petitioner remained in the service until 30th April 1911 when he retired, being over the age of 65 years. On 1st May 1911 he repaid into the consolidated revenue the amount of the compensation paid to him in 1880. *Held*, that the petitioner was a person appointed since the passing of the Act No. 710 and therefore was not entitled under section 99 of the *Public Service Act* 1883 to a pension or superannuation allowance on his retirement in 1911. *Held*, also, that section 22 of the *Public Service Act* 1893 conferred on the petitioner no right which he had not under section 99 of the *Public Service Act* 1883. *Casey* v. *The King*, (1912) 16 C.L.R., 92 ; 18 A.L.R., 558. H.C. *Griffith*, *C.J.*, *Barton* and *Isaacs*, *JJ.*

Railways Act 1890 (No. 1135), sec. 93—Railway employee — Retiring allowance, whether assignable—Liability to be recalled to service—Civil Service Act 1862 (No. 160), secs. 42, 43, 44.]—An employee of the Victorian Railways Commissioners, who held office before the passing of the *Victorian Railways Commissioners Act* 1883, was permitted by the Governor-in-Council to retire from the service with a retiring allowance, on the ground of incapacity to discharge the duties of his office by reason of infirmity of body. *Held*, that the employee was not liable to be recalled to service, and that the allowance was therefore assignable. *Brown* v. *Victorian Railways Commissioners*, 3 C.L.R , 316 ; 12 A.L.R., 1, applied. *Crouch* v. *Victorian Railways Commissioners*, (1907) V.L.R., 80 ; 28 A.L.T., 141 ; 12 A.L.R., 574. F.C. *a'Beckett*, *A.C.J.*, *Hodges* and *Cussen*, *JJ.*

Pension—Whether assignable—Liability of pensioner to be recalled to duty—Police Regulation Act 1890 (No. 1127), secs. 20, 24.]—*See* POLICE AND POLICE REGULATION ACT. *In re Hilliard ; Ex parte Tinkler*, (1907) V.L.R., 375 ; 28 A.L.T., 204 ; 13 A.L.R., 138.

Railways Act 1890 (No. 1135), secs. 70, 86-88, 93—Compensation, when employee entitled to—Employee not ready and willing to perform his contract—Removal of such employee—Ways in which contract with employee may be terminated.]—*See* RAILWAYS. *Noonan* v. *Victorian Railways Commissioners*, 4 C.L.R., 1668 ; 13 A.L.R., 593.

Railways Act 1890 (No. 1135), sec. 93—Compensation, meaning of—Who entitled to—Employee deprived of his office through no fault of his own.]—*See* RAILWAYS. *Noonan* v. *Victorian Railways Commissioners*, 4 C.L.R., 1668 ; 13 A.L.R., 593.

Public Service Act 1890 (No. 1133), sec. 3—Provision that Act shall not apply to certain officers—Appointment of such officer to position under Public Service Act, validity of.]—Section 3 of the *Public Service Act* 1890, which provides that the Act shall not apply to certain named classes of persons, does not prevent a member of any such class or classes from being validly appointed under the *Public Service Act* 1890. *Rex* v. *Turnbull*, (1907) V.L.R., 11 ; 28 A.L.T., 103 ; 12 A.L.R., 551. *Cussen*, *J.*

Barrister and solicitor—Articled clerk—Leave to serve in Crown Law Department during service under articles of clerkship—Rules of Council of Legal Education of 27th November 1905.] — Leave granted to an articled clerk to act as clerk in the Public Service, Crown Law Department, while articled to Crown solicitor. *Re Shelton*, 32 A.L.T., 135 ; *a'Beckett*, *Hodges* and *Hood*, *JJ.* (1910).

Solicitor—Clerk articled to Crown Solicitor—Covenant by Crown Solicitor to teach " if he shall continue Crown Solicitor . . . . to the extent of his official opportunities and so far as the exigencies of the Public Service and the relative status of the parties as members of the Public Service of Victoria will permit "—Admission granted.]—*In re Clarke*, 12 A.L.R. (C.N.), 18. *The Judges* (1906).

PURE FOOD ACTS.

Pure Food Act 1905 (No. 2010), secs. 3, 35 —Sale for human consumption or use— Sale for analysis.]—*Quaere*, whether section 35 of the *Pure Food Act* 1905 refers to a sale for analysis. *Rider* v. *Dunn*, (1908) V.L.R., 377 ; 29 A.L.T., 279 ; 14 A.L.R., 245. *Cussen, J.*

Pure Food Act 1905 (No. 2010), sec. 41 (2) —Cleanliness and freedom from contamination of articles of food—Regulation, validity of — Reasonableness — Certainty.] — *See* HEALTH (PUBLIC), cols. 628, 629. *Robertson* v. *Abadee*, (1907) V.L.R., 235 ; 28 A.L.T., 184 ; 13 A.L.R., 137.

Pure Food Act 1905 (No. 2010), sec. 23— Sale of adulterated article of food—Article taken for analysis—Justices requested at hearing to send part for analysis—No part in existence—Compliance with request, whether a condition precedent to conviction.]—*See* HEALTH (PUBLIC), col. 630. *Gunner* v. *Payne*, (1908) V.L.R., 363 ; 29 A.L.T., 264 ; 14 A.L.R., 243.

Public health—Pure Food Act 1905 (No. 2010), sec. 41 (2)—Regulations of 28th June 1907 —Transport of milk—Secure closing of milk cans—Method of closing—Departmental approval—Delivery by producer personally.] —*See* HEALTH (PUBLIC), col. 629. *O'Connor* v. *Anderson*, (1909) V.L.R., 1 ; 30 A.L.T., 145 ; 15 A.L.R., 22.

Pure Food Act 1905 (No. 2010), sec. 32— Proof of reasonable precautions against committing offence—Whether necessary where special exculpatory provisions exist—Health Act 1890 (No. 1098), sec. 71.]—Where there are special provisions in the *Health Acts* as in section 71 of the *Health Act* 1890, exculpating a defendant on proof of certain facts, section 32 of the *Pure Food Act* 1905 does not apply. *Rider* v. *Dunn*, (1908) V.L.R., 377 ; 29 A.L.T., 279 ; 14 A.L.R., 245. *Cussen, J.*

Pure Food Act 1905 (No. 2010), sec. 32 (1) (a)—Sale of adulterated article of food— Reasonable precautions against committing an offence, what are—Health Act 1890 (No.

1098), sec. 71.]—*See* HEALTH (PUBLIC), cols. 632, 633. *Rider* v. *Dunn*, (1908) V.L.R., 377 ; 29 A.L.T., 279 ; 14 A.L.R., 245.

Health Act 1890 (No. 1098), secs. 43, 71— Article purchased as same in nature substance and quality as demanded by prosecutor— Written warranty—Exculpatory provisions, when available—Pure Food Act 1905 (No. 2010), sec. 35.]—*See* HEALTH (PUBLIC), col. 632. *Rider* v. *Dunn*, (1908) V.L.R., 377 ; 29 A.L.T., 279 ; 14 A.L.R., 245.

Pure Food Act 1905 (No. 2010), secs. 3, 33, 35—Sale of article of food which is adulterated —Purchase of with warranty—What amounts to—When a complete defence—Health Act 1890 (No. 1098), secs. 43, 47, 49, 71.]—*See* HEALTH (PUBLIC), col. 630, 631. *O'Connor* v. *McKimmie*, (1909) V.L.R., 166 ; 30 A.L.T., 179 ; 15 A.L.R., 118.

Health Act 1890 (No. 1098), sec. 71—Warranty that article same in nature, substance and quality as that demanded by prosecutor.]— *See* HEALTH (PUBLIC), cols 630, 631. *O'Connor* v. *McKimmie*, (1909) V.L.R., 166 ; 30 A.L.T., 179 ; 15 A.L.R., 118.

Health Act 1890 (No. 1098), sec. 71—Warranty incomplete and indefinite.]—*See* HEALTH (PUBLIC), col. 631. *O'Connor* v. *McKimmie*, (1909) V.L.R., 166 ; 30 A.L.T., 179 ; 15 A.L.R., 118.

Pure Food Act 1903 (No. 2010), secs. 32, 35, 36—Adulterated article of food, sale of—Sale by servant—Reasonable precautions by master against committing an offence.]—*See* HEALTH (PUBLIC), cols. 631, 632. *O'Connor* v. *Jenner*, (1909) V.L.R., 468 ; 31 A.L.T., 71 ; 15 A.L.R., 519.

Pure Food Act 1905 (No. 2010), sec. 23— Pure Food—Adulteration—Division of article taken into parts—Request to justices to send part to Board—Request made after close of evidence—Whether too late.]—*See* HEALTH (PUBLIC), col 630. *Gunner* v. *Payne*, (1910) V.L.R., 45 ; 31 A.L.T., 138 ; 16 A.L.R., 29

Health Act 1890 (No. 1098), secs. 53, 54— Unwholesome food—Prosecution for having such food under control for purpose of sale for human consumption — Prima facie case proved by informant—Burden of proof that food not intended for sale—Effect of statements made by the defendant elicited on cross-examination of informant's witnesses.]—*See* HEALTH (PUBLIC). *Mellis* v. *Jenkins*, (1910) V.L.R., 380; 32 A.L.T., 36; 16 A.L.R., 430.

Crimes Act 1891 (No. 1231), sec. 34 (3)—Witness on own behalf—Cross-examination as to credit, when admitted—Evidence as to good character in the particular class of transactions in • issue—Prosecution under Health Acts.]—*See* EVIDENCE, col. 509. *Gunner* v. *Payne*, (1910) V.L.R., 45; 31 A.L.T., 138; 16 A.L.R., 29.

Pure Food Act 1905 (No. 2010), sec. 35—Article of food—Keeping for sale an adulterated article of food—Several offences alleged on one day—Conviction for one offence.]—*See* HEALTH (PUBLIC), col. 629. *O'Connor* v. *Bini*, (1908) V.L.R., 567; 30 A.L.T., 74; 14 A.L.R., 537.

" Second offence," what is—Pure Food Act 1905 (No. 2010), sec. 36.]—*See* CRIMINAL LAW, cols. 367, 368. *O'Connor* v. *Bini*, (1908) V.L.R., 567; 30 A.L.T., 74; 14 A.L.R., 537.

RABBITS.

See VERMIN DESTRUCTION ACT.

RACECOURSE.

See GAMING AND WAGERING.

RAILWAYS.

I.—NEGLIGENCE.

Negligence — Railway — Level crossing — Duty of persons crossing and of owners of railway respectively.]—Where a railway crosses a road at a level crossing without gates and an approaching train is visible from all material positions to persons about to pass over the crossing, it is the duty of the owners of the railway to take reasonable precautions to prevent such persons from being injured by trains. It is equally the duty of such persons to look for approaching trains, and they are not excused from looking by the omission of precautions on the part of the owners of the railway. *Fraser* v. *Victorian Railways Commissioners*, (1909) 8 C.L.R., 54; 15 A.L.R., 93. H.C.

Negligence— Railway crossing — Accident due to negligence of plaintiff or defendant—Evidence consistent with either view.]—In an action in the County Court by the representative of a man, who had been killed by a train at a railway crossing, against the Victorian Railways Commissioners alleging that the death of the deceased had been caused by the negligence of the defendants, at the close of the plaintiff's case the plaintiff was non-suited. *Held*, that the evidence being equally consistent with the death of the deceased having been caused by the omission of the engine driver to sound a whistle, and with its having been caused by the negligence of the deceased in that he did not look, or if he did look, voluntarily undertook the risk of crossing, the plaintiff was properly non-suited. *Wakelin* v. *London and South Western Railway Co.*, 12 App. Cas., 41, applied. *Dublin, Wicklow and Wexford Railway Co.* v. *Slattery*, 3 App. Cas., 1155; *Smith* v. *South Eastern Railway Co.*, (1896) 1 Q.B., 178, and *Toronto Railway Co.* v. *King*, (1908) A.C., 260, distinguished. *Fraser* v. *The Victorian Railways Commissioners*, (1909) 8 C.L.R., 54; 15 A.L.R., 93, H.C., *Griffith*, *C.J.*, *Barton* and *O'Connor*. *JJ.* (*Isaacs*, *J.*, dissenting).

Negligence—Evidence equally consistent with negligence of either party—Whether case to be left to jury.]—In an action for negligence where the evidence called for the plaintiff is equally consistent with the wrong complained of having been caused by the negligence of the plaintiff and with its having been caused by the negligence of the defendant, the case should not be left to the jury. *Fraser* v. *Victorian Railways Commissioners*, (1909) 8 C.L.R., 54; 15 A.L.R., 93. H.C.

Negligence—Evidence—Railway — Regulation of owners of railway requiring whistle to be sounded—Omission to sound.]—A regulation issued by the owners of the railway directing their engine-drivers to sound a whistle when approaching a level crossing without gates, is evidence that the sounding of the whistle is a reasonable precaution to be taken in such circumstances, and the omission to sound a whistle is evidence of negligence. *Fraser* v. *Victorian Railways Commissioners*, (1909) 8 C.L.R., 54; 15 A.L.R., 93. H.C.

Railways—Damages by sparks—Fire on land between railway fences—Occupation by licensee—Reservation of control by Railways Commissioners — Negligence — Omission to burn off grass.]—By an agreement with the Victorian Railways Commissioners A. was allowed permission to use certain land between the Commissioners' railway fences for grazing purposes at reasonable times and under the control of the officer of the Commissioners in charge of the section of the railway line in which such land was situated, and A. agreed to take every precaution to prevent the spreading of fire on the land, and also to allow the Commissioners by their officers or servants to enter upon the land and burn off the grass should they consider it necessary. *Held*, that the agreement did not relieve the Commissioners from the liability which, according to *Dennis* v. *Victorian Railways Commissioners*, 28 V.L.R., 576; 24 A.L.T., 196; 9 A.L.R., 69, attaches to them for damages arising from their negligent omission to burn or clear off grass naturally growing within their railway fences, with the result that sparks from a railway engine sets fire to such grass and the fire spreads to adjoining land. *Victorian Railways Commissioners* v. *Campbell*, 4 C.L.R., 1446; 13 A.L.R., 403. H.C., *Griffith, C.J., Barton Isaacs* and *Higgins, JJ.* (1907).

Railway—Water—Railway embankment—Flood water blocked—Diversion of water—Damage to adjoining land—Board of Land and Works—Constructing authority—Exercise of statutory powers—Subsequent vesting in Railways Commissioners—Negligence—Railways Act 1891 (No. 1250), secs. 4, 5.]—The *Railways Act* 1891, sec. 4, provides that :—" The Board of Land and Works . . . shall construct and complete all lines of railway which Parliament may hereafter authorise to be constructed." Sec. 5 provides that when a railway line is completed it is to be transferred to the Victorian Railways Commissioners, and when transferred shall vest in them and shall be supervised and maintained by them and all further powers duty authority or responsibility of the Board in regard to such line shall cease the settlement of past contracts alone excepted. The Board under statutory authority constructed a railway line in a district subject to occasional floods from the river Murray. The line when completed was duly transferred to and vested in the Commissioners, in pursuance of the above-mentioned Act. The plaintiff suffered damage by reason of floods water from the Murray being obstructed by the railway embankment, and thus diverted on to his land. The diversion of the flood waters and the consequent damage could not have been avoided except by a radical alteration in the construction of the line. *Held*, in an action against the Commissioners for damage by the flooding, that the defendants were not liable. *Bourchier* v. *Victorian Railways Commissioners*, (1910) V.L.R., 385; 32 A.L.T., 48; 16 A.L.R., 396. F.C., *a'Beckett, Hodges* and *Cussen, JJ.* (1910).

Railways Act 1896 (No. 1439), sec. 21—Order XXX., r. 2 (Rules of 1906)—Practice—Summons for directions—Action against Railways Commissioners for losses caused by sparks from railway engine—Order on summons—Arbitration.]—The only order which can be made upon a summons for directions in an action brought against the Victorian Railways Commissioners for losses caused by sparks from railway engines is an order referring the action to arbitration under sec. 21 of the *Railways Act* 1896. *Roach* v. *Victorian Railways Commissioners*, (1910) V.L.R., 314; 32 A.L.T., 10; 16 A.L.R., 302. *Hodges, J.* (1910).

II.—By-Law.

Railways Act 1890 (No. 1135), secs. 33, 105 —By-law—Validity—Repugnancy to Act of Parliament—Taking seat with intent to evade payment of fare.]—Where by an act of Parliament the doing of an act with a fraudulent intent is made punishable, a by-law, imposing a penalty on the doing of the same Act irrespective of the intent, is repugnant to the Act of Parliament and therefore invalid. *Held*, accordingly, that a by-law, made by the Victorian Railways Commissioners imposing a penalty on any person who should travel in a railway carriage without a pass or ticket entitling him to enter or travel therein, was invalid, inasmuch as it was repugnant to sec. 33 of the *Railways Act* 1890, which provides that, if any person take a seat in any carriage without having a free pass or a ticket entitling him to such seat, with intent to evade payment of his fare, he shall forfeit a sum not exceeding Twenty pounds. *Borsum v. Smith*, (1907) V.L.R., 72; 28 A.L.T., 89; 12 A.L.R., 495. F.C., *Hodges, Hood*, and *Chomley, JJ.* (1906).

III.—Officers and Employees; Dismissal; Retirement; Compensation; Retiring Allowance.

Railways Act 1890 (No. 1135), secs. 70, 86-88, 93—Compensation, when employee entitled to—Employee not ready and willing to perform his contract—Removal of such employee—Ways in which contract with employee may be terminated.]—*Per Griffith, C.J., Barton* and *Isaacs, JJ.*—Under secs. 70 and 93 of the *Railways Act* 1890, the Railways Commissioners may dispense with the services of an employee, who was appointed before the passing of the *Railways Commissioners Act* 1883, and who is no longer ready and willing to discharge or who becomes incapable of performing his duties, without being liable to pay compensation to such employee. *Per Higgins, J.* (dissenting). —There are only two ways of discharging an employee in the Railways. He may be dismissed for breach of regulations, &c., under secs. 86-88, or he may be removed upon grounds irrespective of misconduct, but at the will of the Commissioners under sec. 70.

If the latter course is adopted the employee is entitled to compensation. *Noonan v. Victorian Railways Commissioners*, 4 C.L.R., 1668; 13 A.L.R., 593. (1907).

Railways Act 1890 (No. 1135), sec. 93— Compensation, meaning of—Who entitled to— Employee deprived of his office through no fault of his own.]—The word " compensation " in sec. 93 of the *Railways Act* 1890 means an indemnity given to an employee who is deprived of his office through no fault of his own. Any default or failure on the part of an employee which at common law would disentitle him to claim to be retained in the service of the Railways Commissioners is such a fault as to disentitle him to compensation. *Noonan v. Victorian Railways Commissioners*, 4 C.L.R., 1668; 13 A.L.R., 593. H.C., *Griffith, C.J., Barton* and *Isaacs, JJ., Higgins, J.*, dissenting (1907).

Railways Act 1890 (No. 1135), sec. 93— Compensation or retiring allowance—Officer employed at the time of the passing of the Victorian Railways Commissioners Act 1883 —Services of officer dispensed with for physical unfitness—Held entitled to compensation.]—*See Gleeson v. Victorian Railways Commissioners*, (1907) V.L.R., 129. F.C., *a'Beckett, A.C.J., Hodges* and *Chomley, JJ.*

Railways Act 1890 (No. 1135), sec. 93— Railway employee — Retiring allowance, whether assignable—Liability to be recalled to service—Civil Service Act 1862 (No. 160), secs. 42, 43, 44.]—An employee of the Victorian Railways Commissioners, who held office before the passing of the *Victorian Railways Commissioners Act* 1883, was permitted by the Governor-in-Council to retire from the service with a retiring allowance, on the ground of incapacity to discharge the duties of his office by reason of infirmity of body. *Held*, that the employee was not liable to be recalled to service, and that the allowance was therefore assignable. *Brown v. Victorian Railways Commissioners*, 3 C.L.R., 316; 12 A.L.R., 1, applied. *Crouch v. Victorian Railways Commissioners*, (1907) V.L.R., 80; 28 A.L.T., 141; 12 A.L.R., 574. F.C., *a'Beckett, A.-C.J., Hodges* and *Cussen, JJ.*

RATES.

See LOCAL GOVERNMENT.

REAL PROPERTY ACTS.

As to proceedings to establish Title under the *Transfer of Land Act* 1904, *see* cols. 849, 850.

Limitations, Statutes of—Rates—Charge upon land—Local Government Act 1903 (No. 1893), secs. 2, 341—Local Government Act 1891 (No. 1243), sec. 64—Local Government Act 1890 (No. 1112), sec. 235.]—The *Real Property Act* 1890 (No. 1136), sec. 47, is no bar to the enforcement of a charge under section 341 of the *Local Government Act* 1903. *Mayor, &c., of Richmond* v. *The Federal Building Society*, (1909) V.L.R., 413 ; 31 A.L.T., 52 ; 15 A.L.R., 439. F.C., *Madden, C.J., Hodges* and *Cussen, JJ.*

Real Property Act 1907 (No. 2086), secs. 3, 4—Arrears of interest—Statute of Limitations.]—*Cussen, J.* : " The wording of those sections seems to make it perfectly clear that the legislature is placing the same limitations on the recovery of interest whether payable in respect of money charged on land or not. I do not think you can recover more than six years' interest." *The Land Mortgage Bank of Victoria Ltd.* v. *Reid*, (1909) V.L.R., 284, at p. 286.

Real Property Act 1890 (No. 1136), sec. 23—Adverse possession—Statutory period, when time begins to run—Tenancy at will—Creation of new tenancy—Permission of owner, acknowledgment by tenant that he holds by.]—*See* LIMITATIONS (STATUTES OF), col. 845. *Wilson* v. *Equity Trustees Executors &c. Co. Ltd.*, (1911) V.L.R., 481 ; 33 A.L.T., 89 ; 17 A.L.R., 523.

Real Property Act 1890 (No. 1136), secs. 18, 23—Adverse possession—Period of limitation, commencement of—New tenancy at will, what will create—Request for transfer of land.]—*See* LIMITATIONS (STATUTES OF), col. 845. *Wilson* v. *Equity Trustees Executors &c. Co. Ltd.*, (1911) V.L.R., 481 ; 33 A.L.T., 89 ; 17 A.L.R., 523.

Possession—Land of two owners within one fence—Presumption of possession—Possession follows title—Equivocal acts of possession—Intention.]—*See* LIMITATIONS (STATUTES OF), col. 846. *Clement* v. *Jones*, 8 C.L.R., 133 ; 15 A.L.R., 158.

Real Property Act 1890 (No. 1136), Part II.—Transfer of Land Act 1904 (No. 1931), secs. 10, 11—Title by adverse possession—Land of several owners—Enclosed by common fence—Common use—Presumption of possession—Equivocal acts of possession—Intention.]—*See* LIMITATIONS (STATUTES OF), cols. 846, 847. *Clement* v. *Jones*, 8 C.L.R., 133 ; 15 A.L.R., 158.

Possession—Adverse possession—Land of two owners within one fence—Re-entry of registered proprietor—Cutting firewood—Renewal of survey marks on boundaries, effect of.]—*See* LIMITATIONS (STATUTES OF), col. 847. *Clement* v. *Jones*, 8 C.L.R., 113 ; 15 A.L.R., 158.

Mortgagor and mortgagee—Recovery of money secured by mortgage barred by determination of period of limitation—Mortgagee in possession—Power of sale, whether exercise of also barred—Real Property Act 1890 (No. 1136), secs. 18, 43, 47—Transfer of Land Act 1890 (No. 1149), secs. 114, 116.]—A mortgagee's power of sale under the *Transfer of Land Act* 1890, where he has entered into possession of the mortgaged land, and is in receipt of the rents and profits thereof, is not affected by reason only that his right to recover by suit or action the money secured by the mortgage is barred by sec. 47 of the *Real Property Act* 1890. *Ex parte The Australian Deposit and Mortgage Bank Ltd.*, (1907) V.L.R., 348 ; 28 A.L.T., 192 ; 13 A.L.R., 132. F.C., *Madden, C.J., Hodges* and *Hood, JJ.*

Real Property Act 1890 (No. 1136), sec. 47—" Other proceeding," meaning of—Mortgagee's power of sale.]—The " other proceeding " mentioned in sec. 47 of the *Real Property Act* 1890 is *ejusdem generis* with " action or suit " and does not include the exercise of a mortgagee's power of sale. *Ex parte The Australian Deposit and Mortgage*

Bank Ltd., (1907) V.L.R., 348 ; 28 A.L.T., 192 ; 13 A.L.R , 132. F.C., Madden, C.J., Hodges and Hood, JJ.

Mortgagor and mortgagee—Real Property Act 1890 (No. 1136), secs. 18, 43, 47—Exercise of power of sale—Whether barred by expiration of period of limitation.]—Sec. 43 of the Real Property Act 1890 is to be read with sec. 18 and not with sec. 47. Ex parte The Australian Deposit and Mortgage Bank Ltd., (1907) V.L.R., 348 ; 28 A.L.T., 192 ; 13 A.L.R., 132. F.C., Madden, C.J., Hodges and Hood, JJ.

Death of registered proprietor—Next of kin unknown—Possession of widow.]—See LIMITATIONS (STATUTES OF), col. 847. Lambourn v. Hosken, (1912) V.L.R., 394 ; 34 A.L.T., 101 ; 18 A.L.R., 371.

Transfer of Land Act 1904 (No. 1931), sec. 10—Adverse possession—Registered proprietor dead before commencement of adverse possession—No administration of his estate—Next of kin unknown—Duration of adverse possession.]—See LIMITATIONS (STATUTES OF), col. 849. Lambourn v. Hosken, (1912) V.L.R., 394 ; 34 A.L.T., 101 ; 18 A.L.R., 371.

Real Property Act 1890 (No. 1136), secs. 64, 90—Settled estate—Petition—Power of Court to authorise leases—" Manifest intention " of settlor as to use of estate—" Manifest intention " that power of Court shall not be exercised.]—See SETTLEMENTS. In re Staughton, (1909) V.L.R., 174 ; 30 A.L.T., 184 ; 15 A.L.R., 148.

RECEIVING.
See CRIMINAL LAW.

REGISTRATION OF BIRTHS, DEATHS AND MARRIAGES.

Evidence—Date of birth—Certificates of death and of burial.]—Certificates of death and of burial containing the age of a deceased person are prima facie evidence of the date of birth. In re Osmand ; Bennett v. Booty,

(1908) V.L.R., 67 ; 29 A.L.T., 168 ; 13 A.L.R., 728. F.C., a' Beckett, A.-C.J., Hodges and Hood, JJ. (1908) affirming Cussen, J. (1906) V.L.R., 455 ; 27 A.L.T., 218 ; 12 A.L.R., 256.

REGISTRATION OF FIRMS ACT.

Insolvency — Partnership — Joint executors carrying on business of testator—Partnership Act 1891 (No. 1222), sec. 5—Registration of Firms Act 1892 (No. 1256), sec. 4.]—See EXECUTORS AND ADMINISTRATORS, col. 560. In re Whitelaw ; Savage v. The Union Bank of Australia Ltd. ; Whitelaw v. The Same, (1906) 3 C.L.R., 1170 ; 12 A.L.R., 285.

RES JUDICATA.

Res Judicata—Judgment—Finding of fact, whether conclusive in other proceedings against another party—Finding of fact as to status—Prohibited immigrant—Immigration Restriction Act 1901 (No. 17).]—See EVIDENCE, col. 500. Christie v. Ah Sheung, (1906) 3 C.L.R., 998 ; 12 A.L.R., 432.

Supreme Court Act 1890 (No. 1142), sec. 231—Privy Council—Appealable amount—" Matter in issue," what is—Assumption that contention of unsuccessful party was correct—Res judicata—Uncontradicted affidavits.]—See APPEAL, cols. 15, 16. In re " Maizo ' and "Maizena " Trade Marks ; Robert Harper & Co. v. National Starch Co., (1906) V.L.R., 246 ; 27 A.L.T., 168 ; 12 A.L.R., 164.

Marriage Act 1890 (No. 1166), secs. 42, 43—Illegitimate child without adequate means of support—Dismissal of previous complaint.]—Semble.—That the mere fact that a complaint against a father for leaving his child without adequate means of support has been dismissed, does not entitle the defendant to plead res judicata to a similar complaint subsequently laid against him. Russ v. Carr, 30 A.L.T., 131. Hodges, J. (1908).

Justices Act 1890 (No. 1105), secs. 4, 59 (3)—Complaint for detention of goods—Refusal to make order—Dismissal—Second com-

plaint for same cause of action—Estoppel.]—
See JUSTICES OF THE PEACE, cols. 790, 791.
McMahon v. *Johnson*, (1909) V.L.R., 376;
31 A.L.T., 36; 15 A.L.R., 371.

REVENUE.

I.—CUSTOMS AND EXCISE.

**Customs Tariff 1908 (No. 7 of 1908), secs. 3,
4, 5, 7—Duties collected under proposed tariff
—Proposed tariff different from tariff enacted
by Parliament—Right to recover money back
—" Duties of Customs collected pursuant to
any Tariff or Tariff alteration "—Commonwealth Constitution, sec. 55—Imposing taxation.]**—*See* CUSTOMS., cols. 374, 375. *Sargood Bros.* v. *The Commonwealth*, (1910) 11
C.L.R., 258; 16 A.L.R., 483.

**Customs Act 1901 (No. 6)—Whether a
taxing Act.]**—*See* CUSTOMS, col. 375. *Sargood Bros.* v. *The Commonwealth*, (1910) 11
C.L.R., 258; 16 A.L.R., 483.

**Customs Act 1901 (No. 6), sec. 167—Cus-
toms Tariff 1908 (No. 7), sec. 7—Duties collected under proposed tariff—Proposed tariff
different from tariff enacted—Payment without protest—Recovery back of money paid—
Money exacted colore officii—Deposit of
amount demanded under sec. 167 of the Customs Act 1901—Whether the only remedy—
" Dispute," what is.]**—*See* CUSTOMS, col.
375. *Sargood Bros.* v. *The Commonwealth*,
(1910) 11 C.L.R., 258; 16 A.L.R., 483.

**Customs duties—Tariff—Manufactures of
paper for advertising purposes—" Pictures
(not being advertising) "—Customs Tariff
1902 (No. 14 of 1902), Schedule, Division
XIII., Items 122, 123 and Exemption (k)—
Construction of taxing Statute.]**—*See* CUS-
TOMS, cols, 375, 376. *Chandler* v. *Collector
of Imposts*, 4 C.L.R., 1719; 13 A.L.R., 617.

**Customs Act 1901 (No. 6), sec. 154 (a)—
Value of goods for purposes of duty—Outside
packages containing goods dutiable ad valorem—Whether packages accessories to
goods—Whether value of packages to be
included in that of goods.]**—*See* CUSTOMS, col.
376. *Sargood Bros.* v. *The Commonwealth*,
(1910) 11 C.L.R., 258; 16 A.L.R., 483.

**Customs Act 1901 (No. 6 of 1901), secs. 229,
233—Unlawful possession of goods—Unlawful
importation—Possession unconnected with importation—Knowledge—Prohibited imports.]**
—*See* CUSTOMS, col. 377. *Lyons* v. *Smart*,
(1908) 6 C.L.R., 143; 14 A.L.R., 328.

**Offences against Customs laws—Intent to
defraud the revenue—Reduction of penalty—
Customs Act 1901 (No. 6 of 1901), secs. 234,
240 and 241.]**—*See* CUSTOMS, col. 377. *Lewis*
v. *The King*, (1912) 14 C.L.R., 183; 18
A.L.R., 239. H.C., *Griffith, C.J., Barton
and Isaacs, JJ.*

**The Constitution (63 & 64 Vict. c. 12), secs.
51 (ii.), 99—Taxation, power of Commonwealth with respect to—Discrimination between States or parts of States—Preference to
one State over another State—Excise Tariff
1906 (No. 16 of 1906), whether ultra vires.]**—
See COMMONWEALTH OF AUSTRALIA CONSTITU-
TION, cols. 116, 117. *The King* v. *Barger*;
The Commonwealth v. *McKay*, (1908) 6
C.L.R., 41; 14 A.L.R., 374.

**The Constitution (63 & 64 Vict. c. 12), sec.
51—Legislative powers of Commonwealth—
—Validity of Act, principles to be observed
in determining question of—Form of Act—
Substance of Act—Direct and indirect effect—
Motive and object of legislation—Interference
with domestic affairs of State—Taxation—
Excise Tariff 1906 (No. 16 of 1906).]**—*See*
COMMONWEALTH OF AUSTRALIA CONSTITU-
TION, cols. 115, 116. *The King* v. *Barger*;
The Commonwealth v. *McKay*, (1908) 6
C.L.R., 41; 14 A.L.R., 374.

**The Constitution (63 & 64 Vict. c. 12), sec.
51 (ii.)—Legislative powers of the Commonwealth — Taxation — Regulative legislation,
what is—Excise Tariff 1906 (No. 16 of 1906),
whether a taxing or a regulative Act.]**—*See*
COMMONWEALTH OF AUSTRALIA CONSTITU-

TION, cols. 117, 118. *The King* v. *Barger*; *The Commonwealth* v. *McKay*, (1908) 6 C.L.R., 41; 14 A.L.R., 374.

The Constitution (63 & 64 Vict. c. 12), sec. 55—Laws imposing taxation—To deal only with imposition of taxation—Excise Tariff 1906 (No. 16 of 1906), whether it deals with matters other than excise duty.]—*See* COMMONWEALTH OF AUSTRALIA CONSTITUTION, co. 118. *The King* v. *Barger*; *The Commonwealth* v. *McKay*, (1908) 6 C.L.R., 41; 14 A.L.R., 374.

II.—DUTIES ON THE ESTATES OF DECEASED PERSONS.

Administration and Probate Act 1903 (No. 1815), sec. 13—Duty—General power of appointment—By will only—Property subject to power, whether dutiable.]—*See* DUTIES ON ESTATES OF DECEASED PERSONS, cols. 414, 415. *In re McCracken*; *Webb* v. *McCracken*, 3 C.L.R., 1018; 12 A.L.R., 313.

Administration and Probate Act 1907 (No. 2089), sec. 3—Exemption from duty—Public charitable bequest or settlement—Institution for the promotion of science and art, what is.]—*See* DUTIES ON THE ESTATES OF DECEASED PERSONS, col. 415. *Edgar* v. *Greenwood*, (1910) V.L.R., 137; 31 A.L.T., 132: 16 A.L.R., 6.

Settlement, duty on—Trusts or dispositions to take effect after the death of settlor—Trust to come into operation on death of survivor of settlor or his wife—Death of settlor before his wife—Administration and Probate Act 1890 (No. 1060), sec. 112—Administration and Probate Act 1903 (No. 1815), sec. 8.]—*See* DUTIES ON THE ESTATES OF DECEASED PERSONS, cols. 415, 416. *In re Rosenthal*; *Rosenthal* v. *Rosenthal*, (1910) 11 C.L.R., 87; 16 A.L.R., 455.

Administration and Probate Act 1890 (No. 1060), sec. 112—Administration and Probate Act 1903 (No. 1815), secs. 8, 9—Settlement—Duty—Trusts and dispositions to take effect after death.]—*See* DUTIES ON THE ESTATES OF DECEASED PERSONS, col. 416. *Whiting* v. *McGinnis*, (1909) V.L.R., 250; 30 A.L.T., 207; 15 A.L.R., 203.

Administration and Probate Act 1903 (No. 1815), sec. 11—Probate duty—Liability for —Gifts purporting to act as immediate gift inter vivos—Donor continuing in possession under lease at full rental from donee—Whether bona fide possession and enjoyment immediately assumed and retained to the exclusion of donor or of any benefit to him by contract or otherwise.]—*See* DUTIES ON THE ESTATES OF DECEASED PERSONS, cols. 416, 417. *Lang* v. *Webb*, (1911) 13 C.L.R., 503; 18 A.L.R., 49.

Administration and Probate Act 1890 (No. 1060), sec. 112—Settlement containing trusts which may take effect either before or after settlor's death—Property transferred in lifetime of settlor—Whether duty payable in respect of.]—*See* DUTIES ON THE ESTATES OF DECEASED PERSONS, col. 417. *In re Rosenthal*; *Rosenthal* v. *Rosenthal*, (1911) V.L.R., 55; 32 A.L.T., 46; 16 A.L.R., 399.

Will—Probate duty—Voluntary transfer by testator during lifetime—Duty chargeable upon property transferred, how to be paid—Administration and Probate Act 1903 (No. 1815), sec. 11.]—*See* DUTIES ON THE ESTATES OF DECEASED PERSONS, cols. 417, 418. *In re Draper*; *Graham* v. *Draper*, (1910) V.L.R., 376; 32 A.L.T., 34; 16 A.L.R., 370.

Administration and Probate Act 1907 (No. 2120), sec. 3—Administration and Probate Act 1903 (No. 1815), sec. 11—Probate duty on property voluntarily transferred in lifetime of deceased—Whether payable out of residue.]—*See* DUTIES ON THE ESTATES OF DECEASED PERSONS, col. 418. *In re Draper*; *Graham* v. *Draper*, (1910) V.L.R., 376; 32 A.L.T., 34; 16 A.L.R., 370.

Will — Construction — Direction to pay funeral and testamentary expenses and debts—Probate duty in respect of property transferred by testator in his lifetime—Administration and Probate Act 1903 (No. 1815), sec. 11.]—*See* DUTIES ON THE ESTATES OF DECEASED PERSONS, col. 418. *In re Draper*; *Graham* v. *Draper*, (1910) V.L.R., 376; 32 A.L.T., 34; 16 A.L.R., 370.

Probate duty, how payment to be apportioned—Direction that each beneficiary shall pay duty in respect of his interest—Tenants for life and remaindermen.]—*See* DUTIES ON THE ESTATES OF DECEASED PERSONS, cols. 418, 419. *In re Buckhurst*; *Equity Trustees, Executors and Agency Co. Ltd.* v. *Buckhurst*, (1907) V.L.R., 252; 28 A.L.T., 190; 13 A.L.R., 74.

Administration and Probate Act 1907 (No. 2120), sec. 3—Administration and Probate Act 1890 (No. 1060), sec. 103—Probate duty—Apportionment—Tenant for life and remainder man—Whether legislation retrospective.]—*See* DUTIES ON THE ESTATES OF DECEASED PERSONS, col. 419. *In re Staughton*; *Oliver* v. *Staughton*, (1910) V.L.R., 415; 32 A.L.T., 63; 16 A.L.R., 443.

Probate duty—Apportionment—Tenant for life and remainderman—Mistake of law—Agreement between executors and tenant for life as to apportionment of duty based on wrong principle—Duty of executors.]—*See* DUTIES ON THE ESTATES OF DECEASED PERSONS, cols. 419, 420. *In re Staughton*; *Oliver* v. *Staughton*, (1910) V.L.R., 415; 32 A.L.T., 63; 16 A.L.R., 443.

Will and codicil—General direction in will exempting legacies from probate duty—Further legacies given in codicil without reference to exemption from probate duty.]—*See* WILL. *In re Stroud*; *Bell* v. *Stroud*. (1908) V.L.R., 33; 29 A.L.T., 104; 13 A.L.R., 645.

Probate duty—Testamentary expenses—Estate for life devised subject to payment thereof—Tenant for life, refusal of payment by—No income from realty available—Payment by trustees of probate duty and testamentary expenses out of personalty bequeathed to other beneficiaries—Mortgage of real estate to recoup such beneficiaries—Whether a breach of trust.]—*See* TRUSTS AND TRUSTEES. *Crout* v. *Beissel*, (1909) V.L.R., 207; 30 A.L.T., 185; 15 A.L.R., 143.

Administration and Probate Act 1890 (No. 1060), secs. 100, 112, 116—Administration and Probate Act 1903 (No. 1815), secs. 9 (2), 15 (2)—Second Schedule—"Total value of the property"—Settlement—Rate at which duty payable—Whether based on the value of all

the settled property.]—*See* DUTIES ON THE ESTATES OF DECEASED PERSONS, cols. 420, 421. *Edgar* v. *Greenwood*, (1910) V.L.R., 137; 31 A.L.T., 132; 16 A.L.R., 6.

Function imposed upon tribunal by Legislature—No machinery provided—Power of Court—Ascertainment of amount of duty payable—Administration and Probate Act 1903 (No. 1815), secs. 9 (2), 15 (2)—Second Schedule.]—*See* DUTIES ON THE ESTATES OF DECEASED PERSONS, col. 421. *Edgar* v. *Greenwood*, (1910) V.L.R., 137; 31 A.L.T., 132; 16 A.L.R., 6.

Administration and Probate Act 1890 (No. 1060), sec. 99—Probate duty—Procedure on assessment—Valuation of assets—Summons by master, when it may be issued.]—*See* DUTIES ON THE ESTATES OF DECEASED PERSONS, col. 421. *Brookes* v. *The King*, (1911) V.L.R., 371; 33 A.L.T., 91; 17 A.L.R., 402.

Administration and Probate Act 1890 (No. 1060), sec. 98—Case stated—Right to begin.]—*See* DUTIES ON THE ESTATES OF DECEASED PERSONS, col. 421. *In re McCracken*, 27 A.L.T., 233; 12 A.L.R., 303.

Costs—Taxation—Appendix N.—Drawing pleadings and other documents—Accounts, statements, etc., for Judge's Chambers—Statement for duty.]—*See* COSTS, col. 270. *In re Duke's Will*, (1907) V.L.R., 632; 29 A.L.T., 50; 13 A.L.R., 477.

III.—INCOME TAX.

Income tax—Profits of company, what are—Assets taken over for realization—Valuation of assets—Decrease in value—Reduction of capital—Surplus over valuation on realization—Income Tax Act 1903 (No. 1819), sec. 9.]—*See* INCOME TAX ACTS, cols. 674, 675. *Webb* v. *Australian Deposit and Mortgage Bank Ltd.*, (1910) 11 C.L.R., 223; 16 A.L.R., 446.

Income tax—Company formed to realize assets—Income Tax Act 1903 (No. 1819), sec. 9 (1).]—*See* INCOME TAX ACTS, cols. 675, 676. *Commissioner of Income Tax* v. *Melbourne Trust Ltd.*, (1914) A.C., 1001.

Income Tax Act 1903 (No. 1819), sec. 9—Company—Registered in Victoria—Purchase and sale of land in New South Wales on behalf of company to be formed—Transactions of company in Victoria—Profit, whether earned in Victoria—Re-sales of land by promoter of company—Contracts taken over by company—Purchase moneys payable by instalments—Taxation on sums not yet received.]—*See* INCOME TAX ACTS, cols. 676, 677. *In re Income Tax Acts; Ex parte Quat Quatta Co.,* (1907) V.L.R., 54; 28 A.L.T., 100; 12 A.L.R., 526.

Income Tax Act 1895 (No. 1374), sec. 9 (1), (14)—" Dividends or profits or part of capital credited to any member or shareholder of any company "—Mining company—Proceeds of sale of land—Dividends payable out of profits only—" Outgoings," what may be deducted.]—*See* INCOME TAX ACTS, cols. 677, 678. *In re Income Tax Acts; The Seven Hills Estate Company's Case,* (1906) V.L.R., 225; 27 A.L.T., 175; 12 A.L.R., 188.

Income Tax Act 1903 (No. 1819), sec. 9 (1)—" Profits " of company, what are—Mutual benefit association incorporated as a company—Profits from Club established for benefit of members and other persons—Subscriptions by members to benefit funds—Interest on investment of benefit funds—Income Tax Act 1895 (No. 1374), secs. 2, 7 (e)—Companies Act 1890 (No. 1074), sec. 181.]—*See* INCOME TAX ACTS. cols. 678, 679. *In re Income Tax Acts,* (1907) V.L.R., 185; 28 A.L.T., 168; 13 A.L.R., 31.

Income Tax Act 1903 (No. 1819), sec. 9—Companies Act 1896 (No. 1482), sec. 88—Profits of company—Reduction of capital—Receipts in excess of amount of reduced capital—Whether such receipts may be capital.]—*See* INCOME TAX ACTS, col. 679. *Webb* v. *Australian Deposit and Mortgage Bank Ltd.,* (1910). 11 C.L.R., 223; 16 A.L.R., 446.

Company—Income tax — " Profits " of company, what are—Income Tax Act 1903 (No. 1819), sec. 9.]—*See* INCOME TAX ACTS, col. 679. *Webb* v. *Australian Deposit and Mortgage Bank Ltd.,* (1910) 11 C.L.R., 223; 16 A.L.R., 446.

Income Tax Act 1903 (No. 1819), sec. 9 (1), (2)—Whether tax payable by trading company only—" Profits," meaning of—Income Tax Act 1895 (No. 1374), secs. 2, 7 (e).]—*See* INCOME TAX ACTS, col. 679. *In re Income Tax Acts,* (1907) V.L.R., 185; 28 A.L.T., 168; 13 A.L.R., 31.

Income Tax Act 1903 (No. 1819), sec. 11 (1)—Companies Act 1890 (No. 1074), sec. 334—Income of life assurance company—Premiums in respect of insurances or assurances—Consideration for annuities.]—*See* INCOME TAX ACTS, col. 680. *In re Income Tax Acts; In re Australian Mutual Provident Society,* (1913) V.L.R., 42; 34 A.L.T., 118; 18 A.L.R., 524.

Commonwealth of Australia Constitution Act (63 & 64 Vict. c. 12)—Interference by State with legislative or executive authority of Commonwealth—Implied prohibition—Income Tax Acts, validity of.]—*See* INCOME TAX ACTS, col. 680. *Baxter* v. *Commissioners of Taxation; Flint* v. *Webb,* 4 C.L.R., 1087, 1178; 13 A.L.R., 313 (1907).

Commonwealth of Australia Constitution (63 & 64 Vict. c. 12)—Income of Federal officer—Whether liable to income tax imposed by State—Power of State Legislature—Whether restricted by Commonwealth Constitution.]—*See* INCOME TAX ACTS, cols. 680, 681. *Webb* v. *Outtrim,* (1907) A.C., 81; 13 A.L.R., (C.N.), 1.

Practice—Special leave to appeal to Privy Council from judgment of High Court—State income tax—Liability of Commonwealth officers.]—*See* APPEAL, cols. 12, 13. *Webb* v. *Crouch; Same* v. *Flint,* (1908) A.C., 214.

Income tax—Assessment—Deduction—Outgoings incurred in production of income—Disbursements or expenses wholly and exclusively laid out or expended for purposes of trade—Commonwealth land tax—Income Tax Act 1895 (No. 1374), sec. 9.]—*See* INCOME TAX ACTS, cols. 681, 682. *Moffatt* v. *Webb,* 1913] 16 C.L.R., 120; 19 A.L.R., 190.

Income Tax Act 1903 (No. 1819), secs. 5, 9—Taxation of company—Deductions, authority for making—Income Tax Act 1895 (No. 1374),

sec. 9—Income Tax Act 1896 (No. 1467), sec.
6.]—*See* INCOME TAX ACTS, col. 682. *Re
Income Tax Acts*, (1907) V.L.R., 327 ; 28
A.L.T., 196 : 13 A.L.R., 154.

Income tax—Deductions—Company formed
for one venture—Profits from venture—De-
ductions of promotion expenses.]—*See* IN-
COME TAX ACTS, col. 682. *In re Income
Tax Acts* ; *Ex parte Quat Quatta Co.*, (1907)
V.L.R., 54 ; 28 A.L.T., 100 ; 12 A.L.R., 526.

Income Tax Act 1903 (No. 1819), secs. 5, 9—
Taxation of company—Deductions—Depreciation of machinery.]—*See* INCOME TAX ACTS,
col. 682. *Re Income Tax Acts*, (1907)
V.L.R., 327 ; 28 A.L.T., 196 ; 13 A.L.R.,
154.

Income Tax Act 1903 (No. 1819), secs. 5, 9—
Taxation of company—Interest on borrowed
capital—Interest on bills given for purchase of
stock in trade.]—*See* INCOME TAX ACTS, cols.
682, 683. *Re Income Tax Acts*, (1907)
V.L.R., 327 ; 28 A.L.T., 196 ; 13 A.L.R., 154.

Income Tax Act 1895 (No. 1374), secs. 2, 5, 9
(1)—Profit on Victorian station property—Loss
on New South Wales station property—
Whether such loss a proper deduction—Income
derived from property within Victoria—Losses
and outgoings incurred in Victoria.]—*See*
INCOME TAX ACTS, col. 683. *Re Income Tax
Acts*, (1907) V.L.R., 358 ; 28 A.L.T., 215 ;
13 A.L.R., 151.

Income tax—Income derived from trust
estate—Trade carried on by trustees—Income
from personal exertion or income the produce
of property—Income Tax Act 1895 (No. 1374),
secs. 2, 8, 9, 12 — Income Tax Act 1896 (No.
1467), secs. 4, 12.]—*See* INCOME TAX ACTS,
cols. 683, 684, 685. *Webb* v. *Syme*, 10 C.L.R.,
482 ; 17 A.L.R., 18.

Income Tax Act 1896 (No. 1467), sec. 12 (d)
—Income derived by trustee—No other person
presently entitled in actual receipt and liable
as taxpayer in respect thereof—Beneficiaries
contingently entitled—Whether tax payable
on whole amount or on each interest separately
—Income Tax Act 1895 (No. 1374), sec. 2—
Person liable in representative character.]—
See INCOME TAX ACTS, col. 685. *Re Income*

Tax Acts, (1907) V.L.R., 358 ; 28 A.L.T.,
215 ; 13 A L R., 151.

Income tax—Scheme of Income Tax Acts—
Income Tax Act 1895 (No. 1374), secs. 2, 8, 9,
12—Income Tax Act 1896 (No. 1467), secs.
4, 12.]—*See* INCOME TAX ACTS, col. 685.
Webb v. *Syme*, 10 C.L.R., 482 ; 17 A.L.R.,
18.

Commonwealth of Australia Constitution
(63 & 64 Vict. c. 12)—Power of Victorian
Legislature (18 & 19 Vict. c. 55)—Income
tax—Right of appeal from Supreme Court to
Privy Council—Whether Commonwealth Par-
liament may take away.]—*See* INCOME TAX
ACTS, cols. 685, 686. *Webb* v. *Outrim*, (1907)
A.C., 81 ; 13 A.L.R. (C.N.), 1.

Commonwealth of Australia Constitution
(63 & 64 Vict. c. 12)—The Constitution, secs.
73, 74, 76, 77—Question as to limits inter se
of constitutional powers of Commonwealth
and State, what is—Question raised by defence
whether State tax on Federal salary an interference with powers of Commonwealth—
Exercise of Federal jurisdiction by Court of
Petty Sessions—Appeal to High Court, competency of—Judiciary Act 1903 (No. 6 of 1903),
sec. 39.]—*See* APPEAL, cols. 19, 20. *Baxter*
v. *Commissioners of Taxation* ; *Flint* v.
Webb, 4 C.L.R., 1087, 1178 ; 13 A.L.R.,
313.

Income Tax Act 1895 (No. 1374), sec. 27—
Special case for opinion of Supreme Court—
Number of counsel who may be heard.]—*See*
INCOME TAX ACTS, col. 686. *In re Income
Tax Acts*, (1907) V.L.R., 358. F.C.

IV.—LAND TAX.

Land Tax Assessment Act 1910 (No. 22 of
1910), sec. 11—Several parcels of land—
Number of deductions of £5,000 to be al-
lowed.]—*See* LAND TAX, cols. 819, 820.
Bailey v. *Federal Commissioner of Land
Tax*, (1911) 13 C.L.R., 302.

Land Tax Assessment Act 1910 (No. 22 of
1910), secs. 11, 33, 35, 38, 43—Deductions—
Owner of several parcels of land—One of
several joint owners—Secondary tax payer—
Deductions to prevent double taxation.]—*See*

LAND TA‚X col. 820. *Bailey* v. *Federal Commissioner of Land Tax*, (1911) 13 C.L.R., 302.

Vendor and purchaser—Contract of sale—Provision for apportionment of federal land tax—Validity—Interpretation—Land Tax Assessment Act 1910 (No. 22 of 1910), secs. 37, 63.]—*See* VENDOR AND PURCHASER. *Patterson* v. *Farrell*, (1912) 14 C.L.R., 348 ; 18 A.L.R., 237.

Income tax—Assessment—Deduction—Outgoings incurred in production of income—Disbursements or expenses wholly and exclusively laid out or expended for purposes of trade—Commonwealth land tax—Income Tax Act 1895 (No. 1374), sec. 9.]—*See* INCOME TAX ACTS, cols. 681, 682. *Moffatt* v. *Webb*, (1913) 16 C.L.R., 120 ; 19 A.L.R., 190.

V.—STAMP DUTIES ; COURT FEES.

Stamps Act 1892 (No. 1274), Schedule, Division VIII.—" Deed of Settlement "—Liability to tax, how to be determined—Whether necessary that instrument should create new beneficial interests.]—*See* STAMPS ACTS. *Davidson* v. *Chirnside*, (1908) 7 C.L.R., 324 ; 14 A.L.R., 686.

Stamps Act 1892 (No. 1274), secs. 4, 28—Schedule, Part VIII.—Settlement, meaning of—Special power of appointment created by instrument executed prior to passing of Act—Power exercised after passing of Act—Fee simple appointed to certain of objects of power.]—*See* STAMPS ACTS. *Davidson* v. *Armytage*, 4 C.L.R., 205 ; 12 A.L.R., 538.

Stamps Act 1892 (No. 1274), secs. 27, 28, Schedule, Division VIII.—Settlement in pursuance of power in will—Trustees of settlement holding upon same trusts as trustees of will—No new beneficial interests created—Deed of settlement, whether liable to duty—Instrument of appointment.]—*See* STAMPS ACTS. *Davidson* v. *Chirnside*, (1908) 7 C.L.R., 324 ; 14 A.L.R., 686

Stamps Act 1892 (No. 1274), sec. 28—" Power of appointment," what is—" Instrument of appointment."]—*See* STAMPS ACTS. *Davidson* v. *Chirnside*, (1908) 7 C.L.R., 324 ; 14 A.L.R., 686.

Stamps Act 1892 (No. 1274), Schedule, Part VIII.—Settlement or gift, deed of—Instrument upon valuable consideration—Sale of land, what is.]—*See* STAMPS ACTS. *Kelly* v. *Collector of Imposts*, 29 A.L.T., 91 ; 13 A.L.R., 613.

Stamps Act 1892 (No. 1274), Schedule, Part VIII.—Settlement or Gift, deed of—Consideration other than bona fide adequate consideration.]—*See* STAMPS ACTS. *Kelly* v. *Collector of Imposts*, 29 A.L.T., 91 ; 13 A.L.R., 613.

Stamps—Family arrangement — Exchange and partition on division—Conveyance or transfer on sale—Stamps Act 1890 (No. 1140), secs. 93, 95, 97, Schecule III.—Stamps Act 1892 (No. 1274), sec. 17, Schedule V.]—*See* STAMPS ACTS. *Davies* v. *Collector of Imposts*, (1908) V.L.R., 272 ; 29 A.L.T., 233 ; 14 A.L.R., 149.

Stamps Act 1890 (No. 1140), sec. 81, Third Schedule—Stamps Act 1892 (No. 1274), Schedule—" Promissory note " — Mortgage debenture charging property and providing means for enforcement of security.]—*See* STAMPS ACTS. *In re Stamps Acts*, (1906) V.L.R., 364 ; 27 A.L.T., 204 ; 12 A.L.R., 186.

Stamps Act 1892 (No. 1274), Schedule—Duty—Amount of—Basis of calculation—" Value of the property," meaning of.]—*See* STAMPS ACTS. *Davidson* v. *Armytage*, 4 C.L.R., 205 ; 12 A.L.R., 538.

Stamp duty—Conveyance or transfer on sale of real property—Property conveyed to purchaser in separate parts by different instruments—Part of land under Transfer of Land Act and part under general law—Exemption of first £50—Stamps Act 1890 (No. 1140), secs. 32, 34, 98 (1)—Third Schedule III. (A), (B).]—*See* STAMPS ACTS. *Hendy* v. *Collector of Imposts*, (1907) V.L.R., 704 ; 29 A.L.T., 89 ; 13 A.L.R., 612.

Special case—Right to begin—Stamps Act 1890 (No. 1140), sec. 71.]—*See* STAMPS ACTS. *Armytage* v. *Collector of Imposts*, (1906) V.L.R., 504 ; 28 A.L.T., 9 ; 12 A.L.R., 305

Stamps Act 1890 (No. 1140), sec. 23—Stamps—Offence—Fraudulently affixing stamp removed from another document—Fraudulently affixing adhesive stamps to other documents.]—*See* STAMPS ACTS. *Burvett* v. *Moody*, (1909) V.L.R., 126; 30 A.L.T., 160; 15 A.L.R., 91.

Costs — Taxation — Appendix N.—Drawing pleadings and other documents—Accounts, statements, etc. for Judge's Chambers—Statement for duty.]—*See* COSTS, col. 270. *In re Duke's Will*, (1907) V.L.R., 632; 29 A.L.T., 50; 13 A.L.R., 477.

Appendix O* Rules of Supreme Court 1884 — Trustees — Passing accounts — Accounts agreed upon between parties—Fees chargeable.]—*See* COSTS, col. 280. *In re Winter*; *Winter-Irving* v. *Winter*, (1908) V.L.R., 74; 29 A.L.T., 144; 13 A.L.R., 701.

Rules of Supreme Court 1884, Order LXXIII.—Appendix O.—Court fees and percentages—Attendance of officer on production of document.]—*See* COSTS, cols. 280, 281. *Daniel* v. *McNamara*, 17 A.L.R. (C.N.), 9.

ROYAL COMMISSION.

See EVIDENCE.

SALE OF GOODS.

See also, LICENSING.

Sale of goods—Memorandum in writing, whether necessary—Contract itself in writing —Sale of Goods Act 1896 (No. 1422), sec. 9.] —A. signed and sent to B. a letter offering to sell him goods of the value of £10 and upwards on conditions therein specified. B. by a subsequent letter, accepted A.'s offer. *Held*, that the provisions of section 9 (1) of the *Sale of Goods Act* 1896 requiring a note or memorandum of the contract did not preclude B. from enforcing the agreement to sell. *Patterson* v. *Dolman*, (1908) V.L.R., 354; 29 A.L.T., 256; 14 A.L.R., 240. F.C. *a'Beckett*, *Hodges* and *Cussen*, JJ.

Sale of goods—Restrictions in regard to the use or sale of goods—Running with goods.]—*Per* Lord Shaw of Dunfermline: The owner of ordinary goods bought and sold may use and dispose of these as he thinks fit. He may have made a certain contract with the person from whom he bought, and to such a contract he must answer. Simply, however, in his capacity as owner, he is not bound by any restrictions in regard to the use or sale of the goods and it is out of the question to suggest that restrictive conditions run with the goods. The judgment of *Swinfen Eady*, J. in *Taddy* v. *Sterious*, (1904) 1 Ch., 358, is plainly sound. *National Phonograph Co. of Australia Ltd.* v. *Menck*, L.R. (1911) A.C., 336 (P.C.), at p. 347; 17 A.L.R., 94, at p. 96.

Sale of goods—Patented articles sold to dealers—Conditions imposed upon dealer.]— *See* PATENT. *National Phonohraph Co. of Australia Ltd.* v. *Menck*, L.R. (1911) A.C., 336 (P.C.); 17 A.L.R., 94.

Conversion—Sale of stolen goods—Recovery of value of goods from purchaser— Payment by cheque—Proceeds afterwards coming to hands of owner of goods—Obligation to elect to affirm or disaffirm sale.]— If a man, having received a sum of money which is identified as being in fact the proceeds of goods of his that have been sold without his authority, afterwards becomes aware of the fact, he is, as between himself and the purchaser of such goods, *prima facie* bound to elect whether he will affirm or disaffirm the sale, and the obligation to elect continues until the happening of some new fact which would alter his position to his prejudice if he were still called upon to elect. If a man, whose servant has stolen his goods and has also stolen his money, afterwards receives from the police money found upon the thief, he is not entitled, without inquiry as to the source of the money, to appropriate it in satisfaction of the stolen money, to the prejudice of the purchaser of the stolen goods, so as to exclude the obligation to elect above stated. *Creak* v. *James Moore & Sons Proprietary Ltd.*, (1912) 15 C.L.R., 426; 18 A.L.R., 542. *Griffith*, C.J. and *Barton*, J., *Isaacs*, J. dissenting.

Pounds Act 1890 (No. 1129), secs. 21, 22—Sale by poundkeeper—Provisions of Act duly observed—Title of purchaser.]—*See* POUNDS AND IMPOUNDING. *Doig* v. *Keating*, (1908) V.L.R., 118; 29 A.L.T., 171; 14 A.L.R., 20.

Pounds Act 1890 (No. 1129), secs. 21, 22—Sale by poundkeeper—Failure to observe provisions of the Act—Title of purchaser.]—*See* POUNDS AND IMPOUNDING. *Doig* v. *Keating*, (1908) V.L.R., 118; 29 A.L.T., 171; 14 A.L.R., 20.

Sale of goods to be shipped from one port to another—Price payable at certain place on delivery of shipping documents—Bill of lading stating goods shipped by vendor and deliverable to his order or assigns—Property in goods, passing of—Delivery, when effected.]—*See* CONTRACT OR AGREEMENT, cols. 224, 225. *Alexander Cross & Sons Ltd.* v. *Hasell*, (1908) V.L.R., 194; 29 A.L.T., 179; 14 A.L.R., 44.

Stipulations as to place of delivery—Whether conditions precedent or warranties—Symbolical delivery elsewhere than place of actual delivery.]—*See* CONTRACT OR AGREEMENT, col. 225. *Alexander Cross & Sons Ltd.* v. *Hasell*, (1908) V.L.R., 194; 29 A.L.T., 179; 14 A.L.R., 44.

Agreement to sell goods—Goods to be shipped from Glasgow and delivered at a certain place at Melbourne—Price payable in London on receipt of proper bill of lading—Place of delivery in bill of lading different from place provided by agreement—Place of completion of contract—Delivery of shipping documents in accordance with agreement—Whether a condition precedent—Right of rescission.]—*See* CONTRACT OR AGREEMENT, col. 224. *Alexander Cross & Sons Ltd.* v. *Hasell*, (1908) V.L.R., 194; 29 A.L.T., 179; 14 A.L.R., 44.

Husband and wife—Agency—Destitute wife—Sale of husband's goods to purchase necessaries—Authority of wife.]—*See* HUSBAND AND WIFE, col. 664. *Moreno* v. *Slinn*, (1910) V.L.R., 457; 32 A.L.T., 66; 16 A.L.R., 503.

SAVINGS BANK.

See BANKER AND CUSTOMER.

SECRET COMMISSION PROHIBITION ACT.

Secret Commissions Prohibition Act 1905 (No. 1974), sec. 2—Corruptly giving valuable consideration to agent—Secret giving, presumption as to corruptness arising from.]—The fact that a secret commission has been given raises the presumption that it was given " corruptly " within the meaning of section 2 of the *Secret Commissions Prohibition Act* 1905. *Rex* v. *Scott*, (1907) V.L.R., 471; 29 A.L.T., 60; 13 A.L.R., 143. *Cussen, J.*

Secret Commissions Prohibition Act 1905 (No. 1974), sec. 2—" Corruptly," meaning of.]—" Corruptly " in the *Secret Commissions Prohibition Act* 1905 does not mean merely the doing of an act prohibited by the Statute, but the doing of that act with some wrongful intention. *Rex* v. *Stevenson*, (1907) V.L.R., 475; 29 A.L.T., 62; 13 A.L.R., 383. *Hood, J.* (1907).

Secret Commissions Prohibition Act 1905 (No. 1974), sec. 2—Giving of valuable consideration to agent—Tendency to influence agent to show favour.]—On a presentment for an offence under section 2 of the *Secret Commissions Prohibition Act* 1905 charging the prisoner with unlawfully and corruptly giving a valuable security to an agent the receipt of which would tend to influence the agent to show favour to the prisoner in relation to his principal's affairs or business, it is for the jury to decide whether the giving of the valuable security would not so tend to influence the agent. *Rex* v. *Scott*, (1907) V.L.R., 471; 29 A.L.T., 60; 13 A.L.R., 143. *Cussen, J.*

Secret Commission Prohibition Act 1905 (No. 1974), secs. 2, 14—Giving money to agent without principal's knowledge—Burden of proof.]—Where without his principal's knowledge money is given to an agent the receipt of which would tend to influence the agent to show favour to the donor in relation to the principal's business, the donor is guilty of an offence under section 2 of the *Secret Commissions Prohibition Act* 1905, unless he proves that when he gave the money he did not intend to influence the agent. *Rex* v. *Stevenson*, (1907) V.L.R., 475; 29 A.L.T., 62; 13 A.L.R., 383. *Hood, J.* (1907).

SECURITY.

See COSTS, EXECUTORS AND ADMIN-ISTRATORS, INSOLVENCY.

SERVICE.

See also, SERVICE AND EXECUTION OF PROCESS ACT.

Appeal—Jurisdiction—Discretion of Judge of County Court—Order enlarging time for taking any step—County Court Rules 1891, r. 424.]—*See* COUNTY COURT, col. 328. *Armstrong* v. *Great Southern Gold Mining Co., No Liability*, (1911) 12 C.L.R., 382; 17 A.L.R., 377.

Practice—Service of summons—Time—Whether time for service may be abridged—Defendant, whether a party to action before service of plaint summons.]—*See* COUNTY COURT, cols. 301, 302. *Newnham* v. *Lobb*, 27 A.L.T. (Supplement), 15; 12 A.L.R. (C.N.), 10.

Marriage Act 1890 (No. 1166), sec. 52—Marriage Act 1900 (No. 1684), sec. 7—Applications to quash, etc.—Orders under the Marriage Acts—Service of notices.]—*See* GENERAL SESSIONS, col. 619. *In re Applications to Quash, &c.*, 31 A.L.T. (Supplement), 10; 15 A.L.R. (C.N.), 25.

Justices Act 1890 (No. 1105), sec. 23 (1)—Service of summons—Service on person other than defendant—Defendant unaware of service—Hearing case in his absence.]—*See* JUSTICES OF THE POLICE, col. 783. *Hunter* v. *Stewart*, (1907) V.L.R., 619; 29 A.L.T., 39; 13 A.L.R., 440.

Justices—Service of summons—Summons left at last place of abode—Defendant absent in England—Justices Act 1890 (No. 1105), sec. 23 (1).]—*See* JUSTICES OF THE PEACE, col. 783. *Rees* v. *Downer*, (1910) V.L.R., 5; 31 A.L.T., 97; 15 A.L.R., 630.

Justices—Service of summons—Summons left at last place of abode—Defendant absent in England—Objection to service taken before Justices—Order to review—Renewal of objection—Justices Act 1890 (No. 1105), secs. 23 (1). 146.]—*See* JUSTICES OF THE PEACE, col. 803. *Rees* v. *Downer*, (1910) V.L.R., 5; 31 A.L.T., 97; 15 A.L.R., 630.

Imprisonment of Fraudulent Debtors Act 1890 (No. 1100), sec. 15—County Court Act 1890 (No. 1078), sec. 31—Judgment debtor's summons—Service of judgment—Certified extract from Register.]—*See* DEBTORS ACT, col. 384. *The Royal Finance Co.* v. *Summers*, 30 A.L.T. (Supplement), 24: 15 A.L.R. (C.N.), 9.

Marriage Act 1890 (No. 1166), secs. 43, 51—Maintenance order—Necessity for service of order before proceedings to enforce.]—*See* MAINTENANCE AND MAINTENANCE ORDERS, col. 886. *Cohen* v. *MacDonough*, (1907) V.L.R., 7; 28 A.L.T., 119; 12 A.L.R., 566.

Service of copy of maintenance order—Proof of, by affidavit—Proceedings for disobedience of order—Marriage Act 1890 (No. 1166), sec. 51—Justices Act 1890 (No. 1105), sec. 74.]—*See* MAINTENANCE AND MAINTENANCE ORDERS, col. 888. *Cohen* v. *MacDonough (or O'Donough)*, (1906) V.L.R., 521; 28 A.L.T., 97; 12 A.L.R., 447.

SERVICE AND EXECUTION OF PROCESS ACT.

Bill of exchange—Action upon under Instruments Act 1890—Writ—Service out of jurisdiction—Indorsement by Prothonotary—Necessity for Judge's Order for such indorsement—Instruments Act 1890 (No. 1103), sec. 92—Service and Execution of Process Act 1901 (No. 11 of 1901), secs. 5, 8.]—*Sternberg* v *Egan*, 18 A.L.R. (C.N.), 20. *Hood, J.* (1912).

Service and Execution of Process Act 1901 (No. 11), sec. 10—Writ of summons served in another State—Security for costs—Discretion.]—Section 10 of the *Service and Execution of Process Act* 1901 leaves the Court entirely at large as to the ground upon which it may exercise or ought to exercise its discretion to order that security for costs of a defendant who has been served under that Act with a writ of summons should be given by the plaintiff, and the Court must be guided in each particular case by the facts. In *Evans* v. *Sneddon*, 24 A.L.T., 79 ; 28 V.L.R., 396 : 8 A.L.R., 215, the Full Court did not attempt to enumerate all the circumstances which might influence the Court in granting or refusing an application under that section. *Smith* v. *Chisholm*, (1908) V.L.R., 579 ; 30 A.L.T., 48 ; 14 A.L.R., 471. *Hodges, J.* (1908).

Service and Execution of Process Act 1901 (No. 11), sec. 11—Writ—Service in another State—No appearance entered—Application for leave to proceed—Affidavit of service—Particulars.]—In an application under section 11 of the *Service and Execution of Process Act* 1901 for leave to proceed when no appearance has been entered or made by the defendant within the time limited for appearance, the affidavit relied on as to service of the writ should show how the deponent knew the person served to be the defendant, and what was done at the time of effecting service ; and a statement merely that the deponent personally served the defendant with the writ is insufficient. *Jarrett* v. *Brown*, (1908) V.L.R., 478 ; 30 A.L.T., 17 ; 14 A.L.R., 349. *Madden, C.J.* (1908).

Practice—Service of process—Subpoena—Application for leave to serve beyond State—Affidavit in support—Service and Execution of Process Act 1901 (No. 11 of 1901), sec. 16 (1).]—Leave to serve a subpoena upon a person in any other State, or part of the Commonwealth will not be granted under section 16 (1) of the *Service and Execution of Process Act* 1901 where the affidavit filed in support of the application for such leave does not show what facts the witness is likely to prove. *Trapp Couche & Co.* v. *H.*

McKenzie Limited, 30 A.L.T., 200 ; 15 A.L.R., 179. *Hood, J.* (1909).

Service and Execution of Process Act 1901 (No. 11), sec. 16—Evidence Act 1890 (No. 1088), secs. 4, 10—Commission for examination of witness out of Victoria—Whether commission may issue in case of witness whose attendance can be enforced.]—*See* EVIDENCE, col. 511. *National Mutual Life Association of Australasia Ltd.* v. *Australian Widows' Fund, &c. Society Ltd.,* (1910) V.L.R., 411 ; 32 A.L.T., 51 ; 16 A.L.R., 460.

Service and Execution of Process Act 1901 (No. 11), sec. 18—Person apprehended on warrant issued in another State—Duty of Justice of Peace before whom such person is brought.]—When a person apprehended under a warrant issued in another State which has been indorsed under section 18 (1), (2) of the *Service and Execution of Process Act* 1901 is brought before a Justice of the Peace, on the production of the warrant the Justice of the Peace should order the return of such person either in custody or on bail unless the defendant satisfies such Justice that on one of the grounds specified in section 18 (4) he should be discharged or otherwise dealt with as provided by that section. *O'Donnell* v. *Heslop ; The King* v. *Cresswell ; Ex parte Heslop,* (1910) V.L.R., 162 ; 31 A.L.T., 173 ; 16 A.L.R., 168. F.C. *Madden, C.J., Hodges* and *Cussen, JJ.*

Service and Execution of Process Act 1901 (No. 11), sec. 18 (4)—Person arrested on warrant issued in another State—Return of such person to such other State, whether unjust or oppressive—Dispute as to facts alleged in defence—Bona fide assurance of dispute by prosecutor.]—Where the defendant proves facts which unless contradicted would be a good defence to the charge, if the prosecutor *bona fide* assures the Bench that such evidence will be contradicted at the trial it is not " unjust or oppressive " to return the defendant to the place where the charge was laid. *O'Donnell* v. *Heslop ; The King* v. *Cresswell, Ex parte Heslop,* (1910) V.L.R., 162 ; 31 A.L.T., 173 ; 16 A.L.R., 168. F.C. *Madden, C.J., Hodges* and *Cussen, JJ.*

Service and Execution of Process Act 1901 (No. 11), sec. 18—Person charged with offence in another State—Execution of warrant in Victoria — Power to discharge accused — Whether it may be exercised after his admission to bail to appear and answer the charge.] —The provisions of section 18 (4) of the *Service and Execution of Process Act* 1901 empowering a Justice of the Peace or a Judge to " discharge the person either absolutely or on bail, &c., &c.," apply not only to cases where there is an order that such person shall be returned in custody but also to cases where he has been admitted to bail to appear and answer the charge in the State in which the warrant was issued. *O'Donnell* v. *Heslop; The King* v. *Cresswell, Ex parte Heslop,* (1910) V.L.R., 162; 31 A.L.T., 173; 16 A.L.R., 168. F.C. *Madden, C.J., Hodges* and *Cussen, JJ.*

Service and Execution of Process Act 1901 (No. 11), sec. 18 (4)—Application to Judge— Jurisdiction—Whether original or appellate.] —*Per Cussen, J.*—The jurisdiction of a Judge under section 18 (4) of the *Service and Execution of Process Act* 1901 is rather original than appellate. The Judge has power to hear fresh evidence where the application has been made in the first instance to a Justice of the Peace and may exercise his jurisdiction although no application has been made. *O'Donnell* v. *Heslop ; The King* v. *Cresswell, Ex parte Heslop,* (1910) V.L.R., 162; 31 A.L.T., 173; 16 A.L.R., 168.

Service and Execution of Process Act 1901 (No. 11 of 1901), sec. 18—Warrant endorsed for execution in another State—Apprehension of accused on unsustainable charge—Discharge of accused—Exercise of discretion by Justice or Judge—Jurisdiction of Judge—Review of Justice's discretion by Judge.]—Where, in the case of a person who has been apprehended in Victoria under the provisions of section 18 of the *Service and Execution of Process Act* 1901, in consequence of the issue in another State of a warrant for his apprehension upon a charge of having committed an offence within such other State, it appears to the Justice of the Peace before whom he is brought in Victoria or to a Judge of this State, that, if the accused were put on trial upon the charge alleged against him, he ought on the undisputed facts to be acquitted, the Justice or Judge ought to discharge him. A Judge of this State has jurisdiction under section 18 (4) of the *Service and Execution of Process Act* 1901 to discharge the accused person absolutely, although a Justice of the Peace has previously finally dealt with the matter and has made an order under section 18 (3). *In re George,* (1909) V.L.R., 15; 30 A.L.T., 141; 15 A.L.R., 27. *a' Beckett, J.*

Service and Execution of Process Act 1901 (No. 11), sec. 18 (4)—Practice—Application to Judge for discharge of prisoner, how made.] —The application to a Judge under section 18 (4) of the *Service and Execution of Process Act* 1901 should be by way of order *nisi* calling on the informant or his representative in the State to show cause why the defendant should not be discharged absolutely or admitted to bail as the case may be on any of the grounds mentioned in section 18 (4). The time for the return of the order *nisi* is in the discretion of the Judge. *O'Donnell* v. *Heslop; The King* v. *Cresswell, Ex parte Heslop,* (1910) V.L.R., 162; 31 A.L.T. 173; 16 A.L.R., 168. F.C. *Madden, C.J., Hodges* and *Hood, JJ.*

Service and Execution of Process Act 1901 (No. 11), sec. 18 (4)—Warrant—Execution— Application for discharge of person apprehended—Procedure—Form of Order.]—Upon an application under section 18 (4) of the *Service and Execution of Process Act* 1901 for the discharge of a person who is held under a warrant issued in another State on which a Justice of the Peace in Victoria has made an indorsement authorizing the execution thereof within Victoria, the order should in the first instance be in the nature of an order *nisi* calling upon the informant to show cause on a subsequent day why the order applied for should not be made. *In re George,* (1908) V.L.R., 734; 30 A.L.T., 113; 14 A.L.R., 699. *a' Beckett, J.* (1908).

Service and Execution of Process Act 1901 (No. 11), sec. 18—Execution of warrant issued in another State—Order of Justice of Peace directing return of accused—Review of order

by Judge—Costs, jurisdiction to award.]—Upon review of the decision of a Justice of the Peace ordering an accused person to be returned to the State in which the warrant for his apprehension was issued a Judge has no jurisdiction to award costs. *In re George*, (1909) V.L.R., 15; 30 A.L.T., 141; 15 A.L.R., 27. *a' Beckett, J.*

SET-OFF.

Deposit receipt, security by way of—Contract to supply goods to Crown—Security for due performance of contract—Deposit receipt in name of servant of Crown procured by contractor and delivered to such servant—Contractor's account with bank over-drawn—Contract duly performed—Whether amount of deposit receipt a debt due by Crown to contractor—Money had and received—Set-off of bank's claim against contractor, whether justifiable.]—*See* BANKER AND CUSTOMER, cols. 70, 71, 72. *The King* v. *Brown*, (1912) 14 C.L.R., 17; 18 A.L.R., 111.

Order LXV., r. 14 (Rules of 1906)—Several causes of action—Set-off of costs recovered by defendant against damages and costs recovered by plaintiff—Complication of evidence and argument on several causes of action.]—*See* COSTS, col. 260. *O'Sullivan* v. *Morton*, (1911) V.L.R., 249; 32 A.L.T., 198; 17 A.L.R., 201.

SETTLED ESTATES AND SETTLED LANDS ACT.

Settled Estates and Settled Lands Act 1909 (No. 2235), secs. 51, 124—Sale of settled land —Tenant for life, person having the power of sale of—Person entitled in fee simple with executory limitation over in a certain event.]—A testator devised lands to an infant absolutely, with the proviso that should she marry without the consent of the executors of the will before attaining the age of twenty-one the gift should be absolutely null and void, and with a direction for the application of the rents and profits of such lands for her maintenance and education during her minority or until her marriage with such consent. *Held*, that the devisee was entitled to an estate in fee simple subject to an executory limitation over in the event of her marrying without the consent of the executors, and had, therefore, by virtue of section 124 (1) (II) of the *Settled Estates and Settled Lands Act* 1909, the powers of a tenant for life under Part II. of that Act. *In re Cheke or Akehurst*; *Cheke* v. *Hamilton*, (1910) V.L.R., 310; 32 A.L.T., 5; 16 A.L.R., 246. *Hodges, J.*

Settled Estates and Settled Lands Act 1909 (No. 2235), sec. 124—Sale of settled land—Person with powers of tenant for life—Estate or interest in possession, what is.]—In section 124 of the *Settled Estates and Settled Lands Act* 1909 the word " possession " is used as contra-distinguished from reversion or remainder. *In re Morgan*, 24 C.D., 114, followed. *In re Cheke or Akehurst*; *Cheke* v. *Hamilton*, (1910) V.L.R., 310; 32 A.L.T., 5; 16 A.L.R., 246. *Hodges, J.*

Settled Estates and Settled Lands Act 1909 (No. 2235), secs. 50, 51, 99—Settled lands—Devise to trustees—Will containing only power to let or lease—Sale by tenant for life—Trustees without power to consent—" Trustees of the settlement."]—A testatrix devised lands to trustees upon trust for her daughter for life and after her death for the children then living of such daughter, and the only power given to the trustees in respect of the land was to let or lease it. *Held*, that the trustees had no power, under and by virtue of the *Settled Estates and Settled Lands Act* 1909, to consent to a sale of the land by the tenant for life, as they were not trustees of the settlement within the meaning of section 51 of that Act. *Beardsley* v. *Harris*, (1911) V.L.R., 152; 32 A.L.T., 161; 17 A.L.R., 112. *Hodges, J.*

Settled Estates and Settled Lands Act 1909 (No. 2235), secs. 127, 128—Contract of sale—Purchase in names of infants—Settled estate —Tenant for life—Settlement—Appointment of trustees—Trustees to exercise powers of infant tenants for life.]—W. entered into contracts for the purchase of land in which he named his sons as co-purchasers, and died before payment of the balance of the purchase money. By his will he appointed his two elder sons executors and provided that his property should be divided among his four sons equally. Two of the sons being infants and a sale of the land becoming desirable, application was made for the purpose of effecting such a sale under the *Settled Estates and Settled Lands Act* 1909. *Held,* that under the Act the infants' interests in the land were " settled land " and that the infants were " tenants for life " thereof, and that there was a " settlement " within the Act ; and the two elder brothers were appointed trustees of the settlement and a direction was given that the powers of the infants as such tenants for life might be exercised by such trustees by selling or concurring in selling the land without further application to the Court. Form of order in *In re Simpson*, (1897) 1 Ch., 256, adopted. *In re Weir*, (1912) V.L.R., 77 ; 33 A.L.T., 162 ; 18 A.L.R., 26. *Cussen, J.*

Settled Estates and Settled Lands Act 1909 (No. 2235), secs. 50, 51, 98, 101, 117, 118, 121, 124, 127, 128, 132—Will—Devise to trustees—Power of sale given to trustees—Power to carry on testator's business—Settled estate—Persons with powers of tenant for life—Infants.]—By his will and codicil, a testator devised his real estate to trustees on trust to sell the same, and declared that no sale was to be made until the youngest of his children attained twenty-one, and after providing in the will that the trustees were to divide the net income between X and the testator's five children (some of whom were still infants) during their respective lives—the issue of children dying leaving issue to take the parents' share of the income and the shares of income of children dying without issue to go to the other children, and on X's death, X's share to go to the surviving children, and issue of dead children—be declared in the codicil that subject to the provision as to X's income the trustees should, upon the youngest of the children attaining twenty-one hold the corpus of the estate in trust for his child or children living at the period of distribution, and the issue of children then dead *per stirpes* as tenants in common. There

was also a provision empowering the trustees to carry on testator's farming and grazing business, and for that purpose to use his farm land and such of his residuary personal estate and of the income of his real estate as they should think desirable. As the farm land was causing a loss to the trust estate, the trustees and X and testator's adult children desired the sale of such land, and the trustees applied for an order under the *Settled Estates and Settled Lands Act* 1909 authorizing the sale of it. *Held,* that such trustees were trustees of the settlement created by the will and codicil in such land within the meaning of Part II. of the said Act, and that X. and the testator's five children had the powers of a tenant for life of such land under Part II., and that the power of sale conferred on a tenant for life by sec. 51 might be exercised by X. and the adult children and the trustees on behalf of the infants ; and an order was made that X., the adult children and the trustees be at liberty to sell such land, and enter into contracts of sale for that purpose, and that the trustees might execute the necessary instruments under the Transfer of Land Acts for the purpose of transferring the land to the purchaser. By virtue of sec. 101 of the Act, there is a person with the powers of a tenant for life in every class of settlement within the meaning of the Act. *Semble.*— Land is not subject to a " trust or direction for sale " within the meaning of sec. 132 if the power of sale is postponed. *Semble.*—If sec. 117 of that Act applies to a case where under sec. 101 the trustees are not to be " a tenant for life " but to be deemed to " have the powers of a tenant for life " it is impossible for a testator or settlor to prevent his land from being sold. Form of order settled. *In re Snowball*, (1912) V.L.R., 176 ; 33 A.L.T., 172 ; 18 A.L.R., 65. *Cussen, J.* (But see the *Conveyancing Act* 1912 (No. 2440), sec. 15).

Settled Estates and Settled Lands Act 1909 (No. 2235), secs. 51, 124, 127—Sale of settled land—Infant being person with powers of tenant for life—Appointment of persons to exercise such powers.]—Where under a will an infant took such an interest in land that, by virtue of sec. 124 of the *Settled Estates and Settled Lands Act* 1909, she had the powers of a tenant for life, the Court appointed the executors of the will to exercise the power of sale under the Act. *In re Cheke or Akehurst*; *Cheke* v. *Hamilton*, (1910) V.L.R., 310; 32 A.L.T., 5; 16 A.L.R., 246. *Hodges, J.*

SETTLEMENTS.

See also, INSOLVENCY ; SETTLED ESTATES AND SETTLED LANDS ACT ; TENANT FOR LIFE AND REMAINDERMAN ; TRUSTS AND TRUSTEES ; WILL.

I.—REGISTRATION.

Settlement by widow on children—Non-registration—Validity of settlement—Insolvency Act 1897 (No. 1513), sec. 100.]—A settlement by a widow upon her children does not come within sec. 100 of the *Insolvency Act* 1897, and therefore need not be registered under that section in order to make it valid, and to protect it in the event of the insolvency of the settlor. *Lorimer* v. *Smail*, (1911) 12 C.L.R., 504; 17 A.L.R., 441. *Griffith, C.J., Barton* and *O'Connor, JJ.*

II.—INTERPRETATION OF PARTICULAR INSTRUMENTS.

Will — Settlement — Annuity — Charge, whether on corpus or income—Order of Court —Transfer of Land Statute 1866 (No. 301), sec. 86.]—By a marriage settlement made in 1877, the settlor, the intended husband, gave a term of 99 years in certain land to his trustees, who were directed " out of the rents and profits " thereof to raise the annual sum of £500 and pay it to the intended wife during her life. The settlor subsequently by his will devised the land to certain beneficiaries subject to the charge created by the settlement. After the settlor's death, viz., in 1882, by order of the Supreme Court, an instrument of charge under the *Transfer of Land Statute* 1866 to secure the annuity was executed, which had the effect of rendering the corpus as well as the income of the land liable to satisfy the accruing payments of the annuity. The land was subsequently sold pursuant to an order of the Court and the proceeds of sale were invested. An order of Court was afterwards made directing the trustees of the settlor's will to set aside a certain sum to answer the " rent charge " on the land and to pay the residue of the proceeds of sale to the beneficiaries entitled thereto. This order was never carried into effect, as the income from the investments representing the proceeds of sale had become insufficient to pay the annuity, which fell into arrear. *Held*, that whether under the settlement the annuity was or was not a charge upon the corpus as well as the income of the land, it became so by virtue of the instrument of charge under the *Transfer of Land Statute* 1866 ; that it was too late to have the charge corrected if it was inadvertently made ; that that charge equally attached to the proceeds of the sale of the land ; that nothing which had subsequently happened diminished the extent of that charge ; and therefore that the annuitant was entitled to an order for payment of arrears of the annuity out of the corpus of the investments representing the proceeds of the sale of the land. *Brown* v. *Abbott*, (1908) 5 C.L.R., 487. H.C., *Griffith, C.J., O'Connor* and *Isaacs, JJ.*

Settlement—Appointment of fund—New appointment—Revocation— Substituted gifts —Construction.]—In execution of the powers reserved by a marriage settlement, a revocable appointment was made by deed whereby the appointors, the husband and wife, directed the trustees to hold the net purchase moneys already received and to be received in respect of a certain contract of sale upon trust on the death of the survivor of the appointors as to three several sums of £15,000 for each of three of their daughters, and as to £12,500 for their fourth daughter (to whom had already been advanced £2,500), and as to the " remainder " one moiety to each of their two sons. The contract of sale referred to was of certain land subject to the settlement, and was for a sum of £100,000 ; of which £20,000 had already been paid. The deed also contained appointments of two pieces of land, which had been bought out of the £20,000, one to a daughter and the other to a son. The contract of sale was subsequently rescinded on the purchaser paying a further sum of £20,000. Out of the balance of the £40,000 paid in respect of the contract of sale, other lands were afterwards purchased, and certain advances were made to one of the appointors and to some of the beneficiaries, leaving a balance of £7,600. The appointors thereupon made a new appointment whereby they revoked the appointments of the prior deed as to the net purchase money therein referred to " but so far only as may be necessary to the validity of the directions and appointments hereinafter contained and not further or otherwise." They then appointed the land the subject of the contract of sale to their four daughters equally as tenants in common ; they appointed a sum of £1,000 (part of the £40,000) to one daughter ; they revoked the appointment of the land appointed to one daughter and appointed it to one of the sons ; they revoked the residuary appointment " but so far only &c." (as before); they appointed two other pieces of land to a son and a daughter respectively ; they appointed all debts due by one of the settlors to one of the sons with a gift over to the other ; they appointed all debts owing by either son to that son ; and they appointed that the trustees should stand possessed of the moneys in their possession or under their control subject to the trusts of the settlement " of which no other appointment is made " by the first deed " or by these presents " upon trust as to two-thirds to one son and as to one third to the other. Each of these appointments was to take effect on the death of the survivor of the appointors. Held (per Griffith, C.J. and Barton, J., Isaacs, J., dissenting), that, having regard to the known state of the trust funds, under the second deed, the appointment to the two sons of the moneys in the hands or under the control of the trustees, etc., could only apply to the £7,600, that no other appointment of that sum was made by either deed, or within the

meaning of the second deed, and therefore that the two sons were entitled to it in the proportions of two-thirds and one-third to the exclusion of the daughters. *a' Beckett v. The Trustees Executors &c. Co. Ltd.,* (1908) 5. C.L.R., 512.

Settlement—Trustee and cestui que trust—Appointment—Gifts out of specific fund—Gift of residue—Failure of fund—Abatement.] —In execution of the powers received by a marriage settlement, a revocable appointment was made by deed whereby the appointors, the husband and wife, directed the trustees to hold the net purchase money already received and to be received in respect of a certain contract of sale upon trust, on the death of the survivor of the appointors, as to three several sums of £15,000 for each of three of their daughters, and as to £12,500 for their fourth daughter (to whom they had already advanced £2,500) and as to the " remainder " one moiety to each of their two sons. The contract of sale referred to was of certain land subject to the settlement, and was for a sum of £100,000 of which £20,000 had already been paid. The deed also contained appointments of two pieces of land, which had been bought out of the £20,000, one to a daughter and the other to a son. The contract of sale was subsequently rescinded on the purchaser paying a further sum of £20,000. *Held (per Griffith, C.J. and Barton, J.),* that in the events which had happened the principle that, where a person disposing of a sum among different persons acts on the assumption that he is dealing with a fund of specific amount, and gives a part of the fund to one or more persons and the residue to another, if the fund falls short, all the gifts abate proportionately, would not apply, and therefore the sons would get nothing under the gift of the " remainder." *Per Isaacs, J.—* That principle would have applied to the appointment as it stood before the rescission of the contract of sale, and what happened afterwards would not alter the construction of the appointment. *Page v. Leapingwell,* 18 Ves., 463, distinguished. *a' Beckett v. Trustees Executors &c. Co. Ltd.,* (1908) 5 C.L.R., 512. H.C.

Husband and wife—Marriage settlement—Restraint on anticipation—Second marriage—Revival of restraint.]—By an ante-nuptial settlement certain property of the intended wife was assigned to trustees upon trust to pay the income thereof to her for her sole and separate use independently of the intended husband (who was mentioned by name), and of his debts, control, and engagements, with a restraint on anticipation, and after the death of the settlor to stand possessed of the trusts funds and income in trust for other persons. The marriage took place, and upon the death of the husband named in the settlement, the settlor married again. *Held*, that the restraint on anticipation was not confined to the life of the husband named in the settlement, but revived on the second marriage. *Stroud* v. *Edwards*, 77 L.T. (N.S.), 280, followed; *Re Gaffee*, 1 Mac. & G., 541, discussed. *Trustees Executors and Agency Co. Ltd.* v. *Webster*, (1907) V.L.R., 318; 28 A.L.T., 225; 13 A.L.R., 188. *Cussen, J.*

Settlement, construction of—Life estate to A.—Remainder to children of A.—Gift over of share of child dying without issue—Rule against perpetuities—Gift void by—Subsequent limitation whether also void—Gift over in default of grandchildren—Whether it includes gift over in default of children.]—By a settlement land was granted to the grantee to uses to the use of A. the wife of B. for her life, after her decease to the use of the child or children of A. and B. as A. should appoint, in default of appointment " To the use of all and every the said children and child their his and her heirs and assigns and if more than one in equal shares as tenants in common. And if any one or more of the said children shall die without issue then to the use of the other or others of the said children their heirs and assigns, and if more than one in equal shares. And in default of such issue to the right heirs of the said A. for ever." A. died never having had a child. *Held*, that the words " in default of issue " contemplated the failure of the grandchildren who were to take the ultimate fee, and that the rule against perpetuities invalidating the gift over to the grandchildren invalidated also the gift over to the right heirs of A. *Held*, also,

that the gift over in the event of the default of grandchildren could not be split up so as to make the gift over take effect in the event, which had happened but was not specifically and separately provided for, of A. dying without ever having had a child. *In re Bence*, (1891) 3 Ch., 242, followed. *Milligan* v. *Shaw*, (1907) V.L.R., 668; 29 A.L.T., 75; 13 A.L.R., 545. *a' Beckett, J.* (1907).

III.—LEASING; SALE.

Settled estate—Power of Court to authorise leases—" Manifest intention " of settlor as to use of estate—" Manifest intention " that power of Court shall not be exercised—Real Property Act 1890 (No. 1136), secs. 64, 90.]—The provision in sec. 90 of the *Real Property Act* 1890, with regard to the exercise by the Court of any of the powers conferred on it by Part V. of the Act, that " no such powers shall be exercised if an expressed declaration *or manifest intention* that they shall not be exercised is contained in the settlement or may reasonably be inferred therefrom " means that there must be something in the settlement which shows that the settlor was intentionally providing against those powers being called in aid by the trustees of the settlement. The fact that a manifest intention is shown in the settlement that the settled estate should be used in a particular way (which did not include the power to lease the property) does not under sec. 90 of the Act negative the exercise of the power given to the Court by sec. 64 to authorise leases of the settled estate. *In re Staughton*, (1909) V.L.R., 174; 30 A.L.T., 184; 15 A.L.R., 148. *Hodges, J.*). (NOTE.—Part V. of the *Real Property Act* 1890 is repealed by the *Settled Estates and Settled Lands Act* 1909 (No. 2235); but similar powers are conferred on the Court by Part I. of the latter Act. The words italicised in the above quotation do not appear in sec. 35—the corresponding section—of the *Settled Estates and Settled Lands Act* 1909).

Practice—Originating summons—Payment of costs out of estate—Order for sale of settled properties.]—*See* COSTS, col. 266. *In re Lees*; *Lees* v. *National Trustees Co.*, (1908) V.L.R., 211; 30 A.L.T., 26; 14 A.L.R., 147.

IV.—STAMP AND PROBATE DUTY.

Stamps Act 1892 (No. 1274), secs. 4, 28—Schedule, Part VIII.—Settlement, meaning of—Special power of appointment created by instrument executed prior to passing of Act—Power exercised after passing of Act—Fee simple appointed to certain of objects of power.]—*See* STAMPS ACTS. *Davidson* v. *Armytage,* 4 C.L.R., 205 ; 12 A.L.R., 538.

Stamps Act 1892 (No. 1274), sec. 28—" Power of appointment," what is—" Instrument of appointment."]—*See* STAMPS ACTS. *Davidson* v. *Chirnside,* (1908) 7 C.L.R., 324 ; 14 A.L.R., 686.

Stamps Act 1892 (No. 1274), Schedule, Division VIII.—" Deed of settlement "—Liability to tax, how to be determined—Whether necessary that instrument should create new beneficial interests.]—*See* STAMPS ACTS. *Davidson* v. *Chirnside,* (1908) 7 C.L.R., 324 ; 14 A.L.R., 686.

Stamps Act 1892 (No. 1274), secs. 27, 28, Schedule, Division VIII.—Settlement in pursuance of power in will—Trustees of settlement holding upon same trusts as trustees of will—No new beneficial interests created—Deed of settlement, whether liable to duty—Instrument of appointment.]—*See* STAMPS ACTS. *Davidson* v. *Chirnside,* (1908) 7 C.L.R., 324 ; 14 A.L.R., 686.

Stamps Act 1892 (No. 1274), Schedule, Division VIII.—Settlement or gift, deed of—Instrument upon valuable consideration—Sale of land, what is.]—*See* STAMPS ACTS. *Kelly* v. *Collector of Imposts,* 29 A.L.T., 91 ; 13 A.L.R., 613.

Stamps Act 1892 (No. 1274), Schedule, Division VIII.—Settlement or gift, deed of—Consideration other than bona fide adequate pecuniary consideration.]—*See* STAMPS ACTS. *Kelly* v. *Collector of Imposts,* 29 A.L.T., 91 ; 13 A.L.R., 613.

Administration and Probate Duties Act 1907 (No. 2089), sec. 3—Exemption from duty—Public charitable bequest or settlement—Institution for the promotion of science and art, what is.]—*See* DUTIES ON THE ESTATES OF DECEASED PERSONS, col. 415. *Edgar* v.

Greenwood, (1910) V.L.R., 137 ; 31 A.L.T., 132 ; 16 A.L.R., 6.

Settlement, duty on—Trusts or dispositions to take effect after the death of the settlor—Trust to come into operation on death of survivor of settlor or his wife—Death of settlor before his wife—Administration and Probate Act 1890 (No. 1060), sec. 112—Administration and Probate Act 1903 (No. 1815) sec. 8.]—*See* DUTIES ON THE ESTATES OF DECEASED PERSONS, cols. 415, 416. *In re Rosenthal* ; *Rosenthal* v. *Rosenthal,* (1910) 11 C.L.R., 87 ; 16 A.L.R., 455.

Administration and Probate Act 1890 (No. 1060), sec. 112—Administration and Probate Act 1903 (No. 1815), secs. 8 and 9—Settlement—Duty—Trusts and dispositions to take effect after death.]—*See* DUTIES ON ESTATES OF DECEASED PERSONS, col. 416. *Whiting* v. *McGinnis,* (1909) V.L.R., 250 ; 30 A.L.T., 207 ; 15 A.L.R., 203.

Administration and Probate Act 1890 (No. 1060), sec. 112—Settlement containing trusts which may take effect either before or after settlor's death—Property transferred in lifetime of settlor—Whether duty payable in respect of.]—*See* DUTIES ON THE ESTATES OF DECEASED PERSONS, col. 417. *In re Rosenthal* ; *Rosenthal* v. *Rosenthal* (1911) V.L.R, 55 ; 32 A.L.T., 46 ; 16 A.L.R., 399.

Administration and Probate Act 1890 (No. 1060), secs. 100, 112, 116—Administration and Probate Act 1903 (No. 1815), secs. 9 (2), 15 (2)—Second Schedule—" Total value of the property "—Settlement—Rate at which duty payable—Whether based on the value of all the settled property.]—*See* DUTIES ON THE ESTATES OF DECEASED PERSONS, cols. 420, 421. *Edgar* v. *Greenwood,* (1910) V.L.R., 137 ; 31 A.L.T., 132 ; 16 A.L.R., 6.

Function imposed upon tribunal by legislature—No machinery provided—Power of Court—Ascertainment of amount of duty payable—Administration and Probate Act 1903 (No. 1815), secs. 9 (2), 15 (2)—Second Schedule.]—*See* DUTIES ON THE ESTATES OF DECEASED PERSONS, col. 421. *Edgar* v. *Greenwood,* (1910) V.L.R., 137 ; 31 A.L.T., 132 ; 16 A.L.R., 6.

SETTLEMENT OF LANDS ACT 1893
(No. 1311).

See LANDS ACTS.

SHARES.

See COMPANY.

SHAREHOLDER.

See COMPANY.

SHEEP.

See STOCK DISEASES ACT.

SHERIFF.

Attachment of person—Sheriff, duty of—Writ of attachment regular on its face.]—*See* ATTACHMENT, cols. 64, 65. *Peterson* v. *M'Lennan*, (1907) V.L.R., 94; 28 A.L.T., 135; 12 A.L.R., 577.

Order LII., r. 11—Order LXVII.*, r. 9—Writ of attachment—Sheriff, refusal of to execute—Execution, how enforced—Whether mandamus may issue.]—*See* ATTACHMENT, col. 64. *Peterson* v. *M'Lennan*, (1907) V.L.R., 94; 28 A.L.T., 135; 12 A.L.R., 577.

SHIP AND SHIPPING.

Ship—Bill of lading—Exception, construction of—Heat of holds—Neglect of master, mariners or others in service of owners—Fruit damaged by negligent omission to admit air to hold.]—Fruit was shipped at Naples in good order and condition, fit for travelling, and properly packed, to be delivered under the bill of lading at Melbourne "in the like good order and condition," but arrived in a damaged condition owing to the negligence of the servants of the shipowners in not admitting sufficient air to the hold in which the fruit was carried. The bill of lading exempted the shipowners from liability for any loss or damage from certain causes or perils, including *inter alia* "effects of climate," "heat of holds" and "neglect, default, or error in judgment of the master, mariners, engineers, or others in the service of the owners." In an action by the shippers against the shipowners, *Held*, that on the true construction of the bill of lading the "neglect" should not be limited to subject matters other than those previously specified and that the shipowners were exempted from liability for any neglect or default of any of their servants in the discharge of any of their duties connected with bringing the ship and its cargo from port to port. *Henty* v. *Orient Steam Navigation Co. Ltd.*, 29 A.L.T., 48; 13 A.L.R., 516. *Hodges, J.* (1907).

Order XXXVI., rr. 4, 6 (Rules of 1884)—Right to jury—Negligence in navigating ship—Collision.]—An action to recover damages for negligence in the navigation of the defendant's ship whereby it collided with that of the plaintiff is within Order XXXVI., r. 6 of the *Rules of the Supreme Court* 1884, and either party is entitled to have it tried with a jury. *Union Steamship &c. Co.* v. *The Melbourne Harbour Trust Commissioners*, (1907) V.L.R., 204; 29 A.L.T., 63; 13 A.L.R., 136. (*Hood, J.*).

Operation of the Constitution and laws of the Commonwealth—Commonwealth Conciliation and Arbitration Act 1904 (No. 13 of 1904)—Jurisdiction of Court of Conciliation and Arbitration—Industrial dispute—" Ships whose first port of clearance and whose port of destination are in the Commonwealth "—Commonwealth of Australia Constitution Act (63 & 64 Vict. c. 12), sec. V.]—*See* COMMONWEALTH OF AUSTRALIA CONSTITUTION, col. 123. *Merchant Service Guild of Australasia* v. *Archibald Currie & Co.*, (1908) 5 C.L.R., 737; 14 A.L.R., 438.

Principal and agent—Agent for foreign shipping company—Sale of passenger's ticket—Failure by principal to carry passenger on terms mentioned in ticket—Liability of agent—No undertaking by agent that passenger should be so carried.]—*See* CONTRACT OR AGREEMENT, col. 214. *Cheong* v. *Lohmann*, (1907) V.L.R., 571; 28 A.L.T., 252; 13 A.L.R., 269.

SLANDER.

See DEFAMATION.

SOLICITOR.

I. ARTICLED CLERKS; ADMISSION TO PRACTICE.

Barrister and solicitor—Articled clerk—Leave to serve as clerk in Crown Law Department, during service under articles of clerkship—Rules of the Council of Legal Education of 28th November, 1905.]—Leave granted to an articled clerk to act as clerk in the Public Service, Crown Law Department, while articled to the Crown Solicitor. *Re Shelton*, 32 A.L.T., 135. *a' Beckett, Hodges* and *Hood, JJ.* (1910).

Admission—Clerk articled to Crown Solicitor—Covenant by Crown Solicitor to teach " if he shall continue Crown Solicitor . . . to the extent of his official opportunities and so far as the exigencies of the Public Service and the relative Status of the parties as members in common of the Public Service of Victoria will permit "—Admission granted.]—*In re Clarke*, 12 A.L.R. (C.N.), 18. *The Judges* (1906).

Practice—Barrister and solicitor, admission of—Articles of clerkship—Engaging in other employment—" Coaching " in legal subjects —Rules for the Admission of Barristers and Solicitors, 28th November, 1905—23 & 24 Vict. c. 127, sec. 10.]—The fact that an articled clerk, during the period of his articles, " coaches " law students outside of office hours, and so as not to interfere with his service under the articles, does not constitute a breach of the prohibition in sec. 10 of 23 & 24 Vict. c. 127, against engaging in any employment other than the employment of clerk to his employer during the term of service. *In re Eager*, 32 A.L.T., 145; 17 A.L.R., 90. *Madden, C.J., a' Beckett* and *Hodges, JJ.* (1911).

Barrister and solicitor, admission of— Articles of clerkship—Engaging in other employment—Teaching—Rules for the Admission of Barristers and Solicitors, 28th November, 1905—23 & 24 Vict. c. 127, sec. 10.]—An articled clerk during his term of service under articles with the consent and approval of the solicitor to whom he was articled taught elocution out of office hours, for three hours a week. The teaching did not interfere with his work as an articled clerk. On appeal from the refusal by the Board of Examiners to grant him a certificate for admission as a barrister and solicitor, *Held*, that, having regard to the practice of the Court, such teaching did not disentitle the clerk to a certificate. *In re Eager*, 32 A.L.T., 145; 17 A.L.R., 90, approved. *In re Bloom*, (1911) V.L.R., 313; 33 A.L.T., 26; 17 A.L.R., 331. *The Judges, Madden, C.J., a' Beckett, Hodges, Hood* and *Cussen, JJ.*

Barrister and solicitor—Application for admission—Misconduct of applicant—Previous practice of solicitor in name of qualified solicitor—22 Geo. II., c. 46, sec. 11.]—A person who had carried on, whilst unqualified, the business of a solicitor in a country town, in the name of a duly qualified Melbourne solicitor, having otherwise qualified as a barrister and solicitor, applied to the Board of Examiners for a certificate that he was a fit and proper person to be admitted. The Board refused his application on the ground of his misconduct in having carried on such business under the name of another person who was a solicitor. *Held*, on appeal, that such misconduct made the applicant not a fit and proper person to be admitted, but that it should not necessarily be for ever a bar against admission. *Re X.*, (1907) V.L.R., 305; 29 A.L.T., 3; 13 A.L.R., 268. *Madden, C.J., Hood* and *Cussen, JJ.*

Legal Practitioners Reciprocity Act 1903 (No. 1887), sec. 2—Rules for the Admission of Barristers and Solicitors, 16th February, 1905, r. 11—Rules of the Supreme Court of New South Wales, 19th December, 1904, r. 484—Admission of New South Wales practitioner still practising in New South Wales.]— A legal practitioner of New South Wales is not entitled to be admitted as a barrister and solicitor in Victoria under the *Legal Practitioners Reciprocity Act* 1903, unless he has ceased to practice in New South Wales, inasmuch as under rule 484 of the *Rules of the Supreme Court of New South Wales*, 19th December 1904 a Victorian practitioner cannot be admitted in New South Wales unless he has ceased to practise in Victoria. *In re Tietyens*, (1906) V.L.R., 354; 27 A.L.T., 206; 12 A.L.R. (C.N.), 9. *The Judges of the Supreme Court.*

Legal Practitioners Reciprocity Act (No. 1887), secs. 2, 7—Rules for the Admission of Barristers and Solicitors (February 16th, 1905), rr. 11, 12—Admission of practitioner from other State—Determination that reciprocity exists—Council of Legal Education—Whether it may impose terms and conditions.]— Although the Council of Legal Education has determined that there exists a reciprocal right of admission of Victorian barristers and solicitors to practise in another State, it has power to impose terms and conditions in regard to the admission of practitioners from that State. *Re Pirani*, (1907) V.L.R., 310; 29 A.L.T., 66; 13 A.L.R., 306. *Madden, C.J., Hood* and *Cussen, JJ.*

Legal Practitioners Reciprocity Act 1903 (No. 1887)—Barrister and solicitor, admission of—Rules for Admission of Barristers and Solicitors (February 16th, 1905), r. 11—Fees payable on admission—Whether Council of Legal Education may fix.]— The Council of Legal Education has no power to fix the fees payable on the admission of a barrister and solicitor to practice. Rule 11 of the *Rules*

for the Admission of Barristers and Solicitors of February 16th, 1905, is, accordingly, *ultra vires* in so far as it fixes the fees so payable. *Re Burgess*, (1907) V.L.R., 307; 29 A.L.T., 60; 13 A.L.R., 272. *Madden, C.J., Hood* and *Cussen, JJ.*

II.—SOLICITOR AND CLIENT.

Divorce—Practice—Alimony—No claim for alimony in petition—Service of summons for alimony after decree nisi—Retainer of respondent's proctor.]— After a decree *nisi* for dissolution of marriage has been granted on the petition of a wife which contains no claim for alimony, the proctor who was retained by the respondent to defend the suit has no authority by virtue of such retainer to accept service of a summons asking for an order that the respondent pay alimony to the petitioner. *Richardson* v. *Richardson*, (1909) V.L.R., 448; 31 A.L.T., 66; 15 A.L.R., 515. *Hood, J.*

Statute of Limitations—Acknowledgment—Solicitor acting in connection with claim — Whether debtor's agent to make an acknowledgment.]— *Quaere*, whether a mere general statement that solicitors are acting for a client in connection with a certain claim, and nothing more, is sufficient evidence that such solicitors are agents of the debtor to make an acknowledgment of debt. *Holden* v. *Lawes Wittewronge*, (1912) V.L.R., 82; 33 A.L.T., 153; 18 A.L.R., 28. *Cussen, J.*

Legal Profession Practice Act 1891 (No. 1216)—Solicitor, responsibility of—Whether protected by counsel's advice.]— *Quaere*, whether counsel's advice is any protection to a solicitor since the *Legal Profession Practice Act* 1891, even on points of law. *Garrick* v. *Garrick*; *Sutton, Co-respondent*, (1908) V.L.R., 420; 30 A.L.T., 21; 14 A.L.R., 312 *Hood, J.*

III.—RIGHT OF AUDIENCE; PRIVILEGE.

Justices Act 1890 (No. 1105), sec. 77 (11)—Ordering witnesses out of Court at request of party—Discretion of Justices—Counsel and solicitor of opposite party subpoenaed as witnesses—Permission to remain in Court, effect of.]— The provisions of sec. 77 (11) of the *Justices Act* 1890 do not necessarily make it improper for Justices to permit the counsel and solicitor appearing for a party to remain in Court, although the opposite party has subpoenaed them as witnesses, and has requested that all witnesses be ordered out of Court. Even if it were an error to permit them to remain, the proceedings would not thereby be invalidated, if it were evident that the request for their removal was made for the purpose of obstruction, and that the denial of the request in no way resulted in a denial of justice or prevented a proper hearing of the case. *Barry* v. *Cullen*, (1906) V.L.R., 393 ; 27 A.L.T., 227 ; 12 A.L.R., 235. *a' Beckett, A.-C.J.* (1906).

Interrogatories — Privilege — Communications between solicitor and client—Abuse of process—Allegation of fraud.]—The plaintiff sued the defendants for malicious arrest and for abuse of the process of the Court. The plaintiff administered interrogatories to the defendants as to whether the defendants had obtained from their solicitor before they arrested the plaintiff any advice as to his liability. *Held*, that if the arrest was unlawful, the unlawful proceeding did not begin until after the advice had been given, and that as the communications between the defendants and their solicitor were not shown to have been made in furtherance of an illegal object, they were privileged, and that leave to appeal from the decision of the Supreme Court (reported at (1910) V.L.R., 289 ; 31 A.L.T., 179 ; 16 A.L.R., 137) should be refused. *Varawa* v. *Howard Smith & Co. Ltd.*, (1910) 10 C.L.R., 382 ; 16 A.L.R., 526. H.C., *Griffith, C.J., O'Connor* and *Isaacs, JJ.*

IV.—PARTNERSHIP.

Partnership—Contract with individual who afterwards takes another into partnership—Election to hold firm liable on contract—Solicitors—Liability for fraud of co-partner.]—Plaintiff, having agreed to purchase a piece of land, instructed B. to act as his solicitor, and do what was necessary for completing the purchase. While the business was pending, B. took the defendant into partnership, one of the terms of the partnership agreement being that all outstanding costs owing to

B. should become part of the assets of the firm. Plaintiff knew of the partnership, and while the business was still pending, received a bill of costs from and in the name of the firm, paid part of the bill—amounting to £4 10s.—to defendant at the firm offices by cheque payable to the firm or bearer, and was given a receipt by defendant in the firm name. Shortly afterwards plaintiff called at the offices of the firm, and asked for B. who was out. He waited until B. returned, and then paid him a cheque for £105 representing the balance of the purchase money which was outstanding on mortgage, and a cheque for one guinea for costs of the release. Both the latter cheques were payable to B. or bearer. The cheques for £4 10s. and one guinea were each paid into the firm's business account, but the £105 was paid by B. into his private account and misappropriated by him. The work in respect of which the costs were paid was never in fact done either by B. or by the firm. B.'s estate was subsequently sequestrated. *Held*, that the plaintiff had not elected to continue to employ B. alone, but had treated the firm as his solicitors, and the defendant had treated him as a client of the firm and was liable for B.'s fraud. *Held*, also, that defendant was liable to refund the amounts paid for costs. *British Homes Assurance Corporation* v. *Paterson*, (1902) 2 Ch., 404, distinguished. *Reid* v. *Silberberg*, (1906) V.L.R., 126. *a' Beckett, J.*

V.—SOLICITOR ACTING AS TRUSTEE.

Solicitor—Trustee—Trustee member of a firm of solicitors—Charges for non-professional work—Collection of rents.]—By his will testator appointed one of his trustees who was a member of a firm of solicitors " to be the solicitor of my trust property " and directed " that he shall conduct all the legal business of my estate and shall be entitled to make and receive all such charges and emoluments for business, whether of an ordinary professional or any other character done by him in relation to the administration of my estate or the execution of the trusts of this my will as he would have been entitled to make and receive in respect of such business as if he had not been a trustee or executor." Testator also provided that his trustees might deduct and retain a commission or allowance for their trouble. *Held*, that the trustees were authorized to charge against the estate moneys paid to the solicitor-trustee's firm for work which the trustees without express authority would have been justified in employing a stranger to the trust to do. But, *semble*, they would not be authorized to charge the estate in respect of a payment to the solicitor-trustee in relation to work which ordinarily he would have been bound to do as trustee without payment. *Swanson* v. *Emmerton*, (1909) V.L.R., 387; 31 A.L.T., 28; 15 A.L.R., 368. *Cussen, J.*

VI.—APPOINTMENT OF COUNSEL AND SOLICITOR FOR DEFENCE OF PERSON COMMITTED FOR TRIAL.

Judiciary Act 1903 (No. 6 of 1903), sec. 69 (3)—Indictable offences against the Commonwealth—Committal for trial—Appointment of counsel for defence—Application—Materials in support—" Interests of justice."]—In an application under sec. 69 (3) of the *Judiciary Act* 1903 the affidavit in support should state the facts with regard to the means of the accused in such a way as to enable the Judge to decide that the applicant is without adequate means to provide for his defence. A mere general statement by the solicitor for the accused, that he believes it would be unsafe for the accused to be tried without being represented by counsel to argue points of law which deponent believes can be raised in favour of accused, is not sufficient to enable the Judge to decide whether it is desirable in the interests of justice than an appointment of counsel for the defence should be made. In deciding whether such appointment should be made, the Judge should contrast what would or might occur if counsel were not present at the trial, with what might be expected to arise if counsel were present. Facts and circumstances which may render the appointment of counsel for the defence desirable in the interests of justice considered. *Rex* v. *Forrest*, (1912) V.L.R., 466; 34 A.L.T., 95; 18 A.L.R., 495. *Cussen, J.* (1912).

Judiciary Act 1903 (No. 6 of 1903), sec. 69—(3)—Legal assistance for defence of prisoner—Whether solicitor as well as counsel may be provided.]—*Semble.*—Under sec. 69 (3) the Attorney-General has power to provide not only counsel for the defence, but also a solicitor to instruct such counsel. *Rex* v. *Forrest*, (1912) V.L.R., 466; 34 A.L.T., 95; 18 A.L.R., 495. *Cussen, J.* (1912).

VII.—CONVEYANCING BY UNQUALIFIED PERSON.

Supreme Court Act 1890 (No. 1142), sec. 261—Conveyancing by unqualified persons—" Conveyance or other deed or instrument in writing relating to real estate "—Agreement between father and son for transfer of land after father's death in consideration of son's support.]—Sec. 261 of the *Supreme Court Act* 1890 in prohibiting unqualified persons from drawing or preparing for any fee, gain or reward " any conveyance or other deed or instrument in writing relating to real estate " is confined in its operation to something akin in its nature to what is commonly known as conveyancing. A document which is really in its essence an agreement between father and son that, in consideration of the son's supporting the father during the latter's lifetime certain land owned by the father is to be transferred to the son after the father's death, does not come within the section. *In re Wayth*, 5 V.L.R. (L.), 389; 1 A.L.T., 97, followed. *In re Simpson and Fricke*; *Ex parte Robinson*, (1910) V.L.R., 177; 31 A.L.T., 163; 16 A.L.R., 125. *Hood, J.*

VIII.—COSTS.

(a) Bills of Costs.

Supreme Court Act 1890 (No. 1142), sec. 209—Solicitor—Client—Bill of costs—Order for delivery—Discretion of Court.]—Under sec. 209 of the *Supreme Court Act* 1890 the Court has discretion to refuse to order the delivery of a bill of costs. *Bear* v. *Waxman*, (1912) V.L.R., 292; 34 A.L.T., 6; 18 A.L.R., 269. *F.C., Madden, C.J., Hood* and *Cussen, JJ.*

Taxation—Solicitor and client—Bill of costs, what is—Moneys paid to solicitors in England in respect of appeal to Privy Council—Account of balance of lump sum so paid attached to bill of costs—" Moderation " of charges—

Whether amount paid to English solicitors "moderated" or "taxed"—Jurisdiction to review decision of Taxing Master.]—Attached to B. and H.'s bill of costs, which was signed and dated, was a cash account in which the balance of a lump sum was charged as payment to solicitors in England acting in connection with an application for leave to appeal to the Privy Council from the decision in the action in which the costs set out in the bill were incurred. The order of the Court directing taxation did not expressly provide for liberty to charge all sums paid by the solicitors to or on account of the client. The Taxing Master during the taxation in fact dealt with the payment made to the English solicitors, and, to enable him to do so, B. and H. gave him details of the charges of those solicitors. The client had provided the moneys to pay the costs of the English solicitors. *Held*, that the balance charged as payment of the English solicitors did not form part of the bill of costs. *Held*, also, that, under the circumstances, the Taxing Master had not taxed the English solicitor's charges as part of the bill, but had "moderated" them as if they had been charges made by a commission agent. *Semble*, the Court had no jurisdiction to review the Taxing Master's decision. *In re Lamrock, Brown and Hall's Costs*, (1908) V.L.R., 238; 29 A.L.T., 214; 14 A.L.R., 81. *Cussen, J.*

(b) *Agreements for Remuneration of Solicitors.*

Supreme Court Act 1890 (No. 1142), sec. 262—Solicitor—Client—Costs—Agreement as to solicitor's remuneration—Agreement to pay lump sum for work wholly past.]—Sec. 262 of the *Supreme Court Act* 1890 does not relate to agreements between solicitor and client as to the amount of the solicitor's professional remuneration for work wholly past. Such agreements are governed by the rules of common law and equity. *Bear v. Waxman*, (1912) V.L.R., 292; 34 A.L.T., 6; 18 A.L.R., 269. F.C., *Madden, C.J., Hood and Cussen, JJ.*

(c) *Taxation.*

For complete statement, *see* COSTS, cols. 268 *et seq.*

Order LXV., r. 27 (38a) (Rules of 1906)—Taxation—Costs increased by misconduct or negligence of solicitor—Report of Taxing officer—Duty of Judge, nature of.]—On a report by the Taxing Officer under Order LXV., r. 27 (38A) the jurisdiction of the Judge is not disciplinary, but in the nature of a review of taxation. *Woolf v. Willis*, (1911) 13 C.L.R., 23; 17 A.L.R., 454. H.C., *Griffith, C.J., Barton and O'Connor, JJ.*

Order LXV., r. 27 (38a), (Rules of 1906)—Taxation—Costs increased by misconduct or negligence of solicitor—Burden of proof.]—Where it is alleged under Order LXV., r. 27 (38A) that costs have been increased by the misconduct or negligence of the solicitor the onus is upon the client to establish that he has been damnified and to what extent. *Woolf v. Willis*, (1911) 13 C.L.R., 23; 17 A.L.R., 454. H.C., *Griffith, C.J., Barton and O'Connor, JJ.*

Taxation—Solicitor and client—Country solicitor—Attendance at trial at Melbourne—Costs of, when an unusual expense—Knowledge of client that they may not be allowed as between party and party—Necessity of proving.]—B. and H. were a firm of solicitors carrying on business at Melbourne and Benalla. H. resided in Melbourne and did the firm's business there and B. did the firm's business at Benalla. H. attended at the trial of an action in Melbourne and the scale fee for such attendance was claimed in the bill of costs and allowed. B., also, attended at the trial. *Held*, that the costs of B.'s attendance and travelling expenses were an unusual expense and that such costs should not be allowed unless the solicitor proved that before they were incurred the client knew that they would not or might not be allowed as between solicitor and client. *In re Lamrock, Brown & Hall's Costs*, (1908) V.L.R., 238; 29 A.L.T., 214; 14 A.L.R., 81. *Cussen, J.*

Taxation—Unusual work—Making copy of witness's evidence for his use—Request of client—Charge for unusual work—When client protected against.]—A charge for making a copy, at the client's request, of a statement made by a very old and important witness for the use of such witness, is not the kind of charge against which the client needs protection as being for unusual work. That kind of charge usually relates to some matter suggested by the solicitor, and which the client may regard as so much part of the controversial proceedings that success will usually mean an order for payment by the other side. *In re Duke's Will*, (1907) V.L.R., 632 ; 29 A.L.T., 50 ; 13 A.L.R., 477. *Cussen, J.*

Taxation—Solicitor and client—Unusual charges, payment of by solicitor—Client's knowledge of unusual character of charges—Knowledge not obtained from solicitor.]— Where an amount above the ordinary or scale fees is paid by a solicitor on behalf and with the sanction of his client, who knows that the amount is unusual and may not or will not be allowed on taxation between party and party, such payment may be properly chargeable by the solicitor against the client although the client's knowledge was not based on the information of the solicitor. *Re Duke's Will*, (1907) V.L.R., 632 ; 29 A.L.T., 50 ; 13 A.L.R., 477. *Cussen, J.* (1907).

County Court — Costs—Counsel's fees—Practitioner conducting trial on behalf of his client.]—Where a party's practitioner attends Court and conducts the trial on behalf of his client he is not entitled to counsel's fee on brief as set out in Item 11 of the Scale of Costs. His fees for the first and subsequent days of the trial are governed by Items 17 and 44 of such Scale. *O'Brien* v. *Victorian Railways Commissioners*, 27 A.L.T. (Supplement), 11 ; 12 A.L.R. (C.N.), 6. *Judge Eagleson* (1906).

County Court—Costs—Solicitor plaintiff—Acting professionally on his own behalf—Costs of perusing documents—Perusing interrogatories—Schedule of Scale of Costs, Item 28.]—Where the plaintiff, a solicitor, obtains judgment with costs in an action wherein he acted as solicitor on his own behalf, he is entitled to the fee fixed by the Schedule of Scale of Costs for the perusal of all necessary documents, and he accordingly may charge under Item 28 for perusing the defendant's interrogatories. *Hopkins* v. *Forster*, 32

A.L.T. (Supplement), 5 ; 16 A.L.R. (C.N.), 6. *Judge Chomley* (1910).

County Court—Costs—Taxation—Solicitor party to action acting professionally on own behalf—Solicitor called as witness—" Attending Court "—Witnesses' expenses—Schedule of Scale of Costs (The County Court Rules 1891), Items 14, 15, 16.]—A solicitor was party to an action in which he acted professionally on his own behalf and was also called as a witness. *Held*, that he was entitled to be allowed his charge for " attending Court " under Items 14, 15 and 16 of the Schedule of Scale of Costs, or his expenses as a witness, whichever allowance was the higher, but not both. *Hopkins* v. *Forster*, 32 A.L.T. (Supplement), 5 ; 16 A.L.R. (C.N.), 6. *Judge Chomley* (1910).

(d) Lien.

Solicitor to trustee of deceased person's estate—Lien for costs.]—A solicitor to the trustee of the estate of a deceased person is not a solicitor to the estate and therefore does not acquire a lien over the trust property for his costs. *In re Nolan*, (No. 2), 30 A.L.T. (Supplement), 1 ; 14 A.L.R. (C.N.), 25. *Judge Moule* (1908).

Court of Mines—Company in liquidation—Delivery up of Company's property to the liquidator—Costs—Solicitor's lien—Companies Act 1890 (No. 1074), sec. 274.]—An order made under sec. 274 of the *Companies Act 1890* for delivery up to the liquidator of any books, documents or property belonging or relating to the company in the possession of a solicitor deprives the solicitor of his lien thereon for costs. *Re Mount Murphy Wolfram Co., No Liability*, 29 A.L.T. (Supplement), 19 ; 14 A.L.R. (C.N.), 6. *Judge Box* (1908).

SPECIAL CASE.

See also, DUTIES ON THE ESTATES OF DECEASED PERSONS ; GENERAL SESSIONS ; INCOME TAX ACTS ; STAMPS ACTS.

Case stated.—Right to begin.]—The person who began in the Court below should begin upon a special case stated. *Mooney* v. *Lucas,*

(1909) V.L.R., 333 ; 15 A.L.R., 296, *sub nomine In re Lucas, Ex parte Mooney*, 31 A.L.T., 3. F.C., *Hodges* and *Hood, JJ.* (*a' Beckett, J., dissentiente*).

SPECIFIC PERFORMANCE.

See VENDOR AND PURCHASER.

STAMPS ACTS.

Stamps Act 1890 (No. 1140), sec. 81, Third Schedule—Stamps Act 1892 (No. 1274), Schedule—" Promissory note " — Mortgage debenture charging property and providing means for enforcement of security.]—A document purporting to be a " First Mortgage Debenture " issued by a company incorporated under the Companies Acts and charging certain of its property with the payment of the moneys thereby secured, and providing, amongst other things, means for the enforcement of the security and the appointment of a receiver, is not a " promissory note " within the meaning of sec. 81 of the *Stamps Act* 1890. *Hickling* v. *Todd*, 15 V.L.R., 154 ; 10 A.L.T., 236, followed. *In re the Stamps Acts*, (1906) V.L.R., 364 ; 27 A.L.T., 204 ; 12 A.L.R., 186. *a' Beckett, J.* (1906).

Stamps Act 1892 (No. 1274), Schedule, Part VIII.—Settlement or gift, deed of—Instrument upon valuable consideration—Sale of land, what is.]—The elements necessary for a sale of land are two persons with opposing interests, one trying to get the land for as little as he can, and the other trying to get as much for the land as he can. *Kelly* v. *Collector of Imposts*, 29 A.L.T., 91 ; 13 A.L.R., 613. F.C., *Hodges, Hood* and *Cussen, JJ.* (1907).

Stamps Act 1892 (No. 1274), Schedule, Part VIII.—Settlement or Gift, deed of—Consideration other than bona fide adequate pecuniary consideration.]—By a transfer under the *Transfer of Land Act* 1890 a father aged 75 years transferred to his son land admitted to be worth £9,000, the consideration being the payment of about £5,500 to the father, and a verbal promise to pay the sum of £400 to a brother of the transferree and to maintain the father for the rest of his life. *Held*, that the transfer was not for *bona fide* adequate pecuniary consideration, and that the instrument of transfer was liable to duty under Part VIII. of the Schedule to the *Stamps Act* 1892. *Davidson* v. *Armytage*, 4 C.L.R., 205 ; 12 A.L.R., 538, discussed. *Kelly* v. *Collector of Imposts*, 29 A.L.T., 91 ; 13 A.L.R., 613. F.C., *Hodges, Hood* and *Cussen, JJ.* (1907).

Stamps—Family arrangement— Exchange and partition or division—Conveyance or transfer on sale—Stamps Act 1890 (No. 1140), secs. 93, 95, 97, Schedule III.—Stamps Act 1892 (No. 1274), sec. 17, Schedule V.]—Three sisters, A, B, and C, being owners as tenants in common in equal shares of certain property consisting of land mortgages marketable securities and money agreed that A. should take her share of the property so held. In order to carry out this agreement, instruments were executed vesting certain of the mortgages and securities in A. solely, and transferring to B. and C. the interest of A in the rest of the property, including the land, which was valued as a whole at £3,517 5s. 9d., *Held*, that these instruments were taxable as a conveyance or transfer on sale of real property within the meaning of the *Stamps Act* 1890, Schedule IIIA. at an amount based on £1,172 8s. 7d., the value of A's third share in the land. *Davies* v. *Collector of Imposts*, (1908) V.L.R., 272 ; 29 A.L.T., 233 ; 14 A.L.R., 149. *Cussen, J.* (1908).

Stamps Act 1892 (No. 1274), secs. 4, 28—Schedule, Part VIII.—Settlement, meaning of—Special power of appointment created by instrument executed prior to passing of Act—Power exercised after passing of Act—Fee simple appointed to certain of the objects of the power.]—By an instrument executed before the passing of the *Stamps Act* 1892, certain lands were settled, subject to the life estate of A., upon trust for all, or such one or more exclusively of the others, of H., F. and B. for such estates or interests and in such manner as A. should by deed or will appoint, and in default of appointment for H., F. and B. as tenants in common. After the passing of the said Act, A., by two deeds appointed the lands to F. and B. in fee subject to the life estate. *Held*, that such deeds were chargeable with duty as settlements within the meaning of Part VIII. of the Schedule of the *Stamps Act* 1892. *Moffat v. Collector of Imposts*, 22 V.L.R., 164 ; 18 A.L.T., 144 ; 2 A.L.R., 255, approved. *Davidson* v. *Armytage*, 4 C.L.R., 205 ; 12 A.L.R., 538. H.C., *Griffith, C.J., Barton* and *O'Connor, JJ.* (1906).

Stamps Act 1892 (No. 1274), Schedule, Part VIII. — " Deed of settlement " — Liability to tax, how to be determined—Whether necessary that instrument should create new beneficial interests.]—The question whether an instrument is or is not taxable under the *Stamps Act* 1892 must be determined by an examination of the instrument itself, and not upon extrinsic evidence. Any instrument which on its face purports to be a charter of future rights and obligations with respect to the property comprised in it, and which contains such limitations as are ordinarily contained in settlements, is a settlement or an agreement to settle within the meaning of Part VIII. of the Schedule to the *Stamps Act* 1892, whether these rights and obligations could have been established *aliunde* or not. An instrument may be a deed of settlement within Part VIII., although it does not create a new beneficial interest in any person. *Wiseman* v. *Collector of Imposts*, 21 V.L.R., 743 ; 17 A.L.T., 251, overruled. *Davidson* v. *Chirnside*, (1908) 7 C.L.R., 324 ; 14 A.L.R., 686. H.C., *Griffith, C.J., Barton O'Connor, Isaacs* and *Higgins, JJ.*

Stamps Act 1892 (No. 1274), secs. 27, 28, Schedule, Part VIII. — Settlement in pursuance of power in will—Trustees of settlement holding upon same trusts as trustees of will—No new beneficial interests created—Deed of settlement, whether liable to duty —Instrument of appointment.]—A testator by his will directed his trustees to set aside a fund on certain trusts, and he authorized them in their discretion to cause the fund to be settled upon trustees to be nominated by them upon trusts corresponding with those previously declared. The trustees of the will executed an indenture which recited the trusts of the fund and that the trustees of the will would, on execution of the deed by the other parties thereto, pay the fund to those other parties. The indenture then witnessed that the trustees of the will appointed the other parties to be trustees of the fund, and that those trustees of the fund should hold the fund upon the trusts declared in the will, and upon no other trusts whatever. The indenture then continued " it being the purport and intent of these presents only to nominate or constitute trustees of . . . the fund to hold the same upon the trusts in the said will declared concerning the same and not to create or affect any new or existing beneficial interests therein." *Held*, that the indenture was a deed of settlement within the meaning of Part VIII. of the Schedule to the *Stamps Act* 1892, but was also an instrument of appointment in favour of persons specially named in the will as the objects of a power of appointment within the meaning of section 28 of that Act, and that as duty had been paid on the property in respect of which the power of appointment was given, the indenture was exempted from taxation under the Act. *Davidson* v. *Armytage*, 4 C.L.R., 205 ; 12 A.L.R., 538, explained and distinguished. *Davidson* v. *Chirnside*, (1908) 7 C.L.R., 324 ; 14 A.L.R., 686. H.C., *Griffith, C.J., Barton, O'Connor, Isaacs* and *Higgins, JJ.*

Stamps Act 1892 (No. 1274), sec. 28— " Power of appointment," what is—" Instrument of appointment."]—*Per Griffith, C.J., Barton, O'Connor, Isaacs* and *Higgins, JJ.*— The words " power of appointment " in sec. 28 of the *Stamps Act* 1892 include any authority, in whatever form conferred, to make a disposition of property by deed or other writing, in order to give full effect to the will of the settlor or testator, and the words " instrument of appointment " include any instrument by which such a disposition is made. *Per Higgins, J.*—An instrument operates as an appointment if it prescribe or declare the destination of property apart from any right of ownership that the appointor may have. *Davidson* v. *Chirnside*, (1908) **7** C.L.R., 324 ; 14 A.L.R., 686.

Stamp duty—Conveyance or transfer on sale of real property—Property conveyed to purchaser in separate parts by different instruments—Part of land under Transfer of Land Act and part under general law—Exemption of first £50—Stamps Act 1890 (No. 1140), secs. 32, 34, 98 (1)—Third Schedule, Schedule III. (a) (b).]—Where land, part of which was under the *Transfer of Land Act* 1890, and part not, was contracted to be sold for one consideration for the whole, but was conveyed and transferred to the purchaser in separate parts by different conveyances and instruments of transfer, a specific portion of the total consideration being appropriated to each part so conveyed or transferred, *Held*, that an exemption was allowable in the assessment of duty under the *Stamps Act* 1890 in respect of the first £50 stated as consideration in each instrument of conveyance or transfer. *Hendy* v. *Collector of Imposts*, (1907) V.L.R., 704 ; 29 A.L.T., 89 ; 13 A.L.R., 612. F.C., *Madden, C.J., Hodges* and *Cussen, JJ.*

Duty—Amount of—Basis of calculation— " Value of the property," meaning of— Stamps Act 1892 (No. 1274), Schedule.]— The value of the actual interest dealt with in a settlement is the basis on which duty is to be assessed. Accordingly, a deed exercising a power to appoint lands subject to a life interest is chargeable with duty computed on the value of the expectant interest in remainder. *Davidson* v. *Armytage*, 4 C.L.R., 205 ; 12 A.L.R., 538. H.C., *Griffith, C.J., Barton* and *O'Connor, JJ.* (1906).

Special case—Right to begin—Stamps Act 1890 (No. 1140), sec. 71.]—Upon a special case stated under the *Stamps Act* 1890, the alleged taxpayer has the right to begin. *Armytage* v. *Collector of Imposts*, (1906) V.L.R., 504 ; 28 A.L.T., 9 ; 12 A.L.R., 305. F.C., *a'Beckett, A.-C.J., Hodges* and *Hood, JJ.* (1906).

Stamps Act 1890 (No. 1140), sec. 23—Stamps —Offence—Fraudulently affixing stamp removed from another document—Fraudulently affixing adhesive stamp to other documents.]— It is an offence under sec. 23 of the *Stamps Act* 1890 for a person fraudulently to affix to a document or paper an adhesive stamp which has been removed either fraudulently or innocently from another document. *Burvett* v. *Moody*, (1909) V.L.R., 126 ; 30 A.L.T., 160 ; 15 A.L.R., 91. *Madden, C.J.* (1909).

STATE COURT.

See CONSTITUTIONAL LAW.

STATEMENT OF CLAIM.

See PRACTICE AND PLEADING.

STATE SCHOOL TEACHER.

Local Government Act 1903 (No. 1893), sec. 249 (1)—Rates—Rateable property—" Land the property of His Majesty used for public purposes "—Teacher's residence attached to school.]—*See* LOCAL GOVERNMENT, cols. 858, 859. *Ferntree Gully, President, &c. of* v. *Johnston*, (1909) V.L.R., 113 ; 30 A.L.T., 194 ; 15 A.L.R., 62.

STATUTE.

See also INTERPRETATION, cols. 744 *et seq.*

Interpretation of Statute—Punctuation, effect of.]—The punctuation of Statutes does not control the sense if the meaning is otherwise reasonably clear. *Charlton, President &c. of Shire of* v. *Ruse*, (1912) 14 C.L.R., 220 ; 18 A.L.R., 207 ; H.C., *Griffith, C.J., Barton* and *Isaacs, JJ.*

Patents Act 1903 (No. 21 of 1903),—Forms of expression adopted from English Patent Acts—In what sense used by Commonwealth Parliament.]—*See* PATENT. *National Phonograph Co. of Australia* v. *Mencke*, 7 C.L.R., at p. 529 ; 15 A.L.R., at p. 13.

STATUTE OF FRAUDS.

I.—MEMORANDUM, SUFFICIENCY OF.

Instruments Act 1890 (No. 1103), secs. 208, 209—Statutue of Frauds (29 Car. II. c. 3)—Contract for sale of land—Signature to note or memorandum—Signature by amanuensis in presence and by direction of party to be charged, whether sufficient.]—To satisfy the requirements of secs. 208 and 209 of the *Instruments Act* 1890, there must be a personal signature by the hand of the party to be charged, or a signature by an agent authorised in writing by the party to be charged, and the signature by an amanuensis, in the presence by the direction and with the name of the party to be charged, cannot be regarded as a signature by that party with his own hand, and is therefore insufficient. *Thomson* v. *McInnis*, (1911) 12 C.L.R., 562 ; 17 A.L.R., 354. H.C., *Griffith*, *C.J.*, *Barton* and *O'Connor*, *JJ.*

Sale of goods—Memorandum of agreement, whether necessary—Contract itself in writing—Sale of Goods Act 1896 (No. 1422), sec. 9.]—A signed and sent to B a letter offering to sell him goods of the value of £10 and upwards on conditions therein specified. B, by a subsequent letter, accepted A's offer. *Held*, that the provisions of sec. 9 (1) of the *Sale of Goods Act* 1896 requiring a note or memorandum of the contract did not preclude B from enforcing the agreement to sell. *Patterson* v. *Dolman*, (1908) V.L.R., 354 ; 29 A.L.T., 256 ; 14 A.L.R., 240. F.C., *a'Beckett*, *Hodges* and *Cussen*, *JJ.*

Instruments Act 1890 (No. 1103), sec. 208—Memorandum of contract contained in several documents—Agreement to act as manager of company—Agreement implied from Articles of Association and conduct of parties.]—Article 55 of the P company's Articles of Association was to the following effect :—" B.G. shall be the first managing director of the P company and shall hold such office for the term of ten years from August 1st, 1900. B.G. shall be entitled as such managing director to receive out of the funds of the company during his tenure of office the sum of £500 per annum payable by weekly instalments. The remuneration of B.G. after the expiration of the said term of ten years from August 1st 1900 or any other managing director appointed in his stead shall be fixed by the directors." For a period of over four years B.G. acted as managing director of the P company, without any objection by any director or officer or member of the company, and during all that period from August 1st, 1900, was paid for his services at the rate mentioned in the Articles of Association. B.G. signed a consent to act and in the directors' report was returned as managing director. On February 15th, 1905, B.G. wrote a letter to the secretary of the P. company in the following terms :—" Take notice that I claim by virtue of clause 55 of the Articles of Association of the above company and every other right enabling me so to do to be retained in my position as managing director of the P. company for the period of ten years from August 1st, 1900, at the remuneration of £500 as therein provided and that any sale of the company's business assets and goodwill to the D company must be subject to my claim or its equivalent in money." On the next day the secretary wrote in reply as follows :—" In reply to your letter of the 15th which was submitted to my board of directors at their meeting held to-day I am instructed to inform you that the contemplated sale of this company's assets to the D company will carry with it the obligation to carry out the contract with you so far as regards the salary of £500 per annum for the balance of term of ten years from August 1st, 1900." The minutes of the P company showed that the secretary was instructed by the board of directors to write the above letter, and that a copy of that letter was submitted to the board on March 2nd and again approved. In an action by B.G. against the P company for breach of contract to employ him, *Held*, that there was sufficient evidence that a contract was in fact made between the P company and B.G. to employ him for the time and on the terms stated in

Article 55 of the Articles of Association, and that a memorandum of such contract sufficient to comply with the *Statute of Frauds* (*Instruments Act* 1890, sec. 208) was contained in the various documents referred to. *Glass* v. *Pioneer Rubber Works of Australia Ltd.*, (1906) V.L.R., 754 ; 28 A.L.T., 64 ; 12 A.L.R., 529. F.C., *a' Beckett, A.-C.J., Hodges* and *Chomley, JJ.*

Statute of Frauds—Conveyancing Act 1904 (No. 1953), sec. 75—Charge—Parol declaration.]—An equitable charge under sec. 75 of the *Conveyancing Act* 1904 may be created by parol. *In re Smith* ; *Smith* v. *Smith*, (1909) V.L.R., 91 ; 30 A.L.T., 214 ; 15 A.L.R., 25. *Hood, J.*

II.—PAROL EVIDENCE.

Instruments Act 1890 (No. 1103), sec. 208—Sale of land—Note or memorandum—Several documents—Parol evidence, when admissible to connect—Reference to document—Reference to transaction in which document may or may not have been written.]—Where the memorandum of a contract is sought to be constituted from several documents, the reference in the document signed by the party to be charged must be to some other document the identity of which may be proved by parol evidence, and not merely to some transaction in the course of which another document may or may not have been written. *Held*, therefore, that the words, " purchase money " in a receipt given by the vendor of land for a sum of money " being a deposit and first part purchase money " could not refer to another document and that parol evidence was not admissible. *Thomson* v. *Mc Innes*, (1911) 12 C.L.R., 562 ; 17 A.L.R., 354. H.C., *Griffith, C.J., Barton* and *O'Connor, JJ.*

Written contract—Parol evidence to identify subject matter, admissibility of—Latent ambiguity—Language apt to express a specific article of a class or any article of that class—Statute of Frauds.]—Where a written contract for the sale of a particular chattel is couched in general terms equally apt to express the sale of any article of a certain class or the sale of a specific article of that class, parol evidence is admissible to show that a specific article was contracted for and to ascertain and identify that specific article. *Bank of New Zealand* v. *Simpson*, (1900) A.C., 182, followed. *Smith* v. *Jeffryes*, 15 M. & W., 561, and *Wilkie* v. *Hunt*, 1 W.W. & A'B. (L.), 66, distinguished. *Bruton* v. *Farm and Dairy Machinery Co. Proprietary Ltd.*, (1910) V.L.R., 196 ; 31 A.L.T., 200 ; 16 A.L.R., 241. F.C., *Madden, C.J., a' Beckett* and *Hood, JJ.*

Instruments Act 1890 (No. 1103), sec. 208—Parol lease for less than three years—Lessee in possession of premises under existing tenancy.]—An agreement to lease for less than three years premises of which the lessee is already in possession under an existing tenancy, may be proved by parol, and is not affected by the *Statute of Frauds*. The existing tenancy is surrendered by operation of law and the possession of the lessee is referable to the new tenancy. *Knott* v. *Mc Kendrick*, 28 A.L.T. (Supplement), 4 ; 12 A.L.R. (C.N.), 23. *Judge Box* (1906).

Statute of Frauds—Conveyancing Act 1904 (No. 1953), sec. 75—Charge—Parol declaration.]—*See, ante*, I., MEMORANDUM, SUFFICIENCY OF. *In the Will of Smith* ; *Smith* v. *Smith*, (1909) V.L.R., 91 ; 30 A.L.T., 214 ; 15 A.L.R., 25.

STAY OF PROCEEDINGS.

See also, APPEAL, ARBITRATION, COUNTY COURT, PRACTICE AND PLEADING.

Practice—Staying proceedings—Cause of action arising out of jurisdiction.]—Where an action was brought within the jurisdiction of the Supreme Court in respect of a cause of action which arose out of the jurisdiction, *Held*, that a stay was properly refused, the injustice which would be occasioned to the plaintiffs by a stay being as great as that which would be occasioned to the defendants by allowing the action to proceed. *Logan* v. *Bank of Scotland* (*No. 2*), (1906) 1 K.B., 141 ; and *Egbert* v. *Short*, (1907) 2 Ch., 205, considered and applied. *Maritime Insurance Co. Ltd.* v. *Geelong Harbor Trust Commis-*

sioners, (1908) 6 C.L.R., 194; 14 A.L.R., 424. H.C., *Griffith*, *C.J.*, *Barton*, *O'Connor* and *Higgins*, *JJ.*

Practice—Appeal to High Court from Supreme Court—Stay by Supreme Court of proceedings under judgment—Conditions— Order LVIII., r. 16.]—*See* APPEAL, cols. 25, 26. *Howard Smith & Co. Ltd.* v. *Varawa*, (1910) 10 C.L.R., 607.

Judiciary Act 1903 (No. 6), sec. 37—Appeal to High Court from Supreme Court—Cause remitted to Supreme Court for execution of judgment of High Court—Duty of Supreme Court—Stay of proceedings.]—*See* APPEAL, cols. 30, 31. *Peacock* v. *Osborne*, (1907) 4 C.L.R., 1564 ; 13 A.L.R., 565.

Practice—Money paid into Court under Order XIV., r. 6—Defendant successful at trial —Order for payment out of money to defendant—Appeal to High Court—" Execution of the judgment appealed from ''—Stay of execution—High Court Appeal Rules 1903, r. 19.] —*See* APPEAL, col. 27. *Christie* v. *Robinson*, (1907) V.L.R., 118.

STOCK DISEASES ACT.

Stock Diseases Act 1890 (No. 1141), sec. 7 —Travelling sheep—Minimum daily distance not travelled—Lawful excuse—Condition of Sheep.]—On a charge under sec. 74 of the *Stock Diseases Act* 1890 for not driving travelling sheep the minimum daily distance, it is a lawful excuse that the sheep were on the particular day physically unfit to travel the distance. *McCure* v. *Fraser*, (1908) V.L.R., 678 ; 30 A.L.T., 94 ; 14 A.L.R., 561. F.C , *a'Beckett*, *Hodges* and *Cussen*, *JJ.*

Stock Diseases Act 1890 (No. 1141), sec. 74—Travelling sheep—Rate of travelling— " Destination," what is—Ultimate destination—Camping place for a particular night.]— Where travelling sheep are being driven on a journey to a particular place, their " destination " under sec. 74 of the *Stock Diseases Act* 1890 is that place, and is not a place previously fixed upon as a mere camping place for a particular night during the course of

such journey. *McCure* v. *Watts*, (1908) V.L.R., 327 ; 29 A.L.T., 238 ; 14 A.L.R., 219. *Hodges*, *J.*

Stock Diseases Act 1890 (No. 1141), sec. 74 —Travelling sheep—Sheep driven less than six miles—Lawful excuse.]—*Semble*, a lawful excuse for driving sheep less than six miles on a particular day would be established, if the driver proved that they were in poor condition and were stopped for the purpose of being fed. *McCure* v. *Watts*, (1908) V.L.R., 327 ; 29 A.L.T., 238 ; 14 A.L.R., 219. *Hodges*, *J.*

Stock Diseases Act 1890 (No. 1141), sec. 74 —Travelling sheep—Rate of travelling on each day—Meaning of " on each day ''— Offence by person in charge of such sheep for part of a day.]—In sec. 74 of the *Stock Diseases Act* 1890 (which provides that every person who drives travelling sheep on certain lands &c., shall drive such sheep in the direct course so far as practicable of their destination a distance of not less than six miles on each day whilst on their journey), the expression " on each day " refers to each day of the week—such day being computed from midnight on the one day to midnight on the other and the section aims at travelling the sheep not less than six miles towards their real destination on each day. A drover who is in charge of such sheep on a day on which they have not made such progress is liable to a penalty under that section, although he has not been in charge of them during the whole of that day, unless he can show lawful excuse. *West* v. *Armstrong*, (1908) V.L.R., 685 ; 30 A.L.T., 92 ; 14 A.L.R., 562. *Madden*, *C.J.*

STOCK MORTGAGE.

See INSTRUMENTS ACTS.

STREET.

See LOCAL GOVERNMENT, POLICE OFFENCES ACTS.

STREET BETTING SUPPRESSION ACT.

See GAMING AND WAGERING, AND POLICE OFFENCES ACTS.

SUNDAY.

21 Geo. III., c. 49 (Sunday Observance Act), secs. 1, 3—Public entertainment in room—Admission to room free—Admission to portion of room upon payment of money—House, room or other place to which persons admitted by payment of money—Advertising Sunday entertainment.]—In a large room a public entertainment within the meaning of 21 Geo. III., c. 49, was given on Sunday. Portion of the room containing about two-thirds of of the seating accommodation was railed off and in this portion the seats were more comfortable than those in the rest of the room, and it was the best part of the room for hearing and seeing the entertainment. The only entrance to the railed-off portion of the room was from the other portion. There was only one entrance to the room from the outside, and any person might enter there without payment and participate in the entertainment. There was a charge for entering the railed off portion of the room. *Held (per Griffith, C.J., Barton and O'Connor, JJ., Isaacs and Higgins, JJ., dissenting),* that neither the room itself nor the railed off portion was a " house room or place . . . open or used for public entertainment or amusement " upon Sunday and to which persons were " admitted by the payment of money " within the meaning of sec. 1 of 21 Geo., c. 49, and also that the advertising of an entertainment to be given under such circumstances were not within sec. 3 of that Act. *Scott* v. *Cawsey,* 5 C.L.R., 132 ; 13 A.L.R., 568. H.C. (1907).

21 Geo. III., c. 49 (Sunday Observance Act) —Whether in force in Victoria.]—The Act 21 Geo. III., c. 49, is in force in Victoria. *Scott* v. *Cawsey,* 5 C.L.R., 132 ; 13 A.L.R., 568. H.C., *Griffith, C.J., Barton, O'Connor, Isaacs* and *Higgins, JJ.* (1907).

Licensing Act 1906 (No. 2068), sec. 91— " Hours during which the sale of liquor to the public is prohibited "—Whether the whole of Sunday included—Persons found on licensed premises within such hours.]—*See* LICENSING, col. 838. *M'Gee* v. *Wolfenden,* (1907) V.L.R., 195 ; 28 A.L.T., 163 ; 13 A.L.R., 51.

Licensing Act 1906 (No. 2068), sec. 78 (2)— Licensing Act 1890 (No. 1111), sec. 134— Being found in licensed premises when they should not be open for sale of liquor to public— Sunday, whether a time when premises should not be so open.]—*See* LICENSING, col. 837. *Biggs* v. *Lamley,* (1907) V.L.R., 300 ; 28 A.L.T., 202 ; 13 A.L.R., 144.

SUNDAY TRADING.

See LICENSING.

SUPREME COURT ACT.

See PRACTICE AND PLEADING.

SURETY.

See EXECUTORS AND ADMINISTRATORS ; FRAUD AND MISREPRESENTATION.

TELEPHONE.

See POST AND TELEGRAPH ACTS.

TENANCY AT WILL.

See LIMITATIONS (STATUTES OF), col. 845.

TENANCY FROM YEAR TO YEAR.

See LANDLORD AND TENANT, cols. 810, 811.

TENANCY IN COMMON.

Mortgage — Registration — Contributing mortgage—Money advanced by mortgagees in unequal shares—Tenancy in common—Transfer of Land Act 1890 (No. 1149), secs. 57, 65, 113, 229, 240.]—See TRANSFER OF LAND ACT. *Drake* v. *Templeton*, (1913) 16 C.L.R., 153; 19 A.L.R., 93.

TENANT FOR LIFE AND REMAINDERMAN.

I.—APPORTIONMENT OF TRUST FUNDS
 BETWEEN CAPITAL AND INCOME.

Tenant for life and remainderman—Apportionment, basis of—Mortgage effected by testator—Trustee authorised to invest on similar securities—Proceeds of sale of mortgaged property insufficient to pay principal and interest.]—The rule in *Cooper* v. *Cooper*, 26 V.L.R., 649; 22 A.L.T., 215; 7 A.L.R., 147, as to apportionment between tenants for life and remaindermen, where trust funds have been invested on mortgage, and the mortgaged property is sold and the proceeds are insufficient to pay principal and interest due, applies to mortgages effected by a testator, and continued by his trustee after his death, if they are of a class of investments the trustee is authorised to make, and if there are no special reasons why the trustee should have realised them earlier. *In re Earl of Chesterfield's Estate*, 24 Ch. D., 643, distinguished. *Holmes* v. *Holmes*, 28 A.L.T., 22; 12 A.L.R., 409. *a'Beckett, J.* (1906).

Tenant for life and remainderman—Trust funds invested upon mortgage—Proceeds of sale of mortgaged property insufficient to pay principal and interest due—Apportionment of proceeds—Rate of interest.]—Trust funds were invested on mortgage. Upon sale by the mortgagees the proceeds were insufficient to pay principal and interest due, and had to be apportioned between the tenant for life and remaindermen on the basis established by *Cooper* v. *Cooper*, 26 V.L.R., 649; 22 A.L.T., 215; 7 A.L.R., 147. *Held*, that no special circumstances being shown, the rate of interest to be adopted in making the apportionment should not be left to the discretion of the trustees, but should be the rate fixed by the mortgage, that is to say, the ordinary and not the penal rate. *Holmes* v. *Holmes*, 28 A.L.T., 22; 12 A.L.R., 409. *a'Beckett, J.* (1906).

Investment on mortgage—Apportionment of proceeds of realization—Interest on cost of sewerage—Rate of interest upon mortgage.]—Trust moneys having been lent on mortgage by the trustees and the mortgagee being unable to pay the interest, the trustees took possession of the mortgaged property, and expended out of the income of the estate certain sums in sewering the property pursuant to the *Melbourne and Metropolitan Board of Works Act*. The trustees subsequently sold the property for less than the principal sum advanced and interest thereon. On apportionment of the proceeds of sale between corpus and income. *Held*, that before apportionment corpus was chargeable with interest on the sums so expended out of income up to the date of repayment to the life tenants. *In re Morley*, (1895) 2 Ch., 738, followed. On such apportionment the life tenant is entitled to interest on the principal owing under the mortgage from the date when the mortgagee ceased paying interest at the rate (but not the penal rate) fixed by the mortgage, unless it is shown that such rate of interest was higher than the current rates during the period over which the arrears extend. *Cooper* v. *Cooper*, 26 V.L.R., 649; 22 A.L.T., 215; 7 A.L.R., 147, explained and followed. *Macartney* v. *Macartney*, 33 A.L.T., 183; 18 A.L.R., 1. *Madden, C.J.* (1912).

Station property—Management of by trustees—Tenant for life and remainderman—Capital and income, distinction between—Preservation of capital.]—No general principle can be laid down by which station properties in Australia should be managed by trustees having powers of management thereof, or by which the share of profits which would belong to the tenant for life as against the remainderman should be ascertained, as to how capital should be preserved, or as to what are to be regarded as profits or what as capital in any given instance. The whole must depend upon the wise and prudent discretion of those who have the management of the station for the time being. *Re McGaw*, 4 N.S.W. S.R., 591, discussed and disapproved. *In re Moore; Fanning* v. *Fanning*, (1907) V.L.R., 639; 29 A.L.T., 138; 13 A.L.R., 507. *Madden, C.J.*

Excess of expenditure over income—Deficiency met by drawing on capital—Life tenant entitled to income on capital so used—Recoupment of capital out of income—Tenant for life and remainderman.]—The duty of trustees to recoup out of income the excess of expenditure over income occasioned by extraordinary circumstances in particular years, and provided out of other capital to the income of which the life tenant was also entitled, discussed. *In re Moore; Fanning* v. *Fanning*, (1907) V.L.R., 639; 29 A.L.T., 138; 13 A.L.R., 507. *Madden, C.J.*

Tenant for life and remainderman—Income, what is—Shares in insurance company—Dividends paid out of fund accumulated as provision for life assurance liabilities—Dividends paid out of contingency fund to provide against depreciation of securities.]—An insurance company had a " life assurance fund " built up of accumulated profits, to provide for life assurance liabilities. The company had also a " contingency fund " formed by transfers from the " profit and loss account " to " provide for any shrinkage in the value of securities." In the lifetime of the testatrix neither of these funds had been dealt with as available for distribution. By her will and codicil the testatrix created a trust of the " proceeds " of 728 shares in the company,

upon its being wound up, in favour of certain beneficiaries, giving the " annual income from the company " to one of them. After the death of the testatrix the company paid annual dividends on the shares, partly out of profits, but mainly out of moneys transferred to the " profit and loss account " from the " life assurance fund," to which in some cases money had previously been transferred from the " contingency fund." *Held*, that that portion of the dividends, which represented moneys taken from the " life assurance fund " itself, was not, but that the remainder was income within the meaning of the will and codicil. *In re Longley; Reid* v. *Silke*, (1906) V.L.R., 641; 28 A.L.T., 82; 12 A.L.R., 499. *Cussen, J.*

Tenant for life and remainderman—Dividends declared by company, whether capital or income.]—The rule laid down in *Bouche* v. *Sproule*, 12 App. Cas., 385, at pp. 397, 401, to the effect that, where a company has power to determine whether profits reserved and temporarily devoted to capital purposes shall be distributed as dividends or permanently added to capital the conflicting interests of a life tenant and remainderman depend on the decision of the company, is not of universal application, the question being mainly one of fact in each case. *In re Longley; Reid* v. *Silke*, (1906) V.L.R., 641; 28 A.L.T., 82; 12 A.L.R., 499. *Cussen, J.*

Will—Construction—Shares in company owned by testator—Bequest to life tenant of dividends and to remainderman absolutely——Bonus declared by company on shares—New shares issued and offered to shareholders—Bonus applicable in payment therefor—Whether bonus capital or income.]—A testator who held 1,000 shares in a company limited by shares bequeathed them to his trustees to pay the dividends thereof to A. during his life and after his death upon trust for X. and Y. absolutely as tenants in common. Before the testator's death, while he held the shares in question, the company reduced its capital by writing 5s. per share off its issued shares, such shares having been fully paid up to £1 each. Some years after the testator's death the directors were duly authorized by the company to issue part of its unissued capital divided into shares of 15s. each, and to offer the new shares to the shareholders of the company at par in proportion to the number of shares held by each shareholder, and also to declare a bonus of 5s. per share to be paid to the shareholders in respect of their original shares, such bonus being intended as a restoration to them of the capital so written off. Having declared this bonus the directors, in offering the new shares to the shareholders, suggested that the latter should authorize the application of the bonus in payment for the new shares. The company had power under its Articles of Association to declare dividends or bonus to be paid to its members—dividends being payable only out of the company's profits—and also to set aside out of such profits a reserve fund. On a conflict of claims by A. as against X and Y. in respect of the bonus, *Held*, that the company had the power either to distribute its profits as dividends or to convert them into capital, and had validly exercised the latter power ; that, therefore, the bonus was capital and not income, and that A. was entitled to the income arising from the investment of the bonus in the new shares for his lifetime, and X. and Y. had an interest in remainder according to the will as tenants in common after the determination of A.'s life. *Bouch* v. *Sproule*, 12 App. Cas., 385 ; 29 Ch. D., 635, applied. *In re Smith* ; *Edwards* v. *Smith*, 29 A.L.T., 173 ; 14 A.L.R., 22. *Hodges, J.* (1907).

Tenant for life and remainderman—Licensed premises part of estate—Compensation for deprivation of licence—Apportionment—Licensing Act 1890 (No. 1111), secs. 31-44.]—A testator was the owner of and held a licensed victualler's licence in respect of certain premises. He left all his real and personal property to his widow for life with remainder over. The premises were let and the licence transferred to the lessee. Subsequently, under the provisions of Part II. of the *Licensing Act* 1890 the number of licenses in the Licensing District in which such premises were situated was reduced and the premises were deprived of their licence

and the compensation due to the owner and occupier was assessed under sec. 44. *Held*, that the compensation due to the owner formed part of the corpus of the estate. *McKee* v. *Ballarat Trustees Executors &c. Co. Ltd.*, (1910) V.L.R., 358 ; 32 A.L.T., 22 ; 16 A.L.R., 323. *Cussen, J.*

Will—Tenant for life and remainderman—Capital and income—Payment of annuities—Apportionment—Rate of interest.]—J.M.S. who died in 1898, by his will left his property to his trustees upon trusts for conversion, with power of postponement, and as to £800 a year to apply this sum, or such part as the trustees should think fit, for the maintenance and support or otherwise for the benefit of his daughter A.S., the unpaid portion to fall into residue, and as to £500 a year to pay the same to his daughter E.C. during her life, and as to all the residue and ultimate surplus upon trust for his son V.S. and his daughter L.S. in equal shares absolutely. Under the will of L.S., who died in 1903, her trustees were given a discretionary power to pay such sums as they might think fit in and towards the maintenance and support of her sister A.S., the residue of the income to be paid to the appellant C. M. G. Cock, and the corpus to go in equal shares to his children on his death. The question arose whether, in the administration of the trusts of the will of L.S. half the burden of the payments made in satisfaction of those annuities should be borne by the tenant for life under the will of L.S or should be apportioned between the tenant for life and the persons entitled in remainder. *Held*, that for the purpose of determining the income of the estate of L.S. as between the tenant for life and the persons entitled in remainder under her will, it should be ascertained what sum would have been required at the death of L.S. to provide an annuity of £800 during the life of A.S., and an annuity of £500 during the life of E.C., that one half of the interest at 4½ per cent. upon the sums so acertained should be deducted in every year from the income of the estate of L.S. during the respective lives of A.S. and E.C., and that subject to such deductions, the actual net income of the estate of L.S. was payable to the tenant for life under the will of L.S.

Cock v. *Aitken*, (1911) 13 C.L.R., 461 ; 18 A.L.R., 337. H.C., *Griffith*, *C.J.*, *Barton* and *O'Connor*, *JJ.*

Will—Interpretation—Corpus and income— Annuity, gift of—Residue.]—*See* WILL. *Cock* v. *Aitken*, (1908) 6 C.L.R., 290 ; 14 A.L.R., 361.

II.—INCIDENCE OF EXPENSES AND CHARGES AS BETWEEN CAPITAL AND INCOME.

(a) *Power of Trustee to Determine.*

Trustees—Apportionment of charges between capital and income—Apportionment between income takers—Power of trustees to decide questions of apportionment.]—Testator by his will provided as follows—" And I declare that the said trustees or trustee shall have the fullest powers of apportioning blended funds and of determining whether any moneys are to be treated as capital or income and whether any expense outgoings or other payments ought to be paid out of capital or income and generally of determining all matters as to which any doubt, difficulty or question may arise under or in relation to the trusts of this my will or any codicil hereto. And I declare that every determination of the said trustees or trustee in relation to any of the matters aforesaid, whether made upon a question formally or actually raised or implied in any of the acts or proceedings of the said trustees or trustee in relation to the premises shall bind all persons interested under this my will and shall not be objected or questioned upon any ground whatsoever." *Held*, that this provision authorised the trustees to determine that the amount chargeable for certain skilled assistance in the administration of the estate should be borne by income instead of capital, and that as between the takers of income it should be borne rateably. *Swanson* v. *Emmerton*, (1909) V.L.R., 387 ; 31 A.L.T., 28 ; 15 A.L.R., 368. *Cussen, J.*

(b) *Repairs* ; *Improvements* ; *Upkeep of Home* ; *Insurance.*

Life tenant and remainderman—Repairs to trust property—Corpus and income—Appor- tionment—**Trustee with power of management—Bare trustee distinguished as to power to repair.**]—Where property consisting of land and houses is vested in trustees with powers of management in trust for a tenant for life, and for a remainderman, the trustees may make such repairs as are necessary to keep the property in a good state of preservation for the remainderman. The cost of effecting ordinary recurring repairs, which last only a short time, such as painting and papering is to be borne by income. The cost of structural repairs of such a character that both the life tenant and the remainderman will derive substantial benefit therefrom are to be apportioned between income and corpus in such a manner as the trustees in their discretion think fit. The cost of structural repairs of such a character that the remainderman alone will derive substantial benefit therefrom are to be borne wholly by corpus. Bare trustees, without active duties to perform, have no power to apply trust funds in effecting repairs except in a case of salvage. *Wilkie* v. *The Equity Trustees Executors and Agency Co. Ltd.*, (1909) V.L.R., 277 ; 30 A.L.T., 211 ; 15 A.L.R., 208. F.C., *Madden*, *C.J.*, *a'Beckett* and *Hodges, JJ.*

Equitable tenant for life—Expenses for repairs—Whether payable out of corpus or income.] — Where property was held by trustees upon trust to pay the income produced by such property to A. for life with remainder over and no power of management was given, *Held*, that A. was in the position of an equitable tenant for life and under no obligation to repair, and that sums properly expended by the trustees for repairs to and caretaking of the trust property to preserve it from deterioration were payable out of corpus and not out of income. *In re Hotchkys*, 32 Ch. D., 408 ; *Trustees, Executors &c. Co.* v. *Jope*, 27 V.L.R., 706 ; 24 A.L.T., 30 ; 8 A.L.R. (C.N.), 21, and *Reid* v. *Deane*, (1906) V.L.R., 138 ; 27 A.L.T., 153 ; 12 A.L.R., 46, followed ; *Re Folk*, 6 W.W. & A'B. (Eq.), 171, disapproved. *In re Tong* ; *Tong* v. *Trustees, Executors and Agency Co. Ltd.*, (1907) V.L.R., 338 ; 28 A.L.T., 200 ; 13 A.L.R., 119. *a'Beckett, J.*

Improvements to station property — Expenditure, adjustment between capital and income — Tenant for life and remainderman.]—In the management of a station property the trustees expended capital moneys for the purpose of making certain improvements which were necessary for the good management of the station, and likely to enhance its general value, and would be of great use to those having the life interest. *Held*, that such expenditure was properly chargeable to capital ; that capital might properly be recouped by annual charges of ten per cent. on income ; but that on the sale of the property before such recoupment had been fully made, no further recoupment out of income need be made. *In re Moore ; Fanning v. Fanning*, (1907) V.L.R., 639 ; 29 A.L.T., 138 ; 13 A.L.R., 507. *Madden, C.J.*

Trustee—Settled land—Cost of fencing—Apportionment between corpus and income—Sinking fund.]—The cost of fencing land, part of a settled estate, was ordered to be paid out of capital, and a sinking fund established out of income for repayment of amount to capital in fifteen years—the estimated life of fences. *In re Staughton*, (1909) V.L.R., 174 ; 30 A.L.T., 184 ; 15 A.L.R., 148. *Hodges, J.*

Trusts Act 1896 (No. 1421), sec. 11—Trustee—Power to compromise—Agreement between trustee and tenant for life—Compromise as to future liability of tenant for life for repairs—Disadvantage of the estate—Mistake of law, effect of.]—A tenant for life had claims against the estate and the estate had claims against him. The trustee of the estate and tenant for life agreed to compromise all such claims upon certain terms, and mutual releases were given in respect of such claims. One of the terms of the agreement was that the trustee should be at liberty to deduct from the income of the tenant for life from the estate a specified sum per annum during his life, such sum to be spent by the trustee in effecting any necessary repairs to the trust property. *Held*, that, under the *Trusts Act* 1896, the trustee had power to insert in the agreement for compromise the term limiting the liability of the tenant for life in respect of future repairs, as part of a *bona fide* compromise, though such term might have been agreed to under a mistake of law, and would work out to the disadvantage of the estate ; and that, therefore, the obligation of the tenant for life to contribute to the cost of such repairs was limited to the amount specified in the agreement. *In re Tong ; Tong v. Trustees Executors &c. Co. Ltd.*, (1910) V.L.R., 110 ; 31 A.L.T., 169 ; 16 A.L.R., 87. *Hood, J.*

Trustees, duty of—Tenant for life—Repairs.] —*See* TRUSTS AND TRUSTEES. *Carrodus v. Carrodus*, (1913) V.L.R., 1 ; 34 A.L.T., 125 ; 18 A.L.R., 529.

Investment on mortgage—Apportionment of proceeds of realization—Interest on cost of sewerage—Rate of interest upon mortgage.]—*See, ante*, I. APPORTIONMENT OF TRUST FUNDS BETWEEN CAPITAL AND INCOME. *Macartney v. Macartney*, 33 A.L.T., 183 ; 18 A.L.R., 1.

Will—Interpretation—Expenses of upkeep of house—Whether payable out of corpus or income.]—A testatrix directed her trustees to convert her property into money, and to stand possessed of the residuary trust moneys upon trust, after payment thereout of certain sums for the upkeep of C., to pay the residue of the income to one of the appellants. By a codicil the testatrix recited that she had given her estate to her trustees upon trust, after payment for the upkeep of C., to pay the residue of the income of the trust premises to the above-named appellant. *Held*, that it appeared from the codicil that the testatrix intended that the payment for the upkeep of C. should come out of income. *Cock v. Aitken*, (1911) 13 C.L.R., 461 ; 18 A.L.R. 337. H.C., *Griffith, C.J., Barton* and *O'Connor, JJ.*

Will—Construction—" Upkeep and maintenance and carrying on of " house as a home and residence — What expenses included therein—Household expenses—Repairs—Rates and taxes—Outgoings.]—*See* WILL. *In re Stroud ; Bell v. Stroud*, (1908) V.L.R., 33 ; 29 A.L.T., 104 ; 13 A.L.R., 645.

Tenant for life and remainderman—Fire premiums paid prior to the Trusts Act 1896 (No. 1421)—Whether chargeable to income or corpus.]—Fire insurance premiums were paid by trustees prior to the *Trusts Act* 1896 in respect of properties held on trust to let. *Held,* that such premiums were chargeable against income. *Holmes* v. *Holmes,* 28 A.L.T., 22; 12 A.L.R., 409. *a' Beckett, J.* (1906).

Insurance of trust property—Premiums, whether payable out of corpus or income— Trusts Act 1896 (No. 1421), sec. 28.]—Sec. 28 of the *Trusts Act* 1896 governs the incidence of payments made thereunder by trustees for insuring buildings on the trust property. *In re Tong; Tong* v. *Trustees, Executors and Agency Co. Ltd.,* (1907) V.L.R., 338; 28 A.L.T., 200; 13 A.L.R., 119. *a' Beckett, J.*

(c) Probate Duty; Costs; Administration Expenses.

Probate duty, how payment to be apportioned—Direction that each beneficiary shall pay duty payable in respect of his interest— Tenants for life and remaindermen.]—The testator by his will made certain specific bequests and devises and created various life estates with remainders. He also directed that each beneficiary should " pay the legacy probate or succession duty payable in respect of his or her interest." *Held,* that the direction as to payment of duty meant no more than that one beneficiary should not be called upon to pay the duty assessed in respect of the gift to another, and that this would be attained by following the rules laid down in the case of *Murphy* v. *Ainslie,* (1905) V.L.R., 350; 26 A.L.T., 202; 11 A.L.R., 163. *In re Buckhurst; Equity Trustees Executors and Agency Co.* v. *Buckhurst,* (1907) V.L.R., 252; 28 A.L.T., 190; 13 A.L.R., 74. *Cussen, J.*

Administration and Probate Act 1907 (No. 2120), sec. 3—Administration and Probate Act 1890 (No. 1060), sec. 103—Probate duty— Apportionment—Tenant for life and remainderman—Whether legislation retrospective.]—Sec. 3 of the *Administration and Probate Act* 1907 is not retrospective. *In re*

Staughton; Oliver v. *Staughton,* (1910) V.L.R., 415; 32 A.L.T., 63; 16 A.L.R., 443. *a' Beckett, J.*

Probate duty—Apportionment—Tenant for life and remainderman—Mistake of law— Agreement between executors and tenant for life as to apportionment of duty based on wrong principle—Duty of executors.]—A testator by his will left a life interest in the bulk of his estate and specifically devised to her certain properties. The probate duty having been paid on the testator's estate by his executors, they obtained an actuarial valuation of the widow's life interest, and took this valuation as the basis of her contribution to probate duty in respect to such life interest. The widow not being able to provide for immediate payment of the share of duty apportioned on such basis, an arrangement, which was embodied in a deed, was made between her and the executors for payment by her of her proportion of the duty by instalments. At that time the law as to how the burden of probate duty should be borne and apportioned was not settled. Subsequently the case of *Murphy* v. *Ainslie,* (1905) V.L.R., 350; 26 A.L.T., 202; 11 A.L.R., 163, was decided. *Held,* that the executors should exercise their powers under sec. 103 of the *Administration and Probate Act* 1890 as interpreted by the judgment in *Murphy* v. *Ainslie,* notwithstanding the execution of the deed by the widow, and without reference to any payment they had received thereunder attributable to the amount she was charged in respect of her life interest, and that the moneys she had so paid should be returned to her out of the money realised by the exercise of the powers conferred by sec. 103. *In re Staughton; Oliver* v. *Staughton,* (1910) V.L.R., 415; 32 A.L.T., 63; 16 A.L.R., 443. *a' Beckett, J.*

Trustee—Life tenant and remainderman— Corpus and income—Costs paid by trustees under order of High Court—Decision of High Court reversed on appeal by one party to Privy Council—Effect on rights of parties not appealing—Indemnity of trustees—Rights of assignee of life tenant.]—An action was brought in the Supreme Court by a life tenant under the will of A. against the trustees of A.'s estate and the trustees of B.'s estate, claiming against the latter trustees in respect of breaches of trust whereby the income of A.'s estate was diminished, and against the former trustees the determination of the respective rights of himself and the remaindermen. The Court having dismissed the action with costs the High Court on appeal gave relief against both sets of trustees and directed the costs of the plaintiff and of the remaindermen to be provided for out of the corpus of A.'s estate. The trustees of B.'s estate appealed to the Privy Council against so much only of the order of the High Court as applied to them. The Privy Council reversed the order of the High Court, directed the judgment of the Supreme Court to be restored and dismissed the action with costs in both Courts. The plaintiff before bringing the the action had assigned his interest in A.'s estate by way of mortgage. Prior to the appeal to the Privy Council the trustees of A's estate, pursuant to the judgment of the High Court, had paid certain costs to the plaintiff, had retained certain of their own costs, and had incurred certain other costs in taking accounts in connection with the claim against the trustees of A.'s estate. *Held*, that, notwithstanding the order of the Privy Council, the trustees of A.'s estate were entitled to be indemnified for such costs, except such of the plaintiff's costs as were attributable to the plaintiff's appeal to the High Court in respect of his claim against the trustees of B.'s estate, out of the corpus and not out of the income of A.'s estate. By *Griffith, C.J.* and *Barton, J.*, on the ground that, although the order of the High Court must be treated as non-existent, the order of the Privy Council left the rights of the trustees of A.'s estate open to determination. By *Isaacs, J.*, on the ground that the order of the Privy Council, although it authorized the trustees of A.'s estate to apply the income to the payment of the costs, did not permit the income to be applied to the disadvantage of the plaintiff's assignee. *Cock* v. *Aitken*, (1912) 15 C.L.R., 373; 18 A.L.R., 576. H.C.

Costs—Trustees—Corpus and income interested—Mathematical adjustment of burden of costs impossible—Burden divided equally.]—See *Macartney* v. *Macartney*, (1909) V.L.R., 183; 30 A.L.T., 172; 15 A.L.R., 139. *Hodges, J.*

Trustees—Will—Testamentary expenses—Estate for life in realty subject to payment thereof—Tenant for life refuses to pay—No income from realty available—Payment by trustees out of personalty bequeathed to other beneficiaries—Mortgage of real estate to recoup such beneficiaries—Whether a breach of trust.]—See TRUSTS AND TRUSTEES. *Crout* v. *Beissel*, (1909) V.L.R., 207; 30 A.L.T., 185; 15 A.L.R., 143.

(d) Annuities.

Will — Settlement — Annuity — Charge, whether on corpus or income—Order of Court —Transfer of Land Statute 1866 (No. 301), sec. 86.]—By a marriage settlement made in 1887 the settlor, the intended husband, gave a term of 99 years in certain land to his trustees who were directed "out of the rents and profits" thereof to raise the annual sum of £500 and pay it to the intended wife during her life. The settlor by his will subsequently devised the land to certain beneficiaries subject to the charge created by the settlement. After the settlor's death, viz., in 1882, by order of the Supreme Court an instrument of charge under the *Transfer of Land Statute* 1866 to secure the annuity was executed, which had the effect of rendering the corpus as well as the income of the land liable to satisfy the accruing payments of the annuity. The land was subsequently sold pursuant to an order of the Court and the proceeds of sale were invested. An order of the Court was afterwards made directing the trustees of the settlor's will to set aside a certain sum to answer the "rent charge" on the land and to pay the residue of the proceeds of sale to the beneficiaries entitled thereto. This order was never carried into effect, as the income from the investments representing the proceeds of sale had become insufficient to pay the annuity which fell into arrear. *Held*, that whether under the settlement the annuity was or was not a charge upon the corpus as well as the income of the land, it became so by virtue of the instrument of charge under the *Transfer of Land Statute 1866*; that it was too late to have the charge corrected if it had been inadvertently made; that that charge equally attached to the proceeds of the sale of the land; that nothing which had subsequently happened diminished the extent of that charge; and therefore that the annuitant was entitled to an order for payment of arrears of the annuity out of the corpus of the investments representing the proceeds of the sale of the land. *Brown v. Abbott*, (1908) 5 C.L.R., 487. H.C., *Griffith, C.J., O'Connor* and *Issacs, JJ.*

Will—Construction — Annuity — Whether charged on corpus—Legacies—" In the first place "—" In the next place "—Whether priority of enumeration or in order or method of payment or of rights or interests.]—*See* WILL. *Perpetual Executors and Trustees Association of Australia Ltd. v. Knowles,* 32 A.L.T., 163; 16 A.L.R., 582.

III.—SALE OF TRUST ESTATE; ANTICIPATION
PERIOD OF DISTRIBUTION.

Settled Estates and Settled Lands Act 1909 (No. 2235), secs. 51, 124—Sale of settled land —Tenant for life, persons having the powers of sale of—Person entitled in fee simple with executory limitation over in a certain event.]— *See* SETTLED ESTATES AND SETTLED LANDS ACT. *In re Akehurst or Cheke; Cheke v. Hamilton,* (1910) V.L.R., 310; 32 A.L.T., 5; 16 A.L.R , 246.

Settled Estates and Settled Lands Act 1909 (No. 2235), sec. 124—Sale of settled land— Person with powers of tenant for life—Estate or interest in possession, what is.]—*See* SETTLED ESTATES AND SETTLED LANDS ACT. *In re Akehurst or Cheke; Cheke v. Hamilton,* (1910) V.L.R., 310; 32 A.L.T., 5; 16 A.L.R., 246.

Settled Estates and Settled Lands Act 1909 (No. 2235), secs. 50, 51, 99—Settled lands— Devise to trustees—Will containing only power to let or lease—Sale by tenant for life— Trustees without power to consent.—Trustees of the Settlement.]—*See* TRUSTS AND TRUS-

TEES. *Beardsley v. Harris,* (1911) V.L.R., 152; 32 A.L.T., 161; 17 A.L.R., 112.

Settled Estates and Settled Lands Act 1909 (No. 2235), secs. 127, 128—Contract of sale— Purchase in name of infants—Settled estate— Tenant for life—Settlement—Appointment of trustees—Trustees to exercise powers of infant tenants for life.]—*See* SETTLED ESTATES AND SETTLED LANDS ACT. *In re Weir,* (1912) V.L.R., 77; 33 A.L.T., 162; 18 A.L.R., 26.

Settled Estates and Settled Lands Act 1909 (No. 2235), secs. 50, 51, 98, 101, 117, 118, 121, 124, 127, 128, 132—Will—Devise to trustees —Power of sale given to trustees—Power to carry on testator's business—Settled estate —Persons with powers of tenant for life— Infants.]—*See* SETTLED ESTATES AND SETTLED LANDS ACT. *In re Snowball,* (1912) V.L.R., 176; 33 A.L.T., 172; 18 A.L.R., 65.

Settled Estates and Settled Lands Act 1909 (No. 2235), secs. 51, 124, 127—Sale of settled land—Infant being person with powers of tenant for life—Appointment of persons to exercise such powers.]—*See* SETTLED ESTATES AND SETTLED LANDS ACT. *In re Akehurst or Cheke; Cheke v. Hamilton,* (1910) V.L.R., 310; 32 A.L.T., 5; 16 A.L.R., 246.

Will—Gift to daughter with remainder to her children—Gift over upon default of children—Forfeiture of daughter's share— Daughter childless and past child-bearing— When share distributable.]—*See* WILL. *In re Lyons; Grant v. Trustees Executors &c. Co. Ltd.,* (1908) V.L.R., 190; 29 A.L.T., 202; 14 A.L.R., 147.

Declaration that woman past child-bearing.] —Declaration made that a woman in her fifty-sixth year was past child-bearing, where on her statements and their own observations two medical practitioners stated that they were satisfied that the woman would never have a child. *In re Lyons; Grant v. Trustees Executors &c. Co. Ltd.,* (1908) V.L.R., 190; 29 A.L.T., 202; 14 A.L.R., 147. *a' Beckett, J.*

Declaration that woman is past child-bearing —Circumstances in which Court will make.]— The circumstances in which the Court will declare a woman to be past child-bearing considered, and a declaration refused in the case of a woman in her forty-sixth year, though two medical practitioners stated that in their opinion, it was beyond all reasonable probability that the woman would bear a child. *In re Lees*; *Lees* v. *National Trustees Co.*, (1908) V.L.R., 211; 30 A.L.T., 26; 14 A.L.R., 147. *a'Beckett, J.*

TENDER.

Instruments Act 1890 (No. 1103), sec. 142— Bill of sale—Caveat—Tender of amount due to caveator—Refusal to accept—Removal of caveat—Jurisdiction of Judge to order.]—*See* Bill of Sale, col. 76. *In re Coburn*, 28 A.L.T. (Supplement), 3; 12 A.L.R. (C.N.), 17.

THEATRE.

See SUNDAY; TRADE MARKS AND TRADE NAMES; WORDS.

THISTLE ACT.

Thistle Act 1890 (No. 1145), sec. 4—Notice to destroy thistles—Sufficiency of.]—The notice to destroy thistles under sec. 4 of the *Thistles Act* 1890 should be such as to convey to the person served with the notice as a reasonably intelligent man the fact that thistles are growing on the land at the time of the service of the notice. A notice to the following effect was served on the defendant: —Take notice that unless the plants commonly known as thistles (the names of which are indorsed hereon) shall be effectually destroyed off the land being allotment 13 sec. 4 township of Leongatha, situated in the parish of Leongatha, of which you are occupier within fourteen days from the service hereof proceedings will be taken against you in accordance with the Statute 54 Victoria, No. 1145, sec. 4. After the expiration of fourteen days from the service of the

notice the defendant was charged with not effectually destroying within fourteen days after service of such notice certain plants commonly known as ragwort then growing upon the land so occupied by him. Ragwort was one of the plants named on the back of the notice. *Held*, that the notice was insufficient. *Murphy* v. *Shiells*, (1908) V.L.R., 513; 30 A.L.T., 20; 14 A.L.R., 410. *Cussen, J.*

Thistle Act 1890 (No. 1145), sec. 4— Thistle Act 1893 (No. 1337)—Notice to destroy thistles—Foundation of offence—Insufficient notice—Objection first taken in Order nisi to review.]—As the giving of the notice under sec. 4 of the *Thistles Act* 1890 is the foundation of the offence, an objection that no sufficient notice was given to the defendant as required by sec. 4 of the *Thistle Act* 1890 may be taken for the first time in an order *nisi* to review the conviction of the defendant under that section. *Murphy* v. *Shiells*, (1908) V.L.R., 513; 30 A.L.T., 20; 14 A.L.R., 410. *Cussen, J.*

Thistle Act 1890 (No. 1145), sec. 4—Notice calling upon defendant to destroy thistles— Notice to produce, whether necessary— Secondary evidence—Offence constituted by disobedience to notice.]—In proceedings under sec. 4 of the *Thistle Act* 1890 for not effectually destroying thistles after written notice, secondary evidence of such notice is admissible, although notice to produce it has not been given. *Sanderson* v. *Nicholson*, (1906) V.L.R., 371; 27 A.L.T., 215; 12 A.L.R., 208. *a'Beckett, A.-C.J.*

TIME.

See also, COUNTY COURT; PRACTICE AND PLEADING.

" Clear days."] — When reference is made to " clear days " in a rule which is for the advantage of the party who has to take action, it may be a maximum. When the rule is for the protection of another party it is a minimum. In either case it denotes a limit. When it is a minimum, two days, one before and one after the period are excluded from reckoning. But when a thing has to be done within a certain number of days, the end of the last day is the furthest limit. *Armstrong* v. *Great Southern Gold Mining Co., No Liability*, (1911) 12 C.L.R., 382 17 A.L.R., 377. H.C., *Griffith, C.J., Barton and O'Connor, JJ.*

TIME PAYMENT AGREEMENT.

See CONTRACT OR AGREEMENT, col. 203.

TORT.

See NEGLIGENCE; WRONGS ACT.

TRADE MARKS AND TRADE NAMES.

I.—REGISTRATION.

(a) *Registrable Trade Marks.*

Trade Marks Act 1890 (No. 2) (No. 1183), secs. 16, 17—Registration—" Calculated to deceive "—Distinctive."] — A trade mark consisting of a label containing the words " Mowling's Best " with a representation of three stars between those words, and in another line the words " Three Stars " followed by a blank, *Held*, to be distinctive and not to be calculated to deceive within the meaning of sec. 16 (2) or sec. 17 of the *Trade Marks Act* 1892 (No. 2) with respect to a registered trade mark consisting of the word " Starlight " or an unregistered trade mark consisting of a female figure surrounded by stars and the word " Starlight." *Lever Brothers* v. *G. Mowling & Son*, (1908) 6 C.L.R., 136; 14 A.L.R., 296. H.C., *Griffith, C.J., Barton, Isaacs and Higgins, JJ.*

Trade mark—Registration—Similarity of marks — " Honest concurrent user " — " Special circumstances "—Trade Marks Act 1905 (No. 20 of 1905), secs. 8, 9, 16, 25, 28.]— An application for registration of a trade mark having been opposed by the registered proprietor of a trade mark limited to New South Wales, was granted subject to a limitation to the States other than New South Wales. On appeal by the applicant to the High Court, *Held*, on the evidence that the mark of the applicant and that of the opponent were not the same or nearly identical, that, even if they were, there had been honest concurrent user of the marks in New South Wales, and that there were special circumstances within the meaning of sec. 28 of the *Trade Marks Act* 1905, and consequently that the applicant was entitled to registration in New South Wales. *Bedggood & Co.* v. *Graham*, (1909) 7 C.L.R., 752. H.C., *Griffith, C.J., O'Connor and Isaacs, JJ.*

Trade mark—Rectification of register— " Calculated to deceive," meaning of—Trade Marks Act 1890 (No. 2) (No. 1183), secs. 16 (2), 29 (1).]—A trade mark is calculated to deceive " within the meaning of sec. 16 (2) of the *Trade Marks Act* 1890 (No. 2) when the resemblance between it and a previously registered trade mark is such as may not improbably deceive the average ordinary unwary purchaser. *In re Trade Marks Act* 1890 (*No. 2*); *Lysaght Ltd.* v. *Reid Brothers & Russell Proprietary Ltd.*, (1907) V.L.R., 432; 28 A.L.T., 223; 13 A.L.R., 241. F.C., *Madden, C.J., a'Beckett and Hood, JJ.*

Trade mark—Rectification of register— —Entry made without sufficient cause— Trade mark so resembling trade mark already on register as to be calculated to deceive— Trade Marks Act 1890 (No. 2), (No. 1183), secs. 16 (2), 29 (1).]—An entry of a trade mark calculated to deceive is an entry made without sufficient cause within the meaning of sec. 29 (1) of the *Trade Marks Act* 1890 (No. 2). *In re Trade Marks Act* 1890 (*No. 2*); *Lysaght Ltd.* v. *Reid Brothers & Russell Proprietary Ltd.*, (1907) V.L.R., 432; 28 A.L.T., 223; 13 A.L.R., 241. F.C., *Madden, C.J., a'Beckett and Hood, JJ.*

Trade Marks Act 1890 (No. 2) (No. 1183), sec. 8—Distinctive label—Words having reference to the character or quality of the goods.]—A word or representation having reference to the character or quality of the goods may form part of a distinctive label. *Lever Bros. Ltd.* v. *Mowling & Son*, (1909) V.L.R., 59; 30 A.L.T., 115; 14 A.L.R., 726. F.C., *a'Beckett, Hodges* and *Cussen, JJ.*

Trade Marks Act 1890 (No. 2) (No. 1183), secs. 8, 16, 17—Restrictions on registration—"Same . . . description of goods," meaning of—Mark already on register with respect to such goods—Classes of goods set out in regulations of Governor in Council.]—*Quaere,* whether decisions relating to associated goods based on the words "the same description of goods" in sec. 16 of the *Trade Marks Act* 1890 (*No. 2*) have any application to the various classes and sub-classes of goods set out in the regulations made by the Governor-in-Council. *Lever Bros. Ltd.* v. *Mowling & Son*, (1909) V.L.R., 59; 30 A.L.T., 115; 14 A.L.R., 726. F.C., *a'Beckett, Hodges* and *Cussen, JJ.*

Trade mark—Effect of registration—Presence on register for five years, how far conclusive.] The presence on the register of a trade mark makes it *prima facie* good for five years. After that period has expired, it becomes conclusive evidence that it is such a trade mark, provided it is possible for it to be a trade mark at all. *In re Trade Marks Act* 1890 (*No. 2*): *Lysaght Ltd.* v. *Reid Brothers & Russell Proprietary Ltd.*, (1907) V.L.R., 432; 28 A.L.T., 223; 13 A.L.R., 241. F.C., *Madden, C.J., a'Beckett* and *Hood, JJ.* (1907).

(b) Practice.

Trade mark registered in an Australian State—Application for registration under Commonwealth Act — Procedure — Trade Marks Act 1905, secs. 8, 32.]—All applications for registration of trade marks under the *Trade Marks Act* 1905, including those pursuant to secs. 8 and 9 are made under sec. 32. Therefore the Registrar is not entitled to refuse an application which purports to be made under sec. 32 merely because the mark is already registered as a trade mark under the Trade Marks Act of a State, but he must deal with the application on its merits, and give to the applicant such registration as he is entitled to. *Ex parte Salvitis Proprietary Co.*, 4 C.L.R., 941; 13 A.L.R., 93. H.C., *Griffith, C.J., O'Connor, Isaacs* and *Higgins, JJ.* (1907).

Trade Marks Act 1905 (No. 20 of 1905), sec. 105—Trade Marks Regulations 1906, regs. 27, 28—Application for registration—Notice by Registrar—Failure of applicant to reply—Extension of time for reply—Power of Registrar.]—If the Registrar is satisfied that the failure of an applicant to answer the notice referred to in regulations 27 and 28 arises from circumstances for which the applicant should be excused, he may, under sec. 105 of the Act extend the time for so answering and, in considering whether he should or should not extend the time, the Registrar is bound to exercise his discretion. *The King (on the prosecution of Waters)* v. *Registrar of Trade Marks*, (1908) 5 C.L.R., 604; 14 A.L.R., 141. H.C., *Griffith, C.J., O'Connor, Isaacs* and *Higgins, JJ.*

Application for registration—Allegation that applicant registered under another name—Duty of Registrar.]—It was alleged that the applicants, a Joint Stock Company, were identical with a company originally registered under another name, but which had lawfully changed its name. *Held,* that this was a matter of fact to be ascertained by the examiner in dealing with the application, and that if the fact were proved he must proceed with the application on its merits. *Ex parte Salvitis Proprietary Co.*, 4 C.L.R. 941; 13 A.L.R., 93. H.C., *Griffith, C.J., O'Connor, Isaacs* and *Higgins, JJ.* (1907).

Trade Marks Act 1905 (No. 20 of 1905), secs. 33, 37, 41, 46, 94—Trade Marks Regulations 1906, regs. 27, 28—Application for registration—Notice by Registrar—Failure of applicant to reply—Abandonment of application—Validity of regulation—Extension of time for reply—Power of Registrar.]—*Per Griffith, C.J., O'Connor* and *Isaacs, JJ.* (*Higgins, J.,* doubting).—Regulation 28 of the *Trade Mark Regulations* 1906 in so far as it provides for an application being deemed to be abandoned in a certain event, is a lawful exercise of the power conferred by sec. 94 of the *Trade Marks Act* 1905 and is not inconsistent with sec. 37. *The King (on the prosecution of Waters)* v. *Registrar of Trade Marks,* (1908) 5 C.L.R., 604 ; 14 A.L.R., 141.

Trade Marks Act 1905 (No. 20 of 1905), secs. 6, 14—Trade Marks Act 1890 (No. 2) (No. 1183), sec. 13—Application for registration pending at passing of Federal Act—Transfer of administration—Appeal to Federal Attorney-General—Reference of appeal to Supreme Court by Federal Attorney-General—Appeal from Supreme Court, jurisdiction to hear—Whether Supreme Court exercised administrative jurisdiction only.]—An application for the registration of a trade mark was pending at the time the *Trade Marks Act* 1905 (Commonwealth) came into operation, and pursuant to sec. 6 of that Act and sec. 13 of the *Trade Marks Act* 1890 (*No.* 2) an appeal from the Commonwealth Registrar of Trade Marks to the Attorney-General of the Commonwealth was by him referred to the Supreme Court. *Held*, that the reference to the Supreme Court was authorized and that an appeal lay from a decision of that Court to the High Court. *Lever Brothers* v. *G. Mowling & Son*, (1908) 6 C.L.R., 136 ; 14 A.L.R. 296. H.C., *Griffith, C.J., Barton, Isaacs* and *Higgins, JJ.*

Trade mark—Practice—Costs—Award of costs by law officer—Discretion—Appeal to High Court—Trade Marks Act 1905 (No. 20 of 1905), secs. 95, 96.]—The High Court has jurisdiction to entertain an appeal as to the costs awarded by the law officer on an appeal to him from the Registrar of Trade Marks. But on such an appeal the Court will not over-rule his order unless there has been a disregard of principle or a misapprehension of facts. *In re Gilbert* ; *Gilbert* v. *Huddlestone*, 28 Ch. D., 549, applied. *Alexander Ferguson & Co.* v. *Daniel Crawford & Co.*, (1909) 10 C.L.R., 207. H.C., *Griffith, C.J., O'Connor* and *Isaacs, JJ.*

Commonwealth Trade Marks Act 1905 (No. 20 of 1905), sec. 46—Registration of trade mark—Notice of opposition by person not resident in Australia—Security for costs—High Court—Jurisdiction.]—The Court has no jurisdiction under sec. 46 of the *Trade Marks Act* 1905 to order security for costs of an application pending before the Registrar of Trade Marks to be given by a person not resident in Australia who has given notice of opposition to the application. *Ex parte Carroll*, 15 A.L.R., 295. *Isaacs, J.* (1909).

High Court—Practice—Declaratory judgment—Abstract question of law in decision of which rights of parties are not involved—Whether High Court will decide—Rules of High Court 1903, Part I., Order III., r. 1—Trade Marks Act 1905 (No. 20), Part VII., constitutionality of.]—*See* HIGH COURT (PRACTICE), cols. 638, 639. *Bruce* v. *Commonwealth Trade Marks Label Association*, (1907) 4 C.L.R., 1569 ; 13 A.L.R., 582.

II.—PASSING-OFF ; TRADE AND BUSINESS NAMES.

Trade name—Name adopted by company—Similarity to name of another company—Both companies carrying on same business—Likelihood of confusion—Burden of proof.]—In an action by one company to prevent another company from using a name so like that of the plaintiff company as to be likely to deceive, the plaintiff company must show that it is reasonably certain that what the defendant company is about to do will cause imminent and substantial damage to the plaintiff company. *Royal Insurance Co. Ltd.* v. *Midland Insurance Co. Ltd.*, 26 R.P.C 95, followed. *Held*, that the name of the appellant company was not so like that of the respondent company as to render it reasonably certain that anyone intending to employ the respondent company and make them trustees under a will or settlement or employ them as agents would be led to believe the appellant company was the respondent company. *The Bendigo and Country Districts Trustees &c. Co. Ltd.* v. *The Sandhurst and Northern District Trustees &c. Co. Ltd.*, (1909) 9 C.L.R., 474 ; 15 A.L.R., 565. H.C., *Griffith, C.J., O'Connor* and *Isaacs, JJ.*

Trade name—Similarity of names—Mining companies—Names taken from locality of

mining operations—Injunction.]—The name of a mining company called after the locality in which it is carrying on mining operations may be sufficiently distinctive to be entitled to protection. A mining company carrying on operations at Mount Balfour, in Tasmania, was registered under Part II. of the *Companies Act* 1890 as the "Mount Balfour Copper Mines No Liability." A few months later a company carrying on mining operations in the same locality was registered under the name of the "Mount Balfour Mines No Liability." Evidence was given that it would be necessary for the plaintiff to enlarge the subscribed capital by the issue of shares to the public; that owing to the similarity of the names of the two companies, there was a likelihood of the one company being mistaken by members of the public for the other, and consequently under certain circumstances such confusion would depreciate the value of the shares of the first named company and prevent them from being taken up by the public. *Held*, granting an injunction to restrain the defendant from carrying on business under its name as above set out; that the name of the plaintiff company was sufficiently distinctive to entitle it to protection, that members of the public who would be likely to invest on the plaintiff's shares might be deceived as to the identity of the two companies, and damage would be likely to result to the plaintiff from the mistake thereby occasioned. *Mount Balfour Copper Mines No Liability* v. *Mount Balfour Mines No Liability*, (1909) V.L.R., 542; 31 A.L.T., 122; 15 A.L.R., 556. *Cussen, J.*

Trade Marks Act 1905 (No. 20 of 1905)— Trade mark—Infringement—User not as a trade mark—Trade name—Name adopted by company—Similarity to name of another company—Likelihood of confusion—Class of Business carried on—Actual and prospective —Injunction.]—Where a person has innocently applied to his goods a word which is the registered trade mark of another, not as a trade mark, but merely as a distinguishing or shipping mark, and on learning of the trade mark, has, before action, offered to remove the mark from his goods and not again to apply it, an injunction will not be granted

at the instance of the owner of the trade mark. When one incorporated company seeks to restrain a second incorporated company from trading under or using such second company's name on the ground that it is so like the first company's name as to cause a likelihood of deception and confusion, it is in every case a question of fact whether there is such a likelihood, and it is material in considering whether in fact there is such a likelihood to consider the real objects of, and the nature of the business carried on by, the two companies. Where the two companies are in fact engaged in different classes of trade, it is not sufficient for the first company to point to clauses in its memorandum of association which will enable it to extend its operations to numerous classes of trade (embracing almost all the classes of trade in which the second company either actually trades, or may by its memorandum of association trade), unless it can satisfy the Court that it either has carried on or really proposes within a limited time to carry on, business in such other classes of trade. *Austral Canning Co. Proprietary Ltd.* v. *Austral Grain and Produce Proprietary Ltd.*, 34 A.L.T., 37; 18 A.L.R., 354. *a'Beckett, J.* (1912).

Title to a play—Proprietary rights in— Injunction restraining infringement—Performing rights, assignment of—"Theatre," meaning of.]—The plaintiff, who had by licence from the registered proprietor the exclusive right to perform in any theatre in Australia a play entitled "The Fatal Wedding," produced the play under that title at a theatre in Melbourne from March 17th to April 15th, 1906, with success. On May 5th, 1906, the defendant produced a different play under substantially the same title at the South Melbourne Town Hall, and later on, in the same month the defendant, notwithstanding written protests by the plaintiff, produced her play twice at suburban halls, and under the same title. *Held*, that the plaintiff was entitled to an interlocutory injunction restraining the defendant from producing a play under the title of "The Fatal Wedding" or any similar title, and that this would be so even without regard to the licence from the registered proprietor. *Held*, also, that the word " theatre " in such licence is not restricted to licensed theatres, but means the places where the play is performed *Meynell* v. *Pearce*, (1906) V.L.R., 447; 27 A.L.T., 226; 12 A.L.R., 282. *Cussen, J.* (1906).

Trade mark—Falsely applying trade mark—Defence—No intention to defraud—Trade Marks Act 1905 (No. 20 of 1905), sec. 87.]—The words " intent to defraud " in sec. 87 of the *Trade Marks Act* 1905 mean intent to induce the purchaser to believe that goods to which a trade mark is falsely applied, and which are manufactured by the seller, are manufactured by some person other than the seller. And, where an information for an offence under the section had been dismissed, *Held*, that the evidence justified the Justices in finding that the defendant had no intent to defraud. *Jones* v. *Gedye*, (1909) 9 C.L.R., 262. H.C., *Griffith, C.J., O'Connor* and *Isaacs, JJ.*

TRADES UNION.

Commonwealth Conciliation and Arbitration Act 1904 (No. 13 of 1904), sec. 68 — Association registered as organization—Rules — Levies imposed on branches—Liability of members of association.]—See COMMON-WEALTH CONCILIATION AND ARBITRATION ACT, col. 110. *Prentice* v. *Amalgamated Mining Employees Association of Victoria and Tasmania,* (1912) 15 C.L.R., 235; 18 A.L.R., 343.

Action, cause of — Inducing employer to discharge employee from his employment—Interference—Lawful justification or excuse —Intention to injure—Malice—Self interest—Trades union—Secretary.]—See EMPLOYER AND EMPLOYEE, cols. 450, 451. *Bond* v. *Morris,* (1912) V.L.R., 351; 34 A.L.T., 52; 18 A.L.R., 348.

TRAMWAYS ACT.

Information, who may lay—Tramways Act 1890 (No. 1148), sec. 5, Second Schedule, Part II., clause 17—Tramway fare, penalty for avoiding payment of—Delegation of authority of municipal council—Whether delegate may enforce penalty.]—See LOCAL GOVERNMENT, col. 872. *Cochrane* v. *Tuthill,* (1908) V.L.R., 549; 30 A.L.T., 50; 14 A.L.R., 453.

Tramways Act 1890 (No. 1148), Second Schedule, Part II., clause 17—" Avoiding " payment of fare—Refusal to pay full fare—Honest belief that full fare not payable—Mens rea.]—See LOCAL GOVERNMENT, cols. 870, 871. *Cochrane* v. *Tuthill,* (1908) V.L.R., 549; 30 A.L.T., 50; 14 A.L.R., 453.

Tramways Act 1890 (No. 1148),—Tramways tickets sold subject to condition that they shall not be available on holidays—Whether available on half-holidays.]—See LOCAL GOVERN-MENT, col. 871. *Cochrane* v. *Tuthill,* (1908) V.L.R., 549; 30 A.L.T., 50; 14 A.L.R., 453.

TRANSFER OF LAND ACT.

I.—BRINGING LAND UNDER THE ACT.

See also, *post*, IV. CAVEATS ; V. RECTI-FICATION OF CERTIFICATES.

Application to bring land under Transfer of Land Act—Sale of land for non-payment of rates under decree of County Court—Dead owner made defendant—Order for substituted service—Commissioner of Titles acting upon records in the office—Refusal to issue certifi-cate of title—Local Government Act 1903

(No. 1893), secs. 324, 341, 342, 343, 704.]—
An applicant to bring land under the operation of the *Transfer of Land Act* 1890 made title under a conveyance from the Registrar of the County Court at Melbourne and lodged in support of his application the conveyance and an office copy of a decree for sale of such land made in a suit in such Court. The suit had been brought by a municipality against H.M., who appeared by a registered conveyance to be the owner of the land, to obtain a declaration that certain unpaid rates were a charge on the land and for an order for sale in default of payment. An order for substituted service of the summons in the said suit had been obtained. From papers relating to the land in question in the Office of Titles the Commissioner discovered that H.M. had died long before the institution of the suit. He therefore refused the application on the ground that the decree of the County Court was ineffectual to bind the owner of the land. *Held* (*per a' Beckett, Hodges* and *Hood, JJ.*) that the Commissioner was right in refusing to direct the Registrar of Titles to issue a certificate. *Per Hood, J.*—Sec. 704 of the *Local Government Act* 1903 is merely an evidence section and does not enable a plaintiff to escape making the owner or occupier a party by merely inserting the name of a person who is dead as defendant. *In re the Transfer of Land Act; Ex parte Anderson*, (1911) V.L.R., 397; 33 A.L.T., 78; 17 A.L.R., 399.

Transfer of Land Act 1890 (No. 1149), sec. 21—Lunacy Act 1890 (No. 1113), sec. 130—Lunatic so found by inquisition in England—Lunatic's land in Victoria—Bringing land under Act—Committee may be authorised.]—
Semble.—There is jurisdiction under sec. 130 of the *Lunacy Act* 1890 to authorise a committee to bring land under the Act. *In re A.B., a lunatic*, (1909) V.L.R., 100; 30 A.L.T., 158; 15 A.L.R., 85. *a' Beckett, J.*

Transfer of land Act 1890 (No. 1149), sec. 28—Bringing land under the Act—Land sought to be brought under Act in excess of land shown in Crown grant—Occupation, necessity for.]—*Semble*, on an application to bring land under the *Transfer of Land Act*, occupation by the applicant, or those claiming under him, is a necessary condition under sec. 28, when the land sought to be brought under the Act is in excess of the land shown in the Crown grant. *National Trustees Executors &c. Co. of Australasia Ltd.*, v. *Hassett and the Registrar of Titles*, (1907) V.L.R., 404; 28 A.L.T., 232; 13 A.L.R., 208. *Cussen, J.*

Application to bring land under Act—Field notes, date of.]—Where field notes are submitted in support of an application to bring land under the Act, it is desirable that the office should show at what date the field work was done. *National Trustees Executors &c. Co. of Australasia Ltd.* v. *Hassett and the Registrar of Titles*, (1907) V.L.R., 404; 28 A.L.T., 232; 13 A.L.R., 208. *Cussen, J.*

Trustee—Bringing land under Transfer of Land Act 1890—Mortgage of trust estate to pay costs of—Breach of trust.]—See Trusts and Trustees. *Crout* v. *Beissel*, (1909) V.L.R., 207; 30 A.L.T., 185; 15 A.L.R., 143.

II.—Certificates of Title and Registration.

Transfer of Land Act 1890 (No. 1149), secs. 69, 74—Certificate of title, how far conclusive—Same land included in two certificates—Subsequent certificate, when it may be conclusive.]—Sec. 69 of the *Transfer of Land Act* 1890 does not in any way negative or limit the effect of the exceptions contained in sec. 74, which must be read as a proviso to sec. 69. Where the same piece of land is included in two certificates of title, it is the prior certificate which usually has the conclusive effect mentioned in sec. 69; but where there has been a wrong description of boundaries, or where there are rights acquired by adverse possession, the prior certificate may not be conclusive in whole or in part, and the subsequent certificate may then have the conclusive effect. *National Trustees, Executors, &c. Co. of Australasia Ltd.* v. *Hassett and the Registrar of Titles*, (1907) V.L.R., 404; 28 A.L.T., 232; 13 A.L.R., 208. *Cussen, J.*

Transfer of Land Act 1890 (No. 1149), —Certificate of title, effect of—Error in survey —Land under general law owned by person other than registered proprietor included in certificate—Whether registered proprietor entitled to land so included.]—Where by an error in survey land under the general law owned and occupied by B. is included in a certificate of title issued to A., A. does not thereby acquire any estate or interest in such land. *National Trustees Executors, &c., Co. of Australasia Ltd.* v. *Hassett and the Registrar of Titles,* (1907) V.L.R., 404 ; 28 A.L.T., 232 ; 13 A.L.R., 208. *Cussen, J.*

Transfer of Land Act 1890 (No. 1149), secs. 22, 24, 25, 26, 28, 29, 31, 33, 34, 69, 74, 164, 165, 174 to 185, 194, 199, 200, 205, 210—Real Property Act 1890 (No. 1136), secs. 215, 216—Transfer of Land Act 1904 (No. 1931), sec. 10 et seq.—Certificate of title—Same land included in two grants—Difference in dates—Prior certificate not conclusive—Wrong description of parcels or boundaries—Adverse possession—Measurements in Crown grant not in accord with land actually granted—Application to amend certificate by owner and occupier—Action to restrain—Powers of Commissioner.]—Before the year 1858 A. and B. were Crown grantees of adjoining blocks of land, that of B. being to the south of that of A, and the grant of A. being earlier in date. In neither case did the land marked out on the ground correspond with the measurements in the grant, but B.'s block as marked out on the ground was in fact the very land granted by his Crown grant and was subsequently included in the certificate of title issued to him. Along the northern boundary of B.'s block as so marked out a fence had been erected in the year 1857, and this fence remained in the same position up till the time of the action. The foot reserve, afterwards referred to, was always on B.'s side of the fence, and, apart from his right to it as being included in the Crown grant, B. having been in occupation since the year 1858, had acquired a title to it by adverse possession long prior to the year 1891, when A. obtained his certificate of title. A. subdivided his land, and had purported to set out a road along his southern boundary, with a foot reserve between the road and B.'s land, but owing to a surveyor's error, there was not in fact sufficient land for this purpose on the north of the fence and the foot reserve ran along the south side of the fence upon the land owned and occupied by B. In the year 1891 A.'s administratrix made an application to bring A.'s land under the *Transfer of Land Act,* and, owing to errors in survey and to statements as to the extent of the land owned and occupied by her, a certificate of title was issued showing as her southern boundary a line which would include the foot reserve south of the fence. B. afterwards brought his land under the Act, and a certificate of title issued to him also including the foot reserve of which he was still in occupation. The executor of B. applied to have his certificate amended by having the land in it described as abutting on the road set out by A. The administrator *de bonis non* of A.'s estate lodged a caveat and brought an action to recover possession of the foot reserve, and claiming an injunction restraining the executor of B. and the Registrar of Titles from proceeding with the application to amend. The facts were found as above set out. *Held,* that as the land in dispute had been included in plaintiff's certificate by a wrong description of parcels or boundaries and also because of B.'s rights acquired by adverse possession, the plaintiff was not entitled to recover possession. *Held,* also, that as the Commissioner might in the absence of a caveat have granted the application to amend, and as the land in dispute was owned and occupied by the defendant, the plaintiff was not entitled to an injunction. *National Trustees Executors &c. Co. of Australasia Ltd.* v. *Hassett and the Registrar of Titles,* (1907) V.L.R., 404 ; 28 A.L.T., 232 ; 13 A.L.R., 208. *Cussen, J.*

Allegation by plaintiff that he is seised of land in fee—Denial by defence—Certificate of title produced by plaintiff in proof of allegation —Whether defendant may show certificate not conclusive owing to land being included by wrong description of boundaries.]—Where the plaintiff alleges that he is seised in fee of certain land and uses a certificate of title to prove it, it is open to the defendant, who has simply denied the allegations in his defence, to show that the certificate is not conclusive owing to the land in question being included therein by wrong description of boundaries. *National Trustees, Executors &c. Co. of Australasia* v. *Hassett and the Registrar of Titlrs*, (1907) V.L.R., 404 ; 28 A.L.T., 232 ; 13 A.L.R., 208. *Cussen, J.*

III.—DEALINGS WITH LAND.

(a) *Transfers.*

(1) Executors and Administrators.

Transfer of Land Act 1890 (No. 1149), secs. 186, 194, 209—Administrator—Sale of land more than twenty years after death of intestate —Registration of transfer—Registrar of Titles, powers of.]—Where a transfer by an administrator of land of his intestate was lodged for registration twenty-five years after the death of the intestate, *Held*, that the Registrar of Titles was not entitled to require the administrator to justify the sale by adducing evidence that debts of the intestate remained unpaid or that the sale was authorized by the next-of-kin or other persons beneficially entitled to the land. *Blake* v. *Bayne*, (1908) A.C., 371 ; 14 A.L.R., 317, explained ; *Cooper* v. *Cooper*, L.R. 7 H.L., 53, followed. *In re Transfer of Land Act ; Ex parte Equity Trustees Executors &c. Co. Ltd.*, (1911) V.L.R., 197 ; 32 A.L.T., 183 ; 17 A.L.R., 154. F.C., *Madden, C.J., a'Beckett* and *Hood, JJ.*

Transfer of Land Act 1890 (No. 1149), secs. 89, 91—Transfer of Land, registration of— Transfer by administrator as such to himself in his own right—Whether an instrument fit for registration.]—The Registrar of Titles has no power to refuse to register a transfer upon the mere ground that it is a transfer by an executor or administrator as such to himself in his own right. *Ex parte Wisewould*, 16 V.L.R., 149 ; 11 A.L.T., 182, approved. *In re Transfer of Land Act ; Ex parte Danaher*, (1911) V.L.R., 214 ; 32 A.L.T., 190 ; 17 A.L.R., 160. F.C., *Madden, C.J.,* and *a'Beckett, J.* (*Hood, J.,* dissenting).

Transfer of Land Act 1890 (No. 1149), Part IV.—Gift to person standing in fiduciary relation to donor—Transfer by administrator as such to himself in his own right—Assign- ment by next-of-kin of their interests to administrator—Whether Commissioner entitled to call for proof that next-of-kin had independent advice and understood nature of transaction.**]—D., the registered proprietor of certain land, died intestate, and J., one of D.'s next-of-kin, administered to his estate and became registered proprietor of the land as his administrator. J. lodged for registration a transfer of the land by himself as administrator to himself personally and also produced a deed under the general law conveying to him all the estate and interest of all the other next-of-kin who were all *sui juris*. There was no suggestion that any of such other next of kin were insane or had changed their minds. *Held* (*per Madden, C.J.,* and *a'Beckett, J.*) that the Commissioner was not entitled to require, as a condition to registering the transfer, proof that such other next-of-kin had had independent advice and thoroughly understood the nature and effect of the assignment. *In re Transfer of Land Act ; Ex parte Danaher*, (1911) V.L.R., 214 ; 32 A.L.T., 190 ; 17 A.L.R., 160. F.C.

Commissioner of Titles—Matters involving consideration of trust—Power to question.]— *Per a'Beckett, J.* (delivering the judgment of the Court) :—" As to the Commissioner questioning matters involving considerations of trust, we have been urged to say that he should not do so. I think that to say that would be most dangerous. He must frequently have to question documents which would come before him in connection with dealings by trustees. We do not say that he is bound to concern himself with their fiduciary positions, but we decline to say that he is not entitled to do so." *In re Transfer of Land Act 1890 : Ex parte Edmonds and Harrison,* 34 A.L.T., 105 ; 18 A.L.R., 41. F.C., *a'Beckett, Hodges* and *Cussen, JJ.* (1912).

(2) Easements.

Transfer of Land Act 1890 (No. 1149), sec. 89—Conveyancing Act 1904 (No. 1953, sec. 6 Vendor and purchaser—Former unity of title and possession—Implied grant—Quasi-easement—Rainwater flowing over surface— Adjoining owners—Natural servitude—Altera-

tion of surface.]—Upon transfer by A. to B. of one of two allotments owned by A., subject to the *Transfer of Land Act*, and so situated that rainwater flowed from the allotment sold to B. upon the allotment retained by A., there being no grant expressed in the transfer of or implied from the circumstances attending the transfer of a servitude *ne facias* or a negative easement restraining A. from preventing the rainwater from flowing on to the allotment retained by him. *Held*, that such a servitude or easement was not passed by vitue of the general words in sec. 6 of the *Conveyancing Act* 1904, and sec. 89 of the *Transfer of Land Act* 1890. *Nelson* v. *Walker*, (1910) 10 C.L.R. 560; 16 A.L.R., 285. H.C., *Griffith, C.J., O'Connor, Isaacs* and *Higgins, JJ.*

Transfer of Land Act 1890 (No. 1149), secs. 74, 75, 89—Quasi-easement—Severance of unity of possession and title.—Implied grant—Derogation from grant.]—The foundation of the doctrine of implied grant in the case of a conveyance of part of a parcel of land, the vendor retaining the rest, is that having regard to all the circumstances of the case, it must (not may) have been in the contemplation of the parties that the grantor should not use the land which he retains in such a way as to preclude any use of the land which he sells or that use for which he knows he is selling it to the purchaser. *Quaere, per Griffith, C.J.*, whether the doctrine of such implied grant is at all applicable to land under the *Transfer of Land Act. Semble.* — No such grant is to be implied (so as to bind successors in title) from circumstances not referred to in the transfer. *Nelson* v. *Walker*, (1910) 10 C.L.R., 560; 16 A.L.R., 285. H.C., *Griffith, C.J., Isaacs* and *Higgins, JJ.*

Transfer of Land Act 1890 (No. 1149), secs. 74, 140—Rain water flowing over surface—Natural right on the part of adjoining proprietor to the flow.]—*Quaere, per Higgins, J.*, whether land held under the *Transfer of Land Act* 1890 is subject to a natural right on the part of the proprietor of land to the uninterrupted flow of water over adjoining land. *Nelson* v. *Walker*, (1910) 10 C.L.R., 560; 16 A.L.R., 285. H.C., *Griffith, C.J., O'Connor, Isaacs* and *Higgins, JJ.*

(3) Title ; Conditions of Sale.

Title with apparent flaw—Existence of flaw negatived by proof of facts—Whether purchaser may be compelled to accept title—Transfer of Land Act—Land under, whether same rule applicable to.]—By the general law a title, which has what would appear to be a flaw until negatived by proof of disputable facts, can be forced on an unwilling purchaser, and that rule applies to land under the *Transfer of Land Act. In re Kenna and Ritchie's Contract,* (1907) V.L.R., 386; 28 A.L.T., 218; 13 A.L.R., 191. *a' Beckett, J.*

Sale of land—Restrictive covenant running with land—Covenant notified as an encumbrance on certificate of title—Purchaser of part of land not in part affected by covenant—Whether purchaser bound to accept title—Proof of facts showing covenant does not affect part of land sold—Costs, of how borne.]—R., who owned an estate, as to which there existed a restrictive covenant running with the land limiting the amount of water which might be discharged from it on to adjoining land, subdivided the estate and sold part of it to K. The rights of the persons claiming under the deed creating this restrictive covenant were notified as an encumbrance on the certificate of title to the whole estate. A requisition was made for an undertaking by R. that a certificate of title to the part sold should issue to K. free from the encumbrance. R. refused to give his undertaking and K. took out a summons claiming rescission. The Judge found that by reason of the contour and natural features of the part purchased by K. and of the adjoining lands, the restrictive covenant did not in fact affect such part. *Held*, that K, was entitled to demand satisfactory evidence that the covenant in question did not affect the land purchased by him, which evidence should have been furnished at the cost of R., but that the encumbrance on the certificate of title did not constitute a valid objection to title. *In re Kenna and Ritchie's Contract,* (1907) V.L.R., 386; 28 A.L.T., 218; 13 A.L.R., 191. *a' Beckett, J.*

Vendor and purchaser—Contract for sale of land—Requisition on title—Vendor unable or

unwilling to comply with requisition—Right of vendor to annul sale—Transfer of Land Act 1890 (No. 1149), Schedule XXV., Table A (4).]—*See* VENDOR AND PURCHASER. *West* v. *Hedgeland.* (1909) V.L.R., 178; 30 A.L.T., 175; 15 A.L.R., 123.

Vendor and purchaser—Agreement to give possession on a certain day—Condition that vendor may annul sale if unable or unwilling to comply with requisition—Inability or unwillingness, what is—Knowledge of vendor of his inability to comply with terms of contract—Specific performance, so far as possible, with compensation—Whether purchaser entitled to—Transfer of Land Act 1890 (No. 1149), Schedule XXV., Condition 4.]—*See* VENDOR AND PURCHASER. *McGavin* v. *Gerraty*, 32 A.L.T., 151; 17 A.L.R., 85.

Vendor and purchaser—Conditions of sale—Production of certificate of title—Place of production.]—*See* VENDOR AND PURCHASER. *Morrison* v. *Richardson*, (1907) V.L.R., 218; 28 A.L.T., 166; 13 A.L.R., 94.

(4) Costs.

Conveyancing Act 1904 (No. 1953), secs. 1, 3, 4 (6), (9)—Vendor and purchaser—Perusal fees, legality of contract for payment of by purchaser—Land under Transfer of Land Act—Transfer.]—*See* CONVEYANCING ACT, col. 241. *Re Stewart and Parke's Contract*, (1907) V.L.R., 31; 28 A.L.T., 133; 12 A.L.R., 553.

Conveyancing Act 1904 (No. 1953), sec. 4 (6)—Whether applicable to land under Transfer of Land Act—"Conveyance," "transfer"—Contract of sale by auction—Stipulation that purchaser shall pay vendor's costs of perusal of conveyance.]—Sec. 4 (6) of the *Conveyancing Act* 1904 applies to sales by auction of land under the *Transfer of Land Act* 1890. *Re Stewart and Park's Contract*, (1907) V.L.R., 31; 28 A.L.T., 133; 12 A.L.R. 553, followed. *Re Rodgers and Rodd's Contract*, (1907) V.L.R., 511; 29 A.L.T., 13; 13 A.L.R., 312. *Madden, C.J.* (1907).

(b) Mortgages and Annuities.

Transfer of Land Act 1890 (No. 1149), secs. 74, 89, 95, 121, 124, 129, 130, 230—Mortgage

—Foreclosure—Whether, after foreclosure, mortgagee may sue on the covenant to pay —Extinguishment of mortgage debt.]—On foreclosure under secs. 129 and 130 of the *Transfer of Land Act* 1890 the title of the mortgagee, when, pursuant to sec. 130, he is registered as proprietor of the mortgaged land, is, in the absence of fraud, absolute and unimpeachable, and, by reason of the provision in sec. 130 that the mortgagee shall be deemed a transferree of the mortgaged land, and of the other provisions of the Act defining the obligations incurred by a transferree of mortgaged land with respect to the mortgage debt, the mortgage debt is extinguished, and, therefore, no action will lie subsequently by the mortgagee upon the covenant in the mortgage to repay the mortgage debt. *In re Premier Permanent Building Land and Investment Association*; *Ex parte Lyell*, 25 V.L.R., 77; 21 A.L.T., 67; 5 A.L.R., 209, overruled. *Fink* v. *Robertson*, 4 C.L.R., 864; 13 A.L.R., 157. H.C., *Griffith, C.J., Barton* and *O'Connor, JJ., Higgins, J.,* dissenting (1907).

Mortgagor and mortgagee—Recovery of money secured by mortgage barred by determination of period of limitation—Mortgagee in possession—Power of sale, whether exercise of also barred—Real Property Act 1890 (No. 1136), secs. 18, 43, 47—Transfer of Land Act 1890 (No. 1149), secs. 114, 116.]—A mortgagee's power of sale under the *Transfer of Land Act* 1890, where he has entered into possession of the mortgaged land and is in receipt of the rents and profits thereof, is not affected by reason only that his right to recover by suit or action the money secured by the mortgage is barred by sec. 47 of the *Real Property Act* 1890. *Ex parte The Australian Deposit and Mortgage Bank Ltd.*, (1907) V.L.R., 348; 28 A.L.T., 192; 13 A.L.R., 132. F.C., *Madden, C.J., Hodges* and *Hood, JJ.*

Mortgage—Registration—Covenant by persons not parties to the mortgage guaranteeing repayment of principal—Mortgage otherwise in statutory form—Whether Registrar bound to register—Transfer of Land Act 1890 (No. 1149), secs. 113, 240.]—The Registrar of

Titles is not justified in refusing to register a mortgage, otherwise in the ordinary statutory form, of land under the *Transfer of Land Act* 1890 on the ground that there is added to it a covenant by persons not parties to the mortgage guaranteeing repayment of the mortgage money. *Perpetual Executors and Trustees Association, &c. Ltd.* v. *Hosken*, (1912) 14 C.L.R., 286; 18 A.L.R., 201. H.C., *Griffith, C.J., Barton* and *Isaacs, JJ.*

Mortgage—Registration—Improper refusal to register—Mandamus, whether mortgagee has a remedy by—Existence of another remedy—Transfer of Land Act 1890 (No. 1149), sec. 209).]—Where the Registrar improperly refuses to register a mortgage the mortgagee has a remedy by mandamus to compel registration, notwithstanding that right is specifically given by the *Transfer of Land Act* 1890, sec. 209, to the owner or proprietor of the land to summon the Registrar to substantiate the grounds of his refusal before the Supreme Court. *Perpetual Executors and Trustees Association &c. Ltd.* v. *Hosken*, (1912) 14 C.L.R., 286; 18 A.L.R., 201. H.C., *Griffith, C.J., Barton* and *Isaacs, JJ.*

Mortgage — Registration — Contributing mortgage—Money advanced by mortgagees in unequal shares—Tenancy in common—Transfer of Land Act 1890 (No. 1149), secs. 57, 65, 113, 229, 240.]—By an instrument of mortgage a mortgagor mortgaged land under the *Transfer of Land Act* 1890 to the mortgagees The instrument, after setting out the usual covenants, contained a number of provisoes. At the end of the first proviso, which related to the postponement of the time of payment of the principal in the event of punctual payment of interest and due performance of the covenants, was a clause stating that "it is hereby agreed" that the principal sum "belongs to" the two mortgagees in unequal specified proportions. The Registrar of Titles refused to register the instrument. *Held*, that the mortgage was a mortgage to the mortgagees as several owners, and not as joint owners, that there was nothing in the Act prohibiting the registration of such a mortgage, and, therefore, that the Registrar

should have registered it. *Drake* v. *Templeton*, (1913) 16 C.L.R., 153; 19 A.L.R., 93. H.C., *Griffith, C.J., Barton, Isaacs* and *Duffy, JJ.*

Transfer of Land Act 1890 (No. 1149), sec. 59—Companies Act 1890 (No. 1074), sec. 235—Mortgage by mining company—Registration, sufficiency of—Land under the general law.]—Where a mining company gives a mortgage over land under the *Transfer of Land Act* registration of the instrument under that Act is the only registration necessary in order to comply with the requirements of sec. 235 of the *Companies Act* 1890. The provision requiring registration with the Registrar-General applies only to land under the general law. *In re Transfer of Land Act; Ex parte Coronation Gold Mining Co. No Liability*, (1911) V.L.R., 78; 32 A.L.T., 129; 17 A.L.R., 39. F.C., *a' Beckett, Hodges* and *Hood, JJ.*

Transfer of Land Act 1890 (No. 1149), sec. 140—Mortgage by trustee in breach of trust—Absence of fraud or dishonesty—Actual notice of breach—Mortgage not lodged for registration until after issue of writ.]—Where trustees in breach of trust mortgaged trust realty to a person who had actual notice of the breach, and the mortgage though registered was not lodged for registration until after the issue of the writ in the action for breach of trust. *Held*, that as there was nothing on the part of any of the persons concerned which the Court would call fraud or which was in fact dishonest, the mortgage was valid. *Crout* v. *Beissel*, (1909) V.L.R., 207; 30 A.L.T., 185; 15 A.L.R., 143. *a' Beckett, J.*

Transfer of Land Act 1890 (No. 1149), secs. 4, 113, 240, Thirteenth Schedule—Charge of land—Registration—Annuity charged on land to secure performance of contract—Annuity ceasing to be payable in certain events.]—By an instrument in writing A. purported to charge certain land with an annuity of £150 a year for three years payable by equal monthly instalments in favor of B. The instrument contained a provision whereby it was expressly agreed as to any instalment of the annuity that if throughout the month immediately preceding the due date for payment of such instalment the whole of the covenants of A. with B. should have been duly observed and performed B. should give A. a release in respect of that instalment. The instrument then contained certain covenants on the part of A., including covenants to use the premises on the land as a hotel only, to keep in force the licence for the hotel, to perform and observe all the provisions of the Licensing Acts, and to purchase from B. at certain prices all colonial beer, etc., sold in the hotel. *Held,* that that which was called an annuity in the instrument was an annuity within the meaning of sec. 4 of the *Transfer of Land Act* 1890, and that the instrument was a charge within sec. 113 and the Thirteenth Schedule of that Act, and therefore that the Registrar was not justified in refusing to register the instrument as a charge. *Perpetual Executors and Trustees Association of Australia Ltd.* v. *Hosken,* 14 C.L.R., 286 ; 18 A.L.R., 201, followed. *Mahoney* v. *Hosken,* 14 C.L.R., 379 ; 18 A.L.R., 205. H.C., *Griffith, C.J., Barton* and *Isaacs, J.* (1912).

Will—Settlement — Annuity — Charge, whether on corpus or income—Order of Court —Transfer of Land Statute 1866 (No. 301), sec. 86.]—*See* SETTLEMENT. *Brown* v. *Abbott,* (1908) 5 C.L.R., 487.

IV.—CAVEATS.

Application to bring land under the Act— Caveat—Action by caveator to assert right— Action dismissed without determination of merits—Right of applicant to have caveat removed—Transfer of Land Act 1890 (No. 1149), secs. 33, 34.]—Where a caveatrix had taken proceedings under sec. 34 of the *Transfer of Land Act* 1890 to establish her title, and those proceedings had been dismissed for want of prosecution consequent on her inability to give security for costs, the Court ordered the removal of the caveat. *In re McNaughton* ; *In re Transfer of Land Act,* (1909) V.L.R., 398 ; 31 A.L.T., 47 ; 15 A.L.R., 406. F.C., *Madden, C.J.,* and *Hodges, J.* (*Cussen, J.* dissenting), (1909).

Transfer of Land Act 1890 (No. 1149), sec. 33—Removal of caveat—Discretion of Court.] —On an application under sec. 33 of the *Transfer of Land Act* 1890 for the removal of a caveat, the Court has a discretion whether or not it will grant the application. *In re McNaughton* ; *In re Transfer of Land Act,* 1909) V.L.R., 398 ; 31 A.L.T., 47 ; 15 A.L.R., 406. F.C., *Madden, C.J., Hodges* and *Cussen, JJ.* (1909).

V.—RECTIFICATION OF CERTIFICATES.

Transfer of Land Act 1890 (No. 1149), secs. 28-31, Part IX.—Rectification of certificates— Commissioner of Titles, powers of—Whether limited to rectification of mistakes of officers— Judicial functions of Commissioner of Titles.] —The powers of rectification of the Commissioner are not confined to mistakes entirely due to his officers, but extend to mistakes induced by acts of an applicant. His powers are not limited to obvious blunders. He is a judicial officer with a wide jurisdiction over boundaries. *National Trustees Executors &c. Co. of Australasia Ltd.* v. *Hassett and the Registrar of Titles,* (1907) V.L.R., 404 ; 28 A.L.T., 232 ; 13 A.L.R., 208. *Cussen, J.*

Transfer of Land Act 1890 (No. 1149), secs. 28, 29, 176, 183—Rectification of certificate —Limitation of power of rectification to discrepancies referred to in sec. 29.]—*Semble,* sec. 29 of the *Transfer of Land Act* 1890 is a limitation of the powers possessed by the Commissioner of Titles under secs. 28, 176, and 183. *National Trustees Executors &c. Co. of Australasia Ltd.* v. *Hassett and the Registrar of Titles,* (1907) V.L.R., 404 ; 28 A.L.T., 232 ; 13 A.L.R., 208. *Cussen, J.*

Transfer of Land Act 1890 (No. 1149), sec. 183—Rectification of certificates—" Determined in a contested proceeding," meaning of.]—*Semble,* sec. 183 should be read as if the words " against the applicant " were inserted after the word " determined." *National Trustees Executors &c. Co. of Australasia Ltd.* v. *Hassett and the Registrar of Titles,* (1907) V.L.R., 404 ; 28 A.L.T., 232 ; 13 A.L.R., 208. *Cussen, J.*

Rectification of certificates—Crown grant—Evidence of the land to which it relates—Long and unchallenged occupancy.]—In the absence of survey marks there can be no better indication of the land to which a Crown grant relates than long and unchallenged occupancy. *National Trustees Executors &c. Co. of Australasia Ltd.* v. *Hassett and the Registrar of Titles*, (1907) V.L.R., 404 ; 28 A.L.T., 232 ; 13 A.L.R., 208. *Cussen, J.*

VI.—VESTING ORDERS ; TRANSMISSION.

Trusts Act 1890 (No. 1150), secs. 34, 36—Transfer of Land Act 1890 (No. 1149), sec. 188—Appointment of new trustee—Vesting order—Land under the Act.]—Where a sole trustee of land under the *Transfer of Land Act* 1890 dies out of the jurisdiction, and no administration of his estate nor probate of his will is applied for, the Court has power to appoint a new trustee in his place, and to make an order that the land the subject matter of the trust vest in him for all the estate that the deceased trustee had in him at the time of his death. *In re Fink*, (1910) V.L.R., 337 ; 32 A.L.T., 26 ; 16 A.L.R., 352. *a' Beckett, J.*

Two trustees—One incapable—Appointment of new trustee by other trustee—Estate including land under Transfer of Land Act—Vesting order—Trusts Act 1890 (No. 1150), sec. 4—Trusts Act 1896 (No. 1421), sec. 7—Transfer of Land Act 1890 (No. 1149), sec. 188.]—*See* TRUSTS AND TRUSTEES. *Re Hope*, (1910) V.L.R., 492 ; 32 A.L.T., 71 ; 16 A.L.R., 581.

Transfer of Land Act 1890—Real estate of deceased testator—Executor dying without having registered as proprietor—Executorial duties—Administration de bonis non c.t.a. when granted—Administration and Probate Act 1890 (No. 1060), sec. 8.]—Where a testator has left land of which he was registered proprietor, it is the duty of his executor to procure himself to be registered as proprietor of the land as executor and until that is done his executorial duties are not completed. Where an administrator *c.t.a.* having administered the personal estate, died without becoming registered proprietor of the land as administrator of the real estate of the testator, administration *de bonis non c.t.a.* of the estate of the original testator was granted to his daughter. *In re Allan*, (1912) V.L.R., 286 ; 34 A.L.T., 2 ; 18 A.L.R., 217. *Madden, C.J.*

VII.—PROCEEDINGS TO ESTABLISH TITLE UNDER TRANSFER OF LAND ACT 1904.

Transfer of Land Act 1904 (No. 1931), sec. 10—Adverse possession — Registered proprietor dead before commencement of Adverse possession—No administration of his estate—Next of kin unknown—Duration of adverse possession.]—The provisions of sec. 10 of the *Transfer of Land Act* 1904 were not intended to alter the conditions necessary to the acquisition of a title by adverse possession to land. Consequently, where the registered proprietor has died intestate, and no administration of his estate has been granted, and it is not known whether he left any next of kin, a title cannot be acquired under sec. 10 of the *Transfer of Land Act* 1904 by adverse possession commencing after the death of the registered proprietor, until such possession has continued for thirty years. Where the widow of such registered proprietor continues in possession of the land from his death, her possession will be deemed adverse possession although she has purported to hold the land by virtue of the Crown grants in her possession. *Lambourn* v. *Hosken*, (1912) V.L.R., 394 ; 34 A.L.T., 101 ; 18 A.L.R., 371. *a' Beckett, J.*

Transfer of Land Act 1904 (No. 1931), secs. 10, 11—Land alienated after 1st October, 1862—Crown grant not registered—Adverse possession.]—The *Transfer of Land Act* 1904 (sec. 10) applies only where the adverse possession is in derogation of the estate of a deceased proprietor. It does not apply where there has never been a registered proprietor of the land. *Burns* v. *The Registrar of Titles*, (1912) V.L.R., 29 ; 18 A.L.R., 47. *Cussen, J.*

Transfer of Land Act 1904 (No. 1931), sec. 10—Title by adverse possession against registered proprietor—Declaratory judgment sought

—Action brought too soon—Liberty to apply at future date.]—Where an action under sec. 10 of the *Transfer of Land Act* 1904 had been brought too soon, no declaration as to title was made, but on the evidence it was declared that the plaintiff and those through whom he claimed had since the death of the registered proprietor been in undisturbed possession of the land adversely to the rightful owners thereof, and the plaintiff was given liberty to apply at any time to obtain the declaration sought in the action. *Lambourn v. Hosken*, (1912) V.L.R., 394; 34 A.L.T., 101; 18 A.L.R., 371. *a'Beckett, J.*

Transfer of Land Act 1904 (No. 1931), sec. 10—Supreme Court Rules 1906, Chapter VIII., rule 2.—Adverse possession, title by— Vesting order—Registered proprietor deceased —Practice.]—In proceedings to establish title by adverse possession under the *Transfer of Land Act* 1904, sec. 10, where the person who was registered proprietor, and whose name remains on the register is dead, the plaintiff is not bound to adopt the procedure prescribed by the *Supreme Court Rules*, Chapter VIII. *Marriott* v. *Hosken*, (1911) V.L.R., 54; 32 A.L.T., 115; 16 A.L.R., 604. *a'Beckett, J.*

Transfer of Land Act 1904 (No. 1931), sec. 10—Rules of the Supreme Court 1906, Ch. VIII., r. 2—Adverse possession against registered proprietor—Procedure—Registered proprietor deceased.]—The rules in Chapter VIII. of the *Rules of the Supreme Court* 1906, other than rule 2, apply to a case where the registered proprietor is dead. *Marriott* v. *Hosken*, (1911) V.L.R., 54; 32 A.L.T., 115; 16 A.L.R., 604, explained. *Lambourn* v. *Hosken*, (1912) V.L.R., 394; 34 A.L.T., 101; 18 A.L.R., 371. *a'Beckett, J.*

TRAVELLING STOCK.

See STOCK DISEASES ACT.

TRESPASS.

Trespass—Fiduciary relationship—Employer and employee—Servant secretly procuring

determination of master's tenancy and a lease for himself—Exclusion of master from premises.]—The defendant, who was requested to assist his employer, the plaintiff, whose manager the defendant was, in the sale of his business as a going concern, nevertheless unknown to the plaintiff and while the business was still unsold, procured the landlord to determine the plaintiff's tenancy and to give the defendant a lease of the premises for six years. *Held*, that an action for trespass would not lie against the defendant for excluding the plaintiff from the premises after the defendant had entered into possession under the lease. *Prebble* v. *Reeves*, (1910) V.L.R., 88; 31 A.L.T., 114; 15 A.L.R., 631. F.C., *Madden, C.J., Hood* and *Cussen, JJ.*

Trespass to land—Entry by person entitled to possession—Trespass committed before entry but after right to enter arose—Reference back of actual entry to time when right arose— Right of action for trespass.]—For an instance of the application of the rule that the entry upon land by a person having the right to enter has reference to the time at which such right arose, and entitles such person to bring an action for a trespass committed before his actual entry provided that the trespass was subsequent to the right to enter, *see Ebbels* v. *Rewell*, (1908) V.L.R., 261; 29 A.L.T., 252; 14 A.L.R., 121. *Hodges, J.* (1908).

Trespass to land—Possession—Two persons on land each asserting land to be his—Right of person with title.]—For an instance of the application of the rule that, where two persons are on land each asserting that the land is his and each doing some act in assertion of his right of possession, the one who has the title is in actual possession, and has a right of action against the other for trespass, *see Ebbels* v. *Rewell*, (1908) V.L.R., 261; 29 A.L.T., 252; 14 A.L.R., 121. *Hodges, J.* (1908).

TRIAL.

See PRACTICE AND PLEADING.

TRUSTS ACTS.

See TRUSTS AND TRUSTEES.

TRUSTS AND TRUSTEES.

I.—CREATION AND DECLARATION OF TRUSTS.

(a) Express Trusts.

**Will—Precatory trust—" Believing that she
will do justice to my relatives."**]—Testator
devised and bequeathed all his real and personal estate to his executors and trustees and
directed " that the whole of my estate be
given to T.   . believing that she
will do justice to my relatives." *Held,* that
there was no trust and T. took the whole
estate absolutely. *In re Warren ; Verga
v. Taylor,* (1907) V.L.R., 325 ; 28 A.L.T.,
201 ; 13 A.L.R., 118. *a'Beckett, J.*

**Will—Interpretation—" Any balance to be
left as my executor may direct "—Power of
appointment—Trust—Uncertainty.**]—By her
will testatrix, after appointing G. as her
executor and directing payment of debts and
funeral expenses and giving certain legacies
provided that any balance was " to be left
as my executor may direct " and appointed
P. also as executor. *Held,* that the provision
as to the balance created, not a general power
of appointment in the executors, but a trust
which was void for uncertainty and that the
balance accordingly passed to the next of
kin. *Fenton v. Nevin,* 31 L.R. Ir., 478, followed. *In re Lewis ; Gollan v. Pyle,* 29
A.L.T., 36 ; 13 A.L.R., 431. *Hood, J.*
(1907).

Will — Construction — Precatory trust — " Hoping that he will secure."]—*See* WILL. *In re Lord* ; *Hall* v. *Grimshaw*, (1910) V.L.R., 477 ; 32 A.L.T., 90 ; 16 A.L.R., 509.

Will — Construction — Gift to testator's widow—" To be used by her as she may think proper for the benefit of herself and our children " — Whether trust created.]—*See* WILL. *In re Lawn* ; *Ballarat Trustees &c. Co.* v. *Perry*, (1911) V.L.R., 318 ; 33 A.L.T., 25 ; 17 A.L.R., 311.

Partnership agreement—Share payable on death of partner—Whether at his absolute disposal or in trust for widow and children.]— By a deed of partnership between the members of a firm of solicitors it was provided that in the event of the death or retirement of any of the partners the future profits of the business should be liable to the payment to his widow, child or children, or some one or other of them as he might by writing under his hand direct or to himself (as the case might be) of the sum of £2,500. *Held*, that in the event of the death of a partner a trust was created in favour of his widow and children or such of them as he should have appointed. *England* v. *Bayles*, (1906) V.L.R., 94 ; 27 A.L.T., 181 ; 12 A.L.R., 122. *Madden, C.J.* (1906).

Will — Construction — Charitable trust— Trust to pay passage money to immigrants— Relief of poverty—Validity of trust.]—*See* WILL. *In re Wallace* ; *Trustees Executors and Agency Co. Ltd.* v. *Fatt*, (1908) V.L.R., 636 ; 30 A.L.T., 100 ; 14 A.L.R., 502.

Will—Construction—Gift of residue—Trust for " charitable purposes "—Trust for " religious purposes "—Whether valid—Uncertainty.]—*See* WILL. *In re Dobinson* ; *Maddock* v. *Attorney-General*, (1911) V.L.R., 300 ; 33 A.L.T., 20 ; 17 A.L.R., 280.

Trust for accumulation, whether created— Restrictions upon operation of such trusts— —Wills Act 1890 (No. 1159), sec. 35—Trust for accumulation during minorities of persons who if of full age would be entitled to income—

Two periods of accumulation—Accumulation directed during a life with possible further period covering minorities—No person who would be entitled to income if of full age.] —Where by a will an accumulation during the life of each of the testator's daughters of the surplus income of a share in his residuary estate was directed following a direction for partial accumulation during a period of twenty years from testator's death, and the income was disposed of otherwise than as accessory to the gift of corpus, and the children of each daughter, who were to take the corpus and the accumulation of income, did not constitute a class which could be deemed to be closed when a child attained twenty-one years of age or being a female married, and there was accordingly no ascertained person or persons who could say that he or they had a vested indefeasible right to the surplus income, it was held that there was created a trust for accumulation during the life of each daughter which could not be upheld as a provision for accumulation " during the respective minorities only of any persons who under the uses or trusts of the . . . will . would for the time being if of full age be entitled unto the . . . annual produce so directed to be accumulated," and was void after twenty-one years from the testator's death. *In re Watson* ; *Cain* v. *Watson*, (1910) V.L.R., 256 ; 31 A.L.T., 242 ; 16 A.L.R., 76. *Cussen, J.*

Several trusts declared in respect of fund— Impossibility of first trust taking effect— Whether existence of subsequent trusts affected.]—Where a trust fund is in existence and several trusts affecting it are fully declared the later trusts may take effect although the first trust cannot possibly arise. *In re Munro* ; *National Trustees Executors &c. Co. of Australasia Ltd.* v. *Dunbar*, (1910) V.L.R., 395 ; 32 A.L.T., 41 ; 16 A.L.R., 363. *a' Beckett, J.*

Wills Act 1890 (No. 1159), sec. 35—Will, interpretation — Trust for accumulation, whether created—Absolute gift—Invalid attempt to cut down, effect of.]—*See* WILL. *In re Watson* ; *Cain* v. *Watson*, (1910) V.L.R., 256 ; 31 A.L.T., 212 ; 16 A.L.R., 76.

Will — Construction — Perpetuities, rule against—Remoteness—Trust for maintenance and education—Validity.]—*See* Will. *In re Stevens ; Trustees Executors and Agency Co. Ltd.* v. *Teague,* (1912) V.L.R., 194 ; 33 A.L.T., 233 ; 18 A.L.R., 195.

Will — Construction — Accumulations — Income of residuary estate, direction to accumulate beyond period allowed—Gift to grandchildren upon youngest attaining twenty-one —After-born grandchildren—Intestacy—Wills Act 1890 (No. 1159), sec. 35.]—*See* Will. *In re Stevens ; Trustees Executors and Agency Co. Ltd.* v. *Teague,* (1912) V.L.R., 194 ; 33 A.L.T., 233 ; 18 A.L.R., 195.

(b) Implied and Constructive Trusts.

Illegal contract—Transfer of land to defeat creditors—No proof that creditors defeated—Resulting trust.]—In an action by which the plaintiff alleges and proves that land, which stands in the defendant's name, was bought with the plaintiff's money, and was transferred to, and is held by, the defendant as trustee for the plaintiff, and seeks to compel the defendant to transfer the land to the plaintiff, it is not a defence that the land was originally transferred to the defendant in order to defeat the plaintiff's creditors unless it is also alleged and proved that that object was wholly or partly carried into effect. *Quaere,* whether such proof would be sufficient. *Payne* v. *McDonald,* (1908) 6 C.L.R., 208 ; 14 A.L.R., 366. H.C., *Griffith, C.J., O'Connor* and *Higgins, JJ.*

Parent and child—Purchase by parent in name of child—Presumption of advancement, when rebutted—Retention of life interest by parent—Real property, rule applicable to.]— Where property is purchased by a parent in the name of a child the presumption that the purchase is by way of advancement of the child is rebutted if it be shown that the parent intended to reserve a life interest to himself. This applies to both real and personal property. *McKie* v. *McKie,* 23 V.L.R., 489 ; 19 A.L.T., 190 ; 4 A.L.R., 98, followed. *Stuckey* v. *Trustees Executors and Agency Co. Ltd.,* (1910) V.L.R., 55 ; 31 A.L.T., 157 ; 16 A.L.R., 65. *Madden, C.J.*

Conveyancing Act 1904 (No. 1953), sec. 75—Equitable charge upon land, how created —Investment of trust money by agent in purchase of land—Parol evidence.]—A charge under sec. 75 of the *Conveyancing Act* 1904 may be created by parol. When any person in a fiduciary position, including an agent, has invested trust money in the purchase of land, the beneficial owner may have a charge on the property for the amount of the trust money, and trust money may be followed into the land on parol evidence. *In re Smith ; Smith* v. *Smith,* (1909) V.L.R., 91 ; 30 A.L.T., 214 ; 15 A.L.R., 25. *Hood, J.*

Constructive trustee — Employer and employee—Fiduciary relationship—Servant employed to sell business as a going concern— Servant secretly procuring determination of master's tenancy and a lease for himself.]—The plaintiff who carried on business in premises held on a monthly tenancy requested the defendant, his manager, who lived upon the premises, to help him in finding a purchaser for the business as a going concern. While so employed, acting secretly as regards the plaintiff and in breach of his duty, and in his own interest, the defendant procured the landlord to determine the plaintiff's tenancy, and to give the defendant a lease of the premises for six years. *Held,* that the defendant was a trustee for the plaintiff of the lease thus obtained. *Davis* v. *Hamlin,* 48 Am. R., 541 ; *Gower* v. *Andrew,* 43 Am. R., 242, and *Grumley* v. *Webb,* 100 Am. Dec., 304, approved. *Prebble* v. *Reeves,* (1910) V.L.R., 88 ; 31 A.L.T., 114 ; 15 A.L.R., 631. F.C., *Madden, C.J., Hood* and *Cussen, JJ.*

Employee under contract to devote whole time to employer's service—Employee entering service of another person—Duties towards other person inconsistent with service of employer—Knowledge and consent of employer— Right of employer to remuneration received by employee from other person—Constructive trust.]—*See* Employer and Employee, col. 433. *Reid* v. *MacDonald,* (1907) 4 C.L.R., 1572.

II.—Maintenance and Education of
Infants.

**Trusts Act 1896 (No. 1421), sec. 19—Infant
—Maintenance and education—Trust fund—
Breaking into corpus—Advancement.]**—The
Court will direct the application of the
corpus of a trust fund to the education of an
infant beneficiary when satisfied that it is
for the infant's benefit. *In re English,* (1909)
V.L.R., 430; 31 A.L.T., 74; 15 A.L.R.,
517. *Hood, J.*

**Trust—Corpus in trust for infant—Breaking
into in order to provide University fees—
Trusts Act 1896 (No. 1421), sec. 19.]**—By his
will a testator directed his trustees to pay the
net income of his estate to his widow and two
children until the youngest attained the age
of twenty-one, when the property was to be
realised and equally distributed amongst the
widow and children. The estate was of the
value of £1,650 and produced an income of
£48 a year. The elder child, a girl of seven-
teen, had won a scholarship entitling her to
five years' residence and tuition at an educa-
tional convent. As she had already passed
the Senior Public Examination, she would
not be able to avail herself of the scholarship
unless she undertook a University course
entailing an annual expenditure of £13 13s.
in fees. *Held,* that the circumstances
justified an allowance out of the corpus for
the payment of University fees. *Re Keam
(or Kean),* (1911) V.L.R., 165; 32 A.L.T.,
159; 17 A.L.R., 130. *Hodges, J.* (1911).

**Infant—Application for maintenance by
breaking into corpus—Heading of papers, form
of.]**—In applications respecting the maintenance of infants by breaking into corpus
and otherwise, the heading of the papers
should be simply:—" In the matter of A. an
infant." *Re Smith,* 12 A.L.R. (C N.), 5.
a'Beckett, J. (1906).

**Will — Construction — Contingent legacies
—Interim interest, whether infant contingent
legatees entitled to—Trusts Act 1896 (No.
1421), sec. 18.]**—*See* WILL. *In re Thompson; Brahe* v. *Mason,* (1910) V.L.R., 251;
31 A.L.T., 210; 16 A.L.R., 215.

III.—Retirement, Removal and Appointment of New Trustees; Vesting
Orders.

**Trusts Act 1890 (No. 1150), sec. 34—Ap-
pointment of new trustee, whether expedient—
Husband's banking account in wife's name—
Death of wife intestate—Letters of administration not taken out.]**—A married woman
died intestate leaving no property other than
certain moneys deposited in her name in
a bank. Her husband claimed that all
moneys paid into the bank to the credit of
his wife had been held by her in trust for him,
and his claim was not disputed by the wife's
next-of-kin. Upon an application by the
husband under sec. 34 of the *Trusts Act*
1890 for the appointment of a trustee in place
of his wife, *Held,* that it was not a case in
which it was expedient to make an order
under sec. 34, but that the proper course was
for the husband to apply for administration
of his wife's estate. *In re Ethell,* (1908)
V.L.R., 271; 29 A.L.T., 236; 14 A.L.R.,
180. *a'Beckett, J.*

**Appointment of new trustee—Retirement of
two trustees—Appointment of single trustee
in their place, sufficiency of—Trustee company—Trusts Act 1896 (No. 1421), sec. 4—
National Trustees, &c., Company's Act (51
Vict. No. 938), sec. 10.]**—A trustee company
cannot for the purposes of the provisions of
sec. 4 of the *Trusts Act* 1896 be treated as the
equivalent of two trustees. *In re Ritchie;
Murray* v. *Ritchie,* 28 V.L.R., 255; 24
A.L.T., 62; 8 A.L.R., 211, and *In re Fenessy,* 8 A.L.R., 211 (*n*), distinguished. *In re
Transfer of Land Act* 1890; *Ex parte Edmonds and Harrison,* 34 A.L.T., 105; 18
A.L.R., 41. F.C., *a'Beckett, Hodges* and
Cussen, JJ. (1912).

**Trustee—Will—No power of appointing
new trustees—Appointment by two trustees of
a trustee company as new trustee—Validity of
appointment—National Trustee, &c., Company's Act (51 Vict. No. 938), sec. 7.]**—Sec.
7 of the private Act (No. 938) of the National
Trustees, Executors and Agency Co. of Australasia Limited provides that in all cases
in which any person or persons having authority or power to appoint the Company as

trustee, it shall be lawful for the company to be appointed, and to act until removed from office as such trustee, and to perform and discharge all acts and duties pertaining to the office. *Held*, that that section merely provides for the competence of the company to fill the office of trustee, and imposes on it the responsibility for its acts when lawfully appointed, and does not enable trustees to terminate their responsibilities as such in a manner not contemplated by the instrument appointing them. When the trustees of a will, which contained no provision for the appointment of a new trustee, purported to act under that section, and to appoint the company as sole trustee in their place. *Held*, that the appointment was invalid. *In re The Transfer of Land Act* 1890; *Rx parte Edmonds and Harrison*, 34 A.L.T., 105; 18 A.L.R., 41. F.C., *a'Beckett, Hodges* and *Cussen, JJ.* (1912).

" **Equity Trustees Executors and Agency Company Limited Act** " (**No. 978**), **sec. 9— Appointment of company under, effect of.**]— *Quaere*, whether under sec. 9 of the "*Equity Trustees Executors and Agency Company Limited Act*" (No. 978) an executor, administrator or trustee can permanently appoint the company to act in his stead. *In re Hoarey*, (1906) V.L R., 437; 28 A.L.T., 93; 12 A.L.R., 450. *Cussen, J.*

Administration and Probate Act 1907 (No. 2120), sec. 7—Authority to trustee company to apply for probate—Revocation—Form of authority—Form of application.]—*See* EXECUTORS AND ADMINISTRATORS, col. 532. *In re Synot*, (1912) V.L.R., 99; 33 A.L.T., 182; 18 A.L.R., 82.

Practice—Grant of administration—Trustee company authorised by next-of-kin to obtain administration — Complicated transactions between next-of-kin and intestate—Discretion of Court to refuse application of trustee company.]—*See* EXECUTORS AND ADMINISTRATORS, col. 532. *In re Forbes*, (1909) V.L.R., 485; 31 A.L.T., 95; 15 A.L.R., 627.

Intestacy—Next-of-kin entitled to administration resident abroad—Authority to trustee company to obtain administration—Form of grant to company.]—*See* EXECUTORS AND ADMINISTRATORS, col. 533. *In re Morris*, (1909) V.L.R., 425; 31 A.L.T., 61; 15 A.L.R., 446.

Executors — Renunciation — Appointment of a trustee company—Power of sole remaining executor—" The Union Trustees Executors and Administrators' Act " (No. 839), sec. 3.]—*See* EXECUTORS AND ADMINISTRATORS, cols. 532, 533. *In re Gilbert*, 27 A.L.T., 241; 12 A.L.R., 528.

National Trustees Executors and Agency Company of Australasia Limited Act (No. 938), sec. 10—Appointment with consent of Court of company to perform administrator's duties—Title of administrator not perfected— Letters of administration not issued.]—*See* EXECUTORS AND ADMINISTRATORS, cols. 533, 534. *In re Moriarty*, (1907) V.L.R., 315; 29 A.L.T., 65; 13 A.L.R., 307.

Administration and Probate Act 1907 (No. 2120), sec. 5—Executors—Discharge of one co-executor—Appointment of administrator in his place—Discharge by Judge.]—*See* EXECUTORS AND ADMINISTRATORS, cols. 544, 545. *In re Coverdale*, (1909) V.L.R., 248; 30 A.L.T., 199; 15 A.L.R., 233.

Administration and Probate Act 1907 (No. 2120), sec. 5—Administration—Executor of executor—Right to renounce as to original testator's estate.]—*See* EXECUTORS AND ADMINISTRATORS, col. 545. *In re Keys*, (1909) V.L.R., 325; 31 A:L.T., 1; 15 A.L.R., 304.

Administration and Probate Act 1907 (No. 2120), sec. 5 (1) (2)—Executor, removal of— Summons, parties to—Application to Judge to indicate parties to be served.]—*See* EXECUTORS AND ADMINISTRATORS, col. 545. *In re Mitchell*, (1910) V.L.R., 44; 31 A.L.T., 113; 15 A.L.R., 643.

Administration and Probate Act 1907 (No. 2120), sec. 5—Executors—Discharge of one co-executor—Vesting order.]—*See* EXECUTORS AND ADMINISTRATORS, col. 545. *In re Coverdale*, (1909) V.L.R., 248; 30 A.L.T., 199; 15 A.L.R., 233.

40

Trusts Act 1890 (No. 1150), secs. 34, 36—Transfer of Land Act 1890 (No. 1149), sec. 188—Appointment of new trustee—Death of trustee out of jurisdiction—No administration of estate or probate of will—Vesting order—Land under the Act.]—Where a sole trustee of land under the *Transfer of Land Act* 1890 dies out of the jurisdiction, and no administration of his estate or probate of his will is applied for, the Court has power to appoint a new trustee in his place, and to make an order that the land the subject matter of the trust vest in him for all the estate that the deceased trustee had in him at the time of his death. *In re Fink*, (1910) V.L.R., 337; 32 A.L.T., 26; 16 A.L.R., 352. *a'Beckett, J.*

Two trustees—One incapable—Appointment of new trustee by other trustee—Estate including land under Transfer of Land Act—Vesting order—Trusts Act 1890 (No. 1150), sec. 4—Trusts Act 1896 (No. 1421), sec. 7—Transfer of Land Act 1890 (No. 1149), sec. 188.]—A trust estate consisted partly of land under the *Transfer of Land Act* 1890 and partly of land not under the Act. One of the two trustees became incapable and the other trustee appointed a new trustee and made a declaration vesting in the new trustee and himself the land not under the Act. On petition the Court made an order under sec. 4 of the *Trusts Act* 1890 similarly vesting the land under the *Transfer of Land Act*. *Re Hope*, (1910) V.L.R., 492; 32 A.L.T., 71; 16 A.L.R., 581. *a'Beckett, J.*

Trusts Act 1890 (No. 1150), sec. 17—Trustee dying without next-of-kin—Vesting order, subject to mortgage.]—V. for valuable consideration covenanted to transfer the whole of his property including a Crown lease to C. In pursuance of that covenant V. afterwards executed a transfer of the Crown lease. The lease was subject to a mortgage, and the mortgagees paid up the balance of the moneys owing to the Crown in respect of the land and obtained the registration under the provisions of the *Transfer of Land Act* 1890 of the Crown grant in V.'s name for an estate in fee simple. The mortgagees were willing that the land should be transferred to C. subject to the mortgage. V. died without

having executed a transfer of the fee simple to C. So far as was known V. had no relatives. Upon petition by C. under sec. 17 of the *Trusts Act* 1890 an order was made without any notice vesting the land in C. subject to the mortgage. *In re Thornhill*, 3 W.W. & a'B. (E.), 110, followed. *In re Vance; Ex parte Carr*, (1906) V.L.R., 664; 28 A.L.T., 62; 12 A.L.R., 439. *Cussen, J.*

IV.—ADMINISTRATION.

(a) Recovery and Protection of Assets.

Administrator — Transfer of assets to sureties to administration bond to be administered by them—Breach of trust—Recovery of control of assets by administrator.]—See EXECUTORS AND ADMINISTRATORS, col. 539. *Ackerly* v. *Palmer*, (1910) V.L.R., 339; 32 A.L.T., 23; 16 A.L.R., 326.

Attachment of debts—Garnishee order—judgment debtor a trustee of the money attached—Appearance of judgment debtor before Justices to protect fund—Justices Act 1890 (No. 1105), sec. 117.]—A judgment debtor who is a trustee of moneys sought to be attached by a garnishee order *nisi* for payment of a judgment debt due by him personally, has a right and is under a duty to appear before the Justices on the garnishee proceedings to show that the moneys are trust moneys and ought not therefore to be attached. *Roberts* v. *Death*, 8 Q.B.D., 319, followed. *Regina* v. *Justices of Heywood*, 21 V.L.R., 654; 17 A.L.T., 238, 2 A.L.R., 135, distinguished. *Richards* v. *Jager*, (1909) V.L.R., 140; 30 A.L.T., 163; 15 A.L.R., 119. *Madden, C.J.*

Attachment of debts—Action for unlawfully attaching trust funds.]—No action will lie for unlawfully having caused moneys standing to the credit of a trust account in the name of the plaintiff to be attached for his personal debt. *Jager* v. *Richards*, (1909) V.L.R., 181; 30 A.L.T., 199; 15 A.L.R., 123. *Cussen, J.*

(b) Sale and Mortgage of Trust Property.

Direction for sale—" With all convenient speed "—Duty of trustee—Whether sale may be postponed.]—A trust to sell " with all convenient speed " is inconsistent with a power to postpone the sale. The trustees are not bound to sell immediately at a sacrifice, but it is their duty to sell at the first favourable opportunity. *In re Watson; Cain* v. *Watson*, (1910) V.L.R., 256; 31 A.L.T., 212; 16 A.L.R., 76. *Cussen, J.*

Calls on shares in no-liability company— Power in will to postpone sale of personal property—Retention of shares by trustees— Whether liable for calls paid by them.]— Where under a will trustees are given a discretion to postpone the sale of testator's personal property, which includes shares in a no-liability company, and they retain such shares in the honest exercise of their discretion, they will be allowed payments for calls on the shares. *Grunden* v. *Nissen*, (1911) V.L.R., 267; 33 A.L.T., 11; 17 A.L.R., 260. F.C., *Madden, C.J., Hodges* and *Hood, JJ.*

Will— Interpretation — Life estate — Gift over in event of life tenant leaving no children —Intestacy—Power of sale.]—*See* WILL. *Alston* v. *Equity Trustees &c. Co. Ltd.*, (1912) 14 C.L.R., 341; 18 A.L.R., 316.

Trustees—Will—Testamentary expenses— Estate for life in realty subject to payment thereof—Tenant for life refuses to pay— No income from realty available— Payment by trustees out of personalty bequeathed to other beneficiaries—Mortgage of real estate to recoup such beneficiaries—Whether a breach of trust.]—Where under a will a beneficiary was entitled for life to the use and enjoyment free from rent of the real estate of the testator, subject to his paying testamentary expenses, and he refused to do so, and, there being no income from the real estate available, the trustees applied the personal estate which was bequeathed to other beneficiaries to pay those expenses including probate duty, *Held*, that under the circumstances it was not a breach of trust to mortgage the real estate to pay the persons entitled to the personal estate the amount so applied. *Crout* v. *Beissel*, (1909) V.L.R., 207; 30 A.L.T., 185; 15 A.L.R., 143. *a'Beckett, J.*

Trustees—Mortgage—Mortgagee asks to be paid off—Money for payment raised by mortgage for larger sum than actually required for that purpose—Not a breach of trust.]—*Per a'Beckett, J.*—"Mortgagees are not always willing to lend broken sums exactly to the amount trustees require, and the raising of £350 to discharge a mortgage of £300 is not necessarily a breach of trust." *Crout* v. *Beissel*, (1909) V.L.R., 207, at p. 212; 30 A.L.T., 185, at p. 187; 15 A.L.R., 143, at p. 145. *a'Beckett, J.*

Executors, money lent to—Absence of inquiry as to purposes for which money wanted—Misapplication by executors—Securities for loan—Contract to give security.]—*See* EXECUTORS AND ADMINISTRATORS, col. 559. *Crout* v. *Beissel*, (1909) V.L.R., 207; 30 A.L.T., 185; 15 A.L.R., 143.

Settled Estates and Settled Lands Act 1909 (No. 2235), secs. 50, 51, 99—Settled lands— Devise to trustees—Will containing only power to let or lease—Sale by tenant for life— Trustees without power to consent—" Trustees of the settlement."—A testatrix devised land to trustees upon trust for her daughter for life and after her death for the children then living of such daughter, and the only power given to the trustees in respect of the land was to let or lease it. *Held*, that the trustees had no power, under and by virtue of the *Settled Estates and Settled Lands Act 1909*, to consent to a sale of the land by the tenant for life, as they were not " trustees of the settlement " within the meaning of sec. 51 of that Act. *Beardsley* v. *Harris*, (1911) V.L.R., 152; 32 A.L.T., 161; 17 A.L.R., 112. *Hodges, J.*

Settled estate—Power of Court to authorize leases—" Manifest intention " of settlor as to use of estate—" Manifest intention " that power of the Court shall not be exercised— Real Property Act 1890 (No. 1136), secs. 64, 90.]—*See* SETTLEMENTS, col. 1164. *In re Staughton*, (1909) V.L.R., 174; 30 A.L.T., 184; 15 A.L.R., 148.

Settled Estates and Settled Lands Act 1909 (No. 2235), secs. 51, 124, 127—Sale of settled land—Infant being person with powers of

tenant for life—Appointment of persons to exercise such powers.]—*See* SETTLED ESTATES AND SETTLED LANDS ACT, cols. 1158, 1159. *In re Cheke or Akehurst* ; *Cheke* v. *Hamilton*, (1910) V.L.R., 310 ; 32 A.L.T., 5 ; 16 A.L.R., 246.

Settled Estates and Settled Lands Act 1909 (No. 2235), secs. 51, 124—Sale of settled land —Tenant for life, person having powers of sale of—Person entitled in fee simple with executory limitation over in a certain event.]— *See* SETTLED ESTATES AND SETTLED LANDS ACT, cols. 1155, 1156. *In re Cheke or Akehurst* ; *Cheke* v. *Hamilton*, (1910) V.L.R., 310 ; 32 A.L.T., 5 ; 16 A.L.R., 246.

Settled Estates and Settled Lands Act 1909 (No. 2235), sec. 124—Sale of settled land— Person with powers of tenant for life—Estate or interest in possession, what is.]— *See* SETTLED ESTATES AND SETTLED LANDS ACT, col. 1156. *In re Cheke or Akehurst* ; *Cheke* v. *Hamilton*, (1910) V.L.R., 310 ; 32 A.L.T., 5 ; 16 A.L.R., 246.

Settled Estates and Settled Lands Act 1909 (No. 2235), secs. 127, 128—Contract of sale— Purchase in names of infants—Settled estate— Tenant for life—Settlement—Appointment of trustees—Trustees to exercise powers of infant tenant for life.]— *See* SETTLED ESTATES AND SETTLED LANDS ACT, cols. 1156, 1157. *In re Weir*, (1912) V.L.R., 77 ; 33 A.L.T., 162 ; 18 A.L.R., 26.

Settled Estates and Settled Lands Act 1909 (No. 2235), secs, 50, 51, 98, 101, 117, 118, 121, 124, 127, 128, 132—Will—Devise to trustees—Power of sale given to trustees— Power to carry on testator's business— Settled estate—Persons with powers of tenant for life—Infants.]— *See* SETTLED ESTATES AND SETTLED LANDS ACT, cols. 1157, 1158. *In re Snowball*, (1912) V.L.R., 176 ; 33 A.L.T., 172 ; 18 A.L.R., 65.

(c) *Repairs* ; *Improvements* ; *Erection of Tombstone*.

See also, post, (l) *Capital and Income*.

Repairs—Whether bare trustee may expend trust funds upon.]— Bare trustees, without active duties to perform, have no power to apply trust funds in effecting repairs except in a case of salvage. *Wilkie* v. *The Equity Trustees Executors and Agency Co. Ltd.*, (1909) V.L.R., 277 ; 30 A.L.T., 211 ; 15 A.L.R., 208. F.C., *Madden, C.J.*, *a'Beckett* and *Hodges, JJ.*

Trustee, duty of—Tenant for life—Repairs.] —The testator by his will devised his real estate to the trustees and executors of his will upon trust to allow S. to receive and take the rents, issues and profits thereof for her absolute use and benefit for the term of her natural life, she keeping . . . the whole of the said real estate in good and tenantable order and condition. There was a gift over on the death of S. *Held*, that in the absence of gross and palpable disregard by S. of the obligation to keep the devised property in good tenantable order and condition the trustees were under no duty to compel S. to fulfil the obligation. *Carrodus* v. *Carrodus*, (1913) V.L.R., 1 ; 34 A.L.T., 125 ; 18 A.L.R., 529. *a'Beckett, J.*

Will—Construction—" Upkeep and maintenance and carrying on of " house " as a home and residence "—What expenses included therein—Household expenses—Repairs —Rates and taxes—Outgoings.]— *See* WILL. *In re Stroud* ; *Bell* v. *Stroud*, (1908) V.L.R., 33 ; 29 A.L.T., 104 ; 13 A.L.R., 645.

Trustee—Bringing land under Transfer of Land Act 1890—Mortgage of trust estate to pay costs of—Breach of trust.]— Where there is no income available with which to pay the costs of bringing under the *Transfer of Land Act*, land held upon a possessory title, trustees are not justified in mortgaging the land to pay these costs, even though the estate has benefited by the consequent increase in price and avoidance of legal difficulties upon sale. *Crout* v. *Beissel*, (1909) V.L.R., 207 ; 30 A.L.T., 185 ; 15 A.L.R., 143. *a'Beckett, J.*

Breach of trust—House unfinished at death of testator—Completion of and necessary additions thereto—Payment for, not expressly authorized by will.]— A testator died possessed of certain real estate on which stood an unfinished house, intended to be used as a country residence, and portion of which he had had ploughed for an orchard. After the testator's death, his trustees expended money belonging to the estate in completing the house, adding outbuildings and planting the orchard. Portion of the expenditure was for work ordered to be done by the testator in his lifetime, but unfinished at his death, and the rest for the outbuildings, without which the house could not have been used, and for the planting, without which the money spent on ploughing would have been thrown away. The testator's infant children and his widow, who were beneficially entitled, occupied the house after his decease, and asked that some of the additions should be made. The expenditure was complained of as a breach of trust, there being no express provision in the will authorising the expenditure by the trustees, though it was not suggested that too much was paid or that what was done was not beneficial. *Held*, that regarding the special purpose for which the property was purchased, its condition at the testator's death, the amount of compulsory expenditure required, the character of the voluntary expenditure, and the use made of the property, the expenditure should be sanctioned, the Court being satisfied on the evidence that it had been beneficial. *Grunden* v. *Nissen*, (1911) V.L.R., 97 ; 32 A.L.T., 117 ; 16 A.L.R., 636. *a' Beckett, J.*

Breach of trust—Tombstone over testator's grave—How far trustees may expend money in erection of.]—Executors may, without express authority, erect a tombstone over the grave of the testator at a cost regulated by the amount usually expended on tombstones of persons dying in the same condition of life and by the amount available for funeral expenses. *Grunden* v. *Nissen*, (1911) V.L.R., 267 ; 33 A.L.T., 11 ; 17 A.L.R., 260. F.C., *Madden, C.J., Hodges* and *Hood, JJ.*

(d) Carrying on Business.

Trust to carry on business of oyster saloon— Moneys expended in treating customers— Whether trustees may be allowed.]—Trustees, who in pursuance of their trust carried on the business of an oyster saloon were allowed payments made by them in treating customers in order to promote business. *Nissen* v. *Grunden*, (1912) 14 C.L.R., 297 ; 18 A.L.R., 254. H.C., *Griffith, C.J., Barton* and *Isaacs, JJ.*

Station property—Management of by trustees—Tenant for life and remainderman— Capital and income, distinction between— Preservation of capital.]—No general principle can be laid down by which station properties in Australia should be managed by trustees having powers of management thereof, or by which the share of profits which would belong to the tenant for life as against the remainderman should be ascertained, as to how capital should be preserved, or as to what are to be regarded as profits or what as capital in any given instance. The whole must depend upon the wise and prudent discretion of those who have the management of the station for the time being. *Re McGaw*, 4 N.S.W. S.R., 591, discussed, and disapproved. *In re Moore* ; *Fanning* v. *Fanning*, (1907) V.L.R., 639 ; 29 A.L.T., 138 ; 13 A.L.R., 507. *Madden, C.J.*

Will—Interpretation—Carrying on business —Discretion of trustees.]—By his will testator provided :—" My said trustees shall under the management of my son H. A. continue and carry on the business now carried on by me　　　　　　and the usual process of taking stock and making up a balance-sheet shall be taken and made every six months and such business shall be continued so long as my said son H.A. can show and pay a net profit of 6 per centum per annum upon the amount of capital invested therein, which amount of profits my said trustees shall stand possessed of to be divided among etc. . . . my said trustees shall and may after the first six months of the carrying on by them of my said business at such time and in such manner and at such price and prices and upon such terms and conditions as they shall think and consider necessary or expedient and shall upon any balance-sheet taken as aforesaid of the said business showing a loss of £1,000 or a loss during the prior six months of £600 sell and dispose of the said business, &c." *Held*, that so long as H.A. showed and paid a net profit of 6 per centum per annum, the trustees were bound to carry on the business ; that if he failed to show 6 per centum they had a discretion as to carrying on the business ; but if the loss of £1,000 was made in the business, or if a loss of £600 was made in one half-year, it was their duty to sell the business. *Union Bank of Australia Ltd.* v. *Whitelaw,* (1906) V.L.R., 711 ; 28 A.L.T., 17 ; 12 A.L.R., 393. *Hodges, J.*

Will—Trustees—Emergency not contemplated by testator—Departure from terms of will—Authority given by Court—General authority—Authority for specific departure from will.]—A testator by his will appointed A. B. & C., his executors and trustees, and directed them to carry on his business for the period of ten years. B. and C. were, together with D., the managers of the business at the time of testator's death, and by his will he directed that they should receive a certain fixed salary, plus a percentage of the profits of the business. The business increased considerably in extent, and was bringing in much greater profits than it did during the lifetime of the testator. *Held,* that the executors were not at liberty to increase at their discretion the remuneration given to the managers of the business. *Attorney-General* v. *Dean of Christchurch,* (1826) 2 Russ., 321, distinguished. But, *held,* that, as the managers would not continue to act at their present remuneration, the Court would, in order to save the trust property from ruin, sanction a departure from the terms of the trust by authorizing a specific increase in their remuneration. *In re New,* (1901) 2 Ch., 534, applied. *Fomsgard* v. *Fomsgard,* (1912) V.L.R., 209 ; 34 A.L.T., 11 ; 18 A.L.R., 220. *Hodges, J.*

Insolvency Act 1890 (No. 1102), sec. 37— " Secured debt," what is—Business of testator carried on by executors under terms of will— Debt properly incurred—Right of executors to indemnity out of assets of estate—Petitioning creditor having security over property used in business—Whether such security must be given up or valued.]—*See* EXECUTORS AND ADMINISTRATORS, cols. 566, 567. *In re Whitelaw ; Savage* v. *The Union Bank of Australia Ltd. ; Whitelaw* v. *The Same,* 3 C.L.R., 1170 ; 12 A.L.R., 285.

(e) *Compromise of Claims.*

Trusts Act 1896 (No. 1421), sec. 11—Trustee —Power to compromise—Agreement between trustee and tenant for life—Compromise as to future liability of tenant for life for repairs— Disadvantage of the estate—Mistake of law, effect of.]—A tenant for life had claims against the estate and the estate had claims against him. The trustee of the estate and the tenant for life agreed to compromise all such claims upon certain terms, and mutual releases were given in respect of such claims. One of the terms of the agreement was that the trustee should be at liberty to deduct from the tenant for life's income from the estate a specified sum per annum during his life, such sum to be spent by the trustee in effecting any necessary repairs to the trust property. *Held,* that under the *Trusts Act* 1896, the trustee had power to insert in the agreement for compromise the term limiting the liability of the tenant for life in respect of future repairs, as part of a *bona fide* compromise, though such term might have been agreed to under a mistake of law, and would work out to the disadvantage of the estate ; and that, therefore, the obligation of the tenant for life to contribute to the cost of such repairs was limited to the amount specified in the agreement. *In re Tong ; Tong* v. *Trustees Executors &c. Co. Ltd.,* (1910) V.L.R., 110 ; 31 A.L.T., 169 ; 16 A.L.R., 87. *Hood, J.*

Will—Charity, gift to—Compromise, jurisdiction of Court to sanction—Attorney-General, consent of.]—By his will testator left a house and land known as " Goodrest " together with the furniture therein to the Melbourne Hospital upon trust " to be used for hospital purposes and as a convalescent home for the convalescent patients of the said Hospital " with power to the trustees of the Hospital from time to time to alter and repair and erect buildings on such land provided however that such land and the tenements at any time erected thereon should be maintained and kept by the trustees of the Hospital " for hospital purposes and as a convalescent home as hereinbefore specified and for such purposes only." There was a gift of the testator's residuary real and personal estate. To make " Goodrest " suitable for hospital purposes or for a convalescent home would have required a great deal of money. The trustees of the Melbourne Hospital had no money for these purposes, and, being engaged in erecting new hospital buildings, were unable to make up their minds whether to take the gift or not. They then entered into an agreement with the persons entitled under the gift of the residue to sell " Goodrest " and divide the proceeds of the sale into two moieties—one to go to the Melbourne Hospital to be applied for hospital purposes, and the other to go into the residuary estate. *Held*, that the Court had jurisdiction to sanction the compromise, and, the compromise being modified so as to provide that the moiety going to the Melbourne Hospital should be spent in the erection of a building for convalescent hospital patients, and the Attorney-General consenting to the compromise, that the sanction of the Court should be given. *In re Buckhurst; Melbourne Hospital* v. *Equity Trustees Executors &c. Co. Ltd.*, (1911) V.L.R., 61; 32 A.L.T., 165; 17 A.L.R., 63. *Cussen, J.*

(f) Investment of Trust Funds.

Direction as to investment of trust funds in certain named securities—Power to invest in securities authorised by Trusts Acts—Trusts Act 1890 (No. 1150), secs. 88, 90—Trusts Act 1896 (No. 1421), sec. 22—Trusts Act 1906 (No. 2022), sec. 4.]—A testator by his will directed his trustees to invest trust moneys in certain named securities. *Held*, that they were not precluded from investing the trust moneys in any of the securities authorised by the Trusts Acts. *In re Meagher; Trustees Executors and Agency Co. Ltd.* v. *Meagher*, (1910) V.L.R., 407; 32 A.L.T., 69; 16 A.L.R., 551. *a'Beckett, J.*

Trustees of will empowered to purchase station property—Power to raise money out of estate for such purpose—Income to be paid to certain persons—Purchase of station property impracticable—Persons entitled to income—Testator's intention to benefit—Whether it can be given effect to by investment otherwise than by purchase of station property.]—A testator by his will declared that it should be lawful for his trustees on the happening of a certain event to agree for the purchase on account of his son D. of a station and stock in Australia or New Zealand, and for that purpose to raise out of testator's estate the sum of £10,000, and to lay out such sum in part payment of the purchase money of such station and stock, the balance of the purchase money to be secured by mortgage of the purchased property and to be paid out of the profits thereof exclusively and after payment of the said sum of £10,000 testator's estate to be discharged from all further liability in respect of such purchase. When purchased the station and stock were to be held in trust for testator's widow for life, and after her death in trust to be settled in such manner as should be most effectual for securing to D. the personal receipt and enjoyment of the rents and profits during his life inalienably, and after D.'s death in trust for his children. The testator died in 1881. The event specified in the will happened in 1907, when the trustees found that owing to the rise in value of such properties it was impracticable, having regard to the prescribed limit of price, to purchase such a " station " as was contemplated in the will except in districts where a considerable risk of the entire sacrifice of the remaindermen's interests would be involved. *Held*, that the testator's object was that D and his children should have the benefit of £10,000 through the medium of a station, and that, as by force of circumstances, that medium had become impracticable, the trustees were at liberty to raise that sum out of the testator's estate, and invest it in any of the forms of investment authorised by the Trusts Acts, and settle it upon the trusts declared in regard to the station and stock. *In re Johnson; Perpetual Executors and Trustees Association of Australia* v. *Johnson*, (1907) V.L.R., 596; 29 A.L.T., 101; 13 A.L.R., 437. *a'Beckett, J.* (1907).

(g) Employment of Agents.

Collection of rent from trust properties—Numerous properties—Employment of agents—Payment of commission to agents.]—A trustee may employ an agent to collect the rents of numerous trust properties, and may charge the estate with the commission paid to such agent. *In re Corsellis*, 34 Ch. D., 675, followed. *Macartney* v. *Macartney*, (1909) V.L.R., 183; 30 A.L.T., 172: 15 A.L.R., 139. *Hodges, J.*

Employment of agents—Keeping accounts of estate—Collection of rents.]—Whether trustees are justified in obtaining skilled assistance in keeping the trust accounts and collecting the rents of the trust estate, and charging the estate for such assistance, depends on the consideration whether such action on the part of the trustees is reasonable or not. *Held*, on the facts that the trustees might charge the estate for such assistance. *Swanson* v. *Emmerton*, (1909) V.L.R., 387; 31 A.L.T., 128; 15 A.L.R., 368.

Trustee-solicitor—Trustee member of firm of solicitors—Charge for non-professional work.]—*See, post, (m) Dealings by Trustee to his own Advantage.* *Swanson* v. *Emmerton*, (1909) V.L.R., 387; 31 A.L.T., 28; 15 A.L.R., 368.

(h) Powers as to Maintenance and Education of Cestui que Trust, Exercise of.

Suit for contribution—Trustees under two different wills—Discretionary power to provide maintenance for the same legatee—Separate and independent obligation—No right of contribution.]—Discretionary power was given to the appellants as trustees under a will to pay the testator's daughter £800 a year, the unpaid portion thereof to fall into the residue of his estate. A like power was given to one of the appellants, and a respondent as trustees under the will of her sister to pay such sums as they might think fit in and towards her maintenance, the residue of the income of the testatrix's estate to be paid to her nephew, the corpus to go in equal shares to his children on his death. The trustees under the first will paid £400 a year to the daughter, but on the death of the testatrix they reduced the allowance to £100 a year, while the trustees of the second will paid from £700 to £800 a year. In a suit by the said nephew and the trustee of his insolvent estate for an order that the said daughter's maintenance should be provided for by a proportionate contribu-

tion from the two estates, *Held*, that there was no common obligation and no right to contribution. The trusts were different in their terms to be exercised at the discretion of different trustees, and the resulting obligations were separate and different. *Smith* v. *Cock*, (1911) A.C., 317; 17 A.L.R., 99. Privy Council.

Will—Construction—Real estate devised to testator's son for life on attaining twenty-five—Subsequent direction as to son acquiring a profession before getting possession of estate—Whether condition precedent—Direction to trustees to see that son acquires profession, effect of.]—*See* WILL. *In re Meagher; Trustees Executors and Agency Co. Ltd.* v. *Meagher*, (1910) V.L.R., 407; 32 A.L.T., 69; 16 A.L.R., 551.

(i) Income Tax.

Income Tax Act 1896 (No. 1467), sec. 12 (d)—Income derived by trustee—No other person presently entitled in actual receipt and liable as taxpayer in respect thereof—Beneficiaries contingently entitled—Whether tax payable on whole amount or on each interest separately—Income Tax Act 1895 (No. 1374), sec. 2—Person liable in representative character.]—*See* INCOME TAX ACTS, col. 685. *Re Income Tax Acts*, (1907) V.L.R., 358; 28 A.L.T., 215; 13 A.L.R., 151.

Income Tax—Income derived from trust estate—Trade carried on by trustees—Income from personal exertion or income the produce of property—Income Tax Act 1895 (No. 1374), secs. 2, 8, 9 and 12—Income Tax Act 1896 (No. 1467), secs. 4 and 12.]—*See* INCOME TAX ACTS, cols. 683, 684, 685. *Webb* v. *Syme*, 10 C.L.R., 482; 17 A.L.R., 18.

(j) Advice of Judge of Supreme Court under Sec. 60 of Trusts Act 1890.

Trusts Act 1890 (No. 1150), sec. 60—Petition for advice—Jurisdiction—Small estate—Further inquiries as to next of kin—Expense of inquiries nearly equal to value of estate.]—On a petition for advice under sec. 60 of the *Trusts Act* 1890 a Judge has jurisdiction to advise whether certain alleged facts should be further investigated and whether certain inquiries should be made; and where an intestate estate consisted of a small sum of money and the expense of making further inquiries as to the next of kin would have amounted to nearly the whole of such sum, the administrator was advised that it was not necessary to make any further inquiries. *In re Cave-Brown-Cave*, (1906) V.L.R., 283; 27 A.L.T., 183; 12 A.L.R., 167. *Cussen, J.* (1906).

Trusts Act 1890 (No. 1150), sec. 60—Petition for advice—Distribution of intestate estate on footing of death of certain persons before intestate—Value of interests involved.]—On a petition by the administrator of an intestate estate for advice whether the estate might be distributed on the footing that two persons had pre-deceased the intestate, each of whom, if he survived the intestate, would be entitled to the sum of £718 as one of the next-of-kin. *Held*, that, having regard to the value of the interests involved, no advice should be given. *In the matter of O'Grady*, 26 V.L.R., 171; 6 A.L.R., 162, followed; *In the matter of Cave-Brown-Cave*, (1906) V.L.R., 283; 27 A.L.T., 183; 12 A.L.R., 167, explained. *In re Cavin*, (1906) V.L.R., 517; 28 A.L.T., 39; 12 A.L.R., 333. *Cussen, J.*

(k) *Advice of Counsel.*

Clause empowering trustees to act on advice of counsel—Liability of trustees so acting.]—A will contained a clause providing that in all cases in which a question of law or equity should arise in relation to the estate on the construction of the will, the trustees might settle and arrange the same in such manner as they might be advised by counsel. Acting upon counsel's advice as to the proper construction of the will which was afterwards held by the Court to be erroneous, the trustees paid the income of a fund to certain contingent legatees instead of to the residuary legatees. *Held*, that all such payments made in the past were good for all purposes and gave no rights against the trustees or the contingent legatees. *In re Thompson*; *Brahe* v. *Mason*, (1910) V.L.R., 251; 31 A.L.T., 210; 16 A.L.R., 215. *a'Beckett, J.*

(l) *Capital and Income.*

(1) RECEIPTS.

Trustees—Apportionment of charges between capital and income—Apportionment between income takers—Power of trustees to decide questions of apportionment.]—*See* TENANT FOR LIFE AND REMAINDERMAN. *Swanson* v. *Emmerton*, (1909) V.L.R., 387; 31 A.L.T., 28; 15 A.L.R., 368.

Tenant for life and remaindermen—Licensed premises part of testator's estate—Compensation for deprivation of licence—Apportionment—Licensing Act 1890 (No. 1111), secs. 31-44.]—*See* LICENSING, cols. 828, 829. *McKee* v. *Ballarat Trustees Executors &c. Co. Ltd.*, (1910) V.L.R., 358; 32 A.L.T., 22; 16 A.L.R., 323.

Tenant for life and remainderman—Income what is—Shares in insurance company—Dividend paid out of fund accumulated as provision for life assurance liabilities—Dividend paid out of contingency fund to provide against depreciation of securities.]—*See* TENANT FOR LIFE AND REMAINDERMAN, cols. 1197, 1198. *In re Longley*; *Reid* v. *Silke*, (1906) V.L.R., 641; 28 A.L.T., 82; 12 A.L.R., 499.

Tenant for life and remainderman—Dividends declared by company, whether capital or income.]—*See* TENANT FOR LIFE AND REMAINDERMAN, col. 1198. *In re Longley*; *Reid* v. *Silke*, (1906) V.L.R., 641; 28 A.L.T., 82; 12 A.L.R., 499.

Will—Construction—Shares in company owned by testator—Bequest to life tenant of dividends and to remainderman absolutely—Bonus declared by company on shares—New shares issued and offered to shareholders—Bonus applicable in payment therefor—Whether bonus capital or income.]—*See* TENANT FOR LIFE AND REMAINDERMAN, cols. 1198, 1199. *In re Smith*; *Edwards* v. *Smith*, 29 A.L.T., 173; 14 A.L.R., 22.

(2) EXPENDITURE.

(a) Repairs and Improvements.

Repairs to trust property—Life tenant and remainderman—Corpus and income—Apportionment—Trustee with power of management

and bare trustee distinguished as to power to repair.]—Where property consisting of land and houses is vested in trustees with powers of management in trust for a tenant for life and for a remainderman, the trustees may make such repairs as are necessary to keep the property in a good state of preservation for the remainderman. The cost of effecting ordinary recurring repairs, which last only a short time, such as painting and papering, is to be borne by income. The cost of structural repairs of such a character that both the life tenant and the remainderman will derive substantial benefit therefrom are to be apportioned between income and corpus in such a manner as the trustees in their discretion think fit. The cost of structural repairs of such a character that the remainderman alone will derive substantial benefit therefrom are to be borne wholly by corpus. *Wilkie* v. *The Equity Trustees Executors and Agency Co. Ltd.,* (1909) V.L.R., 277 ; 30 A.L.T., 211 ; 15 A.L.R., 208. F.C., *Madden, C.J., a' Beckett* and *Hodges, JJ.*

Equitable tenant for life—Repairs to preserve property from deterioration—Expenses, whether payable out of corpus or income.]— Where property was held by trustees upon trust to pay   ·. the income produced by such property to A. for life with remainder over and no power of management was given, *Held,* that A. was in the position of an equitable tenant for life and under no obligation to repair, and that sums properly expended by the trustees for repairs to and caretaking of the trust property to preserve it from deterioration were payable out of corpus and not out of income. *In re Hotchkys,* 32 Ch. D., 408 ; *Trustees Executors &c. Co.* v. *Jope,* 27 V.L.R., 706 ; 24 A.L.T., 30 ; 8 A.L.R. (C.N.), 21, and *Reid* v. *Deane,* (1906) V.L.R., 138 ; 27 A.L.T., 153 ; 12 A.L.R., 46, followed. *Re Folk,* 6 W.W. & A'B. (Eq.), 171, disapproved. *In re Tong* ; *Tong* v. *Trustees, Executors and Agency Co. Ltd.,* (1907) V.L.R., 338 ; 28 A.L.T., 200 ; 13 A.L.R., 119. *a' Beckett, J.*

Improvements to station property—Expenditure, adjustment of between capital and income—Tenant for life and remainderman.]—

In the management of a station property, the trustees expended capital moneys for the purpose of making certain improvements which were necessary for the good management of the station, and likely to enhance its general value, and would be of great use to those having the life interest. *Held,* that such expenditure was properly chargeable to capital ; that capital might properly be recouped by annual charges of ten per cent. on income ; but that on the sale of the property before such recoupment had been fully made no further recoupment out of income need be made. *In re Moore* ; *Fanning* v. *Fanning,* (1907) V.L.R., 639 ; 29 A.L.T., 138 ; 13 A.L.R., 507. *Madden, C.J.*

Life tenant and remainderman—Income and corpus—Repairs to trust property—Sewerage.] The expense of sewerage is exclusively the liability of corpus. *Wilkie* v. *Equity Trustees &c. Co.,* (1909) V.L.R., 277 ; 30 A.L.T., 211 ; 15 A.L.R., 208, followed. *Reid* v. *Deane,* (1906) V.L.R., 138 ; 27 A.L.T., 153 ; 12 A.L.R., 46, not followed. *Macartney* v. *Macartney,* 33 A.L.T., 183 ; 18 A.L.R., 1. *Madden, C.J.* (1912).

Trustee—Settled lands—Cost of fencing—Apportionment between corpus and income—Sinking fund.]—*See* TENANT FOR LIFE AND REMAINDERMAN, col. 1203. *In re Staughton,* (1909) V.L.R., 174 ; 30 A.L.T., 184 ; 15 A.L.R., 148.

(*b*) Insurance.

Tenant for life and remainderman—Fire premiums paid prior to the Trusts Act 1896 (No. 1421)—Whether chargeable to income or corpus.]—Fire insurance premiums were paid by trustees prior to the *Trusts Act* 1896 in respect of properties held on trust to let. *Held* that such premiums were chargeable against income *Holmes* v. *Holmes,* 28 A.L.T., 22 ; 12 A.L.R., 409. *a' Beckett, J.* (1906).

Insurance of trust property—Premiums, whether payable out of income or corpus—Trusts Act 1896 (No. 1421), sec. 28.]—Sec. 28 of the *Trusts Act* 1896 governs the incidence of payments made thereunder by trusstees for insuring buildings on the trust property. *In re Tong ; Tong* v. *Trustees Executors and Agency Co. Ltd.,* (1907) V.L.R., 338 ; 28 A.L.T., 200 ; 13 A.L.R., 119. *a' Beckett, J.*

(c) Probate Duty.

Probate duty, how payment to be apportioned—Direction that each beneficiary shall pay duty payable in respect of his interest—Tenants for life and remaindermen.]—*See* DUTIES ON THE ESTATES OF DECEASED PERSONS, cols. 418, 419. *In re Buckhurst ; Equity Trustees Executors and Agency Co.* v. *Buckhurst,* (1907) V.L.R., 252 ; 28 A.L.T., 190 ; 13 A.L.R., 74.

Administration and Probate Act 1907 (No. 2120), sec. 3—Administration and Probate Act 1890 (No. 1060), sec. 103—Probate duty—Apportionment—Tenant for life and remainderman—Whether legislation retrospective.] —*See* DUTIES ON THE ESTATES OF DECEASED PERSONS, col. 419. *In re Staughton ; Oliver* v. *Staughton,* (1910) V.L.R., 415 ; 32 A.L.T., 63 ; 16 A.L.R., 443.

Probate duty—Apportionment—Tenant for life and remainderman—Mistake of law—Agreement between executors and tenant for life as to apportionment of duty based on wrong principle—Duty of executors.]—*See* DUTIES ON THE ESTATES OF DECEASED PERSONS, col. 419, 420. *In re Staughton ; Oliver* v. *Staughton,* (1910) V.L.R., 415 ; 32 A.L.T., 63 : 16 A.L.R., 443.

(d) Annuities.

Will—Settlement — Annuity — Charge, whether on corpus or income—Order of Court —Transfer of Land Statute 1866 (No. 301), sec. 86.]—*See* SETTLEMENTS, cols. 1159, 1160. *Brown* v. *Abbott,* (1908) 5 C.L.R., 487.

Will—Interpretation—Corpus and income—Annuity, gift of — Residue.]—*See* WILL. *Cock* v. *Aitken,* (1908) 6 C.L.R., 290 ; 14 A.L.R., 361.

Will — Construction — Annuity, whether charged on corpus—Legacies—" In the first place," " in the next place "—Whether priority in enumeration or in order or method of payment or of rights or interests.]—*See*

WILL. *Perpetual Executors and Trustees Association of Australia Ltd.* v. *Knowles,* 32 A.L.T., 163 ; 16 A.L.R., 582.

(e) Costs.

Costs—Trustees—Corpus and income interested—Mathematical adjustment of burthen of costs impossible—Burden divided equally.]— *See Macartney* v. *Macartney,* (1909) V.L.R., 183 ; 30 A.L.T., 172 ; 15 A.L.R., 139. *Hodges, J.*

Trustee—Life tenant and remainderman—Corpus and income—Costs paid by trustees under order of High Court—Decision of High Court reversed on appeal by one party to Privy Council—Effect on rights of parties not appealing—Indemnity of trustees—Rights of assignee of life tenant.]—*See* TENANT FOR LIFE AND REMAINDERMAN, cols. 1206, 1207. *Cock* v. *Aitken,* (1912) 15 C.L.R., 373 ; 18 A.L.R., 576.

(3) ADJUSTMENT OF ACCOUNTS BETWEEN BENEFICIARIES.

Tenant for life and remainderman—Apportionment, basis of—Mortgage effected by testator—Trustee authorised to invest on similar securities—Proceeds of sale of mortgaged property insufficient to pay principal and interest.]—The rule in *Cooper* v. *Cooper,* 26 V.L.R., 649 ; 22 A.L.T., 215 ; 8 A.L.R., 212, as to apportionment between tenants for life and remaindermen, where trust funds have been invested on mortgage and the mortgaged property is sold and the proceeds are insufficient to pay principal and interest due, applies to mortgages effected by a testator and continued by his trustee after his death, if they are of a class of investments the trustee is authorised to make and if there are no special reasons why the trustee should have realised them earlier. *In re Earl of Chesterfield's Estate,* 24 Ch. D., 643, distinguished. *Holmes* v. *Holmes,* 28 A.L.T., 22 ; 12 A.L.R., 409. *a' Beckett, J.*

Tenant for life and remainderman—Trust funds invested upon mortgage—Proceeds of sale of mortgaged property insufficient to pay principal and interest—Apportionment of proceeds—Rate of interest.]—Trust funds were invested on mortgage. Upon sale by the mortgagees the proceeds were insufficient to pay principal and interest due and had to be apportioned between the tenant for life and remainderman on the basis established by *Cooper v. Cooper*, 26 V.L.R., 649 ; 22 A.L.T., 215 ; 8 A.L.R., 212. *Held*, that, no special circumstances being shown, the rate of interest to be adopted in making the apportionment should not be left to the discretion of the trustees, but should be the rate fixed by the mortgage, that is to say, the ordinary and not the penal rate. *Holmes v. Holmes*, 28 A.L.T., 22 ; 12 A.L.R., 409. *a' Beckett, J.* (1906).

Trustee and cestui que trust—Tenant for life and remainderman—Investment on mortgage—Apportionment of proceeds of realization—Interest on cost of sewerage—Rate of interest upon mortgage.]—Trust moneys having been lent on mortgage by the trustees, and the mortgagor being unable to pay the interest, the trustees took possession of the mortgaged property, and expended out of the income of the estate certain sums on sewering the property pursuant to the *Melbourne and Metropolitan Board of Works Act*. The trustees subsequently sold the property for less than the principal sum advanced and interest thereon. On apportionment of the proceeds of sale between corpus and income : *Held*, that before apportionment corpus was chargeable with interest on the sums so expended out of income up to the date of repayment to the life tenants. *In re Morley*, (1895) 2 Ch., 738, followed. On such apportionment, the life tenant is entitled to interest on the principal owing under the mortgage from the date when the mortgagor ceased paying interest at the rate (but not the penal rate) fixed by the mortgage, unless it is shown that such rate of interest was higher than the current rates during the period over which the arrears extend. *Cooper v. Cooper*, 26 V.L.R , 649 ; 22 A.L.T., 215 ; 7 A.L.R., 147, explained and followed. *Macartney v. Macartney*, 33 A.L.T., 183 ; 18 A.L.R., 1. *Madden, C.J.* (1912).

Trustee—Overpayment by mistake to life tenant—Right to recoup from income payable to life tenant, how exercised—Control of Court —Gradual deductions—Amount of deduction.]—Where a trustee has by mistake overpaid a beneficiary he has no absolute right in all circumstances to lay his hands on anything under his control belonging to the beneficiary and to apply it to replace the money paid away by his own mistake, but he may obtain the sanction of the Court to an adjustment of such overpayments. Where the interest of the beneficiary consists of an annuity required for maintenance the Court will not permit the trustee suddenly to stop payment of the annuity, but will direct a gradual deduction which will in general be at the rate of 10 per cent of the income payable to the annuitant. *Perpetual Executors and Trustees Association v. Simpson*, 27 A.L.T., 179 ; 12 A.L.R., 95. *a' Beckett, J.* (1906).

Excess of expenditure over income—Deficiency met by drawing on capital—Life tenant entitled to income on capital so used—Recoupment of capital out of income—Tenant for life and remainderman.]—The duty of trustees to recoup out of income the excess of expenditure over income occasioned by extraordinary circumstances in particular years, and provided out of other capital to the income of which the life tenant was also entitled, discussed. *In re Moore ; Fanning v. Fanning*, (1907) V.L.R. 639 ; 29 A.L.T., 138 ; 18 A.L.R., 507. *Madden, C.J.*

Will—Tenant for life and remainderman—Capital and income—Payment of annuities—Apportionment—Rate of interest.]—*See* TENANT FOR LIFE AND REMAINDERMAN, cols. 1200, 1201. *Cock v. Aitken*, (1911) 13 C.L.R., 461 ; 18 A.L.R., 337.

(m) Dealings by Trustee to his own Advantage.

Profit made by trustee out of estate—Goods supplied to testator for purposes of his business—Person supplying goods appointed trustee of testator's estate—Continued supply of goods after appointment—Whether a breach of trust.]—A testator appointed as one of two trustees, who were given power to carry on his business, a person who at a profit to himself had been in the habit of supplying the testator with meals for the employees in the business, and that person, while he and his co-trustee were carrying on the business, continued to supply such meals and charged the estate such a price for them as to give him a reasonable profit. *Semble*, that such charge might properly be allowed. *Nissen* v. *Grunden*, (1912) 14 C.L.R., 297 ; 18 A.L.R., 254. H.C., *Griffith, C.J., Barton* and *Isaacs, JJ.*

Removal of trustee—Retirement of trustee and appointment of new trustee—Employment of retired trustee at a salary.]—Two trustees N. and P., who were carrying on their testator's business under a direction contained in the will, with power to appoint a salaried manager, employed one of themselves, P. as manager, and paid him a salary for so acting On objection being taken on behalf of beneficiaries that this was wrong, P. retired from his trusteeship, and appointed S. to act as trustee in his place, and thereafter continued to act as manager, and received a salary as before. *Held*, that the appointment of S. was not improper, and that he should not be removed. *Nissen* v. *Grunden*, (1912) 14 C.L.R., 297 ; 18 A.L.R., 254. H.C., *Griffith, C.J., Barton* and *Isaacs, JJ.*

Trustees and cestui que trust—Profit made by trustee in connection with trust estate—Conflict between trustee's interest and duty.]—A trustee must not place himself in a position where his personal interests may be in conflict with his duty to his *cestui que trust*. Rule laid down in *Broughton* v. *Broughton*, 5 DeG. M. & G., 160, at p. 164, applied. *Macartney* v. *Macartney*, (1909) V.L.R., 183 ; 30 A.L.T., 172 ; 15 A.L.R., 139. *Hodges, J.*

Profit made by trustee in connection with trust estate—Insurance of trust properties by trustee, an insurance broker—Commission allowed by insurance companies to brokers—Provision that no part of commission be paid to insured—Obligation of trustee to account for commission received.]—X., a trustee, who was a member of a firm of insurance brokers, effected insurances of trust properties with certain insurance companies, members of an association which had an arrangement with brokers that the latter should receive commission on all insurances effected by them.

It was part of the arrangement that no part of the commission so received should be paid to the persons insured. Under this arrangement X. received commission. *Held*, that he was not entitled to retain the same, but must account therefor to the estate. The rule laid down in *Broughton* v. *Broughton*, 5 DeG. M. & G., 160, at p. 164, applied. *Macartney* v. *Macartney*, (1909) V.L.R., 183 ; 30 A.L.T., 172 ; 15 A.L.R., 139. *Hodges, J.*

Trustee—Solicitor—Trustee member of firm of solicitors—Charges for non-professional work.]—By his will testator appointed one of his trustees, who was a member of a firm of solicitors " to be the solicitor of my trust property " and directed " that he shall conduct all the legal business of my estate and shall be entitled to make and receive all such charges and emoluments for business whether of an ordinary professional or any other character done by him in relation to the administration of my estate or the execution of the trusts of this my will as he would have been entitled to make and receive in respect of such business as if he had not been a trustee or executor." Testator also provided that his trustees might deduct and retain a commission or allowance for their trouble *Held*, that the trustees were authorised to charge against the estate, moneys paid to the solicitor-trustee firm for work which the trustees, without express authority, would have been justified in employing a stranger to the trust to do. But, *semble*, they would not be authorised to charge the estate in respect of a payment to the solicitor trustee in relation to work which ordinarily he would have been bound to do as trustee , without payment. *Swanson* v. *Emmerton*, (1909) V.L.R., 387 ; 31 A.L.T., 28 ; 15 A.L.R., 368. *Cussen, J.*

Transfer of Land Act 1890 (No. 1149), Part IV.—Gift to person standing in fiduciary relation to donor—Transfer by administrator as such to himself in his own right—Assignment by next-of-kin of their interests to administrator—Whether Commissioner entitled to call for proof that next-of-kin had independent legal advice and understood nature of transaction.]—*See* TRANSFER OF LAND

ACT, cols. 1227, 1228. *In re Transfer of Land Act*; *Ex parte Danaher*, (1911) V.L.R., 214; 32 A.L.T., 190; 17 A.L.R., 160.

Commissioner of Titles—Matters involving consideration of trust—Power to question.]— *See* TRANSFER OF LAND ACT, col. 1228. *In re Transfer of Land Act*; *Ex parte Edmonds and Harrison*, 34 A.L.T., 105; 18 A.L.R., 41.

(n) *Liabilities of Third Parties in Respect of Breaches of Trust or Loss Incurred in Administration.*

Fiduciary relation—Undue influence, presumption of—Whether principle confined to voluntary dealings.]—*Per Hodges, J.—*" I think that the principle enunciated in *Huguenin* v. *Baseley*, 14 Ves., 273, has gone beyond purely voluntary transactions, but I can find no case where it has been applied to an ordinary business transaction such as this, where the person suing (*i.e.*, a bank which had made advances) has had nothing to do with the procuring of the guarantee, and where the surety (the person alleged to have been subject to undue influence) has had a direct personal pecuniary interest in the business which is being conducted by means of the account guaranteed, and has for years derived all the benefits that accrued from the account." *Union Bank of Australia Ltd.* v. *Whitelaw*, (1906) V.L.R., 711; 28 A.L.T., 17: 12 A.L.R., 393.

" Undue concealment "—Business carried on by trustees in breach of trust—Moneys advanced to trustees on guarantee of beneficiaries — Ordinary business transaction— Whether creditor under duty to inform himself and beneficiaries as to conduct of trustees.]—The trustees of a will who were in fact carrying on the business of their testator in breach of trust were pressed by their banker to reduce their indebtedness to the bank by means of the sale of some of the goods of the business. The trustees objected to this and it was arranged, on their suggestion, that they should get their account guaranteed by the beneficiaries, who, under the will, were interested in the business, and that then the bank would make further advances. The trustees accordingly procured and handed to the bank guarantees signed by the bene-

ficiaries, and further advances were made. The banker had, through balance-sheets and a copy of the will, the means of knowing, but had not applied his mind to the question, and did not in fact know of the breach of trust. The only matter with which he concerned himself was to see the bank protected, and it never occurred to him to question the legality of the acts of the trustees. The bank took no part in the procuring of the guarantees. An action to enforce the guarantees was resisted on the ground of " undue concealment." *Held*, that there was no duty imposed on the bank to search after the persons who proposed to become surety, and to inform them of the conduct or behaviour of those for whom they proposed to become surety, such conduct being outside the dealing between the creditor and the principal debtor, and that there was no "undue concealment." *Union Bank of Australia Ltd.* v. *Whitelaw*, (1906) V.L.R., 711; 28 A.L.T., 17; 12 A.L.R., 393. *Hodges J.*

Undue influence—Parent and child — Trustee and cestui que trust—Whether transaction may be set aside against a third party— Ordinary business transaction—Beneficiary surety for trustees—Independent advice.]— The trustees of a will, who were carrying on the business of the testator in trust to divide the profits between the beneficiaries named in the will, were pressed by their bank to reduce their indebtedness to the bank by means of the sale of some of the goods of the business. The trustees objected to do so and asked for further advances for the purposes of the business, and on their suggestion it was arranged that their account should be guaranteed by the beneficiaries and that then the bank should allow the trustees more accommodation. The trustees accordingly procured and handed to the bank guarantees signed by the beneficiaries, and further advances were made. One of the trustees was the mother and another of the trustees was the elder brother of the beneficiaries. The bank manager was aware of facts from which, had he adverted to them, he must have inferred that some of the beneficiaries were not much over 21 years of age. The bank had nothing to do with the procuring of the guarantees. *Held*, that, even if as between the trustees and the beneficiaries the guarantees were of no avail until the trustees proved that the beneficiaries had had independent advice, it was not necessary for the bank to give such proof before it could enforce the guarantees against the beneficiaries. *Semble*, it would have been otherwise if the bank had procured the guarantees from the beneficiaries, or had been in any way mixed up in the obtaining of them, or if the guarantees had been simply to secure a past debt and not to procure future advances, or if the beneficiaries had had no direct interest in the business. *Union Bank of Australia Ltd.* v. *Whitelaw*, (1906) V.L.R., 711; 28 A.L.T., 17; 12 A.L.R., 393. *Hodges, J.*

Assignment of interest in trust estate— Liability subsequently incurred by cestui que trust—Whether liabilities may be discharged out of trust estate to disadvantage of assignee.]—Where in an action by a *cestui que trust* an order is made against him whereby the income of his interest in the trust estate becomes applicable to payment and recoupment of the costs of the other party, such order does not enable such payment and recoupment to be made to the disadvantage of a person to whom the *cestui que trust* before the bringing of the action assigned his interest in the estate by way of mortgage. *Cock* v. *Aitken*, (1912) 15 C.L.R., 373; 18 A.L.R., 576. *Isaacs, J.*

(o) Attachment for Breach of Trust.

Insolvency Act 1890 (No. 1102), secs. 76, 113—Execution of process or judgment, stay of—Debt due by insolvent to creditor— Trust moneys which are or ought to be in hands of trustee—Trustee ordered to pay money into Court—Disobedience of order— Attachment.]—Secs. 76 and 113 of the *Insolvency Act* 1890 are both directed to process for the enforcement of the payment of money as a debt due by the insolvent to a creditor. The insolvency of a person who, in the position of a trustee has not accounted for money he once had and still ought to have, and who has been ordered to pay such money into Court, does not operate as a

stay upon process of attachment against him for non-compliance with the order for payment into Court. *Peterson* v. *M'Lennan*, (1907) V.L.R., 94; 28 A.L.T., 135; 12 A.L.R., 577. *Cussen, J.*

(p) Completion of Administration.

Administration bond—Duration of sureties' liability—Title of beneficiaries to the residue— Completion of the administration.] — *See* EXECUTORS AND ADMINISTRATORS, col. 538. *Bayne* v. *Blake*, (1908) A.C., 371; 14 A.L.R., 317.

(q) Remuneration of Trustees; Passing Accounts.

(1) Commission, Allowance of; Amount of, How Estimated.

Commission — Jurisdiction of Supreme Court to grant—Whether limited to applications in a summary way—Administration action—Future commission—Supreme Court Act 1890 (No. 1142), sec. 21—Administration and Probate Act 1890 (No. 1060), sec. 26.]— The Supreme Court has, under sec. 21 of the *Supreme Court Act* 1890 (sec. 16 of 15 Vict. No. 10) jurisdiction to grant commission, both past and future, to executors, administrators and trustees for their pains and trouble and this jurisdiction is not limited in its exercise by the provisions of sec. 26 of the *Administration and Probate Act* 1890 empowering the Court to grant commission in a summary way to executors administrators and trustees on passing their accounts; an order granting such commission may be made in an administration action. *Nissen* v. *Grunden*, (1912) 14 C.L.R., 297: 18 A.L.R., 254. H.C., *Griffith, C.J., Barton* and *Isaacs, JJ.*

Administration and Probate Act 1890 (No. 1060), sec. 26—Commission—Retainer out of estate without order of Court—Breach of trust.]—It is a breach of trust for executors to retain commission out of an estate without obtaining an order of the Court. *Crout* v. *Beissel*, (1909) V.L.R., 207; 30 A.L.T., 185; 15 A.L.R., 143. *a'Beckett, J.*

Commission—Whether trustee may safely help himself.]—Executors and trustees may not safely help themselves to commission.

Crout v. *Beissel*, (1909) V.L.R., 207 ; 30 A.L.T., 185 ; 15 A.L.R., 143, followed. *Grunden* v. *Nissen*, (1911) V.L.R., 97 ; 32 A.L.T., 117 ; 16 A.L.R., 636. *a' Beckett, J.*

Executor's commission—Commission given to executors by will as remuneration—Further remuneration—Administration and Probate Act 1890 (No. 1060), sec. 26.]—Although by a will the executors are given a definite commission as remuneration, the Court, if it thinks that such commission is inadequate, ought, in the exercise of its jurisdiction under sec. 26 of the *Administration and Probate Act* 1890, to allow them an additional sum by way of commission, taking into account in estimating such additional sum the amount of the commission given by the will. *Re Millin*, 2 V.L.R. (I. P. & M.), 58, 86 and *Re Lee*, 28 V.L.R., 510 ; 22 A.L.T., 117 ; 6 A.L.R., 235, approved. *In re Howell*, (1906) V.L.R., 223 ; 27 A.L.T., 172 ; 12 A.L.R., 92. F.C., *Holroyd, A.-C.J., a' Beckett* and *Hodges*, JJ. (1906).

Administration and Probate Act 1890 (No. 1060), sec. 26—Remuneration of executors and trustees—Legacy given as remuneration for pains and trouble—Allowance of commission.]—See EXECUTORS AND ADMINISTRATORS, 562, 563. *In re Winter* ; *Winter-Irving* v. *Winter*, (1907) V.L.R., 546 ; 29 A.L.T., 4 ; 13 A.L.R., 298.

Executor—Commission—Probate in Scotland and Victoria—Victorian executors also attorneys of trustees of will in Scotland—Agreement as to commission—Costs of executor passing accounts—Administration and Probate Act 1890 (No. 1060), sec. 26.]—See EXECUTORS AND ADMINISTRATORS, cols. 563-564. *Cattanach* v. *Macpherson*, (1908) V.L.R., 390 ; 29 A.L.T., 259 ; 14 A.L.R., 214.

Administration and Probate Act 1890 (No. 1060), sec. 26—Remuneration of executors administrators and trustees—Agreement as to amount of, effect of.]—See EXECUTORS AND ADMINISTRATORS, cols. 563. *Cattanach* v. *Macpherson*, (1908) V.L.R., 390 ; 29 A.L.T., 259 ; 14 A.L.R., 214.

Executor's commission—Amount of, how calculated—Administration and Probate Act 1890 (No. 1060), sec. 26.]—Where lands and houses form parts of the estate which are to remain unconverted under the management of executors until transferred to beneficiaries ultimately entitled, the value of these lands and houses is not to be estimated as part of the amount upon which they are entitled to commission. *Crout* v. *Beissel*, (1909) V.L.R., 207 ; 30 A.L.T., 185 ; 15 A.L.R., 143. *a' Beckett, J.*

Trustee — Commission — Trusts not fully completed—Part only of the trust estate sold—Administration and Probate Act 1890 (No. 1060), sec. 26.]—The Court may allow a trustee commission on corpus the proceeds of the sale of real estate before the same is disposed of in accordance with the trusts. *In re Johnson* ; *Perpetual Executors and Trustees Association &c. Ltd.* v. *Johnson*, (1911) V.L.R., 263 ; 32 A.L.T., 179 ; 17 A.L.R, 187. *a' Beckett, J.*

Trustee—Investment on mortgage—Realization of mortgage—Commission on proceeds of realization.]—When trustees have received commission on portion of the trust fund, which has been invested by them on mortgage, neither they nor their successors are entitled to further commission on the proceeds of realization of the mortgaged property. *Crowley* v. *Crane*, 21 V.L.R., 258 ; 17 A.L.T., 43 ; 1 A.L.R., 101, followed. *Macartney* v. *Macartney*, 33 A.L.T., 183 ; 18 A.L.R., 1. *Madden, C.J.* (1912).

Trustees— Commission — Employment of agents at the expense of the estate to do work which trustees cannot be expected to do personally—Commission on work done by such agents—Special circumstances—Maximum percentage allowed—Administration and Probate Act 1890 (No. 1060), sec. 26.]—See *Macartney* v. *Macartney*, (1909) V.L.R., 183 ; 30 A.L.T., 172 ; 15 A.L.R., 139. *Hodges, J.*

(2) Practice ; Costs ; Court Fees.

Executors—Commission—Order for upon passing accounts—Originating summons—Administration and Probate Act 1890 (No. 1060), sec. 26.]—See EXECUTORS AND ADMINISTRATORS, col. 566. *Re Garrett* ; *Smith*

v. *Garrett*, (1910) V.L.R., 287; 31 A.L.T., 203; 16 A.L.R., 215.

Administration and Probate Act 1890 (No. 1060), sec. 26—Trustees of will—Commission —Individual trustee and trustee company— Prospective order for allowance of commission and passing accounts—Existing accounts passed by Judge.]—*See* EXECUTORS AND ADMINISTRATORS, col. 565. *Sharp* v. *Hobson*, (1911) V.L.R., 321; 33 A.L.T., 18; 17 A.L.R., 274.

Trustees—Passing accounts and allowance of commission—Costs of trustee—Summons for sole purpose of obtaining leave to pass accounts and commission.]—Trustees seeking leave by originating summons to pass their accounts and obtain commission out of the testator's estate on passing accounts, may be allowed their costs out of the estate, even though no other questions are asked by the summons. *In re Foulkes*; *Ford* v. *Foulkes*, 30 A.L.T., 108; 14 A.L.R., 729. *Madden*, *C.J.* (1908).

Costs—Trustees—Passing accounts and allowance of commission—Order for in action— Trustees' costs of obtaining commission— Whether chargeable against estate —Administration and Probate Act 1890 (No. 1060), sec. 26.]—Where under an order in an action trustees of a will are authorised to pass their accounts and apply for commission, they are entitled to charge the estate with the costs incurred by them in relation to commission, as well as in regard to passing their accounts. *Abbott* v. *Morris*, 24 A.L.T., 228; 9 A.L.R., 96, not followed on one point. *Macartney* v. *Kesterson*, (1907) V.L.R., 226; 28 A.L.T., 170; 13 A.L.R., 14. *Hodges, J.*

Executor or trustee passing accounts— Costs—Whether payable out of estate.]— Although ordinarily an executor or trustee is entitled to have his costs of passing his accounts and obtaining his discharge paid out of the estate, yet, if in so doing he seeks to cast an unnecessary burden on the estate, he must abide those costs himself. *Cattanach* v. *Macpherson*, (1908) V.L.R., 390; 29 A.L.T., 259; 14 A.L.R., 214. *Madden*, *C.J.* (1908).

Administration and Probate Act 1890 (No. 1060), sec. 26—Practice—Executors and trustees—Passing Accounts before Chief Clerk— Costs of executors and trustees—Objection to allowance thereof—Time to take.]—Where beneficiaries desire to object that executors and trustees should not be allowed their costs of the proceedings before the Chief Clerk for the passing of accounts and allowance of commission, they should ask the Chief Clerk to certify specially upon the matter, and then raise the question upon further consideration before the Judge on the certificate. *In re Dingwall*; *Ross* v. *Ross*, 34 A.L.T., 137; 18 A.L.R., 584. *a' Beckett, J.* (1912).

Appendix O*, Rules of Supreme Court 1884 — Trustees — Passing accounts — Accounts agreed upon between parties—Fees chargeable.]—Where trustees are ordered by the Court to pass their accounts before the Chief Clerk the fees prescribed for " taking accounts " by Appendix O* to the *Rules of the Supreme Court* 1884 are chargeable, although the parties agree among themselves not to dispute the accounts presented by the trustees and the Chief Clerk accordingly accepts them as proper accounts. There is also chargeable 10s. per hour for each hour occupied by the Chief Clerk in inquiring as to the commission to be allowed the trustees. *Re Hutchison*, 32 W.R., 392, approved and applied. *In re Winter*; *Winter- Irving* v. *Winter*, (1908) V.L.R., 74; 29 A.L.T., 144; 13 A.L.R., 701. F.C., *Madden, C.J.*, *a' Beckett* and *Cussen*, *JJ.* (1907).

V.—ACTIONS BY AND AGAINST TRUSTEES.

(a) Parties; *Evidence*; *Form of Writ*.

Practice—Joinder of parties—Administration action—Trustee sued as representative— Refusal of trustee to appeal—Judgment not yet drawn up—Joinder of cestui que trustent— Order XVI., r. 8 (Rules of 1906).]—Where a trustee is sued as a representative of his *cestui que trustent*, and a judgment adverse to them is given from which the trustee refuses to appeal, the *cestui que trustent*, before the judgment is drawn up are entitled *ex debito justitiae* to be added as parties so that they may appeal. *Connolly* v. *Macartney*,

41

(1908) 7 C.L.R., 48 ; 14 A.L.R., 558. H.C., *Griffith, C.J., Barton, O'Connor* and *Isaacs, JJ.*

Order XVI. (Rules of 1906)—Parties—Administrator—Assets transferred by administrator in breach of trust—Action by administrator to recover—Whether beneficiaries necessary parties.]—*See* PRACTICE PLEADING, col. 1039. *Ackerly* v. *Palmer,* (1910) V.L.R., 339 ; 32 A.L.T., 23 ; 16 A.L.R., 326.

Burden of proof—Land held in fee simple to be used only for a public racecourse—Member of public claiming right to enter land—Victoria Racing Club Act 1871 (No. 398), secs. 7-20.]—As to the burden of proof, where the plaintiff, a member of the public, claims the right to enter on race days land on which a racecourse is situated, and the defendant is the legal owner in fee simple, but, under a Statute, holds the land to be used as a public racecourse and for that purpose only, *see Colman* v. *Miller,* (1906) V.L.R., 622 ; 28 A.L.T., 35 ; 12 A.L.R., 386. F.C., *Hodges, Hood* and *Chomley, JJ.* (1906).

Administration action—Writ of summons—Form of heading.]—*See* PRACTICE AND PLEADING, col. 1028. *Cameron* v. *Cameron,* (1906) V.L.R., 13 ; 28 A.L.T., 169 ; 13 A.L.R., 10.

(b) *Costs.*

Costs—Trustees—Unsuccessful appeal.]—The costs of trustees, unsuccessful appellants, were in the special circumstances allowed out of the estate. *In re Rosenthal ; Rosenthal* v. *Rosenthal,* (1910) 11 C.L.R., 87 ; 16 A.L.R., 455. H.C., *Griffith, C.J.,* and *Isaacs, J.* (*Higgins, J.,* dissenting)

Costs—Appeal in administration action—Costs of trustee—Whether trustee entitled to be indemnified out of estate.]—Trustees who have been guilty of breaches of trust in respect of which an order has been made in an administration action by a Court of first instance but who, in respect of the matters in question upon an appeal from that order, are blameless, are entitled to be indemnified out of the estate for their costs of such appeal.

Nissen v. *Grunden,* 14 C.L.R., 297 ; 18 A.L.R., 254. H.C., *Griffith, C.J., Barton* and *Isaacs, JJ.*

Appeal—Costs—Order directing trustees to pay costs—Supreme Court Act 1890 (No. 1142), sec. 60.]—An appeal lies from an order directing a trustee to pay costs in an action for administration, because it is a settled rule that such an order cannot be made unless the occasion of the suit has arisen from something in the nature of the trustee's own misconduct. It is also settled that the question, whether a trustee has been guilty of such misconduct as to justify the Court in ordering him to pay costs, is appealable. *Amos* v. *Fraser,* 4 C.L.R., 78 ; 12 A.L.R., 481. H.C., *Griffith, C.J., Barton* and *O'Connor, JJ.* (1906).

Trustee—Life tenant and remainderman—Capital and income—Costs paid by trustees under order of High Court—Decision of High Court reversed on appeal by one party to Privy Council—Effect on rights of parties not appealing—Indemnity of trustees—Rights of assignee of life tenant.]—*See* TENANT FOR LIFE AND REMAINDERMAN, cols. 1206, 1207. *Cock* v. *Aitken,* (1912) 15 C.L.R., 373 ; 18 A.L.R., 576.

Solicitor to trustee of deceased person's estate—Lien for costs.]—*See* COSTS, col. 293. *In re Nolan (No.* 2), 30 A.L.T. (Supplement), 1 ; 14 A.L.R. (C.N.), 25. *Judge Moule* (1908).

VI.—CRIMINAL MATTERS.

Embezzlement — Secretary of friendly society—Moneys of trustees—No relation of master and servant.]—*See* CRIMINAL LAW, col. 336. *Rex* v. *McAuslan,* (1907) V.L.R., 710 ; 29 A.L.T., 83 ; 13 A.L.R., 609.

Larceny—Money of friendly society — Money in possession of treasurer—Felonious taking by trustee—In whom property should be laid—Friendly Societies Act 1890 (No. 1094), sec. 16 (iii.), (vi.).]—*See* CRIMINAL LAW. cols. 338, 339. *Rex* v. *Watson,* (1908) V.L.R., 103 ; 29 A.L.T., 146 ; 13 A.L.R., 724

Friendly Societies Act 1890 (No. 1094), sec. 16 (iii.), (vi.))—Property of society. legal proceedings concerning—Owners, who may be named as—Trustees.]—*See* CRIMINAL LAW, col. 339. *Rex* v. *Watson,* (1908) V.L.R., 103; 29 A.L.T., 146; 13 A.L.R., 724.

Criminal law—Larceny—Property, in whom to be laid—Trustees of friendly society—Friendly Societies Act 1890 (No. 1094), sec. 16 (vi.)]—*See* CRIMINAL LAW, col. 339. *Rex* v. *Watson,* 13 A.L.R., at p. 725.

ULTRA VIRES.

See APPEAL, FRIENDLY SOCIETIES, POST AND TELEGRAPH ACTS.

UNCONSCIONABLE BARGAIN.

See MONEY LENDERS ACT, cols. 924 *et seq.*

UNDUE INFLUENCE.

See FRAUD AND MISREPRESENTA-TION; WILL.

UNLAWFULLY USING.

See CRIMINAL LAW, col. 344

VACCINATION.

Vaccination—Duty of parent to have child vaccinated—No public vaccinator — Notice specifying when and where public vaccinator will attend—Parent attending with child at time and place specified—Health Act 1890 (No. 1098), secs. 191, 204—Eighteenth Schedule.]—*See* HEALTH (PUBLIC), cols. 633, 634. *Thornton* v. *Kelly,* (1910) V.L.R., 156; 31 A.L.T., 197; 16 A.L.R., 142.

Health Act 1890 (No. 1098), Part IX., Eighteenth Schedule—Vaccination—Notice of requirement of vaccination—Notification of place of attendance of public vaccinator for the district—" District," meaning of—Place of attendance outside district of Registrar of Births and Deaths causing notice to be given.] —*See* HEALTH (PUBLIC), col. 634. *O'Malley* v. *Russell,* (1908) V.L.R., 545; 30 A.L.T., 39; 14 A.L.R., 462.

Information—Allegation as to date of offence incorrect—Health Act 1890 (No. 1098), Part IX.—Vaccination—Justices Act—1890 (No. 1105), sec. 73 (3).]—*See* HEALTH (PUBLIC), col. 634. *O'Malley* v. *Russell,* (1908) V.L.R., 545; 30 A.L.T., 39; 14 A.L.R., 462.

Information, sufficiency of—Charge against father for not having child vaccinated—Allegation that vaccination notice given by Registrar of district in which father resided—Who may properly give such notice — Health Act 1890 (No. 1098), Part IX.]—*See* HEALTH (PUBLIC). cols. 634, 635. *O'Malley* v. *Russell,* (1908) V.L.R., 545; 30 A.L.T., 39; 14 A.L.R., 462.

VENDOR AND PURCHASER.

I.—CONTRACT OF SALE.

(a) *Offer and Acceptance; Legality.*

See also, post, V. COSTS.

Sale of land—Contract—Offer—Acceptance—Formal contract to be signed—Statute of Frauds—Instruments Act 1890 (No. 1103), sec. 208.]—Plaintiff wrote to defendant—" As I am anxious to dispose of my property in Faraday Street, Carlton, I should be glad if you would favour me with an offer by return post ." Four days afterwards the defendant wrote in reply—" In answer to yours I can offer you £1,450 for your property in Faraday Street, Carlton." On the same day the plaintiff wrote in reply—" I accept your offer of this day's date to purchase my properties, Nos. 156-162 Faraday Street, Carlton, for the sum of £1,450 cash, formal contract to be signed." *Held*, that the defendant's letter amounted to an offer, and that the plaintiff's second letter was an acceptance of that offer, the words " formal contract to be signed " not being a term of the assent, and therefore that there was a binding contract enforceable by the plaintiff. *Bruen* v. *Smith*, 30 A.L.T., 149 ; 14 A.L.R., 700. *a' Beckett, J.* (1908).

Vendor and purchaser—Contract of sale—Provision for apportionment of Federal Land Tax—Validity—Interpretation—Land Tax Assessment Act 1910 (No. 22 of 1910), secs. 37, 63.]—See CONTRACT OR AGREEMENT, cols. 220, 221. *Patterson* v. *Farrell*, (1912) 14 C.L.R., 348 ; 18 A.L.R., 237. *Griffith, C.J., Barton* and *Isaacs, JJ.*

(b) Statute of Frauds.

Instruments Act 1890 (No. 1103), secs. 208, 209—Statute of Frauds (29 Car. II. c. 3)—Contract for sale of land—Signature to note or memorandum—Signature by amanuensis in presence and by direction of party to be charged, whether sufficient.]—See CONTRACT OR AGREEMENT, col. 194. *Thomson* v. *McInnes*, (1911) 12 C.L.R., 562 ; 17 A.L.R., 354.

Instruments Act 1890 (No. 1103), sec. 208—Sale of land—Note or memorandum—Several documents—Parol evidence, when admissible to connect—Reference to document—Reference to transaction in which document may or may not have been written.]—See CONTRACT OR AGREEMENT, col. 196. *Thomson* v. *McInnes*, (1911) 12 C.L.R., 562 ; 17 A.L.R., 354.

(c) Interpretation.

(1) Description of Land.

Contract of sale—Construction—Sale of land under name by which it is known—Words stating measurements, whether words of estimate or of warranty.]—In a contract of sale the particulars described the property sold as being " that property known as Nos. 420 and 422 Church Street Richmond Victoria and having a frontage of about 40 feet by a depth of 130 feet to a right of way on which are erected two shops." *Semble*, what was sold by the contract was the property known as Nos. 420 and 422 Church Street, Richmond, and the words " about 40 feet " were words of estimate and not of warranty. *In re Cook and Preece's Contract*, (1910) V.L.R., 328 ; 32 A.L.T., 17 ; 16 A.L.R., 324 *Hodges, J.* (1910).

(2) Conditions of Sale.

Vendor and purchaser—Specific performance—Time limited for production of title—Notice to produce—Deficiency of area—Annulment of contract—Land Act 1901 (No. 1749), secs. 35, 49 (6), 56 (6).]—By a contract of sale of seven specified Crown allotments of land described therein as containing 2,131 acres or thereabouts, the titles to which were Crown leases of grazing areas granted under the *Land Act* 1901, the vendors agreed that they would apply to select two of the allotments as agricultural allotments and a third as a grazing allotment, and to have issued to them a lease under section 49 (6) of the Act in respect of such two allotments, and a lease under sec. 56 (6) in respect of such third allotment. It was also agreed that " the two last-mentioned leases " and the leases of the other grazing areas should be produced " to the purchaser or his solicitor within eight months from the day of sale and a copy thereof may be made by the purchaser or his solicitor on application in that behalf to the vendors or their solicitor," and that in the event of non-production of the leases it shall be lawful for either the vendors or the purchaser to annul the sale It was further provided that if any mistake should be made in the description or area of the property or any other error should appear in the particulars, such mistake or error should not annul the sale, but compensation should be fixed by referees. It was finally provided that time should be of the essence of the contract in all respects. The two allotments agreed to be selected as agricultural allotments were comprised in a single Crown lease and together contained more land by about 30 acres than could under the Act be so selected, and the allotment agreed to be selected as a grazing allotment contained more land by about 3 acres than could under the Act be so selected, and the leases issued in respect of such selections were of correspondingly smaller areas. The price was at the rate of 5s. per acre for the land agreed to be selected as agricultural allotments, and 10s. per acre for the rest. *Held*, that in order to enable the vendors to rely on the non-production of the leases within the specified period, they must before the expiration of that period have asked for production. *Held*, also, that the deficiency in the area of the land selected was not a ground for resisting specific performance of the contract, but was a matter for compensation under the contract. *Cox* v. *Hoban*, (1911) 12 C.L.R., 256 ; 17 A.L.R., 195. H.C., *Griffith, C.J., O'Connor* and *Isaacs, JJ.*

Contract of sale of land—Construction—Provisions for annulment and compensation, whether mutually exclusive—Objections to title or matter in particulars—Power to annul if objection to title " or otherwise "—Error in particulars—Deficiency in frontage.]—In a contract of sale of land the particulars described the property sold as " having a frontage of about 40 feet." As a matter of fact, the frontage was 33 feet 3 inches. One of the conditions of sale contained in the contract required the purchaser within a certain time to deliver to the vendor a statement in writing of all objections to the title or " concerning any matter appearing on the particulars." In the next condition the vendor was empowered to annul the sale if the purchaser made any objection to the title " or otherwise " which the vendor was unable or unwilling to remove ; and then followed a condition providing that any mistake in the description or error in the particulars of the property should not annul the sale but, that compensation, to be settled by arbitration, should be given or taken as the case might require. *Held*, that the conditions as to annulment and compensation were

not mutually exclusive, and that, objection having been raised by the purchaser as to the deficiency of frontage, such objection was an objection concerning a " matter appearing on the particulars," and that, consequently, the vendor was entitled to annul the contract. *In re Cook and Preece's Contract*, (1910) V.L.R., 328 ; 32 A.L.T., 17 ; 16 A.L.R., 324. *Hodges, J.*

Vendor and purchaser—Contract for sale of land—Requisition on title—Vendor unable or unwilling to comply with requisition—Right of vendor to annul sale—Transfer of Land Act 1890 (No. 1149), Schedule XXV., Table A. (4).] —Where the purchaser under a contract of sale of land in his requisitions on title persists in making requisitions of such a nature that the vendor by complying or partly complying therewith may complicate matters, the vendor may avail himself of a condition in the contract entitling him to annul a sale which is substantially the same as condition 4 in Schedule XXV. Table A. of the *Transfer of Land Act* 1890. *West* v. *Hedgeland*, (1909) V.L.R., 178 ; 30 A.L.T., 175 ; 15 A.L.R., 123. *a'Beckett J.*

Vendor and purchaser—Agreement to give possession on a certain day—Condition that vendor may annul sale if unable or unwilling to comply with requisition—Inability or unwillingness, what is—Knowledge by vendor of his inability to comply with term of contract—Specific performance so far as possible, with compensation—Whether purchaser entitled to —Transfer of Land Act 1890 (No. 1149), Schedule XXV., Table A., Condition 4.]—The vendor under a contract for the sale of land made in April, 1909, agreed to give possession to the purchaser on May 17th, 1910. The contract contained the following condition :—" In case the purchaser shall . . . make any objection to or requisition on the title or otherwise which the vendor shall be unable or unwilling to remove or comply with and such objection or requisition be insisted on it shall be lawful for the vendor (whether he shall have attempted to remove such objection or to comply with such requisition or not) at any time by notice in writing to annul the sale, and within one week after giving such notice to repay to the purchaser the amount of the purchase money or so much thereof as shall have been paid in full satisfaction of all claims and demands whatsoever by the purchaser, and also to return all unpaid acceptances given by the purchaser, but without any interest, costs, or damages of any description." At the time the contract was made a tenant was in possession of the premises under a lease expiring on May 13th, 1910, with an option of renewal for a term of eleven years. The purchaser at the time of entering into the contract was unaware of this option, and the vendor who never made any real effort to procure possession had been refused vacant possession by the lessee at the end of her then current term. The lessee exercised her option and obtained a renewal of her lease for a term of eleven years from May 13th, 1910. The purchaser made requisitions on title including a demand for vacant possession on May 17th, 1910. This demand was refused by the vendor, and the purchaser persisting in it the vendor gave formal notice that he annulled the sale purporting to act under the condition above set forth. In an action by the purchaser against the vendor claiming specific performance or specific performance so far as possible with damages, *Held*, that the vendor's inability or unwillingness to give possession was not covered by the condition above set out and that he was not entitled to annul the sale ; and that the purchaser was entitled to specific performance, so far as possible, with compensation for loss of possession. *McGavin* v. *Gerraty*, 32 A.L.T., 151 ; 17 A.L.R., 85. *Madden, C.J.* (1911).

Vendor and purchaser—Conditions of sale—Production of certificate of title—Place of production.]—One of the conditions in a contract for the sale of land situated in the neighbourhood of Kerang, provided that " the certificate of title to the property sold shall be produced and a copy thereof may be made by the purchaser or his solicitor on application in that behalf to the vendor or his solicitor." No place for the production of the certificate of title was specified. The vendor lived near Kerang, and it was a condition of the contract that the vendor's solicitor was M. O. of Kerang. *Held*, that the certificate of title should be produced at some place reasonably convenient to Kerang, it might be the land itself or the place of residence or business of the vendor or his solicitor and that the production of the certificate at Melbourne was not a compliance with the condition. *Morrison* v. *Richardson*, (1907) V.L.R., 218 ; 28 A.L.T., 166 ; 13 A.L.R., 94. *Hodges, J.*

Vendor and purchaser—Contract for sale of land—Deposit to be paid to G. " as agent for the vendor "—Deposit to be paid over to vendor on acceptance of title—Contract rescinded by mutual consent—Title not accepted—Whether vendor liable to repay deposit to purchaser—Money had and received—Stakeholder.]—One of the conditions of a contract in writing for the sale of certain land and stock provided that the purchasers should, on the signing of the contract pay " a deposit of £500 " to G. " as agent for the vendor." Another condition provided that as soon as the purchasers accepted the title " the deposit shall be paid over to the vendor." There was another condition enabling the vendor in certain circumstances to annul the sale and prescribing that he should " repay " the purchase money already paid. The £500 deposit was paid by the purchasers to G. but was not paid by him to the vendor. Subsequently the purchasers and the vendor by agreement in writing rescinded the contract, title never having been accepted. In an action by the purchasers against the vendor to recover the £500 deposit as money had and received, *Held* (by *Griffith, C.J., O'Connor* and *Higgins, JJ., Isaacs, J.*, dissenting), that G. was the agent of the vendor and not a stakeholder, and that the purchasers were entitled to recover the £500 from the vendor. *Christie* v. *Robinson*, 4 C.L.R., 1338 ; 13 A.L.R., 288 (1907).

II.—TITLE.

See also, *ante*, I.—CONTRACT OF SALE. (c) INTERPRETATION. (2) CONDITIONS OF SALE.

Local Government Act 1903 (No. 1893), secs. 341, 342—County Court Rules 1891, r. 103—

Rates—Charge on Land—Proceedings to enforce—Death of owner—Parties—Executor of executor—Order for sale—Title.]—The purchaser of land at a sale made pursuant to an order in an action under section 342 of the *Local Government Act* 1903 (No. 1893) wherein the executor of the executor of the registered proprietor of the land is defendant will acquire a good title to the land. *Moorabbin Shire* v. *Soldi*, (1912) V.L.R., 389; 34 A.L.T., 93; 18 A.L.R., 493. F.C. *a'Beckett, Hodges* and *Cussen, JJ.* (1912).

Title with apparent flaw—Existence of flaw negatived by proof of facts—Whether purchaser may be compelled to accept title—Transfer of Land Act—Land under, whether same rule applicable to.]—By the general law a title having what would appear to be a flaw until negatived by proof of disputable facts, can be forced on an unwilling purchaser, and that rule applies to land under the *Transfer of Land Act*. *In re Kenna and Ritchie's Contract*, (1907) V.L.R., 386; 28 A.L.T., 218; 13 A.L.R., 191. *a'Beckett, J.*

Sale of land—Restrictive covenant running with land—Covenant notified as an encumbrance on certificate of title—Purchaser of part of land not in fact affected by covenant—Whether purchaser bound to accept title—Proof of facts showing covenant does not affect part of land sold—Costs of, how borne.]—R., who owned an estate, as to which there existed a restrictive covenant running with the land limiting the amount of water which might be discharged from it on to adjoining land, subdivided the estate and sold part of it to K. The rights of the persons claiming under the deed creating this restrictive covenant were notified as an encumbrance on the certificate of title to the whole estate. A requisition was made for an undertaking by R. that a certificate of title to the part sold should issue to K. free from the incumbrance. R. refused to give his undertaking and K. took out a summons claiming rescission. The Judge found that by reason of the contour and natural features of the part purchased by K. and of the adjoining lands, the restrictive covenant would not in fact affect such part. *Held,*

that K. was entitled to demand satisfactory evidence that the covenant in question did not affect the land purchased by him, which evidence should have been furnished at the cost of R., but that the encumbrance on the certificate of title did not constitute a valid objection to title. *In re Kenna and Ritchie's Contract*, (1907) V.L.R., 386; 28 A.L.T., 218; 13 A.L.R., 191. *a'Beckett, J.*

Vendor and purchaser—Title—Executor of an administrator—Conveyance by—Devolution of estate—Administration and Probate Act 1890 (No. 1060), sec. 6.]—Persons deriving title to the beneficial interest in land from the devisees, and procuring the conveyance of the legal estate from the person in whom it is vested under section 6 of the *Administration and Probate Act* 1890, can make good title without completing the chain of representation of the original testator. *In re Thomas and McKenzie's Contract*, (1912) V.L.R., 1; 33 A.L.T., 141; 17 A.L.R., 451. *a'Beckett, J.* (1911).

Landlord and Tenant Act 1890 (No. 1108), sec. 92—Eighth Schedule—Notice of owner's intention to apply to justices to recover possession—Statement that tenement held over and detained from purchaser—Legal estate still in vendor—Whether equitable owner might himself obtain warrant.]—*See* LANDLORD AND TENANT, cols. 816, 817. *Equity Trustees Executors and Agency Co. Ltd.* v. *Harston*, (1908) V.L.R., 23; 29 A.L.T., 131; 13 A.L.R., 686.

III.—EASEMENT, IMPLIED GRANT OF.

Vendor and purchaser—Derogation from grant—Implied grant—Quasi-easement—Rain-water flowing over surface—Adjoining owners—Natural servitude—Alteration of surface—Transfer of Land Act 1890 (No. 1149), sec. 89—Conveyancing Act 1904 (No. 1953), sec. 6.]—Where the proprietor of land under the *Transfer of Land Act* 1890, comprising two adjoining town allotments, and lying upon a slope, sells and transfers the upper allotment, the rain water falling on which naturally flowed at the time of transfer on to the other or lower allotment, no grant of a quasi-easement to allow the rainwater to continue so to flow is to be implied from the transfer in favour of the transferree as against the transferror. By creating an embankment to prevent the flow, the transferror is not derogating from his grant. *Vinnicombe* v. *MacGregor*, 29 V.L.R., 32; 28 V.L.R., 144; 24 A.L.T., 200; 24 A.L.T., 15; 9 A.L.R., 60; 8 A.L.R., 141, disapproved, *per Griffith, C.J.,* and *O'Connor, J. Nelson* v. *Walker*, (1910) 10 C.L.R., 560; 16 A.L.R., 285. H.C., *Griffith, C.J., O'Connor, Isaacs* and *Higgins, JJ.*

Vendor and purchaser—Sale of part of a parcel of land—Retention by vendor of balance—Implied grant of easement.]—In order that the grant to a purchaser of a right in the nature of an easement in respect of land of the vendor may be implied from a conveyance of part of a parcel of land of which the vendor retains the balance, it must appear, having regard to all the circumstances of the case, to have been in the contemplation of the parties that the grantor should not use the land which he retains in a manner inconsistent with the enjoyment of the alleged easement. *Nelson* v. *Walker*, (1910) 10 C.L.R., 560; 16 A.L.R., 285. H.C. *Griffith, C.J., O'Connor, Isaacs* and *Higgins, JJ.*

Quasi-easement—Severance of unity of possession and title—Implied grant—Derogation from grant.]—The foundation of the doctrine of implied grant in the case of conveyance of part of a parcel of land, the vendor retaining the rest, is that having regard to all the circumstances of the case it must (not may) have been in the contemplation of the parties that the grantor should not use the land which he retains in such a way as to preclude any use of the land which he sells or that use for which he knows he is selling it to the purchaser. *Semble.*—No such grant is to be implied (so as to bind successors in title) from circumstances not referred to in the transfer or conveyance. *Nelson* v. *Walker*, (1910) 10 C.L.R., 560; 16 A.L.R., 285. H.C. *Griffith, C.J., O'Connor, Isaacs* and *Higgins, JJ.*

IV.—SPECIFIC PERFORMANCE.

See, ante, I.—CONTRACT OF SALE. (*c*) INTERPRETATION. (2) CONDITIONS OF SALE and II.—TITLE.

V.—COSTS.

Conveyancing Act 1904 (No. 1953), secs. 1, 3, 4 (6), (9)—Vendor and purchaser—Perusal fees, legality of contract for payment of by purchaser—Land under Transfer of Land Act—Transfer.]—Sub-sec. 6 of sec. 4 of the *Conveyancing Act* 1904, is effective, notwithstanding sub-sec. 9, and it applies to all land sold by auction whether under the *Transfer of Land Act* or under the general law. *Re Stewart and Park's Contract*, (1907) V.L.R., 31; 28 A.L.T., 133; 12 A.L.R., 553. *Hood, J.* (1906).

Conveyancing Act 1904 (No. 1953), sec. 4 (6), (9)—Interpretation—Repugnant clauses—Insertion of words to give effect to clear intention of Statute.]—Sub-sec. 9 of sec. 4 of the *Conveyancing Act* 1904 should be read as though it contained some words excluding sub-sec. 6 from its operation. *Re Stewart and Park's Contract*, (1907) V.L.R., 31; 28 A.L.T., 133; 12 A.L.R., 553. *Hood, J.* (1906).

Conveyancing Act 1904 (No. 1953), sec. 4 (6)—Whether applicable to land under Transfer of Land Act—" Conveyance," " transfer "—Contract of sale by auction—Stipulation that purchaser shall pay vendor's costs of perusal of conveyance.]—Sec. 4 (6) of the *Conveyancing Act* 1904 applies to sales by auction of land under the *Transfer of Land Act* 1890. *Re Stewart and Park's Contract*, (1907) V.L.R., 31; 28 A.L.T., 133; 12 A.L.R., 553, followed. *Re Rogers and Rodd's Contract*, (1907) V.L.R., 511; 29 A.L.T., 13; 13 A.L.R., 312. *Madden, C.J.* (1907).

Conveyancing Act 1904 (No. 1953), sec. 4 (6)—Auction Sales Act 1890 (No. 1065), secs. 3, 29—Sale of land by Sheriff under fi. fa.—Whether a " sale by auction "—Sheriff's costs of perusal of conveyance—Stipulation in contract of sale for payment by purchaser, legality of.]—A sale of land by auction conducted by the Sheriff under a writ of *fi. fa.* is, notwithstanding the provisions of the *Auction*

Sales Act 1890 excusing the Sheriff from the responsibilities imposed by that Act, a sale by auction within the meaning of sec. 4 (6) of the *Conveyancing Act* 1904, and a clause in the contract of sale charging the purchaser with the payment of the Sheriff's costs of perusal of the conveyance is accordingly illegal. *Re Rogers' and Rodd's Contract*, (1907) V.L.R., 511 ; 29 A.L.T. 13 ; 13 A.L.R., 312. *Madden, C.J.* (1907).

Conveyancing Act 1904 (No. 1953), secs. 4 (6), (9), 10—Auction—Sale of land—Contract of sale—Costs of perusal and of obtaining execution of conveyance—Stipulation for payment by purchaser—Waiver by signing contract—Procedure for declaration of illegality of stipulation—Existence of contract.]—A clause in a contract of sale by auction of land stating that sec. 4 (6) of the *Conveyancing Act* 1904 shall not apply to the contract and stipulating for the payment by the purchaser to the vendor or his solicitor of the costs of perusal of the conveyance or of obtaining the execution thereof is illegal, and the purchaser does not waive the benefit of the provision in that section of the Act by signing a contract containing such a clause. Where a purchaser has signed a contract containing such a clause he may apply on summons under sec. 10 of the *Conveyancing Act* 1904 for a declaration that the clause is illegal and void, as the illegal stipulation may be disregarded and the contract still subsists. *In re Stewart and Park's Contract*, (1907) V.L.R., 31 ; 28 A.L.T., 133 ; 12 A.L.R., 553, and *In re Rogers and Rodd's Contract*, (1907) V.L.R., 511 ; 29 A.L.T., 13 ; 13 A.L.R., 312, followed. *In re Crook's Contract*, (1909) V.L.R., 12 ; 30 A.L.T., 108 ; 14 A.L.R., 698. *a'Beckett, J.* (1908).

Conveyancing Act 1904 (No. 1953) sec. 4 (6)—Contract for sale of land—Sale by auction—Costs—Exclusive of perusal and obtaining execution of transfer—Purchaser to pay—Validity—Condition.]—A provision in a contract made at the sale of land by auction " that the purchaser shall pay the vendor's costs and expenses of and incidental to the transfer exclusive of perusal and of obtaining the execution of the transfer " is not void

under sec. 4 (6) of the *Conveyancing Act* 1904. The expression " costs of perusal of the conveyance or of obtaining the execution thereof " in sec. 4 (6) of the *Conveyancing Act* 1904 does not include the costs of all matters connected with the transfer of the land sold. Perusal means reading the conveyance to see if it expresses what it is intended to express. *In re Sutton and the Federal Building Society's Contract*, (1909) V.L.R., 473 ; 31 A.L.T., 75 ; 15 A.L.R., 560. *Cussen, J.*

Sale of land—Restrictive covenant running with land—Covenant notified as encumbrance on certificate of title—Purchaser of part of land not in fact affected by covenant—Whether purchaser bound to accept title—Proof of facts showing covenant does not affect part of land sold—Costs of, how to be borne.]—*See, ante,* II.—TITLE. *In re Kenna and Ritchie's Contract*, (1907) V.L.R., 386 ; 28 A.L.T., 218 ; 18 A.L.R., 191.

VENUE.

See CRIMINAL LAW, col. 361.

VERMIN.

Vermin Destruction Act 1890 (No. 1153), sec. 22—Recovery of expenses incurred by inspector—" Owner "—Liability of vendor when sale is not completed.]—The registered proprietor of land who has sold it and given possession to the purchaser but who has not received the whole of the purchase money is an " owner " of the land within sec. 22 of the *Vermin Destruction Act* 1890, and is therefore liable for the expenses incurred by an inspector in destroying rabbits on the land. *Moore* v. *Irvine*, (1913) V.L.R., 14 ; 34 A.L.T., 107 ; 18 A.L.R., 526. F.C. *a'Beckett, Hodges* and *Cussen, JJ.* (1912).

Vermin Destruction Act 1890 (No. 1153), sec. 20—Service of notice by registered letter —Addressee's name mis-spelt—Name on letter sounding the same as addressee's name.] —Service by registered letter of a notice under the *Vermin Destruction Act* 1890 is not invalid although the addressee's name is mis-spelt, provided that the name, as spelt, is *idem sonans. McCallum* v. *Purvis*, (1906) V.L.R., 578; 28 A.L.T., 31; 12 A.L.R., 329. *Hood, J.* (1906).

Vermin Destruction Act 1890 (No. 1153), sec. 20—Service of notice by registered letter effect of—Notice never received by addressee.]—Proof of the posting of a notice under the *Vermin Destruction Act* 1890 in a registered letter properly addressed is proof of service of the notice for the purposes of the Act, although it is proved that the notice never reached the addressee. *McCallum* v. *Purvis*, (1906) V.L.R., 578; 28 A.L.T., 31; 12 A.L.R., 329. *Hood, J.* (1906).

Vermin Destruction Act 1890 (No. 1153), sec. 26—Costs incurred by inspector in destroying vermin—Certificate of amount, how far conclusive.]—The certificate of the inspector under sec. 26 of the *Vermin Destruction Act* 1890 does not preclude evidence to show that the charges were not reasonably incurred. *McCallum* v. *Purvis*, (1906) V.L.R., 578; 28 A.L.T., 31; 12 A.L.R., 329. *Hood, J.* (1906).

VICTORIA RACING CLUB.

Burden of proof—Land held in fee simple to be used only for a public racecourse—Member of public claiming right to enter land—Victoria Racing Club Act 1871 (No. 398), secs. 7-20.]—As to the burden of proof, where the plaintiff, a member of the public, claims the right to enter on race days land on which a race-course is situated, and the defendant is the legal owner in fee simple, but, under a Statute, holds the land to be used as a public racecourse and for that purpose only, *See Colman* v. *Miller*, (1906) V.L.R., 622; 28 A.L.T., 35; 12 A.L.R., 386. F.C. *Hodges, Hood* and *Chomley, JJ.* (1906).

By-law — Validity — Unreasonableness and uncertainty—Regulation of "bookmaking" on public racecourse—Victoria Racing Club Act 1871 (No. 398), secs. 7-20.]—*See* GAMING AND WAGERING, cols. 603, 604. *Colman* v. *Miller*, (1906) V.L.R., 622; 28 A.L.T., 35; 12 A.L.R., 386.

" Bookmaking " on racecourse—How far lawful—By-law regulating " bookmaking."—Validity of.]—*Per Hood, J.*—Provided that in doing so he violates no Statute law nor interferes unduly with others, any person lawfully on a racecourse may make wagers either privately with his friends or publicly as a business. Public betting as a business may become a nuisance or an annoyance, and by-laws designed to prevent this should be supported if possible, but, like all by-laws interfering with private rights, they must be reasonable and certain. *Colman* v. *Miller*, (1906) V.L.R., 622; 28 A.L.T., 35; 12 A.L.R., 386.

WAIVER.

See also, COMPANY.

Contract—Breach in performance of—Steps taken by party not in default to minimise loss—Whether new contract or waiver of rights to be inferred.]—Steps taken by a party not in default for the purpose of minimising loss should not of themselves be taken as evidencing any intention to enter into a new agreement or to waive any of his rights. *Alexander Cross & Sons Ltd.* v. *Hasell*, (1908) V.L.R., 194; 29 A.L.T., 179; 14 A.L.R., 44. *Cussen, J.*

Director with contractual rights against company—Concurrence in acts rendering company unable to perform contract — Whether a waiver of rights of director.]—The mere concurrence of a person in his capacity of director of a company in acts, which render such company unable to perform a contract then existing between him and the company, does not amount to a waiver by him of his personal rights in respect of a breach of contract by the company resulting from such acts. *Glass* v. *Pioneer Rubber Works of Australasia Ltd*, (1906) V.L.R., 754; 28 A.L.T., 64; 12 A.L.R., 529. F.C. *a'Beckett, A.C.J., Hodges* and *Chomley, JJ.*

Mines Act 1897 (No. 1514), sec. 75—Mining on private property—Compensation—Agreement with owner—Necessity for writing

—**Waiver.**]—*See* MINES AND MINING, col. 911. *Armstrong* v. *The Duke of Wellington G. M. Co. No Liability*, (1906) V.L.R., 145; 27 A.L.T., 146; 12 A.L.R., 67.

Building contract—Provision for appointment of architect to certify for payment to contractor—No architect appointed—Waiver —Payment of whole of contract price— Subsequent discovery of defects—Architect's certificate, effect of.]—*See* CONTRACT OR AGREEMENT, col. 234. *Hopper* v. *Meyer*, (1906) V.L.R., 235; 27 A.L.T., 185; 12 A.L.R., 146.

Landlord and Tenant Act 1890 (No. 1108), secs. 92, 93—Notice to quit—Second notice effect of—Offer of new tenancy—Non-acceptance—Whether second notice a waiver of the first.]—*See* LANDLORD AND TENANT, col. 815. *Green* v. *Summers*, 29 A.L.T., 245; 14 A.L.R., 218.

Juryman, alleged misconduct of—Evidence on oath to prove misconduct—Denial of juryman not on oath accepted by Judge—Denial in nature of plea of not guilty—No objection raised—Waiver.]—*See* JURY, cols. 768, 769. *David Syme & Co.* v. *Swinburne*, 10 C.L.R., 43; 16 A.L.R., 93.

WARD.

See INFANT, cols. 690, 691.

WATER.

Flow of water—Owners of adjoining lands —Former unity of title and possession— Upper and lower—Country and town—Artificial alteration of natural surface—Obligation to receive—Transfer of Land Act 1890 (No. 1149).]—By *Griffith*, *C.J.* and *O'Connor*, *J.* (contra by *Isaacs*, *J.* and *Higgins*, *J.*) :— If the principle that an owner is bound to receive the rain water naturally flowing over the surface of the adjoining higher land is part of the common law, it applies to the case of land the surface of which has been altered by the hand of man or otherwise during unity of title and possession and before severance, as well as to land the

original natural surface of which has been altered. By *Griffith*, *C.J.* and *O'Connor*, *J.* :—That principle, if it is part of the common law, applies only to country lands and not to town lands. By *O'Connor*, *J.* (*semble* by *Griffith*, *C.J.*) :—That principle is not part of the common law and the owner of the lower land may prevent such water from flowing on to his land. By *Higgins*, *J.*—*Quaere*, Whether land held under the *Transfer of Land Act* 1890 is subject to a natural right on the part of the proprietor of adjoining land to the flow of water. By *Higgins*, *J.* :—If there is any right such as is declared in *Vinnicombe* v. *MacGregor*, it must be confined as in the case of a defined stream to water spreading over the natural surface of the land, but under the words " natural " surfaces (or river beds) which have changed beyond living memory should be included. *Vinnicombe* v. *MacGregor*, 29 V.L.R., 32; 28 V.L.R., 144; 24 A.L.T., 200; 24 A.L.T., 15; 9 A.L.R., 60; 8 A.L.R., 141, discussed and (*per Griffith*, *C.J.* and *O'Connor*, *J.*) disapproved. *Nelson* v. *Walker*, (1910) 10 C.L.R., 560; 16 A.L.R., 285. H.C. *Griffith*, *C.J.*, *O'Connor*, *Isaacs* and *Higgins*, *JJ.*

Negligence—Overflow of water from lavatory in upper upper floor—Malicious act of third party—Liability in respect of.]—*See* NEGLIGENCE, col. 939. *Rickards* v. *Lothian*, (1913) A.C., 263; 19 A.L.R., 105.

Processes of nature—Natural user of land —Injury arising from combined effect of.]— Injury arising from the combined effect of the processes of nature and the natural user of property does not give rise to an actionable wrong. *Glenelg*, *Shire of* v *Grills*; *Matheson* v. *Grills*, (1907) V.L.R., 673; 29 A.L.T., 67; 13 A.L.R., 550. F.C. *a'Beckett*, *Hood* and *Cussen*, *JJ.*

Water—Natural user of land—Dividing fence and hedge—Bed of creek filled up by processes of nature—Consequent overflow of water of creek—Water deflected by hedge and fence on to land of another.]—A. and B. were adjoining owners, A.'s land forming the northern boundary of B.'s land. A creek ran in a southerly direction through A.'s and B.'s land. A post and rail fence had been erected along B.'s northern boundary and a hedge grown. The fence and hedge did not in any way obstruct the bed of the creek. Many years after the erection of the fence and the growth of the hedge the creek silted up, and, as a result, in times of flood, the water overflowed its banks at a point in A.'s land and flowed southerly until it came to the hedge and fence on B.'s northern boundary and there in course of time a bank of silt was formed which prevented the water flowing on to B.'s land, and diverted its flow in a westerly direction on to the road of the plaintiff Shire and the land of the plaintiff Matheson. The plaintiffs brought an action for damages and for an injunction for the removal of the hedge and fence. *Held* (*per a' Beckett* and *Cussen, JJ* *Hood, J.* dissenting on the facts) that the erection of the fence and the growth of the hedge in the first place was a natural user of the land and that the subsequent deflection by the hedge and fence of flood water on to the plaintiff's land did not give the plaintiffs a right of action. *Glenelg, Shire of* v. *Grills* ; *Matheson* v. *Grills,* (1907) V.L.R., 673 ; 29 A.L.T., 67 ; 13 A.L.R., 550.

Railway — Water — Railway embankment —Flood water blocked—Diversion of water— Damage to adjoining land—Board of Land and Works—Constructing authority—Exercise of statutory powers—Subsequent vesting in Railways Commissioners—Negligence— Railways Act 1891 (No. 1250), secs. 4, 5.]— *See* NEGLIGENCE, cols. 940, 941. *Bourchier* v. *Victorian Railways Commissioners,* (1910) V.L.R., 385 ; 32 A.L.T., 48 ; 16 A.L.R., 396.

Water Act 1905 (No. 2016), sec. 231— Compensation for land taken for works— Principles in awarding compensation—Municipal valuation of block of land as a whole— Part only of block taken.]—Where land taken as a site for a channel for the conveyance and distribution of water forms portion of a block of land of the same owner which has been valued as a whole by the municipal authority, the value of the land so taken must, for the purpose of ascertaining the compensation payable in respect of such land, be estimated at an amount bearing the same proportion to the value of the whole block as the area of such land bears to that of such block. *In re Godfrey and the Board of Land and Works,* (1910) V.L.R., 83 ; 31 A.L.T., 152 ; 16 A.L.R., 51. *Madden, C.J.* (1910).

Water Act 1905 (No. 2016), sec. 231— Compensation in respect of land taken— Injury to other land of same owner—Compensation in respect of, whether it may be given.]—In assessing compensation in respect of land taken under the *Water Act* 1905 compensation may be awarded for other land of the same owner injuriously affected by the taking of the land required. *In re Godfrey and the Board of Land and Works,* (1910) V.L.R., 83 ; 31 A.L.T., 152 ; 16 A.L.R., 51. *Madden, C.J.* (1910).

Water Act 1905 (No. 2016), sec. 231— Compensation in respect of land taken— Principles in awarding—" Channels for the conveyance and distribution of water."]—In sec. 231 of the *Water Act* 1905 the words " channels for the conveyance and distribution of water " include main irrigation channels as well as distributing channels. *In re Godfrey and the Board of Land and Works,* (1910) V.L.R., 83 ; 31 A.L.T., 152 ; 16 A.L.R., 51. *Madden, C.J.* (1910).

WEIGHTS AND MEASURES.

See also, BAKERS AND MILLERS ACT, col. 69.

Weights and Measures Act 1890 (No. 1158), sec. 54—False weights, etc.—" Possession," meaning of—Prima facie evidence of use.]—The word " possession " in sec. 54 of the *Weights and Measures Act* 1890 (which makes it an offence for any person to have in his possession certain weights) means " possession for the purpose of use.' The possession of weights and scales in the ordinary way in a shop on the counter is *prima facie* evidence of use. *Montgomery* v. *Ah Luey,* 2 A.L.R., 207, distinguished. *English* v. *Potter,* (1908) V.L.R., 632 ; 30 A.L.T., 91 ; 14 A.L.R., 559. *Hood, J.*

WIDOWS AND YOUNG CHILDREN MAINTENANCE ACT.

Widows and Young Children Maintenance Act 1906 (No. 2074), sec. 3—Disposition of property by will—Widow and children left without sufficient means for maintenance—Provision for maintenance by order of Court—Discretion, how exercised.]—In the exercise of its jurisdiction under *Widows and Young Children Maintenance Act* the Court will disturb testamentary dispositions only where it is necessary to do so. The mere fact that the testator might have disposed of his property more beneficially will not justify the exercise by the Court of its discretion. *In re Read*, (1910) V.L.R., 68 ; 31 A.L.T., 154 ; 16 A.L.R., 60. *a' Beckett, J.*

Widows and Young Children Maintenance Act 1906 (No. 2074)—Purpose of Act—Capricious and unreasonable testamentary dispositions.]—The *Widows and Young Children Maintenance Act* 1906 does not warrant an interference with a man's will where there is no capricious unreasonable testamentary disposition. *In re McGoun*, (1910) V.L.R., 153 ; 31 A.L.T., 193 ; 16 A.L.R., 141. *a' Beckett, J.*

Widows and Young Children Maintenance Act 1906 (No. 2074), secs. 3, 9—Widow's maintenance—Application for further provision—Widow's interest under testator's will—Limit on amount of provision.]—Where a testator has by his will given to his widow more than the income or interest on such portion of his estate as she would have been entitled to had he died intestate, the Court has no power under the *Widows and Young Children Maintenance Act* 1906 to order any further provision to be made for her out of the estate. *In re Maslin*, (1908) V.L.R., 641 ; 30 A.L.T., 70 ; 14 A.L.R., 499. *Hodges, J.*

Widows and Young Children Maintenance Act 1906 (No. 2074), secs. 3, 9—Insufficient provision by testator for the maintenance of widow—Application by widow for further allowance—Limit of amount of provision Court may allow.]—Upon an application by the widow of a testator under sec. 3 of the *Widows and Young Children Maintenance Act* 1906 that provision should be made out of the estate of the testator in or towards her maintenance, the Court, by sec. 9 (2) of the Act is prohibited from giving the widow more than the income or interest of what would have been her share upon intestacy. The Court has no power under the Act to order the payment to the widow of a lump sum in lieu of such income or interest. *In re Mailes*, (1908) V.L.R., 269 ; 29 A.L.T., 263 ; 14 A.L.R., 181, explained. *In re Bennett*, (1909) V.L.R., 205 ; 30 A.L.T., 181 ; 15 A.L.R., 141. *a' Beckett, J.*

Widows and Young Children Maintenance Act 1906 (No. 2074), sec. 3—Disposition of property by will—Provision for widow and children—" Sufficient means for their maintenance and support," what are.]—A bare subsistence allowance is not " sufficient means " for the maintenance and support of a widow or children within the meaning of sec. 3 of the *Widows and Young Children Maintenance Act* 1906. In determining whether applicants under that section have been left without sufficient means for maintenance and support the Court will take into consideration the position of the applicants during the testator's lifetime and the extent of the testator's estate. *In re Read*, (1910) V.L.R., 68 ; 31 A.L.T., 154 ; 16 A.L.R., 60. *a' Beckett, J.*

Widows and Young Children Maintenance Act 1906 (No. 2074), secs. 3, 8, 9 — Maintenance—Application by widow—Husband and wife separated—Misconduct of wife—Widow left destitute.]—For many years prior to his death a testator had lived apart from his wife. The separation was caused by his belief, for which he had good grounds, that she had committed adultery. During the separation he had contributed nothing to her support, and on two occasions Justices had refused to grant her application for an order for maintenance. The testator died leaving a large estate, and made no provision by his will for his widow, who was destitute. *Held*, that no order should be made in her favour under sec. 3 of the *Widows and Young Children Maintenance Act* 1906.

In re McGoun, (1910) V.L.R., 153; 31 A.L.T., 193; 16 A.L.R., 141. *a' Beckett, J.*

Widows and Young Children Maintenance Act 1906 (No. 2074), secs. 3, 7, 8 (2)—Maintenance—Application by widow—Order making provision for widow assignable—Small estate.]—On an application by the widow of a testator for an allowance out of his estate under the *Widows and Young Children Maintenance Act* 1906 an order was made that one-third of the estate, which was a small one, should be set aside and invested, and the income thereof paid to the widow or her assigns for her life. The order expressly made the interest of the widow assignable so that she and the beneficiaries under the will might, if so disposed, come to an arrangement by which she would receive a lump sum in settlement of the provision for her. *In re Mailes*, (1908) V.L.R., 269; 29 A.L.T., 263; 14 A.L.R., 181. *a' Beckett, J.*

WILL.

I.—TESTAMENTARY CAPACITY; UNDUE INFLUENCE.

Will—Testamentary capacity—Delusions.]—Delusions are only material to the question of testamentary capacity if they are connected with the dispositions made by the will. *Tipper* v. *Moore*, (1911) 13 C.L.R.,

248; 18 A.L.R., 341. H.C., *Griffith, C.J., Barton* and *O'Connor, JJ.*

Will—Revocation—Mental capacity.]—The revocation of a will requires the same degree of mental capacity as the making of a will. *In re Richards*, (1911) V.L.R., 284; 33 A.L.T., 38. *a'Beckett, J.*

"Undue influence," what is.]—"Undue influence" is the improper use of the ascendancy acquired by one person over another for the benefit of the ascendant person himself or someone else, so that the acts of the person influenced are not, in the fullest sense of the word, his free voluntary acts. *Union Bank of Australia Ltd.* v. *Whitelaw*, (1906) V.L.R., 711; 28 A.L.T., 17; 12 A.L.R., 393. *Hodges, J.*

II.—TESTAMENTARY DOCUMENTS.

Draft will—Clauses omitted from engrossed will in error—Omission unknown to testator—Probate of both documents.]—A testator duly executed a draft will appointing certain persons as executors, but being in some doubt as to whether he should change his executors, he left that question open for further consideration. He afterwards instructed his solicitor to change the executors. An engrossment was then made which the solicitor told the testator was to the same effect as the draft will already executed, with the exception of the alterations in the executorship which the testator had directed. Acting upon that statement the testator duly executed the engrossment without reading it. After the testator's death it was discovered that certain important clauses contained in the draft will had been omitted from the engrossed will. *Held*, that, as the omitted clauses were omitted without the testator's knowledge or consent and purely in error, and as the true intention of the testator was expressed by reading the draft will and the engrossed will together, both documents should be admitted to probate. *In re Porter*, 28 A.L.T., 92; 12 A.L.R., 496. *Chomley, J.* (1906).

Probate—Of what documents—Will dealing with whole of testator's property—Codicil dealing with English property only and appoint- ing separate executor therefor—Whether documents independent or interdependent.]—Testator made a will in Melbourne disposing of the whole of his property, and appointing A. as executor thereof. Subsequently he executed in England a testamentary paper commencing with the words "This is a codicil to the will made in Melbourne." By this testamentary paper the testator, after reciting certain provisions of the will including the bequest of a legacy to his son B., appointed B. to be the sole executor of his "said will" so far as it related to his property in the United Kingdom, and devised and bequeathed to B. all his property in the United Kingdom upon trust, after payment thereout of debts due to persons in the United Kingdom, and the expenses incurred by B. in the administration of testator's estate in the United Kingdom or wherever situated, to appropriate to himself the said legacy "in my said will" specified. *Held*, that the two documents were not independent but interdependent, and that probate of both should be granted, the Melbourne will by itself not being entitled to probate. *In re Butler*, 32 A.L.T., 8; 16 A.L.R., 283. *Hodges, J.* (1910).

Wills Act 1890 (No. 1159), secs. 3, 18—Testamentary disposition, what amounts to—Letter declaring intention to revoke legacies executed in same manner as a will.]—By instructions to his solicitor for a will executed in conformity with the requirements for the execution of a valid will, testator directed certain legacies to be given to G. and Y. respectively. But by letter of the same date similarly executed and addressed to the same solicitor the testator expressed his desire that G. and Y. should receive the sums which he had directed to be given to them as legacies, and requested the solicitor to pay to them out of certain moneys due to him, such sums, and "if they should receive the amounts prior to my death such legacies as I have directed must be revoked by a codicil to my will if same is executed by me." No formal will was drawn up, and the sums mentioned were paid to G. and Y. in the testator's life time. *Held*, that the letter came within sec. 18 of the *Wills Act* 1890, and operated as a conditional revocation of the legacies, and that, the condition having been fulfilled, the letter must be annexed to the grant of administration. The Court directed that the grant should not be operative until G. and Y. had been served with notice of the Court's intention to annex the letter to the grant. *In re Johnston, deceased,* (1912) V.L.R., 55; 33 A.L.T., 151; 18 A.L.R., 7. *Cussen, J.*

III.—EXECUTION OF WILL.

Will—Signature of testator and witnesses in margin—Validity—Wills Act 1890 (No. 1159), secs. 7, 8.]—The various dispositions and the attestation clause of what purported to be the last will of M. took up almost the whole of one side of a sheet of paper with the exception of a margin so that very little room was left at the bottom for the signatures of M. and the witnesses. Accordingly, the signature of M. was written lengthwise in the margin opposite and at right angles only to the earlier dispositions. The signatures of the witnesses were written lengthwise in the margin at right angles to the attestation clause, and the last provision. *Held,* that the document should be admitted to probate. *In re Mathew,* (1906) V.L.R., 531; 28 A.L.T., 7; 12 A.L.R., 417. *a'Beckett, A.-C.J.*

Wills Act 1890 (No. 1159), secs. 7, 8—Will—Execution—Foot or end of will—Will written on first, third and second pages—Testator's signature on second page.]—A will was written on a sheet of paper which was doubled so as to make four pages. The will commenced on the first page, and was continued on the third page at the foot of which was a blank space. On the second page were the concluding six words of the will, the signature of the testator, the attestation clause, and the signature of witnesses. There were no new beneficial interests created by the words on the second page which simply created part of the machinery for carrying into effect the trusts contained in the will. *Held,* that the will was signed at the foot or end thereof within the meaning of the *Wills Act* 1890. *In the Goods of Wotton,* L.R. 3 P. & D., 159, followed. *In re Hall,* (1910)

V.L.R., 14; 31 A.L.T., 132; 16 A.L.R., 15. *a'Beckett, J.*

Will—Execution—Wills Act 1890 (No. 1159), sec. 7—Witnesses " shall attest and shall subscribe the will," meaning of.]—Sec. 7 of the *Wills Act* 1890 requires that the two witnesses in whose presence the testator has signed or acknowledged a document as his will shall thereafter subscribe the will. A signed a document as his will in the presence of B., who signed the document as attesting witness. A crossed out his signature and again signed the document in the presence of B. and C. C. signed his name as attesting witness to the second signature of A., but B. did not again sign. *Held,* that the requirement of sec. 7 had not been complied with. *In re Burr,* (1912) V.L.R., 246; 33 A.L.T., 237; 18 A.L.R., 212.

IV.—PROBATE AND ADMINISTRATION

(a) *Persons Entitled to Grant.*

Administration, grant of—Discretion of Court—Effect of English practice.]—*See* EXECUTORS AND ADMINISTRATORS, col. 530. *In re Hoarey,* (1906) V.L.R., 437; 28 A.L.T., 93; 12 A.L.R., 450.

Administration, right to—Next-of-kin of deceased woman—Executor of deceased's widower—Discretion of Court.]—*See* EXECUTORS AND ADMINISTRATORS, col. 530. *In re Hoarey,* (1906) V.L.R., 437; 28 A.L.T., 93; 12 A.L.R., 450.

Administration cum testamento annexo—Right of corporation aggregate, a beneficiary, to administer—Grant to syndic of corporation aggregate.]—*See* EXECUTORS AND ADMINISTRATORS, col. 530. *In re Basse,* (1909) V.L.R., 313; 31 A.L.T., 17; 15 A.L.R., 302.

Probate, to whom granted—Several testamentary documents—Revocation by subsequent document of appointment of executor in previous document.]—*See* EXECUTORS AND ADMINISTRATORS, col. 530. *In re Porter,* 28 A.L.T., 92; 12 A.L.R., 496.

Administration, grant of—Discretion of Court, matters affecting exercise of—Application by party who has parted with his interest

—Party with major interest.]—*See* Executors and Administrators, cols. 530, 531.
In re Hoarey, (1906) V.L.R., 437; 28 A.L.T.,
93; 12 A.L.R., 450.

Administration and probate—Practice—Administration—Grant of joint administration
when made.]—*See* Executors and Administrators, col.531. *In re McMurchy*, (1909)
V.L.R., 359; 31 A.L.T., 2; 15 A.L.R., 328.

Will—Executor predeceasing testator—No
beneficiary within jurisdiction entitled to
apply for administration c.t.a.—Beneficiaries
outside jurisdiction not notified of their
rights—Power of Court to take goods of
deceased into its own hands.]—*See* Executors
and Administrators, col. 531. *In re Basse*
(1909) V.L.R., 313; 31 A.L.T., 17; 15
A.L.R., 302.

(b) *Delegation of Right to Grant.*

Administration and Probate Act 1907 (No.
2120), sec. 7—Authority of trustee company
to apply for probate—Revocation—Form of
authority—Form of application.]—*See* Executors and Administrators, col. 532. *In
re Synot*, (1912) V.L.R., 99; 33 A.L.T., 182;
18 A.L.R., 82.

Practice—Grant of administration—Trustee
company authorized by next-of-kin to obtain
administration—Complicated transactions between next-of-kin and intestate—Discretion of
Court to refuse application of trustee company.]—*See* Executors and Administrators, col. 532. *In re Forbes*, (1909) V.L.R.,
485; 31 A.L.T., 95; 15 A.L.R., 627.

Executors—Renunciation—Appointment of
trustee company—Power of sole remaining
executor—" The Union Trustees Executors
and Administrators' Act " (No. 839), sec. 3.]
—*See* Executors and Administrators, cols.
532, 533. *In re Gilbert*, 27 A.L.T., 241; 12
A.L.R., 528.

" Equity Trustees Executors and Agency
Company Limited Act " (No. 978), sec. 9—
Appointment of Company under, effect of.]—
See Executors and Administrators, col.
533. *In re Hoarey*, (1906) V.L.R., 437; 28
A.L.T., 93; 12 A.L.R., 450.

Intestacy—Next-of-kin entitled to administration—Resident abroad—Authority to trustee company to obtain administration—Form
of grant to company—" The Perpetual Executors and Trustees Association Act " (No.
840), sec. 4.]—*See* Executors and Administrators, col. 533. *In re Morris*, (1909)
V.L.R., 425; 31 A.L.T., 61; 15 A.L.R., 446.

" National Trustees Executors and Agency
Company of Australasia Ltd. Act " (No. 938),
s. 10—Appointment with consent of Court of
Company to perform administrator's duties—
Title of administrator not perfected—Letters
of administration not issued.]—*See* Execu-
tors and Administrators, cols. 533, 534.
In re Moriarty, (1907) V.L.R., 315; 29
A.L.T., 65; 13 A.L.R., 307. *a'Beckett, J.*
(1907).

Administration, application for grant of—
Advertisement of intention to apply—Person
named in advertisement not entitled to grant
—Authority of person not named in adver-
tisement, effect of.]—*See* Executors and
Administrators, col. 534. *In re Hoarey*,
(1906) V.L.R., 437; 28 A.L.T., 93; 12
A.L.R., 450.

Administration, application for grant of—
Power of attorney, interpretation of—Whether
attorney under power authorised to support
application—General words, effect of on
special powers.]—*See* Executors and Administrators, col. 534. *In re Hoarey*,
(1906) V.L.R., 437; 28 A.L.T., 93; 12
A.L.R., 450.

(c) *Certain Limited Grants.*

Administration ad litem—Application under
peculiar circumstances—Proposed action under
Wrongs Act for benefit of widow and children
of deceased—Time for bringing action about
to expire—Poverty of widow the applicant
for administration—Wrongs Act 1890 (No.
1160), secs. 14, 15, 16.]—*See* Executors and
Administrators, cols. 534, 535. *Greenway
v. McKay*, (1911) 12 C.L.R., 310; 17 A.L.R.,
350.

Probate—Grant limited as to performance
of particular duties—Executors appointed by
will—Executors of will and another person

42

appointed executors of codicil—Limitation of grant to carry out purpose of codicil.]—*See* EXECUTORS AND ADMINISTRATORS, col. 535. *In re Graham*, (1910) V.L.R., 16; 31 A.L.T., 130; 16 A.L.R., 15.

Administration—Will disposing of real property out of the jurisdiction—Real and personal estate within the jurisdiction undisposed of—Grant of letters of administration—Form.]—*See* EXECUTORS AND ADMINISTRATORS, cols. 535, 536. *In re Trethewie*, (1913) V.L.R., 26; 34 A.L.T., 136; 18 A.L.R., 560.

(*d*) *Delay in Making Application, Effect of.*

Probate—Stale will—Making title.]—*See* EXECUTORS AND ADMINISTRATORS, col. 536. *In re Smith*, (1907) V.L.R., 717; 29 A.L.T., 89; 13 A.L.R., 615.

Administration—Death of intestate in 1864 —Intestate entitled to estate in land in remainder after life estate and to no other property—Death of life tenant in 1905. Application for administration after death of life tenant.]—*See* EXECUTORS AND ADMINISTRATORS, col. 536. *In re Ghillmetei*, (1907) V.L.R., 657; 29 A.L.T., 81; 13 A.L.R., 519.

Practice—Administration with will annexed—Delay—Death of testator in 1870—Executrix dying without proving in 1907—Application after death of executrix.]—*See* EXECUTORS AND ADMINISTRATORS, col. 536. *In re Smith*, (1907) V.L.R., 717; 29 A.L.T., 89; 13 A.L.R., 615.

Practice—Administration de bonis non—Death of executor—Executorial duties all performed—Real property—Legal estate outstanding—Trusts declared in respect of real property—Unadministered estate, what is.]—*See* EXECUTORS AND ADMINISTRATORS, cols. 536, 537. *In re Graham*, (1910) V.L.R., 466; 32 A.L.T., 68; 16 A.L.R., 512.

Administration de bonis non c.t.a. when granted — Unadministered estate — Executor registered as proprietor of land under Transfer of Land Act 1890 (No. 1149).]—*See* EXECUTORS AND ADMINISTRATORS, col. 537. *In re Martin*, (1912) V.L.R., 206; 34 A.L.T., 1; 18 A.L.R., 216.

Administration de bonis non c.t.a. when granted—Unadministered estate—Real estate —Executorial duties—Executor not registered as proprietor under Transfer of Land Act 1890—Administration and Probate Act 1890 (No. 1060), sec. 8.]—*See* EXECUTORS AND ADMINISTRATORS, cols. 537, 538. *In re Allan*, (1912) V.L.R., 286; 34 A.L.T., 2; 18 A.L.R., 217.

(*e*) *Bonds and Sureties.*

Administration bond—Duration of sureties liability—Title of beneficiaries to the residue —Completion of administration.]—*See* EXECUTORS AND ADMINISTRATORS. *Bayne v. Blake*, (1908) A.C., 371; 14 A.L.R., 317. Privy Council.

Administration bond—Sureties—Deed of indemnity by beneficiaries, validity of.]—*See* EXECUTORS AND ADMINISTRATORS, cols. 538, 539. *Bayne v. Blake*, 4 C.L.R., 1; 12 A.L.R., 454.

Administration and Probate Act 1890 (No. 1060), secs. 15, 16—Administration bond—Jurisdiction to dispense with, whether Court has.]—*See* EXECUTORS AND ADMINISTRATORS. *In re Allen*, (1908) V.L.R., 20; 29 A.L.T., 164; 14 A.L.R., 28.

Sureties to administration bond—Evidence in support of application to dispense with—Consent of beneficiary—Necessity for proving beneficiary fully aware of his rights and of the risk he runs—Administration and Probate Act 1890 (No. 1060), sec. 16.]—*See* EXECUTORS AND ADMINISTRATORS, col. 539. 34 A.L.T., 86; 18 A.L.R. (C.N.), 20.

Administrator—Transfer of assets to sureties to administration bond to be administered by them—Breach of trust—Recovery of control of assets by administrator.]—*See* EXECUTORS AND ADMINISTRATORS, col. 539. *Ackerly v. Palmer*, (1910) V.L.R., 339; 32 A.L.T., 23; 16 A.L.R., 326.

(*f*) *Proof in Solemn Form, Whether Necessary.*

Probate—Practice—Valid will executed by testator—Later document purporting to be a will—Application for probate of valid will—Affidavits showing invalidity of later document—Consent of beneficiaries under later document—No intention to apply for probate of later document—Proof in solemn form, whether necessary.]—*See* EXECUTORS AND ADMINISTRATORS, col. 540. *In re Munro*, (1911) V.L.R., 20; 32 A.L.T., 107; 16 A.L.R., 603.

Application for probate of document purporting to be a will—Caveat—Order nisi—Testamentary incapacity — Proof by propounders—Evidence on affidavit—Summary hearing.]—*See* EXECUTORS AND ADMINISTRATORS, col. 540. *In re Sabelberg*, (1911) V.L.R., 157; 32 A.L.T., 182; 17 A.L.R., 142.

Will and codicils—Subsequent document purporting to be last will believed by executor to have been executed when testatrix not of sound mind—Same executor in will and codicils and in subsequent document—Application for probate of will and codicils notwithstanding the existence of subsequent document —Order nisi calling on beneficiaries under subsequent document to show cause why probate of will and codicils should not be granted —Form of order nisi.]—*See* EXECUTORS AND ADMINISTRATORS, cols. 540, 541. *In re Suter*, 12 A.L.R. (C.N.), 1. *Holroyd, J.* (1906).

(g) *Caveat, Who May Lodge.*

Administration and Probate Act 1890 (No. 1060), sec. 18—Will—Caveat, who may lodge — Infant — Next friend — Appointment of guardian as—Form of caveat where both next friend and infant interested in estate.]— *See* EXECUTORS AND ADMINISTRATORS, col. 541. *In re Siméon*, (1910) V.L.R., 335; 32 A.L.T., 25; 16 A.L.R., 362.

(h) *Evidence; Discovery of Documents.*

Probate—Order nisi—Affidavit of attesting witness made on application for probate— Whether it can be used on hearing of an order nisi.]—*See* EXECUTORS AND ADMINISTRATORS, col. 541. *Gair* v. *Bowers*; *Falconar* v. *Bowers*; *Gair* v. *Falconar*, (1909) 9 C.L.R., 510; 15 A.L.R., 494.

Will—Execution—Evidence—Will not produced—Presumption of due execution.]—*See*

EXECUTORS AND ADMINISTRATORS, cols. 541, 542. *Gair* v. *Bowers*; *Falconar* v. *Bowers*; *Gair* v. *Falconar*, (1909) 9 C.L.R., 510; 15 A.L.R., 494.

Will—Execution—Evidence—Statements by testator after execution.]—*See* EXECUTORS AND ADMINISTRATORS, col. 542. *Gair* v. *Bowers*; *Falconar* v. *Bowers*; *Gair* v. *Falconar*, (1909) 9 C.L.R., 510; 15 A.L.R., 494

Will—Revocation by subsequent will—Subsequent will not produced.]—The revocation of a will which has been duly executed will not be established by the execution of a subsequent will which is not produced, unless the latter will is clearly proved to have contained an express revocation of the earlier will or dispositions inconsistent with those in the earlier will. *Cutts* v. *Gilbert*, 9 Moo. P.C.C., 131, followed. *Gair* v. *Bowers*; *Falconar* v. *Bowers*; *Gair* v. *Falconar*, (1909) 9 C.L.R., 510; 15 A.L.R., 494. H.C. *Griffith, C.J., O'Connor, Isaacs* and *Higgins, JJ.*

Discovery of documents—Probate—Caveat —Testamentary incapacity and undue influence alleged—Discovery by caveator, how limited—Rules of Supreme Court 1906 (Probate), Rule 32.]—*See* EXECUTORS AND ADMINISTRATORS, col. 543. *Re Baker*, (1907) V.L.R., 234; 28 A.L.T., 189; 13 A.L.R., 121

Practice — Probate — Discovery — Testamentary scripts—English practice, whether applicable.]—*See* EXECUTORS AND ADMINISTRATORS, cols. 542, 543. *In re Cotter*, (1907) V.L.R., 78; 28 A.L.T., 106; 12 A.L.R., 550.

(i) *Parties.*

Administration cum testimento annexo— Application by beneficiary—Right of Curator of Intestate Estates to appear on such application.]—*See* EXECUTORS AND ADMINISTRATORS, col. 543. *In re Basse*, (1909) V.L.R., 313; 31 A.L.T., 17; 15 A.L.R., 302.

(j) *Citations; Notices; Advertisements.*

Administration cum testimento annexo— Application by beneficiary—Notice to beneficiary with prior right.]—*See* EXECUTORS

AND ADMINISTRATORS, col. 543. *In re Basse*, (1909) V.L.R., 313; 31 A.L.T., 17; 15 A.L.R., 302.

Administration ad litem—Notice of intention to apply, necessity for—Application under peculiar circumstances—Administration and Probate Act 1890 (No. 1060), secs. 14, — Probate and Administration Rules 1906, rr. 4, 15.]—*See* EXECUTORS AND ADMINISTRATORS cols. 543, 544. *Greenway* v. *Mc Kay*, (1911) 12 C.L.R., 310; 17 A.L.R., 350.

Administration and Probate Act 1911 (No. 2342), secs. 3, 4—Executors—Claim against testator's estate—Notice of—Contemplated proceedings for revocation of probate—Notice to claimant—Application by executor for order to bar or disregard claim.]—*See* EXECUTORS AND ADMINISTRATORS, col. 544. *In re Timm*, (1912) V.L.R., 460; 34 A.L.T., 97; 18 A.L.R., 496.

Probate and Administration Rules 1906, r. 4—Practice—Advertisement of intention to apply for probate—Number of codicils must be mentioned in advertisement.]—*See* EXECUTORS AND ADMINISTRATORS, col. 544. *In re Blake*, (1912) V.L.R., 59; 33 A.L.T., 155; 18 A.L.R., 7.

(k) Discharge or Removal of Executor or Administrator.

Administration and Probate Act 1907 (No. 2120), sec. 5—Executors—Discharge of one co-executor—Appointment of administrator in his place—Discharge by Judge.]—*See* EXECUTORS AND ADMINISTRATORS, cols. 544, 545. *In re Coverdale*, (1909) V.L.R., 248; 30 A.L.T., 199; 15 A.L.R., 233.

Administration and Probate Act 1907 (No. 2120), sec. 5—Administration—Executor of executor—Right to renounce as to original testator's estate.]—*See* EXECUTORS AND ADMINISTRATORS, col. 545. *In re Keys*, (1909) V.L.R., 325; 31 A.L.T., 1; 15 A.L.R., 304. *Madden, C.J.*

Administration and Probate Act 1907 (No. 2120), sec. 5 (1) (2)—Executor, removal of—Summons, parties to—Application to Judge to indicate parties to be served.]—*See* EXECUTORS

AND ADMINISTRATORS, col. 545. *In re Mitchell*, (1910) V.L.R., 44; 31 A.L.T., 113; 15 A.L.R., 643.

Administration and Probate Act 1907 (No. 2120), sec. 5—Executors—Discharge of one co-executor—Vesting order.]—*See* EXECUTORS AND ADMINISTRATORS, col. 545. *In re Coverdale*, (1909) V.L.R., 248; 30 A.L.T., 199; 15 A.L.R., 233.

(l) Revocation of Grant.

Administration ad litem — Revocation — Whether defendant in proposed action may apply for.]—*See* EXECUTORS AND ADMINISTRATORS, cols. 545, 546. *Greenway* v. *Mc Kay* (1911) 12 C.L.R., 310; 17 A.L.R., 350.

Revocation of grant of administration—Practice—Consent of administrator.]—*See* EXECUTORS AND ADMINISTRATORS, col. 546. *In re Sutherland*, (1910) V.L.R., 118; 31 A.L.T., 150; 16 A.L.R., 63. *Cussen, J.*

(m) Appeal.

Appeal to High Court—Appealable amount —Order nisi for probate—Interest of caveator less than £300—Judiciary Act 1903 (No. 6 of 1903), sec. 35.]—*See* APPEAL, col. 24. *Tipper* v. *Moore*, (1911) 13 C.L.R., 248; 18 A.L.R., 341.

(n) Costs.

Costs — Probate — Will — Caveat — Withdrawal before motion—Costs against caveator.] —*See* EXECUTORS AND ADMINISTRATORS, col. 546. *In re Johnson*, (1909) V.L.R., 324; 31 A.L.T., 2; 15 A.L.R., 304.

Will — Probate — Caveat — Costs — Administration and Probate Act 1890 (No. 1060), sec. 21.]—*See* EXECUTORS AND ADMINISTRATORS, col. 546. *In re Millar*, (1908) V.L.R., 682; 30 A.L.T., 106; 14 A.L.R., 564.

Order nisi for revocation of probate—Probate revoked on ground of want of testamentary capacity—Reasonable belief by executor in validity of will—Executor allowed his costs as between solicitor and client out of estate, including costs of propounding the will originally.]— *In re Keane*, (1909) V.L.R., 231; 30 A.L.T., 216; 15 A.L.R., 198.

Will—Party supporting invalid revocation —Costs.]—*See* EXECUTORS AND ADMINIS-TRATORS, col. 547. *In re Richards*, (1911) V.L.R., 284 ; 33 A.L.T., 38.

Taxation—Attendance on Registrar of Probates—What should be allowed for.]—*See* EXECUTORS AND ADMINISTRATORS, col. 547. *In re Duke's Will*, (1907) V.L.R., 632 : 29 A.L.T. 50; 13 A.L.R. 477.

Order LXV., r. 28 (Rules of 1906)—Whether applicable to probate matters—Appeal from taxing officer's decision on " Instructions for Brief "—Discretion of Judge.]—*See* EXECUTORS AND ADMINISTRATORS, col. 547. *Re Duke's Will*, (1907) V.L.R., 632 ; 29 A.L.T., 50 ; 13 A.L.R., 477.

Costs — Taxation — Appendix N.—Drawing pleadings and other documents—Accounts, statements, etc. for Judge's Chambers—Statement for duty.]—*See* EXECUTORS AND ADMINISTRATORS, col. 547. *In re Duke's Will*, (1907) V.L.R., 632 ; 29 A.L.T., 50 ; 13 A.L.R., 477.

V.—CONSTRUCTION AND INTERPRETATION.

(a) *Generally.*

Will—Rule against perpetuities—Meaning of will doubtful—Construction to effectuate intention of testator.]—Where the meaning of words in a will is doubtful, the Court is entitled, even on a question of remoteness, to give some weight to the consideration that it is better to effectuate rather than to destroy the intention of the testator. *In re Hobson* ; *Hobson* v. *Sharp*, (1907) V.L.R., 724 ; 29 A.L.T., 125 ; 13 A.L.R , 703. *Cussen, J.*

Will—Interpretation — Subject matter of gift, how determined—Matters which testator may presumably have known, right of Court to consider.]—For the purpose of ascertaining what is the subject matter of a gift the Court is entitled to place itself in the position of the testator and to consider what he may reasonably be presumed to have known. *Higgins* v. *Dawson*, (1902) A.C., 1, applied. *In re Longley* ; *Reid* v. *Silk*, (1906) V.L.R., 641 ; 28 A.L.T., 82 ; 12 A.L.R., 499. *Cussen, J.*

Will—Interpretation—Extrinsic evidence, admissibility of—Facts known to testator at time of making will.]—For the purpose of ascertaining the object of a testator's bounty the Court has a right to ascertain all the facts known to the testator at the time he made his will ; and such evidence is always admissible to explain what the testator has written whether an ambiguity is raised by the will or not. *Charter* v. *Charter*, L.R. 7 H.L., 364, applied ; *Re Ely* ; *Tottenham* v. *Ely*, 65 L.T., 452 and *In re Whorwood* ; *Ogle* v. *Lord Sherborne*, 34 Ch. D., 446, distinguished. *In re Loughlin* ; *Acheson* v. *O'Meara*, (1906) V.L.R., 597 ; 28 A.L.T., 28 ; 12 A.L.R., 411. *Hood, J.*

Evidence — Will — Ambiguity — Parol evidence, admissibility of—Language ordinarily used by testatrix in referring to certain of her property—Intention of testatrix expressed in conversation.]—The only land which testatrix had was a block of 145 acres in the Parish of Waaia divided into three paddocks containing 45, 38½ and 61½ acres respectively. By her will testatrix devised " unto W. 40 acres of land situated in the Parish of Waaia being part of . . 140 land . . . and to my grandchildren the remaining one hundred acres." The question before the Court being what was meant by the devise to W. of " 40 acres." *Held*, that evidence that testatrix used to speak of the 38½ acre paddock as " the forty acre block " or " the forty acre paddock " was admissible, but that evidence that testatrix when she asked W. to draw up her will told him she wished him to have the 38½ acre paddock, and that the testatrix intended the words used in the will to describe that paddock, was inadmissible. *In re Leaf* ; *Donaldson* v. *Leaf*, (1907) V.L.R., 278 ; 29 A.L.T., 54 ; 13 A.L.R., 148. *a'Beckett, J.*

Will—Construction—Gift to class—Mis-statement of number of persons constituting a class—Falsa demonstratio—Gift to " the child " of a niece—How gift construed.]— *See post,* B. (2) CLASS GIFTS. *In re McNicol* ; *Herron* v. *McNicol*, (1909) V.L.R., 311 ; 30 A.L.T., 220 ; 15 A.L.R., 308.

Will—Construction—Division of residue into forty-three parts—Gift of forty-two parts—Allotment of parts to specified beneficiaries—One part unallotted—Mistake—Intestacy as to unallotted part.]—*See post*, (*c*) BEQUESTS AND DEVISES. (1) WHAT PROPERTY WILL PASS BY PARTICULAR WORDS AND DESCRIPTIONS. *Trustees Executors and Agency Co. Ltd.* v. *Sutherland*, (1909) V.L.R., 223; 30 A.L.T., 182; 15 A.L.R., 179.

Gift of " the following twelve properties "—Eleven properties only enumerated—Accidental omission, whether Court may supply—Ambiguity.]—*See post*, (*c*) BEQUESTS AND DEVISES. (1) WHAT PROPERTY WILL PASS BY PARTICULAR WORDS AND DESCRIPTIONS. *In re Green*; *Crowson* v. *Wild*, (1907) V.L.R., 284; 28 A.L.T., 206; 13 A.L.R., 121.

Will—Construction—When codicil may be used to interpret will.]—A will and codicil being all one testament, the language of the codicil may be used to interpret that of the will if the latter is capable of two constructions. *Jenkins* v. *Stewart*, 3 C.L.R., 799; 12 A.L.R., 370. H.C. *Griffith, C.J., Barton* and *O'Connor, JJ.* (1906).

Will—Limitation in will—Whether legal or equitable—Administration and Probate Act 1890 (No. 1060), secs. 6, 8, 9.]—*See post*, (*c*) BEQUESTS AND DEVISES. (7) PERPETUITIES; RESTRAINT ON ACCUMULATION. *In re Malin*; *National Trustees &c. Co.* v. *Loughnan*, (1912) V.L.R., 259; 34 A.L.T., 30; 18 A.L.R., 274.

Will and codicil—Construction—Revocation by codicil.]—If there is a gift by will the person who asserts that there is a revocation of that gift by codicil must show a plain revocation. Further, the revocation extends only so far as the will is inconsistent with the codicil. *In re Stroud*; *Bell* v. *Stroud*, (1908) V.L.R., 33; 29 A.L.T., 104; 13 A.L.R., 645. *Cussen, J.*

Clause empowering trustees to act on advice of counsel—Liability of trustees so acting.]—A will contained a clause providing that in all cases in which a question of law or equity should arise in relation to the estate or the construction of the will the trustees might settle and arrange the same in such manner as they might be advised by counsel. Acting upon counsel's advice as to the proper construction of the will which was afterwards held by the Court to be erroneous, the trustees paid the income of a fund to certain contingent legatees instead of to the residuary legatees. *Held*, that all such payments made in the past were good for all purposes and gave no rights against the trustees or the contingent legatees. *In re Thompson*; *Brahe* v. *Mason*, (1910) V.L.R., 251; 31 A.L.T., 210; 16 A.L.R., 215. *a' Beckett, J.* (1910).

(*b*) *Devisees and Legatees.*

(1) Donees in Particular Cases.

Will—Interpretation—Misnomer of legatee—Description of legatee—Legacy to nonexistent person—Object of testator's bounty ascertainment of — Extrinsic evidence.]—A testator in his will directed his trustees to pay a certain sum " to each of my godchildren living at my death " naming four, including one " Archibald Martin O'Meara son of John Joseph O'Meara.'' The only god-child answering both to the above name and to the above description had died nine years prior to the date of the will, but at its date there was living a god-child of the testator named Martin Henry O'Meara who was a brother of the deceased god-child and survived the testator. *Held*, that evidence was admissible to show that the testator was aware of the death of one god-child and of the existence of the other prior to making his will, and that the bequest went to Martin Henry O'Meara who through an error was misnamed by the testator in the will. *In re M. Loughlin*; *Acheson* v. *O'Meara*, (1906) V.L.R., 597; 28 A.L.T., 28; 12 A.L.R., 411. *Hood, J.*

Will—Interpretation—Devise to " right heirs "—Will made since the Act No. 230.]—Where in a will executed after the passing of the *Intestates Real Estate Act* 1864 (No. 230) the testator makes an ultimate devise to his " right heirs," such expression will be construed to mean his " next-of-kin." *In re Goodman's Trust*, 6 V.L.R. (Eq.), 181;

and *Morrice* v. *Morrice*, 14 N.S.W.L.R. (Eq.), 211, followed. *In re Connell*; *National Trustees Executors &c. Co. of Australasia Ltd.* v. *Connell*, (1910) V.L.R., 471; 32 A.L.T., 83; 16 A.L.R., 504. *Madden, C.J.*

Will — Construction — Rule against perpetuities—Gift to father for life—Gift over to "all his children" who shall attain the age of twenty-five years—Context showing intention to benefit only certain children then in being.]—*See post,* (c) BEQUESTS AND DEVISES. (7) PERPETUITIES; RESTRAINT ON ACCUMULATION. *In re Hobson*; *Hobson* v. *Sharp,* (1907) V.L.R., 724; 29 A.L.T., 125; 13 A.L.R., 703.

(2) Class Gifts; Time of Ascertaining Donees.

Will—Interpretation—Gift to named perons and to their children or to the survivors—Death of named persons before testator—Whether an intestacy—Gift to class ascertainable at testator's death.] — Testator directed his trustees to expend all the produce and profits arising from the residue of his property for the benefit and use of his four sisters and his brother, all of whom he named, and also " for the benefit and use of the children of the above-named sisters and brother or the survivors of my said sisters and brother and their children as herein directed and in the proportions herein mentioned." He then directed that each of the above-named sisters and brother or the survivors of them should take in the proportion of four parts, and each of the children of the above-named sisters and brother or the survivors of them in the proportion of one part. Testator's brother survived him but all his sisters predeceased him. Ten children, the sons and daughters of the deceased sisters and of the brother, also survived the testator. *Held,* that the gift was to a class ascertainable at the testator's death, and that his brother was entitled to four-fourteenths and each of the ten children was entitled to one-fourteenth of the residue of testator's estate. *In re Stead*; *McArthur* v. *Stead,* (1908) V.L.R.,

10; 29 A.L.T., 155; 13 A.L.R., 683. *Cussen, J.*

Will—Construction—Gift of legacy to each member of a class who shall attain twenty-one years of age—When class to be ascertained.] —A testatrix devised and bequeathed her residuary estate to trustees upon trust for sale and conversion and out of the proceeds to pay a legacy of one thousand pounds to each child of A. who should attain the age of twenty-one years and subject to such and other payments directed that her residuary estate should be divided into certain shares and held in trust for certain persons. *Held,* that a child of A. born after the death of the testatrix would not become entitled to a legacy in any event. *Rogers* v. *Mutch,* 10 Ch. D., 25, followed. *In re Thompson*; *Brahe* v. *Mason,* (1910) V.L.R., 251; 31 A.L.T. 210; 16 A.L.R., 215. *a'Beckett, J.* (1910).

Will—Construction—Gift to class—Gift to testator's brother and his sister's children—Division per capita.]—A will contained a residuary gift " in equal shares unto my brother G. J. and the children of my sister S. O." *Held,* that the brother and the sister's children took equally *per capita*. *Kingsbury* v. *Walter,* (1901) A.C., 187, distinguished. *In re Jones*; *Harris* v. *Jones,* (1910) V.L.R., 306; 32 A.L.T., 3; 16 A.L.R., 266. *Cussen, J.*

Gift to a class after determination of life estate—Plan of distribution.]—Where after the determination of the life estate there was a gift over to a class the plan of distribution settled in *In re Knapp's Settlement*; *Knapp* v. *Vassall,* (1895) 1 Ch., 91, was adopted. *In re Hobson*; *Hobson* v. *Sharp,* (1907) V.L.R.. 724; 29 A.L.T., 125; 13 A.L.R., 703. *Cussen, J.*

Vesting—If A. shall die without issue then to B., C. and D. as tenants in common—Death of B. in lifetime of A.]—Testator devised certain real property to his trustees on trust for his daughter M. for life with remainder to her children and declared that in the event of M. dying without leaving lawful issue the said property should go and belong to her three brothers, E., P. and D. as tenants in common in equal shares. E., P., D. and M. all survived the testator, but P. predeceased M. who died without issue. *Held,* that the representatives of P. were entitled to share in the said property. *In re Gleeson; Gleeson* v. *Gleeson,* (1910) V.L.R., 181; 31 A.L.T., 194; 16 A.L.R., 143 *a' Beckett, J.*

Will—Construction—Devise to two persons their heirs and assigns as tenants in common —" If either shall die without leaving lawful issue," his share to go to survivor—Whether gift over limited to death without lawful issue before testator.]—A testator devised certain lands unto and to the use of his two sons E. and P. their heirs and assigns as tenants in common in equal shares and declared that if either of his said sons should die without leaving lawful issue, the share to which he would be entitled under the will should go and belong to the survivor of his said two sons E. and P. Both of them having survived the testator, and P. having died without leaving issue. *Held,* that, as there was nothing either in the provisions of the will above referred to or in the context showing that the testator intended to limit the condition upon which the gift over was to take effect to the case of the death of either of the sons during the testator's lifetime, E. was entitled to the whole of the said lands. *In re Hayward,* 19 Ch. D., 470, distinguished. *In re Gleeson; Gleeson* v. *Gleeson,* (1910) V.L.R., 181; 31 A.L.T., 194; 16 A.L.R., 143. *a' Beckett, J.*

Will—Construction—Gift of income equally among several—Life estate—Right of survivorship.]—*See post,* (b) BEQUESTS AND DEVISES. (3) WHAT ESTATE OR INTEREST PASSES. *Macartney* v. *Macartney,* 30 A.L.T., 77; 14 A.L.R., 492.

Will — Construction — Accumulations — Income of residuary estate, direction to accumulate beyond period allowed—Gift to grandchildren upon youngest attaining twenty-one—After-born grandchildren—Intestacy—Wills Act 1890 (No. 1159), sec. 35.]—*See post,* (c) BEQUESTS AND DEVISES. (7) PERPETUITIES; RESTRAINT ON ACCUMULATION.

In re Stevens; Trustees, &c. Co. Ltd. v. *Teague,* (1912) V.L.R., 194; 33 A.L.T., 233; 18 A.L.R., 195.

Will—Construction—Gift to a class—Misstatement of number of persons constituting a class—Falsa demonstratio—Gift to " the child " of a niece—How gift construed.]—Where a will read as a whole shows the dominant idea of the testator to be to benefit a class, the misstatement of the number of persons constituting the class is mere *falsa demonstratio* and will be rejected, and the actual members of the class will take even in the case where only one person is referred to by the will. A testator by his will gave the residue of his estate to the child of his niece, who had in fact two children. *Held,* on the true construction of the will, that the two children were each entitled to a half-share in the residue. *In re McNicol; Herron* v. *McNicol,* (1909) V.L.R., 311; 30 A.L.T., 220; 15 A.L.R., 308. *Madden, C.J.*

(3) Precatory, Charitable and Other Trusts.

Will—Precatory trust—" Believing that she will do justice to my relatives."]—Testator devised and bequeathed all his real and personal estate to his executors and trustees, and directed " that the whole of my estate be given to T. . . . believing that she will do justice to my relatives." *Held,* there was no trust and T. took the whole estate absolutely. *In re Warren; Verga* v. *Taylor,* (1907) V.L.R., 325; 28 A.L.T., 201; 13 A.L.R., 118. *a' Beckett, J.*

Will — Construction — Precatory trust — "Hoping that he will secure."]—The will of the testatrix contained a gift in the following words :—" Next I give to John Lord brother of my husband the sum of £1,500 hoping he will secure it to the children of his daughter Alice Leach Lord." This was followed by a series of pecuniary legacies amounting to £1,600 to the children of brothers and sisters of the testatrix, and there was no gift of any fund to any trustee. The estate was of the value of about £3,000. *Held,* that the children of Alice Leach Lord took no interest under the will, for there was no precatory trust of the £1,500 legacy. *In re*

Lord ; Hall v. Grimshaw, (1910) V.L.R., 477 ; 32 A.L.T., 90 ; 16 A.L.R., 509. Hood, J.

Will — Construction — Charitable trust — Trust to pay passage money for immigrants— Relief of poverty—Validity of trust.]—A testatrix in her will directed the expenditure of certain income of her estate " in paying the passage money to Victoria of immigrants of good character " from her native town in England, such immigrants to be selected by a certain person. Held, that a valid charitable trust had been created, as it clearly appeared that the bequest was intended for the relief of poverty. Re Sidney ; Hingeston v. Sidney, (1908) 1 Ch., 126, 488, distinguished. In re Wallace ; Trustees Executors and Agency Co. Ltd. v. Fatt, (1908) V.L.R., 636 ; 30 A.L.T., 100 ; 14 A.L.R., 502. Hood, J.

Will—Construction—Gift of residue—Trust for " charitable purposes "—Trust for " religious purposes "—Whether valid—Uncertainty.]—By her will testatrix bequeathed to her trustee the residue of her estate and directed him to hold it " upon trust to dispose of one moiety of the same for such charitable uses or purposes as he shall in his absolute and uncontrolled discretion think fit, and to dispose of the other moiety of the same for such religious uses or purposes as he shall in his absolute and uncontrolled discretion think fit." Held, that the bequest of the moiety for charitable uses or purposes was a good charitable bequest, but that the bequest of the other moiety for religious uses and purposes was void for uncertainty. In re Dobinson ; Maddock v. Attorney-General, (1911) V.L.R., 300 ; 33 A.L.T., 20 ; 17 A.L.R., 280.

Will — Construction — Gift to testator's widow—" To be used by her as she may think proper for the benefit of herself and our children "—Whether trust created.]—A testator devised and bequeathed all his real and personal estate to his widow " to be used by her as she may think proper for the benefit of herself and our children." Held, that no trust was created, but that the widow took an absolute interest. McAlinden v. McAlin-

den, 11 Ir. R. Eq., 219 and Lambe v. Eames, L.R. 6 Ch., 597, followed. Raikes v. Ward, 1 Hare, 445, commented on. In re Lawn ; Ballarat Trustees &c. Co. v. Perry, (1911) V.L.R., 318 ; 33 A.L.T., 25 ; 17 A.L.R., 311.

Will—Interpretation—" Any balance to be left as my executor may direct "—Power of appointment — Trust — Uncertainty.]—By her will testatrix, after appointing G. as her executor and directing the payment of debts and funeral expenses and giving certain legacies, provided that any balance was " to be left as my executors may direct " and appointed P. also as executor. Held, that the provision as to the balance created, not a general power of appointment in the executors, but a trust which was void for uncertainty and that the balance accordingly passed to the next of kin. Fenton v. Nevin, 31 L.R. Ir., 478, followed. In re Lewis ; Gollan v. Pyle, 29 A.L.T., 36 ; 13 A.L.R., 431. Hood, J. (1907).

(c) Bequests and Devises.

(1) What Property Will Pass by Particular Words and Descriptions.

Will—Construction—Devise of " 40 acres " —Uncertainty as to which 40 acres intended.]—By her will testatrix made the following devises, " unto W. 40 acres of land situated in the parish of Waaia being part of . . 140 land . I also give and bequeath unto my grandchildren . . . the remaining one hundred acres." The only land which testatrix had was a block of land in the parish of Waaia, consisting of two Crown allotments under separate grants—one being a paddock containing 45 acres, and the other being divided into two paddocks containing about 38½ and 61½ acres respectively. Evidence was admitted to show that she used to speak of the 38½ acre paddock as the " 40 acre block " or " the 40 acre paddock." Held, that there was nothing in the will or in the facts to indicate which part of the land was meant by the expression " 40 acres of land "; that W. was not given the right to select any forty acres ; and that both the devise to W. and the devise to the grandchildren were void for uncertainty.

Asten v. *Asten*, (1894) 3 Ch., 260, followed.
In re Leaf; *Donaldson* v. *Leaf*, (1907)
V.L.R., 278 ; 29 A.L.T., 54 ; 13 A.L.R., 148.
a' Beckett, J.

**Gift of " the following twelve properties "
—Eleven properties only enumerated—Accidental omission, whether Court may supply
—Ambiguity.**]—Testator by his will devised
to his daughter " the following twelve properties," and then enumerated not twelve
properties but eleven. Evidence was given
that in the draft will prepared under the
testator's instructions a twelfth property
had been included in the list of properties
given to the testator's daughter, but that it
had been accidentally omitted therefrom in
the will as executed. The twelfth property
was nowhere mentioned in the will. *Held*,
that no words in the will required interpretation, and the wrong enumeration of twelve
could not be corrected by adding to the
properties specified another property. *Harter*
v. *Harter*, L.R. 3 P. & D., 11, applied. *In
re Green*; *Crowson* v. *Wild*, (1907) V.L.R.,
284 ; 28 A.L.T., 206 ; 13 A.L.R., 121.
a' Beckett, J. (1907).

**Will — Construction — Division of residue
into forty-three parts—Gift of forty-two parts
—Allotment of parts to specified beneficiaries
—One part unallotted—Mistake—Intestacy as
to unallotted part.**]—A testator directed that
the residue of his estate should be divided
into forty-three equal parts and distributed
among sixteen charitable institutions who
were named with the number of parts to be
given to each. The total number of parts
so allotted was forty-two. *Held*, that there
was an intestacy as to the part undisposed of
Trustees Executors and Agency Co. Ltd. v.
Sutherland, (1909) V.L.R., 223 ; 30 A.L.T.,
182 ; 15 A.L.R., 179. *Hood, J.*

**Will — Construction — " Homestead,"
meaning of.**]—A gift of a " homestead,"
Held, on the evidence, not to refer to a
grazing paddock, which was the only real
estate of the testatrix, and which was about
a mile from the house in which the testatrix
lived. *In re Anderson*; *Longstaff* v. *Anderson*, (1908) V.L.R., 593 ; 30 A.L.T., 30 ; 14
A.L.R., 412. *Madden, C.J.*

**Will — Construction — " Any moneys
remaining."**]—By her will testatrix gave,
after the payment of all her just debts
funeral and testamentary expenses, a number
of pecuniary legacies and directed a certain
sum to be expended in the erection of a
tombstone and then gave to F. the homestead and " any moneys remaining." *Held*,
that under the bequest of " any moneys
remaining " F. took the residuary personal
estate. *In re Anderson*; *Longstaff* v.
Anderson, (1908) V.L.R., 593 ; 30 A.L.T.,
30 ; 14 A.L.R., 412. *Madden, C.J.*

**Gift of " free use of all my property "—
What property passes—Things consumed by
use.**]—By his will testator gave to his nephew
" the free use of all my property " except a
certain township allotment of land. *Held*,
that " all my property " included stock and
implements, if unsold, on a farm belonging
to the testator, and, if sold, the proceeds
thereof, but not the things which are consumed by use. *In re Nilen*; *Kidd* v. *Nilen*,
(1908) V.L.R., 332 ; 29 A.L.T., 225 ; 14
A.L.R., 176. *Cussen, J.*

**Will—Construction—Bequest of " moneys
and securities for moneys "—Money on fixed
deposit in bank—Money in Savings Bank.**]—
A bequest of " all moneys and securities for
moneys " will not include moneys on fixed
deposit in a bank, but will include moneys
in a Savings Bank. *Young* v. *Ormiston*, 11
V.L.R., 285, followed ; *In re Williamson*;
Price v. *Williamson*, 26 A.L.T., 91 ; 10
A.L.R., 197, distinguished. *In re Reed*;
Reed v. *Reed*, (1911) V.L.R., 232 ; 32 A.L.T.,
168 ; 17 A.L.R., 164. *a' Beckett, J.*

**Will — Construction — " Seised," whether
used in its technical sense.**]—The context
may show that the word " seised " in a will
is not to be restricted to its strict legal
meaning. *In re Gleeson*; *Gleeson* v. *Gleeson*,
(1910) V.L.R., 181 ; 31 A.L.T., 194 ; 16
A.L.R., 143. *a' Beckett, J.*

**Will—Interpretation—Life estate—Gift over
in event of life tenant leaving no children—
Intestacy—Power of sale.**]—A testator by his
will gave the whole of his real and personal
estate to trustees upon trust to sell his sheep

and all other his personal estate and effects and to invest the moneys to arise therefrom upon real securities. He directed the trustees to finish the erection of a shop on certain land in Melbourne. He directed that the trustees " do and shall stand possessed of the said trust moneys securities rents and all other the premises in trust for my daughter E.B.   until she shall attain the age of twenty-one years or marry under that age with the consent of her guardian." He directed the trustees during E.B.'s minority " to pay and apply all or any part of the interest and annual produce of the expectant portion of my said daughter " towards her maintenance and education. The will then went on—" Provided always and I hereby declare that if my said daughter shall marry and have any child or children and shall die leaving such child or children her surviving that they my said trustees or trustee for the time being do and shall stand possessed of my said real and personal estate and effects " upon trust to divide the proceeds among such of her children as being sons should attain the age of twenty-one years or being daughters marry under that age, " and in case there shall be no child or issue of my said daughter who under the trusts hereinbefore contained shall become entitled to the said trust moneys and securities then and in such case my said trustees or trustee shall stand possessed thereof " in trust for the testator's brothers and sister. E.B. died never having had any children. *Held*, that in the events which had happened the testator's brothers and sister or their legal personal representatives were entitled to the testator's real estate, and that there was a power of sale of the real estate given to the trustees which had arisen. *Altson* v. *Equity Trustees &c. Co. Ltd.*, (1912) 14 C.L.R., 341 ; 18 A.L.R., 316. H.C. *Griffith, C.J., Barton* and *Isaacs, JJ.*

Tenant for life and remainderman—Dividends declared by company, whether capital or income.]—The rule laid down in *Bouche* v. *Sproule*, 12 App. Cas., 385, at pp. 397, 401, to the effect that, where a company has power to determine whether profits reserved and temporarily devoted to capital purposes shall be distributed as dividends or permanently added to capital the conflicting interests of a life tenant and remainderman depend on the decision of the company, is not of universal application, the question being mainly one of fact in each case. *In re Longley* ; *Reid* v. *Silke*, (1906) V.L.R., 641 ; 28 A.L.T., 82 ; 12 A.L.R., 499. *Cussen, J.*

Tenant for life and remainderman—Income, what is—Shares in insurance company—Dividends paid out of fund accumulated as provision for life assurance liabilities—Dividends paid out of contingency fund to provide against depreciation of securities.]—An insurance company had a " life assurance fund " built up of accumulated profits, to provide for life assurance liabilities. The company had also a " contingency fund " formed by transfer from the " profit and loss account " to " provide for shrinkage in the value of securities." In the lifetime of the testatrix neither of these funds had been dealt with as available for distribution. By her will and codicil the testatrix created a trust of the " proceeds " of 728 shares in the company, upon its being wound up, in favour of certain beneficiaries, giving the " annual income from the company " to one of them. After the death of the testatrix the company paid annual dividends on the shares, partly out of profits, but mainly out of moneys transferred to the " profit and loss account " from the " life assurance fund," to which in some cases moneys had previously been transferred from the " contingency fund." *Held*, that that portion of the dividends, which represented moneys taken from the " life assurance fund," was not, but that the remainder was income within the meaning of the will and codicil. *In re Longley* ; *Reid* v. *Silke*, (1906) V.L.R., 641 ; 28 A.L.T., 82 ; 12 A.L.R., 499. *Cussen, J.*

Will—Construction—Shares in company owned by testator—Bequest to life tenant of dividends and to remaindermen absolutely—Bonus declared by company on shares—New shares issued and offered to shareholders—Bonus applicable in payment therefor—Whether bonus capital or income.]—*See*

TENANT FOR LIFE AND REMAINDERMAN. *In re Smith*; *Edwards* v. *Smith*, 29 A.L.T., 173; 14 A.L.R., 22.

(2) Interest on Legacies; Income of Fund.

Gift of residuary personal property—Whether it carries intermediate income—Intention of testator.]—The rule that a gift of residuary personal property, even if on a future contingency, carries with it the intermediate income subject to the statutory provisions against accumulations, like all other rules of construction, yields to sufficient evidence of a contrary intention. *In re Watson*; *Cain* v. *Watson*, (1910) V.L.R., 256; 31 A.L.T., 212; 16 A.L.R., 76. *Cussen, J.*

Will and codicil—Interest directed to be paid on legacies to legatees under will—No general direction—Further legacies under codicil without direction as to interest.]—Testator by his will gave a number of pecuniary legacies and directed that " the respective legatees . . . shall until payment to them respectively of the said legacies respectivly given or bequeathed to them be entitled to receive as from my death . . · interest thereon　　　　at the rate of 5 per cent. per annum." By a codicil he gave a number of legacies to legatees not mentioned in the will, but gave no direction as to payment of interest. *Held*, that the direction as to payment of interest, inasmuch as it was not a general direction but referred to particular persons only, did not apply to the legacies under the codicil. *In re Stroud*; *Bell* v. *Stroud*, (1908) V.L.R., 33; 29 A.L.T., 104; 13 A.L.R., 645. *Cussen, J.*

Will—Construction—Contingent legacies—Interim interest, whether infant contingent legatees entitled to—Trusts Act 1896 (No. 1421), sec. 18.]—By a will the whole of the residuary estate after payment of debts, probate duty, and pecuniary legacies, was given to trustees upon trust to pay a number of legacies including a legacy of one thousand pounds to each child of A. who should attain the age of twenty-one years, with the residue to named persons. *Held*, that there was no direction to set apart a fund for the payment of the legacies to the children of A. so as to operate in effect as a gift of the income to the legatees; that therefore the legacies to the children of A. did not carry interest, and that the income of a sum set apart to provide for such legacies was not applicable for the maintenance of such children, but belonged to the residuary legatees. *In re Inman*, (1893) 3 Ch., 518, followed. *In re Thompson*; *Brahe* v. *Mason*, (1910) V.L.R., 251; 31 A.L.T., 210; 16 A.L.R., 215. *a'Beckett, J.*

Will and codicil—Interest on legacies—From what time payable—Rate of interest.]—Certain legatees under a will were given interest on their legacies at the rate of 5 per cent. per annum from the death of the testator. The greater part of the estate in the hands of the trustees was returning 5 per cent. per annum. *Held*, that the general legacies under a codicil carried interest at the rate of 5 per cent. per annum from a year after testator's death. *In re Stroud*; *Bell* v. *Stroud*, (1908) V.L.R., 33; 29 A.L.T., 104; 13 A.L.R., 645. *Cussen, J.*.

Legacy—Interest—Date from which payable—Death of testator presumed—Lapse of considerable time between presumed date of death and grant of probate—Infants—Maintenance clause—Executor's year.]—Testator was a passenger by the s.s. " Waratah " which left Durban on or about 27th July 1909 and was never afterwards heard of. Probate to testator's will was granted in September 1910, the Court presuming that he died on 27th July 1909. *Held*, that interest on legacies to infants, for whose maintenance during infancy provision was made in the will, should run from the presumed date of testator's death, and on other legacies from one year after that date. *In re Black*; *Black* v. *Melbourne Hospital*, (1911) V.L.R., 280; 33 A.L.T., 2; 17 A.L.R., 240. F.C. *Madden, C.J.*, *Hodges* and *Hood, JJ.*

Interest on legacies—Rate of—Order LV., r. 64 (Rules of 1906).]—Upon an originating summons enquiring as to the rate of interest to be paid on certain legacies, *Held*, that the rate should be such as the executors might expect to get upon investments of the estate, and that, accordingly, interest on the legacies should be at the rate of 4 per cent. per annum. *National Trustees Executors &c. Co.* v. *McCracken*, 19 A.L.T., 175; 4 A.L.R., 31, discussed. *In re Black; Black* v. *Melbourne Hospital*, (1911) V.L.R., 280; 33 A.L.T., 2; 17 A.L.R., 240. F.C. *Madden, C.J., Hodges* and *Hood, JJ.*

Will—Tenant for life and remainderman—Capital and income—Payment of annuities—Apportionment—Rate of interest.]—*See* TENANT FOR LIFE AND REMAINDERMAN. *Cock* v. *Aitken*, (1911) 13 C.L.R., 461; 18 A.L.R., 337.

Will—Construction—Maintenance of infants out of income—Whether to be treated as a common fund or separate shares—Income directed to form part of the capital of the share when it arose.]—A testator by his will directed the sale and conversion and investment of seven-ninths of the estate which he styled his trust property, and then further directed his trustees " to pay out of the net annual income actually produced by my trust property, howsoever constituted or invested, such sum or sums as my trustees shall in their absolute discretion think fit for the maintenance clothing education and personal support of my son L.M. until he attains the age of twenty-one years and of my daughters J.M. and A.M. until they respectively attain the age of twenty-one years or marry under that age with the consent of my said trustees and my said wife and I direct my said trustees to invest and accumulate any unapplied income in the way of compound interest upon any of the securities hereby authorized with power from time to time to resort to such accumulations for all or any of the purposes aforesaid which shall form part the capital of the share whence the same income shall have arisen." The seven-ninths were afterwards divided, three-ninths to the son and two-ninths to each daughter. *Held*, that the sums advanced for each child should be treated as taken from the share of such child and not as withdrawals from a common fund. *In re Munro; National Trustees Executors &c. Co. of Australasia Ltd.* v. *Dunbar*, (1910) V.L.R., 395; 32 A.L.T., 41; 16 A.L.R., 363. *a'Beckett, J.*

(3) What Estate or Interest Passes.

Absolute gift—Invalid attempt to cut down—Whether the gift remains absolute except in so far as validly cut down.]—For an application of the principle that, where there is an absolute gift to a legatee in the first place, and trusts are engrafted or imposed on that absolute interest which fail, either from lapse or invalidity or for any other reason, then the absolute gift takes effect so far as the trusts have failed to the exclusion of the residuary legatee, or next-of-kin, as the case may be, *See In re Watson; Cain* v. *Watson*, (1910) V.L.R., 256; 31 A.L.T., 212; 16 A.L.R., 76. *Cussen, J.*

Several trusts declared in respect of fund—Impossibility of first trust taking effect—Whether existence of subsequent trusts affected.]—Where a trust fund is in existence and several trusts affecting it are fully declared the later trusts may take effect although the first trust cannot possibly arise. *In re Munro; National Trustees Executors &c. Co. of Australasia Ltd.* v. *Dunbar*, (1910) V.L.R., 395; 32 A.L.T., 41; 16 A.L.R., 363. *a'Beckett, J.*

Will—Construction—Absolute gift—Subsequent limitation to life estate with void gift over—Appointment in excess of power—Whether appointment wholly void.]—*See post*, (6) POWERS OF APPOINTMENT. *England* v. *Bayles*, (1906) V.L.R., 94; 27 A.L.T., 181; 12 A.L.R., 122.

Will—Construction—Gift to two persons for life—Gift to their issue after their death or the death of either of them—Rule in Shelley's Case—Tenancy in common—Real Property Act 1890 (No. 1136), sec. 108.]—Lands were devised to trustees upon trust to sell at a favourable time, and invest the proceeds in the purchase of real estate, and to pay the income arising from such investment to A. and B. during their lives " and after their decease or the decease of either of them unto their issue." *Held*, that A. and B. took an equitable estate in fee as tenants in common in the lands devised. *In re Coleman; Equity Trustees &c. Co. Ltd.* v. *Coleman*, 29 A.L.T., 277; 14 A.L.R., 182. *Madden, C.J.* (1908).

Gift over in event of beneficiary dying without leaving wife or children—Whether contingency limited to death in testator's lifetime—Codicil used to explain will.]—By a will property was given to A. with a gift over in the event of his dying without leaving a wife or children, and the question was whether the contingency was limited to the death of A. before that of the testator, or whether it referred to the death of A. at any time. A codicil to the will contained language which showed that the testator thought he had given an estate to A. which would be absolute if A. survived him. *Held*, that A., having survived the testator, took an absolute estate. *Jenkins* v. *Stewart*, 3 C.L.R., 799 ; 12 A.L.R., 370. H.C. *Griffith, C.J., Barton* and *O'Connor, JJ.* (1906).

Gift of interest for life determinable in certain events during life—Gift over on happening of such events—No gift over in event of death —Implied gift over in that event.]—Testator by his will directed that A., in consideration of the payment by him of testator's debts, should have the free use of a farm of the testator for such time as A. should retain possession of his property adjoining such farm, but that in the event of his disposing of his property adjoining the farm or refusing to pay testator's debts the farm should be sold and the proceeds divided amongst certain beneficiaries. The will did not say what was to happen if A. died without having disposed of his property or refused to pay testator's debts. *Held*, that the gift to A. was confined to an uncertain period included in his life and that the gift over took effect on his death as well as in the events specified in the will. *In re Tredwell*, (1891) 2 Ch., 640, distinguished. *In re Nilen* ; *Kidd* v. *Nilen*, (1908) V.L.R., 332 ; 29 A.L.T., 284 ; 14 A.L.R., 277. F.C. *a'Beckett, Hodges* and *Hood, JJ.*

Will—Construction—Devise to widow with gift over in event of re-marriage—Wills Act 1890 (No. 1159), sec. 26.]—By his will testator devised and bequeathed " all my real and personal estate unto my dear wife . . . but in the event of her marrying she forfeits all claims to the said estate which then be-

comes the property of my children." *Held*, that the widow took an estate in fee simple determinable on her re-marriage, and that the children had merely a remainder on the happening of that event. *In re Hoare* ; *Quinlan* v. *Hoare*, (1908) V.L.R., 369 ; 29 A.L.T., 251 ; 14 A.L.R., 276. *Hood, J.* (1908)

Will—Interpretation—No devise in express terms—Devise by implication—Whether intention of testator on the whole will sufficiently declared to justify implication—Devise of property for life with remainder to children of life tenant—Gift of other properties to life tenant " upon the same condition " as properties hereinbefore mentioned are to be given—Whether children take in remainder.] —Testator gave all his real and personal property to his executors, and directed them to give his daughter all the proceeds arising from all rents after deduction of all rates and insurance premiums and costs of all necessary repairs of the properties A, B, and C, during her lifetime . . . and after her decease to give the properties A, B and C, in equal shares to her surviving children. Testator also directed his executors to give to X. during his lifetime property D with remainder over after X.'s death to testator's daughter " upon the same condition as properties A, B, and C are to be given," and to give life interests in other properties to other beneficiaries with like remainders over to testator's daughter. *Held*, that the words " upon the same condition " were fully satisfied by importing into the gift to testator's daughter of property D the deductions for rates, &c. which were directed as to properties A, B, and C ; and that the surviving children of testator's daughter did not take property D upon the death of their mother, there being no express devise over to them and the intention of the testator not being sufficiently declared by the will to justify a devise by implication. *Towns* v. *Wentworth*, 11 Moo. P.C., 526, applied ; *Sweeting* v. *Prideaux*, 2 Ch. D., 413, distinguished. *In re Green* ; *Crowson* v. *Wild*, (1907) V.L.R., 284 ; 28 A.L.T., 206 ; 13 A.L.R., 121. *a'Beckett, J.* (1907).

Gift by implication—Gift to parent—Postponement of gift over until child attains twenty-one—Whether child entitled contingently on attaining twenty-one.]—By his will testator directed his trustees on his son attaining twenty-one as to three-ninths part of his estate to stand possessed of the income thereof and to pay the same to his son until he attained the age of thirty, and upon his son attaining thirty he directed his trustees to stand possessed of the capital, income and accumulations as to two-ninths in trust for his son absolutely " but in case he shall die before attaining that age without issue who shall live to attain twenty-one " then in trust for testator's daughters in equal shares. The son died before attaining thirty and left an infant daughter. *Held*, that there was no gift by implication to the infant daughter of the son on her attaining twenty-one. *In re Rawlins' Trusts*, 45 Ch., 299; (1892) A.C., 342, applied. *In re Munro; National Trustees Executors &c. Co. of Australasia Ltd.*, v. *Dunbar*, (1910) V.L.R., 395; 32 A.L.T., 41; 16 A.L.R., 363. *a'Beckett, J.*

Will—Construction—Trust to hold for infants until they shall have attained 21—Interest of infants.]—A testator devised and bequeathed all his real and personal estate to a person to hold the same upon trust for that person's two infant children until they should have attained the age of 21 years respectively. *Held*, that the infants took a beneficial interest in the whole estate. *In re Hedley's Trust*, 25 W.R., 529, distinguished. *In re Vickers; Vickers* v. *Vickers*, (1912) V.L.R., 385; 34 A.L.T., 133; 18 A.L.R., 521. *Hood, J.*

Will—Construction—Gift of income equally among several—Life estate—Right of survivorship.]—By his will a testator gave the residue of his real and personal estate to trustees upon trust to pay the rents, issues and profits thereof to his daughters (of whom he left six him surviving) in equal shares for their separate use with a restraint on anticipation, and he directed that " in case any of my said daughters shall die leaving issue then as to the share or shares which my said daughter or daughters so dying would have

acquired if she had lived upon trust for the issue of such deceased daughter or daughters in equal shares if more than one who being a son or sons should attain the age of 21 years or a daughter or daughters should attain that age or marry previously and so that the issue of such daughter or daughters may take in equal shares the share or respective shares only which the parent or respective parents would if living have taken." He further directed that " from and after the decease of my last surviving daughter and the attainment of his majority by my youngest grandchild being a male at the decease of my last surviving daughter or the attainment of that age or previous marriage if such grandchild be a female," the trustees should sell and convert and stand possessed of the fund so created " together with any accumulations thereof in trust for the issue then living of my daughter or daughters and also the issue of my grandchildren who shall be dead to be divided amongst them so that the issue of my said daughters may receive the share of or to which their mother would be entitled if living in equal shares and the issue of such grandchildren may receive in like manner to be equally divided between them the share of or to which their parent would have become entitled under this my will if he or she were living." *Held, per Hood* and *Cussen, JJ.*, (*a'Beckett, J.*, dissenting) that the six daughters took life estates as tenants in common in the income, and that on the death of a daughter without issue the income was distributable equally among the surviving daughters. *Macartney* v. *Macartney*, (1908) V.L.R., 649; 30 A.L.T., 77; 14 A.L.R., 492. *F.C.*

Vesting—Death before time fixed for acquisition of capital—Gift of income up to that time, effect of—Whether gift of capital vested or contingent.]—By his will testator directed his trustees to sell convert and invest seven-ninths of his estate and out of the net annual income to pay such sums as they should think fit for the maintenance education and support of his son until he attained twenty-one and of his two daughters until they attained that age or married and to invest and accumulate unapplied income in the way of compound interest upon any of the authorised securities with power to resort to such accumulations " for all or any of the purposes aforesaid which shall form part of the capital of the share whence the same income shall have arisen." Four-ninths were afterwards given to the daughters and as to the other three ninths the testator directed his trustees on his son attaining twenty-one " to stand possessed of the income thereof and to pay the same to my son until he attains the age of thirty and upon my son attaining thirty I direct my trustees to stand possessed of the capital, rents income and accumulations as to two-ninths in trust for my son absolutely but in case he shall die before attaining that age without issue who shall live to attain twenty-one then in trust for my daughters in equal shares." The son survived the testator, but died before attaining thirty leaving an infant daughter. *Held*, that the two-ninths vested in the son and the gift was not contingent on his attaining thirty. *In re Gossling*, (1902) 1 Ch., 945 ; (1903) 1 Ch., 448, applied. *In re Munro* ; *National Trustees Executors &c. Co. of Australasia Ltd. v. Dunbar*, (1910) V.L.R., 395 ; 32 A.L.T., 41 ; 16 A.L.R., 363. *a' Beckett, J.*

Will—Construction—Trust to permit widow to use and occupy house for a home—Whether widow entitled to life estate—Occupation of house by person other than widow—Payment to widow in consideration of such occupation.] —A testator by his will directed his trustees to stand possessed of his residence known as " Goodrest " and the furniture and fittings therein upon trust " to permit my said wife to use and occupy the same for a home for my said wife during her life," and upon her death to convey and transfer it to the Melbourne Hospital. In several gifts in the will life estates were created in the ordinary way. *Held*, that the widow did not have a life estate in ' Goodrest '' and had no other right than to use and occupy it as a home. *Quaere*, whether the trustees would be doing wrong in permitting " Goodrest " to be occupied by a person willing to pay something to the widow in consideration of her not insisting on her right to use and occupy. *In re Buck-*

hurst ; *Equity Trustees Executors and Agency Co. v. Buckhurst*, (1907) V.L.R., 252 ; 28 A.L.T., 190 ; 13 A.L.R., 74. *Cussen, J.*

Will—Interpretation—Corpus and income —Annuity, gift of—Residue.]—By his will a testator gave his property to trustees upon trust (*inter alia*) as to £800 a year during the life of his daughter A.S., upon trust from time to time to apply the same or such part as they should think fit for the personal maintenance and support or otherwise for the personal benefit of A.S., or to pay the same or such part as they should think fit to her or to any other person to be so applied, or, at the option of the trustees, to pay the whole or such part to his executors to be applied as part of the residue of the estate. The testator gave the residue of his estate equally between his son J. M. V. S. and his daughter L.S. The trustees, during the life of L.S. and after her death, applied only portion of the annuity of £800, for the benefit of A.S. *Held*, that one half of any portion of the annuity which in any year after the death of L.S. was not applied for the benefit of A.S. came to the estate of L.S. as portion of the corpus of the estate of the testator and was part of the corpus of the estate of L.S. *Cock v. Aitken*, (1908) 6 C.L.R., 290 ; 14 A.L.R., 361. H.C., *Barton, Isaacs* and *Higgins, JJ.*

Suit for contribution—Trustees under two different wills—Discretionary power to provide maintenance for the same legatee—Separate and independent obligation—No. right of contribution.]—*See* TRUSTS AND TRUSTEES. *Smith v. Cock*, (1911) A.C., 317 ; 17 A.L.R., 99.

(4) Direction as to Priority of Payment of Legacy.

Will—Construction—Annuity — Whether charged on corpus—Legacies—" In the first place," " in the next place "—Whether priority of enumeration or in order or method of payment or priority of rights or interests.]— A testator by his will gave to his wife all his furniture effects and jewellery, to his brother A. K. the sum of £50, and to his nephew the sum of £10, and then directed his executors to realise all property not producing income and after payment of debts, funeral and testamentary expenses and the previously mentioned legacies, to hold all the residue of his personal estate and all his real estate upon trust " to receive the income and the rents and profits arising therefrom and thereout in the first place to pay to my wife the sum of five pounds per week then in the next place to pay to my brother the said A. K the sum of fifty pounds per annum to commence from one year after my death by yearly half-yearly or quarterly payments (less the expenses of transmission) as my executors may think fit and in the last place to pay the residue (if any) of such income rents and profits to my said wife." Upon the death of his wife the testator directed his executors to sell and convert all his real and personal estate and divide the proceeds equally among several named relatives. *Held* (1) that the annuities were not charged on the corpus ; (2) that on the language of the will the wife's annuity had priority over that of A. K. *Perpetual Executors and Trustees Association of Australia Ltd.* v. *Knowles*, 32 A.L.T., 163 ; 16 A.L.R., 582 *Cussen, J.* (1910).

(5) Conditions ; Particular Divesting Provisions.

Will—Construction—Gift of free use of land so long as donee retained possession of adjoining land—Conditional limitation or condition.]—A testator by his will directed that all his debts should be immediately paid by his nephew, and that in consideration thereof the nephew should have " the free use of all my property " . . . " for such time as he shall retain possession of his property adjoining mine but in the event of " his " disposing of his property which adjoins mine . . . then the whole of my property " . . . " shall be sold and . . shall be disposed of " as directed in the will. The nephew owned land adjoining testator's farm. *Held*, that upon his paying the debts the nephew was entitled, not to an estate in fee simple in the testator's property but only to the free use of it so long as he lived and retained the ownership or possession of the adjoining land. *Held*,

also, that by leasing or ceasing personally to occupy his adjoining land he would not determine his interest. *In re Nilen ; Kidd* v. *Nilen*, (1908) V.L.R., 332 ; 29 A.L.T., 284 ; 14 A.L.R., 277. F.C., *a' Beckett, Hodges* and *Hood, JJ.*

Will—Construction — Gift — Limitation — Condition subsequent—Wife living apart from husband.]—By her will a testatrix gave to her daughter a certain house " so long as she lives at Osborne Flat and not with her husband." At the date of the will and of the death of the testatrix the daughter was living in the house apart from her husband who had deserted her some years previously. *Held*, that there was a gift of a life estate in the house to the daughter subject to conditions subsequent, and that the condition that the daughter should live apart from her husband was void as being illegal or uncertain. *In re Anderson ; Longstaff* v. *Anderson*, (1908) V.L.R., 593 ; 30 A.L.T., 30 ; 14 A.L.R., 412. *Madden, C.J.*

Will — Construction — Conditions — Validity of—Restraint of marriage—Motive of testator.]—A condition in a will in general restraint of marriage is void, unless the motive of the testator in imposing the restraint is an interest personal to the object of his bounty, and not a general objection to marriage. A testator devised real estate to trustees upon trust to allow S. " to receive and take the rents and profits thereof for her absolute use and benefit for the term of her natural life she nevertheless remaining unmarried conducting herself with propriety and respectability and keeping the whole of the said estate in good tenantable order and condition." The will contained no gift over until after the determination of the life estate of S. *Held*, that the condition as to her remaining unmarried was in general restraint of marriage and within the general rule, and therefore void. *Held*, further, that as there was no gift over upon breach of the condition, S. was not divested of her interest upon her marriage. *Carrodus* v. *Carrodus*, (1913) V.L.R., 1 ; 34 A.L.T., 125 ; 18 A.L.R., 529. *a' Beckett, J.*

Will—Construction—Real estate devised to testator's son for life on attaining twenty-five

43

—Subsequent direction as to son acquiring profession before getting possession of estate—Whether condition precedent—Direction to trustees to see that son acquires profession, effect of.]—By his will testator devised real estate to his son to be held in trust for him until he attained the age of twenty-five years, when he was to get possession of the said real estate and to hold the same and to receive the rents and profits thereof for his life. In a later part of the will testator directed that before his son got possession of such real estate he should acquire and learn a profession, and that his trustees should see that his son so learned and acquired a profession. *Held*, that there was a concluded gift to the son and that the acquiring of a profession was not a condition precedent to his taking possession ; that the duty imposed on the trustees was merely to afford the son the means and opportunity of acquiring a profession. *In re Meagher* ; *Trustees Executors and Agency Co. Ltd.* v. *Meagher*, (1910) V.L.R., 407 ; 32 A.L.T., 69 ; 16 A.L.R., 551. *a'Beckett, J.*

Will—Gift to daughter with remainder to her children—Gift over upon default of children —Forfeiture of daughter's share—Daughter childless and past child-bearing—When share distributable.]—The testator, who died in 1883, by his will gave a share of his property to F. B. his daughter, for life, with a clause of forfeiture upon attempted alienation ; with a gift over after her death or the determination of her interest to her children ; and with a gift over in the event of F. B. dying without children, to the testator's other children or their issue. There was no disposition in the will of the income of the share in the event of it being forfeited and F. B. having no children. In 1901 the Court declared that the share of F. B. had become forfeited, and, F. B. having no children, directed the trustee of the will to accumulate the income (but for not more than twenty-one years) for the benefit of the persons ultimately entitled. In 1907 it was proved that F. B. had no children and was past child-bearing. *Held*, that the persons entitled to F. B.'s share could only be ascertained at her death, and that the trustee would not be justified in distributing her share before that time. *Stanford* v. *Stanford*, (1886) 34 Ch. D., 362, and *In re Akeroyd's Settlement* ; *Roberts* v. *Akeroyd*, (1893) 3 Ch., 363, distinguished. *In re Lyons* ; *Grant* v. *Trustees Executors &c. Co. Ltd.*, (1908) V.L.R., 190 ; 29 A.L.T., 202 ; 14 A.L.R., 147. *a'Beckett, J.*

Will—Construction—Legacy, lapse of — Death of beneficiary " before he shall have become entitled," meaning of.]—A testator devised his real estate upon trust for the use of his brother J. B. until his youngest surviving brother or sister should attain twenty-one years, and afterwards to the use of J. B. absolutely, charged, however, with the payment of certain legacies to each of certain named brothers and sisters ; and testator directed that " in the event of any of my said brothers or sisters dying before he or they shall have become entitled under this my will the share or shares of such of my said brothers and sisters so dying as aforesaid shall be divided equally amongst those of my brothers and sisters them surviving with the exception of my said brother " J. B. *Held*, that by the word " entitled " the testator meant entitled in " possession." *Held*, therefore, that where one of the sisters of the testator had died before his youngest brother had attained the age of twenty one, the legacy so left her as above-mentioned was not payable to her executor. *In re Borger* ; *Sandhurst & Northern District Trustees Co. Ltd.* v. *Golden*, (1912) V.L.R., 310 ; 34 A.L.T., 27 ; 18 A.L.R., 279. *Hodges J.*

Will—Construction—Divesting of legacy—Uncertainty—Gift over of legacy in case of death before legatee " shall have actually received " the legacy.]—A gift over of residue in the case of the death of the legatee before actually receiving the legacy is void for uncertainty. *In re Hudson* ; *Trustees Executors, &c., Co.* v. *Eastwood*, (1912) V.L.R., 140 ; 33 A.L.T., 212 ; 18 A.L.R., 149. *a'Beckett, J.*

(6) Powers of Appointment.

Will—Construction—Absolute gift—Subsequent limitation to life estate with void gift over—Appointment in excess of power—

Whether appointment wholly void.]—By a deed of partnership between the members of a firm of solicitors it was provided that in the event of the death or retirement of any of the partners the future profits of the business should be liable to the payment of the sum of £2,500 to his widow, child or children, or some one or other of them as he might by writing direct. The deed also provided that in the event of the death of a partner he should not be entitled to receive anything in respect of the goodwill of the business. By his will a deceased partner provided that his goodwill of the business was to form part of the residue of his estate and that the residue should be held as to one-half and the income thereof for one of his daughters and as to the other half and the income thereof for another daughter in accordance with the trusts thereinafter declared, which were that each share should be invested and the income paid to each daughter respectively for life and that on the death of a daughter her share should be held in trust for such persons as she should by will appoint and in default of appointment for her children. *Held*, that by his gift of the goodwill the testator intended to and did dispose of the £2,500; that the clause cutting down the gift to each daughter to a life estate and the gift over to objects not within the power were both inoperative and that each daughter took a half-share of the residue absolutely. *Trustees Executors and Agency Co. v. Jenner*, 22 V.L.R., 584; 18 A.L.T., 255; 3 A.L.R., 138, followed. *England* v. *Bayles*, (1906) V.L.R., 94; 27 A.L.T., 181; 12 A.L.R., 122. *Madden, C.J.* (1906).

Will—Power of appointment of certain land to testator's children—Appointment to testator's sons—Legacies to daughter out of his own estate—If such estate insufficient to pay legacies payment to extent of deficiency charged on land—Validity of charge.]—Under the will of his deceased father a son had a power to appoint by will certain land belonging to the father's estate, to such uses and for such estates and in such manner for the benefit of all or any one or more of the son's children as he should think fit. The son died leaving a will by which he devised such land in trust for his sons in equal shares in fee simple, and out of the residue of his own property he gave to his daughters legacies of £200 each, and directed, if his own estate should be insufficient to pay those legacies, they should to the extent of the deficiency be a charge upon the above-mentioned land. *Held*, that the charge was valid and within the terms of the power of appointment. *In re Connell*; *National Trustees Executors &c. Co. of Australasia Ltd.* v. *Connell*, (1910) V.L.R., 471; 32 A.L.T., 83; 16 A.L.R., 504. *Madden, C.J.* (1910).

Rule against perpetuities—Power of appointment void for remoteness—Limitations over in default of appointment, whether valid.]—See, *post*, (7) PERPETUITIES; RESTRAINT ON ACCUMULATION. *In re Hobson*; *Hobson* v. *Sharp*, (1907) V.L.R., 724; 29 A.L.T., 125; 13 A.L.R., 703

Power of appointment—Possibility of exercising power in breach of rule against perpetuities—Power to select so as to make valid appointment.]—See, *post*, (7) PERPETUITIES RESTRAINT ON ACCUMULATION *In re Hobson*; *Hobson* v. *Sharp*, (1907) V.L.R., 724; 29 A.L.T., 125; 13 A.L.R., 703.

Will—Interpretation—" Any balance to be left as my executor may direct "—Power of appointment — Trust — Uncertainty.]—See, *ante*, (b) DEVISEES AND LEGATEES; (3) PRECATORY, CHARITABLE AND OTHER TRUSTS. *In re Lewis*; *Gollan* v. *Pyle*, 29 A.L.T., 36; 13 A.L.R, 431.

(7) Perpetuities; Restraint on Accumulation.

Will — Construction — Rule against perpetuities — Legal contingent remainder, applicability of rule to—Rule against double possibilities—Devise to next of kin of unborn person after life estate to such unborn person.]—A devise by way of legal contingent remainder to the next of kin of an unborn person after a life estate given to such unborn person is void. *Per a' Beckett* and *Hood, JJ.*—Because it offends against the rule against perpetuities, which rule is applicable to legal contingent remainders. *In re Frost*, 43 Ch. D., 246 ; *In re Ashforth*, (1905) 1 Ch., 535, followed. *Per Cussen, J.*—Because, although the rule against perpetuities is not as such applicable to legal estates in remainder still that rule defines the furthest limit allowed to restraints on alienation by the common law, and this devise exceeds that limit, and secondly, because this devise (apart altogether from the rule against perpetuities) was void at common law, which would not have permitted a limitation involving such a double personal contingency. *In re Malin* ; *National Trustees &c. Co.* v. *Loughnan*, (1912) V.L.R., 259 ; 34 A.L.T., 30 ; 18 A.L.R., 274. F.C., *a' Beckett*, *Hood* and *Cussen, JJ.*

Will—Limitation in will—Whether legal or equitable—Administration and Probate Act 1890 (No. 1060), secs. 6, 8 and 9.]—*Per a' Beckett, J.*—*Semble*, in a will a limitation of estates in land, although legal in form, is, by reason of the *Administration and Probate Act* 1890, not a limitaton of legal but of equitable interests. *In re Malin* ; *National Trustees &c. Co.* v. *Loughnan*, (1912) V.L.R., 259 ; 34 A.L.T., 30 . 18 A.L.R., 274. F.C., *a' Beckett*, *Hood* and *Cussen, JJ.*

Rule against perpetuities—Power of appointment void for remoteness—Limitations over in default of appointment, whether valid.]—Limitations in default of appointment under a power which is void for remoteness are not invalid, unless they themselves contravene the rule against perpetuities. *In re Hobson* ; *Hobson* v. *Sharp*, (1907) V.L.R., 724 ; 29 A.L.T., 125 ; 13 A.L.R., 703. *Cussen, J.*

Power of appointment—Possibility of exercising power in breach of rule against perpetuities—Power to select so as to make valid appointment.]—The possibility of a power being exercised so as to infringe the rule against perpetuities does not make the power void if there is a power to select, and if those to whom a valid appointment may be made may be selected. *In re Hobson* ; *Hobson* v. *Sharp*, (1907) V.L.R., 724 ; 29 A.L.T., 125 ; 13 A.L.R., 703. *Cussen, J.*

Will—Construction—Rule against perpetuities—Gift to father for life—Gift over to " all his children " who shall attain the age of twenty-five years—Context showing intention to benefit only certain children then in being.]—A testatrix by her will gave property to trustees in trust for her only son for life and after his death in trust for " all his children . . . who being male shall attain the age of 25 years or being female shall attain that age or marry." It appeared that at the time of making her will the testatrix was well acquainted with the members of her son's family ; and there were directions given elsewhere in the will which showed that the expression " all her children " in the gift over should be confined to those of her son's children previously named in the will who were living at her death. *Held*, that the gift over was not void for remoteness. *In re Hobson* ; *Hobson* v. *Sharp*, (1907) V.L.R., 724 ; 29 A.L.T., 125 ; 13 A.L.R., 703. *Cussen, J.*

Will — Construction — Perpetuity — Gift void for remoteness—Direction to hold land until extension of railway definitely settled.]—Testator by his will directed that a certain allotment of land should be held " until such time as the extension of the Alexandra Road railway into the township of Alexandra shall have been definitely settled and it shall then be sold " and the proceeds devoted as he then directed. It was uncertain whether such extension would ever be made. *Held*, that the gift was void for remoteness. *In re Nilen* ; *Kidd* v. *Nilen*, (1908) V.L.R., 332 ; 29 A.L.T., 225 ; 14 A.L.R., 176. *Cussen, J.*

Will — Construction — Perpetuities, rule against—Remoteness—Trust for maintenance and education — Validity.] — A testator directed his trustees " to pay and apply the yearly sum of £250 to or for the maintenance and advancement in life of all the children of my son E. J. S., who being sons shall be under the age of eighteen years or being daughters shall be spinsters." *Held*, that the trustees had no discretion or power of apportioning the annuity among the children, and that, therefore, the whole gift was not void on the ground of remoteness. *Williams*

v. *Papworth*, (1900) A.C., p. 566, followed. *Held,* further, that the fact that the increment accruing on the marriage of any daughter might fall in at uncertain date did not invalidate the gift. *In re Stevens*; *Trustees Executors and Agency Co. Ltd.* v. *Teague,* (1912) V.L.R., 194; 33 A.L.T., 233; 18 A.L.R., 195. *Hood, J.*

Wills Act 1890 (No. 1159), sec. 36—Restriction upon accumulations—Exceptions—Provision for raising portions for children taking interest under will, what is—Accumulation of uncertain portion of income from share of residue—Accumulated fund to be added to such share and aggregate divided amongst children—Parent of children entitled to interest in such share.]—A direction in a will that an uncertain portion of the income from a share of the residuary estate is to be accumulated and added to the share from which such income proceeded, the aggregate fund or the two funds together being divided amongst the children of a specified parent, is not a provision for raising portions, even though the share was originally given to the parent absolutely, and though under the later provisions of the will the parent takes a life interest in portion of the income from such share of the residue. *In re Watson*; *Cain* v. *Watson,* (1910) V.L.R., 256; 31 A.L.T., 212; 16 A.L.R., 76. *Cussen, J.*

Wills Act 1890 (No. 1159), sec. 35—Restriction upon accumulations—Exceptions—Trust for accumulation during minorities of persons who if of full age would be entitled to income—Two periods of accumulation—Accumulation directed during a life with possible further period covering minorities—No person who would be entitled to income if of full age.]—Where by a will an accumulation during the life of each of the testator's daughters of the surplus income of a share in his residuary estate was directed following a direction for partial accumulation during a period of twenty years from testator's death, and the income was disposed of otherwise than as accessory to the gift of the corpus, and the children of each daughter, who were to take the corpus and the accumulation of income, did not constitute a class which could be deemed to be closed when a child attained twenty-one years of age or being a female married, and there was accordingly no ascertained person or persons who could say that he or they had a vested indefeasible right to the surplus income, it was held that there was created a trust for accumulation during the life of each daughter which could not be upheld as a provision for accumulation " during the respective minorities only of any persons who under the uses or trusts of the . . . will . . . would for the time being if of full age be entitled unto the . . . annual produce so directed to be accumulated," and was void after twenty-one years from the testator's death. *In re Watson*; *Cain* v. *Watson,* (1910) V.L.R., 256; 31 A.L.T., 212; 16 A.L.R., 76. *Cussen, J.*

Wills Act 1890 (No. 1159), sec. 35—Will, interpretation — Trust for accumulation, whether created—Absolute gift—Invalid attempt to cut down, effect of.]—Testator, by his will directed his trustees to hold his residuary trust estate in trust for his children living at the expiration of twenty years from his death as tenants in common the shares of his sons to be paid immediately. He declared that his trustees should retain the share or shares to which each or any daughter of his acquiring an absolutely vested interest should become entitled upon trust to pay half of the annual income of such share or shares to each of his daughters except J. M. who he directed should be paid a specified sum per annum and no more out of the income of her share " any surplus income from her share to be invested and accumulated for her children in equal shares." Subject to the trusts aforesaid he directed that the share of each daughter original and accruing should be held in trust for the children of such daughter who being sons should attain the age of twenty-one years or being daughters should attain that age or marry under that age and if more than one in equal shares. With regard to the share of each daughter except J. M. he directed his trustees to invest and accumulate the surplus income by way of compound interest and to add the accumulations to such share. *Held,* (a) that there was no effective trust to accumulate the surplus income of .I. M.'s share and that therefore sec. 35 of the *Wills Act* 1890 had no application ; (*b*) that there was an accumulation directed during the life of each of the other daughters of the surplus income of her share which direction was void after twenty-one years from the testator's death : (*c*) and, upon the construction of the whole will, that the surplus income of the share of each of such other daughters went to her under the gift to the daughters, which was absolute so far as not validly cut down. *Hancock v. Watson*, (1902) A.C., 14, at p. 22, applied. *In re Watson* ; *Cain v. Watson*, (1910) V.L.R., 256 ; 31 A.L.T., 212 ; 16 A.L.R., 76. *Cussen, J.*

Will — Construction — Accumulations — Wills Act 1890 (No. 1159),sec. 35.]—Where an accumulation is directed for an excessive period, and there is no disposition of the property until the expiration of that period, the *Wills Act* 1890, sec. 35 in stopping the accumulation beyond the period allowed, does not accelerate the disposition, but the effect is to withdraw the subsequent income from the disposition of the rest of the property. The subsequent income until the disposition takes effect will then pass under the residuary disposition in the will ; or, if the disposition from which such income is withdrawn be a residuary disposition, it will pass as undisposed of. *In re Stevens, deceased* ; *The Trustees Executors and Agency Co. Ltd. v. Teague*, (1912) V.L.R., 194 ; 33 A.L.T., 233 ; 18 A.L.R., 195. *Hood, J.*

Will—Construction — Accumulations — Income of residuary estate, direction to accumulate, beyond period allowed—Gift to grandchildren upon youngest attaining twenty-one— After-born grandchildren—Intestacy—Wills Act 1890 (No. 1159), sec. 35.]—A testator directed his trustees to stand possessed of the corpus of his residuary estate and the interest and the income to arise therefrom upon trust to invest the same at interest until the youngest of his grandchildren attained the age of twenty-one years, and then to distribute the same amongst all his grand-children in equal shares *per capita*. *Held*, that the gift included all the testator's grandchildren whenever born. *Held*, further, that the direction to accumulate the income until the youngest of the testator's grand-children attained the age of twenty-one violated sec. 35 of the *Wills Act* 1890 ; that, therefore, the direction was only effective for twenty-one years from testator's death, and that there was an intestacy as to the income derived from the residuary estate for the period between twenty-one years after the testator's death and the time when the youngest grand-child attained twenty-one. *In re Stevens* ; *Trustees Executors and Agency Co. Ltd. v. Teague*, (1912) V.L.R., 194 ; 33 A.L.T., 233 ; 18 A.L.R., 195. *Hood, J.*

(8) Directions as to Payment of Duty, Upkeep of Property and the Like.

Direction that each beneficiary shall pay duty payable in respect of his interest—Probate duty, how payment to be apportioned— Tenant for life and remainderman.]—The testator by his will made certain specific bequests and devises and created various life estates with remainders. He also directed that each beneficiary should " pay the legacy probate or succession duty payable in respect of his or her interest." *Held*, that the direction as to payment of duty meant no more than that one beneficiary should not be called upon to pay the duty assessed in respect of the gift to another, and that this would be attained by following the rules laid down in the case of *Murphy v. Ainslie*, (1905) V.L.R., 350 ; 26 A.L.T., 202 ; 11 A.L.R., 163. *In re Buckhurst* ; *Equity Trustees Executors and Agency Co. Ltd. v. Buckhurst*, (1907) V.L.R., 252 ; 28 A.L.T., 190 ; 13 A.L.R., 74. *Cussen, J.*

Will and codicil—General direction in will exempting legacies from probate duty—Further legacies given in codicil without reference to exemption from probate duty.]—By his will the testator directed that probate duty should be paid out of his residuary estate and that in respect of such duty no deduction should be made " from or in respect of any devise bequest or legacy coming under this my will to my said wife or to the several persons hereinafter mentioned or referred." By a codicil " in addition to any other bequest or legacy hereinbefore or by my said will given " he gave a number of legacies to legatees not mentioned in the will but gave no direction as to exempting such legacies from probate duty. *Held*, that the provision that no deduction in respect of probate duty should be made from any legacy applied also to legacies under the codicil. *Re Sealey*; *Tomkins* v. *Tucker*, 85 L.T., 451, applied. *In re Stroud*: *Bell* v. *Stroud*, (1908) V.L.R., 33; 29 A.L.T., 104; 13 A.L.R., 645. *Cussen, J.*

Will — Construction — Direction to pay funeral and testamentary expenses and debts—Probate duty in respect of property transferred by testator in his lifetime—Administration and Probate Act 1903 (No. 1815), sec. 11.]— A direction by a testator to his executors to pay his funeral and testamentary expenses and debts out of his residuary estate does not authorise the payment of probate duty on property the subject of a voluntary transfer made chargeable with that duty under sec. 11 of the *Administration and Probate Act* 1903. *National Trustees Executors &c. Co.* v. *O'Hea*, 29 V.L.R., 814; 25 A.L.T., 230; 10 A.L.R., 81, applied. *In re Draper*; *Graham* v. *Draper*, (1910) V.L.R., 376; 32 A.L.T., 34; 16 A.L.R., 370. *a'Beckett, J.*

Will—Tenant for life of realty subject to payment of testamentary expenses but refuses to pay—No income of realty available for payment—Payment by trustees of probate duty and testamentary expenses out of personalty bequeathed to other beneficiaries—Mortgage of real estate to recoup such beneficiaries—Whether a breach of trust.]— See TRUSTS AND TRUSTEES. *Crout* v. *Beissel*, (1909) V.L.R., 207; 30 A.L.T., 185; 15 A.L.R., 143.

Will—Interpretation—Payment for upkeep of property—Whether out of corpus or income.]— A testatrix directed her trustees to convert her property into money and to stand possessed of the residuary trust moneys upon trust, after payment thereout of certain sums for the upkeep of C., to pay the residue of the income to one of the appellants. By a codicil the testatrix recited that she had

given her estate to her trustees upon trust, after payment for the upkeep of C., to pay the residue of the income of the trust premises to the one of the appellants above referred to. *Held*, that it appeared from the codicil that the testatrix intended that payment of the upkeep of C. should come out of income. *Cock* v. *Aitken*, (1911) 13 C.L.R., 461: 18 A.L.R., 337. H.C., *Griffith, C.J., Barton* and *O'Connor, JJ.*

Trustee — Skilled assistance — Apportionment of charges between capital and income—Apportionment between income takers.]— Testator by his will provided as follows :— " And 1 declare that the said trustees or trustee shall have the fullest power of apportioning blended trust funds and of determining whether any moneys are to be treated as capital or income and whether any expense outgoings or other payments ought to be made out of capital or income and generally of determining all matters as to which any doubt difficulty or question may arise under or in relation to the trusts of this my will or any codicil thereto. And I declare that every determination of the said trustees or trustee in relation to any of the matters aforesaid whether made upon a question formally or actually raised or implied in any of the acts or proceedings of the said trustees or trustee in relation to the premises shall bind all persons interested under this my will and shall not be objected to or questioned upon any ground whatsoever.'' *Held*, that this provision authorised the trustees to determine that the amount chargeable for such skilled assistance as the trustees might properly charge the estate for should be borne by income instead of capital and that as between the takers of income it should be borne rateably. *Swanson* v. *Emmerton*, (1909) V.L.R., 387; 31 A.L.T., 28; 15 A.L.R., 368. *Cussen, J.*

Will—Construction—" Upkeep and maintenance and carrying on of '' house " as a home and residence ''—What expenses included therein—Household expenses—Repairs—Rates and taxes—Outgoings.]— A testator by his will devised a house to his trustees upon trust for his wife for life " she paying all rates taxes and other outgoings payable during her life in respect thereof," and keeping it insured and in repair. He gave her £1,000 a year until the trustees should have set aside and invested a sum which they were directed to set aside and invest and pay to the widow the income therefrom made up, in case of deficiency, to £1,000 a year. By a codicil he revoked the trusts as to the income of the sum to be set aside, and directed that such portion or portions thereof as the trustees should from time to time consider reasonably requisite should be applied to the " upkeep " of the said house " and the maintenance and carrying on of the same as a home for and residence of my said wife during her life." *Held*, that the expression " upkeep and the maintenance and carrying on of the same as a home for and residence " included the ordinary and usual housekeeping expenses of the widow, and that after the trustees had set aside the sum mentioned, she would not be under any obligation to keep the house in repair and would then be liable to pay only such rates as were in the nature of proprietary rates imposed on the property as property, and, *semble*, that she would not be under any obligation to keep the house insured. *In re Stroud* ; *Bell* v. *Stroud*, (1908) V.L.R., 33 ; 29 A.L.T., 104 ; 13 A.L.R., 645. *Cussen, J.*

Trustees, duty of—Tenant for life—Repairs.]—Testator by his will devised his real estate to the trustees and executors of his will upon trust to allow S. to receive and take the rents issues and profits thereof for her absolute use and benefit for the term of her natural life she keeping   . the whole of the said real estate in good and tenantable order and condition. There was a gift over on the death of S. *Held*, that in the absence of gross and palpable disregard by S. of the obligation to keep the devised property in good tenantable order and condition the trustee was under no duty to compel S. to fulfil the obligation. *Carrodus* v. *Carrodus*, (1913) V.L.R., 1 ; 34 A.L.T., 125 ; 18 A.L.R., 529. *a'Beckett, J.*

Will — Interpretation — Carrying on business—Discretion of trustees.]—*See* TRUSTS AND TRUSTEES. *Union Bank of Australia Ltd.* v. *Whitelaw*, (1906) V.L.R., 711 ; 28 A.L.T., 17 ; 12 A.L.R., 393.

(9) Powers of Sale and Investment.

Direction for sale—" With all convenient speed "—Duty of trustee—Whether sale may be postponed.]—A trust to sell " with all convenient speed " is inconsistent with a power to postpone the sale. The trustees are not bound to sell immediately at a sacrifice, but it is their duty to sell at the first favourable opportunity. *In re Watson* ; *Cain* v. *Watson*, (1910) V.L.R., 256 ; 31 A.L.T., 212 ; 16 A.L.R., 76. *Cussen, J.*

Will—Interpretation—Life estate—Gift over in event of life tenant leaving no children—Intestacy—Power of sale.]—*See, ante,* (1) WHAT PROPERTY WILL PASS BY PARTICULAR WORDS AND DESCRIPTIONS. *Altson* v. *Equity Trustees &c. Co. Ltd.*, (1912) 14 C.L.R. 341 ; 18 A.L.R., 316.

Direction as to investment of trust funds in certain named securities—Power to invest in securities authorised by Trusts Acts—Trusts Act 1890 (No. 1150), secs. 88, 90—Trusts Act 1896 (No. 1421), sec. 22—Trusts Act 1906 (No. 2022), sec. 4.]—A testator by his will directed his trustees to invest trust moneys in certain named securities. *Held*, that they were not precluded from investing the trust moneys in any of the securities authorised by the Trusts Acts. *In re Meagher* ; *Trustees Executors and Agency Co. Ltd.* v. *Meagher*, (1910) V.L.R., 407 ; 32 A.L.T., 69 ; 16 A.L.R., 551. *a'Beckett, J.*

Will—Construction—Trustees empowered to purchase station property—Power to raise money out of estate for such purchase—Income to be paid to certain persons—Purchase of station property impracticable—Persons entitled to income—Testator's intention to benefit—Whether it can be given effect to by investment otherwise than by purchase of station property.]—A testator by his will declared that it should be lawful for his trustees on the happening of a certain event to agree for the purchase on account of his son D. of a station and stock in Australia or New Zealand, and for that purpose to raise out of the testator's estate the sum of £10,000, and to lay out such sum in part payment of the purchase money of such station and stock, the balance of the purchase money to be secured by mortgage of the purchased property and to be paid out of the profits thereof exclusively, and after payment of the said sum of £10,000 testator's estate to be discharged from all further liability in respect of such purchase. When purchased the station and stock were to be held in trust for testator's widow for life, and after her death in trust to be settled in such manner as should be most effectual for securing to D. the personal receipt and enjoyment of the rents and profits during his life inalienably, and after D.'s death in trust for his children. The testator died in 1881. The event specified in the will happened in 1907, when the trustees found that owing to the rise in value of such properties, it was impracticable, having regard to the prescribed limit of price, to purchase such a "station" as was contemplated in the will except in districts where a considerable risk of the entire sacrifice of the remaindermen's interests would be involved. *Held*, that the testator's object was that D. and his children should have the benefit of £10,000 through the medium of a station, and that, as by force of circumstances that medium had become impracticable, the trustees were at liberty to raise that sum out of the testator's estate, and invest it in any of the forms of investment authorised by the Trusts Acts, and settle it upon the trusts declared in regard to the station and stock. *In re Johnson*; *Perpetual Executors and Trustees Association of Australia* v. *Johnson*, (1907) V.L.R., 596; 29 A.L.T., 101; 13 A.L.R., 437. *a'Beckett, J..*

Calls on shares in No-Liability company—Power in will to postpone sale of personal property—Retention of shares by trustees—Whether liable for calls paid by them.]—See Trusts and Trustees. *Grunden* v. *Nissen*, (1911) V.L.R., 267; 33 A.L.T., 11; 17 A.L.R., 260.

(10) Lapse ; Ademption.

Will and codicil—Gift of residue by will—Gift by codicil of property forming part of
residue—**Failure of gift by codicil—Whether an intestacy—Intention of testator.]—**Where property is taken out of a residuary gift and disposed of by a devise which fails, it will fall into the residue, unless there is an expression of intention by the testator that it shall not do so. *In re Bagot*; *Paton* v. *Ormerod*, (1893) 3 Ch., 348, and *In re Fraser*; *Lowther* v. *Fraser*, (1904) 1 Ch., 726, followed. *Skrymsher* v. *Northcote*, 1 Swanst., 566, distinguished *In re Stead*; *McArthur* v. *Stead*, (1908) V.L.R., 10; 29 A.L.T., 155; 13 A.L.R., 683. *Cussen, J.*

Will and codicil—Gift of residue by will—Gift by codicil of property forming part of residue—Lapse of gift by codicil—Whether lapsed gift falls into residue.]—A testator by his will, after making certain specific bequests and devises, gave the whole of the residue of his real and personal estate to his trustees upon certain trusts. By a codicil to his will he revoked the will so far as the same was inconsistent with the two devises which he then made in favour of his brother X. of certain properties which formed part of the residue, and confirmed his will except so far as it was affected by the codicil. X. predeceased the testator. *Held*, that the two properties devised to X. by the codicil fell into the residue. *In re Stead*; *McArthur* v. *Stead*, (1908) V.L.R., 10; 29 A.L.T., 155; 13 A.L.R., 683. *Cussen, J.*

Ademption—Pecuniary legacy to be applied in uncontrolled discretion of trustees to several purposes—Subsequent gift by testatrix towards one of such purposes which was only imperfectly accomplished at death—Statements as to her intention made by testatrix subsequently to gifts.]—By her will a testatrix gave £2,500 to be applied by her executors in their uncontrolled discretion in or towards the erection of a Presbyterian Church, including all necessary fittings and accessories, and a manse at Daylesford. Subsequently to the execution of the will a Presbyterian Church was built at Daylesford at a cost of £2,270, of which the testatrix contributed £1,700, and she also gave £306 towards erecting an organ in the Church. Owing to insufficiency of funds the Church was not completed in accordance with the original design, and the testatrix knew of this. The testatrix made statements showing that it was her intention that the legacy should stand notwithstanding the gifts made after its date, and that she considered none of the purposes designated in her will as satisfactorily achieved. There was a manse attached to the Church, but it was old and dilapidated. *Held*, that, even if the evidence as to the statements of the testatrix were disregarded, the legacy was not on the facts adeemed in whole or *pro tanto* by the gifts. *In re Leggatt*; *Griffith* v. *Calder*, (1908) V.L.R., 385; 30 A.L.T., 34; 14 A.L.R., 314. *a'Beckett, J.*

Evidence — Legacy — Ademption — Gifts made for same purpose as legacy—Statements by donor made subsequently to gifts as to intention in making gifts.]—Where a pecuniary legacy was given by a will for particular purposes, and the testatrix subsequently during her lifetime made gifts of money towards the same purposes, statements made by her subsequently to the gifts are admissible to negative any intention that the gifts should reduce or supersede the legacy. *In re Leggatt*; *Griffith* v. *Calder*, (1908) V.L.R., 385; 30 A.L.T., 34; 14 A.L.R., 314. *a'Beckett, J.* (1908).

(11) Other Matters.

Declaration that woman is past child-bearing—Circumstances in which Court will make.]—The circumstances in which the Court will declare a woman to be past child-bearing considered, and a declaration refused in the case of a woman in her forty-sixth year, though two medical practitioners stated that in their opinion it was beyond all reasonable probability that the woman would bear a child. *In re Lees*; *Lees* v. *National Trustees Co.*, (1908) V.L.R., 211; 30 A.L.T., 26; 14 A.L.R., 147. *a'Beckett, J.*

Declaration that woman past child-bearing.]—Declaration made that a woman in her fifty-sixth year was past child-bearing, where on her statements and their own observations two medical practitioners stated that they were satisfied that the woman would never have a child. *In re Lyons*; *Grant* v.

Trustees Executors &c. Co. Ltd., (1908) V.L.R., 190; 29 A.L.T., 202; 14 A.L.R., 147. *a'Beckett, J.*

VI.—Widows and Young Children Maintenance Act.

Widows and Young Children Maintenance Act 1906 (No. 2074), secs. 3, 9—Widow's maintenance—Application for further provision—Widow's interest under testator's will—Limit on amount of provision.]—*See* Widows and Young Children Maintenance Act. *In re Maslin*, (1908) V.L.R., 641; 30 A.L.T., 70; 14 A.L.R., 499.

Widows and Young Children Maintenance Act 1906 (No. 2074), secs. 3, 9—Insufficient provision by testator for maintenance of widow—Application by widow for further allowance—Limit of amount of provision Court may allow.]—*See* Widows and Young Children Maintenance Act. *In re Bennett*, (1909) V.L.R., 205; 30 A.L.T., 181; 15 A.L.R., 141.

Widows and Young Children Maintenance Act 1906 (No. 2074), sec. 3—Disposition of property by will—Provision for widow and children—" Sufficient means for their maintenance and support," what are.] — *See* Widows and Young Children Maintenance Act. *In re Read*, (1910) V.L.R., 68; 31 A.L.T., 154; 16 A.L.R., 60.

Widows and Young Children Maintenace Act 1906 (No. 2074). sec. 3—Disposition of property by will—Widow and young children left without sufficient means for maintenance—Provision for maintenance by order of Court—Discretion, how exercised.]—*See* Widows and Young Children Maintenance Act. *In re Read*, (1910) V.L.R., 68; 31 A.L.T., 154; 16 A.L.R., 60.

Widows and Young Children Maintenance Act 1906 (No. 2074)—Purpose of Act—Capricious and unreasonable testamentary dispositions.]—*See* Widows and Young Children Maintenance Act. *In re McGoun*, (1910) V.L.R., 153; 31 A.L.T., 193; 16 A.L.R., 141.

Widows and Young Children Maintenance Act 1906 (No. 2074), secs. 3, 8, 9 (5)—Maintenance—Application by widow—Husband and wife separated**—**Misconduct of wife**—**Widow left destitute.**]—*See* WIDOWS AND YOUNG CHILDREN MAINTENANCE ACT. *In re Mc-Goun.* (1910) V.L.R., 153 : 31 A.L.T., 193 ; 16 A.L.R., 141.

Widows and Young Children Maintenance Act 1906 (No. 2074), secs. 3, 7, 8 (2)—**Maintenance**—**Application by widow**—**Order making provision for widow assignable**—**Small estate.**] —*See* WIDOWS AND YOUNG CHILDREN MAINTENANCE ACT. *In re Mailes,* (1908) V.L.R., 269 ; 29 A.L.T., 263 ; 14 A.L.R., 181.

VII.—DUTIES ON THE ESTATES OF DECEASED PERSONS.

See cols. 414 *et seq.*

VIII.—MANAGEMENT OF ESTATE ; ADJUSTMENT OF ACCOUNTS BETWEEN BENEFICIARIES.

See EXECUTORS AND ADMINISTRATORS ; TENANT FOR LIFE AND REMAINDERMAN ; TRUSTS AND TRUSTEES.

WORDS.

" **Affix a stamp so removed.** "]—For meaning of these words in sec. 23 of *Stamps Act* 1890 (No. 1140), *see* Stamps Acts, cols. 1185, 1186. *Burvett* v. *Moody.* (1909) V.L.R., 126 ; 30 A.L.T., 160 ; 15 A.L.R., 91.

" **Approach** " **to a bridge.**]—Meaning discussed. *See Daniel* v. *Benalla President &c. of,* (1906) V.L.R., 101 ; 27 A.L.T., 141 : 12 A.L.R., 16.

" **Avoid.** "]—For a consideration of what is meant by " avoiding " payment of a tramway fare under the *Tramways Act* 1890, Second Schedule, Part II., clause 17, *see* LOCAL GOVERNMENT, cols. 870, 871. *Cochrane* v. *Tuthill,* (1908) V.L.R., 549 ; 30 A.L.T., 50 ; 14 A.L.R., 453. *Madden, C.J.* (1908).

" **Becoming insolvent.** "]—The words " becoming insolvent " in sub-sec. (v.) of sec. 141 of the *Insolvency Act* 1890 are used in the same sense as the words " became insolvent " in sec. 145 of that Act and refer to the order

actually making the person insolvent. *In re O'Hanlon,* 30 A.L.T. (Supplement), 8 ; 14 A.L.R. (C.N.), 33. *Judge Moule* (1908).

" **Book debts.** "]—*See* BOOK DEBTS, cols. 81, 82. *Shackell* v. *Howe, Thornton and Palmer,* (1909) 8 C.L.R., 170 ; 15 A.L.R., 176.

" **Bridge.** "] — Meaning discussed. *See Daniell* v. *Benalla, President, &c. of,* (1906) V.L.R., 101 ; 27 A.L.T., 141 ; 12 A.L.R., 16.

" **Brothel.** "]—For a discussion of the meaning of this word, *see* POLICE OFFENCES ACTS, col. 993. *Appleby* v. *Reddan,* (1912) V.L.R., 270 ; 34 A.L.T., 28 ; 18 A.L.R., 326.

" **Business.** "]—Meaning of in *Book Debts Act* 1896 (No. 1424). *See* BOOK DEBTS ACT, cols. 80, 81. *Schroder* v. *Hebbard,* (1907) V.L.R., 107 ; 29 A.L.T., 1 ; 13 A.L.R., 141.

" **Clear days.** "]—*See* TIME, cols. 1212, 1213. *Armstrong* v. *Great Southern Gold Mining Co. No Liability,* (1911) 12 C.L.R., 382 ; 17 A.L.R., 377.

" **Comment.** "]—*See* DEFAMATION, col. 395. *Clarke* v. *Norton,* (1910) V.L.R., 494. ; 32 A.L.T., 109 ; 16 A.L.R., 544.

" **Corruptly.** "]—For a discussion of the meaning of this word in the *Secret Commissions Prohibition Act* 1905, *see* CRIMINAL LAW, col. 344. *Rex* v. *Scott,* (1907) V.L.R., 471 : 29 A.L.T., 60 ; 13 A.L.R., 143. *Cussen, J.*

" **Corruptly.** "] — " Corruptly " in the *Secret Commissions Prohibition Act* 1905 does not mean merely the doing of an act prohibited by the Statute, but the doing of that act with some wrongful intention. *Rex* v. *Stevenson,* (1907) V.L.R., 475 ; 29 A.L.T., 62 ; 13 A.L.R., 383. *Hood, J.* (1907).

" **Crop of grass.** "]—*See* CRIMINAL LAW, col. 340. *Rex* v. *Philbey,* (1906) V.L.R., 290 ; 27 A.L.T., 186 : 12 A.L.R., 188.

" **Decision.** "]—In sec. 74 of the Australian Constitution the term " decision " is not equivalent to " judgment, decree, order or sentence." It means the declaration of law as affirmed by the High Court. *Baxter v. Commissioners of Taxation* : *Flint v. Webb*, 4 C.L.R., 1087 ; 1178 ; 13 A.L.R., 313 (1907).

" **Destination.**"]—For the meaning of this word, see STOCK DISEASES ACT, 1191, 1192. *McCure* v. *Watts*, (1908) V.L.R., 327 ; 29 A.L.T., 238 ; 14 A.L.R., 219.

" **Dishonest.**"]—The word " dishonest " is generally used in connection with acts which are either crimes at common law or are made crimes by Statute. *Green v. Jones*, (1910) V.L.R., 284 ; 31 A.L.T., 203 ; 16 A.L.R., 304. *Cussen, J.* (1910).

" **Dispute.**"]—The meaning of this word in sec. 167 of the *Customs Act* 1901 (No. 6) discussed. *Sargood Bros.* v. *The Commonwealth*, (1910) 11 C.L.R., 258 ; 16 A.L.R., 483.

" **Divine service.**"]—*See* POLICE OFFENCES ACTS, col. 988. *Goodson* v. *M'Namara*, (1907) V.L.R., 89 ; 28 A.L.T., 115 ; 12 A.L.R., 547.

" **Duly summoned.**"]—For the meaning of this expression in sec. 40 (1) of the *Police Offences Act* 1890, see *Wilson* v. *Travers*, (1906) V.L.R., 734 ; 28 A.L.T., 56 ; 12 A.L.R., 413.

" **Fence.**"]—A creek may be a substantial fence within the meaning of sec. 9 of the *Pounds Act* 1890. *Helding* v. *Davis*, (1911) V.L.R., 74 ; 32 A.L.T., 188 ; 17 A.L.R., 72. *Hood, J.* (1911).

" **First offence.**"]—*Semble*, In the *Street Betting Suppression Act* 1896 (No. 1436), sec. 7, the words " first offence " include all offences up to the time of the first conviction and probably all offences where it is not proved that there has been a prior conviction. *Knox v. Thomas Bible* ; *Knox v. J. L. Bible*, (1907) V.L.R., 485 ; 29 A.L.T., 23 ; 13 A.L.R., 352. *Cussen, J.*

" **Foreign.**"]—A lottery got up in Tasmania is not in Victoria a " foreign " lottery within the meaning of 6 Geo. II., c. 35. *The Attorney-General* v. *Moses*, (1907) V.L.R., 130; 28 A.L.T., 125 ; 12 A.L.R., 606. F.C., *a' Beckett, A.-C.J., Hodges* and *Chomley, JJ.*

" **Forthwith.**"]—The word " forthwith " in sec. 20 of the *Justices Act* 1904 (No. 1959) means " at once " without the lapse of any interval of time. *Adams* v. *Rogers*, (1907) V.L.R., 245 ; 28 A.L.T., 180 ; 13 A.L.R., 71. *Hood, J.*

" **Fraudulent.**"]—Meaning of in sec. 141 (xiii.) of the *Insolvency Act* 1890, discussed. *See* INSOLVENCY, col. 731. *Re Cohen*, (1908) V.L.R., 171 ; 29 A.L.T., 187 ; 14 A.L.R., 74.

" **Frequent.**"]—For the meaning of this word in the expression " frequent convictions for crime " in sec. 74 (c) of the *Marriage Act* 1890, see HUSBAND AND WIFE, col. 651. *Kemp* v. *Kemp*, (1907) V.L.R., 718 ; 29 A.L.T., 92. 13 A.L.R., 615.

" **Goods.**"]—The word " goods " in sec. 58 of the *Police Regulation Act* 1890 includes money. *McKenna* v. *Dent and Williamson*, (1912) V.L.R., 150 ; 33 A.L.T., 202 ; 18 A.L.R., 148. *a' Beckett, J.*

" **Immigrant.**"]—Meaning in Immigration Restriction Acts discussed. *See* IMMIGRATION RESTRICTION ACTS, col. 670. *Ah Sheung* v. *Lindberg*, (1906) V.L.R., 323 ; 27 A.L.T., 189 ; *sub nom.*, *Rex* v. *Ah Sheung*, 12 A.L.R., 190.

" **Improver.**"]—*See* FACTORIES AND SHOPS ACTS, col. 582. *Hines* v. *Phillips*, (1906) V.L.R., 417 ; 28 A.L.T., 1 ; 12 A.L.R., 249.

" **Inadvertence.**"]—A deliberate omission on mistaken grounds is not an omission arising from " inadvertence " within the meaning of rule 270 of the *Insolvency Rules* 1898. *In re McGee*, 28 A.L.T. (Supplement), 12 ; 13 A.L.R. (C.N.), 7. *Judge Molesworth* (1907).

" **Indentures of apprenticeship.**"] — *See* FACTORIES AND SHOPS ACTS, col. 582. *Hines* v. *Phillips*, (1906) V.L.R., 417 ; 28 A.L.T., 1 ; 12 A.L.R., 249.

" **Industry.**"]—For the meaning of this word in the *Commonwealth Conciliation and Arbitration Act* 1904, see EMPLOYER AND EMPLOYEE, cols. 437, 438. *Federated Engine*

Drivers and Firemen's Association of Australasia v. *Broken Hill Proprietary Co. Ltd.,* (1911) 12 C.L.R., 398 ; 17 A.L.R., 285.

" **Information or advice.**"]—For a discussion of the meaning of these words in sec. 22 of the *Lotteries Gaming and Betting Act* 1906, see *O'Donnell* v. *Smart,* (1907) V.L.R., 439 ; 28 A.L.T., 245 ; 13 A.L.R., 255.

" **Insolvent estate** " **in sec. 139 of the Insolvency Act 1890 (sec. 1102).**]—*See* INSOLVENCY, col. 727. *In re Wood,* 29 A.L.T. (Supplement), 21 ; 14 A.L.R. (C.N.), 9.

" **In the first place,**" " **in the next place.**" —For a consideration of the question whether these phrases in a will signify priority of enumeration or in time, order or method of payment, or of rights and interests, *see Perpetual Executors and Trustees Association of Australia Ltd.* v. *Knowles,* 32 A.L.T., 163 ; 16 A.L.R., 582. *Cussen, J.* (1910).

" **Invention.**"]—The meaning of " invention " as the object of the verb " vend " cannot be limited to the idea itself but extends to the product of the invention. Dictum of *Griffith, C.J.,* approved on appeal. *National Phonograph Co. of Australia Ltd.* v. *Menck,* 7 C.L.R., at p. 512 ; 15 A.L.R., at p. 6. On appeal, (1911) A.C., 336, at p. 348 ; 17 A.L.R., at p. 97.

" **Liquor.**"]—For meaning of in *Licensing Act* 1890, see LICENSING, cols. 831, 832. *Gleeson* v. *Hobson,* (1907) V.L.R., 148 ; 28 A.L.T., 151 ; 13 A.L.R., 10.

" **Living wage.**"]—For a consideration of the meaning of this expression, see FACTORIES AND SHOPS ACTS, col. 577. *In re the Starch Board,* 13 A.L.R., 558.

" **Living wage.**"]—The term " living wage" as used in sec. 122 of the *Factories and Shops Act* 1905 (No. 1975) refers to the personal living wage, and not to the family living wage, *i.e.,* such a wage as will support a man and his wife and family in frugal comfort. *In re the Fellmongers. Board,* 15 A.L.R., 225. Court of Industrial Appeals *a' Beckett, J.* (1909).

" **May.**"]—For a discussion of the meaning of this word in sec. 38 (1) of the *Lotteries Gaming and Betting Act* 1906 (No. 2055), see GAMING AND WAGERING, col. 610. *In re Lotteries Gaming and Betting Act* 1906 ; *Ex parte Gleeson,* (1907) V.L.R., 368 ; 28 A.L.T., 228 ; 13 A.L.R., 146. *Cussen, J.*

" **May amend.**"]—For meaning of these words in sec. 187 of the *Justices Act* 1890 (No. 1105) see INFORMATION, col. 697. *Burvett* v. *Moody,* (1909) V.L.R., 126 ; 30 A.L.T., 160 ; 15 A.L.R., 91.

" **Mineral.**"]—" Bluestone " is a mineral within the meaning of sec. 67 of the *Mines Act* 1897 (No. 1514). *Cairns* v. *O'Hanlon,* 17 A.L.R. (C.N.), 6. *Judge Moule* (1911).

" **Necessary for the public convenience.**"]—For meaning of these words in sec. 7 of *Licensing Act* 1890 (No. 1111), see LICENSING, col. 824. *Lucas* v. *Mooney,* (1909) 9 C.L.R., 231 ; 15 A.L.R., 490.

" **Neighbourhood.**"]—For meaning of this word in sec. 7 of *Licensing Act* (No. 1111), see LICENSING, col. 823. *Lucas* v. *Mooney,* (1909) 9 C.L.R., 231 ; 15 A.L.R., 490.

" **Obstruction.**"]—For a consideration of the meaning of this word in sec. 6 of the *Police Offences Act* 1890, see POLICE OFFENCES ACTS, cols. 986, 987. *Haywood* v. *Mumford,* (1908) 7 C.L.R., 133 ; 14 A.L.R., 555.

" **Occupier.**"]—For a discussion of the meaning of this word for rating purposes, see LOCAL GOVERNMENT, col. 859. *Poowong, Shire of* v. *Gillen,* 28 A.L.T., 123 ; 12 A.L.R., 522.

" **On the trial.**"]—For the meaning of these words in sec. 481 of the *Crimes Act* 1890, see CRIMINAL LAW, col. 365. *Rex* v. *Turnbull.* (1907) V.L.R., 11 ; 28 A.L.T., 103 ; 12 A.L.R., 551.

" **Outgoings.**"]—*See* WILL. *In re Stroud* ; *Bell* v. *Stroud,* (1908) V.L.R., 33 ; 29 A.L.T., 104 ; 13 A.L.R., 645.

" **Owner.**"]—For a consideration of the meaning of this word in the *Vermin Destruction Act* 1890 (No. 1153), see VERMIN. *Moore*

v. *Irvine*, (1913) V.L.R., 14 ; 34 A.L.T., 107 ;
18 A.L.R., 526.

" **Person.**"]—*Quaere*, whether " the Clerk
of Petty Sessions " *eo nomine* is a " person "
within the meaning of sec. 43 of the *Marriage
Act* 1890. *Cohen* v. *MacDonough* (*or
O'Donough*), (1906) V.L.R., 521 ; 28 A.L.T.,
97 ; 12 A.L.R., 447. *Cussen, J.*

" **Place.**"]—For a discussion of the meaning of this word in 21 Geo. III., c. 49 (*Sunday
Observance Act*), see *Scott* v. *Cawsey*, 5 C.L.R.,
132 ; 13 A.L.R., 568. H.C. (1907).

" **Place.**"]—See GAMING AND WAGERING,
cols. 606, 607. *McCann* v. *Morgan*, (1912)
V.L.R., 303 ; 34 A.L.T., 43 ; 18 A.L.R., 334.

" **Place of public resort.**"]—See POLICE
OFFENCES ACTS, col. 993. *Howard* v.
Murphy ; *Sainsbury* v. *Palmer*, 28 A.L.T.
(Supplement), 10 ; 13 A L.R. (C.N.), 3.

" **Possession.**"]—Used as contra-distin-
guished from reversion or remainder in the
Settled Estates and Settled Lands Act 1909.
In re Cheke or Akehurst ; Cheke v. *Hamilton*,
(1910) V.L.R., 310 ; 32 A.L.T., 5 ; 16
A.L.R., 246. *Hodges, J.*

" **Preparing . . . for sale.**"]—For the
meaning of these words in sec. 5 of the
Factories and Shops Act 1905 (No. 1975), *see
Alderson* v. *Gold*, (1909) V.L.R., 219 ; 30
A.L.T., 189 ; 15 A.L.R., 180. (But *see Henry
Bull & Co. Ltd.* v. *Holden*, (1912) 13 C.L.R.,
569).

" **Presented by a Company.**"]—*Per* Judge
Chomley : " In my opinion the words ' if
presented by a Company ' in sec. 253 of the
Companies Act 1890 ' refer to the company
proposed to be wound up and not to a com-
pany which is presenting the petition either
as a creditor or shareholder." *Re the Mount
Lyell Consols Mining Corporation No Liability
(No. 2)*, 30 A.L.T. (Supplement), 17 ; 14
A.L.R. (C.N.), 41.

" **Printing.**"]—Typewriting is not " printing " within the meaning of sec. IV., r. 16,
of the Appeal Rules under the *High Court
Procedure Act. Peacock* v. *Osborne & Co.*,
13 A.L.R., 254. *Barton, J.* (1907).

" **Privy.**"—For a consideration of the
meaning of this word in the *Opium Smoking
Prohibition Act* 1905, see OPIUM SMOKING
PROHIBITION, cols. 959, 960. *Stapleton* v.
Davis ; Stapleton v. *Bell*, (1908) V.L.R., 114 ;
29 A.L.T., 162 ; 14 A.L.R., 26.

" **Profits.**"]—For a discussion of the
meaning of this word in sec. 9 of the *Income
Tax Act* 1903 (No. 1819), *see Webb* v.
Australian Deposit and Mortgage Bank Ltd.,
(1910) 11 C.L.R., 223 ; 16 A.L.R., 446.

" **Public place.**"]—For a discussion of the
meaning of this phrase, see *Richardson* v.
Austin, (1911) 12 C.L.R., 463 ; 17 A.L.R.,
324.

" **Recklessly.**"]—For a discussion of the
meaning of this term in sec. 10 of the *Motor
Car Act* 1909, see *Kane* v. *Dureau*, (1911)
V.L.R., 293 ; 33 A.L.R., 15 ; 17 A.L.R.,
277.

" **Required.**"]—For the meaning of " required " in sec. 40 (1) of the *Police Offences
Act* 1890, *see Wilson* v. *Travers*, (1906)
V.L.R., 734 ; 28 A.L.T., 56 ; 12 A.L.R.,
413.

" **Sale.**"]—The meaning of this word in
the Stamps Acts discussed. *See* STAMPS
ACTS, col. 1182. *Davies* v. *Collector of Imposts*, (1908) V.L.R., 272 ; 29 A.L.T., 233 ;
14 A.L.R., 149. *Cussen, J.*

" **Second offence.**"]—*Semble* : In sec. 7
of the *Street Betting Suppression Act* 1896
(No. 1436), sec. 7, " a second offence " means
any offence where it is proved that the act
was done after a prior conviction for a former
offence. *Knox* v. *Thomas Bible ; Knox* v.
J. L. Bible, (1907) V.L.R., 485 ; 29 A.L.T.,
23 ; 13 A.L.R., 352. *Cussen, J.*

" **Second offence,**" what is—**Pure Food Act**
1905 (No. 2010), sec. 36.]—See CRIMINAL LAW,
cols. 367, 368. *O'Connor* v. *Bini*, (1908)
V.L.R., 567 ; 30 A.L.T., 74 ; 14 A.L.R., 537.

" **Settled hopeless expectation of immediate**
death."]—See CRIMINAL LAW, col. 354.
Rex v. *Florence Hope*, (1909) V.L.R., 149,
p. 165 ; 30 A.L.T., 167, p. 171 ; 15 A.L.R.,
87, p. 90. F.C.

" **Settlement.** "]—For a discussion of the meaning of this word, *see Davidson v. Army-taqe*, 4 C.L.R., 205 ; 12 A.L.R., 538. H.C , *Griffith*, *C.J.*, *Barton* and *O'Connor, JJ.* (1906).

" **Shop.** "]—*See* FACTORIES AND SHOPS, col. 511. *Mackinnon v. Hannay*, (1906) V.L.R., 604 ; 28 A.L.T., 33 ; 12 A.L.R., 381.

" **Shop.** "]—For a discussion of the meaning of this word, *see Richardson v. Austin*, (1911) 12 C.L.R., 463 ; 17 A.L.R., 324.

" **Special reasons** " within the meaning of the Insolvency Act 1897 (No. 1513), sec. 92.]—*See* INSOLVENCY, col. 727. *In re Moulton*, 30 A.L.T. (Supplement), 4 ; 14 A.L.R. (C.N.), 29.

" **Theatre.** "]—The registered proprietor of the performing rights in a play gave to X. " the exclusive licence to perform the said play in any theatre in any part of Australia." *Held*, that the word " theatre " was not restricted in meaning to licensed theatres, but meant the places where the play was performed. *Meynell v. Pearce*, (1906) V.L.R., 447 ; 27 A.L.T., 226 ; 12 A.L.R., 282. *Cussen, J.* (1906).

" **The betting,** " " **betting.** "]—For a discussion of the meaning of these words, *see O'Donnell v. Smart*, (1907) V.L.R., 439 ; 28 A.L.T., 245 ; 13 A.L.R., 255.

" **The manager** " of a bank.]—The expression " the manager " of a bank held to mean the manager of a branch of the bank, *see Union Bank of Australia Ltd. v. Whitelaw*, (1906) V.L.R., 711 ; 28 A.L.T., 17 ; 12 A.L.R., 393.

" **True in substance and in fact.** "]—*See* DEFAMATION, col. 395. *Clarke v. Norton*, (1910) V.L.R , 494 ; 32 A.L.T., 109 ; 16 A.L.R., 544.

" **Unable.** "]—The meaning of this word in sec. 708 of the *Local Government Act* 1903 discussed. *See* LOCAL GOVERNMENT, cols. 873, 874. *Leeder v. Ballarat East, Mayor &c. of*, (1908) V.L.R., 214 ; 29 A.L.T., 192 ; 14 A.L.R., 124.

" **Upkeep.** "]—*See* WILL. *In re Stroud* ; *Bell v. Stroud*, (1908) V.L.R., 33 ; 29 A.L.T., 104 ; 13 A.L.R., 645.

" **Vehicle.** "]—A traction engine is a " vehicle " within the meaning of sec. 197 (29) of the *Local Government Act* 1903. *Tungamah, President, &c. of the Shire of v. Merrett*, (1912) 15 C.L.R., 407 ; 18 A.L.R., 511. H.C., *Griffith*, *C.J.* and *Barton, J.* (*Isaacs, J.* doubting).

" **Vehicle.** "]—For meaning of this word in *Local Government Act* 1903 (No. 1893), sec. 197 (29), *see* LOCAL GOVERNMENT, col. 855. *Ahern v. Cathcart*, (1909) V.L.R., 132 ; 30 A.L.T., 156 ; 15 A.L.R., 67.

" **Vehicle.** "]—A cable tram-car is a " vehicle " within the meaning of Regulation 2 (3) of the Motor Car Regulations 1910. *Gillin v. Malmgren*, (1912) V.L.R., 26 ; 33 A.L.T., 118 ; 17 A.L.R., 564. *a'Beckett, J.* (1911).

" **Visible means of support.** "]—For the meaning of this expression in sec. 40 (1) of the *Police Offences Act* 1890, *see Wilson v. Travers*, (1906) V.L.R., 734 ; 28 A.L.T., 56 ; 12 A.L.R., 413.

" **With all convenient speed.** "]—For the meaning of these words in connection with a direction to trustees to sell, *see* TRUSTS AND TRUSTEES. *In re Watson* ; *Cain v. Watson*, (1910) V.L.R., 256 ; 31 A.L.T., 212 ; 16 A.L.R., 76.

" **With a view to prefer** "—Meaning in Insolvency Act 1890 (No. 1102), sec. 73.]—*See* INSOLVENCY, col. 710. *Muntz v. Smail*, 8 C.L.R., 262 ; 15 A.L.R., 162.

" **Work.** "]—For the meaning of this word in sec. 42 of the *Factories and Shops Act* 1905, (No. 1975) *see* FACTORIES AND SHOPS ACTS, cols. 573, 574. *Ingham v. Hie Lee*, (1912) 15 C.L.R., 267 ; 18 A.L.R., 453.

————

WORK AND LABOUR DONE.

See MEDICAL MAN, cols. 901, 902.

WRONGS ACT.

Wrongs Act 1890 (No. 1160), sec. 5—Rules of the Supreme Court 1906, XXII., r. 1—Practice—Libel action against newspaper proprietor—Defence—Payment into Court with denial of liability—Defence under Wrongs Act and payment into Court thereunder.]—In an action against a proprietor of a newspaper for the recovery of damages for libel, the defendant pleaded in one paragraph of his defence payment into Court of £10 with a denial of liability, and in another paragraph thereof, whilst denying the meanings ascribed by the plaintiff to the words complained of, he pleaded a defence and a payment into Court as under sec. 5 of the *Wrongs Act* 1890. Only one sum of £10 was paid into Court by the defendant. *Held,* that the words denying the innuendoes should be struck out of the latter paragraph, and a second sum of £10 should be brought into Court as under that paragraph. *Kiel* v. *Clark,* (1908) V.L.R., 627; 30 A.L.T., 86; 14 A.L.R., 500. *Madden, C.J.* (1908).

Order XIX., r. 27—Pleading—Tendency to embarrass—Libel contained in public newspaper—Allegation of apology and absence of malice and gross negligence—No payment into Court—Wrongs Act 1890 (No. 1160), sec. 5.]—*See* DEFAMATION, col. 397. *Wilson* v. *Dun's Gazette Ltd.,* (1912) V.L.R., 342; 34 A.L.T., 77; 18 A.L.R., 327.

County Court Act 1890 (No. 1078), sec. 51—County Court Rules 1891, rr. 155, 424—Wrongs Act 1890 (No. 1160)—Remitted action—Action for libel—Notice of special defence under the Wrongs Act 1890—Enlargement of time for serving and filing such notice—Power of Court to grant.]—*See* DEFAMATION, cols. 397, 398. *Bayne* v. *Wilson and Mackinnon,* 31 A.L.T. (Supplement), 2

Administration ad litem—Application under peculiar circumstances—Proposed action under Wrongs Act for benefit of widow and children of deceased—Time for bringing action about to expire—Poverty of widow the applicant for administration—Wrongs Act 1890 (No. 1160), secs. 14, 15, 16.]—*See* EXECUTORS AND ADMINISTRATORS, cols. 534, 535. *Greenway* v. *McKay,* (1911) 12 C.L.R., 310; 17 A.L.R., 350.

9 789353 86